Contemporary Mathematics

FOR BUSINESS AND CONSUMERS

Robert Brechner and George Bergeman

 CENGAGE

Australia • Brazil • Mexico • Singapore • United Kingdom • United States

CENGAGE

Contemporary Mathematics for Business and Consumers, 9th Edition

Robert A. Brechner, George W. Bergeman

Senior Vice President, Higher Ed Product, Content, and Market Development: Erin Joyner

Vice President, Product Management: Mike Schenk

Senior Product Director: Joe Sabatino

Senior Product Manager: Aaron Arnsparger

Senior Learning Designer: Brandon Foltz

Senior Content Manager: D. Jean Bora

Product Assistant: Christian Wood

Marketing Manager: Chris Walz

Associate Program Manager, WebAssign: Jessica Galloway

Associate Subject Matter Expert: Nancy Marchant

Senior Digital Delivery Lead: Mark Hopkinson

Production Service: SPi Global

Designer: Chris Doughman

Cover Image: Cico/ShutterStock.com

Internal Image: spainter_vfx/Shutterstock.com

Intellectual Property Analyst: Reba Frederics

Intellectual Property Project Manager: Betsy Hathaway

For product information and technology assistance, contact us at
Cengage Customer & Sales Support, 1-800-354-9706
or **support.cengage.com.**

For permission to use material from this text or product, submit all requests online at **www.cengage.com/permissions.**

Library of Congress Control Number: 2018962212

ISBN: 978-0-357-02644-1

Cengage
20 Channel Center Street
Boston, MA 02210
USA

Cengage is a leading provider of customized learning solutions with employees residing in nearly 40 different countries and sales in more than 125 countries around the world. Find your local representative at **www.cengage.com**.

Cengage products are represented in Canada by Nelson Education, Ltd.

To learn more about Cengage platforms and services, register or access your online learning solution, or purchase materials for your course, visit **www.cengage.com**.

Printed at CLDPC, USA, 01-21

Contemporary Mathematics, 9e
Real Business. Real Math. Real Life.

> Contemporary Mathematics, 9e helps students overcome math anxiety and confidently master key business and mathematics concepts!

SECTION I — 8 MARKUP BASED ON COST

Determining an appropriate selling price for a company's goods or services is an extremely important function in business. The price must be attractive to potential customers, yet sufficient to cover expenses and provide the company with a reasonable profit.

In business, expenses are separated into two major categories. The first is the **cost of goods sold**. To a manufacturer, this expense would be the cost of production; to a wholesaler or retailer, the expense is the price paid to a manufacturer or distributor for the merchandise. The second category includes all the other expenses required to operate the business, such as salaries, rent, utilities, taxes, insurance, advertising, and maintenance. These expenses are known as **operating expenses**, overhead expenses, or simply **overhead**.

The amount added to the cost of an item to cover the operating expenses and profit is known as the **markup, markon, or margin**. It is the difference between the cost and the selling price of an item. Markup is applied at all levels of the marketing channels of distribution. This chapter deals with the business math applications involved in the pricing of goods and services.

cost of goods sold The cost of the merchandise sold during an operating period. One of two major expense categories of a business.

operating expenses, or **overhead** All business expenses, other than cost of merchandise, required to operate a business, such as payroll, rent, utilities, and insurance.

markup, markon, or **margin** The amount added to the cost of an item to cover the operating expenses and profit. It is the difference between the cost and the selling price.

8-1 UNDERSTANDING AND USING THE RETAILING EQUATION TO FIND COST, AMOUNT OF MARKUP, AND SELLING PRICE OF AN ITEM

The fundamental principle on which business operates is to sell goods and services for a price high enough to cover all expenses and provide the owners with a reasonable profit. The formula that describes this principle is known as the **retailing equation**. The equation states that the selling price of an item is equal to the cost plus the markup.

retailing equation The selling price of an item is equal to the cost plus the markup.

$$\text{Selling price} = \text{Cost} + \text{Markup}$$

Using the abbreviations C for cost, M for markup, and SP for selling price, the formula is written as

FROM MOTIVATION TO MASTERY

Brechner's **accessible and engaging style** begins with a business-oriented review of basic math operations, including whole numbers, fractions, and decimals. After students master these operations, they move to basic equations and their use in solving business problems. These tools form a strong foundation enabling students to succeed as they study the wide range of business math topics presented in subsequent chapters.

REFLECTING THE LATEST IN REAL BUSINESS

Brechner incorporates numerous **realistic** and **current** problems that are designed to develop problem-solving and critical thinking skills.

- Coverage of personal finances addresses the newest ways to manage finances, including online bills and banking, debit cards, and e-management of accounts.

- Realistic business and government forms, checks, bank statements, financial statements, credit card statements, and invoices are featured throughout.

- Stock, bond, and mutual fund tables are taken from *The Wall Street Journal Online*.

STEP INTO THE REAL BUSINESS WORLD

Brechner's unique modular approach **breaks each chapter into separate learning components**, allowing you to customize the material and order of coverage to meet the specific learning needs of your students.

WEBASSIGN
From Cengage

ENHANCE YOUR LEARNING

Built by educators and very widely used, the WebAssign course management system includes components that provide the tools you need to master topics in your course efficiently. Features such as Read It, Watch It (videos by author George Bergeman), and Master It provide extra help if and when you need it.

A Proven Step-by-step Learning System Powers Learning

Each chapter is broken into discrete performance objectives. For each objective, the text guides students to mastery by way of a carefully designed learning system that includes these components:

DETERMINING RATE OF INCREASE OR DECREASE

In calculating the rate of increase or decrease of something, we use the same percentage formula concepts as before. Rate of change means percent change; therefore, the *rate* is the unknown. Once again we use the formula $R = P \div B$. Rate of change situations contain an original amount of something, which either increases or decreases to a new amount.

In solving these problems, the original amount is always the base. The amount of change is the portion. The unknown, which describes the percent change between the two amounts, is the rate.

$$\text{Rate of change (Rate)} = \frac{\text{Amount of change (Portion)}}{\text{Original amount (Base)}}$$

STEPS FOR DETERMINING THE RATE OF INCREASE OR DECREASE

STEP 1. Identify the original and the new amounts and find the *difference* between them.

STEP 2. Using the rate formula $R = P \div B$, substitute the difference from Step 1 for the portion and the original amount for the base.

STEP 3. Solve the equation for R. Remember, your answer will be in decimal form, which must be converted to a percent.

An **EXPLANATION** of the topic

A **STEP BOX** clearly describing the solution steps

An **EXAMPLE** with a complete step-by-step solution

A **TRY-IT EXERCISE** with solution so students can immediately test their understanding

EXAMPLE16 FINDING THE RATE OF CHANGE

Last year Iberia Furniture had a work force of 360 employees. This year there are 504 employees. What is the rate of change in the number of employees?

▶SOLUTIONSTRATEGY

The key to solving this problem is to properly identify the variables. The problem asks "what is the rate?"; therefore, the rate is the unknown. The original amount, 360 employees, is the base. The difference between the two amounts, $504 - 360 = 144$, is the portion. Now apply the rate formula.

$$R = \frac{P}{B} = \frac{144}{360} = .4 = 40\%$$

40% Increase in employees

▶TRYITEXERCISE 16

Solve the following problem for the rate of increase or decrease. Round to the nearest tenth of a percent when necessary.

When Mike Veteramo was promoted from supervisor to manager, he received a salary increase from $450 to $540 per week. What was the percent change in his salary?

CHECK YOUR ANSWER WITH THE SOLUTION ON PAGE 182.

Step into the Real Business World

Special features engage students and connect business math topics to issues and concerns encountered in everyday life as well as in business settings.

New Federal Debit Card – The U.S. Treasury now provides a debit card that people without traditional bank accounts can use to access federal benefits such as Social Security and disability payments.

Federal payments are credited to the cards each month, enabling users to make free withdrawals from ATMs in the government's Direct Express network.

In The Business World

Useful and interesting notes provide connections to the real business world. Many have useful information to help students manage their own personal finance situations.

Note that *markdown percent* calculations are an application of *rate of decrease*, covered in Chapter 6.

In the percentage formula, the markdown (portion) represents the amount of the decrease and the original selling price (base) represents the original amount.

Learning Tips

Helpful mathematical hints, shortcuts, and reminders enhance students' understanding of the chapter material.

Dollars and Sense

Opportunity cost is the sacrifice of benefits from the next-best alternative when you make a financial or economic decision. To fully evaluate how much a checking account with a required minimum balance costs, calculate the opportunity cost.

Consider a bank that requires an average monthly balance of $1,500. If you can earn 3% a year in interest on an investment maintaining this checking account means giving up $45 in potential interest income.

Business Profiles

Accompanying selected exercises, photos and brief business-related profiles provide perspective, historical data, and other information to connect problems to the real world.

Business Math Journal

Appearing every three chapters, these pages provide current news items, cartoons, famous business and inspirational quotes, career information, and many other interesting facts and figures related to business topics.

Dollars and Sense

This feature stimulates student curiosity with current news items and statistics related to chapter topics. "Dollars and Sense" provides students with numerous personal finance and business money tips.

Additional Features and Tools Further Prepare You for the Real World

END-OF-CHAPTER FEATURES

- A **Chapter Summary Chart** provides a comprehensive review of each performance objective. The chart emphasizes important chapter concepts, steps, formulas, and illustrative examples with worked-out solutions.

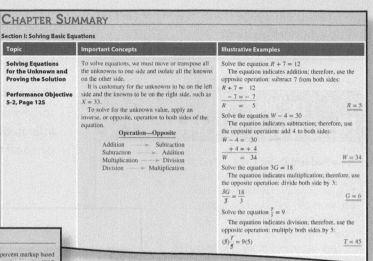

CHAPTER SUMMARY

Section I: Solving Basic Equations

Topic	Important Concepts	Illustrative Examples
Solving Equations for the Unknown and Proving the Solution **Performance Objective 5-2, Page 125**	To solve equations, we must move or transpose all the unknowns to one side and isolate all the knowns on the other side. 　It is customary for the unknowns to be on the left side and the knowns to be on the right side, such as $X = 33$. 　To solve for the unknown value, apply an inverse, or opposite, operation to both sides of the equation. 　　Operation—Opposite Addition → Subtraction Subtraction → Addition Multiplication → Division Division → Multiplication	Solve the equation $R + 7 = 12$ 　The equation indicates addition; therefore, use the opposite operation: subtract 7 from both sides: $R + 7 = 12$ $\underline{-7 = -7}$ $R = 5$　　$R = 5$ Solve the equation $W - 4 = 30$ 　The equation indicates subtraction; therefore, use the opposite operation: add 4 to both sides: $W - 4 = 30$ $\underline{+4 = +4}$ $W = 34$　　$W = 34$ Solve the equation $3G = 18$ 　The equation indicates multiplication; therefore, use the opposite operation: divide both side by 3: $\frac{3G}{3} = \frac{18}{3}$　　$G = 6$ Solve the equation $\frac{T}{5} = 9$ 　The equation indicates division; therefore, use the opposite operation: multiply both sides by 5: $(5)\frac{T}{5} = 9(5)$　　$T = 45$

CONCEPT REVIEW

1. The retailing equation states that the selling price is equal to the _____ plus the _____. (8-1)

   cost, markup

2. In business, expenses are separated into two major categories. The cost of _____ sold and _____ expenses. (8-1)

   goods, operating or overhead

3. There are two ways of expressing markup as a percent: based on _____ and based on _____. (8-2)

   cost, selling price

4. Write the formula for calculating the selling price when markup is based on cost. (8-3)

   Selling price = Cost(100% + Percent markup on cost)

5. To calculate cost, we divide the _____ price by 100% plus the percent markup based on cost. (8-4)

   selling

6. The percent markup based on selling price is equal to the _____ divided by the selling price. (8-5)

   markup

7. When markup is based on selling price, the _____ price is the base and represents _____ percent. (8-6)

9. To convert percent markup based on cost to percent markup based on selling price, we divide percent markup based on cost by 100% _____ the percent markup based on cost. (8-8)

   plus

10. To convert percent markup based on selling price to percent markup based on cost, we divide percent markup based on selling price by 100% _____ the percent markup based on selling price. (8-8)

    minus

11. A price reduction from the original selling price of merchandise is called a(n) _____. (8-9)

    markdown

12. Write the formula for calculating the sale price after a markdown. (8-10)

    Sale price = Original selling price(100% − MD%)

13. In calculating a series of markups and markdowns, each calculation is based on the previous _____ price. (8-11)

    selling

14. Products that have a certain shelf life and then no value at all, such as fruit, vegetables, flowers, and dairy products, are known as _____. (8-12)

    perishable goods

- **Concept Review** fill-in questions test students' comprehension of the basic concepts and important vocabulary of each chapter.

Also at the end of each chapter…

- An **Assessment Test** includes exercises with multiple parts that build on previous answers and previously-learned material to encourage critical thinking and problem-solving.

- A **Collaborative Learning Activity** provides practice working in teams while enhancing students' comprehension of the chapter topics and their relevance in real-world scenarios.

SUPPLEMENTAL TOOLS FOR STUDENTS

- **Jump Start Solutions** provide worked-out solutions to the first question in each new topic set in the section exercises.

- **Excel® Templates** corresponding to problems in the text are presented at three levels of difficulty.

- An **Excel® Guide and Workbook** helps students learn spreadsheet basics.

- **Author Videos** (new for this edition) by George Bergeman accompany each objective and walk students through detailed step-by-step solutions to sample problems.

- A **Financial Calculator Guide and Workbook** provides keystroke-by-keystroke instruction on using a business calculator.

Students access these tools by going to www.cengage.com/decisionsciences/brechner/cmbc/9e.

Acknowledgments

Contemporary Mathematics for Business and Consumers benefited from the valuable input of instructors throughout the country. We would like to especially thank those who responded to our questions about how they teach business math and those who reviewed various parts of the manuscript and/or allowed this book to be tested by their classes.

Reviewers:

Alton Amidon,
Pamlico Community College

Carol Baker,
Napa Valley
Community College

Sara Barritt,
Northeast Community College

Michael J. Batali,
Yakima Valley
Community College

Leon G. Bean,
International Business College
El Paso, Texas

Christine F. Belles,
Macomb Community College

Robert Bennett,
Delaware County
Community College

Ellen A. Benowitz,
Mercer Country
Community College

George H. Bernard,
Professor, Seminole
Community College

Tom Bilyeu,
Southwestern
Illinois College

Yvonne Block,
College of Lake County

Don Boyer,
Jefferson College

Cindy Brown,
South Plains College

Sylvia Brown,
Mountain Empire
Community College

Steven Bruenjes,
Dover Business College

Barry Bunn,
Professor, Business, Valencia
Community College

Celestino Caicoya,
Miami Dade Community
College Education

Natalie Card,
Utah Valley State College

Jesse Cecil,
College of the Siskiyou

Janet P. Ciccarelli,
Professor, Herkimer County
Community College

Milton Cohen,
Fairfax Community Adult
Education

Ron Cooley,
South Suburban College

F. Bruce Creech,
Sampson Community College

Sue Courtney,
Business Professor,
Kansas City,
Kansas Community College

Samantha Cox,
Wake Technical
Community College

Toby F. Deal,
Patrick Henry Community
College, Martinsville, VA

Frank DiFerdinando,
Hudson County
Community College

Mary Jo Dix,
Jamestown Business College

Elizabeth Domenico,
Gaston College

Gary M. Donnelly

J.D. Dulgeroff,
San Bernardino Valley
Community College

Donna N. Dunn,
Beaufort County
Community College

Michael E. Durkee,
San Diego Miramar
Community College

Acie B. Earl,
Black Hawk
Community College

Susan Emens,
Kent State University –
Trumbull Campus

Gregory G. Fallon,
College of St. Joseph in
Vermont

Marty Franklin,
Wilkes Community College

Robert S. Frye,
Polk State College

Rene Garcia,
Miami-Dade Community
College, Wolfson Campus

Patricia Gardner,
San Bernardino Valley College

Glen Gelderloos,
Grand Rapids
Community College

Cecil Green,
Riverside Community College

Stephen W. Griffin,
Tarrant County Junior College,
South Campus

James Grigsby,
Lake Sumter
Community College

Paul Grutsis,
San Bernardino Valley College

Julie Hall,
Napa Valley
Community College

Giselle Halpern,
El Camino Community College

Ronnie R. Hector,
Briarcliff College

John Heinsius,
Modesto Junior College

Brenda Henry,
McLennan
Community College

Jana Hosmer,
Blue Ridge
Community College

Jan Ivansek,
Lakeland
Community College

Diane Jacobson,
Ridley-Lowell Business &
Technical Institute

Ed Kavanaugh,
Schoolcraft College

Deanna R. Knight,
Daytona State College

Dr. Harry T. Kolendrianos,
Danville Community College,
Danville, VA

Sky Kong,
PRCC

Phil C. Kopriva,
San Francisco Community
College District

Jeffrey Kroll,
Assistant Professor,
Brazosport College

Joe D. DiCostanzo,
Johnson County
Community College

Stephen Ernest,
Baton Rouge School of
Computers

Carol Ferguson,
Rock Valley College

Mark Finger,
Madison Area
Technical College

Dennis Franklin,
Culinary Arts Institute

Rachael Freuche,
Indiana Business College

Rick Gallardo,
International Business College

Miriam Gateley,
Valencia Community
College

Cynthia Gerber,
Indiana Business College

Jeff Gordon,
San Joaquin Valley College

Carolyn Green,
Universal Business & Media
School

Bob Grenier,
Vatterott College

Ray Hale,
Rets Medical & Business
Institute

Michael Hlebik,
Erie Business School

Bill Holbrook,
Owensboro Junior College of
Business

Brenda Holmes,
Northwest Mississippi
Community College

John Hudson,
National Business College

Jared Jay,
American Commercial College

Joanne Kaufman,
Metro Business College

Patti Koluda,
Yakima Valley County College

Janice Lawrence,
Northwestern Business
College

Suzann Lewison,
Southwestern WI
Technical College

Marvin Mai,
Empire College

Jackie Marshall,
Ohio Business College

Faye Massey,
Northwest Mississippi
Community College

Cheryl McGahee,
Guilford Community College

Mary Jo McKinney,
American School of Business

Hugh McNiece,
Lincolnland County College

Rose Miller,
Milwaukee Area
Technical College

Charlene Mulleollan,
Dubois Business College

Jim Murray,
Western WI Technical College

Steve O'Rourke,
Newcastle Business School

Peggy Peterson,
Rasmussen College

Barbara Portzen,
Mid State Technical College

Edward Pratowski,
Dorsey Business School

Rose Ramirez,
MTL Business College of
Stockton

Bill Rleodarmer,
Haywood County College

Linda Rockwall,
Ridley Lowell Business &
Technical Institute

Steve Shaw,
Tidewater Tech

Susan Shaw,
Southwestern Business College

Chuck Sherryll,
Community College of Aurora

Forrest Simmons,
Portland Community College

Eileen Snyder,
Harrisburg Area
Community College

Adina Solomon,
Vatterott College

Walter Soroka,
Newcastle School of Trade

Teresa Stephenson,
Indianapolis Business
School

Mary Susa,
Mid-State Technical
College

Kermit Swanson,
Rasmussen College

Paula Terrones,
College of Office
Technology

Arthur Walter,
Suffolk Community College

Winston Wrenn,
Draughton Junior College

Gaylon Wright,
Angelina College

Sandra Young,
Business Institute of
Pennsylvania

Many thanks to the academic, business, and other professionals who have provided contributions and support for the development of this text and package over many years:

Nancy Aiello
Santiago Alan
Bob Albrecht
John Aldrich
John Anderson
Vince Arenas
Marcie Bader
Christine Balmori
Robert Barton
Charlie Beavin
Jessica Bergeman
Ed Blakemore
Joan Braverman

Martha Cavalaris
Gilbert S. Cohen
Patricia Conroy
Dave Cook
Ralph Covert
Nancy De La Vega
Elliott Denner
George DiOrio
John Dunham
Ivan Figueroa
Mario Font
Butch Gemin
John Godlewski

Abdul Hamza
Lionel Howard
Scott Isenberg
Al Kahn
Joseph Kreutle
Kimberly Lipscomb
Jaime Lopez
Marvin Mai
Jane Mangrum
Jim McHugh
Noemi McPherson
Sharon Meyer
Rolando Montoya

Joseph Moutran
Sylvia Ratner
Cheryl Robinson
Brian Rochlin
Michael Rohrer
Joyce Samuels
Howard Schoninger
Steven Steidel
Bill Taylor
Richard Waldman
Joseph Walzer
Kathryn Warren
Larry Zigler

Also, thanks to the corporate and government organizations that were used as examples and sources of information in preparing and developing this book:

7-Eleven	Dow Jones, Inc.,	New York Times	Toys "R" Us, Inc.
AAMCO	The Wall Street Journal	Nike	Transamerica Life Companies
Ace Hardware	eBay	Nissan	Transocean
Aetna	Federal Express	Office Depot	Travelocity.com
Amazon.com	General Motors/Saturn	Olive Garden	Tribune
AMR Corporation	Goodrich	On the Border	TruValue Hardware
Ann Taylor	Google	Panasonic	Tupperware
Apple	Harley-Davidson	Pizza Hut	U. S. Census Bureau
Arthur Andersen & Company	Home Depot	Popular Bank of Florida	U.S. Department of Commerce
AutoZone	Hotels.com	Radio Shack	U.S. Department of Housing
Bank of America	Insurance Information Institute	Red Lobster	and Urban Development
Baskin & Robbins	Internal Revenue Service	Reebok, Inc.	U.S. Government Printing
Best Buy	Jiffy Lube	Ryder	Office, Statistical Abstract of
Board of Governors, Federal	Kellogg	Sea Ray Boats	the United States
Reserve System	KFC	Sirius Satellite Radio	U.S. Postal Service
Brinker International	Kinko's	Smith Barney Shearson	U.S. Timber
Bureau of Labor Statistics	Kodak	Sony	U-Haul
CarMax	Long John Silver	Sprint/Nextel	USA Today
Center	Lowe's Home Improvement	Starbucks	Wall Street Journal
Chili's	Center	State of Florida, Department of	Wall Street Journal Online
Circuit City	Macaroni Grill	Revenue	Wal-Mart, Inc.
Citicorp Financial Services	Macy's	Taco Bell	Walt Disney Company
Dairy Queen	MasterCard International	Target	Wendy's
Darden Restaurants	McDonald's	Time, Inc., Fortune Magazine	West Marine
Dell	The Miami Herald	Town & Country	XM Satellite Radio
Domino's Pizza	Microsoft	Toyota Motors	Yum Brands

I would like to gratefully acknowledge and thank the editorial, production, and marketing teams at Cengage Learning for their insights and skillful support of the ninth edition. It has been a great pleasure working with them.

Special thanks to Aaron Arnsparger, Senior Product Manager; Brandon Foltz, Senior Learning Designer; Chris Walz, Senior Marketing Manager; Chris Doughman, Designer; Nancy Marchant, Associate Subject Matter Expert; and Jessica Galloway, Associate Program Manager (WebAssign). D. Jean Bora, Senior Content Manager, was my daily connection to Cengage, and I very much appreciate the care and speedy efficiency Jean provided throughout the entire development process.

Thanks to Thivya Nathan, Senior Executive (SPi Global) for her excellent support in the production phase of this text. Thanks also to Mike Gordon and Fernando Rodriquez for their creativity, business acumen, and wonderful research.

I wish to convey my love and thanks to my daughter, Jessy Bergeman, for her assistance with the development of the software components to accompany each of the past editions as well as her help with various aspects of the current edition of the text itself.

Bob Brechner worked tirelessly to develop the first six editions of this text, and he was both a good friend and an esteemed colleague. He is keenly missed, and I very much appreciate my good fortune in having had the opportunity to collaborate with him for more than sixteen years. I am also grateful to have the continuing support and friendship of Bob's wife, Shari Brechner, who has positively impacted this text from its very first edition.

Finally, I wish to express my love and gratitude to my wife, Clarissa. She has provided encouragement and support over many years, and I offer her my heartfelt thanks.

George Bergeman
November, 2018

About the Authors

Robert Brechner

Robert Brechner was Professor Emeritus, School of Business, at Miami Dade College. For 42 years he taught business math, principles of business, marketing, advertising, public relations, management, and personal finance. He was also Adjunct Professor at Florida Atlantic University, Boca Raton, International Fine Arts College, Miami, and Florida International University School of Journalism and Mass Communications.

In professional work outside the classroom, he consulted widely with industrial companies. In addition to authoring the first six editions of *Contemporary Mathematics*, Professor Brechner authored several other successful texts highlighting annuities, management, business math, and applied math.

Bob and his wife, Shari, were avid travelers and enjoyed a wide range of activities together and in the company of friends. In many ways, both professional and otherwise, Bob's legacy remains an enduring inspiration for his colleagues, his friends, and his students.

Photo by Shari Brechner

George Bergeman

George Bergeman's teaching career of over twenty-five years began at a small college in West Africa as a Peace Corps Volunteer and continued at Northern Virginia Community College, one of the largest multi-campus colleges in the country. Teaching awards included Faculty Member of the Year honors at his campus.

George is the author of numerous packages developed to provide targeted and effective support for instruction. His first package was a statistics software/workbook combination published in 1985, and since then he has developed a variety of software packages to support statistics, calculus, developmental math, and finite math including math of finance. Developing the software components formerly known as MathCue.Business for use with *Contemporary Mathematics for Business and Consumers* has been a focal point for George for more than eighteen years. During that time, he worked closely with Bob Brechner to develop and refine the package, and he coauthored the text beginning with the seventh edition.

Photo by Clarissa Bergeman

George lives with his wife, Clarissa, near Washington, D.C. Their daughter, Jessy, completed grad school in Colorado and lives in Denver after previously working in San Francisco, Boston, and Brazil. In his free time, George enjoys accompanying his wife and their young corgi, Simon, on various adventures and on training sessions in preparation for dog shows. Other hobbies include photography and videography, and these activities frequently intersect with dog training and dog shows. Along those lines, George and his wife produced a dog-sport training video which has been distributed throughout the United States and several other countries.

BRIEF CONTENTS

CONTENTS

CHAPTER 1   Whole Numbers

PERFORMANCE OBJECTIVES

Numbers are one of the primary tools used in business. The ability to read, comprehend, and manipulate numbers is an essential part of the everyday activity in today's complex business world. To be successful, business students should become competent and confident in dealing with numbers.

We will begin our study of business mathematics with whole numbers and their basic operations—addition, subtraction, multiplication, and division. The material in this chapter is based on the assumption that you have a basic working knowledge of these operations. Our goal is to review these fundamentals and build accuracy and speed. This arithmetic review will set the groundwork for our study of fractions, decimals, and percentages. Most business math applications involve calculations using these components.

1-1 READING AND WRITING WHOLE NUMBERS IN NUMERICAL AND WORD FORM

decimal number system A system using the 10 Hindu-Arabic symbols 0 through 9. In this place value system, the position of a digit to the left or right of the decimal point affects its value.

decimal point A dot written in a decimal number that separates the whole number part from the fractional part of the number.

whole numbers Any numbers 0 or greater that do not contain a decimal or fraction. Whole numbers are found to the left of the decimal point. Also known as an integer. For example, 6, 25, and 300 are whole numbers.

The number system most widely used in the world today is known as the Hindu-Arabic numeral system, or **decimal number system**. This system is far superior to any other for today's complex business calculations. It derives its name from the Latin words *decimus*, meaning 10th, and *decem*, meaning 10. The decimal system is based on 10s, with the starting point marked by a dot known as the **decimal point**. The decimal system uses the 10 familiar Hindu-Arabic symbols or digits:

$$0, 1, 2, 3, 4, 5, 6, 7, 8, 9$$

The major advantage of our decimal system over previous systems is that the position of a digit to the left or right of the decimal point affects its value. This enables us to write any number with only the 10 single-digit numbers, 0 through 9. For this reason, we have given names to the places or positions. In this chapter, we work with places to the left of the decimal point, **whole numbers**. The next two chapters are concerned with the places to the right of the decimal point, fractions, and decimals.

When whole numbers are written, a decimal point is understood to be located on the right of the number. For example, the number **27** is actually

27.

The decimal point is not displayed until we write a decimal number or dollars and cents, such as 27.25 inches or $27.25.

Pressmaster/Shutterstock.com

Skills you acquire in this course will be applied frequently in your roles as a consumer and a businessperson.

Exhibit 1-1 illustrates the first 15 places, and five groups, of the decimal number system. Note that our system is made up of groups of three places, separated by commas, each with its own name. Whole numbers start at the understood decimal point and increase in value from right to left. Each group contains the same three places: ones, tens, and hundreds. Note that each place increases by a factor of "times 10." The group names are units, thousands, millions, billions, and trillions.

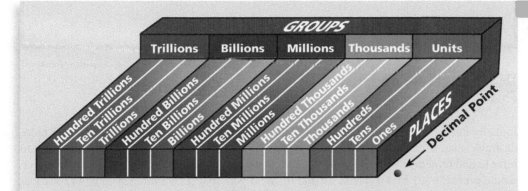

Whole Number Place Value Chart

STEPS FOR READING AND WRITING WHOLE NUMBERS

STEP 1. Beginning at the right side of the number, insert a comma after every three digits to mark the groups.

STEP 2. Beginning from left to right, name the digits and the groups. The units group and groups that have all zeros are not named.

STEP 3. When writing whole numbers in word form, the numbers from 21 to 99 are hyphenated, except for the decades (e.g., thirty). For example, 83 would be written as eighty-three.

Note: The word *and* should *not* be used in reading or writing whole numbers. It represents the decimal point and will be covered in Chapter 3.

Learning Tip

Whole numbers with four digits may be written with or without a comma. For example, 3,400 or 3400 are both correct.

EXAMPLE 1   READING AND WRITING WHOLE NUMBERS

Read and write the following whole numbers in numerical and word form.

a. 14296   b. 560

c. 2294857   d. 184910

e. 3004959001   f. 24000064

►SOLUTIONSTRATEGY

Following the steps above, we insert the commas to mark the groups, then read and write the numbers from left to right.

Number	Numerical Form	Word Form
a. 14296	14,296	fourteen thousand, two hundred ninety-six
b. 560	560	five hundred sixty
c. 2294857	2,294,857	two million, two hundred ninety-four thousand, eight hundred fifty-seven
d. 184910	184,910	one hundred eighty-four thousand, nine hundred ten
e. 3004959001	3,004,959,001	three billion, four million, nine hundred fifty-nine thousand, one
f. 24000064	24,000,064	twenty-four million, sixty-four

IN THE Business World

In text, large numbers, in the millions and greater, may be easier to read by writing the "zeros portion" in words. For example, 44,000,000,000,000 may be written as 44 trillion.

1-2   ROUNDING WHOLE NUMBERS TO A SPECIFIED PLACE VALUE

rounded numbers Numbers that are approximations or estimates of exact numbers. For example, 50 is the rounded number of the exact number 49.

estimate To calculate approximately the amount or value of something. The number 50 is an estimate of 49.

rounding all the way A process of rounding numbers to the first (i.e., the leftmost) digit. Used to prework a problem to an estimated answer. For example, 2,865 rounded all the way is 3,000.

In many business applications, the use of an approximation of an exact number may be more desirable than using the number itself. Approximations, or **rounded numbers**, are easier to refer to and remember. For example, if a grocery store carries 9,858 items on its shelves, you would probably say that it carries 10,000 items. If you drive 1,593 miles, you would say that the trip is 1,600 miles. Another rounding application in business involves money. If your company has profits of $1,302,201, you might refer to this exact amount by the rounded number $1,300,000. Money amounts are usually rounded to the nearest cent, although they could also be rounded to the nearest dollar.

Rounded numbers are frequently used to **estimate** an answer to a problem before that problem is worked. Estimation approximates the exact answer. By knowing an estimate of an answer in advance, you will be able to catch many math errors. When using estimation to prework a problem, you can generally round off to the first (i.e., the leftmost) digit, which is called **rounding all the way**.

Once you have rounded to the first digit, perform the indicated math procedure. This can often be done quickly and will give you a ballpark or general idea of the actual answer. In the example below, the estimated answer of 26,000 is a good indicator of the "reasonableness" of the actual answer.

Original Calculation	Estimated Solution (rounding all the way)	Actual Solution
19,549	20,000	19,549
+ 6,489	+ 6,000	+ 6,489
	26,000	26,038

If, for example, you had mistakenly added for a total of 23,038 instead of 26,038, your estimate would have immediately indicated that something was wrong.

STEPS FOR ROUNDING WHOLE NUMBERS TO A SPECIFIED PLACE VALUE

STEP 1. Determine the place to which the number is to be rounded.

STEP 2a. If the digit to the right of the place being rounded is 5 or more, increase the digit in that place by 1.

STEP 2b. If the digit to the right of the place being rounded is 4 or less, do not change the digit in the place being rounded.

STEP 3. Change all digits to the right of the place being rounded to zeros.

Dollars AND Sense

Pricey Diplomas

In the past five decades, college costs[1] have increased nearly tenfold at private schools and sixfold at public ones.

■ Private four-year
■ Public (in-state) four-year

1978–79
$4,610
$2,145

1988–89
$11,660
$4,455

1998–99
$20,462
$7,769

2008–09
$34,132
$14,333

2016–17
$45,370
$20,090

1. Figures include tuition, fees, and room and board and are not adjusted for inflation.
Source: *The College Board*

EXAMPLE 2 ROUNDING WHOLE NUMBERS

Round the following numbers to the indicated place.

a. 1,867 to tens
b. 760 to hundreds
c. 129,338 to thousands
d. 293,847 to hundred thousands
e. 97,078,838,576 to billions
f. 85,600,061 all the way

SOLUTIONSTRATEGY

Following the steps on page 4, locate the place to be rounded, use the digit to the right of that place to determine whether to round up or leave it as is, and change all digits to the right of the place being rounded to zeros.

		Place Indicated	Rounded Number
a.	1,867 to tens	1,867	1,870
b.	760 to hundreds	760	800
c.	129,338 to thousands	129,338	129,000
d.	293,847 to hundred thousands	293,847	300,000
e.	97,078,838,576 to billions	97,078,838,576	97,000,000,000
f.	85,600,061 all the way	85,600,061	90,000,000

TRYITEXERCISE 2

Round the following numbers to the indicated place.

a. 51,667 to hundreds
b. 23,441 to tens
c. 175,445,980 to ten thousands
d. 59,561 all the way
e. 14,657,000,138 to billions
f. 8,009,070,436 to ten millions

CHECK YOUR ANSWERS WITH THE SOLUTIONS ON PAGE 25.

REVIEW EXERCISES

1   SECTION I

Read and write the following whole numbers in numerical and word form.

	Number	Numerical Form	Word Form
1.	22938	22,938	Twenty-two thousand, nine hundred thirty-eight
2.	1573	_____	_____
3.	184	_____	_____
4.	984773	_____	_____
5.	2433590	_____	_____
6.	49081472	_____	_____

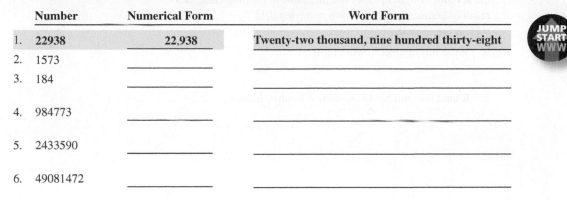

JUMP
START
WWW

Write the following whole numbers in numerical form.

| 7. One hundred eighty-three thousand, six hundred twenty-two | 183,622 |

8. Two million, forty-three thousand, twelve _____

9. According to Globo's G1 website, expenses in preparation for the 2014 World Cup in Brazil reached forty billion dollars. Write this number in numerical form.

_____

Match the following numbers in word form with the numbers in numerical form.

| 10. One hundred two thousand, four hundred seventy   __b__ | | a. 12,743 |

11. One hundred twelve thousand, seven hundred forty-three _____   b. 102,470

12. Twelve thousand, seven hundred forty-three _____   c. 11,270

13. Eleven thousand, two hundred seventy _____   d. 112,743

14. Write the word form: 790,324

Round the following numbers to the indicated place.

| 15. 1,757 to tens | 1,760 |

16. 32,475 to thousands _____

17. 812,461 to hundreds _____

18. 6,971,506 to hundred thousands _____

19. 25,812,922 to millions _____

20. 45,699 all the way _____

21. 1,325,669,226 to hundred millions _____

22. 23,755 all the way _____

23. According to the American Wind Energy Association, Texas has the highest operating wind capacity, 8,797 megawatts. Iowa is second with 3,053 megawatts capacity.

    a. Write each of these numbers in word form.

    b. Round each of these numbers to the nearest hundred.

24. According to the *Financial Times*, in a recent recession, outstanding consumer credit in the United States fell to $2,460,000,000,000— the seventh straight monthly decline. Most of the drop came as a result of consumers paying down revolving debt such as credit cards.

    a. Write this number in word form.

    b. Round this number to the nearest hundred billion.

iStock.com/MarsBars

BUSINESS DECISION: UP OR DOWN?

25. You are responsible for writing a monthly stockholders' report about your company. Your boss has given you the flexibility to round the numbers to tens, hundreds, thousands, and so on, or not at all, depending on which is most beneficial for the company's image. For each of the following monthly figures, make a rounding choice and explain your reasoning.

    a. 74,469—number of items manufactured   _____

    b. $244,833—your department's net sales for the month   _____

    c. 5,648—defective items manufactured   _____

    d. $649,341—total company profit   _____

    e. 149 new customers   _____

ADDITION AND SUBTRACTION OF WHOLE NUMBERS

1 **SECTION II**

Addition and subtraction are the most basic mathematical operations. They are used in almost all business calculations. In business, amounts of things or dollars are often combined or added to determine the total. Likewise, subtraction is frequently used to determine an amount of something after it has been reduced in quantity.

ADDING WHOLE NUMBERS AND VERIFYING YOUR ANSWERS

1-3

Addition is the mathematical process of computing sets of numbers to find their sum, or total. The numbers being added are known as **addends**, and the result or answer of the addition is known as the **sum**, **total**, or **amount**. The "+" symbol represents addition and is called the **plus sign**.

$$
\begin{array}{r}
1{,}932 \quad \text{addend} \\
2{,}928 \quad \text{addend} \\
+\ 6{,}857 \quad \text{addend} \\
\hline
11{,}717 \quad \text{total}
\end{array}
$$

addition The mathematical process of computing sets of numbers to find their sum, or total.

addends Any of a set of numbers being added in an addition problem. For example, 4 and 1 are the addends of the addition problem $4 + 1 = 5$.

sum, total, or amount The result or answer of an addition problem. The number 5 is the sum, or total, of $4 + 1 = 5$.

plus sign The symbol "+" represents addition.

STEPS FOR ADDING WHOLE NUMBERS

STEP 1. Write the whole numbers in columns so that you line up the place values—units, tens, hundreds, thousands, and so on.

STEP 2. Add the digits in each column, starting on the right with the units column.

STEP 3. When the total in a column is greater than nine, write the units digit and carry the tens digit to the top of the next column to the left.

iStock.com/Nikada

VERIFYING ADDITION

Generally, when adding the digits in each column, we add from top to bottom. An easy and commonly used method of verifying your addition is to add the numbers again, but this time from bottom to top. By adding the digits in the *reverse* order, you will reduce the chance of making the same error twice.

For illustrative purposes, addition verification will be rewritten in reverse. In actuality, you do not have to rewrite the numbers; just add them from bottom to top. As mentioned earlier, you will achieve speed and accuracy with practice.

Learning Tip

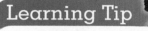

Once you become proficient at verifying addition, you can speed up your addition by recognizing and combining two numbers that add up to 10, such as $1 + 9$, $2 + 8$, $6 + 4$, and $5 + 5$. After you have mastered combining two numbers, try combining three numbers that add up to 10, such as $3 + 3 + 4$, $2 + 5 + 3$, and $4 + 4 + 2$.

B-A-C-O/Shutterstock.com

Addition	Verification
8	6
3	3
+ 6	+ 8
17	17

A WORD ABOUT WORD PROBLEMS

In business math, calculations are only a part of the story! Most importantly, business math requires the ability to (1) understand and analyze the facts of business situations, (2) determine what information is given and what is missing, (3) decide what strategy and procedure is required to solve for an answer, and (4) verify your answer. Business application word problems are an important part of each chapter's subject matter. As you progress through the course, your ability to analyze and solve these business situations will improve. Now start slowly and relax!

EXAMPLE3 ADDING WHOLE NUMBERS

Add the following sets of whole numbers. Verify your answers by adding in reverse.

a.   40,562
    29,381
 + 60,095

b. $2{,}293 + 121 + 7{,}706 + 20 + 57{,}293 + 4$

c. Galaxy Industries, a furniture manufacturing company, has 229 employees in the design and cutting department, 439 employees in the assembly department, and 360 employees in the finishing department. There are 57 warehouse workers, 23 salespeople, 4 bookkeepers, 12 secretaries, and 5 executives. How many people work for this company?

▶SOLUTIONSTRATEGY

a.

Step 1. Write the numbers in columns so that the place values line up. In this example, they are already lined up.

   40,562
   29,381
+ 60,095
  130,038 ◄

Verification:

  60,095
  29,381
+ 40,562
  130,038 ─

Step 2. Add the digits in each column, starting with the units column.

Units column: $2 + 1 + 5 = 8$ Enter the 8 under the units column.

Tens column: $6 + 8 + 9 = 23$ Enter the 3 under the tens column and carry the 2 to the hundreds column.

Hundreds column: $2 + 5 + 3 + 0 = 10$ Enter the 0 under the hundreds column and carry the 1 to the thousands column.

Thousands column: $1 + 0 + 9 + 0 = 10$ Enter the 0 under the thousands column and carry the 1 to the ten thousands column.

Ten thousands column: $1 + 4 + 2 + 6 = 13$ Enter the 3 under the ten thousands column and the 1 under the hundred thousands column.

b.

Addition	Verification
2,293	4
121	57,293
7,706	20
20	7,706
57,293	121
+ 4	+ 2,293
67,437 ◄────	──── 67,437

c.

Addition	Verification
229	5
439	12
360	4
57	23
23	57
4	360
12	439
+ 5	+ 229
1,129 ◄────	──── 1,129

▶TRYITEXERCISE 3

Add the following sets of whole numbers and verify your answers.

a.   39,481
       5,594
    + 11,029

b. 6,948 + 330 + 7,946 + 89 + 5,583,991 + 7 + 18,606

c. Anthony's Italian Restaurant served 183 meals on Monday, 228 meals on Tuesday, 281 meals on Wednesday, 545 meals on Thursday, and 438 meals on Friday. On the weekend, it served 1,157 meals. How many total meals were served that week?

CHECK YOUR ANSWERS WITH THE SOLUTIONS ON PAGE 25.

SUBTRACTING WHOLE NUMBERS AND VERIFYING YOUR ANSWERS

1-4

Subtraction is the mathematical computation of taking away, or deducting, an amount from a given number. Subtraction is the opposite of addition. The original or top number is the **minuend**; the amount we are subtracting from the original number is the **subtrahend**; and the answer is the **difference** (sometimes called the "remainder" although "difference" is preferred). The "−" symbol represents subtraction and is called the **minus sign**.

$$
\begin{array}{rl}
2{,}495 & \text{minuend} \\
-\quad 320 & \text{subtrahend} \\
\hline
2{,}175 & \text{difference}
\end{array}
$$

subtraction The mathematical process of taking away, or deducting, an amount from a given number.

minuend In subtraction, the original number. The amount from which another number, the subtrahend, is subtracted. For example, 5 is the minuend of the subtraction problem 5 − 1 = 4.

subtrahend The amount being taken or subtracted from the minuend. For example, 1 is the subtrahend of 5 − 1 = 4.

difference The number obtained when one number is subtracted from another. The answer or result of subtraction. For example, 4 is the difference of 5 − 1 = 4.

minus sign The symbol "−" represents subtraction.

STEPS FOR SUBTRACTING WHOLE NUMBERS

STEP 1. Write the whole numbers in columns so that the place values line up.

STEP 2. Starting with the units column, subtract the digits.

STEP 3. When a column cannot be subtracted, you must "borrow" a digit from the column to the left of the one you are working in.

VERIFYING SUBTRACTION

An easy and well-known method of verifying subtraction is to add the difference and the subtrahend. If you subtracted correctly, this total will equal the minuend.

Subtraction	Verification
200 minuend	150 difference
− 50 subtrahend	+ 50 subtrahend
150 difference	200 minuend

EXAMPLE4 SUBTRACTING WHOLE NUMBERS

Subtract the following whole numbers and verify your answers.

a. 4,968
   − 192

b. 189,440 − 1,347

c. On Monday morning, Appliance Depot had 165 microwave ovens in inventory. During the week, the store had a clearance sale and sold 71 of the ovens. How many ovens remain in stock for next week?

iStock.com/Nikada

Learning Tip

Because each place value increases by a factor of 10 as we move from right to left (units, tens, hundreds, etc.), when we borrow a digit, we can think of it as borrowing a 10.

B-A-C-O/Shutterstock.com

▶ SOLUTIONSTRATEGY

a.

$$
\begin{array}{r}
4,\cancel{9}68 \\
- \quad 192 \\
\hline
4,776
\end{array}
$$

Verification:

$$
\begin{array}{r}
4,776 \\
+ \quad 192 \\
\hline
4,968
\end{array}
$$

Write the numbers in columns so that the place values are lined up. In this problem, they are already lined up.

Starting with the units column, subtract the digits.

Units column: 8 − 2 = 6. Enter the 6 under the units column.

Tens column: 6 − 9 can't be subtracted, so we must borrow a digit, 10, from the hundreds column of the minuend. This reduces the 9 to an 8 and gives us a 10 to add to the 6, making it 16.

Now we can subtract 9 from 16 to get 7. Enter the 7 under the tens column.

Hundreds column: 8 − 1 = 7. Enter the 7 under the hundreds column.

Thousands column: This column has no subtrahend, so just bring down the 4 from the minuend to the answer line.

b. **Subtraction**	**Verification**		c. **Subtraction**	**Verification**
189,$\cancel{440}$	188,093		$\cancel{1}$65	94
− 1,347	+ 1,347		− 71	+ 71
188,093	189,440		94	165

▶ TRYITEXERCISE 4

Subtract the following whole numbers and verify your answers.

a. 98,117
    − 7,682

b. 12,395 − 5,589

c. Joe Montgomery has $4,589 in his checking account. If he writes a check for $344, how much will be left in the account?

CHECK YOUR ANSWERS WITH THE SOLUTIONS ON PAGE 25.

SECTION II **1** **REVIEW EXERCISES**

Add the following numbers.

1.	45	2.	548	3.	339	4.	2,359	5.	733
	27		229		1,236		8,511		401
	+ 19		4,600		5,981		+ 14,006		1,808
	91		+ 62,660		3,597				24,111
					+ 8,790				+ 10,595

6. 2,339 + 118 + 3,650 + 8,770 + 81 + 6 = _____

7. 12,554 + 22,606 + 11,460 + 20,005 + 4,303 = _____

Estimate the following by rounding each number all the way; then add to find the exact answer.

		Estimate	Rounded Estimate	Exact Answer
8.	288	300	6,800	6,694
	512	500		
	3,950	4,000		
	+ 1,944	+ 2,000		
	6,694	6,800		
9.	27,712		_____	_____
	5,281			
	+ 368			
10.	318,459		_____	_____
	+ 283,405			

11. City traffic engineers in Canmore are doing an intersection traffic survey. On Tuesday, a counter placed at the intersection of Armstrong Place and Three Sisters Blvd. registered the following counts: morning, 2,594; afternoon, 2,478; and evening, 1,863.
    a. Round each number to the nearest hundred and add to get an *estimate* of the traffic count for the day.

    b. What was the *exact* amount of traffic for the day?

12. A service station's record of gallons of gasoline sold per day over a 4-day period produced the figures below. What was the total number of gallons sold?
    717; 1,389; 1,226; 1,029

13. The following chart shows the April, May, and June sales figures by service categories for Pandora's Beauty Salon. Total each row to get the category totals. Total each column to get the monthly totals. Calculate the grand total for the 3-month period.

Pandora's Beauty Salon

Service Category	April	May	June	Category Totals
Cutting, Styling, Coloring	$13,515	$12,350	$14,920	_____
Manicure, Pedicure, Waxing	5,418	7,640	5,756	_____
Facials and Makeup	4,251	6,125	6,740	_____
Beauty Supplies	8,690	7,254	10,346	_____
Monthly Totals	_____	_____	_____	**Grand Total** _____

Service Sector According to the *CIA World Factbook*, service sector businesses such as beauty salons and dry cleaners account for 79.6% of the U.S. economy's gross domestic product. Other sectors include industrial at 19.2% and agriculture at 1.2%.

Romaset/Shutterstock.com

14. At Cherry Valley Farms, a farmer plants 350 acres of soybeans, 288 acres of corn, 590 acres of wheat, and 43 acres of assorted vegetables. In addition, the farm has 9 acres for grazing and 4 acres for the barnyard and farmhouse. What is the total acreage of the farm?

15. Service Masters Carpet Cleaners pays its sales staff a salary of $575 per month, plus commissions. Last month Alex Acosta earned commissions of $129, $216, $126, $353, and $228. What was Alex's total income for the month?

Subtract the following numbers.

16.	354	17.	5,596	18.	6,309 − 2,229	19.	339,002	20.	2,000,077
	− 48		− 967		6,309		− 60,911		− 87,801
	306				− 2,229				

21. $185 minus $47

22. 67,800 − 9,835

23. $127 less $33

24. Subtract 5,868 from 10,918

25. Subtract 8,906,000 from 12,396,700

26. The beginning inventory of the Designer Shoe Salon for August was 850 pairs of shoes. On the 9th, it received a shipment from the factory of 297 pairs. On the 23rd, another shipment of 188 pairs arrived. When inventory was taken at the end of the month, there were 754 pairs left. How many pairs of shoes were sold that month?

Dollars AND Sense

27. An electrician, Sparky Wilson, starts the day with 650 feet of wire on his truck. In the morning, he cuts off pieces 26, 78, 45, and 89 feet long. During lunch, he goes to an electrical supply warehouse and buys another 250 feet of wire. In the afternoon, he uses lengths of 75, 89, and 120 feet. How many feet of wire are still on the truck at the end of the day?

28. Use the U.S. Postal Service Mail Volume graph on the next page to answer the following questions.
   a. How many pieces were delivered in 2005 and 2006 combined?

   b. How many fewer pieces were delivered in 2009 than in 2007?

   c. Write the number of pieces of mail for 2008 in numerical form.

U.S. Postal Service Plunging Mail Volume

Rapidly Decreasing Postal Volume This chart illustrates the dramatic decrease in U.S. postal mail volume as e-mail and other electronic transfers of information became more widely used.
Source: *U.S. Postal Service*

29. Eileen Townsend is planting her flower beds. She initially bought 72 bedding plants at Home Depot.
   a. If she plants 29 in the front bed, how many plants remain unplanted?

   b. Eileen's remaining flower beds have room for 65 bedding plants. How many more plants must she buy to fill up the flower beds?

   c. How many total plants did she buy?

30. An Allied Vans Lines moving truck picks up loads of furniture weighing 5,500 pounds, 12,495 pounds, and 14,562 pounds. The truck weighs 11,480 pounds, and the driver weighs 188 pounds. If a bridge has a weight limit of 42,500 pounds, is the truck within the weight limit to cross the bridge?

BUSINESS DECISION: PERSONAL BALANCE SHEET

31. A *personal balance sheet* is the financial picture of how much "wealth" you have accumulated as of a certain date. It specifically lists your *assets* (i.e., what you own) and your *liabilities* (i.e., what you owe). Your current *net worth* is the difference between the assets and the liabilities.

> **Net worth = Assets − Liabilities**

   Tom and Carol Jackson have asked for your help in preparing a personal balance sheet. They have listed the following assets and liabilities: current value of home, $144,000; audio/video equipment, $1,340; automobiles, $17,500; personal property, $4,350; computer, $3,700; mutual funds, $26,700; 401(k) retirement plan, $53,680; jewelry, $4,800; certificates of deposit, $19,300; stock investments, $24,280; furniture and other household goods, $8,600; balance on Walmart and Sears charge accounts, $4,868; automobile loan balance, $8,840; home mortgage

balance, $106,770; Visa and MasterCard balances, $4,211; savings account balance, $3,700; Carol's night school tuition loan balance, $2,750; checking account balance, $1,385; signature loan balance, $6,350.

Use the data provided and the personal balance sheet on page 14 to calculate the following for the Jacksons.

a. Total assets

b. Total liabilities

c. Net worth

d. Explain the importance of the personal balance sheet. How often should this information be updated?

Just as with corporate statements, **personal financial statements** are an important indicator of your financial position. The balance sheet, income statement, and cash flow statement are most commonly used. When compared over a period of time, they tell a story of where you have been and where you are going financially.

PERSONAL BALANCE SHEET

ASSETS		LIABILITIES	
CURRENT ASSETS		**CURRENT LIABILITIES**	
Checking account	_____	Store charge accounts	_____
Savings account	_____	Credit card accounts	_____
Certificates of deposit	_____	Other current debt	_____
Other	_____	**Total Current Liabilities**	_____
Total Current Assets	_____	**LONG-TERM LIABILITIES**	
LONG-TERM ASSETS		Home mortgage	_____
Investments		Automobile loan	_____
Retirement plans	_____	Education loan	_____
Stocks	_____	Other loan	_____
Bonds	_____	Other loan	_____
Mutual funds	_____	**Total Long-Term Liabilities**	_____
Other	_____	**TOTAL LIABILITIES**	══════
Personal			
Home	_____		
Automobiles	_____		
Furniture	_____		
Personal property	_____		
Jewelry	_____		
Other	_____	**NET WORTH**	
Other	_____	Total Assets	_____
Total Long-Term Assets	_____	Total Liabilities	_____
TOTAL ASSETS	══════	**NET WORTH**	══════

SECTION III · 1 · MULTIPLICATION AND DIVISION OF WHOLE NUMBERS

Multiplication and division are the next two mathematical procedures used with whole numbers. Both are found in business as often as addition and subtraction. In reality, most business problems involve a combination of procedures. For example, invoices, which are a detailed list of goods and services sold by a company, require multiplication of items by the price per item and then addition to reach a total. From the total, discounts are frequently subtracted or transportation charges are added.

MULTIPLYING WHOLE NUMBERS AND VERIFYING YOUR ANSWERS

Multiplication of whole numbers is actually a shortcut method for addition. Let's see how this works. If a clothing store buys 12 pairs of jeans at $29 per pair, what is the total cost of the jeans? One way to solve this problem is to add $29 + $29 + . . ., 12 times. It's not hard to see how tedious this repeated addition becomes, especially with large numbers. By using multiplication, we get the answer in one step: $12 \times 29 = \$348$.

Multiplication is the combination of two whole numbers in which the number of times one is represented is determined by the value of the other. These two whole numbers are known as factors. The number being multiplied is the **multiplicand**, and the number by which the multiplicand is multiplied is the **multiplier**. The answer to a multiplication problem is the **product**. Intermediate answers are called partial products.

258	multiplicand or factor
$\times$ 43	multiplier or factor
774	partial product 1
10 32	partial product 2
11,094	product

In mathematics, the **times sign**—represented by the symbols "$\times$" or "$\cdot$" or "$(\ )$"—is used to indicate multiplication. For example, 12 times 18 can be expressed as

$$12 \times 18 \qquad 12 \cdot 18 \qquad (12)(18) \qquad 12(18)$$

Note: The raised symbol $\cdot$ is *not* a decimal point.

multiplication The combination of two numbers in which the number of times one is represented is determined by the value of the other.

multiplicand In multiplication, the number being multiplied. For example, 5 is the multiplicand of $5 \times 4 = 20$.

multiplier The number by which the multiplicand is multiplied. For example, 4 is the multiplier of $5 \times 4 = 20$.

product The answer or result of multiplication. The number 20 is the product of $5 \times 4 = 20$.

times sign The symbol "$\times$" represents multiplication. Also represented by a raised dot "$\cdot$" or parentheses "$(\ )$".

STEPS FOR MULTIPLYING WHOLE NUMBERS

STEP 1. Write the factors in columns so that the place values line up.

STEP 2. Multiply each digit of the multiplier, starting with units, times the multiplicand. Each will yield a partial product whose units digit appears under the corresponding digit of the multiplier.

STEP 3. Add the digits in each column of the partial products, starting on the right with the units column.

iStock.com/Nikada

MULTIPLICATION SHORTCUTS

The following shortcuts can be used to make multiplication easier and faster.

1. **When multiplying any number times 0**, the resulting product is *always* 0. For example,
$$573 \times 0 = 0 \qquad 0 \times 34 = 0 \qquad 1,254,779 \times 0 = 0$$

2. **When multiplying a number times 1, the product is that number itself.** For example,
$$1,844 \times 1 = 1,844 \qquad 500 \times 1 = 500 \qquad 1 \times 894 = 894$$

3. **When a number is multiplied by 10, 100, 1,000, 10,000, 100,000, and so on,** simply attach the zeros of the multiplier to the end of that number. For example,
$$792 \times 100 = 79,200 \qquad 9,345 \times 1,000 = 9,345,000$$

4. **When the multiplier has a 0 in one or more of its middle digits,** there is no need to write a whole line of zeros as a partial product. Simply place a 0 in the next partial product row directly below the 0 in the multiplier and go on to the next digit in the multiplier. The next partial product will start on the same row one place to the left of the 0 and directly below its corresponding digit in the multiplier. For example, consider 554 times 103.

Shortcut:	554	*Long way:*	554
	$\times$ 103		$\times$ 103
	1 662		1 662
	55 40		0 00
	57,062		55 4
			57,062

5. **When the multiplicand and/or the multiplier have zeros at the end,** multiply the two numbers without the zeros and attach that number of zeros to the product. For example,

$$130 \times 90 = 11,700$$

Note: $13 \times 9 = 117$, and we attach two zeros (and include a comma).

$$5,800 \times 3,400 = 19,720,000$$

Note: $58 \times 34 = 1,972$, and we attach four zeros (and adjust the commas).

VERIFYING MULTIPLICATION

To check your multiplication for accuracy, divide the product by the multiplier. If the multiplication was correct, this will yield the multiplicand. For example,

Multiplication	Verification	Multiplication	Verification
48		527	
× 7		× 18	
336	336 ÷ 7 = 48	4 216	
		5 27	
		9,486	9,486 ÷ 18 = 527

EXAMPLE 5 MULTIPLYING WHOLE NUMBERS

Multiply the following numbers and verify your answers by division.

a. 2,293   b. 59,300   c. 436 × 2,027   d. 877 × 1   e. 6,922 × 0
    ×   45   ×   180

f. Maytag Industries has a new aluminum parts molding machine that produces 85 parts per minute. How many parts can this machine produce in an hour? If a company has 15 of these machines and they run for 8 hours per day, what is the total output of parts per day?

SOLUTIONSTRATEGY

a.
```
    2,293
  ×    45
   11 465
   91 72
  103,185
```
This is a standard multiplication problem with two partial products. Always be sure to keep your columns lined up. The answer, 103,185, can be verified by division: $103,185 \div 45 = 2,293$

b.
```
     593
   ×  18
   4 744
   5 93
10,674 + "000" = 10,674,000
```
In this problem, we remove the three zeros, multiply, and then add back the zeros.
Verification: $10,674 \div 18 = 593$

c.
```
    2,027
  ×   436
   12 162
   60 81
   810 8
  883,772
```
This is another standard multiplication problem. Note that the larger number was made the multiplicand (top) and the smaller number became the multiplier. This makes the problem easier to work.
Verification: $883,772 \div 436 = 2,027$

d. $877 \times 1 = 877$ Remember, any number multiplied by 1 is that number.

e. $6,922 \times 0 = 0$ Remember, any number multiplied by 0 is 0.

f. 85 parts per minute × 60 minutes per hour = 5,100 parts per hour

   5,100 parts per hour × 15 machines = 76,500 parts per hour, all machines

   76,500 parts per hour × 8 hours per day = 612,000 parts per day, total output

Learning Tip

In multiplication, the factors are interchangeable. For example, 15 times 5 gives the same product as 5 times 15.

Multiplication is usually expressed with the larger factor on top as the multiplicand and the smaller factor placed under it as the multiplier.

B-A-C-O/Shutterstock.com

▶TRYITEXERCISE 5

Multiply the following numbers and verify your answers.

a.   8,203   b.   5,400   c.   3,370   d. 189 × 169
   × 508   × 250   ×4,002

e. Howard Martin, a plasterer, can finish 150 square feet of interior wall per hour. If he works 6 hours per day
   • How many square feet can he finish per day?
   • If a contractor hires four plasterers, how many feet can they finish in a 5-day week?

CHECK YOUR ANSWERS WITH THE SOLUTIONS ON PAGE 26.

DIVIDING WHOLE NUMBERS AND VERIFYING YOUR ANSWERS

1-6

Just as multiplication is a shortcut for repeated addition, division is a shortcut for repeated subtraction. Let's say while shopping you want to know how many $5 items you can purchase with $45. You could get the answer by finding out how many times 5 can be subtracted from 45. You would begin by subtracting 5 from 45 to get 40, then subtracting 5 from 40 to get 35, subtracting 5 from 35 to get 30, and so on, until you get 0. Quite tedious, but it does give you the answer, 9. By using division, we simply ask how many $5 are contained in $45. By dividing 45 by 5, we get the answer in one step ($45 \div 5 = 9$). Because division is the opposite of multiplication, we can verify our answer by multiplying 5 times 9 to get 45.

Division of whole numbers is the process of determining how many times one number is contained within another number. The number being divided is called the **dividend**, the number doing the dividing is called the **divisor**, and the answer is known as the **quotient**. When the divisor has only one digit, as in 100 divided by 5, it is called short division. When the divisor has more than one digit, as in 100 divided by 10, it is known as long division.

The "÷" symbol represents division and is known as the **division sign**. For example, $12 \div 4$ is read "12 divided by 4." Another way to show division is

$$\frac{12}{4}$$

This is also read as "12 divided by 4." To actually solve the division, we use the sign $\overline{)}$. The problem is then written as $4\overline{)12}$. As in addition, subtraction, and multiplication, proper alignment of the digits is very important.

$$\frac{\text{Dividend}}{\text{Divisor}} = \text{Quotient} \qquad \text{Divisor} \overline{)\text{Dividend}}^{\text{Quotient}}$$

When the divisor divides evenly into the dividend, it is known as even division. When the divisor does not divide evenly into the dividend, the answer then becomes a quotient plus a **remainder**. The remainder is the amount left over after the division is completed. This is known as uneven division. In this chapter, a remainder of 3, for example, is expressed as R 3. In Chapter 2, remainders will be expressed as fractions, and in Chapter 3, remainders will be expressed as decimals.

VERIFYING DIVISION

To verify even division, multiply the quotient by the divisor. If the problem was worked correctly, this will yield the dividend. To verify uneven division, multiply the quotient by the divisor and add the remainder to the product. If the problem was worked correctly, this will yield the dividend.

division The mathematical process of determining how many times one number is contained within another number.

dividend In division, the quantity being divided. For example, 20 is the dividend of $20 \div 5 = 4$.

divisor The quantity by which another quantity, the dividend, is being divided. The number doing the dividing. For example, 5 is the divisor of $20 \div 5 = 4$.

quotient The answer or result of division. The number 4 is the quotient of $20 \div 5 = 4$.

division sign The symbol "÷" represents division.

remainder In uneven division, the amount left over after the division is completed. For example, 2 is the remainder of $22 \div 5 = 4$, R 2.

EVEN DIVISION ILLUSTRATED

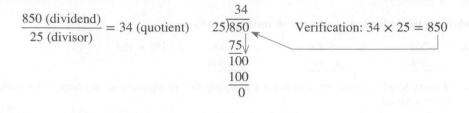

$$\frac{850 \text{ (dividend)}}{25 \text{ (divisor)}} = 34 \text{ (quotient)}$$

$$\begin{array}{r} 34 \\ 25\overline{)850} \\ 75 \\ \hline 100 \\ 100 \\ \hline 0 \end{array}$$

Verification: $34 \times 25 = 850$

UNEVEN DIVISION ILLUSTRATED

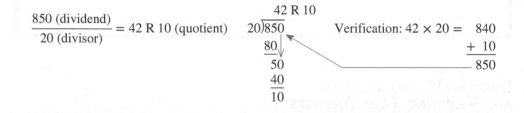

$$\frac{850 \text{ (dividend)}}{20 \text{ (divisor)}} = 42 \text{ R } 10 \text{ (quotient)}$$

$$\begin{array}{r} 42 \text{ R } 10 \\ 20\overline{)850} \\ 80 \\ \hline 50 \\ 40 \\ \hline 10 \end{array}$$

Verification: $42 \times 20 = \quad 840$
$$+ \quad 10$$
$$\overline{850}$$

STEPS FOR DIVIDING WHOLE NUMBERS

STEP 1. Determine the first group of digits in the dividend that the divisor will divide into at least once. Divide and place the partial quotient over the last digit in that group.

STEP 2. Multiply the partial quotient by the divisor. Place it under the first group of digits and subtract.

STEP 3. From the dividend, bring down the next digit after the first group of digits.

STEP 4. Repeat Steps 1, 2, and 3 until all of the digits in the dividend have been brought down.

iStock.com/Nikada

EXAMPLE6 DIVIDING WHOLE NUMBERS

Divide the following numbers and verify your answers.

a. $210 \div 7$ b. $185 \div 9$ c. $\dfrac{1,508}{6}$ d. $\dfrac{14,000}{3,500}$

e. On an assembly line, a packing machine uses rolls of rope containing 650 feet. How many 8-foot pieces can be cut from each roll?

▶SOLUTIONSTRATEGY

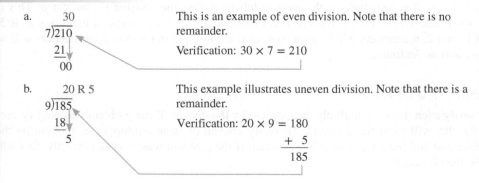

a.
$$\begin{array}{r} 30 \\ 7\overline{)210} \\ 21 \\ \hline 00 \end{array}$$

This is an example of even division. Note that there is no remainder.

Verification: $30 \times 7 = 210$

b.
$$\begin{array}{r} 20 \text{ R } 5 \\ 9\overline{)185} \\ 18 \\ \hline 5 \end{array}$$

This example illustrates uneven division. Note that there is a remainder.

Verification: $20 \times 9 = 180$
$$+ \quad 5$$
$$\overline{185}$$

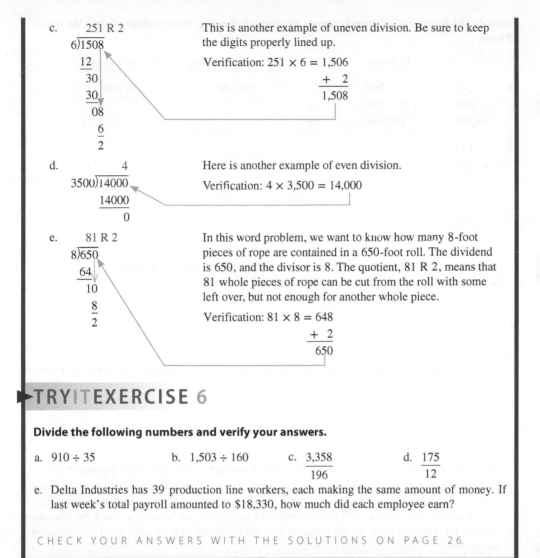

c.
$$\begin{array}{r} 251\text{ R }2 \\ 6\overline{)1508} \\ \underline{12} \\ 30 \\ \underline{30} \\ 08 \\ \underline{6} \\ 2 \end{array}$$

This is another example of uneven division. Be sure to keep the digits properly lined up.

Verification: 251 × 6 = 1,506
$$\begin{array}{r} +\ \ 2 \\ \hline 1,508 \end{array}$$

d.
$$\begin{array}{r} 4 \\ 3500\overline{)14000} \\ \underline{14000} \\ 0 \end{array}$$

Here is another example of even division.

Verification: 4 × 3,500 = 14,000

e.
$$\begin{array}{r} 81\text{ R }2 \\ 8\overline{)650} \\ \underline{64} \\ 10 \\ \underline{8} \\ 2 \end{array}$$

In this word problem, we want to know how many 8-foot pieces of rope are contained in a 650-foot roll. The dividend is 650, and the divisor is 8. The quotient, 81 R 2, means that 81 whole pieces of rope can be cut from the roll with some left over, but not enough for another whole piece.

Verification: 81 × 8 = 648
$$\begin{array}{r} +\ \ 2 \\ \hline 650 \end{array}$$

►TRYITEXERCISE 6

Divide the following numbers and verify your answers.

a. 910 ÷ 35

b. 1,503 ÷ 160

c. $\dfrac{3,358}{196}$

d. $\dfrac{175}{12}$

e. Delta Industries has 39 production line workers, each making the same amount of money. If last week's total payroll amounted to $18,330, how much did each employee earn?

CHECK YOUR ANSWERS WITH THE SOLUTIONS ON PAGE 26.

REVIEW EXERCISES

1 **SECTION III**

Multiply the following numbers and verify your answers.

1.
$$\begin{array}{r} 589 \\ \times\ \ 19 \\ \hline 11,191 \end{array}$$

2.
$$\begin{array}{r} 1,292 \\ \times\ \ 158 \end{array}$$

3.
$$\begin{array}{r} 327 \\ \times\ \ 900 \end{array}$$

4.
$$\begin{array}{r} 76,000 \\ \times\ \ 45 \end{array}$$

5.
$$\begin{array}{r} 56,969 \\ \times\ \ 1,000 \end{array}$$

JUMP START WWW

6. $4 by 501.

7. 6,702 × 82

8. What is 475 times 12?

Estimate the following by rounding each number all the way; then multiply to get the exact answer.

		Estimate	Rounded Estimate	Exact Answer
9.	202 × 490 98,980	200 × 500 100,000	100,000	98,980
10.	515 × 180		_____	_____
11.	17 × 11		_____	_____

12. Dazzling Designs made custom drapery for a client using 30 yards of material.
    a. At $5 per yard, what is the cost of the material?

    b. If the company received 4 more orders of the same size, how much material will be needed to fill the orders?

Xavier MARCHANT/Shutterstock.com

13. The U.S. Department of Transportation has a rule designed to reduce passenger discomfort and inconvenience. It states that airlines must let passengers off domestic flights when they have waited 3 hours without taking off. Airlines that don't comply can be fined up to $27,500 per passenger.
    If a Premium Airlines 767 aircraft with 254 passengers on board was fined the maximum penalty for waiting 4 hours on the tarmac at JFK before takeoff last Tuesday, what was the amount of the fine?

14. There are 34 stairs from bottom to top in each of 5 stairways in the football bleachers at Waycross Stadium. If each track team member is to run 4 complete sets up and down each stairway, how many stairs will be covered in a workout?

15. To earn extra money while attending college, you work as a cashier in a restaurant.
    a. Find the total bill for the following food order: 3 sirloin steak dinners at $12 each; 2 baked chicken specials at $7 each; 4 steak burger platters at $5 each; 2 extra salads at $2 each; 6 drinks at $1 each; and tax of $7.

    b. How much change will you give back if the check is paid with a $100 bill?

16. Bob Powers, a consulting electrical engineer, is offered two different jobs. Abbott Industries has a project that pays $52 per hour and will take 35 hours to complete. Micro Systems has a project that pays $44 per hour and will take 45 hours to complete. Which offer has a greater gross income and by how much?

Divide the following numbers.

17. **4,500 ÷ 35**

$$
\begin{array}{r}
128 \text{ R } 20 \\
35\overline{)4500} \\
\underline{35} \\
100 \\
\underline{70} \\
300 \\
\underline{280} \\
20
\end{array}
$$

18. 1,317 ÷ 16

19. $\dfrac{6,000}{25}$

20. $\dfrac{2,365}{43}$

Estimate the following by rounding each number to hundreds; then divide to get the exact answer.

	Estimate	Rounded Estimate	Exact Answer
21. 890 ÷ 295	$\dfrac{900}{300}$	3	3 R 5
22. 1,499 ÷ 580		_____	_____
23. 68,246 ÷ 112		_____	_____

24. Tip-Top Roofing has 50,640 square feet of roofing material on hand. If the average roof requires 8,440 square feet of material, how many roofs can be installed?

25. A calculator uses 8 circuit boards, each containing 450 parts. A company has 421,215 parts in stock.
    a. How many calculators can it manufacture?

    b. How many parts will be left over?

26. Eric Shotwell borrows $24,600 from the Mercantile Bank and Trust Co. The interest charge amounts to $8,664. What equal monthly payments must Eric make in order to pay back the loan, with interest, in 36 months?

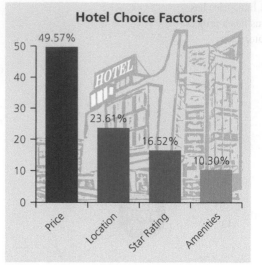

Hotels.com Survey When selecting a hotel, what do you consider most important?
Source: Hotels.com

27. A 16-person college basketball team is going to a tournament in Boston. As the team manager, you are trying to find the best price for hotel rooms. The Windsor Hotel is quoting a price of $108 for 2 people in a room and $10 for each extra person. The Royale Hotel is quoting a price of $94 for 2 people in a room and $15 for each extra person. If the maximum number of people allowed in a room is 4, which hotel would be more economical?

28. You have just purchased a 65-acre ranch for a price of $780 per acre. In addition, the house was valued at $125,000 and the equipment amounted to $22,300.

    a. What was the total price of your purchase?

    b. Since the owner was anxious to sell, he offered to finance the ranch for you with a no-interest mortgage loan. What would your monthly payments be to pay off the loan in 10 years?

    c. Besides the mortgage payment, you are required to make monthly property tax and insurance payments. If property tax is $3,000 per year and insurance is $2,400 per year, how much would these items add to your monthly expenses for the ranch?

29. As the IT manager for FastNet Enterprises, you have maintained records of the average prices you've paid for PCs over the years, and you are reviewing your records from the first 7 years during your company's initial growth phase. In year 1, you purchased 12 laptop computers and 15 desktop computers for your office staff. Using the graph Average PC Prices, answer the following:

    a. What was the total amount of the purchase for these computers in year 1?

    b. In year 7, you replaced all of the computers with new ones. What was the total amount of the purchase for these computers?

    c. In total, how much did you save in year 7 compared to year 1 because of falling computer prices?

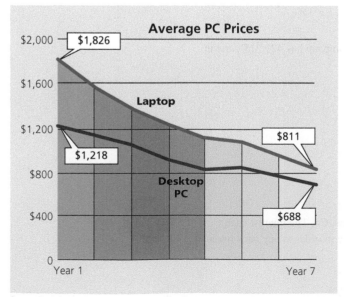

Source: By Julie Snider, USA TODAY

BUSINESS DECISION: ESTIMATING A TILE JOB

30. You are the owner of Decorama Flooring. Todd and Claudia have asked you to give them an estimate for tiling four rooms of their house. The living room is 15 feet × 23 feet, the dining room is 12 feet × 18 feet, the kitchen is 9 feet × 11 feet, and the study is 10 feet × 12 feet.

    a. How many square feet of tile are required for each room? (Multiply the length by the width.)

    b. What is the total number of square feet to be tiled?

    c. If the tile for the kitchen and study costs $4 per square foot and the tile for the living and dining rooms costs $3 per square foot, what is the total cost of the tile?

    d. If your company charges $2 per square foot for installation, what is the total cost of the tile job?

    e. If Todd and Claudia have saved $4,500 for the tile job, by how much are they over or under the amount needed?

CHAPTER SUMMARY

Section I: The Decimal Number System: Whole Numbers

Topic	Important Concepts	Illustrative Examples
Reading and Writing Whole Numbers in Numerical and Word Form **Performance Objective 1-1, Page 2**	1. Insert the commas every three digits to mark the groups, beginning at the right side of the number. 2. From left to right, name the digits and the units group. The units group and groups that have all zeros are not named. 3. When writing whole numbers in word form, the numbers from 21 to 99 are hyphenated, except for the decades (e.g., thirty). *Note:* The word *and* should not be used in reading or writing whole numbers.	Write each number in numerical and word form. The number 15538 takes on the numerical form 15,538 and is read, "fifteen thousand, five hundred thirty-eight." The number 22939643 takes on the numerical form 22,939,643 and is read, "twenty-two million, nine hundred thirty-nine thousand, six hundred forty-three." The number 1000022 takes on the numerical form 1,000,022 and is read, "one million, twenty-two."
Rounding Whole Numbers to a Specified Place Value **Performance Objective 1-2, Page 4**	1. Determine the place to which the number is to be rounded. 2a. If the digit to the right of the one being rounded is 5 or more, increase the digit in the place being rounded by 1. 2b. If the digit to the right of the one being rounded is 4 or less, do not change the digit in the place being rounded. 3. Change all digits to the right of the place being rounded to zeros.	Round as indicated. 1,449 to tens = 1,450 255 to hundreds = 300 345,391 to thousands = 345,000 68,658,200 to millions = 69,000,000 768,892 all the way = 800,000

Section II: Addition and Subtraction of Whole Numbers

Topic	Important Concepts	Illustrative Examples
Adding Whole Numbers and Verifying Your Answers **Performance Objective 1-3, Page 7**	1. Write the whole numbers in columns so that the place values line up. 2. Add the digits in each column, starting on the right with the units column. 3. When the total in a column is greater than 9, write the units digit and carry the tens digit to the top of the next column to the left. To verify addition, add the numbers in reverse, from bottom to top.	Add 2 11 1,931 addend 2,928 addend + 5,857 addend 10,716 sum ← Verification: 2 11 5,857 2,928 + 1,931 10,716
Subtracting Whole Numbers and Verifying Your Answers **Performance Objective 1-4, Page 9**	1. Write the whole numbers in columns so that the place values line up. 2. Starting with the units column, subtract the digits. 3. When a column cannot be subtracted, borrow a digit from the column to the left of the one you are working in. To verify subtraction, add the difference and the subtrahend; this should equal the minuend.	Subtract 34,557 minuend ← − 6,224 subtrahend 28,333 difference Verification: 28,333 + 6,224 34,557

Section III: Multiplication and Division of Whole Numbers

Topic	Important Concepts	Illustrative Examples
Multiplying Whole Numbers and Verifying Your Answers **Performance Objective 1-5, Page 15**	1. Write the multiplication factors in columns so that the place values are lined up. 2. Multiply each digit of the multiplier, starting with units, times the multiplicand. Each will yield a partial product whose units digit appears under the corresponding digit of the multiplier. 3. Add the digits in each column of the partial products, starting on the right, with the units column. To verify multiplication, divide the product by the multiplier. If the multiplication is correct, it should yield the multiplicand.	Multiply 258×43 $\begin{array}{r} 258 \text{ multiplicand or factor} \\ \times \quad 43 \text{ multiplier or factor} \\ \hline 774 \text{ partial product 1} \\ 10\,32 \text{ partial product 2} \\ \hline 11{,}094 \text{ product} \end{array}$ Verification: $$\frac{11{,}094}{43} = 258$$
Dividing Whole Numbers and Verifying Your Answers **Performance Objective 1-6, Page 17**	1. The number being divided is the dividend. The number by which we are dividing is the divisor. The answer is known as the quotient. $$\frac{\text{Quotient}}{\text{Divisor)Dividend}}$$ 2. If the divisor does not divide evenly into the dividend, the quotient will have a remainder. To verify division, multiply the divisor by the quotient and add the remainder. If the division is correct, it will yield the dividend.	Divide 650 by 27 $650 \div 27 = \dfrac{650}{27} = 27\overline{)650}$ $\begin{array}{r} 24 \text{ R } 2 \\ \hline 54 \\ \hline 110 \\ 108 \\ \hline 2 \end{array}$ Verification: $27 \times 24 = 648 + 2 = 650$

TRY IT: EXERCISE SOLUTIONS FOR CHAPTER 1

	Numerical Form	Word Form
1a.	49,588	Forty-nine thousand, five hundred eighty-eight
1b.	804	Eight hundred four
1c.	1,928,837	One million, nine hundred twenty-eight thousand, eight hundred thirty-seven
1d.	900,015	Nine hundred thousand, fifteen
1e.	6,847,365,911	Six billion, eight hundred forty-seven million, three hundred sixty-five thousand, nine hundred eleven
1f.	2,000,300,007	Two billion, three hundred thousand, seven

2a. 51,700   **2b.** 23,440   **2c.** 175,450,000   **2d.** 60,000   **2e.** 15,000,000,000   **2f.** 8,010,000,000

3a.
$\begin{array}{r} 39{,}481 \\ 5{,}594 \\ +\,11{,}029 \\ \hline 56{,}104 \end{array}$
  Verify:
$\begin{array}{r} 11{,}029 \\ 5{,}594 \\ +\,39{,}481 \\ \hline 56{,}104 \end{array}$

3b.
$\begin{array}{r} 6{,}948 \\ 330 \\ 7{,}946 \\ 89 \\ 5{,}583{,}991 \\ 7 \\ +\,18{,}606 \\ \hline 5{,}617{,}917 \end{array}$
  Verify:
$\begin{array}{r} 18{,}606 \\ 7 \\ 5{,}583{,}991 \\ 89 \\ 7{,}946 \\ 330 \\ +\,6{,}948 \\ \hline 5{,}617{,}917 \end{array}$

3c.
$\begin{array}{r} 183 \\ 228 \\ 281 \\ 545 \\ 438 \\ +\,1{,}157 \\ \hline 2{,}832 \text{ Meals} \end{array}$
  Verify:
$\begin{array}{r} 1{,}157 \\ 438 \\ 545 \\ 281 \\ 228 \\ +\,183 \\ \hline 2{,}832 \text{ Meals} \end{array}$

4a.
$\begin{array}{r} 98{,}117 \\ -\,7{,}682 \\ \hline 90{,}435 \end{array}$
  Verify:
$\begin{array}{r} 90{,}435 \\ +\,7{,}682 \\ \hline 98{,}117 \end{array}$

4b.
$\begin{array}{r} 12{,}395 \\ -\,5{,}589 \\ \hline 6{,}806 \end{array}$
  Verify:
$\begin{array}{r} 6{,}806 \\ +\,5{,}589 \\ \hline 12{,}395 \end{array}$

4c.
$\begin{array}{r} \$4{,}589 \\ -\,344 \\ \hline \$4{,}245 \text{ Left in account} \end{array}$
  Verify:
$\begin{array}{r} \$4{,}245 \\ +\,344 \\ \hline \$4{,}589 \end{array}$

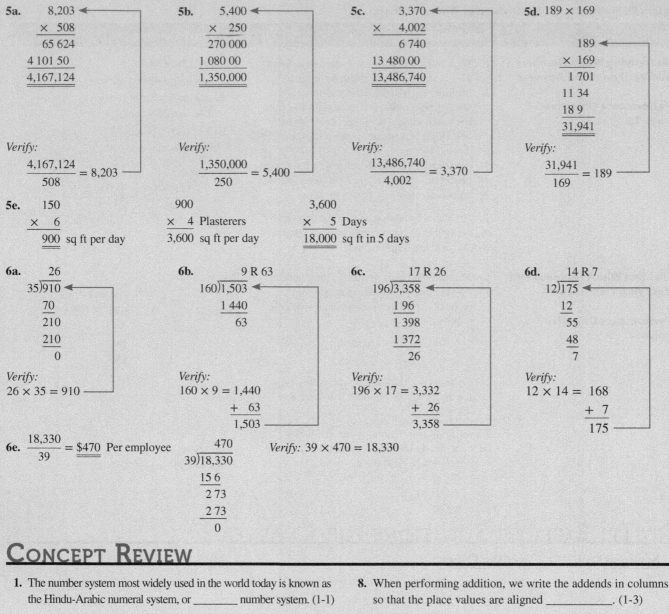

5a.
$$
\begin{array}{r}
8{,}203 \\
\times\ 508 \\
\hline
65\ 624 \\
4\ 101\ 50 \\
\hline
4{,}167{,}124
\end{array}
$$

Verify:
$$\frac{4{,}167{,}124}{508} = 8{,}203$$

5b.
$$
\begin{array}{r}
5{,}400 \\
\times\ 250 \\
\hline
270\ 000 \\
1\ 080\ 00 \\
\hline
1{,}350{,}000
\end{array}
$$

Verify:
$$\frac{1{,}350{,}000}{250} = 5{,}400$$

5c.
$$
\begin{array}{r}
3{,}370 \\
\times\ 4{,}002 \\
\hline
6\ 740 \\
13\ 480\ 00 \\
\hline
13{,}486{,}740
\end{array}
$$

Verify:
$$\frac{13{,}486{,}740}{4{,}002} = 3{,}370$$

5d. 189×169

$$
\begin{array}{r}
189 \\
\times\ 169 \\
\hline
1\ 701 \\
11\ 34 \\
18\ 9 \\
\hline
31{,}941
\end{array}
$$

Verify:
$$\frac{31{,}941}{169} = 189$$

5e.
$$
\begin{array}{r}
150 \\
\times\ 6 \\
\hline
900
\end{array}
\ \text{sq ft per day}
$$

$$
\begin{array}{r}
900 \\
\times\ 4 \\
\hline
3{,}600
\end{array}
\ \text{Plasterers}
\quad
\text{sq ft per day}
$$

$$
\begin{array}{r}
3{,}600 \\
\times\ 5 \\
\hline
18{,}000
\end{array}
\ \text{Days}
\quad
\text{sq ft in 5 days}
$$

6a.
$$
\begin{array}{r}
26 \\
35\overline{)910} \\
70 \\
\hline
210 \\
210 \\
\hline
0
\end{array}
$$

Verify:
$$26 \times 35 = 910$$

6b.
$$
\begin{array}{r}
9\ R\ 63 \\
160\overline{)1{,}503} \\
1\ 440 \\
\hline
63
\end{array}
$$

Verify:
$$160 \times 9 = 1{,}440$$
$$+\ 63$$
$$1{,}503$$

6c.
$$
\begin{array}{r}
17\ R\ 26 \\
196\overline{)3{,}358} \\
1\ 96 \\
\hline
1\ 398 \\
1\ 372 \\
\hline
26
\end{array}
$$

Verify:
$$196 \times 17 = 3{,}332$$
$$+\ 26$$
$$3{,}358$$

6d.
$$
\begin{array}{r}
14\ R\ 7 \\
12\overline{)175} \\
12 \\
\hline
55 \\
48 \\
\hline
7
\end{array}
$$

Verify:
$$12 \times 14 =\ 168$$
$$+\ 7$$
$$175$$

6e. $\dfrac{18{,}330}{39} = \$470$ Per employee

$$
\begin{array}{r}
470 \\
39\overline{)18{,}330} \\
15\ 6 \\
\hline
2\ 73 \\
2\ 73 \\
\hline
0
\end{array}
$$

Verify: $39 \times 470 = 18{,}330$

Concept Review

1. The number system most widely used in the world today is known as the Hindu-Arabic numeral system, or _____ number system. (1-1)

2. Our number system utilizes the 10 Hindu-Arabic symbols _____ through _____ to write any number. (1-1)

3. The set of numbers 1, 2, 3, 4, . . . are known as _____ numbers. (1-1)

4. On the place value chart, whole numbers appear to the _____ of the decimal point. (1-1)

5. A(n) _____ number is an approximation or estimate of an exact number. (1-2)

6. Rounding all the way is a process of rounding numbers to the _____ digit. (1-2)

7. In addition, the numbers being added are known as _____; the answer is known as the _____. (1-3)

8. When performing addition, we write the addends in columns so that the place values are aligned _____. (1-3)

9. The mathematical process of taking away, or deducting, an amount from a given number is known as _____. (1-4)

10. In subtraction, when a column cannot be subtracted, we must _____ a digit from the column to the left. (1-4)

11. In multiplication, the product of any number and 0 is _____. (1-5)

12. In multiplication, the product of any number and _____ is the number itself. (1-5)

13. The amount left over after division is completed is known as the _____. (1-6)

14. Show four ways to express 15 divided by 5. (1-6)

Assessment Test

CHAPTER 1

Read and write the following whole numbers in numerical and word form.

Number	Numerical Form	Word Form

1. 200049 _____ _____

2. 52308411 _____ _____

Write the following whole numbers in numerical form.

3. Three hundred sixteen thousand, two hundred twenty-nine

4. Four million, five hundred sixty thousand

Round the following numbers to the indicated place.

5. 18,334 to hundreds

6. 450,191 all the way

7. 256,733 to ten thousands

Perform the indicated operation for the following.

8.
```
  1,860
  2,391
    133
+ 1,009
```

9.
```
  927
− 828
```

10.
```
    207
 ×  106
```

11. $42\overline{)1876}$

12.
```
  3,505
×   290
```

13.
```
   6,800
     919
     201
+ 14,338
```

14. $150,000 \div 188$

15. $1,205 − 491$

16. The following chart shows the number of meals served at the Gourmet Diner last week. Use addition and subtraction to fill in the blank spaces. What is the week's grand total?

Gourmet Diner

	Monday	Tuesday	Wednesday	Thursday	Friday	Saturday		Total Units
Breakfast	82	___	68	57	72	92		427
Lunch	29	69	61	___	82	75		___
Dinner	96	103	71	108	112	159		___
Daily Totals	___	___	___	223	___	___	**Grand Total**	___

17. You are the bookkeeper for the Gourmet Diner in Exercise 16. If breakfasts average $6 each, lunches average $9 each, and dinners average $13 each, calculate the total dollar sales for last week.

Although the peak years for diners have long since passed, many diners still exist and other restaurants have taken the inspiration from the original diners.

18. The stadium parking lot at Fairview College contained 5,949 cars last Saturday for the homecoming football game.

    a. If there are 3 entrances to the lot, what was the average number of cars that came through each entrance?

    b. If, on average, each car brought 4 people and 2,560 people walked to the stadium from the dormitories and fraternity houses, how many people attended the game?

EXCEL 1

19. Camp Minnewonka, a summer camp in the Rocky Mountains, has budgeted $85,500 for a new fleet of sailboats. The boat selected is a deluxe model costing $4,500.

    a. How many boats can be purchased by the camp?

    b. If, instead, a standard model was chosen costing $3,420, how many boats could be purchased?

20. Facebook reported that for one 3-month period, approximately 2.1 billion photos were uploaded to their site each week. That averages to about 3,500 photographs per second!

    a. At that rate, how many photographs are uploaded per hour?

    b. Write the number of photographs per hour in word form.

21. You are in charge of organizing the annual stockholders' meeting and luncheon for your company, Tundra Industries, Inc. The meal costs $13 per person, entertainment costs $2,100, facility rental is $880, invitations and annual report printing costs are $2,636, and other expenses come to $1,629. If 315 stockholders plan to attend,

    a. What is the total cost of the luncheon?

    b. What is the cost per stockholder?

facebook

Facebook helps you connect and share with the people in your life.

Facebook Facebook's company information indicates that it is now available in more than 100 languages. Approximately 80% of their monthly active users are outside the United States and Canada.

Tom K Photo/Shutterstock.com

22. A study tracking the history of home-schooling found that 2,040,000 students were home-schooled at the end of the study compared with 850,000 students when the study began. How many more students were home-schooled at the end of the study compared to the number at the study's beginning?

23. Katie Jergens had $868 in her checking account on April 1. During the month, she wrote checks for $15, $123, $88, $276, and $34. She also deposited $45, $190 and $436. What is the balance in her checking account at the end of April?

CHAPTER
1

24. A banana nut bread recipe calls for 2 cups of flour. If 4 cups of flour weigh a pound, how many recipes can be made from a 5-pound bag of flour?

25. Brian Hickman bought 2,000 shares of stock at $62 per share. Six months later he sold the 2,000 shares at $87 per share. If the total stockbroker's commission was $740, how much profit did he make on this transaction?

26. The Canmore Mining Company produces 40 tons of ore in an 8-hour shift. The mine operates continuously—3 shifts per day, 7 days per week. How many tons of ore can be extracted in 6 weeks?

27. Last week the *More Joy,* a commercial fishing boat in Alaska, brought in 360 pounds of salmon, 225 pounds of halibut, and 570 pounds of cod. At the dock, the catch was sold to Pacific Seafood Wholesalers. The salmon brought $3 per pound; the halibut, $4 per pound; and the cod, $5 per pound. If fuel and crew expenses amounted to $1,644, how much profit did Captain Bob make on this trip?

Courtesy of Bob Brechner

Alaskan Fishing Boats
According to the Alaska Department of Fish & Game, Alaska supports one of the most productive commercial fishing economies in the world, with more than 9,600 licensed vessels as well as 20,500 licensed crewmembers.

Alaskan fishermen typically receive well over $1 billion for their catch, while the value of Alaskan seafood sold at first wholesale easily tops $2 billion per year.

28. The Iberia Corporation purchased a new warehouse for $165,000. After a down payment of $45,600, the balance was paid in equal monthly payments, with no interest.
a. If the loan was paid off in 2 years, how much were the monthly payments?

b. If the loan was paid off in 5 years, how much *less* were the monthly payments?

29. A flatbed railroad car weighs 150 tons empty and 420 tons loaded with 18 equal-weight trailers. How many tons does each trailer weigh?

30. The Spring Creek Police Department has been asked to provide protection support for a visiting politician. If it has to provide 2 officers at the airport for motorcycle escort, 7 officers for intersection control along the planned route of travel, and 14 officers at the high school auditorium during the speech,

a. How many officers are to be assigned to the protection detail?

b. If each officer is to be paid $75 extra for this duty, what is the total officer payroll for the protection detail?

31. The following ad for Tire King shows the original and sale prices of certain tires. If 2 tires of each size are to be bought, what will be the total amount saved by purchasing at the sale prices rather than at the original prices?

Tire Size	Original Price	Sale Price
14 in.	$36	$32
15 in.	$40	$34

32. John Rock has narrowed down his selection of a new cell phone to two models with similar features. Model 800 is plug-compatible with his existing car charger and remote earbud/ microphone and will cost $140. There is a $35 mail-in rebate for the Model 800. His other choice is the Model 300, which is not plug-compatible with his existing accessories. The price of the Model 300 is $89, and it has a $20 mail-in rebate. But if he buys the Model 300, he will also have to buy the car charger for $30 and an earbud/microphone for $23.

a. All considered, which model would be the least expensive choice? By how much?

b. For either cell phone choice, the monthly charge will be $34 per month with a $5 rebate if fewer than 250 minutes are used during the month. Government fees and taxes will be $9, the access fee is $7, and the Internet connection charge is $15. Based on last year's usage, John estimates that he will use fewer than 250 minutes in May, June, August, and October. If John's service starts on January 1, how much will he spend in the next year on cell phone services?

BUSINESS DECISION: CIRQUE DU SOLEIL—ACROBATIC MAGIC

33. As a professional event planner, you have been hired to put together a family reunion at a local performance of Cirque du Soleil. There will be 25 adults, 30 children, and 15 senior citizens attending the reunion.

   a. Assuming a ticket budget of $6,500, use the price schedule below to determine the *best* ticket level available for the reunion without going over the budget.

Ticket Prices

Ticket Level	Adult	Child	Senior
1—Premium	$125	$88	$115
2—Standard	$95	$66	$85
3—Budget	$85	$59	$76

   b. In addition to the tickets, each person is expected to average $8 in food costs and $29 in bus transportation charges. Your service fee is $250. Calculate the total cost of the reunion.

Cirque du Soleil Cirque du Soleil (French for "Circus of the Sun," in English pronounced Serk-doo-Solay) is a Canadian entertainment company, self-described as a "dramatic mix of circus arts and street entertainment." Starting with 20 street performers and 73 employees in 1984, Cirque du Soleil today employs more than 4,000 people from 40 different countries.

Since 1984, Cirque shows have visited more than 200 cities around the world. Nearly 200 million people have seen at least one Cirque du Soleil show.

COLLABORATIVE LEARNING ACTIVITY

Using Math in Business

1. As a team, discuss and list the ways that math is used in the following types of business. Report your findings to the class.

   a. Supermarket
   b. Car dealership
   c. Beauty salon
   d. Dog-walking service
   e. Restaurant
   f. Additional team choice _____

CHAPTER 2 Fractions

PERFORMANCE OBJECTIVES

UNDERSTANDING AND WORKING WITH FRACTIONS

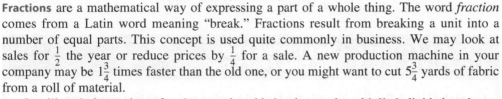

2 SECTION I

Fractions are a mathematical way of expressing a part of a whole thing. The word *fraction* comes from a Latin word meaning "break." Fractions result from breaking a unit into a number of equal parts. This concept is used quite commonly in business. We may look at sales for $\frac{1}{2}$ the year or reduce prices by $\frac{1}{4}$ for a sale. A new production machine in your company may be $1\frac{3}{4}$ times faster than the old one, or you might want to cut $5\frac{3}{4}$ yards of fabric from a roll of material.

Just like whole numbers, fractions can be added, subtracted, multiplied, divided, and even combined with whole numbers. This chapter introduces you to the various types of fractions and shows you how they are used in the business world.

fractions A mathematical way of expressing a part of a whole thing. For example, $\frac{1}{4}$ is a fraction expressing one part out of a total of four parts.

DISTINGUISHING AMONG THE VARIOUS TYPES OF FRACTIONS

2-1

Technically, fractions express the relationship between two numbers set up as division. The **numerator** is the number on the top of the fraction. It represents the dividend in the division. The **denominator** is the bottom number of the fraction. It represents the divisor. The numerator and the denominator are separated by a horizontal or slanted line, known as the **division line**. This line means "divided by." For example, the fraction 2/3 or $\frac{2}{3}$, read as "two-thirds," means 2 divided by 3, or 2 ÷ 3.

$$\frac{\text{Numerator}}{\text{Denominator}} \quad \frac{2}{3}$$

Remember, fractions express parts of a whole unit. The unit may be dollars, feet, ounces, or anything else. The denominator describes how many total parts are in the unit. The numerator represents how many of the total parts we are describing or referring to. For example, an apple pie (the whole unit) is divided into eight slices (total equal parts, denominator). As a fraction, the whole pie would be represented as $\frac{8}{8}$. If five of the slices were eaten (parts referred to, numerator), what fraction represents the part that was eaten? The answer would be the fraction $\frac{5}{8}$, read "five-eighths." Because five slices were eaten out of a total of eight, three slices, or $\frac{3}{8}$, of the pie is left.

numerator The number on top of the division line of a fraction. It represents the dividend in the division. In the fraction $\frac{1}{4}$, 1 is the numerator.

denominator The number on the bottom of the division line of a fraction. It represents the divisor in the division. In the fraction $\frac{1}{4}$, 4 is the denominator.

division line The horizontal or slanted line separating the numerator from the denominator. The symbol representing "divided by" in a fraction. In the fraction $\frac{1}{4}$, the line between the 1 and the 4 is the division line.

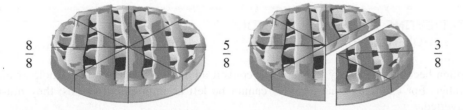

$$\frac{8}{8} \qquad \frac{5}{8} \qquad \frac{3}{8}$$

Fractions such as $\frac{3}{8}$ and $\frac{5}{8}$, in which the numerator is smaller than the denominator, represent less than a whole unit and are known as **common** or **proper fractions**. Some examples of proper fractions are

$$\frac{3}{16} \text{ three-sixteenths} \qquad \frac{1}{4} \text{ one-fourth} \qquad \frac{9}{32} \text{ nine-thirty-seconds}$$

When a fraction's denominator is equal to or less than the numerator, it represents one whole unit or more and is known as an **improper fraction**. Some examples of improper fractions are

$$\frac{9}{9} \text{ nine-ninths} \qquad \frac{15}{11} \text{ fifteen-elevenths} \qquad \frac{19}{7} \text{ nineteen-sevenths}$$

common or proper fractions Fractions in which the numerator is less than the denominator. Represent less than a whole unit. The fraction $\frac{1}{4}$ is a common or proper fraction.

improper fraction A fraction in which the denominator is equal to or less than the numerator. Represents one whole unit or more. The fraction $\frac{4}{1}$ is an improper fraction.

mixed number A number that combines a whole number with a proper fraction. The fraction $10\frac{1}{4}$ is a mixed number.

A number that combines a whole number with a proper fraction is known as a **mixed number**. Some examples of mixed numbers are

$$3\frac{1}{8} \text{ three and one-eighth} \qquad 7\frac{11}{16} \text{ seven and eleven-sixteenths}$$

$$46\frac{51}{60} \text{ forty-six and fifty-one-sixtieths}$$

EXAMPLE 1 IDENTIFYING AND WRITING FRACTIONS

For each of the following, identify the type of fraction and write it in word form.

a. $\dfrac{45}{16}$ b. $14\dfrac{2}{5}$ c. $\dfrac{11}{12}$

SOLUTION STRATEGY

a. $\dfrac{45}{16}$ This is an improper fraction because the denominator, 16, is less than the numerator, 45. In word form, we say "forty-five-sixteenths." It could also be read as "45 divided by 16" or "45 over 16."

b. $14\dfrac{2}{5}$ This is a mixed number because it combines the whole number 14 with the fraction $\dfrac{2}{5}$. In word form, this is read "fourteen and two-fifths."

c. $\dfrac{11}{12}$ This is a common or proper fraction because the numerator, 11, is less than the denominator, 12. This fraction is read "eleven-twelfths." It could also be read "11 over 12" or "11 divided by 12."

TRY IT EXERCISE 1

For each of the following, identify the type of fraction and write it in word form.

a. $76\dfrac{3}{4}$ b. $\dfrac{3}{5}$ c. $\dfrac{18}{18}$ d. $\dfrac{33}{8}$

CHECK YOUR ANSWERS WITH THE SOLUTIONS ON PAGE 61.

Learning Tip

A **complex fraction** is one in which the numerator, the denominator, or both are fractions.

Examples: $\dfrac{\frac{2}{3}}{\frac{9}{6}}, \dfrac{\frac{7}{8}}{\frac{3}{4}}, \dfrac{\frac{7}{8}}{\frac{1}{4}}$

Can you simplify them?

(Answers: $\frac{1}{9}, 12, 3\frac{1}{2}$)

2-2 CONVERTING IMPROPER FRACTIONS TO WHOLE OR MIXED NUMBERS

It often becomes necessary to change or convert an improper fraction to a whole or mixed number. For example, final answers cannot be left as improper fractions; they must be converted.

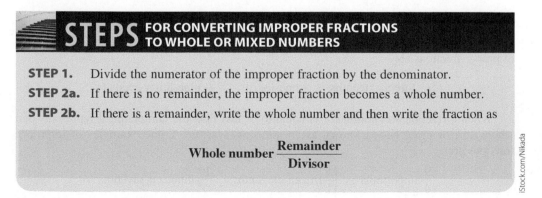

STEPS FOR CONVERTING IMPROPER FRACTIONS TO WHOLE OR MIXED NUMBERS

STEP 1. Divide the numerator of the improper fraction by the denominator.

STEP 2a. If there is no remainder, the improper fraction becomes a whole number.

STEP 2b. If there is a remainder, write the whole number and then write the fraction as

$$\text{Whole number} \frac{\text{Remainder}}{\text{Divisor}}$$

EXAMPLE2 CONVERTING FRACTIONS

Convert the following improper fractions to whole or mixed numbers.

a. $\dfrac{30}{5}$ b. $\dfrac{9}{2}$

►SOLUTIONSTRATEGY

a. $\dfrac{30}{5} = \underline{6}$ When we divide the numerator, 30, by the denominator, 5, we get the whole number 6. There is no remainder.

b. $\dfrac{9}{2} = 2\overline{)9} = \underline{4\dfrac{1}{2}}$ This improper fraction divides 4 times with a remainder of 1; therefore, it will become a mixed number. In this case, the 4 is the whole number. The remainder, 1, becomes the numerator of the new fraction; the divisor, 2, becomes the denominator.

►TRYITEXERCISE 2

Convert the following improper fractions to whole or mixed numbers.

a. $\dfrac{8}{3}$ b. $\dfrac{25}{4}$ c. $\dfrac{39}{3}$

CHECK YOUR ANSWERS WITH THE SOLUTIONS ON PAGE 61.

CONVERTING MIXED NUMBERS TO IMPROPER FRACTIONS

2-3

STEPS FOR CONVERTING A MIXED NUMBER TO AN IMPROPER FRACTION

STEP 1. Multiply the denominator by the whole number.

STEP 2. Add the numerator to the product from Step 1.

STEP 3. Place the total from Step 2 as the "new" numerator.

STEP 4. Place the original denominator as the "new" denominator.

EXAMPLE3 CONVERTING FRACTIONS

Convert the following mixed numbers to improper fractions.

a. $5\dfrac{2}{3}$ b. $9\dfrac{5}{6}$

►SOLUTIONSTRATEGY

a. $5\dfrac{2}{3} = \dfrac{17}{3}$ In this example, we multiply the denominator, 3, by the whole number, 5, and add the numerator, 2, to get 17 ($3 \times 5 + 2 = 17$). We then place the 17 over the original denominator, 3.

b. $9\dfrac{5}{6} = \dfrac{59}{6}$ In this example, we multiply the denominator, 6, by the whole number, 9, and add the numerator, 5, to get 59 ($6 \times 9 + 5 = 59$). We then place the 59 over the original denominator, 6.

IN THE Business World

Certain calculators have a fraction key, $a\frac{b}{c}$, that allows you to enter fractions. For example, $\frac{2}{3}$ would be entered as [2] [$a\frac{b}{c}$] [3] and would appear as 2 ⌐ 3.

The mixed fraction $25\frac{2}{3}$ would be entered as [25] [$a\frac{b}{c}$] [2] [$a\frac{b}{c}$] [3] and would appear as 25 ⌐2⌐ 3.

Fraction calculators express answers in fractional notation and are a handy tool for measuring materials without having to convert fractions to decimals. They are particularly useful in the construction, medical, and food industries.

iStock.com/Nikada

rguest/Shutterstock.com

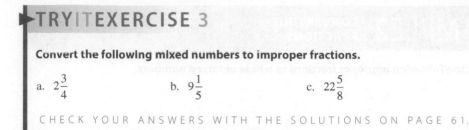

▶TRYITEXERCISE 3

Convert the following mixed numbers to improper fractions.

a. $2\frac{3}{4}$ b. $9\frac{1}{5}$ c. $22\frac{5}{8}$

CHECK YOUR ANSWERS WITH THE SOLUTIONS ON PAGE 61.

2-4 REDUCING FRACTIONS TO LOWEST TERMS

Reducing a fraction means finding whole numbers, called common divisors or common factors, that divide evenly into both the numerator and denominator of the fraction. For example, the fraction $\frac{24}{48}$ can be reduced to $\frac{12}{24}$ by the common divisor 2. The new fraction, $\frac{12}{24}$, can be further reduced to $\frac{4}{8}$ by the common divisor 3 and to $\frac{1}{2}$ by the common divisor 4. When a fraction has been reduced to the point where there are no common divisors left, other than 1, it is said to be **reduced to lowest terms**.

The largest number that is a common divisor of a fraction is known as the **greatest common divisor**. It reduces the fraction to lowest terms in one step. In the example of $\frac{24}{48}$ above, we could have used 24, the greatest common divisor, to reduce the fraction to $\frac{1}{2}$.

reduced to lowest terms The process of having divided whole numbers, known as common divisors or common factors, into both the numerator and denominator of a fraction. Used for expressing fractions as final answers. For example, $\frac{5}{20}$ is reduced to $\frac{1}{4}$ by the common divisor 5.

greatest common divisor The largest number that is a common divisor of a fraction. Used to reduce a fraction to lowest terms in one step. For example, 5 is the greatest common divisor of $\frac{5}{20}$.

A. REDUCING FRACTIONS BY INSPECTION

Reducing fractions by inspection or observation is often a trial-and-error procedure. Sometimes a fraction's common divisors are obvious; other times they are more difficult to determine. The following rules of divisibility may be helpful:

RULES OF DIVISIBILITY

A Number Is Divisible by	Conditions
2	If the last digit is 0, 2, 4, 6, or 8.
3	If the sum of the digits is divisible by 3.
4	If the last two digits are divisible by 4.
5	If the last digit is 0 or 5.
6	If the number is divisible by 2 and 3 or if it is even and the sum of the digits is divisible by 3.
8	If the last three digits are divisible by 8.
9	If the sum of the digits is divisible by 9.
10	If the last digit is 0.

Construction workers must accurately measure and calculate various lengths of building materials by using fractions.

EXAMPLE4 REDUCING FRACTIONS TO LOWEST TERMS USING INSPECTION

Use observation and the rules of divisibility to reduce $\frac{48}{54}$ to lowest terms.

▶SOLUTIONSTRATEGY

$\frac{48}{54} = \frac{48 \div 2}{54 \div 2} = \frac{24}{27}$ Because the last digit of the numerator is 8 and the last digit of the denominator is 4, they are both divisible by 2.

$\frac{24}{27} = \frac{24 \div 3}{27 \div 3} = \frac{8}{9}$ Because the sum of the digits of the numerator, 2 + 4, and the denominator, 2 + 7, are both divisible by 3, the fraction is divisible by 3.

$\frac{48}{54} = \frac{8}{9}$ Because no numbers other than 1 divide evenly into the new fraction $\frac{8}{9}$, it is now reduced to lowest terms.

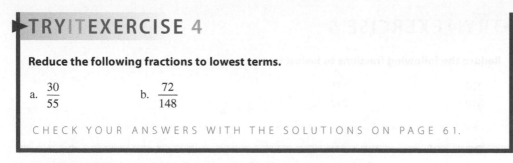

▶TRYITEXERCISE 4

Reduce the following fractions to lowest terms.

a. $\dfrac{30}{55}$ b. $\dfrac{72}{148}$

CHECK YOUR ANSWERS WITH THE SOLUTIONS ON PAGE 61.

B. REDUCING FRACTIONS BY USING THE GREATEST COMMON DIVISOR

A good method for reducing a fraction to lowest terms is to divide the numerator and the denominator by the greatest common divisor because this accomplishes the task in one step. When the greatest common divisor is not obvious to you, use the following steps to determine it:

STEPS FOR DETERMINING THE GREATEST COMMON DIVISOR OF A FRACTION

STEP 1. Divide the numerator of the fraction into the denominator.

STEP 2. Examine the remainder.

- If it is 0, stop. The divisor is the greatest common divisor.
- If it is 1, stop. The fraction cannot be reduced and is therefore in lowest terms.
- If it is another number, divide the remainder into the divisor.

STEP 3. Repeat Step 2 as needed.

EXAMPLE5 REDUCING FRACTIONS TO LOWEST TERMS USING THE GREATEST COMMON DIVISOR METHOD

Reduce the fraction $\dfrac{63}{213}$ by finding the greatest common divisor.

▶SOLUTIONSTRATEGY

$$\begin{array}{r} 3 \\ 63\overline{)231} \\ \underline{189} \\ 42 \end{array}$$

Divide the numerator, 63, into the denominator, 231. This leaves a remainder of 42.

$$\begin{array}{r} 1 \\ 42\overline{)63} \\ \underline{42} \\ 21 \end{array}$$

Next, divide the remainder, 42, into the previous divisor, 63. This leaves a remainder of 21.

$$\begin{array}{r} 2 \\ 21\overline{)42} \\ \underline{42} \\ 0 \end{array}$$

Then divide the remainder, 21, into the previous divisor, 42. Because this leaves a remainder of 0, the last divisor, 21, is the greatest common divisor of the original fraction.

$$\dfrac{63 \div 21}{231 \div 21} = \dfrac{3}{11}$$

By dividing both the numerator and the denominator by the greatest common divisor, 21, we get the fraction, $\frac{3}{11}$, which is the original fraction reduced to lowest terms.

► TRYITEXERCISE 5

Reduce the following fractions to lowest terms.

a. $\dfrac{270}{810}$ b. $\dfrac{175}{232}$

CHECK YOUR ANSWERS WITH THE SOLUTIONS ON PAGE 61.

2-5   RAISING FRACTIONS TO HIGHER TERMS

raise to higher terms The process of multiplying the numerator and denominator of a fraction by a common multiple. Sometimes needed in addition and subtraction of fractions. For example, $\frac{5}{20}$ is the fraction $\frac{1}{4}$ raised to higher terms, twentieths, by the common multiple 5.

common multiple Whole number used to raise a fraction to higher terms. The common multiple 5 raises the fraction $\frac{1}{4}$ to $\frac{5}{20}$.

Raising a fraction to higher terms is a procedure sometimes needed in addition and subtraction. It is the opposite of reducing fractions to lower terms. In reducing, we used common divisors; in raising fractions, we use common multiples. To **raise to higher terms**, simply multiply the numerator and denominator of a fraction by a **common multiple**.

For example, if we want to raise the numerator and denominator of the fraction $\frac{3}{4}$ by factors of 7, multiply the numerator and the denominator by 7. This procedure raises the fraction to $\frac{21}{28}$.

$$\frac{3 \times 7}{4 \times 7} = \frac{21}{28}$$

It is important to remember that the value of the fraction has not changed by raising it; we have simply divided the "whole" into more parts.

STEPS   FOR RAISING A FRACTION TO A NEW DENOMINATOR

STEP 1.   Divide the original denominator into the new denominator. The resulting quotient is the common multiple that raises the fraction.

STEP 2.   Multiply the numerator and the denominator of the original fraction by the common multiple.

EXAMPLE 6   RAISING FRACTIONS TO HIGHER TERMS

Raise the following fractions to higher terms as indicated.

a. $\dfrac{2}{3}$ to fifteenths   b. $\dfrac{3}{5}$ to fortieths

► SOLUTIONSTRATEGY

a. $\dfrac{2}{3} = \dfrac{?}{15}$ In this example, we are raising the fraction $\frac{2}{3}$ to the denominator 15.

$15 \div 3 = 5$ Divide the original denominator, 3, into 15. This yields the common multiple 5.

$\dfrac{2 \times 5}{3 \times 5} = \dfrac{10}{15}$ Now multiply both the numerator and the denominator by the common multiple, 5.

b. $\dfrac{3}{5} = \dfrac{?}{40}$ Here the indicated denominator is 40.

$40 \div 5 = 8$ Dividing 5 into 40, we get the common multiple 8.

$\dfrac{3 \times 8}{5 \times 8} = \dfrac{24}{40}$ Now raise the fraction by multiplying the numerator, 3, and the denominator, 5, by 8.

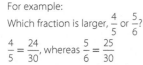

Learning Tip

Sometimes it is difficult to determine which of two fractions is the larger or smaller number. By converting them to **like fractions** (same denominator), the answer will become evident.

For example:
Which fraction is larger, $\frac{4}{5}$ or $\frac{5}{6}$?

$\frac{4}{5} = \frac{24}{30}$, whereas $\frac{5}{6} = \frac{25}{30}$

Therefore, $\frac{5}{6}$ is larger than $\frac{4}{5}$.

►TRYITEXERCISE 6

Raise the following fractions to higher terms as indicated.

a. $\dfrac{7}{8}$ to sixty-fourths   b. $\dfrac{3}{7}$ to thirty-fifths

CHECK YOUR ANSWERS WITH THE SOLUTIONS ON PAGE 61.

REVIEW EXERCISES

2 SECTION I

For each of the following, identify the type of fraction and write it in word form.

1. $23\dfrac{4}{5}$ 2. $\dfrac{12}{12}$ 3. $\dfrac{15}{9}$ 4. $\dfrac{7}{16}$ 5. $2\dfrac{1}{8}$

$\underline{\underline{\text{Mixed}}}$
Twenty-three
and four-fifths

Convert the following improper fractions to whole or mixed numbers.

6. $\dfrac{26}{8} = 3\dfrac{2}{8} = 3\underline{\underline{\dfrac{1}{4}}}$ 7. $\dfrac{20}{6}$ 8. $\dfrac{92}{16}$

9. $\dfrac{27}{7}$ 10. $\dfrac{88}{11}$ •   11. $\dfrac{33}{31}$

Convert the following mixed numbers to improper fractions.

12. $6\dfrac{1}{2} = \underline{\underline{\dfrac{13}{2}}}$ 13. $11\dfrac{4}{5}$ 14. $25\dfrac{2}{3}$
$(6 \times 2 + 1 = 13)$

15. $12\dfrac{3}{8}$ 16. $1\dfrac{5}{9}$ 17. $250\dfrac{1}{4}$

Use inspection or the greatest common divisor to reduce the following fractions to lowest terms.

18. $\dfrac{21}{35}$ 19. $\dfrac{9}{12}$ 20. $\dfrac{18}{48}$ 21. $\dfrac{216}{920}$

$\dfrac{21 \div 7}{35 \div 7} = \underline{\underline{\dfrac{3}{5}}}$

22. $\dfrac{24}{40}$ 23. $\dfrac{14}{112}$ 24. $\dfrac{9}{42}$ 25. $\dfrac{95}{325}$

26. $\dfrac{8}{23}$ 27. $\dfrac{78}{96}$ 28. $\dfrac{30}{150}$ 29. $\dfrac{85}{306}$

Raise the following fractions to higher terms as indicated.

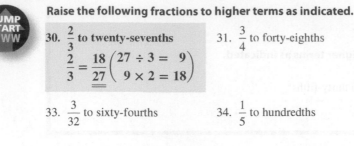

30. $\dfrac{2}{3}$ to twenty-sevenths

$$\dfrac{2}{3} = \dfrac{18}{27} \left(\begin{array}{l} 27 \div 3 = 9 \\ 9 \times 2 = 18 \end{array} \right)$$

31. $\dfrac{3}{4}$ to forty-eighths

32. $\dfrac{7}{20}$ to eightieths

33. $\dfrac{3}{32}$ to sixty-fourths

34. $\dfrac{1}{5}$ to hundredths

35. $\dfrac{3}{7}$ to ninety-eighths

36. $\dfrac{3}{5} = \dfrac{}{25}$

37. $\dfrac{5}{8} = \dfrac{}{64}$

38. $\dfrac{5}{6} = \dfrac{}{360}$

39. $\dfrac{9}{13} = \dfrac{}{182}$

40. What fraction represents the laptops in this group of computers?

41. What fraction represents the screwdrivers in this group of tools?

42. A wedding cake was cut into 40 slices. If 24 of the slices were eaten, what fraction represents the eaten portion of the cake? Reduce your answer to lowest terms.

43. Jasmine Marley's swimming pool holds 16,000 gallons of water, and her spa holds 2,000 gallons of water. Of all the water in the pool and spa,
    a. What fraction is the spa water?

    b. What fraction is the pool water?

44. You work in the tool department at The Home Depot. Your manager asks you to set up a point-of-purchase display for a set of 10 wrenches that are on sale this week. He asks you to arrange them in order from smallest to largest on the display board. When you open the box, you find the following sizes in inches: $\dfrac{9}{32}, \dfrac{5}{8}, \dfrac{5}{16}, \dfrac{1}{2}, \dfrac{3}{16}, \dfrac{3}{4}, \dfrac{7}{8}, \dfrac{5}{32}, \dfrac{1}{4}, \dfrac{3}{8}$.
    a. Rearrange the wrenches by size from smallest to largest.

    b. Next your manager tells you that the sale will be "1/3 off" the regular price of $57 and has asked you to calculate the sale price to be printed on the sign.

Courtesy of Bob Brechner

The Home Depot is the largest home improvement chain in the world with approximately 2,250 stores in the United States, Puerto Rico, Canada, Mexico, and China.

Lowe's is number two with about 1,650 stores.

c. After the sale is over, your manager asks you for the sales figures on the wrench promotion. If 150 sets were sold that week, what amount of revenue will you report?

d. If $6,000 in sales was expected, what reduced fraction represents sales attained?

BUSINESS DECISION: EVALUATING THE QUESTION

45. You are on an academic committee tasked to evaluate state employment math test questions. The following question has come to the attention of the committee.

> "Each of the four digits 2, 4, 6, and 9 is placed in one of the boxes to form a fraction. The numerator and the denominator are two-digit whole numbers. What is the smallest value of all the common fractions that can be formed? Express your answer as a reduced fraction."

Adapted from the NCTM Calendar, November 2004.

Some committee members contend this is not a valid question. Solve the problem and explain the solution to prove (or disprove) the question's validity.

ADDITION AND SUBTRACTION OF FRACTIONS

Adding and subtracting fractions occurs frequently in business. Quite often we must combine or subtract quantities expressed as fractions. To add or subtract fractions, the denominators must be the same. If they are not, we must find a common multiple, or **common denominator**, of all the denominators in the problem. The most efficient common denominator to use is the least common denominator, or LCD. By using the LCD, you avoid raising fractions to terms higher than necessary.

common denominator A common multiple of all the denominators in an addition or subtraction of fractions problem. A common denominator of the fractions $\frac{1}{4} + \frac{3}{5}$ is 40.

DETERMINING THE LEAST COMMON DENOMINATOR (LCD) OF TWO OR MORE FRACTIONS

2-6

The **least common denominator (LCD)** is the smallest number that is a multiple of each of the given denominators. We can often find the LCD by inspection (i.e., mentally) just by using the definition. For example, if we want to find the LCD of $\frac{1}{4}$ and $\frac{1}{6}$, we think (or write out, if we wish):

Multiples of 4 are 4, 8, 12, 16, 20, 24, and so on

Multiples of 6 are 6, 12, 18, 24, 30, and so on

By looking at these two lists, we see that 12 is the smallest multiple of both 4 and 6. Thus, 12 is the LCD.

Sometimes, especially when we have several denominators or the denominators are relatively large numbers, it is easier to use prime numbers to find the LCD. A **prime number** is a whole number greater than 1 that is evenly divisible only by itself and 1. Following are prime numbers:

$$2, 3, 5, 7, 11, 13, 17, 19, 23, 29, 31, \text{ and so on}$$

least common denominator (LCD) The smallest and, therefore, most efficient common denominator in addition or subtraction of fractions. The least common denominator of the fractions $\frac{1}{4} + \frac{3}{5}$ is 20.

prime number A whole number greater than 1 that is divisible only by itself and 1. For example, 2, 3, 5, 7, and 11 are prime numbers.

STEPS FOR DETERMINING THE LEAST COMMON DENOMINATOR OF TWO OR MORE FRACTIONS USING PRIME NUMBERS

STEP 1. Write all the denominators in a row.

STEP 2. Find a prime number that divides evenly into any of the denominators. Write that prime number to the left of the row and divide. Place all quotients and undivided numbers in the next row down.

STEP 3. Repeat this process until the new row contains all ones.

STEP 4. Multiply all the prime numbers on the left to get the LCD of the fractions.

EXAMPLE7 DETERMINING THE LEAST COMMON DENOMINATOR (LCD)

Determine the least common denominator of the fractions $\frac{3}{4}, \frac{1}{5}, \frac{4}{9},$ and $\frac{5}{6}$.

SOLUTIONSTRATEGY

The following chart shows the solution. Note that the first row contains the original denominators. The first prime number, 2, divides evenly into the 4 and the 6. The quotients, 2 and 3, and the non-divisible numbers, 5 and 9, are brought down to the next row.

The same procedure is repeated with the prime numbers 2, 3, 3, and 5. When the bottom row becomes all ones, we multiply all the prime numbers to get the LCD, 180.

Prime Number	Denominators			
2	4	5	9	6
2	2	5	9	3
3	1	5	9	3
3	1	5	3	1
5	1	5	1	1
	1	1	1	1

$2 \times 2 \times 3 \times 3 \times 5 = \underline{180} = \text{LCD}$

TRYITEXERCISE 7

Determine the least common denominator of the fractions $\frac{3}{8}, \frac{4}{5}, \frac{4}{15},$ and $\frac{11}{12}$.

CHECK YOUR ANSWER WITH THE SOLUTION ON PAGE 61.

Learning Tip

Answers to fraction problems should be reduced to lowest terms.

B-A-C-O/Shutterstock.com

iStock.com/Nikada

2-7 ADDING FRACTIONS AND MIXED NUMBERS

Now that you have learned to convert fractions to higher and lower terms and find least common denominators, you are ready to add and subtract fractions. We will learn to add and subtract fractions with the same denominator, fractions with different denominators, and mixed numbers.

ADDING FRACTIONS WITH THE SAME DENOMINATOR

like fractions Proper fractions that have the same denominator. For example, $\frac{1}{4}$ and $\frac{3}{4}$ are like fractions.

Proper fractions that have the same denominator are known as **like fractions**.

STEPS FOR ADDING LIKE FRACTIONS

STEP 1. Add all the numerators and place the total over the original denominator.

STEP 2. If the result is a proper fraction, reduce it to lowest terms.

STEP 3. If the result is an improper fraction, convert it to a whole or mixed number.

iStock.com/Nikada

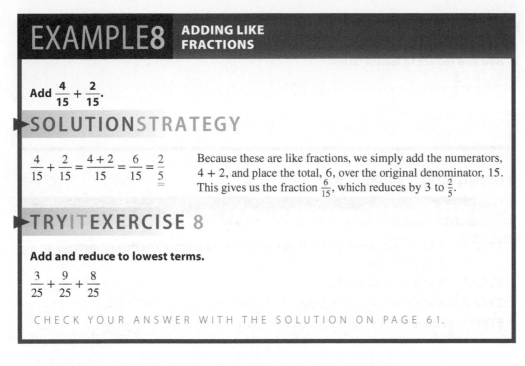

EXAMPLE8 ADDING LIKE FRACTIONS

Add $\frac{4}{15} + \frac{2}{15}$.

▶SOLUTIONSTRATEGY

$\frac{4}{15} + \frac{2}{15} = \frac{4+2}{15} = \frac{6}{15} = \underline{\underline{\frac{2}{5}}}$ Because these are like fractions, we simply add the numerators, 4 + 2, and place the total, 6, over the original denominator, 15. This gives us the fraction $\frac{6}{15}$, which reduces by 3 to $\frac{2}{5}$.

▶TRYITEXERCISE 8

Add and reduce to lowest terms.

$\frac{3}{25} + \frac{9}{25} + \frac{8}{25}$

CHECK YOUR ANSWER WITH THE SOLUTION ON PAGE 61.

ADDING FRACTIONS WITH DIFFERENT DENOMINATORS

Proper fractions that have different denominators are known as **unlike fractions**. Unlike fractions must be converted to like fractions before they can be added.

unlike fractions Proper fractions that have different denominators. For example, $\frac{1}{4}$ and $\frac{1}{3}$ are unlike fractions.

STEPS FOR ADDING UNLIKE FRACTIONS

STEP 1. Find the least common denominator of the unlike fractions.

STEP 2. Raise all fractions to the terms of the LCD, making them like fractions.

STEP 3. Follow the same procedure used for adding like fractions.

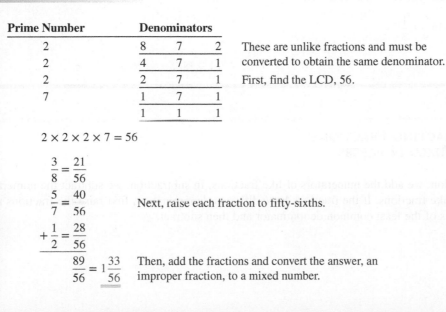

EXAMPLE9 ADDING UNLIKE FRACTIONS

Add $\frac{3}{8} + \frac{5}{7} + \frac{1}{2}$.

▶SOLUTIONSTRATEGY

Prime Number	Denominators		
2	8	7	2
2	4	7	1
2	2	7	1
7	1	7	1
	1	1	1

These are unlike fractions and must be converted to obtain the same denominator.

First, find the LCD, 56.

$2 \times 2 \times 2 \times 7 = 56$

$\frac{3}{8} = \frac{21}{56}$

$\frac{5}{7} = \frac{40}{56}$

Next, raise each fraction to fifty-sixths.

$+\frac{1}{2} = \frac{28}{56}$

$\frac{89}{56} = 1\frac{33}{56}$ Then, add the fractions and convert the answer, an improper fraction, to a mixed number.

Dollars AND Sense

Regular Gasoline	294 $\frac{9}{10}$
Plus Gasoline	304 $\frac{9}{10}$
Premium Gasoline	314 $\frac{9}{10}$
Diesel #2	341 $\frac{9}{10}$

When buying gas, the price per gallon is frequently quoted as a fraction. The price of 294 $\frac{9}{10}$ is read as "two dollars, ninety-four and nine-tenths cents."

iStock.com/Nikada

Jason Stitt/Shutterstock.com

iStock.com/vreemous

▶TRYITEXERCISE 9

Add and reduce to lowest terms.

$\dfrac{1}{6} + \dfrac{3}{5} + \dfrac{2}{3}$

CHECK YOUR ANSWER WITH THE SOLUTION ON PAGE 61.

ADDING MIXED NUMBERS

STEPS FOR ADDING MIXED NUMBERS

STEP 1. Add the fractional parts. If the sum is an improper fraction, convert it to a mixed number.

STEP 2. Add the whole numbers.

STEP 3. Add the fraction from Step 1 to the whole number from Step 2.

STEP 4. Reduce the answer to lowest terms if necessary.

EXAMPLE10 ADDING MIXED NUMBERS

Add $15\dfrac{3}{4} + 18\dfrac{5}{8}$.

▶SOLUTIONSTRATEGY

$15\dfrac{3}{4} = 15\dfrac{6}{8}$

$+18\dfrac{5}{8} = 18\dfrac{5}{8}$

$\overline{\qquad 33\dfrac{11}{8} = 33 + 1\dfrac{3}{8} = 34\dfrac{3}{8}}$

First, add the fractional parts using 8 as the LCD. Because $\dfrac{11}{8}$ is an improper fraction, convert it to the mixed number $1\dfrac{3}{8}$.

Next, add the whole numbers: $15 + 18 = 33$. Then add the fraction and the whole number to get the answer, $34\dfrac{3}{8}$.

▶TRYITEXERCISE 10

Add and reduce to lowest terms.

$45\dfrac{1}{4} + 16\dfrac{5}{9} + \dfrac{1}{3}$

CHECK YOUR ANSWER WITH THE SOLUTION ON PAGE 61.

2-8 SUBTRACTING FRACTIONS AND MIXED NUMBERS

In addition, we add the numerators of like fractions. In subtraction, we subtract the numerators of like fractions. If the fractions have different denominators, first raise the fractions to the terms of the least common denominator and then subtract.

STEPS FOR SUBTRACTING LIKE FRACTIONS

STEP 1. Subtract the numerators and place the difference over the original denominator.

STEP 2. Reduce the answer to lowest terms if necessary.

EXAMPLE11 SUBTRACTING LIKE FRACTIONS

Subtract $\frac{9}{16} - \frac{5}{16}$.

▶SOLUTIONSTRATEGY

$$\frac{9}{16} - \frac{5}{16} = \frac{9-5}{16}$$
$$= \frac{4}{16} = \underline{\underline{\frac{1}{4}}}$$

In this example, the denominators are the same; so we simply subtract the numerators, $9 - 5$, and place the difference, 4, over the original denominator, 16. Then we reduce the fraction $\frac{4}{16}$ to lowest terms, $\frac{1}{4}$.

▶TRYITEXERCISE 11

Subtract $\frac{11}{25} - \frac{6}{25}$.

CHECK YOUR ANSWER WITH THE SOLUTION ON PAGE 61.

SUBTRACTING FRACTIONS WITH DIFFERENT DENOMINATORS

Unlike fractions must be converted to like fractions before they can be subtracted.

STEPS FOR SUBTRACTING UNLIKE FRACTIONS

STEP 1. Find the least common denominator.

STEP 2. Raise each fraction to the denominator of the LCD.

STEP 3. Follow the same procedure used to subtract like fractions.

EXAMPLE12 SUBTRACTING UNLIKE FRACTIONS

Subtract $\frac{7}{9} - \frac{1}{2}$.

▶SOLUTIONSTRATEGY

$$\frac{7}{9} = \frac{14}{18}$$

In this example, we must first find the least common denominator. By inspection, we can see that the LCD is 18.

$$-\frac{1}{2} = \frac{9}{18}$$
$$\frac{5}{18}$$

Next, raise both fractions to eighteenths. Now subtract the numerators, $14 - 9$, and place the difference, 5, over the common denominator, 18. Because it cannot be reduced, $\frac{5}{18}$ is the final answer.

▶TRYITEXERCISE 12

Subtract $\frac{5}{12}-\frac{2}{9}$.

CHECK YOUR ANSWER WITH THE SOLUTION ON PAGE 61.

SUBTRACTING MIXED NUMBERS

STEPS FOR SUBTRACTING MIXED NUMBERS

STEP 1. If the fractions of the mixed numbers have the same denominator, subtract the fractions and reduce to lowest terms.

STEP 2. If the fractions do not have the same denominator, raise them to the denominator of the LCD and subtract.

Note: When the numerator of the fraction in the minuend is less than the numerator of the fraction in the subtrahend, we must *borrow* one whole unit from the whole number of the minuend. This will be in the form of the LCD/LCD and is added to the fraction of the minuend.

STEP 3. Subtract the whole numbers.

STEP 4. Add the difference of the whole numbers and the difference of the fractions.

EXAMPLE13   SUBTRACTING MIXED NUMBERS

Subtract.

a. $15\frac{2}{3} - 9\frac{1}{5}$

b. $7\frac{1}{8} - 2\frac{3}{4}$

▶SOLUTIONSTRATEGY

a.
$$15\frac{2}{3} = 15\frac{10}{15}$$
$$-9\frac{1}{5} = -9\frac{3}{15}$$
$$\overline{6\frac{7}{15}}$$

In this example, raise the fractions to fifteenths; LCD = 5 × 3 = 15.

Then subtract the fractions to get $\frac{7}{15}$.

Now subtract the whole numbers, 15 − 9, to get the whole number 6.

By combining the 6 and the $\frac{7}{15}$, we get the final answer $6\frac{7}{15}$.

b.
$$7\frac{1}{8} = \quad 7\frac{1}{8} = 6\frac{1}{8} + \frac{8}{8} = 6\frac{9}{8}$$
$$-2\frac{3}{4} = -2\frac{6}{8} = \qquad -2\frac{6}{8}$$
$$\overline{\qquad\qquad 4\frac{3}{8}}$$

In this example, after raising $\frac{3}{4}$ to $\frac{6}{8}$, we find that we cannot subtract $\frac{6}{8}$ from $\frac{1}{8}$. We must *borrow* one whole unit, $\frac{8}{8}$, from the whole number 7, making it a 6 (8 ÷ 8 = 1).

By adding $\frac{8}{8}$ to $\frac{1}{8}$, we get $\frac{9}{8}$.

Now we can subtract $\frac{9}{8} - \frac{6}{8}$ to get $\frac{3}{8}$.

We now subtract the whole numbers 6 − 2 = 4.
By combining the whole number 4 and the fraction $\frac{3}{8}$, we get the final answer $4\frac{3}{8}$.

Learning Tip

Remember, when you borrow "one" in subtraction, you are borrowing a whole unit expressed in terms of the common denominator.

For example, $\frac{4}{4}, \frac{5}{5}, \frac{8}{8}, \frac{24}{24}$

Don't forget to add this to the existing fraction.

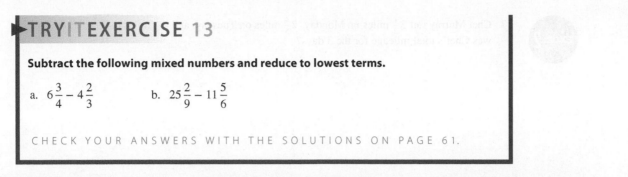

► TRY IT EXERCISE 13

Subtract the following mixed numbers and reduce to lowest terms.

a. $6\dfrac{3}{4} - 4\dfrac{2}{3}$ b. $25\dfrac{2}{9} - 11\dfrac{5}{6}$

CHECK YOUR ANSWERS WITH THE SOLUTIONS ON PAGE 61.

REVIEW EXERCISES

2   SECTION II

Find the least common denominator for the following groups of fractions. For problems 1–3, try finding the LCD by inspection (i.e., mentally) first, then use the prime-number method.

1. $\dfrac{4}{5}, \dfrac{2}{3}, \dfrac{8}{15}$

$$\begin{array}{c|ccc} 3 & 5 & 3 & 15 \\ \hline 5 & 5 & 1 & 5 \\ \hline & 1 & 1 & 1 \end{array}$$

$3 \times 5 = \underline{\underline{15}}\ \text{LCD}$

2. $\dfrac{4}{9}, \dfrac{3}{4}$

3. $\dfrac{5}{6}, \dfrac{11}{12}, \dfrac{1}{4}, \dfrac{1}{2}$

4. $\dfrac{1}{6}, \dfrac{19}{24}, \dfrac{2}{3}, \dfrac{3}{5}$

5. $\dfrac{21}{25}, \dfrac{9}{60}, \dfrac{7}{20}, \dfrac{1}{3}$

6. $\dfrac{5}{12}, \dfrac{9}{14}, \dfrac{2}{3}, \dfrac{7}{10}$

Add the following fractions and reduce to lowest terms.

7. $\dfrac{5}{6} + \dfrac{1}{2}$

$$\begin{array}{r} \dfrac{5}{6} \\ +\dfrac{3}{6} \\ \hline \dfrac{8}{6} = 1\dfrac{2}{6} = 1\underline{\underline{\dfrac{1}{3}}} \end{array}$$

8. $\dfrac{1}{3} + \dfrac{4}{5}$

9. $\dfrac{5}{8} + \dfrac{13}{16}$

10. $\dfrac{9}{32} + \dfrac{29}{32}$

11. $\dfrac{1}{3} + \dfrac{1}{4} + \dfrac{5}{12}$

12. $\dfrac{1}{4} + \dfrac{3}{8} + \dfrac{3}{16}$

13. $\dfrac{11}{12} + \dfrac{3}{5} + \dfrac{19}{30}$

14. $5\dfrac{4}{7} + \dfrac{2}{3}$

15. $7\dfrac{1}{2} + 2\dfrac{7}{8} + 1\dfrac{1}{6}$

16. $13\dfrac{5}{9} + 45\dfrac{1}{3} + 9\dfrac{7}{27}$

17. Chet Murray ran $3\frac{1}{2}$ miles on Monday, $2\frac{4}{5}$ miles on Tuesday, and $4\frac{1}{8}$ miles on Wednesday. What was Chet's total mileage for the 3 days?

18. Crate and Barrel shipped three packages to New York weighing $45\frac{1}{5}$, $126\frac{3}{4}$, and $88\frac{3}{8}$ pounds. What was the total weight of the shipment?

19. At the Fresh Market, you buy $6\frac{3}{10}$ pounds of yams and $4\frac{1}{3}$ pounds of corn. What is the total weight of the purchase?

20. BrewMasters Coffee Co. purchased $12\frac{1}{2}$ tons of coffee beans in January, $15\frac{4}{5}$ tons in February, and $34\frac{7}{10}$ tons in March. What was the total weight of the purchases?

Subtract the following fractions and reduce to lowest terms.

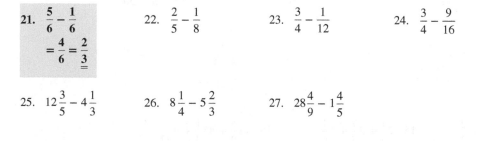

21. $\dfrac{5}{6} - \dfrac{1}{6}$

$= \dfrac{4}{6} = \dfrac{2}{3}$

22. $\dfrac{2}{5} - \dfrac{1}{8}$

23. $\dfrac{3}{4} - \dfrac{1}{12}$

24. $\dfrac{3}{4} - \dfrac{9}{16}$

25. $12\frac{3}{5} - 4\frac{1}{3}$

26. $8\frac{1}{4} - 5\frac{2}{3}$

27. $28\frac{4}{9} - 1\frac{4}{5}$

28. $12\frac{1}{6} - 4\frac{1}{3}$

29. Casey McKee sold $18\frac{4}{5}$ of his $54\frac{2}{3}$ acres of land. How many acres does Casey have left?

30. A particular dress requires $3\frac{1}{4}$ yards of fabric for manufacturing. If the matching jacket requires $\frac{5}{6}$ yard less fabric, how much fabric is needed for both pieces?

31. Robert Burkart bought a frozen, factory-processed turkey that included the giblets and neck. The package weighed $22\frac{3}{4}$ pounds. Robert thawed the bird and then removed and weighed the giblets and neck, which totaled $1\frac{1}{8}$ pounds. The liquid that he drained from the package weighed $\frac{1}{2}$ pound. How much did the turkey weigh going into the oven?

Bochkarev Photography/Shutterstock.com

32. Brady White weighed $196\frac{1}{2}$ pounds when he decided to join a gym to lose some weight. At the end of the first month, he weighed $191\frac{3}{8}$ pounds.
   a. How much did he lose that month?

   b. If his goal is $183\frac{3}{4}$ pounds, how much more does he have to lose?

33. Hot Shot Industries manufactures metal heat shields for light fixture assemblies. What is the length, x, on the heat shield?

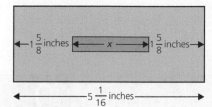

34. Tim Kenney, a painter, used $6\frac{4}{5}$ gallons of paint on the exterior of a house and $9\frac{3}{4}$ gallons on the interior.
    a. What is the total amount of paint used on the house?

    b. If an additional $8\frac{3}{5}$ gallons was used on the garage, what is the total amount of paint used on the house and garage?

    c. Rounding your answer from part b up to the next whole gallon, calculate the total cost of the paint if you paid $23 for each gallon.

BUSINESS DECISION: THE RED-EYE EXPRESS

35. You are an executive with the Varsity Corporation in Atlanta, Georgia. The company president was scheduled to make an important sales presentation tomorrow afternoon in Seattle, Washington, but has now asked you to take his place.

    The trip consists of a $2\frac{1}{2}$-hour flight from Atlanta to Dallas, a $1\frac{1}{4}$-hour layover in Dallas, and then a $3\frac{3}{4}$-hour flight to Portland. There is a $1\frac{1}{2}$-hour layover in Portland and then a $\frac{3}{4}$-hour flight to Seattle. Seattle is on Pacific Time, which is 3 hours earlier than Eastern Time in Atlanta.
    a. If you depart Atlanta tonight at 11:30 P.M. and all flights are on schedule, what time will you arrive in Seattle?

    b. If your return flight is scheduled to leave Seattle at 10:10 P.M. tomorrow night, with the same flight times and layovers in reverse, what time are you scheduled to arrive in Atlanta?

    c. If the leg from Dallas back to Atlanta is $\frac{2}{3}$ of an hour longer than scheduled due to headwinds, what time will you actually arrive?

SECTION III   **2**   MULTIPLICATION AND DIVISION OF FRACTIONS

In addition and subtraction, we were concerned with common denominators; however, in multiplication and division, common denominators are not required. This simplifies the process considerably.

MULTIPLYING FRACTIONS AND MIXED NUMBERS

2-9

STEPS FOR MULTIPLYING FRACTIONS

STEP 1. Multiply all the numerators to form the new numerator.

STEP 2. Multiply all the denominators to form the new denominator.

STEP 3. Reduce the answer to lowest terms if necessary.

A procedure known as **cancellation** can serve as a useful shortcut when multiplying fractions. Cancellation simplifies the numbers with which we are dealing and often leaves the answer in lowest terms.

STEPS FOR APPLYING CANCELLATION

STEP 1. Find a common factor that divides evenly into at least one of the denominators and one of the numerators.

STEP 2. Divide that common factor into the denominator and numerator, thereby reducing it.

STEP 3. Repeat this process until there are no more common factors.

STEP 4. Multiply the fractions as before.

cancellation When multiplying fractions, cancellation is the process of finding a common factor that divides evenly into at least one numerator and one denominator. The common factor 2 can be used to cancel

$$\frac{1}{\overset{}{\underset{2}{\cancel{4}}}} \times \frac{\overset{3}{\cancel{6}}}{7} \text{ to } \frac{1}{2} \times \frac{3}{7}.$$

EXAMPLE 14 — MULTIPLYING FRACTIONS

Multiply the following fractions.

a. $\dfrac{5}{7} \times \dfrac{3}{4}$

b. $\dfrac{2}{3} \times \dfrac{7}{8}$

SOLUTION STRATEGY

a. $\dfrac{5}{7} \times \dfrac{3}{4}$ In this example, there are no common factors between the numerators and the denominators; therefore, we cannot use cancellation.

$\dfrac{5 \times 3}{7 \times 4} = \dfrac{15}{28}$ Multiply the numerators, 5×3, to form the new numerator 15 and multiply the denominators, 7×4, to form the new denominator 28. This fraction does not reduce.

b. $\dfrac{2}{3} \times \dfrac{7}{8}$ In this example, the 2 in the numerator and the 8 in the denominator have the common factor of 2.

$\dfrac{\overset{1}{\cancel{2}}}{3} \times \dfrac{7}{\underset{4}{\cancel{8}}}$ Dividing each by the common factor reduces the 2 to a 1 and the 8 to a 4.

$\dfrac{1 \times 7}{3 \times 4} = \dfrac{7}{12}$ Now multiply the simplified numbers; 1×7 forms the numerator 7 and 3×4 forms the denominator 12. The resulting product is $\frac{7}{12}$.

TRY IT EXERCISE 14

Multiply and reduce to lowest terms.

$$\frac{12}{21} \times \frac{7}{8}$$

CHECK YOUR ANSWER WITH THE SOLUTION ON PAGE 61.

Learning Tip

4 Out of 3 People Have Trouble with Fractions! For additional help with fractions, check out www.math.com, www.tutorvista.com, and your textbook's CengageNOW with MathCue step-by-step tutorial software.

MULTIPLYING MIXED NUMBERS

STEPS FOR MULTIPLYING MIXED NUMBERS

STEP 1. Convert all mixed numbers to improper fractions.

Note: When multiplying fractions by whole numbers, change the whole numbers to fractions by placing them over 1.

STEP 2. Multiply as before, using cancellation wherever possible.

STEP 3. If the answer is an improper fraction, convert it to a whole or mixed number.

STEP 4. Reduce the answer to lowest terms if necessary.

EXAMPLE 15   MULTIPLYING MIXED NUMBERS

Multiply.

a. $3\frac{3}{4} \times 5\frac{1}{2}$

b. $12\frac{5}{6} \times 4$

►SOLUTIONSTRATEGY

a. $3\frac{3}{4} \times 5\frac{1}{2}$ In this example, convert the mixed numbers to improper fractions; $3\frac{3}{4}$ becomes $\frac{15}{4}$, and $5\frac{1}{2}$ becomes $\frac{11}{2}$.

$\frac{15}{4} \times \frac{11}{2}$

$\frac{15 \times 11}{4 \times 2} = \frac{165}{8} = 20\frac{5}{8}$ After multiplying the numerators together and the denominators together, we get the improper fraction $\frac{165}{8}$, which converts to the mixed number $20\frac{5}{8}$.

b. $12\frac{5}{6} \times 4$ This example demonstrates a mixed number multiplied by a whole number.

$\frac{77}{6} \times \frac{4}{1}$ The mixed number $12\frac{5}{6}$ converts to the improper fraction $\frac{77}{6}$. The whole number 4 expressed as a fraction becomes $\frac{4}{1}$.

$\frac{77}{\overset{}{\underset{3}{6}}} \times \frac{\overset{2}{4}}{1}$ Before multiplying, cancel the 4 in the numerator and the 6 in the denominator by the common factor 2.

$\frac{77 \times 2}{3 \times 1} = \frac{154}{3} = 51\frac{1}{3}$ After multiplying, convert the improper fraction $\frac{154}{3}$ to the mixed number $51\frac{1}{3}$.

►TRYITEXERCISE 15

Multiply and reduce to lowest terms.

a. $8\frac{2}{5} \times 6\frac{1}{4}$

b. $45 \times \frac{4}{9} \times 2\frac{1}{4}$

CHECK YOUR ANSWERS WITH THE SOLUTIONS ON PAGE 61.

DIVIDING FRACTIONS AND MIXED NUMBERS

2-10

In division of fractions, it is important to identify which fraction is the dividend and which is the divisor. In whole numbers, we found that a problem such as $12 \div 5$ is read "12 divided by 5." Therefore, the 12 is the dividend and the 5 is the divisor. Fractions work in the same way. The number *after* the "÷" sign is the divisor. In the problem $\frac{3}{4} \div \frac{2}{3}$, for example, $\frac{3}{4}$ is the dividend and $\frac{2}{3}$ is the divisor.

$$\text{Dividend} \div \text{Divisor} = \frac{\text{Dividend}}{\text{Divisor}} = \text{Divisor} \overline{)\text{Dividend}}$$

Division of fractions requires that we **invert** the divisor. To invert means to turn upside down. By inverting a fraction, the numerator becomes the denominator and the denominator becomes the numerator. For example, the fraction $\frac{5}{12}$ becomes $\frac{12}{5}$ when inverted. These fractions are also known as **reciprocals**. Therefore, $\frac{5}{12}$ and $\frac{12}{5}$ are reciprocals of each other.

As in multiplication, division requires that mixed numbers be converted to improper fractions.

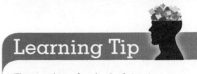

Learning Tip

The number *after* the "÷" sign is the divisor.
　This is the number that gets inverted when dividing.

invert To turn upside down. For example, $\frac{1}{4}$ inverted becomes $\frac{4}{1}$. In division of fractions, the divisor is inverted.

reciprocals Numbers whose product is 1. Inverted numbers are also known as reciprocals of each other. The fractions $\frac{1}{4}$ and $\frac{4}{1}$ are reciprocals because $\frac{1}{4} \times \frac{4}{1} = 1$.

STEPS FOR DIVIDING FRACTIONS

STEP 1. Identify the fraction that is the divisor and invert.

STEP 2. Change the "divided by" sign, ÷, to a "multiplied by" sign, ×.

STEP 3. Multiply the fractions.

STEP 4. Reduce the answer to lowest terms if necessary.

EXAMPLE16 DIVIDING FRACTIONS

Divide the following fractions.

a. $\frac{4}{5} \div \frac{2}{3}$
b. $6\frac{3}{8} \div 2\frac{1}{2}$
c. $12\frac{1}{6} \div 3$

SOLUTIONSTRATEGY

a. $\frac{4}{5} \div \frac{2}{3} = \frac{4}{5} \times \frac{3}{2}$ 　　In this example, invert the divisor, $\frac{2}{3}$, to form its reciprocal, $\frac{3}{2}$, and change the sign from "÷" to "×."

$\frac{\overset{2}{\cancel{4}}}{5} \times \frac{3}{\underset{1}{\cancel{2}}} = \frac{6}{5} = 1\frac{1}{5}$ 　　Now multiply in the usual manner. Note that the 4 in the numerator and the 2 in the denominator can be reduced by the common factor 2. The answer, $\frac{6}{5}$, is an improper fraction and must be converted to the mixed number $1\frac{1}{5}$.

b. $6\frac{3}{8} \div 2\frac{1}{2} = \frac{51}{8} \div \frac{5}{2}$ 　　First, convert the mixed numbers to the improper fractions $\frac{51}{8}$ and $\frac{5}{2}$; then state them again as division.

$\frac{51}{8} \times \frac{2}{5}$ 　　Next, invert the divisor, $\frac{5}{2}$, to its reciprocal, $\frac{2}{5}$, and change the sign from "÷" to "×."

$\frac{51}{\underset{4}{\cancel{8}}} \times \frac{\overset{1}{\cancel{2}}}{5} = \frac{51}{20} = 2\frac{11}{20}$ 　　Now multiply in the usual way. Note that the 2 in the numerator and the 8 in the denominator can be reduced by the common factor 2. The answer, $\frac{51}{20}$, is an improper fraction and must be converted to the mixed number $2\frac{11}{20}$.

IN THE Business World

According to *The Wall Street Journal*, the problem below was a question on the Jersey City High School admissions exam in June 1885! Try this for practice:

Divide the difference between 37 hundredths and 95 thousandths by 25 hundred-thousandths and express the result in words.

Answer: one thousand, one hundred

c. $12\frac{1}{6} \div 3 = \frac{73}{6} \div \frac{3}{1}$ In this example, we have a mixed number that must be converted to the improper fraction $\frac{73}{6}$ and the whole number 3, which converts to $\frac{3}{1}$.

$\frac{73}{6} \times \frac{1}{3}$ The fraction $\frac{3}{1}$ is the divisor and must be inverted to its reciprocal, $\frac{1}{3}$. The sign is changed from "÷" to "×."

$\frac{73}{6} \times \frac{1}{3} = \frac{73}{18} = 4\frac{1}{18}$ The answer is the improper fraction $\frac{73}{18}$, which converts to the mixed number $4\frac{1}{18}$.

▶ TRYITEXERCISE 16

Divide the following fractions and mixed numbers.

a. $\dfrac{14}{25} \div \dfrac{4}{5}$ b. $11\dfrac{3}{16} \div 8\dfrac{2}{3}$ c. $18 \div 5\dfrac{3}{5}$

CHECK YOUR ANSWERS WITH THE SOLUTIONS ON PAGE 62.

SECTION III   2   REVIEW EXERCISES

JUMP START WWW

Multiply the following fractions and reduce to lowest terms. Use cancellation whenever possible.

1. $\dfrac{2}{3} \times \dfrac{4}{5} = \dfrac{8}{15}$ 2. $\dfrac{2}{11} \times \dfrac{5}{7}$ 3. $\dfrac{1}{2} \times \dfrac{4}{9}$ 4. $\dfrac{7}{8} \times \dfrac{1}{3} \times \dfrac{4}{7}$

5. $\dfrac{16}{19} \times \dfrac{5}{8}$ 6. $\dfrac{25}{51} \times \dfrac{2}{5}$ 7. $\dfrac{8}{11} \times \dfrac{33}{40} \times \dfrac{4}{1}$ 8. $\dfrac{2}{3} \times \dfrac{2}{3} \times \dfrac{6}{1}$

9. $8\dfrac{1}{5} \times 2\dfrac{2}{3}$ 10. $\dfrac{1}{2} \times \dfrac{2}{3} \times \dfrac{4}{5} \times \dfrac{3}{4} \times \dfrac{5}{1}$ 11. $\dfrac{1}{5} \times \dfrac{1}{5} \times \dfrac{1}{5}$

EXCEL 1   12. $\dfrac{2}{3} \times 5\dfrac{4}{5} \times 9$

13. A recent market research survey showed that $\frac{3}{8}$ of the people interviewed preferred decaffeinated coffee over regular.

   a. What fraction of the people preferred regular coffee?

   b. If 4,400 people were interviewed, how many preferred regular coffee?

14. Wendy Wilson planned to bake a triple recipe of chocolate chip cookies for her office party. If the recipe calls for $1\frac{3}{4}$ cups of flour, how many cups will she need?

15. A driveway requires $9\frac{1}{2}$ truckloads of gravel. If the truck holds $4\frac{5}{8}$ cubic yards of gravel, how many total cubic yards of gravel are used for the driveway?

Marketing Research Market and survey researchers gather information about what people think. They help companies understand what types of products and services people want and at what price. By gathering statistical data on competitors and examining prices, sales, and methods of marketing and distribution, they advise companies on the most efficient ways of marketing their products.

According to the U.S. Bureau of Labor Statistics, overall employment of market and survey researchers is projected to grow 23% from 2016 to 2026. Median annual salaries for market researchers in 2017 was $63,230.

ESB Professional/Shutterstock.com

16. Melissa Silva borrowed \$4,200 from the bank. If she has already repaid $\frac{3}{7}$ of the loan, what is the remaining balance owed to the bank?

17. Amy Richards' movie collection occupies $\frac{5}{8}$ of her computer's hard drive. Her photography takes up $\frac{1}{6}$ of the drive. The operating system, application software, and miscellaneous files take up another $\frac{1}{12}$ of the drive. If her hard drive's capacity is 120 gigabytes, how many gigabytes of free space remain on the hard drive?

18. Three partners share a business. Max owns $\frac{3}{8}$, Sherry owns $\frac{2}{5}$, and Duane owns the rest. If the profits this year are \$150,000, how much does each partner receive?

Divide the following fractions and reduce to lowest terms.

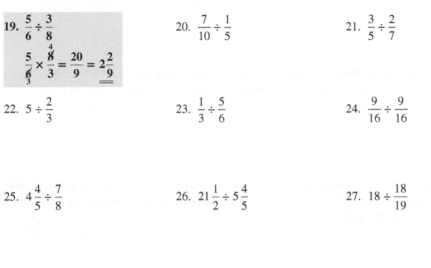

19. $\frac{5}{6} \div \frac{3}{8}$

$$\frac{5}{\cancel{6}_{3}} \times \frac{\cancel{8}^{4}}{3} = \frac{20}{9} = 2\frac{2}{9}$$

20. $\frac{7}{10} \div \frac{1}{5}$

21. $\frac{3}{5} \div \frac{2}{7}$

22. $5 \div \frac{2}{3}$

23. $\frac{1}{3} \div \frac{5}{6}$

24. $\frac{9}{16} \div \frac{9}{16}$

25. $4\frac{4}{5} \div \frac{7}{8}$

26. $21\frac{1}{2} \div 5\frac{4}{5}$

27. $18 \div \frac{18}{19}$

28. $12 \div 1\frac{3}{5}$

29. $\frac{15}{60} \div \frac{7}{10}$

30. $1\frac{1}{5} \div 10$

31. Frontier Homes, Inc., a builder of custom homes, owns $126\frac{1}{2}$ acres of undeveloped land. If the property is divided into $2\frac{3}{4}$-acre pieces, how many homesites can be developed?

32. An automobile travels 365 miles on $16\frac{2}{3}$ gallons of gasoline.
    a. How many miles per gallon does the car get on the trip?

Grzegorz Czapski/Shutterstock.com

b. How many gallons would be required for the car to travel 876 miles?

33. Pier 1 Imports purchased 600 straw baskets from a wholesaler.
   a. In the first week, $\frac{2}{5}$ of the baskets are sold. How many are sold?

   b. By the third week, only $\frac{3}{20}$ of the baskets remain. How many baskets are left?

34. At the Cattleman's Market, $3\frac{1}{2}$ pounds of hamburger meat are to be divided into 7 equal packages. How many pounds of meat will each package contain?

35. Super Value Hardware Supply buys nails in bulk from the manufacturer and packs them into $2\frac{4}{5}$-pound boxes. How many boxes can be filled from 518 pounds of nails?

36. The chef at the Sizzling Steakhouse has 140 pounds of sirloin steak on hand for Saturday night. If each portion is $10\frac{1}{2}$ ounces, how many sirloin steak dinners can be served? Round to the nearest whole dinner. (There are 16 ounces in a pound.)

37. Regal Reflective Signs makes speed limit signs for the state department of transportation. By law, these signs must be displayed every $\frac{5}{8}$ of a mile. How many signs will be required on a new highway that is $34\frac{3}{8}$ miles long?

38. Engineers at Triangle Electronics use special silver wire to manufacture fuzzy logic circuit boards. The wire comes in 840-foot rolls that cost $1,200 each. Each board requires $4\frac{1}{5}$ feet of wire.
   a. How many circuit boards can be made from each roll?

   b. What is the cost of wire per circuit board?

39. At Celtex Manufacturing, a chemical etching process reduces $2\frac{13}{16}$-inch copper plates by $\frac{35}{64}$ of an inch.

    a. What is the thickness of each copper plate after the etching process?

    b. How many etched copper plates can fit in a box 25 inches high?

BUSINESS DECISION: DINNER SPECIAL

40. You are the owner of The Gourmet Diner. On Wednesday nights, you offer a special of "Buy one dinner, get one free dinner—of equal or lesser value." Michael and Wayne come in for the special. Michael chooses chicken Parmesan for $15, and Wayne chooses a $10 barbecue-combo platter.

    a. Excluding tax and tip, how much should each pay for his proportional share of the check?

    b. If sales tax and tip amount to $\frac{1}{5}$ of the total of the two dinners, how much is that?

    c. If they decide to split the tax and tip in the same ratio as the dinners, how much more does each owe?

CHAPTER SUMMARY

Section I: Understanding and Working with Fractions

Topic	Important Concepts	Illustrative Examples
Distinguishing among the Various Types of Fractions **Performance Objective 2-1, Page 33**	**Common or proper fraction:** A fraction representing less than a whole unit where the numerator is less than the denominator. **Improper fraction:** A fraction representing one whole unit or more where the denominator is equal to or less than the numerator. **Mixed number:** A number that combines a whole number with a proper fraction.	Proper fraction $\dfrac{4}{7}, \dfrac{2}{3}, \dfrac{93}{124}$ Improper fraction $\dfrac{5}{4}, \dfrac{7}{7}, \dfrac{88}{51}, \dfrac{796}{212}, \dfrac{1{,}200}{1{,}200}$ Mixed number $12\dfrac{2}{5}, 4\dfrac{5}{9}, 78\dfrac{52}{63}$
Converting Improper Fractions to Whole or Mixed Numbers **Performance Objective 2-2, Page 34**	**To convert improper fractions to whole or mixed numbers:** 1. Divide the numerator of the improper fraction by the denominator. 2a. If there is no remainder, the improper fraction becomes a whole number. 2b. If there is a remainder, write the whole number and then write the fraction as $$\text{Whole Number } \dfrac{\text{Remainder}}{\text{Divisor}}$$	Convert the following to whole or mixed numbers. a. $\dfrac{68}{4} = 17$ b. $\dfrac{127}{20} = 6\dfrac{7}{20}$
Converting Mixed Numbers to Improper Fractions **Performance Objective 2-3, Page 35**	**To covert mixed numbers to improper fractions:** 1. Multiply the denominator by the whole number. 2. Add the numerator to the product from Step 1. 3. Place the total from Step 2 as the "new" numerator. 4. Place the original denominator as the "new" denominator.	Convert $15\dfrac{3}{4}$ to an improper fraction. $15\dfrac{3}{4} = \dfrac{(15 \times 4) + 3}{4} = \dfrac{63}{4}$
Reducing Fractions to Lowest Terms by Inspection **Performance Objective 2-4a, Page 36**	**Reducing a fraction** means finding whole numbers, called common divisors or common factors, that divide evenly into both the numerator and denominator of the fraction. When a fraction has been reduced to the point where there are no common divisors left other than 1, it is said to be **reduced to lowest terms**.	Reduce $\dfrac{24}{120}$ to lowest terms by inspection. $\dfrac{24}{120} = \dfrac{24 \div 3}{120 \div 3} = \dfrac{8}{40}$ $\dfrac{8}{40} = \dfrac{8 \div 2}{40 \div 2} = \dfrac{4}{20}$ $\dfrac{4}{20} = \dfrac{4 \div 4}{20 \div 4} = \dfrac{1}{5}$

Finding the Greatest Common Divisor (Reducing Shortcut)
 	
Performance Objective 2-4b, Page 37
	The largest number that is a common divisor of a fraction is known as the **greatest common divisor (GCD)**. It reduces the fraction to lowest terms in one step.
	
	To find the GCD:
	1. Divide the numerator of the fraction into the denominator.
	2. Examine the remainder.
	  • If it is 0, stop. The divisor is the greatest common divisor.
	  • If it is 1, stop. The fraction cannot be reduced and is therefore in lowest terms.
	  • If it is another number, divide the remainder into the divisor.
	3. Repeat Step 2 as needed.
		What greatest common divisor will reduce the fraction $\dfrac{48}{72}$?
		
		$\begin{array}{cc} 1 & 2 \\ 48\overline{)72} & 24\overline{)48} \\ \underline{48} & \underline{48} \\ 24 & 0 \end{array}$
		
		The greatest common divisor is 24.

Topic	Important Concepts	Illustrative Examples
Raising Fractions to Higher Terms **Performance Objective 2-5, Page 38**	**To raise a fraction to a new denominator:** 1. Divide the original denominator into the new denominator. The resulting quotient is the common multiple that raises the fraction. 2. Multiply the numerator and the denominator of the original fraction by the common multiple.	Raise $\frac{5}{8}$ to forty-eighths. $\frac{5}{8} = \frac{?}{48}$ $48 \div 8 = 6$ $\frac{5 \times 6}{8 \times 6} = \frac{30}{48}$

Section II: Addition and Subtraction of Fractions

Topic	Important Concepts	Illustrative Examples
Understanding Prime Numbers **Performance Objective 2-6, Page 41**	A **prime number** is a whole number greater than 1 that is divisible only by 1 and itself. Prime numbers are used to find the least common denominator of two or more fractions.	Examples of prime numbers: 2, 3, 5, 7, 11, 13, 17, 19, 23, 29
Determining the Least Common Denominator (LCD) of Two or More Fractions **Performance Objective 2-6, Page 41**	*Note*: The LCD can often be found by inspection by mentally calculating the smallest number that is a multiple of each denominator. When this approach is difficult, use these steps: 1. Write all the denominators in a row. 2. Find a prime number that divides evenly into any of the denominators. Write that prime number to the left of the row and divide. Place all quotients and undivided numbers in the next row down. 3. Repeat this process until the new row contains all ones. 4. Multiply all the prime numbers on the left to get the LCD of the fractions.	Find the LCD of $\frac{2}{9}, \frac{5}{6}, \frac{1}{4}$, and $\frac{4}{5}$. **Prime Number** **Denominators** $\begin{array}{c\|cccc} 3 & 9 & 6 & 4 & 5 \\ 2 & 3 & 2 & 4 & 5 \\ 2 & 3 & 1 & 2 & 5 \\ 3 & 3 & 1 & 1 & 5 \\ 5 & 1 & 1 & 1 & 5 \\ & 1 & 1 & 1 & 1 \end{array}$ $LCD = 3 \times 2 \times 2 \times 3 \times 5 = 180$
Adding Like Fractions **Performance Objective 2-7, Page 42**	1. Add all the numerators and place the total over the original denominator. 2. If the result is a proper fraction, reduce it to lowest terms. 3. If the result is an improper fraction, convert it to a whole or mixed number.	Add $\frac{8}{9}, \frac{4}{9}$, and $\frac{1}{9}$. $\frac{8 + 4 + 1}{9} = \frac{13}{9} = 1\frac{4}{9}$
Adding Unlike Fractions **Performance Objective 2-7, Page 43**	1. Find the least common denominator of the unlike fractions. 2. Raise each fraction to the terms of the LCD, thereby making them like fractions. 3. Add the like fractions.	Add $\frac{2}{3} + \frac{5}{7}$. $LCD = 3 \times 7 = 21$ $\frac{2 \times 7}{21} + \frac{5 \times 3}{21} = \frac{14 + 15}{21} = \frac{29}{21} = 1\frac{8}{21}$
Adding Mixed Numbers **Performance Objective 2-7, Page 44**	1. Add the fractional parts. If the sum is an improper fraction, convert it to a mixed number. 2. Add the whole numbers. 3. Add the fraction from Step 1 to the whole number from Step 2. 4. Reduce the answer to lowest terms if necessary.	Add $3\frac{3}{4} + 4\frac{1}{8}$. $\frac{3}{4} + \frac{1}{8} = \frac{6}{8} + \frac{1}{8} = \frac{7}{8}$ $3 + 4 = 7$ $7 + \frac{7}{8} = 7\frac{7}{8}$
Subtracting Like Fractions **Performance Objective 2-8, Page 44**	1. Subtract the numerators and place the difference over the original denominator. 2. Reduce the fraction to lowest terms if necessary.	Subtract $\frac{11}{12} - \frac{5}{12}$. $\frac{11 - 5}{12} = \frac{6}{12} = \frac{1}{2}$
Subtracting Unlike Fractions **Performance Objective 2-8, Page 45**	1. Find the least common denominator. 2. Raise each fraction to the denominator of the LCD. 3. Subtract the like fractions.	Subtract $\frac{7}{8} - \frac{2}{3}$. $LCD = 8 \times 3 = 24$ $\frac{21}{24} - \frac{16}{24} = \frac{5}{24}$

Topic	Important Concepts	Illustrative Examples
Subtracting Mixed Numbers **Performance Objective 2-8, Page 46**	1. If the fractions of the mixed numbers have the same denominator, subtract them and reduce to lowest terms. 2. If the fractions do not have the same denominator, raise them to the denominator of the LCD and subtract. 3. Subtract the whole numbers. 4. Add the difference of the whole numbers and the difference of the fractions.	Subtract $15\frac{5}{8} - 12\frac{1}{2}$. $15\frac{5}{8} = \quad 15\frac{5}{8}$ $-12\frac{1}{2} = -12\frac{4}{8}$ $\quad\quad\quad = \quad 3\frac{1}{8}$
Subtracting Mixed Numbers Using Borrowing **Performance Objective 2-8, Page 46**	When the numerator of the fraction in the minuend is less than the numerator of the fraction in the subtrahend, we must borrow one whole unit from the whole number of the minuend. This will be in the form of the LCD/LCD and is added to the fraction of the minuend. Then subtract as before.	Subtract $6\frac{1}{7} - 2\frac{5}{7}$. $6\frac{1}{7} = 5\frac{7}{7} + \frac{1}{7} = 5\frac{8}{7}$ $-2\frac{5}{7} \quad\quad\quad\quad -2\frac{5}{7}$ $\quad\quad\quad\quad\quad = 3\frac{3}{7}$

Section III: Multiplication and Division of Fractions

Topic	Important Concepts	Illustrative Examples
Multiplying Fractions **Performance Objective 2-9, Page 50**	1. Multiply all the numerators to form the new numerator. 2. Multiply all the denominators to form the new denominator. 3. Reduce the answer to lowest terms if necessary.	Multiply $\frac{5}{8} \times \frac{2}{3}$. $\frac{5}{8} \times \frac{2}{3} = \frac{10}{24} = \frac{5}{12}$
Multiplying Fractions Using Cancellation **Performance Objective 2-9, Page 52**	Cancellation simplifies the numbers and leaves the answer in lowest terms. 1. Find a common factor that divides evenly into at least one of the denominators and one of the numerators. 2. Divide that common factor into the denominator and the numerator, thereby reducing it. 3. Repeat this process until there are no more common factors. 4. Multiply the fractions. The resulting product will be in lowest terms.	Use cancellation to solve the multiplication problem above. Cancellation Method: $\frac{5}{8} \times \frac{2}{3} = \frac{5}{\overset{}{8}_{4}} \times \frac{\overset{1}{2}}{3} = \frac{5}{12}$
Multiplying Mixed Numbers **Performance Objective 2-9, Page 52**	1. Convert all mixed numbers to improper fractions. 2. Multiply using cancellation wherever possible. 3. If the answer is an improper fraction, convert it to a whole or mixed number. 4. Reduce the answer to lowest terms if necessary. *Note*: When multiplying fractions by whole numbers, change the whole numbers to fractions by placing them over 1.	Multiply $3\frac{1}{2} \times 2\frac{3}{8}$. $3\frac{1}{2} = \frac{7}{2} \quad\quad 2\frac{3}{8} = \frac{19}{8}$ $\frac{7}{2} \times \frac{19}{8} = \frac{133}{16} = 8\frac{5}{16}$
Dividing Fractions and Mixed Numbers **Performance Objective 2-10, Page 53**	Division of fractions requires that we invert the divisor, or turn it upside down. The inverted fraction is also known as a reciprocal. **Dividing fractions:** 1. Convert all mixed numbers to improper fractions. 2. Identify the fraction that is the divisor and invert it. 3. Change ÷ to ×. 4. Multiply the fractions. 5. Reduce the answer to lowest terms if necessary.	Divide $\frac{11}{12} \div \frac{2}{3}$. $\frac{11}{12}$ is the dividend. $\frac{2}{3}$ is the divisor. $\frac{11}{12} \div \frac{2}{3} = \frac{11}{12} \times \frac{3}{2}$ $\frac{11}{\overset{}{12}_{4}} \times \frac{\overset{1}{3}}{2} = \frac{11}{8} = 1\frac{3}{8}$

TRY IT: EXERCISE SOLUTIONS FOR CHAPTER 2

1a. Mixed fraction   Seventy-six and three-fourths

1b. Common or proper fraction   Three-fifths

1c. Improper fraction   Eighteen-eighteenths

1d. Improper fraction   Thirty-three-eighths

2a. $8 \div 3 = 2\dfrac{2}{3}$

2b. $25 \div 4 = 6\dfrac{1}{4}$

2c. $39 \div 3 = \underline{\underline{13}}$

3a. $\dfrac{11}{4}$
$(2 \times 4 + 3 = 11)$

3b. $\dfrac{46}{5}$
$(9 \times 5 + 1 = 46)$

3c. $\dfrac{181}{8}$
$(22 \times 8 + 5 = 181)$

4a. $\dfrac{30 \div 5}{55 \div 5} = \dfrac{6}{11}$

4b. $\dfrac{72 \div 2}{148 \div 2} = \dfrac{36 \div 2}{74 \div 2} = \dfrac{18}{37}$

5a. $\dfrac{270 \div 270}{810 \div 270} = \dfrac{1}{3}$

$$270\overline{)810} \quad \begin{array}{r} 3 \\ 810 \\ \hline 0 \end{array}$$

5b. At lowest terms

$$\begin{array}{r} 1 \\ 175\overline{)232} \\ 175 \\ \hline 57 \end{array}$$

$$\begin{array}{r} 3 \\ 57\overline{)175} \\ 171 \\ \hline 4 \end{array}$$

$$\begin{array}{r} 14 \\ 4\overline{)57} \\ 4 \\ \hline 17 \\ 16 \\ \hline 1 \end{array}$$

6a. $\dfrac{7 \times 8}{8 \times 8} = \dfrac{56}{64}(64 \div 8 = 8)$

6b. $\dfrac{3 \times 5}{7 \times 5} = \dfrac{15}{35}(35 \div 7 = 5)$

7.
$$\begin{array}{r|cccc}
2 & 8 & 5 & 15 & 12 \\
2 & 4 & 5 & 15 & 6 \\
2 & 2 & 5 & 15 & 3 \\
3 & 1 & 5 & 15 & 3 \\
5 & 1 & 5 & 5 & 1 \\
& 1 & 1 & 1 & 1
\end{array}$$
$2 \times 2 \times 2 \times 3 \times 5 = \underline{120 = LCD}$

8. $\dfrac{3}{25} + \dfrac{9}{25} + \dfrac{8}{25} = \dfrac{3+9+8}{25} = \dfrac{20}{25} = \dfrac{4}{5}$

9.
$$\begin{array}{l}
\dfrac{1}{6} = \dfrac{5}{30} \\[6pt]
\dfrac{3}{5} = \dfrac{18}{30} \\[6pt]
+\dfrac{2}{3} = +\dfrac{20}{30} \\[6pt]
\hline
\dfrac{43}{30} = 1\dfrac{13}{30}
\end{array}$$

10.
$$\begin{array}{l}
45\dfrac{1}{4} = 45\dfrac{9}{36} \\[6pt]
16\dfrac{5}{9} = 16\dfrac{20}{36} \\[6pt]
+\dfrac{1}{3} = +\dfrac{12}{36} \\[6pt]
\hline
61\dfrac{41}{36} = 61 + 1\dfrac{5}{36} = 62\dfrac{5}{36}
\end{array}$$

11.
$$\begin{array}{l}
\dfrac{11}{25} \\[6pt]
-\dfrac{6}{25} \\[6pt]
\hline
\dfrac{5}{25} = \dfrac{1}{5}
\end{array}$$

12.
$$\begin{array}{l}
\dfrac{5}{12} = \dfrac{15}{36} \\[6pt]
-\dfrac{2}{9} = -\dfrac{8}{36} \\[6pt]
\hline
\dfrac{7}{36}
\end{array}$$

13a.
$$\begin{array}{l}
6\dfrac{3}{4} = 6\dfrac{9}{12} \\[6pt]
-4\dfrac{2}{3} = -4\dfrac{8}{12} \\[6pt]
\hline
2\dfrac{1}{12}
\end{array}$$

13b.
$$25\dfrac{2}{9} = \quad 25\dfrac{4}{18} = 24\dfrac{18}{18} + \dfrac{4}{18} = 24\dfrac{22}{18}$$
$$-11\dfrac{5}{6} = \quad -11\dfrac{15}{18} = \qquad\qquad -11\dfrac{15}{18}$$
$$\hline$$
$$13\dfrac{7}{18}$$

14. $\dfrac{12}{21} \times \dfrac{7}{8} = \dfrac{1}{2}$

15a. $8\dfrac{2}{5} \times 6\dfrac{1}{4} = \dfrac{42}{5} \times \dfrac{25}{4} = \dfrac{105}{2} = 52\dfrac{1}{2}$

15b. $45 \times \dfrac{4}{9} \times 2\dfrac{1}{4} = \dfrac{45}{1} \times \dfrac{4}{9} \times \dfrac{9}{4} = \dfrac{45}{1} = 45$

16a. $\dfrac{14}{25} \div \dfrac{4}{5} = \dfrac{\overset{7}{\cancel{14}}}{\underset{5}{\cancel{25}}} \times \dfrac{\overset{1}{\cancel{5}}}{\underset{2}{\cancel{4}}} = \dfrac{7}{10}$

16b. $11\dfrac{3}{16} \div 8\dfrac{2}{3} = \dfrac{179}{16} \div \dfrac{26}{3} = \dfrac{179}{16} \times \dfrac{3}{26} = \dfrac{537}{416} = 1\dfrac{121}{416}$

16c. $18 \div 5\dfrac{3}{5} = \dfrac{18}{1} \div \dfrac{28}{5} = \dfrac{\overset{9}{\cancel{18}}}{1} \times \dfrac{5}{\underset{14}{\cancel{28}}} = \dfrac{45}{14} = 3\dfrac{3}{14}$

CONCEPT REVIEW

1. In fractions, the number above the division line is the _____; the number below the division line is the _____. (2-1)

2. The numerator of a proper fraction is _____ than the denominator. (2-1)

3. To convert an improper fraction to a whole or mixed number, we _____ the numerator by the denominator. (2-2)

4. To convert a mixed number to an improper fraction, we begin by multiplying the denominator by the _____ number. (2-3)

5. A fraction can be reduced to lowest terms by inspection or by the greatest common _____ method. (2-4)

6. Common multiples are whole numbers used to raise fractions to _____ terms. (2-5)

7. In addition and subtraction of fractions, the most efficient common denominator is the _____ common denominator. It is abbreviated _____. (2-6)

8. A whole number divisible only by itself and 1 is a(n) _____ number. The first five of these numbers are _____, _____, _____, _____, and _____. (2-6)

9. Like fractions have the same _____. (2-7)

10. When adding unlike fractions, we begin by finding the _____ common denominator of those fractions. (2-7)

11. When subtracting like fractions, we subtract the numerators and place the difference over the original _____. (2-8)

12. When subtracting unlike fractions, we _____ each fraction to the denominator of the LCD. (2-8)

13. When multiplying fractions, cancellation is the shortcut process of finding common factors that _____ evenly into at least one of the numerators and one of the denominators. (2-9)

14. When dividing fractions, we _____ the fraction that is the divisor and then _____ the fractions. (2-10)

ASSESSMENT TEST

Identify the type of fraction and write it in word form.

1. $\dfrac{18}{11}$

2. $4\dfrac{1}{6}$

3. $\dfrac{13}{16}$

Convert to whole or mixed numbers.

4. $\dfrac{33}{6}$

5. $\dfrac{125}{5}$

Convert to improper fractions.

6. $7\dfrac{4}{5}$

7. $21\dfrac{2}{3}$

Reduce to lowest terms.

8. $\dfrac{96}{108}$

9. $\dfrac{26}{65}$

Convert to higher terms as indicated.

10. $\dfrac{4}{5}$ to twenty-fifths

11. $\dfrac{3}{13} = \dfrac{}{78}$

Find the least common denominator for the following fractions.

12. $\dfrac{3}{4}, \dfrac{19}{20}, \dfrac{1}{6}, \dfrac{3}{5}, \dfrac{8}{15}$

Solve the following problems and reduce to lowest terms.

13. $\dfrac{5}{6} - \dfrac{3}{4}$

14. $\dfrac{2}{3} + \dfrac{1}{6} + \dfrac{11}{12}$

15. $\dfrac{2}{3} \div \dfrac{1}{8}$

16. $\dfrac{5}{6} \times \dfrac{1}{4}$

17. $\dfrac{2}{5} \times 5\dfrac{3}{8} \times 2$

18. $6\dfrac{5}{6} - \dfrac{17}{18}$

19. $4\dfrac{1}{2} + 5\dfrac{5}{6} + 3$

20. $25\dfrac{1}{2} \div 1\dfrac{2}{3}$

21. The Bean Counters, an accounting firm, has 161 employees. If $\dfrac{3}{7}$ of them are certified public accountants, how many CPAs are there?

CHAPTER 2

22. Ventura Coal mined $6\frac{2}{3}$ tons on Monday, $7\frac{3}{4}$ tons on Tuesday, and $4\frac{1}{2}$ tons on Wednesday. If the goal is to mine 25 tons this week, how many more tons must be mined?

23. A blueprint of a house has a scale of 1 inch equals $4\frac{1}{2}$ feet. If the living room wall measures $5\frac{1}{4}$ inches on the drawing, what is the actual length of the wall?

24. If $\frac{3}{8}$ of a 60-pound bag of ready-mix concrete is Portland cement, how many pounds of other materials are in the bag?

25. The total length of an extension cord measures $18\frac{9}{16}$ inches. The plug end measures $2\frac{3}{4}$ inches, and the receptacle end measures $5\frac{3}{8}$ inches. What is the length of the wire portion of the extension cord?

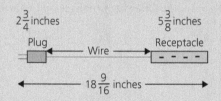

26. During a spring clearance sale, Walmart advertises $\frac{1}{4}$ off the list price of Model II microwave ovens and an additional $\frac{1}{5}$ off the sale price for ovens that are scratched or dented.

   a. If the list price of a Model II is $240, what is the sale price?

   b. What is the price of a scratched one?

27. You are a sales representative for Boater's Paradise. Last year you sold $490,000 in marine products.

   a. If this year you expect to sell $\frac{1}{5}$ more, how much will your sales be?

   b. If you are paid a commission of $\frac{1}{12}$ of sales, how much will you earn this year?

CHAPTER
2

28. A developer owns three lots measuring $1\frac{2}{3}$ acres each, four lots measuring $2\frac{1}{2}$ acres each, and one lot measuring $3\frac{3}{8}$ acres.

   a. What is the total acreage owned by the developer?

   b. If each acre is worth $10,000, what is the total value of the properties?

   c. If the company plans to build 8 homes per acre, how many homes will it build?

29. A house has 4,400 square feet. The bedrooms occupy $\frac{2}{5}$ of the space, the living and dining rooms occupy $\frac{1}{4}$ of the space, the garage represents $\frac{1}{10}$ of the space, and the balance is split evenly among three bathrooms and the kitchen.

   a. How many square feet are in each bath and the kitchen?

   b. If the owner wants to increase the size of the garage by $\frac{1}{8}$, how many total square feet will the new garage have?

30. Among other ingredients, a recipe for linguini with red sauce calls for the following: 24 ounces linguini pasta, $6\frac{2}{5}$ tablespoons minced garlic, 5 cups fresh tomatoes, and 10 tablespoons Parmesan cheese. If the recipe serves 8 people, recalculate the quantities to serve 5 people.

Pasta:

Garlic:

Tomatoes:

Cheese:

Rod Ferris/Shutterstock.com

Chefs and cooks measure, mix, and cook ingredients according to recipes, using a variety of pots, pans, cutlery, and other kitchen equipment.

A working knowledge of fractions is one of the job requirements for people employed in the culinary arts. Most foods and other recipe ingredients are measured and combined using fractions.

31. You are an engineer with Ace Foundations, Inc. Your company has been hired to build a 165-foot foundation wall for the construction of a house. You have calculated that the drainage line around the wall will take 1 cubic yard of gravel for every 5 feet of wall.

    a. If a contractor's wheelbarrow has a $\frac{1}{3}$ cubic yard capacity, how many wheelbarrow loads of gravel will be needed?

    b. If your company typically builds this type of a wall at an average rate of $7\frac{1}{2}$ feet per hour, how many hours will it take to build the foundation wall?

    c. Each load of gravel costs $4. The wall materials cost $13 per foot, and labor costs $62 per hour. If $2,700 profit is to be added to the job, how much is the total charge to build the foundation wall?

BUSINESS DECISION: THE CUTTING EDGE

32. You have been given the job of cutting a supply of 2" × 4" pieces of lumber for a frame house. Each piece is to be $14\frac{1}{2}$ inches long. Each cut is $\frac{1}{8}$ inch wide. At Home Depot and Lowe's, the choices of stock length are 10 feet, 12 feet, and 14 feet. You have been asked to choose the length of stock that will have the least amount of waste after you cut as many pieces as you can from it. Which length of stock should you choose?

COLLABORATIVE LEARNING ACTIVITY

Knowing Fractions Is Half the Battle

As a team, investigate and share with the class how fractions are used in the following areas.

a. Cooking
b. Sports
c. Medicine or pharmacy
d. Architecture or building construction
e. Additional team choice _____
f. Additional team choice _____

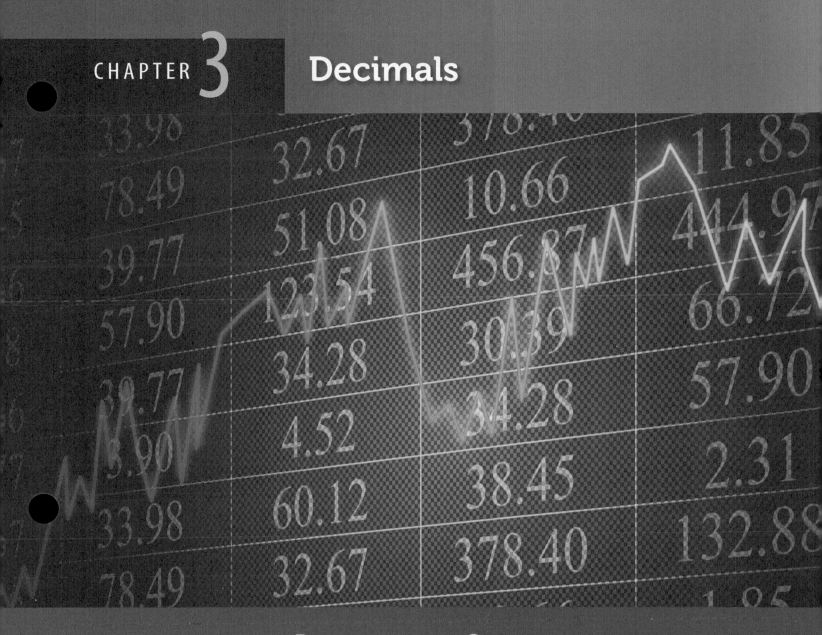

CHAPTER 3 Decimals

PERFORMANCE OBJECTIVES

In Chapter 1, we learned that the position of the digits in our number system affects their value. In whole numbers, we dealt with the positions, or places, to the left of the decimal point. In decimal numbers, we deal with the places to the right of the decimal point. These places express values that are less than whole numbers.

As with fractions, decimals are a way of expressing *parts* of a whole thing. Decimals are used extensively in business applications. In this chapter, you will learn to read, write, and work problems involving all types of decimal numbers.

3-1 READING AND WRITING DECIMAL NUMBERS IN NUMERICAL AND WORD FORM

decimal numbers, or **decimals** Amounts less than whole, or less than one. For example, .44 is a decimal number.

decimal point A dot written in a decimal number to indicate where the place values change from whole numbers to decimal numbers.

mixed decimals Decimals written in conjunction with whole numbers. For example, 2.44 is a mixed decimal.

By definition, **decimal numbers**, or **decimals**, are amounts less than whole, or less than one. They are preceded by a dot known as the **decimal point** and are written .31 or 0.31, for example. The zero is used to ensure that the decimal point is not missed. Often, decimals are written in conjunction with whole numbers. These are known as **mixed decimals**. In mixed decimals, the decimal point separates the whole numbers from the decimal, such as 4.31.

The place value chart shown in Exhibit 3-1 expands the whole number chart from Chapter 1 to include the places representing decimals. In decimals, the value of each place starting at the decimal point and moving from left to right decreases by a factor of 10. The names of the places on the decimal side end in *ths*; they are tenths, hundredths, thousandths, ten-thousandths, hundred-thousandths, millionths, and so on.

To read or write decimal numbers in words, you must read or write the decimal part as if it were a whole number, then name the place value of the last digit on the right. For example, .0594 would be read as "five hundred ninety-four ten-thousandths."

In reading and writing mixed decimals, the decimal point should be read as "and." For example, 81.205 would be read as "eighty-one and two hundred five thousandths." If the

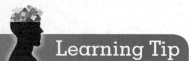

Learning Tip

When reading numbers, remember that decimals start with the *tenths* place as we move left to right starting from the decimal point, whereas whole numbers start with the *ones* place as we move right to left starting from the decimal point.

Also, don't forget that the word "and" is used to represent the decimal point.

B-A-C-O/Shutterstock.com

Margin of Victory Decimals are used in all forms of racing to express the time differences among the competitors. The closest NASCAR finish to date occurred at the Darlington Raceway in 2003 when Ricky Craven finished ahead of Kurt Bush by a mere 0.002 of a second in the Carolina Dodge Dealers 400.

Action Sports Photography/Shutterstock.com

EXHIBIT 3-1

Decimal Numbers Place Value
Chart

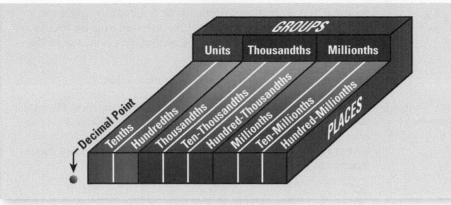

decimal has a fraction at the end, simply read them together using the place value of the last digit of the decimal. For example, $.12\frac{1}{2}$ would be read as "twelve and one-half hundredths."

When a dollar sign ($) precedes a number, the whole number value represents dollars and the decimal value represents cents. The decimal point is read as "and." For example, $146.79 would be read as "one hundred forty-six dollars and seventy-nine cents."

EXAMPLE1 READING AND WRITING DECIMALS

Read and write the following numbers in word form.

a. .18   b. .0391   c. .00127   d. 34.892   e. 1,299.008   f. $.328\frac{2}{3}$

Read and write the following numbers in numerical form.

g. Three hundred seventy-two ten-thousandths

h. Sixteen thousand and forty-one hundredths

i. Twenty-five and sixty-three and one-half thousandths

►SOLUTIONSTRATEGY

a. .18

Strategy: In this example, write the number eighteen. Because the last digit, 8, is in the hundredths place, the decimal would be written:

Eighteen hundredths

b. .0391

Strategy: Write the number three hundred ninety-one. The last digit, 1, is in the ten-thousandths place; therefore, the decimal would be written:

Three hundred ninety-one ten-thousandths

c. .00127

Strategy: Write the number one hundred twenty-seven. The last digit, 7, is in the hundred-thousandths place; therefore, the decimal would be written:

One hundred twenty-seven hundred-thousandths

d. 34.892

Strategy: This example is a mixed decimal. First, write the whole number: thirty-four. The decimal point is represented by the word *and*. Now write the decimal part as the number eight hundred ninety-two. The last digit, 2, is in the thousandths place; therefore, the mixed decimal is written:

Thirty-four and eight hundred ninety-two thousandths

e. 1,299.008

Strategy: This example is also a mixed decimal. Start by writing the whole number: one thousand, two hundred ninety-nine. Write *and* for the decimal point and write the number eight. Because the last digit, 8, is in the thousandths place, the mixed decimal is written:

One thousand, two hundred ninety-nine and eight thousandths

f. $.328\frac{2}{3}$

Strategy: This decimal has a fraction at the end. Start by writing the number three hundred twenty-eight. Write *and*; then write the fraction, two-thirds. Because the last digit of the decimal, 8, is in the thousandths place, it is written.

Three hundred twenty-eight and two-thirds thousandths

g. Three hundred seventy-two ten-thousandths

Strategy: Write three hundred seventy-two in numerical form. Place the last digit, 2, in the ten-thousandths place. Because ten thousand has four zeros, this is four places to the right of the decimal point. Note that we have to add a zero in the tenths place for the last digit, 2, to be in the ten-thousandths place.

.0372

h. Sixteen thousand and forty-one hundredths

Strategy: Write the whole number sixteen thousand. Place the decimal point for the word *and*. Write the number forty-one and place the last digit, 1, in the hundredths place. Note that hundred has two zeros; therefore, the hundredths place is two places to the right of the decimal point.

16,000.41

i. Twenty-five and sixty-three and one-half thousandths

Strategy: Write the whole number twenty-five. Place the decimal point for the word *and*. Write the number sixty-three and place the fraction one-half after it. Write the last digit, 3, in the thousandths place, three places to the right of the decimal point. Note that we have to add a zero in the tenths place for the last digit, 3, to be in the thousandths place.

$25.063\frac{1}{2}$

▶TRYITEXERCISE 1

Read and write the following numbers in word form.

a. .64   b. .492   c. .10019   d. 579.0004   e. 26.708   f. $.33\frac{1}{3}$

Write the following numbers in numerical form.

g. Twenty-one thousandths

h. Two hundred seventy-two and ninety-four hundred-thousandths

i. Eleven and three and one-quarter thousandths

CHECK YOUR ANSWERS WITH THE SOLUTIONS ON PAGE 88.

3-2   ROUNDING DECIMAL NUMBERS TO A SPECIFIED PLACE VALUE

Rounding decimals is important in business because numbers frequently contain more decimal places than necessary. For monetary amounts, we round to the nearest cent, or hundredth place. For other business applications, we usually do not go beyond thousandths as a final answer.

STEPS TO ROUND DECIMALS TO A SPECIFIED PLACE VALUE

STEP 1. Determine the place to which the decimal is to be rounded.

STEP 2a. If the digit to the right of the one being rounded is 5 or more, increase the digit in the place being rounded by 1.

STEP 2b. If the digit to the right of the one being rounded is 4 or less, do not change the digit in the place being rounded.

STEP 3. Delete all digits to the right of the digit being rounded.

EXAMPLE2 ROUNDING DECIMALS

Round the following numbers to the indicated place.

a. .0292 to hundredths

b. .33945 to thousandths

c. 36.798 to tenths

d. 177.0212782 to hundred-thousandths

e. $46.976 to cents

f. $66.622 to dollars

SOLUTIONSTRATEGY

Decimal Number	Indicated Place	Rounded Number
a. .0292	.0292	.03
b. .33945	.33945	.339
c. 36.798	36.798	36.8
d. 177.0212782	177.0212782	177.02128
e. $46.976	$46.976	$46.98
f. $66.622	$66.622	$67

TRYITEXERCISE 2

Round the following numbers to the indicated place.

a. 5.78892 to thousandths

b. .004522 to ten-thousandths

c. $345.8791 to cents

d. 76.03324 to hundredths

e. $766.43 to dollars

f. 34,956.1229 to tenths

CHECK YOUR ANSWERS WITH THE SOLUTIONS ON PAGE 88.

Learning Tip

Most business calculators, such as the Texas Instruments BA II Plus, store numeric values internally to an accuracy of 13 digits, but you can specify the number of decimal places you want to display. When using the "floating-decimal" option, the calculator displays up to 10 digits.

Changing the number of decimal places affects the display only. Except for certain business applications such as amortization and depreciation results, the calculator does not round internal values. To round the internal value, you must use the "round" function.

REVIEW EXERCISES

3 SECTION I

Write the following numbers in word form.

1. .21

   Twenty-one hundredths

2. 2.48

3. .081

4. 14.659

5. 98,045.045

6. .000033

7. .00938

8. $36.99\frac{2}{3}$

9. $.00057\frac{1}{2}$

10. $2,885.59

JUMP START WWW

Write the following numbers in numerical form.

11. **Eight tenths**

    .8

12. Twenty-nine thousandths

JUMP START WWW

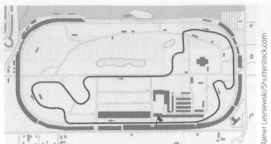

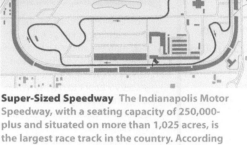

Super-Sized Speedway The Indianapolis Motor Speedway, with a seating capacity of 250,000-plus and situated on more than 1,025 acres, is the largest race track in the country. According to *The Wall Street Journal*, the property could hold about 40 Yankee Stadiums, 12 Wimbledon tennis campuses, or two Vatican Cities!

13. Sixty-seven thousand, three hundred nine and four hundredths

14. Two hundred two and eight thousand, seven hundred ninety-three ten-thousandths

15. On three consecutive laps at the Indianapolis Motor Speedway, a race car was timed at 41.507 seconds, 41.057 seconds, and 41.183 seconds. List these times in ascending order, from shortest to longest.

16. On an assembly line quality control test at Hi-Volt Electronics, silver wire measured 0.9 inches, 0.962 inches, 0.098 inches, and 0.9081 inches in diameter. List these measurements in descending order, from largest to smallest.

Round the following numbers to the indicated place.

JUMP
START
WWW

17. **.448557 to hundredths**

   $0.448557 = 0.45$

18. 123.0069 to thousandths

19. .4813501 to ten-thousandths

20. .0100393 to hundred-thousandths

21. $688.75 to dollars

22. $14.59582 to cents

23. 88.964 to tenths

EXCEL**1**

24. 43.0056 to hundredths

25. 1.344 to hundredths

26. 45.80901 to a whole number

A *micrometer* is a device used in science and engineering for precisely measuring minute distances or thicknesses.

A *micron* (also known as a *micrometer*) is a unit of length in the metric system equal to one-millionth of a meter. The diameter of a human hair measures 80–100 microns.

A *millimeter* (symbol mm) is a unit of length in the metric system equal to one-thousandth of a meter. One inch is equal to 25.4 mm.

A *centimeter* (symbol cm) is a unit of length in the metric system equal to one-hundredth of a meter. One inch is equal to 2.54 cm.

For complete coverage of business measurements and the metric system, see Chapter 22 on your text's website.

BUSINESS DECISION: TECH TALK

27. You are the assistant to the production manager for All American Industries. When you arrived at work, there was a message on your answering machine from an important client with a rush order. It stated the following:

   Hi! This is Lee Perry from Precision Fabricators. We need sixteen of the three and three-quarter-inch Wedgebands with a gap of fifty-seven thousandths; twenty of the four and three-eighth-inch Wedgebands with a gap of two hundred forty-nine ten-thousandths of an inch; and twenty-five Wedgeband connectors with clamps that adjust from one and twenty-three hundredths inches to five and three hundred seventy-six thousandths. Please bill and ship the order to the usual address. Thanks.

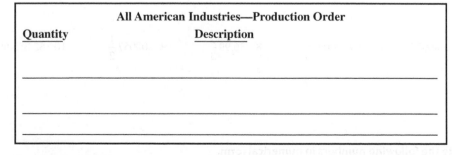

All American Industries—Production Order	
Quantity	**Description**

a. Write this order in numerals for the production department to process.

b. Comparing the $3\frac{3}{4}''$ Wedgeband and the $4\frac{3}{8}''$ Wedgeband, which has the smaller gap?

DECIMAL NUMBERS AND THE FUNDAMENTAL PROCESSES

3 | **SECTION II**

In business, working with decimals is an everyday occurrence. As you will see, performing the fundamental processes of addition, subtraction, multiplication, and division on decimal numbers is very much like performing them on whole numbers. As before, the alignment of the numbers is very important. The difference is in the handling and placement of the decimal point.

ADDING AND SUBTRACTING DECIMALS

3-3

In adding and subtracting decimals, we follow the same procedure as we did with whole numbers. As before, be sure that you line up all the place values, including the decimal points.

STEPS FOR ADDING AND SUBTRACTING DECIMALS

STEP 1. Line up all the decimal points vertically.

STEP 2. (Optional) Add zeros to the right of the decimal numbers that do not have enough places.

STEP 3. Perform the addition or subtraction, working from right to left.

STEP 4. Place the decimal point in the answer in the same position (column) as in the problem.

EXAMPLE3 ADDING AND SUBTRACTING DECIMALS

a. Add 45.3922 + .0019 + 2.9 + 1,877.332
b. Add $37.89 + $2.76

c. Subtract 87.06 − 35.2
d. Subtract $67.54 from $5,400

SOLUTIONSTRATEGY

These examples are solved by lining up the decimal points, then performing the indicated operation as if they were whole numbers.

a.
$$
\begin{array}{r}
45.3922 \\
.0019 \\
2.9000 \\
+\,1,877.3320 \\
\hline
1,925.6261
\end{array}
$$

b.
$$
\begin{array}{r}
\$37.89 \\
+\ \ 2.76 \\
\hline
\$40.65
\end{array}
$$

c.
$$
\begin{array}{r}
87.06 \\
-\,35.20 \\
\hline
51.86
\end{array}
$$

d.
$$
\begin{array}{r}
\$5,400.00 \\
-\ \ \ \ 67.54 \\
\hline
\$5,332.46
\end{array}
$$

TRYITEXERCISE 3

Perform the indicated operation.

a. 35.7008 + 311.2 + 84,557.54
b. $65.79 + $154.33

c. Subtract 57.009 from 186.7
d. $79.80 minus $34.61

CHECK YOUR ANSWERS WITH THE SOLUTIONS ON PAGE 88.

IN THE Business World

Did you know the Romans called the total of addition problems *res summa*, the highest thing. Later this was shortened to *summa*, which is why we call addition answers *sums*.

When adding, the Romans always added a column of numbers starting from the bottom, putting the total at the top! This explains why we still say "to add up."

iStock.com/Nikada

rtguest/Shutterstock.com

3-4 MULTIPLYING DECIMALS

Decimals are multiplied in the same way as whole numbers except we must now deal with placing the decimal point in the answer. The rule is that there must be as many decimal places in the product as there are total decimal places in the two factors, the multiplier and the multiplicand. This may require adding zeros to the product.

STEPS FOR MULTIPLYING DECIMALS

STEP 1. Multiply the numbers as if they were whole numbers. Disregard the decimal points.

STEP 2. Total the number of decimal places in the two factors, the multiplier and the multiplicand.

STEP 3. Insert the decimal point in the product, giving it the same number of decimal places as the total from Step 2.

STEP 4. If necessary, place zeros to the left of the product to provide the correct number of digits.

EXAMPLE4 MULTIPLYING DECIMALS

a. **Multiply 125.4 by 3.12.**

▶SOLUTIONSTRATEGY

```
    125.4  1 decimal place
 ×  3.12   2 decimal places
   2 508
  12 54
 376 2
 391.248   3 decimal places
```

b. **Multiply .0004 by 6.3.**

▶SOLUTIONSTRATEGY

```
   6.3   1 decimal place
 × .0004  4 decimal places
  .00252  5 decimal places
```

Here, we had to add two zeros to the left of the product to make five decimal places.

Multiplication Shortcut

Whenever you are multiplying a decimal by a power of 10, such as 10, 100, 1,000, or 10,000, count the number of zeros in the multiplier and move the decimal point in the multiplicand the same number of places to the right. If necessary, add zeros to the product to provide the required places.

c. **Multiply 138.57 by 10, 100, 1,000, and 10,000.**

▶SOLUTIONSTRATEGY

$138.57 \times 10 = \underline{1,385.7}$	Decimal moved 1 place to the right
$138.57 \times 100 = \underline{13,857}$	Decimal moved 2 places to the right
$138.57 \times 1,000 = \underline{138,570}$	Decimal moved 3 places to the right—1 zero added
$138.57 \times 10,000 = \underline{1,385,700}$	Decimal moved 4 places to the right—2 zeros added

iStock.com/Nikada

▶ **TRYITEXERCISE 4**

Multiply the following numbers.

a.   876.66
     × .045

b.   4,955.8
     ×   2.9

c. $65.79
     ×   558

d.   .00232 by 1,000

CHECK YOUR ANSWERS WITH THE SOLUTIONS ON PAGE 88.

DIVIDING DECIMALS   3-5

In division of decimals, be aware of the decimal points. The basic rule is that you cannot divide with a decimal in the divisor. If there is a decimal, you must convert it to a whole number before dividing.

STEPS FOR DIVIDING DECIMALS IF THE DIVISOR IS A WHOLE NUMBER

STEP 1. Place the decimal point in the quotient directly above the decimal point in the dividend.

STEP 2. Divide the numbers. Zeros may be added to the right of the dividend as needed.

EXAMPLE 5A   DIVIDING DECIMALS

Divide: 8.50 ÷ 25.

▶ SOLUTION STRATEGY

$$
\begin{array}{r}
.34 \\
8.50 \div 25 = 25)\overline{8.50} \\
7\,5 \\
\overline{1\,00} \\
1\,00 \\
\overline{0}
\end{array}
$$

In this example, the divisor, 25, is a whole number; so we place the decimal point in the quotient directly above the decimal point in the dividend and then divide. The answer is .34.

STEPS FOR DIVIDING DECIMALS IF THE DIVISOR IS A DECIMAL NUMBER

STEP 1. Move the decimal point in the divisor to the right until it becomes a whole number.

STEP 2. Move the decimal point in the dividend the same number of places as you moved it in the divisor. It may be necessary to add zeros to the right of the dividend if there are not enough places.

STEP 3. Place the decimal point in the quotient directly above the decimal point in the dividend.

STEP 4. Divide the numbers.

Note: All answers involving money should be rounded to the nearest cent. This means dividing until the quotient has a thousandths place and then rounding back to hundredths. For example, $45.671 = $45.67 and $102.879 = $102.88.

Learning Tip

When adding, subtracting, multiplying, or dividing decimals, numbers should not be rounded until the final answer—unless you are estimating.

If the situation involves money, final answers should be rounded to the nearest cent.

EXAMPLE5B   DIVIDING DECIMALS

Divide: 358.75 ÷ 17.5.

►SOLUTIONSTRATEGY

$358.75 \div 17.5 =$

$17.5)\overline{358.75}$

$175)\overline{3587.5}$

In this example, the divisor, 17.5, is a decimal with one place. To make it a whole number, move the decimal point one place to the right.

Then move the decimal point in the dividend one place to the right and place the decimal point in the quotient above the decimal point in the dividend.

Now divide the numbers. The answer is 20.5.

$$
\begin{array}{r}
20.5 \\
175)\overline{3587.5} \\
\underline{350} \\
87\ 5 \\
\underline{87\ 5} \\
0
\end{array}
$$

Division Shortcut

Whenever you divide a decimal by a power of 10, such as 10, 100, 1,000, or 10,000, count the number of zeros in the divisor and move the decimal point in the dividend the same number of places to the left. It may be necessary to add zeros to provide the required places.

EXAMPLE5C   DIVIDING DECIMALS BY A POWER OF 10

Divide 43.78 by 10, 100, 1,000, and 10,000.

►SOLUTIONSTRATEGY

$43.78 \div 10 = 4.378$	Decimal moved 1 place to the left
$43.78 \div 100 = .4378$	Decimal moved 2 places to the left
$43.78 \div 1,000 = .04378$	Decimal moved 3 places to the left—1 zero added
$43.78 \div 10,000 = .004378$	Decimal moved 4 places to the left—2 zeros added

►TRYITEXERCISE 5

Divide the following decimals.

a. $716.8 \div 16$ b. $21.336 \div .007$ c. $\$3,191.18 \div 42.1$ d. $2.03992 \div 1,000$

CHECK YOUR ANSWERS WITH THE SOLUTIONS ON PAGE 88.

SECTION II   3   REVIEW EXERCISES

Perform the indicated operation for the following.

1. $2.03 + 56.003$

$$
\begin{array}{r}
2.030 \\
+56.003 \\
\hline
58.033
\end{array}
$$

2. $.006 + 12.33$

3. $24.66 + $19.72 + $.89

4. 54.669 + 121.3393 + 7.4

5. .000494 + 45.776 + 16.008 + 91

6. 495.09 − 51.05

7. 58.043 − 41.694

8. $70.55 − $12.79

9. $2.54 − $.95

10. 61.58 − 13.214

11. Add seventy-five and twenty-six hundredths and forty-one and eighteen thousandths. Express your answer in numerical and word form.

12. Subtract fifteen and eighty-eight ten-thousandths from thirty-six. Express your answer in numerical and word form.

13. On a recent trip, Tony Segretto filled up his gas tank four times with the following quantities of gasoline: 23.4 gallons, 19.67 gallons, 21.008 gallons, and 16.404 gallons. How many gallons did Tony buy?

14. In 1 week of training for the San Francisco Marathon, Jessy Bergeman had training runs of 4.3 miles, 9.7 miles, 5.9 miles, 18.4 miles, and 5.4 miles. What was the total distance for these training runs?

iStock.com/Sawayasu Tsuji

15. On the way home from work, Bill Kingman stopped at Chicken Delight to purchase dinner for the family. The chicken was $12.79. Drinks came to $4.84. Side dishes totaled $7.65, and desserts amounted to $4.97.

    a.   What was the total cost of the food?

b. If Bill had a coupon for "$2.50 off any purchase over $15," how much did he pay?

16. Last week Kate Burke ran a 5-kilometer race in 26.696 minutes. This week she ran a race in 24.003 minutes. What is the difference in Kate's times?

17. Jason Carlage needed a few groceries. At E-Z Shop Market, he bought a loaf of cinnamon raisin bread for $2.29, a quart of milk for $1.78, a bunch of bananas for $1.83, and a pound of butter for $2.96. How much change did he receive from a $20 bill?

18. Faith Sherlock received her monthly pension check of $1,348.26. From that amount, she transferred $180 to a savings account and paid the electricity bill for $156.33, the gas bill for $9.38, the water bill for $98.42, and the cable television bill for $48.54. How much remained of Faith's monthly pension?

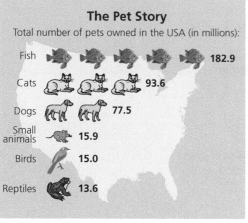

The Pet Story

Total number of pets owned in the USA (in millions):

Fish	182.9
Cats	93.6
Dogs	77.5
Small animals	15.9
Birds	15.0
Reptiles	13.6

Source: American Pet Product Manufacturers Association

19. Use the chart "The Pet Story" to answer the following questions.

a. How many fewer birds are there than small animals? Express your answer in numerical form.

b. How many more fish are there than cats and dogs combined? Express your answer in numerical form.

Multiply the following numbers.

20. $\begin{array}{r} 45.77 \\ \times\ \ \ 12 \\ \hline 549.24 \end{array}$

21. $\begin{array}{r} 508.02 \\ \times\ \ \ .61 \\ \hline \end{array}$

22. $\begin{array}{r} 4.711 \\ \times\ \ 2.4 \\ \hline \end{array}$

23. $\begin{array}{r} 112.005 \\ \times\ \ 10,000 \\ \hline \end{array}$

24. $\begin{array}{r} .00202 \\ \times\ \ \ 24 \\ \hline \end{array}$

25. 3.861×5.2

26. $45.0079 \times 1,000$

27. $.3309 \times 100,000$

Divide the following numbers. Round to hundredths when necessary.

28. $24.6 \div 19$
$1.294 = \underline{\underline{1.29}}$

29. $1,864.2 \div 12.31$

30. $25.64 \div 1,000$

31. $\$24.50 \div 9$

32. $72\overline{)266.4}$

33. $23.18\overline{)139.08}$

34. $.04\overline{)62.2}$

35. $4.6\overline{)1000}$

36. Sam Estero received a $50 gift card to iTunes for his birthday. If he downloaded 12 songs at $0.99 per song, 5 songs at $1.29 per song, and 4 apps for his iPhone at $1.99 per app, how much credit remained on the gift card?

37. Ben Whitney bought a car at Auto Nation for $14,566.90. The sticker price was $17,047.88.

    a. How much did Ben save from the sticker price?

    b. The tax was $957.70, and the registration and license plate cost $65.40. What is the total cost of the car?

    c. If Ben makes a down payment of $4,550 and gets an interest-free car loan from the dealer, what will the equal monthly payments be for 48 months?

38. Jimmie Masters earns $4,825.50 per month as a manager at Berries Restaurant.

    a. How much does he earn in a year?

    b. If Jimmie gets a raise of $2,865 per year, what is his new annual and monthly salary?

39. *USA Today* reported that Ethiopian Airlines had confirmed a $3 billion order for 12 A350 aircrafts from Airbus.

    a. What was the average cost per plane?

    b. It was also reported that Airbus planned large wingtip devices on the A320 aircraft, reducing fuel burn by 3.5% and saving about $220,000 a year per plane. How much will these fuel savings per year amount to for a fleet of 12 of these aircraft?

Airbus is an aircraft manufacturing subsidiary of EADS, a European aerospace company. Based in Toulouse, France, and with significant activity across Europe, the company produces about half of the world's jet airliners.

Airbus employs more than 50,000 people in four European Union countries: Germany, France, the United Kingdom, and Spain.

40. Last week, you worked 18 hours and earned $256.50. What was your hourly rate?

41. Matt Menke purchased 153.6 square yards of carpeting on sale for $13.70 per yard.

    a. What was the cost of the carpet?

b. Normally, this carpeting sells for $19.69 per yard. How much did Matt save by purchasing during the sale?

42. Edward Nolan has room for 26 bedding plants in his garden. He can get pansies for $1.89 each, marigolds for $1.29 each, and zinnias for $0.84 each. He plans to buy 10 of one type and 8 each of the other two types of plants.

a. What is the minimum Edward will have to spend?

b. What is the maximum Edward could spend?

43. Southern Telecom is offering a prepaid phone card that contains 200 minutes of time for 8 cents per minute. What is the cost of the card?

44. A developer, Fiesta Valley Homes, is building 13 townhouses at one time. Each roof measures 45.7 feet by 68.55 feet.

a. What is the total square feet per roof? (Multiply length by width.)

b. What is the total square feet of roof for the entire project?

c. If the roofing company charges $4.15 per square foot, what is the total cost of the roofs?

45. Tim Meekma owns a PepsiCo vending truck that holds 360 quarts of soda. Last Saturday at a carnival, Tim sold out completely. He sells a 10-ounce Pepsi for $1.25. There are 16 ounces in a pint and 2 pints in a quart.

a. How many drinks did he serve?

Cola Wars! Coke was created in 1896 and Pepsi followed twelve years later. Together these companies typically spend more than $3 billion annually on advertising and account for more than two-thirds of U.S. soft drink revenues.

b. How much revenue did he take in for the day?

c. For the next carnival, Tim is considering switching to either a 12-ounce drink for $1.65 or a 16-ounce drink for $1.95. As his business adviser, what size do you recommend, assuming each would be a sellout?

BUSINESS DECISION: ADMINISTERING A GOVERNMENT PROGRAM

46. According to the Food and Nutrition Service of the U.S. Department of Agriculture, in one school year the National School Lunch Program (NSLP) served 31.2 million school lunches. Of these, 16.1 million were free lunches, 3.2 million were lunches at reduced price, and 11.9 million were full-priced lunches.

    The federal government reimburses school districts $2.68 for each free lunch, $2.28 for each reduced-price lunch, and $0.25 for each paid lunch. In addition to cash reimbursements, schools are entitled to receive USDA foods called "entitlement" foods at a value of 19.50 cents for each lunch served.

    You are the administrator in charge of the school lunch program for your school district. Last month the schools in your district served 25,000 free lunches, 15,000 "reduced-price" lunches, and 50,000 regular-priced lunches.

    a. Calculate the amount of reimbursement you expect to receive from the NSLP for last month.

    b. In addition to the lunch reimbursement, the NSLP program pays your district $.035 per one-half pint of milk served with each meal. If each meal averaged 1 one-half pint of milk per meal, calculate the total amount of milk reimbursement you expect for last month.

    c. **The Bottom Line –** What is the total amount of reimbursement your district will receive for last month?

    d. **Red Tape –** The government paperwork you must submit requires that you report the average reimbursement per meal for both lunch and milk combined last month. Calculate this amount.

The National School Lunch Program (NSLP) is a federally assisted meal program operating in public and nonprofit private schools and residential child care institutions. It provides nutritionally balanced, low-cost or free lunches to children each school day. The program was established under the National School Lunch Act and signed by President Harry Truman in 1946

CONVERSION OF DECIMALS TO FRACTIONS AND FRACTIONS TO DECIMALS

3   SECTION III

Changing a number from decimal form to its fractional equivalent or changing a number in fractional form to its decimal equivalent is common in the business world. For example, a builder or an architect may use fractions when dealing with the measurements of a project but convert to decimals when calculating the cost of materials.

CONVERTING DECIMALS TO FRACTIONS   3-6

Keep in mind that decimals are another way of writing fractions whose denominators are powers of 10 (10, 100, 1,000, …). When you are converting a mixed decimal, the whole number is added to the new fraction, resulting in a mixed fraction.

STEPS FOR CONVERTING DECIMALS TO THEIR FRACTIONAL EQUIVALENT

STEP 1. Write the numerator of the fraction as the decimal number, without the decimal point.

STEP 2. Write the denominator as 1 followed by as many zeros as there are decimal places in the original decimal number.

STEP 3. Reduce the fraction to lowest terms.

EXAMPLE6 CONVERTING DECIMALS TO FRACTIONS

Convert the following numbers to their reduced fractional equivalent.

a. .64   b. .125   c. .0457   d. 17.31

SOLUTIONSTRATEGY

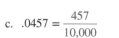

a. $.64 = \dfrac{64}{100} = \dfrac{16}{25}$

In this example, 64 becomes the numerator. Because there are two decimal places, the denominator is 1 with two zeros. Then reduce the fraction.

b. $.125 = \dfrac{125}{1,000} = \dfrac{1}{8}$

Once again, the decimal becomes the numerator, 125. This decimal has three places; therefore, the denominator will be 1 followed by three zeros. The resulting fraction is then reduced to lowest terms.

c. $.0457 = \dfrac{457}{10,000}$

This fraction does not reduce.

d. $17.31 = 17 + \dfrac{31}{100} = 17\dfrac{31}{100}$

This mixed decimal results in a mixed fraction. It cannot be reduced.

TRYITEXERCISE 6

Convert the following decimals to their fractional equivalent, reducing where possible.

a. .875   b. 23.076   c. .0004   d. 84.75

CHECK YOUR ANSWERS WITH THE SOLUTIONS ON PAGE 88.

Learning Tip

When converting decimals to fractions, verbally say the decimal and then write down what you said as a fraction. For example:

- .85 would be verbally stated as "eighty-five hundredths" and written as $\dfrac{85}{100}$.

- .655 would be verbally stated as "six hundred fifty-five thousandths" and written as $\dfrac{655}{1,000}$.

3-7 CONVERTING FRACTIONS TO DECIMALS

In Chapter 2, we learned that fractions are actually a way of expressing division, with the line separating the numerator and the denominator representing "divided by."

$$\frac{\textbf{Numerator (dividend)}}{\textbf{Denominator (divisor)}} = \textbf{Denominator } \overline{)\textbf{Numerator}}$$

In business, decimal numbers are usually rounded to three places (thousandths) or less. When expressing money, round to the nearest hundredth, or cent.

STEPS FOR CONVERTING FRACTIONS TO DECIMALS

STEP 1. Divide the numerator by the denominator.

STEP 2. Add a decimal point and zeros, as necessary, to the numerator (dividend).

Learning Tip

Try this for practice:
You are driving to a new restaurant in an unfamiliar area. A highway billboard directs you to make a right turn at an intersection $4\frac{3}{5}$ miles ahead. If your odometer reads 16,237.8, at what mileage should you make the turn?

Solution: $4\frac{3}{5} = 4.6$ 16,237.8 + 4.6 = 16,242.4 miles

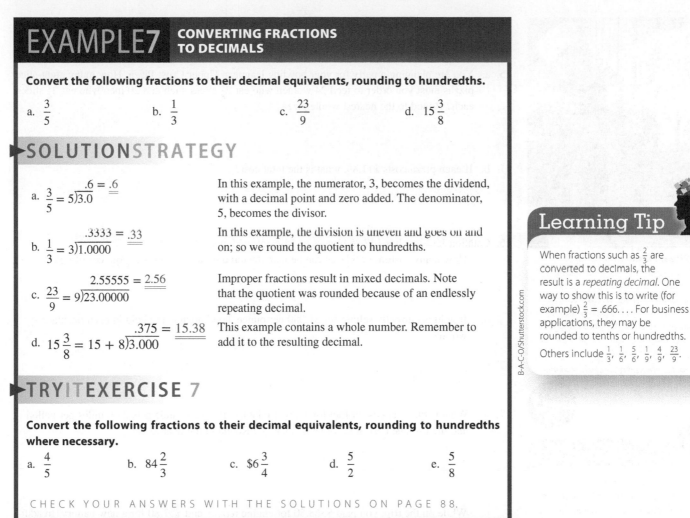

EXAMPLE7 CONVERTING FRACTIONS TO DECIMALS

Convert the following fractions to their decimal equivalents, rounding to hundredths.

a. $\dfrac{3}{5}$ b. $\dfrac{1}{3}$ c. $\dfrac{23}{9}$ d. $15\dfrac{3}{8}$

▶SOLUTIONSTRATEGY

a. $\dfrac{3}{5} = 5\overline{)3.0}^{\,.6} = .6$

In this example, the numerator, 3, becomes the dividend, with a decimal point and zero added. The denominator, 5, becomes the divisor.

b. $\dfrac{1}{3} = 3\overline{)1.0000}^{\,.3333} = .33$

In this example, the division is uneven and goes on and on; so we round the quotient to hundredths.

c. $\dfrac{23}{9} = 9\overline{)23.00000}^{\,2.55555} = 2.56$

Improper fractions result in mixed decimals. Note that the quotient was rounded because of an endlessly repeating decimal.

d. $15\dfrac{3}{8} = 15 + 8\overline{)3.000}^{\,.375} = 15.38$

This example contains a whole number. Remember to add it to the resulting decimal.

Learning Tip

When fractions such as $\frac{2}{3}$ are converted to decimals, the result is a *repeating decimal*. One way to show this is to write (for example) $\frac{2}{3} = .666....$ For business applications, they may be rounded to tenths or hundredths.

Others include $\frac{1}{3}, \frac{1}{6}, \frac{5}{6}, \frac{1}{9}, \frac{4}{9}, \frac{23}{9}.$

▶TRYITEXERCISE 7

Convert the following fractions to their decimal equivalents, rounding to hundredths where necessary.

a. $\dfrac{4}{5}$ b. $84\dfrac{2}{3}$ c. $\$6\dfrac{3}{4}$ d. $\dfrac{5}{2}$ e. $\dfrac{5}{8}$

CHECK YOUR ANSWERS WITH THE SOLUTIONS ON PAGE 88.

REVIEW EXERCISES   3   SECTION III

Convert the following decimals to fractions and reduce to lowest terms.

1. .125
$$\dfrac{125}{1,000} = \dfrac{1}{8}$$

2. 4.75   3. .016   4. 93.614   5. 14.82

JUMP START WWW

Convert the following fractions to decimals. Round the quotients to hundredths when necessary.

6. $\dfrac{9}{16}$
$$.5625 = .56$$

7. $5\dfrac{2}{3}$ 8. $24\dfrac{1}{8}$ 9. $\dfrac{55}{45}$ 10. $\dfrac{8}{5}$

JUMP START WWW

For the following numbers, perform the indicated operation. Give the result in decimal form.

11. $34.55 + 14.08 + 9\dfrac{4}{5}$

12. $565.809 - 224\dfrac{3}{4}$

Pizza, Pizza! According to industry sources, each man, woman, and child in America eats an average of 46 slices (23 pounds) of pizza per year. The equivalent of 100 acres of pizza is consumed daily, or about 350 slices per second.

Source: www.pmq.com, *Pizza Magazine*

Learning Tip

When a fraction is found at the end of a decimal number, convert the fraction to a decimal and place the decimal at the end of the original decimal number.

In Exercise 17a: $2.50\dfrac{9}{10} = \$2.509$

13. $12\dfrac{1}{2} \div 2.5$

14. $\$35.88 \times 21\dfrac{1}{4}$

15. a. You are planning a party for your bowling league at Upper Crust Pizza. How many eight-slice pizzas must you order to feed 24 women who eat $2\dfrac{1}{8}$ slices each and 20 men who eat $3\dfrac{3}{4}$ slices each? Round to the nearest whole pizza.

    b. If each pizza costs $11.89, what is the total cost?

16. Catalina Jewelers has 147.25 ounces of 14-carat gold in stock.
    a. How many custom necklaces can be manufactured if each requires $2\dfrac{3}{8}$ ounces of gold?

    b. If gold is currently selling for $1,050 per ounce, how much is the gold in each necklace worth?

17. a. What is the total cost of fuel for a 4,602 mile trip if your vehicle gets 23.6 miles per gallon and the average cost of gasoline is $3.40\dfrac{9}{10}$? Round to the nearest cent.

    b. While on the trip, you paid $368.50 for engine repairs and $37.80 for a new battery. In addition, tolls amounted to $45.75 and parking averaged $4.50 per day for nine days. What was the cost per mile for the trip? Round to the nearest tenth of a cent.

18. Ever Ready taxicabs charge $1.20 for the first $\dfrac{1}{4}$ of a mile and $0.35 for each additional $\dfrac{1}{4}$ of a mile. What is the cost of a trip from the airport to downtown, a distance of $8\dfrac{3}{4}$ miles?

19. You are the purchasing manager for Five Star Graphics, a company that uses specially treated photo paper. The yellow paper costs $.07\dfrac{1}{5}$ per sheet, and the blue paper costs $.05\dfrac{3}{8}$ per sheet. If you order 15,000 yellow sheets and 26,800 blue sheets, what is the total cost of the order?

20. You are the manager of Rally Rent-a-Car. A customer, Sandy Furrow, has asked you for an estimate of charges for a nine-day rental of an SUV. She expects to drive 670 miles. If Rally charges $53.50 per day plus $18\frac{1}{2}$ cents per mile for this category of vehicle, what would be the total rental charge for Sandy's trip?

BUSINESS DECISION: QUALIFYING FOR A MORTGAGE

21. You are a loan officer at the West Elm Savings and Loan. Mr. and Mrs. Brady are in your office to apply for a mortgage loan on a house they want to buy. The house has a market value of $180,000. Your bank requires $\frac{1}{5}$ of the market value as a down payment.

  a. What is the amount of the down payment?

  b. What is the amount of the mortgage for which the Bradys are applying?

  c. Your bank offers the Bradys a 30-year mortgage with a rate of 5%. At that rate, the monthly payments for principal and interest on the loan will be $5.37 for every $1,000 financed. What is the amount of the principal and interest portion of the Bradys' monthly payment?

  d. What is the total amount of interest that will be paid over the life of the loan?

  e. Your bank also requires that the monthly mortgage payments include property tax and homeowners insurance payments. If the property tax is $1,710 per year and the property insurance is $1,458 per year, what is the total monthly payment for PITI (principal, interest, taxes, and insurance)?

  f. To qualify for the loan, bank rules state that mortgage payments cannot exceed $\frac{1}{4}$ of the combined monthly income of the family. If the Bradys earn $3,750 per month, will they qualify for this loan?

  g. What monthly income would be required to qualify for this size mortgage payment?

CHAPTER SUMMARY

Section I: Understanding Decimal Numbers

Topic	Important Concepts	Illustrative Examples
Reading and Writing Decimal Numbers in Numerical and Word Form **Performance Objective 3-1, Page 68**	In decimals, the value of each place starting at the decimal point and moving from left to right decreases by a factor of 10. The names of the places end in *ths*; they are tenths, hundredths, thousandths, ten-thousandths, hundred-thousandths, millionths, and so on. 1. To write decimal numbers in words, write the decimal part as a whole number; then add the place value of the last digit on the right. 2. When writing mixed decimals, the decimal point should be read as "and." 3. If the decimal ends in a fraction, read them together using the place value of the last digit of the decimal. 4. When a dollar sign ($) precedes a number, the whole number value represents dollars, the decimal value represents cents, and the decimal point is read as "and."	*Decimal Numbers* .0691 is six hundred ninety-one ten-thousandths Twenty-one ten-thousandths is .0021 *Mixed Decimals* 51.305 is fifty-one and three hundred five thousandths Eighteen and thirty-six thousandths is 18.036 *Decimals with Fractions* $.22\frac{1}{2}$ is twenty-two and one-half hundredths Seventeen and one-half hundredths is $.17\frac{1}{2}$ *Dollars and Cents* $946.73 is nine hundred forty-six dollars and seventy-three cents Six dollars and twelve cents is $6.12
Rounding Decimal Numbers to a Specified Place Value **Performance Objective 3-2, Page 70**	1. Determine the place to which the decimal is to be rounded. 2a. If the digit to the right of the one being rounded is 5 or more, increase the digit in the place being rounded by 1. 2b. If the digit to the right of the one being rounded is 4 or less, do not change the digit in the place being rounded. 3. Delete all digits to the right of the one being rounded.	Round as indicated: .645 rounded to hundredths is .65 42.5596 rounded to tenths is 42.6 .00291 rounded to thousandths is .003 $75.888 rounded to cents is $75.89

Section II: Decimal Numbers and the Fundamental Processes

Topic	Important Concepts	Illustrative Examples
Adding and Subtracting Decimals **Performance Objective 3-3, Page 73**	1. Line up all the place values, including the decimal points. 2. The decimal point in the answer will appear in the same position (column) as in the problem. 3. You may add zeros to the right of the decimal numbers that do not have enough places.	Addition: $$\begin{array}{r} 2{,}821.049 \\ 12.500 \\ +\ 143.008 \\ \hline 2{,}976.557 \end{array}$$ Subtraction: $$\begin{array}{r} 194.1207 \\ -\ 45.3400 \\ \hline 148.7807 \end{array}$$
Multiplying Decimals **Performance Objective 3-4, Page 74**	1. Multiply the numbers as if they were whole numbers, disregarding the decimal points. 2. Total the number of decimal places in the multiplier and the multiplicand. 3. Insert the decimal point in the product, giving it the same number of decimal places as the total from Step 2. 4. If necessary, place zeros to the left of the product to provide the correct number of digits. *Note:* If the situation involves money, answers should be rounded to the nearest cent.	Multiply 224.5 by 4.53. $$\begin{array}{r} 224.5 \text{ 1 decimal place} \\ \times\ 4.53 \text{ 2 decimal places} \\ \hline 6\ 735 \\ 112\ 25 \\ 898\ 0 \\ \hline 1{,}016.985 \text{ 3 decimal places} \end{array}$$

Topic	Important Concepts	Illustrative Examples
Multiplication Shortcut: Powers of 10 **Performance Objective 3-4, Page 74**	When multiplying a decimal by a power of 10 (such as 10, 100, 1,000, or 10,000): 1. Count the number of zeros in the multiplier and move the decimal point in the multiplicand the same number of places to the right. 2. If necessary, add zeros to the product to provide the required places.	Multiply $.064 \times 10 = .64$ 1 place to the right $.064 \times 100 = 6.4$ 2 places to the right $.064 \times 1,000 = 64$ 3 places to the right $.064 \times 10,000 = 640$ 4 place to the right $.064 \times 100,000 = 6,400$ 5 places to the right
Dividing Decimals **Performance Objective 3-5, Page 75**	*If the divisor is a whole number:* 1. Place the decimal point in the quotient directly above the decimal point in the dividend. 2. Divide the numbers. *If the divisor is a decimal number:* 1. Move the decimal point in the divisor to the right until it becomes a whole number. 2. Move the decimal point in the dividend the same number of places you moved it in the divisor. It may be necessary to add zeros to the right of the dividend if there are not enough places. 3. Place the decimal point in the quotient directly above the decimal point in the dividend. 4. Divide the numbers. *Note:* All answers involving money should be rounded to the nearest cent.	Divide: $9.5 \div 25$ $\begin{array}{r} .38 \\ 25\overline{)9.50} \\ 75 \\ \hline 200 \\ 200 \\ \hline 0 \end{array}$ Divide: $14.3 \div 2.2$ $2.2\overline{)14.3}$ $\begin{array}{r} 6.5 \\ 22\overline{)143.0} \\ 132 \\ \hline 110 \\ 110 \\ \hline 0 \end{array}$
Division Shortcut: Powers of 10 **Performance Objective 3-5, Page 75**	When dividing a decimal by a power of 10 (such as 10, 100, 1,000, or 10,000): 1. Count the number of zeros in the divisor and move the decimal point in the dividend the same number of places to the left. 2. It may be necessary to add zeros to provide the required number of decimal places.	Divide $21.69 \div 10 = 2.169$ 1 place to the left $21.69 \div 100 = .2169$ 2 places to the left $21.69 \div 1,000 = .02169$ 3 places to the left $21.69 \div 10,000 = .002169$ 4 places to the left

Section III: Conversion of Decimals to Fractions and Fractions to Decimals

Topic	Important Concepts	Illustrative Examples
Converting Decimals to Fractions **Performance Objective 3-6, Page 81**	1. Write the numerator of the fraction as the decimal number without the decimal point. 2. Write the denominator as "1" followed by as many zeros as there are decimal places in the original decimal number. 3. Reduce the fraction to lowest terms.	$.88 = \dfrac{88}{100} = \dfrac{22}{25}$ $5.57 = 5 + \dfrac{57}{100} = 5\dfrac{57}{100}$
Converting Fractions to Decimals **Performance Objective 3-7, Page 82**	1. Divide the numerator by the denominator. 2. Add a decimal point and zeros, as necessary, to the numerator.	$\dfrac{4}{5} = 5\overline{)4.0}^{\;.8}$ $\dfrac{22}{4} = 4\overline{)22.0}^{\;5.5}$

TRY IT: EXERCISE SOLUTIONS FOR CHAPTER 3

1. a. Sixty-four hundredths

b. Four hundred ninety-two thousandths

c. Ten thousand nineteen hundred-thousandths

d. Five hundred seventy-nine and four ten-thousandths

e. Twenty-six and seven hundred eight thousandths

f. Thirty-three and one-third hundredths

g. .021

h. 272.00094

i. $11.003\frac{1}{4}$

2. a. $5.78892 = 5.789$

b. $.004522 = .0045$

c. $\$345.8791 = \$345.88$

d. $76.03324 = 76.03$

e. $\$766.43 = \$766$

f. $34,956.1229 = 34,956.1$

3. a.
$$\begin{array}{r} 35.7008 \\ 311.2000 \\ + 84,557.5400 \\ \hline 84,904.4408 \end{array}$$

b.
$$\begin{array}{r} 65.79 \\ + 154.33 \\ \hline \$220.12 \end{array}$$

c.
$$\begin{array}{r} 186.700 \\ - 57.009 \\ \hline 129.691 \end{array}$$

d.
$$\begin{array}{r} 79.80 \\ - 34.61 \\ \hline \$45.19 \end{array}$$

4. a.
$$\begin{array}{r} 876.66 \\ \times\ .045 \\ \hline 4\,38330 \\ 35\,0664 \\ \hline 39.44970 \end{array}$$

b.
$$\begin{array}{r} 4,955.8 \\ \times\quad 2.9 \\ \hline 4\,460\,22 \\ 9\,911\,6 \\ \hline 14,371.82 \end{array}$$

c.
$$\begin{array}{r} 65.79 \\ \times\ 558 \\ \hline 526\,32 \\ 3\,289\,5 \\ 32\,895 \\ \hline \$36,710.82 \end{array}$$

d. $.00232 \times 1,000 = 2.32$

5. a.
$$\begin{array}{r} 44.8 \\ 16\overline{)716.8} \\ \underline{64} \\ 76 \\ \underline{64} \\ 12\,8 \\ \underline{12\,8} \\ 0 \end{array}$$

b.
$$\begin{array}{r} 3048 \\ 7\overline{)21336} \\ \underline{21} \\ 33 \\ \underline{28} \\ 56 \\ \underline{56} \\ 0 \end{array}$$

c.
$$\begin{array}{r} 75.8 = \$75.80 \\ 421\overline{)31911.8} \\ \underline{2947} \\ 2441 \\ \underline{2105} \\ 336\,8 \\ \underline{336\,8} \\ 0 \end{array}$$

d. $2.03992 \div 1,000 = .00203992$

6. a. $\dfrac{875}{1,000} = \dfrac{7}{8}$

b. $23\dfrac{76}{1,000} = 23\dfrac{19}{250}$

c. $\dfrac{4}{10,000} = \dfrac{1}{2,500}$

d. $84\dfrac{75}{100} = 84\dfrac{3}{4}$

7. a. $\dfrac{4}{5} = .8$

$$\begin{array}{r} .8 \\ 5\overline{)4.0} \\ \underline{4\,0} \\ 0 \end{array}$$

b. $84\dfrac{2}{3} = 84.67$

$$\begin{array}{r} .666 \\ 84 + 3\overline{)2.000} \\ \underline{1\,8} \\ 20 \\ \underline{18} \\ 20 \\ \underline{18} \\ 2 \end{array}$$

c. $\$6\dfrac{3}{4} = \$6.75$

$$\begin{array}{r} .75 \\ 6 + 4\overline{)3.00} \\ \underline{2\,8} \\ 20 \\ \underline{20} \\ 0 \end{array}$$

d. $\dfrac{5}{2} = 2.5$

$$\begin{array}{r} 2.5 \\ 2\overline{)5.0} \\ \underline{4} \\ 1\,0 \\ \underline{1\,0} \\ 0 \end{array}$$

e. $\dfrac{5}{8} = .63$

$$\begin{array}{r} .625 \\ 8\overline{)5.000} \\ \underline{4\,8} \\ 20 \\ \underline{16} \\ 40 \\ \underline{40} \\ 0 \end{array}$$

CONCEPT REVIEW

1. As with fractions, _____ are a way of expressing parts of a whole thing. (3-1)

2. The _____ _____ separates the whole number part from the decimal part of a mixed decimal. It is read as the word _____. (3-1)

3. When rounding decimals, we delete all digits to the _____ of the digit being rounded. (3-2)

4. When rounding monetary amounts, we round to the nearest _____, or _____ place. (3-2)

5. When adding or subtracting decimals, we begin by lining up all the _____ _____ vertically. (3-3)

6. When adding or subtracting decimals, we work from _____ to _____. (3-3)

7. In the multiplication of decimals, the product has as many decimal places as the total number of decimal places in the two _____, the multiplier and the multiplicand. (3-4)

8. When multiplying a decimal by a power of 10, as a shortcut, move the decimal point to the right the same number of places as there are _____ in the power of 10. (3-4)

9. When dividing decimals, the basic rule is that you cannot divide with a decimal in the _____. (3-5)

10. When dividing a decimal by a power of 10, as a shortcut, move the decimal point in the dividend to the _____ the same number of places as there are zeros in the divisor. (3-5)

11. When converting a decimal to a fraction, we commonly _____ the fraction to lowest terms. (3-6)

12. To convert a fraction to a decimal, we divide the _____ by the _____. (3-7)

ASSESSMENT TEST

Write the following numbers in word form.

1. .61 **2.** 34.581 **3.** $119.85 **4.** $.09\frac{3}{7}$ **5.** .0495

Write the following numbers in numerical form.

6. Nine hundred sixty-seven ten-thousandths

7. Five and fourteen thousandths

8. Eight hundred forty-three and two tenths

9. Sixteen dollars and fifty-seven cents

Round the following numbers to the indicated place.

10. .44857 to hundredths

11. 995.06966 to thousandths

12. $127.94 to dollars

13. 4.6935 to tenths

Perform the indicated operation for the following.

14. 6.03 + 45.168

15. $.81 + $2.03 + $12.88 + $80.50

16. .0031 + 69.271 + 193.55 + 211

17. 23.0556 − 15.35

CHAPTER
3

18. $78.14 − $9.52

19. .802 − .066

20. 21.46
   × 15

21.   .008
   × .024

22. .9912 × 100,000

23. .503 ÷ 1.2575

24. 79.3 ÷ 10,000

25. $150.48 ÷ 7.5

Convert the following decimals to fractions and reduce to lowest terms.

26. 12.035

27. .0441

Convert the following fractions to decimals. Round the quotients to hundredths.

28. $\frac{15}{16}$

29. $7\frac{5}{9}$

30. $\frac{95}{42}$

31. Gary Scott can buy a box of 40 Blu-ray discs for $18.99 and a box of 40 jewel cases for $9.98. Alternatively, he can purchase two boxes of 20 Blu-ray discs already in jewel cases for $16.95 each. Which is the better buy, and by how much—the box of 40 Blu-ray discs and a box of 40 cases or the two boxes of 20 Blu-ray discs with jewel cases included?

32. Two Wheeler-Dealer Bike Shop has a 22-inch off-road racer on sale this month for $239.95. If the original price of the bike was $315.10, how much would a customer save by purchasing it on sale?

33. The chief financial officer of Allied Corporation is setting up two production work shift pay schedules. Swing shift workers are to receive $\frac{1}{12}$ more pay than day shift workers. If the day shift workers are to receive average pay of $18.36 per hour, what is the average pay for the swing shift workers?

34. A spindle of 50 blank DVD discs costs $16.90. How much does each disc cost? Do not round your answer.

35. Liz Thorton has signed up for a one-semester class that meets twice a week. The semester is 16 weeks long. She knows that she will miss three classes during her vacation. She has a choice of buying a semester parking pass for $41.50, or she can pay $1.75 daily for parking. How much will Liz save if she buys the parking pass?

36. At Mager's Market, a 24-bottle case of spring water is on sale for $5.99. If the regular price for the case is $6.97,

   a. How much is saved if a customer buys the case at the sale price?

   b. What is the sale price per bottle? Round to the nearest cent.

   c. Which sales strategy earns more revenue for Mager's Market, selling 400 cases of water per week at the sale price or selling 300 cases per week at the regular price?

Mager's Market

37. Maria Lopez shares an apartment with a friend. They divide all expenses evenly. Maria's monthly take-home pay is $2,792.15. The apartment expenses this month are $985.50 for rent, $192.00 for maintenance fees, $56.31 for electricity, and $28.11 for telephone. How much remains from Maria's check after she pays her share of the monthly rent and expenses?

38. Ryan Miller wanted to make some money at a flea market. He purchased 55 small orchids from a nursery for a total of $233.75, three bags of potting soil for $2.75 each, and 55 ceramic pots at $4.60 each. After planting the orchids in the pots, Ryan sold each plant for $15.50 at the flea market.

   a. What was his total cost per potted plant?

   b. How much profit did Bill make on this venture?

Anneka/Shutterstock.com

Maersk Line is the core liner shipping activity of the A.P. Moller–Maersk Group and the leading container shipping company in the world. Maersk employs about 16,900 and has 7,600 seafarers.

   The Maersk Line fleet comprises more than 500 vessels and a number of containers corresponding to more than 2 million TEU (twenty-foot equivalent unit—a container 20 feet long).

39. A cargo ship, *The Caribbean Trader*, has a cargo area of 23,264 cubic feet.

   a. How many 145.4 cubic foot storage containers can the ship hold?

   b. The shipping cost per storage container is $959.64 for a trip from Miami to Nassau. What is the cost per cubic foot?

40. As the food manager for a local charity, you are planning a fund-raising pasta party. Spaghetti sells for $1.79 per 16-ounce box.

   a. If the average adult serving is $5\frac{3}{4}$ ounces and the average child eats $3\frac{1}{2}$ ounces, how many boxes will you have to purchase to serve 36 adults and 46 children?

CHAPTER 3

b. What is the total cost of the spaghetti?

BUSINESS DECISION: THE
INTERNATIONAL BUSINESS TRIP

41. U.S. dollars are legal currency only in the United States. International investment, travel, and trade require that dollars be exchanged for foreign currency. In today's global economy, a floating exchange rate system is used to value major currencies compared to each other. Because the values of these currencies vary continually, exchange rate tables are published daily by numerous business sources. The information below is taken from one such exchange-rate table.

Currency Exchange Rates

Country – Currency	Dollar	Euro	Pound	SFranc	Peso	Yen	CdnDlr
Canada – Canadian dollar	1.0625	1.5793	1.7663	1.0445	0.0814	0.0120	....
Japan – Yen	88.777	132.08	147.70	87.277	6.8018	....	83.537
Mexico – Peso	13.052	19.411	21.701	12.830	....	0.1470	12.280
Switzerland – Swiss Franc	1.0170	1.5132	1.6924	....	0.0779	0.0115	0.9580
Britain – Pound	0.6010	0.8941	....	0.5911	0.0461	0.0068	0.5659
Euro – Euro	0.6721	....	1.1187	0.6610	0.0515	0.0076	0.6334
U.S. – Dollar	....	1.4877	1.6639	0.9839	0.0767	0.0113	0.9420

For example, on that date, 100 U.S. dollars was worth 67.21 euros.

$$\$100 \times 0.6721 = 67.21 \text{ euros}$$

STEPS TO CONVERT BETWEEN FOREIGN CURRENCIES

STEP 1. Locate the *currency exchange rate* at the intersection of the column of the currency you are changing from (old currency) and the row of the currency you are changing to (new currency).

STEP 2. Multiply the number of units you are changing from (old currency) by the currency exchange rate.

New currency = Old currency × Currency exchange rate

Dollars AND Sense

Up-to-the-minute currency exchange rates can be found at **www.xe.com**.

iStock.com/vreemous

iStock.com/Nikada

You are the sales manager of Republic Enterprises, Inc., a company that sells motor parts in many countries. For the next 2 weeks, you are going on a selling trip to Canada and the United Kingdom. Your airline fare and hotel bill will be charged on company credit cards. Your boss has allotted an additional $2,500 for out-of-pocket expenses during the trip. Use the currency exchange rate table above to perform the following calculations.

a. A few days before your trip, you exchange the 2,500 U.S. dollars for British pounds to be used while you are in London. How many pounds will you have for the British portion of your trip? Round to the nearest pound.

b. When you finish your business in London, you have 800 pounds left. Your next stop is Toronto, Canada. How many Canadian dollars will those British pounds purchase? Round to the nearest Canadian dollar.

c. After completing your business in Canada, you have 375 Canadian dollars left. How many U.S. dollars will those Canadian dollars purchase? Round to the nearest U.S. dollar.

d. Before you left on the trip, you price-checked a particular camera at Best Buy for $358. You then used the Internet to find that the same camera model is available in London for 266 British pounds and in Toronto for 362 Canadian dollars. Where should you buy the camera to get the lowest price—at home or in one of the cities on the trip? Round each figure to the nearest U.S. dollar.

COLLABORATIVE LEARNING ACTIVITY

Sports Math

As a team, choose two sports.

a. Investigate how fractions and decimals are used in their record keeping and statistics.
b. Prepare a visual presentation of your findings to share with the class.

Tips for Taking Math Tests

Before the Test
- Know what material will be covered on the test and pace your study schedule accordingly.
- Get a good night's sleep. (Don't study all night.)
- Get up earlier than usual on test day to review your notes.
- Have a positive mental attitude about doing well on the test.
- Bring all necessary materials—calculator, pencils, erasers, paper, ruler, etc.

During the Test
- Listen to all verbal instructions. If you have a question or don't understand something, ask for clarification.
- If you feel nervous, close your eyes and take a few deep breaths.
- Read all written directions carefully.
- If there is an answer sheet, make sure you write your answers in the proper place.
- Budget your time. Spend the most time on those portions of the test that are worth the most points.
- Skip questions you don't know and come back to them. Place a check mark next to the questions you must return to.
- Be sure your answers are logical. On multiple-choice tests, eliminate the answers you know can't be right and work from there.
- If time permits, double-check your answers.

After the Test
- If you did well, reward yourself.
- If you didn't do so well, reward yourself for a good effort and learn from your mistakes.

Overcoming Anxiety in Business Math

Math! It makes throats lumpy, stomachs queasy, and palms sweaty. Each year in thousands of classrooms around the country, math causes anxiety in many students.

What can you do? To begin, understand that math isn't just another course you have to take in school and then not deal with any more. On the contrary, math skills, particularly in business, are an integral part of what it takes to build a successful career.

HomeStudio/Shutterstock.com

Even as a consumer, today's complex marketplace requires math skills if you are to function in an informed and prudent manner. Make the commitment—Learn It Now!

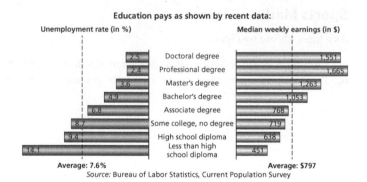

Education pays as shown by recent data:

Unemployment rate (in %)	Education category	Median weekly earnings (in $)
2.5	Doctoral degree	1,551
2.4	Professional degree	1,665
3.6	Master's degree	1,263
4.9	Bachelor's degree	1,053
6.8	Associate degree	768
8.7	Some college, no degree	719
9.4	High school diploma	638
14.1	Less than high school diploma	451

Average: 7.6%   **Average: $797**

Source: Bureau of Labor Statistics, Current Population Survey

Issues & Activities

1. Use the chart above to:
   a. Calculate the annual earnings for each education category.
   b. Calculate the annual difference in earnings between the categories: some college, associate degree, and bachelor's degree.
2. Locate the most recent edition of the *Current Population Survey* published by the Bureau of Labor Statistics. For the associate degree and bachelor's degree categories, calculate the difference in annual earnings found in the chart above and in the latest figures.
3. In teams, research the Internet to find current trends in "value of education" statistics. List your sources and visually report your findings to the class.

Brainteaser—"Get the Point"

What mathematical symbol can you place between the number 1 and the number 2 to yield a new number larger than 1 but less than 2?

See the end of Appendix A for the solution.

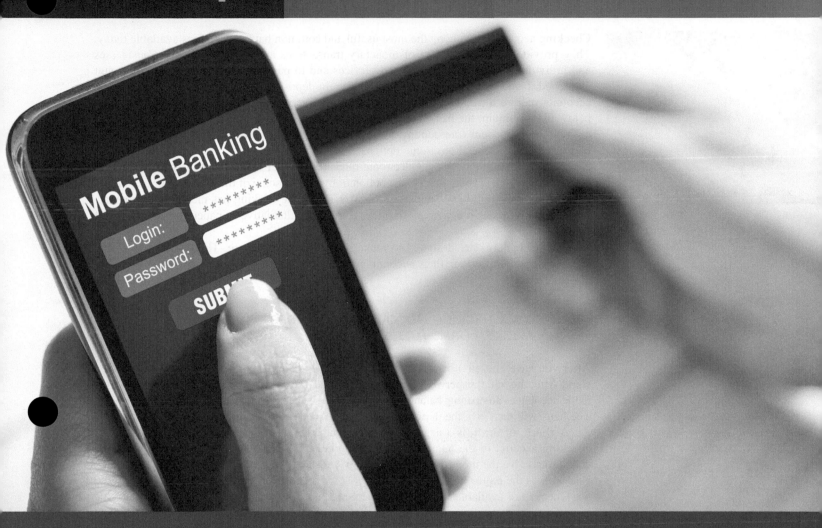

CHAPTER 4 Checking Accounts

The percentage of internet users who banked online was 12% in 1998. Just fifteen years later it reached 61%, and it continues to rise rapidly each year. (Pew Research Center)

Checking accounts are among the most useful and common banking services available today. They provide a detailed record of monetary transactions and are used by most businesses and individuals to purchase goods and services and to pay bills. When a checking account is opened, banks often require an initial minimum deposit of $50 or $100. Certain types of accounts require a minimum *average monthly balance* in the account. If the balance falls below the minimum, the bank may charge a fee.

Checking account transactions are processed in our banking system using a combination of paper checks and electronic options such as automated teller machines (ATMs), debit cards, automatic bill paying, and electronic funds transfer (EFT). Online banking uses today's technology to give account holders the option of bypassing some of the time-consuming paper-based aspects of traditional banking (Exhibit 4-1). Online banking has increased in popularity in recent years as it is a green-friendly, convenient alternative to paper-based methods of banking.

Several features are designed to make mobile banking secure. These include viewing accounts by name rather than account number and using encryption to mask sensitive information.

4-1 OPENING A CHECKING ACCOUNT AND UNDERSTANDING HOW VARIOUS FORMS ARE USED

deposits Funds added to a checking account.

depositor A person who deposits money in a checking account.

check, or **draft** A written order to a bank by a depositor to pay the amount specified on the check from funds on deposit in a checking account.

payee The person or business named on the check to receive the money.

payor The person or business issuing the check.

After you have chosen a bank, the account is usually opened by a new accounts officer or a clerk. After the initial paperwork has been completed, the customer places an amount of money in the account as an opening balance. Funds added to a checking account are known as **deposits**. The bank will then give the **depositor** a checkbook containing checks and deposit slips.

A **check**, or **draft**, is a negotiable instrument ordering the bank to pay money from the checking account to the name written on the check. The person or business named on the check to receive the money is known as the **payee**. The person or business issuing the check is known as the **payor**.

Checks are available in many sizes, colors, and designs; however, they all contain the same fundamental elements. Exhibit 4-2 shows a check with the major parts labeled. Look at the illustration carefully and familiarize yourself with the various parts of the check.

iStock.com/YinYang

EXHIBIT 4-1
Preferred Banking Method—This chart shows that by 2013 visits to bank branches had become only a small part of banking transactions.

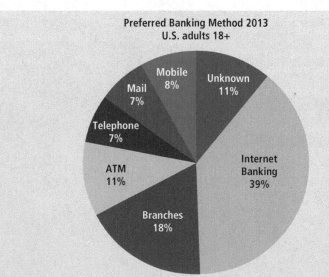

Preferred Banking Method 2013
U.S. adults 18+

- Mobile 8%
- Mail 7%
- Unknown 11%
- Telephone 7%
- ATM 11%
- Internet Banking 39%
- Branches 18%

Source: American Bankers Association and Ipsos Public Affairs. The annual telephone survey of more than 1,000 randomly-selected consumers was conducted for ABA by Ipsos Public Affairs, an independent market research firm.

Deposit slips, or deposit tickets, are printed forms with the depositor's name, address, account number, and space for the details of the deposit. Deposit slips are used to record money, both cash and checks, being *added* to the checking account. They are presented to the bank teller along with the items to be deposited. When a deposit is completed, the depositor receives a copy of the deposit slip as a receipt, or proof of the transaction. The deposit should also be recorded by the depositor on the current check stub or in the check register. Exhibit 4-3 is an example of a deposit slip.

Either **check stubs** or a **check register** can be used to keep track of the checks written, the deposits added, and the current account balance. It is very important to keep these records accurate and up to date. This will prevent the embarrassing error of writing checks with insufficient funds in the account.

Check stubs, with checks attached by perforation, are usually a bound part of the checkbook. A sample check stub with a check is shown in Exhibit 4-4. Note that the check number is preprinted on both the check and the attached stub. Each stub is used to record the issuing of its corresponding check and any deposits made on that date.

Check registers are the alternative method for keeping track of checking account activity. They are a separate booklet of forms rather than stubs attached to each check. A sample check register is shown in Exhibit 4-5. Note that space is provided for all the pertinent information required to keep an accurate and up-to-date running balance of the account.

deposit slips Printed forms with the depositor's name, address, account number, and space for the details of the deposit. Used to record money, both cash and checks, being added to the checking account.

check stubs A bound part of the checkbook attached by perforation to checks. Used to keep track of the checks written, deposits, and current account balance of a checking account.

check register A separate booklet of blank forms used to keep track of all checking account activity. An alternative to the check stub.

EXHIBIT 4-2 Check

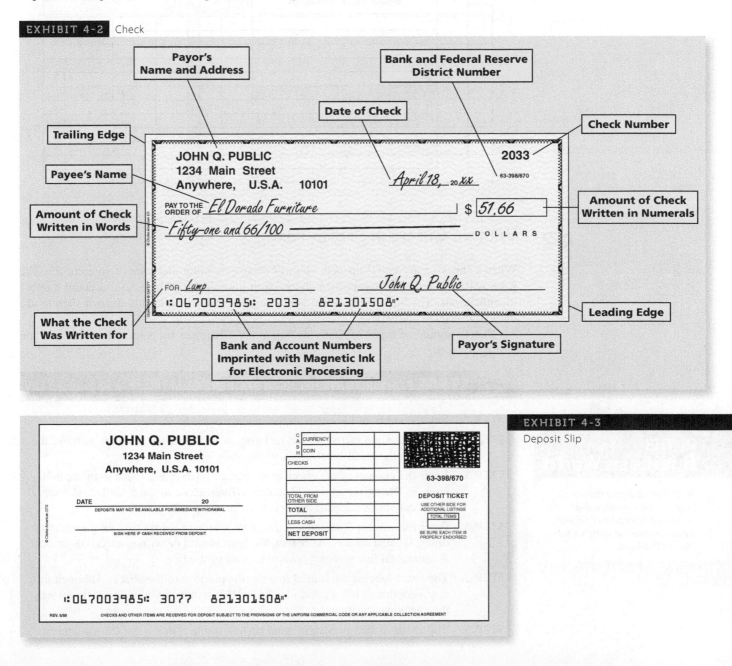

EXHIBIT 4-3

Deposit Slip

EXHIBIT 4-4 Check Stub with Check

IF TAX DEDUCTIBLE CHECK HERE ☐	$

3078

_____ 20___

TO _____

FOR _____

BAL. FWD.	DOLLARS	CENTS
DEPOSIT		
DEPOSIT		
TOTAL		
THIS ITEM		
SUB-TOTAL		
OTHER DEDUCT. (IF ANY)		
BAL. FWD.		

JOHN Q. PUBLIC   3078
1234 Main Street
Anywhere,   U.S.A.   10101   _____ 20_____   63-398/670

PAY TO THE
ORDER OF _____ $ _____

_____ D O L L A R S

FOR _____   _____

⑆067003985⑆ 3078 821301508⑈

EXHIBIT 4-5

Check Register

						BALANCE FORWARD
		PLEASE BE SURE TO **DEDUCT** ANY BANK CHARGES THAT APPLY TO YOUR ACCOUNT.				
CHECK NUMBER	DATE	DESCRIPTION OF TRANSACTION	AMOUNT OF PAYMENT OR WITHDRAWAL (−)	✓	AMOUNT OF DEPOSIT OR INTEREST (+)	
		To				
		For		.		Bal.
		To				
		For				Bal.
		To				
		For				Bal.
		To				
		For				Bal.
		To				
		For				Bal.
		To				
		For				Bal.

4-2   WRITING CHECKS IN PROPER FORM

When a checking account is opened, you will choose the color and style of your checks. The bank will then order custom-printed checks with your name, address, and account number identifications. The bank will provide you with some blank checks and deposit slips to use until your printed ones arrive.

Checks should be typed or neatly written in ink. There are six parts to be filled in when writing a check.

IN THE Business World

When there is a discrepancy between the numerical and written word amount of a check, banks consider the _written word amount_ as official.

STEPS FOR WRITING CHECKS IN PROPER FORM

STEP 1. Enter the _date_ of the check in the space provided.

STEP 2. Enter the name of the person or business to whom the check is written, the payee, in the space labeled _pay to the order of._

STEP 3. Enter the amount of the check in numerical form in the space with the dollar sign, $. The dollar amount should be written close to the $ so that additional digits cannot be added. The cents may be written as xx/100 or .xx.

STEP 4. Enter the amount of the check, this time written in word form, on the next line down, labeled _dollars._ As before, the cents should be written as xx/100 or .xx. A horizontal line is then drawn to the end of the line.

STEP 5. The space labeled _for_ is used to write the purpose of the check. Although this step is optional, it's a good idea to use this space so you will not forget why the check was written.

STEP 6. The space in the lower right-hand portion of the check is for the signature.

EXAMPLE1 WRITING A CHECK

Write a check for Walter Anderson to the Falcon Tire Center for a front-end alignment in the amount of $83.73 on June 7, 20xx.

SOLUTIONSTRATEGY

Here is the check for Walter Anderson written in proper form. Note that the amount, $83.73, is written $83 and 73/100 and the name is signed as it is printed on the check.

```
John Q. Public                                              181
1234 Main Street
Anywhere, U.S.A. 10101          June 7  20 xx      63-398/670

PAY TO THE
ORDER OF   Falcon Tire Center _____ | $  83.73

Eighty-Three and 73/100 _____ DOLLARS


FOR  Front-end alignment _____      Walter Anderson _____

⑈067003985A⑈  181  710290497⑈
```

TRYITEXERCISE 1

1. Use the following blank to write a check for Natalie Eldridge to Whole Foods for a party platter in the amount of $41.88 on April 27.

```
Cindy J. Citizen                                           206
1234 Main Street
Anywhere, U.S.A. 10101        _____ 20 _____   63-398/670

PAY TO THE
ORDER OF _____ | $ _____

_____ DOLLARS


FOR _____        _____

⑈067003985⑈  206  821451902⑈
```

CHECK YOUR ANSWER WITH THE SOLUTION ON PAGE 120.

CHECK YOUR ANSWER WITH THE SOLUTION ON PAGE 120.

ENDORSING CHECKS BY USING BLANK, RESTRICTIVE, AND FULL ENDORSEMENTS

4-3

When you receive a check, you may cash it, deposit it in your account, or transfer it to another party. The **endorsement** on the back of the check instructs the bank on what to do. Federal regulations require that specific areas of the reverse side of checks be designated for the payee and bank endorsements. Your endorsement should be written within the $1\frac{1}{2}$-inch space at the trailing edge of the check, as shown in Exhibit 4-6. The space is usually labeled "ENDORSE HERE."

There are three types of endorsements with which you should become familiar: blank endorsements, restrictive endorsements, and full endorsements, which are shown in Exhibits 4-7, 4-8, and 4-9, respectively.

Learning Tip

Don't forget, when writing the amount of a check in word form, the word *and* represents the decimal point.

IN THE Business World

New Federal Debit Card – The U.S. Treasury now provides a debit card that people without traditional bank accounts can use to access federal benefits such as Social Security and disability payments.

Federal payments are credited to the cards each month, enabling users to make free withdrawals from ATMs in the government's Direct Express network.

endorsement The signature and instructions on the back of a check instructing the bank on what to do with that check.

EXHIBIT 4-6
Endorsement Space

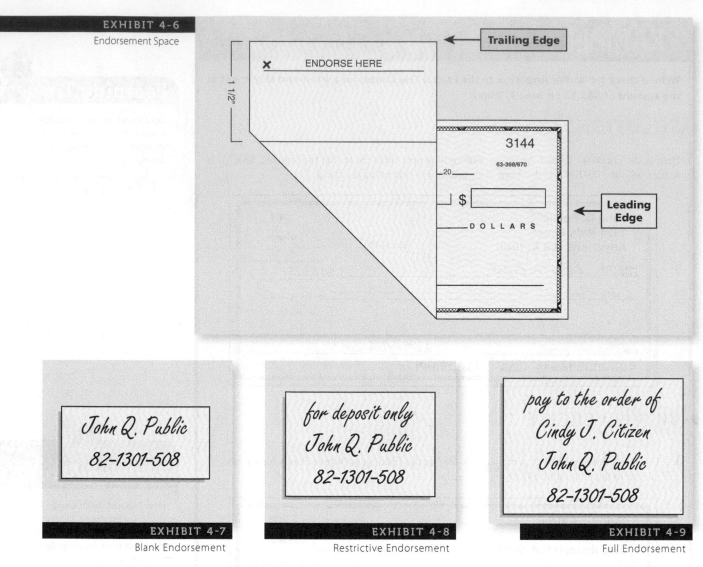

EXHIBIT 4-7
Blank Endorsement

EXHIBIT 4-8
Restrictive Endorsement

EXHIBIT 4-9
Full Endorsement

blank endorsement An endorsement used when the payee wants to cash a check.

restrictive endorsement An endorsement used when the payee wants to deposit a check in his or her account.

full endorsement An endorsement used when the payee wants to transfer a check to another party.

A **blank endorsement** is used when you want to cash the check. You, as the payee, simply sign your name exactly as it appears on the front of the check and write your account number. Once you have endorsed a check in this manner, anyone who has possession of the check can cash it. For this reason, you should use blank endorsements cautiously.

A **restrictive endorsement** is used when you want to deposit the check in your account. In this case, you endorse the check "for deposit only," sign your name as it appears on the front, and write your account number.

A **full endorsement** is used when you want to transfer the check to another party. In this case, you endorse the check "pay to the order of," write the name of the person or business to whom the check is being transferred, sign your name, and write your account number.

EXAMPLE2   ENDORSING A CHECK

You have just received a check. Your account number is #2922-22-33-4. Write the following endorsements and identify what type they are.

a. Allowing you to cash the check.

b. Allowing you to deposit the check in your checking account.

c. Allowing the check to be transferred to your partner Sam Johnson.

▶SOLUTIONSTRATEGY

a.

> Blank Endorsement
> *Your Signature*
> *2922-22-33-4*

b.

> Restrictive Endorsement
> *for deposit only*
> *Your Signature*
> *2922-22-33-4*

c.

> Full Endorsement
> *pay to the order*
> *of Sam Johnson*
> *Your Signature*
> *2922-22-33-4*

▶TRYITEXERCISE 2

You have just received a check. Your account number is #696-339-1028. Write the following endorsements in the space provided and identify what type they are.

a. Allowing the check to be transferred to your friend Roz Reitman.

b. Allowing you to cash the check.

c. Allowing you to deposit the check in your checking account.

a.

b.

c.

CHECK YOUR ANSWERS WITH THE SOLUTIONS ON PAGE 120.

Taking the place of checks or credit cards in some situations, smartphone apps such as Apple Pay and Google Pay let users make payments using tap-to-pay on their smartphone or smartwatch.

Primakov/Shutterstock.com

PREPARING DEPOSIT SLIPS IN PROPER FORM

4-4

Deposit slips are filled out and presented to the bank along with the funds being deposited. They are dated and list the currency, coins, individual checks, and total amount of the deposit. Note on the sample deposit slip, Exhibit 4-10, that John Q. Public took $100 in cash out of the deposit, which required him to sign the deposit slip.

EXHIBIT 4-10
Completed Deposit Slip

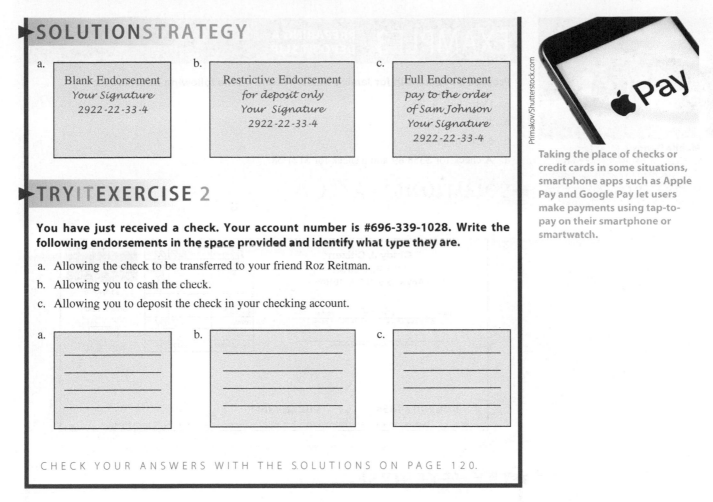

JOHN Q. PUBLIC
1234 Main Street
Anywhere, U.S.A. 10101

CASH CURRENCY	121	00
CASH COIN	16	10
CHECKS	237	55
	500	00

63-398/670

DATE *April 18*, 20XX
DEPOSITS MAY NOT BE AVAILABLE FOR IMMEDIATE WITHDRAWAL

John Q. Public
SIGN HERE IF CASH RECEIVED FROM DEPOSIT

TOTAL FROM OTHER SIDE		
TOTAL	874	65
LESS CASH	100	00
NET DEPOSIT	774	65

DEPOSIT TICKET
USE OTHER SIDE FOR ADDITIONAL LISTINGS
TOTAL ITEMS

BE SURE EACH ITEM IS PROPERLY ENDORSED

© Clarke American 07S

⑈067003985⑈ 821301508⑈

REV. 6/88 CHECKS AND OTHER ITEMS ARE RECEIVED FOR DEPOSIT SUBJECT TO THE PROVISIONS OF THE UNIFORM COMMERCIAL CODE OR ANY APPLICABLE COLLECTION AGREEMENT

Mobile Deposit Most large banks now allow checks to be deposited by using a smartphone app. Part of the process involves sending photos of both sides of the check after it has been endorsed.

EXAMPLE3 PREPARING A DEPOSIT SLIP

Prepare a deposit slip for Jamie McCallon based on the following information.

a. Date: June 4, 20xx.

b. $127 in currency.

c. $3.47 in coins.

d. A check for $358.89 and a check for $121.68.

▶ SOLUTIONSTRATEGY

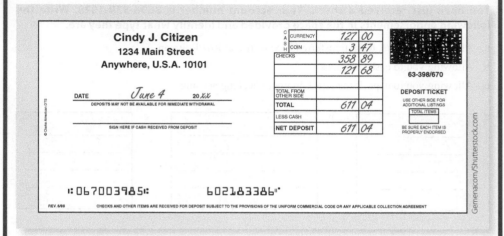

▶ TRYITEXERCISE 3

Fill out the deposit slip for Hi-Volt Electronics based on the following information.

a. Date: November 11, 20xx.

b. $3,549 in currency.

c. 67 quarters, 22 dimes, and 14 nickels.

d. A check for $411.92 and a check for $2,119.56.

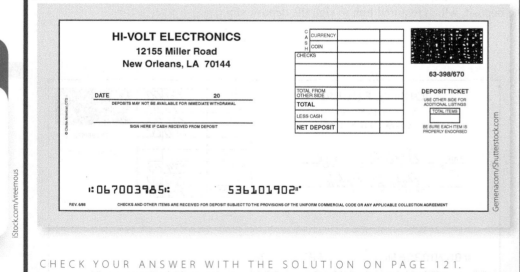

CHECK YOUR ANSWER WITH THE SOLUTION ON PAGE 121.

Dollars AND Sense

It's Your Money

It is important to keep accurate checkbook records and reconcile the account balance each month. Banks can and do make mistakes!

Inaccurate record keeping on the part of the account holder can cause embarrassment due to incorrect balances, as well as service charges for bounced checks.

USING CHECK STUBS OR CHECKBOOK REGISTERS TO RECORD ACCOUNT TRANSACTIONS

4-5

In Performance Objective 4-1, we learned that some people use check stubs to keep records and some use check registers. Exhibit 4-11 shows a check and its corresponding stub properly filled out. Note that the check number is printed on the stub. The stub is used to record the amount of the check, the date, the payee, and the purpose of the check. In addition, the stub also records the balance forwarded from the last stub, deposits made since the previous check, and the new balance of the account after the current check and any other charges are deducted.

Check registers record the same information as the stub but in a different format. Exhibit 4-12 shows a check register properly filled out. The starting balance is located in the upper right-hand corner. In keeping a check register, it is your option to write it single spaced or double spaced. Remember, in reality, you would use *either* the check stub or the checkbook register.

EXHIBIT 4-11 Check with Filled-Out Stub

IF TAX DEDUCTIBLE CHECK HERE ☐	$ *183.12*		
3078			
May 26 20 *XX*			
TO *Walmart*			
FOR *Stereo*			
	DOLLARS	CENTS	
BAL. FWD.	1,240	89	
DEPOSIT	300	00	
DEPOSIT			
TOTAL	1,540	89	
THIS ITEM	183	12	
SUB-TOTAL	1,357	77	
OTHER DEDUCT. (IF ANY)			
BAL. FWD.	1,357	77	

JOHN Q. PUBLIC
1234 Main Street
Anywhere, U.S.A. 10101   3078

63-398/670

May 26 20 *XX*

PAY TO THE ORDER OF *Walmart* $ 183.72

One Hundred Eighty-Three and 12/100 ——— DOLLARS

FOR *Stereo*   *Rick Ungerman*

⑆067003985⑆ 3078 53678792⑈

EXHIBIT 4-12

Filled-Out Check Register

PLEASE BE SURE TO **DEDUCT** ANY BANK CHARGES THAT APPLY TO YOUR ACCOUNT.

CHECK NUMBER	DATE	DESCRIPTION OF TRANSACTION	AMOUNT OF PAYMENT OR WITHDRAWAL (−)	✓	AMOUNT OF DEPOSIT OR INTEREST (+)	BALANCE FORWARD
						560 00
450	1/6	To *MasterCard*	34 60			
		For			Bal.	525 40
451	1/8	To *Allstate Insurance*	166 25			
		For			Bal.	359 15
	1/12	To *Electronic Payroll Deposit*			340 00	
		For			Bal.	699 15
452	1/13	To *CVS Pharmacy*	15 50			
		For			Bal.	683 65
	1/15	To *Deposit*			88 62	
		For			Bal.	772 27
	1/17	To *ATM—Withdrawal*	100 00			
		For			Bal.	672 27
	1/21	To *Debit Card—AMC Theater*	24 15			
		For			Bal.	648 12

EXAMPLE4   RECORDING ACCOUNT TRANSACTIONS

From the following information, complete the two check stubs and the check register in proper form.

a. Starting balance $1,454.21.

b. January 14, 20xx, check #056 in the amount of $69.97 issued to Paints & Pails Hardware for a ladder.

c. January 19, 20xx, deposit of $345.00.

d. February 1, 20xx, check #057 in the amount of $171.55 issued to Northern Power & Light for electricity bill.

e. February 1, 20xx, debit card purchase—groceries, $77.00.

▶ SOLUTIONSTRATEGY

Below are the properly completed stubs and register. Note that the checks were subtracted from the balance and that the deposits were added to the balance.

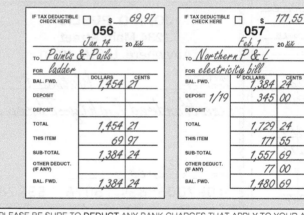

▶ TRYITEXERCISE 4

From the following information, complete the two check stubs and the check register in proper form.

a. Starting balance $887.45.

b. March 12, 20xx, check #137 issued to Nathan & David Hair Stylists for a permanent and manicure in the amount of $55.75.

c. March 16, 20xx, deposits of $125.40 and $221.35.

d. March 19, 20xx, check #138 issued to Complete Auto Service for car repairs in the amount of $459.88.

e. March 20, 20xx, debit card purchase—post office, $53.00.

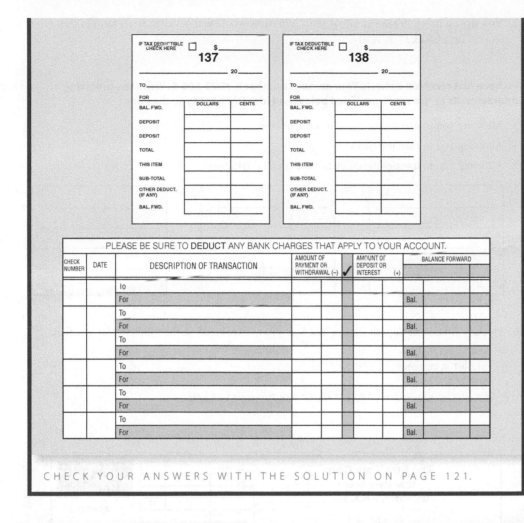

IF TAX DEDUCTIBLE CHECK HERE ☐ $ _____		
137		
_____ 20 ____		
TO _____		
FOR		
BAL. FWD.	DOLLARS	CENTS
DEPOSIT		
DEPOSIT		
TOTAL		
THIS ITEM		
SUB-TOTAL		
OTHER DEDUCT. (IF ANY)		
BAL. FWD.		

IF TAX DEDUCTIBLE CHECK HERE ☐ $ _____		
138		
_____ 20 ____		
TO _____		
FOR		
BAL. FWD.	DOLLARS	CENTS
DEPOSIT		
DEPOSIT		
TOTAL		
THIS ITEM		
SUB-TOTAL		
OTHER DEDUCT. (IF ANY)		
BAL. FWD.		

PLEASE BE SURE TO **DEDUCT** ANY BANK CHARGES THAT APPLY TO YOUR ACCOUNT.

CHECK NUMBER	DATE	DESCRIPTION OF TRANSACTION	AMOUNT OF PAYMENT OR WITHDRAWAL (−)	✓	AMOUNT OF DEPOSIT OR INTEREST (+)	BALANCE FORWARD	
		To					
		For				Bal.	
		To					
		For				Bal.	
		To					
		For				Bal.	
		To					
		For				Bal.	
		To					
		For				Bal.	
		To					
		For				Bal.	

C H E C K   Y O U R   A N S W E R S   W I T H   T H E   S O L U T I O N   O N   P A G E   1 2 1 .

REVIEW EXERCISES

4 | SECTION I

You are the owner of the Busy Bee Launderette. Using the blanks provided, write out the following checks in proper form.

1. **Check #2550, September 14, 20xx, in the amount of $345.54 to the Silky Soap Company for 300 gallons of liquid soap.**

BUSY BEE LAUNDERETTE   **2550**
1234 Main Street
Anywhere, U.S.A. 10101   *Sept. 14* 20 *xx*   63-398/670

PAY TO THE ORDER OF _____ *Silky Soap Company* _____ $ *345.54*

Three Hundred Forty-Five and⁵⁴/₁₀₀ ———— D O L L A R S

FOR _____ *300 gals. Soap* _____ *Your Signature*

⑈067003985⑈ 2550 821301508⑈"

Dollars AND Sense

The Federal Deposit Insurance Corporation (FDIC) insures every depositor for at least $250,000 at each insured bank. People with more than $250,000 can split their cash among insured banks to remain fully protected. The FDIC insures more than 8,000 banks nationwide.

Source: Federal Deposit Insurance Corporation (FDIC), https://www.fdic.gov/

EXCEL 1

EXCEL 2

Dollars AND Sense

Safe-deposit boxes are a type of safe usually located inside a bank vault or in the back of a bank or post office. These boxes are typically used to store things such as valuable gemstones, precious metals, currency, or important documents. In the typical arrangement, a renter pays the bank a fee for the use of the box, which can be opened only with the assigned key, the bank's key, the proper signature, or perhaps a code of some sort.

The contents of the safe-deposit boxes are not insured unless you cover them in your homeowner's or renter's insurance policy.

A "cyber backup" is a good way to protect your important documents. Banks and online vendors offer "virtual safe-deposit boxes," where digital copies of documents can be stored.

Source: *AARP The Magazine*, "Not-so-safe deposits," Nov./Dec. 2009, page 20.

2. You write a check to cover a bill of $8,072.75. How would you write the word form of this amount on a check?

You have just received a check. Your account number is #099-506-8. Write the following endorsements in the space provided below and identify what type they are.

3. Allowing you to deposit the check in your account.

4. Allowing you to cash the check.

5. Allowing you to transfer the check to your friend David Sporn.

3.   4.   5.

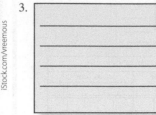

6. Properly fill out the deposit slip for The Star Vista Corp. based on the following information:
   a. Date: July 9, 20xx.
   b. $1,680 in currency.
   c. $62.25 in coins.
   d. Checks in the amount of $2,455.94, $4,338.79, and $1,461.69.

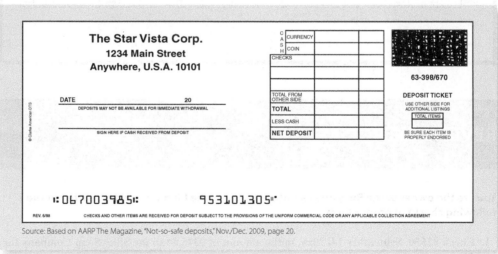

	CURRENCY	
CASH	COIN	
	CHECKS	

The Star Vista Corp.
1234 Main Street
Anywhere, U.S.A. 10101

DATE _____ 20____
DEPOSITS MAY NOT BE AVAILABLE FOR IMMEDIATE WITHDRAWAL

SIGN HERE IF CASH RECEIVED FROM DEPOSIT

TOTAL FROM OTHER SIDE
TOTAL
LESS CASH
NET DEPOSIT

63-398/670

DEPOSIT TICKET
USE OTHER SIDE FOR ADDITIONAL LISTINGS
TOTAL ITEMS
BE SURE EACH ITEM IS PROPERLY ENDORSED

⑆067003985⑆   953101305⑈

REV. 6/88   CHECKS AND OTHER ITEMS ARE RECEIVED FOR DEPOSIT SUBJECT TO THE PROVISIONS OF THE UNIFORM COMMERCIAL CODE OR ANY APPLICABLE COLLECTION AGREEMENT

Source: Based on AARP The Magazine, "Not-so-safe deposits," Nov./Dec. 2009, page 20.

7. Properly fill out the deposit slip for Howard Lockwood based on the following information:
   a. Date: December 18, 20xx.
   b. A check for $651.03.
   c. $150 cash withdrawal.

JOHN Q. PUBLIC
1234 Main Street
Anywhere, U.S.A. 10101

	CURRENCY		
CASH	COIN		
CHECKS			

63-398/670

DATE _____ 20 ____

DEPOSITS MAY NOT BE AVAILABLE FOR IMMEDIATE WITHDRAWAL

_____
SIGN HERE IF CASH RECEIVED FROM DEPOSIT

TOTAL FROM OTHER SIDE		
TOTAL		
LESS CASH		
NET DEPOSIT		

DEPOSIT TICKET
USE OTHER SIDE FOR
ADDITIONAL LISTINGS
TOTAL ITEMS
BE SURE EACH ITEM IS
PROPERLY ENDORSED

© Clarke American DTS

⑆067003985⑆ 450912507⑈

REV. 6/88 CHECKS AND OTHER ITEMS ARE RECEIVED FOR DEPOSIT SUBJECT TO THE PROVISIONS OF THE UNIFORM COMMERCIAL CODE OR ANY APPLICABLE COLLECTION AGREEMENT

8. From the following information, complete the three check stubs on page 103 in proper form.
   a. Starting balance $265.73.
   b. February 12, 20xx, check #439 in the amount of $175.05 to The Fidelity Bank for a car payment.
   c. February 15, deposit of $377.10.
   d. February 18, check #440 in the amount of $149.88 to Apex Fitness Equipment for a set of dumbbells.
   e. February 22, deposit of $570.00.
   f. February 27, check #441 in the amount of $23.40 to Royalty Cleaners for dry cleaning.
   g. March 3, debit card purchase—tires, $225.10.

IF TAX DEDUCTIBLE CHECK HERE ☐ $ _____		
439		
_____ 20 ____		
TO _____		
FOR _____		
	DOLLARS	CENTS
BAL. FWD.		
DEPOSIT		
DEPOSIT		
TOTAL		
THIS ITEM		
SUB-TOTAL		
OTHER DEDUCT. (IF ANY)		
BAL. FWD.		

IF TAX DEDUCTIBLE CHECK HERE ☐ $ _____		
440		
_____ 20 ____		
TO _____		
FOR _____		
	DOLLARS	CENTS
BAL. FWD.		
DEPOSIT		
DEPOSIT		
TOTAL		
THIS ITEM		
SUB-TOTAL		
OTHER DEDUCT. (IF ANY)		
BAL. FWD.		

IF TAX DEDUCTIBLE CHECK HERE ☐ $ _____		
441		
_____ 20 ____		
TO _____		
FOR _____		
	DOLLARS	CENTS
BAL. FWD.		
DEPOSIT		
DEPOSIT		
TOTAL		
THIS ITEM		
SUB-TOTAL		
OTHER DEDUCT. (IF ANY)		
BAL. FWD.		

9. From the following information, complete the checkbook register:
   a. Starting balance $479.20.
   b. April 7, 20xx, deposit of $766.90.
   c. April 14, 20xx, debit card purchase in the amount of $45.65 to Mario's Market for groceries.
   d. April 16, ATM withdrawal, $125.00.
   e. April 17, check #1208 in the amount of $870.00 to Banyan Properties, Inc., for rent.
   f. April 21, 20xx, electronic payroll deposit of $1,350.00.
   g. April 27, check #1209 in the amount of $864.40 to Elegant Decor for a dining room set.

EXCEL 3

PLEASE BE SURE TO **DEDUCT** ANY BANK CHARGES THAT APPLY TO YOUR ACCOUNT.

CHECK NUMBER	DATE	DESCRIPTION OF TRANSACTION	AMOUNT OF PAYMENT OR WITHDRAWAL (–)	✔	AMOUNT OF DEPOSIT OR INTEREST (+)	BALANCE FORWARD	
		To					
		For				Bal.	
		To					
		For				Bal.	
		To					
		For				Bal.	
		To					
		For				Bal.	
		To					
		For				Bal.	
		To					
		For				Bal.	

10. Find the amount of the balance forward that would result following these transactions:

   a. Starting balance: $2,476.80

   b. May 2; check #791; to Dreamscape Landscaping; amount of $334.99

   c. Deposit: May 12; amount of $487.73

   d. May 20; check #792; to cheng's Lumber; amount of $67.95

NUMBER	DATE	DESCRIPTION	PAYMENT/ WITHDRAWAL	DEPOSIT/ INTEREST	BALANCE	

BUSINESS DECISION: TELLER TRAINING

11. You are the training director for tellers at a large local bank. As part of a new training program that you are developing, you have decided to give teller trainees a "sample" deposit slip, check, and check register with common errors on them. The trainees must find and correct the errors. Your task is to create the three documents.

   a. On a separate sheet of paper, list some "typical errors" that bank customers might make on a deposit slip, a check, and a check register.

   b. Use the following blank deposit slip, check, and check register to create "filled-out" versions, each with one error you named for that document in part **a**. You make up all the details: names, dates, numbers, etc.

   c. After completing part **b**, exchange documents with another student in the class and try to find and correct the errors. (If this is a homework assignment, bring a copy of each document you created to class for the exchange. If this is an in-class assignment, temporarily trade documents with the other student after completing part **b**.)

iStock.com/ MarsBars

Stockbyte/Getty Images

Bank Teller According to the U.S. Department of Labor, bank tellers make up 28% of bank employees and conduct most of a bank's routine transactions.

In hiring tellers, banks seek people who enjoy public contact and have good numerical, clerical, and communication skills. Banks prefer applicants who have had courses in mathematics, accounting, bookkeeping, economics, and public speaking.

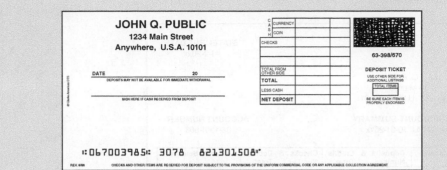

CHECK NUMBER	DATE	DESCRIPTION OF TRANSACTION	AMOUNT OF PAYMENT OR WITHDRAWAL (–)	✓	AMOUNT OF DEPOSIT OR INTEREST (+)	BALANCE FORWARD	
		To					
		For				Bal.	
		To					
		For				Bal.	
		To					
		For				Bal.	
		To					
		For				Bal.	
		To					
		For				Bal.	
		To					
		For				Bal.	

PLEASE BE SURE TO **DEDUCT** ANY BANK CHARGES THAT APPLY TO YOUR ACCOUNT.

BANK STATEMENT RECONCILIATION

4 · SECTION II

Your monthly **bank statement** gives you a detailed review of the activity in your account for a specific period of time. It's your best opportunity to make sure your records match the bank's records. Be prepared to "match up" every activity (credits and debits) on the statement with your checkbook.

It is important that you review the bank statement in a timely fashion. If you find any discrepancies in ATM, debit card, or other electronic transactions, you must report them to the bank within 60 days of the date of the statement or the bank has no obligation to conduct an investigation. Another important reason to reconcile your checkbook with the statement is to look for debits you didn't make that might indicate that someone has access to your account.

bank statement A monthly summary of the activities in a checking account, including debits, credits, and beginning and ending balance. Sent by the bank to the account holder.

UNDERSTANDING THE BANK STATEMENT

4-6

Bank statements vary widely in style from bank to bank; however, most contain essentially the same information. Exhibit 4-13 illustrates typical online and printed bank statements. Note that it shows the balance brought forward from the last statement, the deposits and

EXHIBIT 4-13   Paper and Electronic Bank Statements

STATEMENT DATE
11-2-20xx

John Q. Public
1234 Main St.
Anywhere, U.S.A. 10101

CHECKING ACCOUNT SUMMARY   **ACCOUNT NUMBER**
10-1-20xx THRU 10-31-20xx   82-1301-508

Previous Balance	Deposits & Credits Number	Total	Checks & Debits Number	Total	Current Balance
775.20	3	3,228.11	7	2,857.80	1,145.51

CHECKING ACCOUNT TRANSACTIONS

DATE	AMOUNT	DESCRIPTION	BALANCE
10-2	125.00	Check #445	650.20
10-4	357.18	Deposit	1,007.38
10-7	884.22	Debit Purchase	123.16
10-13	1,409.30	EFT Payroll Deposit	1,532.46
10-15	12.95	Debit Card Purchase	1,519.51
10-16	326.11	Check #446	1,193.40
10-22	200.00	ATM Withdrawal	993.40
10-25	1,461.63	Deposit	2,455.03
10-27	1,294.52	Check #447	1,160.51
10-31	15.00	Service Charge	1,145.51

pacentalbank.com   pacentalbank.com

File   Edit   View   Favorites   Tools   Help

Log Out | ATM/Branch Locator | Calculators | Help Center | Contact Us | Privacy Policy

July 22, 2015   Home   **On Your Accounts**   Bank One for You   Bank One for Your Business

→ Special Offers   → Borrow Money   → Reward Yourself

Account Summary > **Account Activity**

Account Activity

🖶 Print   🔋 Help With This Page

| 🖃 CHECKING | **Current Balance** | $8,404.67 | Select Action ▾ | GO |

Displaying 41 transactions for account XXXXXXXXX1234.

This 🖃 icon beside any transaction description means a copy of the cancelled check or deposit slip is available online. Click the icon to view the image. To sort your transactions by date, description, amount or type, just click the column heading.

Note: If a check image is no longer available online, you may order a paper copy. Deposit slip images are only available online at this time.

Date▼	Description	Amount	Type
07/12/2008	CHECK #1456 🖃 view	$-23.27	CHK
07/12/2008	CHECK #1457 🖃 view	$-179.00	CHK
07/12/2008	CHECK #1455 🖃 view	$-675.14	CHK
07/09/2008	ONLINE TRF FROM CHEC	$-563.00	W/D
07/09/2008	ATM WITHDRAWAL	$-360.00	W/D
07/08/2008	DEPOSIT 🖃 view	$200.00	DEP
07/05/2008	AMOCO OIL 079104	$-41.00	W/D
07/02/2008	ATM WITHDRAWAL	$-20.00	W/D
07/02/2008	JUBILEE JUICE & FOOD	$-33.36	W/D
07/02/2008	CHICAGO SUN TIMES 70	$-99.00	W/D
07/01/2008	LEONA S HYDE PARK IL	$-25.94	W/D

Electronic statement

credits that have been added to the account during the month, the checks and debits that have been subtracted from the account during the month, any service charges assessed to the account, and the current or ending balance.

Credits are additions to the account, such as interest earned, notes collected, and electronic funds transfers of direct deposit payroll checks. **Debits** are subtractions from the account, such as ATM withdrawals, debit card transactions, monthly service charges, check printing charges, nonsufficient fund (NSF) fees, and returned items. A **nonsufficient fund (NSF) fee** is a fee charged by the bank when a check is written without sufficient funds in the account to cover the amount of that check. **Returned items** are checks from others that you deposited in your account but were returned to your bank unpaid because the person or business issuing the check had insufficient funds in its account to cover the check. Banks usually charge a returned item fee when this occurs.

credits Additions to a checking account, such as deposits and interest earned.

debits Subtractions from a checking account, such as service charges.

nonsufficient fund (NSF) fee A fee charged by the bank when a check is written without sufficient funds in the account to cover the amount of that check.

returned items Checks that you deposited but were returned to your bank unpaid because the person or business issuing the checks had insufficient funds to cover them.

PREPARING A BANK STATEMENT RECONCILIATION

4-7

When the statement arrives from the bank each month, the depositor must compare the bank balance with the balance shown in the checkbook. Usually, the balances are not the same because during the month, some account activity has taken place without being recorded by the bank and other activities have occurred without being recorded in the checkbook. The process of adjusting the bank and checkbook balances to reflect the actual current balance is known as **bank statement reconciliation**. When we use the word *checkbook* in this chapter, we are actually referring to the records kept by the depositor on the check stubs or in the checkbook register.

Before a statement can be reconciled, you must identify and total all the checks that have been written but have not yet reached the bank. These are known as **outstanding checks**. Outstanding checks are found by comparing and checking off each check in the checkbook with those shown on the statement. Any checks not appearing on the statement are outstanding checks.

Sometimes deposits are made close to the statement date or by mail and do not clear the bank in time to appear on the current statement. These are known as **deposits in transit**. Just like outstanding checks, deposits in transit must be identified and totaled. Once again, this is done by comparing and checking off the checkbook records with the deposits shown on the bank statement.

A bank statement is reconciled when the **adjusted checkbook balance** is equal to the **adjusted bank balance**. Most bank statements have a form on the back to use in reconciling the account. Exhibit 4-14 is an example of such a form and is used in this chapter.

bank statement reconciliation The process of adjusting the bank and checkbook balances to reflect the actual current balance of the checking account.

outstanding checks Checks that have been written but have not yet reached the bank and therefore do not appear on the current bank statement.

deposits in transit Deposits made close to the statement date or by mail that do not clear in time to appear on the current bank statement.

adjusted checkbook balance The checkbook balance minus service charges and other debits plus interest earned and other credits.

adjusted bank balance The bank balance minus outstanding checks plus deposits in transit.

STEPS FOR PREPARING A BANK STATEMENT RECONCILIATION

STEP 1. Calculate the adjusted checkbook balance:
   a. Look over the bank statement and find any credits not recorded in the checkbook, such as interest earned or notes collected, and *add* them to the checkbook balance to get a subtotal.
   b. From the bank statement, locate any charges or debits such as service charges, NSF fees, or returned items that have not been recorded in the checkbook and *subtract* them from the subtotal from Step 1a.

STEP 2. Calculate the adjusted bank balance:
   a. Locate all of the deposits in transit and *add* them to the statement balance to get a subtotal.
   b. Locate and total all outstanding checks and *subtract* them from the subtotal from Step 2a.

STEP 3. Compare the adjusted balances:
   a. If they are equal, the statement has been reconciled.
   b. If they are not equal, an error exists that must be found and corrected. The error is either in the checkbook or on the bank statement.

EXHIBIT 4-14   Bank Statement Reconciliation Form

CHECKBOOK BALANCE	$	STATEMENT BALANCE	$
Add: Interest Earned & Other Credits		Add: Deposits in Transit	
SUBTOTAL		SUBTOTAL	
Deduct: Service Charges & Other Debits		Deduct: Outstanding Checks	
ADJUSTED CHECKBOOK BALANCE		ADJUSTED STATEMENT BALANCE	

Checks Outstanding

No.	Amount	
Total		

Reconciled Balances

Learning Tip

When a bank statement arrives, the balance on that statement will not agree with the checkbook balance until the account has been *reconciled*. Remember that *both* balances need to be adjusted.

To determine which balance, the checkbook or the bank, gets adjusted for various situations, ask "Who didn't know?" For example,

- The bank "*didn't know*" about outstanding checks and deposits in transit; therefore, these adjustments are made to the bank balance.
- The checkbook "*didn't know*" the amount of the service charges and other debits or credits. These adjustments are made to the checkbook.

B-A-C-O/Shutterstock.com

EXAMPLE5   RECONCILING A BANK STATEMENT

Prepare a bank reconciliation for Anita Gomberg from the bank statement and checkbook records below.

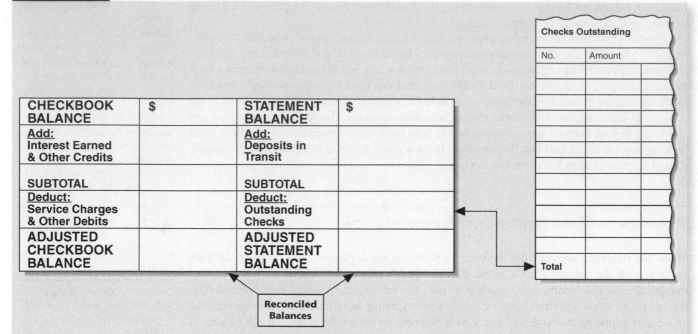

STATEMENT DATE
8-2-20xx

CINDY J. CITIZEN
1234 Main Street
Anywhere, U.S.A. 10101

CHECKING ACCOUNT SUMMARY
7-1-20xx THRU 7-31-20xx

ACCOUNT NUMBER
82-1301-508

Previous Balance	Deposits & Credits Number	Total	Checks & Debits Number	Total	Current Balance
1,233.40	3	2,445.80	7	2,158.92	1,520.28

CHECKING ACCOUNT TRANSACTIONS

DATE	AMOUNT	DESCRIPTION	BALANCE
7-3	450.30	Check #1209	783.10
7-6	500.00	Deposit	1,283.10
7-10	47.75	Check #1210	1,235.35
7-13	1,300.00	EFT Payroll Deposit	2,535.35
7-15	312.79	Check #1212	2,222.56
7-17	547.22	Check #1214	1,675.34
7-22	350.00	ATM Withdrawal	1,325.34
7-24	645.80	Deposit	1,971.14
7-28	430.86	Debit Card Purchase	1,540.28
7-30	20.00	Service Charge	1,520.28

CHECK NUMBER	DATE	DESCRIPTION OF TRANSACTION	AMOUNT OF PAYMENT OR WITHDRAWAL (−)	✓	AMOUNT OF DEPOSIT OR INTEREST (+)	BALANCE FORWARD 1,233 40
		PLEASE BE SURE TO **DEDUCT** ANY BANK CHARGES THAT APPLY TO YOUR ACCOUNT				
1209	7/1	To Home Shopping Network	450 30			
		For				Bal. 783 10
	7/6	To Deposit			500 00	
		For				Bal. 1,283 10
1210	7/8	To Food Spot	47 75			
		For				Bal. 1,235 35
1211	7/10	To Delta Air Lines	342 10			
		For				Bal. 893 25
	7/13	To Payroll Deposit			1,300 00	
		For				Bal. 2,193 25
1212	7/13	To Hyatt Hotel	312 79			
		For				Bal. 1,880 46
1213	7/15	To Wall Street Journal	75 00			
		For				Bal. 1,805 46
1214	7/15	To Fashionista	547 22			
		For				Bal. 1,258 24
	7/21	To ATM Withdrawal	350 00			
		For				Bal. 908 24
	7/24	To Deposit			645 80	
		For				Bal. 1,554 04
	7/28	To J. Crew — Debit Card	430 86			
		For				Bal. 1,123 18
	7/31	To Deposit			550 00	
		For				Bal. 1,673 18

▶SOLUTIONSTRATEGY

The properly completed reconciliation form is on page 109. Note that the adjusted checkbook balance equals the adjusted bank statement balance. The balances are now reconciled. After some practice, the format will become familiar to you and you should no longer need the form.

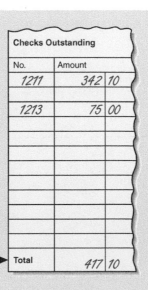

CHECKBOOK BALANCE	$ 1,673.18	STATEMENT BALANCE	$ 1,520.28
Add: Interest Earned & Other Credits		**Add:** Deposits in Transit	550.00
SUBTOTAL	1,673.18	SUBTOTAL	2,070.28
Deduct: Service Charges & Other Debits	20.00	**Deduct:** Outstanding Checks	417.10
ADJUSTED CHECKBOOK BALANCE	1,653.18	ADJUSTED STATEMENT BALANCE	1,653.18

Reconciled Balances

Checks Outstanding

No.	Amount
1211	342 10
1213	75 00
Total	417 10

▶TRYITEXERCISE 5

Using the form provided, reconcile the following bank statement and checkbook records for Max Mangones.

	STATEMENT DATE
	4-3-20xx

JOHN Q. PUBLIC
1234 Main Street
Anywhere, U.S.A. 10101

CHECKING ACCOUNT SUMMARY   **ACCOUNT NUMBER**
3-1-20xx THRU 3-31-20xx   097440

Previous Balance	Deposits & Credits Number	Total	Checks & Debits Number	Total	Current Balance
625.40	3	1,790.00	8	690.00	1,725.40

CHECKING ACCOUNT TRANSACTIONS

DATE	AMOUNT	DESCRIPTION	BALANCE
3-2	34.77	**Debit Card Purchase**	590.63
3-6	750.00	**Payroll-EFT Deposit**	1,340.63
3-10	247.05	**Check #340**	1,093.58
3-13	390.00	**Deposit**	1,483.58
3-15	66.30	**Check #342**	1,417.28
3-17	112.18	**Check #343**	1,305.10
3-22	150.00	**ATM Withdrawal**	1,155.10
3-24	650.00	**Deposit**	1,805.10
3-28	50.00	**Check #345**	1,755.10
3-30	17.70	**Check Printing Charge**	1,737.40
3-31	12.00	**Service Charge**	1,725.40

PLEASE BE SURE TO **DEDUCT** ANY BANK CHARGES THAT APPLY TO YOUR ACCOUNT.

CHECK NUMBER	DATE	DESCRIPTION OF TRANSACTION	AMOUNT OF PAYMENT OR WITHDRAWAL (−)	✓	AMOUNT OF DEPOSIT OR INTEREST (+)	BALANCE FORWARD
						625 40
	3/2	To Naples Pet Shop — Debit Card	34 77			
		For				Bal. 590 63
	3/5	To Electronic Payroll Deposit			750 00	
		For				Bal. 1,340 63
339	3/5	To Alison Company	19 83			
		For				Bal. 1,320 80
340	3/9	To Tennis Warehouse	247 05			
		For				Bal. 1,073 75
	3/12	To Deposit			390 00	
		For				Bal. 1,463 75
341	3/12	To The Book Shelf	57 50			
		For				Bal. 1,406 25
342	3/13	To Walmart	66 30			
		For				Bal. 1,339 95
343	3/15	To Sports Authority	112 18			
		For				Bal. 1,227 77
	3/22	To ATM Withdrawal	150 00			
		For				Bal. 1,077 77
	3/24	To Deposit			650 00	
		For				Bal. 1,727 77
344	3/24	To Foot Locker	119 32			
		For				Bal. 1,608 45
345	3/28	To Cablevision, Inc.	50 00			
		For				Bal. 1,558 45
	3/30	To Deposit			240 23	
		For				Bal. 1,798 68

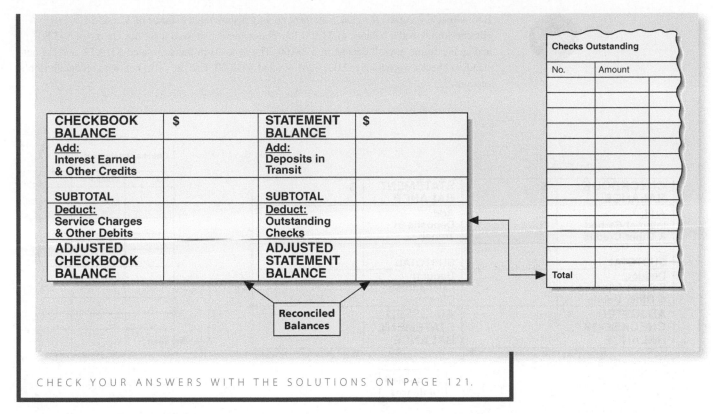

CHECKBOOK BALANCE	$	STATEMENT BALANCE	$
Add: Interest Earned & Other Credits		Add: Deposits in Transit	
SUBTOTAL		SUBTOTAL	
Deduct: Service Charges & Other Debits		Deduct: Outstanding Checks	
ADJUSTED CHECKBOOK BALANCE		ADJUSTED STATEMENT BALANCE	

Reconciled Balances

Checks Outstanding		
No.	Amount	
Total		

CHECK YOUR ANSWERS WITH THE SOLUTIONS ON PAGE 121.

REVIEW EXERCISES

4   SECTION II

1. On April 3, Erin Gardner received her bank statement showing a balance of $2,087.93. Her checkbook showed a balance of $1,922.47. Outstanding checks were $224.15, $327.80, $88.10, $122.42, and $202.67. The account earned $21.43. Deposits in transit amount to $813.11, and there is a service charge of $8.00. Use the form below to calculate the reconciled balance.

EXCEL 1

CHECKBOOK BALANCE	$	STATEMENT BALANCE	$
Add: Interest Earned & Other Credits		Add: Deposits in Transit	
SUBTOTAL		SUBTOTAL	
Deduct: Service Charges & Other Debits		Deduct: Outstanding Checks	
ADJUSTED CHECKBOOK BALANCE		ADJUSTED STATEMENT BALANCE	

Reconciled Balances

Checks Outstanding		
No.	Amount	
Total		

2. Bob Albrecht received his bank statement on July 5 showing a balance of $2,663.31. His checkbook had a balance of $1,931.83. The statement showed a service charge of $15.80 and an electronic payroll deposit of $200.00. The deposits in transit totaled $314.12, and the outstanding checks were for $182.00, $261.40, and $418.00. Use the form below to reconcile Bob's account.

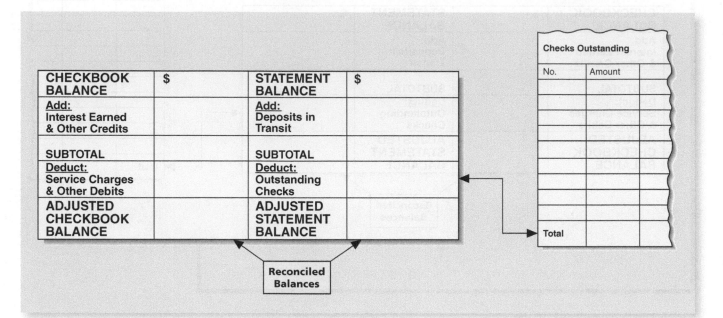

CHECKBOOK BALANCE	$	STATEMENT BALANCE	$
Add: Interest Earned & Other Credits		Add: Deposits in Transit	
SUBTOTAL		SUBTOTAL	
Deduct: Service Charges & Other Debits		Deduct: Outstanding Checks	
ADJUSTED CHECKBOOK BALANCE		ADJUSTED STATEMENT BALANCE	

Reconciled Balances

Checks Outstanding

No.	Amount	
Total		

3. On December 2, John Leahy received his bank statement showing a balance of $358.97. His checkbook showed a balance of $479.39. There was a check printing charge of $13.95, and interest earned was $6.40. The outstanding checks were for $22.97, $80.36, $19.80, and $4.50. The deposits in transit totaled $240.50. Use the form below to reconcile John's account.

CHECKBOOK BALANCE	$	STATEMENT BALANCE	$
Add: Interest Earned & Other Credits		Add: Deposits in Transit	
SUBTOTAL		SUBTOTAL	
Deduct: Service Charges & Other Debits		Deduct: Outstanding Checks	
ADJUSTED CHECKBOOK BALANCE		ADJUSTED STATEMENT BALANCE	

Reconciled Balances

Checks Outstanding

No.	Amount	
Total		

BUSINESS DECISION: CHOOSING A BANK

iStock.com/ MarsBars

4. You are looking for a bank in which to open a checking account for your new part-time business. You estimate that in the first year, you will be writing 30 checks per month and will make three debit transactions per month. Your average daily balance is estimated to be $900 for the first six months and $2,400 for the next six months.

   Use the following information to solve the problem.

Bank	Monthly Fees and Conditions
Intercontinental Bank	$15.00 with $1,000 min. daily balance -or- $25.00 under $1,000 min. daily balance
City National Bank	$4.50 plus $0.50 per check over 10 checks monthly $1.00 per debit transaction
Bank of America	$6 plus $0.25 per check $2.00 per debit transaction
First Union Bank	$9 plus $0.15 per check $1.50 per debit transaction

a. Calculate the cost of doing business with each bank for a year.

   Intercontinental Bank:

   City National Bank:

   Bank of America:

   First Union Bank:

b. Which bank should you choose for your checking account?

Taking a Toll

175
150
125
100
75
50
25
0
2008   2009   2010

In the two-year period from 2008 to 2010, U.S. bank failures increased dramatically as part of the global financial crisis.

Source: FDIC

CHAPTER SUMMARY

Section I: Understanding and Using Checking Accounts

Topic	Important Concepts	Illustrative Examples

Checks
 	
Performance Objectives 4-1 and 4-2, Pages 96–98
	Checks, or drafts, are negotiable instruments ordering the bank to pay money from the checking account to the name written on the check.
	
	    The person or business named on the check to receive the money is known as the payee.
	
	    The person or business issuing the check is known as the payor.
		See Check with Parts Labeled, Exhibit 4-2, p. 98

Deposit Slips
 	
Performance Objective 4-1, Page 96
 	
Performance Objective 4-4, Page 101
	Deposit slips, or deposit tickets, are printed forms with the depositor's name, address, account number, and space for the details of the deposit.
	
	    Deposit slips are used to record money, both cash and checks, being added to the checking account. They are presented to the bank teller along with the items to be deposited.
	
	    When a deposit is completed, the depositor receives a copy of the deposit slip as a receipt or proof of the transaction.
		See Deposit Slip, Exhibit 4-3, p. 98
		
		See Completed Deposit Slip, Exhibit 4-10, p. 102

Check Stubs
 	
Performance Objective 4-1, Page 96
 	
Performance Objective 4-5, Page 103
	Check stubs, with checks attached by perforation, are a bound part of the checkbook.
	
	    The check number is preprinted on both the check and the attached stub.
	
	    Each stub is used to record the issuing of its corresponding check and any deposits made on that date.
		See Check Stub with Check, Exhibit 4-4, p. 99

Check Registers **Performance Objective 4-1, Page 96** **Performance Objective 4-5, Page 103**	Check registers are the alternative method for keeping track of checking account activities. They are a separate booklet of forms rather than stubs attached to each check. Space is provided for all the pertinent information required to keep an accurate and up-to-date running balance of the account.	See Check Register, Exhibit 4-5, p. 99
Endorsements **Performance Objective 4-3, Page 99**	When you receive a check, you may cash it, deposit it in your account, or transfer it to another party. The endorsement on the back of the check tells the bank what to do. Your endorsement should be written within the $1\frac{1}{2}$-inch space at the trailing edge of the check.	See Endorsement Space, Exhibit 4-6, p. 101

Topic	Important Concepts	Illustrative Examples
Blank Endorsement **Performance Objective 4-3, Page 99**	A blank endorsement is used when you want to cash the check. You, as the payee, simply sign your name exactly as it appears on the front of the check and write your account number. Once you have endorsed a check in this manner, anyone who has possession of the check can cash it.	See Blank Endorsement, Exhibit 4-7, p. 101 *John Q. Public* *82-1301-508*
Restrictive Endorsement **Performance Objective 4-3, Page 99**	A restrictive endorsement is used when you want to deposit the check in your account. In this case, you endorse the check "for deposit only," sign your name as it appears on the front, and write your account number.	See Restrictive Endorsement, Exhibit 4-8, p. 101 *for deposit only* *John Q. Public* *82-1301-508*
Full Endorsement **Performance Objective 4-3, Page 99**	A full endorsement is used when you want to transfer the check to another party. In this case, you endorse the check "pay to the order of," write the name of the person or business to whom the check is being transferred, sign your name, and write your account number.	See Full Endorsement, Exhibit 4-9, p. 101 *pay to the order of* *Cindy J. Citizen* *John Q. Public* *82-1301-508*

Section II: Bank Statement Reconciliation

Topic	Important Concepts	Illustrative Examples
Bank Statements **Performance Objective 4-6, Page 99**	Bank statements are a recap of the checking account activity for the month. They show the balance brought forward from the last statement, the deposits and credits that have been added to the account during the month, the checks and debits that have been subtracted from the account during the month, service charges assessed to the account, and the current or ending balance.	See Paper Bank Statement, Exhibit 4-13, p. 111 STATEMENT DATE 11-2-20xx John Q. Public 1234 Main St. Anywhere, U.S.A. 10101 CHECKING ACCOUNT SUMMARY 10-1-20xx THRU 10-31-20xx ACCOUNT NUMBER 82-1301-508 Previous Balance 775.20 | Deposits & Credits Number 3 Total 3,228.11 | Checks & Debits Number 7 Total 2,857.80 | Current Balance 1,145.51 CHECKING ACCOUNT TRANSACTIONS DATE / AMOUNT / DESCRIPTION / BALANCE 10-2 / 125.00 / Check #445 / 650.20 10-4 / 357.18 / Deposit / 1,007.38 10-7 / 884.22 / Debit Purchase / 123.16 10-13 / 1,409.30 / EFT Payroll Deposit / 1,532.46 10-15 / 12.95 / Debit Card Purchase / 1,519.51 10-16 / 326.11 / Check #446 / 1,193.40 10-22 / 200.00 / ATM Withdrawal / 993.40 10-25 / 1,461.63 / Deposit / 2,455.03 10-27 / 1,294.52 / Check #447 / 1,160.51 10-31 / 15.00 / Service Charge / 1,145.51

Topic	Important Concepts	Illustrative Examples

Bank Statement Reconciliation
 	
Performance Objective 4-7, Page 111
	1. Calculate the adjusted checkbook balance:
	  a. Locate any credits on the statement not recorded in the checkbook, such as interest earned or notes collected, and add them to the checkbook balance to get a subtotal.
	  b. Subtract any debits or charges such as service charges, NSF fees, or returned items from the subtotal above.
	
	2. Calculate the adjusted bank balance:
	  a. Locate all the deposits in transit and add them to the bank statement balance to get a subtotal.
	  b. Locate all outstanding checks and subtract them from the subtotal above.
	
	3. Compare the adjusted balances:
	  a. If they are equal, the statement has been reconciled.
	  b. If they are *not* equal, an error exists that must be found and corrected. The error is either in the checkbook or on the bank statement.
		See Bank Statement Reconciliation Form, Exhibit 4-14, p. 113 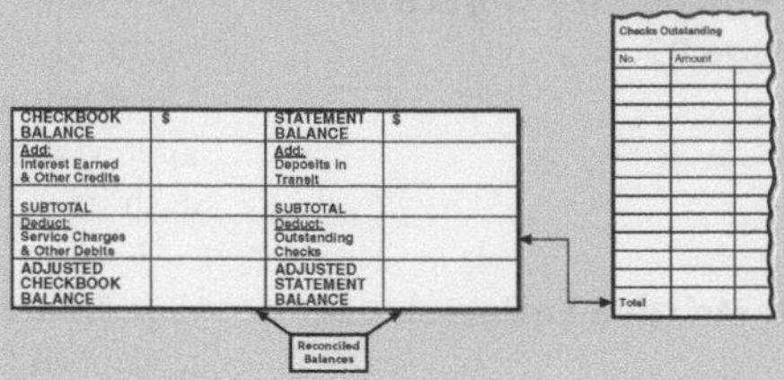

TRY IT: EXERCISE SOLUTIONS FOR CHAPTER 4

1.

2. a.

| Pay to the order of |
| Roz Reitman |
| Your Signature |
| 696-339-1028 |

Full Endorsement

b.

| Your Signature |
| 696-339-1028 |
| |
| |

Blank Endorsement

c.

| for deposit only |
| Your Signature |
| 696-339-1028 |
| |

Restrictive Endorsement

CHAPTER 4

3.

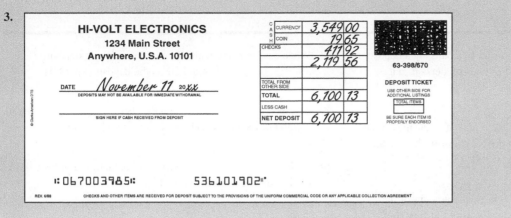

HI-VOLT ELECTRONICS
1234 Main Street
Anywhere, U.S.A. 10101

DATE *November 11* 20 xx

DEPOSITS MAY NOT BE AVAILABLE FOR IMMEDIATE WITHDRAWAL

SIGN HERE IF CASH RECEIVED FROM DEPOSIT

C A S H	CURRENCY	3,549	00
	COIN	19	65
	CHECKS	411	92
		2,119	56

63-398/670

TOTAL FROM OTHER SIDE		
TOTAL	6,100	13
LESS CASH		
NET DEPOSIT	6,100	13

DEPOSIT TICKET
USE OTHER SIDE FOR ADDITIONAL LISTINGS
TOTAL ITEMS
BE SURE EACH ITEM IS PROPERLY ENDORSED

⑆067003985⑆ 536101902⑈

REV. 6/98   CHECKS AND OTHER ITEMS ARE RECEIVED FOR DEPOSIT SUBJECT TO THE PROVISIONS OF THE UNIFORM COMMERCIAL CODE OR ANY APPLICABLE COLLECTION AGREEMENT

© Clarke American DTS

4.

IF TAX DEDUCTIBLE CHECK HERE ☐	$	55.75

137
March 12 20 xx
TO *Nathan & David*
FOR *perm & manicure*

	DOLLARS	CENTS
BAL. FWD.	887	45
DEPOSIT		
DEPOSIT		
TOTAL	887	45
THIS ITEM	55	75
SUB-TOTAL	831	70
OTHER DEDUCT. (IF ANY)		
BAL. FWD.	831	70

IF TAX DEDUCTIBLE CHECK HERE ☐	$	459.88

138
March 19 20 xx
TO *Complete Auto Service*
FOR *Car repairs*

	DOLLARS	CENTS
BAL. FWD.	831	70
DEPOSIT 3/16	125	40
DEPOSIT 3/16	221	35
TOTAL	1,178	45
THIS ITEM	459	88
SUB-TOTAL	718	57
OTHER DEDUCT. (IF ANY)	53	00
BAL. FWD.	665	57

PLEASE BE SURE TO **DEDUCT** ANY BANK CHARGES THAT APPLY TO YOUR ACCOUNT.

CHECK NUMBER	DATE	DESCRIPTION OF TRANSACTION	AMOUNT OF PAYMENT OR WITHDRAWAL (−)	✓	AMOUNT OF DEPOSIT OR INTEREST (+)	BALANCE FORWARD	
						887	45
137	3/12	To *Nathan & David Hair Stylists*	55	75			
		For				Bal. 831	70
	3/16	To *Deposit*			125	40	
		For				Bal. 957	10
	3/16	To *Deposit*			221	35	
		For				Bal. 1,178	45
138	3/19	To *Complete Auto Service*	459	88			
		For				Bal. 718	57
	3/20	To *Debit Card — Post Office*	53	00			
		For				Bal. 665	57

5.

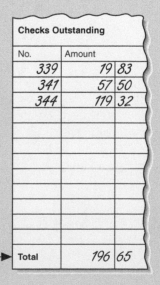

Checks Outstanding

No.	Amount	
339	19	83
341	57	50
344	119	32
Total	**196**	**65**

CHECKBOOK BALANCE	$ 1,798.68	STATEMENT BALANCE	$ 1,725.40
Add: Interest Earned & Other Credits		**Add:** Deposits in Transit	240.23
SUBTOTAL	1,798.68	SUBTOTAL	1,965.63
Deduct: Service Charges & Other Debits	17.70 12.20	**Deduct:** Outstanding Checks	196.65
ADJUSTED CHECKBOOK BALANCE	1,768.98	ADJUSTED STATEMENT BALANCE	1,768.98

Reconciled Balances

CONCEPT REVIEW

1. A(n) _____ is a written order to a bank by a depositor to pay the amount specified from funds on deposit in a checking account. (4-1)

2. On a check, the _____ is the person or business issuing the check; the _____ is the person or business named on the check to receive the money. (4-1)

3. When a(n) _____ card is used, the amount of the transaction is deducted electronically from the checking account. (4-1)

4. Write the word form of $52.45 as it would appear on a check. (4-2)

5. The signature and instructions on the back of a check are known as the _____. (4-3)

6. There are three types of endorsements used on checks: the blank, the restrictive, and the _____ endorsement. (4-3)

7. The form used to record money being added to the checking account is a called a(n) _____. (4-4)

8. When cash is being withdrawn at the time of a deposit, a(n) _____ is required on the deposit slip. (4-4)

9. Attached by perforation to checks, check _____ are one method of tracking checking account activity. (4-5)

10. A check _____ is a separate booklet used to keep track of checking account activity. (4-5)

11. A bank _____ is a monthly summary of activities in a checking account. (4-6)

12. Additions to a checking account are called _____; subtractions from a checking account are called _____. (4-6)

13. A bank statement is reconciled when the adjusted checkbook balance _____ the adjusted bank balance. (4-7)

14. Checks that have not yet reached the bank are called _____ checks. Deposits that have not reached the bank are called deposits in _____. (4-7)

ASSESSMENT TEST

1. As the purchasing manager for Fuzzy Logic Industries, write a check dated April 29, 20xx, in the amount of $24,556.00, to Outback Electronics, Inc., for circuit boards.

```
┌──────────────────────────────────────────────────────────────┐
│  FUZZY LOGIC INDUSTRIES                            206         │
│  1234 Main Street                                             │
│  Anywhere, U.S.A. 10101              _____ 20____  63-398/670│
│                                                               │
│  PAY TO THE                                                   │
│  ORDER OF _____  $ _____        │
│                                                               │
│  _____ DOLLARS          │
│                                                               │
│                                                               │
│  FOR _____      _____            │
│  ⑆067003985⑆  206  731021807⑈                                 │
└──────────────────────────────────────────────────────────────┘
```

2. You have just received a check. Your account number is #9299-144-006. Write the following endorsements in the space provided below and identify what type they are.
   a. Allowing the check to be transferred to Expo, Inc.
   b. Allowing you to cash the check.
   c. Allowing you to deposit the check in your account.

a.

b.

c.

3. As cashier for Cellini's Pizza, it is your responsibility to make the daily deposits. Complete the deposit slip below based on the following information.

a. Date: January 20, 20xx.
b. Checks totaling $344.20.
c. Currency of $547.00
d. Coins: 125 quarters, 67 dimes, 88 nickels, and 224 pennies.

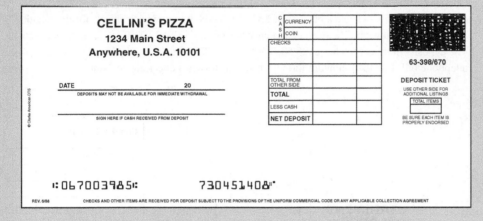

4. Simon Fitzrowdy checked his checking account online on Tuesday morning, and it showed a balance of $1,472.38. During a morning shopping trip, he used his debit card to buy gasoline for $48.92, groceries for $77.10, and a shirt for $34.98. He used his smartphone and his mobile-banking app to deposit a check for $150. What will his balance be the next morning?

5. From the following information, complete the two check stubs and the check register below.

a. Starting balance: $463.30.
b. April 15, 20xx, check #450 issued to the Keystone Market for groceries in the amount of $67.78.
c. April 17, debit card purchase of $250.
d. April 19, deposit of $125.45.
e. April 20, deposit of $320.00.
f. April 27, check #451 in the amount of $123.10 to Ace Appliance, Inc., for refrigerator repair.

Dollars AND Sense

Rewards Checking

Recently, a new type of checking account has been offered by banks and credit unions. These accounts, known as rewards checking, promise to pay high interest rates and are without any fees. Rewards checking accounts typically require that you use your debit card at least 10 times per month and that you give up paper bank statements in favor of online ones.

You can research various checking account offers at such sites as:

- www.bankrate.com
- www.bankdeals.com
- www.bankingmyway.com

iStock.com/Vreemous

CHAPTER
4

CHECK NUMBER	DATE	DESCRIPTION OF TRANSACTION	AMOUNT OF PAYMENT OR WITHDRAWAL (−)	✓	AMOUNT OF DEPOSIT OR INTEREST (+)	BALANCE FORWARD	
		To					
		For				Bal.	
		To					
		For				Bal.	
		To					
		For				Bal.	
		To					
		For				Bal.	
		To					
		For				Bal.	
		To					
		For				Bal.	

PLEASE BE SURE TO **DEDUCT** ANY BANK CHARGES THAT APPLY TO YOUR ACCOUNT.

6. On October 1, Jessica Clay received her bank statement showing a balance of $374.52. Her checkbook records indicate a balance of $338.97. There was a service charge for the month of $4.40 on the statement. The outstanding checks were for $47.10, $110.15, $19.80, and $64.10. The deposits in transit totaled $125.50. There was a $75.70 debit for automatic payment of her telephone bill. Use the following form to reconcile Jessica's checking account.

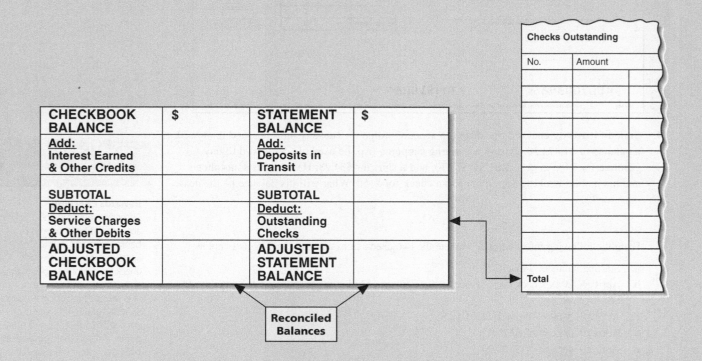

CHECKBOOK BALANCE	$	STATEMENT BALANCE	$
Add: Interest Earned & Other Credits		**Add:** Deposits in Transit	
SUBTOTAL		SUBTOTAL	
Deduct: Service Charges & Other Debits		**Deduct:** Outstanding Checks	
ADJUSTED CHECKBOOK BALANCE		**ADJUSTED STATEMENT BALANCE**	

Reconciled Balances

Checks Outstanding

No.	Amount	
Total		

CHAPTER
4

7. Using the form on page 121, prepare a bank reconciliation for Kali Loi from the following checkbook records and bank statement.

CHECK NUMBER	DATE	DESCRIPTION OF TRANSACTION	AMOUNT OF PAYMENT OR WITHDRAWAL (−)	✓	AMOUNT OF DEPOSIT OR INTEREST (+)	BALANCE FORWARD 879 36
801	10/1	To H & H Jewelers	236 77			
		For				Bal. 642 59
	10/6	To Deposit			450 75	
		For				Bal. 1,093 34
802	10/8	To L.L. Bean	47 20			
		For				Bal. 1,046 14
803	10/10	To Cashé	75 89			
		For				Bal. 970 25
	10/13	To Deposit			880 34	
		For				Bal. 1,850 59
804	10/13	To Four Seasons Hotel	109 00			
		For				Bal. 1,741 59
805	10/15	To American Express	507 82			
		For				Bal. 1,233 77
	10/20	To ATM Withdrawal	120 00			
		For				Bal. 1,113 77
	10/24	To Deposit			623 50	
		For				Bal. 1,737 27
	10/27	To Deposit			208 40	
		For				Bal. 1,945 67
	10/28	To Home Depot — Debit Card	48 25			
		For				Bal. 1,897 42

PLEASE BE SURE TO **DEDUCT** ANY BANK CHARGES THAT APPLY TO YOUR ACCOUNT.

STATEMENT DATE
11-2-20xx

CHECKING ACCOUNT SUMMARY
10-1-20xx THRU 10-31-20xx

ACCOUNT NUMBER
449-56-7792

Previous Balance	Deposits & Credits Number	Deposits & Credits Total	Checks & Debits Number	Checks & Debits Total	Current Balance
879.36	3	1,954.59	7	1,347.83	1,486.12

CHECKING ACCOUNT TRANSACTIONS

DATE	AMOUNT	DESCRIPTION	BALANCE
10-3	236.77	Check #801	642.59
10-6	450.75	Deposit	1,093.34
10-10	324.70	Returned Item	768.64
10-13	880.34	EFT Payroll Deposit	1,648.98
10-15	75.89	Check #803	1,573.09
10-17	507.82	Check #805	1,065.27
10-22	120.00	ATM Withdrawal	945.27
10-24	623.50	Deposit	1,568.77
10-28	48.25	Debit Card Purchase	1,520.52
10-30	34.40	Check Printing Charge	1,486.12

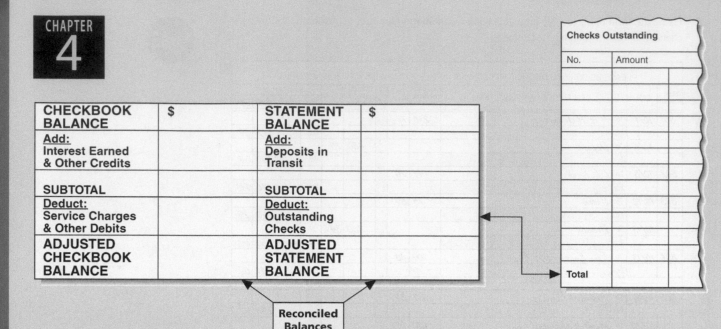

Dollars AND Sense

Opportunity cost is the sacrifice of benefits from the next-best alternative when you make a financial or economic decision. To fully evaluate how much a checking account with a required minimum balance costs, calculate the opportunity cost.

Consider a bank that requires an average monthly balance of $1,500. If you can earn 3% a year in interest on an investment maintaining this checking account means giving up $45 in potential interest income.

BUSINESS DECISION: CHOOSING A BANK WITH INTEREST

8. Sometimes banks offer checking accounts that earn interest on the average daily balance of the account each month. This interest is calculated using a formula known as the simple interest formula. The formula is written as:

$$\text{Interest} = \text{Principal} \times \text{Rate} \times \text{Time} \quad I = PRT$$

The formula states that the amount of **interest** earned on the account is equal to the **principal** (average daily balance) multiplied by the **rate** (interest rate per year—expressed as a decimal) multiplied by the **time** (expressed in years—use $\frac{1}{12}$ to represent one month of a year).

a. If you have not already done so, complete the Business Decision, Choosing a Bank on page **112**.

b. Use the simple interest formula to calculate the amount of interest you would earn per month if the Intercontinental Bank was offering 1.5% (.015) interest per year on checking accounts. (Note that your average daily balance changes from $900 to $2,400 in the last six months of the year.) Round monthly amounts to the nearest cent when necessary. How much interest would you earn for the year?

c. How much interest would you earn per month at Bank of America if it were offering 1% (.01) interest per year on checking accounts? How much interest would you earn for the year?

d. Recalculate the cost of doing business with Intercontinental Bank and Bank of America for a year.

Largest U.S. Banks by Assets ($ trillions)	
JPMorgan Chase & Co. (JPM)	2.53
Bank of America Corp. (BAC)	2.28
Wells Fargo & Co (WFC)	1.95
Citigroup Inc. (C)	1.84

e. Based on this new information, which of the four banks should you choose for your checking account?

COLLABORATIVE LEARNING ACTIVITY

Choosing a Checking Account

Have each team member research a local bank, a credit union, or another financial institution offering checking accounts to find the types of checking accounts they have and other banking services they offer. As a team, look over the material and answer the following:

a. How do the accounts compare regarding online and/or mobile banking options, monthly service charges, interest paid, account minimums, debit and ATM charges, and other rules and regulations?

b. Do the banks offer any incentives such as a no-fee Visa or MasterCard, bounce-proof checking, or a line of credit?

c. Based on your team's research, which bank would you recommend for each of the following:
   - College student. Why?
   - Small business. Why?
   - Family with three teenagers. Why?

d. Because many banks have failed in recent years, check your bank's health by looking up its "star rating" at www.bauerfinancial.com or www.bankrate.com. Also look over your bank's financial statements filed quarterly with the government at www.fdic.gov. What can you conclude from your findings?

CHAPTER 5

Using Equations to Solve Business Problems

PERFORMANCE OBJECTIVES

SECTION I: Solving Basic Equations

5-1: Understanding the concept, terminology, and rules of equations (p. 129)

5-2: Solving equations for the unknown and proving the solution (p. 130)

5-3: Writing expressions and equations from written statements (p. 136)

SECTION II: Using Equations to Solve Business-Related Word Problems

5-4: Setting up and solving business-related word problems by using equations (p. 139)

5-5: Understanding and solving ratio and proportion problems (p. 143)

Monkey Business Images/Shutterstock.com

SOLVING BASIC EQUATIONS

One of the primary objectives of business mathematics is to describe business situations and solve business problems. Many business problems requiring a mathematical solution have been converted to formulas. A **formula** is a mathematical statement describing a real-world situation in which letters represent number quantities. A typical example of a formula follows:

Business situation: Revenue less expenses is profit

Mathematical formula: Revenue − Expenses = Profit

or

$$R - E = P$$

By knowing the numerical value of any two of the three parts, we can use the formula to determine the unknown part. Formulas are a way of standardizing repetitive business situations. They are used in almost every aspect of business activity and are an essential tool for the businessperson. Later in the book, we see formulas applied to topics such as markup and markdown, percents, interest rates, financial ratios, inventory, and depreciation.

As valuable and widespread as formulas are, they cannot anticipate all business situations. Today businesspeople must have the ability to analyze the facts of a situation and devise custom-made formulas to solve business problems. These formulas are actually mathematical **equations**.

In this important chapter, you learn to write and solve equations. At first, some of the concepts may seem a bit strange. Equations use letters of the alphabet as well as numbers. Do not be intimidated! After some practice, you will be able to write and solve equations comfortably.

formula A mathematical statement describing a real-world situation in which letters represent number quantities. An example is the simple interest formula $I = PRT$, where *interest* equals *principal* times *rate* times *time*.

equations Mathematical statements expressing a relationship of equality; usually written as a series of symbols that are separated into left and right sides and joined by an equal sign. $X + 7 = 10$ is an equation.

UNDERSTANDING THE CONCEPT, TERMINOLOGY, AND RULES OF EQUATIONS

5-1

In English, we write by using words to form complete thoughts known as sentences. Equations convert written sentences describing business situations into mathematical sentences. When the statement contains an equal sign (=), it is an equation. If it does not contain an equal sign, it is simply an **expression**. Equations express business problems in their simplest form. There are no adjectives or words of embellishment, just the facts.

$S + 12$ is an *expression* $S + 12 = 20$ is an *equation*

An equation is a mathematical statement using numbers, letters, and symbols to express a relationship of equality. Equations have an expression on the left side and an expression on the right side connected by an equal sign.

Letters of the alphabet are used to represent unknown quantities in equations and are called **variables**. In the equation above, S is the variable, or the **unknown**. The 12 and the 20 are the **constants**, or **knowns**. Variables and constants are also known as the **terms** of the equation. The plus sign and the equal sign separate the terms and describe the relationship between them.

To **solve an equation** means to find the numerical value of the unknown that makes the equation true. From our equation $S + 12 = 20$, what value of S would make the equation true? Is it 6? No, 6 plus 12 is 18, and 18 does not equal 20. Is it 10? No, 10 plus 12 is 22, and 22 does not equal 20. How about 8? Yes, 8 plus 12 does equal 20.

$$S + 12 = 20$$
$$8 + 12 = 20$$
$$20 = 20$$

By substituting 8 for the variable, S, we have found the value of the unknown that satisfies the equation and makes it true: 20 equals 20. The numerical value of the variable that makes the equation true (in this case, 8) is known as the **solution**, or **root**, of the equation.

expression A mathematical operation or a quantity stated in symbolic form, not containing an equal sign. $X + 7$ is an expression.

variables, or unknowns The parts of an equation that are not given. In equations, the unknowns, or variables, are represented by letters of the alphabet. In the equation $X + 7 = 10$, X is the unknown, or variable.

constants, or knowns The parts of an equation that are given. In equations, the knowns are constants (numbers), which are quantities having a fixed value. In the equation $X + 7 = 10$, 7 and 10 are the knowns, or constants.

terms The knowns (constants) and unknowns (variables) of an equation. In the equation $X + 7 = 10$, the terms are X, 7, and 10.

solve an equation To find the numerical value of the unknown in an equation that makes the equation true.

solution, or root The numerical value of the unknown that makes the equation true. In the equation $X + 7 = 10$, for example, 3 is the solution because $3 + 7 = 10$.

5-2   SOLVING EQUATIONS FOR THE UNKNOWN AND PROVING THE SOLUTION

suhendri/Shutterstock.com

Today managers must have the ability to analyze the facts of a business problem and devise custom-made formulas to solve them.

coefficient A number or quantity placed before another quantity, indicating multiplication. For example, 4 is the coefficient in the expression 4C. This indicates 4 multiplied by C.

transpose To move a term from one side of an equation to the other. Whenever addition or subtraction is used for moving the term, a corresponding change of sign occurs.

In solving equations, we use the same basic operations we used in arithmetic: addition, subtraction, multiplication, and division. The meanings of the signs $+$, $-$, $\times$, and $\div$ are still the same. Equations have a few new designations, however, that we must learn.

Multiplication of 5 times Y, for example, may be written as

$$5 \times Y$$
$$5 \cdot Y$$
$$5(Y)$$
$$5Y$$

The number 5 in the term $5Y$ is known as the **coefficient** of the term. In cases in which there is no numerical coefficient written, such as W, the coefficient is understood to be a 1. Therefore,

$$1W = W.$$

Division in equations is indicated by the fraction bar, just as in Chapter 2. For example, the term 5 divided by Y would be written as

$$\frac{5}{Y}$$

It is important to remember that an equation is a statement of *equality*. To solve an equation, we must move or **transpose** all the unknowns to one side and all the knowns to the other side. We accomplish this by performing the same operation on <u>both</u> sides of the equation. By doing the same thing on both sides of the equation, we create a new equation that has the same solution as the original equation. It is customary for the unknowns to be on the left side and the knowns to be on the right side, such as $X = 7$.

Transposing involves the use of inverse, or opposite, operations. To transpose a term in an equation, (1) note the operation indicated and (2) apply the *opposite* operation to both sides of the equation as follows:

Operation Indicated		Opposite Operation
Addition	$\longrightarrow$	Subtraction
Subtraction	$\longrightarrow$	Addition
Multiplication	$\longrightarrow$	Division
Division	$\longrightarrow$	Multiplication

STEPS FOR SOLVING EQUATIONS AND PROVING THE SOLUTION

STEP 1. Transpose all the *unknowns* to the left side of the equation and all the *knowns* to the right side of the equation by using the following operation order for solving equations.

- *Parentheses*, if any, must be cleared before any other operations are performed. To clear parentheses, multiply the coefficient by each term inside the parentheses. For example:

$$3(5C + 4) = 2 \quad 3(5C) + 3(4) = 2 \quad 15C + 12 = 2$$

- To solve equations with more than one operation:
  - First, apply opposite operations using additions and subtractions.
  - Then apply opposite operations using multiplications and divisions.

STEP 2. Prove the solution by substituting your answer for the letter or letters in the original equation. If the left and right sides are *equal*, the equation is true and your answer is correct.

iStock.com/Nikada

EXAMPLE1 SOLVING EQUATIONS

Solve the equation $X + 4 = 15$ and prove the solution.

▶ SOLUTIONSTRATEGY

The equation $X + 4 = 15$ indicates addition (+4). To solve for X, apply the opposite operation, subtraction. Subtract 4 from each side.

$$
\begin{array}{r}
X + 4 = 15 \\
\underline{-4 \quad -4} \\
X \quad = 11 \\
\underline{X = 11}
\end{array}
$$

Proof: The solution can easily be proven by substituting our answer (11) for the letter or letters in the original equation. If the left and right sides are equal, the equation is true and the solution is correct.

$$
\begin{array}{r}
X + 4 = 15 \\
11 + 4 = 15 \\
\underline{15 = 15}
\end{array}
$$

▶ TRYITEXERCISE 1

Solve the following equations for the unknown and prove your solutions.

a.   a. $W + 10 = 25$ b. $Q + 30 = 100$

CHECK YOUR ANSWERS WITH THE SOLUTIONS ON PAGE 154.

EXAMPLE2 SOLVING EQUATIONS

Solve the equation $H - 20 = 44$ and prove the solution.

▶ SOLUTIONSTRATEGY

The equation $H - 20 = 44$ indicates subtraction (−20). To solve for H, apply the opposite operation, addition. Add 20 to each side of the equation.

$$
\begin{array}{r}
H - 20 = \quad 44 \\
\underline{+20 \quad +20} \\
H \quad = \quad 64 \\
\underline{H = 64}
\end{array}
$$

Proof: Substitute 64 for H.

$$
\begin{array}{r}
H - 20 = 44 \\
64 - 20 = 44 \\
\underline{44 = 44}
\end{array}
$$

▶ TRYITEXERCISE 2

Solve the following equations for the unknown and prove your solutions.

a.   a. $A - 8 = 40$ b. $L - 3 = 7$

CHECK YOUR ANSWERS WITH THE SOLUTIONS ON PAGE 154.

Learning Tip

Remember, an equation is a statement of "equality." The left side must equal the right side for the equation to be true. The word *equation*, in fact, is derived from the word *equal*.

IN THE Business World

The equal sign, two parallel lines (=), was invented in the sixteenth century by Robert Recorde. He stated, "Nothing can be more equal than parallel lines!"

Other related mathematical symbols are:

$\approx$ is approximately equal to
$\neq$ is not equal to
$\geq$ is greater than or equal to
$\leq$ is less than or equal to

EXAMPLE3 SOLVING EQUATIONS

Solve the equation $9T = 36$ and prove the solution.

▶SOLUTIONSTRATEGY

The equation $9T = 36$ indicates multiplication. $9T$ means 9 times T. To solve for T, apply the opposite operation. Divide both sides of the equation by 9.

$$9T = 36$$
$$\frac{\cancel{9}T}{\cancel{9}} = \frac{36}{9}$$
$$\underline{T = 4}$$

Proof:

$$9T = 36$$
$$9(4) = 36$$
$$\underline{36 = 36}$$

▶TRYITEXERCISE 3

Solve the following equations for the unknown and prove your solutions.

a.   a. $15L = 75$ b. $16F = 80$

CHECK YOUR ANSWERS WITH THE SOLUTIONS ON PAGE 154.

EXAMPLE4 SOLVING EQUATIONS

Solve the equation $\dfrac{M}{5} = 4$ and prove the solution.

▶SOLUTIONSTRATEGY

The equation $\dfrac{M}{5} = 4$ indicates division. To solve for M, do the opposite operation. Multiply both sides of the equation by 5.

$$(\cancel{5})\frac{M}{\cancel{5}} = 4(5)$$
$$\underline{M = 20}$$

Proof:

$$\frac{M}{5} = 4$$
$$\frac{20}{5} = 4$$
$$\underline{4 = 4}$$

▶TRYITEXERCISE 4

Solve the following equations for the unknown and prove your solutions.

a.   a. $\dfrac{Z}{8} = 2$ b. $\dfrac{C}{9} = 9$

CHECK YOUR ANSWERS WITH THE SOLUTIONS ON PAGE 154.

EXAMPLE5 — SOLVING EQUATIONS CONTAINING MULTIPLE OPERATIONS

Solve the equation $7R - 5 = 51$ and prove the solution.

►SOLUTIONSTRATEGY

The equation $7R - 5 = 51$ indicates subtraction and multiplication. Following the operation order for solving equations, begin by adding 5 to each side of the equation.

$$
\begin{aligned}
7R - 5 &= 51 \\
+5 \quad &+5 \\
\hline
7R &= 56 \\
7R &= 56
\end{aligned}
$$

Next, divide both sides of the equation by 7.

$$\frac{7R}{7} = \frac{56}{7}$$

$$\underline{\underline{R = 8}}$$

Proof:

$$
\begin{aligned}
7R - 5 &= 51 \\
7(8) - 5 &= 51 \\
56 - 5 &= 51 \\
\underline{\underline{51 &= 51}}
\end{aligned}
$$

►TRYITEXERCISE 5

Solve the following equations for the unknown and prove the solutions.

a.

a. $12N + 14 = 50$ b. $3W - 4 = 26$

CHECK YOUR ANSWERS WITH THE SOLUTIONS ON PAGE 154.

EXAMPLE6 — SOLVING EQUATIONS CONTAINING MULTIPLE OPERATIONS

Solve the equation $\dfrac{X}{2} + 20 = 34$ and prove the solution.

►SOLUTIONSTRATEGY

The equation $\dfrac{X}{2} + 20 = 34$ indicates addition and division. Following the operation order for solving equations begin by subtracting 20 from each side.

$$
\begin{aligned}
\frac{X}{2} + 20 &= 34 \\
-20 \quad &-20 \\
\hline
\frac{X}{2} &= 14 \\
\frac{X}{2} &= 14
\end{aligned}
$$

Next, multiply each side by 2.

$$(2)\,\frac{X}{2} = 14(2)$$

$$\underline{\underline{X = 28}}$$

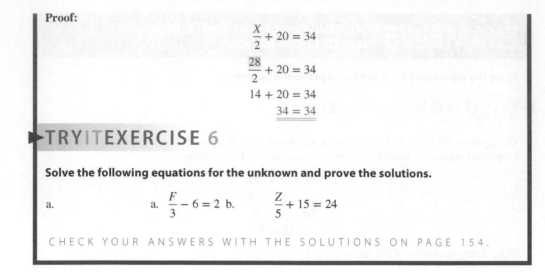

Proof:

$$\frac{X}{2} + 20 = 34$$

$$\frac{28}{2} + 20 = 34$$

$$14 + 20 = 34$$

$$\underline{34 = 34}$$

▶TRYITEXERCISE 6

Solve the following equations for the unknown and prove the solutions.

a.   a. $\dfrac{F}{3} - 6 = 2$ b. $\dfrac{Z}{5} + 15 = 24$

CHECK YOUR ANSWERS WITH THE SOLUTIONS ON PAGE 154.

PARENTHESES

Sometimes parentheses are used in equations. They contain a number just outside the left-hand parentheses known as the coefficient and two or more terms inside the parentheses. An example is $5(3X + 6) = 20$.

PARENTHESES RULE

In solving equations, parentheses must be removed before any other operations are performed. To remove parentheses, multiply the coefficient by each term inside the parentheses.

To apply this rule to the example above,

$$5(3X + 6) = 20$$
$$5(3X) + 5(6) = 20$$
$$15X + 30 = 20$$

EXAMPLE7 SOLVING EQUATIONS CONTAINING PARENTHESES

Solve the equation $8(2K - 4) = 48$ and prove the solution.

▶SOLUTIONSTRATEGY

Because this equation contains parentheses, we must begin there. Following the rule for removing parentheses, multiply the coefficient, 8, by each term inside the parentheses.

$$8(2K - 4) = 48$$
$$8(2K) - 8(4) = 48$$
$$16K - 32 = 48$$

Now solve the equation as before by isolating the unknown, K, on the left side of the equal sign. Remember, add and subtract first, then multiply and divide.

$$16K - 32 = \quad 48$$
$$\underline{\quad + 32 \quad + 32}$$
$$16K \quad = \quad 80$$

$$16K = 80$$

$$\frac{\cancel{16}K}{\cancel{16}} = \frac{80}{16}$$

$$\underline{K = 5}$$

Proof:

$$8(2K - 4) = 48$$
$$8(2\{5\} - 4) = 48$$
$$8(10 - 4) = 48$$
$$8(6) = 48$$
$$\underline{48 = 48}$$

▶TRYITEXERCISE 7

Solve the following equations for the unknown and prove the solutions.

a.

a. $4(5G + 6) = 64$ b. $6(3H - 5) = 42$

CHECK YOUR ANSWERS WITH THE SOLUTIONS ON PAGE 154.

When equations contain unknowns that appear two or more times, they must be combined.

STEPS FOR COMBINING MULTIPLE UNKNOWNS

STEP 1. To combine unknowns, they must be on the same side of the equation. If they are not, move them all to the same side.

$$5X = 12 + 2X$$
$$5X - 2X = 12$$

STEP 2. Once the unknowns are on the same side of the equation, add or subtract their coefficients as indicated.

$$5X - 2X = 12$$
$$3X = 12$$

EXAMPLE8   SOLVING EQUATIONS WHEN THE UNKNOWN OCCURS MORE THAN ONCE

Solve the equation $4C + 7 - C = 25 - 6C$ and prove the solution.

▶SOLUTIONSTRATEGY

To solve this equation, we begin by combining the two terms on the left side that contain C: $4C - C = 3C$. This leaves

$$3C + 7 = 25 - 6C$$

Next, move the $-6C$ to the left side by adding $+6C$ to both sides of the equation.

$$3C + 7 = 25 - 6C$$
$$\underline{+6C \qquad\qquad +6C}$$
$$9C + 7 = 25$$

Now that all the terms containing the unknown, C, have been combined, we can solve the equation.

$$9C + 7 = 25$$
$$\underline{-7 \quad -7}$$
$$9C \quad\ = 18$$
$$\frac{9C}{9} = \frac{18}{9}$$
$$C = 2$$

Proof:

$$4C + 7 - C = 25 - 6C$$
$$4(2) + 7 - 2 = 25 - 6(2)$$
$$8 + 7 - 2 = 25 - 12$$
$$\underline{13 = 13}$$

▶TRYITEXERCISE 8

Solve the following equations for the unknown and prove the solutions.

a. $X + 3 = 18 - 4X$ b. $9S + 8 - S = 2(2S + 8)$

CHECK YOUR ANSWERS WITH THE SOLUTIONS ON PAGE 154.

5-3 WRITING EXPRESSIONS AND EQUATIONS FROM WRITTEN STATEMENTS

Expressions and equations are created from written statements by identifying the unknowns and the knowns and then determining the mathematical relationship between them. The variables are assigned letters of the alphabet. The letter X is commonly used to represent the unknown. The relationship between the knowns and the unknowns involves addition, subtraction, multiplication, or division or a combination of two or more of these.

STEPS FOR WRITING EXPRESSIONS AND EQUATIONS

STEP 1. Read the written statement carefully.

STEP 2. Using the following list, identify and underline the key words and phrases.

STEP 3. Convert the words to numbers and mathematical symbols.

Learning Tip

Think of equations as complete mathematical sentences. Equations include the verb "is" or another verb similar to those listed under "Equal Sign" in the table to the right. When no such verb is present, the statement is an expression.

Key Words and Phrases for Creating Equations

Equal Sign	Addition	Subtraction	Multiplication	Division	Parentheses
is	and	less	of	divide	times the quantity of
are	added to	less than	multiply	divided by	
was	totals	smaller than	times	divided into	
equals	the sum of	minus	product of	quotient of	
gives	plus	difference	multiplied by	ratio of	
giving	more than	decreased by	twice		
leaves	larger than	reduced by	double		
results in	increased by	take away	triple		
produces	greater than	loss of	at		
yields	exceeds	fewer than	@		

EXAMPLE 9 WRITING EXPRESSIONS

For the following statements, underline the key words and translate into *expressions*.

a. A number increased by 18
b. 19 times W
c. 12 less than S
d. $\frac{2}{3}$ of Y
e. 9 more than 2 times R
f. 4 times the quantity of X and 8

►SOLUTIONSTRATEGY

Key Words	Expression
a. A number increased by 18	$N + 18$
b. 19 times W	$19W$
c. 12 less than S	$S - 12$
d. $\frac{2}{3}$ of Y	$\frac{2}{3}Y$
e. 9 more than 2 times R	$2R + 9$
f. 4 times the quantity of X and 8	$4(X + 8)$

▶TRYITEXERCISE 9

For the following statements, underline the key words and translate into *expressions*.

a. The sum of twice E and 9

b. 6 times N divided by Z

c. 8 less than half of F

d. \$45.75 more than the product of X and Y

e. The difference of Q and 44

f. R times A times B

CHECK YOUR ANSWERS WITH THE SOLUTIONS ON PAGE 155.

EXAMPLE10 WRITING EQUATIONS

For the following statements, underline the key words and translate into *equations*.

a. A number decreased by 14 is 23.

b. 8 less than $3D$ leaves 19.

c. A number totals 4 times the quantity of V and N.

d. The cost of X lb at \$3 per lb is \$12.

e. Cost is the product of price and quantity.

f. The sum of liabilities and capital is assets.

▶SOLUTIONSTRATEGY

Key Words	Equation
a. A number <u>decreased by</u> 14 <u>is</u> 23.	$X - 14 = 23$
b. 8 <u>less than</u> $3D$ <u>leaves</u> 19.	$3D - 8 = 19$
c. A number <u>totals</u> 4 <u>times the quantity of</u> V <u>and</u> N.	$X = 4(V + N)$
d. The cost of X lb <u>at</u> \$3 per lb <u>is</u> \$12.	$3X = 12$
e. Cost <u>is</u> the <u>product of</u> price and quantity.	$C = PQ$
f. The <u>sum of</u> liabilities <u>and</u> capital <u>is</u> assets.	$L + C = A$

▶TRYITEXERCISE 10

For the following statements, underline the key words and translate into *equations*.

a. What number increased by 32 yields 125?

b. 21 less than twice C gives 9.

c. 5 more than 6 times a number plus 3 times that number is 25.

d. The cost of G gallons at \$1.33 per gallon equals \$34.40.

e. The area of a rectangle is the length times the width.

f. (Challenge) What number less 12 is the average of A, B, and C?

CHECK YOUR ANSWERS WITH THE SOLUTIONS ON PAGE 155.

REVIEW EXERCISES   5 | SECTION I

Solve the following equations for the unknown and prove your solutions.

1. $B + 11 = 24$
   $B = \underline{13}$

2. $D - 32 = 40$

3. $S + 35 = 125$

4. $M - 58 = 12$ 5. $21K = 63$ 6. $\dfrac{Z}{3} = 45$

7. $50Y = 375$ 8. $\dfrac{L}{5} = 8$ 9. $6G + 5 = 29$

10. $\dfrac{C}{4} - 3 = 10$ 11. $25A - 11 = 64$ 12. $\dfrac{R}{5} + 33 = 84$

13. $5(2S + 1) = 35$ 14. $C + 5 = 26 - 2C$ 15. $12(2D - 4) = 72$

16. $14V + 5 - 5V = 4(V + 5)$ 17. $Q + 20 = 3(9 - 2Q)$

For the following statements, underline the key words and translate into *expressions*.

18. **5 <u>times</u> G <u>divided by</u> R**   19. The sum of 5 times F and 33

$$\underline{\underline{\dfrac{5G}{R}}}$$

20. 6 less than one-fourth of C 21. 550 more than the product of H and P

22. T times B times 9   23. The difference of $8Y$ and 128

24. 7 times the quantity of X and 7   25. 40 more than $\frac{3}{4}$ of B

For the following statements, underline the key words and translate into *equations*.

26. **A number <u>increased by</u> 24 <u>is</u> 35.**   27. A number totals 5 times B and C.

$$\underline{\underline{X + 24 = 35}}$$

28. 12 less than $4G$ leaves 33.   29. The cost of R at \$5.75 each is \$28.75.

30. 5 times the sum of X and 30 equals 320

31. 4 more than 5 times a number plus 2 times that number is that number increased by 40.

BUSINESS DECISION: GROUPING SYMBOLS

32. Grouping symbols are used to arrange numbers, variables, and operations. In this chapter, you learned to use the grouping symbols known as parentheses ( ). In addition to parentheses, other symbols used for grouping are brackets [ ] and braces { }. When solving equations with multiple grouping symbols, always start with the innermost symbols and work to the outside.

    In business, you may encounter situations that require you to set up equations with more than just parentheses. For practice, solve the following equation.

$$X = 6\{2 + 3[2(9 - 3) + (8 + 1) - 4]\}$$

USING EQUATIONS TO SOLVE BUSINESS-RELATED WORD PROBLEMS

5   SECTION II

In business, most of the math encountered is in the form of business-situation word problems. Variables such as profits, production units, inventory, employees, money, customers, and interest rates are constantly interacting mathematically. Your boss will not ask you simply to add, subtract, multiply, or divide, but will ask for information requiring you to perform these functions in a business context. Business students must be able to analyze a business situation requiring math, set up the situation in a mathematical expression or equation, and work it out to a correct solution.

Learning Tip

This is the real "bottom line" of equations: the ability to analyze a business situation, convert it to an equation, and solve it. Proficiency will come with practice.

B-A-C-O/Shutterstock.com

SETTING UP AND SOLVING BUSINESS-RELATED WORD PROBLEMS BY USING EQUATIONS

5-4

In Section I of this chapter, we learned to create and solve equations from written statements. Let's see how to apply these skills in business situations. You will learn a logical procedure for setting up and solving business-related word problems. Some problems have more than one way to arrive at an answer. The key, once again, is not to be intimidated. Learning to solve word problems requires practice, and the more you do it, the easier it will become and the more comfortable you will feel with it.

STEPS FOR SETTING UP AND SOLVING WORD PROBLEMS

STEP 1. **Understand the situation.** If the problem is written, read it carefully, perhaps a few times. If the problem is verbal, write down the facts of the situation.

STEP 2. **Take inventory.** Identify all the parts of the situation. These parts can be any variables, such as dollars, people, boxes, tons, trucks, anything! Separate them into knowns and unknowns.

STEP 3. **Make a plan—create an equation.** The object is to solve for the unknown. Ask yourself what math relationship exists between the knowns and the unknowns. Use the chart of key words and phrases on page 131 to help you write the equation.

STEP 4. **Work out the plan—solve the equation.** To solve an equation, you must move the unknowns to one side of the equal sign and the knowns to the other side.

STEP 5. **Check your solution.** Does your answer make sense? Is it exactly correct? It is a good idea to estimate an approximate answer by using rounded numbers. This will let you know if your answer is in the correct range. If it is not, either the equation is set up incorrectly or the solution is wrong. If this occurs, you must go back and start again.

iStock.com/Nikada

EXAMPLE 11   SOLVING BUSINESS-RELATED EQUATIONS

On Tuesday, Double Bubble Car Wash took in $360 less in wash business than in wax business. If the total sales for the day were $920, what were the sales for each service?

▶SOLUTIONSTRATEGY

Reasoning: Wax sales <u>plus</u> wash sales <u>equals</u> the total sales, $920.

$$\text{Let } X = \$ \text{ amount of wax sales}$$
$$\text{Let } X - 360 = \$ \text{ amount of wash sales}$$
$$X + X - 360 = 920$$
$$\underline{+\ 360 \qquad +\ 360}$$
$$X + X \qquad = 1{,}280$$

Learning Tip

Frequently, the left side of an equation represents the "interaction" of the variables and the right side shows the "result" of that interaction.

In this example, the left side is the interaction (in this case, addition) of the wax and wash sales. The right side is the result, or total.

$$\underset{X + X - 360}{\underbrace{\text{Interaction}}} = \underset{920}{\underbrace{\text{Result}}}$$

$$2X = 1,280$$
$$\frac{2X}{2} = \frac{1,280}{2}$$
$$X = 640 \quad \underline{\text{Wax sales} = \$640}$$
$$X - 360 = 640 - 360 = 280 \quad \underline{\text{Wash sales} = \$280}$$

Proof:

$$X + X - 360 = 920$$
$$640 + 640 - 360 = 920$$
$$920 = 920$$

▶TRYITEXERCISE 11

Don and Chuck are salespeople for Security One Alarms. Last week Don sold 12 fewer alarm systems than Chuck did. Together they sold 44. How many did each sell?

CHECK YOUR ANSWER WITH THE SOLUTION ON PAGE 155.

EXAMPLE 12 SOLVING BUSINESS-RELATED EQUATIONS

Dynamic Industries, Inc., spends $\frac{1}{4}$ of total revenue on employee payroll expenses. If last week's payroll amounted to $5,000, what was the revenue for the week?

▶SOLUTIONSTRATEGY

Reasoning: $\underset{=}{\frac{1}{4}}$ of revenue $\underset{=}{\text{is}}$ the week's payroll, $5,000.

$$\text{Let } R = \text{revenue for the week}$$

$$\frac{1}{4} R = 5,000$$

$$(4)\frac{1}{4} R = 5,000(4)$$

$$R = 20,000 \quad \underline{\text{Revenue for the week} = \$20,000}$$

Proof:

$$\frac{1}{4} R = 5,000$$

$$\frac{1}{4}(20,000) = 5,000$$

$$5,000 = 5,000$$

▶TRYITEXERCISE 12

One-third of the checking accounts at the Community Bank earn interest. If 2,500 accounts are this type, how many total checking accounts does the bank have?

CHECK YOUR ANSWER WITH THE SOLUTION ON PAGE 155.

IN THE Business World

Formulas are a part of our lives. Whether you drive a car and need to calculate the distance of travel or need to work out the volume in a milk container, you use algebraic formulas every day without even realizing it.

Let's say, for example, that you have a total of $100 to spend on video games. When you go to the game store, you find that each game sells for $20. How many games can you buy? This scenario provides the equation $20X = 100$, where X is the number of games you can buy. Most people don't realize that this type of calculation is algebra; they just subconsciously do it!

EXAMPLE 13 SOLVING BUSINESS-RELATED EQUATIONS

United Dynamics, Inc., has 25 shareholders. If management decides to split the $80,000 net profit equally among the shareholders, how much will each receive?

▶SOLUTIONSTRATEGY

Reasoning: Profit per shareholder is the net profit, $80,000, divided by the number of shareholders.

$$\text{Let } P = \text{Profit per shareholder}$$

$$P = \frac{80,000}{25}$$

$$P = 3,200 \quad \underline{\text{Profit per shareholder} = \$3,200}$$

Proof:

$$P = \frac{80,000}{25}$$

$$3,200 = \frac{80,000}{25}$$

$$\underline{\underline{3,200 = 3,200}}$$

▶TRYITEXERCISE 13

Century Manufacturing, Inc., fills an order for 58 cartons of merchandise weighing a total of 7,482 pounds. What is the weight per carton?

CHECK YOUR ANSWER WITH THE SOLUTION ON PAGE 155.

EXAMPLE14 SOLVING BUSINESS-RELATED EQUATIONS

A local Best Buy store sold 144 TVs last week. If five times as many LCD models sold as compared to plasma models, how many of each were sold?

▶SOLUTIONSTRATEGY

Reasoning: Plasma models plus LCD models equals total TVs sold, 144.

$$\text{Let } X = \text{plasma models}$$

$$\text{Let } 5X = \text{LCD models}$$

$$X + 5X = 144$$

$$6X = 144$$

$$\frac{6X}{6} = \frac{144}{6}$$

$$X = 24 \qquad \underline{\text{Plasma models sold} = 24}$$

$$5X = 5(24) = 120 \quad \underline{\text{LCD models sold} = 120}$$

Proof:

$$X + 5X = 144$$

$$24 + 5(24) = 144$$

$$24 + 120 = 144$$

$$\underline{144 = 144}$$

▶TRYITEXERCISE 14

Dollar Discount Department Store sells three times as much in soft goods, such as clothing and linens, as it sells in hard goods, such as furniture and appliances. If total store sales on Saturday were $180,000, how much of each category was sold?

CHECK YOUR ANSWER WITH THE SOLUTION ON PAGE 155.

iStock.com/Michael Phillips

Best Buy was founded in 1966. Originally called Sound of Music, the name changed to Best Buy in 1983.

The company now has over 1,000 stores in the U.S., Canada, and Mexico, and its total annual revenue typically exceeds $42 billion.

Source: Adapted from information at https://corporate.bestbuy.com/about-best-buy/

Municipal solid waste (MSW)— more commonly known as garbage—consists of everyday items we throw away. According to the U.S. Environmental Protection Agency (EPA), in a recent year Americans generated about 250 million tons of trash and recycled and composted 83 million tons of this material. On average, we recycled and composted 1.5 pounds of our individual waste generation of 4.5 pounds per person per day.

Recycling and composting 83 million tons of MSW saved 1.3 quadrillion Btu of energy, the equivalent of more than 10.2 billion gallons of gasoline and reduced CO_2 emissions by 182 million metric tons, comparable to the annual emissions from more than 33 million passenger vehicles.

Source: www.epa.gov

EXAMPLE 15 SOLVING BUSINESS-RELATED EQUATIONS

Yesterday the Valley Vista recycling van picked up a total of 4,500 pounds of material. If newspaper weighed three times as much as aluminum cans and aluminum weighed twice as much as glass, what was the weight of each material?

SOLUTION STRATEGY

Reasoning: Glass plus aluminum plus newspaper amounts to the total material, 4,500 pounds.

Hint: Let the least (smallest) element equal X. That way the larger ones will be multiples of X. By doing this, you avoid having fractions in your equation.

$$\text{Let } X = \text{pounds of glass}$$
$$\text{Let } 2X = \text{pounds of aluminum}$$
$$\text{Let } 3(2X) = \text{pounds of newspaper}$$
$$X + 2X + 3(2X) = 4,500$$
$$X + 2X + 6X = 4,500$$
$$9X = 4,500$$
$$\frac{9X}{9} = \frac{4,500}{9}$$
$$X = 500 \qquad \underline{\text{Glass collected} = 500 \text{ pounds}}$$
$$2X = 2(500) = 1,000 \qquad \underline{\text{Aluminum collected} = 1,000 \text{ pounds}}$$
$$3(2X) = 3(1,000) = 3,000 \qquad \underline{\text{Newspaper collected} = 3,000 \text{ pounds}}$$

Proof:
$$X + 2X + 3(2X) = 4,500$$
$$500 + 2(500) + 3(2[500]) = 4,500$$
$$500 + 1,000 + 3,000 = 4,500$$
$$\underline{4,500 = 4,500}$$

TRY IT EXERCISE 15

Last week Comfy Cozy Furniture sold 520 items. It sold twice as many sofas as chairs and four times as many chairs as tables. How many were sold of each product?

CHECK YOUR ANSWER WITH THE SOLUTION ON PAGE 156.

EXAMPLE 16 SOLVING BUSINESS-RELATED EQUATIONS

Chicken Delight sells whole chicken dinners for $12 and half chicken dinners for $8. Yesterday it sold a total of 400 dinners and took in $4,200. How many of each size dinner were sold? What were the dollar sales of each size dinner?

SOLUTION STRATEGY

Reasoning: The sum of the price multiplied by the quantity of each item is total sales, $4,200.

Hint: This type of problem requires that we multiply the price of each item by the quantity. We know that a total of 400 dinners were sold; therefore,

$$\text{Let } X = \text{quantity of whole chicken dinners}$$
$$\text{Let } 400 - X = \text{quantity of half chicken dinners}$$

Note: By letting X equal the quantity related to the more expensive item, we avoid dealing with negative numbers.

$$\text{Price times quantity of whole chicken dinners} = \$12X$$
$$\text{Price times quantity of half chicken dinners} = \$8(400 - X)$$

$$12X + 8(400 - X) = 4,200$$
$$12X + 3,200 - 8X = 4,200$$
$$4X + 3,200 = 4,200$$
$$\underline{-3,200 \qquad -3,200}$$
$$\overline{4X \qquad\qquad = 1,000}$$
$$\frac{\cancel{4}X}{\cancel{4}} = \frac{1,000}{4}$$
$$X = 250 \qquad \underline{\text{Quantity of whole chicken dinners} = 250}$$
$$400 - X = 400 - 250 = 150 \qquad \underline{\text{Quantity of half chicken dinners} = 150}$$

Proof:

$$12X + 8(400 - X) = 4,200$$
$$12(250) + 8(400 - 250) = 4,200$$
$$3,000 + 8(150) = 4,200$$
$$3,000 + 1,200 = 4,200$$
$$\underline{4,200 = 4,200}$$

Now that we have calculated the quantity sold of each size dinner, we can find the dollar sales.

Reasoning: Dollar sales <u>are</u> the price per dinner <u>multiplied by</u> the quantity sold.

Let S = dollar sales

Whole chicken dinners: $S = \$12(250) = \underline{\$3,000 \text{ in sales}}$

Half chicken dinners: $S = \$8(150) = \underline{\$1,200 \text{ in sales}}$

▶**TRYITEXERCISE** 16

REI (Recreational Equipment Incorporated) sells a 35-liter backpack for $110 and an 18-liter backpack for $70. If a store sold 40 packs yesterday for a total of $3,400, how many of each type backpack were sold? What were the dollar sales of each type?

CHECK YOUR ANSWER WITH THE SOLUTION ON PAGE 156.

REI (Recreational Equipment Incorporated) began as a group of 23 mountain climbing friends and today is the largest consumer cooperative in the nation. As a co-op, REI relies upon sales of memberships for investment capital while giving members 10% back on most purchases.

UNDERSTANDING AND SOLVING RATIO AND PROPORTION PROBLEMS

5-5

Many business problems and situations are expressed as ratios. A **ratio** is a fraction that describes a comparison of two numbers or quantities. In business, numbers often take on much more meaning when compared with other numbers in the form of a ratio.

For example, a factory has an output of 40 units per hour. Is this good or bad? If we also know that the industry average is 20 units per hour, we can set up a ratio of our factory, 40, compared with the industry average, 20.

$$\frac{\text{Factory}}{\text{Industry}} = \frac{40}{20} = 40:20 \qquad \text{Expressed verbally, we say, "40 to 20."}$$

Because ratios are fractions, we can reduce our fraction and state that our factory output is 2 to 1 over the industry average. If the industry average changed to 40, the ratio would be $\frac{40}{40}$, or 1 to 1. Had the industry average been 80, the ratio would have been $\frac{40}{80}$, or 1 to 2.

Ratios can compare anything: money, weights, measures, output, or individuals. The units do not have to be the same. If we can buy 9 ounces of shampoo for $2, this is actually a ratio of ounces to dollars, or 9:2.

A **proportion** is a statement indicating that two ratios are equal. Proportions are equations, with *as* representing the equal sign. For example, we could say, "9 is to 2 as 18 is to 4."

$$\frac{9}{2} = \frac{18}{4} \qquad \text{or} \qquad 9:2 = 18:4$$

ratio A fraction that describes a comparison of two numbers or quantities. For example, five cats for every three dogs is a ratio of 5 to 3, written as 5:3.

proportion A mathematical statement showing that two ratios are equal. For example, 9 is to 3 as 3 is to 1, written as 9:3 = 3:1.

Learning Tip

Remember, when setting up a proportion, the variables of both ratios must be in the same "order"— numerator to denominator. For example:

$$\frac{\text{dollars}}{\text{doughnuts}} = \frac{\text{dollars}}{\text{doughnuts}}$$

This means that if we can buy 9 ounces for $2, we can buy 18 ounces for $4. Proportions with three knowns and one unknown become a very useful business tool. For example, if we can buy 9 ounces for $2, how many ounces can we buy for $7? This proportion, 9 is to 2 as X is to 7, would be written as

$$\frac{9 \text{ ounces}}{\$2} = \frac{X \text{ ounces}}{\$7} \quad \text{or} \quad 9{:}2 = X{:}7$$

STEPS FOR SOLVING PROPORTION PROBLEMS USING CROSS-MULTIPLICATION

STEP 1. Assign a letter to represent the unknown quantity.

STEP 2. Set up the proportion with one ratio (expressed as a fraction) on each side of the equal sign.

STEP 3. Multiply the numerator of the first ratio by the denominator of the second and place the product on one side of the equal sign.

STEP 4. Multiply the denominator of the first ratio by the numerator of the second and place the product on the other side of the equal sign. (Steps 3 and 4 taken together are called "cross-multiplication" for reasons that will be clear in our first example.)

STEP 5. Solve for the unknown.

EXAMPLE 17 SOLVING PROPORTIONS

On a recent trip, a car used 16 gallons of gasoline to travel 350 miles. At that rate, how many gallons of gasoline would be required to complete a trip of 875 miles?

▶SOLUTIONSTRATEGY

This situation can be solved by setting up and solving a proportion. The proportion reads:

"16 gallons is to 350 miles as X gallons is to 875 miles"

$$\frac{16}{350} = \frac{X}{875}$$

Using cross-multiplication to solve the proportion,

$$350X = 16(875)$$
$$350X = 14{,}000$$
$$X = \frac{14{,}000}{350}$$
$$\underline{X = 40 \text{ Gallons}}$$

▶TRYITEXERCISE 17

If Steve earns $87.50 for 7 hours of work, how much can he expect to earn in a 35-hour week?

CHECK YOUR ANSWER WITH THE SOLUTION ON PAGE 156.

Dollars AND Sense

Most high-tech employers expect their employees to be able to do the fundamentals of algebra. If you want to do any advanced training, you will have to be fluent in the concept of letters and symbols used to represent quantities.

REVIEW EXERCISES

Set up and solve equations for the following business situations.

1. **Kathy and Karen work in a boutique. During a sale, Kathy sold eight fewer dresses than Karen did. If together they sold 86 dresses, how many did each sell?**

$$X + X - 8 = 86 \qquad \frac{2X}{2}$$

Karen = X
$$2X - 8 = 86$$
Kathy = X − 8
$$\frac{+8 \quad +8}{2X \qquad = 94} \qquad X = 47 \text{ Karen's sales}$$

$$X - 8 = 47 - 8 = \underline{39} \text{ Kathy's sales}$$

2. One-fifth of the employees of Delta Industries, Inc., work in the Southeastern region. If the company employs 252 workers in that region, what is the total number of employees working for the company?

3. Walter's salary this year is $23,400. If this is $1,700 more than he made last year, what was his salary last year?

4. The Book Nook makes four times as much revenue on paperback books as on hardcover books. If last month's sales totaled $124,300, how much was sold of each type book?

5. An online store sells two types of speaker docks for smartphones. The higher-priced speaker dock sells for $190 and the lower-priced speaker dock sells for $80. Last week the store sold three times as many lower-priced speaker docks as higher-priced speaker docks. Combined sales totaled $3,440. How many lower-priced speaker docks did it sell?

Digital Music The Apple iPod first went on the market in 2001, selling 125,000 units. Only 10 years later, 304 million units had been sold. These sales helped cause an explosion in the digital delivery of music which, in turn, led phone makers to incorporate music capabilities into their products. Speaker docks allow music from smartphones to be heard throughout a room.

Source: About.com

6. You are moving to a new home and have rented a truck to assist you with the move. Trailside Truck Rentals charges $39.95 per day plus 68 cents per mile. You will need the truck for 3 days and will travel 460 miles. If you have budgeted $400 for the truck rental, will this amount be sufficient to cover the cost?

7. Kid's Kingdom, a retail toy chain, placed a seasonal order for stuffed animals from Stuffed Stuff, a distributor. Large animals cost $20, and small ones cost $14.

   a. If the total cost of the order was $7,320 for 450 pieces, how many of each size were ordered?

   b. What was the dollar amount of each size ordered?

8. PC Solutions sells regular keyboards for $84 and wireless keyboards for $105. Last week the store sold three times as many regular keyboards as wireless. If total keyboard sales were $4,998, how many of each type were sold?

9. An estate is to be distributed among a wife, three children, and two grandchildren. The children will each receive three times as much as each grandchild, and the wife will receive four times as much as each child. If the estate amounts to $115,000, how much will each person receive?

10. Pitt's Pit Stop sold $15,496.50 worth of gasoline yesterday. Regular sold for $3.30 a gallon and premium sold for $3.45 a gallon. If the station sold 380 more gallons of regular than premium,

    a. How many gallons of each type of gasoline were sold?

    b. If the profit on regular gas is $0.15 per gallon and on premium is $0.18 per gallon, what was the station's total profit?

11. Yesterday Tween Teen Fashions had seven less than three-fourths of its sales transactions paid for by credit cards. If 209 transactions were charged, how many total transactions took place?

12. You are the administrator of an annual essay contest scholarship fund. This year a $48,000 college scholarship is being divided between the top two contestants so that the winner receives three times as much as the runner-up. How much will each contestant receive?

13. The Cookie Monster sells oatmeal cookies for $1.30 per pound and peanut butter cookies for $1.60 per pound.
    a. If total cookie sales last week amounted to 530 pounds, valued at $755, how many pounds of each type of cookie were sold?

    b. What dollar amount of each type was sold?

Bed Bath & Beyond Inc., together with its subsidiaries, operates a chain of retail stores. It sells a range of domestic merchandise (e.g., bed linens and related items, bath items, and kitchen textiles) and home furnishings, including kitchen and tabletop items, fine tabletop, basic housewares, and general home furnishings.

Bed Bath & Beyond has more than 1,000 stores ranging in size from 20,000 to 50,000 square feet with several stores exceeding 80,000 square feet.

Source: Based on Bed, Bath & Beyond website

14. If a 48-piece set of stainless steel flatware costs $124.80 at Bed Bath & Beyond, what is the cost per piece?

15. The U.S. Congress has a total of 535 members. If the number of representatives is 65 less than five times the number of senators, how many senators and how many representatives are in Congress?

16. One-ninth of Polymer Plastics' sales are made in New England. If New England sales amount to $600,000, what are the total sales of the company?

17. You are the shipping manager for World Imports. Calculate the total cost to ship an order of glassware weighing 1,860 pounds if the breakdown is $0.04 per pound for packing, $0.02 per pound for insurance, $0.13 per pound for transportation, and $132.40 for the crate.

FedEx Office (formerly FedEx Kinko's and earlier simply Kinko's) is a chain of stores that provides a retail outlet for FedEx Express and FedEx Ground shipping as well as printing, copying, and binding services. Many stores also provide videoconferencing facilities.

The primary clientele consists of small business and home office clients. There are more than 2,000 centers in Asia, Australia, Europe, and North America. FedEx reports $43 billion in annual revenues and has more than 300,000 team members. FedEx Office's primary competitors include The UPS Store, OfficeMax, Alpha Graphics, Staples, Sir Speedy, and VistaPrint.

Source: Based on www.fedex.com

18. Scott Mason purchased a 4-unit apartment building as an investment before he retired. From the rent he collects each month, Scott pays out $600 for expenses. How much rent must he charge for each of the 4 apartments if he wants to make $500 profit each month? The amount of rent is the same for each of the apartments.

19. You are the facilities director of the Carnival Shopping Mall. You have been asked to rope off a rectangular section of the parking lot for a car show next weekend. The area to be roped off is 250 feet long by 300 feet wide. Rubber traffic cones are to be placed every 25 feet around the lot. How many cones are needed?

Use ratio and proportion to solve the following business situations.

20. If a bulk order of 1,600 blouses costs $41,600, how much would 2,000 blouses cost?

21. At Fancy Fruit Distributors, Inc., the ratio of fruits to vegetables sold is 5 to 3. If 1,848 pounds of vegetables are sold, how many pounds of fruit are sold?

22. A local FedEx Office store has a press that can print 5,800 brochures per hour. How many can be printed during a $3\frac{1}{4}$-hour run?

23. A recipe for turkey stuffing calls for three eggs for every $12\frac{1}{2}$ ounces of corn bread. If a dinner party requires $87\frac{1}{2}$ ounces of corn bread for stuffing, how many eggs should be used?

24. An architect uses a scale of $\frac{3}{4}$ inch to represent 1 foot on a blueprint for a building. If the east wall of the building is 36 feet long, how long will the line be on the blueprint?

25. Following a recent election, it was reported that 300,000 people applied for 7,000 available jobs in the new president's administration. At that rate, on average, how many people had applied for each job? Round to the nearest whole person.

26. If auto insurance costs $6.52 per $1,000 of coverage, what is the cost to insure a car valued at $17,500?

27. Blue Sky International Airport handles passenger to cargo traffic in a ratio of 8 to 5. If 45 cargo planes landed yesterday, how many passenger flights came in?

28. Eighty ounces of Lazy Lawn fertilizer covers 1,250 square feet of lawn.
    a. How many ounces would be required to cover a 4,000-square-foot lawn?

    b. If Lazy Lawn costs $1.19 for a 32-ounce bag, what is the total cost to fertilize the lawn?

29. You have just been hired as advertising manager of *The Daily Chronicle*, a not-very-successful newspaper. In the past, *The Chronicle* contained one-half advertising and one-half news stories. Current industry research indicates a newspaper must have three times as much advertising as news stories to make money. In addition, the advertising must be divided in the following ratio: 5 to 3 to 1, retail advertising to national advertising to classified advertising. *The Chronicle* is typically 48 pages in length.
    a. How many pages should be advertising, and how many should be news stories?

    b. Based on the industry ratios, how should the pages be divided among the three types of advertising?

c.   After you made the changes in the advertising distributions ratios, your newspaper began making a profit—for the first time in years. If last year's total advertising revenue was $810,000, how much was earned by each type of advertising?

d.   When you accepted the job of advertising manager, in addition to your salary, you were promised a $\frac{1}{50}$ share of each year's revenue from retail and classified advertising and a $\frac{1}{75}$ share for national. What bonus will you receive for last year's sales?

BUSINESS DECISION: HELPING CAR MANUFACTURERS—SAVING THE PLANET!

30. In a move to provide additional sales for U.S. car manufacturers, the White House announced the purchase of 17,600 new fuel-efficient vehicles for the federal fleet. The new fleet, which includes 2,500 hybrid sedans, will cost $285 million.

As an accountant in the White House Budget Office (WHBO), you have been asked to calculate the following:

a.   If each hybrid vehicle will have an average cost of $24,000, what will be the average cost per non-hybrid vehicle? Round to the nearest whole dollar.

b.   Furthermore, the White House said that by replacing less efficient vehicles, the government will reduce gasoline consumption by 1.3 million gallons per year and prevent 26 million pounds of carbon dioxide from entering the atmosphere. On average, how many gallons of gasoline and how many pounds of carbon dioxide will be "saved" per year per vehicle? Round to the nearest whole gallon and whole pound.

CHAPTER SUMMARY

Section I: Solving Basic Equations

Topic	Important Concepts	Illustrative Examples
Solving Equations for the Unknown and Proving the Solution **Performance Objective 5-2, Page 129**	To solve equations, we must move or transpose all the unknowns to one side and isolate all the knowns on the other side. It is customary for the unknowns to be on the left side and the knowns to be on the right side, such as $X = 33$. To solve for the unknown value, apply an inverse, or opposite, operation to both sides of the equation. **Operation—Opposite** Addition $\longrightarrow$ Subtraction Subtraction $\longrightarrow$ Addition Multiplication $\longrightarrow$ Division Division $\longrightarrow$ Multiplication	Solve the equation $R + 7 = 12$ The equation indicates addition; therefore, use the opposite operation: subtract 7 from both sides: $$\begin{aligned} R + 7 &= 12 \\ -7 &= -7 \\ \hline R &= 5 \end{aligned}$$ $\underline{\underline{R = 5}}$ Solve the equation $W - 4 = 30$ The equation indicates subtraction; therefore, use the opposite operation: add 4 to both sides: $$\begin{aligned} W - 4 &= 30 \\ +4 &= +4 \\ \hline W &= 34 \end{aligned}$$ $\underline{\underline{W = 34}}$ Solve the equation $3G = 18$ The equation indicates multiplication; therefore, use the opposite operation: divide both side by 3: $$\frac{\cancel{3}G}{\cancel{3}} = \frac{18}{3}$$ $\underline{\underline{G = 6}}$ Solve the equation $\frac{T}{5} = 9$ The equation indicates division; therefore, use the opposite operation: multiply both sides by 5: $$(\cancel{5})\frac{T}{\cancel{5}} = 9(5)$$ $\underline{\underline{T = 45}}$
Solving Equations Containing Multiple Operations **Performance Objective 5-2, Page 133**	Operation order for solving equations: To solve equations with more than one operation, transpose the terms by applying opposite operations using *additions* and *subtractions* first, then using *multiplications* and *divisions*.	Solve the equation $5X - 4 = 51$ $$\begin{aligned} 5X - 4 &= 51 \\ +4 &= +4 \\ \hline 5X &= 55 \end{aligned}$$ $$\frac{\cancel{5}X}{\cancel{5}} = \frac{55}{5}$$ $\underline{\underline{X = 11}}$
Solving Equations Containing Parentheses **Performance Objective 5-2, Page 134**	To remove parentheses, multiply the coefficient by each term inside the parentheses. Sign Rules: When like signs are multiplied, the result is positive. For example, $5(5) = 25$ and $-5(-5) = 25$. When unlike signs are multiplied, the result is negative. For example, $5(-5) = -25$.	Solve the equation $3(4S - 5) = 9$ To remove the parentheses, multiply the coefficient, 3, by both terms inside the parentheses: $$\begin{aligned} 3(4S - 5) &= 9 \\ 3(4S) - 3(5) &= 9 \\ 12S - 15 &= 9 \\ 12S &= 24 \end{aligned}$$ $\underline{\underline{S = 2}}$
Solving Equations When the Unknown Occurs More Than Once **Performance Objective 5-2, Page 135**	To combine unknowns in an equation, add or subtract their coefficients and retain their common variable. For example, $6B + 4B = 10B$. If the unknowns are on opposite sides of the equal sign, first move them all to one side.	Solve the equation $3B + 5 - B = 7$ $$\begin{aligned} 3B + 5 - B &= 7 \\ 2B + 5 &= 7 \\ 2B &= 2 \end{aligned}$$ $\underline{\underline{B = 1}}$

Topic	Important Concepts	Illustrative Examples

Writing Expressions and Equations from Written Statements
 	
Performance Objective 5-3, Page 136
	Expressions and equations are created from written statements by identifying the unknowns and the knowns and determining the mathematical relationship between them.
	    The variables are assigned letters of the alphabet.
	The relationship between the knowns and the unknowns involve addition, subtraction, multiplication,
	and division or a combination of two or more.
	    Key words indicate what relationship exists between the terms (see list, page 131).
	    If the written statement has a verb such as *is*, the statement is an equation.
		A number increased by 44 $X + 44$
		
		6 more than 3 times U $3U + 6$
		
		3 times the sum of C and 9 $3(C + 9)$
		
		7 less than 4 times M leaves 55. $4M - 7 = 55$
		
		2 less than 5 times a number
		
		 plus 9 times that number is 88. $5X - 2 + 9X = 88$

Section II: Using Equations to Solve Business-Related Word Problems

Topic	Important Concepts	Illustrative Examples

Solving Business-Related Equations
 	
Performance Objective 5-4, Page 139
	Example 1:
	Mary and Beth sell furniture at Contempo Designs. Last week Mary sold eight fewer recliner chairs than Beth sold. Together they sold 30. How many chairs did each sell?
		Solution:
		Reasoning: Beth's sales plus Mary's sales equals total sales, 30.
		
		   Let X = Beth's sales
		 Let $X - 8$ = Mary's sales
		$X + X - 8 = 30$
		    $2X - 8 = 30$
		        $2X = 38$
		           $X = 19$ Chairs—Beth's sales
		     $X - 8 = 11$ Chairs—Mary's sales

	Example 2:
	One-fourth of the employees at Atlas Distributors work in the accounting division. If there are 45 workers in this division, how many people work for Atlas?
		Solution:
		Reasoning: $\frac{1}{4}$ of the total employees are in accounting, 45.
		
		   Let X = total employees
		
		  Let $\frac{1}{4}X$ = accounting employees
		
		    $\frac{1}{4}X = 45$
		
		  $(4)\frac{1}{4}X = 45(4)$
		
		      $X = 180$ Total employees

	Example 3:
	Frontier Industries, a small manufacturing company, made a profit of \$315,000 last year. If the nine investors decide to evenly split this profit, how much will each receive?
		Solution:
		Reasoning: Each investor's share is the total profit divided by the number of investors.
		
		   Let X = each investor's share
		
		  $X = \dfrac{315,000}{9}$
		
		  $X = \$35,000$ Each investor's share

Section II (continued)

Topic	Important Concepts	Illustrative Examples
	Example 4: The Pet Carnival sells four times as much in cat supplies as in fish supplies. If total sales last week were $6,800, how much of each category was sold?	Solution: *Reasoning*: Fish supplies plus cat supplies equals total, $6,800. Let X = fish supplies Let $4X$ = cat supplies $X + 4X = 6,800$ $X + 4X = 6,800$ $5X = 6,800$ $X = \$1,360$ Fish supplies $4X = \$5,440$ Cat supplies
	Example 5: The Male Image, a clothing store, sells suits for $275 and sport coats for $180. Yesterday it made 20 sales, for a total of $4,360. a. How many suits and how many sport coats were sold? b. What were the dollar sales of each?	Solution a: *Reasoning*: The sum of the price multiplied by the quantity of each item is the total sales, $4,360. Let X = suit sales Let $20 - X$ = sport coat sales $275X + 180(20 - X) = 4,360$ $275X + 3,600 - 180X = 4,360$ $95X + 3,600 = 4,360$ $95X = 760$ $X = 8$ Number of suits sold $20 - X = 12$ Number of sports coats sold Solution b: 8 suits × $275 each = $2,200 Suits sales 12 coats × $180 each = $2,160 Coats sales
Understanding and Solving Ratio and Proportion Problems **Performance Objective 5-5, Page 143**	A ratio is a fraction that describes a comparison of two numbers or quantities. A proportion is a statement showing that two ratios are equal. Proportions are equations with "as" being the equal sign and "is to" being the division bar. Proportion problems are solved by cross-multiplication: 1. Let X represent the unknown quantity. 2. Set up the equation with one ratio on each side of the equal sign. 3. Multiply the numerator of the first ratio by the denominator of the second and place the product to the left of the equal sign. 4. Multiply the denominator of the first ratio by the numerator of the second and place the product to the right of the equal sign. 5. Solve the equation for X.	Example 1: 12 is to 42 as 6 is to X $\dfrac{12}{42} = \dfrac{6}{X}$ $12X = 42(6)$ $12X = 252$ $X = 21$ Example 2: If Larry works 6 hours for $150, how much can he expect to earn in a 42-hour week? $\dfrac{6}{150} = \dfrac{42}{X}$ $6X = 150(42)$ $6X = 6,300$ $X = \$1,050$ Larry's salary for 42 hours of work

TRY IT: EXERCISE SOLUTIONS FOR CHAPTER 5

1a.
$$W + 10 = 25$$
$$W + 10 = 25$$
$$\underline{\quad - 10 \quad -10}$$
$$W \quad = \quad 15$$
$$W = 15$$

Proof:
$$W + 10 = 25$$
$$15 + 10 = 25$$
$$\underline{25 = 25}$$

1b.
$$Q + 30 = 100$$
$$Q + 30 = 100$$
$$\underline{\quad - 30 \quad -30}$$
$$Q \quad = \quad 70$$
$$Q = 70$$

Proof:
$$Q + 30 = 100$$
$$70 + 30 = 100$$
$$\underline{100 = 100}$$

2a.
$$A - 8 = 40$$
$$A - 8 = 40$$
$$\underline{\quad + 8 \quad +8}$$
$$A \quad = \quad 48$$
$$A = 48$$

Proof:
$$A - 8 = 40$$
$$48 - 8 = 40$$
$$\underline{40 = 40}$$

2b.
$$L - 3 = 7$$
$$L - 3 = 7$$
$$\underline{\quad + 3 \quad +3}$$
$$L \quad = \quad 10$$
$$L = 10$$

Proof:
$$L - 3 = 7$$
$$10 - 3 = 7$$
$$\underline{7 = 7}$$

3a.
$$15L = 75$$
$$\frac{\cancel{15}L}{\cancel{15}} = \frac{75}{15}$$
$$L = 5$$

Proof:
$$15L = 75$$
$$15(5) = 75$$
$$\underline{75 = 75}$$

3b.
$$16F = 80$$
$$\frac{\cancel{16}F}{\cancel{16}} = \frac{80}{16}$$
$$F = 5$$

Proof:
$$16F = 80$$
$$16(5) = 80$$
$$\underline{80 = 80}$$

4a.
$$\frac{Z}{8} = 2$$
$$(8)\frac{Z}{\cancel{8}} = 2(8)$$
$$Z = 16$$

Proof:
$$\frac{Z}{8} = 2$$
$$\frac{16}{8} = 2$$
$$\underline{2 = 2}$$

4b.
$$\frac{C}{9} = 9$$
$$(9)\frac{C}{\cancel{9}} = 9(9)$$
$$C = 81$$

Proof:
$$\frac{C}{9} = 9$$
$$\frac{81}{9} = 9$$
$$\underline{9 = 9}$$

5a.
$$12N + 14 = 50$$
$$12N + 14 = 50$$
$$\underline{\quad - 14 \quad -14}$$
$$12N \quad = \quad 36$$
$$\frac{\cancel{12}N}{\cancel{12}} = \frac{36}{12}$$
$$N = 3$$

Proof:
$$12N + 14 = 50$$
$$12(3) + 14 = 50$$
$$36 + 14 = 50$$
$$\underline{50 = 50}$$

5b.
$$3W - 4 = 26$$
$$3W - 4 = 26$$
$$\underline{\quad + 4 \quad +4}$$
$$3W \quad = \quad 30$$
$$\frac{\cancel{3}W}{\cancel{3}} = \frac{30}{3}$$
$$W = 10$$

Proof:
$$3W - 4 = 26$$
$$3(10) - 4 = 26$$
$$30 - 4 = 26$$
$$\underline{26 = 26}$$

6a.
$$\frac{F}{3} - 6 = 2$$
$$\frac{F}{3} - 6 = 2$$
$$\underline{\quad + 6 \quad +6}$$
$$\frac{F}{3} \quad = \quad 8$$
$$(3)\frac{F}{\cancel{3}} = 8(3)$$
$$F = 24$$

Proof:
$$\frac{F}{3} - 6 = 2$$
$$\frac{24}{3} - 6 = 2$$
$$8 - 6 = 2$$
$$\underline{2 = 2}$$

6b.
$$\frac{Z}{5} + 15 = 24$$
$$\frac{Z}{5} + 15 = 24$$
$$\underline{\quad - 15 \quad -15}$$
$$\frac{Z}{5} \quad = \quad 9$$
$$(5)\frac{Z}{\cancel{5}} = 9(5)$$
$$Z = 45$$

Proof:
$$\frac{Z}{5} + 15 = 24$$
$$\frac{45}{5} + 15 = 24$$
$$9 + 15 = 24$$
$$\underline{24 = 24}$$

7a.
$$4(5G + 6) = 64$$
$$20G + 24 = 64$$
$$20G + 24 = 64$$
$$\underline{\quad - 24 \quad -24}$$
$$20G \quad = \quad 40$$
$$\frac{\cancel{20}G}{\cancel{20}} = \frac{40}{20}$$
$$G = 2$$

Proof:
$$4(5G + 6) = 64$$
$$4(5\{2\} + 6) = 64$$
$$4(10 + 6) = 64$$
$$4(16) = 64$$
$$\underline{64 = 64}$$

7b.
$$6(3H - 5) = 42$$
$$18H - 30 = 42$$
$$18H - 30 = 42$$
$$\underline{\quad + 30 \quad +30}$$
$$18H \quad = \quad 72$$
$$\frac{\cancel{18}H}{\cancel{18}} = \frac{72}{18}$$
$$H = 4$$

Proof:
$$6(3H - 5) = 42$$
$$6(3\{4\} - 5) = 42$$
$$6(12 - 5) = 42$$
$$6(7) = 42$$
$$\underline{42 = 42}$$

8a.
$$X + 3 = 18 - 4X$$
$$X + 3 = 18 - 4X$$
$$\underline{+ 4X \qquad\qquad + 4X}$$
$$5X + 3 = 18$$
$$5X + 3 = 18$$
$$\underline{\quad - 3 \quad - 3}$$
$$5X \quad = \quad 15$$
$$\frac{\cancel{5}X}{\cancel{5}} = \frac{15}{5}$$
$$X = 3$$

Proof:
$$X + 3 = 18 - 4X$$
$$3 + 3 = 18 - 4(3)$$
$$6 = 18 - 12$$
$$\underline{6 = 6}$$

8b.
$$9S + 8 - S = 2(2S + 8)$$
$$9S + 8 - S = 4S + 16$$
$$8S + 8 = 4S + 16$$
$$8S + 8 = 4S + 16$$
$$\underline{- 4S \qquad - 4S}$$
$$4S + 8 = \qquad + 16$$
$$4S + 8 = 16$$
$$\underline{\quad - 8 \quad - 8}$$
$$4S \quad = \quad 8$$
$$\frac{\cancel{4}S}{\cancel{4}} = \frac{8}{4}$$
$$S = 2$$

Proof:
$$9S + 8 - S = 2(2S + 8)$$
$$9(2) + 8 - 2 = 2(2\{2\} + 8)$$
$$18 + 8 - 2 = 2(4 + 8)$$
$$24 = 2(12)$$
$$\underline{24 = 24}$$

9a. The sum of twice E and 9

$$2E + 9$$

9b. 6 times N divided by Z

$$\frac{6N}{Z}$$

9c. 8 less than half of F

$$\frac{1}{2}F - 8$$

9d. \$45.75 more than the product of X and Y

$$XY + \$45.75$$

9e. The difference of Q and 44

$$Q - 44$$

9f. R times A times B

$$RAB$$

10a. What number increased by 32 yields 125?

$$X + 32 = 125$$

10b. 21 less than twice C gives 9.

$$2C - 21 = 9$$

10c. 5 more than 6 times a number plus 3 times that number is 25.

$$6X + 5 + 3X = 25$$

10d. The cost of G gallons at \$1.33 per gallon equals \$34.40.

$$\$1.33G = \$34.40$$

10e. The area of a rectangle is the length times the width.

$$A = LW$$

10f. What number less 12 is the average of A, B, and C?

$$X - 12 = \frac{A + B + C}{3}$$

11. *Reasoning:* Don's sales and Chuck's sales equal total sales, 44.

Let X = Chuck's sales
Let $X - 12$ = Don's sales
$$X + X - 12 = 44$$
$$2X - 12 = 44$$
$$2X = 56$$
$$\frac{2X}{2} = \frac{56}{2}$$
$$X = 28 \quad \text{Chuck's sales} = 28 \text{ Alarm systems}$$
$$X - 12 = 28 - 12 = 16 \quad \text{Don's sales} = 16 \text{ Alarm systems}$$

Proof:
$$X + X - 12 = 44$$
$$28 + 28 - 12 = 44$$
$$44 = 44$$

12. *Reasoning:* $\frac{1}{3}$ of the total checking accounts are interest-earning, 2,500.

Let C = total checking accounts
$$\frac{1}{3}C = 2,500$$
$$(3)\frac{1}{3}C = 2,500(3)$$
$$C = 7,500$$
Total checking accounts = 7,500

Proof:
$$\frac{1}{3}C = 2,500$$
$$\frac{1}{3}(7,500) = 2,500$$
$$2,500 = 2,500$$

13. *Reasoning:* Weight per carton equals the total weight divided by the number of cartons.

Let W = weight per carton
$$W = \frac{7,482}{58}$$
$$W = 129$$

Weight per carton = 129 pounds

Proof:
$$W = \frac{7,482}{58}$$
$$129 = \frac{7,482}{58}$$
$$129 = 129$$

14. *Reasoning:* Soft goods plus hard goods equals total store sales, \$180,000.

Let X = hard goods
Let $3X$ = soft goods
$$X + 3X = \$180,000$$
$$4X = 180,000$$
$$\frac{4X}{4} = \frac{180,000}{4}$$
$$X = 45,000 \quad \text{Hard goods} = \$45,000$$
$$3X = 3(45,000) = 135,000 \quad \text{Soft goods} = \$135,000$$

Proof:
$$X + 3X = 180,000$$
$$45,000 + 3(45,000) = 180,000$$
$$45,000 + 135,000 = 180,000$$
$$180,000 = 180,000$$

15. *Reasoning:* Tables <u>plus</u> chairs <u>plus</u> sofas <u>equals</u> total items sold, 520.

Let X = tables

Let $4X$ = chairs   *Proof:*

Let $2(4X)$ = sofas
$$X + 4X + 2(4X) = 520$$
$X + 4X + 2(4X) = 520$ $40 + 4(40) + 2(4\{40\}) = 520$

$X + 4X + 8X = 520$ $40 + 160 + 2(160) = 520$

$13X = 520$ $40 + 160 + 320 = 520$

$$\frac{\cancel{13}X}{\cancel{13}} = \frac{520}{13}$$ $520 = 520$

$X = 40$ Tables sold = 40

$4X = 4(40) = 160$ Chairs sold = 160

$2(4X) = 2(4\{40\}) = 2(160) = 320$ Sofas sold = 320

16. *Reasoning:* The <u>sum of</u> the price of each item <u>multiplied by</u> the quantity of each item <u>is</u> the total sales, \$3,400.

Remember: Let <u>X</u> equal the more expensive item, thereby avoiding negative numbers.

Let X = Quantity of 35-liter backpacks

Let $40 - X$ = Quantity of 18-liter backpacks   *Proof:*

Price times quantity of 35-liter backpacks = \$110X $110X + 70(40 - X) = 3,400$

Price times quantity of 18-liter backpacks = \$70$(40 - X)$ $110(15) + 70(40 - 15) = 3,400$

$110X + 70(40 - X) = 3,400$ $1,650 + 70(25) = 3,400$

$110X + 2,800 - 70X = 3,400$ $1,650 + 1,750 = 3,400$

$40X + 2,800 = 3,400$ $3,400 = 3,400$

$40X = 600$

$$\frac{\cancel{40}X}{\cancel{40}} = \frac{600}{40}$$

$X = 15$ Quantity of 35-liter backpacks = 15

$40 - X = 40 - 15 = 25$ Quantity of 18-liter backpacks = 25

Now that we have calculated the quantity of each backpack, we can find the dollar sales.

Reasoning: Dollar sales <u>are</u> the price per backpack <u>multiplied by</u> the quantity sold.

Let S = dollar sales

35-liter backpack: $S = \$110(15) = \$1,650$ in sales

18-liter backpack: $S = \$70(25) = \$1,750$ in sales

17. $\dfrac{87.50}{7} = \dfrac{X}{35}$ *Proof:* $\dfrac{87.50}{7} = \dfrac{X}{35}$

$7X = 87.50(35)$ $\dfrac{87.50}{7} = \dfrac{437.50}{35}$

$7X = 3,062.50$

$\dfrac{\cancel{7}X}{\cancel{7}} = \dfrac{3,062.50}{7}$ $12.50 = 12.50$

$X = 437.50$ Steve would earn \$437.50 for 35 hours of work.

CONCEPT REVIEW

1. A(n) _____ is a mathematical statement describing a real-world situation in which letters represent number quantities. (5-1)

2. A mathematical statement expressing a relationship of equality is known as a(n) _____. (5-1)

3. The parts of an equation that are *given* are called the constants, or _____. (5-1)

4. The variables, or unknowns, of an equation are represented by letters of the _____. (5-1)

5. The numerical value of the unknown that makes an equation true is called the _____, or _____. (5-1)

6. A coefficient is a number or quantity placed before another quantity, indicating _____. (5-2)

7. To transpose means to bring a term from one side of an equation to the other. When addition or subtraction is used for moving the term, a corresponding change of _____ occurs. (5-2)

8. List the operation order for solving equations. (5-2)

9. To prove the solution of an equation, we substitute the solution for the _____ in the original equation. (5-2)

10. When writing an equation from a written statement, a verb such as *is* represents the _____ _____ in the equation. (5-3)

11. When writing an equation from a written statement, the word *difference* means _____, while the word *of* means _____. (5-3)

12. A comparison of two quantities by division is known as a(n) _____. (5-5)

13. A mathematical statement showing that two ratios are equal is known as a(n) _____. (5-5)

14. Proportions are solved using a process known as _____ multiplication. (5-5)

ASSESSMENT TEST

Solve the following equations for the unknown and prove your solutions.

1. $W + 10 = 53$

2. $G - 24 = 75$

3. $11K = 165$

4. $3(2C - 5) = 45$

5. $8X - 15 = 49$

6. $\dfrac{S}{7} = 12$

7. $B + 5 = 61 - 6B$

8. $\dfrac{N}{4} - 7 = 8$

9. $4(3X + 8) = 212$

For the following statements, underline the key words and translate into *expressions*.

10. 15 less than one-ninth of P

11. The difference of $4R$ and 108

12. 3 times the quantity of H less 233

13. 24 more than the product of Z and W

For the following statements, underline the key words and translate into *equations*.

14. A number increased by 11 is 32.

15. A number totals 4 times C and L.

16. The cost of Q at $4.55 each is $76.21.

17. 14 less than $3F$ leaves 38.

18. The sum of 2 more than 6 times a number and 7 times that number is that number decreased by 39.

Set up and solve equations for each of the following business situations.

19. At a recent boat show, Boater's Paradise sold five more boats than Pelican Marine sold. If together they sold 33 boats, how many were sold by each company?

CHAPTER
5

EXCEL 2

20. At TelePower Plus, long-distance phone calls to China cost $0.59 for the first minute and $0.25 for each additional minute plus an additional roaming charge of $2.50. If the total charge of a call to Beijing was $11.84, how long did the call last?

EXCEL 2

21. Discount Electronics ordered three dozen cell phones from the manufacturer. If the total order amounted to $1,980, what was the cost of each phone?

22. The Cupcake Café makes $4\frac{1}{2}$ times as much revenue on doughnuts as muffins. If total sales were $44,000 for May, what dollar amount of each was sold?

23. A regular lightbulb uses 20 watts less than twice the power of an energy-saver lightbulb. If the regular bulb uses 170 watts, how much does the energy-saver bulb use?

24. Do It Best Hardware is offering a 140-piece mechanic's tool set plus a $65 tool chest for $226. What is the cost per tool?

Nordroden/Shutterstock.com

25. En Vogue Menswear ordered short-sleeve shirts for $23.00 each and long-sleeve shirts for $28.50 each from Hugo Boss.
   a. If the total order amounted to $9,862.50 for 375 shirts, how many of each were ordered?

Do it Best Corp. engages in the wholesale distribution of hardware, lumber, builder supplies, and related products. The company is a member-owned cooperative and is guided by the members of the board of directors. This group is entirely composed of and elected by Do it Best Corp. stockholders—those hardware, lumber, and home center store owners who make up the 4,100 member-retailers in the United States and in 45 countries around the world.

Sources: www.doitbestcorp.com and www.businessweek.com

   b. What was the dollar amount of each type of shirt ordered?

26. Austin and Kaitlyn Kojan invested $195,000 in a business venture. If Kaitlyn invested $2\frac{1}{4}$ times as much as Austin invested, how much did each invest?

27. You are planning to advertise your boat for sale on the Internet. *The Boat Mart* charges $1.30 for a photo plus $0.12 per word. *Boat Bargains* charges $1.80 for a photo plus $0.10 per word. For what number of words will the charges be the same?

28. A Cold Stone Creamery ice cream shop sells sundaes for $3.60 and banana splits for $4.25. The shop sells four times as many sundaes as banana splits.
    a. If total sales amount to $3,730 last weekend, how many of each dish were sold?

    b. What were the dollar sales of each?

Use ratio and proportion to solve the following business situations.

29. At Trident Sporting Goods, the inventory ratio of equipment to clothing is 8 to 5. If the clothing inventory amounts to $130,000, what is the amount of the equipment inventory?

30. You are interested in purchasing a wide-screen TV set at Target. On this type of TV, the ratio of the width of the screen to the height of the screen is 16 to 9. If a certain model you are considering has a screen width of 64 inches, what would be the height of this screen?

Target Since 1946, Target has consistently given 5% of its income back to communities for betterment programs in education and volunteerism. A few years ago, Target achieved the milestone of giving more than $3 million dollars back per week.

Source: Target.com

31. The directions on a bag of powdered driveway sealant call for the addition of 5 quarts of water for every 30 pounds of sealant. How much water should be added if only 20 pounds of sealant will be used?

32. Angela Hatcher is planting flower bulbs in her garden for this coming summer. She intends to plant 1 bulb for every 5 square inches of flower bed.
    a. How many flower bulbs will she need for an area measuring 230 square inches?

    b. If the price is $1.77 for every 2 bulbs, how much will she spend on the flower bulbs?

CHAPTER 5

33. The Pizza Palace makes 30 pizzas every 2 hours to accommodate the lunch crowd.
   a. If lunch lasts 3 hours, how many pizzas does Pizza Palace make?

   b. If each pizza can serve 4 people, how many people are served during the 3-hour lunch period?

BUSINESS DECISION: DETERMINING THE "BEST BUY"

34. One special type of ratio is known as a *rate*. A rate is a ratio that compares two quantities that have different units, such as miles per hour, calories per serving, pounds per square inch, and price per unit. In consumer economics, expressing prices as "price per unit" allows us to determine the "best buy" when comparing various shopping choices. All else being equal, the best buy is the choice with the *lowest* price per unit (unit price).

   Donna Kelsch is comparing dry cat food brands for her cats Nicki and Nasty. If Nicki and Nasty's favorite, Funny Fish, comes in the three sizes listed below, which size is the best buy?
   Hint: Determine the unit price for each size. Round to the nearest cent if necessary.

Size	Price	Unit Price
5 pounds	$12.25	
10 pounds	$21.90	
20 pounds	$38.50	

COLLABORATIVE LEARNING ACTIVITY

Using Formulas in Business

Have each member of the team speak with someone in one of the following professions to determine how the person uses standardized formulas in his or her business.

a. Store owner or manager
b. Real estate or insurance salesperson
c. Advertising or marketing manager
d. Production manager
e. Accountant
f. Banker
g. Stockbroker
h. Additional choice: _____

CHAPTER 6

Percents and Their Applications in Business

Monkey Business Images/Shutterstock.com

PERFORMANCE OBJECTIVES

Percents are commonly used in retailing to advertise discounts.

Source: Based on Supermarket News

percent A way of representing the parts of a whole. Percent means "per hundred" or "parts per hundred."

percent sign The symbol, %, used to represent percents. For example, 1 percent would be written as 1%.

It takes only a glance at the business section of a newspaper or an annual report of a company to see how extensively percents are applied in business. Percents are the primary way of measuring change among business variables. For example, a business might report "revenue is up 6% this year" or "expenses have been cut by 2.3% this month." Interest rates, commissions, and many taxes are expressed in percent form. You may have heard phrases like these: "Sunnyside Bank charged 12% on the loan," "A real estate broker made 5% commission on the sale of the property," or "The state charges a $6\frac{1}{2}\%$ sales tax." Even price changes are frequently advertised as percents, "Sears Dishwasher Sale—All Models, 25% off!"

To this point, we have learned that fractions and decimals are ways of representing parts of a whole. Percents are another way of expressing quantity with relation to a whole. **Percent** means "per hundred" or "parts per hundred" and is represented by the **percent sign**, **%**.

Percents are numbers equal to a fraction with a denominator of 100. Five percent, for example, means five parts out of 100 and may be written in the following ways:

5 percent　　　　5%　　　　5 hundredths　　　$\frac{5}{100}$　　　.05

Before performing any mathematical calculations with percents, they must be converted to either decimals or fractions. Although this function is performed automatically by the percent key on a calculator, Section I of this chapter covers the procedures for making these conversions manually. Sections II and III introduce you to some important applications of percents in business.

6-1 CONVERTING PERCENTS TO DECIMALS AND DECIMALS TO PERCENTS

Because percents are numbers expressed as parts per 100, the percent sign, %, mean multiplication by $\frac{1}{100}$. Therefore, 25% means

$$25\% = 25 \times \frac{1}{100} = \frac{25}{100} = .25$$

STEPS FOR CONVERTING A PERCENT TO A DECIMAL

Learning Tip

To divide a number by 100, move the decimal point two places to the left. Add zeros as needed.

Remember, if there is no decimal point, it is understood to be to the right of the digit in the ones place. (24 = 24.)

STEP 1. Remove the percent sign.

STEP 2. Divide by 100.

Note: If the percent is a fraction such as $\frac{3}{8}\%$ or a mixed number such as $4\frac{3}{4}\%$, change the fraction to a decimal; then follow Steps 1 and 2 above.

$$\frac{3}{8}\% = .375\% = .00375 \qquad 4\frac{3}{4}\% = 4.75\% = .0475$$

Note: If the percent is a fraction such as $\frac{2}{3}\%$, which converts to a repeating decimal, .66666, round the decimal to hundredths, .67; then follow Steps 1 and 2 above.

$$\frac{2}{3}\% = .67\% = .0067$$

EXAMPLE 1　CONVERTING PERCENTS TO DECIMALS

Convert the following percents to decimals.

a.　44%　　b.　233%　　c.　56.4%　　d.　.68%　　e.　$18\frac{1}{4}\%$　　f.　$\frac{1}{8}\%$　　g.　$9\frac{1}{3}\%$

SOLUTIONSTRATEGY

Remove the percent sign and move the decimal point two places to the left.

a. $44\% = .44$ b. $233\% = 2.33$ c. $56.4\% = .564$ d. $.68\% = .0068$

e. $18\frac{1}{4}\% = 18.25\% = .1825$ f. $\frac{1}{8}\% = .125\% = .00125$ g. $9\frac{1}{3}\% = 9.33\% = .0933$

▶TRYITEXERCISE 1

Convert the following percents to decimals.

a. 27% b. 472% c. 93.7% d. $.81\%$ e. $12\frac{3}{4}\%$ f. $\frac{7}{8}\%$

CHECK YOUR ANSWERS WITH THE SOLUTIONS ON PAGE 189.

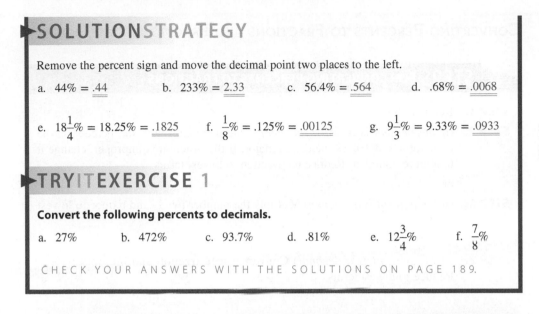

STEPS FOR CONVERTING A DECIMAL OR WHOLE NUMBER TO A PERCENT

STEP 1. Multiply by 100.

STEP 2. Write a percent sign after the number.

STEP 3. If there are fractions involved, such as $\frac{3}{4}$, convert them to decimals first; then proceed with Steps 1 and 2 above.

$$\frac{3}{4} = .75 = 75\%$$

EXAMPLE2 CONVERTING DECIMALS TO PERCENTS

Convert the following decimals or whole numbers to percents.

a. $.5$ b. 3.7 c. $.044$ d. $.09\frac{3}{5}$ e. 7 f. $6\frac{1}{2}$

▶SOLUTIONSTRATEGY

Move the decimal point two places to the right and add a percent sign.

a. $.5 = 50\%$ b. $3.7 = 370\%$ c. $.044 = 4.4\%$

d. $.09\frac{3}{5} = .096 = 9.6\%$ e. $7 = 700\%$ f. $6\frac{1}{2} = 6.5 = 650\%$

▶TRYITEXERCISE 2

Convert the following decimals or whole numbers to percents.

a. $.8$ b. 1.4 c. $.0023$ d. $.016\frac{2}{5}$ e. 19 f. $.57\frac{2}{3}$

CHECK YOUR ANSWERS WITH THE SOLUTIONS ON PAGE 189.

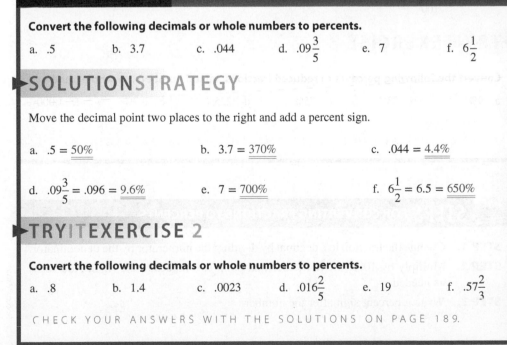

Learning Tip

To multiply a number by 100, move the decimal point two places to the right. Add zeros as needed. As a "navigational aid" to the direction of the decimal point, consider the words *decimal* and *percent* as written alphabetically, with *decimal* preceding *percent*.

- When converting from decimal to percent, the decimal moves **right**

  decimal → percent

- When converting from percent to decimal, the decimal moves **left**

  decimal ← percent

6-2 CONVERTING PERCENTS TO FRACTIONS AND FRACTIONS TO PERCENTS

STEPS FOR CONVERTING PERCENTS TO FRACTIONS

STEP 1. Remove the percent sign.

STEP 2. (*If the percent is a whole number*) Write a fraction with the percent as the numerator and 100 as the denominator. If that fraction is improper, change it to a mixed number. Reduce the fraction to lowest terms.

or

STEP 2. (*If the percent is a fraction*) Multiply the number by $\frac{1}{100}$ and reduce to lowest terms.

or

STEP 2. (*If the percent is a decimal*) Convert it to a fraction and multiply by $\frac{1}{100}$. Reduce to lowest terms.

Dollars AND Sense

If you have not already done so and your instructor allows it, this would be a good time to purchase a business calculator. There are many choices available today in the $10 to $40 price range. Popular brands include Hewlett-Packard and Texas Instruments. Calculators are also available from Canon, Sharp, Casio, and others.

To help you choose a calculator, go to www.shopzilla.com and enter *business calculators* in the "I'm Shopping for" box.

EXAMPLE3 CONVERTING PERCENTS TO FRACTIONS

Convert the following percents to reduced fractions, mixed numbers, or whole numbers.

a. 3%   b. 57%   c. $2\frac{1}{2}$%   d. 150%   e. 4.5%   f. 600%

▶SOLUTIONSTRATEGY

a. $3\% = \frac{3}{100}$ b. $57\% = \frac{57}{100}$ c. $2\frac{1}{2}\% = \frac{5}{2} \times \frac{1}{100} = \frac{5}{200} = \frac{1}{40}$

d. $150\% = \frac{150}{100} = 1\frac{50}{100} = 1\frac{1}{2}$ e. $4.5\% = 4\frac{1}{2}\% = \frac{9}{2} \times \frac{1}{100} = \frac{9}{200}$

f. $600\% = \frac{600}{100} = 6$

▶TRYITEXERCISE 3

Convert the following percents to reduced fractions, mixed numbers, or whole numbers.

a. 9%   b. 23%   c. 75%   d. 225%   e. 8.7%   f. 1,000%

CHECK YOUR ANSWERS WITH THE SOLUTIONS ON PAGE 189.

STEPS FOR CONVERTING FRACTIONS TO PERCENTS

STEP 1. Change the fraction to a decimal by dividing the numerator by the denominator.

STEP 2. Multiply by 100. (Move the decimal point two places to the right. Add zeros as needed.)

STEP 3. Write a percent sign after the number.

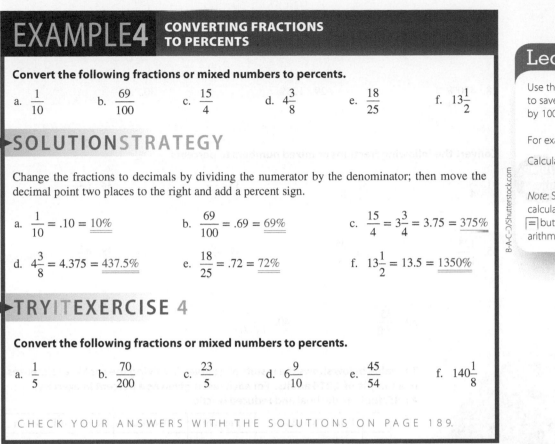

EXAMPLE4 CONVERTING FRACTIONS TO PERCENTS

Convert the following fractions or mixed numbers to percents.

a. $\dfrac{1}{10}$ b. $\dfrac{69}{100}$ c. $\dfrac{15}{4}$ d. $4\dfrac{3}{8}$ e. $\dfrac{18}{25}$ f. $13\dfrac{1}{2}$

▶SOLUTIONSTRATEGY

Change the fractions to decimals by dividing the numerator by the denominator; then move the decimal point two places to the right and add a percent sign.

a. $\dfrac{1}{10} = .10 = \underline{\underline{10\%}}$

b. $\dfrac{69}{100} = .69 = \underline{\underline{69\%}}$

c. $\dfrac{15}{4} = 3\dfrac{3}{4} = 3.75 = \underline{375\%}$

d. $4\dfrac{3}{8} = 4.375 = \underline{\underline{437.5\%}}$

e. $\dfrac{18}{25} = .72 = \underline{\underline{72\%}}$

f. $13\dfrac{1}{2} = 13.5 = \underline{\underline{1350\%}}$

▶TRYITEXERCISE 4

Convert the following fractions or mixed numbers to percents.

a. $\dfrac{1}{5}$ b. $\dfrac{70}{200}$ c. $\dfrac{23}{5}$ d. $6\dfrac{9}{10}$ e. $\dfrac{45}{54}$ f. $140\dfrac{1}{8}$

CHECK YOUR ANSWERS WITH THE SOLUTIONS ON PAGE 189.

Learning Tip

Use the % key on your calculator to save the step of multiplying by 100.

For example: $\dfrac{44}{50} = .88 = 88\%$.

Calculator sequence:

$44 \boxed{\div} 50 \boxed{\%} = 88$

Note: Scientific and business calculators require pushing the $\boxed{=}$ button after the % key; common arithmetic calculators do not.

B-A-C-O/Shutterstock.com

REVIEW EXERCISES

6 SECTION I

Convert the following percents to decimals.

1. 28%
.28

2. 63%

3. 13.4%

4. 121%

5. 42.68%

6. $26\dfrac{1}{2}\%$

7. .05%

8. $\dfrac{3}{5}\%$

9. $125\dfrac{1}{6}\%$

10. 2,000%

Convert the following decimals or whole numbers to percents.

11. 3.5
350%

12. .27

13. 46

14. $.34\dfrac{1}{2}$

15. .0052

16. $.9\dfrac{3}{4}$

17. 164

18. .04

19. 5.33

20. $1.15\dfrac{5}{8}$

Convert the following percents to reduced fractions, mixed numbers, or whole numbers.

21. 5%
$$\dfrac{5}{100} = \dfrac{1}{20}$$

22. 75%

23. 89%

24. 230%

25. 38%   26. 37.5%   27. $62\frac{1}{2}\%$

28. 450%   29. 125%   30. .8%

Convert the following fractions or mixed numbers to percents.

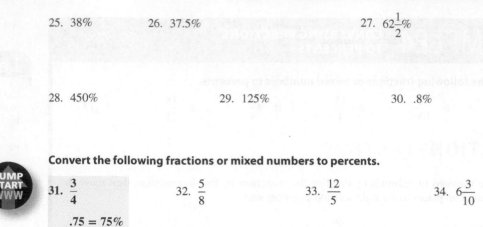

31. $\frac{3}{4}$ 32. $\frac{5}{8}$ 33. $\frac{12}{5}$ 34. $6\frac{3}{10}$

$.75 = \underline{75\%}$

35. $\frac{125}{100}$ 36. $\frac{35}{8}$ 37. $\frac{3}{16}$ 38. $4\frac{1}{5}$

39. $\frac{35}{100}$ 40. $\frac{375}{1,000}$

The table below shows the results of a survey involving the cookie preferences of a sample of 1,214 adults. For each result given as a percent in exercises 41-45, find the decimal and reduced fraction.

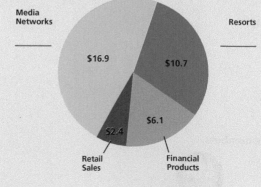

Sergio33/Shutterstock.com

	Type of Cookie	Percent	Decimal	Reduced Fraction
41.	Chocolate chip	57%		
42.	Peanut butter	16%		
43.	Oatmeal	15%		
44.	Sugar/shortbread	7%		
45.	Other	5%		

iStock.com/
MarsBars

BUSINESS DECISION: ENHANCING THE PIE

Fosteral Enterprises

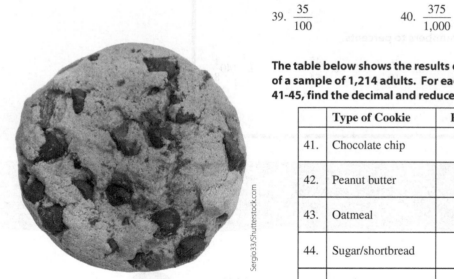

Fosteral Enterprises Segment Revenue ($millions)

Media Networks ____

Resorts ____

$16.9

$10.7

$2.4

$6.1

Retail Sales ____

Financial Products ____

Source: Disney Enterprises, Inc.

46. You have been asked to make a presentation about Fosteral Enterprises. In your research, you locate the accompanying pie chart, which shows Fosteral revenue by segment expressed in millions of dollars.

To enhance your presentation, you have decided to convert the dollar amounts to percents and display both numbers.

a. What is the total revenue?

b. What percent (rounded to the nearest tenth percent) does each segment contribute to the total revenue?

Media Networks   Resorts

Retail Sales   Financial Products

USING THE PERCENTAGE FORMULA TO SOLVE BUSINESS PROBLEMS

6 SECTION II

Now that we have learned to manipulate percents, let's look at some of their practical applications in business. Percent problems involve the use of equations known as the percentage formulas. These formulas have three variables: the **base**, the **portion**, and the **rate**. In business situations, two of the variables will be given and are the *knowns*; one of the variables will be the *unknown*.

Once the variables have been properly identified, the equations are simple to solve. The variables have the following characteristics, which should be used to help identify them:

BASE: The base is the number that represents 100%, or the *whole thing*. It is the starting point, the beginning, or total value of something. The base is often preceded by the word *of* in the written statement of the situation because it is multiplied by the rate.

PORTION: The portion is the number that represents a *part* of the base. The portion is always in the same terms as the base. For example, if the base is dollars, the portion is dollars; if the base is people, the portion is people; if the base is production units, the portion will be production units. The portion often has a "unique characteristic" that is being measured or compared with the base. For example, if the base is the total number of cars in a parking lot, the portion could be the part of the total cars that are convertibles (the unique characteristic).

RATE: The rate is easily identified. It is the number with the *percent sign* or the word *percent*. It defines what part the portion is of the base. If the rate is less than 100%, the portion is less than the base. If the rate is 100%, the portion is equal to the base. If the rate is more than 100%, the portion is greater than the base.

base The variable of the percentage formula that represents 100%, or the whole thing.

portion The variable of the percentage formula that represents a part of the base.

rate The variable of the percentage formula that defines how much or what part the portion is of the base. The rate is the number with the percent sign.

The following percentage formulas are used to solve percent problems:

Portion = Rate × Base	$P = R \times B$
Rate = $\dfrac{\textbf{Portion}}{\textbf{Base}}$	$R = \dfrac{P}{B}$
Base = $\dfrac{\textbf{Portion}}{\textbf{Rate}}$	$B = \dfrac{P}{R}$

STEPS FOR SOLVING PERCENTAGE PROBLEMS

STEP 1. Identify the two knowns and the unknown.

STEP 2. Choose the formula that solves for that unknown.

STEP 3. Solve the equation by substituting the known values for the letters in the formula.

Hint: By remembering the one basic formula, $P = R \times B$, you can derive the other two by using your knowledge of solving equations from Chapter 5. Because multiplication is indicated, we isolate the unknown by performing the inverse, or opposite, operation, division.

Learning Tip

Don't confuse the word *percentage* with the percent, or rate. The *percentage* means the portion, not the rate.

iStock.com/Nikada

B-A-C-O/Shutterstock.com

To solve for rate, R, divide both sides of the equation by B:

$$P = R \times B \longrightarrow \frac{P}{B} = \frac{R \times \cancel{B}}{\cancel{B}} \longrightarrow \frac{P}{B} = R$$

To solve for base, B, divide both sides of the equation by R:

$$P = R \times B \longrightarrow \frac{P}{R} = \frac{\cancel{R} \times B}{\cancel{R}} \longrightarrow \frac{P}{R} = B$$

Another method for remembering the percentage formulas is by using the Magic Triangle.

The Magic Triangle

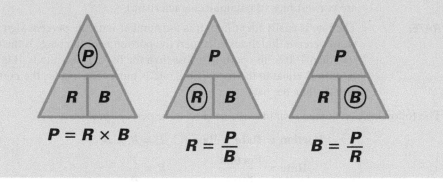

The triangle is divided into three sections representing the portion, rate, and base. By circling or covering the letter in the triangle that corresponds to the *unknown* of the problem, the triangle will "magically" reveal the correct formula to use.

$$P = R \times B \qquad\qquad R = \frac{P}{B} \qquad\qquad B = \frac{P}{R}$$

6-3   SOLVING FOR THE PORTION

Remember, the portion is a part of the whole and will always be in the same terms as the base. It is found by multiplying the rate times the base: $P = R \times B$. The following examples will demonstrate solving for the portion.

$$P = R \times B$$

EXAMPLE5   SOLVING FOR THE PORTION

What is the portion if the base is $400 and the rate is 12%?

►SOLUTIONSTRATEGY

Substitute the knowns for the letters in the formula Portion = Rate × Base. In this problem, 12% is the rate and $400 is the base. Do not forget to convert the percent (rate) to a decimal by deleting the % sign and moving the decimal point two places to the left (12% = .12).

$$P = R \times B$$
$$P = 12\% \times 400 = .12 \times 400 = 48$$
$$\underline{\text{Portion} = \$48}$$

TRYITEXERCISE 5

Solve the following for the portion.

What is the portion if the base is 980 and the rate is 55%?

CHECK YOUR ANSWER WITH THE SOLUTION ON PAGE 189.

EXAMPLE6 USING THE PERCENTAGE FORMULA

What number is 43.5% of 250?

SOLUTIONSTRATEGY

In this problem, the rate is easily identified as the term with the % sign. The base, or whole amount, is preceded by the word *of*. We use the formula Portion = Rate × Base, substituting the knowns for the letters that represent them.

$$P = R \times B$$
$$P = 43.5\% \times 250 = .435 \times 250 = 108.75$$
$$\underline{108.75}$$

TRYITEXERCISE 6

Solve the following for the portion.

What number is 72% of 3,200?

CHECK YOUR ANSWER WITH THE SOLUTION ON PAGE 189.

EXAMPLE7 USING THE PERCENTAGE FORMULA

Republic Industries produced 6,000 stoves last week. If 2% of them were defective, how many defective stoves were produced?

SOLUTIONSTRATEGY

To solve this problem, we must first identify the variables. Because 2% has the percent sign, it is the rate. The terms are stoves; the total number of stoves (6,000) is the base. The unique characteristic of the portion, the unknown, is that they were defective.

$$P = R \times B$$
$$P = 2\% \times 6,000 = .02 \times 6,000 = 120$$
$$\underline{120} = \text{Number of defective stoves last week}$$

> ▶**TRYITEXERCISE** 7
>
> **Solve the following for the portion.**
>
> a. Premier Industries has 1,250 employees. 16% constitute the sales staff. How many employees are in sales?
>
> b. Aventura Savings & Loan requires a 15% down payment on a mortgage loan. What is the down payment needed to finance a $148,500 home?
>
> CHECK YOUR ANSWERS WITH THE SOLUTIONS ON PAGE 189.

6-4 SOLVING FOR THE RATE

$$R = \frac{P}{B}$$

The rate is the variable that describes what part of the base is represented by the portion. It is *always* the term with the percent sign. When solving for the rate, your answer will be a decimal. Be sure to convert the decimal to a percent by moving the decimal point two places to the right and adding a percent sign. We use the formula

$$\text{Rate} = \frac{\text{Portion}}{\text{Base}} \quad \text{or} \quad R = \frac{P}{B}$$

The following examples demonstrate solving for the rate.

Learning Tip

Remember, the rate expresses "what part" the portion is of the base.

- When the rate is less than 100%, the portion is *less* than the base.
- When the rate is more than 100%, the portion is *more* than the base.
- When the rate is 100%, the portion *equals* the base.

B-A-C-O/Shutterstock.com

> **EXAMPLE8** **SOLVING FOR THE RATE**
>
> **What is the rate if the base is 160 and the portion is 40?**
>
> ▶**SOLUTIONSTRATEGY**
>
> Substitute the knowns for the letters in the formula.
>
> $$\text{Rate} = \frac{\text{Portion}}{\text{Base}}$$
>
> $$R = \frac{P}{B}$$
>
> $$R = \frac{40}{160} = .25 = 25\%$$
>
> $$\underline{\text{Rate} = 25\%}$$
>
> ▶**TRYITEXERCISE 8**
>
> **Solve the following for the rate. Round to the nearest tenth when necessary.**
>
> What is the rate if the base is 21 and the portion is 9?
>
> CHECK YOUR ANSWER WITH THE SOLUTION ON PAGE 189.

EXAMPLE9 USING THE PERCENTAGE FORMULA

What percent of 700 is 56?

SOLUTIONSTRATEGY

This problem asks what percent, indicating that the rate is the unknown. The 700 is preceded by the word *of* and is therefore the base. The 56 is part of the base and is therefore the portion. Once again we use the formula $R = P \div B$, substituting the knowns for the letters that represent them.

$$R = \frac{P}{B}$$

$$R = \frac{56}{700} = .08 = 8\%$$

$$\underline{\underline{8\%}}$$

▶TRYITEXERCISE 9

Solve the following for the rate. Round to the nearest tenth when necessary.

67 is what percent of 142?

CHECK YOUR ANSWER WITH THE SOLUTION ON PAGE 189.

EXAMPLE10 USING THE PERCENTAGE FORMULA

Pet Supermarket placed an order for 560 fish tanks. If only 490 tanks were delivered, what percent of the order was received?

SOLUTIONSTRATEGY

The first step in solving this problem is to identify the variables. The statement asks "what percent"; therefore, the rate is the unknown. Because 560 is the total order, it is the base; 490 is a part of the total and is therefore the portion. Note that the base and the portion are in the same terms, fish tanks; the unique characteristic of the portion is that 490 tanks *were delivered*.

$$R = \frac{P}{B}$$

$$R = \frac{490}{560} = .875 = 87.5\%$$

$$\underline{87.5\% = \text{Percent of the order received}}$$

Note: Because 560 is the total order, it is the base and therefore represents 100% of the order. If 87.5% of the tanks were received, then 12.5% of the tanks were not received.

$$100\% - 87.5\% = \underline{12.5\% \text{ not received}}$$

▶TRYITEXERCISE 10

Solve the following for the rate. Round to the nearest tenth when necessary.

a. A contract called for 18,000 square feet of tile to be installed in a shopping mall. In the first week, 5,400 square feet of tile was completed.

What percent of the job has been completed?

What percent of the job remains?

b. During a recent sale, Sir John, a men's boutique, sold $5,518 in business suits. If total sales amounted to $8,900, what percent of the sales were suits?

CHECK YOUR ANSWERS WITH THE SOLUTIONS ON PAGE 189.

6-5   SOLVING FOR THE BASE

To solve business situations in which the whole or total amount is the unknown, we use the formula

$$\text{Base} = \frac{\text{Portion}}{\text{Rate}} \quad \text{or} \quad B = \frac{P}{R}$$

The following examples illustrate solving for the base.

$$B = \frac{P}{R}$$

Learning Tip

Percentage problems can also be solved by using proportion. Set up the proportion

$$\frac{\text{Rate}}{100} = \frac{\text{Portion}}{\text{Base}}$$

and cross-multiply to solve for the unknown.

For example, at an electronics store last week, 70 televisions were sold with built-in DVD players. If this represents 20% of all TVs sold, how many total TVs were sold?

$$\frac{20}{100} = \frac{70}{\text{Base (total TVs)}}$$
$$20B = 100(70)$$
$$20B = 7,000$$
$$B = 350 \text{ Total TVs}$$

B-A-C-O/Shutterstock.com

EXAMPLE 11   SOLVING FOR THE BASE

What is the base if the rate is 21% and the portion is 58.8?

▶ SOLUTION STRATEGY

In this basic problem, we simply substitute the known values for the letters in the formula. Remember, the rate must be converted from a percent to a decimal.

$$B = \frac{P}{R}$$
$$B = \frac{58.8}{21\%} = \frac{58.8}{.21} = 280$$
$$\underline{\text{Base} = 280}$$

▶ TRY IT EXERCISE 11

Solve the following for the base. Round to hundredths or the nearest cent when necessary.

What is the base if the rate is 40% and the portion is 690?

CHECK YOUR ANSWER WITH THE SOLUTION ON PAGE 189.

EXAMPLE 12   USING THE PERCENTAGE FORMULA

75 is 15% of what number?

▶ SOLUTION STRATEGY

Remember, the base is usually identified as the value preceded by *of* in the statement. In this case, that value is the unknown. Because 15 has the percent sign, it is the rate, and 75 is the part of the whole, or the portion.

$$B = \frac{P}{R}$$
$$B = \frac{75}{15\%} = \frac{75}{.15} = 500$$
$$\underline{500}$$

▶TRYITEXERCISE 12

Solve the following for the base. Round to hundredths or the nearest cent when necessary.

$550 is 88% of what amount?

CHECK YOUR ANSWER WITH THE SOLUTION ON PAGE 189.

EXAMPLE13   USING THE PERCENTAGE FORMULA

All Star Sporting Goods reports that 28% of total shoe sales are from Nike products. If last week's Nike sales were $15,400, what was the total amount of sales for the week?

▶SOLUTIONSTRATEGY

In this problem, the total amount of sales, the base, is unknown. Because 28% has the percent sign, it is the rate and $15,400 is the portion. Note again, the portion is in the same terms as the base, dollar sales; however, the unique characteristic is that the portion represents Nike sales.

$$B = \frac{P}{R}$$

$$B = \frac{15,400}{28\%} = \frac{15,400}{.28} = 55,000$$

$55,000 Total sales for the week

▶TRYITEXERCISE 13

Solve the following for the base. Round to hundredths or the nearest cent when necessary.

a. In a machine shop, 35% of the motor repairs are for broken shafts. If 126 motors had broken shafts last month, how many total motors were repaired?

b. At Office Mart, 75% of the copy paper sold is letter size. If 3,420 reams of letter size were sold, how many total reams of copy paper were sold?

CHECK YOUR ANSWERS WITH THE SOLUTIONS ON PAGE 189.

REVIEW EXERCISES

6   SECTION II

Solve the following for the portion. Round to hundredths when necessary.

1. 15% of 380 is _____

   $P = R \times B = .15 \times 380 = \underline{57}$

2. 10.5% of 1,400 is _____

3. 200% of 45 is _____

4. $5\frac{1}{2}$% of $600 is _____

5. What is the portion if the base is 450 and the rate is 19%?

6. What is the portion if the base is 1,650 and the rate is 150%?

7. What number is 35.2% of 184?

8. What number is .8% of 500?

9. What is $8\frac{4}{5}\%$ of 200?   10. What number is 258% of 2,500?

Solve the following for the rate. Round to the nearest tenth of a percent when necessary.

11. 40 is _____ % of 125   12. _____ % of 50 is 23   13. 600 is _____ % of 240

$$R = \frac{P}{B} = \frac{40}{125} = .32 = \underline{\underline{32\%}}$$

14. What is the rate if the base is 288 and the portion is 50?

15. What is the rate if the portion is 21.6 and the base is 160?

16. What is the rate if the base is $24,500 and the portion is $5,512.50?

17. What percent of 77 is 23?   18. What percent of 1,600 is 1,900?

19. 52 is what percent of 840?   20. $7.80 is what percent of $58.60?

Solve the following for the base. Round to hundredths when necessary.

21. 69 is 15% of _____   22. 360 is 150% of _____   23. 6.45 is $18\frac{1}{2}\%$ of _____

$$B = \frac{P}{R} = \frac{69}{.15} = \underline{\underline{460}}$$

24. What is the base if the rate is 16.8% and the portion is 451?

25. What is the base if the portion is 10 and the rate is $2\frac{3}{4}\%$?

26. What is the base if the portion is $4,530 and the rate is 35%?

27. 60 is 15% of what number?   28. 160 is 130% of what number?

29. $46.50 is $86\frac{2}{3}\%$ of what number?   30. .84 is 62.5% of what number?

Travel Agent According to data from the U.S. Bureau of Labor Statistics, overall employment of travel agents is expected to decline somewhat in the years ahead. The job prospects are best for travel agents who specialize in either specific types of travelers, such as corporate travelers, or particular destinations. The median annual wage for a travel agent is roughly $2,000 less than the median wage for all occupations.

Subbotina Anna/Shutterstock.com

Solve the following word problems for the portion, rate, or base.

31. Alicia Kirk owns 37% of a travel agency.
   a. If the total worth of the business is $160,000, how much is Alicia's share?

   b. Last month Alicia's agency booked $14,500 in airline fares on Orbit Airline. If Orbit pays agencies a commission of 4.1%, how much commission should the agency receive?

32. The sales force at a certain company successfully closed 72 out of 200 sales calls. What was their percent success rate?

33. A recent report on a financial website noted that for the first time in more than a decade, the size of the average newly built American house had shrunk to 2,065 square feet, or 93% of its original size. What was the original size before the decline? Round to the nearest square foot.

34. 52% of the students at a college are from in-state. If 3,250 students are from in-state, how many students attend the college?

35. A computer chip manufacturer made 210,000 chips last week. If 6% of them were defective, how many defective chips were made?

36. As part of a report you are writing that compares living expenses in various cities, use the chart "Cities with the highest average monthly utility bills" to calculate the following:

    a. What percent is the Baltimore utility bill of the Las Vegas bill? Round to the nearest whole percent.

    b. What percent is the Orlando utility bill of the Dallas bill? Round to the nearest tenth of a percent.

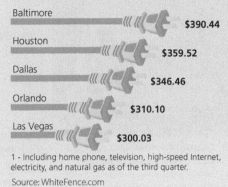

Cities with the highest average monthly utility bills[1]

Baltimore	$390.44
Houston	$359.52
Dallas	$346.46
Orlando	$310.10
Las Vegas	$300.03

1 - Including home phone, television, high-speed Internet, electricity, and natural gas as of the third quarter.

Source: WhiteFence.com

37. Thirty percent of the inventory of a Nine West shoe store is high heels. If the store has 846 pairs of high heels in stock, how many total pairs of shoes are in the inventory?

38. Municipal Auto Sales advertised a down payment of $1,200 on a Mustang valued at $14,700. What is the percent of the down payment? Round to the nearest tenth of a percent.

39. According to *The Miami Herald* for every dollar of tip left at South Florida restaurants, 74% went to the server, 5% went to the host, 6% went to the bartender, and 15% went to the busser. One night a large party spent $750 on dinner and left a 20% tip.

    a. How much tip was left?

    b. Use the research percents to distribute the tip between the server, the host, the bartender, and the busser.

40. A quality control process finds 17.2 defects for every 8,600 units of production. What percent of the production is defective?

41. The Parker Company employs 68 part-time workers. If this represents 4% of the total work force, how many individuals work for the company?

Century Mutual Fund – Investments
($ billions)

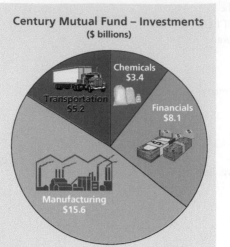

42. A medical insurance policy requires Ana to pay the first $100 of her hospital expense. The insurance company will then pay 80% of the remaining expense. Ana is expecting a short surgical stay in the hospital, for which she estimates the total bill to be about $4,500. How much will Ana's portion of the bill amount to?

43. A corporation earned $457,800 last year. If its tax rate is $13\frac{3}{8}\%$, how much tax was paid?

44. In June, the New York Yankees won 15 games and lost 9. What percent of the games did they win? (*Hint:* Use total games played as the base.)

Use the pie chart "Century Mutual Fund – Investments" for Exercises 45 and 46.

45. What is the total amount invested in the Century Mutual Fund?

46. What percent does each investment category represent? Round your answers to the nearest tenth of a percent.

Nuptial Numbers According to the Bridal Association of America, in a recent year there were over 2.3 million weddings in the United States, with a market value of over $72 billion. The average cost of a wedding was almost $31,000, with 169 guests. The average engagement time was 17 months.

In 1960, an American bride was typically 20 years old and a groom was 23. Today the average age of wedding couples is 26 for the bride and 28 for the groom. Approximately 75% of all wedding receptions take place at a hotel, country club, or catering facility.

47. Ford Motor Co. announced that it planned to sell a new police cruiser vehicle in the United States to replace its Crown Victoria "Police Interceptor." Ford sells about 45,000 police vehicles a year, or about 75% of all police vehicles sold in the United States. Based on this information, what is the total number of police vehicles sold in the United States each year?

48. Elwood Smith attends a college that charges $1,400 tuition per semester for 12 credit hours of classes. If tuition is raised by 9% next year:

a. How much more will he pay for two semesters of classes with the same course load?

b. If Elwood works at a car wash earning $8 per hour and pays 15% in taxes, how many extra hours must he work to make up for the tuition increase? Round to the nearest whole hour.

BUSINESS DECISION: THE PARTY PLANNER

49. You are the catering manager for the Imperial Palace Hotel. Last Saturday your staff catered a wedding reception in the main ballroom, during which 152 chicken dinners, 133 steak dinners, and 95 fish dinners were served. All dinners are the same price. The hotel charges "per person" for catered events.

a. What percent of the total meals served was each type of dinner?

b. If $13,300 was charged for all the meals, how much revenue did each type produce?

c. If a 20% price increase goes into effect next month, what will be the new price per meal?

d. When photographers, florists, DJs, bands, and other outside vendors are booked through your office for events at the hotel, a $5\frac{1}{2}\%$ "finder's fee" is charged. Last year $175,000 of such services were booked. How much did the hotel make on this service?

e. If your boss is expecting $11,000 in "finder's fee" revenue next year, what amount of these services must be booked?

SOLVING OTHER BUSINESS PROBLEMS INVOLVING PERCENTS

6 SECTION III

In addition to the basic percentage formulas, percents are used in many other ways in business. Measuring increases and decreases, comparing results from one year with another, and reporting economic activity and trends are just a few of these applications.

The ability of managers to make correct decisions is fundamental to success in business. These decisions require accurate and up-to-date information. Measuring percent changes in business activity is an important source of this information. Percents often describe a situation in a more informative way than do the raw data alone.

For example, a company reports a profit of $50,000 for the year. Although the number $50,000 is correct, it does not give a perspective of whether that amount of profit is good or bad. A comparison to last year's figures using percents might reveal that profits are up 45% over last year or profits are down 66.8%. Significant news!

Learning Tip

It is important to remember when solving percentage problems that involve "change" from an original number to a new number, the original number is always the *base* and represents 100%.

DETERMINING RATE OF INCREASE OR DECREASE

6-6

In calculating the rate of increase or decrease of something, we use the same percentage formula concepts as before. Rate of change means percent change; therefore, the *rate* is the unknown. Once again we use the formula $R = P \div B$. Rate of change situations contain an original amount of something, which either increases or decreases to a new amount.

In solving these problems, the original amount is always the base. The amount of change is the portion. The unknown, which describes the percent change between the two amounts, is the rate.

$$\text{Rate of change (Rate)} = \frac{\text{Amount of change (Portion)}}{\text{Original amount (Base)}}$$

Tropical Storm Force Wind Speed Probabilities
For the 120 hours (5 days) from 8 am EDT Thu Aug 27 to 8 am EDT Tue Sep 1

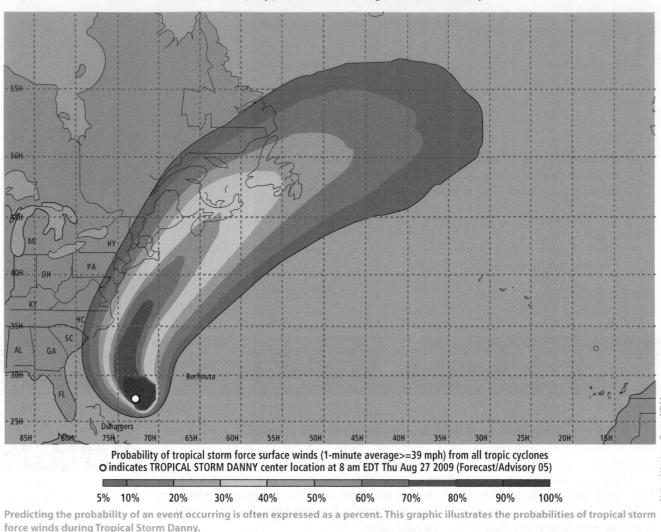

National Hurricane Center-NOAA

Probability of tropical storm force surface winds (1-minute average>=39 mph) from all tropic cyclones
O indicates TROPICAL STORM DANNY center location at 8 am EDT Thu Aug 27 2009 (Forecast/Advisory 05)

5% 10%   20%   30%   40%   50%   60%   70%   80%   90%   100%

Predicting the probability of an event occurring is often expressed as a percent. This graphic illustrates the probabilities of tropical storm force winds during Tropical Storm Danny.

iStock.com/Nikada

STEPS FOR DETERMINING THE RATE OF INCREASE OR DECREASE

STEP 1. Identify the original and the new amounts and find the *difference* between them.

STEP 2. Using the rate formula $R = P \div B$, substitute the difference from Step 1 for the portion and the original amount for the base.

STEP 3. Solve the equation for R. Remember, your answer will be in decimal form, which must be converted to a percent.

EXAMPLE14   FINDING THE RATE OF INCREASE

If a number increases from 60 to 75, what is the rate of increase?

►SOLUTIONSTRATEGY

In this basic situation, a number changes from 60 to 75 and we are looking for the percent change; in this case, it is an increase. The original amount is 60; the new amount is 75.

The portion is the difference between the amounts, $75 - 60 = 15$, and the base is the original amount, 60. We now substitute these values into the formula.

$$R = \frac{P}{B} = \frac{15}{60} = .25 = 25\%$$

Rate of increase = 25%

►TRYITEXERCISE 14

Solve the following problem for the rate of increase or decrease. Round to the nearest tenth of a percent when necessary.

If a number increases from 650 to 948, what is the rate of increase?

CHECK YOUR ANSWER WITH THE SOLUTION ON PAGE 189.

EXAMPLE15 FINDING THE RATE OF DECREASE

A number decreased from 120 to 80. What is the rate of decrease?

►SOLUTIONSTRATEGY

This problem illustrates a number decreasing in value. The unknown is the rate of decrease. We identify the original amount as 120 and the new amount as 80.

The difference between them is the portion: $120 - 80 = 40$. The original amount, 120, is the base. Now apply the rate formula.

$$R = \frac{P}{B} = \frac{40}{120} = .333 = 33.3\%$$

Rate of decrease = 33.3%

►TRYITEXERCISE 15

Solve the following problem for the rate of increase or decrease. Round to the nearest tenth of a percent when necessary.

If a number decreases from 21 to 15, what is the rate of decrease?

CHECK YOUR ANSWER WITH THE SOLUTION ON PAGE 189.

EXAMPLE16 FINDING THE RATE OF CHANGE

Last year Iberia Furniture had a work force of 360 employees. This year there are 504 employees. What is the rate of change in the number of employees?

►SOLUTIONSTRATEGY

The key to solving this problem is to properly identify the variables. The problem asks "what is the rate?"; therefore, the rate is the unknown. The original amount, 360 employees, is the base. The difference between the two amounts, $504 - 360 = 144$, is the portion. Now apply the rate formula.

$$R = \frac{P}{B} = \frac{144}{360} = .4 = 40\%$$

40% Increase in employees

►TRYITEXERCISE 16

Solve the following problem for the rate of increase or decrease. Round to the nearest tenth of a percent when necessary.

When Mike Veteramo was promoted from supervisor to manager, he received a salary increase from $450 to $540 per week. What was the percent change in his salary?

CHECK YOUR ANSWER WITH THE SOLUTION ON PAGE 189.

EXAMPLE 17   FINDING THE RATE OF CHANGE

Over-the-Top Roofing had revenue of $122,300 in May and $103,955 in June. What is the percent change in revenue from May to June?

▶ SOLUTIONSTRATEGY

In this problem, the rate of change, the unknown, is a decrease. The original amount, $122,300, is the base. The difference between the two amounts, $122,300 − $103,955 = $18,345, is the portion. Now apply the rate formula.

$$R = \frac{P}{B} = \frac{18,345}{122,300} = .15 = 15\%$$

<u>15% Decrease in revenue</u>

▶ TRYITEXERCISE 17

Solve the following problem for the rate of increase or decrease. Round to the nearest tenth of a percent when necessary.

You are the production manager for the Berkshire Corporation. After starting a quality control program on the production line, the number of defects per day dropped from 60 to 12. Top management was very pleased with your results but wanted to know what percent decrease this change represented. Calculate the percent change in the number of defects per day.

CHECK YOUR ANSWER WITH THE SOLUTION ON PAGE 189.

6-7

DETERMINING AMOUNTS IN INCREASE OR DECREASE SITUATIONS

FINDING THE NEW AMOUNT AFTER A PERCENT CHANGE

Sometimes the original amount of something and the rate of change will be known and the new amount, after the change, will be the unknown. For example, if a store sold $5,000 in merchandise on Tuesday and 8% more on Wednesday, what are Wednesday's sales?

Keep in mind that the original amount, or beginning point, is always the base and represents 100%. Because the new amount is the total of the original amount, 100%, and the amount of increase, 8%, the rate of the new amount is 108% (100% + 8%). If the rate of change had been a decrease instead of an increase, the rate would have been 8% less than the base, or 92% (100% − 8%).

The unknown in this situation, the new amount, is the portion; therefore, we use the formula Portion = Rate × Base.

Learning Tip

Remember
- If the rate of change is an increase, *add* that rate to 100%.
- If the rate of change is a decrease, *subtract* that rate from 100%.

B-A-C-O/Shutterstock.com

STEPS FOR DETERMINING THE NEW AMOUNT AFTER A PERCENT CHANGE

STEP 1. In the formula Portion = Rate × Base, substitute the original amount, or starting point, for the base.

STEP 2. If the rate of change is an increase, add that rate to 100% to get the rate.

or

STEP 2. If the rate of change is a decrease, subtract that rate from 100% to get the rate.

STEP 3. Solve the equation for the portion.

iStock.com/Nikada

EXAMPLE 18 — FINDING THE NEW AMOUNT AFTER A PERCENT CHANGE

Affiliated Insurance estimated that the number of claims on homeowner's insurance would increase by 15% this year. If the company received 1,240 claims last year, how many can it expect this year?

▶ SOLUTION STRATEGY

Last year's claims, the original amount, is the base. Because the rate of change is an increase, we find the rate by adding that change to 100% (100% + 15% = 115%). Now, substitute these values in the portion formula.

$$P = R \times B$$
$$P = 115\% \times 1{,}240 = 1.15 \times 1{,}240 = 1{,}426$$
$$\underline{1{,}426 \text{ Homeowners' claims expected this year}}$$

▶ TRY IT EXERCISE 18

Solve the following business situation for the new amount after a percent change.

Worldwide Imports had a computer with a 525 gigabyte hard drive. If it was replaced with a new model containing 60% more capacity, how many gigabytes would the new hard drive have?

CHECK YOUR ANSWER WITH THE SOLUTION ON PAGE 189.

EXAMPLE 19 — FINDING THE NEW AMOUNT AFTER A PERCENT CHANGE

Mel's Drive-in Restaurant sold 25% fewer milk shakes this week than last week. If the drive-in sold 380 milk shakes last week, how many did it sell this week?

▶ SOLUTION STRATEGY

Because this situation represents a percent decrease, the rate is determined by subtracting the rate of decrease from 100% (100% − 25% = 75%). As usual, the base is the original amount.

$$P = R \times B$$
$$P = 75\% \times 380 = .75 \times 380 = 285$$
$$\underline{285 \text{ Milk shakes sold this week}}$$

▶ TRY IT EXERCISE 19

Solve the following business situation for the new amount after a percent change.

Overland Express has delivery trucks that cover 20% fewer miles per week during the winter snow season. If the trucks average 650 miles per week during the summer, how many miles can be expected per week during the winter?

CHECK YOUR ANSWER WITH THE SOLUTION ON PAGE 189.

FINDING THE ORIGINAL AMOUNT BEFORE A PERCENT CHANGE

In another business situation involving percent change, the new amount is known and the original amount, the base, is unknown. For example, a car dealer sold 42 cars today. If this represents a 20% increase from yesterday, how many cars were sold yesterday? Solving for the original amount is a base problem; therefore, we use the formula

$$\text{Base} = \frac{\text{Portion}}{\text{Rate}}$$

STEPS FOR DETERMINING THE ORIGINAL AMOUNT BEFORE A PERCENT CHANGE

STEP 1.   In the formula Base = Portion ÷ Rate, substitute the new amount for the portion.

STEP 2.   If the rate of change is an increase, add that rate to 100% to get the rate.

or

STEP 2.   If the rate of change is a decrease, subtract that rate from 100% to get the rate.

STEP 3.   Solve the equation for the base.

Costco Wholesale Corporation operates an international chain of membership warehouses, mainly under the "Costco Wholesale" name, that carry brand name merchandise at substantially lower prices than are typically found at conventional wholesale or retail sources.

Costco has over 400 stores in more than 40 states and in Puerto Rico. Typical annual revenues exceed $70 billion.

EXAMPLE 20   FINDING THE ORIGINAL AMOUNT

At Costco, the price of a Sony HD camcorder dropped by 15% to $425. What was the original price?

SOLUTION STRATEGY

Because this situation represents a percent decrease, the rate is determined by subtracting the rate of decrease from 100%. 100% − 15% = 85%. The portion is the new amount, $425. The original price, the base, is the unknown. Using the formula for the base,

$$B = \frac{P}{R}$$

$$B = \frac{425}{85\%} = \frac{425}{.85} = 500$$

$$\underline{\underline{\$500}}$$

▶TRY IT EXERCISE 20

Solve the following business situation for the original amount before a percent change.

The water level in a large holding tank decreased to 12 feet. If it is down 40% from last week, what was last week's level?

CHECK YOUR ANSWER WITH THE SOLUTION ON PAGE 189.

EXAMPLE 21   FINDING THE ORIGINAL AMOUNT

Viking Technologies found that after an advertising campaign, business in April increased 12% over March. If April sales were $53,760, how much were the sales in March?

▶SOLUTION STRATEGY

April's sales, the new amount, is the portion. Because the rate of change is an increase, we find the rate by adding that change to 100%. 100% + 12% = 112%.

$$B = \frac{P}{R}$$

$$B = \frac{53,760}{112\%} = \frac{53,760}{1.12} = 48,000$$

$$\underline{\underline{\$48,000}}$$

▶ **TRYITEXERCISE** 21

Solve the following business situation for the original amount before a percent change.

A John Deere harvester can cover 90 acres per day with a new direct-drive system. If this represents an increase of 20% over the conventional chain-drive system, how many acres per day were covered with the old chain-drive?

CHECK YOUR ANSWER WITH THE SOLUTION ON PAGE 189.

UNDERSTANDING AND SOLVING PROBLEMS INVOLVING PERCENTAGE POINTS

6-8

Percentage points are a way of expressing a change from an original amount to a new amount without using a percent sign. When percentage points are used, it is assumed that the original amount of percentage points is the base amount, or the whole to which the change is compared. For example, if a company's market share increased from 40% to 44% of a total market, this is expressed as an increase of 4 percentage points.

The actual percent change in business, however, is calculated by using the following formula:

$$\text{Rate of change} = \frac{\text{Change in percentage points}}{\text{Original amount of percentage points}}$$

In this illustration, the change in percentage points is 4 and the original amount of percentage points is 40; therefore,

$$\text{Rate of change} = \frac{4}{40} = .10 = \underline{10\% \text{ Increase in market share}}$$

percentage points A way of expressing a change from an original amount to a new amount without using a percent sign.

> **Learning Tip**
>
> Calculating percentage points is an application of the rate formula, Rate = Portion ÷ Base, with the change in percentage points as the *portion* and the original percentage points as the *base*.

B-A-C-O/Shutterstock.com

EXAMPLE22 SOLVING A PERCENTAGE POINTS PROBLEM

When a competitor built a better mouse trap, a company's market share dropped from 55% to 44% of the total market, a drop of 11 percentage points. What percent decrease in market share did this represent?

▶ **SOLUTIONSTRATEGY**

In this problem, the change in percentage points is 11 and the original market share is 55. Using the formula to find rate of change:

$$\text{Rate of change} = \frac{\text{Change in percentage points}}{\text{Original amount of percentage points}}$$

$$\text{Rate of change} = \frac{11}{55} = .2 = 20\%$$

<u>20% Decrease in market share</u>

▶ **TRYITEXERCISE** 22

Prior to an election, a political research firm announced that a candidate for mayor had gained 8 percentage points in the polls that month, from 20% to 28% of the total registered voters. What is the candidate's actual percent increase in voters?

CHECK YOUR ANSWER WITH THE SOLUTION ON PAGE 189.

SECTION III **6** **Review Exercises**

Solve the following increase or decrease problems for the unknown. Round decimals to hundredths and percents to the nearest tenth.

1. If a number increases from 320 to 440, what is the rate of increase?

   Portion = Increase = 440 − 320 = 120

   Base = Original number = 320 $R = \dfrac{P}{B} = \dfrac{120}{320} = .375 = \underline{\underline{37.5\%}}$

2. If a number decreases from 88 to 55, what is the rate of decrease?

3. What is the rate of change if the price of an item rises from $123 to $154?

4. What is the rate of change if the number of employees in a company decreases from 133 to 89?

5. 50 increased by 20% = _____   6. 750 increased by 60% = _____

   Rate = 100% + 20% = 120%
   Base = Original number = 50
   $P = R \times B = 1.2 \times 50 = \underline{\underline{60}}$

7. 25 decreased by 40% = _____   8. 3,400 decreased by 18.2% = _____

9. 820 increased by 400% = _____   10. $46 decreased by $10\frac{1}{2}\%$ = _____

11. Juan manages an appliance store. In July, sales were $141,800. In August, sales were $104,223. What was the rate of change? That is, what was the percent increase or percent decrease?

12. Sales at LL Boutique decreased 10% this month compared to last month. If sales this month were $166,581, what were the sales last month?

13. At a Sports King store, 850 tennis racquets were sold last season.
    a. If racquet sales are predicted to be 30% higher this season, how many racquets should be ordered from the distributor?

b. If racquet sales break down into 40% metal alloy and 60% graphite, how many of each type should be ordered?

14. At a Safeway Supermarket, the price of yellow onions dropped from $.59 per pound to $.45 per pound.

    a. What is the percent decrease in the price of onions?

    b. Tomatoes are expected to undergo the same percent decrease in price. If they currently sell for $1.09 per pound, what will be the new price of tomatoes?

Supermarket Revenues A milestone was reached in 2012 when, for the first time in history, each of the 75 companies in *Supermarket News'* list of Top 75 Food Retailers in North America had annual sales exceeding $1 billion.

Source: Based on Supermarket News

15. According to the American Association of Retired Persons, AARP, without healthcare reform, the number of people in the United States without healthcare insurance would have reached 61 million in 2020. This represents a 24.5% increase from 2010. How many people were uninsured in 2010? Round to the nearest million.

16. Housing prices in Foster County have increased by 28.5% over the price of houses five years ago.

    a. If $240,000 was the average price of a house five years ago, what is the average price of a house today?

    b. Economists predict that next year housing prices will drop by 5% in this area. Based on your answer from part **a**, what will the average price of a house be next year?

17. At Camper's Paradise, sales have increased 15%, 20%, and 10% over the past 3 years; that is, 15% 3 years ago, 20% 2 years ago, and 10% 1 year ago. If sales this year are $1,000,000, how much were sales 3 years ago? Round each year's sales to the nearest dollar.

18. According to the U.S. Census Bureau, in 1950, 39.3 million families had a child under 18 at home. A recent study found that number had decreased by 9.4%. How many families had a child under 18 at home according to this study? Round the number of millions to the nearest tenth.

19. Shareholders in an electronics company were informed that the company's market share increased from 5.4% to 8.1%, a rise of 2.7 percentage points. What percent increase in sales does this represent?

20. The chart "Chip Rivalry" illustrates the results from a survey of Intel and AMD processing chips shipped to PC makers in the years before tablet computers became very popular. Use this chart to answer the following questions:
   a. From 2004 to 2009, Intel's market share in this survey dropped by 3.7 percentage points. What percent decrease in market share does this represent? Round to the nearest tenth percent.

   b. From 2004 to 2009, AMD's market share in the survey increased by 4.7 percentage points. What percent increase in market share does this represent? Round to the nearest tenth percent.

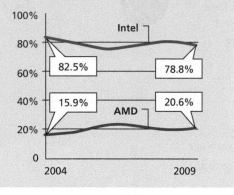

Chip Rivalry before Tablet Computers

Source: IDC

21. Economic reports indicate that during a recent manufacturing slowdown, unemployment in River Valley increased from 7.4% to 9.8%, an increase of 2.4 percentage points.
   a. What percent increase does this represent? Round to the nearest tenth of a percent.

   b. As manufacturing picked up, unemployment dropped from 9.8% to 8.1%, a decrease of 1.7 percentage points. What percent decrease does this represent? Round to the nearest hundredth of a percent.

BUSINESS DECISION: CREATING AN ECONOMIC SNAPSHOT

22. In the year 2008, the United States was just entering a major recession. You are researching how various consumer prices changed in the ten-year period starting in 2008 and ending in 2018. You have located the following chart listing various consumer purchases and their costs in 2008 and 2018, as well as the percentage change based on the 2008 prices. Unfortunately, portions of the chart are missing.

Fill in the blank spaces to complete the chart for your story. Round percent answers to the nearest tenth of a percent. Round dollar amount answers to the nearest whole dollar.

	Consumer Purchase	2008	2018	Percent Change
	Single-Family Home Median resale price (month of July)	$237,300	$290,800	_____
	Toyota Camry MSRP for the LE – manual transmission	$20,600	_____	13.2%
	Pair of Jeans Gap's Easy Fit, stonewashed	$44.50	$59.95	_____
	McDonald's Big Mac Average price at company-owned restaurants	$2.97	$3.99	_____

CHAPTER FORMULAS

The Percentage Formula

Portion = Rate × Base

Rate = Portion ÷ Base

Base = Portion ÷ Rate

Rate of Change

$$\text{Rate of change (Rate)} = \frac{\text{Amount of change (Portion)}}{\text{Original amount (Base)}}$$

Percentage Points

$$\text{Rate of change} = \frac{\text{Change in percentage points}}{\text{Original amount of percentage points}}$$

CHAPTER SUMMARY

Section I: Understanding and Converting Percents

Topic	Important Concepts	Illustrative Examples
Converting a Percent to a Decimal **Performance Objective 6-1, Page 162**	1. Remove the percent sign. 2. Move the decimal point two places to the left. *Note:* If the percent is a fraction such as $\frac{4}{5}\%$ or a mixed number such as $9\frac{1}{2}\%$, change the fraction part to a decimal; then follow Steps 1 and 2.	$28\% = .28 \qquad \frac{4}{5}\% = .8\% = .008$ $159\% = 1.59 \qquad 9\frac{1}{2}\% = 9.5\% = .095$ $.37\% = .0037$
Converting a Decimal or Whole Number to a Percent **Performance Objective 6-1, Page 163**	1. Move the decimal point two places to the right. 2. Write a percent sign after the number. *Note:* If there are fractions involved, convert them to decimals first; then proceed with Steps 1 and 2.	$.8 = 80\% \qquad 3 = 300\%$ $2.9 = 290\% \qquad \frac{1}{2} = .5 = 50\%$ $.075 = 7.5\%$
Converting a Percent to a Fraction **Performance Objective 6-2, Page 164**	1. Remove the percent sign. 2. *(If the percent is a whole number)* Write a fraction with the percent as the numerator and 100 as the denominator. Reduce to lowest terms. or 2. *(If the percent is a fraction)* Multiply the number by $\frac{1}{100}$ and reduce to lowest terms. or 2. *(If the percent is a decimal)* Convert it to a fraction and multiply by $\frac{1}{100}$. Reduce to lowest terms.	$7\% = \frac{7}{100}$ $60\% = \frac{60}{100} = \frac{3}{5}$ $400\% = \frac{400}{100} = 4$ $2.1\% = 2\frac{1}{10}\% = \frac{21}{10} \times \frac{1}{100} = \frac{21}{1,000}$ $5\frac{3}{4}\% = \frac{23}{4} \times \frac{1}{100} = \frac{23}{400}$
Converting a Fraction or Mixed Number to a Percent **Performance Objective 6-2, Page 164**	1. Change the fraction to a decimal by dividing the numerator by the denominator. 2. Move the decimal point two places to the right. 3. Write a percent sign after the number.	$\frac{1}{8} = .125 = 12.5\%$ $\frac{16}{3} = 5.333 = 533.3\%$ $12\frac{3}{4} = 12.75 = 1,275\%$

Section II: Using the Percentage Formula to Solve Business Problems

Topic	Important Concepts	Illustrative Examples
Solving for the Portion Performance Objective 6-3, Page 168	The portion is the number that represents a part of the base. To solve for portion, use the formula $$\text{Portion} = \text{Rate} \times \text{Base}$$	15% of Kwik-Mix Concrete employees got raises this year. If 1,800 individuals work for the company, how many got raises? $$P = .15 \times 1,800 = 270$$ 270 Employees got raises this year
Solving for the Rate Performance Objective 6-4, Page 170	The rate is the variable that describes what part of the base is represented by the portion. It is always the term with the percent sign. To solve for rate, use the formula $$\text{Rate} = \frac{\text{Portion}}{\text{Base}}$$	28 out of 32 warehouses owned by Metro Distributors passed safety inspection. What percent of the warehouses passed? $$\text{Rate} = \frac{28}{32} = .875 = 87.5\%$$ 87.5% Passed inspection
Solving for the Base Performance Objective 6-5, Page 172	Base is the variable that represents 100%, the starting point, or the whole thing. To solve for base, use the formula $$\text{Base} = \frac{\text{Portion}}{\text{Rate}}$$	34.3% of Thrifty Tile's sales are from customers west of the Mississippi River. If those sales last year were $154,350, what are the company's total sales? $$\text{Base} = \frac{154,350}{.343} = \$450,000$$ Total sales = $450,000

Section III: Solving Other Business Problems Involving Percents

Topic	Important Concepts	Illustrative Examples
Determining Rate of Increase or Decrease Performance Objective 6-6, Page 177	1. Identify the original and the new amounts and find the difference between them. 2. Using the rate formula $R = P \div B$, substitute the difference from Step 1 for the portion and the original amount for the base. 3. Solve the equation for R. $$\text{Rate of change } (R) = \frac{\text{Amount of change } (P)}{\text{Original amount } (B)}$$	A price rises from $45 to $71. What is the rate of increase? $$\text{Portion} = 71 - 45 = 26$$ $$\text{Rate} = \frac{P}{B} = \frac{26}{45} = .5778 = 57.8\%$$ What is the rate of decrease from 152 to 34? $$\text{Portion} = 152 - 34 = 118$$ $$\text{Rate} = \frac{P}{B} = \frac{118}{152} = .776 = 77.6\%$$
Determining New Amount after a Percent Change Performance Objective 6-7, Page 180	Solving for the new amount is a portion problem; therefore, we use the formula $$\text{Portion} = \text{Rate} \times \text{Base}$$ 1. Substitute the original amount for the base. 2. If the rate of change is an increase, add that rate to 100%. or 2. If the rate of change is a decrease, subtract that rate from 100%.	Prestige Plastics projects a 24% increase in sales for next year. If sales this year were $172,500, what sales can be expected next year? $$\text{Rate} = 100\% + 24\% = 124\%$$ $$P = R \times B = 1.24 \times 172,500$$ $$P = 213,900$$ Projected sales = $213,900
Determining Original Amount before a Percent Change Performance Objective 6-7, Page 182	Solving for the original amount is a base problem; therefore, we use the formula $$\text{Base} = \frac{\text{Portion}}{\text{Rate}}$$ 1. Substitute the new amount for the portion. 2. If the rate of change is an increase, add that rate to 100%. or 2. If the rate of change is a decrease, subtract that rate from 100%.	If a DVD was marked down by 30% to $16.80, what was the original price? $$\text{Portion} = 100\% - 30\% = 70\%$$ $$\text{Base} = \frac{P}{R} = \frac{16.80}{.7} = 24$$ Original price = $24

Section III (continued)

Topic	Important Concepts	Illustrative Examples
Solving Problems Involving Percentage Points **Performance Objective 6-8, Page 183**	Percentage points are a way of expressing a change from an original amount to a new amount without using the percent sign. When percentage points are used, it is assumed that the base amount, 100%, stays constant. The actual percent change in business, however, is calculated by using the formula Rate of change = $\dfrac{\text{Change in percentage points}}{\text{Original percentage points}}$	After an intensive advertising campaign, General Industries' market share increased from 21 to 27%, an increase of 6 percentage points. What percent increase in business does this represent? % change = $\dfrac{6}{21}$ = .2857 = 28.6% % increase in business = 28.6%

TRY IT: EXERCISE SOLUTIONS FOR CHAPTER 6

1a. 27% = .27

1b. 472% = 4.72

1c. 93.7% = .937

1d. .81% = .0081

1e. $12\dfrac{3}{4}\%$ = 12.75% = .1275

1f. $\dfrac{7}{8}\%$ = .875% = .00875

2a. .8 = 80%

2b. 1.4 = 140%

2c. .0023 = .23%

2d. $.016\dfrac{2}{5}$ = .0164 = 1.64%

2e. 19 = 1,900%

2f. $.57\dfrac{2}{3}$ = .5767 = 57.67%

3a. 9% = $\dfrac{9}{100}$

3b. 23% = $\dfrac{23}{100}$

3c. 75% = $\dfrac{75}{100} = \dfrac{3}{4}$

3d. 225% = $\dfrac{225}{100} = 2\dfrac{25}{100} = 2\dfrac{1}{4}$

3e. 8.7% = $8\dfrac{7}{10}\% = \dfrac{87}{10} \times \dfrac{1}{100} = \dfrac{87}{1,000}$

3f. 1,000% = $\dfrac{1,000}{100}$ = 10

4a. $\dfrac{1}{5}$ = .2 = 20%

4b. $\dfrac{70}{200}$ = .35 = 35%

4c. $\dfrac{23}{5} = 4\dfrac{3}{5}$ = 4.6 = 460%

4d. $6\dfrac{9}{10}$ = 6.9 = 690%

4e. $\dfrac{45}{54}$ = .8333 = 83.33%

4f. $140\dfrac{1}{8}$ = 140.125 = 14,012.5%

5. $P = R \times B$ = .55 × 980 = 539

6. $P = R \times B$ = .72 × 3,200 = 2,304

7a. $P = R \times B$ = .16 × 1,250 = 200 Salespeople

7b. $P = R \times B$ = .15 × 148,500 = $22,275 Down payment

8. $R = \dfrac{P}{B} = \dfrac{9}{21}$ = .4285 = 42.9%

9. $R = \dfrac{P}{B} = \dfrac{67}{142}$ = .4718 = 47.2%

10a. $R = \dfrac{P}{B} = \dfrac{5,400}{18,000}$ = .3 = 30% Completed

100% − 30% = 70% Remains

10b. $R = \dfrac{P}{B} = \dfrac{5,518}{8,900}$ = .62 = 62% Suits

11. $B = \dfrac{P}{R} = \dfrac{690}{.4}$ = 1,725

12. $B = \dfrac{P}{R} = \dfrac{550}{.88}$ = $625

13a. $B = \dfrac{P}{R} = \dfrac{126}{.35}$ = 360 Motors

13b. $B = \dfrac{P}{R} = \dfrac{3,420}{.75}$ = 4,560 Reams of paper

14. Portion = Increase = 948 − 650 = 298

Base = Original number = 650

$R = \dfrac{P}{B} = \dfrac{298}{650}$ = .45846 = 45.8% Increase

15. Portion = Decrease = 21 − 15 = 6

Base = Original number = 21

$R = \dfrac{P}{B} = \dfrac{6}{21}$ = .2857 = 28.6% Decrease

16. Portion = Increase = $540 − $450 = $90

Base = Original number = $450

$R = \dfrac{P}{B} = \dfrac{90}{450}$ = .2 = 20% Increase

17. Portion = Decrease = 60 − 12 = 48

Base = Original number = 60

$R = \dfrac{P}{B} = \dfrac{48}{60}$ = .8 = 80% Decrease

18. Rate $= 100\% + 60\% = 160\%$

$P = R \times B = 1.6 \times 525 = \underline{840}$ Gigabytes

19. Rate $= 100\% - 20\% = 80\%$

$P = R \times B = .8 \times 650 = \underline{520}$ Miles per week

20. Rate $= 100\% - 40\% = 60\%$

$B = \dfrac{P}{R} = \dfrac{12}{.6} = \underline{20}$ Feet

21. Rate $= 100\% + 20\% = 120\%$

$B = \dfrac{P}{R} = \dfrac{90}{1.2} = \underline{75}$ Acres per day

22. $R = \dfrac{P}{B} = \dfrac{8}{20} = .4 = \underline{40\%}$ Increase in voters

CONCEPT REVIEW

1. A percent is a way of expressing a part of a(n)_____. (6-1)

2. In previous chapters, we expressed these parts as _____ and _____. (6-1)

3. Percent means "parts per _____." The percent sign is written as _____. (6-1)

4. To convert a percent to a decimal, we remove the percent sign and _____ by 100. (6-1)

5. To convert a decimal to a percent, we multiply by 100 and write a(n) _____ sign after the number. (6-1)

6. To convert a percent to a fraction, we remove the percent sign and place the number over _____. (6-2)

7. List the steps for converting a fraction to a percent. (6-2)

8. The three basic parts of the percentage formula are the _____, _____, and _____. (6-3)

9. The percentage formula is written as _____ . (6-3)

10. In the percentage formula, the _____ is the variable with the percent sign or the word *percent*. (6-4)

11. In the percentage formula, the _____ represents 100%, or the whole thing. In a sentence, it follows the word _____. (6-5)

12. Write the formula for the rate of change. (6-6)

13. When calculating amounts in percent change situations, the rate of change is added to 100% if the change is a(n) _____ and subtracted from 100% if the change is a(n) _____. (6-7)

14. Percentage _____ are a way of expressing a change from an original amount to a new amount without using a percent sign. (6-8)

ASSESSMENT TEST

Convert the following percents to decimals.

1. 76%

2. $3\dfrac{3}{4}\%$

3. 59.68%

4. 422%

5. $\dfrac{9}{16}\%$

Convert the following decimals or whole numbers to percents.

6. 12.6

7. .681

8. 53

9. $24\dfrac{4}{5}$

10. .0929

Convert the following percents to reduced fractions, mixed numbers, or whole numbers.

11. 19%   **12.** 217%   **13.** 7.44%   **14.** 126%   **15.** $25\frac{2}{5}\%$

Convert each of the following fractions or mixed numbers to percents.

16. $\frac{4}{5}$ **17.** $\frac{5}{9}$ **18.** $\frac{33}{4}$ **19.** $56\frac{3}{10}$ **20.** $\frac{745}{100}$

Solve the following for the portion, rate, or base, rounding decimals to hundredths and percents to the nearest tenth when necessary.

21. 32% of 5,500 =   **22.** 56 is _____ % of 125   **23.** 91 is 88% of _____

24. What number is 45% of 680?   **25.** $233.91 is what percent of $129.95?

26. 1,450 is 125% of _____   **27.** 60 increased by 15% = _____

28. If a number increases from 47 to 70.5, what is the rate of increase?

29. What is the base if the portion is 444 and the rate is 15%?

EXCEL 2

30. What is the portion if the base is 900 and the rate is $12\frac{3}{4}\%$?

EXCEL 3

31. What is 100% of 1,492?   **32.** 340 decreased by 35% = _____

Solve the following word problems for the unknown. Round decimals to hundredths and percents to the nearest tenth when necessary.

33. An ad for Target reads, "This week only, all electronics 35% off!" If a television set normally sells for $449.95, what is the amount of the savings?

34. If 453 runners out of 620 completed a marathon, what percent of the runners finished the race?

EXCEL 2

35. Last year Keystone's corporate jet required $23,040 in maintenance and repairs.

   a. If this represents 32% of the total operating costs of the airplane, what was the total cost to fly the plane for the year?

b. If the plane flew 300,000 miles last year, what is the cost per mile to operate the plane?

c. Sky King Leasing offered a deal whereby it would operate the plane for Keystone for only $0.18 per mile. What is the percent decrease in operating expense per mile being offered by Sky King?

Jets for Sale

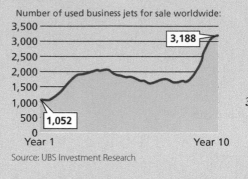

Number of used business jets for sale worldwide:

3,188

1,052

Year 1   Year 10

Source: UBS Investment Research

d. In one ten-year period, the sales of used business jets rose and fell and then rose again. Use the chart "Jets for Sale" to calculate the rate of increase of jets sold in year 10 compared to year 1. Round to the nearest whole percent.

36. A letter carrier can deliver mail to 112 homes per hour by walking and 168 homes per hour by driving.

   a. By what percent is productivity increased by driving?

   b. If a new ZIP Code system improves driving productivity by 12.5%, what is the new number of homes per hour for driving?

37. Last year the Tundra Corporation had sales of $343,500. If this year's sales are forecast to be $415,700, what is the percent increase in sales?

38. After a 12% pay raise, Kristen Fischer now earns $31,360. What was her salary before the raise?

39. According to Autodata research, in a recent year, Toyota sold 130,307 vehicles in the United States in the month of November.

   a. If November sales increased 2.6% one year later, how many vehicles were sold in that month.

   b. The research also indicated that in that same year Toyota's November U.S. market share increased from 17.4% to 17.9%, an increase of 0.5 percentage points. What percent does this increase represent?

40. Three of every seven sales transactions at Dollar Discount are on credit cards. What percent of the transactions are *not* credit card sales?

41. A pre-election survey shows that an independent presidential candidate has increased his popularity from 26.5% to 31.3% of the electorate, an increase of 4.8 percentage points. What percent does this increase represent?

42. By what percent is a 100-watt lightbulb brighter than a 60-watt bulb?

43. In 1998, a 30-second television advertisement on the Super Bowl telecast cost $1.3 million. In 2010, the price of a 30-second ad had increased by 132% over the 1998 price. How much was a Super Bowl ad in 2010? Write your answer in numerical form.

44. Michael Reeves, an ice cream vendor, pays $17.50 for a five-gallon container of premium ice cream. From this quantity, he sells 80 scoops at $0.90 per scoop. If he sold smaller scoops, he could sell 98 scoops from the same container; however, he could charge only $0.80 per scoop. As his accountant, you are asked the following questions.

  a. If Michael switches to the smaller scoops, by how much will his profit per container go up or down? (Profit = Sales − Expenses)

  b. By what percent will the profit change? Round to the nearest tenth of a percent.

45. An insurance adjuster for UPS found that 12% of a shipment was damaged in transit. If the damaged goods amounted to $4,870, what was the total value of the shipment?

46. Morley Fast, a contractor, built a warehouse complex in Canmore for the following costs: land, $12,000; concrete and steel, $34,500; plumbing and electrical, $48,990; general carpentry and roof, $42,340; and other expenses, $34,220.

  a. What percent of the total cost is represented by each category of expenses?

  b. When the project was completed, Morley sold the entire complex for 185% of its cost. What was the selling price of the complex?

Use the chart "The Rise of E-Books in Education" for Exercises 47–49.

47. What was the rate of change in education e-book sales from 2008 to 2013? Round to the nearest tenth of a percent.

48. What were the sales of education e-books in 2009 if they were 10.3% higher than 2008? Round to the nearest tenth of a million.

49. If the 2013 figure represents a 19.6% increase from 2012, what are the projected education e-book sales for 2012? Round to the nearest tenth of a million.

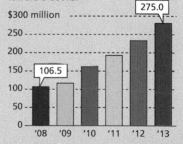

The Rise of E-Books in Education
This chart shows historical data reflecting the beginnings of a significant trend toward e-books.

Source: Albert N. Greco, Fordham Graduate School of Business Administration

BUSINESS DECISION: ALLOCATING OVERHEAD EXPENSES

50. You are the owner of a chain of three successful restaurants with the following number of seats in each location: airport, 340 seats; downtown, 218 seats; and suburban, 164 seats.

    a. If the liability insurance premium is $16,000 per year, how much of that premium should be allocated to each of the restaurants based on percent of total seating capacity? Round each percent to the nearest tenth.

    b. If you open a fourth location at the beach that has 150 seats and the liability insurance premium increases by 18%, what is the new allocation of insurance premium among the four locations? If necessary round percents to the nearest tenth.

    c. (Optional) What other expenses could be allocated to the four restaurants?

    d. (Optional) What other ways, besides seating capacity, could you use to allocate expenses?

COLLABORATIVE LEARNING ACTIVITY

Percents—The Language of Business

For emphasis and illustration, business percentage figures, when printed, are frequently presented in circle, bar, and line chart format. Charts add a compelling element to otherwise plain "numbers in the news."

As a team, search business publications, annual reports, and the Internet to find 10 interesting and varied examples of business percentage figures being presented in chart form. Share your findings with the class.

Business Math JOURNAL

Green Numbers – The Power of One

According to Jim Hackler, theurbaneenvironmentalist.com, "the people of the United States represent less than 5 percent of the world's population—yet that 5 percent consumes more than a quarter of our planet's resources. If the rest of the world rose to the U.S. level of consumption, four additional planets would be needed to supply the resources and absorb the waste!"

Here's a look at some of Jim's intriguing findings, "how a single act can help (or hurt) the environment—especially when it's shared by millions."

It's too Darn Hot

If the thermostat in every house in America were lowered **1 degree Fahrenheit** during the winter, the nation would save **230 million barrels of crude oil**—enough to fill an oil tanker 400 times.

Shower Power

If 40 million people were to spend **one minute less** each day in the shower over their lifetime, they would save **4 trillion gallons** of water—the total amount of snow and rain that falls over the entire lower 48 states in a day.

Straight Flush

If home builders had installed **one dual-flush toilet** instead of a standard low-flow toilet in every new house they built in 2008, they would have saved **1.65 billion gallons of water** a year.

In the Can

One soft drink can recycled by each elementary school student in America would save **24.8 million cans**. That would be enough aluminum to create 21 Boeing 737 airplanes.

Virtual Payment

If every American switched to receiving just **one bill** as an electronic statement instead of a paper statement, the one-time savings would be **217,800,000 sheets**—enough to blanket the island of Key West in a single layer of paper.

Wrapacious

One out of every 3 pounds of the waste that Americans generate is for packaging, which each year adds up to **77 million tons**—enough to fill the Louisiana Superdome 37 times.

Arthimedes/Shutterstock.com

Bath Party

If every American collected **1 gallon of water** once a week while waiting for the shower or bathwater to get hot and used it to water his or her houseplants, the total saved would be **15.8 billion gallons of water** a year—enough to fill the Reflecting Pool at the National Mall in Washington, D.C. 2,338 times.

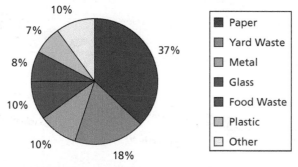

Composition of an Average Dump

- Paper — 37%
- Yard Waste — 18%
- Metal — 10%
- Glass — 10%
- Food Waste — 8%
- Plastic — 7%
- Other — 10%

Source: Green Numbers, "The Power of 1," Jim Hackler, *Sky Magazine*, March 2008, pages 48–51

Issues & Activities

1. Assume that a dump received a total of 750,000 pounds of waste last week. Use the chart above to allocate the number of pounds of waste for each category.
2. If recycling one glass bottle or jar saves enough electricity to light a 100-watt bulb for four hours, how many bottles or jars will it take to light the bulb for a year?
3. Americans use 4 million plastic bottles every hour, but only 25% of plastic bottles are recycled. At that rate, how many plastic bottles are recycled in a week?
4. In teams, research the Internet to find current trends in "greening of America" statistics. List your sources and visually report your findings to the class.

Brainteaser – "Buy the Numbers"

You recently purchased a 100-unit apartment building. As part of a fix-up project, you have decided to install new numbers on each front door. If the apartments are numbered from 1 to 100, how many nines will you need to buy?

See the end of Appendix A for the solution.

Invoices, Trade Discounts, and Cash Discounts

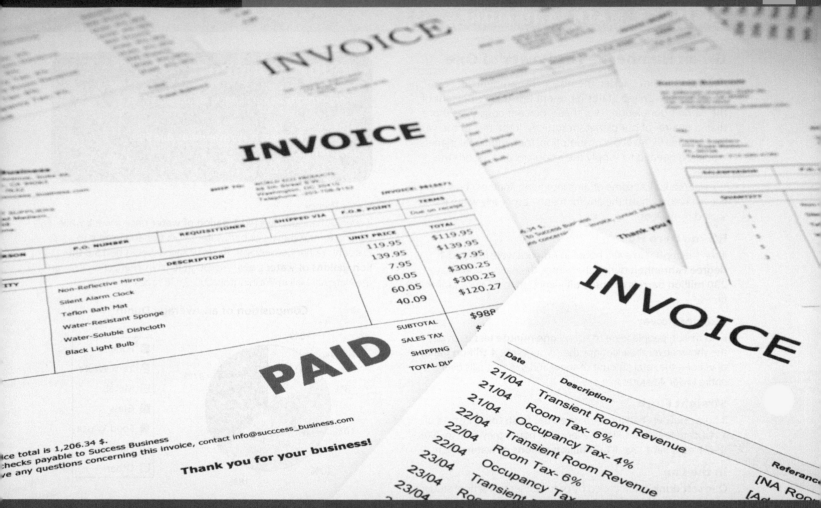

PERFORMANCE OBJECTIVES

THE INVOICE

In business, merchandise is bought and sold many times as it passes from the manufacturer through wholesalers and retailers to the final consumer. A bill of sale, or an **invoice**, is a business document used to keep track of these sales and purchases. From the seller's point of view, they are sales invoices; from the buyer's point of view, they are purchase invoices or purchase orders.

Invoices are a comprehensive record of a sales transaction. They show what merchandise or services have been sold, to whom, in what quantities, at what price, and under what conditions and terms. They vary in style and format from company to company, but most contain essentially the same information. Invoices are used extensively in business, and it is important to be able to read and understand them. In this chapter, you learn how businesses use invoices and the math applications that relate to them.

invoice A document detailing a sales transaction that contains a list of goods shipped or services rendered with an account of all costs.

READING AND UNDERSTANDING THE PARTS OF AN INVOICE

7-1

Exhibit 7-1 shows a typical format used in business for an invoice. The important parts have been labeled and are explained in Exhibit 7-2. Some of the terms have page references, which direct you to the sections in this chapter that further explain those terms and their business math applications. Exhibit 7-2 also presents some of the most commonly used invoice abbreviations. These pertain to merchandise quantities and measurements.

With some practice, these terms and abbreviations will become familiar to you. Take some time to look them over before you continue reading.

SHIPPING TERMS

Two frequently used shipping terms that you should become familiar with are **F.O.B. shipping point** and **F.O.B. destination**. **F.O.B.** means "free on board" or "freight on board." These terms define the shipping charges and when the title (ownership) of the goods is transferred from the seller to the buyer. Ownership becomes important when insurance claims must be filed due to problems in shipment.

F.O.B. Shipping Point   When the terms are F.O.B. shipping point, the buyer pays the shipping company directly. The merchandise title is transferred to the buyer at the manufacturer's factory or at a shipping point such as a railroad freight yard or air freight terminal. From this point, the buyer is responsible for the merchandise. It is common for the seller to prepay the freight and add the amount to the invoice.

F.O.B. Destination   When the shipping terms are F.O.B. destination, the seller is responsible for prepaying the shipping charges to the destination. The destination is usually the buyer's store or warehouse. Unless prices are quoted as "delivered," the seller then bills the buyer on the invoice for the shipping charges.

Sometimes the freight terms are stated as F.O.B. with the name of a city. For example, if the seller is in Fort Worth and the buyer is in New York, F.O.B. Fort Worth means the title is transferred in Fort Worth and the buyer pays the shipping charges from Fort Worth to New York. If the terms are F.O.B. New York, the seller pays the shipping charges to New York and then bills the buyer for those charges on the invoice. Exhibit 7-3, Shipping Terms, on page 200, illustrates these transactions.

F.O.B. shipping point The buyer pays all transportation charges from the vendor's location.

F.O.B. destination The seller pays all the shipping charges to the buyer's store or warehouse and then bills the buyer for these charges on the invoice.

F.O.B. Term used in quoting shipping charges meaning "free on board" or "freight on board."

Franck Boston/Shutterstock.com

When companies ship and receive merchandise, invoices and purchase orders are used to record the details of the transaction.

EXHIBIT 7-1 Typical Invoice Format

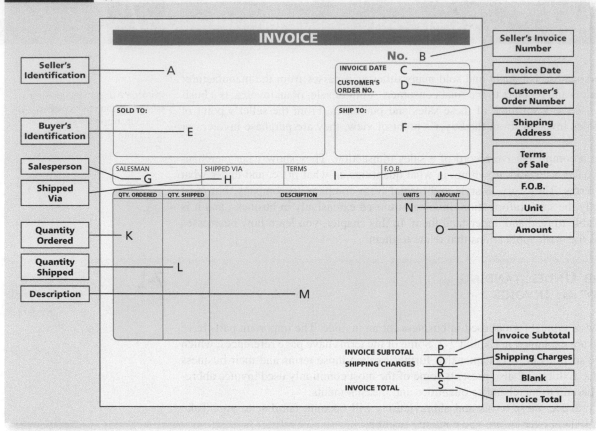

EXHIBIT 7-2 Invoice Terminology and Abbreviations

Invoice Terminology

A   Seller's Identification— Name, address, and logo or corporate symbol of the seller

B   Seller's Invoice Number— Seller's identification number of the transaction

C   Invoice Date—Date the invoice was written

D   Customer's Order Number— Buyer's identification number of the transaction

E   Buyer's Identification—Name and mailing address of the buyer

F   Shipping Address—Address where merchandise will be shipped

G   Salesperson—Name of salesperson credited with the sale

H   Shipped Via—Name of shipping company handling the shipment

I   Terms—Terms of sale— Section detailing date of payment and cash discount

J   F.O.B.—"Free on board"— Section detailing who pays the shipping company and when title is transferred

K   Quantity Ordered—Number of units ordered

L   Quantity Shipped—Number of units shipped

M   Description—Detailed description of the merchandise, including model numbers

N   Unit—Price per unit of merchandise

O   Amount—Extended total—Quantity in units times the unit price for each line

P   Invoice Subtotal—Total of the Amount column— Merchandise total

Q   Shipping Charges—Cost to physically transport the merchandise from the seller to the buyer

R   Blank Line—Line used for other charges such as insurance or handling

S   Invoice Total—Total amount of the invoice—Includes merchandise plus all other charges

Invoice Abbreviations

ea	each	pr	pair	in.	inch	oz	ounce
dz or doz	dozen	dm or drm	drum	ft	foot	g or gr	gram
gr or gro	gross	bbl	barrel	yd	yard	kg	kilogram
bx	box	sk	sack	mm	millimeter	pt	pint
cs	case	@	at	cm	centimeter	qt	quart
ct or crt	crate	C	100 items	m	meter	gal	gallon
ctn or cart	carton	M	1,000 items	lb	pound	cwt	hundred weight

EXAMPLE 1 — IDENTIFYING PARTS OF AN INVOICE

From the following Whole Grain Cereal Co. invoice, identify the indicated parts.

a. Seller _____
b. Invoice number _____
c. Invoice date _____
d. Customer order # _____
e. Buyer _____
f. Terms of sale _____
g. Shipping address

h. Salesperson _____
i. Shipped via _____
j. Insurance _____
k. Shipping charges _____
l. Invoice subtotal _____
m. Unit price—Fruit and Nut Flakes _____
n. Invoice total

▶ SOLUTION STRATEGY

a. Seller — Organic Grain Cereal Co.
b. Invoice number — 2112
c. Invoice date — August 19, 20XX
d. Customer order # — B-1623
e. Buyer — Kroger Supermarkets
f. Terms of sale — Net - 45 days

g. Shipping address — 1424 Peachtree Rd

h. Salesperson — H. L. Mager
i. Shipped via — Terminal Transport
j. Insurance — $33.00
k. Shipping charges — $67.45
l. Invoice subtotal — $2,227.05
m. Unit price—Fruit and Nut Flakes — $19.34
n. Invoice total — $2,327.50

Dollars AND Sense

The U.S. Department of Transportation's Maritime Administration has published a comprehensive "Glossary of Shipping Terms" that you may encounter in your business when dealing with shipping companies. This Glossary can be found at www.marad.dot.gov/documents/Glossary_final.pdf

Note: The *G* in *Glossary* is case-sensitive.

iStock.com/vreemous

INVOICE

Organic Grain Cereal Co.
697 Canyon Road
Boulder, CO 80304

No. 2112

| INVOICE DATE | August 19, 20XX |
| CUSTOMER'S ORDER NO. | B-1623 |

SOLD TO:
KROGER SUPERMARKETS
565 North Avenue
Atlanta, Georgia 30348

SHIP TO:
DISTRIBUTION CENTER
1424 Peachtree Road
Atlanta, Georgia 30341

SALESMAN	SHIPPED VIA	TERMS	F.O.B.
H. L. Mager	Terminal Transport	Net - 45 Days	Boulder, CO

QTY. ORDERED	QTY. SHIPPED	DESCRIPTION		UNIT	AMOUNT	
55 cs.	55 cs.	Corn Crunchies	24 ounce	$22.19	$1220	45
28 cs.	28 cs.	Fruit and Nut Flakes	24 ounce	19.34	541	52
41 cs.	22 cs.	Rice and Wheat Flakes	16 ounce	21.14	465	08

INVOICE SUBTOTAL	2,227.05
SHIPPING CHARGES	67.45
INSURANCE	33.00
INVOICE TOTAL	$2,327.50

▶ TRY IT EXERCISE 1

From the following FotoFair invoice, identify the indicated parts.

a. Buyer _____
b. Invoice number _____
c. Invoice date _____
d. Amount—Pocket Pro 55 _____
e. Seller _____
f. Terms of sale _____
g. Shipping address _____

h. Salesperson _____
i. Shipped via _____
j. F.O.B. _____
k. Shipping charges _____
l. Invoice subtotal _____
m. Unit price—Pocket Pro 75 _____
n. Invoice total _____

CHECK YOUR ANSWERS WITH THE SOLUTIONS ON PAGE 231.

INVOICE

FotoFair Distributors
3900 Crescent Way
Knoxville, TN 37996

No. 44929

INVOICE DATE	November 27, 20XX
CUSTOMER'S ORDER NO.	09022

SOLD TO:	SHIP TO:
SHUTTERBUG CAMERA SHOPS 1518 N.W. 123rd Street Chicago, Illinois 60613	Warehouse 1864 N.W. 123rd Street Chicago, Illinois 60613

SALESMAN	SHIPPED VIA	TERMS	F.O.B.
J. Herman	Federal Express	Net - 30 Days	Knoxville, TN

QTY. ORDERED	QTY. SHIPPED	DESCRIPTION	UNIT	AMOUNT
12	12	Pocket Pro 55—digital camera	$260.00	$3,120 00
6	6	Pocket Pro 75—digital camera	345.00	2,070 00
15	15	Compact flash memory cards	24.40	366 00
8	8	Tripods	9.60	76 80

Invoice Subtotal	5,632.80
Shipping Charges	125.00
Invoice Total	$5,757.80

7-2 EXTENDING AND TOTALING AN INVOICE

invoice subtotal The amount of all merchandise or services on the invoice before adjustments.

invoice total The final amount due from the buyer to the seller.

Extending an invoice is the process of computing the value in the Total or Amount column for each line of the invoice. This number represents the total dollar amount of each type of merchandise or service being purchased. The **invoice subtotal** is the amount of all items on the invoice before shipping and handling charges; insurance; and other adjustments such as discounts, returns, and credits. The **invoice total** is the final amount due from the buyer to the seller.

EXHIBIT 7-3 Shipping Terms

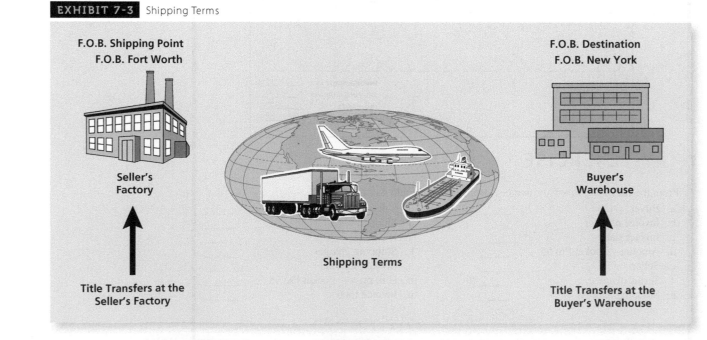

F.O.B. Shipping Point
F.O.B. Fort Worth

F.O.B. Destination
F.O.B. New York

Seller's Factory

Buyer's Warehouse

Shipping Terms

Title Transfers at the Seller's Factory

Title Transfers at the Buyer's Warehouse

STEPS TO EXTEND AND TOTAL AN INVOICE

STEP 1. For each line of the invoice, multiply the number of items by the cost per item.

Extended total = Number of items × Cost per item

STEP 2. Add all extended totals to get the invoice subtotal.

STEP 3. Calculate the invoice total by adding the freight charges, insurance, and any other charges to the subtotal.

EXAMPLE2 EXTENDING AND TOTALING AN INVOICE

From the following invoice for Computer Mart, extend each line to the Total column and calculate the invoice subtotal and total.

Stock #	Quantity	Unit	Merchandise Description	Unit Price	Total
4334	17	ea.	13" Monitors	$244.00	_____
1217	8	ea.	17" Monitors	525.80	_____
2192	2	doz.	USB Cables	24.50	_____
5606	1	bx.	Blu-ray Discs	365.90	_____
				Invoice Subtotal	
				Shipping Charges	$244.75
				Invoice Total	_____

►SOLUTIONSTRATEGY

					Total
13" Monitors	17	×	$244.00	=	$4,148.00
17" Monitors	8	×	525.80	=	4,206.40
USB Cables	2	×	24.50	=	49.00
Blu-ray Discs	1	×	365.90	=	365.90
			Invoice Subtotal		$8,769.30
			Shipping Charges		+ 244.75
			Invoice Total		$9,014.05

►TRYITEXERCISE 2

From the following invoice for The Kitchen Connection, extend each line to the Total column and calculate the invoice subtotal and total.

Stock #	Quantity	Unit	Merchandise Description	Unit Price	Total
R443	125	ea.	Food Processors	$89.00	_____
B776	24	ea.	Microwave Ovens	225.40	_____
Z133	6	doz.	12" Mixers	54.12	_____
Z163	1	bx.	Mixer Covers	166.30	_____
				Invoice Subtotal	
				Shipping Charges	$194.20
				Invoice Total	_____

CHECK YOUR ANSWERS WITH THE SOLUTIONS ON PAGE 231.

iStock.com/Nikada

SECTION I 7 REVIEW EXERCISES

What word is represented by each of the following abbreviations?

1. bx.   Box   2. pt _____   3. drm. _____   4. kg _____
5. gro.   Gross   6. oz _____   7. M. _____   8. cwt _____

Using the Panorama Products invoice below, extend each line to the Amount column and calculate the subtotal and total. Then answer Questions 9–22. (*Note:* Although 26 boxes of 2" reflective tape were ordered, only 11 boxes were shipped. Charge only for the boxes shipped.)

9. Seller   **Panorama Products**   10. Invoice number   **R-7431**

11. Invoice date   _____   12. Cust. order #   _____

13. Buyer   _____   14. Terms of sale   _____

15. Shipping address   _____   16. Salesperson   _____

17. Shipped via   _____   18. Insurance   _____

19. Shipping charges   _____   20. Unit price—2" Tape   _____

21. Invoice subtotal   _____   22. Invoice total   _____

IN THE Business World

Frequently, merchandise that is ordered from vendors is "out of stock" and goes into back-order status.

As a general rule, companies charge only for the merchandise that is shipped.

rrguest/Shutterstock.com

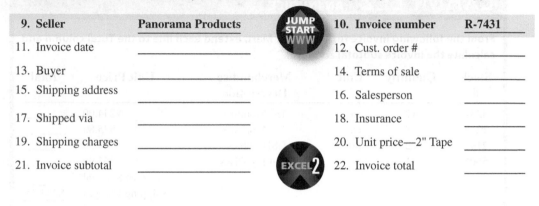

INVOICE				

No. R-7431

Panorama Products
486 5th Avenue
Eureka, CA 95501

INVOICE DATE   June 16, 20XX
CUSTOMER'S ORDER NO.   12144

SOLD TO:
J. M. Hardware Supply
2051 West Adams Blvd.
Lansing, MI 48901

SHIP TO:
SAME

SALESMAN	SHIPPED VIA	TERMS	F.O.B.
H. Marshall	Gilbert Trucking	Net 30 Days	Effingham, IL

QTY. ORDERED	QTY. SHIPPED	DESCRIPTION	UNIT	AMOUNT
16 cases	16 cases	Masking Tape 1/2" Standard	$21.90	
12 cases	12 cases	Masking Tape 1 1/2" Standard	26.79	
26 boxes	11 boxes	2" Reflective Tape	88.56	
37 cases	37 cases	Sandpaper Assorted	74.84	

INVOICE SUBTOTAL _____
SHIPPING CHARGES $61.45
_____
INVOICE TOTAL _____

23.

Stock #	Quantity	Unit	Description	Unit Price	Total
424	11	ea.	24" Bird Feeder	$23.00	_____
121	31	10 lbs.	Standard Feed	11.00	_____
504	37	ea.	Wren House	12.00	_____
				Invoice Subtotal	_____
				Shipping Charges	$47.00
				Invoice Total	_____

BUSINESS DECISION: MANAGING MERCHANDISE

24. You are the store manager for The Bedding Warehouse. The invoice below is due for payment to one of your vendors, Hamilton Mills.

   a. Check the invoice for errors and correct any you find.

   b. Your warehouse manager reports that there were three king-size sheets and five queen-size sheets returned, along with four packages of queen pillow cases. Calculate the revised total due.

   c. The vendor has offered a 4% early payment discount that applies only to the merchandise, not the shipping or insurance. What is the amount of the discount?

   d. What is the new balance due after the discount?

Retail store managers manage stores that specialize in selling a specific line of merchandise, such as groceries, meat, liquor, apparel, furniture, automobile parts, electronic items, or household appliances.

INVOICE

Hamilton Mills
115 Rock Creek Road
Charlotte, North Carolina 28235

No. 49485

INVOICE DATE July 9, 20XX

CUSTOMER'S ORDER NO. 49485

SOLD TO:

The Bedding Warehouse
406 Maple Road
Franklin, VA 23851

SHIP TO:

SAME

SALESMAN	SHIPPED VIA	TERMS	F.O.B.
	Federal Express	Net 30 Days	Charlotte, N.C.

QTY. ORDERED	QTY. SHIPPED	DESCRIPTION	UNIT	AMOUNT
42	ea.	Sheets, king	$45.10	$1,894 20
65	ea.	Sheets, queen	$37.60	$2,444 00
26	pkg.	Pillow Cases, queen	$17.85	$464 10
55	pkg.	Pillow Cases, std.	$14.35	$789 25
8	ea.	Shams	$33.25	$366 00

INVOICE SUBTOTAL	$5,957.55
SHIPPING CHARGES	$132.50
INSURANCE	$21.15
INVOICE TOTAL	$6,111.20

SECTION II 7 TRADE DISCOUNTS—SINGLE

trade discounts Reductions from the manufacturer's list price given to businesses that are "in the trade" for performance of marketing functions.

list price Suggested retail selling price of an item set by the manufacturer or supplier. The original price from which discounts are taken.

The path merchandise travels as it moves from the manufacturer through wholesalers and retailers to the ultimate consumer is known as a channel of distribution or trade channel. The businesses that form these channels are said to be "in the trade." In today's complex economy, a number of different trade channels are used to move goods and services efficiently.

Trade discounts are reductions from the manufacturer's suggested **list price**. They are given to businesses at various levels of the trade channel for the performance of marketing functions. These functions may include activities such as selling, advertising, storage, service, and display.

Manufacturers print catalogs showcasing their merchandise. Often these catalogs contain the manufacturer's suggested list or retail prices. Businesses in the trade receive price sheets from the manufacturer listing the trade discounts in percent form associated with each item in the catalog. By issuing updated price sheets of trade discounts, manufacturers have the flexibility of changing the prices of their merchandise without the expense of reprinting the entire catalog.

Trade discounts are sometimes quoted as a single discount and sometimes as a series or chain of discounts. The number of discounts is dependent on the extent of the marketing services performed by the channel member.

CALCULATING THE AMOUNT OF A SINGLE TRADE DISCOUNT

The amount of a single trade discount is calculated by multiplying the list price by the trade discount rate.

> **Trade discount = List price × Trade discount rate**

EXAMPLE3 **CALCULATING THE AMOUNT OF A SINGLE TRADE DISCOUNT**

What is the amount of the trade discount on merchandise with a list price of $2,800 and a trade discount rate of 45%?

▶**SOLUTIONSTRATEGY**

Trade discount = List price × Trade discount rate
Trade discount = 2,800 × .45 = $1,260

▶**TRYITEXERCISE 3**

Gifts Galore, a retail gift shop, buys merchandise with a list price of $7,600 from a wholesaler of novelty items and toys. The wholesaler extends a 30% trade discount rate to the retailer. What is the amount of the trade discount?

CHECK YOUR ANSWER WITH THE SOLUTION ON PAGE 231.

CALCULATING NET PRICE BY USING THE NET PRICE FACTOR, COMPLEMENT METHOD

The **net price** is the amount a business actually pays for the merchandise after the discount has been deducted. It may be calculated by subtracting the amount of the trade discount from the list price.

net price The amount a business actually pays for the merchandise after the discount has been deducted.

> **Net price = List price − Trade discount**

Frequently, merchants are more interested in knowing the net price of an item than the amount of the trade discount. In that case, the net price can be calculated directly from the list price without first finding the amount of the discount.

The list price of an item is considered to be 100%. If, for example, the trade discount on an item is 40% of the list price, the net price will be 60% because the two must equal 100%. This 60%, the complement of the trade discount rate (100% − 40%), is the portion of the list price that *is* paid. Known as the **net price factor**, it is usually written in decimal form.

net price factor The percent of the list price a business pays for merchandise. It is the multiplier used to calculate the net price.

B-A-C-O/Shutterstock.com

Learning Tip

Complements are two numbers that add up to 100%. The trade discount rate and the net price factor are complements of each other. This means that if we know one of them, the other can be found by subtracting from 100%.

STEPS TO CALCULATE NET PRICE BY USING THE NET PRICE FACTOR

STEP 1. Calculate the net price factor, complement of the trade discount rate.

$$\text{Net price factor} = 100\% - \text{Trade discount rate}$$

STEP 2. Calculate the net price.

$$\text{Net price} = \text{List price} \times \text{Net price factor}$$

Note: This procedure can be combined into one step by the formula.

$$\text{Net price} = \text{List price} \,(100\% - \text{Trade discount rate})$$

iStock.com/Nikada

EXAMPLE4   CALCULATING THE NET PRICE

Calculate the net price of merchandise at Astana Imports listing for **$900** less a trade discount rate of **45%**.

▶SOLUTIONSTRATEGY

$$\text{Net price} = \text{List price} \,(100\% - \text{Trade discount rate})$$
$$\text{Net price} = 900 \,(100\% - 45\%)$$
$$\text{Net price} = 900 \,(.55) = \underline{\$495}$$

▶TRYITEXERCISE 4

Central Hardware Store bought paint supplies listing for $2,100 with a single trade discount rate of 35%. What is the net price of the order?

CHECK YOUR ANSWER WITH THE SOLUTION ON PAGE 231.

7-5 CALCULATING TRADE DISCOUNT RATE WHEN LIST PRICE AND NET PRICE ARE KNOWN

The trade discount rate can be calculated by using the now-familiar percentage formula Rate = Portion ÷ Base. For this application, the amount of the trade discount is the portion, or numerator, and the list price is the base, or denominator.

$$\text{Trade discount rate} = \frac{\text{Trade discount}}{\text{List price}}$$

STEPS FOR CALCULATING TRADE DISCOUNT RATE

STEP 1. Calculate the amount of the trade discount.

$$\text{Trade discount} = \text{List price} - \text{Net price}$$

STEP 2. Calculate the trade discount rate.

$$\text{Trade discount rate} = \frac{\text{Trade discount}}{\text{List price}}$$

iStock.com/Nikada

EXAMPLE5 CALCULATING THE SINGLE TRADE DISCOUNT AND RATE

Sterling Manufacturing sells tools to American Garden Supply. In a recent transaction, the list price of an order was $47,750 and the net price of the order was $32,100. Calculate the amount of the trade discount. What was the trade discount rate? Round your answer to the nearest tenth percent.

▶SOLUTIONSTRATEGY

$$\text{Trade discount} = \text{List price} - \text{Net price}$$

$$\text{Trade discount} = 47{,}750 - 32{,}100 = \underline{\$15{,}650}$$

$$\text{Trade discount rate} = \frac{\text{Trade discount}}{\text{List price}}$$

$$\text{Trade discount rate} = \frac{15{,}650}{47{,}750} = .3277 = \underline{\underline{32.8\%}}$$

▶TRYITEXERCISE 5

Wilson Sporting Goods recently sold tennis rackets listing for $109,500 to The Sports Authority. The net price of the order was $63,300. What was the amount of the trade discount? What was the trade discount rate? Round your answer to the nearest tenth percent.

CHECK YOUR ANSWERS WITH THE SOLUTIONS ON PAGE 231.

REVIEW EXERCISES

7 SECTION II

Calculate the following trade discounts. Round all answers to the nearest cent.

	List Price	Trade Discount Rate	Trade Discount
1.	$860.00	30%	$258.00
	Trade discount = 860.00 × .30 = $258.00		
2.	125.50	12%	_____
3.	41.75	19%	_____
4.	395.00	7%	_____
5.	88.25	50%	_____

Calculate the following trade discounts and net prices to the nearest cent.

	List Price	Trade Discount Rate	Trade Discount	Net Price
6.	$286.00	25%	$71.50	$214.50
7.	134.79	40%	_____	_____
8.	21.29	18%	_____	_____
9.	1,250.00	45%	_____	_____

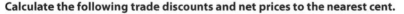

Calculate the following net price factors and net prices by using the complement method. Round all answers to the nearest cent.

	List Price	Trade Discount Rate	Net Price Factor	Net Price
10.	$3,499.00	37%	63%	$2,204.37
11.	565.33	24%		
12.	1,244.25	45.8%		
13.	4.60	$12\frac{3}{4}\%$		

Calculate the following trade discounts and trade discount rates. Round answers to the nearest tenth of a percent.

	List Price	Trade Discount	Trade Discount Rate	Net Price
14.	$4,500.00	$935.00	20.8%	$3,565.00
15.	345.50			$225.00
16.	2.89			$2.15

17. Find the amount of a trade discount of 30% on a television set that has a list price of $799.95.

18. A boutique buys some merchandise with a list price of $3,600. If the wholesaler extends a 40% trade discount rate, find the trade discount.

19. What is the amount of a trade discount of 45% on a dining room table that lists for $395.50?

20. Whole Foods Market ordered 12 cases of organic vegetable soup with a list price of $18.90 per case and 8 cases of organic baked beans with a list price of $33.50 per case. The wholesaler offered Whole Foods a 39% trade discount.

   a. What is the total extended list price of the order?

   b. What is the total amount of the trade discount on this order?

   c. What is the total net amount Whole Foods owes the wholesaler for the order?

21. La Bella, a chain of clothing boutiques, purchased merchandise with a total list price of $25,450 from Sandy Sport, a manufacturer. The order has a trade discount of 34%.

   a. What is the amount of the trade discount?

   b. What is the net amount LaBella owes Sandy Sport for the merchandise?

22. Sharma Kennels buys some items with a list price of $4,500. The supplier extends a 40% trade discount rate. What is the net price?

23. Nathan and David Beauty Salon places an order for beauty supplies from a wholesaler. The list price of the order is $2,800. If the vendor offers a trade discount of 46%, what is the net price of the order?

A number of supermarkets now make supporting local growers and producers a priority. Whole Foods, one such store, opened in 1980 and four years later began expanding rapidly.

Today, there are more than 310 stores in North America and the United Kingdom, and Whole Foods has acquired more than 10 natural food store chains. It is the world's leading supermarket emphasizing natural and organic foods and America's first national "Certified Organic" grocer.

24. A business supply store bought some merchandise with a list price of $13,200. The wholesaler extended a trade discount that made the net price $9,900. Find the trade discount rate.

25. Nutrition Central pays $11.90 net price for a bottle of 60 multivitamins. The price represents a 30% trade discount from the manufacturer. What is the list price of the vitamins?

26. You are the buyer for the housewares department of the Galleria Department Store. A number of vendors in your area carry similar lines of merchandise. On sets of microwavable serving bowls, Kitchen Magic offers a list price of $400 per dozen less a 38% trade discount. Pro-Chef offers a similar set for a list price of $425 less a 45% trade discount.

    a. Which vendor is offering the lower net price?

    b. If you order 500 dozen sets of the bowls, how much money will be saved by using the lower-priced vendor?

BUSINESS DECISION: QUANTITY DISCOUNT

27. You are the purchasing manager for Tiger Electronics, a company that manufactures scanners and other computer peripherals. Your vendor for scanner motors, Enfield Industries, is now offering "quantity discounts" in the form of instant rebates and lower shipping charges as follows:

Quantity	Net Price	Rebate	Shipping
1–500 motors	$16	none	$1.30
501–1,000 motors	16	$1.20	.90
1,001–2,000 motors	16	1.80	.60

    a. Calculate the cost of the motors, including shipping charges, for each category.

    b. If you usually purchase 400 motors per month, what percent would be saved per motor by ordering 800 every two months? Round to the nearest tenth of a percent.

    c. What percent would be saved per motor by ordering 1,200 every three months? Round to the nearest tenth of a percent.

d. How much money can be saved in a year by purchasing the motors every three months instead of every month?

e. (Optional) What other factors besides price should be considered before changing your purchasing procedures?

chain or series trade discounts Term used when a vendor offers a buyer more than one trade discount.

Trade discounts are frequently offered by manufacturers to wholesalers and retailers in a series of two or more, known as **chain** or **series trade discounts**. For example, a series of 25% and 10% is verbally stated as "25 and 10." It is written 25/10. A three-discount series is written 25/10/5. Multiple discounts are given for many reasons. Some of the more common ones follow.

Position or Level in the Channel of Distribution   A manufacturer might sell to a retailer at a 30% trade discount, whereas a wholesaler in the same channel might be quoted a 30% and a 15% trade discount.

Learning Tip

Remember, when calculating the net price by using a series of trade discounts, you *cannot* simply add the trade discounts together. Each discount must be applied to a successively lower base.

Volume Buying   Many manufacturers and wholesalers grant an extra discount for buying a large volume of merchandise. For example, any purchase more than 5,000 units at one time may earn an extra 7% trade discount. Retailers with many stores or those with large storage capacity can enjoy a considerable savings (additional trade discounts) by purchasing in large quantities.

Advertising and Display   Additional discounts are often given to retailers and wholesalers who heavily advertise and aggressively promote a manufacturer's line of merchandise.

Competition   Competitive pressures often cause extra trade discounts to be offered. In certain industries such as household products and consumer electronics, price wars are not an uncommon occurrence.

7-6   CALCULATING NET PRICE AND THE AMOUNT OF A TRADE DISCOUNT BY USING A SERIES OF TRADE DISCOUNTS

Dollars AND Sense

An **industry trade group**, also known as a **trade association**, is an organization founded and funded by businesses that operate in a specific industry. An industry trade association participates in public relations activities such as advertising, education, political donations, lobbying, and publishing, but its main focus is collaboration between companies, or standardization.

Associations may offer other services, such as sponsoring conferences, providing networking, hosting charitable events, or offering classes or educational materials.

A directory of trade associations may be found at http://dir.yahoo.com/Business_and_Economy/organizations/trade_associations

Finding net price with a series of trade discounts is accomplished by taking each trade discount, one at a time, from the previous net price until all discounts have been deducted. Note that you *cannot* simply add the trade discounts together. They must be calculated individually unless the net price factor method—a handy shortcut—is used. Trade discounts can be taken in any order, although they are usually listed and calculated in descending order.

For illustrative purposes, let's begin with an example of how to calculate a series of trade discounts one at a time; then we will try the shortcut method.

EXAMPLE6   CALCULATING NET PRICE AND THE AMOUNT OF A TRADE DISCOUNT

Calculate the net price and trade discount for merchandise with a list price of $2,000 less trade discounts of 30/20/15.

▶SOLUTIONSTRATEGY

$2,000	$2,000	$1,400	$1,400	$1,120	$1,120
× .30	− 600	× .20	− 280	× .15	− 168
$600	$1,400	$280	$1,120	$168	$952 = Net price

►TRY**IT**EXERCISE 6

Northwest Publishers sold an order of books to The Bookworm, Inc., a chain of bookstores. The list price of the order was $25,000. The Bookworm buys in volume from Northwest. The Bookworm also prominently displays and heavily advertises Northwest's books. Northwest, in turn, gives The Bookworm a series of trade discounts amounting to 35/20/10. Calculate the net price of the order and the amount of the trade discount.

CHECK YOUR ANSWERS WITH THE SOLUTIONS ON PAGE 231.

CALCULATING THE NET PRICE OF A SERIES OF TRADE DISCOUNTS BY USING THE NET PRICE FACTOR, COMPLEMENT METHOD

7-7

As a shortcut, the net price can be calculated directly from the list price, bypassing the trade discount, by using the net price factor as before. Remember, the net price factor is the complement of the trade discount rate. With a series of discounts, we must find the complement of each trade discount to calculate the net price factor of the series.

The net price factor indicates to buyers what percent of the list price they actually *do* pay. For example, if the net price factor of a series of discounts is calculated to be .665, this means that the buyer is paying 66.5% of the list price.

STEPS FOR CALCULATING NET PRICE BY USING THE NET PRICE FACTOR

STEP 1. Find the complement of the trade discount rates in the series by subtracting each from 100% and converting them to decimal form.

STEP 2. Calculate the net price factor of the series by multiplying all the decimals together.

STEP 3. Calculate the net price by multiplying the list price by the net price factor.

Net price = List price × Net price factor

EXAMPLE7 CALCULATING NET PRICE FACTOR AND NET PRICE

The Crystal Gallery purchased merchandise from a manufacturer in Italy. The merchandise had a list price of $37,000 less trade discounts of 40/25/10. Calculate the net price factor and the net price of the order.

►SOLUTION**STRATEGY**

Step 1. Subtract each trade discount from 100% and convert to decimals.

100%	100%	100%
− 40%	− 25%	− 10%
60% = .6	75% = .75	90% = .9

Step 2. Multiply all the complements together to get the net price factor.

Net price factor = .6 × .75 × .9
Net price factor = .405

Step 3.

Net price = List price × Net price factor
Net price = 37,000 × .405
Net price = $14,985

▶TRYITEXERCISE 7

Something's Fishy, a pet shop, always gets a 30/20/12 series of trade discounts from the Clearview Fish Tank Company. In June, the shop ordered merchandise with a list price of $3,500. In September, the shop placed an additional order listing for $5,800.

a. What is the net price factor for the series of trade discounts?

b. What is the net price of the merchandise purchased in June?

c. What is the net price of the merchandise purchased in September?

CHECK YOUR ANSWERS WITH THE SOLUTIONS ON PAGE 231.

7-8   CALCULATING THE AMOUNT OF A TRADE DISCOUNT BY USING A SINGLE EQUIVALENT DISCOUNT

single equivalent discount A single trade discount that equates to all the discounts in a series or chain.

Sometimes retailers and wholesalers want to know the one single discount rate that equates to a series of trade discounts. This is known as the **single equivalent discount**. We have already learned that the trade discounts *cannot* simply be added together.

Here is the logic: The list price of the merchandise is 100%. If the net price factor is the part of the list price that is paid, then 100% minus the net price factor is the part of the list price that is the trade discount. The single equivalent discount, therefore, is the complement of the net price factor (100% − Net price factor percent).

STEPS TO CALCULATE THE SINGLE EQUIVALENT DISCOUNT AND THE AMOUNT OF A TRADE DISCOUNT

STEP 1. Calculate the net price factor as before by subtracting each trade discount from 100% and multiplying them all together in decimal form.

STEP 2. Calculate the single equivalent discount by subtracting the net price factor in decimal form from 1.

Single equivalent discount = 1 − Net price factor

STEP 3. Find the amount of the trade discount by multiplying the list price by the single equivalent discount.

Trade discount = List price × Single equivalent discount

EXAMPLE8   CALCULATING THE SINGLE EQUIVALENT DISCOUNT AND THE AMOUNT OF A TRADE DISCOUNT

Calculate the single equivalent discount and amount of the trade discount on merchandise listing for $10,000 less trade discounts of 30/10/5.

▶SOLUTIONSTRATEGY

Step 1. Calculate the net price factor.

$$
\begin{array}{ccccc}
100\% & & 100\% & & 100\% \\
-\ 30\% & & -\ 10\% & & -\ 5\% \\
\hline
.70 & \times & .90 & \times & .95
\end{array}
= .5985 = \text{Net price factor}
$$

Step 2. Calculate the single equivalent discount.

Single equivalent discount = 1 − Net price factor

Single equivalent discount = 1 − .5985 = .4015

Note: 40.15% is the single equivalent discount of the series 30%, 10%, and 5%.

Step 3. Calculate the amount of the trade discount.

Trade discount = List price × Single equivalent discount

Trade discount = 10,000 × .4015 = $4,015

▶ TRYITEXERCISE 8

The Rainbow Appliance Center purchased an order of dishwashers and ovens listing for $36,800. The manufacturer allows Rainbow a series of trade discounts of 25/15/10. What are the single equivalent discount and the amount of the trade discount?

CHECK YOUR ANSWERS WITH THE SOLUTIONS ON PAGE 232.

REVIEW EXERCISES

7 SECTION III

Calculate the following net price factors and net prices. For convenience, round net price factors to five decimal places when necessary.

	List Price	Trade Discount Rates	Net Price Factor	Net Price
1.	**$360.00**	12/10	.792	$285.12
2.	425.80	18/15/5	_____	_____
3.	81.75	20/10/10	_____	_____
4.	979.20	15/10/5	_____	_____
5.	7.25	25/15/10½	_____	_____
6.	.39	20/9/8	_____	_____

Calculate the following net price factors and single equivalent discounts. Round to five places when necessary.

	Trade Discount Rates	Net Price Factor	Single Equivalent Discount
7.	15/10	.765	.235
8.	20/15/12	_____	_____
9.	25/15/7	_____	_____
10.	30/5/5	_____	_____
11.	35/15/7.5	_____	_____

Complete the following table. Round net price factors to five decimal places when necessary.

	List Price	Trade Discount Rates	Net Price Factor	Single Equivalent Discount	Trade Discount	Net Price
12.	**$7,800.00**	15/5/5	.76713	.23287	$1,816.39	$5,983.61
13.	1,200.00	20/15/7	_____	_____	_____	_____
14.	560.70	25/15/5	_____	_____	_____	_____
15.	883.50	18/12/9	_____	_____	_____	_____
16.	4.89	12/10/10	_____	_____	_____	_____
17.	2,874.95	30/20/5.5	_____	_____	_____	_____

18. What is the net price factor of a 25/15 series of trade discounts?

19. What is the net price factor of a 35/20/15 series of discounts?

20. Kathi's Katering buys some items with a list price of $5,000. If the supplier extends trade discount rates of 40/25/15, find the net price using the net price factor, complement method.

Satellite radio, also called digital radio, receives radio signals broadcast from a network of satellites more than 22,000 miles above the earth. In contrast, traditional radio reception is usually limited to 50–100 miles.

Sirius XM Radio, Inc., offers a programming lineup of 135 channels of commercial-free music, sports, news, talk, entertainment, traffic, and weather. Subscribers can listen on more than 800 different types of devices for boats, cars, home, office, or a number of types of mobile devices. Sirius has agreements for the installation of satellite radio in vehicles with every major automaker.

Curtis Barnard/Shutterstock.com

EXCEL**1**

21. Legacy Designs places an order for furniture listing for $90,500 less trade discounts of 25/20.

   a. What is the net price factor?

   b. What is the net price of the order?

22. Audio Giant received an order of Sirius XM satellite radios listing for $9,500 with trade discounts of 25/13/8.

   a. What is the net price factor?

   b. What is the single equivalent discount?

   c. What is the amount of the trade discount?

   d. What is the net price of the order?

EXCEL**2**

23. The Speedy Auto Service Center can buy auto parts from Southeast Auto Supply at a series discount of 20/15/5 and from Northwest Auto Supply for 25/10/8.

   a. Which auto parts supplier offers a better discount to Speedy?

   b. If Speedy orders $15,000 in parts at list price per month, how much will it save in a year by choosing the lower-priced supplier?

24. Picture Perfect Photography buys some merchandise with a list price of $7,000. If the supplier offers trade discount rates of 35/20/15, find the trade discount. (Find the single equivalent discount first.)

25. Midtown Market received the following items at a discount of 25/20/10: 18 cases of canned peaches listing at $26.80 per case and 45 cases of canned pears listing at $22.50 per case.

    a. What is the total list price of this order?

    b. What is the amount of the trade discount?

    c. What is the net price of the order?

The Pharmacy and Drug Store Industry in the United States retails a range of prescription and over-the-counter products. These include medicines; apothecaries; health and beauty items such as vitamin supplements, cosmetics, and toiletries; and photo processing services.

Top U.S. drug retailers include Rite Aid, CVS, Target, Kmart, Kroger, Safeway, Duane Reade, Supervalu, Walgreens, and Walmart.

26. Shopper's Mart purchased the following items. Calculate the extended total after the trade discounts for each line, the invoice subtotal, and the invoice total.

Quantity	Unit	Merchandise	Unit List	Trade Discounts	Extended Total
150	ea.	Blenders	$59.95	20/15/15	_____
400	ea.	Toasters	$39.88	20/10/10	_____
18	doz.	Coffee Mills	$244.30	30/9/7	_____
12	doz.	Juicers	$460.00	25/10/5	_____
				Invoice subtotal	_____
		Extra $5\frac{1}{2}$% volume discount on total order			_____
				Invoice total	_____

27. Referring back to Exercise 26, you have just been hired as the buyer for the kitchen division of Shopper's Mart, a general merchandise retailer. After looking over the discounts offered to the previous buyer by the vendor, you decide to ask for better discounts.

    After negotiating with the vendor's salesperson, you now can buy blenders at trade discounts of 20/20/15 and juicers at 25/15/10. In addition, the vendor has increased the volume discount to $6\frac{1}{2}$%.

    a. How much would have been saved with your new discounts based on the quantities of the previous order (Exercise 26)?

    b. As a result of your negotiations, the vendor has offered an additional discount of 2% of the total amount due if the invoice is paid within 15 days instead of the usual 30 days. What would be the amount of this discount?

BUSINESS DECISION: THE ULTIMATE TRADE DISCOUNT

28. A General Motors incentive program designed to reduce inventory of certain low-selling models offers a $7,000 extra dealer incentive for each of these vehicles that the dealer moved into its rental or service fleets.

   As the accountant for a dealership with a number of these vehicles left in stock, your manager has asked you to calculate certain invoice figures. The normal trade discount from GM is 18%. If the average sticker price (list price) of these remaining vehicles at your dealership is $23,500, calculate the following.

   a. What is the amount of the trade discount, including the incentive?

   b. What is the trade discount rate? Round to the nearest tenth of a percent.

   c. What is the net price (invoice price) to your dealership?

   d. If the cars were then sold from the fleets at $1,000 over "invoice" (net price), what is the total percentage savings to the consumer based on the list price? Round to the nearest tenth of a percent.

   e. (Optional) Although these incentive prices reflect extraordinary discounts to the consumer, what other factors should a consumer consider before purchasing a "discontinued" brand of vehicle?

SECTION IV   7   CASH DISCOUNTS AND TERMS OF SALE

terms of sale The details of when an invoice must be paid and if a cash discount is being offered.

credit period The time period that the seller allows the buyer to pay an invoice.

net date, or due date The last day of the credit period.

cash discount An extra discount offered by the seller as an incentive for early payment of an invoice.

invoice date The date an invoice is written. The beginning of the discount and credit periods when ordinary dating is used.

cash discount period The time period in which a buyer can take advantage of the cash discount.

discount date The last day of the discount period.

As merchandise physically arrives at the buyer's back door, the invoice ordinarily arrives by mail through the front door. Today more and more arrive by e-mail. What happens next? The invoice has a section entitled **terms of sale**. The terms of sale are the details of when the invoice must be paid and whether any additional discounts will be offered.

Commonly, manufacturers allow wholesalers and retailers 30 days or even longer to pay the bill. In certain industries, the time period is as much as 60 or 90 days. This is known as the **credit period**. This gives the buyer time to unpack and check the order and, more important, begin selling the merchandise. This credit period clearly gives the wholesaler and retailer an advantage. They can generate revenue by selling merchandise that they have not paid for yet.

To encourage them to pay the bill earlier than the **net date**, or **due date**, sellers frequently offer buyers an optional extra discount over and above the trade discounts. This is known as a **cash discount**. Cash discounts are an extra few percent offered as an incentive for early payment of the invoice, usually within 10 to 15 days after the **invoice date**. This is known as the **cash discount period**. The last date for a buyer to take advantage of a cash discount is known as the **discount date**.

THE IMPORTANCE OF CASH DISCOUNTS

Both buyers and sellers benefit from cash discounts. Sellers get their money much sooner, which improves their cash flow, whereas buyers get an additional discount, which lowers their merchandise cost, thereby raising their margin or gross profit.

Cash discounts generally range from an extra 1% to 5% off the net price of the merchandise. A 1% to 5% discount may not seem significant, but it is. Let's say that an invoice is due in 30 days; however, a distributor would like payment sooner. It might offer the retailer a cash discount of 2% if the bill is paid within 10 days rather than 30 days. If the retailer chooses to take the cash discount, he or she must pay the bill by the 10th day after the date of the invoice. Note that this is *20 days* earlier than the due date. The retailer is therefore receiving a 2% discount for paying the bill 20 days early.

The logic: There are 18.25 twenty-day periods in a year (365 days divided by 20 days). By multiplying the 2% discount by the 18.25 periods, we see that on a yearly basis, 2% cash discounts can *theoretically* amount to 36.5%. Very significant!

> ### Dollars AND Sense
>
> Cash discounts are so important to wholesalers' and retailers' "profit picture" that frequently they borrow the money on a short-term basis to take advantage of the cash discount savings. This procedure is covered in Chapter 10, "Simple Interest."

CALCULATING CASH DISCOUNTS AND NET AMOUNT DUE

7-9

Cash discounts are offered in the terms of sale. A transaction with no cash discount would have terms of sale of net 30, for example. This means the **net amount** of the invoice is due in 30 days. If a cash discount is offered, the terms of sale would be written as 2/10, n/30. This means a 2% cash discount may be taken if the invoice is paid within 10 days; if not, the net amount is due in 30 days. (See Exhibit 7-4.)

Exhibit 7-5 shows a time line of the discount period and credit period on an invoice dated October 15. The 2/10, n/30 terms of sale stipulate a cash discount if the bill is paid within 10 days. If not, the balance is due in 30 days. As you can see, the cash discount period runs for 10 days from the invoice date, October 15 to October 25. The credit period, 30 days, extends from the invoice date through November 14.

Sometimes two cash discounts are offered, such as 3/15, 1/25, n/60. This means a 3% cash discount is offered if the invoice is paid within 15 days, a 1% cash discount if the invoice is paid within 25 days, with the net amount due in 60 days.

Cash discounts cannot be taken on shipping charges or returned goods, only on the net price of the merchandise. If shipping charges are included in the amount of an invoice, they must be subtracted before the cash discount is taken. After the cash discount has been deducted, the shipping charges are added back to get the invoice total.

net amount The amount of money due from the buyer to the seller.

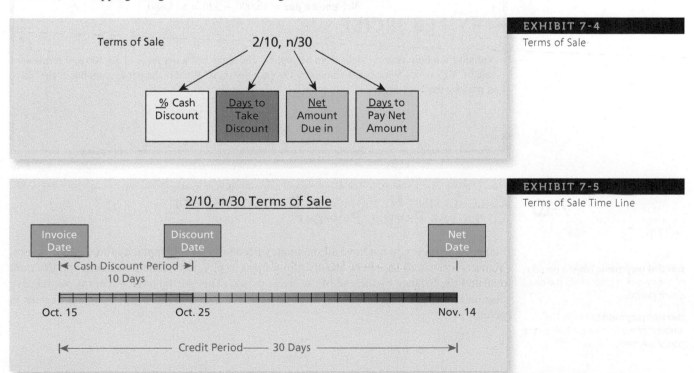

EXHIBIT 7-4
Terms of Sale

EXHIBIT 7-5
Terms of Sale Time Line

If arriving merchandise is damaged or is not what was ordered, those goods will be returned to the vendor. The amount of the returned goods must also be subtracted from the amount of the invoice. They are no longer a part of the transaction.

STEPS TO CALCULATE CASH DISCOUNT AND NET AMOUNT DUE

STEP 1. Calculate the amount of the cash discount by multiplying the cash discount rate by the net price of the merchandise.

$$\text{Cash discount} = \text{Net price} \times \text{Cash discount rate}$$

STEP 2. Calculate the net amount due by subtracting the amount of the cash discount from the net price.

$$\text{Net amount due} = \text{Net price} - \text{Cash discount}$$

Note: As with trade discounts, buyers are frequently more interested in the net amount due than the amount of the discount. When that is the case, we can simplify the calculation by using the complement method to determine the net amount due.

$$\text{Net amount due} = \text{Net price} (100\% - \text{Cash discount rate})$$

EXAMPLE9 CALCULATING CASH DISCOUNT AND NET AMOUNT DUE

Rugs.com buys merchandise with an invoice amount of $16,000 from Karistan Carpet Mills. The terms of sale are 2/10, n/30. What is the amount of the cash discount? What is the net amount due on this order if the bill is paid by the 10th day?

SOLUTIONSTRATEGY

Cash discount = Net price × Cash discount rate

$$\text{Cash discount} = 16,000 \times .02 = \underline{\$320}$$

$$\text{Net amount due} = \text{Net price} - \text{Cash discount}$$

$$\text{Net amount due} = 16,000 - 320 = \underline{\underline{\$15,680}}$$

TRYITEXERCISE 9

Valiant Plumbing ordered sinks from a supplier. The sinks had a net price of $8,300 and terms of sale of 3/15, n/45. What is the amount of the cash discount? What is the net amount due if the bill is paid by the 15th day?

CHECK YOUR ANSWERS WITH THE SOLUTIONS ON PAGE 232.

7-10 CALCULATING NET AMOUNT DUE, WITH CREDIT GIVEN FOR PARTIAL PAYMENT

partial payment When a portion of the invoice is paid within the discount period.

partial payment credit The amount of the invoice paid off by the partial payment.

Sometimes buyers do not have all the money needed to take advantage of the cash discount. Manufacturers and suppliers usually allow them to pay part of the invoice by the discount date and the balance by the end of the credit period. This **partial payment** earns partial cash discount credit. In this situation, we must calculate how much **partial payment credit** is given.

Here is how it works: Assume a cash discount of 4/15, n/45 is offered to a retailer. A 4% cash discount means that the retailer will pay 96% of the bill (100% − 4%) and receive 100% credit. Another way to look at it is that every $0.96 paid toward the invoice earns $1.00 credit. We must determine how many $0.96s are in the partial payment. This will tell us how many $1.00s of credit we receive.

STEPS TO CALCULATE PARTIAL PAYMENT CREDIT AND NET AMOUNT DUE

STEP 1. Calculate the amount of credit given for a partial payment by dividing the partial payment by the complement of the cash discount rate.

$$\text{Partial payment credit} = \frac{\text{Partial payment}}{100\% - \text{Cash discount rate}}$$

STEP 2. Calculate the net amount due by subtracting the partial payment credit from the net price.

$$\text{Net amount due} = \text{Net price} - \text{Partial payment credit}$$

IN THE
Business World

The extension of partial payment credit by vendors is important to small retailers who don't always have the cash flow to take advantage of the full cash discount.

EXAMPLE 10 CALCULATING NET AMOUNT DUE AFTER A PARTIAL PAYMENT

Happy Feet, a chain of children's shoe stores, receives an invoice from a tennis shoe manufacturer on September 3 with terms of 3/20, n/60. The net price of the order is $36,700. Happy Feet wants to send a partial payment of $10,000 by the discount date and the balance on the net date. How much credit does Happy Feet get for the partial payment? What is the remaining net amount due to the manufacturer?

►SOLUTIONSTRATEGY

$$\text{Partial payment credit} = \frac{\text{Partial payment}}{100\% - \text{Case discount rate}}$$

$$\text{Partial payment credit} = \frac{10,000}{100\% - 3\%} = \frac{10,000}{.97} = \underline{\$10,309.28}$$

$$\text{Net amount due} = \text{Net price} - \text{Partial payment credit}$$

$$\text{Net amount due} = \$36,700.00 - \$10,309.28 = \underline{\$26,390.72}$$

►TRYITEXERCISE 10

All Pro Sports Center purchases $45,300 in baseball gloves from Spaulding on May 5. Spaulding allows 4/15, n/45. If All Pro sends a partial payment of $20,000 on the discount date, how much credit will be given for the partial payment? What is the net amount still due on the order?

CHECK YOUR ANSWERS WITH THE SOLUTIONS ON PAGE 232.

iStock.com/Nikada

rtguest/Shutterstock.com

7-11   DETERMINING DISCOUNT DATE AND NET DATE BY USING VARIOUS TERMS OF SALE DATING METHODS

To determine the discount date and net date of an invoice, you must know how many days are in each month or use a calendar.

Here is a rhyme to help you remember how many days are in each month:

Thirty days has September
April, June, and November
All the rest have thirty-one
Except February,
which has twenty-eight
(twenty-nine in leap years).

Remember, in a leap year, February has 29 days. Leap years occur when the year is evenly divisible by 4 except if the year is also evenly divisible by 400. Therefore, 2016, 2020, and 2024 are examples of leap years, while 2000 was not a leap year.

Another way to find these dates is to use the days-in-a-year calendar shown in Exhibit 7-6. In Chapter 10, you will be able to use this calendar again to find future dates and calculate the number of days of a loan.

STEPS TO FINDING A FUTURE DATE USING A DAYS-IN-A-YEAR CALENDAR

STEP 1. Find the "day number" of the starting date.

Note: In leap years, add 1 to the day numbers beginning with March 1.

STEP 2. Add the number of days of the discount or credit period to that day number.

Note: If the new day number is over 365, subtract 365. This means the future date is in the next year.

STEP 3. Find the date by looking up the new day number from Step 2.

iStock.com/Nikada

EXAMPLE11   FINDING THE NET DATE

If an invoice dated April 14 is due in 75 days, what is the net date?

▶SOLUTIONSTRATEGY

Step 1. From the calendar, April 14 is day number 104.

Step 2. $104 + 75 = 179$

Step 3. From the calendar, day number 179 is <u>June 28</u>.

▶TRYITEXERCISE 11

If an invoice dated September 12 is due in 60 days, what is the net date?

CHECK YOUR ANSWER WITH THE SOLUTION ON PAGE 232.

EXHIBIT 7-6 Days-in-a-Year Calendar

Day of month	Jan.	Feb.	Mar.	Apr.	May	June	July	Aug.	Sept.	Oct.	Nov.	Dec.
1	1	32	60	91	121	152	182	213	244	274	305	335
2	2	33	61	92	122	153	183	214	245	275	306	336
3	3	34	62	93	123	154	184	215	246	276	307	337
4	4	35	63	94	124	155	185	216	247	277	308	338
5	5	36	64	95	125	156	186	217	248	278	309	339
6	6	37	65	96	126	157	187	218	249	279	310	340
7	7	38	66	97	127	158	188	219	250	280	311	341
8	8	39	67	98	128	159	189	220	251	281	312	342
9	9	40	68	99	129	160	190	221	252	282	313	343
10	10	41	69	100	130	161	191	222	253	283	314	344
11	11	42	70	101	131	162	192	223	254	284	315	345
12	12	43	71	102	132	163	193	224	255	285	316	346
13	13	44	72	103	133	164	194	225	256	286	317	347
14	14	45	73	104	134	165	195	226	257	287	318	348
15	15	46	74	105	135	166	196	227	258	288	319	349
16	16	47	75	106	136	167	197	228	259	289	320	350
17	17	48	76	107	137	168	198	229	260	290	321	351
18	18	49	77	108	138	169	199	230	261	291	322	352
19	19	50	78	109	139	170	200	231	262	292	323	353
20	20	51	79	110	140	171	201	232	263	293	324	354
21	21	52	80	111	141	172	202	233	264	294	325	355
22	22	53	81	112	142	173	203	234	265	295	326	356
23	23	54	82	113	143	174	204	235	266	296	327	357
24	24	55	83	114	144	175	205	236	267	297	328	358
25	25	56	84	115	145	176	206	237	268	298	329	359
26	26	57	85	116	146	177	207	238	269	299	330	360
27	27	58	86	117	147	178	208	239	270	300	331	361
28	28	59	87	118	148	179	209	240	271	301	332	362
29	29		88	119	149	180	210	241	272	302	333	363
30	30		89	120	150	181	211	242	273	303	334	364
31	31		90		151		212	243		304		365

During a leap year, add 1 to the day numbers beginning with March 1.

TERMS OF SALE—DATING METHODS

ORDINARY DATING

When the discount period and the credit period start on the date of the invoice, this is known as **ordinary dating**. It is the most common method of dating the terms of sale. The last day to take advantage of the cash discount, the discount date, is found by adding the number of days in the discount period to the date of the invoice. For example, to receive a cash discount, an invoice dated November 8 with terms of 2/10, n/30 should be paid no later than November 18 (November 8 + 10 days). The last day to pay the invoice, the net date, is found by adding the number of days in the credit period to the invoice date. With terms of 2/10, n/30, the net

ordinary dating When the discount period and credit period start on the invoice date.

date would be December 8 (November 8 + 30 days). If the buyer does not pay the bill by the net date, the seller may impose a penalty charge for late payment.

EXAMPLE12 USING ORDINARY DATING

AccuCare Pharmacy receives an invoice dated August 19 from Bristol Drug Wholesalers for merchandise. The terms of sale are 3/10, n/45. If AccuCare elects to take the cash discount, what is the discount date? If AccuCare does not take the cash discount, what is the net date?

▶SOLUTIONSTRATEGY

Find the discount date by adding the number of days in the discount period to the date of the invoice.

$$\text{Discount date} = \text{August } 19 + 10 \text{ days} = \underline{\text{August } 29}$$

If the discount is not taken, find the net date by adding the number of days in the credit period to the invoice date.

$$\text{August } 19 + 45 \text{ days} = \begin{array}{l} 12 \text{ days left in August } (31-19) \\ + \ 30 \text{ days in September} \\ + \ \ 3 \text{ days in October} \\ \hline 45 \text{ days} \end{array}$$

The net date, the 45th day, is October 3.

▶TRYITEXERCISE 12

Great Impressions Printing buys ink and paper from a supplier. The invoice date of the purchase is June 11. If the terms of sale are 4/10, n/60, what are the discount date and the net date of the invoice?

CHECK YOUR ANSWERS WITH THE SOLUTIONS ON PAGE 232.

EOM OR PROXIMO DATING

EOM dating End-of-month dating. Depending on invoice date, terms of sale start at the end of the month of the invoice or the end of the following month.

proximo, or prox Another name for EOM dating. Means "in the following month."

EOM dating, or end-of-month dating, means that the terms of sale start *after* the end of the month of the invoice. Another name for this dating method is **proximo**, or **prox**. Proximo means "in the following month." For example, 2/10 EOM, or 2/10 proximo, means that a 2% cash discount will be allowed if the bill is paid 10 days after the *end of the month* of the invoice. This is the case for any invoice dated from the 1st to the 25th of a month. If an invoice is dated after the 25th of the month, the terms of sale begin *after* the end of the *following* month. Unless otherwise specified, the net amount is due *20 days* after the discount date.

EXAMPLE13 USING EOM DATING

As the shipping manager for World Imports, answer the following questions.

a. What are the discount date and the net date of an invoice dated March 3 with terms of 3/15 EOM?

b. What are the discount date and the net date of an invoice dated March 27 with terms of 3/15 EOM?

SOLUTIONSTRATEGY

a. Because the invoice date is between the 1st and the 25th of the month, March 3, the discount date on terms of 3/15 EOM would be 15 days *after* the end of the month of the invoice. The net date would be 20 days later.

$$\text{Discount date} = 15 \text{ days after the end of March} = \underline{April\ 15}$$
$$\text{Net date} = April\ 15 + 20 \text{ days} = \underline{\underline{May\ 5}}$$

b. Because the invoice date is after the 25th of the month, March 27, the discount date on terms of 3/15 EOM would be 15 days *after* the end of the month *following* the invoice month. The net date would be 20 days later.

$$\text{Discount date} = 15 \text{ days after the end of April} = \underline{May\ 15}$$
$$\text{Net date} = May\ 15 + 20 \text{ days} = \underline{\underline{June\ 4}}$$

▶TRYITEXERCISE 13

As the accounts receivable manager for River Bend Industries, answer the following questions.

a. What are the discount date and the net date of an invoice dated November 18 with terms of 3/15 EOM?

b. What are the discount date and the net date of an invoice dated November 27 with terms of 3/15 EOM?

CHECK YOUR ANSWERS WITH THE SOLUTIONS ON PAGE 232.

ROG DATING

Receipt of goods dating, or **ROG dating**, is a common method used when shipping times are long, such as with special or custom orders. When ROG dating is used, the terms of sale begin the day the goods are received at the buyer's location. With this method, the buyer does not have to pay for the merchandise before it arrives. An example would be 2/10 ROG. As usual, the net date is 20 days after the discount date.

ROG dating Receipt of goods dating. Terms of sale begin on the date the goods are received by the buyer.

EXAMPLE14 USING ROG DATING

What are the discount date and the net date for an invoice dated June 23 if the shipment arrives on August 16 and the terms are 3/15 ROG?

▶SOLUTIONSTRATEGY

In this case, the discount period starts on August 16, the date the shipment arrives. The net date will be 20 days after the discount date.

$$\text{Discount date} = August\ 16 + 15 \text{ days} = \underline{August\ 31}$$
$$\text{Net date} = August\ 31 + 20 \text{ days} = \underline{\underline{September\ 20}}$$

▶TRYITEXERCISE 14

What are the discount date and the net date of an invoice dated October 11 if the shipment arrives on December 29 and the terms are 2/20 ROG?

CHECK YOUR ANSWERS WITH THE SOLUTIONS ON PAGE 232.

EXTRA DATING

Extra, Ex, or X dating The buyer receives an extra discount period as an incentive to purchase slow-moving or out-of-season merchandise.

The last dating method commonly used in business today is called **Extra, Ex,** or **X dating**. With this dating method, the seller offers an extra discount period to the buyer as an incentive for purchasing slow-moving or out-of-season merchandise, such as Christmas goods in July and bathing suits in January. An example would be 3/10, 60 extra. This means the buyer gets a 3% cash discount in 10 days plus 60 *extra* days, or a total of 70 days. Once again, unless otherwise specified, the net date is 20 days after the discount date.

EXAMPLE15   USING EXTRA DATING

What are the discount date and the net date of an invoice dated February 9 with terms of 3/15, 40 Extra?

►SOLUTIONSTRATEGY

These terms, 3/15, 40 Extra, give the retailer 55 days (15 + 40) from February 9 to take the cash discount. The net date will be 20 days after the discount date.

$$\text{Discount date} = \text{February } 9 + 55 \text{ days} = \underline{\text{April } 5}$$
$$\text{Net date} = \text{April } 5 + 20 \text{ days} = \underline{\text{April } 25}$$

►TRYITEXERCISE 15

What are the discount date and the net date of an invoice dated February 22 with terms of 4/20, 60 Extra?

CHECK YOUR ANSWERS WITH THE SOLUTIONS ON PAGE 232.

Learning Tip

Remember, when using extra dating, unless otherwise specified, the net date is 20 days after the discount date.

B-A-C-O/Shutterstock.com

Calculate the cash discount and the net amount due for each of the following transactions.

	Amount of Invoice	Terms of Sale	Cash Discount	Net Amount Due
1.	$15,800.00	3/15, n/30	$474.00	$15,326.00
2.	12,660.00	2/10, n/45	_____	_____
3.	2,421.00	4/10, n/30	_____	_____
4.	6,010.20	4/10, n/30	_____	_____
5.	9,121.44	$3\frac{1}{2}$/15, n/60	_____	_____

For the following transactions, calculate the credit given for the partial payment and the net amount due on the invoice.

	Amount of Invoice	Terms of Sale	Partial Payment	Credit for Partial Payment	Net Amount Due
6.	$8,303.00	2/10, n/30	$2,500	$2,551.02	$5,751.98
7.	1,344.60	3/10, n/45	460	_____	_____
8.	5,998.20	4/15, n/60	3,200	_____	_____
9.	7,232.08	$4\frac{1}{2}$/20, n/45	5,500	_____	_____

Using the ordinary dating method, calculate the discount date and the net date for the following transactions.

	Date of Invoice	Terms of Sale	Discount Date(s)	Net Date
10.	November 4	2/10, n/45	Nov. 14	Dec. 19
11.	August 18	2/24, n/55		
12.	August 11	3/20, n/45		
13.	January 29	2/10, 1/20, n/60		
14.	July 8	4/25, n/90		

Using the EOM, ROG, and Extra dating methods, calculate the discount date and the net date for the following transactions. Unless otherwise specified, the net date is 20 days after the discount date.

	Date of Invoice	Terms of Sale	Discount Date	Net Date
15.	December 5	2/10, EOM	Jan. 10	Jan. 30
16.	June 27	3/15, EOM		
17.	September 1	3/20, ROG		
		Rec'd Oct. 3		
18.	February 11	2/10, 60 Extra		
19.	May 18	4/25, EOM		
20.	October 26	2/10, ROG		
		Rec'd Nov. 27		

21. The Apollo Company received an invoice from a vendor on April 12 in the amount of $1,420. The terms of sale were 2/15, n/45. The invoice included shipping charges of $108. The vendor sent $250 in merchandise that was not ordered. These goods will be returned by Apollo. (Remember, no discounts on shipping charges or returned goods.)

    a. What are the discount date and the net date?

    b. What is the amount of the cash discount?

    c. What is the net amount due?

22. An invoice is dated August 21 with terms of 4/18 EOM.

    a. What is the discount date?   b. What is the net date?

23. An invoice dated January 15 has terms of 3/20 ROG. The goods are delayed in shipment and arrive on March 2.

    a. What is the discount date?   b. What is the net date?

24. A retailer buys merchandise from a supplier with an invoice amount of $12,900. The terms of the sale are 5/20, n/30. What is the net amount due on the order if the bill is paid by the 20th day?

25. What payment should be made on an invoice in the amount of $3,400 dated August 7 if the terms of sale are 3/15, 2/30, n/45 and the bill is paid on

   a. August 19?

   b. September 3?

26. Vu Video purchases some merchandise with an invoice price of $20,900 and terms of sale of 5/15, n/45. What is the net amount due on the order if a partial payment of $10,800 is made on the 15th day?

27. Red Tag Furniture received a SeaLand container of sofas from Thailand on April 14. The invoice, dated March 2, was for $46,230 in merchandise and $2,165 in shipping charges. The terms of sale were 3/15 ROG. Red Tag Furniture made a partial payment of $15,000 on April 27.

   a. What is the net amount due?

   b. What is the net date?

28. City Cellular purchased $28,900 in cell phones on April 25. The terms of sale were 4/20, 3/30, n/60. Freight terms were F.O.B. destination. Returned goods amounted to $650.

   a. What is the net amount due if City Cellular sends the manufacturer a partial payment of $5,000 on May 20?

   b. What is the net date?

   c. If the manufacturer charges a $4\frac{1}{2}$% late fee, how much would City Cellular owe if it did not pay the balance by the net date?

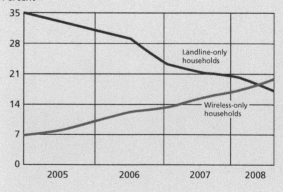

When cell phones passed landlines in use in U.S. homes.

Percent

Landline-only households

Wireless-only households

2005 2006 2007 2008

In 2008, for the first time, the number of U.S. households opting for only cell phones outnumbered those that had just traditional landlines, and the trend has continued since that time.

Source: National Center for Health Statistics

BUSINESS DECISION: THE EMPLOYMENT TEST

29. As part of the employment interview for an accounting job at Sound Design, you have been asked to answer the questions below, based on an invoice from one of Sound Design's vendors, Target Electronic Wholesalers.

TARGET ELECTRONIC WHOLESALERS
1979 N.E. 123 Street
Jacksonville, Florida 32204

Sold to: Sound Design
480 McDowell Rd.
Phoenix, AZ 85008

Invoice Date: June 28, 20XX

Terms of Sale: 3/15, n/30 ROG

Stock #	Description	Unit Price	Amount
4811V	Stereo Receivers	50 × $297.50 =	_____
511CX	Blu-ray Players	25 × $132.28 =	_____
6146M	Home Theater Systems	40 × $658.12 =	_____
1031A	LCD TVs	20 × $591.00 =	_____

Merchandise Total		_____
Insurance + Shipping		$1,150.00
Invoice Total		_____

a. Extend each line and calculate the merchandise total and the total amount of the invoice, using the space provided on the invoice.

b. What are the discount date and the net date if the shipment arrived on July 16?

c. While in transit, five Blu-ray players and four LCD TVs were damaged and will be returned. What is the amount of the returned merchandise? What is the revised merchandise total?

d. What are the amount of the cash discount and the net amount due if the discount is taken?

e. If Sound Design sends in a partial payment of $20,000 within the discount period, what is the net balance still due?

CHAPTER 7

CHAPTER FORMULAS

The Invoice

Extended total = Number of items × Cost per item

Trade Discounts—Single

Trade discount = List price × Trade discount rate

Net price = List price − Trade discount

Net price = List price (100% − Trade discount rate)

$$\text{Trade discount rate} = \frac{\text{Trade discount}}{\text{List price}}$$

Trade Discounts—Series

Net price = List price × Net price factor

Single equivalent discount = 1 − Net price factor

Trade discount = List price × Single equivalent discount

Cash Discounts and Terms of Sale

Net amount due = Net price (100% − Cash discount rate)

$$\text{Partial payment credit} = \frac{\text{Partial payment}}{100\% - \text{Cash discount rate}}$$

Net amount due = Net price − Partial payment credit

CHAPTER SUMMARY

Section I: The Invoice

Topic	Important Concepts	Illustrative Examples
Reading and Understanding the Parts of an Invoice **Performance Objective 7-1, Page 197**	Refer to Exhibits 7-1 to 7-3.	

Extending and Totaling an Invoice
 	
Performance Objective 7-2, Page 200
		The Great Subversion, a sandwich shop, ordered 25 lb of ham at $3.69 per pound and 22 lb of cheese at $4.25 per pound. There is a $7.50 delivery charge. Extend each item and find the invoice subtotal and invoice total.
		
		25 × 3.69 = $92.25 Ham
		22 × 4.25 = 93.50 Cheese
		         $185.75 Subtotal
		         + 7.50 Delivery charge
		         $193.25 Invoice total

Section II: Trade Discounts—Single

Topic	Important Concepts	Illustrative Examples
Calculating the Amount of a Single Trade Discount **Performance Objective 7-3, Page 205**	Trade discounts are reductions from the manufacturer's list price given to businesses in the trade for the performance of various marketing functions.	Sunglass King ordered merchandise with a list price of $12,700 from a manufacturer. Because it is in the trade, Sunglass King gets a 35% trade discount. What is the amount of the trade discount? Trade discount = 12,700 × .35 = $4,445

Section II (continued)

Topic	Important Concepts	Illustrative Examples
Calculating Net Price by Using the Net Price Factor, Complement Method **Performance Objective 7-4, Page 205**		From the previous problem, use the net price factor to find the net price of the order for Sunglass King. Net price $= 12,700\,(100\% - 35\%)$ Net price $= 12,700 \times .65 = \underline{\$8,255}$
Calculating Trade Discount Rate When List Price and Net Price Are Known **Performance Objective 7-5, Page 206**		Cycle World Bike Shop orders merchandise listing for $5,300 from Schwinn. The net price of the order is $3,200. What is the trade discount rate? Trade discount $= 5,300 - 3,200 = \$2,100$ Trade discount rate $= \dfrac{2,100}{5,300} = \underline{\underline{39.6\%}}$

Section III: Trade Discounts—Series

Topic	Important Concepts	Illustrative Examples
Calculating Net Price and the Amount of a Trade Discount by Using a Series of Trade Discounts **Performance Objective 7-6, Page 210**	Net price is found by taking each trade discount in the series from the succeeding net price until all discounts have been deducted.	An invoice with merchandise listing for $4,700 was entitled to trade discounts of 20% and 15%. What is the net price and the amount of the trade discount? $4,700 \times .20 = 940$ $4,700 - 940 = 3,760$ $3,760 \times .15 = 564$ $3,760 - 564 = \underline{\$3,196}$ Net price Trade discount $= 4,700 - 3,196 = \underline{\underline{\$1,504}}$
Calculating Net Price of a Series of Trade Discounts by Using the Net Price Factor, Complement Method **Performance Objective 7-7, Page 211**	Net price factor is found by subtracting each trade discount rate from 100% (complement) and multiplying these complements together.	Use the net price factor method to verify your answer to the previous problem. $\begin{array}{cc} 100\% & 100\% \\ -\ 20\% & -\ 15\% \\ \hline .80\ \times & .85\ = .68 \end{array}$ Net price factor Net price $= 4,700 \times .68 = \underline{\$3,196}$
Calculating the Amount of a Trade Discount by Using a Single Equivalent Discount **Performance Objective 7-8, Page 212**		What is the single equivalent discount and the amount of the trade discount in the previous problem? Use this to verify your trade discount answer. Single equivalent discount $= 1 - .68 = \underline{.32}$ Trade discount $= 4,700 \times .32 = \underline{\$1,504}$

Section IV: Cash Discounts and Terms of Sale

Topic	Important Concepts	Illustrative Examples
Calculating Cash Discounts and Net Amount Due **Performance Objective 7-9, Page 217**	Terms of sale specify when an invoice must be paid and if a cash discount is offered. Cash discount is an extra discount offered by the seller as an incentive for early payment of an invoice.	Action Auto Parts orders merchandise for $1,800, including $100 in freight charges. Action gets a 3% cash discount. What is the amount of the cash discount and the net amount due? $1,800 - 100 = \$1,700$ Net price Cash discount $= 1,700 \times .03 = \underline{\$51}$ $1,700 - 51 =$ 1,649 $\underline{+\ 100}$ Shipping charge $\underline{\underline{\$1,749}}$ Net amount due
Calculating Net Amount Due, with Credit Given for Partial Payment **Performance Objective 7-10, Page 218**		Elite Fashions makes a partial payment of $3,000 on an invoice of $7,900. The terms of sale are 3/15, n/30. What is the amount of the partial payment credit, and how much does Elite Fashions still owe on the invoice? Part pmt credit $= \dfrac{3,000}{100\% - 3\%} = \underline{\$3,092.78}$ Net amount due $=$ 7,900.00 $\underline{-\ 3,092.78}$ $\underline{\underline{\$4,807.22}}$
Determining Discount Date and Net Date by Using Various Terms of Sale Dating Methods **Performance Objective 7-11, Page 220**	Discount date: last date to take advantage of a cash discount. Net date: last date to pay an invoice without incurring a penalty charge.	
Ordinary Dating Method **Performance Objective 7-11, Page 221**	Ordinary dating: discount period and the credit period start on the date of the invoice.	Galaxy Jewelers receives an invoice for merchandise on March 12 with terms of 3/15, n/30. What are the discount date and the net date? Disc. date $=$ March 12 + 15 days $= \underline{\text{March 27}}$ Net date $=$ March 12 + 30 days $= \underline{\text{April 11}}$

EOM or Proximo Dating Method
 	
Performance Objective 7-11, Page 222
	EOM means end of month. It is a dating method in which the terms of sale start *after* the end of the month of the invoice.
	    If the invoice is dated after the 25th of the month, the terms of sale start *after* the end of the *following* month.
	    Unless otherwise specified, the net date is *20 days* after the discount date.
	    Proximo, or prox, is another name for EOM dating. It means "in the following month."
		Majestic Cleaning Service buys supplies with terms of sale of 2/10, EOM. What are the discount date and the net date if the invoice date is
		
		a. May 5?
		b. May 27?
		
		a. May 5 invoice terms start *after* the end of May:
		
		   Discount date $= \underline{\text{June 10}}$
		   Net date $=$ June 10 + 20 days $= \underline{\text{June 30}}$
		
		b. May 27 invoice terms start *after* the end of the *following* month, June:
		
		   Discount date $= \underline{\text{July 10}}$
		   Net date $=$ July 10 + 20 days $= \underline{\text{July 30}}$

Topic	Important Concepts	Illustrative Examples
ROG Dating Method **Performance Objective 7-11, Page 223**	ROG means receipt of goods. It is a dating method in which the terms of sale begin on the date the goods are received rather than the invoice date. This is used to accommodate long shipping times. Unless otherwise specified, the net date is *20 days* after the discount date.	An invoice dated August 24 has terms of 3/10 ROG. If the merchandise arrives on October 1, what are the discount date and the net date? Disc. date = October 1 + 10 days = October 11 Net date = October 11 + 20 days = October 31
Extra Dating Method **Performance Objective 7-11, Page 224**	Extra, Ex, or X is a dating method in which the buyer receives an extra period of time before the terms of sale begin. Vendors use extra dating as an incentive to entice buyers to purchase out-of-season or slow-moving merchandise. Unless otherwise specified, the net date is *20 days* after the discount date.	Sugar Pine Candy Company buys merchandise from a vendor with terms of 3/15, 60 Extra. The invoice is dated December 11. What are the discount date and the net date? Disc. date = December 11 + 75 days = February 24 Net date = February 24 + 20 days = March 16

TRY IT: EXERCISE SOLUTIONS FOR CHAPTER 7

1. **a.** Shutterbug Camera Shops   **h.** J. Herman

    b. 44929   **i.** Federal Express

    c. November 27, 20XX   **j.** Knoxville, TN

    d. $3,120.00   **k.** $125.00

    e. FotoFair Distributors   **l.** $5,632.80

    f. Net - 30 days   **m.** $345.00

    g. 1864 N.W. 123rd St., Chicago, IL 60613   **n.** $5,757.80

2.

Stock #	Quantity	Unit	Merchandise Description	Unit Price	Total
R443	125	ea.	Food Processors	$89.00	$11,125.00
B776	24	ea.	Microwave Ovens	$225.40	$5,409.60
Z133	6	doz.	12" Mixers	$54.12	$324.72
Z163	1	bx.	Mixer Covers	$166.30	$166.30
				Invoice Subtotal	$17,025.62
				Shipping Charges	+ $194.20
				Invoice Total	$17,219.82

3. Trade discount = List price × Trade discount rate
    Trade discount = 7,600 × .30 = $2,280

4. Net price = List price (100% − Trade discount rate)
    Net price = 2,100 (100% − 35%)
    Net price = 2,100 × .65 = $1,365

5. Trade discount = List price − Net price
    Trade discount = 109,500 − 63,300 = $46,200

    Trade discount rate = $\dfrac{\text{Trade discount}}{\text{List price}}$ = $\dfrac{46,200}{109,500}$ = .4219 = 42.2%

6.

25,000	25,000	16,250	16,250	13,000	13,000
× .35	− 8,750	× .20	− 3,250	× .10	− 1,300
8,750	16,250	3,250	13,000	1,300	$11,700 = Net price

Trade discount = 25,000 − 11,700 = $13,300

7. **a.**

100%		100%		100%	
− 30%		− 20%		− 12%	
.7	×	.8	×	.88	= .4928 = Net price factor

b. Net price = List price × Net price factor
Net price = 3,500 × .4928 = $1,724.80

c. Net price = List price × Net price factor
Net price = 5,800 × .4928 = $2,858.24

8.   100%   100%   100%
        $-\ 25\%$ $-\ 15\%$ $-\ 10\%$
        .75 $\times$ .85 $\times$ .9   = .57375 = Net price factor

Single equivalent discount = 1 – Net price factor
Single equivalent discount = 1 – .57375 = .42625
Trade discount = List price $\times$ Single equivalent discount
Trade discount = 36,800 $\times$ .42625 = $15,686

9. Cash discount = Net price $\times$ Cash discount rate
Cash discount = 8,300 $\times$ .03 = $249
Net amount due = Net price – Cash discount
Net amount due = 8,300 – 249 = $8,051

10. Partial payment credit = $\dfrac{\text{Partial payment}}{100\% - \text{Cash discount rate}}$

Partial payment credit = $\dfrac{20,000}{100\% - 4\%} = \dfrac{20,000}{.96} = \$20,833.33$

Net amount due = Net price – Partial payment credit
Net amount due = 45,300.00 – 20,833.33 = $24,466.67

11. From the calendar, September 12 is day number 255.

255 + 60 = 315

From the calendar, day number 315 is November 11.

12. Discount date = June 11 + 10 days = June 21
Net date = June 11 + 60 days
        30 Days in June
       $-\ 11$ Discount date
        19 June
        31 July
       $+\ 10$ Aug. $\longrightarrow$ August 10
        60 Days

13. a.   Discount date = 15 days after end of November = December 15
            Net date = December 15 + 20 days = January 4

   b.   Discount date = 15 days after end of December = January 15
            Net date = January 15 + 20 days = February 4

14. Discount date = December 29 + 20 days = January 18
Net date = January 18 + 20 days = February 7

15. Discount date = February 22 + 80 days = May 13
Net date = May 13 + 20 days = June 2

CONCEPT REVIEW

1. The document detailing a sales transaction is known as a(n) _____. (7-1)

2. F.O.B. shipping point and F.O.B. destination are shipping terms that specify where the merchandise _____ is transferred. (7-1)

3. To extend an invoice, for each line, we multiply the number of items by the _____ per item. (7-2)

4. To calculate the amount of a single trade discount, we multiply the _____ price by the trade discount rate. (7-3)

5. The _____ price is the amount a business actually pays for merchandise after the discount has been deducted. (7-4)

6. To calculate the net price factor, we subtract the trade discount rate from _____ . (7-4)

7. Write the formula for the trade discount rate. (7-5)

8. In a chain or _____ of trade discounts, we calculate the final net price by taking each discount one at a time from the previous net price. (7-6)

9. As a shortcut, we can use the net price _____ method to calculate the net price. (7-7)

10. To calculate the net price factor, we subtract each trade discount rate from 100% and then _____ all the complements together. (7-7)

11. A single trade discount that equates to all the discounts in a series or chain is called a single _____ discount. (7-8)

12. The "_____ of sale" specify when an invoice must be paid and if a(n) _____ discount is being offered. (7-9)

13. To calculate the credit given for a partial payment, we divide the amount of the partial payment by 100% _____ the cash discount rate. (7-10)

14. The most common method for dating an invoice is when the discount period and the credit period start on the date of the invoice. This method is known as _____ dating. (7-11)

ASSESSMENT TEST

Answer the following questions based on the Leisure Time Industries invoice at the bottom of the page.

1. Who is the vendor?

2. What is the date of the invoice?

3. What is the stock number of rocker chairs?

4. What does dz. mean?

5. What is the unit price of plastic lounge covers?

6. What is the destination?

7. What is the extended total for chaise lounges with no armrest?

8. Who pays the freight if the terms are F.O.B. shipping point?

9. What is the invoice subtotal?

10. What is the invoice total?

LEISURE TIME INDUSTRIES
LTI

Patio Furniture Manufacturers
1930 Main Street
Fort Worth, Texas 76102

DATE: November 2, 20XX

SOLD TO: Patio Magic Stores
3386 Fifth Avenue
Raleigh, NC 27613

INVOICE # B-112743

TERMS OF SALE: Net 30 days

SHIPPING INFO: FedEx Freight

STOCK #	QUANTITY	UNIT	MERCHANDISE DESCRIPTION	UNIT PRICE	TOTAL
1455	40	ea.	Chaise Lounges with armrest	$169.00	_____
1475	20	ea.	Chaise Lounges—no armrest	$127.90	_____
4387	24	ea.	Rocker Chairs	$87.70	_____
8100	3	dz.	Plastic Lounge Covers	$46.55	_____

INVOICE SUBTOTAL: _____
Packing and Handling: $125.00
Shipping Charges: $477.50

INVOICE TOTAL: _____

11. The Fortunate Filly dress shop receives an invoice for the purchase of merchandise with a list price of $9,500 and receives a trade discount of 22%. What is the amount of the trade discount?

12. Stone Implement Supply buys chain saws that list for $395.95 less a 28% trade discount.
   a. What is the amount of the trade discount?

   b. What is the net price of each lawn mower?

13. Shorty's BBQ Restaurant places an order listing for $1,250 with a meat and poultry supplier. Shorty's receives a trade discount of $422 on the order. What is the trade discount rate on this transaction?

14. Fantasia Florist Shop purchases an order of imported roses with a list price of $2,375 less trade discounts of 15/20/20.
   a. What is the amount of the trade discount?

   b. What is the net amount of the order?

15. All-American Sports can purchase sneakers for $450 per dozen less trade discounts of 14/12 from Ideal Shoes. Fancy Footwear is offering the same sneakers for $435 less trade discounts of 18/6. Which supplier offers a lower net price?

16. **a.** What is the net price factor for trade discounts of 25/15/10?

   b. Use that net price factor to find the net price of a TV listing for $600.

17. **a.** What is the net price factor of the trade discount series 20/15/11?

   b. What is the single equivalent discount?

The U.S. Carpet Industry
According to the Carpet and Rug Institute, carpet covers nearly 60% of all floors in the United States. Ninety percent of all domestic carpet is manufactured in Georgia, representing a significant economic impact to the state. Nationwide, the industry employs over 70,000 workers.

18. The Empire Carpet Company orders merchandise for $17,700, including $550 in shipping charges, from Mohawk Carpet Mills on May 4. Carpets valued at $1,390 will be returned because they are damaged. The terms of sale are 2/10, n/30 ROG. The shipment arrives on May 26, and Empire wants to take advantage of the cash discount.
   a. By what date must Empire pay the invoice?

   b. As the bookkeeper for Empire, how much will you send to Mohawk?

19. Lazy Days Laundry receives an invoice for detergent. The invoice is dated April 9 with terms of 3/15, n/30.

    a. What is the discount date?

    c. If the invoice terms are changed to 3/15 EOM, what is the new discount date?

    b. What is the net date?

    d. What is the new net date?

20. Ned's Sheds purchases building materials from Timbertown Lumber for $3,700 with terms of 4/15, n/30. The invoice is dated October 17. Ned's decides to send in a $2,000 partial payment.

    a. By what date must the partial payment be sent to take advantage of the cash discount?

    b. What is the net date?

    c. If partial payment was sent by the discount date, what is the balance still due on the order?

21. A new sound system is being installed at Club Falcon. The invoice, dated June 9, shows the total cost of the equipment as $16,480. Shipping charges amount to $516, and insurance is $81.20. Terms of sale are 2/10 prox. If the invoice is paid on July 9, what is the net amount due?

Chuck Wagner/Shutterstock.com

BUSINESS DECISION: THE BUSY EXECUTIVE

22. You are a salesperson for Victory Lane Wholesale Auto Parts. You have just taken a phone order from one of your best customers, Champion Motors. Because you were busy when the call came in, you recorded the details of the order on a notepad.

Phone Order Notes

- The invoice date is April 4, 20XX.
- The customer order no. is 443B.
- Champion Motors's warehouse is located at 7011 N.W. 4th Avenue, Columbus, Ohio 43205.
- Terms of sale—3/15, n/45.
- The order will be filled by D. Watson.
- The goods will be shipped by truck.
- Champion Motors's home office is located next to the warehouse at 7013 N.W. 4th Avenue.
- Champion ordered 44 car batteries, stock #394, listing for $69.95 each and 24 truck batteries, stock #395, listing for $89.95 each. These items get trade discounts of 20/15.
- Champion also ordered 36 cases of 10W/30 motor oil, stock #838-W, listing for $11.97 per case, and 48 cases of 10W/40 super-oil, stock #1621-S, listing for $14.97 per case. These items get trade discounts of 20/20/12.
- The shipping charges for the order amount to $67.50.
- Insurance charges amount to $27.68.

    a. Transfer your notes to the invoice on the next page, extend each line, and calculate the total.

    b. What is the discount date of the invoice?

c. If Champion sends a partial payment of $1,200 by the discount date, what is the balance due on the invoice?

d. What is the net date of the invoice?

e. Your company has a policy of charging a 5% late fee if invoice payments are more than five days late. What is the amount of the late fee that Champion will be charged if it fails to pay the balance due on time?

INVOICE

Victory Lane
Wholesale Auto Parts
422 Riverfront Road
Cincinnati, Ohio 45244

Invoice #

Invoice Date:

Sold To:

Ship To:

Customer Order No.	Salesperson	Ship via	Terms of Sale	Filled by

Quantity Ordered	Stock Number	Description	Unit List Price	Trade Discounts	Extended Amount

Invoice Subtotal   _____
Shipping Charges   _____
Insurance   _____
Invoice Total   _____

COLLABORATIVE LEARNING ACTIVITY

Comparing Invoices and Discounts

1. As a team, collect invoices from a number of businesses in different industries in your area.

   a. How are they similar?

   b. How are they different?

2. Have each member of the team speak with a wholesaler or a retailer in your area.

   a. What are the typical trade discounts in that industry?

   b. What are the typical terms of sale in that industry?

CHAPTER 8 Markup and Markdown

PERFORMANCE OBJECTIVES

8

MARKUP BASED ON COST

cost of goods sold The cost of the merchandise sold during an operating period. One of the two major expense categories of a business.

operating expenses or **overhead** All business expenses, other than the cost of merchandise, required to operate a business, such as payroll, rent, utilities, and insurance.

markup, markon, or margin The amount added to the cost of an item to cover the operating expenses and profit. It is the difference between the cost and the selling price.

Determining an appropriate selling price for a company's goods or services is an extremely important function in business. The price must be attractive to potential customers, yet sufficient to cover expenses and provide the company with a reasonable profit.

In business, expenses are separated into two major categories. The first is the **cost of goods sold**. To a manufacturer, this expense would be the cost of production; to a wholesaler or retailer, the expense is the price paid to a manufacturer or distributor for the merchandise. The second category includes all the other expenses required to operate the business, such as salaries, rent, utilities, taxes, insurance, advertising, and maintenance. These expenses are known as **operating expenses**, overhead expenses, or simply **overhead**.

The amount added to the cost of an item to cover the operating expenses and profit is known as the **markup, markon,** or **margin**. It is the difference between the cost and the selling price of an item. Markup is applied at all levels of the marketing channels of distribution. This chapter deals with the business math applications involved in the pricing of goods and services.

8-1 UNDERSTANDING AND USING THE RETAILING EQUATION TO FIND COST, AMOUNT OF MARKUP, AND SELLING PRICE OF AN ITEM

retailing equation The selling price of an item is equal to the cost plus the markup.

The fundamental principle on which business operates is to sell goods and services for a price high enough to cover all expenses and provide the owners with a reasonable profit. The formula that describes this principle is known as the **retailing equation**. The equation states that the selling price of an item is equal to the cost plus the markup.

$$\text{Selling price} = \text{Cost} + \text{Markup}$$

Using the abbreviations C for cost, M for markup, and SP for selling price, the formula is written as

$$SP = C + M$$

To illustrate, if a camera costs a retailer $60 and a $50 markup is added to cover operating expenses and profit, the selling price of the camera would be $110.

$$\$60 \text{ (cost)} + \$50 \text{ (markup)} = \$110 \text{ (selling price)}$$

In Chapter 5, we learned that equations are solved by isolating the unknowns on one side and the knowns on the other. Using this theory, when the amount of markup is the unknown, the equation can be rewritten as

$$\text{Markup} = \text{Selling price} - \text{Cost} \qquad M = SP - C$$

When the cost is the unknown, the equation becomes

$$\text{Cost} = \text{Selling price} - \text{Markup} \qquad C = SP - M$$

The following examples illustrate how these formulas are used to determine the dollar amount of cost, markup, and selling price.

EXAMPLE1 FINDING THE SELLING PRICE

Mementos Gift Shop pays $8.00 for a picture frame. If a markup of $6.50 is added, what is the selling price of the frame?

▶SOLUTIONSTRATEGY

Because selling price is the unknown variable, we use the formula $SP = C + M$ as follows:

$$SP = C + M$$
$$SP = 8.00 + 6.50 = 14.50$$
$$\text{Selling price} = \underline{\$14.50}$$

▶TRYITEXERCISE 1

For the following, use the basic retailing equation to solve for the unknown.

Hairbrushes cost the manufacturer $6.80 per unit to produce. If a markup of $9.40 is added to the cost, what is the selling price per brush?

CHECK YOUR ANSWER WITH THE SOLUTION ON PAGE 264.

EXAMPLE2 FINDING THE AMOUNT OF MARKUP

Reliable Office Supply buys printing calculators from Taiwan for $22.50 each. If they are sold for $39.95, what is the amount of the markup?

▶SOLUTIONSTRATEGY

Because the markup is the unknown variable, we use the formula $M = SP - C$ as follows:

$$M = SP - C$$
$$M = 39.95 - 22.50 = 17.45$$
$$\text{Markup} = \underline{\$17.45}$$

▶TRYITEXERCISE 2

For the following, use the basic retailing equation to solve for the unknown.

The 19th Hole sells a dozen golf balls for $28.50. If the distributor was paid $16.75, what is the amount of the markup?

CHECK YOUR ANSWER WITH THE SOLUTION ON PAGE 264.

EXAMPLE3 FINDING THE COST

Safeway Supermarkets sell Corn Crunchies for $3.29 per box. If the markup on this item is $2.12, how much did the store pay for the cereal?

▶SOLUTIONSTRATEGY

Because the cost is the unknown variable in this problem, we use the formula $C = SP - M$.

$$C = SP - M$$
$$C = 3.29 - 2.12 = 1.17$$
$$\text{Cost} = \underline{\$1.17}$$

▶TRYITEXERCISE 3

For the following, use the basic retailing equation to solve for the unknown.

After a wholesaler adds a markup of $75 to a television set, it is sold to a retail store for $290. What is the wholesaler's cost?

CHECK YOUR ANSWER WITH THE SOLUTION ON PAGE 264.

8-2 CALCULATING PERCENT MARKUP BASED ON COST

markup based on cost When cost is 100% and the markup is expressed as a percent of that cost.

In addition to being expressed in dollar amounts, markup is frequently expressed as a percent. There are two ways of representing markup as a percent: based on cost and based on selling price. Manufacturers and most wholesalers use cost as the base in calculating the percent markup because cost figures are readily available to them. When markup is based on cost, the cost is 100%, and the markup is expressed as a percent of that cost. Retailers, however, use selling price figures as the base of most calculations, including percent markup. In retailing, the selling price represents 100%, and the markup is expressed as a percent of that selling price.

In Chapter 6, we used the percentage formula Portion = Rate × Base. To review these variables, portion is a *part* of a whole amount; base is the *whole amount*; and rate, as a percent, describes what part the portion is of the base. When we calculate markup as a percent, we are actually solving a rate problem using the formula Rate = Portion ÷ Base.

When the markup is based on cost, the percent markup is the rate; the dollar amount of markup is the portion; and the cost, representing 100%, is the base. The answer will describe what percent the markup is of the cost; therefore, it is called percent **markup based on cost**. We use the formula:

Learning Tip

A shortcut for calculating the factors of the retailing equation is to use the **markup table**. The cells represent cost, markup, and selling price in both dollars and percents.

Markup Table

	$	%
C		
+ MU		
SP		

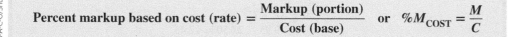

$$\text{Percent markup based on cost (rate)} = \frac{\text{Markup (portion)}}{\text{Cost (base)}} \quad \text{or} \quad \%M_{\text{COST}} = \frac{M}{C}$$

Learning Tip

Step 1. Fill in the given information using 100% for the base and *X* for this unknown. (orange)

Step 2. Calculate the figure for the remaining cell (red) in the column without the *X*.

$89.60 − $56.00 = $33.60

	$	%
C	56.00	100
+ MU	**33.60**	**X**
SP	89.60	

Then form a box. **(yellow)**

(continued on next page)

EXAMPLE4 CALCULATING PERCENT MARKUP BASED ON COST

Blanco Industries produces stainless steel sinks at a cost of $56.00 each. If the sinks are sold to distributors for $89.60 each, what are the amount of the markup and the percent markup based on cost?

▶SOLUTIONSTRATEGY

$$M = SP - C$$
$$M = 89.60 - 56.00 = 33.60$$
$$\text{Markup} = \underline{\$33.60}$$

$$\%M_{\text{COST}} = \frac{M}{C}$$

$$\%M_{\text{COST}} = \frac{33.60}{56.00} = .6$$

$$\text{Percent markup based on cost} = \underline{60\%}$$

►TRYITEXERCISE 4

The Light Source buys lamps for $45 and sells them for $63. What are the amount of the markup and the percent markup based on cost?

CHECK YOUR ANSWERS WITH THE SOLUTIONS ON PAGE 264.

(continued from previous page)

The figures in the box form a proportion.

$$\frac{56}{33.60} = \frac{100}{X}$$

Step 3. Solve the proportion for X by cross-multiplying the corner figures in the box.

$$56X = 33.60 \,(100)$$
$$X = \frac{3,360}{56} = 60\%$$

CALCULATING SELLING PRICE WHEN COST AND PERCENT MARKUP BASED ON COST ARE KNOWN

8-3

From the basic retailing equation, we know that the selling price is equal to the cost plus the markup. When the markup is based on cost, the cost equals 100%, and the selling price equals 100% plus the percent markup. If, for example, the percent markup is 30%, then

Selling price = Cost + Markup
Selling price = 100% + 30%
Selling price = 130% *of* the cost

Because *of* means multiply, we multiply the cost by (100% plus the percent markup).

Selling price = Cost (100% + Percent markup based on cost)

$$SP = C \,(100\% + \%M_{COST}).$$

EXAMPLE5 CALCULATING THE SELLING PRICE

A wallet costs $50 to produce. If the manufacturer wants a 70% markup based on cost, what should be the selling price of the wallet?

►SOLUTIONSTRATEGY

$$SP = C \,(100\% + \%M_{COST})$$
$$SP = 50 \,(100\% + 70\%)$$
$$SP = 50 \,(170\%) = 50 \,(1.7) = 85$$
Selling price = $\underline{\underline{\$85}}$

	+		= 170%
		$	%
C			
+ MU			
SP		X	170

Note: When the brown box has six cells, use the four corner figures to form the proportion.

$$100X = 50 \,(170)$$
$$X = \underline{\underline{\$85}}$$

►TRYITEXERCISE 5

Superior Appliances buys toasters for $38. If a 65% markup based on cost is desired, what should be the selling price of the toaster?

CHECK YOUR ANSWER WITH THE SOLUTION ON PAGE 264.

8-4 CALCULATING COST WHEN SELLING PRICE AND PERCENT MARKUP BASED ON COST ARE KNOWN

To calculate cost when selling price and percent markup on cost are known, let's use our knowledge of solving equations from Chapter 5. Because we are dealing with the same three variables from the last section, simply solve the equation $SP = C (100\% + \%M_{COST})$ for the cost. Cost, the unknown, is isolated on one side of the equation by dividing both sides by (100% + Percent markup).

$$\text{Cost} = \frac{\text{Selling price}}{100\% + \text{Percent markup on cost}} \qquad C = \frac{SP}{100\% + \%M_{COST}}$$

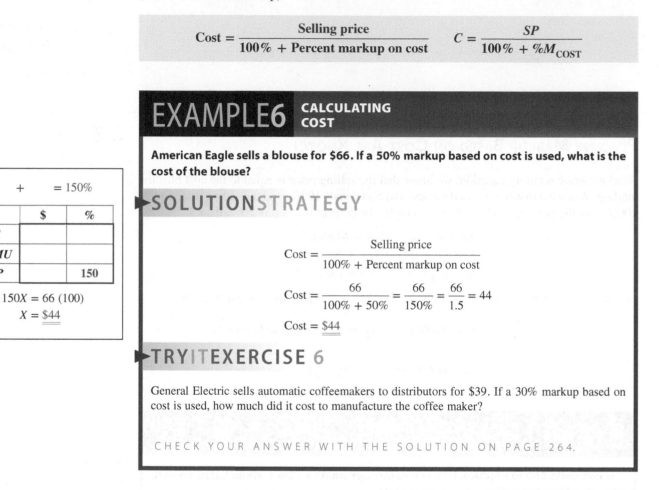

EXAMPLE 6   CALCULATING COST

American Eagle sells a blouse for $66. If a 50% markup based on cost is used, what is the cost of the blouse?

SOLUTIONSTRATEGY

$$\text{Cost} = \frac{\text{Selling price}}{100\% + \text{Percent markup on cost}}$$

$$\text{Cost} = \frac{66}{100\% + 50\%} = \frac{66}{150\%} = \frac{66}{1.5} = 44$$

$$\text{Cost} = \$44$$

TRYITEXERCISE 6

General Electric sells automatic coffeemakers to distributors for $39. If a 30% markup based on cost is used, how much did it cost to manufacture the coffee maker?

CHECK YOUR ANSWER WITH THE SOLUTION ON PAGE 264.

Table alongside example:

	$	%
C		
+ MU		
SP		150

+ = 150%

$150X = 66 (100)$

$X = \$44$

SECTION I   8   REVIEW EXERCISES

For the following items, calculate the missing information. Round dollars to the nearest cent and percents to the nearest tenth of a percent.

JUMP START WWW

	Item	Cost	Amount of Markup	Selling Price	Percent Markup Based on Cost
1.	Television set	$161.50	$138.45	$299.95	85.7%
2.	Bookcase	$32.40	$21.50		
3.	Automobile		$5,400.00	$12,344.80	
4.	Dress	$75.00			80%
5.	Vacuum cleaner			$249.95	60%

Item	Cost	Amount of Markup	Selling Price	Percent Markup Based on Cost
6. Hat	$46.25	$50.00	$96.25	108.1%
7. Computer	$1,350.00	_____	$3,499.00	_____
8. Treadmill	_____	$880.00	$2,335.00	_____
9. 1 lb potatoes	$.58	_____	_____	130%
10. Wallet	_____	_____	$44.95	75%

Solve the following word problems. Round dollars to the nearest cent and percents to the nearest tenth of a percent.

11. Alarm clocks cost the manufacturer $56.10 per unit to produce. If a markup of $29.80 is added to the cost, what is the selling price per clock?

12. LooLoo Clothing Emporium sells scarves for $19.95. If the cost per scarf is $12.50, what is the amount of the markup?

13. After a wholesaler adds a markup of $420 to a TV, it sold for $949. What is the cost of the TV?

14. A wholesaler sells a guitar for $1,248.90. What is the percent markup based on cost if the whole-saler paid $690 for the guitar?

15. The Holiday Card Shop purchased stationery for $2.44 per box. A $1.75 markup is added to the stationery.

    a. What is the selling price?

    b. What is the percent markup based on cost?

16. Staples adds a $4.60 markup to calculators and sells them for $9.95.

    a. What is the cost of the calculators?

    b. What is the percent markup based on cost?

17. a. What is the amount of markup on a skateboard from Flying Wheels Skate Shop if the cost is $58.25 and the selling price is $118.88?

    b. What is the percent markup based on cost?

Amazon.com, Inc., product categories include books, movies, music, and games; digital downloads; electronics and computers; home and garden; toys, kids, and baby; grocery; apparel, shoes, and jewelry; health and beauty; sports and outdoors; and tools, auto, and industrial products.

The stated mission of Amazon.com is to "be Earth's most customer-centric company for four primary customer sets: consumers, sellers, enterprises, and content creators." In its first year, 1997, Amazon.com's net sales were $148 million. Twenty years later net sales were over $177 billion.

THE CAMERA CONNECTION

$109.99

PowerShooter **1800**

$199.99

CyberShooter **2400**

18. You are the manager of The Camera Connection. Use the advertisement for your store to answer the following questions:

   a. If the PowerShooter 1800 is marked up by $58.50, what is the cost and what is the percent markup based on cost?

   b. If the CyberShooter 2400 has a cost of $88.00, what are the amount of the markup and the percent markup based on cost?

   c. Which camera is more "profitable" to the store? Why?

   d. What other factors should be considered in determining profitability?

19. A wholesaler requires a markup of 35% based on cost for merchandise sold. What should the selling price of a watch be if each watch costs $70?

20. Broadway Carpets sells designer rugs at retail for $875.88. If a 50% markup based on cost is added, what is the cost of the designer rugs?

21. A customer just paid $79.20 for a raincoat. If the percent markup based on cost is 44%, what was the cost?

22. A real-wood filing cabinet from Office Solutions is marked up by $97.30 to $178.88.

   a. What is the cost?

   b. What is the percent markup based on cost?

23. The Green Thumb Garden Shop purchases automatic lawn sprinklers for $12.50 from the manufacturer. If a 75% markup based on cost is added, at what retail price should the sprinklers be marked?

24. a. What is the cost of a desk lamp at Urban Accents if the selling price is $49.95 and the markup is 70% based on the cost?

   b. What is the amount of the markup?

BUSINESS DECISION: KEYSTONE MARKUP

iStock.com/
MarsBars

25. In department and specialty store retailing, a common markup strategy is to double the cost of an item to arrive at the selling price. This strategy is known as **keystoning** the markup and is widely used in apparel, cosmetics, fashion accessories, shoes, and other categories of merchandise.

   The reasoning for the high amount of markup is that these stores have particularly high operating expenses. In addition, they have a continuing need to update fixtures and remodel stores to attract customers.

   You are the buyer in the women's shoe department of the Roma Grande Department Store. You normally keystone your markups on certain shoes and handbags. This amount of markup allows you enough gross margin so that you can lower prices when "sales" occur and still have a profitable department.

   a. If you are looking for a line of handbags that will retail for $120, what is the most you can pay for the bags?

   b. At a women's wear trade show, you find a line of handbags that you like with a suggested retail price of $130. The vendor has offered you trade discounts of 30/20/5. Will this series of trade discounts allow you to keystone the handbags?

   c. (Challenge) The vendor tells you that the first two discounts, 30% and 20%, are fixed, but the 5% is negotiable. What trade discount, rounded to a whole percent, should you request in order to keystone the markup?

Shopping Malls Southdale Center in a suburb of the Twin Cities in Minnesota was the first fully enclosed, climate-controlled shopping center in the United States. It opened in 1956 with approximately 800,000 square feet of retail space.

   Today there are over 1,000 shopping malls in the United States with numerous malls exceeding 2,000,000 square feet of retail space.

   Adapted from information at www.simon.com/mall/southdale-center/about and https://www.worldatlas.com/articles/largest-malls-in-the-us.html

---

MARKUP BASED ON SELLING PRICE

8 SECTION II

In Section I, we calculated markup as a percentage of the cost of an item. The cost was the base and represented 100%. As noted, this method is primarily used by manufacturers and wholesalers. In this section, the markup is calculated as a percentage of the selling price; therefore, the selling price will be the base and represent 100%. This practice is used by most retailers because most retail records and statistics are kept in sales dollars.

CALCULATING PERCENT MARKUP BASED ON SELLING PRICE

8-5

The calculation of percent **markup based on selling price** is the same as that for percent markup based on cost except that the base (the denominator) changes from cost to selling price. Remember, finding percent markup is a rate problem using the now familiar percentage formula Rate = Portion ÷ Base.

markup based on selling price
When selling price is 100% and the markup is expressed as a percent of that selling price.

For this application of the formula, the percent markup based on selling price is the rate, the amount of the markup is the portion, and the selling price is the base. The formula is

$$\text{Percent markup based on selling price (rate)} = \frac{\text{Markup (portion)}}{\text{Selling price (base)}} \quad \text{or} \quad \%M_{SP} = \frac{M}{SP}$$

EXAMPLE7 CALCULATING THE PERCENT MARKUP BASED ON SELLING PRICE

Quality Hardware & Garden Supply purchases electric drills for $60 each. If it sells the drills for $125, what is the amount of the markup and what is the percent markup based on selling price?

►SOLUTIONSTRATEGY

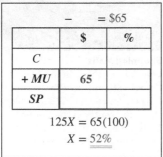

$$M = SP - C$$
$$M = 125 - 60 = 65$$
$$\text{Markup} = \underline{\$65}$$

$$\%M_{SP} = \frac{M}{SP}$$

$$\%M_{SP} = \frac{65}{125} = .52$$

Percent markup based on selling price = 52%

►TRYITEXERCISE 7

Deals on Wheels buys bicycles from the distributor for $94.50 each. If the bikes sell for $157.50, what is the amount of the markup and what is the percent markup based on selling price?

CHECK YOUR ANSWERS WITH THE SOLUTIONS ON PAGE 264.

8-6 CALCULATING SELLING PRICE WHEN COST AND PERCENT MARKUP BASED ON SELLING PRICE ARE KNOWN

When the percent markup is based on selling price, remember that the selling price is the base and represents 100%. This means the percent cost plus the percent markup must equal 100%. If, for example, the markup is 25% of the selling price, the cost must be 75% of the selling price.

$$\text{Cost} + \text{Markup} = \text{Selling price}$$
$$75\% + 25\% = 100\%$$

Because the percent markup is known, the percent cost will always be the complement, or

% Cost = 100% − Percent markup based on selling price

Because the selling price is the base, we can solve for the selling price by using the percentage formula Base = Portion ÷ Rate, where the cost is the portion and the percent cost or (100% − Percent markup on selling price) is the rate.

$$\text{Selling price} = \frac{\text{Cost}}{100\% - \text{Percent markup on selling price}} \quad \text{or} \quad SP = \frac{C}{100\% - \%M_{SP}}$$

EXAMPLE8 CALCULATING SELLING PRICE

High Point Furniture purchases wall units from the manufacturer for $550. If the store policy is to mark up all merchandise 60% based on the selling price, what is the retail selling price of the wall units?

SOLUTIONSTRATEGY

$$SP = \frac{C}{100\% - \%M_{SP}}$$

$$SP = \frac{550}{100\% - 60\%} = \frac{550}{40\%} = 1,375$$

Selling price = $1,375

	$	%
	−	= 40%
C		40
+ MU		
SP	X	

$$40X = 550 (100)$$
$$X = \$1,375$$

►TRYITEXERCISE 8

Grand Prix Menswear buys suits for $169 from the manufacturer. If a 35% markup based on selling price is the objective, what should be the selling price of the suit?

CHECK YOUR ANSWER WITH THE SOLUTION ON PAGE 264.

CALCULATING COST WHEN SELLING PRICE AND PERCENT MARKUP BASED ON SELLING PRICE ARE KNOWN

8-7

Often retailers know how much their customers are willing to pay for an item. The following procedure is used to determine the most a retailer can pay for an item and still get the intended markup.

To calculate the cost of an item when the selling price and percent markup based on selling price are known, we use a variation of the formula used in the last section. To solve for cost, we must isolate cost on one side of the equation by multiplying both sides of the equation by (100% − Percent markup). This yields the equation for cost:

Cost = Selling price (100% − Percent markup on selling price)

$$C = SP (100\% - \%M_{SP})$$

Learning Tip

The percent markup on cost is always *greater* than the corresponding percent markup on selling price because markup on cost uses cost as the base, which is *less* than the selling price. In the percentage formula, the lower the base, the greater the rate.

EXAMPLE9 CALCULATING COST

A buyer for a chain of boutiques is looking for a line of dresses to retail for $120. If a 40% markup based on selling price is the objective, what is the most the buyer can pay for these dresses and still get the intended markup?

►SOLUTIONSTRATEGY

$$C = SP (100\% - \%M_{SP})$$
$$C = 120 (100\% - 40\%) = 120 (.6) = 72$$

Cost = $72

	$	%
	−	= 60%
C	X	60
+ MU		
SP		

$$100X = 120(60)$$
$$X = \$72$$

▶TRYITEXERCISE 9

What is the most a gift shop buyer can pay for a set of wine glasses if he or she wants a 55% markup based on selling price and expects to sell the glasses for $79 at retail?

CHECK YOUR ANSWER WITH THE SOLUTION ON PAGE 264.

8-8   CONVERTING PERCENT MARKUP BASED ON COST TO PERCENT MARKUP BASED ON SELLING PRICE, AND VICE VERSA

CONVERTING PERCENT MARKUP BASED ON COST TO PERCENT MARKUP BASED ON SELLING PRICE

When percent markup is based on cost, it can be converted to percent markup based on selling price by using the following formula:

$$\text{Percent markup based on selling price} = \frac{\text{Percent markup based on cost}}{100\% + \text{Percent markup based on cost}}$$

EXAMPLE10   CONVERTING BETWEEN MARKUP TYPES

If a purse is marked up 60% based on cost, what is the corresponding percent markup based on selling price?

▶SOLUTIONSTRATEGY

$$\text{Percent markup based on selling price} = \frac{\text{Percent markup based on cost}}{100\% + \text{Percent markup based on cost}}$$

$$\text{Percent markup based on selling price} = \frac{60\%}{100\% + 60\%} = \frac{.6}{1.6} = .375$$

$$\text{Percent markup based on selling price} = \underline{37.5\%}$$

▶TRYITEXERCISE 10

A suitcase is marked up 50% based on cost. What is the corresponding percent markup based on selling price?

CHECK YOUR ANSWER WITH THE SOLUTION ON PAGE 264.

Learning Tip

This table provides a shortcut for converting between markup types. As before:

- Fill in the given information and also use 100% for the bases and X for the unknown. (orange)
- Calculate the figure for the remaining cell in the column without the X. (red)

  $100 + 60 = 160$

- Form a proportion and solve for X.

	% C	% SP
C	100	
+ MU	60	X
SP	160	100

$$\frac{60}{160} = \frac{X}{100}$$
$$160X = 60(100)$$
$$X = \underline{37.5\%}$$

CONVERTING PERCENT MARKUP BASED ON SELLING PRICE TO PERCENT MARKUP BASED ON COST

When percent markup is based on selling price, it can be converted to percent markup based on cost by using the following formula:

$$\text{Percent markup based on cost} = \frac{\text{Percent markup based on selling price}}{100\% - \text{Percent markup based on selling price}}$$

EXAMPLE11 CONVERTING BETWEEN MARKUP TYPES

At Walmart, a Panasonic sound system is marked up 25% based on selling price. What is the corresponding percent markup based on cost? Round to the nearest tenth of a percent.

▶ SOLUTIONSTRATEGY

$$\text{Percent markup based on cost} = \frac{\text{Percent markup based on selling price}}{100\% - \text{Percent markup based on selling price}}$$

$$\text{Percent markup based on cost} = \frac{25\%}{100\% - 25\%} = \frac{.25}{.75} = .3333$$

$$\text{Percent markup based on cost} = 33.3\%$$

−		= 75%
	% C	**% SP**
C		75
+ MU		
SP		

$$75X = 25\ (100)$$
$$X = \underline{33.3\%}$$

▶ TRYITEXERCISE 11

At Video Outlet, a PlayStation 4 game is marked up 75% based on selling price. What is the corresponding percent markup based on cost? Round to the nearest tenth of a percent.

CHECK YOUR ANSWER WITH THE SOLUTION ON PAGE 265.

REVIEW EXERCISES

8 SECTION II

For the following items, calculate the missing information. Round dollars to the nearest cent and percents to the nearest tenth of a percent.

	Item	Cost	Amount of Markup	Selling Price	Percent Markup Based on Cost	Percent Markup Based on Selling Price
1.	Sink	$65.00	$50.00	$115.00		43.5%
2.	Textbook	$34.44	_____	$51.50		_____
3.	Telephone	$75.00	_____	_____		45%
4.	Bicycle	_____	_____	$133.50		60%
5.	Magazine				60%	_____
6.	Flashlight				_____	35%
7.	Dollhouse	$71.25	$94.74	$165.99	133%	57.1%
8.	Bar of soap	$1.18	$.79	_____	_____	_____
9.	Truck	$15,449.00	_____	_____		38%
10.	Sofa	_____	_____	$1,299.00		55%
11.	Fan				150%	_____
12.	Drill				_____	47%

Solve the following word problems. Round dollars to the nearest cent and percents to the nearest tenth of a percent.

13. You are the manager of Midtown Hardware. If the EnergyMax batteries in your advertisement have a cost of $3.25, answer the following questions:

    a. What is the amount of the markup on these batteries?

    b. What is your percent markup based on selling price?

    c. If the vendor reduces the cost to $2.90 as a promotional trade discount this week, what is your new amount of markup and what is the percent markup based on selling price?

14. The selling price for a fishing boat is $8,732.39. What percent of the sale price is the markup if the cost of the fishing boat was $6,200?

15. The markup on a TV should be 53% based on selling price. If the seller paid $235 for one, then how much should it be sold for to achieve the desired markup?

16. Video Depot uses a 40% markup based on selling price for its video game systems. On games and accessories, they use a 30% markup based on selling price. (See advertisement.)

    a. What is the cost and the amount of the markup of the video game system?

    b. What is the cost and the amount of the markup of the Sports Package game?

    c. As a promotion this month, the manufacturer is offering its dealers a rebate of $5.50 for each additional remote sold. What is the cost and percent markup (rounded to the nearest tenth of a percent) based on selling price?

17. Galaxy Tools manufactures an 18-volt drill at a cost of $38.32. It imports rechargeable battery packs for $20.84 each. Galaxy offers its distributors a "package deal" that includes a drill and two battery packs. The markup is 36% based on selling price. What is the selling price of the package?

18. The markup on a video game is 25% of the sale price. If the video game sells for $46.67, what was the cost?

19. If the markup on a sofa is 45% based on selling price, what is the corresponding percent markup based on cost?

20. A purchaser paid $379.50 for a TV that cost the seller $230. If the seller's markup was 65% of the $230 cost, then what would be the percent markup based on the selling price?

21. A purse has a cost of $21.50 and a selling price of $51.99.

    a. What is the amount of markup on the purse?

    b. What is the percent markup based on cost?

    c. What is the corresponding percent markup based on selling price?

22. As the manager of Speedy Supermarket, answer the following questions:

    a. If 2-liter Bubbly-Cola products cost Speedy $16.50 per case of 24 bottles, what are the amount of the markup and the percent markup on selling price per case?

    b. If 12-pack Bubbly-Cola products have a markup of $8.25 per case of six 12-packs at Speedy, what are the cost and the percent markup on selling price per case?

    c. Why has Speedy Supermarket chosen to use markup based on selling price?

BUSINESS DECISION: INCREASING THE MARGIN

23. If Costco pays $37.50 for the vacuum cleaner shown here,

    a. What is the percent markup based on selling price?

    b. If Costco pays $1.50 to the insurance company for each product replacement policy sold, what is the percent markup based on selling price of the vacuum cleaner and policy combination?

    c. If 6,000 vacuum cleaners are sold in a season and 40% are sold with the insurance policy, how many additional "markup dollars," the **gross margin**, was made by offering the policy?

    d. (Optional) As a housewares buyer for Costco, what is your opinion of such insurance policies, considering their effect on the "profit picture" of the department? How can you sell more policies?

markdown A price reduction from the original selling price of merchandise.

markdown cancellation Raising prices back to the original selling price after a sale is over.

The original selling price of merchandise usually represents only a temporary situation based on customer and competitor reaction to that price. A price reduction from the original selling price of merchandise is known as a **markdown**. Markdowns are frequently used in retailing because of errors in initial pricing or merchandise selection. For example, the original price may have been set too high or the buyer ordered the wrong styles, sizes, or quantities of merchandise.

Most markdowns should not be regarded as losses but as sales promotion opportunities used to increase sales and profits. When a sale has been concluded, raising prices back to the original selling price is known as a **markdown cancellation**. This section deals with the mathematics of markdowns, a series of markups and markdowns, and the pricing of perishable merchandise.

8-9   DETERMINING THE AMOUNT OF MARKDOWN AND THE MARKDOWN PERCENT

sale price The promotional price of merchandise after a markdown.

A markdown is a reduction from the original selling price of an item to a new **sale price**. To determine the amount of a markdown, we use the following formula:

$$\textbf{Markdown} = \textbf{Original selling price} - \textbf{Sale price}$$

For example, if a sweater was originally marked at $89.95 and then was sale-priced at $59.95, the amount of the markdown would be $30.00 ($89.95 − $59.95 = $30.00).

To find the markdown percent, we use the percentage formula once again, Rate = Portion ÷ Base, where the markdown percent is the rate, the amount of the markdown is the portion, and the original selling price is the base:

$$\textbf{Markdown percent} = \frac{\textbf{Markdown}}{\textbf{Original selling price}}$$

Dollars AND Sense

Become a Prudent Shopper!
The price difference between two items is cash you get to put in your pocket. Even $10 saved this week will buy three dozen eggs next week. And using coupons and sales to save $100 will give you over $265 in 20 years at 5% interest.

Prudent shoppers often spend time comparing products in order to make informed buying decisions.

EXAMPLE12   DETERMINING THE MARKDOWN AND MARKDOWN PERCENT

A blender that originally sold for $60 was marked down and sold for $48. What is the amount of the markdown and the markdown percent?

SOLUTIONSTRATEGY

$$\text{Markdown} = \text{Original selling price} - \text{Sale price}$$

$$\text{Markdown} = 60 - 48 = 12$$

$$\text{Markdown} = \underline{\underline{\$12}}$$

$$\text{Markdown percent} = \frac{\text{Markdown}}{\text{Original selling price}} = \frac{12}{60} = .2$$

$$\text{Markdown percent} = \underline{\underline{20\%}}$$

▶TRYITEXERCISE 12

A tennis racquet that originally sold for $75 was marked down and sold for $56. What are the amount of the markdown and the markdown percent? Round your answer to the nearest tenth of a percent.

CHECK YOUR ANSWERS WITH THE SOLUTIONS ON PAGE 265.

Learning Tip

Note that *markdown percent* calculations are an application of *rate of decrease*, covered in Chapter 6.

In the percentage formula, the markdown (portion) represents the amount of the decrease and the original selling price (base) represents the original amount.

DETERMINING THE SALE PRICE AFTER A MARKDOWN AND THE ORIGINAL PRICE BEFORE A MARKDOWN

8-10

DETERMINING SALE PRICE AFTER A MARKDOWN

In markdown calculations, the original selling price is the base, or 100%. After a markdown is subtracted from that price, the new price represents (100% − Markdown percent) *of* the original price. For example, if a chair is marked down 30%, the sale price would be 70% (100% − 30%) of the original price.

To find the new sale price after a markdown, we use the familiar percentage formula, Portion = Rate × Base, where the sale price is the portion, the original price is the base, and (100% − Markdown percent) is the rate.

> **Sale price = Original selling price (100% − Markdown percent)**

EXAMPLE13 DETERMINING THE SALE PRICE

Fernando's Hideaway, a men's clothing store, originally sold a line of ties for $55 each. If the manager decides to mark them down 40% for a clearance sale, what is the sale price of a tie?

▶SOLUTIONSTRATEGY

Remember, if the markdown is 40%, the sale price must be 60% (100% − 40%) *of* the original price.

Sale price = Original selling price(100% − Markdown percent)

Sale price = $55(100% − 40%) = 55(.6) = 33

Sale price = $33

▶TRYITEXERCISE 13

Craftsman's Village originally sold paneling for $27.50 per sheet. When the stock was almost depleted, the price was marked down 60% to make room for incoming merchandise. What was the sale price per sheet of paneling?

CHECK YOUR ANSWER WITH THE SOLUTION ON PAGE 265.

DETERMINING THE ORIGINAL PRICE BEFORE A MARKDOWN

To find the original selling price before a markdown, we use the sale price formula solved for the original selling price. The original selling price is isolated to one side by dividing both sides of the equation by (100% − Markdown percent). *Note*: This is actually the percentage formula Base = Portion ÷ Rate with the original selling price as the base.

$$\text{Original selling price} = \frac{\text{Sale price}}{100\% - \text{Markdown percent}}$$

EXAMPLE14   DETERMINING THE ORIGINAL SELLING PRICE

What was the original selling price of a backpack at Walmart that is currently on sale for $99 after a 25% markdown?

SOLUTIONSTRATEGY

Reasoning: $99 = 75% (100% − 25%) *of* the original price. Solve for the original price.

$$\text{Original selling price} = \frac{\text{Sale price}}{100\% - \text{Markdown percent}} = \frac{99}{100\% - 25\%} = \frac{99}{.75} = 132$$

Original selling price = $\underline{\underline{\$132}}$

▶TRYITEXERCISE 14

What was the original selling price of a necklace currently on sale for $79 after a 35% markdown? Round your answer to the nearest cent.

CHECK YOUR ANSWER WITH THE SOLUTION ON PAGE 265.

Walmart Stores, Inc., operates more than 5,000 stores across the U.S. and Puerto Rico. Back in 1990, Walmart's net sales were $25 billion. Twenty-five years later net sales had grown to over $487 billion.

Source: http://walmartstores.com

singh_lens/Shutterstock.com

8-11   COMPUTING THE FINAL SELLING PRICE AFTER A SERIES OF MARKUPS AND MARKDOWNS

staple goods Products considered basic and routinely purchased that do not undergo seasonal fluctuations in sales, such as food, tools, and furniture.

seasonal goods Products that undergo seasonal fluctuations in sales, such as fashion apparel and holiday merchandise.

Products that do not undergo seasonal fluctuations in sales, such as food, tools, tires, and furniture, are known as **staple goods**. These products are usually marked up once and perhaps marked down occasionally, on sale. **Seasonal goods**, such as men's and women's fashion items, snow shovels, bathing suits, and holiday merchandise, may undergo many markups and markdowns during their selling season. Merchants must continually adjust prices as the season progresses. Getting caught with an excessive amount of out-of-season inventory can ruin an otherwise bright profit picture. Christmas decorations in January and snow tires in June are virtually useless profit-wise!

EXAMPLE15 COMPUTING A SERIES OF MARKUPS AND MARKDOWNS

In March, Swim and Sport purchased designer bathing suits for $50 each. The original markup was 60% based on selling price. In May, the shop took a 25% markdown by having a sale. After three weeks, the sale was over and all merchandise was marked up 15%. By July, many of the bathing suits were still in stock, so the shop took a 30% markdown to stimulate sales. At the end of August, the balance of the bathing suits were put on clearance sale with a final markdown of another 25%. Compute the intermediate prices and the final selling price of the bathing suits. Round to the nearest cent.

▶SOLUTIONSTRATEGY

When solving a series of markups and markdowns, remember that each should be based on the previous selling price. Use the formulas presented in this chapter and take each step one at a time.

Step 1. Find the original selling price, with markup based on selling price.

$$\text{Selling price} = \frac{\text{Cost}}{100\% - \text{Percent markup}} = \frac{50}{100\% - 60\%} = \frac{50}{.4} = 125$$

Original selling price = $\underline{\$125}$

Step 2. Calculate the 25% markdown in May.
Sale price = Original selling price(100% − Markdown percent)
Sale price = 125(100% − 25%) = 125(.75) = 93.75
Sale price = $\underline{\$93.75}$

Step 3. Calculate the after-sale 15% markup.
Remember, the base is the previous selling price, $93.75.
Selling price = Sale price(100% + Percent markup)
Selling price = 93.75(100% + 15%) = 93.75(1.15) = 107.81
Selling price = $\underline{\$107.81}$

Step 4. Calculate the July 30% markdown.
Sale price = Previous selling price(100% − Markdown percent)
Sale price = 107.81(100% − 30%) = 107.81(.7) = 75.47
Sale price = $\underline{\$75.47}$

Step 5. Calculate the final 25% markdown.
Sale price = Previous selling price(100% − Markdown percent)
Sale price = 75.47(100% − 25%) = 75.47(.75) = 56.60
Final sale price = $\underline{\$56.60}$

▶TRYITEXERCISE 15

In September, Tire Depot in Chicago purchased snow tires from a distributor for $48.50 each. The original markup was 55% based on selling price. In November, the tires were marked down 30% and put on sale. In December, they were marked up 20%. In February, the tires were again on sale at 30% off, and in March, they cleared out with a final 25% markdown. What was the final selling price of the tires? Round to the nearest cent.

CHECK YOUR ANSWER WITH THE SOLUTION ON PAGE 265.

Learning Tip

In a series of markups and markdowns, each calculation is based on the *previous* selling price.

Dollars AND Sense

Spotting Counterfeit Products
A fake designer purse probably won't hurt you, although your pride might be injured if someone discreetly points out that *Gucci* is spelled with two c's.

But counterfeit electrical items can present a serious risk. The unlabeled $1 extension cord at a discount store, for example, could electrocute you! Those holiday lights found at a flea market could catch fire!

Here are some things to watch out for:

· Spelling and grammatical errors on packaging

· No contact information

· Absence of a certification mark such as UL, Underwriters Laboratories

· Products from different manufacturers bundled together

· No-name products

· No UPC bar code

· Unbelievably low prices

Source: *USA Today*, "Watch for spelling errors, no bar code, too-good deals," by Sandra Block, Dec. 18, 2009, page 2B.

B-A-C-O/Shutterstock.com

iStock.com/vreemous

8-12   CALCULATING THE SELLING PRICE OF PERISHABLE GOODS

perishable goods Products that have a certain shelf life and then no value at all, such as fruits, vegetables, flowers, and dairy products.

Out-of-season merchandise still has some value, whereas **perishable goods** (such as fruits, vegetables, flowers, and dairy products) have a certain shelf life and then no value at all. For sellers of this type of merchandise to achieve their intended markups, the selling price must be based on the quantity of products sold at the original price. The quantity sold is calculated as total items less spoilage. For example, if a tomato vendor anticipates a 20% spoilage rate, the selling price of the tomatoes should be calculated based on 80% of the original stock. To calculate the selling price of perishables, use the following formula:

$$\text{Selling price of perishables} = \frac{\text{Total expected selling price}}{\text{Total quantity} - \text{Anticipated spoilage}}$$

EXAMPLE16   CALCULATING THE SELLING PRICE OF PERISHABLE GOODS

The Farmer's Market buys 1,500 pounds of fresh bananas at a cost of $0.60 a pound. If a 15% spoilage rate is anticipated, at what price per pound should the bananas be sold to achieve a 50% markup based on selling price? Round to the nearest cent.

SOLUTIONSTRATEGY

Step 1. Find the total expected selling price: The total expected selling price is found by applying the selling price formula, $SP = C \div (100\% - \%M_{SP})$. The cost will be the total pounds times the price per pound, $1{,}500 \times \$.60 = \$900$.

$$SP = \frac{\text{Cost}}{100\% - \%M_{SP}} = \frac{900}{100\% - 50\%} = \frac{900}{.5} = 1{,}800$$

Total expected selling price = $\underline{\$1{,}800}$

Step 2. Find the anticipated spoilage: To find the amount of anticipated spoilage, use the formula

Anticipated spoilage = Total quantity × Spoilage rate
Anticipated spoilage = $1{,}500 \times 15\% = 1{,}500(.15) = 225$
Anticipated spoilage = $\underline{225 \text{ Pounds}}$

Step 3. Calculate the selling price of the perishables:

$$\text{Selling price of perishables} = \frac{\text{Total expected selling price}}{\text{Total quantity} - \text{Anticipated spoilage}}$$

$$\text{Selling price} = \frac{1{,}800}{1{,}500 - 225} = \frac{1{,}800}{1{,}275} = 1.411$$

Selling price of bananas = $\underline{\$1.41 \text{ Per pound}}$

TRYITEXERCISE 16

Enchanted Gardens, a chain of flower shops, purchases 800 dozen roses for Valentine's Day at a cost of $6.50 per dozen. If a 10% spoilage rate is anticipated, at what price per dozen should the roses be sold to achieve a 60% markup based on selling price? Round to the nearest cent.

CHECK YOUR ANSWER WITH THE SOLUTION ON PAGE 265.

REVIEW EXERCISES

8   SECTION III

For the following items, calculate the missing information. Round dollars to the nearest cent and percents to the nearest tenth of a percent.

JUMP START
WWW

	Item	Original Selling Price	Amount of Markdown	Sale Price	Markdown Percent
1.	Fish tank	$189.95	$28.50	$161.45	15%
2.	Sneakers	$53.88		$37.50	
3.	Cantaloupe		$.39	$1.29	
4.	CD player	$264.95			30%
5.	1 yd carpet			$24.66	40%
6.	Suitcase	$68.00	$16.01	$51.99	23.5%
7.	Chess set	$115.77	$35.50		
8.	Necklace		$155.00	$235.00	
9.	Copier	$1,599.88			35%
10.	Pen			$15.90	25%

Solve the following word problems, rounding dollars to the nearest cent and percents to the nearest tenth of a percent.

11. A home theater system that originally sold for $4,700 was marked down and sold for $3,900.

    a. What is the amount of the markdown?

    b. What is the markdown percent?

12. A jet ski that previously sold for $5,899.99 has been reduced to $3,421.99. What is the markdown percent?

13. a. A notebook that originally sold for $1.69 at Dollar General was marked down to $0.99. What is the amount of the markdown on these notebooks?

    b. What is the markdown percent?

    c. If the sale price is then marked up by 40%, what is the new selling price?

JUMP START
WWW

designs by Jack/Shutterstock.com

What would eventually become Target began in 1902 as Dayton's Dry Goods Company. The company entered the mass-market retail world in 1962, opening the very first Target. In 1995, the first SuperTarget, which includes an in-store grocery, opened. In 1999, architect Michael Graves, the first of more than 75 designers to do so, created an exclusive product line for Target. Typical Target annual revenues now exceed $70 billion.

14. You are shopping for a headset and webcam at the Micro-Electronics Warehouse so that you can video-chat with your friends.

a. Verify the "regular price" (original price) of each headset in the ad and calculate which headset offers the greater markdown percent, the BuddyChat 200 or BuddyChat 300.

b. What is the markdown percent on the BuddyCam HD webcam?

c. You have decided to purchase the headset with the greatest markdown percent and the BuddyCam HD webcam in order to take advantage of an "Extra $15 Rebate" offer when you purchase both. What is the markdown percent on your total purchase including the rebate?

15. If a file cabinet selling for $98 is put on clearance sale at 60% off, what is the selling price?

16. Carousel Toys has Romper Buckaroos, wooden rocking horses for toddlers, on a 30% markdown sale for $72.09. What was the original price before they were marked down? Round to the nearest cent.

17. At a clearance sale, everything has been marked down 30%. How much did a watch originally sell for if its current price is $48.65?

18. From the Office Market coupon shown here,

a. Calculate the markdown percent.

b. If the offer was changed to "Buy 3, Get 2 Free," what would be the new markdown percent?

c. Which offer is more profitable for the store? Explain.

19. The wholesale cost of a birdcage is $55. The original markup was 48% based on selling price. Find the final sale price after the following series of price changes: a markdown of 16% and a markup of 7%.

    (Round each intermediate selling price to the nearest cent.)

20. 700 bags of onions were purchased at $2.57 per bag. The desired markup is 41% based on selling price, but 20% spoilage is expected. What should the selling price per bag be?

21. A microwave oven cost The Appliance Warehouse $141.30 and was initially marked up by 55% based on selling price. In the next few months, the item was marked down 20%, marked up 15%, marked down 10%, and marked down a final 10%. What was the final selling price of the microwave oven?

22. The Flour Power Bakery makes 200 cherry cheesecakes at a cost of $2.45 each. If a spoilage rate of 5% is anticipated, at what price should the cakes be sold to achieve a 40% markup based on cost?

23. You have decided to purchase a set of four Good-Ride tires for your vehicle at the Tire Emporium.

    a. If the original price of these tires is $160.00 each, what are the amount of the markdown with rebate per tire and the markdown percent if you get the rebate and pay cash?

    b. What are the amount of the markdown per tire and the markdown percent if you decide to put the purchase on your Good-Ride credit card and get the double rebate?

TIRE EMPORIUM

Good-Ride Raven GT – Tire Sale

Sale Price: $115 + $20 Rebate

Double rebate when you use your Good-Ride Credit Card

c. When you purchased the set of four tires, you were offered an "Extra 5%" discount on the entire purchase if you also included wheel balancing at $5.75 per tire and a front-end alignment for $65.00. The sales tax in your state is 7.5%. What was the total amount of your purchase if you used your Good-Ride credit card? Use the unrounded markdown percent you found in part b in your calculations.

d. What are the advantages and disadvantages of using the credit card?

BUSINESS DECISION: THE PERMANENT MARKDOWN

24. You are the manager of World Wide Athlete, a chain of six sporting goods shops in your area. The shops sell 12 racing bikes per week at a retail price of $679.99. Recently, you put the bikes on sale at $599.99. At the sale price, 15 bikes were sold during the one-week sale.

    a. What was your markdown percent on the bikes?

    b. What is the percent increase in number of bikes sold during the sale?

    c. How much more revenue would be earned in 6 months by permanently selling the bikes at the lower price rather than having a 1-week sale each month? (6 sale weeks in 26 weeks.)

    d. (Optional) As manager of World Wide Athlete, would you recommend this permanent price reduction? Explain.

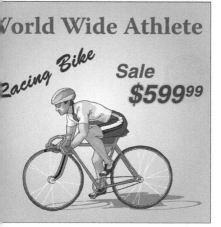

CHAPTER FORMULAS

Markup

Selling price = Cost + Markup

Cost = Selling price − Markup

Markup = Selling price − Cost

$$\text{Percent markup}_{\text{COST}} = \frac{\text{Markup}}{\text{Cost}}$$

$$\text{Percent markup}_{SP} = \frac{\text{Markup}}{\text{Selling price}}$$

Selling price = Cost(100% + %Markup$_{\text{COST}}$)

$$\text{Cost} = \frac{\text{Selling price}}{100\% + \%\text{Markup}_{\text{COST}}}$$

$$\text{Selling price} = \frac{\text{Cost}}{100\% - \%\text{Markup}_{SP}}$$

Cost = Selling price(100% − %Markup$_{SP}$)

$$\%\text{Markup}_{SP} = \frac{\%\text{Markup}_{\text{COST}}}{100\% + \%\text{Markup}_{\text{COST}}}$$

$$\%\text{Markup}_{\text{COST}} = \frac{\%\text{Markup}_{SP}}{100\% - \%\text{Markup}_{SP}}$$

Markdown

Markdown = Original selling price − Sale price

$$\text{Markdown}\% = \frac{\text{Markdown}}{\text{Original price}}$$

Sale price = Original price(100% − Markdown%)

$$\text{Original price} = \frac{\text{Sale price}}{100\% - \text{Markdown}\%}$$

Perishables

$$\text{Selling price}_{\text{Perishables}} = \frac{\text{Expected selling price}}{\text{Total quantity} - \text{Spoilage}}$$

CHAPTER SUMMARY

Section I: Markup Based on Cost

Topic	Important Concepts	Illustrative Examples
Using the Basic Retailing Equation **Performance Objective 8-1, Page 238**	The basic retailing equation is used to solve for selling price (SP), cost (C), and amount of markup (M).	1. What is the selling price of a blender that costs $86.00 and has a $55.99 markup? $SP = 86.00 + 55.99$ Selling price = $\underline{\$141.99}$ 2. What is the cost of a radio that sells for $125.50 and has a $37.29 markup? $C = 125.50 - 37.29$ Cost = $\underline{\$88.21}$ 3. What is the markup on a set of dishes costing $53.54 and selling for $89.95? $M = 89.95 - 53.54$ Markup = $\underline{\$36.41}$

Section I (continued)

Topic	Important Concepts	Illustrative Examples
Calculating Percent Markup Based on Cost **Performance Objective 8-2, Page 240**		A calculator costs $25. If the markup is $10, what is the percent markup based on cost? $$\%M_{COST} = \frac{10}{25} = .4$$ $$\%M_{COST} = \underline{\underline{40\%}}$$
Calculating Selling Price **Performance Objective 8-3, Page 241**		A desk costs $260 to manufacture. What should be the selling price if a 60% markup based on cost is desired? $$SP = 260(100\% + 60\%)$$ $$SP = 260(1.6) = 416$$ Selling price = $\underline{\$416}$
Calculating Cost **Performance Objective 8-4, Page 242**		What is the cost of a leather sofa with a selling price of $250 and a 45% markup based on cost? $$C = \frac{250}{100\% + 45\%} = \frac{250}{1.45}$$ Cost = $\underline{\$172.41}$

Section II: Markup Based on Selling Price

Topic	Important Concepts	Illustrative Examples
Calculating Percent Markup Based on Selling Price **Performance Objective 8-5, Page 245**		What is the percent markup on the selling price of a Hewlett Packard printer with a selling price of $400 and a markup of $188? $$\%M_{SP} = \frac{188}{400} = .47$$ $$\%M_{SP} = \underline{\underline{47\%}}$$
Calculating Selling Price **Performance Objective 8-6, Page 246**		What is the selling price of a marker pen with a cost of $1.19 and a 43% markup based on selling price? $$SP = \frac{1.19}{100\% - 43\%} = \frac{1.19}{.57}$$ $$SP = \underline{\$2.09}$$
Calculating Cost **Performance Objective 8-7, Page 247**		What is the most a hardware store can pay for a drill if it will have a selling price of $65.50 and a 45% markup based on selling price? $$C = 65.50(100\% - 45\%)$$ $$C = 65.50(.55)$$ Cost = $\underline{\$36.03}$
Converting Percent Markup Based on Cost to Percent Markup Based on Selling Price **Performance Objective 8-8, Page 248**		If a hair dryer is marked up 70% based on cost, what is the corresponding percent markup based on selling price? $$\%M_{SP} = \frac{70\%}{100\% + 70\%} = \frac{.7}{1.7}$$ $$\%M_{SP} = .4118 = \underline{\underline{41.2\%}}$$

Section II (continued)

Topic	Important Concepts	Illustrative Examples
Converting Percent Markup Based on Selling Price to Percent Markup Based on Cost **Performance Objective 8-8, Page 248**		If a toaster is marked up 35% based on selling price, what is the corresponding percent markup based on cost? $$\%M_{COST} = \frac{35\%}{100\% - 35\%} = \frac{.35}{.65}$$ $$\%M_{COST} = .5384 = \underline{\underline{53.8\%}}$$

Section III: Markdowns, Multiple Operations, and Perishable Goods

Topic	Important Concepts	Illustrative Examples
Calculating the Amount of Markdown and Markdown Percent **Performance Objective 8-9, Page 252**		Calculate the amount of markdown and the markdown percent of a television set that originally sold for $425.00 and was then put on sale for $299.95. $$\text{Markdown} = 425.00 - 299.95$$ $$\text{Markdown} = \underline{\$125.05}$$ $$MD\% = \frac{125.05}{425.00} = .2942$$ $$\text{Markdown\%} = \underline{\underline{29.4\%}}$$
Determining the Sale Price after a Markdown **Performance Objective 8-10, Page 253**		What is the sale price of a computer that originally sold for $2,500 and was then marked down by 35%? $$\text{Sale} = 2,500(100\% - 35\%)$$ $$\text{Sale} = 2,500(.65) = 1,625$$ $$\text{Sale price} = \underline{\$1,625}$$
Determining the Original Selling Price before a Markdown **Performance Objective 8-10, Page 254**		What is the original selling price of an exercise bicycle, which is currently on sale at Sears for $235.88, after a 30% markdown? $$\text{Original price} = \frac{235.88}{100\% - 30\%} = \frac{235.88}{.7}$$ $$\text{Original price} = \underline{\$336.97}$$
Computing the Final Selling Price after a Series of Markups and Markdowns **Performance Objective 8-11, Page 254**	To solve for the final selling price after a series of markups and markdowns, calculate each step based on the previous selling price.	Compute the intermediate prices and the final selling price of an umbrella costing $27.50 with the following seasonal activity: a. Initial markup, 40% on cost b. 20% markdown c. 15% markdown d. 10% markup e. Final clearance, 25% markdown a. Initial 40% markup: $$SP = C(100\% + \%M_{COST})$$ $$SP = 27.50(100\% + 40\%)$$ $$SP = 27.50(1.4) = 38.50$$ Original price = $\underline{\$38.50}$ b. 20% markdown: $$\text{Sale} = \text{Orig}(100\% - MD\%)$$ $$\text{Sale} = 38.50(100\% - 20\%)$$ $$\text{Sale} = 38.50(.8)$$ Sale price = $\underline{\$30.80}$

Section III (continued)

Topic	Important Concepts	Illustrative Examples
		c.　15% markdown: $$\text{Sale} = \text{Orig}(100\% - MD\%)$$ $$\text{Sale} = 30.80(100\% - 15\%)$$ $$\text{Sale} = 30.80(.85)$$ $$\underline{\text{Sale price} = \$26.18}$$ d.　10% markup: $$SP = \text{sale price}(100\% + M\%)$$ $$SP = 26.18(100\% + 10\%)$$ $$SP = 26.18(1.10)$$ $$\underline{\text{Selling price} = \$28.80}$$ e.　Final 25% markdown: $$\text{Sale} = \text{Orig}(100\% - MD\%)$$ $$\text{Sale} = 28.80(100\% - 25\%)$$ $$\text{Sale} = 28.80(.75)$$ $$\underline{\text{Final selling price} = \$21.60}$$
Calculating the Selling Price of Perishable Goods **Performance Objective 8-12, Page 256**		A grocery store purchases 250 pounds of apples from a wholesaler for $.67 per pound. If a 10% spoilage rate is anticipated, what selling price per pound will yield a 45% markup based on cost? $$\text{Total cost} = 250 \text{ lb @ } \$.67 = \$167.50$$ $$\text{Exp } SP = C(100\% + M_{COST})$$ $$\text{Exp } SP = 167.50(100\% + 45\%)$$ $$\text{Exp } SP = 167.50(1.45) = \$242.88$$ $$SP_{\text{perish}} = \frac{242.88}{250 - 25} = \frac{242.88}{225}$$ $$\underline{SP_{\text{perish}} = \$1.08 \text{ Per pound}}$$

TRY IT: EXERCISE SOLUTIONS FOR CHAPTER 8

1. $SP = C + M = 6.80 + 9.40 = \underline{\$16.20}$

2. $M = SP - C = 28.50 - 16.75 = \underline{\$11.75}$

3. $C = SP - M = 290 - 75 = \underline{\$215}$

4. $M = SP - C = 63 - 45 = \underline{\$18}$

$$\%M_{COST} = \frac{M}{C} = \frac{18}{45} = .4 = 40\%$$

5. $SP = C(100\% + \%M_{COST}) = 38(100\% + 65\%) = 38(1.65) = \underline{\$62.70}$

6. $C = \dfrac{SP}{100\% + \%M_{COST}} = \dfrac{39}{100\% + 30\%} = \dfrac{39}{1.3} = \underline{\$30}$

7. $M = SP - C = 157.50 - 94.50 = \underline{\$63}$

$$\%M_{SP} = \frac{M}{SP} = \frac{63.00}{157.50} = .40 = \underline{40\%}$$

8. $SP = \dfrac{C}{100\% - \%M_{SP}} = \dfrac{169}{100\% - 35\%} = \dfrac{169}{.65} = \underline{\$260}$

9. $C = SP(100\% - \%M_{SP}) = 79(100\% - 55\%) = 79(.45) = \underline{\$35.55}$

10. $\%M_{SP} = \dfrac{\%M_{COST}}{100\% + \%M_{COST}} = \dfrac{50\%}{100\% + 50\%} = \dfrac{.5}{1.5} = .333 = \underline{33.3\%}$

11. $\%M_{COST} = \dfrac{\%M_{SP}}{100\% - \%M_{SP}} = \dfrac{75\%}{100\% - 75\%} = \dfrac{.75}{.25} = 3 = \underline{\underline{300\%}}$

12. Markdown = Original price − Sale price = 75 − 56 = $\underline{\underline{\$19}}$

$MD\% = \dfrac{MD}{\text{Original price}} = \dfrac{19}{75} = .2533 = \underline{\underline{25.3\%}}$

13. Sale price = Original price$(100\% - MD\%) = 27.50(100\% - 60\%) = 27.50(.4) = \underline{\underline{\$11}}$

14. Original price $= \dfrac{\text{Sale price}}{100\% - MD\%} = \dfrac{79}{100\% - 35\%} = \dfrac{79}{.65} = \underline{\underline{\$121.54}}$

15. $SD = \dfrac{C}{100\% - \%M_{SP}} = \dfrac{48.50}{100\% - 55\%} = \dfrac{48.50}{.45} = \$107.78$

    Markdown #1: Original price$(100\% - MD\%) = 107.78(.7) = \$75.45$
    20% markup: $75.45(100\% + 20\%) = 75.45(1.2) = \$90.54$
    Markdown #2: Original price$(100\% - MD\%) = 90.54(.7) = \$63.38$
    Final markdown: Original price$(100\% - MD\%) = 63.38(.75) = \underline{\underline{\$47.54}}$

16. Total cost = 800 dozen @ $6.50 = $5,200

    Expected selling price $= \dfrac{C}{100\% - \%M_{SP}} = \dfrac{5,200}{100\% - 60\%} = \dfrac{5,200}{.4} = \$13,000$

    Selling price$_{\text{Perishables}} = \dfrac{\text{Expected selling price}}{\text{Total quantity} - \text{Spoilage}} = \dfrac{13,000}{800 - 80} = \dfrac{13,000}{720} = \underline{\underline{\$18.06 \text{ per doz}}}$

CONCEPT REVIEW

1. The retailing equation states that the selling price is equal to the _____ plus the _____. (8-1)

2. In business, expenses are separated into two major categories. The cost of _____ sold and _____ expenses. (8-1)

3. There are two ways of expressing markup as a percent: based on _____ and based on _____ _____. (8-2)

4. Write the formula for calculating the selling price when markup is based on cost. (8-3)

5. To calculate cost, we divide the _____ price by 100% plus the percent markup based on cost. (8-4)

6. The percent markup based on selling price is equal to the _____ divided by the selling price. (8-5)

7. When markup is based on selling price, the _____ price is the base and represents _____ percent. (8-6)

8. We use the formula for calculating _____ to find the most a retailer can pay for an item and still get the intended markup. (8-7)

9. To convert percent markup based on cost to percent markup based on selling price, we divide percent markup based on cost by 100% _____ the percent markup based on cost. (8-8)

10. To convert percent markup based on selling price to percent markup based on cost, we divide percent markup based on selling price by 100% _____ the percent markup based on selling price. (8-8)

11. A price reduction from the original selling price of merchandise is called a(n) _____. (8-9)

12. Write the formula for calculating the sale price after a markdown. (8-10)

13. In calculating a series of markups and markdowns, each calculation is based on the previous _____ price. (8-11)

14. Products that have a certain shelf life and then no value at all, such as fruit, vegetables, flowers, and dairy products, are known as _____ _____. (8-12)

CHAPTER

8

ASSESSMENT TEST

Solve the following word problems. Round dollars to the nearest cent and percents to the nearest tenth of a percent.

1. A hair dryer is sold at wholesale for $12.50. If it is sold at retail with a markup of $7.25, what is the sales price?

2. Castle Mountain Furniture sells desks for $346.00. If the desks cost $212.66, what is the amount of the markup?

3. After Sunset Food Wholesalers adds a markup of $15.40 to a case of tomato sauce, it sells for $33.98. What is the wholesaler's cost per case?

4. Wyatt's Western Wear purchases shirts for $47.50 each. A $34.00 markup is added to the shirts.
   a. What is the selling price?

   b. What is the percent markup based on cost?

   c. What is the percent markup based on selling price?

Dollar Depot

Softies Cube 2 ply, Regular 2 ply, or Lotion with Aloe

99¢

Your choice

5. As the manager of Dollar Depot, calculate the amount of the markup and the percent markup based on selling price per case if these Softies products cost your store $5.60 per case of 12 boxes.

6. Saks Fifth Avenue purchases a bracelet for $57.20. If the store policy is to mark up all merchandise in that department 42% based on selling price, what is the retail selling price of the perfume?

7. The Carpet Gallery is looking for a new line of nylon carpeting to retail at $39.88 per square yard. If management wants a 60% markup based on selling price, what is the most that can be paid for the carpeting to still get the desired markup?

8. a. At The Luminary, the markup on a halogen light fixture is 50% based on selling price. What is the corresponding percent markup based on cost?

   b. If the markup on a fluorescent light fixture transformer is 120% based on cost, what is the corresponding percent markup based on selling price?

CHAPTER

8

9. A TV selling for $888 was marked down by $200 for a store-wide sale.

   a. What is the sale price of the TV?

   b. What is the markdown percent?

10. You are shopping for an executive desk chair at The Furniture Gallery.
    a. Calculate the original price and markdown percent of each chair to determine which has the greater markdown percent.

The Furniture Gallery

Save $40
instantly
$79.99

OfficePro
Model 20
High Back
Leather Chair

Save $60
instantly
$89.99

OfficePro
Model 30
High Back
Leather Chair

   b. With the purchase of either chair, The Furniture Gallery is offering a 15% discount on plastic chair mats. You have chosen a mat with an original price of $29.00. You also purchase a 2-year leather protection plan on the chair for $19.95. If you choose the chair with the greater markdown percent and the sales tax in your area is 6.3%, what is the total amount of your purchase?

11. Macy's originally sold designer jackets for $277. If they are put on sale at a markdown of 22%, what is the sale price?

 EXCEL 2

12. What was the original selling price of a treadmill currently on sale for $2,484 after a 20% markdown?

13. Backyard Bonanza advertised a line of inflatable pools for the summer season. The store uses a 55% markup based on selling price.
    a. If they were originally priced at $124.99, what was the cost?

    b. As the summer progressed, they were marked down 25%, marked up 15%, marked down 20%, and cleared out in October at a final 25%-off sale. What was the final selling price of the pools?

THE
WORLD'S
LARGEST
STORE

macy's ★macy's

Joe Ravi/Shutterstock.com

14. Epicure Market prepares fresh gourmet entrees each day. On Wednesday, 80 baked chicken dinners were made at a cost of $3.50 each. A 10% spoilage rate is anticipated.
    a. At what price should the dinners be sold to achieve a 60% markup based on selling price?

 EXCEL 3

    b. If Epicure offers a $1-off coupon in a newspaper advertisement, what markdown percent does the coupon represent?

Macy's is one of the nation's premier retailers, with typical annual sales exceeding $20 billion. The company operates more than 600 Macy's department stores and furniture galleries in 45 states, the District of Columbia, Guam, and Puerto Rico, as well as 40 Bloomingdale's stores in 12 states.

   Macy's diverse workforce includes approximately 130,000 employees. The company also operates macys.com and bloomingdales.com.

Source: www.macysinc.com

15. a. What is the original selling price of the guitar on sale at Music Mania if the $1,999.99 sale price represents 20% off?

b. How much did the store pay for the guitar if the initial markup was 150% based on cost?

c. What is the percent markup based on selling price?

d. If next month the guitar is scheduled to be on sale for $1,599.99, what is the markdown percent from the original price?

BUSINESS DECISION: MAINTAINED MARKUP

16. The markup that a retail store actually realizes on the sale of its goods is called **maintained markup**. It is what is achieved after "retail reductions" (markdowns) have been subtracted from the initial markup. Maintained markup is one of the "keys to profitability" in retailing. It is the difference between the actual selling price and the cost and therefore has a direct effect on net profits.

$$\text{Maintained markup} = \frac{\text{Actual selling price} - \text{Cost}}{\text{Actual selling price}}$$

You are the buyer for Four Aces Menswear, a chain of men's clothing stores. For the spring season, you purchased a line of men's casual shirts with a manufacturer's suggested retail price of $29.50. Your cost was $16.00 per shirt.

a. What is the initial percent markup based on selling price?

b. The shirts did not sell as expected at the regular price, so you marked them down to $21.99 and sold them out. What is the maintained markup on the shirts?

c. When you complained to the manufacturer's sales representative about having to take excessive markdowns in order to sell the merchandise, she offered a $2 rebate per shirt. What is your new maintained markup?

COLLABORATIVE LEARNING ACTIVITY

Retailing and the Demographic Generations

Understanding the shopping and media habits of different age groups can help marketers optimize product assortment, pricing, promotion, and advertising decisions by creating targeted strategies and special offers. As an example, consider the following.

According to *USA Today*, in the book *Gen buY: How Tweens, Teens, and Twenty-Somethings Are Revolutionizing Retail*, authors Kit Yarrow and Jane O'Donnell say Generation Y—today's teens, tweens, and twenty-somethings were the least likely to cut back spending during a recession.

What's more, the authors point out that the 84 million Generation Y'ers, born from 1978 through 2000, are so influential, they've changed shopping for all consumers. They call Gen Y "the taste-makers, influencers, and most enthusiastic buyers of today" who will become "the mature, high-income purchasers of the future."

Because of Gen Y, we now have, among other things:

- More creative, technically advanced websites
- A wide availability of online customer reviews
- A faster stream of product introductions
- Bigger, more comfortable dressing rooms

Source: *USA Today*, "Generation Y forces retailers to keep up with technology, new stuff," by Richard Eisenberg, Sept. 14, 2009, page 6B.

As a team, divide up the four major demographic generations: The Silent Generation: the Baby Boomers, Generation X, and Generation Y (aka the Millennials) to research the following questions and report your findings to the class. Use visual presentations whenever possible and be sure to site your sources.

1. How did each generation get its distinctive name? List any "subgroups" that have been defined, such as Baby Boomers—Young and Baby Boomers—Old.
2. Define each generation in terms of years born, size, income and purchasing power, lifestyle preferences, and particularly consumer buying behavior.
3. How and to what extent does each generation use the Internet?
4. How do manufacturers, retailers, and shopping malls use these demographic distinctions to "target" their marketing efforts to the various generations? Give specific examples.

WEEKLY TIME SHEET

	Mon 6/10	Tue 6/11	Wed 6/12	Thu 6/13
TIME IN	8.00	8.00	8.00	8.00
TIME OUT		16.00	16.00	16
		7	7	
	2	-	-	-
...RS	10	7	7	7
TOTAL				

WEEKLY TOTAL	54

Employee Sig...

PERFORMANCE OBJECTIVES

EMPLOYEE'S GROSS EARNINGS AND INCENTIVE PAY PLANS

Because payroll is frequently a company's largest operating expense, efficient payroll preparation and record keeping are extremely important functions in any business operation. Although today most businesses computerize their payroll functions, it is important for businesspeople to understand the processes and procedures involved.

Employers are responsible for paying employees for services rendered to the company over a period of time. In addition, the company is responsible for withholding certain taxes and other deductions from an employee's paycheck and depositing those taxes with the Internal Revenue Service (IRS) through authorized financial institutions. Other deductions, such as insurance premiums and charitable contributions, are also disbursed by the employer to the appropriate place.

In business, the term **gross pay**, or **gross earnings** means the *total* amount of earnings due an employee for work performed before payroll deductions are withheld. The **net pay**, **net earnings**, or **take-home pay** is the actual amount of the employee's paycheck after all payroll deductions have been withheld. This concept is easily visualized by the formula

gross pay, or **gross earnings** Total amount of earnings due an employee for work performed before payroll deductions are withheld.

net pay, net earnings, or **take-home pay** The actual amount of the employee's paycheck after all payroll deductions have been withheld.

> **Net pay = Gross pay − Total deductions**

This chapter deals with the business math involved in payroll management: the computation of employee gross earnings; the calculation of withholding taxes and other deductions; and the associated governmental deposits, regulations, and record keeping requirements.

PRORATING ANNUAL SALARY ON THE BASIS OF WEEKLY, BIWEEKLY, SEMIMONTHLY, AND MONTHLY PAY PERIODS

9-1

Employee compensation takes on many forms in the business world. Employees who hold managerial, administrative, or professional positions are paid a salary. A **salary** is a fixed gross amount of pay equally distributed over periodic payments without regard to the number of hours worked. Salaries are usually expressed as an annual, or yearly, amount. For example, a corporate accountant might receive an annual salary of $50,000.

salary A fixed gross amount of pay equally distributed over periodic payments without regard to the number of hours worked.

Although salaries may be stated as annual amounts, they are usually distributed to employees on a more timely basis. A once-a-year paycheck would be a real trick to manage! Employees are most commonly paid in one of the following ways:

Weekly	52 paychecks per year	Annual salary ÷ 52
Biweekly	26 paychecks per year	Annual salary ÷ 26
Semimonthly	24 paychecks per year	Annual salary ÷ 24
Monthly	12 paychecks per year	Annual salary ÷ 12

EXAMPLE1   PRORATING ANNUAL SALARY

What is the weekly, biweekly, semimonthly, and monthly amount of gross pay for a corporate accountant with an annual salary of $50,000?

▶SOLUTIONSTRATEGY

The amount of gross pay per period is determined by dividing the annual salary by the number of pay periods per year.

$$\text{Weekly pay} = \frac{50,000}{52} = \$961.54$$

$$\text{Biweekly pay} = \frac{50,000}{26} = \$1,923.08$$

$$\text{Semimonthly pay} = \frac{50,000}{24} = \$2,083.33$$

$$\text{Monthly pay} = \frac{50,000}{12} = \$4,166.67$$

9-2 CALCULATING GROSS PAY BY HOURLY WAGES, INCLUDING REGULAR AND OVERTIME RATES

wages Earnings for routine or manual work, usually based on the number of hours worked.

hourly wage, or **hourly rate** The amount an employee is paid for each hour worked.

overtime According to federal law, the amount an employee is paid for each hour worked over 40 hours per week.

Wages are earnings for routine or manual work, usually based on the number of hours worked. An **hourly wage**, or **hourly rate** is the amount an employee is paid for each hour worked. The hourly wage is the most frequently used pay method and is designed to compensate employees for the amount of time spent on the job. The Fair Labor Standards Act of 1938, a federal law, specifies that a standard work week is 40 hours and **overtime**, amounting to at least $1\frac{1}{2}$ times the hourly rate, must be paid for all hours worked over 40 hours per week. Paying an employee $1\frac{1}{2}$ times the hourly rate is known as time-and-a-half.

Many companies have taken overtime a step farther than required by compensating employees at time-and-a-half for all hours over 8 hours per day instead of 40 hours per week. Another common payroll benefit is when companies pay double time, twice the hourly rate, for holidays, midnight shifts, and weekend hours.

Minimum Wage Laws in the United States

U. S. Department of Labor—Wage and Hour Division (WHD)—July 1, 2018

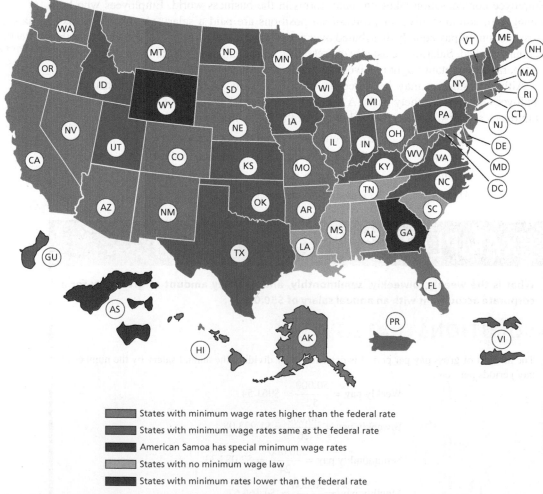

States with minimum wage rates higher than the federal rate
States with minimum wage rates same as the federal rate
American Samoa has special minimum wage rates
States with no minimum wage law
States with minimum rates lower than the federal rate

U. S. Department of Labor

Source: Department of Labor, www.dol.gov/whd/minwage/america.htm

STEPS TO CALCULATE AN EMPLOYEE'S GROSS PAY BY HOURLY WAGES

STEP 1. Calculate an employee's regular gross pay for working 40 hours or less.

Regular pay = Hourly rate × Regular hours worked

STEP 2. Calculate an employee's overtime pay by chain multiplying the hourly rate by the overtime factor by the number of overtime hours.

Overtime pay = Hourly rate × Overtime factor × Overtime hours worked

STEP 3. Calculate total gross pay.

Total gross pay = Regular pay + Overtime pay

EXAMPLE2 CALCULATING HOURLY PAY

Karen Sullivan earns $8 per hour as a checker on an assembly line. If her overtime rate is time-and-a-half, what is her total gross pay for working 46 hours last week?

SOLUTIONSTRATEGY

To find Karen's total gross pay, compute her regular pay plus overtime pay.

Regular pay = Hourly rate × Regular hours worked
Regular pay = 8 × 40 = $320
Overtime pay = Hourly rate × Overtime factor × Overtime hours worked
Overtime pay = 8 × 1.5 × 6 = $72
Total gross pay = Regular pay + Overtime pay
Total gross pay = 320 + 72 = $392

TRYITEXERCISE 2

Rick Morton works as a delivery truck driver for $10.50 per hour with time-and-a-half for overtime and double time on Sundays. What was his total gross pay last week if he worked 45 hours on Monday through Saturday in addition to a four-hour shift on Sunday?

CHECK YOUR ANSWER WITH THE SOLUTION ON PAGE 303.

IN THE Business World

Payroll is a very important business responsibility. Employees must be paid on a regular basis, and accurate records must be kept for government reporting.

- Payroll is usually one of the largest "expense" categories of a company.
- The department responsible for the payroll function may be called Payroll, Personnel, or Human Resources.
- In recent years, companies have evolved that specialize in doing payroll. When a business hires an outside firm to perform a function such as payroll, this is known as *outsourcing*.

CALCULATING GROSS PAY BY STRAIGHT AND DIFFERENTIAL PIECEWORK SCHEDULES

9-3

A **piecework** pay rate schedule is based not on time but on production output. The incentive is that the more units the worker produces, the more money he or she makes. A **straight piecework plan** is when the worker receives a certain amount of pay per unit of output regardless of output quantity. A **differential piecework plan** gives workers a greater incentive to increase output because the rate per unit increases as output goes up. For example, a straight piecework plan might pay $3.15 per unit, whereas a differential plan might pay $3.05 for the first 50 units produced, $3.45 for units 51–100, and $3.90 for any units over 100.

piecework Pay rate schedule based on an employee's production output, not hours worked.

straight piecework plan Pay per unit of output regardless of output quantity.

differential piecework plan Greater incentive method of compensation than straight piecework, where pay per unit increases as output goes up.

STEPS TO CALCULATE GROSS PAY BY PIECEWORK

Straight Piecework:

STEP 1. Multiply the number of pieces or output units by the rate per unit.

Total gross pay = Output quantity × Rate per unit

Differential Piecework:

STEP 1. Multiply the number of output units at each level by the rate per unit at that level.

STEP 2. Find the total gross pay by adding the total from each level.

EXAMPLE3 CALCULATING PIECEWORK PAY

Barb Nelson works on a hat assembly line. Barb gets paid at a straight piecework rate of $0.35 per hat. What was Barb's total gross pay last week if she produced 1,655 hats?

SOLUTIONSTRATEGY

Total gross pay = Output quantity × Rate per unit
Total gross pay = 1,655 × .35 = $579.25

TRYITEXERCISE 3

George Lopez works at a tire manufacturing plant. He is on a straight piecework rate of $0.41 per tire. What was George's total gross pay last week if he produced 950 tires?

CHECK YOUR ANSWER WITH THE SOLUTION ON PAGE 303.

EXAMPLE4 CALCULATING DIFFERENTIAL PIECEWORK PAY

Paula Duke assembled 190 watches last week. Calculate her total gross pay based on the following differential piecework schedule.

Pay Level	Watches Assembled	Rate per Watch
1	1–100	$2.45
2	101–150	$2.75
3	Over 150	$3.10

SOLUTIONSTRATEGY

To find Paula's total gross earnings, we calculate her earnings at each level of the pay schedule and add the totals. In this case, she will be paid for all of level 1, 100 watches; for all of level 2, 50 watches; and for 40 watches at level 3 (190 − 150 = 40).

Level pay = Output × Rate per piece

Level 1 = 100 × 2.45 = $245

Level 2 = 50 × 2.75 = $137.50

Level 3 = 40 × 3.10 = $124

Total gross pay = Level 1 + Level 2 + Level 3

Total gross pay = 245 + 137.50 + 124 = $506.50

▶TRYITEXERCISE 4

You are the payroll manager for Trendy Toys, Inc., a manufacturer of small plastic toys. Your production workers are on a differential piecework schedule as follows.

Pay Level	Toys Produced	Rate per Toy
1	1–300	$0.68
2	301–500	$0.79
3	501–750	$0.86
4	Over 750	$0.94

Calculate last week's total gross pay for the following employees.

Name	Toys Produced	Total Gross Pay
C. Gomez	515	_____
L. Clifford	199	_____
M. Maken	448	_____
B. Nathan	804	_____

CHECK YOUR ANSWERS WITH THE SOLUTIONS ON PAGE 303.

CALCULATING GROSS PAY BY STRAIGHT AND INCREMENTAL COMMISSION, SALARY PLUS COMMISSION, AND DRAWING ACCOUNTS

9-4

STRAIGHT AND INCREMENTAL COMMISSION

Commission is a method of compensation primarily used to pay employees who sell a company's goods or services. **Straight commission** is based on a single specified percentage of the sales volume attained. For example, Delta Distributors pays its sales staff a commission of 8% on all sales. **Incremental commission** is much like the differential piecework rate whereby higher levels of sales earn increasing rates of commission. An example would be 5% commission on all sales up to $70,000, 6% on sales greater than $70,000 and up to $120,000, and 7% commission on any sales greater than $120,000.

commission Percentage method of compensation primarily used to pay employees who sell a company's goods and services.

straight commission Commission based on a specified percentage of the sales volume attained by an employee.

incremental commission Greater incentive method of compensation than straight commission whereby higher levels of sales earn increasing rates of commission.

STEPS TO CALCULATE GROSS PAY BY COMMISSION

Straight Commission:

STEP 1. Multiply the total sales by the commission rate.

Total gross pay = Total sales × Commission rate

Incremental Commission:

STEP 1. Multiply the total sales at each level by the commission rate for that level.

STEP 2. Find the total gross pay by adding the total from each level.

iStock.com/Nikada

EXAMPLE5   CALCULATING COMMISSIONS

Diamond Industries pays its sales force a commission rate of 6% of all sales. What was the total gross pay for an employee who sold $113,500 last month?

▶ SOLUTIONSTRATEGY

$$\text{Total gross pay} = \text{Total sales} \times \text{Commission rate}$$
$$\text{Total gross pay} = 113,500 \times .06 = \$6,810$$

▶ TRYITEXERCISE 5

Alexa Walsh sells for Supreme Designs, a manufacturer of women's clothing. Alexa is paid a straight commission of 2.4%. If her sales volume last month was $233,760, what was her total gross pay?

CHECK YOUR ANSWER WITH THE SOLUTION ON PAGE 303.

EXAMPLE6   CALCULATING INCREMENTAL COMMISSION

Vista Electronics pays its sales representatives on the following incremental commission schedule.

Level	Sales Volume	Commission Rate
1	$1–$50,000	4%
2	$50,001–$150,000	5%
3	Over $150,000	6.5%

What was the total gross pay for a sales rep who sold $162,400 last month?

▶ SOLUTIONSTRATEGY

Using an incremental commission schedule, we find the pay for each level and then add the totals from each level. In this problem, the sales rep will be paid for all of level 1, $50,000; for all of level 2, $100,00; and for $12,400 of level 3 ($162,400 − $150,000 = $12,400).

$$\text{Level pay} = \text{Sales per level} \times \text{Commission rate}$$
$$\text{Level 1 pay} = 50,000 \times .04 = \$2,000$$
$$\text{Level 2 pay} = 100,000 \times .05 = \$5,000$$
$$\text{Level 3 pay} = 12,400 \times .065 = \$806$$
$$\text{Total gross pay} = \text{Level 1} + \text{Level 2} + \text{Level 3}$$
$$\text{Total gross pay} = 2,000 + 5,000 + 806 = \$7,806$$

▶ TRYITEXERCISE 6

Mike Lamb sells copiers for Royal Business Products. He is on an incremental commission schedule of 1.7% of sales up to $100,000 and 2.5% on sales greater than $100,000. What was Mike's total gross pay last month if his sales volume was $184,600?

CHECK YOUR ANSWER WITH THE SOLUTION ON PAGE 303.

IN THE Business World

Companies often give sales managers *override* commissions. This is a small commission on the total sales of the manager's sales force.

Example: Jim and Diane sell for Apex Electronics. They each receive 15% commission on their sales. John, their sales manager, receives a 3% override on their total sales. If Jim sells $20,000 and Diane sells $30,000 in June, how much commission does each person receive?

- Jim: $20,000 × 15% = $3,000
- Diane: $30,000 × 15% = $4,500
- John: $50,000 × 3% = $1,500

rtguest/Shutterstock.com

SALARY PLUS COMMISSION

A variation of straight and incremental commission pay schedules is the **salary plus commission** whereby the employee is paid a guaranteed salary plus a commission on sales over a specified amount. To calculate the total gross pay, find the amount of commission and add it to the salary.

salary plus commission A guaranteed salary plus a commission on sales over a specified amount.

EXAMPLE7 CALCULATING SALARY PLUS COMMISSION

Karie Jabe works on a pay schedule of $1,500 per month salary plus a 3% commission on all sales greater than $40,000. If she sold $60,000 last month, what was her total gross pay?

▶SOLUTIONSTRATEGY

To solve for Karie's total gross pay, add her monthly salary to her commission for the month.

Commission = Commission rate × Sales subject to commission
Commission = 3% (60,000 − 40,000)
Commission = .03 × 20,000 = $600
Total gross pay = Salary + Commission
Total gross pay = 1,500 + 600 = $2,100

▶TRYITEXERCISE 7

Ed Diamond is a sales representative for Jersey Shore Supply, Inc. He is paid a salary of $1,400 per month plus a commission of 4% on all sales greater than $20,000. If he sold $45,000 last month, what was his total gross earnings?

CHECK YOUR ANSWER WITH THE SOLUTION ON PAGE 303.

DRAW AGAINST COMMISSION

In certain industries and at certain times of the year, sales fluctuate significantly. To provide salespeople on commission with at least some income during slack periods of sales, a drawing account is used. A **drawing account**, or **draw against commission**, is a commission paid in advance of sales and later deducted from the commissions earned. If a period goes by when the salesperson does not earn enough commission to cover the draw, the unpaid balance carries over to the next period.

drawing account, or **draw against commission**
Commission paid in advance of sales and later deducted from the commission earned.

EXAMPLE8 CALCULATING DRAW AGAINST COMMISSION

Bill Carpenter is a salesperson for Power Electronics. The company pays 8% commission on all sales and gives Bill a $1,500 per month draw against commission. If he receives his draw at the beginning of the month and then sells $58,000 during the month, how much commission is owed to Bill?

▶SOLUTIONSTRATEGY

To find the amount of commission owed to Bill, find the total amount of commission he earned and subtract $1,500, the amount of his draw against commission.

Commission = Total sales × Commission rate
Commission = 58,000 × 8% = $4,640
Commission owed = Commission − Amount of draw
Commission owed = 4,640 − 1,500 = $3,140

► TRY IT EXERCISE 8

Howard Lockwood sells for Catalina Designs, Inc. He is on a 3.5% straight commission with a $2,000 drawing account. If he is paid the draw at the beginning of the month and then sells $120,000 during the month, how much commission is owed to Howard?

CHECK YOUR ANSWER WITH THE SOLUTION ON PAGE 303.

SECTION I   9   REVIEW EXERCISES

Calculate the gross earnings per pay period for the following pay schedules.

	Annual Salary	Monthly	Semimonthly	Biweekly	Weekly
1.	$15,000	$1,250.00	$625.00	$576.92	$288.46
2.	$44,200	_____	_____	_____	_____
3.	$100,000	_____	_____	_____	_____
4.	$21,600	$1,800.00	$900.00	$830.77	$415.38
5.	_____	_____	$1,450.00	_____	_____
6.	_____	_____	_____	$875.00	_____
7.	_____	_____	_____	_____	$335.00

8. Brianna's semimonthly salary is $3,675. What would be her equivalent biweekly salary?

9. Deb O'Connell is an accounting professional earning a salary of $58,000 at her firm. What is her equivalent weekly gross pay?

10. Jennifer Brunner works 40 hours per week as a chef's assistant. At the rate of $7.60 per hour, what are her gross weekly earnings?

11. Alan Kimball earns $22.34 per hour as a specialty chef at Le Bistro Restaurant. If he worked 53 hours last week and was paid time-and-a-half for weekly hours over 40, what was his gross pay?

12. Paul Curcio earns $8.25 per hour for regular time up to 40 hours, time-and-a-half for overtime, and double time for working on holidays. Find his gross pay if he worked 6 holiday hours in addition to 58 hours Monday through Saturday.

As the payroll manager for Stargate Industries, your task is to complete the following weekly payroll record. The company pays overtime for all hours worked over 40 at the rate of time-and-a-half. Round to the nearest cent when necessary. Note: Do not round the hourly overtime rate before finding the amount of overtime pay.

Employee	M	T	W	T	F	S	S	Hourly Rate	Total Hours	Overtime Hours	Regular Pay	Overtime Pay	Total Pay
13. Peters	7	8	5	8	8	0	0	$8.70	36	0	$313.20	0	$313.20
14. Sands	6	5	9	8	10	7	0	$9.50	___	___	___	___	___
15. Warner	8	6	11	7	12	0	4	$7.25	___	___	___	___	___
16. Lee	9	7	7	7	9	0	8	$14.75	___	___	___	___	___

17. Larry Jefferson gets paid a straight piecework rate of $3.15 for each alternator he assembles for Allied Mechanical Corp. If he assembled 226 units last week, what was his gross pay?

You are the payroll manager for Euro Couture, a manufacturer of women's apparel. Your workers are paid per garment sewn on a differential piecework schedule as follows.

Pay Level	Garments Produced	Rate per Garment
1	1–50	$3.60
2	51–100	$4.25
3	101–150	$4.50
4	Over 150	$5.10

Calculate last week's total gross pay for each of the following employees.

Employee	Garments Produced	Total Gross Pay
18. Goodrich, P.	109	$433.00
19. Walker, A.	83	

20. Rachael has a job assembling a certain car accessory.

Last month she made a total of 424. Calculate her gross pay if she is paid on the following differential piecework schedule:

Pay Level	Item produced	Rate per Item
1	1–160	$9.68
2	Over 160	$11.71

21. Katrina Byrd assembles motor mounts for C-207 executive planes. Her company has established a differential piecework scale as an incentive to increase production due to backlogged orders. The pay scale is $11.50 for the first 40 mounts, $12.35 for the next 30 mounts, $13.00 for the next 20 mounts, and $13.40 for all remaining mounts assembled during the week. Katrina assembled 96 mounts last week. What was her total gross pay?

22. Bob Farrell works for a company that manufactures small appliances. Bob is paid $2.00 for each toaster, $4.60 for each microwave oven, and $1.55 for each food blender he assembles. If he produced 56 toasters, 31 microwave ovens, and 79 blenders, what were his total weekly gross earnings?

23. What is the total gross pay for a salesperson on a straight commission of 4.7% if his or her sales volume is $123,200?

24. Pamela Mello is paid on an incremental commission schedule. She is paid 2.6% on the first $60,000 and 3.4% on any sales over $60,000. If her weekly sales volume was $89,400, what was her total commission?

25. Dory Schrader is a buyer for Oceans of Notions. She is paid a weekly salary of $885 plus a 4% commission on sales over $45,000. If her sales were $62,000 last week, what was her total gross pay?

26. Mary is a sales person for Challenge Furniture. She receives an incremental commission based on the table below. If she sells $25,000 and has already received a draw of $766.15, how much commission is still owed to Mary?

Level	Item produced	Commision Rate
1	1–11,700	3.6%
2	11,701–21,200	4.2%
3	Over 21,200	4.6%

27. Katie Jergens works for Dynamic Designs selling clothing. She is on a salary of $140 per week plus a commission of 7% of her sales. Last week she sold 19 dresses at $79.95 each, 26 skirts at $24.75 each, and 17 jackets at $51.50 each. What were her total gross earnings for the week?

28. Jerry King is a server in a restaurant that pays a salary of $22 per day. He also averages tips of 18% of his total gross food orders. Last week he worked 6 days and had total food orders of $2,766.50. What was his total gross pay for the week?

BUSINESS DECISION: MINIMUM WAGE TIED TO INFLATION

29. In an effort to keep low-wage workers' salaries commensurate with the cost of living, a number of states have amended their constitutions to allow the minimum wage to be adjusted with inflation.

    You are the accountant for Delicious, Inc., a company that owns a chain of 18 fast-food restaurants in a state which adjusts the minimum wage for inflation. Each restaurant employs 35 workers, each averaging 20 hours per week at the current federal minimum wage, $7.25 per hour.

a. How many hours at minimum wage are paid out each week by Delicious?

b. At the current rate of $7.25 per hour, what is the amount of the weekly "minimum wage" portion of the restaurant's payroll?

c. If the inflation rate this year is .7%, calculate the "adjusted" minimum wage rate to be paid next year.

d. How much in "additional wages" will Delicious have to pay out next year at the adjusted rate?

e. (Optional) Go to www.dol.gov/whd/minwage/america.htm and click on your state to find the current minimum wage. Calculate the weekly "minimum wage" portion of the restaurant's payroll assuming the restaurant is located in your state.

f. (Optional) Suggest some ways that the restaurant chain or other small businesses can offset the increase in payroll and subsequent decrease in profit as a result of the minimum wage hike.

EMPLOYEE'S PAYROLL DEDUCTIONS

9 SECTION II

"Hey! What happened to my paycheck?" This is the typical reaction of employees on seeing their paychecks for the first time after a raise or a promotion. As we will see, gross pay is by no means the amount of money the employee takes home.

Employers, by federal law, are required to deduct or withhold certain funds, known as **deductions** or **withholdings**, from an employee's paycheck. Employee payroll deductions fall into two categories: mandatory and voluntary. The three major **mandatory deductions** most workers in the United States are subject to are social security, Medicare, and federal income tax. Other mandatory deductions found only in some states are state income tax and state disability insurance.

In addition to the mandatory deductions, employees may also choose to have **voluntary deductions** taken out of their paychecks. Some examples include payments for life or health insurance premiums, union or professional organization dues, credit union savings deposits or loan payments, stock or bond purchases, and charitable contributions.

After all the deductions have been subtracted from the employee's gross earnings, the remaining amount is known as net, or take-home, pay.

Net pay = Gross pay − Total deductions

deductions or **withholdings** Funds withheld from an employee's paycheck.

mandatory deductions Deductions withheld from an employee's paycheck by law: social security, Medicare, and federal income tax.

voluntary deductions Deductions withheld from an employee's paycheck by request of the employee, such as insurance premiums, dues, loan payments, and charitable contributions.

COMPUTING FICA TAXES, BOTH SOCIAL SECURITY AND MEDICARE, WITHHELD FROM AN EMPLOYEE'S PAYCHECK

9-5

In 1937 during the Great Depression, Congress enacted legislation known as the **Federal Insurance Contribution Act (FICA)** with the purpose of providing monthly benefits to retired and disabled workers and to the families of deceased workers. This social security tax, which is assessed to virtually every worker in the United States, is based on a certain percent of the

Federal Insurance Contribution Act (FICA) Federal legislation enacted in 1937 during the Great Depression to provide retirement funds and hospital insurance for retired and disabled workers. Today FICA is divided into two categories, social security and Medicare.

wage base The amount of earnings up to which an employee must pay social security tax.

social security tax (OASDI) Old Age, Survivors, and Disability Insurance—a federal tax based on a percentage of a worker's income up to a specified limit or wage base for the purpose of providing monthly benefits to retired and disabled workers and to the families of deceased workers.

Medicare tax A federal tax used to provide health care benefits and hospital insurance to retired and disabled workers.

worker's income up to a specified limit or **wage base** per year. When the tax began in 1937, the tax rate was 1% up to a wage base of $3,000. At that time, the maximum a worker could be taxed per year for social security was $30 (3,000 × .01).

Today the FICA tax is divided into two categories. **Social security tax** (OASDI, which stands for Old Age, Survivors, and Disability Insurance) is a retirement plan, and **Medicare tax** is for health care and hospital insurance. The social security wage base changes every year. For the most current information, consult the Internal Revenue Service, *Circular E, Employer's Tax Guide*. As this is written, the following rates and wage base were in effect for the FICA tax and should be used for all exercises in this chapter:

	Tax Rate	Wage Base
Social Security (OASDI)	6.2%	$128,400
Medicare	1.45%	no limit

When an employee reaches the wage base for the year, he or she is no longer subject to the tax. Based on the table on the previous page, the maximum social security tax per year is limited to $7,960.80 (128,400 × .062). There is no limit on the amount of Medicare tax. The 1.45% is in effect regardless of how much an employee earns.

Congress passed the Social Security Act in 1935 and passed Medicare into law in 1965.

Source: ssa.gov

Courtesy of Bob Brechner

EXAMPLE9 CALCULATING SOCIAL SECURITY AND MEDICARE WITHHOLDINGS

What are the withholdings for social security and Medicare for an employee with gross earnings of $650 per week? Round to the nearest cent.

▶SOLUTIONSTRATEGY

To find the withholdings, we apply the tax rates for social security (6.2%) and Medicare (1.45%) to the gross earnings for the week:

$$\text{Social security tax} = \text{Gross earnings} \times 6.2\%$$
$$\text{Social security tax} = 650 \times .062 = \underline{\$40.30}$$
$$\text{Medicare tax} = \text{Gross earnings} \times 1.45\%$$
$$\text{Medicare tax} = 650 \times .0145 = 9.425 = \underline{\$9.43}$$

▶TRYITEXERCISE 9

What are the withholdings for social security and Medicare for an employee with gross earnings of $5,000 per month?

CHECK YOUR ANSWERS WITH THE SOLUTIONS ON PAGE 304.

REACHING THE WAGE BASE LIMIT

In the pay period when an employee's year-to-date (YTD) earnings reach and surpass the wage base for social security, the tax is applied only to the portion of the earnings below the limit.

EXAMPLE10 CALCULATING SOCIAL SECURITY WITH WAGE BASE LIMIT

Vickie Hirsh has earned $125,600 so far this year. Her next paycheck, $5,000, will put her earnings over the wage base limit for social security. What is the amount of Vickie's social security withholdings for that paycheck?

▶SOLUTIONSTRATEGY

To calculate Vickie's social security deduction, first determine how much more she must earn to reach the wage base of $128,400.

(continued)

Earnings subject to tax = Wage base − Year-to-date earnings

Earnings subject to tax = 128,400 − 125,600 = $2,800

Social security tax = Earnings subject to tax × 6.2%

Social security tax = 2,800 × .062 = $173.60

▶TRYITEXERCISE 10

Rick Nicotera has year-to-date earnings of $123,900. If his next paycheck is $6,000, what is the amount of his social security deduction?

CHECK YOUR ANSWER WITH THE SOLUTION ON PAGE 304.

CALCULATING AN EMPLOYEE'S FEDERAL INCOME TAX (FIT) WITHHOLDING BY THE PERCENTAGE METHOD

9-6

In addition to social security and Medicare tax withholdings, an employer is also responsible, by federal law, for withholding an appropriate amount of **federal income tax (FIT)** from each employee's paycheck. This graduated tax allows the government a steady flow of tax revenues throughout the year. Self-employed persons must send quarterly tax payments based on estimated earnings to the Internal Revenue Service. By IRS rules, 90% of the income tax due for a given calendar year must be paid within that year to avoid penalties.

The amount of income tax withheld from an employee's paycheck is determined by his or her amount of gross earnings, marital status, and the number of **withholding allowances**, claimed. Employees are allowed one withholding allowance for themselves, one for their spouse if the spouse does not work, and one for each dependent child or elderly parent living with the taxpayer but not working.

Each employee is required to complete a form called W-4, Employee's Withholding Allowance Certificate. The information provided on this form is used by the employer in calculating the amount of income tax withheld from the paycheck. Employees should keep track of their tax liability during the year and adjust the number of withholding allowances as their personal situations change (i.e., marriage, divorce, or birth of a child).

The **percentage method** for determining the amount of federal income tax withheld from an employee's paycheck is used by companies whose payroll processing is on a computerized system. The amount of tax withheld is based on the amount of gross earnings, the marital status of the employee, and the number of withholding allowances claimed.

The percentage method of calculating federal income tax requires the use of two tables. The first is the Percentage Method Amount for One Withholding Allowance Table, as shown in Exhibit 9-1. This table shows the dollar amount of one withholding allowance for the various payroll periods. The second, as shown in Exhibit 9-2, is the Tables for Percentage Method of Withholding. These tables were in effect as this is written following the significant changes in the income tax laws in 2018 and should be used for the exercises in this chapter.

federal income tax (FIT) A graduated tax based on gross earnings and marital status that is paid by all workers earning over a certain amount in the United States.

withholding allowance An amount that reduces an employee's withholding amount. Employees are allowed one withholding allowance for themselves, one for their spouse if the spouse does not work, and one for each dependent child or elderly parent living with the taxpayer but not working.

percentage method An alternative method to the wage bracket tables used to calculate the amount of an employee's federal income tax withholding.

EXHIBIT 9-1

Percentage Method Amount for One Withholding Allowance

Payroll Period	One Withholding Allowance
Weekly	$ 79.80
Biweekly	159.60
Semimonthly	172.90
Monthly	345.80
Quarterly	1,037.50
Semiannually	2,075.00
Annually	4,150.00
Daily or miscellaneous (each day of the payroll period)	16.00

EXHIBIT 9-2 Tables for Percentage Method of Withholding

Percentage Method Tables for Income Tax Withholding

(For Wages Paid in 20XX)

TABLE 1—WEEKLY Payroll Period

(a) SINGLE person (including head of household)—

If the amount of wages (after subtracting withholding allowances) is: The amount of income tax to withhold is:

Not over $71 ....$0

Over—	But not over—		of excess over—
$71	—$254	......$0.00 plus 10%	—$71
$254	—$815	......$18.30 plus 12%	—$254
$815	—$1,658	......$85.62 plus 22%	—$815
$1,658	—$3,100	......$271.08 plus 24%	—$1,658
$3,100	—$3,917	......$617.16 plus 32%	—$3,100
$3,917	—$9,687	$878.60 plus 35%	—$3,917
$9,687	................................$2,898.10 plus 37%		—$9,687

(b) MARRIED person—

If the amount of wages (after subtracting withholding allowances) is: The amount of income tax to withhold is:

Not over $222 ....$0

Over—	But not over—		of excess over—
$222	—$588	......$0.00 plus 10%	—$222
$588	—$1,711	......$36.60 plus 12%	—$588
$1,711	—$3,395	......$171.36 plus 22%	—$1,711
$3,395	—$6,280	......$541.84 plus 24%	—$3,395
$6,280	—$7,914	......$1,234.24 plus 32%	—$6,280
$7,914	—$11,761	......$1,757.12 plus 35%	—$7,914
$11,761	................................$3,103.57 plus 37%		—$11,761

TABLE 2—BIWEEKLY Payroll Period

(a) SINGLE person (including head of household)—

If the amount of wages (after subtracting withholding allowances) is: The amount of income tax to withhold is:

Not over $142 ....$0

Over—	But not over—		of excess over—
$142	—$509	......$0.00 plus 10%	—$142
$509	—$1,631	......$36.70 plus 12%	—$509
$1,631	—$3,315	......$171.34 plus 22%	—$1,631
$3,315	—$6,200	......$541.82 plus 24%	—$3,315
$6,200	—$7,835	......$1,234.22 plus 32%	—$6,200
$7,835	—$19,373	......$1,757.42 plus 35%	—$7,835
$19,373	................................$5,795.72 plus 37%		—$19,373

(b) MARRIED person—

If the amount of wages (after subtracting withholding allowances) is: The amount of income tax to withhold is:

Not over $444 ....$0

Over—	But not over—		of excess over—
$444	—$1,177	......$0.00 plus 10%	—$444
$1,177	—$3,421	......$73.30 plus 12%	—$1,177
$3,421	—$6,790	......$342.58 plus 22%	—$3,421
$6,790	—$12,560	......$1,083.76 plus 24%	—$6,790
$12,560	—$15,829	......$2,468.56 plus 32%	—$12,560
$15,829	—$23,521	......$3,514.64 plus 35%	—$15,829
$23,521	................................$6,206.84 plus 37%		—$23,521

TABLE 3—SEMIMONTHLY Payroll Period

(a) SINGLE person (including head of household)—

If the amount of wages (after subtracting withholding allowances) is: The amount of income tax to withhold is:

Not over $154 ....$0

Over—	But not over—		of excess over—
$154	—$551	......$0.00 plus 10%	—$154
$551	—$1,767	......$39.70 plus 12%	—$551
$1,767	—$3,592	......$185.62 plus 22%	—$1,767
$3,592	—$6,717	......$587.12 plus 24%	—$3,592
$6,717	—$8,488	......$1,337.12 plus 32%	—$6,717
$8,488	—$20,988	......$1,903.84 plus 35%	—$8,488
$20,988	................................$6,278.84 plus 37%		—$20,988

(b) MARRIED person—

If the amount of wages (after subtracting withholding allowances) is: The amount of income tax to withhold is:

Not over $481 ....$0

Over—	But not over—		of excess over—
$481	—$1,275	......$0.00 plus 10%	—$481
$1,275	—$3,706	......$79.40 plus 12%	—$1,275
$3,706	—$7,356	......$371.12 plus 22%	—$3,706
$7,356	—$13,606	......$1,174.12 plus 24%	—$7,356
$13,606	—$17,148	......$2,674.12 plus 32%	—$13,606
$17,148	—$$25,481	......$3,807.11 plus 35%	—$17,148
$25,481	................................$6,724.11 plus 37%		—$25,481

TABLE 4—MONTHLY Payroll Period

(a) SINGLE person (including head of household)—

If the amount of wages (after subtracting withholding allowances) is: The amount of income tax to withhold is:

Not over $308 ....$0

Over—	But not over—		of excess over—
$308	—$1,102	......$0.00 plus 10%	—$308
$1,102	—$3,533	......$79.40 plus 12%	—$1,102
$3,533	—$7,183	......$371.12 plus 22%	—$3,533
$7,183	—$13,433	......$1,174.12 plus 24%	—$7,183
$13,433	—$16,975	......$2,674.12 plus 32%	—$13,433
$16,975	—$41,975	......$3,807.56 plus 35%	—$16,975
$41,975	................................$12,557.56 plus 37%		—$41,975

(b) MARRIED person—

If the amount of wages (after subtracting withholding allowances) is: The amount of income tax to withhold is:

Not over $963 ....$0

Over—	But not over—		of excess over—
$963	—$2,550	......$0.00 plus 10%	—$963
$2,550	—$7,413	......$158.70 plus 12%	—$2,550
$7,413	—$14,713	......$742.26 plus 22%	—$7,413
$14,713	—$27,213	......$2,348.26 plus 24%	—$14,713
$27,213	—$34,296	......$5,345.26 plus 32%	—$27,213
$34,296	—$50,963	......$7,614.82 plus 35%	—$34,296
$50,963	................................$13,448.27 plus 37%		—$50,963

STEPS TO CALCULATE THE INCOME TAX WITHHELD BY THE PERCENTAGE METHOD

STEP 1. Using the proper payroll period, multiply one withholding allowance, Exhibit 9-1, by the number of allowances claimed by the employee.

STEP 2. Subtract that amount from the employee's gross earnings to find the wages subject to federal income tax.

STEP 3. From Exhibit 9-2, locate the proper segment (Table 1, 2, 3, or 4) corresponding to the employee's payroll period. Within that segment, use the *left* side (a) for single employees and the *right* side (b) for married employees.

STEP 4. Locate the "Over—" and "But not over—" brackets containing the employee's taxable wages from Step 2. The tax is listed to the right as a percent or a dollar amount and a percent.

iStock.com/Nikada

EXAMPLE11 CALCULATING INCOME TAX WITHHOLDING

Lori Fast is a manager for Wayward Wind Travel. She is single and is paid $750 weekly. She claims two withholding allowances. Using the percentage method, calculate the amount of income tax that should be withheld from her paycheck each week.

►SOLUTIONSTRATEGY

From Exhibit 9-1, the amount of one withholding allowance for an employee paid weekly is $79.80. Multiply this amount by the number of allowances claimed, two.

$$79.80 \times 2 = \$159.60$$

Subtract that amount from the gross earnings to get taxable income.

$$750.00 - 159.60 = \$590.40$$

From Exhibit 9-2, find the tax withheld from Lori's paycheck in Table 1(a), Weekly payroll period, Single person. Lori's taxable wages of $598.00 fall in the category "Over $254, but not over $815." The tax, therefore, is $18.30 plus 12% of the excess over $254.

$$\text{Withholding} = 18.30 + .12(590.40 - 254.00)$$
$$\text{Withholding} = 18.30 + .12(336.40)$$
$$\text{Withholding} = 18.30 + 40.37 = \underline{\underline{\$58.67}}$$

►TRYITEXERCISE 11

Jan McMillan is married, claims five withholding allowances, and earns $5,670 per month. As the payroll manager of Jan's company, use the percentage method to calculate the amount of income tax that must be withheld from her paycheck.

CHECK YOUR ANSWER WITH THE SOLUTION ON PAGE 304.

9-7 DETERMINING AN EMPLOYEE'S TOTAL WITHHOLDING FOR FEDERAL INCOME TAX, SOCIAL SECURITY, AND MEDICARE USING THE COMBINED WAGE BRACKET TABLES

combined wage bracket tables IRS tables used to determine the combined amount of income tax, social security, and Medicare that must be withheld from an employee's gross earnings each pay period.

In 2001, the IRS introduced **combined wage bracket tables** that can be used to determine the combined amount of income tax, social security, and Medicare that must be withheld from an employee's gross earnings each pay period. These tables are found in *Publication 15-A, Employer's Supplemental Tax Guide*. This publication contains a complete set of tables for both single and married people, covering weekly, biweekly, semimonthly, monthly, and even daily pay periods.

Exhibit 9-3 shows a portion of the wage bracket tables for Married Persons—Weekly Payroll Period, and Exhibit 9-4 shows a portion of the wage bracket table for Single Persons—Monthly Payroll Period. These tables were in effect as this is written and should be used to solve wage bracket problems in this chapter.

STEPS TO FIND THE TOTAL INCOME TAX, SOCIAL SECURITY, AND MEDICARE WITHHELD USING THE COMBINED WAGE BRACKET TABLE

STEP 1. Based on the employee's marital status and period of payment, find the corresponding table (Exhibit 9-3 or 9-4).

STEP 2. Note that the two left-hand columns, labeled "At least" and "But less than," are the wage brackets. Scan down these columns until you find the bracket containing the gross pay of the employee.

STEP 3. Scan across the row of that wage bracket to the intersection of the column containing the number of withholding allowances claimed by the employee.

STEP 4. The number in that column on the wage bracket row is the amount of combined tax withheld.

EXAMPLE 12 USING THE COMBINED WAGE BRACKET TABLES

Use the combined wage bracket tables to determine the amount of income tax, social security, and Medicare withheld from the monthly paycheck of Erin Lane, a single employee claiming three withholding allowances and earning $2,975 per month.

SOLUTIONSTRATEGY

To find Erin Lane's monthly income tax withholding, choose the table for Single Persons—Monthly Payroll Period, Exhibit 9-4. Scanning down the "At least" and "But less than" columns, we find the wage bracket containing Erin's earnings: "At least 2,965—But less than 3,005."

Next, scan across that row from left to right to the "3" withholding allowances column. The number at that intersection, $409.35, is the total combined tax to be withheld from Erin's paycheck.

▶TRYITEXERCISE 12

Using the combined wage bracket tables, what is the total amount of income tax, social security, and Medicare that should be withheld from Brent Andrus's weekly paycheck of $1,160 if he is married and claims two withholding allowances?

CHECK YOUR ANSWER WITH THE SOLUTION ON PAGE 304.

EXHIBIT 9-3 Payroll Deductions—Married, Paid Weekly

MARRIED Persons—WEEKLY Payroll Period
(For Wages Paid through December 20XX)

And the wages are—		And the number of withholding allowances claimed is—										
At least	But less than	0	1	2	3	4	5	6	7	8	9	10
		The amount of income, social security, and Medicare taxes to be withheld is—										
915	925	146.38	137.38	127.38	118.38	108.38	100.38	92.38	84.38	76.38	70.38	70.38
925	935	149.15	139.15	129.15	120.15	110.15	102.15	94.15	86.15	78.15	71.15	71.15
935	945	150.91	140.91	131.91	121.91	112.91	103.91	95.91	87.91	79.91	71.91	71.91
945	955	152.68	142.68	133.68	123.68	114.68	105.68	97.68	89.68	81.68	73.68	72.68
955	965	154.44	145.44	135.44	125.44	116.44	107.44	99.44	91.44	83.44	75.44	73.44
965	975	156.21	147.21	137.21	128.21	118.21	109.21	101.21	93.21	85.21	77.21	74.21
975	985	158.97	148.97	138.97	129.97	119.97	110.97	102.97	94.97	86.97	78.97	74.97
985	995	160.74	150.74	141.74	131.74	122.74	112.74	104.74	96.74	88.74	80.74	75.74
995	1,005	162.50	152.50	143.50	133.50	124.50	114.50	106.50	98.50	90.50	82.50	76.50
1,005	1,015	164.27	155.27	145.27	135.27	126.27	116.27	108.27	100.27	92.27	84.27	77.27
1,015	1,025	166.03	157.03	147.03	138.03	128.03	119.03	110.03	102.03	94.03	86.03	78.03
1,025	1,035	168.80	158.80	148.80	139.80	129.80	120.80	111.80	103.80	95.80	87.80	79.80
1,035	1,045	170.56	160.56	151.56	141.56	132.56	122.56	113.56	105.56	97.56	89.56	81.56
1,045	1,055	172.33	162.33	153.33	143.33	134.33	124.33	115.33	107.33	99.33	91.33	83.33
1,055	1,065	174.09	165.09	155.09	145.09	136.09	126.09	117.09	109.09	101.09	93.09	85.09
1,065	1,075	175.86	166.86	156.86	147.86	137.86	128.86	118.86	110.86	102.86	94.86	86.86
1,075	1,085	178.62	168.62	158.62	149.62	139.62	130.62	120.62	112.62	104.62	96.62	88.62
1,085	1,095	180.39	170.39	161.39	151.39	142.39	132.39	122.39	114.39	106.39	98.39	90.39
1,095	1,105	182.15	172.15	163.15	153.15	144.15	134.15	125.15	116.15	108.15	100.15	92.15
1,105	1,115	183.92	174.92	164.92	154.92	145.92	135.92	126.92	117.92	109.92	101.92	93.92
1,115	1,125	185.68	176.68	166.68	157.68	147.68	138.68	128.68	119.68	111.68	103.68	95.68
1,125	1,135	188.45	178.45	168.45	159.45	149.45	140.45	130.45	121.45	113.45	105.45	97.45
1,135	1,145	190.21	180.21	171.21	161.21	152.21	142.21	132.21	123.21	115.21	107.21	99.21
1,145	1,155	191.98	181.98	172.98	162.98	153.98	143.98	134.98	124.98	116.98	108.98	100.98
1,155	1,165	193.74	184.74	174.74	164.74	155.74	145.74	136.74	126.74	118.74	110.74	102.74
1,165	1,175	195.51	186.51	176.51	167.51	157.51	148.51	138.51	128.51	120.51	112.51	104.51
1,175	1,185	198.27	188.27	178.27	169.27	159.27	150.27	140.27	131.27	122.27	114.27	106.27
1,185	1,195	200.04	190.04	181.04	171.04	162.04	152.04	142.04	133.04	124.04	116.04	108.04
1,195	1,205	201.80	191.80	182.80	172.80	163.80	153.80	144.80	134.80	125.80	117.80	109.80
1,205	1,215	203.57	194.57	184.57	174.57	165.57	155.57	146.57	136.57	127.57	119.57	111.57
1,215	1,225	205.33	196.33	186.33	177.33	167.33	158.33	148.33	138.33	129.33	121.33	113.33
1,225	1,235	208.10	198.10	188.10	179.10	169.10	160.10	150.10	141.10	131.10	123.10	115.10
1,235	1,245	209.86	199.86	190.86	180.86	171.86	161.86	151.86	142.86	132.86	124.86	116.86
1,245	1,255	211.63	201.63	192.63	182.63	173.63	163.63	154.63	144.63	134.63	126.63	118.63
1,255	1,265	213.39	204.39	194.39	184.39	175.39	165.39	156.39	146.39	137.39	128.39	120.39
1,265	1,275	215.16	206.16	196.16	187.16	177.16	168.16	158.16	148.16	139.16	130.16	122.16
1,275	1,285	217.92	207.92	197.92	188.92	178.92	169.92	159.92	150.92	140.92	131.92	123.92
1,285	1,295	219.69	209.69	200.69	190.69	181.69	171.69	161.69	152.69	142.69	133.69	125.69
1,295	1,305	221.45	211.45	202.45	192.45	183.45	173.45	164.45	154.45	144.45	135.45	127.45
1,305	1,315	223.22	214.22	204.22	194.22	185.22	175.22	166.22	156.22	147.22	137.22	129.22
1,315	1,325	224.98	215.98	205.98	196.98	186.98	177.98	167.98	157.98	148.98	138.98	130.98
1,325	1,335	227.75	217.75	207.75	198.75	188.75	179.75	169.75	160.75	150.75	140.75	132.75
1,335	1,345	229.51	219.51	210.51	200.51	191.51	181.51	171.51	162.51	152.51	143.51	134.51
1,345	1,355	231.28	221.28	212.28	202.28	193.28	183.28	174.28	164.28	154.28	145.28	136.28
1,355	1,365	233.04	224.04	214.04	204.04	195.04	185.04	176.04	166.04	157.04	147.04	138.04
1,365	1,375	234.81	225.81	215.81	206.81	196.81	187.81	177.81	167.81	158.81	148.81	139.81
1,375	1,385	237.57	227.57	217.57	208.57	198.57	189.57	179.57	170.57	160.57	150.57	141.57
1,385	1,395	239.34	229.34	220.34	210.34	201.34	191.34	181.34	172.34	162.34	153.34	143.34
1,395	1,405	241.10	231.10	222.10	212.10	203.10	193.10	184.10	174.10	164.10	155.10	145.10
1,405	1,415	242.87	233.87	223.87	213.87	204.87	194.87	185.87	175.87	166.87	156.87	146.87
1,415	1,425	244.63	235.63	225.63	216.63	206.63	197.63	187.63	177.63	168.63	158.63	149.63
1,425	1,435	247.40	237.40	227.40	218.40	208.40	199.40	189.40	180.40	170.40	160.40	151.40
1,435	1,445	249.16	239.16	230.16	220.16	211.16	201.16	191.16	182.16	172.16	163.16	153.16
1,445	1,455	250.93	240.93	231.93	221.93	212.93	202.93	193.93	183.93	173.93	164.93	154.93
1,455	1,465	252.69	243.69	233.69	223.69	214.69	204.69	195.69	185.69	176.69	166.69	156.69
1,465	1,475	254.46	245.46	235.46	226.46	216.46	207.46	197.46	187.46	178.46	168.46	159.46
1,475	1,485	257.22	247.22	237.22	228.22	218.22	209.22	199.22	190.22	180.22	170.22	161.22
1,485	1,495	258.99	248.99	239.99	229.99	220.99	210.99	200.99	191.99	181.99	172.99	162.99
1,495	1,505	260.75	250.75	241.75	231.75	222.75	212.75	203.75	193.75	183.75	174.75	164.75
1,505	1,515	262.52	253.52	243.52	233.52	224.52	214.52	205.52	195.52	186.52	176.52	166.52
1,515	1,525	264.28	255.28	245.28	236.28	226.28	217.28	207.28	197.28	188.28	178.28	169.28
1,525	1,535	267.05	257.05	247.05	238.05	228.05	219.05	209.05	200.05	190.05	180.05	171.05
1,535	1,545	268.81	258.81	249.81	239.81	230.81	220.81	210.81	201.81	191.81	182.81	172.81
1,545	1,555	270.58	260.58	251.58	241.58	232.58	222.58	213.58	203.58	193.58	184.58	174.58
1,555	1,565	272.34	263.34	253.34	243.34	234.34	224.34	215.34	205.34	196.34	186.34	176.34

EXHIBIT 9-4 Payroll Deductions—Single, Paid Monthly

SINGLE Persons—MONTHLY Payroll Period
(For Wages Paid through December 20XX)

And the wages are—		And the number of withholding allowances claimed is—										
At least	But less than	0	1	2	3	4	5	6	7	8	9	10
		The amount of income, social security, and Medicare taxes to be withheld is—										
2,765	2,805	494.05	453.05	411.05	370.05	328.05	288.05	253.05	219.05	213.05	213.05	213.05
2,805	2,845	502.11	461.11	419.11	378.11	336.11	295.11	260.11	226.11	216.11	216.11	216.11
2,845	2,885	510.17	468.17	427.17	385.17	344.17	302.17	267.17	233.17	219.17	219.17	219.17
2,885	2,925	518.23	476.23	435.23	393.23	352.23	310.23	274.23	240.23	222.23	222.23	222.23
2,925	2,965	526.29	484.29	443.29	401.29	360.29	318.29	281.29	247.29	225.29	225.29	225.29
2,965	3,005	533.35	492.35	450.35	409.35	367.35	326.35	288.35	254.35	228.35	228.35	228.35
3,005	3,045	541.41	500.41	458.41	417.41	375.41	334.41	295.41	261.41	231.41	231.41	231.41
3,045	3,085	549.47	507.47	466.47	424.47	383.47	341.47	302.47	268.47	234.47	234.47	234.47
3,085	3,125	557.53	515.53	474.53	432.53	391.53	349.53	309.53	275.53	240.53	237.53	237.53
3,125	3,165	565.59	523.59	482.59	440.59	399.59	357.59	316.59	282.59	247.59	240.59	240.59
3,165	3,205	572.65	531.65	489.65	448.65	406.65	365.65	323.65	289.65	254.65	243.65	243.65
3,205	3,245	580.71	539.71	497.71	456.71	414.71	373.71	331.71	296.71	261.71	246.71	246.71
3,245	3,285	588.77	546.77	505.77	463.77	422.77	380.77	339.77	303.77	268.77	249.77	249.77
3,285	3,325	596.83	554.83	513.83	471.83	430.83	388.83	347.83	310.83	275.83	252.83	252.83
3,325	3,365	604.89	562.89	521.89	479.89	438.89	396.89	355.89	317.89	282.89	255.89	255.89
3,365	3,405	611.95	570.95	528.95	487.95	445.95	404.95	362.95	324.95	289.95	258.95	258.95
3,405	3,445	620.01	579.01	537.01	496.01	454.01	413.01	371.01	332.01	297.01	262.01	262.01
3,445	3,485	628.07	586.07	545.07	503.07	462.07	420.07	379.07	339.07	304.07	269.07	265.07
3,485	3,525	636.13	594.13	553.13	511.13	470.13	428.13	387.13	346.13	311.13	276.13	268.13
3,525	3,565	645.19	602.19	561.19	519.19	478.19	436.19	395.19	353.19	318.19	283.19	271.19
3,565	3,605	656.25	610.25	568.25	527.25	485.25	444.25	402.25	361.25	325.25	290.25	274.25
3,605	3,645	668.31	618.31	576.31	535.31	493.31	452.31	410.31	369.31	332.31	297.31	277.31
3,645	3,685	680.37	625.37	584.37	542.37	501.37	459.37	418.37	376.37	339.37	304.37	280.37
3,685	3,725	692.43	633.43	592.43	550.43	509.43	467.43	426.43	384.43	346.43	311.43	283.43
3,725	3,765	704.49	641.49	600.49	558.49	517.49	475.49	434.49	392.49	353.49	318.49	286.49
3,765	3,805	715.55	649.55	607.55	566.55	524.55	483.55	441.55	400.55	360.55	325.55	291.55
3,805	3,845	727.61	657.61	615.61	574.61	532.61	491.61	449.61	408.61	367.61	332.61	298.61
3,845	3,885	739.67	664.67	623.67	581.67	540.67	498.67	457.67	415.67	374.67	339.67	305.67
3,885	3,925	751.73	675.73	631.73	589.73	548.73	506.73	465.73	423.73	382.73	346.73	312.73
3,925	3,965	763.79	687.79	639.79	597.79	556.79	514.79	473.79	431.79	390.79	353.79	319.79
3,965	4,005	774.85	698.85	646.85	605.85	563.85	522.85	480.85	439.85	397.85	360.85	326.85
4,005	4,045	786.91	710.91	654.91	613.91	571.91	530.91	488.91	447.91	405.91	367.91	333.91
4,045	4,085	798.97	722.97	662.97	620.97	579.97	537.97	496.97	454.97	413.97	374.97	340.97
4,085	4,125	811.03	735.03	671.03	629.03	588.03	546.03	505.03	463.03	422.03	382.03	348.03
4,125	4,165	823.09	747.09	679.09	637.09	596.09	554.09	513.09	471.09	430.09	389.09	355.09
4,165	4,205	834.15	758.15	686.15	645.15	603.15	562.15	520.15	479.15	437.15	396.15	362.15
4,205	4,245	846.21	770.21	694.21	653.21	611.21	570.21	528.21	487.21	445.21	404.21	369.21
4,245	4,285	858.27	782.27	706.27	660.27	619.27	577.27	536.27	494.27	453.27	411.27	376.27
4,285	4,325	870.33	794.33	718.33	668.33	627.33	585.33	544.33	502.33	461.33	419.33	383.33
4,325	4,365	882.39	806.39	730.39	676.39	635.39	593.39	552.39	510.39	469.39	427.39	390.39
4,365	4,405	893.45	817.45	741.45	684.45	642.45	601.45	559.45	518.45	476.45	435.45	397.45
4,405	4,445	905.51	829.51	753.51	692.51	650.51	609.51	567.51	526.51	484.51	443.51	404.51
4,445	4,485	917.57	841.57	765.57	699.57	658.57	616.57	575.57	533.57	492.57	450.57	411.57
4,485	4,525	929.63	853.63	777.63	707.63	666.63	624.63	583.63	541.63	500.63	458.63	418.63
4,525	4,565	941.69	865.69	789.69	715.69	674.69	632.69	591.69	549.69	508.69	466.69	425.69
4,565	4,605	952.75	876.75	800.75	724.75	681.75	640.75	598.75	557.75	515.75	474.75	432.75
4,605	4,645	964.81	888.81	812.81	736.81	689.81	648.81	606.81	565.81	523.81	482.81	440.81
4,645	4,685	976.87	900.87	824.87	748.87	697.87	655.87	614.87	572.87	531.87	489.87	448.87
4,685	4,725	988.93	912.93	836.93	760.93	705.93	663.93	622.93	580.93	539.93	497.93	456.93
4,725	4,765	1,000.99	924.99	848.99	771.99	713.99	671.99	630.99	588.99	547.99	505.99	464.99
4,765	4,805	1,012.05	936.05	860.05	784.05	721.05	680.05	638.05	597.05	555.05	514.05	472.05
4,805	4,845	1,024.11	948.11	872.11	796.11	729.11	688.11	646.11	605.11	563.11	522.11	480.11
4,845	4,885	1,036.17	960.17	884.17	808.17	737.17	695.17	654.17	612.17	571.17	529.17	488.17
4,885	4,925	1,048.23	972.23	896.23	820.23	745.23	703.23	662.23	620.23	579.23	537.23	496.23
4,925	4,965	1,060.29	984.29	908.29	831.29	755.29	711.29	670.29	628.29	587.29	545.29	504.29
4,965	5,005	1,071.35	995.35	919.35	843.35	767.35	719.35	677.35	636.35	594.35	553.35	511.35
5,005	5,045	1,083.41	1,007.41	931.41	855.41	779.41	727.41	685.41	644.41	602.41	561.41	519.41
5,045	5,085	1,095.47	1,019.47	943.47	867.47	791.47	734.47	693.47	651.47	610.47	568.47	527.47
5,085	5,125	1,107.53	1,031.53	955.53	879.53	803.53	742.53	701.53	659.53	618.53	576.53	535.53
5,125	5,165	1,119.59	1,043.59	967.59	890.59	814.59	750.59	709.59	667.59	626.59	584.59	543.59
5,165	5,205	1,130.65	1,054.65	978.65	902.65	826.65	758.65	716.65	675.65	633.65	592.65	550.65
5,205	5,245	1,142.71	1,066.71	990.71	914.71	838.71	766.71	724.71	683.71	641.71	600.71	558.71
5,245	5,285	1,154.77	1,078.77	1,002.77	926.77	850.77	774.77	732.77	690.77	649.77	607.77	566.77
5,285	5,325	1,166.83	1,090.83	1,014.83	938.83	862.83	785.83	740.83	698.83	657.83	615.83	574.83
5,325	5,365	1,178.89	1,102.89	1,026.89	949.89	873.89	797.89	748.89	706.89	665.89	623.89	582.89

REVIEW EXERCISES

9 SECTION II

Solve the following problems using 6.2%, up to $128,400 for social security tax and 1.45%, no wage limit, for Medicare tax.

1. What are the withholdings for social security and Medicare for an employee with gross earnings of $825 per week?

$825 \times .062 = \underline{\$51.15}$ Social security
$825 \times .0145 = \underline{\$11.96}$ Medicare

2. What are the social security and Medicare withholdings for an executive whose annual gross earnings are $138,500?

3. Brian Hickman is an executive with Westco Distributors. His gross earnings are $11,200 per month.

   a. What are the withholdings for social security and Medicare for Brian in his January paycheck?

   b. In what month will Brian's salary reach the social security wage base limit?

   c. What are the social security and Medicare tax withholdings for Brian in the month named in part b?

4. Kristy Dunaway has biweekly gross earnings of $1,750. What are her total social security and Medicare tax withholdings for a whole year?

As the payroll manager for Freeport Enterprises, it is your task to calculate the monthly social security and Medicare withholdings for the following employees.

Employee	Year-to-Date Earnings	Current Month	Social Security	Medicare
5. Perez, J.	$23,446	$3,422	$212.16	$49.62
6. Graham, C.	$14,800	$1,540	_____	_____
7. Jagger, R.	$105,200	$4,700	_____	_____
8. Andretti, K.	$145,000	$12,450	_____	_____

Use the percentage method of income tax calculation to complete the following payroll roster.

	Employee	Marital Status	Withholding Allowances	Pay Period	Gross Earnings	Income Tax Withholding
9.	Randolph, B.	M	2	Weekly	$594	$21.24
10.	White, W.	S	0	Semimonthly	$1,227	_____
11.	Milian, B.	S	1	Monthly	$4,150	_____

12. David Grange is married and claims 4 withholding allowances. If he is paid biweekly and earns $1,849 per period, use the percentage method to find his income tax withholding each pay period.

Use the combined wage bracket tables, Exhibits 9-3 and 9-4, to solve Exercises 13–19.

13. How much combined tax should be withheld from the paycheck of a married employee earning $1,075 per week and claiming four withholding allowances?

14. How much combined tax should be withheld from the paycheck of a single employee earning $3,185 per month and claiming zero withholding allowances?

15. Jeremy Dunn is single, claims two withholding allowances, and earns $4,025 per month. Calculate the amount of Jeremy's paycheck after his employer withholds social security, Medicare, and federal income tax.

	Employee	Marital Status	Withholding Allowances	Pay Period	Gross Earnings	Combined Withholding
16.	Alton, A.	S	3	Monthly	$4,633	$736.81
17.	Emerson, P.	M	5	Weekly	$937	_____
18.	Reese, S.	M	4	Weekly	$1,172	_____
19.	Benson, K.	S	1	Monthly	$3,128	_____

BUSINESS DECISION: TAKE-HOME PAY

20. You are the payroll manager for the Canyon Ridge Resort. Your daughter (Sarah Boxwood) is the marketing director earning a salary of $43,200 per year, payable monthly. She is married and claims four withholding allowances. Her social security number is 444-44-4444.

    In addition to federal income tax, social security, and Medicare, Sarah pays 2.3% state income tax, $\frac{1}{2}$% for state disability insurance (both based on gross earnings), $23.74 for term life insurance, $122.14 to the credit union, and $40 to the United Way.

    Fill out the following payroll voucher for Sarah for the month of April.

Canyon Ridge Resort
Payroll Voucher

Employee: _____   Tax Filing Status: _____
SSN: _____   Withholding Allowances: ___

Full-time Pay Period From _____ to _____

Primary Withholdings: Additional Withholdings:

Federal income tax   _____   _____

Social security   _____   _____

Medicare   _____   _____

State income tax   _____

State disability   _____

              Gross earnings: _____
          – Total withholdings: _____

              NET PAY   _____

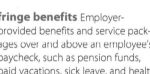

EMPLOYER'S PAYROLL EXPENSES AND SELF-EMPLOYED PERSON'S TAX RESPONSIBILITY

9 | SECTION III

To this point, we have discussed payroll deductions from the employee's point of view. Now let's take a look at the payroll expenses of the employer. According to the Fair Labor Standards Act, employers are required to maintain complete and up-to-date earnings records for each employee.

Employers are responsible for the payment of four payroll taxes: social security, Medicare, state unemployment tax (SUTA), and federal unemployment tax (FUTA). In addition, most employers are responsible for a variety of **fringe benefits** that are offered to their employees. These are benefits over and above an employee's normal earnings and can be a significant expense to the employer. Some typical examples are retirement plans, stock option plans, holiday leave, sick days, health and dental insurance, and tuition reimbursement. This section deals with the calculation of these employer taxes as well as the tax responsibility of self-employed persons.

fringe benefits Employer-provided benefits and service packages over and above an employee's paycheck, such as pension funds, paid vacations, sick leave, and health insurance.

COMPUTING FICA TAX FOR EMPLOYERS AND SELF-EMPLOYMENT TAX FOR SELF-EMPLOYED PERSONS

9-8

FICA TAX FOR EMPLOYERS

Employers are required to *match* all FICA tax payments, both social security and Medicare, made by each employee. For example, if a company withheld a total of $23,000 in FICA taxes from its employee paychecks this month, the company would be responsible for a matching share of $23,000.

EXAMPLE13 | COMPUTING FICA TAX FOR EMPLOYEES AND THE EMPLOYER

Spectrum Engineering has 25 employees, each with gross earnings of $250 per week.

a. What are the total FICA (social security and Medicare) taxes that should be withheld from each employee's weekly paycheck?

b. At the end of the first quarter (13 weeks), what were the accumulated totals of the employee's share and the matching taxes for FICA that Spectrum had sent to the IRS?

▶SOLUTIONSTRATEGY

To solve for the total FICA tax due quarterly from the employees and the employer, calculate the tax due per employee per week, multiply by 25 to find the total weekly FICA for all employees, and multiply by 13 weeks to find the total quarterly amount withheld from all employees. The employer's share will be an equal amount.

a. Social security tax = Gross earnings × 6.2% = 250 × .062 = $15.50
    Medicare tax = Gross earnings × 1.45% = 250 × .0145 = $3.63
    Total FICA tax per employee per week = 15.50 + 3.63 = $19.13

b. Total FICA tax per week = FICA tax per employee × 25 employees
    Total FICA tax per week = 19.13 × 25 = $478.25

    Total FICA tax first quarter = Total FICA tax per week × 13 weeks
    Total FICA tax first quarter = 478.25 × 13 = $6,217.25

    Total FICA tax first quarter—Employee's share = $6,217.25
    Total FICA tax first quarter—Employer's share = $6,217.25

▶TRYITEXERCISE 13

Big Pine Tree Service has 18 employees, 12 with gross earnings of $350 per week and 6 with gross earnings of $425 per week. What are the employee's share and the employer's share of the social security and Medicare tax for the first quarter of the year?

CHECK YOUR ANSWERS WITH THE SOLUTIONS ON PAGE 304.

SELF-EMPLOYMENT TAX

The self-employment tax, officially known as the Self-Employment Contributions Act (SECA) tax, is the self-employed person's version of the FICA tax. It is due on the net earnings from self-employment.

Self-employed persons are responsible for social security and Medicare taxes at twice the rate deducted for employees. Technically, they are the employee and the employer and therefore must pay both shares. For a self-employed person, the social security and Medicare tax rates are twice the normal rates, as follows:

	Tax Rate	Wage Base
Social Security	12.4% (6.2% × 2)	$128,400
Medicare	2.9% (1.45% × 2)	No limit

EXAMPLE14 CALCULATING SELF-EMPLOYMENT TAX

What are the social security and Medicare taxes of a self-employed landscaper with net earnings of $43,800 per year?

▶SOLUTIONSTRATEGY

To find the amount of self-employment tax due, we apply the self-employed tax rates, 12.4% for social security and 2.9% for Medicare, to the net earnings.

Social security tax = Net earnings × Tax rate
Social security tax = 43,800 × .124 = $5,431.20
Medicare tax = Net earnings × Tax rate
Medicare tax = 43,800 × .029 = $1,270.20

► TRYITEXERCISE 14

Les Roberts, a self-employed commercial artist, had total net earnings of $60,000 last year. What was the amount of the social security and Medicare taxes Les was required to send the IRS last year?

CHECK YOUR ANSWERS WITH THE SOLUTIONS ON PAGE 304.

COMPUTING THE AMOUNT OF STATE UNEMPLOYMENT TAX (SUTA) AND FEDERAL UNEMPLOYMENT TAX (FUTA)

9-9

The **Federal Unemployment Tax Act (FUTA)**, together with state unemployment systems, provides for payments of unemployment compensation to workers who have lost their jobs. Most employers are responsible for both a federal and a state unemployment tax.

Generally, an employer can take a credit against the FUTA tax for amounts paid into state unemployment funds. These state taxes are commonly known as the **State Unemployment Tax Act (SUTA)**. This credit cannot be more than 5.4% of the first $7,000 of employees' taxable wages.

SUTA tax rates vary from state to state according to the employment record of the company. These merit-rating systems found in many states provide significant SUTA tax savings to companies with good employment records.

The FUTA may change from year to year. In this chapter, we'll use a FUTA tax rate of .6%. (This assumes an unreduced FUTA tax of 6% for the first $7,000 of wages paid to each employee during the year reduced by a 5.4% SUTA credit. That is, 6% − 5.4% = .6% FUTA tax rate.)

Federal Unemployment Tax Act (FUTA) A federal tax that is paid by employers for each employee to provide unemployment compensation to workers who have lost their jobs.

State Unemployment Tax Act (SUTA) A state tax that is paid by employers for each employee to provide unemployment compensation to workers who have lost their jobs.

EXAMPLE15 CALCULATING SUTA AND FUTA TAXES

Uniphase Industries, Inc., had a total payroll of $50,000 last month. Uniphase pays a SUTA tax rate of 5.4% and a FUTA rate of 6.0% less the SUTA credit. If none of the employees had reached the $7,000 wage base, what is the amount of SUTA and FUTA tax the company must pay?

►SOLUTIONSTRATEGY

To calculate the SUTA and FUTA taxes, apply the appropriate tax rates to the gross earnings subject to the tax, in this case, all the gross earnings.

$$\text{SUTA tax} = \text{Gross earnings} \times 5.4\%$$
$$\text{SUTA tax} = 50,000 \times .054 = \$2,700$$

The FUTA tax rate will be .6%. Remember, it is actually 6.0% less the 5.4% credit.

$$\text{FUTA tax} = \text{Gross earnings} \times .6\%$$
$$\text{FUTA tax} = 50,000 \times .006 = \$300$$

►TRYITEXERCISE 15

Sunshine Catering had a total payroll of $10,000 last month. Sunshine pays a SUTA tax rate of 5.4% and a FUTA rate of 6.0% less the SUTA credit. If none of the employees had reached the $7,000 wage base, what is the amount of SUTA and FUTA tax the company must pay?

CHECK YOUR ANSWERS WITH THE SOLUTIONS ON PAGE 304.

9-10 CALCULATING EMPLOYER'S FRINGE BENEFIT EXPENSES

perquisites, or **perks** Executive-level fringe benefits such as first-class airline travel, company cars, and country club membership.

cafeteria style, or **flexible benefit programs** A plan whereby employees are given a menu of fringe benefits from which to choose up to a specified dollar amount.

IN THE Business World

Although paid vacations and health insurance are still the most popular among company-sponsored benefits, there is a trend today toward more "work-life initiatives." These are benefits that help employees balance their professional and personal lives, such as child-care assistance and flexible work hours.

Paid vacation time is one of the many fringe benefits offered by employers today.

In addition to compensating employees with a paycheck, most companies today offer employee fringe benefit and services packages. These packages include a wide variety of benefits such as pension plans, paid vacations and sick leave, day-care centers, tuition assistance, and health insurance. Corporate executives may receive benefits such as company cars, first-class airline travel, and country club memberships. At the executive level of business, these benefits are known as **perquisites**, or **perks**.

Over the past decade, employee benefits have become increasingly important to workers. They have grown in size to the point where today total benefits may cost a company as much as 40% to 50% of payroll. Frequently, employees are given a *menu* of fringe benefits from which to choose up to a specified dollar amount. These plans are known as **cafeteria style**, or **flexible benefit programs**.

STEPS TO CALCULATE EMPLOYER'S FRINGE BENEFITS EXPENSE

STEP 1. If the fringe benefit is a percent of gross payroll, multiply that percent by the amount of the gross payroll. If the fringe benefit is a dollar amount per employee, multiply that amount by the number of employees.

STEP 2. Find the total fringe benefits by adding all the individual fringe benefit amounts.

STEP 3. Calculate the fringe benefit percent by using the percentage formula Rate = Portion ÷ Base with total fringe benefits as the portion and gross payroll as the base (remember to convert your answer to a percent).

$$\text{Fringe benefit percent} = \frac{\text{Total fringe benefits}}{\text{Gross payroll}}$$

EXAMPLE 16 CALCULATING FRINGE BENEFITS

In addition to its gross payroll of $150,000 per month, Premier Distributors, Inc., with 75 employees, pays 7% of payroll to a retirement fund, 9% for health insurance, and $25 per employee for a stock purchase plan.

a. What are the company's monthly fringe benefit expenses?

b. What percent of payroll does this represent?

▶ SOLUTIONSTRATEGY

a. To solve for monthly fringe benefits, compute the amount of each benefit and add them to find the total.

Retirement fund expense = Gross payroll × 7%
Retirement fund expense = 150,000 × .07 = $10,500

Health insurance expense = Gross payroll × 9%
Health insurance expense = 150,000 × .09 = $13,500

Stock plan expense = Number of employees × $25
Stock plan expense = 75 × 25 = $1,875

Total fringe benefits = Retirement + Health + Stock
Total fringe benefits = 10,500 + 13,500 + 1,875 = $25,875

b. Fringe benefit percent = $\dfrac{\text{Total fringe benefits}}{\text{Gross payroll}} = \dfrac{25,875}{150,000} = .1725 = 17.25\%$

▶TRYITEXERCISE 16

Dynamo Productions employs 250 workers with a gross payroll of $123,400 per week. Fringe benefits are 5% of gross payroll for sick days and holiday leave, 8% for health insurance, and $12.40 per employee for dental insurance.

a. What is the total weekly cost of fringe benefits for Dynamo?

b. What percent of payroll does this represent?

c. What is the cost of these fringe benefits to the company for a year?

CHECK YOUR ANSWERS WITH THE SOLUTIONS ON PAGE 304.

CALCULATING QUARTERLY ESTIMATED TAX FOR SELF-EMPLOYED PERSONS

9-11

By IRS rules, you must pay self-employment tax if you had net earnings of $400 or more as a self-employed person. This is income that is not subject to withholding tax. Quarterly estimated tax is the method used to pay tax on these earnings. You may pay all of your estimated tax by April or in four equal amounts: in April, June, September, and January of the following year.

To calculate the quarterly estimated tax of a self-employed person, we divide the total of social security, Medicare, and income tax by 4. (There are 4 quarters in a year.) Internal Revenue Service form 1040 ES, Quarterly Estimated Tax Payment Voucher, shown in Exhibit 9-5, is used to file this tax with the IRS each quarter.

$$\text{Quarterly estimated tax} = \frac{\text{Social security} + \text{Medicare} + \text{Income tax}}{4}$$

EXHIBIT 9-5 Quarterly Estimated Tax Payment Voucher

Form **1040-ES** Department of the Treasury Internal Revenue Service	**20XX** Payment Voucher **4**		OMB No. 1545-0087
File only if you are making a payment of estimated tax by check or money order. Mail this voucher with your check or money order payable to the **"United States Treasury."** Write your social security number and "20XX Form 1040-ES" on your check or money order. Do not send cash. Enclose, but do not staple or attach, your payment with this voucher.		Calendar year—Due Jan. 15,	
		Amount of estimated tax you are paying by check or money order.	$

	Your first name and initial	Your last name	Your social security number
Type or print	If joint payment, complete for spouse		
	Spouse's first name and initial	Spouse's last name	Spouse's social security number
	Address (number, street, and apt. no.)		
	City, state, and ZIP code (If a foreign address, enter city, province or state, postal code, and country.)		

For Privacy Act and Paperwork Reduction Act Notice, see instructions on page 5.

Page 6

iStock.com/vreemous

EXAMPLE17 CALCULATING QUARTERLY ESTIMATED TAX FOR SELF-EMPLOYED PERSONS

Ben Qualls is a self-employed marketing consultant. His estimated annual earnings this year are $145,000. His social security tax rate is 12.4% up to the wage base, Medicare is 2.9%, and his estimated federal income tax rate is 18%. How much estimated tax must he send to the IRS each quarter?

SOLUTIONSTRATEGY

Note that Ben's salary is above the social security wage base limit.

$$\text{Social security} = 128,400 \times .124 = \$15,921.60$$
$$\text{Medicare} = 145,000 \times .029 = \$4,205$$
$$\text{Income tax} = 145,000 \times .18 = \$26,100$$

$$\text{Quarterly estimated tax} = \frac{\text{Social security} + \text{Medicare} + \text{Income tax}}{4}$$

$$\text{Quarterly estimated tax} = \frac{15,921.60 + 4,205 + 26,100}{4} = \frac{46,226.60}{4} = \underline{\$11,556.65}$$

TRYITEXERCISE 17

Howard Lockwood is a self-employed freelance editor and project director for a large publishing company. His annual salary this year is estimated to be $150,000 with a federal income tax rate of 20%. What is the amount of estimated tax Howard must send to the IRS each quarter?

CHECK YOUR ANSWER WITH THE SOLUTION ON PAGE 304.

SECTION III 9 REVIEW EXERCISES

1. **Westside Auto Supply has 8 delivery truck drivers, each with gross earnings of $570 per week.**

   a. **What are the total social security and Medicare taxes that should be withheld from these employees' paychecks each week?**

   570 × 8 = $4,560 Gross earnings per week
   4,560 × .062 = $282.72 Total social security
   4,560 × .0145 = $66.12 Total Medicare

   b. **What is the employer's share of these taxes for these employees for the first quarter of the year?**
   282.72 × 13 = $3,675.36 Social security for the first quarter
   66.12 × 13 = $859.56 Medicare for the first quarter

2. Fandango Furniture Manufacturing, Inc., has 40 employees on the assembly line, each with gross earnings of $325 per week.

   a. What are the total social security and Medicare taxes that should be withheld from the employees' paychecks each week?

   b. What is the employer's share of these taxes for these employees for the first quarter of the year?

3. Arrow Asphalt & Paving Company has 24 employees, 15 with gross earnings of $345 per week and nine with gross earnings of $385 per week. What is the total social security and Medicare tax the company must send to the Internal Revenue Service for the first quarter of the year?

4. **What are the social security and Medicare taxes due on gross earnings of $53,200 per year for Tricia Marvel, a self-employed commercial artist?**

    $53,200 \times .124 = \underline{\underline{\$6,596.80}}$ **Social security**
    $53,200 \times .029 = \underline{\underline{\$1,542.80}}$ **Medicare**

5. What are the social security and Medicare taxes due on gross earnings of $42,600 per year for a self-employed person?

6. Lee Sutherlin is a self-employed electrical consultant. He estimates his annual net earnings at $38,700. How much social security and Medicare must he pay this year?

7. **Barry Michaels earns $36,500 per year as the housewares manager at the Home Design Center.**

    a. **If the SUTA tax rate is 5.4% of the first $7,000 earned each year, how much SUTA tax must the company pay each year for Barry?**

    $7,000 \times .054 = \underline{\underline{\$378}}$ **SUTA annually**

    b. **If the FUTA tax rate is 6.0% of the first $7,000 earned in a year minus the SUTA tax paid, how much FUTA tax must the company pay each year for Barry?**

    $7,000 \times .006 = \underline{\underline{\$42}}$ **FUTA tax the company must pay annually**

8. Dave O'Bannon earns $41,450 annually as a line supervisor for Redwood Manufacturers.

    a. If the SUTA tax rate is 5.4% of the first $7,000 earned in a year, how much SUTA tax must Redwood pay each year for Dave?

    b. If the FUTA tax rate is 6.0% of the first $7,000 earned in a year minus the SUTA tax paid, how much FUTA tax must the company pay each year for Dave?

9. The SUTA rate for Thomson Temp Agency is 5.4% and its FUTA rate is 6% less the 5.4% SUTA credit.
    If its semimonthly payroll is $138,320 and none was for payments to employees in excess of the $7,000 wage base, then what are the total FUTA and SUTA taxes for the payroll?

10. Amazon Appliance Company has three installers. Larry earns $355 per week, Curly earns $460 per week, and Moe earns $585 per week. The company's SUTA rate is 5.4%, and the FUTA rate is 6.0% minus the SUTA. As usual, these taxes are paid on the first $7,000 of each employee's earnings.

   a. How much SUTA and FUTA tax does Amazon owe for the first quarter of the year?

   b. How much SUTA and FUTA tax does Amazon owe for the second quarter of the year?

11. **Jiffy Janitorial Service employs 48 workers and has a gross payroll of $25,200 per week. Fringe benefits are 6.4% for sick days and holiday leave, 5.8% for health and hospital insurance, and $14.50 per employee per week for uniform allowance.**

   a. **What is the total weekly cost of fringe benefits for Jiffy?**

$$25,200 \times .064 = \$1,612.80$$
$$25,200 \times .058 = 1,461.60$$
$$48 \times 14.50 = 696.00$$
$$\overline{\$3,770.40}$$

   b. **What percent of payroll does this represent?**

$$R = \frac{P}{B} = \frac{3,770.40}{25,200.00} = .1496 = \underline{\underline{15\%}}$$

   c. **What is Jiffy's annual cost of fringe benefits?**

$$3,770.40 \times 52 = \underline{\underline{\$196,060.80}} \text{ Annual cost of fringe benefits}$$

12. North Beach Limousine Service employs 166 workers and has a gross payroll of $154,330 per week. Fringe benefits are $4\frac{1}{2}\%$ of gross payroll for sick days and maternity leave, 7.4% for health insurance, 3.1% for the retirement fund, and $26.70 per employee per week for a stock purchase plan.

   a. What is the total weekly cost of fringe benefits for the company?

   b. What percent of payroll does this represent? Round to the nearest tenth of a percent.

   c. What is the company's annual cost of fringe benefits?

13. National Storage employs 88 workers with a gross monthly payroll of $132,000. Fringe benefits are 8.3% of payroll for a profit sharing plan and $9.24 per employee for life insurance.

    What percent of payroll is the total cost of fringe benefits? Round your answer to the nearest tenth of a percent.

14. Marc Batchelor, a self-employed sales consultant, has estimated annual earnings of $300,000 this year. His social security tax rate is 12.4% up to the wage base, Medicare is 2.9%, and his federal income tax rate is 24%.

    How much estimated tax must Marc send to the IRS each quarter?

BUSINESS DECISION: NEW FRINGE BENEFITS

iStock.com/ MarsBars

15. You are the human resource manager for Sunlink International, a cellular phone company with 800 employees. Top management has asked you to implement three additional fringe benefits that were negotiated with employee representatives and agreed upon by a majority of the employees. These include group term life insurance, a group legal services plan, and a wellness center.

    The life insurance is estimated to cost $260 per employee per quarter. The legal plan will cost $156 semiannually per employee. The company will contribute 40% to the life insurance premium and 75% to the cost of the legal services plan. The employees will pay the balance through payroll deductions from their biweekly paychecks. In addition, they will be charged $\frac{1}{4}$% of their gross earnings per paycheck for maintaining the wellness center. The company will pay the initial cost of $500,000 to build the center. This expense will be spread over 5 years.

    a. What total amount should be deducted *per paycheck* for these new fringe benefits for an employee earning $41,600 per year?

    b. What is the total *annual* cost of the new fringe benefits to Sunlink?

Human resource managers handle or oversee all aspects of human resources work. Typical areas of responsibility include unemployment compensation, fringe benefits, training, and employee relations. They held about 904,900 jobs in 2008, with median annual earnings of $96,130. The middle 50% earned between $73,480 and $126,050.

moodboard/Alamy Stock Photo

CHAPTER FORMULAS

Hourly Wages

Regular pay = Hourly rate × Regular hours worked

Overtime pay = Hourly rate × Overtime factor × Overtime hours worked

Total gross pay = Regular pay + Overtime pay

Piecework

Total gross pay = Output quantity × Rate per unit

Commission

Total gross pay = Total sales × Commission rate

Payroll Deductions

Total deductions = Social security + Medicare + Income tax + Voluntary deductions

Net pay = Gross pay − Total deductions

Fringe Benefits

$$\text{Fringe benefit percent} = \frac{\text{Total fringe benefits}}{\text{Gross payroll}}$$

Quarterly Estimated Tax

$$\text{Quarterly estimated tax} = \frac{\text{Social security} + \text{Medicare} + \text{Income tax}}{4}$$

CHAPTER SUMMARY

Section I: Employee's Gross Earnings and Incentive Pay Plans

Topic	Important Concepts	Illustrative Examples
Prorating Annual Salary to Various Pay Periods **Performance Objective 9-1, Page 271**	Salaried employees are most commonly paid based on one of the following pay schedules: *Weekly:* 52 paychecks per year Annual salary ÷ 52 *Biweekly:* 26 paychecks per year Annual salary ÷ 26 *Semimonthly:* 24 paychecks per year Annual salary ÷ 24 *Monthly:* 12 paychecks per year Annual salary ÷ 12	What are the gross earnings of an employee with an annual salary of $40,000 based on weekly, biweekly, semimonthly, and monthly pay schedules? $\text{Weekly} = \dfrac{40,000}{52} = \$769.233$ $\text{Biweekly} = \dfrac{40,000}{26} = \$1,538.46$ $\text{Semimonthly} = \dfrac{40,000}{24} = \$1,666.67$ $\text{Monthly} = \dfrac{40,000}{12} = \$3,333.33$
Calculating Gross Pay by Regular Hourly Wages and Overtime **Performance Objective 9-2, Page 272**	An hourly wage is the amount an employee is paid for each hour worked. Regular time specifies that a standard work week is 40 hours. Overtime amounting to at least time-and-a-half must be paid for all hours over 40 hours. Some employers pay double time for weekend, holiday, and midnight shifts.	Sami Brady earns $9.50 per hour as a supervisor in a plant. If her overtime rate is time-and-a-half and holidays are double time, what is Sami's total gross pay for working 49 hours last week, including 4 holiday hours? Regular pay = 9.50 × 40 = $380.00 Overtime pay = 9.50 × 1.5 × 5 = $71.25 Double-time pay = 9.50 × 2 × 4 = $76.00 Total gross pay = 380.00 + 71.25 + 76.00 = $527.25

Section I (continued)

Topic	Important Concepts	Illustrative Examples
Calculating Gross Pay by Straight and Differential Piecework Schedules **Performance Objective 9-3, Page 273**	A piecework pay rate schedule is based on production output, not time. Straight piecework pays the worker a certain amount of pay per unit regardless of quantity. In differential piecework, the rate per unit increases as output quantity goes up.	Chemical Labs pays its workers $2.50 per unit of production. What is the gross pay of a worker producing 233 units? Gross pay = 233 × 2.50 = $582.50 Fortune Manufacturing pays its production workers $.54 per unit up to 5,000 units and $.67 per unit above 5,000 units. What is the gross pay of an employee who produces 6,500 units? 5,000 × .54 = 2,700 1,500 × .67 = 1,005 Total gross pay $3,705
Calculating Gross Pay by Straight and Incremental Commission **Performance Objective 9-4, Page 275**	Commission is a method of compensation primarily used to pay employees who sell goods and services. Straight commission is based on a single specified percentage of the sales volume attained. Incremental commission, like differential piecework, is when various levels of sales earn increasing rates of commission.	Horizon Products pays 4% straight commission on all sales. What is the gross pay of an employee who sells $135,000? Gross pay = 135,000 × .04 = $5,400 Discovery Imports pays incremental commissions of 3.5% on sales up to $100,000 and 4.5% on all sales greater than $100,000. What is the gross pay of an employee selling $164,000? 100,000 × .035 = 3,500 64,000 × .045 = 2,880 Gross pay $6,380
Calculating Gross Pay by Salary Plus Commission **Performance Objective 9-4, Page 277**	Salary plus commission is a pay schedule whereby the employee receives a guaranteed salary in addition to a commission on sales over a specified amount.	An employee is paid a salary of $350 per week plus a 2% commission on sales greater than $8,000. If he sold $13,400 last week, how much did he earn? 350 + 2%(13,400 − 8,000) 350 + .02 × 5,400 350 + 108 = $458
Calculating Gross Pay with Drawing Accounts **Performance Objective 9-4, Page 277**	A drawing account, or draw against commission, is a commission paid in advance of sales and later deducted from the commission earned.	Steve Korb sells for a company that pays $6\frac{1}{2}\%$ commission with a $600 per month drawing account. If Steve takes the draw and then sells $16,400 in goods, how much commission is he owed? (16,400 × .065) − 600 1,066 − 600 = $466

Section II: Employee's Payroll Deductions

Topic	Important Concepts	Illustrative Examples
Computing FICA Taxes, Both Social Security and Medicare **Performance Objective 9-5, Page 281**	FICA taxes are divided into two categories: social security and Medicare. When employees reach the wage base for the year, they are no longer subject to the tax. **Tax Rate / Wage Base** Social Security 6.2% $128,400 Medicare 1.45% no limit	What are the FICA tax withholdings for social security and Medicare for an employee with gross earnings of $760 per week? Social security = $760 × 6.2% = $47.12 Medicare = $760 × 1.45% = $11.02
Calculating Federal Income Tax Using Percentage Method	1. Multiply one withholding allowance, in Exhibit 9-1, by the number of allowances the employee claims.	Michelle Wolf is single, earns $1,800 per week as a loan officer for Bank of America, and claims three withholding allowances.

Section II (continued)

Topic	Important Concepts	Illustrative Examples
Performance Objective 9-6, Page 283	2. Subtract that amount from the employee's gross earnings to find the income subject to income tax. 3. Determine the amount of tax withheld from the appropriate section of Exhibit 9-2.	Calculate the amount of federal income tax withheld from Michelle's weekly paycheck. From Exhibit 9-1: $\qquad 79.80 \times 3 = \$239.40$ Taxable income = $\qquad 1,800 - 239.40 = \$1,560.60$ From Exhibit 9-2: Withholding tax = $\qquad 85.62 + .22(1,560.60 - 815)$ $\qquad 85.62 + .22(745.60)$ $\qquad 85.62 + 164.03 = \underline{\underline{\$249.65}}$
Determining an Employee's Total Withholding for Federal Income Tax, Social Security, and Medicare Using the Combined Wage Bracket Tables **Performance Objective 9-7, Page 286**	1. Based on marital status and payroll period, choose either Exhibit 9-3 or 9-4. 2. Scan down the left-hand columns until you find the bracket containing the gross pay of the employee. 3. Scan across the row of that wage bracket to the intersection of that employee's "withholding allowances claimed" column. 4. The number in that column on the wage bracket row is the amount of combined withholding tax.	What amount of combined tax should be withheld from the monthly paycheck of a single employee claiming two withholding allowances and earning $3,495 per month? Use Exhibit 9-4. Scan down the wage brackets to $3,485–$3,525. Scan across to "2" withholding allowances to find the tax, $\underline{\underline{\$553.13}}$.

Section III: Employer's Payroll Expenses and Self-Employed Person's Tax Responsibility

Topic	Important Concepts	Illustrative Examples
Computing FICA Tax for Employers **Performance Objective 9-8, Page 291**	Employers are required to match all FICA tax payments made by each employee.	Last month Midland Services withheld a total of $3,400 in FICA taxes from employee paychecks. What is the company's FICA liability? The company is responsible for a matching amount withheld from the employees, $\underline{\underline{\$3,400}}$.
Computing Self-Employment Tax **Performance Objective 9-8, Page 292**	Self-employed persons are responsible for social security and Medicare taxes at twice the rate deducted for employees. Technically, they are the employee and the employer; therefore, they must pay both shares, as follows:	What are the social security and Medicare taxes due on gross earnings of $4,260 per month for a self-employed person? *Social security* Gross earnings × 12.4% = $\qquad 4,260 \times .124 = \underline{\underline{\$528.24}}$ *Medicare* Gross earnings × 2.9% = $\qquad 4,260 \times .029 = \underline{\underline{123.54}}$
Computing the Amount of State Unemployment Tax (SUTA) and Federal Unemployment Tax (FUTA) **Performance Objective 9-9, Page 293**	SUTA and FUTA taxes provide for unemployment compensation to workers who have lost their jobs. These taxes are paid by the employer. The SUTA tax rate is 5.4% of the first $7,000 of earnings per year by each employee. The FUTA tax rate used in this chapter is 6.0% of the first $7,000 minus the SUTA tax paid (6.0% − 5.4% = 0.6%).	Trans Lux, Inc., had a total payroll of $40,000 last month. If none of the employees has reached the $7,000 wage base, what is the amount of SUTA and FUTA tax due? SUTA = 40,000 × 5.4% = $\underline{\underline{\$2,160}}$ FUTA = 40,000 × .6% = $\underline{\underline{\$240}}$

Section III (continued)

Topic	Important Concepts	Illustrative Examples
Calculating Employer's Fringe Benefit Expenses **Performance Objective 9-10, Page 294**	In addition to compensating employees with a paycheck, most companies offer benefit packages that may include pensions, paid sick days, tuition assistance, and health insurance. Fringe benefits represent a significant expense to employers.	Linear Industries employs 48 workers and has a monthly gross payroll of $120,000. In addition, the company pays 6.8% to a pension fund, 8.7% for health insurance, and $30 per employee for a stock purchase plan. What are Linear's monthly fringe benefit expenses? What percent of payroll does this represent? $120,000 \times 6.8\% =$　　8,160 $120,000 \times 8.7\% =$　10,440 　　$48 \times \$30 \ \ =$　$+ 1,440$ Total fringe benefits $\underline{\$20,040}$ Fringe benefit % $= \dfrac{20,040}{120,000} = \underline{16.7\%}$
Calculating Quarterly Estimated Tax for Self-Employed Persons **Performance Objective 9-11, Page 295**	Each quarter self-employed persons must send to the IRS Form 1040-ES along with a tax payment for social security, Medicare, and income tax.	Amanda Turner is a self-employed decorator. She estimates her annual net earnings at $44,000 for the year. Her income tax rate is 10%. What is the amount of her quarterly estimated tax? $44,000 \times .124 = \$5,456$ Social security $44,000 \times .029 = \$1,276$ Medicare $44,000 \times .10 \ \ = \$4,400$ Income tax Quarterly estimated tax $= \dfrac{5,456 + 1,276 + 4,400}{4}$ $= \dfrac{11,132}{4} = \underline{\underline{\$2,783}}$

TRY IT: EXERCISE SOLUTIONS FOR CHAPTER 9

1. Weekly pay $= \dfrac{\text{Annual salary}}{50} = \dfrac{43,500}{52} = \underline{\$836.54}$

Biweekly pay $= \dfrac{\text{Annual salary}}{26} = \dfrac{43,500}{26} = \underline{\$1,673.08}$

Semimonthly pay $= \dfrac{\text{Annual salary}}{24} = \dfrac{43,500}{24} = \underline{\$1,812.50}$

Monthly pay $= \dfrac{\text{Annual salary}}{12} = \dfrac{43,500}{12} = \underline{\$3,625.00}$

2. Regular pay = Hourly rate × Regular hours worked
Regular pay = 10.50 × 40 = $\underline{\$420}$
Overtime pay
　= Hourly rate × Overtime factor × Hours worked
Overtime pay = 10.50 × 1.5 × 5 = $\underline{\$78.75}$
Double-time pay
　= Hourly rate × Overtime factor × Hours worked
Double-time pay = 10.50 × 2 × 4 = $\underline{\$84}$

Total gross pay = Regular pay + Overtime pay
Total gross pay = 420.00 + 78.75 + 84.00 = $\underline{\$582.75}$

3. Total gross pay = Output quantity × Rate per unit
Total gross pay = 950 × .41 = $\underline{\$389.50}$

4. Level pay = Output rate per piece
Gomez: 300 × .68 = $204.00
　　　　200 × .79 = 　158.00
　　　　 15 × .86 = $+ 12.90$
　　　　　　　　 $\underline{\$374.90}$ Total gross pay

Clifford: 199 × .68 = $\underline{\$135.32}$ Total gross pay

Maken:　300 × .68 = 　$204.00
　　　　148 × .79 = $+ \ 116.92$
　　　　　　　　　 $\underline{\$320.92}$ Total gross pay

Nathan:　300 × .68 = 　$204.00
　　　　　200 × .79 = 　158.00
　　　　　250 × .86 = 　215.00
　　　　　 54 × .94 = $+ \ 50.76$
　　　　　　　　　　 $\underline{\$627.76}$ Total gross pay

5. Total gross pay = Total sales × Commission rate
Total gross pay = 233,760 × .024 = $\underline{\$5,610.24}$

6. Level pay = Sales per level × Commission rate
Level pay = 100,000 × .017 = 　$1,700
　　　　　84,600 × .025 = $+ \ 2,115$
　　　　　　　　　　　 $\underline{\$3,815}$

7. Commission = Commission rate × Sales subject to commission
Commission = 4%(45,000 − 20,000)
Commission = .04 × 25,000 = $1,000

Total gross pay = Salary + Commission
Total gross pay = 1,400 + 1,000 = $\underline{\$2,400}$

8. Commission = Total sales × Commission rate
Commission = 120,000 × 3.5% = $4,200

Commission owed = Commission − Amount of draw
Commission owed = 4,200 − 2,000 = $\underline{\$2,200}$

9. Social security tax = Gross earnings × 6.2%
Social security tax = 5,000 × .062 = $310

Medicare tax = Gross earnings × 1.45%
Medicare tax = 5,000 × .0145 = $72.50

10. Earnings subject to tax = Wage base − Year-to-date earnings
Earnings subject to tax = 128,400 − 123,900 = $4,500

Social security tax = Earnings subject to tax × 6.2%
Social security tax = 4,500 × .062 = $279.00

11. From Exhibit 9-1
Withholding allowance = 1 allowance × Exemptions
Withholding allowance = $345.80 × 5 = $1,729

Taxable income = Gross pay − Withholding allowance
Taxable income = 5,670 − 1,729 = $3,941

From Exhibit 9-2, Table 4(b):
Category $2,550 to $7,413

Withholding Tax = 158.70 + 12% of amount greater than $2,550
Withholding Tax = 158.70 + .12(3,941 − 2,550)
Withholding Tax = 158.70 + .12(1,391)
Withholding Tax = 158.70 + 166.92 = $325.62

12. From Exhibit 9-3
$1,160 Weekly, married, 2 allowances = $174.74

13. *12 employees @ $350*
Social security = 350 × .062 = $21.70
Medicare = 350 × .0145 = $5.08

Total FICA per employee = 21.70 + 5.08 = $26.78
Total FICA per week = 26.78 × 12 employees = $321.36
Total FICA per quarter = 321.36 × 13 weeks = $4,177.68

6 employees @ $425
Social security = 425 × .062 = $26.35
Medicare = 425 × .0145 = $6.16

Total FICA per employee = 26.35 + 6.16 = $32.51
Total FICA per week = 32.51 × 6 employees = $195.06
Total FICA per quarter = 195.06 × 13 weeks = $2,535.78

Total FICA per quarter:
Employees' share = 4,177.68 + 2,535.78 = $6,713.46
Employer's share = 4,177.68 + 2,535.78 = $6,713.46

14. Social security = 60,000 × .124 = $7,440
Medicare = 60,000 × .029 = $1,740

15. SUTA tax = Gross earnings × 5.4%
SUTA tax = 10,000 × .054 = $540

FUTA tax = Gross earnings × .6%
FUTA tax = 10,000 × .006 = $60

16. **a.** Fringe benefits
Sick days = Gross payroll × 5%
Sick days = 123,400 × .05 = $6,170

Health insurance = Gross payroll × 8%
Health insurance = 123,400 × .08 = $9,872

Dental insurance = Number of employees × 12.40
Dental insurance = 250 × 12.40 = $3,100

Total fringe benefits = 6,170 + 9,872 + 3,100 = $19,142

b. Fringe benefit percent = $\dfrac{\text{Total fringe benefit}}{\text{Gross payroll}}$

Fringe benefit percent = $\dfrac{19,142}{123,400}$ = .155 = 15.5%

c. Yearly fringe benefits = Weekly total × 52
Yearly fringe benefits = 19,142 × 52 = $995,384

17. Social security = 128,400 × .124 = $15,921.60
Medicare = 150,000 × .029 = $4,350
Income tax = 150,000 × .2 = $30,000

Quarterly estimated tax = $\dfrac{\text{Social security + Medicare + Income tax}}{4}$

Quarterly estimated tax = $\dfrac{15,921.60 + 4,350 + 30,000}{4}$

$= \dfrac{50,271.60}{4}$ = $12,567.90

CONCEPT REVIEW

1. Gross pay is the amount of earnings before payroll _____ are withheld; net pay is the actual amount of the _____. (9.1)

2. Annual salaries are commonly prorated to be paid weekly, biweekly, _____, and _____. (9-1)

3. Total gross pay includes regular pay and _____ pay, which according to federal law is for hours worked over _____ hours per week. (9-2)

4. When employees are paid on their production output, not hours worked, this is called _____. (9-3)

5. To calculate total gross pay for an employee paid on commission, we multiply the total _____ by the commission rate. (9-4)

6. A draw against commission is commission paid in _____ of sales and later _____ from the commission earned. (9-4)

7. The current employee tax rate for social security is _____ percent of gross earnings; the current tax rate for Medicare is _____ percent of gross earnings. (9-5)

8. The wage base limit for social security used in this chapter is _____. (9-5)

9. In addition to social security and Medicare tax withholdings, an employer is also responsible, by federal law, for withholding an appropriate amount of federal _____ tax from each employee's paycheck. (9-6)

10. The combined wage bracket table is based on the _____ status of the employee and the _____ period used. The columns list the combined taxes to be withheld based on the number of withholding _____ claimed. (9-7)

11. Self-employed persons are responsible for social security and Medicare taxes at _____ the rate deducted for employees. This amounts to _____ percent for social security and _____ percent for Medicare. (9-8)

12. For companies with full and timely payments to the state unemployment system, the SUTA tax rate is _____ percent of gross earnings and the FUTA tax rate is _____ percent of gross earnings. (9-9)

13. A plan whereby employees are given a menu of fringe benefits from which to choose is known as the _____ style or _____ benefit program. (9-10)

14. Write the formula for quarterly estimated tax for self-employed persons. (9-11)

ASSESSMENT TEST

1. Bill Pearson earns $2,800 semimonthly as a congressional aide for a senator in the state legislature.

   a. How much are his annual gross earnings?

   b. If the senator switches pay schedules from semimonthly to biweekly, what will Bill's new gross earnings be per payroll period?

2. Barbara Sultan works 40 hours per week as a registered nurse. At the rate of $31.50 per hour, what are her gross weekly earnings?

3. Eric Shotwell's company pays him $18.92 per hour for regular time up to 40 hours and time-and-a-half for overtime. His time card for Monday through Friday last week had 8.3, 8.8, 7.9, 9.4, and 10.6 hours. What was Eric's total gross pay?

4. Mitch Anderson is a security guard. He earns $7.45 per hour for regular time up to 40 hours, time-and-a-half for overtime, and double time for the midnight shift. If Mitch worked 56 hours last week, including 4 hours on the midnight shift, how much were his gross earnings?

5. Fergie Nelson assembles toasters for the Gold Coast Corporation. She is paid on a differential piecework rate of $2.70 per toaster for the first 160 toasters and $3.25 for each toaster over 160. If she assembled 229 units last week, how much were her gross earnings?

6. You work in the payroll department of Universal Manufacturing. The following piece rate schedule is used for computing earnings for assembly line workers. As an overtime bonus, on Saturdays, each unit produced counts as $1\frac{1}{2}$ units.

1–100	$2.30
101–150	2.60
151–200	2.80
over 200	3.20

Registered nurses (RNs) treat patients, educate patients and the public about various medical conditions, and provide advice and emotional support to patients' family members. RNs record patients' medical histories and symptoms, help perform diagnostic tests and analyze results, operate medical machinery, administer treatment and medications, and help with patient follow-up and rehabilitation.

Overall job opportunities for registered nurses are excellent. Employment of registered nurses is expected to grow by 22% from 2008 to 2018, much faster than the average for all other occupations.

Calculate the gross earnings for the following Universal Manufacturing employees.

	Employee	Mon.	Tues.	Wed.	Thurs.	Fri.	Sat.	Total Units	Gross Earnings
a.	Shane	0	32	16	36	27	12	_____	_____
b.	Gonzales	18	26	24	10	13	0	_____	_____
c.	Bethards	26	42	49	51	34	20	_____	_____

7. Kate Fitzgerald's company pays differential piecework for electronic product manufacturing. Production pay rates for a particular circuit board assembly and soldering are $18.20 per board for the first 14 boards, $19.55 each for boards 15–30, $20.05 each for boards 31–45, and $20.48 each for boards 46 and up. If Kate assembled and soldered 52 boards last week, what was her total gross pay?

8. Foremost Fish Market pays a straight commission of 18% on gross sales, divided equally among the three employees working the counter. If Foremost sold $22,350 in seafood last week, how much was each counter employee's total gross pay?

9. Bryan Vincent booked $431,000 in new sales last month. Commission rates are 1% for the first $150,000, 1.8% for the next $200,000, and 2.3% for amounts over $350,000. What was Bryan's total gross pay?

10. Spencer Morris works in the telemarketing division for a company that pays a salary of $735 per month plus a commission of $3\frac{1}{2}$% of all sales greater than $15,500. If he sold $45,900 last month, what was his total gross pay?

11. Bonnie Woodruff is on a 2.1% straight commission with a $700 drawing account. If she is paid the draw at the beginning of the month and then sells $142,100 during the month, how much commission is owed to Bonnie?

Regardless of what they sell, **telemarketers** are responsible for initiating telephone sales calls to potential clients, using a prepared selling script. They are usually paid on a commission based on the amount of their sales volume or number of new "leads" they generate.

12. Arturo Muina is the captain on a charter fishing boat. He is paid a salary of $140 per day. He also averages tips amounting to 12% of the $475 daily charter rate. Last month during a fishing tournament, Arturo worked 22 days. What were his total gross earnings for the month?

ESB Professional/Shutterstock.com

Solve the following problems using 6.2% up to $128,400 for social security withholding and 1.45% for Medicare.

13. What are the withholdings for social security and Medicare for an employee with gross earnings of $725 per week?

14. Dan Dietrich is an executive with Coronado Distributors. His gross earnings are $17,300 per month.

    a. What are the withholdings for social security and Medicare for Dan's January paycheck?

    b. In what month will his salary reach the social security wage base limit?

    c. What are the social security and Medicare tax withholdings for Dan in the month named in part b?

Use the *percentage method* to solve the following.

15. Larry Alison is single, claims one withholding allowance, and earns $2,450 per month.

    a. What is the amount of Larry's paycheck after his employer withholds social security, Medicare, and income tax?

    b. If Larry gets married and changes to two withholding allowances, what will be the new amount of his paycheck?

Use the *combined wage bracket tables*, Exhibits 9-3 and 9-4, for Exercises 16 and 17.

16. How much combined tax should be withheld from the paycheck of a married employee earning $1,210 per week and claiming three withholding allowances?

17. How much combined tax should be withheld from the paycheck of a single employee earning $4,458 per month and claiming zero withholding allowances?

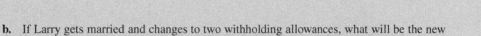

CHAPTER 9

18. Fran Mallory is married, claims five withholding allowances, and earns $3,500 per month. In addition to social security, Medicare, and FIT, Fran pays 2.1% state income tax, $\frac{1}{2}$% for state disability insurance (both based on gross income), $43.11 for life insurance, and $72.30 to the credit union. As payroll manager for Fran's company, calculate her net take-home pay per month.

19. Vanguard Fabricators has 83 employees on the assembly line, each with gross earnings of $329 per week.
    a. What are the total social security and Medicare taxes that should be withheld from the employee paychecks each week?

    b. At the end of the first quarter (13 weeks), what are the accumulated totals of the employee's share and the *matching* taxes for FICA that Vanguard had sent to the IRS?

20. Paul Warren is a self-employed mechanic. Last year he had total gross earnings of $44,260. What are Paul's quarterly social security and Medicare payments due to the IRS?

21. Tim Ries earns $48,320 annually as a supervisor for the Lakeside Bank.
    a. If the SUTA tax rate is 5.4% of the first $7,000 earned in a year, how much SUTA tax must the bank pay each year for Tim?

    b. If the FUTA tax rate is 6.0% of the first $7,000 earned in a year minus the SUTA tax paid, how much FUTA tax must the bank pay each year for Tim?

22. Universal Exporting has three warehouse employees: John Abner earns $422 per week, Anne Clark earns $510 per week, and Todd Corbin earns $695 per week. The company's SUTA tax rate is 5.4%, and the FUTA rate is 6.0% minus the SUTA. As usual, these taxes are paid on the first $7,000 of each employee's earnings.
    a. How much SUTA and FUTA tax did the company pay for these employees in the first quarter of the year?

    b. How much SUTA and FUTA tax did Universal pay in the second quarter of the year?

23. Sky High Crane Company employs 150 workers and has a gross payroll of $282,100 per week. Fringe benefits are $6\frac{1}{2}$% of gross payroll for sick days and holiday leave, 9.1% for health and hospital insurance, 4.6% for the retirement fund, and $10.70 per employee per week for a stock purchase plan.

    a. What is the total weekly cost of fringe benefits for the company?

    b. What percent of payroll does this represent?

    c. What is the company's annual cost of fringe benefits?

24. Ransford Alda is a self-employed security consultant with estimated annual earnings of $90,000. His social security tax rate is 12.4%, Medicare is 2.9%, and his federal income tax rate is 14%.

    a. How much estimated tax must Ransford send to the IRS each quarter?

    b. What form should he use?

BUSINESS DECISION: THE BRIDE, THE GROOM, AND THE TAX MAN

25. Two of your friends, Chuck and Joan, have been dating for a year. Chuck earns $5,000 per month as the manager of an Aeropostale store. Joan is a sophomore in college and is not currently working. They plan to marry but cannot decide whether to get married now or wait a year or two.

    After studying the payroll chapter in your business math class, you inform Chuck that married couples generally pay less income taxes and that if they got married now instead of waiting, he would have less income tax withheld from his paychecks. Chuck's current tax filing status is single, one withholding allowance. If he and Joan got married, he could file as married, two withholding allowances. Use the percentage method and Exhibits 9-1 and 9-2 to calculate the following:

    a. How much income tax is withheld from Chuck's paycheck each month now?

    b. How much income tax would be withheld from Chuck's check if he and Joan got married?

c. To the nearest tenth percent, what would be the percent savings if they got married?

COLLABORATIVE LEARNING ACTIVITY

Researching the Job Market

1. As a team, collect "Help Wanted" ads from the classified section of your local newspaper. (Note: Weekend editions are usually the most comprehensive.) Find examples of various jobs that are paid by salary, hourly rate, piece rate, and commission. Answer the following for similar jobs.

    a. How much do they pay?
    b. What pay periods are used?
    c. What fringe benefits are being offered?

2. As a team, research the Internet or library for the following payroll information. Present your findings to the class. List your sources for the answers.

    a. Starting salaries of employees in various industries and in government occupations.
    b. Personal and household income by area of the country or by state. How does your area or state compare?
    c. Starting salaries by amount of education for various professions.

Business Math JOURNAL

Social Security

Source: Forrester Research

The United States did not have social security on a national level until 1935 when the Social Security Act was passed. It was part of President Franklin Delano Roosevelt's response to the Great Depression which began in 1929 and lasted into the late-1930s.

The act established two social insurance programs: a federal-state program of unemployment compensation and a federal program of old-age retirement insurance.

Upon signing the Social Security Act, President Roosevelt made this comment:

"We can never insure one hundred percent of the population against one hundred percent of the hazards and vicissitudes of life, but we have tried to frame a law which will give some measure of protection to the average citizen and to his family against the loss of a job and against poverty-ridden old age."

The rate of the Social Security tax was originally set at 1% with a $3,000 wage base limit. Increases in social security retirement benefits and wage bases are tied to increases in the Consumer Price Index. Both the number of beneficiaries and the amount of

payments have increased dramatically since the program's inception. This table provides a brief summary of this growth by showing data over 20-year intervals starting in 1950.

Year	Number of beneficiaries	Total dollars paid out (in millions)
1937 (first year)	53,236	$1.28
1950	3,477,243	$961
1970	26,228,629	$31,863
1990	39,832,125	$247,796
2010	54,032,097	$781,128

Source: Adapted from information at www.ssa.gov

Issues & Activities

Use the table to answer these questions:
1. What was the percent increase in the number of beneficiaries in the 40-year period from 1970 to 2010?
2. What was the percent increase in the dollar amount paid from 1970 to 2010?

Medicare

In 1965, Congress enacted the Medicare program providing medical benefits for persons over the age of 65 and an accompanying Medicaid program for the indigent, regardless of age. The initial tax rate was .35%.

Medicare is funded by a 1.45% tax on the earnings of employees, and that amount is matched by the employer. Annual expenditures exceed $700 billion.

Adapted from www.ssa.gov/history and www.ssa.gov/oact/STATS

Brainteaser—"Work, Don't Work"

You have agreed to work under the conditions that you are to be paid $55 for every day you work and you must pay back $66 for every day you don't work. If after 30 days you have earned $924, how many days did you work?

See the end of Appendix A for the solution.

CHAPTER 10 Simple Interest and Promissory Notes

PERFORMANCE OBJECTIVES

UNDERSTANDING AND COMPUTING SIMPLE INTEREST

The practice of borrowing and lending money dates back in history for thousands of years. Today institutions such as banks, savings and loans, and credit unions are specifically in business to borrow and lend money. They constitute a significant portion of the service sector of the American economy.

Interest is the rental fee charged by a lender to a business or an individual for the use of money. The amount of interest charged is determined by three factors: the amount of money being borrowed or invested, known as the **principal**; the percent of interest charged on the money per year, known as the **rate**; and the length of time of the loan, known as **time**. The manner in which the interest is computed is an additional factor that influences the amount of interest. The two most commonly used methods in business today for computing interest are simple and compound.

Simple interest means that the interest is calculated *only once* for the entire time period of the loan. At the end of the time period, the borrower repays the principal plus the interest. Simple interest loans are usually made for short periods of time, such as a few days, weeks, or months. **Compound interest** means that the interest is calculated *more than once* during the time period of the loan. When compound interest is applied to a loan, each succeeding time period accumulates interest on the previous interest in addition to interest on the principal. Compound interest loans are generally for time periods of a year or longer.

This chapter discusses the concepts of simple interest; simple discount, which is a variation of a simple interest loan; and promissory notes. Chapter 11 covers the concepts and calculations related to compound interest and present value.

interest The price or rental fee charged by a lender to a borrower for the use of money.

principal A sum of money, either invested or borrowed, on which interest is calculated.

rate The percent that is charged or earned for the use of money per year.

time Length of time, expressed in days, months, or years, of an investment or loan.

simple interest Interest calculated solely on the principal amount borrowed or invested. It is calculated only once for the entire time period of the loan.

compound interest Interest calculated at regular intervals on the principal and previously earned interest. Covered in Chapter 11.

COMPUTING SIMPLE INTEREST FOR LOANS WITH TERMS OF YEARS OR MONTHS

10-1

Simple interest is calculated by using a formula known as the simple interest formula. It is stated as follows:

$$\text{Interest} = \text{Principal} \times \text{Rate} \times \text{Time}$$
$$I = PRT$$

When using the simple interest formula, the time factor, T, must be expressed in years or a fraction of a year.

SIMPLE INTEREST FORMULA—YEARS OR MONTHS

Years

When the time period of a loan is a year or longer, use the number of years as the time factor, converting fractional parts to decimals. For example, the time factor for a 2-year loan is 2, 3 years is 3, $1\frac{1}{2}$ years is 1.5, $4\frac{3}{4}$ years is 4.75, and so on.

Months

When the time period of a loan is for a specified number of months, express the time factor as a fraction of a year. The number of months is the numerator, and 12 months (1 year) is the denominator. A loan for 1 month would have a time factor of $\frac{1}{12}$; a loan for 2 months would have a factor of $\frac{2}{12}$, or $\frac{1}{6}$; a 5-month loan would use $\frac{5}{12}$ as the factor; a loan for 18 months would use $\frac{18}{12}$, or $1\frac{1}{2}$, written as 1.5.

db mages/Alamy Stock Photo

Banking institutions all over the world are in business specifically to borrow and lend money at a profitable rate of interest.

EXAMPLE1   CALCULATING SIMPLE INTEREST

a. What is the amount of interest for a loan of $8,000 at 9% interest for 1 year?

▶ SOLUTIONSTRATEGY

To solve this problem, we apply the simple interest formula:

$$\text{Interest} = \text{Principal} \times \text{Rate} \times \text{Time}$$
$$\text{Interest} = 8{,}000 \times 9\% \times 1$$
$$\text{Interest} = 8{,}000 \times .09 \times 1$$
$$\text{Interest} = \underline{\$720}$$

b. What is the amount of interest for a loan of $16,500 at $12\frac{1}{2}$% interest for 7 months?

▶ SOLUTIONSTRATEGY

In this example, the rate is converted to .125 and the time factor is expressed as a fraction of a year, $\frac{7}{12}$.

$$\text{Interest} = \text{Principal} \times \text{Rate} \times \text{Time}$$
$$\text{Interest} = 16{,}500 \times .125 \times \frac{7}{12}$$
$$\text{Interest} = \underline{\$1{,}203.13}$$

Calculator Sequence: 16500 ⊠ .125 ⊠ 7 ÷ 12 ═ $\underline{\$1{,}203.13}$

▶ TRYITEXERCISE 1

Find the amount of interest on each of the following loans.

	Principal	Rate	Time
a.	$4,000	7%	$2\frac{1}{4}$ years
b.	$45,000	$9\frac{3}{4}$%	3 months
c.	$130,000	10.4%	42 months

CHECK YOUR ANSWERS WITH THE SOLUTIONS ON PAGE 343.

10-2   CALCULATING SIMPLE INTEREST FOR LOANS WITH TERMS OF DAYS BY USING THE EXACT INTEREST AND ORDINARY INTEREST METHODS

There are two methods for calculating the time factor, T, when applying the simple interest formula using days. Because time must be expressed in years, loans whose terms are given in days must be made into a fractional part of a year. This is done by dividing the days of a loan by the number of days in a year.

SIMPLE INTEREST FORMULA—DAYS

Exact Interest

exact interest Interest calculation method using 365 days (366 in leap year) as the time factor denominator.

The first method for calculating the time factor is known as **exact interest**. Exact interest uses *365 days* as the time factor denominator. This method is used by government agencies, the Federal Reserve Bank, and most credit unions.

$$\text{Time} = \frac{\text{Number of days of a loan}}{365}$$

Ordinary Interest

The second method for calculating the time factor is known as **ordinary interest**. Ordinary interest uses *360 days* as the denominator of the time factor. This method dates back to the time before electronic calculators and computers. In the past, when calculating the time factor manually, a denominator of 360 was easier to use than 365.

   Regardless of today's electronic sophistication, banks and most other lending institutions still use ordinary interest because it yields a somewhat higher amount of interest than does the exact interest method. Over the years, ordinary interest has become known as the **banker's rule**.

ordinary interest or banker's rule Interest calculation method using 360 days as the time factor denominator.

$$\text{Time} = \frac{\text{Number of days of a loan}}{360}$$

EXAMPLE2 CALCULATING EXACT INTEREST

Using the exact interest method, what is the amount of interest on a loan of $4,000 at 7% interest for 88 days?

▶SOLUTIONSTRATEGY

Because we are looking for exact interest, we will use 365 days as the denominator of the time factor in the simple interest formula:

$$\text{Interest} = \text{Principal} \times \text{Rate} \times \text{Time}$$

$$\text{Interest} = 4{,}000 \times .07 \times \frac{88}{365}$$

$$\text{Interest} = 67.506849$$

$$\text{Interest} = \underline{\$67.51}$$

Calculator Sequence: 4000 ✕ .07 ✕ 88 ÷ 365 = $67.51

▶TRYITEXERCISE 2

Joe Hale goes to a credit union and borrows $23,000 at 8% for 119 days. If the credit union calculates interest by the exact interest method, what is the amount of interest on the loan?

CHECK YOUR ANSWER WITH THE SOLUTION ON PAGE 343.

EXAMPLE3 CALCULATING ORDINARY INTEREST

Using the ordinary interest method, what is the amount of interest on a loan of $19,500 at 6% interest for 160 days?

▶SOLUTIONSTRATEGY

Because we are looking for ordinary interest, we will use 360 days as the denominator of the time factor in the simple interest formula:

$$\text{Interest} = \text{Principal} \times \text{Rate} \times \text{Time}$$

$$\text{Interest} = 19{,}500 \times .06 \times \frac{160}{360}$$

$$\text{Interest} = \underline{\$520}$$

Calculator Sequence: 19500 ✕ .06 ✕ 160 ÷ 360 = $520

> ▶**TRYITEXERCISE 3**
>
> Karen Mitroff goes to the bank and borrows $15,000 at $9\frac{1}{2}\%$ for 250 days. If the bank uses the ordinary interest method, how much interest will Karen have to pay?
>
> CHECK YOUR ANSWER WITH THE SOLUTION ON PAGE 343.

10-3 CALCULATING THE MATURITY VALUE OF A LOAN

maturity value The total payback of principal and interest of an investment or a loan.

When the time period of a loan is over, the loan is said to mature. At that time, the borrower repays the original principal plus the interest. The total payback of principal and interest is known as the **maturity value** of a loan. Once the interest has been calculated, the maturity value can be found by using the following formula:

$$\text{Maturity value} = \text{Principal} + \text{Interest}$$
$$MV = P + I$$

For example, if a loan for $50,000 had interest of $8,600, the maturity value would be found by adding the principal and the interest: $50,000 + 8,600 = \$58,600$.

Maturity value can also be calculated directly without first calculating the interest by using the following formula:

$$\text{Maturity value} = \text{Principal} (1 + \text{Rate} \times \text{Time})$$
$$MV = P (1 + RT)$$

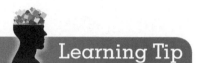

Learning Tip

When using the maturity value formula, $MV = P(1 + RT)$, the order of operation is
- Multiply Rate by Time
- Add the 1
- Multiply by the Principal

B-A-C-O/Shutterstock.com

EXAMPLE4 CALCULATING MATURITY VALUE

What is the maturity value of a loan for $25,000 at 11% for $2\frac{1}{2}$ years?

▶**SOLUTIONSTRATEGY**

Because this example asks for the maturity value, not the amount of interest, we will use the formula for finding maturity value directly, $MV = P (1 + RT)$. Remember to multiply the rate and time first, then add the 1. Note that the time, $2\frac{1}{2}$ years, should be converted to the decimal equivalent 2.5 for ease in calculation.

$$\text{Maturity value} = \text{Principal} (1 + \text{Rate} \times \text{Time})$$
$$\text{Maturity value} = 25,000 (1 + .11 \times 2.5)$$
$$\text{Maturity value} = 25,000 (1 + .275)$$
$$\text{Maturity value} = 25,000 (1.275)$$
$$\text{Maturity value} = \underline{\$31,875}$$

▶**TRYITEXERCISE 4**

a. What is the amount of interest and the maturity value of a loan for $15,400 at $6\frac{1}{2}\%$ simple interest for 24 months? (Use the formula $MV = P + I$.)

b. Apollo Air Taxi Service borrowed $450,000 at 8% simple interest for 9 months to purchase a new airplane. Use the formula $MV = P (1 + RT)$ to find the maturity value of the loan.

CHECK YOUR ANSWERS WITH THE SOLUTIONS ON PAGE 343.

CALCULATING THE NUMBER OF DAYS OF A LOAN

The first day of a loan is known as the **loan date**, and the last day is known as the **due date** or **maturity date**. When these dates are known, the number of days of the loan can be calculated by using the "Days in Each Month" chart and the steps that follow.

loan date The first day of a loan.

due date or maturity date The last day of a loan.

Days in Each Month

28 Days	30 Days	31 Days
February	April	January
(29 leap year)	June	March
	September	May
	November	July
		August
		October
		December

STEPS FOR DETERMINING THE NUMBER OF DAYS OF A LOAN

STEP 1. Determine the number of days remaining in the first month by subtracting the loan date from the number of days in that month.

STEP 2. List the number of days for each succeeding whole month.

STEP 3. List the number of loan days in the last month.

STEP 4. Add the days from Steps 1, 2, and 3.

EXAMPLE5 CALCULATING DAYS OF A LOAN

Kevin Krease borrowed money from the Charter Bank on August 18 and repaid the loan on November 27. What was the number of days of the loan?

SOLUTIONSTRATEGY

The number of days from August 18 to November 27 would be calculated as follows:

Step 1.	Days remaining in first month	Aug. 31		
		Aug. −18		
		13 → August	13 days
Step 2.	Days in succeeding whole months → September	30 days
	→ October	31 days
Step 3.	Days of loan in last month → November	+ 27 days
Step 4.	Add the days	Total 101 days

TRYITEXERCISE 5

a. A loan was made on April 4 and had a due date of July 18. What was the number of days of the loan?

b. Ryan McPherson borrowed $3,500 on June 15 at 11% interest. If the loan was due on October 9, what was the amount of interest on Ryan's loan using the exact interest method?

CHECK YOUR ANSWERS WITH THE SOLUTIONS ON PAGE 343.

Learning Tip

An alternative method for calculating the number of days of a loan is to use the Days-in-a-Year Calendar, Exhibit 7-6, page 213.
- Subtract the "day number" of the loan date from the "day number" of the maturity date.
- If the maturity date is in the next year, add 365 to that day number, then subtract. *Note:* In leap years, add 1 to the day numbers beginning with March 1.

10-5   DETERMINING THE MATURITY DATE OF A LOAN

When the loan date and number of days of the loan are known, the maturity date can be found as follows:

STEPS FOR DETERMINING THE MATURITY DATE OF A LOAN

STEP 1. Find the number of days remaining in the first month by subtracting the loan date from the number of days in that month.

STEP 2. Subtract the days remaining in the first month (Step 1) from the number of days of the loan.

STEP 3. Continue subtracting days in each succeeding whole month until you reach a month with a difference less than the total days in that month. At that point, the maturity date will be the day that corresponds to the difference.

EXAMPLE6   DETERMINING MATURITY DATE OF A LOAN

What is the maturity date of a loan taken out on April 14 for 85 days?

SOLUTIONSTRATEGY

Step 1.	Days remaining in first month	30 Days in April
		−14 Loan date April 14
	Days remaining in April	16
Step 2.	Subtract remaining days in first month from days of the loan	85 Days of the loan
		−16 Days remaining in April
	Difference	69
Step 3.	Subtract succeeding whole months	69 Difference
		−31 Days in May
	Difference	38
		38 Difference
		−30 Days in June
	Difference	8

At this point, the difference, 8, is less than the number of days in the next month, July; therefore, the maturity date is <u>July 8</u>.

TRYITEXERCISE 6

a. What is the maturity date of a loan taken out on September 9 for 125 days?

b. On October 21, Jill Voorhis went to the Regal National Bank and took out a loan for $9,000 at 10% ordinary interest for 80 days. What is the maturity value and maturity date of this loan?

CHECK YOUR ANSWERS WITH THE SOLUTIONS ON PAGE 343.

SECTION I   10   REVIEW EXERCISES

Find the amount of interest on each of the following loans.

	Principal	Rate (%)	Time	Interest
1.	$5,000	8	2 years	$800.00
2.	$60,000	$6\frac{3}{4}$	9 months	_____
3.	$100,000	5.5	18 months	_____

	Principal	Rate (%)	Time	Interest
4.	$80,000	6	$3\frac{1}{2}$ years	_____
5.	$6,440	$5\frac{1}{2}$	7 months	_____
6.	$13,200	9.2	$4\frac{3}{4}$ years	_____

Use the exact interest method (365 days) and the ordinary interest method (360 days) to compare the amount of interest for the following loans.

	Principal	Rate (%)	Time (days)	Exact Interest	Ordinary Interest
7.	$45,000	13	100	$1,602.74	$1,625.00
8.	$184,500	7.75	58	_____	_____
9.	$32,400	8.6	241	_____	_____
10.	$7,230	9	18	_____	_____
11.	$900	$10\frac{1}{4}$	60	_____	_____
12.	$100,000	10	1	_____	_____
13.	$2,500	6	74	_____	_____
14.	$350	14.1	230	_____	_____

15. Find the amount of interest on a loan of $3,000, at 5% interest, for 80 days using the exact interest method.

16. Hernandez Engineering borrows $2,500, at $6\frac{1}{2}$% interest, for 240 days. If the bank uses the ordinary interest method, how much interest will the bank collect?

Find the amount of interest and the maturity value of the following loans. Use the formula $MV = P + I$ to find the maturity values.

	Principal	Rate (%)	Time	Interest	Maturity Value
17.	$54,000	11.9	2 years	$12,852.00	$66,852.00
18.	$125,000	$12\frac{1}{2}$	5 months	_____	_____
19.	$33,750	8.4	10 months	_____	_____
20.	$91,000	$9\frac{1}{4}$	$2\frac{1}{2}$ years	_____	_____
21.	$56,200	10.2	4 years	_____	_____

22. Anny takes out a loan of $1,500, at 6% interest, for 30 months. Use the formula $MV = P + I$ to find the maturity value.

Find the maturity value of the following loans. Use $MV = P(1 + RT)$ to find the maturity values.

	Principal	Rate (%)	Time	Maturity Value
23.	$1,500	9	2 years	$1,770.00
24.	$18,620	$10\frac{1}{2}$	30 months	_____
25.	$1,000,000	11	3 years	_____
26.	$750,000	13.35	11 months	_____
27.	$128,400	8.3	2.5 years	_____
28.	$5,200	7.4	16 months	_____

From the following information, determine the number of days of each loan.

	Loan Date	Due Date	Number of Days
29.	September 5	December 12	98
30.	June 27	October 15	_____
31.	January 23	November 8	_____
32.	March 9	July 30	_____
33.	August 2	September 18	_____
34.	November 18	March 2	_____

From the following information, determine the maturity date of each loan.

	Loan Date	Time of Loan (days)	Maturity Date
35.	October 19	45	December 3
36.	February 5	110	_____
37.	May 26	29	_____
38.	July 21	200	_____
39.	December 6	79	_____
40.	January 13	87	_____
41.	April 27	158	_____

Solve the following problems. Round to the nearest cent when necessary.

42. On April 12, Michelle Lizaro borrowed $5,000 from her credit union at 9% for 80 days. The credit union uses the ordinary interest method.

   a.   What is the amount of interest on the loan?

   b.   What is the maturity value of the loan?

   c.   What is the maturity date of the loan?

Credit unions differ from banks and other financial institutions in that the members who are account holders are the owners of the credit union. Credit unions serve groups that share something in common, such as where they work or where they live. The largest credit union in the United States is Navy Federal Credit Union in Vienna, Virginia, with $36.4 billion in assets and 3.2 million members.

43. What is the maturity value of a $60,000 loan for 100 days at 6.1% interest using the exact interest method?

44. Central Auto Parts borrowed $350,000 at 9% interest on July 19 for 120 days.

   a.   If the bank uses the ordinary interest method, what is the amount of interest on the loan?

   b.   What is the maturity date?

45. Emil Benson missed an income tax payment of $9,000. The Internal Revenue Service charges a 13% simple interest penalty calculated by the exact interest method. If the tax was due on April 15 but was paid on August 19, what was the amount of the penalty charge?

46. At the City National Credit Union, a 7%, $8,000 loan for 180 days had interest charges of $276.16. What type of interest did City National use, ordinary or exact?

47. Kyle Rohrs borrowed $1,080 on June 16 at 9.2% exact interest from the Wells Fargo Bank. On August 10, Kyle repaid the loan. How much interest did he pay?

BUSINESS DECISION: COMPETING BANKS

48. You are the accounting manager for Kool Ragz, Inc., a manufacturer of men's and women's clothing. The company needs to borrow $1,800,000 for 90 days in order to purchase a large quantity of material at "closeout" prices. The interest rate for such loans at your bank, Rimrock Bank, is 11% using ordinary interest.

    a. What is the amount of interest on this loan?

    b. After making a few "shopping" calls, you find that Southside National Bank will lend at 11% using exact interest. What is the amount of interest on this offer?

    c. So that it can keep your business, Rimrock Bank has offered a loan at 10.5% using ordinary interest. What is the amount of interest on this offer?

    d. (Challenge) If Southside National wants to beat Rimrock's last offer (part c) by charging $1,250 less interest, what rate, rounded to the nearest hundredths of a percent, must it quote using exact interest?

iStock.com/ MarsBars

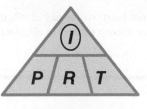 (photo at right)

There are approximately 7,000 commercial banks in the United States. Roughly 25% of these banks have assets in excess of $300 million.

Pavel L Photo and Video/Shutterstock.com

USING THE SIMPLE INTEREST FORMULA

10 SECTION II

In Section I, we used the simple interest formula, $I = PRT$, to solve for the interest. Frequently in business, however, the principal, rate, or time might be the unknown factor. Remember from Chapter 5 that an equation can be solved for any of the variables by isolating that variable to one side of the equation. In this section, we convert the simple interest formula to equations that solve for each of the other variable factors.

If you find this procedure difficult to remember, use the magic triangle, as we did in Chapter 6, to calculate the portion, rate, and base. Remember, to use the Magic Triangle, cover the variable you are solving for and the new formula will "magically" appear!

**Magic Triangle
Simple Interest Formula**

$$I = PRT$$

10-6   SOLVING FOR THE PRINCIPAL

When using the simple interest formula to solve for the principal, P, we isolate the P on one side of the equation by dividing both sides of the equation by RT. This yields the new equation as follows:

$$\text{Principal} = \frac{\text{Interest}}{\text{Rate} \times \text{Time}} \qquad P = \frac{I}{RT}$$

We can also find the formula in the Magic Triangle by covering the unknown variable, P, as follows:

**Magic Triangle
Solving for Principal**

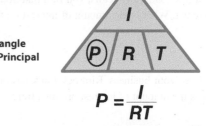

$$P = \frac{I}{RT}$$

Learning Tip

This formula provides a good opportunity to use your calculator's memory keys. Use M+ to store a number in memory and MR to retrieve it.

Some financial and scientific calculators use STO (store) and RCL (recall) keys for the memory function.

EXAMPLE7 — FINDING THE PRINCIPAL OF A LOAN

Allied Bank loaned Checkpoint Industries money at 8% interest for 90 days. If the amount of interest was $4,000, use the ordinary interest method to find the amount of principal borrowed.

►SOLUTIONSTRATEGY

To solve for the principal, we use the formula $P = \dfrac{I}{RT}$.

$P = \dfrac{I}{RT}$ 　　　　　　Substitute the known variables into the equation.

$P = \dfrac{4,000}{.08 \times \dfrac{90}{360}}$ 　　Calculate the denominator first.

　　　　　　　　　Calculator sequence: .08 ✕ 90 ÷ 360 = M+

$P = \dfrac{4,000}{.02}$ 　　　　Next, divide the numerator by the denominator.

　　　　　　　　　Calculator sequence: 4000 ÷ MR = 200,000

Principal = $200,000 　　The company borrowed $200,000 from the bank.

►TRYITEXERCISE 7

Telex Electronics borrowed money at 9% interest for 125 days. If the interest charge was $560, use the ordinary interest method to calculate the amount of principal of the loan.

CHECK YOUR ANSWER WITH THE SOLUTION ON PAGE 343.

SOLVING FOR THE RATE

When we solve the simple formula for rate, the answer will be a decimal that must be converted to a percent. In business, interest rates are always expressed as a percent.

When the rate is the unknown variable, we isolate the R on one side of the equation by dividing both sides of the equation by PT. This yields the new equation as follows:

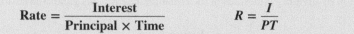

$$\text{Rate} = \frac{\text{Interest}}{\text{Principal} \times \text{Time}} \qquad R = \frac{I}{PT}$$

We can also find the formula in the Magic Triangle by covering the unknown variable, R, as follows:

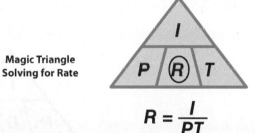

**Magic Triangle
Solving for Rate**

$$R = \frac{I}{PT}$$

EXAMPLE8   FINDING THE RATE OF A LOAN

Using the ordinary interest method, what is the rate of interest on a loan of $5,000 for 125 days if the amount of interest is $166? Round your answer to the nearest hundredth of a percent.

▶SOLUTIONSTRATEGY

To solve for the rate, we use the formula $R = \dfrac{I}{PT}$.

$R = \dfrac{I}{PT}$ Substitute the known variables into the equation.

$R = \dfrac{166}{5{,}000 \times \dfrac{125}{360}}$ Calculate the denominator first.

Calculator sequence: 5000 ⨉ 125 ÷ 360 = M+
Next, divide the numerator by the denominator.

$R = \dfrac{166}{1{,}736.111111}$ *Note:* Don't round the denominator.
Calculator sequence: 166 ÷ MR = .095616

$R = .095616$ Round the answer to the nearest hundredth of a percent.

Rate = 9.56%   The bank charged 9.56% interest.

▶TRYITEXERCISE 8

Using the ordinary interest method, what is the rate of interest on a loan of $25,000 for 245 days if the amount of interest is $1,960? Round your answer to the nearest hundredth of a percent.

CHECK YOUR ANSWER WITH THE SOLUTION ON PAGE 343.

SOLVING FOR THE TIME

When solving the simple interest formula for time, a whole number in the answer represents years and a decimal represents a portion of a year. The decimal should be converted to days by multiplying it by 360 for ordinary interest or by 365 for exact interest. Lending institutions

Learning Tip

Remember, when time, *T*, is calculated, any fraction of a day is rounded up to the next higher day even if it is less than .5.

For example, 25.1 days would round up to 26 days.

consider any part of a day to be a full day. Therefore, any fraction of a day is rounded up to the next higher day even if it is less than .5.

For example, an answer of 3 means 3 years. An answer of 3.22 means 3 years and .22 of the next year. Assuming ordinary interest, multiply the decimal portion of the answer, .22, by 360. This gives 79.2, which represents the number of days. The total time of the loan would be 3 years and 80 days. Remember to always round up any fraction of a day.

When using the simple interest formula to solve for time, *T*, we isolate the *T* on one side of the equation by dividing both sides of the equation by *PR*. This yields the new equation as follows:

$$\text{Time} = \frac{\text{Interest}}{\text{Principal} \times \text{Rate}} \qquad T = \frac{I}{PR}$$

We can also find the formula in the Magic Triangle by covering the unknown variable, *T*, as follows:

Magic Triangle
Solving for Time

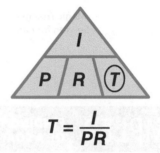

$$T = \frac{I}{PR}$$

EXAMPLE 9   FINDING THE TIME PERIOD OF A LOAN

What would be the time period of a loan for $7,600 at 11% ordinary interest if the amount of interest is $290?

▶ SOLUTIONSTRATEGY

To solve for the time, we use the formula $T = \dfrac{I}{PR}$.

$T = \dfrac{I}{PR}$	Substitute the known variables into the equation.
$T = \dfrac{290}{7{,}600 \times .11}$	Calculate the denominator first. Calculator sequence: 7600 ☒ .11 ▭ M+
$T = \dfrac{290}{836}$	Next, divide the numerator by the denominator. Calculator sequence: 290 ÷ MR ▭ .3468899
$T = .3468899$ years	Because the answer is a decimal, the time is less than 1 year. Using ordinary interest, we multiply the entire decimal by 360 to find the number of days of the loan.
$T = .3468899 \times 360$	Calculator Sequence: .3468899 ☒ 360 ▭ 124.8 or <u>125 days</u>

Time = 124.8 days, or <u>125 days</u>

▶ TRYITEXERCISE 9

What is the time period of a loan for $15,000 at 9.5% ordinary interest if the amount of interest is $650?

CHECK YOUR ANSWER WITH THE SOLUTION ON PAGE 343.

CALCULATING LOANS INVOLVING PARTIAL PAYMENTS BEFORE MATURITY

10-9

Frequently, businesses and individuals who have borrowed money for a specified length of time find that they want to save some interest by making one or more partial payments on the loan before the maturity date. The most commonly used method for this calculation is known as the **U.S. rule**. The rule states that when a partial payment is made on a loan, the payment is first used to pay off the accumulated interest to date and the balance is used to reduce the principal. In this application, the ordinary interest method (360 days) will be used for all calculations.

U.S. rule Method for distributing early partial payments of a loan whereby the payment is first used to pay off the accumulated interest to date, with the balance used to reduce the principal.

STEPS FOR CALCULATING MATURITY VALUE OF A LOAN AFTER ONE OR MORE PARTIAL PAYMENTS

STEP 1. Using the simple interest formula with *ordinary* interest, compute the amount of interest due from the date of the loan to the date of the partial payment.

STEP 2. Subtract the interest from Step 1 from the partial payment. This pays the interest to date.

STEP 3. Subtract the balance of the partial payment after Step 2 from the original principal of the loan. This gives the adjusted principal.

STEP 4. If another partial payment is made, repeat Steps 1, 2, and 3 using the adjusted principal and the number of days since the last partial payment.

STEP 5. The maturity value is computed by adding the interest since the last partial payment to the adjusted principal.

Learning Tip

Remember to use *ordinary interest*, 360 days, for all calculations involving partial payments.

To help you visualize the details of a loan with partial payments, construct a timeline such as the one illustrated in Exhibit 10-1.

EXHIBIT 10-1
Partial Payment Timeline

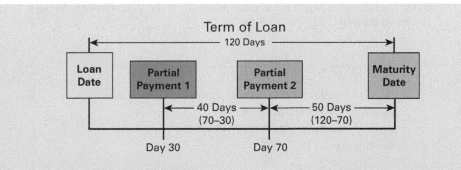

EXAMPLE10 CALCULATING LOANS INVOLVING PARTIAL PAYMENTS

Ray Windsor borrowed $10,000 at 9% interest for 120 days. On day 30, Ray made a partial payment of $2,000. On day 70, he made a second partial payment of $3,000. What is the maturity value of the loan after the partial payments?

▶SOLUTIONSTRATEGY

Step 1. Compute the interest from the date of the loan to the partial payment. In this problem, the first partial payment was made on day 30.

$$I = PRT$$

$$I = 10,000 \times .09 \times \frac{30}{360} = 75$$

$$I = \$75$$

Step 2. Subtract the interest from the partial payment.

$2,000   Partial payment
−   75   Accumulated interest
$1,925   Amount of partial payment left to reduce the principal

Step 3. Reduce the principal.

$10,000   Original principal
− 1,925   Amount of partial payment used to reduce principal
 $8,075   Adjusted principal

Step 4. A second partial payment of $3,000 was made on day 70. We now repeat Steps 1, 2, and 3 to credit the second partial payment properly. Remember, use the adjusted principal and 40 days (70 − 30 = 40) for this calculation.

Step 1.

$$I = PRT$$

$$I = \$8,075 \times .09 \times \frac{40}{360}$$

$I = \$80.75$ Accumulated interest since last partial payment

Step 2.

$3,000.00   Partial payment
−   80.75   Accumulated interest
$2,919.25   Amount of partial payment left to reduce principal

Step 3.

 $8,075.00   Principal
− 2,919.25   Amount of partial payment used to reduce principal
 $5,155.75   Adjusted principal

Step 5. Once all partial payments have been credited, we find the maturity value of the loan by calculating the interest due from the last partial payment to the maturity date and adding it to the last adjusted principal.

Note: The last partial payment was made on day 70 of the loan; therefore, 50 days remain on the loan (120 − 70 = 50 days).

$$I = PRT$$

$$I = \$5,155.75 \times .09 \times \frac{50}{360}$$

$I = \$64.45$ Interest from last partial payment to maturity date

Maturity value = Principal + Interest
Maturity value = $5,155.75 + $64.45
Maturity value = $5,220.20

▶TRYITEXERCISE 10

Rita Peterson borrowed $15,000 at 12% ordinary interest for 100 days. On day 20 of the loan, she made a partial payment of $4,000. On day 60, she made another partial payment of $5,000. What is the maturity value of the loan after the partial payments?

CHECK YOUR ANSWER WITH THE SOLUTION ON PAGE 343.

REVIEW EXERCISES

10 SECTION II

Compute the principal for the following loans. Use ordinary interest when time is stated in days.

	Principal	Rate (%)	Time	Interest
1.	$1,250	12	2 years	$300
2.	_____	9	$1\frac{1}{2}$ years	$675
3.	_____	8	9 months	$3,000
4.	_____	8.6	90 days	$4,950
5.	_____	5	210 days	$917
6.	_____	6	6 months	$2,250

7. Jefferson Bank mode a loan at 7% interest for 226 days. If the amount of interest was $329.58, use the ordinary interest method to find the amount of principal borrowed.

   Round to the nearest whole dollar amount.

Compute the rate for the following loans. Round answers to the nearest tenth of a percent; use ordinary interest when time is stated in days.

	Principal	Rate (%)	Time	Interest
8.	$5,000	8	3 years	$1,200
9.	$1,800	____	5 months	$35
10.	$48,000	____	60 days	$728
11.	$54,000	____	72 days	$732
12.	$125,000	____	2 years	$18,750
13.	$36,700	____	190 days	$2,000

14. What is the rate of interest on a loan of $7,000, for 242 days, if the amount of interest is $329.39, using the ordinary interest method? Round to the nearest tenth of percent.

Use the ordinary interest method to compute the time for the following loans. Round answers to the next higher day when necessary.

	Principal	Rate (%)	Time	Interest
15.	$18,000	12	158 days	$948
16.	$7,900	10.4	_____	$228
17.	$4,500	$9\frac{3}{4}$	_____	$375
18.	$25,000	8.9	_____	$4,450
19.	$7,400	9.6	_____	$200
20.	$41,000	6.4	_____	$3,936

21. Carlos takes out a loan for $10,500, at 8% ordinary interest. If the amount of interest is $504.00, what is the time period of the loan?

    Round any fraction to the next higher day.

Calculate the missing information for the following loans. Round percents to the nearest tenth and days to the next higher day when necessary.

	Principal	Rate (%)	Time (days)	Interest Method	Interest	Maturity Value
22.	$16,000	13	___	Ordinary	$760	_____
23.	_____	9.5	100	Exact	$340	_____
24.	$3,800	___	165	Exact	$220	_____
25.	$25,500	$11\frac{1}{4}$	300	Ordinary	_____	_____
26.	_____	10.4	___	Exact	$4,000	$59,000

Solve the following problems. Round answers to the nearest cent when necessary.

27. Kendall Motors, a Buick dealership, borrowed $225,000 on April 16 to purchase a shipment of new cars. The interest rate was 9.3% using the ordinary interest method. The amount of interest was $9,600.

    a. For how many days was the loan?

    b. What was the maturity date of the loan?

Dollars AND Sense

28. Mike Drago took out a loan for $3,500 at the Gold Coast Bank for 270 days. If the bank uses the ordinary interest method, what rate of interest was charged if the amount of interest was $269? Round your answer to the nearest tenth of a percent.

29. Tiffany Francis borrowed money from her credit union to buy a car at 13.5% simple interest. If the loan was repaid in 2 years and the amount of interest was $2,700, how much did Tiffany borrow?

30. What is the maturity date of a loan for $5,000 at 15% exact interest taken out on June 3? The amount of interest on the loan was $150.

iStock.com/vreemous

31. You are the owner of a Supercuts Hair Salon. What rate of interest were you charged on an ordinary interest loan for $135,000 in equipment if the interest was $4,400 and the time period was from January 16 to April 27? Round your answer to the nearest tenth of a percent.

32. Michelle Payne deposited $8,000 in a savings account paying 6.25% simple interest. How long will it take for her investment to amount to $10,000?

33. The Actor's Playhouse theater borrowed $100,000 at 8% ordinary interest for 90 days to purchase new stage lighting equipment. On day 40 of the loan, the theater made a partial payment of $35,000. What is the new maturity value of the loan?

$$I = PRT - 100,000 \times .08 \times \frac{40}{360} = \$888.89$$

$$\begin{array}{ll} \$35,000.00 \text{ Paid} & \$100,000.00 \\ \underline{-\ 888.89} \text{ Interest} & \underline{-\ 34,111.11} \\ \$34,111.11 & \$65,888.89 \\ & \textbf{Adjusted principal} \end{array}$$

$$MV = P(1 + RT) = 65,888.89 \left(1 + .08 \times \frac{50}{360} \right) = \$66,620.99$$

34. Steve Perry borrowed $10,000 at 12% ordinary interest for 60 days. On day 20 of the loan, Steve made a partial payment of $4,000. What is the new maturity value of the loan?

35. Suppose you take out a loan for 160 days in the amount of $11,000 at 7% ordinary interest. After 50 days, you make a partial payment of $1,500. After another 60 days, you make a second partial payment of $3,000. What is the final amount due on the loan?

36. The Mutt Hut Pet Shop borrowed $60,000 on March 15 for 90 days. The rate was 13% using the ordinary interest method. On day 25 of the loan, The Mutt Hut made a partial payment of $16,000, and on day 55 of the loan, The Mutt Hut made a second partial payment of $12,000.

    a. What is the new maturity value of the loan?

b. What is the maturity date of the loan?

37. a. How many years will it take $5,000 invested at 8% simple interest to double to $10,000?

b. How long will it take if the interest rate is increased to 10%?

iStock.com/
MarsBars

BUSINESS DECISION: THE OPPORTUNITY COST

38. You are the owner of four Taco Bell restaurant locations. You have a business loan with Citizens Bank taken out 60 days ago that is due in 90 days. The amount of the loan is $40,000, and the rate is 9.5% using ordinary interest.

You currently have some excess cash. You have the choice of sending Citizens $25,000 now as a partial payment on your loan or purchasing an additional $25,000 of serving supplies such as food containers, cups, and plastic dinnerware for your inventory at a special discount price that is "10% off" your normal cost of these items.

a. How much interest will you save on this loan if you make the partial payment and don't purchase the additional serving supplies?

QualityHD/Shutterstock.com

Taco Bell serves more than 2 billion consumers each year in more than 7,000 restaurants in the United States. The initial investment to franchise a Taco Bell is $1.3 million–$2.3 million. Franchise fees are $45,000 initial fee, then 5.5% monthly royalty fees, and 4.5% monthly advertising fees.

Yum! Brands, Inc., based in Louisville, Kentucky, is the world's largest restaurant company in terms of system restaurants, with more than 37,000 restaurants in over 110 countries and territories and more than 1 million associates. Yum! is ranked in the top 250 companies on the Fortune 500 list. Four of the restaurant brands—KFC, Pizza Hut, Taco Bell, and Long John Silver's—are the global leaders of the chicken, pizza, Mexican-style food, and quick-service seafood categories, respectively.

b. How much will you save by purchasing the discounted serving supplies and not making the partial payment?

c. (Optional) What other factors should you consider before making this decision?

UNDERSTANDING PROMISSORY NOTES AND DISCOUNTING

Technically, the document that states the details of a loan and is signed by the borrower is known as a **promissory note**. *Promissory* means it is a promise to pay the principal back to the lender on a certain date. *Note* means that the document is a negotiable instrument and can be transferred or sold to others not involved in the original loan. Much like a check, with proper endorsement by the payee, the note can be transferred to another person, company, or lending institution.

Promissory notes are either noninterest-bearing or interest-bearing. When a note is noninterest-bearing, the maturity value equals the principal because there is no interest being charged. With interest-bearing notes, the maturity value equals the principal plus the interest.

Exhibit 10-2 is an example of a typical promissory note with its parts labeled. Notice the similarity between a note and a check. A list explaining the labels follows.

Maker: The person or company borrowing the money and issuing the note.

Payee: The person or institution lending the money and receiving the payment.

Term: The time period of the note, usually stated in days. (Use ordinary interest.)

Date: The date that the note is issued.

Face Value or Principal: The amount of money borrowed.

Interest Rate: The annual rate of interest being charged.

Maturity Date or Due Date: The date when maturity value is due to the payee.

> **promissory note** A debt instrument in which one party agrees to repay money to another within a specified period of time. Promissory notes may be noninterest-bearing at no interest or interest-bearing at a specified rate of interest.

EXHIBIT 10-2 Interest-Bearing Promissory Note

Term		Date

$5,000   Miami, Fla.,   May 21, 20XX

Face Value

Ninety Days   after date   1   promise to pay

to the order of   Travel Adventures   **Payee**

Five Thousand and ^xx/100   Dollars

for value received with interest at   twelve   percent per annum.

Due   Aug. 19, 20XX   Shari Joy

Maturity Date or Due Date   **Interest Rate**   **Maker**

10-10　CALCULATING BANK DISCOUNT AND PROCEEDS FOR A SIMPLE DISCOUNT NOTE

To this point, we have been dealing with *simple interest notes* in which the interest was added to the principal to determine the maturity value. Another way of lending money is to deduct the interest from the principal at the beginning of the loan and give the borrower the difference. These are known as **simple discount notes**. When this method is used, the amount of interest charged is known as the **bank discount** and the amount that the borrower receives is known as the **proceeds**. When the term of the note is over, the borrower will repay the entire principal, or face value, of the note as the maturity value.

For example, Julie goes to a bank and signs a simple interest note for $5,000. If the interest charge amounts to $500, she will receive $5,000 at the beginning of the note and repay $5,500 on maturity of the note. If the bank used a simple discount note for Julie's loan, the bank discount (interest) would be deducted from the face value (principal). Julie's proceeds on the loan would be $4,500, and on maturity she would pay $5,000.

simple discount notes Promissory notes in which the interest is deducted from the principal at the beginning of the loan.

bank discount The amount of interest charged (deducted from the principal) on a discounted promissory note.

proceeds The amount of money that the borrower receives at the time a discounted note is made.

BANK DISCOUNT

Because bank discount is the same as interest, we use the formula $I = PRT$ as before, substituting bank discount for interest, face value for principal, and discount rate for interest rate. *Note:* Use ordinary interest, 360 days, for simple discount notes whose terms are stated in days.

$$\text{Bank discount} = \text{Face value} \times \text{Discount rate} \times \text{Time}$$

PROCEEDS

The proceeds of a note are calculated using the following formula:

$$\text{Proceeds} = \text{Face value} - \text{Bank discount}$$

EXAMPLE 11　CALCULATING BANK DISCOUNT AND PROCEEDS

What are the bank discount and proceeds of a $7,000 note at a 7% discount rate for 270 days?

▶ SOLUTION STRATEGY

$$\text{Bank discount} = \text{Face value} \times \text{Discount rate} \times \text{Time}$$

$$\text{Bank discount} = \$7,000 \times .07 \times \frac{270}{360}$$

$$\text{Bank discount} = \underline{\$367.50}$$

$$\text{Proceeds} = \text{Face value} - \text{Bank discount}$$

$$\text{Proceeds} = \$7,000 - \$367.50$$

$$\text{Proceeds} = \underline{\$6,632.50}$$

▶ TRY IT EXERCISE 11

Erin Lang signed a $20,000 simple discount promissory note at the Sovereign Bank for a student loan. The discount rate is 13%, and the term of the note is 330 days. What is the amount of the bank discount, and what are Erin's proceeds on the loan?

CHECK YOUR ANSWERS WITH THE SOLUTIONS ON PAGE 343.

Dollars AND Sense

Student Aid

The U.S. Department of Education student aid programs are the largest source of student aid in America. The Free Application for Federal Student Aid (FAFSA) is the form used by virtually all two- and four-year colleges, universities, and career schools for federal, state, and college aid.

A number of student loans allow for a grace period before the loan must be repaid. However, interest may accrue during this time. For more information, visit www.fafsa.ed.gov and http://ibrinfo.org.

CALCULATING TRUE, OR EFFECTIVE, RATE OF INTEREST FOR A SIMPLE DISCOUNT NOTE

In a simple interest note, the borrower receives the full face value, whereas with a simple discount note, the borrower receives only the proceeds. Because the proceeds are less than the face value, the stated discount rate is not the true or actual interest rate of the note.

To protect the consumer, the U.S. Congress has passed legislation requiring all lending institutions to quote the **true**, or **effective**, **interest rate** for all loans. Effective interest rate is calculated by substituting the bank discount for interest and the proceeds for principal in the rate formula,

true, or **effective**, **interest rate**
The actual interest rate charged on a discounted note. Takes into account the fact that the borrower does not receive the full amount of the principal.

$$\text{Effective interest rate} = \frac{\text{Bank discount}}{\text{Proceeds} \times \text{Time}}$$

EXAMPLE 12 — CALCULATING EFFECTIVE INTEREST RATE

What is the effective interest rate of a simple discount note for $10,000 at a bank discount rate of 14% for a period of 90 days? Round to the nearest tenth of a percent.

▶ SOLUTIONSTRATEGY

To find the effective interest rate, we must first calculate the amount of the bank discount and the proceeds of the note, then substitute these numbers in the effective interest rate formula.

Step 1. Bank Discount

$$\text{Bank discount} = \text{Face value} \times \text{Discount rate} \times \text{Time}$$

$$\text{Bank discount} = \$10,000 \times .14 \times \frac{90}{360}$$

$$\text{Bank discount} = \$350$$

Step 2. Proceeds

$$\text{Proceeds} = \text{Face value} - \text{Bank discount}$$

$$\text{Proceeds} = 10,000 - 350$$

$$\text{Proceeds} = \$9,650$$

Step 3. Effective Interest Rate

$$\text{Effective interest rate} = \frac{\text{Bank discount}}{\text{Proceeds} \times \text{Time}}$$

$$\text{Effective interest rate} = \frac{350}{9,650 \times \frac{90}{360}}$$

$$\text{Effective interest rate} = \frac{350}{2,412.50}$$

$$\text{Effective interest rate} = .14507, \text{ or } \underline{\underline{14.5\%}}$$

▶ TRYITEXERCISE 12

What is the effective interest rate of a simple discount note for $40,000 at a bank discount rate of 11% for a period of 270 days? Round your answer to the nearest hundredth of a percent.

CHECK YOUR ANSWER WITH THE SOLUTION ON PAGE 343.

DISCOUNTING NOTES BEFORE MATURITY

Frequently in business, companies extend credit to their customers by accepting short-term promissory notes as payment for goods or services. These notes are simple interest and are usually for less than one year. Prior to the maturity date of these notes, the payee (lender) may

discounting a note A process whereby a company or an individual can cash in or sell a promissory note at a discount at any time before maturity.

discount period The time period between the date a note is discounted and the maturity date. Used to calculate the proceeds of a discounted note.

take the note to a bank and sell it. This is a convenient way for a company or an individual to *cash in* a note at any time before maturity. This process is known as **discounting a note**.

When a note is discounted at a bank, the original payee receives the proceeds of the discounted note and the bank (the new payee) receives the maturity value of the note when it matures. The time period used to calculate the proceeds is from the date the note is discounted to the maturity date. This is known as the **discount period**.

Exhibit 10-3 illustrates the timeline for a 90-day simple interest note discounted on the 60th day.

EXHIBIT 10-3

Timeline for Discounted Note

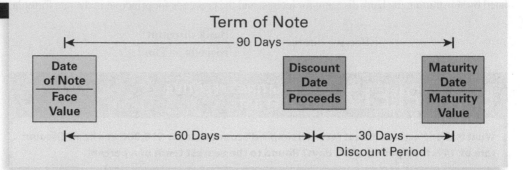

STEPS FOR DISCOUNTING A NOTE BEFORE MATURITY

STEP 1. Calculate the maturity value of the note. If the original note was noninterest-bearing, the maturity value will be the same as the face value. If the original note was interest-bearing, the maturity value should be calculated as usual:

Maturity value = Principal (1 + Rate × Time)

STEP 2. Determine the number of days or months of the discount period. The discount period is used as the numerator of the time in Step 3.

STEP 3. Calculate the amount of the bank discount by using the following formula. *Note*: Use ordinary interest, 360 days, for discounting a note before maturity, when the terms are stated in days.

Bank discount = Maturity value × Discount rate × Time

STEP 4. Calculate the proceeds of the note by using the following formula:

Proceeds = Maturity value − Bank discount

EXAMPLE13 CALCULATING PROCEEDS OF A DISCOUNTED NOTE

Continental Industries received a $15,000 promissory note for 150 days at 12% simple interest from one of its customers. After 90 days, Continental needed cash, so it discounted the note at the InterAmerican Bank at a discount rate of 14%. What are the proceeds Continental will receive from the discounted note?

▶SOLUTIONSTRATEGY

Step 1. Calculate the maturity value of the original note:

Maturity value = Principal (1 + Rate × Time)

$$\text{Maturity value} = 15,000 \left(1 + .12 \times \frac{150}{360}\right)$$

Maturity value = 15,000 (1 + .05) = 15,000(1.05)

Maturity value = $15,750

Step 2. Find the number of days of the discount period: In this example, the note was discounted after 90 days of a 150-day note; therefore, the discount period is 60 days (150 − 90 = 60).

Step 3. Calculate the amount of the bank discount:

$$\text{Bank discount} = \text{Maturity value} \times \text{Discount rate} \times \text{Time}$$

$$\text{Bank discount} = \$15{,}750 \times .14 \times \frac{60}{360}$$

$$\text{Bank discount} = \$367.50$$

Step 4. Calculate the proceeds of the discounted note:

$$\text{Proceeds} = \text{Maturity value} - \text{Bank discount}$$

$$\text{Proceeds} = \$15{,}750.00 - \$367.50$$

$$\text{Proceeds} = \underline{\$15{,}382.50}$$

▶TRYITEXERCISE 13

Legacy Lumber received a $35,000 promissory note at 10% simple interest for 6 months from one of its customers. After 4 months, the note was discounted at the Keystone Bank at a discount rate of 14%. What are the proceeds Legacy will receive from the discounted note?

CHECK YOUR ANSWER WITH THE SOLUTIONS ON PAGE 344.

PURCHASING U.S. TREASURY BILLS

10-13

U.S. Treasury bills, or **T-bills**, are short-term government securities with maturities of 4 weeks, 13 weeks, and 26 weeks. Sold by banks, brokers, and dealers in increments of $1,000, these securities represent loans to the U.S. government and are considered to be among the safest of investments. Just like discounted bank notes, T-bills are sold at a discount from their face value.

U.S. Treasury bills, or **T-bills**
Short-term government securities that represent loans to the U.S. government.

For example, you might pay $970 for a T-bill with a face value of $1,000. When the bill matures, you would be paid its face value, $1,000. Your interest is the difference between the face value and the purchase price—in this example, $30. The interest is determined by the discount rate, which is set when the bills are initially auctioned by the U.S. Treasury.

When comparing T-bills to discounted bank notes, the interest of a T-bill is the equivalent of the bank discount of a note; the face value of a T-bill is the equivalent of the proceeds of a note. Use the following formulas for T-bill calculations:

$$\textbf{Interest} = \textbf{Face value} \times \textbf{Discount rate} \times \textbf{Time}$$

$$\textbf{Purchase price} = \textbf{Face value} - \textbf{Interest}$$

$$\textbf{Effective interest rate} = \frac{\textbf{Interest}}{\textbf{Purchase price} \times \textbf{Time}}$$

EXAMPLE14 PURCHASING U.S. TREASURY BILLS

Peggy Estes purchased $5,000 in U.S. Treasury bills with a discount rate of 4% for a period of 13 weeks.

a. How much interest did Peggy earn on the T-bill investment?

b. How much was the purchase price of Peggy's T-bills?

c. What was the effective interest rate of Peggy's T-bill investment? Round to the nearest hundredth of a percent.

▶SOLUTIONSTRATEGY

a. Interest = Face value × Discount rate × Time

$$\text{Interest} = \$5{,}000 \times .04 \times \frac{13}{52} = \underline{\$50}$$

Dollars AND Sense

For more information about Treasury bills, go to www.ustreas.gov.

iStock.com/vreemous

b. Purchase price = Face value − Interest
   Purchase price = 5,000 − 50 = $4,950

c. Effective interest rate = $\dfrac{\text{Interest}}{\text{Purchase price} \times \text{Time}}$

   Effective interest rate = $\dfrac{50}{4,950 \times \dfrac{13}{52}}$ = .040404 = 4.04%

►TRYITEXERCISE 14

Bob Schaller purchased $10,000 in U.S. Treasury bills with a discount rate of 4.6% for a period of 26 weeks.

a. How much interest did Bob earn on the T-bill investment?

b. How much was the purchase price of Bob's T-bills?

c. What was the effective interest rate of Bob's T-bill investment? Round to the nearest hundredth of a percent.

CHECK YOUR ANSWERS WITH THE SOLUTIONS ON PAGE 344.

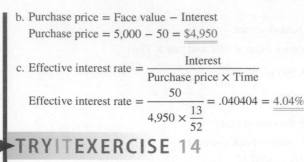

SECTION III **10**   REVIEW EXERCISES

Calculate the bank discount and proceeds for the following simple discount notes. Use the ordinary interest method, 360 days, when applicable.

	Face Value	Discount Rate (%)	Term	Bank Discount	Proceeds
1.	$4,500	13	6 months	$292.50	$4,207.50
2.	$235	11.3	50 days	_____	_____
3.	$2,000	$7\frac{1}{2}$	1 year	_____	_____
4.	$35,000	9.65	11 months	_____	_____

5. You sign a simple discount promissory note for $3,000 at a discount rate of 5%, for 24 months. What are the proceeds?

Using ordinary interest, 360 days, calculate the missing information for the following simple discount notes.

	Face Value	Discount Rate (%)	Date of Note	Term (days)	Maturity Date	Bank Discount	Proceeds
6.	$16,800	10	June 3	80	Aug. 22	$373.33	$16,426.67
7.	$5,000	14.7	April 16	_____	July 9	_____	_____
8.	$800	12.1	Sept. 3	109	_____	_____	_____
9.	$1,300	$9\frac{1}{2}$	Aug. 19	_____	Nov. 27	_____	_____
10.	$75,000	5	May 7	53	_____	_____	_____

Using ordinary interest, 360 days, calculate the bank discount, proceeds, and effective rate for the following simple discount notes. Round effective rate to the nearest hundredth of a percent.

	Face Value	Discount Rate (%)	Term (days)	Bank Discount	Proceeds	Effective Rate (%)
11.	$2,700	14	126	$132.30	$2,567.70	14.72
12.	$6,505	10.39	73			
13.	$3,800	7.25	140			
14.	$95,000	9.7	45			

15. If you sign a discount note for $7,500 at a bank discount rate of 7% for 3 months, what is the effective interest rate? Round to the nearest tenth percent.

The following interest-bearing promissory notes were discounted at a bank by the payee before maturity. Use the ordinary interest method, 360 days, to calculate the missing information.

	Face Value	Interest Rate (%)	Date of Note	Term of Note (days)	Maturity Date	Maturity Value	Date of Discount	Discount Period (days)	Discount Rate (%)	Proceeds
16.	$2,500	12	Mar. 4	70	May 13	$2,558.33	Apr. 15	28	13	$2,532.46
17.	$4,000	10.4	Dec. 12	50			Jan. 19		15	
18.	$850	$13\frac{1}{2}$	June 7	125			Sept. 3		16.5	
19.	$8,000	9	May 10	90			July 5		10.2	
20.	$1,240	7.6	Sept. 12	140			Dec. 5		11.8	

Calculate the interest, purchase price, and effective interest rate of the following Treasury bill (T-bill) purchases. Round effective interest rate to the nearest hundredth of a percent.

	Face Value	Discount Rate (%)	Term (weeks)	Interest	Purchase Price	Effective Rate (%)
21.	$15,000	5.20	13	$195	$14,805	5.27
22.	$50,000	4.40	26			
23.	$80,000	4.82	13			
24.	$35,000	3.80	4			

25. If you purchase $25,000 in U.S. Treasury Bills with a discount rate of 4.1% for a period of 26 weeks, what is the effective interest rate? Round to the nearest hundredth percent.

Use the ordinary interest method, 360 days, to solve the following word problems. Round to the nearest cent when necessary.

26. Roni Lockard signed a $22,500 simple discount promissory note at the Pacific National Bank. The discount rate was 11%, and the note was made on February 17 (not in a leap-year) for 107 days.

   a. What proceeds will Roni receive on the note?

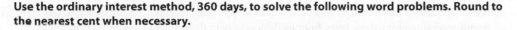

   b. What is the maturity date of the note?

27. Boz Foster signed a $10,000 simple discount promissory note at a bank discount rate of 6%. If the term of the note was 125 days, what was the effective interest rate of the note? Round your answer to the nearest hundredth of a percent.

28. JAB Consulting received a promissory note of $12,500 at 5% simple interest for 15 months from one of its customers. After 6 months, Grove Isle Bank discounted the note at a discount rate of 8% Calculate the proceeds that JAB Consulting will receive from the discounted note.

29. Christy Thomas purchased $150,000 in U.S. Treasury bills with a discount rate of 4.2% for a period of 4 weeks.

   a. How much interest did Christy earn on the T-bill investment?

   b. How much was the purchase price of Christy's T-bills?

   c. What was the effective interest rate of Christy's T-bill investment? Round to the nearest hundredth of a percent.

BUSINESS DECISION: FINANCING THE DEALERS

30. Richie Powers is the owner of American Eagle Boats, a manufacturer of custom pleasure boats. Because of the economic recession and slow boat sales recently, American Eagle has begun accepting promissory notes from its dealers to help finance large orders. This morning American Eagle accepted a 90-day, 9.5% promissory note for $600,000 from Champion Marine, one of its sales dealers.

   You are a manager for Atlantic Bank, and Richie is one of your clients. Atlantic's discount rate is currently 16%. Richie's goal is to discount the note as soon as possible, but not until the proceeds are at least equal to the face value of the note, $600,000.

a.   As his banker, Richie has asked you to "run the numbers" at ten-day intervals starting with day 20 and advise him as to when he can discount the note and still receive his $600,000.

According to the National Marine Manufacturers Association, the top five boating states are Florida, Texas, California, North Carolina, and New York. Typical sales and service expenditures for recreational boating exceed $30 billion annually.

b.   (Challenge) Calculate the exact day the note should be discounted to meet Richie's goal.

CHAPTER FORMULAS

CHAPTER 10

Simple Interest

Interest = Principal × Rate × Time

$$\text{Time (exact interest)} = \frac{\text{Number of days of a loan}}{365}$$

$$\text{Time (ordinary interest)} = \frac{\text{Number of days of a loan}}{360}$$

Maturity value = Principal + Interest

Maturity value = Principal (1 + Rate × Time)

The Simple Interest Formula

$$\text{Principal} = \frac{\text{Interest}}{\text{Rate} \times \text{Time}}$$

$$\text{Rate} = \frac{\text{Interest}}{\text{Principal} \times \text{Time}}$$

$$\text{Time} = \frac{\text{Interest}}{\text{Principal} \times \text{Rate}}$$

Simple Discount Notes

Bank discount = Face value × Discount rate × Time

Proceeds = Face value − Bank discount

$$\text{Effective interest rate} = \frac{\text{Bank discount}}{\text{Proceeds} \times \text{Time}}$$

Discounting a Note before Maturity

Bank discount = Maturity value × Discount rate × Time

Proceeds = Maturity value − Bank discount

Purchasing U.S. Treasury Bills

Interest = Face value × Discount rate × Time

Purchase price = Face value − Interest

$$\text{Effective interest rate} = \frac{\text{Interest}}{\text{Purchase price} \times \text{Time}}$$

CHAPTER SUMMARY

Section I: Understanding and Computing Simple Interest

Topic	Important Concepts	Illustrative Examples
Computing Simple Interest for Loans with Terms of Years or Months **Performance Objective 10-1, Page 313**	Simple interest is calculated by using the formula $I = PRT$. *Note*: Time is always expressed in years or fractions of a year.	What is the amount of interest for a loan of $20,000 at 6% simple interest for 9 months? $$I = 20{,}000 \times .06 \times \frac{9}{12}$$ Interest = $900
Calculating Simple Interest for Loans with Terms of Days by Using the Exact Interest Method **Performance Objective 10-2, Page 314**	Exact interest uses *365 days* as the time factor denominator.	Using the exact interest method, what is the amount of interest on a loan of $5,000 at 8% for 95 days? $$I = PRT$$ $$I = 5{,}000 \times .08 \times \frac{95}{365}$$ Interest = $104.11
Calculating Simple Interest for Loans with Terms of Days by Using the Ordinary Interest Method **Performance Objective 10-2, Page 315**	Ordinary interest uses *360 days* as the time factor denominator.	Using the ordinary interest method, what is the amount of interest on a loan of $8,000 at 9% for 120 days? $$I = PRT$$ $$I = 8{,}000 \times .09 \times \frac{120}{360}$$ Interest = $240
Calculating the Maturity Value of a Loan **Performance Objective 10-3, Page 316**	When the time period of a loan is over, the loan is said to mature. The total payback of principal and interest is known as the maturity value of a loan.	What is the maturity value of a loan for $50,000 at 12% interest for 3 years? $$MV = 50{,}000(1 + .12 \times 3)$$ $$MV = 50{,}000(1.36)$$ Maturity value = $68,000

Calculating the Number of Days of a Loan
 	
Performance Objective 10-4, Page 317
	1. Determine the number of days remaining in the first month by subtracting the loan date from the number of days in that month.
	2. List the number of days for each succeeding whole month.
	3. List the number of loan days in the last month.
	4. Add the days from Steps 1, 2, and 3.
		Steve Adams borrowed money from the Republic Bank on May 5 and repaid the loan on August 19. For how many days was this loan?
		
		  May 31
		− May 5
		     26 Days in May
		     61 June–July
		  +19 August
		  106 Days

Determining the Maturity Date of a Loan
 	
Performance Objective 10-5, Page 318
	1. Determine the number of days remaining in the first month.
	2. Subtract days from Step 1 from number of days in the loan.
	3. Subtract days in each succeeding whole month until you reach a month in which the difference is less than the days in that month. The maturity date will be the day of that month that corresponds to the difference.
		What is the maturity date of a loan taken out on June 9 for 100 days?
		
		June 30 100 Days of the loan
		June −9 − 21 Days in June
		  21 Days in June 79
		               − 31 Days in July
		               48
		               − 31 Days in August
		               17
		At this point, the difference, 17, is less than the days in September; therefore, the maturity date is September 17.

Section II: Using the Simple Interest Formula

Topic	Important Concepts	Illustrative Examples
Solving for the Principal **Performance Objective 10-6, Page 322**	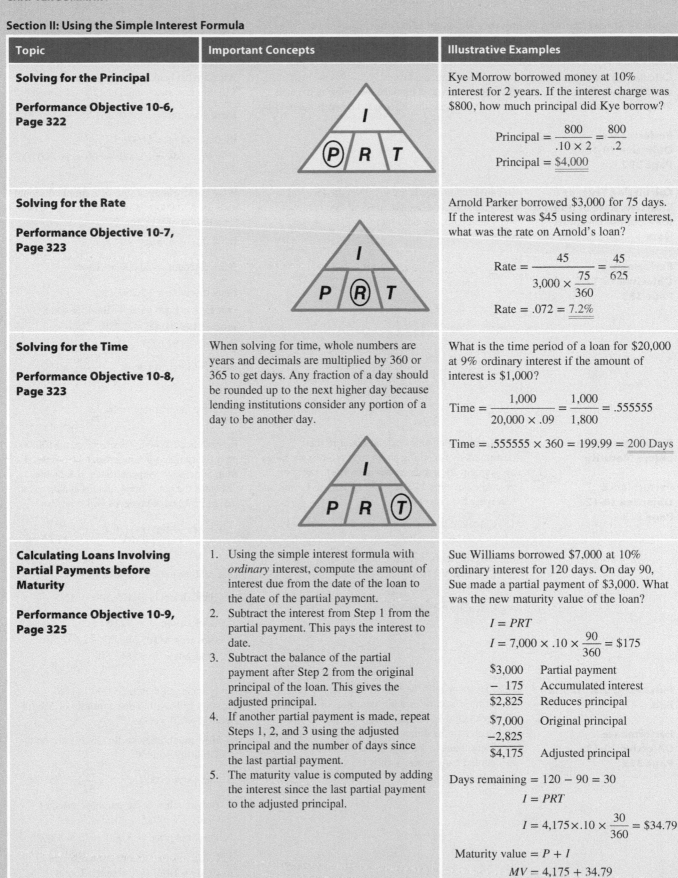	Kye Morrow borrowed money at 10% interest for 2 years. If the interest charge was $800, how much principal did Kye borrow? $$\text{Principal} = \frac{800}{.10 \times 2} = \frac{800}{.2}$$ $$\text{Principal} = \underline{\$4,000}$$
Solving for the Rate **Performance Objective 10-7, Page 323**		Arnold Parker borrowed $3,000 for 75 days. If the interest was $45 using ordinary interest, what was the rate on Arnold's loan? $$\text{Rate} = \frac{45}{3,000 \times \frac{75}{360}} = \frac{45}{625}$$ $$\text{Rate} = .072 = \underline{7.2\%}$$
Solving for the Time **Performance Objective 10-8, Page 323**	When solving for time, whole numbers are years and decimals are multiplied by 360 or 365 to get days. Any fraction of a day should be rounded up to the next higher day because lending institutions consider any portion of a day to be another day.	What is the time period of a loan for $20,000 at 9% ordinary interest if the amount of interest is $1,000? $$\text{Time} = \frac{1,000}{20,000 \times .09} = \frac{1,000}{1,800} = .555555$$ $$\text{Time} = .555555 \times 360 = 199.99 = \underline{200 \text{ Days}}$$
Calculating Loans Involving Partial Payments before Maturity **Performance Objective 10-9, Page 325**	1. Using the simple interest formula with *ordinary* interest, compute the amount of interest due from the date of the loan to the date of the partial payment. 2. Subtract the interest from Step 1 from the partial payment. This pays the interest to date. 3. Subtract the balance of the partial payment after Step 2 from the original principal of the loan. This gives the adjusted principal. 4. If another partial payment is made, repeat Steps 1, 2, and 3 using the adjusted principal and the number of days since the last partial payment. 5. The maturity value is computed by adding the interest since the last partial payment to the adjusted principal.	Sue Williams borrowed $7,000 at 10% ordinary interest for 120 days. On day 90, Sue made a partial payment of $3,000. What was the new maturity value of the loan? $$I = PRT$$ $$I = 7,000 \times .10 \times \frac{90}{360} = \$175$$ $\$3,000$ Partial payment $- \ 175$ Accumulated interest $\overline{\$2,825}$ Reduces principal $\$7,000$ Original principal $-2,825$ $\overline{\$4,175}$ Adjusted principal Days remaining $= 120 - 90 = 30$ $$I = PRT$$ $$I = 4,175 \times .10 \times \frac{30}{360} = \$34.79$$ Maturity value $= P + I$ $$MV = 4,175 + 34.79$$ Maturity value $= \underline{\$4,209.79}$

Section III: Understanding Promissory Notes and Discounting

Topic	Important Concepts	Illustrative Examples
Calculating Bank Discount and Proceeds for a Simple Discount Note **Performance Objective 10-10, Page 332**	With discounting, the interest, known as the bank discount, is deducted from the face value of the loan. The borrower gets the difference, known as the proceeds.	What are the bank discount and proceeds of a $10,000 note discounted at 12% for 6 months? Bank discount $= 10,000 \times .12 \times \dfrac{6}{12}$ Bank discount $= \$600$ Proceeds $= 10,000 - 600 = \underline{\$9,400}$
Calculating True, or Effective, Rate of Interest for a Simple Discount Note **Performance Objective 10-11, Page 333**	Because the proceeds are less than the face value of a loan, the true, or effective, interest rate is higher than the stated bank discount rate.	What is the effective rate of a simple discount note for $20,000 at a bank discount of 15% for a period of 9 months? Bank discount $= FV \times R \times T$ Bank discount $= 20,000 \times .15 \times \dfrac{9}{12}$ Bank discount $= \$2,250$ Proceeds $=$ Face value $-$ Bank discount Proceeds $= 20,000 - 2,250$ Proceeds $= \$17,750$ Effective interest rate $= \dfrac{2,250}{17,750 \times \dfrac{9}{12}}$ Effective interest rate $= \underline{16.9\%}$
Discounting Notes before Maturity **Performance Objective 10-12, Page 333**	Frequently, companies extend credit to their customers by accepting short-term promissory notes as payment for goods or services. These notes can be cashed in early by discounting them at a bank and receiving the proceeds. 1. Calculate the maturity value. 2. Determine the discount period. 3. Calculate the bank discount. 4. Calculate the proceeds.	Reliable Food Wholesalers received a $100,000 promissory note for 6 months at 11% interest from SuperSaver Supermarkets. If Reliable discounts the note after 4 months at a discount rate of 15%, what proceeds will it receive? $MV = 100,000 \left(1 + .11 \times \dfrac{6}{12} \right)$ $MV = \$105,500$ Discount period $= 2$ months $(6 - 4)$ Bank discount $= 105,500 \times .15 \times \dfrac{2}{12}$ Bank discount $= \$2,637.50$ Proceeds $= 105,500.00 - 2,637.50$ Proceeds $= \underline{\$102,862.50}$
Purchasing U.S. Treasury Bills **Performance Objective 10-13, Page 335**	U.S. Treasury bills, or T-bills, are short-term government securities with maturities of 4 weeks, 13 weeks, and 26 weeks. Sold by banks, brokers, and dealers in increments of $1,000, these securities represent loans to the U.S. government. Just like discounted bank notes, T-bills are sold at a discount from their face value.	Cindy Lane purchased $3,000 in U.S. Treasury bills with a discount rate of 5% for a period of 26 weeks. a. How much interest did Cindy earn on the T-bill investment? Interest $= 3,000 \times .05 \times \dfrac{26}{52} = \underline{\$75}$ b. How much was the purchase price of Cindy's T-bills? Purchase price $= 3,000 - 75 = \underline{\$2,925}$ c. What was the effective interest rate of Cindy's T-bill investment? Round to the nearest hundredth of a percent. Effective interest rate $= \dfrac{75}{2,925 \times \dfrac{26}{52}}$ $= .05128 = \underline{5.13\%}$

TRY IT: EXERCISE SOLUTIONS FOR CHAPTER 10

1a. $I = PRT = 4,000 \times .07 \times 2.25 = \underline{\underline{\$630}}$

1b. $I = PRT = 45,000 \times .0975 \times \dfrac{3}{12} = \underline{\underline{\$1,096.88}}$

1c. $I = PRT = 130,000 \times .104 \times \dfrac{42}{12} = \underline{\underline{\$47,320}}$

2. $I = PRT = 23,000 \times .08 \times \dfrac{119}{365} = \underline{\underline{\$599.89}}$

3. $I = PRT = 15,000 \times .095 \times \dfrac{250}{360} = \underline{\underline{\$989.58}}$

4a. $I = PRT = 15,400 \times .065 \times \dfrac{24}{12} = \underline{\underline{\$2,002}}$

$MV = P + I = 15,400 + 2,002 = \underline{\underline{\$17,402}}$

4b. $MV = P(1 + RT) = 450,000 \left(1 + .08 \times \dfrac{9}{12}\right) = \underline{\underline{\$477,000}}$

5a.
$$\begin{array}{ll} 30 & \nearrow 26 \text{ April} \\ \underline{-\ 4} & \quad 61 \text{ May–June} \\ 26 \text{ Days} & \underline{+18} \text{ July} \\ & \underline{105 \text{ Days}} \end{array}$$

5b.
$$\begin{array}{ll} 30 & \nearrow 15 \text{ June} \\ \underline{-15} & \quad 92 \text{ July–Sept.} \\ 15 \text{ Days} & \underline{+9} \text{ Oct.} \\ & \underline{116 \text{ Days}} \end{array}$$

$I = PRT = 3,500 \times .11 \times \dfrac{116}{365} = \underline{\underline{\$122.36}}$

6a.
$$\begin{array}{ll} \text{Days in Sept. } 30 & 125 \text{ Days of loan} \\ \text{Loan date } \underline{-9} & \nearrow \underline{-21} \text{ Days of Sept.} \\ \text{Days of Sept. } 21 & 104 \\ & \underline{-31} \text{ October} \\ & 73 \\ & \underline{-30} \text{ November} \\ & 43 \\ & \underline{-31} \text{ December} \\ & 12 \longrightarrow \text{January 12} \end{array}$$

6b. $MV = P(1 + RT) = 9,000 \left(1 + .10 \times \dfrac{80}{360}\right) = \underline{\underline{\$9,200}}$

$$\begin{array}{ll} 31 & \nearrow 10 \text{ Oct.} \\ \underline{-21} & \quad 61 \text{ Nov.–Dec.} \\ 10 \text{ Days} & \underline{+9} \text{ Jan.} \longrightarrow \text{January 9} \\ & \overline{80 \text{ Days}} \end{array}$$

7. $P = \dfrac{I}{RT} = \dfrac{560}{.09 \times \dfrac{125}{360}} = \underline{\underline{\$17,920}}$

8. $R = \dfrac{I}{PT} = \dfrac{1,960}{25,000 \times \dfrac{245}{360}} = .1152 = \underline{\underline{11.52\%}}$

9. $I = \dfrac{I}{PR} = \dfrac{650}{15,000 \times .095} = \begin{array}{r} .4561404 \\ \times \quad 360 \\ \hline 164.2 = \underline{\underline{165 \text{ Days}}} \end{array}$

10. $I = PRT = 15,000 \times .12 \times \dfrac{20}{360} = \$100$ 1st partial payment = 20 Days

$$\begin{array}{ll} 4,000 \text{ Payment} & 15,000 \\ \underline{-100} \text{ Interest} & \underline{-3,900} \\ 3,900 & 11,100 \text{ Adjustment principal} \end{array}$$

$I = PRT = 11,100 \times .12 \times \dfrac{40}{360} = \$148$ 2nd partial payment = 40 Days $(60 - 20)$

$$\begin{array}{ll} 5,000 \text{ Payment} & 11,100 \\ \underline{-\ 148} \text{ Interest} & \underline{-4,852} \\ 4,852 & 6,248 \text{ Adjustment principal} \end{array}$$ Days remaining = 40 $(100 - 60)$

$I = PRT = 6,248 \times .12 \times \dfrac{40}{360} = \$83.31$

Final due $= P + I = 6,248.00 + 83.31 = \underline{\underline{\$6,331.31}}$

11. Bank discount $= FV \times R \times T = 20,000 \times .13 \times \dfrac{330}{360} = \underline{\underline{\$2,383.33}}$

Proceeds = Face value − Bank discount = 20,000.00 − 2,383.33 = $\underline{\underline{\$17,616.67}}$

12. Bank discount $= FV \times R \times T = 40,000 \times .11 \times \dfrac{270}{360} = \underline{\underline{\$3,300}}$

Proceeds = Face value − Bank discount = 40,000 − 3,300 = $36,700

Effective interest rate $= \dfrac{\text{Bank discount}}{\text{Proceeds} \times \text{Time}} = \dfrac{3,300}{36,700 \times \dfrac{270}{360}} = \underline{\underline{11.99\%}}$

CHAPTER 10

13. $MV = P(1 + RT) = 35{,}000 \left(1 + .10 \times \dfrac{6}{12}\right) = \underline{\$36{,}750}$

$$\begin{array}{r} 6 \text{ months} \\ -\,4 \text{ months} \\ \hline \end{array}$$

Discount period = 2 months

Bank discount $= MV \times R \times T = 36{,}750 \times .14 \times \dfrac{2}{12} = \$857.50$

Proceeds = Maturity value − Bank discount = \$36,750.00 − 857.50 = $\underline{\$35{,}892.50}$

14. a. Interest = Face value × Discount rate × Time $= 10{,}000 \times .046 \times \dfrac{26}{52} = \underline{\$230}$

b. Purchase price = Face value − Interest = 10,000 − 230 = $\underline{\$9{,}770}$

c. Effective interest rate $= \dfrac{\text{Interest}}{\text{Purchase price} \times \text{Time}} = \dfrac{230}{9{,}770 \times \dfrac{26}{52}} = .04708 = \underline{4.71\%}$

CONCEPT REVIEW

1. The price or rental fee charged by a lender to a borrower for the use of money is known as _____. (10-1)

2. List the three factors that determine the amount of interest charged on a loan. (10-1)

3. Interest calculated solely on the principal amount borrowed is known as _____ interest, whereas interest calculated at regular intervals on the principal and previously earned interest is known as _____ interest. (10-1)

4. The interest calculation method that uses 365 days (366 in leap year) as the time factor denominator is known as _____ interest. (10-2)

5. The interest calculation method that uses 360 days as the time factor denominator is known as _____ interest. (10-2)

6. Maturity value is the total payback of principal and interest of a loan. List the two formulas for calculating maturity value. (10-3)

7. The first day of a loan is known as the _____ date; the last day of a loan is known as the _____ date. (10-4, 10-5)

8. Write the formula for calculating simple interest. (10-6)

9. When solving the simple interest formula for principal, rate, or time, the _____ is always the numerator. (10-6, 10-7, 10-8)

10. The U.S. rule states that when a partial payment is made on a loan, the payment is first used to pay off the accumulated _____ to date and the balance is used to reduce the _____. (10-9)

11. The amount of money that the borrower receives at the time a discounted note is made is known as the _____. (10-10)

12. The actual interest rate charged on a discounted note is known as the _____, or _____, interest rate. (10-11)

13. When a note is discounted before maturity, the proceeds are calculated by subtracting the amount of the bank discount from the _____ value of the loan. (10-12)

14. Discounted short-term loans made to the U.S. government are known as U.S. Treasury _____. (10-13)

ASSESSMENT TEST

Using the exact interest method (365 days), find the amount of interest on the following loans.

	Principal	Rate (%)	Time (days)	Exact Interest
1.	$15,000	13	120	_____
2.	$1,700	$12\frac{1}{2}$	33	_____

Using the ordinary interest method (360 days), find the amount of interest on the following loans.

	Principal	Rate (%)	Time (days)	Ordinary Interest
3.	$20,600	6%	98	_____
4.	$286,000	$13\frac{1}{2}$	224	_____

What is the maturity value of the following loans? Use $MV = P(1 + RT)$ to find the maturity values.

	Principal	Rate (%)	Time	Maturity Value
5.	$15,800	7	4 years	_____
6.	$100,000	$6\frac{3}{4}$	7 months	_____

From the following information, determine the number of days of each loan.

	Loan Date	Due Date	Number of Days
7.	April 16	August 1	_____
8.	October 20	December 18	_____

From the following information, determine the maturity date of each loan.

	Loan Date	Time Loan (days)	Maturity Date
9.	November 30	55	_____
10.	May 15	111	_____

Compute the principal for the following loans. Round answers to the nearest cent.

	Principal	Rate (%)	Time	Interest
11.	_____	7	2 years	$2,800
12.	_____	$10\frac{1}{2}$	10 months	$5,900

Compute the rate for the following loans. Round answers to the nearest tenth of a percent.

	Principal	Rate (%)	Time	Interest
13.	$2,200	_____	4 years	$800
14.	$50,000	_____	9 months	$4,500

Use the ordinary interest method to compute the time for the following loans. Round answers to the next higher day when necessary.

	Principal	Rate (%)	Time (days)	Interest
15.	$13,500	6	_____	$350
16.	$7,900	10.4	_____	$625

Calculate the missing information for the following loans. Round percents to the nearest tenth and days to the next higher day when necessary.

	Principal	Rate (%)	Time (days)	Interest Method	Interest	Maturity Value
17.	$13,000	14	_____	Ordinary	$960	_____
18.	_____	12.2	133	Exact	$1,790	_____
19.	$2,500	_____	280	Ordinary	$295	_____

CHAPTER 10

Using ordinary interest, calculate the missing information for the following simple discount notes.

	Face Value	Discount Rate (%)	Date of Note	Term (days)	Maturity Date	Bank Discount	Proceeds
20.	$50,000	13	Apr. 5	_____	Aug. 14	_____	_____
21.	$875,000	$9\frac{1}{2}$	Oct. 25	87	_____	_____	_____

Using ordinary interest (360 days), calculate the bank discount, proceeds, and effective rate for the following simple discount notes. Round effective rate to the nearest hundredth of a percent.

	Face Value	Discount Rate (%)	Term (days)	Bank Discount	Proceeds	Effective Rate (%)
22.	$22,500	$10\frac{1}{2}$	60	_____	_____	_____
23.	$290,000	11.9	110	_____	_____	_____

The following interest-bearing promissory notes were discounted at a bank by the payee before maturity. Use the ordinary interest method (360 days) to solve for the missing information.

	Face Value	Interest Rate (%)	Date of Note	Term of Note (days)	Maturity Date	Maturity Value	Date Note Discounted	Discount Period (days)	Discount Rate (%)	Proceeds
24.	$8,000	11	Jan. 12	83	_____	_____	Mar. 1	_____	15	_____
25.	$5,500	$13\frac{1}{2}$	June 17	69	_____	_____	July 22	_____	13.7	_____

Calculate the interest, purchase price, and effective interest rate of the following Treasury bill (T-bill) purchases. Round effective interest rate to the nearest hundredth of a percent.

	Face Value	Discount Rate (%)	Term (weeks)	Interest	Purchase Price	Effective Rate (%)
26.	$75,000	5.15	4	_____	_____	_____
27.	$28,000	4.90	26	_____	_____	_____

Solve the following word problems. Round to the nearest cent when necessary.

28. On May 23, Samantha Best borrowed $4,000 from the Tri City Credit Union at 13% for 160 days. The credit union uses the exact interest method.

   a. What was the amount of interest on the loan?

   b. What was the maturity value of the loan?

   c. What is the maturity date of the loan?

29. Ronald Brown missed an income tax payment of $2,600. The Internal Revenue Service charges a 15% simple interest penalty calculated by the exact interest method. If the tax was due on April 15 but was paid on July 17, what was the amount of the penalty charge?

30. Katie Chalmers borrowed money from her credit union at 13.2% simple interest to buy furniture. If the loan was repaid in $2\frac{1}{2}$ years and the amount of interest was $1,320, how much did Katie borrow?

31. Ryan Roberts took out a loan for $5,880 at the Linville Ridge Bank for 110 days. The bank uses the ordinary method for calculating interest. What rate of interest was charged if the amount of interest was $152? Round to the nearest tenth of a percent.

32. Alicia Eastman deposited $2,000 in a savings account at the Biltmone Bank paying 6% ordinary interest. How long will it take for her investment to amount to $2,600?

33. Laurie Carron borrowed $16,000 at 14% ordinary interest for 88 days. On day 30 of the loan, she made a partial payment of $7,000. What was the new maturity value of the loan?

34. Euromart Tile Company borrowed $40,000 on April 6 for 66 days. The rate was 14% using the ordinary interest method. On day 25 of the loan, Euromart made a partial payment of $15,000, and on day 45 of the loan, Euromart made a second partial payment of $10,000.

    a. What was the new maturity value of the loan?

    b. What was the maturity date of the loan?

35. Brandi Lee signed a $30,000 simple discount promissory note at the Signature Bank. The discount rate was 13% ordinary interest, and the note was made on August 9 for 95 days.

    a. What proceeds did Brandi receive on the note?

    b. What was the maturity date of the note?

    c. What was the effective interest rate of the note? Round the answer to the nearest hundredth of a percent.

CHAPTER 10

36. Varsity Press, a publisher of college textbooks, received a $70,000 promissory note at 12% ordinary interest for 60 days from one of its customers, Reader's Choice Bookstores. After 20 days, Varsity Press discounted the note at the Grove Isle Bank at a discount rate of 14.5%. The note was made on March 21.

   a. What was the maturity date of the note?

   b. What was the maturity value of the note?

   c. What was the discount date of the note?

   d. What proceeds did Varsity Press receive after discounting the note?

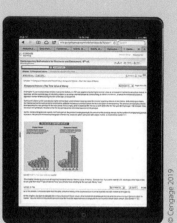

© Cengage 2019

On-campus and online **bookstores** are the main sources of textbooks for college students. Electronic textbooks represent an ever-increasing portion of total textbook sales. Some digital textbooks can be made to expire anywhere from 6 to 18 months after the date of purchase.

37. Fernando Rodriguez purchased $64,000 in U.S. Treasury bills with a discount rate of 4.7% for a period of 13 weeks.

   a. How much interest did Fernando earn on the T-bill investment?

   b. How much was the purchase price of Fernando's T-bills?

   c. What was the effective interest rate of Fernando's T-bill investment? Round to the nearest hundredth of a percent.

BUSINESS DECISION: BORROWING TO TAKE ADVANTAGE OF A CASH DISCOUNT

EXCEL 3

38. You are the accountant for Suite Dreams, a retail furniture store. Recently, an order of sofas and chairs was received from a manufacturer with terms of 3/15, n/45. The order amounted to $230,000, and Suite Dreams can borrow money at 13% ordinary interest.

   a. How much can be saved by borrowing the funds for 30 days to take advantage of the cash discount? (Remember, Suite Dreams must borrow only the net amount due after the cash discount is taken.)

Dollars AND Sense

This Business Decision illustrates an important business concept—borrowing money to take advantage of a cash discount.

Note how much can be saved by taking the cash discount even if the money is borrowed.

For a review of cash discounts, see Section IV in Chapter 7.

iStock.com/vreemous

   b. What would you recommend?

COLLABORATIVE LEARNING ACTIVITY

The Automobile Loan

As a team, choose a particular type of automobile category that you want to research (such as sport utility vehicle, sports car, hybrid, or luxury sedan). Then have each member of the team choose a different manufacturer's model within that category.

   For example, if the team picked sport utility vehicle, individual choices might include Chevy Equinox, Mazda CX-7, Ford Escape, or Honda CRV.

a. From your local newspaper and the Internet, collect advertisements and offers for the purchase of the model you have chosen.

b. Visit or call a dealership for the vehicle you picked. Speak with a salesperson about the types of "deals" currently being offered on that model.

 • What loan rates and terms are available from the dealer?
 • Who is the actual lender?

c. Contact various lending institutions (banks, finance companies, credit unions) and inquire about vehicle loans.

 • What loan rates and terms are being offered?
 • Which lending institution is offering the best deal? Why?
 • How do these rates and terms compare with those from the dealership?

PERFORMANCE OBJECTIVES

COMPOUND INTEREST—THE TIME VALUE OF MONEY

In Chapter 10, we studied simple interest in which the formula $I = PRT$ was applied once during the term of a loan or an investment to find the amount of interest. In business, another common way of calculating interest is by using a method known as *compounding*, or **compound interest**, in which the interest calculation is applied a number of times during the term of the loan or investment.

Compound interest yields considerably higher interest than simple interest does because the investor is earning interest on the interest. With compound interest, the interest earned for each period is reinvested or added to the previous principal before the next calculation or compounding. The previous principal plus interest then becomes the new principal for the next period. For example, $100 invested at 8% interest is worth $108 after the first year ($100 principal + $8 interest). If the interest is not withdrawn, the interest for the next period will be calculated based on $108 principal.

As this compounding process repeats itself each period, the principal keeps growing by the amount of the previous interest. As the number of compounding periods increases, the amount of interest earned grows dramatically, especially when compared with simple interest, as illustrated in Exhibit 11-1.

compound interest Interest that is applied a number of times during the term of a loan or an investment. Interest paid on principal and previously earned interest.

EXHIBIT 11-1 The Time Value of Money

THE VALUE OF COMPOUND INTEREST

The growth of an investment may vary greatly depending on whether simple or compound interest is involved. For example, the chart below shows the growth of $1,000 invested in an account paying 10% annual simple interest versus the same amount invested in an account paying 10% annual compound interest. As this chart shows, compound interest yields more than four times the value generated by simple interest over 30 years.

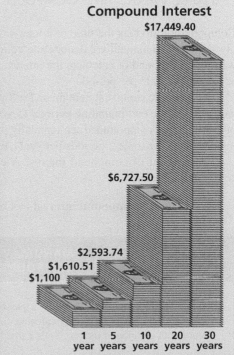

Simple Interest

$4,000
$3,000
$2,000
$1,500
$1,100

| 1 year | 5 years | 10 years | 20 years | 30 years |

Compound Interest

$17,449.40
$6,727.50
$2,593.74
$1,610.51
$1,100

| 1 year | 5 years | 10 years | 20 years | 30 years |

This chapter introduces you to an all-important business concept, the **time value of money**. Consider this: If you were owed $1,000, would you rather have it now or 1 year from now? If you answered "now," you already have a feeling for the concept. Money "now,"

time value of money The idea that money "now," or in the present, is more desirable than the same amount of money in the future because it can be invested and earn interest as time goes by.

compound amount, or future value (FV) The total amount of principal and accumulated interest at the end of a loan or an investment.

present amount, or present value (PV) An amount of money that must be deposited today at compound interest to provide a specified lump sum of money in the future.

or in the *present*, is more desirable than the same amount of money in the *future* because it can be invested and earn interest as time goes by.

In this chapter, you learn to calculate the **compound amount (future value)** of an investment at compound interest when the **present amount (present value)** is known. You also learn to calculate the present value that must be deposited now at compound interest to yield a known future amount. (See Exhibit 11-2.)

EXHIBIT 11-2   Present Value and Future Value at Compound Interest

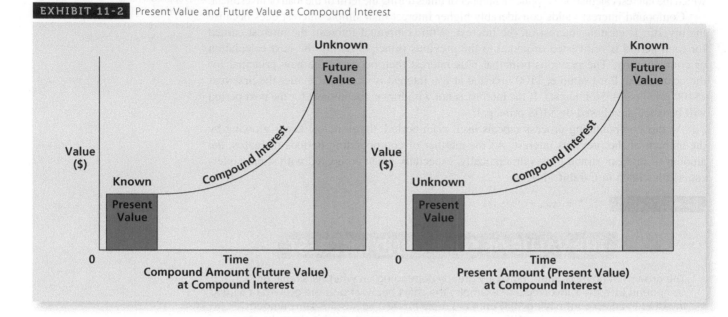

11-1   **MANUALLY CALCULATING COMPOUND AMOUNT (FUTURE VALUE) AND COMPOUND INTEREST**

The Time Value of Money

Compounding divides the time of a loan or an investment into compounding periods or simply periods. To manually calculate the compound amount or future value of an investment, we must compound or calculate the interest as many times as there are compounding periods at the interest rate per period.

For example, an investment made for 5 years at 6% compounded annually (once per year) would have five compounding periods (5 years × 1 period per year), each at 6%. If the same investment was compounded semiannually (two times per year), there would be 10 compounding periods (5 years × 2 periods per year), each at 3% (6% annual rate ÷ 2 periods per year).

The amount of compound interest is calculated by subtracting the principal from the compound amount.

Compound interest = Compound amount − Principal

EXAMPLE1   MANUALLY CALCULATING COMPOUND INTEREST

a. Katie Trotta invested $20,000 in a passbook savings account at 5% interest compounded annually for 2 years. Manually calculate the compound amount of the investment and the total amount of compound interest Katie earned.

▶SOLUTIONSTRATEGY

To solve this compound interest problem manually, we must apply the simple interest formula twice because there are two compounding periods (2 years × 1 period per year). Note how the interest from the first period is reinvested or added to the original principal to earn interest in the second period.

Original principal	$20,000.00	
Interest—period 1	+ 1,000.00	($I = PRT = 20{,}000.00 \times .05 \times 1$)
Principal—period 2	21,000.00	
Interest—period 2	+ 1,050.00	($I = PRT = 21{,}000.00 \times .05 \times 1$)
Compound Amount	$22,050.00	

Compound amount	$22,050.00
Principal	− 20,000.00
Compound Interest Earned	$2,050.00

b. Manually recalculate the compound amount and compound interest from the previous example by using semiannual compounding (two times per year). How much more interest would Katie earn if the bank offered semiannual compounding?

▶SOLUTIONSTRATEGY

To solve this compound interest problem, we must apply the simple interest formula four times because there are four compounding periods (2 years × 2 periods per year). Note that the time factor is now $\frac{6}{12}$, or $\frac{1}{2}$, because semiannual compounding means every 6 months.

Original principal	$20,000.00	
Interest—period 1	+ 500.00	($I = PRT = 20{,}000.00 \times .05 \times \frac{1}{2}$)
Principal—period 2	20,500.00	
Interest—period 2	+ 512.50	($I = PRT = 20{,}500.00 \times .05 \times \frac{1}{2}$)
Principal—period 3	21,012.50	
Interest—period 3	+ 525.31	($I = PRT = 21{,}012.50 \times .05 \times \frac{1}{2}$)
Principal—period 4	21,537.81	
Interest—period 4	+ 538.45	($I = PRT = 21{,}537.81 \times .05 \times \frac{1}{2}$)
Compound Amount	$22,076.26	

Compound amount	$22,076.26
Principal	− 20,000.00
Compound Interest	$2,076.26

For the same investment values, semiannual compounding yields $26.26 more than annual compounding:

Interest with semiannual compounding	2,076.26
Interest with annual compounding	− 2,050.00
	$26.26

▶TRYITEXERCISE 1

Gail Parker invested $10,000 at 6% interest compounded semiannually for 3 years. Manually calculate the compound amount and the compound interest of Gail's investment.

CHECK YOUR ANSWERS WITH THE SOLUTIONS ON PAGE 373.

COMPUTING COMPOUND AMOUNT (FUTURE VALUE) AND COMPOUND INTEREST BY USING COMPOUND INTEREST TABLES

11-2

You do not have to work many compound interest problems manually, particularly those with numerous compounding periods, before you start wishing for an easier way! In actuality, there are two other methods for solving compound interest problems. The first uses a compound interest formula, and the second uses compound interest tables.

The compound interest formula, $A = P(1 + i)^n$, contains an exponent and therefore requires the use of a calculator with an exponential function key. The use of the compound interest formula is covered in Performance Objective 11-5.

A compound interest table, such as Table 11-1 on page 354, is a useful set of factors that represent the future values of $1 at various interest rates for a number of compounding

TABLE 11-1   Compound Interest Table (Future Value of $1 at Compound Interest)

Periods	$\frac{1}{2}\%$	1%	$1\frac{1}{2}\%$	2%	3%	4%	5%	6%	7%	8%	Periods
1	1.00500	1.01000	1.01500	1.02000	1.03000	1.04000	1.05000	1.06000	1.07000	1.08000	1
2	1.01003	1.02010	1.03023	1.04040	1.06090	1.08160	1.10250	1.12360	1.14490	1.16640	2
3	1.01508	1.03030	1.04568	1.06121	1.09273	1.12486	1.15763	1.19102	1.22504	1.25971	3
4	1.02015	1.04060	1.06136	1.08243	1.12551	1.16986	1.21551	1.26248	1.31080	1.36049	4
5	1.02525	1.05101	1.07728	1.10408	1.15927	1.21665	1.27628	1.33823	1.40255	1.46933	5
6	1.03038	1.06152	1.09344	1.12616	1.19405	1.26532	1.34010	1.41852	1.50073	1.58687	6
7	1.03553	1.07214	1.10984	1.14869	1.22987	1.31593	1.40710	1.50363	1.60578	1.71382	7
8	1.04071	1.08286	1.12649	1.17166	1.26677	1.36857	1.47746	1.59385	1.71819	1.85093	8
9	1.04591	1.09369	1.14339	1.19509	1.30477	1.42331	1.55133	1.68948	1.83846	1.99900	9
10	1.05114	1.10462	1.16054	1.21899	1.34392	1.48024	1.62889	1.79085	1.96715	2.15892	10
11	1.05640	1.11567	1.17795	1.24337	1.38423	1.53945	1.71034	1.89830	2.10485	2.33164	11
12	1.06168	1.12683	1.19562	1.26824	1.42576	1.60103	1.79586	2.01220	2.25219	2.51817	12
13	1.06699	1.13809	1.21355	1.29361	1.46853	1.66507	1.88565	2.13293	2.40985	2.71962	13
14	1.07232	1.14947	1.23176	1.31948	1.51259	1.73168	1.97993	2.26090	2.57853	2.93719	14
15	1.07768	1.16097	1.25023	1.34587	1.55797	1.80094	2.07893	2.39656	2.75903	3.17217	15
16	1.08307	1.17258	1.26899	1.37279	1.60471	1.87298	2.18287	2.54035	2.95216	3.42594	16
17	1.08849	1.18430	1.28802	1.40024	1.65285	1.94790	2.29202	2.69277	3.15882	3.70002	17
18	1.09393	1.19615	1.30734	1.42825	1.70243	2.02582	2.40662	2.85434	3.37993	3.99602	18
19	1.09940	1.20811	1.32695	1.45681	1.75351	2.10685	2.52695	3.02560	3.61653	4.31570	19
20	1.10490	1.22019	1.34686	1.48595	1.80611	2.19112	2.65330	3.20714	3.86968	4.66096	20
21	1.11042	1.23239	1.36706	1.51567	1.86029	2.27877	2.78596	3.39956	4.14056	5.03383	21
22	1.11597	1.24472	1.38756	1.54598	1.91610	2.36992	2.92526	3.60354	4.43040	5.43654	22
23	1.12155	1.25716	1.40838	1.57690	1.97359	2.46472	3.07152	3.81975	4.74053	5.87146	23
24	1.12716	1.26973	1.42950	1.60844	2.03279	2.56330	3.22510	4.04893	5.07237	6.34118	24
25	1.13280	1.28243	1.45095	1.64061	2.09378	2.66584	3.38635	4.29187	5.42743	6.84848	25

Periods	9%	10%	11%	12%	13%	14%	15%	16%	17%	18%	Periods
1	1.09000	1.10000	1.11000	1.12000	1.13000	1.14000	1.15000	1.16000	1.17000	1.18000	1
2	1.18810	1.21000	1.23210	1.25440	1.27690	1.29960	1.32250	1.34560	1.36890	1.39240	2
3	1.29503	1.33100	1.36763	1.40493	1.44290	1.48154	1.52088	1.56090	1.60161	1.64303	3
4	1.41158	1.46410	1.51807	1.57352	1.63047	1.68896	1.74901	1.81064	1.87389	1.93878	4
5	1.53862	1.61051	1.68506	1.76234	1.84244	1.92541	2.01136	2.10034	2.19245	2.28776	5
6	1.67710	1.77156	1.87041	1.97382	2.08195	2.19497	2.31306	2.43640	2.56516	2.69955	6
7	1.82804	1.94872	2.07616	2.21068	2.35261	2.50227	2.66002	2.82622	3.00124	3.18547	7
8	1.99256	2.14359	2.30454	2.47596	2.65844	2.85259	3.05902	3.27841	3.51145	3.75886	8
9	2.17189	2.35795	2.55804	2.77308	3.00404	3.25195	3.51788	3.80296	4.10840	4.43545	9
10	2.36736	2.59374	2.83942	3.10585	3.39457	3.70722	4.04556	4.41144	4.80683	5.23384	10
11	2.58043	2.85312	3.15176	3.47855	3.83586	4.22623	4.65239	5.11726	5.62399	6.17593	11
12	2.81266	3.13843	3.49845	3.89598	4.33452	4.81790	5.35025	5.93603	6.58007	7.28759	12
13	3.06580	3.45227	3.88328	4.36349	4.89801	5.49241	6.15279	6.88579	7.69868	8.59936	13
14	3.34173	3.79750	4.31044	4.88711	5.53475	6.26135	7.07571	7.98752	9.00745	10.14724	14
15	3.64248	4.17725	4.78459	5.47357	6.25427	7.13794	8.13706	9.26552	10.53872	11.97375	15
16	3.97031	4.59497	5.31089	6.13039	7.06733	8.13725	9.35762	10.74800	12.33030	14.12902	16
17	4.32763	5.05447	5.89509	6.86604	7.98608	9.27646	10.76126	12.46768	14.42646	16.67225	17
18	4.71712	5.55992	6.54355	7.68997	9.02427	10.57517	12.37545	14.46251	16.87895	19.67325	18
19	5.14166	6.11591	7.26334	8.61276	10.19742	12.05569	14.23177	16.77652	19.74838	23.21444	19
20	5.60441	6.72750	8.06231	9.64629	11.52309	13.74349	16.36654	19.46076	23.10560	27.39303	20
21	6.10881	7.40025	8.94917	10.80385	13.02109	15.66758	18.82152	22.57448	27.03355	32.32378	21
22	6.65860	8.14027	9.93357	12.10031	14.71383	17.86104	21.64475	26.18640	31.62925	38.14206	22
23	7.25787	8.95430	11.02627	13.55235	16.62663	20.36158	24.89146	30.37622	37.00623	45.00763	23
24	7.91108	9.84973	12.23916	15.17863	18.78809	23.21221	28.62518	35.23642	43.29729	53.10901	24
25	8.62308	10.83471	13.58546	17.00006	21.23054	26.46192	32.91895	40.87424	50.65783	62.66863	25

The values in Table 11-1 were generated by the formula $FV = (1 + i)^n$ rounded to five decimal places, where i is the interest rate per period and n is the total number of periods.

Interest Compounded		Compounding Periods per Year
Annually	Every year	1
Semiannually	Every 6 months	2
Quarterly	Every 3 months	4
Monthly	Every month	12
Daily	Every day	365
Continuously		Infinite

EXHIBIT 11-3
Compounding Periods per Year

periods. Because these factors are based on $1, the future values of other principal amounts are found by multiplying the appropriate table factor by the number of dollars of principal.

$$\text{Compound amount (future value)} = \text{Table factor} \times \text{Principal}$$

To use the compound interest tables, we must know the number of compounding periods and the interest rate per period. Exhibit 11-3 above shows the various compounding options and the corresponding number of periods per year. *Note:* The greater the number of compounding periods per year, the higher the interest earned on the investment. Today interest can actually be calculated on a continuous basis—that is, up to the minute. In competitive markets, many banks offer continuous compounding as an incentive to attract new deposits.

To find the number of compounding periods of an investment, multiply the number of years by the number of periods per year.

$$\text{Compounding periods} = \text{Years} \times \text{Periods per year}$$

To find the interest rate per period, divide the annual, or nominal, rate by the number of periods per year.

$$\text{Interest rate per period} = \frac{\text{Nominal rate}}{\text{Period per year}}$$

IN THE Business World

Today most banks, savings and loan institutions, and credit unions pay compound interest on depositors' money. The U.S. government also uses compounding for savings bonds.

rtguest/Shutterstock.com

STEPS FOR USING COMPOUND INTEREST TABLES

STEP 1. Scan across the top row to find the interest rate per period.

STEP 2. Look down that column to the row corresponding to the number of periods.

STEP 3. The table factor at the intersection of the rate-per-period column and the number-of-periods row is the future value of $1 at compound interest. Multiply the table factor by the principal to determine the compound amount.

$$\text{Compound amount} = \text{Table factor} \times \text{Principal}$$

iStock.com/Nikada

EXAMPLE2 USING COMPOUND INTEREST TABLES

John Anderson invested $1,200 in an account at 8% interest compounded quarterly for 5 years. Use Table 11-1 to find the compound amount of John's investment. What is the amount of the compound interest?

►SOLUTIONSTRATEGY

To solve this compound interest problem, we must first find the interest rate per period and the number of compounding periods.

$$\text{Interest rate per period} = \frac{\text{Nominal rate}}{\text{Periods per year}}$$

$$\text{Interest rate per period} = \frac{8\%}{4} = 2\%$$

$$\text{Compounding periods} = \text{Years} \times \text{Periods per year}$$

$$\text{Compounding periods} = 5 \times 4 = 20$$

Dollars AND Sense

The Federal Deposit Insurance Corporation (FDIC) is an independent agency of the U.S. government that protects the funds depositors place in banks and savings associations. FDIC insurance is backed by the full faith and credit of the U.S. government. FDIC insurance covers all deposit accounts, including checking and savings accounts, money market deposit accounts, and certificates of deposit.

The standard insurance amount currently is $250,000 per depositor, per insured bank.

iStock.com/vreemous

Now find the table factor by scanning across the top row of the compound interest table to 2% and down the 2% column to 20 periods. The table factor at that intersection is 1.48595. The compound amount is found by multiplying the table factor by the principal:

$$\text{Compound amount} = \text{Table factor} \times \text{Principal}$$
$$\text{Compound amount} = 1.48595 \times 1,200 = \$1,783.14$$

The amount of interest is found by subtracting the principal from the compound amount.

$$\text{Compound interest} = \text{Compound amount} - \text{Principal}$$
$$\text{Compound interest} = 1,783.14 - 1,200.00 = \$583.14$$

▶TRYITEXERCISE 2

Jenny Chao invested $20,000 at 6% interest compounded semiannually for 8 years. Use Table 11-1 to find the compound amount of her investment. What is the amount of compound interest Jenny earned?

CHECK YOUR ANSWERS WITH THE SOLUTIONS ON PAGE 373.

11-3 CREATING COMPOUND INTEREST TABLE FACTORS FOR PERIODS BEYOND THE TABLE

When the number of periods of an investment is greater than the number of periods provided by the compound interest table, you can compute a new table factor by multiplying the factors for any two periods that add up to the number of periods required. For answer consistency in this chapter, use the two table factors that represent *half*, or values as close as possible to half, of the periods required. For example,

20 periods
20 periods ⟶ 40 periods

20 periods
21 periods ⟶ 41 periods

STEPS FOR CREATING NEW COMPOUND INTEREST TABLE FACTORS

STEP 1. For the stated interest rate per period, find the two table factors that represent *half*, or values as close as possible to half, of the periods required.

STEP 2. Multiply the two table factors from Step 1 to form the new factor.

STEP 3. Round the new factor to five decimal places.

EXAMPLE3 CALCULATING COMPOUND AMOUNT FOR PERIODS BEYOND THE TABLE

Calculate a new table factor and find the compound amount of $10,000 invested at 6% compounded monthly for 3 years.

▶SOLUTIONSTRATEGY

This investment requires a table factor for 36 periods (12 periods per year for 3 years). Because Table 11-1 provides factors only up to 25 periods, we must create one using the steps above.

iStock.com/Nikada

Step 1. At 6% interest compounded monthly, the rate per period is $\frac{1}{2}$%. Because we are looking for 36 periods, we will use the factors for 18 and 18 periods at $\frac{1}{2}$%.

Table factor for 18 periods, $\frac{1}{2}$% = 1.09393

Table factor for 18 periods, $\frac{1}{2}$% = 1.09393

Step 2. Multiply the factors for 18 and 18 periods.

$$1.09393 \times 1.09393 = 1.196682$$

Step 3. Round to five decimal places.

The new table factor for 36 periods is 1.19668.

The compound amount of the $10,000 investment is

Compound amount = Table factor × Principal

Compound amount = 1.19668 × 10,000 = $11,966.80

▶ TRYITEXERCISE 3

Stan Gray invests $3,500 at 8% interest compounded quarterly for 7 years. Calculate a new table factor and find the compound amount of Stan's investment.

CHECK YOUR ANSWERS WITH THE SOLUTIONS ON PAGE 373.

CALCULATING ANNUAL PERCENTAGE YIELD (APY) OR EFFECTIVE INTEREST RATE

11-4

In describing investments and loans, the advertised or stated interest rate is known as the **annual**, or **nominal, rate**. It is also the rate used to calculate the compound interest. Consider, however, what happens to an investment of $100 at 12% nominal interest.

As we learned in Performance Objective 11-2, the greater the number of compounding periods per year, the higher the amount of interest earned. (See Exhibit 11-4.) Although the nominal interest rate is 12%, with monthly compounding, the $100 earns more than 12%. This is why many investment offers today advertise daily or continuous compounding. How much are these investments really earning?

annual, or nominal, rate The advertised or stated interest rate of an investment or loan. The rate used to calculate the compound interest.

Compounding	Interest Earned
Annually	$12.00
Semiannually	$12.36
Quarterly	$12.55
Monthly	$12.68

EXHIBIT 11-4

Compound Interest Earned on $100 at 12%

The **annual percentage yield (APY)**, or **effective rate**, reflects the real rate of return on an investment. APY is calculated by finding the total compound interest earned in 1 year and dividing by the principal. *Note*: This is actually the simple interest formula (from Chapter 10) solved for rate $R = I \div PT$, where T is equal to 1.

$$\text{Annual percentage (APY)} = \frac{\text{Total compound interest earned in 1 year}}{\text{Principal}}$$

annual percentage yield (APY), or effective rate The real or true rate of return on an investment. It is the total compound interest earned in 1 year divided by the principal. The more compounding periods per year, the higher the APY.

From Exhibit 11-4, we can see that the annual percentage yield is the same as the nominal rate when interest is compounded annually; however, it jumps to 12.36% ($12.36) when the compounding is changed to semiannually and to 12.68 % ($12.68) when compounded monthly.

EXAMPLE4   CALCULATING APY

What is the compound amount, compound interest, and annual percentage yield of $4,000 invested for 1 year at 8% compounded semiannually?

▶SOLUTIONSTRATEGY

First, we must find the total compound interest earned in 1 year. We can find the compound amount using the factor for 4%, two periods, from Table 11-1.

$$\text{Compound amount} = \text{Table factor} \times \text{Principal}$$
$$\text{Compound amount} = 1.08160 \times 4,000 = \underline{\$4,326.40}$$

$$\text{Compound interest} = \text{Compound amount} - \text{Principal}$$
$$\text{Compound interest} = 4,326.40 - 4,000 = \underline{\$326.40}$$

$$\text{Annual percentage yield} = \frac{\text{Total compound interest earned in 1 year}}{\text{Principal}}$$

$$\text{Annual percentage yield} = \frac{326.40}{4,000.00} = \underline{8.16\%}$$

▶TRYITEXERCISE 4

Jill Quinn invested $7,000 in a certificate of deposit for 1 year at 6% interest compounded quarterly. What is the compound amount, compound interest, and annual percentage yield of Jill's investment? Round the APY to the nearest hundredth of a percent.

CHECK YOUR ANSWERS WITH THE SOLUTIONS ON PAGE 373.

11-5   CALCULATING COMPOUND AMOUNT (FUTURE VALUE) BY USING THE COMPOUND INTEREST FORMULA

If your calculator has an exponential function key, y^x, you can calculate the compound amount of an investment by using the compound interest formula.

The compound interest formula states:

$$A = P(1 + i)^n$$

where:

A = **Compound amount**

P = **Principal**

i = **Interest rate per period (expressed as a decimal)**

n = **Total compounding periods (years × periods per year)**

STEPS FOR SOLVING THE COMPOUND INTEREST FORMULA

STEP 1. Add the 1 and the interest rate per period, i.

STEP 2. Raise the sum from Step 1 to the nth (number of compounding periods) power by using the y^x key on your calculator.

STEP 3. Multiply the principal, P, by the answer from Step 2.

Calculator Sequence: 1 $+$ i $=$ y^x n $\times$ P $=$ A

EXAMPLE5   USING THE COMPOUND INTEREST FORMULA

Use the compound interest formula to calculate the compound amount of $5,000 invested at 10% interest compounded semiannually for 3 years.

SOLUTIONSTRATEGY

This problem is solved by substituting the investment information into the compound interest formula. It is important to solve the formula using the sequence of steps outlined above. Note that the rate per period, i, is 5% (10% ÷ 2 periods per year). The total number of periods, the exponent n, is 6 (3 years × 2 periods per year).

$$A = P\,(1 + i)^n$$
$$A = 5,000\,(1 + .05)^6$$
$$A = 5,000\,(1.05)^6$$
$$A = 5,000\,(1.3400956) = 6,700.4782 = \$6,700.48$$

Calculator Sequence: 1 $+$ .05 $=$ y^x 6 $\times$ 5000 $=$ $6,700.4782 = \underline{\$6,700.48}$

▶TRYITEXERCISE 5

Use the compound interest formula to calculate the compound amount of $3,000 invested at 8% interest compounded quarterly for 5 years.

CHECK YOUR ANSWER WITH THE SOLUTION ON PAGE 373.

REVIEW EXERCISES

11 SECTION I

For the following investments, find the total number of compounding periods and the interest rate per period.

JUMP START WWW

	Term of Investment	Nominal (Annual) Rate (%)	Interest Compounded	Compounding Periods	Rate per Period (%)
1.	3 years	13	annually	3	13
2.	5 years	4	quarterly		
3.	12 years	8	semiannually		
4.	6 years	6	monthly		
5.	4 years	6	quarterly		
6.	9 years	5.5	semiannually		
7.	9 months	4	quarterly		

Manually calculate the compound amount and compound interest for the following investments.

	Principal	Time Period (years)	Nominal Rate (%)	Interest Compounded	Compound Amount	Compound Interest
8.	$4,000	2	10	annually	$4,840.00	$840.00
9.	$10,000	1	4	quarterly	_____	_____
10.	$8,000	3	8	semiannually	_____	_____

11. Brian invests $10,500, at 6% interest, compounded semiannually for 2 years. Manually calculate the compound amount for his investment.

Using Table 11-1, calculate the compound amount and compound interest for the following investments.

	Principal	Time Period (years)	Nominal Rate (%)	Interest Compounded	Compound Amount	Compound Interest
12.	$7,000	4	13	annually	$11,413.29	$4,413.29
13.	$11,000	6	4	semiannually	_____	_____
14.	$5,300	3	8	quarterly	_____	_____
15.	$67,000	2	18	monthly	_____	_____
16.	$25,000	15	5	annually	_____	_____
17.	$400	2	6	monthly	_____	_____

18. Suppose that you invest $8,000 at 6% interest, compound quarterly, for 5 years. use Table 11-1 to calculate the compound interest on your investment.

The following investments require table factors for periods beyond the table. Create the new table factor, rounded to five places, and calculate the compound amount for each.

	Principal	Time Period (years)	Nominal Rate (%)	Interest Compounded	New Table Factor	Compound Amount
19.	$13,000	3	12	monthly	1.43077	$18,600.01
20.	$19,000	29	9	annually	_____	_____
21.	$34,700	11	4	quarterly	_____	_____
22.	$10,000	40	3	annually	_____	_____

23. Use Table 11-1 to calculate the compound amount on an investment of $4,500 at 8% interest, compounded semiannually, for 15 years.

For the following investments, compute the amount of compound interest earned in 1 year and the annual percentage yield (APY).

	Principal	Nominal Rate (%)	Interest Compounded	Compound Interest Earned in 1 Year	Annual Percentage Yield (APY)
24.	$5,000	10	semiannually	$512.50	10.25%
25.	$2,000	4	annually	_____	_____
26.	$36,000	12	monthly	_____	_____
27.	$1,000	8	quarterly	_____	_____

28. Maria invests $3,500, at 6% interest, compounded quarterly for one year. Use Table 11-1 to calculate the annual percentage yield (APY) for her investment. Note: "Annual percentage yield" is also known as "effective interest rate."

Solve the following problems by using Table 11-1.

29. Sherry Smith invested $3,000 at the Horizon Bank at 6% interest compounded quarterly.

    a. What is the annual percentage yield of this investment?

    b. What will Sherry's investment be worth after 6 years?

30. As a savings plan for college, when their son Bob was born, the Wilburs deposited $10,000 in an account paying 8% compounded annually. How much will the account be worth when Bob is 18 years old?

31. You are the owner of a UPS Store franchise. You have just deposited $12,000 in an investment account earning 12% compounded monthly. This account is intended to pay for store improvements in $2\frac{1}{2}$ years. At that rate, how much will be available in the account for the project?

32. The First National Bank is offering a 6-year certificate of deposit (CD) at 4% interest compounded quarterly; Second National Bank is offering a 6-year CD at 5% interest compounded annually.

    a. If you were interested in investing $8,000 in one of these CDs, calculate the compound amount of each offer.

    b. What is the annual percentage yield of each CD?

c.   (Optional) If Third National Bank has a 6-year CD at 4.5% interest compounded monthly, use the compound interest formula to calculate the compound amount of this offer.

33. A certain animal husbandry program has a flock of sheep that increases in size by 15% every year. If there are currently 48 sheep, how many sheep are expected to be in the flock in 5 years? Round to the nearest whole sheep.

Learning Tip

Compounding Sheep!
The concept of compounding may also be used to compound "other variables" besides money. Use the compound interest table or formula for Exercises 33 and 34.

34. The rate of bacteria growth in a laboratory experiment was measured at 16% per hour. If this experiment is repeated and begins with 5 grams of bacteria, how much bacteria should be expected after 12 hours? Round to the nearest tenth of a gram.

Solve the following problems by using the compound interest formula.

	Principal	Time Period (years)	Nominal Rate (%)	Interest Compounded	Compound Amount	Compound Interest
35.	$5,000	4	4.2	semiannually	$5,904.40	$904.40
36.	$700	8	1.5	monthly	_____	_____
37.	$2,800	$2\frac{1}{2}$	3.1	quarterly	_____	_____

38. You invest $11,000 at 6% interest, compounded monthly, for 2 years. Use the compound interest formula to calculate the compound amount for your investment.

39. Gabriel Hopen, a 32-year-old commercial artist, has just signed a contract with an advertising agency. Gabriel's starting salary is $47,800. The agency has agreed to increase his salary by 8.5% annually. How much will Gabriel's salary be after 5 years? Round to the nearest whole dollar.

40. The FernRod Motorcycle Company invested $250,000 at 4.5% compounded monthly to be used for the expansion of their manufacturing facilities. How much money will be available for the project in $3\frac{1}{2}$ years?

BUSINESS DECISION: DAILY COMPOUNDING

41. As an incentive to attract savings deposits, most financial institutions today offer **daily** and even **continuous compounding**. This means that savings, or passbook, accounts, as well as CDs, earn interest compounded each day or even more frequently, such as every hour or even every minute. (Continuous compounding, in which compounding occurs every instant, involves a different formula that is derived from the formula we've been using.) Let's take a look at daily compounding.

To calculate the compound amount, A, of an investment with daily compounding, use the compound interest formula modified as follows:

- Rate per period (daily) $= \dfrac{i}{365}$ (nominal interest rate, i, divided by 365)

- Number of periods (days), n, $=$ number of days of the investment.

$$A = P\left(1 + \frac{i}{365}\right)^n$$

Calculator Sequence: (1 + (i ÷ 365)) y^x n × P = A

a. On April 19, Thomas Ash deposited \$2,700 in a passbook savings account at 3.5% interest compounded daily. What is the compound amount of his account on August 5?

b. Using daily compounding, recalculate the compound amount for each of the three certificates of deposit in Exercise 32.

PRESENT VALUE   11 SECTION II

In Section I, we learned how to find a future value when the present value was known. Let's take a look at the reverse situation, also commonly found in business. When a future value (an amount needed in the future) is known, the present value is the amount that must be invested today to accumulate with compound interest to that future value. For example, if a corporation wants \$100,000 in 5 years (future value—known) to replace its fleet of trucks, what amount must be invested today (present value—unknown) at 8% compounded quarterly to achieve this goal? (See Exhibit 11-5.)

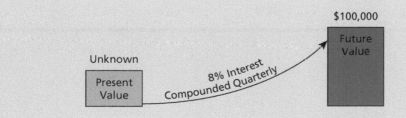

EXHIBIT 11-5
Present Value to Future Value

11-6 CALCULATING THE PRESENT VALUE OF A FUTURE AMOUNT BY USING PRESENT VALUE TABLES

Just as there are compound interest tables to aid in the calculation of compound amounts, present value tables help calculate the present value of a known future amount. Table 11-2 is such a table. Note that this table is similar to the compound interest table in that the table factors are based on the interest rate per period and the number of compounding periods.

STEPS FOR USING PRESENT VALUE TABLES

STEP 1. Scan across the top row to find the interest rate per period.

STEP 2. Look down that column to the row corresponding to the number of periods.

STEP 3. The table factor found at the intersection of the rate-per-period column and the number-of-periods row is the present value of $1 at compound interest. Multiply the table factor by the compound amount to determine the present value.

Present value = Table factor × Compound amount (future value)

EXAMPLE6 CALCULATING PRESENT VALUE

Charlie Watson will need $5,000 in 8 years. Use Table 11-2 to find how much he must invest now at 6% interest compounded semiannually to have $5,000, 8 years from now.

►SOLUTIONSTRATEGY

To solve this present value problem, we will use 3% per period (6% nominal rate ÷ 2 periods per year) and 16 periods (8 years × 2 periods per year).

Step 1. Scan the top row of the present value table to 3%.

Step 2. Look down that column to the row corresponding to 16 periods.

Step 3. Find the table factor at the intersection of Steps 1 and 2 and multiply it by the compound amount to find the present value. Table factor = .62317.

$$\text{Present value} = \text{Table factor} \times \text{Compound amount}$$
$$\text{Present value} = .62317 \times 5{,}000 = \underline{\$3{,}115.85}$$

►TRYITEXERCISE 6

Count Gustav wants to renovate his castle in Boulogne in 3 years. He estimates the cost to be $3,000,000. Use Table 11-2 to find how much Count Gustav must invest now at 8% interest compounded quarterly to have $3,000,000, 3 years from now.

CHECK YOUR ANSWER WITH THE SOLUTION ON PAGE 373.

iStock.com/Nikada

TABLE 11-2 Present Value Table (Present Value of $1 at Compound Interest)

Periods	$\frac{1}{2}$%	1%	$1\frac{1}{2}$%	2%	3%	4%	5%	6%	7%	8%	Periods
1	0.99502	0.99010	0.98522	0.98039	0.97087	0.96154	0.95238	0.94340	0.93458	0.92593	1
2	0.99007	0.98030	0.97066	0.96117	0.94260	0.92456	0.90703	0.89000	0.87344	0.85734	2
3	0.98515	0.97059	0.95632	0.94232	0.91514	0.88900	0.86384	0.83962	0.81630	0.79383	3
4	0.98025	0.96098	0.94218	0.92385	0.88849	0.85480	0.82270	0.79209	0.76290	0.73503	4
5	0.97537	0.95147	0.92826	0.90573	0.86261	0.82193	0.78353	0.74726	0.71299	0.68058	5
6	0.97052	0.94205	0.91454	0.88797	0.83748	0.79031	0.74622	0.70496	0.66634	0.63017	6
7	0.96569	0.93272	0.90103	0.87056	0.81309	0.75992	0.71068	0.66506	0.62275	0.58349	7
8	0.96089	0.92348	0.88771	0.85349	0.78941	0.73069	0.67684	0.62741	0.58201	0.54027	8
9	0.95610	0.91434	0.87459	0.83676	0.76642	0.70259	0.64461	0.59190	0.54393	0.50025	9
10	0.95135	0.90529	0.86167	0.82035	0.74409	0.67556	0.61391	0.55839	0.50835	0.46319	10
11	0.94661	0.89632	0.84893	0.80426	0.72242	0.64958	0.58468	0.52679	0.47509	0.42888	11
12	0.94191	0.88745	0.83639	0.78849	0.70138	0.62460	0.55684	0.49697	0.44401	0.39711	12
13	0.93722	0.87866	0.82403	0.77303	0.68095	0.60057	0.53032	0.46884	0.41496	0.36770	13
14	0.93256	0.86996	0.81185	0.75788	0.66112	0.57748	0.50507	0.44230	0.38782	0.34046	14
15	0.92792	0.86135	0.79985	0.74301	0.64186	0.55526	0.48102	0.41727	0.36245	0.31524	15
16	0.92330	0.85282	0.78803	0.72845	0.62317	0.53391	0.45811	0.39365	0.33873	0.29189	16
17	0.91871	0.84438	0.77639	0.71416	0.60502	0.51337	0.43630	0.37136	0.31657	0.27027	17
18	0.91414	0.83602	0.76491	0.70016	0.58739	0.49363	0.41552	0.35034	0.29586	0.25025	18
19	0.90959	0.82774	0.75361	0.68643	0.57029	0.47464	0.39573	0.33051	0.27651	0.23171	19
20	0.90506	0.81954	0.74247	0.67297	0.55368	0.45639	0.37689	0.31180	0.25842	0.21455	20
21	0.90056	0.81143	0.73150	0.65978	0.53755	0.43883	0.35894	0.29416	0.24151	0.19866	21
22	0.89608	0.80340	0.72069	0.64684	0.52189	0.42196	0.34185	0.27751	0.22571	0.18394	22
23	0.89162	0.79544	0.71004	0.63416	0.50669	0.40573	0.32557	0.26180	0.21095	0.17032	23
24	0.88719	0.78757	0.69954	0.62172	0.49193	0.39012	0.31007	0.24698	0.19715	0.15770	24
25	0.88277	0.77977	0.68921	0.60953	0.47761	0.37512	0.29530	0.23300	0.18425	0.14602	25

Periods	9%	10%	11%	12%	13%	14%	15%	16%	17%	18%	Periods
1	0.91743	0.90909	0.90090	0.89286	0.88496	0.87719	0.86957	0.86207	0.85470	0.84746	1
2	0.84168	0.82645	0.81162	0.79719	0.78315	0.76947	0.75614	0.74316	0.73051	0.71818	2
3	0.77218	0.75131	0.73119	0.71178	0.69305	0.67497	0.65752	0.64066	0.62437	0.60863	3
4	0.70843	0.68301	0.65873	0.63552	0.61332	0.59208	0.57175	0.55229	0.53365	0.51579	4
5	0.64993	0.62092	0.59345	0.56743	0.54276	0.51937	0.49718	0.47611	0.45611	0.43711	5
6	0.59627	0.56447	0.53464	0.50663	0.48032	0.45559	0.43233	0.41044	0.38984	0.37043	6
7	0.54703	0.51316	0.48166	0.45235	0.42506	0.39964	0.37594	0.35383	0.33320	0.31393	7
8	0.50187	0.46651	0.43393	0.40388	0.37616	0.35056	0.32690	0.30503	0.28478	0.26604	8
9	0.46043	0.42410	0.39092	0.36061	0.33288	0.30751	0.28426	0.26295	0.24340	0.22546	9
10	0.42241	0.38554	0.35218	0.32197	0.29459	0.26974	0.24718	0.22668	0.20804	0.19106	10
11	0.38753	0.35049	0.31728	0.28748	0.26070	0.23662	0.21494	0.19542	0.17781	0.16192	11
12	0.35553	0.31863	0.28584	0.25668	0.23071	0.20756	0.18691	0.16846	0.15197	0.13722	12
13	0.32618	0.28966	0.25751	0.22917	0.20416	0.18207	0.16253	0.14523	0.12989	0.11629	13
14	0.29925	0.26333	0.23199	0.20462	0.18068	0.15971	0.14133	0.12520	0.11102	0.09855	14
15	0.27454	0.23939	0.20900	0.18270	0.15989	0.14010	0.12289	0.10793	0.09489	0.08352	15
16	0.25187	0.21763	0.18829	0.16312	0.14150	0.12289	0.10686	0.09304	0.08110	0.07078	16
17	0.23107	0.19784	0.16963	0.14564	0.12522	0.10780	0.09293	0.08021	0.06932	0.05998	17
18	0.21199	0.17986	0.15282	0.13004	0.11081	0.09456	0.08081	0.06914	0.05925	0.05083	18
19	0.19449	0.16351	0.13768	0.11611	0.09806	0.08295	0.07027	0.05961	0.05064	0.04308	19
20	0.17843	0.14864	0.12403	0.10367	0.08678	0.07276	0.06110	0.05139	0.04328	0.03651	20
21	0.16370	0.13513	0.11174	0.09256	0.07680	0.06383	0.05313	0.04430	0.03699	0.03094	21
22	0.15018	0.12285	0.10067	0.08264	0.06796	0.05599	0.04620	0.03819	0.03162	0.02622	22
23	0.13778	0.11168	0.09069	0.07379	0.06014	0.04911	0.04017	0.03292	0.02702	0.02222	23
24	0.12640	0.10153	0.08170	0.06588	0.05323	0.04308	0.03493	0.02838	0.02310	0.01883	24
25	0.11597	0.09230	0.07361	0.05882	0.04710	0.03779	0.03038	0.02447	0.01974	0.01596	25

The values in Table 11-2 were generated by the formula $PV = \dfrac{1}{(1+i)^n}$ rounded to five decimal places, where i is the interest rate per period and n is the total number of periods.

11-7   CREATING PRESENT VALUE TABLE FACTORS FOR PERIODS BEYOND THE TABLE

Just as with the compound interest tables, there may be times when the number of periods of an investment or a loan is greater than the number of periods provided by the present value tables. When this occurs, you can create a new table factor by multiplying the table factors for any two periods that add up to the number of periods required.

For answer consistency in this chapter, use the two table factors that represent *half*, or values as close as possible to half, of the periods required. For example,

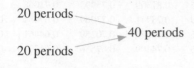

20 periods ⟶ 40 periods ⟵ 20 periods

20 periods ⟶ 41 periods ⟵ 21 periods

STEPS FOR CREATING NEW TABLE FACTORS

STEP 1. For the stated interest rate per period, find the two table factors that represent *half*, or values as close as possible to half, of the periods required.

STEP 2. Multiply the two table factors from Step 1 to form the new factor.

STEP 3. Round the new factor to five decimal places.

Learning Tip

Which table to use— Compound Interest (Table 11-1) or Present Value (Table 11-2)?

Note that the Compound Interest Table factors are all *greater* than 1, whereas the Present Value Table factors are all less than 1.

- When solving for compound amount, a future amount greater than the present value, use the table with factors *greater* than 1—Compound Interest Table.

- When solving for present value, a present amount *less* than the future value, use the table with factors *less* than 1—Present Value Table.

EXAMPLE7   CREATING PRESENT VALUE TABLE FACTORS

Calculate a new table factor and find the present value of $2,000 if the interest rate is 6% compounded quarterly for 8 years.

SOLUTIONSTRATEGY

This investment requires a table factor for 32 periods, four periods per year for 8 years. Because Table 11-2 provides factors only up to 25 periods, we must create one by using the steps above.

Step 1. At 6% interest compounded quarterly, the rate per period is $1\frac{1}{2}\%$. Because we are looking for 32 periods, we will use the factors for 16 and 16 periods at $1\frac{1}{2}\%$.

$$\text{Table factor for 16 periods, } 1\tfrac{1}{2}\% = .78803$$

$$\text{Table factor for 16 periods, } 1\tfrac{1}{2}\% = .78803$$

Step 2. Multiply the factors for 16 and 16 periods:

$$.78803 \times .78803 = .620991$$

Step 3. Rounding to five decimal places, the new table factor for 32 periods is .62099. The present value of the $2,000 investment is

$$\text{Present value} = \text{Table factor} \times \text{Compound amount}$$
$$\text{Present value} = .62099 \times 2,000 = \underline{\$1,241.98}$$

▶TRYITEXERCISE 7

Calculate a new table factor and find the present value of $8,500 if the interest rate is 6% compounded quarterly for 10 years.

CHECK YOUR ANSWERS WITH THE SOLUTIONS ON PAGE 373.

CALCULATING PRESENT VALUE OF A FUTURE AMOUNT BY USING THE PRESENT VALUE FORMULA

11-8

If your calculator has an exponential function key, y^x, you can calculate the present value of an investment by using the present value formula.

The present value formula states:

$$PV = \frac{A}{(1 + i)^n}$$

where:

PV = **Present value**

A – **Compound amount**

i = **Interest rate per period (expressed as a decimal)**

n = **Total compounding periods (years × periods per year)**

STEPS FOR SOLVING THE PRESENT VALUE FORMULA

STEP 1. Add the 1 and the interest rate per period, i.

STEP 2. Raise the sum from Step 1 to the nth power by using the y^x key on your calculator.

STEP 3. Divide the compound amount, A, by the answer from Step 2.

Calculator sequence 1 $+$ i $=$ y^x n $=$ M+ A $\div$ MR $=$ PV

EXAMPLE8 USING THE PRESENT VALUE FORMULA

Use the present value formula to calculate the present value of $3,000 if the interest rate is 8% compounded quarterly for 6 years.

▶SOLUTIONSTRATEGY

This problem is solved by substituting the investment information into the present value formula. It is important to solve the formula using the sequence of steps outlined. Note the rate per period, i, is 2% (8% ÷ 4 periods per year). The total number of periods, the exponent n, is 24 (6 years × 4 periods per year).

$$\text{Present value} = \frac{A}{(1 + i)^n}$$

$$\text{Present value} = \frac{3,000}{(1 + .02)^{24}}$$

$$\text{Present value} = \frac{3,000}{(1.02)^{24}}$$

$$\text{Present value} = \frac{3,000}{1.608437249} = \$1,865.16$$

Calculator Sequence: 1 $+$ .02 $=$ y^x 24 $=$ M+ 3000 $\div$ MR $=$ $\$1,865.16$

▶TRYITEXERCISE 8

Sam and Rosa Alonso want to accumulate $30,000, 17 years from now as a college fund for their baby son, Michael. Use the present value formula to calculate how much they must invest now at an interest rate of 8% compounded semiannually to have $30,000 in 17 years.

CHECK YOUR ANSWER WITH THE SOLUTION ON PAGE 373.

SECTION II 11 REVIEW EXERCISES

For the following investments, calculate the present value (principal) and the compound interest. Use Table 11-2. Round your answers to the nearest cent.

	Compound Amount	Term of Investment	Nominal Rate (%)	Interest Compounded	Present Value	Compound Interest
1.	$6,000	3 years	9	annually	$4,633.08	$1,366.92
2.	$24,000	6 years	4	semiannually		
3.	$650	5 years	8	quarterly		
4.	$2,000	12 years	6	semiannually		
5.	$50,000	25 years	11	annually		
6.	$14,500	18 months	4	semiannually		
7.	$9,800	4 years	12	quarterly		
8.	$100,000	10 years	4	annually		
9.	$250	1 year	6	monthly		

10. Sonia wants to have $9,000 in 9 years. Use Table 11-2 to calculate how much she should invest now at 6% interest, compounded semiannually in order to reach this goal.

The following investments require table factors for periods beyond the table. Create the new table factor rounded to five places and calculate the present value for each.

	Compound Amount	Term of Investment (years)	Nominal Rate (%)	Interest Compounded	New Table Factor	Present Value
11.	$12,000	10	4	quarterly	.67165	$8,059.80
12.	$33,000	38	7	annually		
13.	$1,400	12	6	quarterly		
14.	$1,000	45	3	annually		

15. You wish to have $15,000 in 8 years. Use Table 11-2 to create a new table factor, and then find how much you should invest now at 6% interest, compounded quarterly in order to have $15,000, 8 years from now.

Solve the following problems by using Table 11-2.

16. How much must be invested today at 6% compounded quarterly to have $8,000 in 3 years?

17. Samantha Wimberly is planning a vacation in Europe in 4 years, after graduation. She estimates that she will need $3,500 for the trip.

    a. If her bank is offering 4-year certificates of deposit with 8% interest compounded quarterly, how much must Samantha invest now to have the money for the trip?

b. How much compound interest will be earned on the investment?

18. Pinnacle Homes, a real estate development company, is planning to build five homes, each costing $125,000, in $2\frac{1}{2}$ years. The Galaxy Bank pays 6% interest compounded semiannually. How much should the company invest now to have sufficient funds to build the homes in the future?

19. Tri-Star Airlines intends to pay off a $20,000,000 corporate bond issue that comes due in 4 years. How much must the company set aside now at 6% interest compounded monthly to accumulate the required amount of money?

Corporate bonds are debt obligations, or IOUs, issued by private and public corporations. They are typically issued in multiples of $1,000. Bonds are commonly used to finance company modernization and expansion programs.

When you buy a bond, you are lending money to the corporation that issued it. The corporation promises to return your money (or principal) on a specified maturity date. Until that time, it also pays you a stated rate of interest.

Source: Ford Motor Company

20. Stuart Daniels estimates that he will need $25,000 to set up a small business in 7 years.

a. How much must Stuart invest now at 8% interest compounded quarterly to achieve his goal?

b. How much compound interest will he earn on the investment?

21. Summertime songbird population within the Mid-America flyway is predicted to increase over the next 8 years at the rate of 2% per year. If the songbird population is predicted to reach 55 million in 8 years, how many songbirds are there today? Round to the nearest million.

Learning Tip

Present Value of a Songbird!
Just as with compounding, the concept of present value of a future amount may also be applied to "other variables" besides money. Use the present value table or formula for Exercises 21 and 22.

22. The requirement for computer server capacity at Acme Industries is expected to increase at a rate of 15% per year for the next 5 years. If the server capacity is expected to be 1,400 gigabytes in 5 years, how many gigabytes of capacity are there today? Round to the nearest whole gigabyte.

B-A-C-O/Shutterstock.com

Solve the following problems by using the present value formula.

	Compound Amount	Term of Investment	Nominal Rate (%)	Interest Compounded	Present Value	Compound Interest
23.	$4,500	7 years	3.8	annually	$3,466.02	$1,033.98
24.	$15,000	8 years	4.5	monthly	_____	_____
25.	$18,900	10 years	1.9	semiannually	_____	_____

JUMP START WWW

26. Suppose you wish to have $7,000 in 12 years. Use the present value formula to find how much you should invest now at 6% interest compounded semiannually in order to meet your goal.

27. Alana and Eva Rodriguez are planning a cross-country road trip in 3 years. They estimate $6,000 will be needed to cover expenses. The National Bank of Pinecrest is offering a 3-year CD paying 3.62% interest compounded quarterly.

    a. How much should they set aside now to achieve their goal? Round to the nearest whole dollar.

    b. How much interest will Alana and Eva earn on the CD?

28. Mike Gioulis would like to have $25,000 in 4 years to pay off a balloon payment on his business mortgage. His money market account is paying 1.825% compounded daily. Disregarding leap years, how much money must Mike put in his account now to achieve his goal? Round to the nearest whole dollar.

BUSINESS DECISION: THE INFLATION FACTOR

29. You are the finance manager for Olympia Industries. The company plans to purchase $1,000,000 in new assembly line machinery in 5 years.

    a. How much must be set aside now at 6% interest compounded semiannually to accumulate the $1,000,000 in 5 years?

    b. If the inflation rate on this type of equipment is 4% per year, what will be the cost of the equipment in 5 years, adjusted for inflation?

    c. Use the inflation-adjusted cost of the equipment to calculate how much must be set aside now.

    d. Use the present value formula to calculate how much would be required now if you found a bank that offered 6% interest compounded daily.

Dollars AND Sense

Inflation should be taken into account when making financial plans that cover time periods longer than a year.

iStock.com/MarsBars

iStock.com/vreemous

CHAPTER FORMULAS

Compound Interest

Compound interest = Compound amount − Principal

Compounding periods = Years × Periods per year

$$\text{Interest rate per period} = \frac{\text{Nominal rate}}{\text{Periods per year}}$$

Compound amount = Table factor × Principal

$$\text{Annual percentage yield (APY)} = \frac{\text{Total compound interest earned in 1 year}}{\text{Principal}}$$

Compound amount = Principal(1 + Interest rate per period)^{periods}

Present Value

Present value = Table factor × Compound amount

$$\text{Present value} = \frac{\text{Compound amount}}{(1 + \text{Interest rate per period})^{\text{periods}}}$$

CHAPTER SUMMARY

Section I: Compound Interest—The Time Value of Money

Topic	Important Concepts	Illustrative Examples
Manually Calculating Compound Amount (Future Value) **Performance Objective 11-1, Page 352**	In compound interest, the interest is applied a number of times during the term of an investment. Compound interest yields considerably higher interest than simple interest does because the investor is earning interest on the interest. Interest can be compounded annually, semiannually, quarterly, monthly, daily, and continuously. 1. Determine the number of compounding periods (years × periods per year). 2. Apply the simple interest formula, $I = PRT$, as many times as there are compounding periods, adding interest to principal before each succeeding calculation.	Manually calculate the compound amount of a $1,000 investment at 8% interest compounded annually for 2 years. Original principal 1,000.00 Interest — period 1 + 80.00 Principal — period 2 1,080.00 Interest — period 2 + 86.40 Compound amount $1,166.40
Calculating Amount of Compound Interest **Performance Objective 11-1, Page 352**	Amount of compound interest is calculated by subtracting the original principal from the compound amount.	What is the amount of compound interest earned in the problem above? 1,166.40 − 1,000.00 = $166.40
Computing Compound Amount (Future Value) by Using Compound Interest Tables **Performance Objective 11-2, Page 353**	1. Scan across the top row of Table 11-1 to find the interest rate per period. 2. Look down that column to the row corresponding to the number of compounding periods. 3. The table factor found at the intersection of the rate-per-period column and the number-of-periods row is the future value of $1.00 at compound interest.	Use Table 11-1 to find the compound amount of an investment of $2,000 at 12% interest compounded quarterly for 6 years. Rate = 3% per period (12% ÷ 4) Periods = 24 (6 years × 4) Table factor = 2.03279 Compound amount = 2.03279 × 2,000 = $4,065.58
Creating Compound Interest Table Factors for Periods beyond the Table **Performance Objective 11-3, Page 356**	1. For the stated interest rate per period, find the two table factors that represent *half*, or values as close as possible to half, of the periods required. 2. Multiply the two table factors from Step 1 to form the new factor. 3. Round the new factor to five decimal places.	Create a new table factor for 5% interest for 30 periods. Multiply the 5% factors for 15 and 15 periods from Table 11-1. 5%, 15 periods = 2.07893 5%, 15 periods = × 2.07893 30 periods 4.3219499 New factor rounded = 4.32195

Section I (continued)

Topic	Important Concepts	Illustrative Examples
Calculating Annual Percentage Yield (APY) or Effective Interest Rate **Performance Objective 11-4, Page 357**	To calculate annual percentage yield, divide total compound interest earned in 1 year by the principal.	What is the annual percentage yield of $5,000 invested for 1 year at 12% compounded monthly? 　From Table 11-1, we use the table factor for 12 periods, 1%, to find the compound amount: $1.12683 \times 5,000 = 5,634.15$ Interest = Cmp. amt. − Principal Interest = $5,634.15 − 5,000.00 = 634.15$ $APY = \dfrac{634.15}{5,000} = 12.68\%$
Calculating Compound Amount (Future Value) by Using the Compound Interest Formula **Performance Objective 11-5, Page 358**	In addition to the compound interest tables, another method for calculating compound amount is by using the compound interest formula.	What is the compound amount of $3,000 invested at 8% interest compounded quarterly for 10 years? $A = P(1 + i)^n$ $A = 3,000(1 + .02)^{40}$ $A = 3,000(1.02)^{40}$ $A = 3,000(2.2080396)$ $A = \$6,624.12$

Section II: Present Value

Topic	Important Concepts	Illustrative Examples
Calculating the Present Value of a Future Amount by Using Present Value Tables **Performance Objective 11-6, Page 364**	When the future value, an amount needed in the future, is known, the present value is the amount that must be invested today to accumulate, with compound interest, to that future value. 1. Scan across the top row of Table 11-2 to find the rate per period. 2. Look down that column to the row corresponding to the number of periods. 3. The table factor found at the intersection of the rate-per-period column and the number-of-periods row is the present value of $1 at compound interest.	How much must be invested now at 10% interest compounded semiannually to have $8,000, 9 years from now? Rate = 5% (10% ÷ 2) Periods = 18 (9 years × 2) Table factor = .41552 Present value = .41552 × 8,000 Present value = $3,324.16
Creating Present Value Table Factors for Periods beyond the Table **Performance Objective 11-7, Page 366**	1. For the stated interest rate per period, find the two table factors that represent *half*, or values as close as possible to half, of the periods required. 2. Multiply the two table factors from Step 1 for the new factor. 3. Round the new factor to five decimal places.	Create a new table factor for 6% interest for 41 periods. 　Multiply the 6% factors for 21 and 20 periods from Table 11-2. 　6%, 21 periods　　=　　.29416 　6%, 20 periods　　=　× .31180 　　41 periods　　　　.0917191 New factor rounded = .09172
Calculating Present Value of a Future Amount by Using the Present Value Formula **Performance Objective 11-8, Page 367**	If your calculator has an exponential function key, y^x, you can calculate the present value of an investment by using the present value formula.	How much must be invested now to have $12,000 in 10 years if the interest rate is 12% compounded quarterly? $Present\ value = \dfrac{12,000}{(1 + .03)^{40}}$ $PV = \dfrac{12,000}{(1.03)^{40}} = \dfrac{12,000}{3.2620378}$ Present value = $3,678.68

TRY IT: EXERCISE SOLUTIONS FOR CHAPTER 11

1. 10,000.00 Original principal

  $+ \ 300.00$ $(I = PRT = 10,000 \times .06 \times \frac{1}{2} = 300)$

  10,300.00 Principal period 2

  $+ \ 309.00$ $(I = PRT = 10,300.00 \times .06 \times \frac{1}{2} = 309)$

  10,609.00 Principal period 3

  $+ \ 318.27$ $(I = PRT = 10,609.00 \times .06 \times \frac{1}{2} = 318.27)$

  10,927.27 Principal period 4

  $+ \ 327.82$ $(I = PRT = 10,927.27 \times .06 \times \frac{1}{2} = 327.82)$

  11,255.09 Principal period 5

  $+ \ 337.65$ $(I = PRT = 11,255.09 \times .06 \times \frac{1}{2} = 337.65)$

  11,592.74 Principal period 6

  $+ \ 347.78$ $(I = PRT = 11,592.74 \times .06 \times \frac{1}{2} = 347.78)$

  $\underline{\$11,940.52}$ Compound amount

  Compound Interest $= 11,940.52 - 10,000.00 = \underline{\$1,940.52}$

2. 3%, 16 periods

  Compound amount = Table factor × Principal

  Compound amount $= 1.60471 \times 20,000 = \underline{\$32,094.20}$

  Compound interest = Compound amount − Principal

  Compound interest $= 32,094.20 - 20,000.00 = \underline{\$12,094.20}$

3. Table factor required = 2%, 28 periods

  2%, 14 periods: 1.31948

  2%, 14 periods: $\times \ 1.31948$

    28 periods $1.74102747 = \underline{1.74103}$ New table factor
    2%, 28 periods

  Compound amount $= 1.74103 \times 3,500 = \underline{\$6,093.61}$

4. $1\frac{1}{2}$%, 4 periods

  Compound amount $= 1.06136 \times 7,000 = \underline{\$7,429.52}$

  Compound interest $= 7,429.52 - 7,000.00 = \underline{\$429.52}$

  $\dfrac{\text{Annual}}{\text{percentage yield}} = \dfrac{\text{1 year compound interest}}{\text{Principal}} = \dfrac{429.52}{7,000.00} = \underline{6.14\%}$

5. $A = P (1 + i)^n$ $P = \$3,000$

  $i = \dfrac{8\%}{4} = .02$

  $n = 5 \times 4 = 20$

  $A = 3,000 (1 + .02)^{20}$

  $A = 3,000 (1.02)^{20}$

  $A = 3,000 (1.4859474)$

  $A = \underline{\$4,457.84}$

6. 2%, 12 periods

  Present value = Table factor × Compound amount

  Present value $= .78849 \times 3,000,000 = \underline{\$2,365,470}$

7. Table factor required $= 1\frac{1}{2}$%, 40 periods

  $1\frac{1}{2}$%, 20 periods: .74247

  $1\frac{1}{2}$%, 20 periods: $\times \ .74247$

    40 periods $= .5512617 = \underline{.55126}$ New table factor
      $1\frac{1}{2}$%, 40 periods

  Present value $= .55126 \times 8,500 = \underline{\$4,685.71}$

8. $PV = \dfrac{A}{(1 + i)^n}$ $A = 30,000$

  $i = \dfrac{8\%}{2} = .04$

  $n = 17 \times 2 = 34$

  $PV = \dfrac{30,000}{(1 + .04)^{34}}$

  $PV = \dfrac{30,000}{(1.04)^{34}}$

  $PV = \dfrac{30,000}{3.7943163} = \underline{\$7,906.56}$

CONCEPT REVIEW

1. Interest calculated solely on the principal is known as _____ interest, whereas interest calculated on the principal and previously earned interest is known as _____ interest. (11-1)

2. The concept that money "now," or in the present, is more desirable than the same amount of money in the future because it can be invested and earn interest as time goes by is known as the _____ of money. (11-1)

3. The total amount of principal and accumulated interest at the end of a loan or an investment is known as the _____ amount or _____ value. (11-1)

4. An amount of money that must be deposited today at compound interest to provide a specified lump sum of money in the future is known as the _____ amount or _____ value. (11-1, 11-6)

5. The amount of compound interest is calculated by subtracting the _____ from the compound amount. (11-1)

6. Compound interest is actually the _____ interest formula applied a number of times. (11-1)

7. A compound interest table is a useful set of factors that represent the future value of _____ at various interest rates for a number of compounding periods. (11-2)

8. A shortcut method for calculating approximately how long it takes money to double in value at compound interest is called the Rule of _____. (11-3)

9. Write the formula for calculating the number of compounding periods of a loan or an investment. (11-2)

10. Write the formula for calculating the interest rate per period of a loan or an investment. (11-2)

11. Newly created table factors for compound interest and present value should be rounded to _____ decimal places. (11-3, 11-7)

12. The annual percentage yield (APY) is equal to the total compound interest earned in _____ year divided by the _____. (11-4)

13. When using the compound interest table or the present value table, the factor is found at the intersection of the rate-per-_____ column and the number-of-_____ row. (11-2, 11-6)

14. To use the compound interest formula and the present value formula, you need a calculator with a(n) _____ function (y^x) key. (11-5, 11-8)

ASSESSMENT TEST

Note: Round to the nearest cent when necessary.

Using Table 11-1, calculate the compound amount and compound interest for the following investments.

	Principal	Time Period (years)	Nominal Rate (%)	Interest Compounded	Compound Amount	Compound Interest
1.	$14,000	6	4	semiannually	_____	_____
2.	$7,700	5	6	quarterly	_____	_____
3.	$3,000	1	6	monthly	_____	_____
4.	$42,000	19	11	annually	_____	_____

The following investments require table factors for periods beyond the table. Create the new table factor and calculate the compound amount for each.

	Principal	Time Period (years)	Nominal Rate (%)	Interest Compounded	New Table Factor	Compound Amount
5.	$20,000	11	8	quarterly	_____	_____
6.	$10,000	4	6	monthly	_____	_____

For the following investments, compute the amount of compound interest earned in 1 year and the annual percentage yield. Round APY to the nearest hundredth of a percent.

	Principal	Nominal Rate (%)	Interest Compounded	Compound Interest Earned in 1 Year	Annual Percentage Yield (APY)
7.	$8,500	12	monthly	_____	_____
8.	$1,000,000	8	quarterly	_____	_____

Calculate the present value (principal) and the compound interest for the following investments. Use Table 11-2. Round answers to the nearest cent.

	Compound Amount	Term of Investment	Nominal Rate (%)	Interest Compounded	Present Value	Compound Interest
9.	$150,000	22 years	15	annually	_____	_____
10.	$20,000	30 months	4	semiannually	_____	_____
11.	$900	$1\frac{3}{4}$ years	18	monthly	_____	_____
12.	$5,500	15 months	8	quarterly	_____	_____

The following investments require table factors for periods beyond the table. Create the new table factor and the present value for each.

	Compound Amount	Time Period (years)	Nominal Rate (%)	Interest Compounded	New Table Factor	Present Value
13.	$1,300	4	12	monthly	_____	_____
14.	$100,000	50	5	annually	_____	_____

Solve the following word problems by using Table 11-1 or 11-2. When necessary, create new table factors. Round dollars to the nearest cent and percents to the nearest hundredth of a percent.

15. What is the compound amount and compound interest of $36,000 invested at 12% compounded semiannually for 7 years?

16. What is the present value of $73,000 in 11 years if the interest rate is 8% compounded semiannually?

17. What is the compound amount and compound interest of $15,000 invested at 6% compounded quarterly for 27 months?

18. What is the annual percentage yield of a $10,000 investment for 1 year at 6% interest compounded monthly?

19. City Wide Delivery Service uses vans costing $24,800 each. How much will the company have to invest today to accumulate enough money to buy six new vans at the end of 4 years? City Wide's bank is currently paying 12% interest compounded quarterly.

20. You are the owner of a Jani-King cleaning service franchise. Your accountant has determined that the business will need $27,500 in new equipment in 3 years. If your bank is paying 6% interest compounded monthly, how much must you invest today to meet this financial goal? Round to the nearest whole dollar.

iStock.com/LL28

Jani-King is the world's largest commercial cleaning franchise company with over 12,000 owners worldwide. Jani-King contracts commercial cleaning services for many different facilities including healthcare, office, hotel/resort, manufacturing, restaurant, and sporting venues.

Jani-King has been rated the #1 Commercial Cleaning Franchise Company for 23 years in a row by *Entrepreneur Magazine*. In most regions, one may start a Jani-King franchise for as little as $3,000. Cleaning services is a $100 billion industry and is projected to grow to more than $155 billion. The U.S. Bureau of Labor Statistics reports that professional cleaning specialists will be the fastest-growing occupation in this decade.

CHAPTER
11

21. Valerie Walton invested $8,800 at the Northern Trust Credit Union at 12% interest compounded quarterly.

a. What is the annual percentage yield of this investment?

b. What will Valerie's investment be worth after 6 years?

22. Bob and Joy Salkind want to save $50,000 in $5\frac{1}{2}$ years for home improvement projects. If the Bank of Aventura is paying 8% interest compounded quarterly, how much must they deposit now to have the money for the project?

23. While rummaging through the attic, you discover a savings account left to you by a relative. When you were 5 years old, he invested $20,000 in your name at 6% interest compounded semiannually. If you are now 20 years old, how much is the account worth?

24. Applegate Industries is planning to expand its production facility in a few years. New plant construction costs are estimated to be $4.50 per square foot. The company invests $850,000 today at 8% interest compounded quarterly.

a. How many square feet of new facility could be built after $3\frac{1}{2}$ years? Round to the nearest whole square foot.

b. If the company waits 5 years and construction costs increase to $5.25 per square foot, how many square feet could be built? Round to the nearest whole square foot. What do you recommend?

25. Over the past 10 years, you've made the following investments:
1. Deposited $10,000 at 8% compounded semiannually in a 3-year certificate of deposit.
2. After 3 years, you took the maturity value (principal and interest) of that CD and added another $5,000 to buy a 4-year, 6% certificate compounded quarterly.
3. When that certificate matured, you added another $8,000 and bought a 3-year, 7% certificate compounded annually.

a. What was the total worth of your investment when the last certificate matured?

b. What is the total amount of compound interest earned over the 10-year period?

26. Fred North owns Redlands Farms, a successful strawberry farm. The strawberry plants increase at a compound rate of 12% per year. Each year Fred brings new land under cultivation for the new strawberry plants. If the farm has 50 acres of strawberry plants today, how many acres of strawberry plants will the farm have in 8 years? Round to the nearest whole acre.

Learning Tip

Use tables or formulas to solve Exercises 26 and 27.

B-A-C-O/Shutterstock.com

27. At Reliable Trucking, Inc., annual sales are predicted to increase over the next 3 years at a rate of 6% per year. Sales equate to "fleet miles." If Reliable's fleet miles are predicted to reach 4,4 million in 3 years, what is the number of fleet miles today? Round to the nearest tenth of a million.

Solve the following exercises and word problems using formulas.

	Principal	Time Period (years)	Nominal Rate (%)	Interest Compounded	Compound Amount	Compound Interest
28.	$3,425	11	6.6	monthly	_____	_____
29.	$21,800	6	2.9	semiannually	_____	_____
30.	$400	$2\frac{1}{2}$	4.2	quarterly	_____	_____
31.	$9,630	5	3.1	annually	_____	_____

	Principal	Term of Investment	Nominal Rate (%)	Interest Compounded	Present Value	Compound Interest
32.	$6,300	14 years	6.3	annually	_____	_____
33.	$80,200	9 months	4.8	quarterly	_____	_____
34.	$27,500	10 years	3.6	semiannually	_____	_____
35.	$2,440	5 years	1.5	monthly	_____	_____

36. What is the compound amount and compound interest of a $73,000 investment earning 2.9% interest compounded semiannually for 4 years? Round to the nearest whole dollar.

37. Jorge Rodriguez would like to pay off his condo when he retires. How much must he invest now at 2.3% interest compounded quarterly to have $125,000 in 11 years? Round to the nearest whole dollar.

CHAPTER 11

38. Quinn and Julius inherited $50,000 each from their great-grandmother's estate. Quinn invested her money in a 5-year CD paying 1.6% interest compounded semiannually. Julius deposited his money in a money market account paying 1.05% compounded monthly.

    a. How much money will each have in 5 years? Round to the nearest whole dollar.

    b. How much compound interest will they each have earned at the end of 5 years?

39. Greg and Verena Sava need $20,000 in 3 years to expand their goat cheese business. The Bank of Sutton is offering a 3-year CD paying 3.9% compounded monthly. How much should they invest now to achieve their goal? Round to the nearest whole dollar.

BUSINESS DECISION: PAY ME NOW, PAY ME LATER

40. You are the owner of an apartment building that is being offered for sale for $1,500,000. You receive an offer from a prospective buyer who wants to pay you $500,000 now, $500,000 in 6 months, and $500,000 in 1 year.

    a. What is the actual present value of this offer considering you can earn 12% interest compounded monthly on your money?

    b. If another buyer offers to pay you $1,425,000 cash now, which is a better deal?

Dollars AND Sense

Pay Me Now, Pay Me Later is a good example of how the "time value of money" concept can be applied in business.

    Remember: *When interest can be earned, money today is more desirable than the same amount of money in the future.*

iStock.com/vreemous

    c. Because you understand the "time value of money" concept, you have negotiated a deal with the original buyer from part a whereby you will accept the three-payment offer but will charge 12% interest compounded monthly on the two delayed payments. Calculate the total purchase price under this new arrangement.

    d. Now calculate the present value of the new deal to verify that you will receive the original asking price of $1,500,000 for your apartment building.

COLLABORATIVE LEARNING ACTIVITY

Putting Your Money to Work

As a team, research financial institutions in your area (brick-and-mortar banks), as well as Internet-only institutions (virtual banks and e-banks), to find and list various certificates of deposit currently being offered. Assume that you want to invest $10,000 for 12 months.

a. What interest rates do these CDs pay? How often is interest compounded?
b. What is the early withdrawal penalty?
c. Are these CDs insured? If so, by whom? What is the limit per account?
d. Overall, which institution offers the CD that would earn the most interest after 12 months?

CHAPTER 12 Annuities

PERFORMANCE OBJECTIVES

FUTURE VALUE OF AN ANNUITY: ORDINARY AND ANNUITY DUE

12 **SECTION I**

The concepts relating to compound interest in Chapter 11 were mainly concerned with lump sum investments or payments. Frequently in business, situations involve a series of equal periodic payments or receipts rather than lump sums. These are known as annuities. An **annuity** is the payment or receipt of *equal* cash amounts per period for a specified amount of time. Some common applications are insurance and retirement plan premiums and payouts; loan payments; and savings plans for future events such as starting a business, going to college, or purchasing expensive items (e.g., real estate or business equipment).

In this chapter, you learn to calculate the future value of an annuity, the amount accumulated at compound interest from a series of equal periodic payments. You also learn to calculate the present value of an annuity, the amount that must be deposited now at compound interest to yield a series of equal periodic payments. Exhibit 12-1 graphically shows the difference between the future value of an annuity and the present value of an annuity.

All the exercises in this chapter are of the type known as **simple annuities**. This means that the number of compounding periods per year coincides with the number of annuity payments per year. For example, if the annuity payments are monthly, the interest is compounded monthly; if the annuity payments are made every six months, the interest is compounded semiannually. **Complex annuities** are those in which the annuity payments and compounding periods do not coincide.

As with compound interest, annuities can be calculated manually, by tables, and by formulas. Manual computation is useful for illustrative purposes; however, it is too tedious because it requires a calculation for each period. The table method is the easiest and most widely used and is the basis for this chapter's exercises. As in Chapter 11, there are formulas to calculate annuities; however, they require calculators with the exponential function key, y^x, and the change-of-sign key, $+/-$. These optional Performance Objectives are for students with business, financial, or scientific calculators.

annuity Payment or receipt of equal amounts of money per period for a specified amount of time.

simple annuities Annuities in which the number of compounding periods per year coincides with the number of annuity payments per year.

complex annuities Annuities in which the annuity payments and compounding periods do not coincide.

CALCULATING THE FUTURE VALUE OF AN ORDINARY ANNUITY BY USING TABLES

12-1

Annuities are categorized into annuities certain and contingent annuities. **Annuities certain** are annuities that have a specified number of periods, such as $200 per month for 5 years or $500 semiannually for 10 years. **Contingent annuities** are based on an uncertain time period, such as a retirement plan that is payable only for the lifetime of the retiree. This chapter is concerned only with annuities certain.

annuities certain Annuities that have a specified number of time periods.

contingent annuities Annuities based on an uncertain time period, such as the life of a person.

EXHIBIT 12-1 Timeline Illustrating Present and Future Value of an Annuity

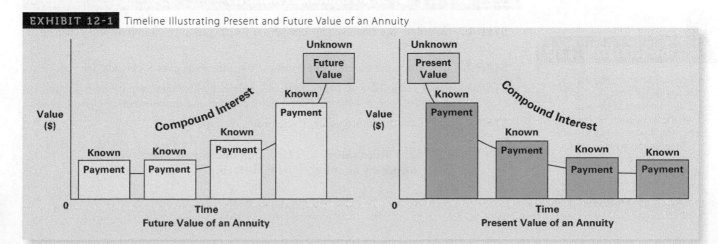

ordinary annuity Annuity that is paid or received at the end of each time period.

annuity due Annuity that is paid or received at the beginning of each time period.

future value of an annuity, or amount of an annuity The total amount of the annuity payments and the accumulated interest on those payments.

When the annuity payment is made at the end of each period, it is known as an **ordinary annuity**. When the payment is made at the beginning of each period, it is called an **annuity due**. A salary paid at the end of each month is an example of an ordinary annuity. A mortgage payment or rent paid at the beginning of each month is an example of an annuity due.

The **future value of an annuity** is also known as the **amount of an annuity**. It is the total of the annuity payments plus the accumulated compound interest on those payments.

For illustrative purposes, consider the following annuity calculated manually.

What is the future value of an ordinary annuity of $10,000 per year for 4 years at 6% interest compounded annually?

Because this is an ordinary annuity, the payment is made at the *end* of each period (in this case, years). Each interest calculation uses $I = PRT$, with $R = .06$ and $T = 1$ year.

Time	Balance	
Beginning of period 1	0	
	+ 10,000.00	First annuity payment (end of period 1)
End of period 1	10,000.00	
Beginning of period 2	10,000.00	
	600.00	Interest earned, period 2 (10,000.00 × .06 × 1)
	+ 10,000.00	Second annuity payment (end of period 2)
End of period 2	20,600.00	
Beginning of period 3	20,600.00	
	1,236.00	Interest earned, period 3 (20,600.00 × .06 × 1)
	+ 10,000.00	Third annuity payment (end of period 3)
End of period 3	31,836.00	
Beginning of period 4	31,836.00	
	1,910.16	Interest earned, period 4 (31,836.00 × .06 × 1)
	+ 10,000.00	Fourth annuity payment (end of period 4)
End of period 4	$43,746.16	Future value of the ordinary annuity

As you can see, calculating annuities this way is tedious. An annuity of 10 years with payments made monthly would require 120 calculations. As with compound interest, we will use tables to calculate the future value (amount) of an annuity.

Learning Tip

The procedure for using the annuity tables, Tables 12-1 and 12-2, is the same as we used with the compound interest and present value tables in Chapter 11.

Table factors are found at the intersection of the rate-per-period column and the number-of-periods row.

STEPS FOR CALCULATING FUTURE VALUE (AMOUNT) OF AN ORDINARY ANNUITY

STEP 1. Calculate the interest rate per period for the annuity (nominal rate ÷ periods per year).

STEP 2. Determine the number of periods of the annuity (years × periods per year).

STEP 3. From Table 12-1 on pages 383–384, locate the ordinary annuity table factor at the intersection of the rate-per-period column and the number-of-periods row.

STEP 4. Calculate the future value of the ordinary annuity.

$$\text{Future value (ordinary annuity)} = \text{Ordinary annuity table factor} \times \text{Annuity payment}$$

TABLE 12-1 Future Value (Amount) of an Ordinary Annuity of $1

Periods	$\frac{1}{2}$%	1%	$1\frac{1}{2}$%	2%	3%	4%	5%	6%	7%	8%	Periods
1	1.00000	1.00000	1.00000	1.00000	1.00000	1.00000	1.00000	1.00000	1.00000	1.00000	1
2	2.00500	2.01000	2.01500	2.02000	2.03000	2.04000	2.05000	2.06000	2.07000	2.08000	2
3	3.01502	3.03010	3.04522	3.06040	3.09090	3.12160	3.15250	3.18360	3.21490	3.24640	3
4	4.03010	4.06040	4.09090	4.12161	4.18363	4.24646	4.31013	4.37462	4.43994	4.50611	4
5	5.05025	5.10101	5.15227	5.20404	5.30914	5.41632	5.52563	5.63709	5.75074	5.86660	5
6	6.07550	6.15202	6.22955	6.30812	6.46841	6.63298	6.80191	6.97532	7.15329	7.33593	6
7	7.10588	7.21354	7.32299	7.43428	7.66246	7.89829	8.14201	8.39384	8.65402	8.92280	7
8	8.14141	8.28567	8.43284	8.58297	8.89234	9.21423	9.54911	9.89747	10.25980	10.63663	8
9	9.18212	9.36853	9.55933	9.75463	10.15911	10.58280	11.02656	11.49132	11.97799	12.48756	9
10	10.22803	10.46221	10.70272	10.94972	11.46388	12.00611	12.57789	13.18079	13.81645	14.48656	10
11	11.27917	11.56683	11.86326	12.16872	12.80780	13.48635	14.20679	14.97164	15.78360	16.64549	11
12	12.33556	12.68250	13.04121	13.41209	14.19203	15.02581	15.91713	16.86994	17.88845	18.97713	12
13	13.39724	13.80933	14.23683	14.68033	15.61779	16.62684	17.71298	18.88214	20.14064	21.49530	13
14	14.46423	14.94742	15.45038	15.97394	17.08632	18.29191	19.59863	21.01507	22.55049	24.21492	14
15	15.53655	16.09690	16.68214	17.29342	18.59891	20.02359	21.57856	23.27597	25.12902	27.15211	15
16	16.61423	17.25786	17.93237	18.63929	20.15688	21.82453	23.65749	25.67253	27.88805	30.32428	16
17	17.69730	18.43044	19.20136	20.01207	21.76159	23.69751	25.84037	28.21288	30.84022	33.75023	17
18	18.78579	19.61475	20.48938	21.41231	23.41444	25.64541	28.13238	30.90565	33.99903	37.45024	18
19	19.87972	20.81090	21.79672	22.84056	25.11687	27.67123	30.53900	33.75999	37.37896	41.44626	19
20	20.97912	22.01900	23.12367	24.29737	26.87037	29.77808	33.06595	36.78559	40.99549	45.76196	20
21	22.08401	23.23919	24.47052	25.78332	28.67649	31.96920	35.71925	39.99273	44.86518	50.42292	21
22	23.19443	24.47159	25.83758	27.29898	30.53678	34.24797	38.50521	43.39229	49.00574	55.45676	22
23	24.31040	25.71630	27.22514	28.84496	32.45288	36.61789	41.43048	46.99583	53.43614	60.89330	23
24	25.43196	26.97346	28.63352	30.42186	34.42647	39.08260	44.50200	50.81558	58.17667	66.76476	24
25	26.55912	28.24320	30.06302	32.03030	36.45926	41.64591	47.72710	54.86451	63.24904	73.10594	25
26	27.69191	29.52563	31.51397	33.67091	38.55304	44.31174	51.11345	59.15638	68.67647	79.95442	26
27	28.83037	30.82089	32.98668	35.34432	40.70963	47.08421	54.66913	63.70577	74.48382	87.35077	27
28	29.97452	32.12910	34.48148	37.05121	42.93092	49.96758	58.40258	68.52811	80.69769	95.33883	28
29	31.12439	33.45039	35.99870	38.79223	45.21885	52.96629	62.32271	73.63980	87.34653	103.96594	29
30	32.28002	34.78489	37.53868	40.56808	47.57542	56.08494	66.43885	79.05819	94.46079	113.28321	30
31	33.44142	36.13274	39.10176	42.37944	50.00268	59.32834	70.76079	84.80168	102.07304	123.34587	31
32	34.60862	37.49407	40.68829	44.22703	52.50276	62.70147	75.29883	90.88978	110.21815	134.21354	32
33	35.78167	38.86901	42.29861	46.11157	55.07784	66.20953	80.06377	97.34316	118.93343	145.95062	33
34	36.96058	40.25770	43.93309	48.03380	57.73018	69.85791	85.06696	104.18375	128.25876	158.62667	34
35	38.14538	41.66028	45.59209	49.99448	60.46208	73.65222	90.32031	111.43478	138.23688	172.31680	35
36	39.33610	43.07688	47.27597	51.99437	63.27594	77.59831	95.83632	119.12087	148.91346	187.10215	36

The values in Table 12-1 were generated by the formula $\dfrac{(1 + i)^n - 1}{i}$ and rounded to five decimal places, where i is the interest rate per period and n is the total number of periods.

TABLE 12-1 Future Value (Amount) of an Ordinary Annuity of $1 *(Continued)*

Periods	9%	10%	11%	12%	13%	14%	15%	16%	17%	18%	Periods
1	1.00000	1.00000	1.00000	1.00000	1.00000	1.00000	1.00000	1.00000	1.00000	1.00000	1
2	2.09000	2.10000	2.11000	2.12000	2.13000	2.14000	2.15000	2.16000	2.17000	2.18000	2
3	3.27810	3.31000	3.34210	3.37440	3.40690	3.43960	3.47250	3.50560	3.53890	3.57240	3
4	4.57313	4.64100	4.70973	4.77933	4.84980	4.92114	4.99338	5.06650	5.14051	5.21543	4
5	5.98471	6.10510	6.22780	6.35285	6.48027	6.61010	6.74238	6.87714	7.01440	7.15421	5
6	7.52333	7.71561	7.91286	8.11519	8.32271	8.53552	8.75374	8.97748	9.20685	9.44197	6
7	9.20043	9.48717	9.78327	10.08901	10.40466	10.73049	11.06680	11.41387	11.77201	12.14152	7
8	11.02847	11.43589	11.85943	12.29969	12.75726	13.23276	13.72682	14.24009	14.77325	15.32700	8
9	13.02104	13.57948	14.16397	14.77566	15.41571	16.08535	16.78584	17.51851	18.28471	19.08585	9
10	15.19293	15.93742	16.72201	17.54874	18.41975	19.33730	20.30372	21.32147	22.39311	23.52131	10
11	17.56029	18.53117	19.56143	20.65458	21.81432	23.04452	24.34928	25.73290	27.19994	28.75514	11
12	20.14072	21.38428	22.71319	24.13313	25.65018	27.27075	29.00167	30.85017	32.82393	34.93107	12
13	22.95338	24.52271	26.21164	28.02911	29.98470	32.08865	34.35192	36.78620	39.40399	42.21866	13
14	26.01919	27.97498	30.09492	32.39260	34.88271	37.58107	40.50471	43.67199	47.10267	50.81802	14
15	29.36092	31.77248	34.40536	37.27971	40.41746	43.84241	47.58041	51.65951	56.11013	60.96527	15
16	33.00340	35.94973	39.18995	42.75328	46.67173	50.98035	55.71747	60.92503	66.64885	72.93901	16
17	36.97370	40.54470	44.50084	48.88367	53.73906	59.11760	65.07509	71.67303	78.97915	87.06804	17
18	41.30134	45.59917	50.39594	55.74971	61.72514	68.39407	75.83636	84.14072	93.40561	103.74028	18
19	46.01846	51.15909	56.93949	63.43968	70.74941	78.96923	88.21181	98.60323	110.28456	123.41353	19
20	51.16012	57.27500	64.20283	72.05244	80.94683	91.02493	102.44358	115.37975	130.03294	146.62797	20
21	56.76453	64.00250	72.26514	81.69874	92.46992	104.76842	118.81012	134.84051	153.13854	174.02100	21
22	62.87334	71.40275	81.21431	92.50258	105.49101	120.43600	137.63164	157.41499	180.17209	206.34479	22
23	69.53194	79.54302	91.14788	104.60289	120.20484	138.29704	159.27638	183.60138	211.80134	244.48685	23
24	76.78981	88.49733	102.17415	118.15524	136.83147	158.65862	184.16784	213.97761	248.80757	289.49448	24
25	84.70090	98.34706	114.41331	133.33387	155.61956	181.87083	212.79302	249.21402	292.10486	342.60349	25
26	93.32398	109.18177	127.99877	150.33393	176.85010	208.33274	245.71197	290.08827	342.76268	405.27211	26
27	102.72313	121.09994	143.07864	169.37401	200.84061	238.49933	283.56877	337.50239	402.03234	479.22109	27
28	112.96822	134.20994	159.81729	190.69889	227.94989	272.88923	327.10408	392.50277	471.37783	566.48089	28
29	124.13536	148.63093	178.39719	214.58275	258.58338	312.09373	377.16969	456.30322	552.51207	669.44745	29
30	136.30754	164.49402	199.02088	241.33268	293.19922	356.78685	434.74515	530.31173	647.43912	790.94799	30
31	149.57522	181.94342	221.91317	271.29261	332.31511	407.73701	500.95692	616.16161	758.50377	934.31863	31
32	164.03699	201.13777	247.32362	304.84772	376.51608	465.82019	577.10046	715.74746	888.44941	1103.49598	32
33	179.80032	222.25154	275.52922	342.42945	426.46317	532.03501	664.66552	831.26706	1040.48581	1303.12526	33
34	196.98234	245.47670	306.83744	384.52098	482.90338	607.51991	765.36535	965.26979	1218.36839	1538.68781	34
35	215.71075	271.02437	341.58955	431.66350	546.68082	693.57270	881.17016	1120.71295	1426.49102	1816.65161	35
36	236.12472	299.12681	380.16441	484.46312	618.74933	791.67288	1014.34568	1301.02703	1669.99450	2144.64890	36

The values in Table 12-1 were generated by the formula $\dfrac{(1+i)^n - 1}{i}$ and rounded to five decimal places, where i is the interest rate per period and n is the total number of periods.

EXAMPLE1 — CALCULATING THE FUTURE VALUE OF AN ORDINARY ANNUITY

Stuart Daniels deposited $3,000 at the *end* of each year for 8 years in his savings account. If his bank paid 5% interest compounded annually, use Table 12-1 to find the future value of Stuart's account.

SOLUTIONSTRATEGY

Step 1. The rate period is 5% (5% ÷ 1 period per year).

Step 2. The number of periods is eight (8 years × 1 period per year).

Step 3. From Table 12-1, the table factor for 5%, eight periods is 9.54911.

Step 4. Future value = Ordinary annuity table factor × Annuity payment

Future value = 9.54911 × 3,000 = <u>$28,647.33</u>

TRYITEXERCISE 1

Freeport Bank is paying 8% interest compounded quarterly. Use Table 12-1 to find the future value of $1,000 deposited at the *end* of every 3 months for 6 years.

CHECK YOUR ANSWER WITH THE SOLUTION ON PAGE 412.

CALCULATING THE FUTURE VALUE OF AN ANNUITY DUE BY USING TABLES

12-2

Once again, for illustrative purposes, let's manually calculate the future value of the annuity. This time, however, it is an annuity due.

> **What is the amount of an annuity due of $10,000 per year for 4 years at 6% interest compounded annually?**

Because this is an annuity due, the payment is made at the *beginning* of each period. Each interest calculation uses $I = PRT$, with $R = .06$ and $T = 1$ year.

Time	Balance	
Beginning of period 1	10,000.00	First annuity payment (beginning of period 1)
	+ 600.00	Interest earned, period 1 (10,000.00 × .06 × 1)
End of period 1	10,600.00	
Beginning of period 2	10,600.00	
	10,000.00	Second annuity payment (beginning of period 2)
	+ 1,236.00	Interest earned, period 2 (20,600.00 × .06 × 1)
End of period 2	21,836.00	
Beginning of period 3	21,836.00	
	10,000.00	Third annuity payment (beginning of period 3)
	+ 1,910.16	Interest earned, period 3 (31,836.00 × .06 × 1)
End of period 3	33,746.16	
Beginning of period 4	33,746.16	
	10,000.00	Fourth annuity payment (beginning of period 4)
	+ 2,624.77	Interest earned, period 4 (43,746.16 × .06 × 1)
End of period 4	<u>$46,370.93</u>	<u>Future value of the annuity due</u>

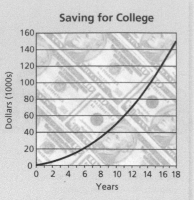

Saving for College

If parents save and invest $10 per workday at 12% interest from the birth date of their child, when the child is 18 and ready for college, the parents would have $150,000 accumulated—through the power of compounding.

When the future value of an annuity due is calculated, the table factor is found by using the same table as ordinary annuities (Table 12-1), with some modifications in the steps. With annuities due, you must *add* one period to the number of periods and *subtract* 1.00000 from the table factor.

STEPS FOR CALCULATING FUTURE VALUE (AMOUNT) OF AN ANNUITY DUE

STEP 1. Calculate the number of periods of the annuity (years × periods per year) and *add* one period to the total.

STEP 2. Calculate the interest rate per period (nominal rate ÷ periods per year).

STEP 3. From Table 12-1, locate the table factor at the intersection of the rate-per-period column and the number-of-periods row.

STEP 4. *Subtract* 1.00000 from the ordinary annuity table factor to get the annuity due table factor.

STEP 5. Calculate the future value of the annuity due.

Future value (annuity due) = Annuity due table factor × Annuity payment

EXAMPLE2 CALCULATING THE FUTURE VALUE OF AN ANNUITY DUE

Chris Manning deposited $60 at the *beginning* of each month for 2 years at his credit union. If the interest rate was 12% compounded monthly, use Table 12-1 to calculate the future value of Chris's account.

►SOLUTIONSTRATEGY

Step 1. Number of periods of the annuity due is 24 (2 × 12) + 1 for a total of 25.

Step 2. Interest rate per period is 1% (12% ÷ 12).

Step 3. The ordinary annuity table factor at the intersection of the rate column and the periods row is 28.24320.

Step 4. Subtract 1.00000 from the table factor:

$$28.24320 \quad \text{ordinary annuity table factor}$$
$$\underline{-1.00000}$$
$$27.24320 \quad \text{annuity due table factor}$$

Step 5. Future value = Annuity due table factor × Annuity payment

Future value = 27.24320 × 60 = $\underline{\$1,634.59}$

►TRYITEXERCISE 2

Vista Savings & Loan is paying 6% interest compounded quarterly. Use Table 12-1 to calculate the future value of $1,000 deposited at the *beginning* of every 3 months for 5 years.

CHECK YOUR ANSWER WITH THE SOLUTION ON PAGE 412.

12-3 CALCULATING THE FUTURE VALUE OF AN ORDINARY ANNUITY AND AN ANNUITY DUE BY FORMULA

Students with financial, business, or scientific calculators may use the following formulas to solve for the future value of an ordinary annuity and the future value of an annuity due.

Future value of an ordinary annuity	Future value of an annuity due
$FV = Pmt \times \dfrac{(1 + i)^n - 1}{i}$	$FV = Pmt \times \dfrac{(1 + i)^n - 1}{i} \times (1 + i)$

where:

FV = **future value**
Pmt = **annuity payment**
   i = **interest rate per period (nominal rate ÷ periods per year)**
   n = **number of periods (years × periods per year)**

Ordinary Annuity
Calculator Sequence: 1 $+$ i $=$ y^x n $-$ 1 $=$ $\div$ i $\times$ Pmt $=$ $FV_{\text{ordinary annuity}}$

Annuity Due
Calculator Sequence: 1 $+$ i $=$ $\times$ $FV_{\text{ordinary annuity}}$ $=$ $FV_{\text{annuity due}}$

EXAMPLE3 USING FORMULAS TO CALCULATE ANNUITIES

a. What is the future value of an ordinary annuity of $100 per month for 3 years at 6% interest compounded monthly?

b. What is the future value of this investment if it is an annuity due?

SOLUTIONSTRATEGY

a. For this future value of an ordinary annuity problem, we use $i = .5\%(6\% \div 12)$ and $n = 36$ periods (3 years × 12 periods per year).

$$FV = Pmt \times \frac{(1 + i)^n - 1}{i}$$

$$FV = 100 \times \frac{(1 + .005)^{36} - 1}{.005}$$

$$FV = 100 \times \frac{(1.005)^{36} - 1}{.005}$$

$$FV = 100 \times \frac{1.196680525 - 1}{.005}$$

$$FV = 100 \times \frac{.196680525}{.005}$$

$$FV = 100 \times 39.336105 = \$3,933.61$$

Calculator Sequence: 1 $+$ .005 $=$ y^x 36 $-$ 1 $=$ $\div$ .005 $\times$ 100 $=$ $\underline{\$3,933.61}$

b. To solve the problem as an annuity due rather than an ordinary annuity, multiply $(1 + i)$, for one extra compounding period, by the future value of the ordinary annuity.

$$FV_{\text{annuity due}} = (1 + i) \times FV_{\text{ordinary annuity}}$$

$$FV_{\text{annuity due}} = (1 + .005) \times 3,933.61$$

$$FV_{\text{annuity due}} = (1.005) \times 3,933.61 = \underline{\$3,953.28}$$

Calculator Sequence: 1 $+$ .005 $=$ $\times$ 3,933.61 $=$ $\underline{\$3,953.28}$

TRYITEXERCISE 3

Katrina Byrd invested $250 at the *end* of every 3-month period for 5 years at 8% interest compounded quarterly.

a. How much is Katrina's investment worth after 5 years?

b. If Katrina had invested the money at the *beginning* of each 3-month period rather than at the end, how much would be in the account?

CHECK YOUR ANSWERS WITH THE SOLUTIONS ON PAGE 412.

SECTION I 12 REVIEW EXERCISES

Note: Round to the nearest cent when necessary.

Use Table 12-1 to calculate the future value of the following ordinary annuities.

	Annuity Payment	Payment Frequency	Time Period (years)	Nominal Rate (%)	Interest Compounded	Future Value of the Annuity
1.	$1,000	every 3 months	4	8	quarterly	$18,639.29
2.	$2,500	every 6 months	5	4	semiannually	_____
3.	$10,000	every year	10	9	annually	_____
4.	$200	every month	2	6	monthly	_____

5. Yolanda deposited $1,100 at the END of each six months for 2 years in a savings account. If the account paid 6% interest, compounded semiannually, use Table 12-1 to find the future value of her account.

Use Table 12-1 to calculate the future value of the following annuities due.

	Annuity Payment	Payment Frequency	Time Period (years)	Nominal Rate (%)	Interest Compounded	Future Value of the Annuity
6.	$400	every 6 months	12	10	semiannually	$18,690.84
7.	$1,000	every 3 months	3	8	quarterly	_____
8.	$50	every month	$2\frac{1}{2}$	6	monthly	_____
9.	$2,000	every year	25	5	annually	_____

10. Your bank pays 6% interest, compounded semiannually. Use Table 12-1 to find the future value of $800 deposited at the BEGINNING of every six months, for 16 years.

Solve the following exercises by using Table 12-1.

11. Paragon Savings & Loan is paying 6% interest compounded monthly. How much will $100 deposited at the *end* of each month be worth after 2 years?

12. Suntech Distributors, Inc. deposits $5,000 at the *beginning* of each 3-month period for 6 years in an account paying 8% interest compounded quarterly.

   a. How much will be in the account at the end of the 6-year period?

   b. What is the total amount of interest earned in this account?

13. Jess Thomas deposits $100 each payday into an account at 6% interest compounded monthly. She gets paid on the last day of each month. How much will her account be worth at the end of 30 months?

14. Jorge Otero has set up an annuity due with the United Credit Union. At the beginning of each month, $170 is electronically debited from his checking account and placed into a savings account earning 6% interest compounded monthly. What is the value of Jorge's account after 18 months?

15. When Ben Taylor was born, his parents began depositing $500 at the *beginning* of every year into an annuity to save for his college education. If the account paid 7% interest compounded annually for the first 10 years and then dropped to 5% for the next 8 years, how much is the account worth now that Ben is 18 years old and ready for college?

Learning Tip

Exercise 15, Solution Hint: Once you have determined the account value after the first 10 years, don't forget to apply 5% compound interest to that value for the remaining 8 years.

Solve the following exercises by using formulas.

Ordinary Annuities

	Annuity Payment	Payment Frequency	Time Period (years)	Nominal Rate (%)	Interest Compounded	Future Value of the Annuity
16.	$2,000	every 6 months	3	3.0	semiannually	$12,459.10
17.	$300	every month	8	6.0	monthly	_____

18. Amishi deposited $500, at the END of each six months for 17 years in a savings account. If the account paid 6% interest, compounded semiannually, use the appropriate formula to find the future value of her account.

Annuities Due

	Annuity Payment	Payment Frequency	Time Period (years)	Nominal Rate (%)	Interest Compounded	Future Value of the Annuity
19.	$675	every month	5	1.5	monthly	$42,082.72
20.	$4,800	every 3 months	3	6.0	quarterly	_____

21. Use the appropriate formula to find the future value of $800 deposited at the BEGINNING of every six months, for 18 years if a bank pays 6% interest, compounded semiannually.

22. To establish a "rainy day" cash reserve account, Bonanza Industries deposits $10,000 of its profit at the end of each quarter into a money market account that pays 1.75% interest compounded quarterly.

a. How much will the account be worth in 3 years?

b. How much will the account be worth in $4\frac{1}{2}$ years?

23. As a part of his retirement planning strategy, Mark Woodson deposits $125 each payday into an investment account at 3% interest compounded monthly. Mark gets paid on the first day of each month.

a. How much will his account be worth in 5 years?

b. How much will his account be worth in 15 years?

24. Hi-Tech Hardware has been in business for a few years and is doing well. The owner has decided to save for a future expansion to a second location. He invests $1,000 at the *end* of every month at 12% interest compounded monthly.

a. How much will be available for the second store after $2\frac{1}{2}$ years?

b. How much would be in the account if the owner saved for 5 years?

c. How much would be in the account after 5 years if it had been an annuity due?

BUSINESS DECISION: PLANNING YOUR NEST EGG

25. As part of your retirement plan, you have decided to deposit $3,000 at the *beginning* of each year into an account paying 5% interest compounded annually.

   a. How much would the account be worth after 10 years?

   b. How much would the account be worth after 20 years?

   c. When you retire in 30 years, what will be the total worth of the account?

   d. If you found a bank that paid 6% interest compounded annually rather than 5%, how much would you have in the account after 30 years?

   e. Use the future value of an annuity due formula to calculate how much you would have in the account after 30 years if the bank in part d switched from annual compounding to monthly compounding and you deposited $250 at the *beginning* of each month instead of $3,000 at the *beginning* of each year.

Dollars AND Sense

In 1950, 16 workers contributed to the Social Security benefit of a single retiree. Today, approximately 2.8 workers pay for a retiree's Social Security benefit and by 2025 that number is projected to fall to just 2.

 **12** SECTION II

PRESENT VALUE OF AN ANNUITY: ORDINARY AND ANNUITY DUE

In Section I of this chapter, we learned to calculate the future value of an annuity. This business situation requires that a series of equal payments be made into an account, such as a savings account. The annuity starts with nothing and accumulates at compound interest to a future amount. Now consider the opposite situation. What if we wanted an account from which we could withdraw a series of equal payments over a period of time? This business situation requires that a lump sum amount be deposited at compound interest now to yield the specified annuity payments. The lump sum that is required up front is known as the **present value of an annuity** present value of an annuity.

Let's look at a business situation using this type of annuity. A company owes $10,000 interest to bondholders at the end of each month for the next 3 years. The company decides to set up an account with a lump sum deposit now, which at compound interest will yield the $10,000 monthly payments for 3 years. After 3 years, the debt will have been paid and the account will be zero.

Just as in Section I, these annuities can be ordinary, whereby withdrawals from the account are made at the *end* of each period, or annuity due, in which the withdrawals are made at the *beginning*. As with the future value of an annuity, we will use tables to calculate the present value of an annuity. Once again, in addition to tables, these annuities can be solved by using formulas requiring a calculator with a y^x key.

present value of an annuity
Lump sum amount of money that must be deposited now to provide a specified series of equal payments (annuity) in the future.

12-4 CALCULATING THE PRESENT VALUE OF AN ORDINARY ANNUITY BY USING TABLES

Table 12-2 on pages 394 and 395 is used to calculate the lump sum required to be deposited now to yield the specified annuity payment.

STEPS FOR CALCULATING PRESENT VALUE OF AN ORDINARY ANNUITY

STEP 1. Calculate the interest rate per period for the annuity (nominal rate ÷ periods per year).

STEP 2. Determine the number of periods of the annuity (years × periods per year).

STEP 3. From Table 12-2, locate the present value table factor at the intersection of the rate-per-period column and the number-of-periods row.

STEP 4. Calculate the present value of the ordinary annuity.

$$\text{Present value (ordinary annuity)} = \frac{\text{Ordinary annuity}}{\text{table factor}} \times \frac{\text{Annuity}}{\text{payment}}$$

EXAMPLE4 CALCULATING THE PRESENT VALUE OF AN ORDINARY ANNUITY

How much must be deposited now at 9% compounded annually to yield an annuity payment of $5,000 at the end of each year for 10 years?

SOLUTIONSTRATEGY

Step 1. The rate per period is 9% (9% ÷ 1 period per year).

Step 2. The number of periods is 10 (10 years × 1 period per year).

Step 3. From Table 12-2, the table factor for 9%, 10 periods is 6.41766.

Step 4. Present value = Ordinary annuity table factor × Annuity payment
Present value = 6.41766 × 5,000 = $32,088.30

TRYITEXERCISE 4

The Broadway Movieplex needs $20,000 at the end of each 6-month movie season for renovations and new projection equipment. How much must be deposited now at 8% compounded semiannually to yield this annuity payment for the next 6 years?

CHECK YOUR ANSWER WITH THE SOLUTION ON PAGE 412.

iStock.com/Nikada

CALCULATING THE PRESENT VALUE OF AN ANNUITY DUE BY USING TABLES

12-5

The present value of an annuity due is calculated by using the same table as ordinary annuities, with some modifications in the steps.

STEPS FOR CALCULATING PRESENT VALUE OF AN ANNUITY DUE

STEP 1. Calculate the number of periods of the annuity (years × periods per year) and *subtract* one period from the total.

STEP 2. Calculate the interest rate per period (nominal rate ÷ periods per year).

STEP 3. From Table 12-2, locate the table factor at the intersection of the rate-per-period column and the number-of-periods row.

STEP 4. *Add* 1.00000 to the ordinary annuity table factor to get the annuity due table factor.

STEP 5. Calculate the present value of the annuity due.

$$\text{Present value (annuity due)} = \text{Annuity due table factor} \times \text{Annuity payment}$$

Learning Tip

The procedure for finding the present value table factor for an annuity due is the *opposite* of that for future value factors. This time you must *subtract* a period and *add* a 1.00000.

EXAMPLE5 CALCULATING THE PRESENT VALUE OF AN ANNUITY DUE

How much must be deposited now at 10% compounded semiannually to yield an annuity payment of $2,000 at the beginning of each 6-month period for 7 years?

SOLUTIONSTRATEGY

Step 1. The number of periods for the annuity due is 14 (7 years × 2 periods per year) less 1 period = 13.

Step 2. The rate per period is 5% (10% ÷ 2 periods per year).

Step 3. From Table 12-2, the ordinary annuity table factor for 5%, 13 periods is 9.39357.

Step 4. Add 1 to the table factor from Step 3 to get 10.39357, the annuity due table factor.

Step 5. Present value (annuity due) = Annuity due table factor × Annuity payment
Present value = 10.39357 × 2,000 = $20,787.14

TRYITEXERCISE 5

You are the accountant at Supreme Lumber, Inc. Based on sales and expense forecasts, you have estimated that $10,000 must be sent to the Internal Revenue Service for income tax payments at the *beginning* of each 3-month period for the next 3 years. How much must be deposited now at 6% compounded quarterly to yield the annuity payment needed?

CHECK YOUR ANSWER WITH THE SOLUTION ON PAGE 412.

TABLE 12-2 Present Value (Amount) of an Ordinary Annuity of $1

Periods	$\frac{1}{2}\%$	1%	$1\frac{1}{2}\%$	2%	3%	4%	5%	6%	7%	8%	Periods
1	0.99502	0.99010	0.98522	0.98039	0.97087	0.96154	0.95238	0.94340	0.93458	0.92593	1
2	1.98510	1.97040	1.95588	1.94156	1.91347	1.88609	1.85941	1.83339	1.80802	1.78326	2
3	2.97025	2.94099	2.91220	2.88388	2.82861	2.77509	2.72325	2.67301	2.62432	2.57710	3
4	3.95050	3.90197	3.85438	3.80773	3.71710	3.62990	3.54595	3.46511	3.38721	3.31213	4
5	4.92587	4.85343	4.78264	4.71346	4.57971	4.45182	4.32948	4.21236	4.10020	3.99271	5
6	5.89638	5.79548	5.69719	5.60143	5.41719	5.24214	5.07569	4.91732	4.76654	4.62288	6
7	6.86207	6.72819	6.59821	6.47199	6.23028	6.00205	5.78637	5.58238	5.38929	5.20637	7
8	7.82296	7.65168	7.48593	7.32548	7.01969	6.73274	6.46321	6.20979	5.97130	5.74664	8
9	8.77906	8.56602	8.36052	8.16224	7.78611	7.43533	7.10782	6.80169	6.51523	6.24689	9
10	9.73041	9.47130	9.22218	8.98259	8.53020	8.11090	7.72173	7.36009	7.02358	6.71008	10
11	10.67703	10.36763	10.07112	9.78685	9.25262	8.76048	8.30641	7.88687	7.49867	7.13896	11
12	11.61893	11.25508	10.90751	10.57534	9.95400	9.38507	8.86325	8.38384	7.94269	7.53608	12
13	12.55615	12.13374	11.73153	11.34837	10.63496	9.98565	9.39357	8.85268	8.35765	7.90378	13
14	13.48871	13.00370	12.54338	12.10625	11.29607	10.56312	9.89864	9.29498	8.74547	8.24424	14
15	14.41662	13.86505	13.34323	12.84926	11.93794	11.11839	10.37966	9.71225	9.10791	8.55948	15
16	15.33993	14.71787	14.13126	13.57771	12.56110	11.65230	10.83777	10.10590	9.44665	8.85137	16
17	16.25863	15.56225	14.90765	14.29187	13.16612	12.16567	11.27407	10.47726	9.76322	9.12164	17
18	17.17277	16.39827	15.67256	14.99203	13.75351	12.65930	11.68959	10.82760	10.05909	9.37189	18
19	18.08236	17.22601	16.42617	15.67846	14.32380	13.13394	12.08532	11.15812	10.33560	9.60360	19
20	18.98742	18.04555	17.16864	16.35143	14.87747	13.59033	12.46221	11.46992	10.59401	9.81815	20
21	19.88798	18.85698	17.90014	17.01121	15.41502	14.02916	12.82115	11.76408	10.83553	10.01680	21
22	20.78406	19.66038	18.62082	17.65805	15.93692	14.45112	13.16300	12.04158	11.06124	10.20074	22
23	21.67568	20.45582	19.33086	18.29220	16.44361	14.85684	13.48857	12.30338	11.27219	10.37106	23
24	22.56287	21.24339	20.03041	18.91393	16.93554	15.24696	13.79864	12.55036	11.46933	10.52876	24
25	23.44564	22.02316	20.71961	19.52346	17.41315	15.62208	14.09394	12.78336	11.65358	10.67478	25
26	24.32402	22.79520	21.39863	20.12104	17.87684	15.98277	14.37519	13.00317	11.82578	10.80998	26
27	25.19803	23.55961	22.06762	20.70690	18.32703	16.32959	14.64303	13.21053	11.98671	10.93516	27
28	26.06769	24.31644	22.72672	21.28127	18.76411	16.66306	14.89813	13.40616	12.13711	11.05108	28
29	26.93302	25.06579	23.37608	21.84438	19.18845	16.98371	15.14107	13.59072	12.27767	11.15841	29
30	27.79405	25.80771	24.01584	22.39646	19.60044	17.29203	15.37245	13.76483	12.40904	11.25778	30
31	28.65080	26.54229	24.64615	22.93770	20.00043	17.58849	15.59281	13.92909	12.53181	11.34980	31
32	29.50328	27.26959	25.26714	23.46833	20.38877	17.87355	15.80268	14.08404	12.64656	11.43500	32
33	30.35153	27.98969	25.87895	23.98856	20.76579	18.14765	16.00255	14.23023	12.75379	11.51389	33
34	31.19555	28.70267	26.48173	24.49859	21.13184	18.41120	16.19290	14.36814	12.85401	11.58693	34
35	32.03537	29.40858	27.07559	24.99862	21.48722	18.66461	16.37419	14.49825	12.94767	11.65457	35
36	32.87102	30.10751	27.66068	25.48884	21.83225	18.90828	16.54685	14.62099	13.03521	11.71719	36

The values in Table 12-2 were generated by the formula $\dfrac{(1 + i)^n - 1}{i(1 + i)^n}$ and rounded to five decimal places, where i is the interest rate per period and n is the total number of periods.

TABLE 12-2 Present Value (Amount) of an Ordinary Annuity of $1   (*Continued*)

Periods	9%	10%	11%	12%	13%	14%	15%	16%	17%	18%	Periods
1	0.91743	0.90909	0.90090	0.89286	0.88496	0.87719	0.86957	0.86207	0.85470	0.84746	1
2	1.75911	1.73554	1.71252	1.69005	1.66810	1.64666	1.62571	1.60523	1.58521	1.56564	2
3	2.53129	2.48685	2.44371	2.40183	2.36115	2.32163	2.28323	2.24589	2.20958	2.17427	3
4	3.23972	3.16987	3.10245	3.03735	2.97447	2.91371	2.85498	2.79818	2.74324	2.69006	4
5	3.88965	3.79079	3.69590	3.60478	3.51723	3.43308	3.35216	3.27429	3.19935	3.12717	5
6	4.48592	4.35526	4.23054	4.11141	3.99755	3.88867	3.78448	3.68474	3.58918	3.49760	6
7	5.03295	4.86842	4.71220	4.56376	4.42261	4.28830	4.16042	4.03857	3.92238	3.81153	7
8	5.53482	5.33493	5.14612	4.96764	4.79877	4.63886	4.48732	4.34359	4.20716	4.07757	8
9	5.99525	5.75902	5.53705	5.32825	5.13166	4.94637	4.77158	4.60654	4.45057	4.30302	9
10	6.41766	6.14457	5.88923	5.65022	5.42624	5.21612	5.01877	4.83323	4.65860	4.49409	10
11	6.80519	6.49506	6.20652	5.93770	5.68694	5.45273	5.23371	5.02864	4.83641	4.65601	11
12	7.16073	6.81369	6.49236	6.19437	5.91765	5.66029	5.42062	5.19711	4.98839	4.79322	12
13	7.48690	7.10336	6.74987	6.42355	6.12181	5.84236	5.58315	5.34233	5.11828	4.90951	13
14	7.78615	7.36669	6.98187	6.62817	6.30249	6.00207	5.72448	5.46753	5.22930	5.00806	14
15	8.06069	7.60608	7.19087	6.81086	6.46238	6.14217	5.84737	5.57546	5.32419	5.09158	15
16	8.31256	7.82371	7.37916	6.97399	6.60388	6.26506	5.95423	5.66850	5.40529	5.16235	16
17	8.54363	8.02155	7.54879	7.11963	6.72909	6.37286	6.04716	5.74870	5.47461	5.22233	17
18	8.75563	8.20141	7.70162	7.24967	6.83991	6.46742	6.12797	5.81785	5.53385	5.27316	18
19	8.95011	8.36492	7.83929	7.36578	6.93797	6.55037	6.19823	5.87746	5.58449	5.31624	19
20	9.12855	8.51356	7.96333	7.46944	7.02475	6.62313	6.25933	5.92884	5.62777	5.35275	20
21	9.29224	8.64869	8.07507	7.56200	7.10155	6.68696	6.31246	5.97314	5.66476	5.38368	21
22	9.44243	8.77154	8.17574	7.64465	7.16951	6.74294	6.35866	6.01133	5.69637	5.40990	22
23	9.58021	8.88322	8.26643	7.71843	7.22966	6.79206	6.39884	6.04425	5.72340	5.43212	23
24	9.70661	8.98474	8.34814	7.78432	7.28288	6.83514	6.43377	6.07263	5.74649	5.45095	24
25	9.82258	9.07704	8.42174	7.84314	7.32998	6.87293	6.46415	6.09709	5.76623	5.46691	25
26	9.92897	9.16095	8.48806	7.89566	7.37167	6.90608	6.49056	6.11818	5.78311	5.48043	26
27	10.02658	9.23722	8.54780	7.94255	7.40856	6.93515	6.51353	6.13636	5.79753	5.49189	27
28	10.11613	9.30657	8.60162	7.98442	7.44120	6.96066	6.53351	6.15204	5.80985	5.50160	28
29	10.19828	9.36961	8.65011	8.02181	7.47009	6.98304	6.55088	6.16555	5.82039	5.50983	29
30	10.27365	9.42691	8.69379	8.05518	7.49565	7.00266	6.56598	6.17720	5.82939	5.51681	30
31	10.34280	9.47901	8.73315	8.08499	7.51828	7.01988	6.57911	6.18724	5.83709	5.52272	31
32	10.40624	9.52638	8.76860	8.11159	7.53830	7.03498	6.59053	6.19590	5.84366	5.52773	32
33	10.46444	9.56943	8.80054	8.13535	7.55602	7.04823	6.60046	6.20336	5.84928	5.53197	33
34	10.51784	9.60857	8.82932	8.15656	7.57170	7.05985	6.60910	6.20979	5.85409	5.53557	34
35	10.56682	9.64416	8.85524	8.17550	7.58557	7.07005	6.61661	6.21534	5.85820	5.53862	35
36	10.61176	9.67651	8.87859	8.19241	7.59785	7.07899	6.62314	6.22012	5.86171	5.54120	36

The values in Table 12-2 were generated by the formula $\dfrac{(1 + i)^n - 1}{i(1 + i)^n}$ and rounded to five decimal places, where i is the interest rate per period and n is the total number of periods.

12-6 CALCULATING THE PRESENT VALUE OF AN ORDINARY ANNUITY AND AN ANNUITY DUE BY FORMULA

Students with financial, business, or scientific calculators may use the following formulas to solve for the present value of an ordinary annuity and the present value of an annuity due. Note that the annuity due formula is the same as the ordinary annuity formula except that it is multiplied by $(1 + i)$. This is to account for the fact that with an annuity due, each payment earns interest for one additional period because payments are made at the beginning of each period, not the end.

Present value of an ordinary annuity	Present value of an annuity due
$$PV = Pmt \times \frac{1 - (1 + i)^{-n}}{i}$$	$$PV = Pmt \times \frac{1 - (1 + i)^{-n}}{i} \times (1 + i)$$

where:

PV = present value (lump sum)

Pmt = annuity payment

i = interest rate per period (nominal rate ÷ periods per year)

n = number of periods (years × periods per year)

Ordinary Annuity

Calculator Sequence: 1 $+$ i $=$ y^x n $+/-$ $=$ M+ 1 $-$ MR $=$ $\div$ i $\times$ Pmt $=$ PV

Annuity Due

Calculator Sequence: 1 $+$ i $=$ $\times$ $PV_{\text{ordinary annuity}}$ $=$ $PV_{\text{annuity due}}$

EXAMPLE6 CALCULATING PRESENT VALUE OF AN ANNUITY BY FORMULA

a. What is the present value of an ordinary annuity of $100 per month for 4 years at 6% interest compounded monthly?

b. What is the present value of this investment if it is an annuity due?

►SOLUTIONSTRATEGY

a. For this present value of an ordinary annuity problem, we use $i = .5\%$ (6% ÷ 12) and $n = 48$ periods (4 years × 12 periods per year).

$$PV = Pmt \times \frac{1 - (1 + i)^{-n}}{i}$$

$$PV = 100 \times \frac{1 - (1 + .005)^{-48}}{.005}$$

$$PV = 100 \times \frac{1 - (1.005)^{-48}}{.005}$$

$$PV = 100 \times \frac{1 - .7870984111}{.005}$$

$$PV = 100 \times \frac{.2129015889}{.005}$$

$$PV = 100 \times 42.58031778 = \underline{\$4,258.03}$$

Calculator Sequence:

1 $+$ .005 $=$ y^x 48 $+/-$ $=$ M+ 1 $-$ MR $=$ $\div$ .005 $\times$ 100 $=$ $\underline{\$4,258.03}$

b. To solve as an annuity due rather than an ordinary annuity, multiply the present value of the ordinary annuity by $(1 + i)$ for one extra compounding period.

$$PV_{\text{annuity due}} = (1 + i) \times PV_{\text{ordinary annuity}}$$

$$PV_{\text{annuity due}} = (1 + .005) \times 4,258.03$$

$$PV_{\text{annuity due}} = (1.005) \times 4,258.03 = \underline{\$4,279.32}$$

Calculator Sequence: 1 $+$ .005 $=$ $\times$ 4,258.03 $=$ $\underline{\$4,279.32}$

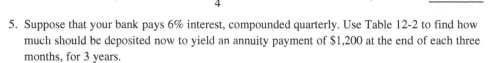

►TRY**IT**EXERCISE 6

Use the present value of an annuity formula to solve the following.

a. Angus McDonald wants $500 at the *end* of each 3-month period for the next 6 years. If Angus's bank is paying 8% interest compounded quarterly, how much must he deposit now to receive the desired ordinary annuity?

b. If Angus wants the payments at the *beginning* of each 3-month period rather than at the end, how much should he deposit?

CHECK YOUR ANSWERS WITH THE SOLUTIONS ON PAGE 412.

REVIEW EXERCISES

12 SECTION II

Note: Round to the nearest cent when necessary.

Use Table 12-2 to calculate the present value of the following ordinary annuities.

	Annuity Payment	Payment Frequency	Time Period (years)	Nominal Rate (%)	Interest Compounded	Present Value of the Annuity
1.	$300	every 6 months	7	10	semiannually	$2,969.59
2.	$2,000	every year	20	7	annually	_____
3.	$4,000	every 3 months	6	8	quarterly	_____
4.	$1,000	every month	$1\frac{3}{4}$	6	monthly	_____

5. Suppose that your bank pays 6% interest, compounded quarterly. Use Table 12-2 to find how much should be deposited now to yield an annuity payment of $1,200 at the end of each three months, for 3 years.

Use Table 12-2 to calculate the present value of the following annuities due.

	Annuity Payment	Payment Frequency	Time Period (years)	Nominal Rate (%)	Interest Compounded	Present Value of the Annuity
6.	$1,400	every year	10	11	annually	$9,151.87
7.	$2,500	every 3 months	5	4	quarterly	_____
8.	$500	every month	$2\frac{1}{4}$	6	monthly	_____
9.	$6,000	every 6 months	15	2	semiannually	_____

10. Use Table 12-2 to find how much should be deposited now at 6% interest, compounded monthly, to yield an annuity payment of $600 at the beginning of each month, for 2 years.

Solve the following exercises by using Table 12-2.

11. Diamond Savings & Loan is paying 6% interest compounded monthly. How much must be deposited now to withdraw an annuity of $400 at the end of each month for 2 years?

12. Jami Minard wants to receive an annuity of $2,000 at the beginning of each year for the next 10 years. How much should be deposited now at 6% compounded annually to accomplish this goal?

13. As the chief accountant for Proline Industries, you have estimated that the company must pay $100,000 income tax to the IRS at the end of each quarter this year. How much should be deposited now at 8% interest compounded quarterly to meet this tax obligation?

14. Ron Sample is the grand prize winner in a college tuition essay contest awarded through a local organization's scholarship fund. The winner receives $2,000 at the beginning of each year for the next 4 years. How much should be invested at 7% interest compounded annually to award the prize?

15. Silver Tip Golf Course management has contracted to pay a golf green maintenance specialist a $680 monthly fee at the end of each month to provide advice on improving the quality of the greens on its 18-hole course. How much should be deposited now into an account that earns 6% compounded monthly to be able to make monthly payments to the consultant for the next year?

16. Analysts at Sky West Airlines did a 3-year projection of expenses. They calculated that the company will need $15,800 at the *beginning* of each 6-month period to buy fuel, oil, lube, and parts for aircraft operations and maintenance. Sky West can get 6% interest compounded semiannually from its bank. How much should Sky West deposit now to support the next 3 years of operations and maintenance expenses?

Solve the following exercises by using formulas.

Present value of an ordinary annuity

	Annuity Payment	Payment Frequency	Time Period (yrs)	Nominal Rate (%)	Interest Compounded	Present Value of the Annuity
17.	$500	every 3 months	$3\frac{1}{4}$	6.0	quarterly	$5,865.77
18.	$280	every month	5	3.0	monthly	_____

19. Kyla wants to have an annuity payment of $700, at the end of each six months. Use the appropriate formula to find how much she should deposit now at 6% interest, compounded semiannually, to yield this payment for 17 years.

Present value of an annuity due

	Annuity Payment	Payment Frequency	Time Period (yrs)	Nominal Rate (%)	Interest Compounded	Present Value of the Annuity
20.	$1,100	every year	5	5.8	annually	$4,929.14
21.	$425	every month	$4\frac{3}{4}$	4.5	monthly	_____

22. A bank pays 6% interest, compounded semiannually. Use the appropriate formula to find how much should be deposited now to yield an annuity payment of $200 at the beginning of each six months, for 17 years.

23. As part of an inheritance, Joan Townsend will receive an annuity of $1,500 at the *end* of each month for the next 6 years. What is the present value of this inheritance at a rate of 2.4% interest compounded monthly?

24. Norm Legend has been awarded a scholarship from Canmore College. For the next 4 years, he will receive $3,500 for tuition and books at the *beginning* of each quarter. How much must the school set aside now in an account earning 3% interest compounded quarterly to pay Norm's scholarship?

BUSINESS DECISION: THE INSURANCE SETTLEMENT

25. Apollo Enterprises has been awarded an insurance settlement of $5,000 at the end of each 6-month period for the next 10 years.

   a. As the accountant, calculate how much the insurance company must set aside now at 6% interest compounded semiannually to pay this obligation to Apollo.

   b. How much would the insurance company have to invest now if the Apollo settlement was changed to $2,500 at the end of each 3-month period for 10 years and the insurance company earned 8% interest compounded quarterly?

c. How much would the insurance company have to invest now if the Apollo settlement was paid at the beginning of each 3-month period rather than at the end?

SECTION III 12 SINKING FUNDS AND AMORTIZATION

sinking funds Accounts used to set aside equal amounts of money at the end of each period at compound interest for the purpose of saving for a future obligation.

amortization A financial arrangement whereby a lump-sum obligation is incurred at compound interest now, such as a loan, and is paid off or liquidated by a series of equal periodic payments for a specified amount of time.

IN THE Business World

Mortgages, which are real estate loans, are a common example of amortization. More detailed coverage, including the preparation of amortization schedules, is found in Chapter 14.

Sinking funds and amortization are two common applications of annuities. In the previous sections of this chapter, the amount of the annuity payment was known and you were asked to calculate the future or present value (lump sum) of the annuity. In this section, the future or present value of the annuity is known and the amount of the payments is calculated.

A sinking fund situation occurs when the future value of an annuity is known and the payment required each period to amount to that future value is the unknown. **Sinking funds** are accounts used to set aside equal amounts of money at the end of each period at compound interest for the purpose of saving for a future obligation. Businesses use sinking funds to accumulate money for such things as new equipment, facility expansion, and other expensive items needed in the future. Another common use is to retire financial obligations such as bond issues that come due at a future date. Individuals can use sinking funds to save for a college education, a car, the down payment on a house, or a vacation.

Amortization is the opposite of a sinking fund. **Amortization** is a financial arrangement whereby a lump-sum obligation is incurred at compound interest now (present value) and is paid off or liquidated by a series of equal periodic payments for a specified amount of time. With amortization, the amount of the loan or obligation is given and the equal payments that will amortize, or pay off, the obligation must be calculated. Some business uses of amortization include paying off loans and liquidating insurance or retirement funds.

In this section, you learn to calculate the sinking fund payment required to save for a future amount and the amortization payment required to liquidate a present amount. We assume that all annuities are ordinary, with payments made at the *end* of each period. As in previous sections, these exercises can be calculated by tables or by formulas.

12-7 CALCULATING THE AMOUNT OF A SINKING FUND PAYMENT BY TABLE

In a sinking fund, the future value is known; therefore, we use the future value of an annuity table (Table 12-1) to calculate the amount of the payment.

STEPS FOR CALCULATING THE AMOUNT OF A SINKING FUND PAYMENT

STEP 1. Using the appropriate rate per period and number of periods of the sinking fund, find the future value table factor from Table 12-2.

STEP 2. Calculate the amount of the sinking fund payment.

$$\text{Sinking fund payment} = \frac{\text{Future value of the sinking fund}}{\text{Future value table factor}}$$

EXAMPLE7 CALCULATING THE AMOUNT OF A SINKING FUND PAYMENT

What sinking fund payment is required at the end of each 6-month period at 6% interest compounded semiannually to amount to $12,000 in 4 years?

▶SOLUTIONSTRATEGY

Step 1. This sinking fund is for 8 periods (4 years × 2 periods per year) at 3% per period (6% ÷ 2 periods per year). From Table 12-1, 8 periods, 3% per period gives a future value table factor of 8.89234.

Step 2. Sinking fund payment = $\dfrac{\text{Future value of the sinking fund}}{\text{Future value table factor}}$

Sinking fund payment = $\dfrac{12{,}000}{8.89234}$ = $\underline{\underline{\$1{,}349.48}}$

▶TRYITEXERCISE 7

Magi Khoo wants to accumulate $8,000 in 5 years for a trip to Europe. If Magi has an investment paying 12% interest compounded quarterly, how much must she deposit at the end of each 3-month period in a sinking fund to reach her desired goal?

CHECK YOUR ANSWER WITH THE SOLUTION ON PAGE 412.

Gilles Lougassi/Shutterstock.com

Sinking funds enable businesses to plan for future purchases of expensive equipment.

CALCULATING THE AMOUNT OF AN AMORTIZATION PAYMENT BY TABLE

12-8

Amortization is the process of "paying off" a financial obligation with a series of equal and regular payments over a period of time. With amortization, the original amount of the loan or obligation is known (present value); therefore, we use the present value table (Table 12-2) to calculate the amount of the payment.

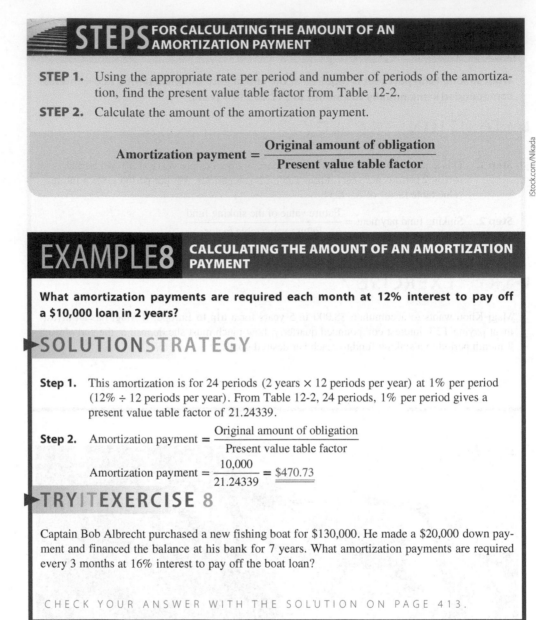

STEPS FOR CALCULATING THE AMOUNT OF AN AMORTIZATION PAYMENT

STEP 1. Using the appropriate rate per period and number of periods of the amortization, find the present value table factor from Table 12-2.

STEP 2. Calculate the amount of the amortization payment.

$$\text{Amortization payment} = \frac{\text{Original amount of obligation}}{\text{Present value table factor}}$$

EXAMPLE 8   CALCULATING THE AMOUNT OF AN AMORTIZATION PAYMENT

What amortization payments are required each month at 12% interest to pay off a $10,000 loan in 2 years?

SOLUTIONSTRATEGY

Step 1. This amortization is for 24 periods (2 years × 12 periods per year) at 1% per period (12% ÷ 12 periods per year). From Table 12-2, 24 periods, 1% per period gives a present value table factor of 21.24339.

Step 2. $\text{Amortization payment} = \dfrac{\text{Original amount of obligation}}{\text{Present value table factor}}$

$\text{Amortization payment} = \dfrac{10,000}{21.24339} = \underline{\$470.73}$

TRYITEXERCISE 8

Captain Bob Albrecht purchased a new fishing boat for $130,000. He made a $20,000 down payment and financed the balance at his bank for 7 years. What amortization payments are required every 3 months at 16% interest to pay off the boat loan?

CHECK YOUR ANSWER WITH THE SOLUTION ON PAGE 413.

12-9 CALCULATING SINKING FUND PAYMENTS BY FORMULA

In addition to using Table 12-1, sinking fund payments may be calculated by using the following formula:

$$\text{Sinking fund payment} = FV \times \frac{i}{(1 + i)^n - 1}$$

where:

FV = **amount needed in the future**

i = **interest rate per period (nominal rate ÷ periods per year)**

n = **number of periods (years × periods per year)**

Calculator Sequence:

1 [+] i [=] [y^x] n [−] 1 [=] [M+] i [÷] [MR] [×] FV [=] Sinking fund payment

EXAMPLE9 CALCULATING SINKING FUND PAYMENTS BY FORMULA

Ocean Air Corporation needs $100,000 in 5 years to pay off a bond issue. What sinking fund payment is required at the end of each month at 12% interest compounded monthly to meet this financial obligation?

▶SOLUTIONSTRATEGY

To solve this sinking fund problem, we use 1% interest rate per period (12% ÷ 12) and 60 periods (5 years × 12 periods per year).

$$\text{Sinking fund payment} = \text{Future value} \times \frac{i}{(1 + i)^n - 1}$$

$$\text{Sinking fund payment} = 100{,}000 \times \frac{.01}{(1 + .01)^{60} - 1}$$

$$\text{Sinking fund payment} = 100{,}000 \times \frac{.01}{.8166967}$$

$$\text{Sinking fund payment} = 100{,}000 \times .0122444 = \$1{,}224.44$$

Calculator Sequence:

1 $+$ .01 $=$ y^x 60 $-$ 1 $=$ M+ .01 $\div$ MR $\times$ 100,000 $=$ $1,224.44

▶TRYITEXERCISE 9

Big Sky Ski Rental Center will need $40,000 in 6 years to replace aging equipment. What sinking fund payment is required at the end of each month at 6% interest compounded monthly to amount to the $40,000 in 6 years?

CHECK YOUR ANSWER WITH THE SOLUTION ON PAGE 413.

CALCULATING AMORTIZATION PAYMENTS BY FORMULA

12-10

In addition to using Table 12-2, amortization payments may be calculated by using the following formula:

$$\textbf{Amortization payment} = PV \times \frac{i}{1 - (1 + i)^{-n}}$$

where:

PV = amount of the loan or obligation

i = interest rate per period (nominal rate ÷ periods per year)

n = number of periods (years × periods per year)

Calculator Sequence:

1 $+$ i $=$ y^x n $+/-$ $=$ M+ 1 $-$ MR $=$ MC M+ i $\div$ MR $\times$ PV $=$ Amortization payment

EXAMPLE10   CALCULATING AMORTIZATION PAYMENTS BY FORMULA

What amortization payment is required each month at 18% interest to pay off $5,000 in 3 years?

▶SOLUTIONSTRATEGY

To solve this amortization problem, we use 1.5% interest rate per period (18% ÷ 12) and 36 periods (3 years × 12 periods per year).

$$\text{Amortization payment} = \text{Present value} \times \frac{i}{1 - (1 + i)^{-n}}$$

$$\text{Amortization payment} = 5{,}000 \times \frac{.015}{1 - (1 + .015)^{-36}}$$

$$\text{Amortization payment} = 5{,}000 \times \frac{.015}{.4149103}$$

$$\text{Amortization payment} = 5{,}000 \times .0361524 = \underline{\$180.76}$$

Calculator Sequence:

1 $+$ .015 $=$ y^x 36 $+/-$ $=$ M+ 1 $-$ MR $=$ MC M+ .015 $\div$ MR $\times$ 5,000 $=$

$$\underline{\$180.76}$$

▶TRYITEXERCISE 10

Apex Manufacturing recently purchased a new computer system for $150,000. What amortization payment is required each month at 12% interest to pay off this obligation in 8 years?

CHECK YOUR ANSWER WITH THE SOLUTION ON PAGE 413.

SECTION III 12 REVIEW EXERCISES

Note: Round to the nearest cent when necessary.

For the following sinking funds, use Table 12-1 to calculate the amount of the periodic payments needed to amount to the financial objective (future value of the annuity).

	Sinking Fund Payment	Payment Frequency	Time Period (years)	Nominal Rate (%)	Interest Compounded	Future Value (Objective)
1.	$2,113.50	every 6 months	8	10	semiannually	$50,000
2.	_____	every year	14	9	annually	$250,000
3.	_____	every 3 months	5	4	quarterly	$1,500
4.	_____	every month	1½	6	monthly	$4,000

5. Choi Home Repair needs to accumulate $23,000 in 6 years to purchase new equipment. What sinking fund payment would they need to make at the end of each three months, at 6% interest compounded quarterly? Use Table 12-1.

You have just been hired as a loan officer at the Eagle National Bank. Your first assignment is to calculate the amount of the periodic payment required to amortize (pay off) the following loans being considered by the bank (use Table 12-2).

	Loan Payment	Payment Period	Term of Loan (years)	Nominal Rate (%)	Present Value (Amount of Loan)
6.	$4,189.52	every year	12	9	$30,000
7.	_____	every 3 months	5	8	$5,500
8.	_____	every month	$1\frac{3}{4}$	6	$10,000
9.	_____	every 6 months	8	6	$13,660

10. What amortization payment would you need to make each month at 6% interest compounded monthly to pay off a loan of $13,000 in 2 years? Use Table 12-2.

Solve the following exercises by using tables.

11. Everest Industries established a sinking fund to pay off a $10,000,000 loan that comes due in 8 years for a corporate yacht.

    a. What equal payments must be deposited into the fund every 3 months at 6% interest compounded quarterly for Everest to meet this financial obligation?

    b. What is the total amount of interest earned in this sinking fund account?

Corporate yachts provide companies with ways to recognize employees; secure the undivided attention of valued clients; perform product launches; hold meetings, conferences, and presentations; and serve as handsome tax write-offs.

12. Jennifer Kaufman bought a used Toyota Prius for $15,500. She made a $2,500 down payment and is financing the balance at Imperial Bank over a 3-year period at 12% interest. As her banker, calculate what equal monthly payments will be required by Jennifer to amortize the car loan.

13. Green Thumb Landscaping buys new lawn equipment every 3 years. It is estimated that $25,000 will be needed for the next purchase. The company sets up a sinking fund to save for this obligation.

    a. What equal payments must be deposited every 6 months if interest is 8% compounded semiannually?

    b. What is the total amount of interest earned by the sinking fund?

14. Paul and Donna Kelsch are planning a Mediterranean cruise in 4 years and will need $7,500 for the trip. They decide to set up a "sinking fund" savings account for the vacation. They intend to make regular payments at the end of each 3-month period into the account that pays 6% interest compounded quarterly. What periodic sinking fund payment will allow them to achieve their vacation goal?

15. Valerie Ross is ready to retire and has saved $200,000 for that purpose. She wants to amortize (liquidate) that amount in a retirement fund so that she will receive equal annual payments over the next 25 years. At the end of the 25 years, no funds will be left in the account. If the fund earns 4% interest, how much will Valerie receive each year?

Solve the following exercises by using the sinking fund or amortization formula.

Sinking fund payment

Sinking Fund Payment	Payment Frequency	Time Period (years)	Nominal Rate (%)	Interest Compounded	Future Value (Objective)
16. $345.97	every 3 months	5	6.0	quarterly	$8,000
17. _____	every month	8	1.5	monthly	$5,500

18. Tara wishes to accumulate $21,000 in 4 years. Use the appropriate formula to find the sinking fund payment she would need to make at the end of each six months, at 6% interest compounded semiannually.

Amortization payment

Loan Payment	Payment Frequency	Time Period (years)	Nominal Rate (%)	Present Value (Amount of Loan)
19. $3,756.68	every year	10	10.6	$22,500
20. _____	every 3 months	4	8.8	$9,000

21. Use the appropriate formula to find the amortization payment you would need to make each month, at 6% interest compounded monthly, to pay off a loan of $3,500 in 2 years.

22. Turnberry Manufacturing has determined that it will need $500,000 in 8 years for a new roof on its southeastern regional warehouse. A sinking fund is established for the roof at 3.4% compounded semiannually. What equal payments are required every 6 months to accumulate the needed funds for the roof?

23. Randy Scott purchased a motorcycle for $8,500 with a loan amortized over 5 years at 7.2% interest. What equal monthly payments are required to amortize this loan?

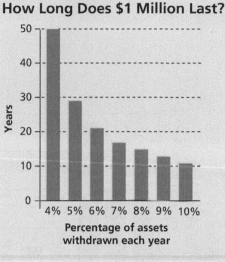

How Long Does $1 Million Last?

24. Betty Price purchased a new home for $225,000 with a 20% down payment and the remainder amortized over a 15-year period at 9% interest.

    a. What amount did Betty finance?

    b. What equal monthly payments are required to amortize this loan over 15 years?

    c. What equal monthly payments are required if Betty decides to take a 20-year loan rather than a 15-year loan?

Dollars AND Sense

This section's Business Decision, "Don't Forget Inflation," illustrates how inflation can affect long-range financial planning in business. Notice how much more the project will cost in 5 years because of rising prices.

At www.bls.gov, the Bureau of Labor Statistics provides an inflation calculator that you can use to enter a year and a dollar amount of buying power and then calculate how much buying power would be required for the same amount of goods or services in a subsequent year after inflation.

25. The Shangri-La Hotel has a financial obligation of $1,000,000 due in 5 years for kitchen equipment. A sinking fund is established to meet this obligation at 7.5% interest compounded monthly.

    a. What equal monthly sinking fund payments are required to accumulate the needed amount?

    b. What is the total amount of interest earned in the account?

BUSINESS DECISION: DON'T FORGET INFLATION!

26. You are the vice president of finance for Neptune Enterprises, Inc., a manufacturer of scuba diving gear. The company is planning a major plant expansion in 5 years. You have decided to start a sinking fund to accumulate the funds necessary for the project. Your company's investments yield 8% compounded quarterly. It is estimated that $2,000,000 in today's dollars will be required; however, the inflation rate on construction costs and plant equipment is expected to average 5% per year for the next 5 years.

    a. Use the compound interest concept from Chapter 11 to determine how much will be required for the project, taking inflation into account.

b. What sinking fund payments will be required at the end of every 3-month period to accumulate the necessary funds?

Forty Years of Changing Inflation Rates

CHAPTER FORMULAS

Future Value of an Annuity

Future value (ordinary annuity) = Ordinary annuity table factor × Annuity payment

$$FV \text{ (ordinary annuity)} = \text{Payment} \times \frac{(1 + i)^n - 1}{i}$$

Future value (annuity due) = Annuity due table factor × Annuity payment

$$FV \text{ (annuity due)} = \text{Payment} \times \frac{(1 + i)^n - 1}{i} \times (1 + i)$$

Present Value of an Annuity

Present value (ordinary annuity) = Ordinary annuity table factor × Annuity payment

$$PV \text{ (ordinary annuity)} = \text{Payment} \times \frac{1 - (1 + i)^{-n}}{i}$$

Present value (annuity due) = Annuity due table factor × Annuity payment

$$PV \text{ (annuity due)} = \text{Payment} \times \frac{1 - (1 + i)^{-n}}{i} \times (1 + i)$$

Sinking Fund

$$\text{Sinking fund payment} = \frac{\text{Future value of the sinking fund}}{\text{Future value table factor}}$$

$$\text{Sinking fund payment} = \text{Future value} \times \frac{i}{(1 + i)^n - 1}$$

Amortization

$$\text{Amortization payment} = \frac{\text{Original amount of obligation}}{\text{Present value table factor}}$$

$$\text{Amortization payment} = \text{Present value} \times \frac{i}{1 - (1 + i)^{-n}}$$

Chapter Summary

Section I: Future Value of an Annuity: Ordinary and Annuity Due

Topic	Important Concepts	Illustrative Examples
Calculating the Future Value of an Ordinary Annuity by Using Tables **Performance Objective 12-1, Page 381**	An annuity is the payment or receipt of *equal* cash amounts per period for a specified amount of time. 1. Calculate the interest rate per period for the annuity (nominal rate ÷ periods per year). 2. Determine the number of periods of the annuity (years × periods per year). 3. From Table 12-1, locate the ordinary annuity table factor at the intersection of the rate column and the periods row. 4. Calculate the future value of an ordinary annuity by	Calculate the future value of an ordinary annuity of $500 every 6 months for 5 years at 12% interest compounded semiannually. Rate per period = 6% (12% ÷ 2 periods per year) Periods = 10 (5 years × 2 periods per year) Table factor 6%, 10 periods = 13.18079 Future value = 13.18079 × 500 Future value = $6,590.40
Calculating the Future Value of an Annuity Due by Using Tables **Performance Objective 12-2, Page 385**	1. Calculate the number of periods of the annuity (years × periods per year) and add one period to the total. 2. Calculate the interest rate per period (nominal rate ÷ periods per year). 3. Locate the table factor at the intersection of the rate column and the periods row. 4. Subtract 1 from the ordinary annuity table factor to get the annuity due table factor. 5. Calculate the future value of an annuity due by	Calculate the future value of an annuity due to $100 per month for 2 years at 12% interest compounded monthly. Periods = (2 × 12) + 1 for a total of 25 Rate per period = 1%, (12% ÷ 12) Table factor 1%, 25 periods = 28.24320 28.24320 − 1 = 27.24320 Future value = 27.24320 × 100 Future value = $2,724.32
Calculating the Future Value of an Ordinary Annuity and an Annuity Due by Formula **Performance Objective 12-3, Page 386**		a. What is the future value of an *ordinary annuity* of $200 per month for 4 years at 12% interest compounded monthly? $$FV = 200 \times \frac{(1 + .01)^{48} - 1}{.01}$$ $FV = 200 \times 61.222608$ $FV = \$12,244.52$ b. What is the future value of this investment if it is an *annuity due*? $FV = 12,244.52 \times (1 + .01)$ $FV = 12,244.52 \times 1.01$ $FV = \$12,366.97$

Section II: Present Value of an Annuity: Ordinary and Annuity Due

Topic	Important Concepts	Illustrative Examples
Calculating the Present Value of an Ordinary Annuity by Using Tables **Performance Objective 12-4, Page 392**	1. Calculate the interest rate per period for the annuity (nominal rate ÷ periods per year). 2. Determine the number of periods of the annuity (years × periods per year). 3. From Table 12-2, locate the present value table factor at the intersection of the rate column and the periods row. 4. Calculate the present value of an ordinary annuity by	How much must be deposited now at 5% compounded annually to yield an annuity payment of $1,000 at the end of each year for 11 years? Rate per period = 5% (5% ÷ 1 period per year) Number of periods = 11 (11 years × 1 period per year) Table factor 5%, 11 periods is 8.30641 Present value = 8.30641 × 1,000 Present value = $8,306.41
Calculating the Present Value of an Annuity Due by Using Tables **Performance Objective 12-5, Page 393**	1. Calculate the number of periods (years × periods per year) and subtract 1 from the total. 2. Calculate rate per period (nominal rate ÷ periods per year). 3. Locate the table factor at the intersection of the rate column and the periods row. 4. Add 1 to the ordinary annuity table factor to get the annuity due table factor. 5. Calculate the present value of an annuity due by	How much must be deposited now at 8% compounded semiannually to yield an annuity payment of $1,000 at the beginning of each 6-month period for 5 years? Number of periods = 10 (5 × 2) less 1 period = 9 Rate per period = 4% (8% ÷ 2) Table factor 4%, 9 periods = 7.43533 7.43533 + 1 = 8.43533 Present value = 8.43533 × 1,000 Present value = $8,435.33
Calculating the Present Value of an Ordinary Annuity and an Annuity Due by Formula **Performance Objective 12-6, Page 396**		a. What is the present value of an ordinary annuity of $100 per month for 5 years at 12% interest compounded monthly? $$PV = 100 \times \frac{1 - (1 + .01)^{-60}}{.01}$$ $$PV = 100 \times 44.955038$$ $$PV = \$4,495.50$$ b. What is the present value of this investment if it is an annuity due? $$PV_{\text{annuity due}} = PV_{\text{ordinary annuity}} \times (1 + i)$$ $$PV = 4,495.50 \times (1 + .01)$$ $$PV = 4,495.50 \times 1.01$$ $$PV = \$4,540.46$$

Section III: Sinking Funds and Amortization

Topic	Important Concepts	Illustrative Examples
Calculating the Amount of a Sinking Fund Payment by Table **Performance Objective 12-7, Page 400**	Sinking funds are accounts used to set aside equal amounts of money at the end of each period at compound interest for the purpose of saving for a known future financial obligation. 1. Using the appropriate rate per period and number of periods, find the future value table factor from Table 12-1. 2. Calculate the amount of the sinking fund payment by	What sinking fund payment is required at the end of each 6-month period at 10% interest compounded semiannually to amount to $10,000 in 7 years? Number of periods = 14 (7 years × 2 periods per year) Rate per period = 5% (10% ÷ 2 periods per year) Table factor 14 periods, 5% = 19.59863 $\text{Payment} = \dfrac{10,000}{19.59863}$ Payment = $510.24
Calculating the Amount of an Amortization Payment by Table **Performance Objective 12-8, Page 401**	Amortization is a financial arrangement whereby a lump-sum obligation is incurred now (present value) and is paid off or liquidated by a series of equal periodic payments for a specified amount of time. 1. Using the appropriate rate per period and number of periods of the amortization, find the present value table factor from Table 12-2. 2. Calculate the amount of the amortization payment by	What amortization payments are required at the end of each month at 18% interest to pay off a $15,000 loan in 3 years? Number of periods = 36 (3 years × 12 periods per year) Rate per period = 1.5% (18% ÷ 12 periods per year) Table factor 36 periods, 1.5% = 27.66068 $\text{Amortization payment} = \dfrac{15,000}{27.66068}$ Amortization payment = $542.29
Calculating Sinking Fund Payments by Formula **Performance Objective 12-9, Page 402**	Sinking fund payments can be calculated by using the following formula	What sinking fund payment is required at the end of each month at 12% interest compounded monthly to amount to $10,000 in 4 years? Rate per period = 1% (12% ÷ 12) Periods = 48 (4 × 12) $Pmt = 10,000 \times \dfrac{.01}{(1 + .01)^{48} - 1}$ $Pmt = 10,000 \times \dfrac{.01}{.6122261}$ $Pmt = 10,000 \times .0163338$ Sinking fund payment = $163.34

Section III (continued)

Topic	Important Concepts	Illustrative Examples
Calculating Amortization Payments by Formula **Performance Objective 12-10, Page 403**	Amortization payments are calculated by using the following formula:	What amortization payment is required each month at 18% interest to pay off $3,000 in 2 years? Rate = 1.5% (18% ÷ 12) Periods = 24 (2 × 12) $Pmt = 3,000 \times \dfrac{.015}{1-(1+.015)^{-24}}$ $Pmt = 3,000 \times \dfrac{.015}{.3004561}$ $Pmt = 3,000 \times .0499241$ Amortization payment = $149.77

TRY IT: EXERCISE SOLUTIONS FOR CHAPTER 12

1. 2%, 24 periods

Future value = Table factor × Annuity payment

Future value = 30.42186 × 1,000 = $30,421.86

2. Periods = 20 (5 × 4) + 1 = 21

$Rate = \dfrac{6\%}{4} = 1\frac{1}{2}\%$

Table factor = 24.47052

$\dfrac{-\ 1.00000}{23.47052}$

Future value = Table factor × Annuity payment

Future value = 23.47052 × 1,000 = $23,470.52

3. a. 2%, 20 periods

$FV = Pmt \times \dfrac{(1+i)^n - 1}{i}$

$FV = 250 \times \dfrac{(1+.02)^{20}-1}{.02} = 250 \times \dfrac{(1.02)^{20}-1}{.02}$

$FV = 250 \times 24.297369 = \$6,074.34$

b. $FV_{\text{annuity due}} = (1+i) \times FV_{\text{ordinary annuity}}$

$FV_{\text{annuity due}} = (1+.02) \times 6,074.34 = \$6,195.83$

4. 4%, 12 periods

Present value = Table factor × Annuity payment

Present value = 9.38507 × 20,000 = $187,701.40

5. Periods = 12 (3 × 4) − 1 = 11

$Rate = \dfrac{6\%}{4} = 1\frac{1}{2}\%$

Table factor = 10.07112

$\dfrac{+\ 1.00000}{11.07112}$

Present value = Table factor × Annuity payment

Present value = 11.07112 × 10,000 = $110,711.20

6. a. 2%, 24 periods

$PV = Pmt \times \dfrac{1-(1+i)^{-n}}{i}$

$PV = 500 \times \dfrac{1-(1+.02)^{-24}}{.02} = 500 \times \dfrac{1-.6217215}{.02}$

$PV = 500 \times 18.913925 = \$9,456.96$

b. $PV_{\text{annuity due}} = (1+i) \times PV_{\text{ordinary annuity}}$

$PV_{\text{annuity due}} = (1+.02) \times 9,456.96 = \$9,646.10$

7. 3%, 20 periods

$\text{Sinking fund payment} = \dfrac{\text{Future value of sinking fund}}{\text{Future value table factor}}$

$\text{Sinking fund payment} = \dfrac{8,000}{26.87037} = \$297.73$

8. Amount financed = 130,000 − 20,000 = $110,000

4%, 28 periods

$$\text{Amortization payment} = \frac{\text{Original amount of obligation}}{\text{Present value table factor}}$$

$$\text{Amortization payment} = \frac{110,000}{16.66306} = \underline{\$6,601.43}$$

9. .5%, 72 periods

$$\text{Sinking fund payment} = FV \times \frac{i}{(1 + i)^n - 1}$$

$$\text{Sinking fund payment} = 40,000 \times \frac{.005}{(1 + .005)^{72} - 1}$$

$$\text{Sinking fund payment} = 40,000 \times .0115729 = \underline{\$462.92}$$

10. 1%, 96 periods

$$\text{Amortization payment} = PV \times \frac{i}{1 - (1 + i)^{-n}}$$

$$\text{Amortization payment} = 150,000 \times \frac{.01}{1 - (1 + .01)^{-96}}$$

$$\text{Amortization payment} = 150,000 \times .0162528 = \underline{\$2,437.93}$$

CONCEPT REVIEW

1. Payment or receipt of equal amounts of money per period for a specified amount of time is known as a(n) _____. (12-1)

2. In a simple annuity, the number of compounding _____ per year coincides with the number of annuity _____ per year. (12-1)

3. An ordinary annuity is paid or received at the _____ of each time period. (12-1, 12-2)

4. An annuity due is paid or received at the _____ of each time period. (12-1, 12-2)

5. The total amount of the annuity payments and the accumulated interest on those payments is known as the _____ value of an annuity. (12-1)

6. The table factor for an annuity due is found by _____ one period to the number of periods of the annuity and then subtracting _____ from the resulting table factor. (12-2)

7. Write the formula for calculating the future value of an ordinary annuity when using a calculator with an exponential function, y^x, key. (12-3)

8. Write the formula for calculating the future value of an annuity due when using a calculator with an exponential function, (y^x), key. (12-3)

9. The lump sum amount of money that must be deposited today to provide a specified series of equal payments (annuity) in the future is known as the _____ value of an annuity. (12-4)

10. The table factor for the present value of an annuity due is found by _____ one period from the number of periods of the annuity and then adding _____ to the resulting table factor. (12-5)

11. A(n) _____ fund is an account used to set aside equal amounts of money at compound interest for the purpose of saving for a future obligation. (12-7)

12. _____ is a financial arrangement whereby a lump-sum obligation is incurred at compound interest now, such as a loan, and is then paid off by a series of equal periodic payments. (12-7, 12-8)

13. Write the formula for calculating a sinking fund payment by table. (12-7)

14. Write the formula for calculating an amortization payment by table. (12-8)

ASSESSMENT TEST

Note: Round to the nearest cent when necessary.

Use Table 12-1 to calculate the future value of the following ordinary annuities.

	Annuity Payment	Payment Frequency	Time Period (years)	Nominal Rate (%)	Interest Compounded	Future Value of the Annuity
1.	$4,000	every 3 months	6	8	quarterly	_____
2.	$10,000	every year	20	5	annually	_____

Use Table 12-1 to calculate the future value of the following annuities due.

	Annuity Payment	Payment Frequency	Time Period (years)	Nominal Rate (%)	Interest Compounded	Future Value of the Annuity
3.	$1,850	every 6 months	12	10	semiannually	_____
4.	$200	every month	$1\frac{3}{4}$	6	monthly	_____

Use Table 12-2 to calculate the present value of the following ordinary annuities.

	Annuity Payment	Payment Frequency	Time Period (years)	Nominal Rate (%)	Interest Compounded	Present Value of the Annuity
5.	$6,000	every year	9	5	annually	_____
6.	$125,000	every 3 months	3	6	quarterly	_____

Use Table 12-2 to calculate the present value of the following annuities due.

	Annuity Payment	Payment Frequency	Time Period (years)	Nominal Rate (%)	Interest Compounded	Present Value of the Annuity
7.	$700	every month	$1\frac{1}{2}$	6	monthly	_____
8.	$2,000	every 6 months	6	4	semiannually	_____

Use Table 12-1 to calculate the amount of the periodic payments needed to amount to the financial objective (future value of the annuity) for the following sinking funds.

	Sinking Fund Payment	Payment Frequency	Time Period (years)	Nominal Rate (%)	Interest Compounded	Future Value (Objective)
9.	_____	every year	13	7	annually	$20,000
10.	_____	every month	$2\frac{1}{4}$	6	monthly	$7,000

Use Table 12-2 to calculate the amount of the periodic payment required to amortize (pay off) the following loans.

	Loan Payment	Payment Period	Term of Loan (years)	Nominal Rate (%)	Interest Compounded	Present Value (Amount of Loan)
11.	_____	every 3 months	8	8	quarterly	$6,000
12.	_____	every month	$2\frac{1}{2}$	6	monthly	$20,000

Solve the following exercises by using tables.

13. How much will $800 deposited into a savings account at the *end* of each month be worth after 2 years at 6% interest compounded monthly?

14. How much will $3,500 deposited at the *beginning* of each 3-month period be worth after 7 years at 12% interest compounded quarterly?

15. What amount must be deposited now to withdraw $200 at the *beginning* of each month for 3 years if interest is 12% compounded monthly?

16. How much must be deposited now to withdraw $4,000 at the *end* of each year for 20 years if interest is 7% compounded annually?

17. Mary Evans plans to buy a used car when she starts college three years from now. She can make deposits at the end of each month into a 6% sinking fund account compounded monthly. If she wants to have $14,500 available to buy the car, what should be the amount of her monthly sinking fund payments?

18. A sinking fund is established by Alliance Industries at 8% interest compounded semiannually to meet a financial obligation of $1,800,000 in 4 years.
   a. What periodic sinking fund payment is required every 6 months to reach the company's goal?

   b. How much greater would the payment be if the interest rate was 6% compounded semiannually rather than 8%?

19. Lucky Strike, a bowling alley, purchased new equipment from Brunswick in the amount of $850,000. Brunswick is allowing Lucky Strike to amortize the cost of the equipment with monthly payments over 2 years at 12% interest. What equal monthly payments will be required to amortize this loan?

CHAPTER
12

EXCEL 3

20. Aaron Grider buys a home for $120,500. After a 15% down payment, the balance is financed at 8% interest for 9 years.
  a. What equal quarterly payments will be required to amortize this mortgage loan?

  b. What is the total amount of interest Aaron will pay on the loan?

Solve the following exercises by using formulas.

Ordinary annuity

	Annuity Payment	Payment Frequency	Time Period (years)	Nominal Rate (%)	Interest Compounded	Future Value of the Annuity
21.	$150	every month	4	3.0	monthly	_____
22.	$5,600	every year	9	1.8	annually	_____

Annuity due

	Annuity Payment	Payment Frequency	Time Period (years)	Nominal Rate (%)	Interest Compounded	Future Value of the Annuity
23.	$500	every 6 months	5	3.0	semiannually	_____
24.	$185	every month	$1\frac{1}{2}$	6.0	monthly	_____

Present value of an ordinary annuity

	Annuity Payment	Payment Frequency	Time Period (years)	Nominal Rate (%)	Interest Compounded	Present Value of the Annuity
25.	$1,500	every month	4	1.5	monthly	_____
26.	$375	every 6 months	2	3	semiannually	_____

Present value of an annuity due

	Annuity Payment	Payment Frequency	Time Period (years)	Nominal Rate (%)	Interest Compounded	Present Value of the Annuity
27.	$2,400	every 3 months	4	10	quarterly	_____
28.	$600	every year	20	4.3	annually	_____

Sinking fund payment

	Sinking Fund Payment	Payment Frequency	Time Period (years)	Nominal Rate (%)	Interest Compounded	Future Value (Objective)
29.	_____	every year	4	3.7	annually	$25,000
30.	_____	every 3 months	3	2	quarterly	$3,600

Amortization payment

	Loan Payment	Payment Frequency	Time Period (years)	Nominal Rate (%)	Present Value (Amount of Loan)
31.	_____	every 6 months	$2\frac{1}{2}$	12.0	$10,400
32.	_____	every month	4	13.5	$2,200

33. The town of Bay Harbor is planning to buy five new hybrid police cars in 4 years. The cars are expected to cost $38,500 each.

    a. What equal quarterly payments must the city deposit into a sinking fund at 3.5% interest compounded quarterly to achieve its goal?

    b. What is the total amount of interest earned in the account?

Hybrid vehicles run off a rechargeable battery and gasoline. With each hybrid burning 20%–30% less gasoline than comparably sized conventional models, they are in great demand by consumers.

34. The Mesa Grande Bank is paying 9% interest compounded monthly.

    a. If you deposit $100 into a savings plan at the beginning of each month, how much will it be worth in 10 years?

    b. How much would the account be worth if the payments were made at the end of each month rather than at the beginning?

35. Sandpiper Savings & Loan is offering mortgages at 7.32% interest. What monthly payments would be required to amortize a loan of $200,000 for 25 years?

BUSINESS DECISION: TIME IS MONEY!

36. You are one of the retirement counselors at the Valley View Bank. You have been asked to give a presentation to a class of high school seniors about the importance of saving for retirement. Your boss, the vice president of the trust division, has designed an example for you to use in your presentation. The students are shown five retirement scenarios and are asked to guess which yields the most money. *Note:* All annuities are *ordinary*. Although some people stop investing, the money remains in the account at 10% interest compounded annually.

    a. Look over each scenario and make an educated guess as to which investor will have the largest accumulation of money invested at 10% over the next 40 years. Then for your presentation, calculate the final value for each scenario.

        • Venus invests $1,200 per year and stops after 15 years.

        • Kevin waits 15 years, invests $1,200 per year for 15 years, and stops.

        • Rafael waits 15 years, then invests $1,200 per year for 25 years.

- Magda waits 10 years, invests $1,500 per year for 15 years, and stops.

- Heather waits 10 years, then invests $1,500 per year for 30 years.

b. Based on the results, what message will this presentation convey to the students?

c. Recalculate each scenario as an annuity due.

d. How can the results be used in your presentation?

COLLABORATIVE LEARNING ACTIVITY

The "Personal" Sinking Fund

1. As a team, design a "personal" sinking fund for something to save for in the future.
   a. What are the amount and the purpose of the fund?
   b. What savings account interest rates are currently being offered at banks and credit unions in your area?
   c. Choose the best rate and calculate what monthly payments would be required to accumulate the desired amount in 1 year, 2 years, and 5 years.

2. As a team, research the annual reports or speak with accountants of corporations in your area that use sinking funds to accumulate money for future obligations. Answer the following questions about those sinking funds.
   a. What is the name of the corporation?
   b. What is the purpose and the amount of the sinking fund?
   c. For how many years is the fund?
   d. How much are the periodic payments?
   e. At what interest rate are these funds growing?

Growing Money

Refer to the "Dollars and Sense" tip on the previous page that discusses how to save for a child's college education. Divide into teams to further research and report to the class on the following.

a. What is the current status of the three tax-free savings plans?
   - 529 plans
   - Coverdell Education Savings Accounts
   - zero coupon bonds

b. What are the current interest rates and contribution limits of the various plans?

c. Speak with a certified financial planner to research other alternatives, such as custodial accounts and IRAs, that are available to those who want to save for their child's college education.

Business Math JOURNAL

Managing Your Money

7 New Rules to Live By

Why is there so much month left at the end of the money? In recent years, our economy has undergone some dramatic changes. The "Great Recession" has significantly altered the financial planning parameters for individuals and families seeking financial freedom.

Here are some new planning guidelines from the editors of *Money* magazine and Bank of America to help you attain your long-term financial goals.

- **Savings**—Save at least 15% (and ideally 20%) of your income for long-term goals. The old rule was 10%, but that was when you could count on pension plans, shorter retirement periods, and better market returns.
- **Debt**—Keep your debt-to-income ratio under 30%. That's down from 36% so that you can direct more cash flow toward emergency and retirement savings. As a cushion, keep a six-month reserve of cash in a high-yield savings account and any additional emergency money in a short-term bond index fund.
- **Home**—Look at refinancing when rates are one percentage point lower than your current rate, not two as in years past when closing costs were higher. You should plan to live in the house for at least as long as it will take to pay off the closing costs and fees with the reduction in payment. (See the Mortgage Refinancing Worksheet in the Review Exercises for Section II of Chapter 14.)
- **Spending**—Keep discretionary spending (clothes, dining out, movies) under 20% of your take-home pay. Before the recession, you could play with up to 30%, but average debt obligations have risen.
- **Investments**—Invest no more than 5% of your portfolio in your company stock or any single stock. The old yardstick was 10%, but you'll be safer with more diversification.
- **Allocation**—To determine how much of your portfolio should be in stocks, subtract your age from 110. The old formula subtracted your age from 100, but rising medical costs and increasing life spans necessitate being more aggressive. If you are comfortable with even more risk, subtract your age from 120.
- **Retirement**—To figure out how big a nest egg you'll need, multiply your ideal annual income by 30. (First, subtract any pension and Social Security income you will receive.) That's up from the previous rule of 25 because of increased longevity.

Helpful Websites

The Internet can be a valuable source of money management information. Some helpful websites are www.bankrate.com, www.creditinfocenter.com, www.moneymanagement.org, www.betterbudgeting.com, and http://moneycentral.msn.com.

create jobs 51/Shutterstock.com

Issues & Activities

1. Use the chart below to:
   a. Distribute the various expenditure categories for a family with annual earnings of $55,000.
   b. Distribute your annual earnings for each expenditure category.
   c. Determine which of your expenditure categories are higher than average and which are lower than average.
   d. List some ways you can save on your annual expenditures.
2. For a family with annual earnings of $64,000, use the "7 New Rules to Live By" to answer the following questions.
   a. Ideally, how much should the family save?
   b. What should the family's debt limit be?
   c. If the family's portfolio amounts to $93,000, what should their limit be on any single stock?
   d. If the family's ideal annual income is $45,000 after pensions and Social Security, how big of a nest egg will they need?
3. In teams, use the websites listed above and other Internet sites to find current trends in "financial planning." List your sources and visually report your findings to the class.

Brainteaser—"Sky-High Debt!"

If a stack of 1,000 thousand dollar bills ($1 million) is 4 inches thick, how high would the stack be if it was equal to $13.72 trillion, the national debt as of December 2010?

See the end of Appendix A for the solution.

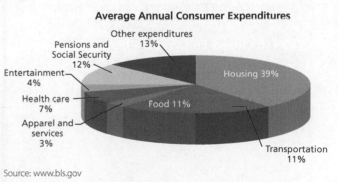

Average Annual Consumer Expenditures

- Other expenditures 13%
- Pensions and Social Security 12%
- Entertainment 4%
- Health care 7%
- Apparel and services 3%
- Housing 39%
- Food 11%
- Transportation 11%

Source: www.bls.gov

CHAPTER 13 Consumer and Business Credit

PERFORMANCE OBJECTIVES

OPEN-END CREDIT—CHARGE ACCOUNTS, CREDIT CARDS, AND LINES OF CREDIT

13 SECTION I

"Buy now, pay later" is a concept that has become an everyday part of the way individuals and businesses purchase goods and services. Merchants in all categories, as well as lending institutions, encourage us to just say "charge it!" Consumers are offered a wide variety of charge accounts with many extra services and incentives attached. Many businesses have charge accounts in the company name. These accounts may be used to facilitate employee travel and entertainment expenses or to fill up the company delivery truck with gasoline without having to deal with cash. Exhibit 13-1 shows a sample credit card and its parts.

Lending and borrowing money comprise a huge portion of the U.S. economic system. Over the years, as the practice became more prevalent, the federal government enacted various legislation to protect the consumer from being misled about credit and finance charges. One of the most important and comprehensive pieces of legislation, known as Regulation Z, covers both installment credit and **open-end credit**.

Regulation Z of the Consumer Credit Protection Act, also known as the Truth in Lending Act, as well as the Fair Credit and Charge Card Disclosure Act, require that lenders fully disclose to the customer, in writing, the cost of the credit and detailed information about their terms. Features such as finance charge, annual percentage rate (APR), cash advances, and annual fees must be disclosed in writing at the time you apply. The **finance charge** is the dollar amount that is paid for the credit. The **annual percentage rate (APR)** is the effective or true annual interest rate being charged. If a card company offers you a written "pre-approved" credit solicitation, the offer must include these terms. Also, card issuers must inform customers if they make certain changes in rates or coverage for credit insurance.

In the past few years, the Federal Reserve implemented a series of amendments to Regulation Z, known as the Credit Card Accountability, Responsibility, and Disclosure Act (the Credit Card Act). These amendments were designed to further protect consumers who

open-end credit A loan arrangement in which there is no set number of payments. As the balance of the loan is reduced, the borrower can renew the amount of the loan up to a pre-approved credit limit. A form of revolving credit.

finance charge Dollar amount that is paid for credit. Total of installment payments for an item less the cost of that item.

annual percentage rate (APR) Effective or true annual interest rate being charged for credit. Must be revealed to borrowers under the Truth in Lending Act.

IN THE Business World

Chip and PIN Credit Cards

In order to combat fraud, chips embedded in these credit cards provide an additional layer of security. Credit card terminals read cryptographic keys contained in the chips and provide further security by asking for a customer's PIN number. Some cards with chips require a signature rather than a PIN and are known as "Chip and Signature Credit Cards."

EXHIBIT 13-1 Parts of a Credit Card

MSSA/Shutterstock.com

unsecured loans Loans that are backed simply by the borrower's "promise" to repay, without any tangible asset pledged as collateral. These loans carry more risk for the lender and therefore have higher interest rates than secured loans.

secured loans Loans that are backed by a tangible asset, such as a car, boat, or home, which can be repossessed and sold if the borrower fails to pay back the loan. These loans carry less risk for the lender and therefore have lower interest rates than do unsecured loans.

revolving credit Loans made on a continuous basis and billed periodically. Borrower makes minimum monthly payments or more and pays interest on the outstanding balance. This is a form of open-end credit extended by many retail stores and credit card companies.

use credit cards from a number of costly and undisclosed bank practices. Exhibit 13-2 outlines the major provisions of these new credit card reforms. Exhibits 13-3 and 13-5 illustrate how these reforms now appear on your monthly credit card statement and bank credit card offer disclosures.

When loans are backed by a simple promise to repay, they are known as **unsecured loans**. Most open-end credit accounts are unsecured. Loans that are backed by tangible assets, such as car and boat loans and home mortgage loans, are known as **secured loans**. These loans are backed, or secured, by an asset that can be repossessed and sold by the lender if the borrower fails to comply with the rules of the loan. Secured loans are covered in Section II of this chapter and also will be discussed in Chapter 14.

Revolving credit is the most popular type of open-end credit. Under this agreement, the consumer has a prearranged credit limit and two payment options. The first option is to use the account as a regular charge account, whereby the balance is paid off at the end of the month with no finance charge. The second option is to make a minimum payment or portion of the payment but less than the full balance. This option leaves a carryover balance, which accrues finance charges by using the following simple interest formula:

$$\text{Interest} = \text{Principal} \times \text{Rate} \times \text{Time}$$

The name *revolving credit* comes from the fact that there is no set number of payments as with installment credit. The account revolves month to month, year to year—technically never being paid off as long as minimum monthly payments are made. Exhibit 13-3 illustrates a typical revolving credit monthly statement.

Using Smartphones for Payment
The use of smartphones to make payments continues to increase and is eventually expected to nearly replace the use of credit cards.

EXHIBIT 13-2   How Credit Card Reforms Affect You

How Credit Card Reforms Affect You

What your credit card company has to tell you
- When they plan to increase your rate or other fees
- How long it will take to pay off your balance

New rules regarding rates, fees, and limits
- No interest rate increases for the first year unless the cardholder goes 60 days past due on the account.
- Promotional rates must remain in effect for at least six months.
- Increased rates apply only to new charges
- Restrictions on over-the-limit transactions
- Caps on high-fee cards
- Protection for underage consumers

Changes to billing and payments
- Standard payment dates and times
- Payments directed to highest interest balances first
- No two-cycle (double-cycle) billing

Reasonable penalty fees and protections
- No fees of more than $25 ($35 in special cases)
- No inactivity fees
- One fee limit for a single transaction
- Explanation of rate increases
- Re-evaluation of increases every six months

13-1   CALCULATING THE FINANCE CHARGE AND NEW BALANCE BY USING THE UNPAID OR PREVIOUS MONTH'S BALANCE METHOD

billing cycles Time periods, usually 28 to 31 days, used in billing revolving credit accounts. Account statements are sent to the borrower after each billing cycle.

Open-end credit transactions are divided into time periods known as **billing cycles**. These cycles are commonly between 28 and 31 days. At the end of a billing cycle, a statement is sent to the account holder much like the one in Exhibit 13-3.

EXHIBIT 13-3   Reformed Bank Credit Card Account Statement

XXX Bank Credit Card Account Statement
Account Number XXXX XXXX XXXX XXXX
February 21, 20XX to March 22, 20XX

Summary of Account Activity

Previous Balance	$535.07
Payments	−$450.00
Other Credits	−$13.45
Purchases	+$529.57
Balance Transfers	+$785.00
Cash Advances	+$318.5
Past Due Amount	+$0.
Fees Charged	+$69.4
Interest Charged	+$10.89
New Balance	$1,784.53
Credit Limit	$2,000.00
Available Credit	$215.47
Statement Closing Date	3/22/20XX
Days in Billing Cycle	30

1

Questions?

Call Customer Service	1-XXX-XXX-XXXX
Lost or Stolen Credit Card	1-XXX-XXX-XXXX

Payment Information

New Balance	$1,784.53
Minimum Payment Due	$53.00
Payment Due Date	4/20/XX

2

Late Payment Warning: If we do not receive your minimum payment by the date listed above, you may have to pay a $35 late fee and your APRs may be increased up to the Penalty APR of 28.99%

3

Minimum Payment Warning: If you make only the minimum payment each period, you will pay more in interest and take you longer to pay off your balance. For example:

4

If you make no additional charges using this card and each month you pay...	You will pay off the balance shown on this statement in about...	And you will end up paying an estimated total of...
Only the minimum payment	10 years	$3,284
$62	3 years	$2,232 (Savings = $1,052)

If you would like information about credit counseling services, call 1-800-XXX-XXXX.

Please send billing inquiries and correspondence to:
PO Box XXXX, Anytown, Anystate XXXXX

Notice of Changes to Your Interest Rates   **5**

You have triggered the Penalty APR of 28.99%.

Current rates will continue to apply to these transactions. However, if you are more than 60 days late on your account, the Penalty APR will apply to those transactions as well.

1) Summary of account activity
   A summary of the transactions on your account—your payments, credits, purchases, balance transfers, cash advances, fees, interest charges, and amounts past due. It will also show your new balance, your available credit, and the last day of the billing period.

2) Payment information
   Your total new balance, the minimum payment amount, and the date your payment is due.

3) Late payment warning
   This section states any additional fees and the higher interest rate that may be charged if your payment is late.

4) Minimum payment warning
   This is an estimate of how long it can take to pay off your credit card balance if you make only the minimum payment each month and an estimate of how much you likely will pay, including interest, in order to pay off your bill in three years.

5) Notice of changes to your interest rates
   If you trigger the penalty rate, your credit card company may notify you that your rates will be increasing. The credit card company must tell you at least 45 days before your rates change.

Source: Federal Reserve

continued

EXHIBIT 13-3 Reformed Bank Credit Card Account Statement *(continued)*

Important Changes to Your Account Terms ⑥

The following is a summary of changes that are being made to your account terms. For more detailed information, please refer to the booklet enclosed with this statement.

As of 5/10/XX, any changes to APRs described below will apply to these transactions.

If you are already being charged a higher Penalty APR for purchases: In this case, any changes to APRs described below will not go into effect at this time. These changes will go into effect when the Penalty APR no longer applies to your account.

Revised Terms, as of 5/10/XX	
APR for Purchases	16.99%

Transactions ⑦

Reference Number	Trans Date	Post Date	Description of Transaction or Credit	Amount
5884186PS0388W6YM	2/22	2/23	Store #1	$133.74
854338203FS8OO0Z5	2/25	2/25	Pymt Thank You	$450.00
564891561545KOSHD	2/25	2/26	Store #2	$247.36
1542202074TWWZV48	2/26	2/26	Cash Advance	$318.00
4545754784KOHUIOS	2/27	3/1	Balance Transfer	$785.00
2564561023184102315	2/28	3/1	Store #3	$34.32
045148714518979874	3/4	3/5	Store #4	$29.45
0547810544898718AF	3/15	3/17	Store #5	$72.25
Fees				
9525156489SFD4545Q	2/23	2/23	Late Fee	$35.00
84151564SADS8745H	2/27	2/27	Balance Transfer Fee	$23.55
256489156189451516L	2/28	2/28	Cash Advance Fee	$10.90
			TOTAL FEES FOR THIS PERIOD	**$69.45**
Interest Charged				
			Interest Charge on Purchases	$6.31
			Interest Charge on Cash Advances	$4.58
			TOTAL INTEREST FOR THIS PERIOD	**$10.89**

⑧

2014 Totals Year-to-Date	
Total fees charged in 20XX	$90.14
Total interest charged in 20XX	$18.27

⑨

Interest Charge Calculation ⑩

Your **Annual Percentage Rate (APR)** is the   interest rate on your account.

Type of Balance	Annual Percentage Rate (APR)	Balance Subject to Interest Rate	Interest Charge
Purchases	14.99% (v)	$512.14	$6.31
Cash Advances	21.99% (v)	$253.50	$4.58
Balance Transfers	0.00%	$637.50	$0.00

(v) = Variable Rate

6) Other changes to your account terms

If your credit card company is going to raise interest rates or fees or make other significant changes to your account, it must notify you at least 45 days before the changes take effect.

7) Transactions

A list of all the transactions that have occurred since your last statement (purchases, payments, credits, cash advances, and balance transfers).

8) Fees and interest charges

Credit card companies must list the fees and interest charges separately on your monthly bill. Interest charges must be listed by type of transaction.

9) Year-to-date totals

This is the total that you have paid in fees and interest charges for the current year. You can avoid some fees, such as over-the-limit fees, by managing how much you charge and by paying on time to avoid late payment fees.

10) Interest charge calculation

A summary of the interest rates on the different types of transactions, account balances, the amount of each, and the interest charged for each type of transaction.

STEPS TO CALCULATE THE FINANCE CHARGE AND NEW BALANCE BY USING THE UNPAID BALANCE METHOD

STEP 1. Divide the annual percentage rate by 12 to find the monthly or periodic interest rate. (Round to the nearest hundredth of a percent when necessary.)

$$\text{Periodic rate} = \frac{\text{Annual percentage rate}}{12}$$

STEP 2. Calculate the finance charge by multiplying the previous month's balance by the periodic interest rate from Step 1.

$$\textbf{Finance charge} = \textbf{Previous month's balance} \times \textbf{Periodic rate}$$

STEP 3. Total all the purchases and cash advances for the month.

STEP 4. Total all the payments and credits for the month.

STEP 5. Use the following formula to determine the new balance:

$$\frac{\textbf{New}}{\textbf{balance}} = \frac{\textbf{Previous}}{\textbf{balance}} + \frac{\textbf{Finance}}{\textbf{charge}} + \frac{\textbf{Purchases and}}{\textbf{cash advances}} - \frac{\textbf{Payments and}}{\textbf{credits}}$$

EXAMPLE 1 CALCULATING THE FINANCE CHARGE AND NEW BALANCE BY USING THE UNPAID BALANCE METHOD

Jake Morrison has a revolving department store credit account with an annual percentage rate of 18%. His balance from last month is $322.40. During the month, he purchased shirts for $65.60 and a baseball bat for $43.25. He returned a tie for a credit of $22.95 and made a $50 payment. If the department store uses the unpaid balance method, what is the finance charge on the account and what is Jake's new balance?

▶ SOLUTIONSTRATEGY

Step 1. Periodic rate $= \dfrac{\text{Annual percentage rate}}{12}$

Periodic rate $= \dfrac{18\%}{12} = 1.5\%$

Step 2. Finance charge = Previous month's balance × Periodic rate
Finance charge = 322.40 × .015
Finance charge = 4.836 = $\underline{\$4.84}$

Step 3. Total the purchases for the month:
$$\$65.60 + \$43.25 = \$108.85$$

Step 4. Total the payments and credits for the month:
$$\$50.00 + \$22.95 = \$72.95$$

Step 5. Find the new balance for Jake's account by using the formula

$$\frac{\text{New}}{\text{balance}} = \frac{\text{Previous}}{\text{balance}} + \frac{\text{Finance}}{\text{charge}} + \frac{\text{Purchases and}}{\text{cash advances}} - \frac{\text{Payments and}}{\text{credits}}$$

$$\frac{\text{New}}{\text{balance}} = \$322.40 + \$4.84 + \$108.85 - \$72.95$$

New balance = $\underline{\$363.14}$

Dollars AND Sense

The Fair Credit Billing Act gives consumers the right to dispute a credit card purchase or billing error.

- Your maximum liability for unauthorized credit card charges: $50.
- Number of days you have to report unauthorized credit card use: no limit.
- Number of days you have to file a billing dispute: 60.
- Number of days the card issuer has to respond: 90.
- Maximum number of days a dispute may drag on: 270.

▶TRYITEXERCISE 1

John Public has a Bank of America account with an annual percentage rate of 15%. His previous month's balance is $214.90. During July, John's account showed the following activity.

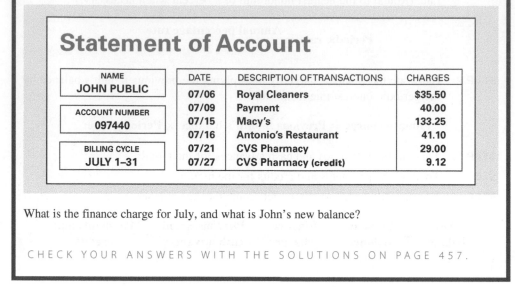

Statement of Account

NAME			
JOHN PUBLIC			

DATE	DESCRIPTION OF TRANSACTIONS	CHARGES
07/06	Royal Cleaners	$35.50
07/09	Payment	40.00
07/15	Macy's	133.25
07/16	Antonio's Restaurant	41.10
07/21	CVS Pharmacy	29.00
07/27	CVS Pharmacy (credit)	9.12

ACCOUNT NUMBER
097440

BILLING CYCLE
JULY 1–31

What is the finance charge for July, and what is John's new balance?

CHECK YOUR ANSWERS WITH THE SOLUTIONS ON PAGE 457.

13-2 CALCULATING THE FINANCE CHARGE AND NEW BALANCE BY USING THE AVERAGE DAILY BALANCE METHOD

average daily balance In revolving credit, the most commonly used method for determining the finance charge for a billing cycle. It is the total of the daily balances divided by the number of days in the cycle.

In business today, the method most widely used to calculate the finance charge on a revolving credit account is known as the **average daily balance**. This method precisely tracks the activity in an account on a daily basis. Each day's balance of a billing cycle is totaled and then divided by the number of days in that cycle. This gives an average of all the daily balances.

For accounts in which many charges are made each month, the average daily balance method results in much higher interest than the unpaid balance method because interest starts accruing on the day purchases are made or cash advances are taken.

STEPS TO CALCULATE THE FINANCE CHARGE AND NEW BALANCE BY USING THE AVERAGE DAILY BALANCE METHOD

STEP 1. Starting with the previous month's balance as the first unpaid balance, multiply each by the number of days that balance existed until the next account transaction.

STEP 2. At the end of the billing cycle, find the sum of all the daily balance figures.

STEP 3. Find the average daily balance.

$$\text{Average daily balance} = \frac{\text{Sum of the daily balances}}{\text{Days in billing cycle}}$$

STEP 4. Calculate the finance charge.

$$\text{Finance charge} = \text{Average daily balance} \times \text{Periodic rate}$$

STEP 5. Compute the new balance as before.

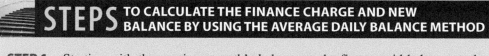

$$\frac{\text{New}}{\text{balance}} = \frac{\text{Previous}}{\text{balance}} + \frac{\text{Finance}}{\text{charge}} + \frac{\text{Purchases and}}{\text{cash advances}} - \frac{\text{Payments and}}{\text{credits}}$$

iStock.com/Nikada

EXAMPLE2 — CALCULATING THE FINANCE CHARGE AND NEW BALANCE BY USING THE AVERAGE DAILY BALANCE METHOD

Cindy Citizen has a Bank of America revolving credit account with a 15% annual percentage rate. The finance charge is calculated by using the average daily balance method. The billing date is the first day of each month, and the billing cycle is the number of days in that month. During the month of March, Cindy's account showed the following activity.

Statement of Account

NAME
CINDY CITIZEN

ACCOUNT NUMBER
1229-3390-0038

BILLING CYCLE
MARCH 1–31

DATE	DESCRIPTION OF TRANSACTIONS	CHARGES
03/01	Previous month's balance	$215.60
03/07	Sports Authority	125.11
03/10	Texaco	23.25
03/12	Payment	75.00
03/17	Amazon.com (credit)	54.10
03/23	H.L. Mager, DDS	79.00
03/23	Texaco	19.43
03/24	Dollar General	94.19

What is the finance charge for March, and what is Cindy's new balance?

SOLUTIONSTRATEGY

Steps 1 and 2. To calculate the daily balances and their sum, set up a chart like the one below that lists the activity in the account by dates and number of days.

Dates	Number of Days	Activity/Amount		Unpaid Balance	Daily Balances (unpaid balance × days)
March 1–6	6	Previous balance		$215.60	$1,293.60
March 7–9	3	Charge	+$125.11	340.71	1,022.13
March 10–11	2	Charge	+23.25	363.96	727.92
March 12–16	5	Payment	−75.00	288.96	1,444.80
March 17–22	6	Credit	−54.10	234.86	1,409.16
March 23	1	Charges	+79.00		
			+19.43	333.29	333.29
March 24–31	8	Charge	+94.19	427.48	3,419.84
	31 days in cycle				Total $9,650.74

Step 3. $\text{Average daily balance} = \dfrac{\text{Sum of the daily balances}}{\text{Days in billing cycle}} = \dfrac{9,650.74}{31} = \$311.31$

Step 4. The periodic rate is 1.25% (15% ÷ 12).

Finance charge = Average daily balance × Periodic rate

Finance charge = 311.31 × .0125 = $3.89

Step 5.

$\text{New balance} = \text{Previous balance} + \text{Finance charge} + \text{Purchases and cash advances} - \text{Payments and credits}$

New balance = $215.60 + $3.89 + $340.98 − $129.10

New balance = $431.37

TRYITEXERCISE 2

John Public has a Bank of America revolving credit account with an 18% annual percentage rate. The finance charge is calculated by using the average daily balance method. The billing date is the first day of each month, and the billing cycle is the number of days in that month. During the month of August, John's account showed the following activity.

Learning Tip

Shortcut

"New Balance" can be calculated by adding the finance charge to the last "Unpaid Balance" of the month.

$427.48 + $3.89 = $431.37

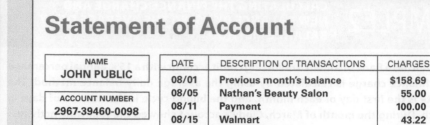

Statement of Account

NAME		DATE	DESCRIPTION OF TRANSACTIONS	CHARGES
JOHN PUBLIC		08/01	Previous month's balance	$158.69
		08/05	Nathan's Beauty Salon	55.00
ACCOUNT NUMBER		08/11	Payment	100.00
2967-39460-0098		08/15	Walmart	43.22
		08/17	Saks Fifth Avenue	54.10
BILLING CYCLE		08/20	eBay.com	224.50
AUGUST 1–31		08/26	Cash Advance	75.00

What is the finance charge for August, and what is John's new balance?

CHECK YOUR ANSWERS WITH THE SOLUTIONS ON PAGE 457.

13-3

CALCULATING THE FINANCE CHARGE AND NEW BALANCE OF BUSINESS AND PERSONAL LINES OF CREDIT

line of credit Pre-approved amount of open-end credit based on borrower's ability to pay.

One of the most useful types of open-end credit is the business or personal **line of credit**. In this section, we investigate the unsecured credit line, which is based on your own merit. In Chapter 14, we will discuss the home equity line of credit, which is secured by a home or another piece of real estate property.

A line of credit is an important tool for ongoing businesses and responsible individuals. For those who qualify, unsecured lines of credit generally range from $2,500 to $250,000. The amount is based on your ability to pay as well as your financial and credit history. This pre-approved borrowing power essentially gives you the ability to become your own private banker. Once the line has been established, you can borrow money by simply writing a check. Lines of credit usually have an annual usage fee of between $50 and $100, and most lenders require that you update your financial information each year.

With credit lines, you pay interest only on the outstanding average daily balance of your loan. For most lines and some credit cards, the interest rate is variable and is based on, or indexed to, the prime rate. The **U.S. prime rate** is the lending rate at which the largest and most creditworthy corporations in the country borrow money from banks. The current prime rate is published daily in the *Wall Street Journal* in a chart entitled "Consumer Rates and Returns to Investors." Exhibit 13-4 shows an example of this chart.

U.S. prime rate Lending rate at which the largest and most creditworthy corporations borrow money from banks. The interest rate of most lines of credit is tied to the movement of the prime rate.

A typical line of credit quotes interest as the prime rate plus a fixed percent, such as "prime + 3%" or "prime + 6.8%." Some lenders have a minimum rate regardless of the prime rate, such as "prime + 3%, minimum 10%." In this case, when the prime is greater than 7%, the rate varies up and down. When the prime falls to less than 7%, the minimum 10% rate applies. This guarantees the lender at least a 10% return on funds loaned. Exhibit 13-5 is an example of a credit card rate disclosure indexed to the prime rate.

Like the calculation of finance charges and new balances on credit cards, the finance charge on a line of credit is based on average daily balance and is calculated by

Finance charge = Average daily balance × Periodic rate

This means that interest begins as soon as you write a check for a loan. Typically, the loan is paid back on a flexible schedule. In most cases, balances of $100 or less must be paid in full. Larger balances require minimum monthly payments of $100 or 2% of the outstanding balance, whichever is greater. As you repay, the line of credit renews itself. The new balance of the line of credit is calculated by

New balance = Previous balance + Finance charge + Loans − Payments

EXHIBIT 13-4

Consumer Money Rates

Consumer Money Rates   Friday, June 29, 2018

Interest Rate	YIELD/RATE (%)		52-WEEK		CHANGE IN PCT. PTS	
	Last	Wk Ago	High	Low	52-Wk	3-Yr
Federal-funds rate target	1.75–2.00	1.75–2.00	1.75	1.00	0.75	1.75
Prime rate*	5.00	5.00	5.00	4.25	0.75	1.75
Money market, annual yield	0.52	0.52	0.52	0.25	0.19	0.18
Five-year CD, annual yield	1.74	1.73	1.74	1.38	0.36	0.29
30-year mortgage, fixed	4.52	4.57	4.69	3.73	0.52	0.33
15-year mortgage, fixed	4.00	4.06	4.14	2.99	0.79	0.63
Jumbo mortgages, $424,100-plus	4.73	4.75	4.96	4.21	0.25	0.23
Five-year adj mortgage (ARM)	4.37	4.48	4.78	3.22	0.95	0.84
New-car loan, 48 month	3.74	3.70	4.28	2.85	0.66	0.78

*Base rate posted by 70% of the nation's largest banks.

Source: SIX Financial Information, WSJ Market Data Group, Bankrate.com

EXAMPLE 3 CALCULATING FINANCE CHARGES ON A LINE OF CREDIT

Shari's Chocolate Shop has a $20,000 line of credit with the Shangri-La National Bank. The annual percentage rate charged on the account is the current prime rate plus 4%. There is a minimum APR on the account of 10%. The starting balance on April 1 was $2,350. On April 9, Shari borrowed $1,500 to pay for a shipment of assorted gift items. On April 20, she made a $3,000 payment on the account. On April 26, she borrowed another $2,500 to pay for air conditioning repairs. The billing cycle for April has 30 days. If the current prime rate is 8%, what is the finance charge on the account and what is Shari's new balance?

►SOLUTIONSTRATEGY

To solve this problem, we must find the annual percentage rate, the periodic rate, the average daily balance, the finance charge, and the new balance.

Annual percentage rate: The annual percentage rate is prime plus 4%, with a minimum of 10%. Because the current prime is 8%, the APR on this line of credit is 12% (8% + 4%).

Periodic rate:

$$\text{Periodic rate} = \frac{\text{Annual percentage rate}}{12 \text{ months}} = \frac{12\%}{12} = 1\%$$

Average daily balance: From the information given, we construct the following chart showing the account activity.

Dates	Number of Days	Activity/Amount	Unpaid Balance	Daily Balances (unpaid balance × days)
April 1–8	8	Previous balance	$2,350	$18,800
April 9–19	11	Borrowed $1,500	3,850	42,350
April 20–25	6	Payment $3,000	850	5,100
April 26–30	5	Borrowed $2,500	3,350	16,750
	30 days in cycle			Total $83,000

$$\text{Average daily balance} = \frac{\text{Sum of the daily balances}}{\text{Days in billing cycle}} = \frac{83,000}{30} = \$2,766.67$$

Finance charge:

$$\text{Finance charge} = \text{Average daily balance} \times \text{Periodic rate}$$
$$\text{Finance charge} = 2,766.67 \times .01 = \underline{\$27.67}$$

New balance:

$$\text{New balance} = \frac{\text{Previous}}{\text{balance}} + \frac{\text{Finance}}{\text{charge}} + \frac{\text{Loan}}{\text{amounts}} - \text{Payments}$$
$$\text{New balance} = \$2,350 + \$27.67 + \$4,000 - \$3,000$$
$$\text{New balance} = \underline{\$3,377.67}$$

page 430, Chapter 13 Consumer and Business Credit

►TRYITEXERCISE 3

Angler Marine has a $75,000 line of credit with Harborside Bank. The annual percentage rate is the current prime rate plus 4.5%. The balance on November 1 was $12,300. On November 7, Angler borrowed $16,700 to pay for a shipment of fishing equipment, and on November 21, it borrowed another $8,800. On November 26, a $20,000 payment was made on the account. The billing cycle for November has 30 days. If the current prime rate is 8.5%, what is the finance charge on the account and what is Angler's new balance?

CHECK YOUR ANSWERS WITH THE SOLUTIONS ON PAGES 457–458.

EXHIBIT 13-5   Reformed Credit Card Rate Disclosure

Interest Rates and Interest Charges	
Annual Percentage Rate (APR) for Purchases ①	**8.99%, 10.99%, or 12.99%** introductory APR for one year, based on your creditworthiness After that, your APR will be **14.99%**. This APR will vary with the market based on the Prime Rate.
APR for Balance Transfers ②	**15.99%** This APR will vary with the market based on the Prime Rate.
APR for Cash Advances ③	**21.99%** This APR will vary with the market based on the Prime Rate.
Penalty APR and When It Applies ④	**28.99%** This APR may be applied to your account if you: 1) Make a late payment. 2) Go over your credit limit. 3) Make a payment that is returned. 4) Do any of the above on another account that you have with us. **How Long Will the Penalty APR Apply?** If your APRs are increased for any of these reasons, the Penalty APR will apply until you make six consecutive minimum payments when due.
How to Avoid Paying Interest on Purchases ⑤	Your due date is at least 25 days after the close of each billing cycle. We will not charge you any interest on purchases if you pay your entire balance by the due date each month.
Minimum Interest Charge ⑥	If you are charged interest, the charge will be no less than $1.50.
For Credit Card Tips from the Federal Reserve Board	To learn more about factors to consider when applying for or using a credit card, visit the website of the Federal Reserve Board at http://www.federalreserve.gov/creditcard.

1) APR for purchases
The interest rate you pay on an annual basis if you carry over balances on purchases from one billing cycle to the next.

2) APR for balance transfers
The interest rate you pay if you transfer a balance from another card. Balance transfer fees may also apply.

3) APR for cash advances
The interest rate you pay if you withdraw a cash advance from your credit card account. Cash advance fees may also apply.

4) Penalty APR and when it applies
Your credit card company may increase your interest rate (with 45 days' advance notice) if you pay your bill late, go over your credit limit, or make a payment that is returned.

How long will the penalty APR apply?
Credit card companies must tell you how long the penalty rates will be in effect. You may be able to go back to regular rates if you pay your bills on time for a period of time.

5) How to avoid paying interest on purchases
You can avoid interest charges on purchases by paying your bill in full by the due date.

6) Minimum interest charge
Credit card companies often have a minimum interest amount. These charges typically range from $0.50 to $2.00 per month.

EXHIBIT 13-5 Reformed Credit Card Rate Disclosure

Fees	
Set-up and Maintenance Fees ⑦	NOTICE: Some of these set-up and maintenance fees will be assessed before you begin using your card and will reduce the amount of credit you initially have available. For example, if you are assigned the minimum credit limit of $250, your initial available credit will be only about $209 (or about $204 if you choose to have an additional card).
• Annual Fee	$20
• Account Set-up Fee	$20 (one-time fee)
• Participation Fee	$12 annually ($1 per month)
• Additional Card Fee	$5 annually (if applicable)
Transaction Fees ⑧	
• Balance Transfer	Either $5 or 3% of the amount of each transfer, whichever is greater (maximum fee: $100).
• Cash Advance	Either $5 or 3% of the amount of each cash advance, whichever is greater.
• Foreign Transaction	2% of each transaction in U.S. dollars.
Penalty Fees ⑨	
• Late Payment	$29 if balance is less than or equal to $1,000; $35 if balance is more than $1,000
• Over-the Credit Limit	$29
• Returned Payment	$35 ⑩

⑪

How We Will Calculate Your Balance: We use a method called "average daily balance (including new purchases)."

⑫

Loss of Introductory APR: We may end your introductory APR and apply the Penalty APR if you become more than 60 days late in paying your bill.

7) Set-up and maintenance fees
Some credit cards offered to people with lower, or subprime, credit scores may charge a variety of fees.

8) Transaction Fees
Credit card companies may charge you a fee (either a fixed dollar amount or a percentage of the transaction) for transferring a balance, getting a cash advance, or making a transaction in a foreign country.

9) Penalty fees
Fee if you pay your bill late, your balance goes over your credit limit, or you make a payment but you don't have enough money in your account to cover the payment.

10) Other fees
Some cards require other fees (known as "account protection") for credit insurance, debt cancellation, or debt suspension coverage.

11) How we will calculate your balance
Credit card companies can use one of several methods to calculate your outstanding balance.
- Adjusted balance method
- Average daily balance method, including new purchases
- Average daily balance method, excluding new purchases
- Previous balance method

12) Loss of Introductory APR
If your card has a special lower rate that is called an "introductory rate," this area will list the ways you can lose this lower rate.

SECTION I **13** **REVIEW EXERCISES**

Calculate the missing information on the following revolving credit accounts. Interest is calculated on the unpaid or previous month's balance.

	Previous Balance	Annual Percentage Rate (APR)	Monthly Periodic Rate	Finance Charge	Purchases and Cash Advances	Payments and Credits	New Balance
1.	$167.88	18%	1.5%	$2.52	$215.50	$50.00	$335.90
2.	$35.00	12%	____	____	$186.40	$75.00	____
3.	$605.42	___	.75%	____	$156.12	$200.00	____
4.	$2,390.00	____	$1\frac{1}{4}\%$	____	$1,233.38	$300.00	____
5.	$3,418.50	9%	____	____	$329.00	$1,200.00	____
6.	$1,028.61	___	1%	____	$322.20	$300.00	____

7. Suppose you have a revolving credit account at an annual percentage rate of 12%, and your previous monthly balance is $384.79. Find your new balance if your account showed the following activity. Use the unpaid balance method.

Statement of Account

Billing cycle: July 1–31

DATE	DESCRIPTION OF TRANSACTIONS	CHARGES
July 04	Kit and Capoodle Pets	$109.08
July 08	Payment	61.00
July 16	Cash advance	93.82
July 22	Mountain Vineyards	31.37
July 29	Vu Video (credit)	99.97

Kathy Hansen has a revolving credit account. The finance charge is calculated on the previous month's balance, and the annual percentage rate is 21%. Complete the following five-month account activity table for Kathy.

	Month	Previous Month's Balance	Finance Charge	Purchases and Cash Advances	Payments and Credits	New Balance End of Month
8.	March	$560.00	_____	$121.37	$55.00	_____
9.	April	_____	_____	$46.45	$65.00	_____
10.	May	_____	_____	$282.33	$105.00	_____
11.	June	_____	_____	$253.38	$400.00	_____
12.	July	_____	_____	$70.59	$100.00	_____

13. **Calculate the average daily balance for November for a revolving credit account with a previous month's balance of $550 and the following activity.**

Date	Activity	Amount
November 6	Purchase	$83.20
November 13	Payment	$150.00
November 19	Purchase	$348.50
November 24	Credit	$75.25
November 27	Cash advance	$200.00

$$\text{Average daily balance} = \frac{20{,}335.25}{30} = \underline{\underline{\$677.84}}$$

14. Calculate the average daily balance for October for a revolving credit account with a previous month's balance of $140 and the following activity.

Date	Activity	Amount
October 3	Cash advance	$50.00
October 7	Payment	$75.00
October 10	Purchase	$26.69
October 16	Credit	$40.00
October 25	Purchase	$122.70

15. Calculate the average daily balance for February for a revolving credit account with a previous month's balance of $69.50 and the following activity.

Date	Activity	Amount
February 6	Payment	$58.00
February 9	Purchase	$95.88
February 15	Purchase	$129.60
February 24	Credit	$21.15
February 27	Cash advance	$100.00

16. Anny has a revolving credit account at an annual percentage rate of 12%. Use the average daily balance method to find the new balance given the following statement of account:

Statement of Account

Billing cycle: July 1–31

DATE	DESCRIPTION OF TRANSACTIONS	CHARGES
July 01	Previous month's balance	$388.99
July 07	Payment	88.00
July 13	Valencia Beauty Salon	111.47
July 19	Choi Home Repair	32.17
July 26	JAB Consulting (credit)	120.61

David Tran Photo/Shutterstock.com

Gap Inc. operates as a specialty retailer. The company offers clothing, accessories, and personal care products for men, women, children, and babies under the Gap, Old Navy, Banana Republic, Piperlime, and Athleta brand names.

The company offers its products through retail stores and catalogs as well as brand name websites. The Gap also franchises agreements with unaffiliated franchisees to operate Gap and Banana Republic stores worldwide. Typical annual sales exceed $14 billion.

17. The Freemont Bank offers a business line of credit that has an annual percentage rate of prime rate plus 5.4%, with a minimum of 11%. What is the APR if the prime rate is

    a. 7%   b. 10.1%   c. 9.25%   d. 5%

    7 + 5.4

    = 12.4%

18. The Jewelry Exchange has a $30,000 line of credit with Nations Bank. The annual percentage rate is the current prime rate plus 4.7%. The balance on March 1 was $8,400. On March 6, the company borrowed $6,900 to pay for a shipment of supplies, and on March 17, it borrowed another $4,500 for equipment repairs. On March 24, a $10,000 payment was made on the account. The billing cycle for March has 31 days. The current prime rate is 9%.

    a. What is the finance charge on the account?

    b. What is the company's new balance?

    c. On April 1, how much credit does the Jewelry Exchange have left on the account?

19. Cook Security Systems has a $37,500 line of credit, which charges an annual percentage rate of prime rate plus 4%. The starting balance on October 1 was $9,800.

    On October 4 they made a payment of $1,900. On October 13 the business borrowed $2,400, and on October 19 they borrowed $4,100. If the current prime rate is 7%, what is the new balance?

Top 6 Credit Card Issuers in the United States
In recent years the top six U.S. credit card issuers (based on outstanding balances) have been:

American Express
Chase
Bank of America
Citibank
Capital One
Discover

BUSINESS DECISION: PICK THE RIGHT PLASTIC

20. On October 22, you plan to purchase a $3,000 computer by using one of your two credit cards. The Silver Card charges 18% interest and calculates interest based on the balance on the first day of the previous month. The Gold Card charges 18% interest and calculates interest based on the average daily balance. Both cards have a $0 balance as of October 1. The closing date is the end of the month for each card.

Your plan is to make a $1,000 payment in November, make a $1,000 payment in December, and pay off the remaining balance in January. All your payments will be received and posted on the 10th of each month. No other charges will be made on the account.

a. Based on this information, calculate the interest charged by each card for this purchase.

b. Which card is the better deal and by how much?

CLOSED-END CREDIT—INSTALLMENT LOANS

13 SECTION II

Closed-end credit in the form of installment loans is used extensively today for the purchase of durable goods such as cars, boats, electronic equipment, furniture, and appliances, as well as services such as vacations and home improvements. An **installment loan** is a lump-sum loan whereby the borrower repays the principal plus interest in a specified number of equal monthly payments. These loans generally range from 6 months to 10 years depending on what is being financed.

When a home or another real estate property is financed, the installment loan is known as a **mortgage**. A mortgage may be for as long as 30 years on a home and even longer on commercial property such as an office building or a factory. These loans, along with home equity loans, will be discussed in Chapter 14.

Many installment loans are secured by the asset for which the loan was made. For example, when a bank makes a car loan for three years, the consumer gets the car to use and monthly payments to make, but the lender still owns the car. Only after the final payment is made on the loan does the lender turn over the title (the proof of ownership document) to the borrower. An additional form of security for the lending institution is that borrowers are often asked to make a down payment as part of the loan agreement.

A **down payment** is a percentage of the purchase price that the buyer must pay in a lump sum at the time of purchase. Down payments on installment loans vary by category of merchandise and generally range from 0% to 30% of the price of the item. Sometimes the amount of the down payment is based on the credit rating of the borrower. Usually, the better the credit, the lower the down payment.

installment loan Loan made for a specified number of equal monthly payments. A form of closed-end credit used for purchasing durable goods such as cars, boats, and furniture and services such as vacations and home improvements.

mortgage An installment loan made for homes and other real estate property.

down payment Portion of the purchase price that the buyer must pay in a lump sum at the time of purchase.

Until the loan on this vehicle is repaid, the lending institution is technically the owner.

Polka Dot Images/Getty Images

13-4   CALCULATING THE TOTAL DEFERRED PAYMENT PRICE AND THE AMOUNT OF THE FINANCE CHARGE OF AN INSTALLMENT LOAN

cash price, or purchase price Price paid for goods and services without the use of financing.

amount financed After the down payment, the amount of money that is borrowed to complete a sale.

IN THE Business World

As with open-end credit, installment loan consumers are protected by Regulation Z of the Truth in Lending Act.

Advertisers of installment loans, such as car dealers and furniture stores, must disclose in the ad and the loan agreement the following information:

- Down payment
- Terms and payments
- Annual percentage rate
- Total payback

Dollars AND Sense

How to improve your credit score:

- Pay your bills on time.
- Have at least three to six active accounts.
- Keep credit card balances low.
- Avoid closing long-standing accounts.
- Avoid applying for new credit.

Source: *USA Today,* Dec. 22, 2009, page 3B, Money.

Let's take a look at some of the terminology of installment loans. When a consumer buys goods or services without any financing, the price paid is known as the **cash price** or **purchase price**. When financing is involved, the **amount financed** is found by subtracting the down payment from the cash or purchase price. Sometimes the down payment will be listed as a dollar amount, and other times it will be expressed as a percent of the purchase price.

Amount financed = Purchase price − Down payment

When the down payment is listed as a percent of the purchase price, it can be found by

Down payment = Purchase price × Down payment percent

A finance charge, which includes simple interest and any loan origination fees, is then added to the amount financed to give the total amount of installment payments.

Total amount of installment payments = Amount financed + Finance charge

The finance charge can be found by subtracting the amount financed from the total amount of installment payments.

Finance charge = Total amount of installment payments − Amount financed

When the amount of the monthly payments is known, the total amount of installment payments can be found by multiplying the monthly payment amount by the number of payments.

$$\text{Total amount of installment payments} = \text{Monthly payment amount} \times \text{Number of monthly payments}$$

The total deferred payment price is the total amount of installment payments plus the down payment. This represents the total out-of-pocket expenses incurred by the buyer for an installment purchase.

Total deferred payment price = Total amount of installment payments + Down payment

EXAMPLE4   CALCULATING INSTALLMENT LOAN VARIABLES

Tracy Hall is interested in buying a computer. At Radio Shack, she picks out a computer and a printer for a total cash price of $2,550. The salesperson informs her that if she qualifies for an installment loan, she may pay 20% now as a down payment and finance the balance with payments of $110 per month for 24 months.

a. What is the finance charge on this loan?

b. What is the total deferred payment price of Tracy's computer?

▶SOLUTIONSTRATEGY

a. Finance charge:

To calculate the finance charge on this loan, we must first find the amount of the down payment, the amount financed, and the total amount of the installment payments.

Down payment = Purchase price × Down payment percent

Down payment = 2,550 × 20% = 2,550 × .2 = $510

Amount financed = Purchase price − Down payment

Amount financed = 2,550 − 510 = $2,040

$$\text{Total amount of installment payments} = \text{Monthly payment amount} \times \text{Number of monthly payments}$$

Total amount of installment payments = 110 × 24 = $2,640

Finance charge = Total amount of installment payments − Amount financed

Finance charge = 2,640 − 2,040

Finance charge = $600

b. Total deferred payment price:

Total deferred payment price = Total amount of installment payments + Down payment

Total deferred payment price = 2,640 + 510

Total deferred payment price = $3,150

▶TRYITEXERCISE 4

Bob Johnson found a car he wanted to buy at Autorama Auto Sales. He had the option of paying $12,500 in cash or financing the car with a 4-year installment loan. The loan required a 15% down payment and equal monthly payments of $309.90 for 48 months.

a. What is the finance charge on the loan?

b. What is the total deferred payment price of Bob's car?

CHECK YOUR ANSWERS WITH THE SOLUTIONS ON PAGE 458.

CALCULATING THE REGULAR MONTHLY PAYMENTS OF AN INSTALLMENT LOAN BY THE ADD-ON INTEREST METHOD

13-5

One of the most common methods of calculating the finance charge on an installment loan is known as **add-on interest**. Add-on interest is essentially the simple interest that we studied in Chapter 10. The term gets its name from the fact that the simple interest is computed and then added to the amount financed to get the total amount of installment payments. The interest or finance charge is computed by using the following simple interest formula:

add-on interest Popular method of calculating the interest on an installment loan. Found by adding the simple interest ($I = PRT$) to the amount financed.

$$
\begin{array}{ccc}
\textbf{Interest} & = & \textbf{Principal} \quad \times \textbf{Rate} \times \textbf{Time} \\
\textit{(finance charge)} & & \textit{(amount financed)}
\end{array}
$$

STEPS TO CALCULATE THE REGULAR MONTHLY PAYMENT OF AN INSTALLMENT LOAN USING ADD-ON INTEREST

STEP 1. Calculate the amount to be financed by subtracting the down payment from the purchase price. *Note:* When the down payment is expressed as a percent, the amount financed can be found by the complement method because the percent financed is 100% minus the down payment percent.

Amount financed = Purchase price (100% − Down payment percent)

STEP 2. Compute the add-on interest finance charge by using $I = PRT$, with the amount financed as the principal.

STEP 3. Find the total amount of installment payments by adding the finance charge to the amount financed.

Total amount of installment payments = Amount financed + Finance charge

STEP 4. Find the regular monthly payments by dividing the total amount of installment payments by the number of months of the loan.

$$
\textbf{Regular monthly payments} = \frac{\textbf{Total amount of installment payments}}{\textbf{Number of months of the loan}}
$$

EXAMPLE5   CALCULATING MONTHLY PAYMENTS

David Kendall bought a new boat with a 7% add-on interest installment loan from his credit union. The purchase price of the boat was $19,500. The credit union required a 20% down payment and equal monthly payments for 5 years (60 months). What are David's monthly payments?

▶SOLUTIONSTRATEGY

Step 1.   Amount financed = Purchase price (100% − Down payment percent)

Amount financed = 19,500 (100% − 20%) = 19,500 × .8

Amount financed = $15,600

Step 2.   Interest   =   Principal   × Rate × Time
       (*finance charge*)   (*amount financed*)

Finance charge = 15,600 × .07 × 5

Finance charge = $5,460

Step 3.   Total amount of installment payments = Amount financed + Finance charge

Total amount of installment payments = 15,600 + 5,460

Total amount of installment payments = $21,060

Step 4.   Regular monthly payments = $\dfrac{\text{Total amount of installment payments}}{\text{Number of months of the loan}}$

Regular monthly payments = $\dfrac{21,060}{60}$

Regular monthly payments = $351

▶TRYITEXERCISE 5

Eileen Townsend bought a bedroom set from El Dorado Furniture with a 6% add-on interest installment loan from her bank. The purchase price of the furniture was $1,500. The bank required a 10% down payment and equal monthly payments for 2 years. What are Eileen's monthly payments?

CHECK YOUR ANSWERS WITH THE SOLUTIONS ON PAGE 458.

13-6   ## CALCULATING THE ANNUAL PERCENTAGE RATE OF AN INSTALLMENT LOAN BY APR TABLES AND BY FORMULA

As we learned in Objective 13-5, the add-on interest calculation for an installment loan is the same as the procedure we used on the simple interest promissory note. Although the interest is calculated the same way, the manner in which the loans are repaid is different. With promissory notes, the principal plus interest is repaid at the end of the loan period. The borrower has the use of the principal for the full time period of the loan. With an installment loan, the principal plus interest is repaid in equal regular payments. Each month in which a payment is made, the borrower has less and less use of the principal.

For this reason, the effective or true interest rate on an installment loan is considerably higher than the simple add-on rate. As we learned in Section I of this chapter, the effective or true annual interest rate being charged on open- and closed-end credit is known as the APR.

The Federal Reserve Board has published APR tables that can be used to find the APR of an installment loan. APR tables, such as Table 13-1, have values representing the finance charge per $100 of the amount financed. To look up the APR of a loan, we must first calculate the finance charge per $100.

TABLE 13-1 Annual Percentage Rate (APR) Finance Charge per $100

ANNUAL PERCENTAGE RATE TABLE FOR MONTHLY PAYMENT PLANS
SEE INSTRUCTIONS FOR USE OF TABLES

FRB-103-M

ANNUAL PERCENTAGE RATE

(FINANCE CHARGE PER $100 OF AMOUNT FINANCED)

NUMBER OF PAYMENTS	10.00%	10.25%	10.50%	10.75%	11.00%	11.25%	11.50%	11.75%	12.00%	12.25%	12.50%	12.75%	13.00%	13.25%	13.50%	13.75%
1	0.83	0.85	0.87	0.90	0.92	0.94	0.96	0.98	1.00	1.02	1.04	1.06	1.08	1.10	1.12	1.15
2	1.25	1.28	1.31	1.35	1.38	1.41	1.44	1.47	1.50	1.53	1.57	1.60	1.63	1.66	1.69	1.72
3	1.67	1.71	1.76	1.80	1.84	1.88	1.92	1.96	2.01	2.05	2.09	2.13	2.17	2.22	2.26	2.30
4	2.09	2.14	2.20	2.25	2.30	2.35	2.41	2.46	2.51	2.57	2.62	2.67	2.72	2.78	2.83	2.88
5	2.51	2.58	2.64	2.70	2.77	2.83	2.89	2.96	3.02	3.08	3.15	3.21	3.27	3.34	3.40	3.46
6	2.94	3.01	3.08	3.16	3.23	3.31	3.38	3.45	3.53	3.60	3.68	3.75	3.83	3.90	3.97	4.05
7	3.36	3.45	3.53	3.62	3.70	3.78	3.87	3.95	4.04	4.12	4.21	4.29	4.38	4.47	4.55	4.64
8	3.79	3.88	3.98	4.07	4.17	4.26	4.36	4.46	4.55	4.65	4.74	4.84	4.94	5.03	5.13	5.22
9	4.21	4.32	4.43	4.53	4.64	4.75	4.85	4.96	5.07	5.17	5.28	5.39	5.49	5.60	5.71	5.82
10	4.64	4.76	4.88	4.99	5.11	5.23	5.35	5.46	5.58	5.70	5.82	5.94	6.05	6.17	6.29	6.41
11	5.07	5.20	5.33	5.45	5.58	5.71	5.84	5.97	6.10	6.23	6.36	6.49	6.62	6.75	6.88	7.01
12	5.50	5.64	5.78	5.92	6.06	6.20	6.34	6.48	6.62	6.76	6.90	7.04	7.18	7.32	7.46	7.60
13	5.93	6.08	6.23	6.38	6.53	6.68	6.84	6.99	7.14	7.29	7.44	7.59	7.75	7.90	8.05	8.20
14	6.36	6.52	6.69	6.85	7.01	7.17	7.34	7.50	7.66	7.82	7.99	8.15	8.31	8.48	8.64	8.81
15	6.80	6.97	7.14	7.32	7.49	7.66	7.84	8.01	8.19	8.36	8.53	8.71	8.88	9.06	9.23	9.41
16	7.23	7.41	7.60	7.78	7.97	8.15	8.34	8.53	8.71	8.90	9.08	9.27	9.46	9.64	9.83	10.02
17	7.67	7.86	8.06	8.25	8.45	8.65	8.84	9.04	9.24	9.44	9.63	9.83	10.03	10.23	10.43	10.63
18	8.10	8.31	8.52	8.73	8.93	9.14	9.35	9.56	9.77	9.98	10.19	10.40	10.61	10.82	11.03	11.24
19	8.54	8.76	8.98	9.20	9.42	9.64	9.86	10.08	10.30	10.52	10.74	10.96	11.18	11.41	11.63	11.85
20	8.98	9.21	9.44	9.67	9.90	10.13	10.37	10.60	10.83	11.06	11.30	11.53	11.76	12.00	12.23	12.46
21	9.42	9.66	9.90	10.15	10.39	10.63	10.88	11.12	11.36	11.61	11.85	12.10	12.34	12.59	12.84	13.08
22	9.86	10.12	10.37	10.62	10.88	11.13	11.39	11.64	11.90	12.16	12.41	12.67	12.93	13.19	13.44	13.70
23	10.30	10.57	10.84	11.10	11.37	11.63	11.90	12.17	12.44	12.71	12.97	13.24	13.51	13.78	14.05	14.32
24	10.75	11.02	11.30	11.58	11.86	12.14	12.42	12.70	12.98	13.26	13.54	13.82	14.10	14.38	14.66	14.95
25	11.19	11.48	11.77	12.06	12.35	12.64	12.93	13.22	13.52	13.81	14.10	14.40	14.69	14.98	15.28	15.57
26	11.64	11.94	12.24	12.54	12.85	13.15	13.45	13.75	14.06	14.36	14.67	14.97	15.28	15.59	15.89	16.20
27	12.09	12.40	12.71	13.03	13.34	13.66	13.97	14.29	14.60	14.92	15.24	15.56	15.87	16.19	16.51	16.83
28	12.53	12.86	13.18	13.51	13.84	14.16	14.49	14.82	15.15	15.48	15.81	16.14	16.47	16.80	17.13	17.46
29	12.98	13.32	13.66	14.00	14.33	14.67	15.01	15.35	15.70	16.04	16.38	16.72	17.07	17.41	17.75	18.10
30	13.43	13.78	14.13	14.48	14.83	15.19	15.54	15.89	16.24	16.60	16.95	17.31	17.66	18.02	18.38	18.74
31	13.89	14.25	14.61	14.97	15.33	15.70	16.06	16.43	16.79	17.16	17.53	17.90	18.27	18.63	19.00	19.38
32	14.34	14.71	15.09	15.46	15.84	16.21	16.59	16.97	17.35	17.73	18.11	18.49	18.87	19.25	19.63	20.02
33	14.79	15.18	15.57	15.95	16.34	16.73	17.12	17.51	17.90	18.29	18.69	19.08	19.47	19.87	20.26	20.66
34	15.25	15.65	16.05	16.44	16.85	17.25	17.65	18.05	18.46	18.86	19.27	19.67	20.08	20.49	20.90	21.31
35	15.70	16.11	16.53	16.94	17.35	17.77	18.18	18.60	19.01	19.43	19.85	20.27	20.69	21.11	21.53	21.95
36	16.16	16.58	17.01	17.43	17.86	18.29	18.71	19.14	19.57	20.00	20.43	20.87	21.30	21.73	22.17	22.60
37	16.62	17.06	17.49	17.93	18.37	18.81	19.25	19.69	20.13	20.58	21.02	21.46	21.91	22.36	22.81	23.25
38	17.08	17.53	17.98	18.43	18.88	19.33	19.78	20.24	20.69	21.15	21.61	22.07	22.52	22.99	23.45	23.91
39	17.54	18.00	18.46	18.93	19.39	19.86	20.32	20.79	21.26	21.73	22.20	22.67	23.14	23.61	24.09	24.56
40	18.00	18.48	18.95	19.43	19.90	20.38	20.86	21.34	21.82	22.30	22.79	23.27	23.76	24.25	24.73	25.22
41	18.47	18.95	19.44	19.93	20.42	20.91	21.40	21.89	22.39	22.88	23.38	23.88	24.38	24.88	25.38	25.88
42	18.93	19.43	19.93	20.43	20.93	21.44	21.94	22.45	22.96	23.47	23.98	24.49	25.00	25.51	26.03	26.55
43	19.40	19.91	20.42	20.94	21.45	21.97	22.49	23.01	23.53	24.05	24.57	25.10	25.62	26.15	26.68	27.21
44	19.86	20.39	20.91	21.44	21.97	22.50	23.03	23.57	24.10	24.64	25.17	25.71	26.25	26.79	27.33	27.88
45	20.33	20.87	21.41	21.95	22.49	23.03	23.58	24.12	24.67	25.22	25.77	26.32	26.88	27.43	27.99	28.55
46	20.80	21.35	21.90	22.46	23.01	23.57	24.13	24.69	25.25	25.81	26.37	26.94	27.51	28.08	28.65	29.22
47	21.27	21.83	22.40	22.97	23.53	24.10	24.68	25.25	25.82	26.40	26.98	27.56	28.14	28.72	29.31	29.89
48	21.74	22.32	22.90	23.48	24.06	24.64	25.23	25.81	26.40	26.99	27.58	28.18	28.77	29.37	29.97	30.57
49	22.21	22.80	23.39	23.99	24.58	25.18	25.78	26.38	26.98	27.59	28.19	28.80	29.41	30.02	30.63	31.24
50	22.69	23.29	23.89	24.50	25.11	25.72	26.33	26.95	27.56	28.18	28.80	29.42	30.04	30.67	31.29	31.92
51	23.16	23.78	24.40	25.02	25.64	26.26	26.89	27.52	28.15	28.78	29.41	30.05	30.68	31.32	31.96	32.60
52	23.64	24.27	24.90	25.53	26.17	26.81	27.45	28.09	28.73	29.38	30.02	30.67	31.32	31.98	32.63	33.29
53	24.11	24.76	25.40	26.05	26.70	27.35	28.00	28.66	29.32	29.98	30.64	31.30	31.97	32.63	33.30	33.97
54	24.59	25.25	25.91	26.57	27.23	27.90	28.56	29.23	29.91	30.58	31.25	31.93	32.61	33.29	33.98	34.66
55	25.07	25.74	26.41	27.09	27.77	28.44	29.13	29.81	30.50	31.18	31.87	32.56	33.26	33.95	34.65	35.35
56	25.55	26.23	26.92	27.61	28.30	28.99	29.69	30.39	31.09	31.79	32.49	33.20	33.91	34.62	35.33	36.04
57	26.03	26.73	27.43	28.13	28.84	29.54	30.25	30.97	31.68	32.39	33.11	33.83	34.56	35.28	36.01	36.74
58	26.51	27.23	27.94	28.66	29.37	30.10	30.82	31.55	32.27	33.00	33.74	34.47	35.21	35.95	36.69	37.43
59	27.00	27.72	28.45	29.18	29.91	30.65	31.39	32.13	32.87	33.61	34.36	35.11	35.86	36.62	37.37	38.13
60	27.48	28.22	28.96	29.71	30.45	31.20	31.96	32.71	33.47	34.23	34.99	35.75	36.52	37.29	38.06	38.83

continued

TABLE 13-1 Annual Percentage Rate (APR) Finance Charge per $100   (continued)

ANNUAL PERCENTAGE RATE TABLE FOR MONTHLY PAYMENT PLANS
SEE INSTRUCTIONS FOR USE OF TABLES

FRB-104-M

NUMBER OF PAYMENTS	14.00%	14.25%	14.50%	14.75%	15.00%	15.25%	15.50%	15.75%	16.00%	16.25%	16.50%	16.75%	17.00%	17.25%	17.50%	17.75%
					(FINANCE CHARGE PER $100 OF AMOUNT FINANCED)											
1	1.17	1.19	1.21	1.23	1.25	1.27	1.29	1.31	1.33	1.35	1.37	1.40	1.42	1.44	1.46	1.48
2	1.75	1.78	1.82	1.85	1.88	1.91	1.94	1.97	2.00	2.04	2.07	2.10	2.13	2.16	2.19	2.22
3	2.34	2.38	2.43	2.47	2.51	2.55	2.59	2.64	2.68	2.72	2.76	2.80	2.85	2.89	2.93	2.97
4	2.93	2.99	3.04	3.09	3.14	3.20	3.25	3.30	3.36	3.41	3.46	3.51	3.57	3.62	3.67	3.73
5	3.53	3.59	3.65	3.72	3.78	3.84	3.91	3.97	4.04	4.10	4.16	4.23	4.29	4.35	4.42	4.48
6	4.12	4.20	4.27	4.35	4.42	4.49	4.57	4.64	4.72	4.79	4.87	4.94	5.02	5.09	5.17	5.24
7	4.72	4.81	4.89	4.98	5.06	5.15	5.23	5.32	5.40	5.49	5.58	5.66	5.75	5.83	5.92	6.00
8	5.32	5.42	5.51	5.61	5.71	5.80	5.90	6.00	6.09	6.19	6.29	6.38	6.48	6.58	6.67	6.77
9	5.92	6.03	6.14	6.25	6.35	6.46	6.57	6.68	6.78	6.89	7.00	7.11	7.22	7.32	7.43	7.54
10	6.53	6.65	6.77	6.88	7.00	7.12	7.24	7.36	7.48	7.60	7.72	7.84	7.96	8.08	8.19	8.31
11	7.14	7.27	7.40	7.53	7.66	7.79	7.92	8.05	8.18	8.31	8.44	8.57	8.70	8.83	8.96	9.09
12	7.74	7.89	8.03	8.17	8.31	8.45	8.59	8.74	8.88	9.02	9.16	9.30	9.45	9.59	9.73	9.87
13	8.36	8.51	8.66	8.81	8.97	9.12	9.27	9.43	9.58	9.73	9.89	10.04	10.20	10.35	10.50	10.66
14	8.97	9.13	9.30	9.46	9.63	9.79	9.96	10.12	10.29	10.45	10.67	10.78	10.95	11.11	11.28	11.45
15	9.59	9.76	9.94	10.11	10.29	10.47	10.64	10.82	11.00	11.17	11.35	11.53	11.71	11.88	12.06	12.24
16	10.20	10.39	10.58	10.77	10.95	11.14	11.33	11.52	11.71	11.90	12.09	12.28	12.46	12.65	12.84	13.03
17	10.82	11.02	11.22	11.42	11.62	11.82	12.02	12.22	12.42	12.62	12.83	13.03	13.23	13.43	13.63	13.83
18	11.45	11.66	11.87	12.08	12.29	12.50	12.72	12.93	13.14	13.35	13.57	13.78	13.99	14.21	14.42	14.64
19	12.07	12.30	12.52	12.74	12.97	13.19	13.41	13.64	13.86	14.09	14.31	14.54	14.76	14.99	15.22	15.44
20	12.70	12.93	13.17	13.41	13.64	13.88	14.11	14.35	14.59	14.82	15.06	15.30	15.54	15.77	16.01	16.25
21	13.33	13.58	13.82	14.07	14.32	14.57	14.82	15.06	15.31	15.56	15.81	16.06	16.31	16.56	16.81	17.07
22	13.96	14.22	14.48	14.74	15.00	15.26	15.52	15.78	16.04	16.30	16.57	16.83	17.09	17.36	17.62	17.88
23	14.59	14.87	15.14	15.41	15.68	15.96	16.23	16.50	16.78	17.05	17.32	17.60	17.88	18.15	18.43	18.70
24	15.23	15.51	15.80	16.08	16.37	16.65	16.94	17.22	17.51	17.80	18.09	18.37	18.66	18.95	19.24	19.53
25	15.87	16.17	16.46	16.76	17.06	17.35	17.65	17.95	18.25	18.55	18.85	19.15	19.45	19.75	20.05	20.36
26	16.51	16.82	17.13	17.44	17.75	18.06	18.37	18.68	18.99	19.30	19.62	19.93	20.24	20.56	20.87	21.19
27	17.15	17.47	17.80	18.12	18.44	18.76	19.09	19.41	19.74	20.06	20.39	20.71	21.04	21.37	21.69	22.02
28	17.80	18.13	18.47	18.80	19.14	19.47	19.81	20.15	20.48	20.82	21.16	21.50	21.84	22.18	22.52	22.86
29	18.45	18.79	19.14	19.49	19.83	20.18	20.53	20.88	21.23	21.58	21.94	22.29	22.64	22.99	23.35	23.70
30	19.10	19.45	19.81	20.17	20.54	20.90	21.26	21.62	21.99	22.35	22.72	23.08	23.45	23.81	24.18	24.55
31	19.75	20.12	20.49	20.87	21.24	21.61	21.99	22.37	22.74	23.12	23.50	23.88	24.26	24.64	25.02	25.40
32	20.40	20.79	21.17	21.56	21.95	22.33	22.72	23.11	23.50	23.89	24.28	24.68	25.07	25.46	25.86	26.25
33	21.06	21.46	21.85	22.25	22.65	23.06	23.46	23.86	24.26	24.67	25.07	25.48	25.88	26.29	26.70	27.11
34	21.72	22.13	22.54	22.95	23.37	23.78	24.19	24.61	25.03	25.44	25.86	26.28	26.70	27.12	27.54	27.97
35	22.38	22.80	23.23	23.65	24.08	24.51	24.94	25.36	25.79	26.23	26.66	27.09	27.52	27.96	28.39	28.83
36	23.04	23.48	23.92	24.35	24.80	25.24	25.68	26.12	26.57	27.01	27.46	27.90	28.35	28.80	29.25	29.70
37	23.70	24.16	24.61	25.06	25.51	25.97	26.42	26.88	27.34	27.80	28.26	28.72	29.18	29.64	30.10	30.57
38	24.37	24.84	25.30	25.77	26.24	26.70	27.17	27.64	28.11	28.59	29.06	29.53	30.01	30.49	30.96	31.44
39	25.04	25.52	26.00	26.48	26.96	27.44	27.92	28.41	28.89	29.38	29.87	30.36	30.85	31.34	31.83	32.32
40	25.71	26.20	26.70	27.19	27.69	28.18	28.68	29.18	29.68	30.18	30.68	31.18	31.68	32.19	32.69	33.20
41	26.39	26.89	27.40	27.91	28.41	28.92	29.44	29.95	30.46	30.97	31.49	32.01	32.52	33.04	33.56	34.08
42	27.06	27.58	28.10	28.62	29.15	29.67	30.19	30.72	31.25	31.78	32.31	32.84	33.17	33.90	34.44	34.97
43	27.74	28.27	28.81	29.34	29.88	30.42	30.96	31.50	32.04	32.58	33.13	33.67	34.22	34.76	35.31	35.86
44	28.42	28.97	29.52	30.07	30.62	31.17	31.72	32.28	32.83	33.39	33.95	34.51	35.07	35.63	36.19	36.76
45	29.11	29.67	30.23	30.79	31.36	31.92	32.49	33.06	33.63	34.20	34.77	35.35	35.92	36.50	37.08	37.66
46	29.79	30.36	30.94	31.52	32.10	32.68	33.26	33.84	34.43	35.01	35.60	36.19	36.78	37.37	37.96	38.56
47	30.48	31.07	31.66	32.25	32.84	33.44	34.03	34.63	35.23	35.83	36.43	37.04	37.64	38.25	38.86	39.46
48	31.17	31.77	32.37	32.98	33.59	34.20	34.81	35.42	36.03	36.65	37.27	37.88	38.50	39.13	39.75	40.37
49	31.86	32.48	33.09	33.71	34.34	34.96	35.59	36.21	36.84	37.47	38.10	38.74	39.37	40.01	40.65	41.29
50	32.55	33.18	33.82	34.45	35.09	35.73	36.37	37.01	37.65	38.30	38.94	39.59	40.24	40.89	41.55	42.20
51	33.25	33.89	34.54	35.19	35.84	36.49	37.15	37.81	38.46	39.12	39.79	40.45	41.11	41.78	42.45	43.12
52	33.95	34.61	35.27	35.93	36.60	37.27	37.94	38.61	39.28	39.96	40.63	41.31	41.99	42.67	43.36	44.04
53	34.65	35.32	36.00	36.68	37.36	38.04	38.72	39.41	40.10	40.79	41.48	42.17	42.87	43.57	44.27	44.97
54	35.35	36.04	36.73	37.42	38.12	38.82	39.52	40.22	40.92	41.63	42.33	43.04	43.75	44.47	45.18	45.90
55	36.05	36.76	37.46	38.17	38.88	39.60	40.31	41.03	41.74	42.47	43.19	43.91	44.64	45.37	46.10	46.83
56	36.76	37.48	38.20	38.92	39.65	40.38	41.11	41.84	42.57	43.31	44.05	44.79	45.53	46.27	47.02	47.77
57	37.47	38.20	38.94	39.68	40.42	41.16	41.91	42.65	43.40	44.15	44.91	45.66	46.42	47.18	47.94	48.71
58	38.18	38.93	39.68	40.43	41.19	41.95	42.71	43.47	44.23	45.00	45.77	46.54	47.32	48.09	48.87	49.65
59	38.89	39.66	40.42	41.19	41.96	42.74	43.51	44.29	45.07	45.85	46.64	47.42	48.21	49.01	49.80	50.60
60	39.61	40.39	41.17	41.95	42.74	43.53	44.32	45.11	45.91	46.71	47.51	48.31	49.12	49.92	50.73	51.55

TABLE 13-1 Annual Percentage Rate (APR) Finance Charge per $100 (continued)

ANNUAL PERCENTAGE RATE TABLE FOR MONTHLY PAYMENT PLANS
SEE INSTRUCTIONS FOR USE OF TABLES

FRB-105-M

NUMBER OF PAYMENTS	18.00%	18.25%	18.50%	18.75%	19.00%	19.25%	19.50%	19.75%	20.00%	20.25%	20.50%	20.75%	21.00%	21.25%	21.50%	21.75%
					(FINANCE CHARGE PER $100 OF AMOUNT FINANCED)											
1	1.50	1.52	1.54	1.56	1.58	1.60	1.62	1.65	1.67	1.69	1.71	1.73	1.75	1.77	1.79	1.81
2	2.26	2.29	2.32	2.35	2.38	2.41	2.44	2.48	2.51	2.54	2.57	2.60	2.63	2.66	2.70	2.73
3	3.01	3.06	3.10	3.14	3.18	3.23	3.27	3.31	3.35	3.39	3.44	3.48	3.52	3.56	3.60	3.65
4	3.78	3.83	3.88	3.94	3.99	4.04	4.10	4.15	4.20	4.25	4.31	4.36	4.41	4.47	4.52	4.57
5	4.54	4.61	4.67	4.74	4.80	4.86	4.93	4.99	5.06	5.12	5.18	5.25	5.31	5.37	5.44	5.50
6	5.32	5.39	5.46	5.54	5.61	5.69	5.76	5.84	5.91	5.99	6.06	6.14	6.21	6.29	6.36	6.44
7	6.09	6.18	6.26	6.35	6.43	6.52	6.60	6.69	6.78	6.86	6.95	7.04	7.12	7.21	7.29	7.38
8	6.87	6.96	7.06	7.16	7.26	7.35	7.45	7.55	7.64	7.74	7.84	7.94	8.03	8.13	8.23	8.33
9	7.65	7.76	7.87	7.97	8.08	8.19	8.30	8.41	8.52	8.63	8.73	8.84	8.95	9.06	9.17	9.20
10	8.43	8.55	8.67	8.79	8.91	9.03	9.15	9.27	9.39	9.51	9.63	9.75	9.88	10.00	10.12	10.24
11	9.22	9.35	9.49	9.62	9.75	9.88	10.01	10.14	10.28	10.41	10.54	10.67	10.80	10.94	11.07	11.20
12	10.02	10.16	10.30	10.44	10.59	10.73	10.87	11.02	11.16	11.31	11.45	11.59	11.74	11.88	12.02	12.17
13	10.81	10.97	11.12	11.28	11.43	11.59	11.74	11.90	12.05	12.21	12.36	12.52	12.67	12.83	12.99	13.14
14	11.61	11.78	11.95	12.11	12.28	12.45	12.61	12.78	12.95	13.11	13.28	13.45	13.62	13.79	13.95	14.12
15	12.42	12.59	12.77	12.95	13.13	13.31	13.49	13.67	13.85	14.03	14.21	14.39	14.57	14.75	14.93	15.11
16	13.22	13.41	13.60	13.80	13.99	14.18	14.37	14.56	14.75	14.94	15.13	15.33	15.52	15.71	15.90	16.10
17	14.04	14.24	14.44	14.64	14.85	15.05	15.25	15.46	15.66	15.86	16.07	16.27	16.48	16.68	16.89	17.09
18	14.85	15.07	15.28	15.49	15.71	15.93	16.14	16.36	16.57	16.79	17.01	17.22	17.44	17.66	17.88	18.09
19	15.67	15.90	16.12	16.35	16.58	16.81	17.03	17.26	17.49	17.72	17.95	18.18	18.41	18.64	18.87	19.10
20	16.49	16.73	16.97	17.21	17.45	17.69	17.93	18.17	18.41	18.66	18.90	19.14	19.38	19.63	19.87	20.11
21	17.32	17.57	17.82	18.07	18.33	18.58	18.83	19.09	19.34	19.60	19.85	20.11	20.36	20.62	20.87	21.13
22	18.15	18.41	18.68	18.94	19.21	19.47	19.74	20.01	20.27	20.54	20.81	21.08	21.34	21.61	21.88	22.15
23	18.98	19.26	19.54	19.81	20.09	20.37	20.65	20.93	21.21	21.49	21.77	22.05	22.33	22.61	22.90	23.18
24	19.82	20.11	20.40	20.69	20.98	21.27	21.56	21.86	22.15	22.44	22.74	23.03	23.33	23.62	23.92	24.21
25	20.66	20.96	21.27	21.57	21.87	22.18	22.48	22.79	23.10	23.40	23.71	24.02	24.32	24.63	24.94	25.25
26	21.50	21.82	22.14	22.45	22.77	23.09	23.41	23.73	24.04	24.36	24.68	25.01	25.33	25.65	25.97	26.29
27	22.35	22.68	23.01	23.34	23.67	24.00	24.33	24.67	25.00	25.33	25.67	26.00	26.34	26.67	27.01	27.34
28	23.20	23.55	23.89	24.23	24.58	24.92	25.27	25.61	25.96	26.30	26.65	27.00	27.35	27.70	28.05	28.40
29	24.06	24.41	24.77	25.13	25.49	25.84	26.20	26.56	26.92	27.28	27.64	28.00	28.37	28.73	29.09	29.46
30	24.92	25.29	25.66	26.03	26.40	26.77	27.14	27.52	27.89	28.26	28.64	29.01	29.39	29.77	30.14	30.52
31	25.78	26.16	26.55	26.93	27.32	27.70	28.09	28.47	28.86	29.25	29.64	30.03	30.42	30.81	31.20	31.59
32	26.65	27.04	27.44	27.84	28.24	28.64	29.04	29.44	29.84	30.24	30.64	31.05	31.45	31.85	32.26	32.67
33	27.52	27.93	28.34	28.75	29.16	29.57	29.99	30.40	30.82	31.23	31.65	32.07	32.49	32.91	33.33	33.75
34	28.39	28.81	29.24	29.66	30.09	30.52	30.95	31.37	31.80	32.23	32.67	33.10	33.53	33.96	34.40	34.83
35	29.27	29.71	30.14	30.58	31.02	31.47	31.91	32.35	32.79	33.24	33.68	34.13	34.58	35.03	35.47	35.92
36	30.15	30.60	31.05	31.51	31.96	32.42	32.87	33.33	33.79	34.25	34.71	35.17	35.63	36.09	36.56	37.02
37	31.03	31.50	31.97	32.43	32.90	33.37	33.84	34.32	34.79	35.26	35.74	36.21	36.69	37.16	37.64	38.12
38	31.92	32.40	32.88	33.37	33.85	34.33	34.82	35.30	35.79	36.28	36.77	37.26	37.75	38.24	38.73	39.23
39	32.81	33.31	33.80	34.30	34.80	35.30	35.80	36.30	36.80	37.30	37.81	38.31	38.82	39.32	39.83	40.34
40	33.71	34.22	34.73	35.24	35.75	36.26	36.78	37.29	37.81	38.33	38.85	39.37	39.89	40.41	40.93	41.46
41	34.61	35.13	35.66	36.18	36.71	37.24	37.77	38.30	38.83	39.36	39.89	40.43	40.96	41.50	42.04	42.58
42	35.51	36.05	36.59	37.13	37.67	38.21	38.76	39.30	39.85	40.40	40.95	41.50	42.05	42.60	43.15	43.71
43	36.42	36.97	37.52	38.08	38.63	39.19	39.75	40.31	40.87	41.44	42.00	42.57	43.13	43.70	44.27	44.84
44	37.33	37.89	38.46	39.03	39.60	40.18	40.75	41.33	41.90	42.48	43.06	43.64	44.22	44.81	45.39	45.98
45	38.24	38.82	39.41	39.99	40.58	41.17	41.75	42.35	42.94	43.53	44.13	44.72	45.32	45.92	46.52	47.12
46	39.16	39.75	40.35	40.95	41.55	42.16	42.76	43.37	43.98	44.58	45.20	45.81	46.42	47.03	47.65	48.27
47	40.08	40.69	41.30	41.92	42.54	43.15	43.77	44.40	45.02	45.64	46.27	46.90	47.53	48.16	48.79	49.42
48	41.00	41.63	42.26	42.89	43.52	44.15	44.79	45.43	46.07	46.71	47.35	47.99	48.64	49.28	49.93	50.58
49	41.93	42.57	43.22	43.86	44.51	45.16	45.81	46.46	47.12	47.77	48.43	49.09	49.75	50.41	51.08	51.74
50	42.86	43.52	44.18	44.84	45.50	46.17	46.83	47.50	48.17	48.84	49.52	50.19	50.87	51.55	52.23	52.91
51	43.79	44.47	45.14	45.82	46.50	47.18	47.86	48.55	49.23	49.92	50.61	51.30	51.99	52.69	53.38	54.08
52	44.73	45.42	46.11	46.80	47.50	48.20	48.89	49.59	50.30	51.00	51.71	52.41	53.12	53.83	54.55	55.26
53	45.67	46.38	47.08	47.79	48.50	49.22	49.93	50.65	51.37	52.09	52.81	53.53	54.26	54.98	55.71	56.44
54	46.62	47.34	48.06	48.79	49.51	50.24	50.97	51.70	52.44	53.17	53.91	54.65	55.39	56.14	56.88	57.63
55	47.57	48.30	49.04	49.78	50.52	51.27	52.02	52.76	53.52	54.27	55.02	55.78	56.54	57.30	58.06	58.82
56	48.52	49.27	50.03	50.78	51.54	52.30	53.06	53.83	54.60	55.37	56.14	56.91	57.68	58.46	59.24	60.02
57	49.47	50.24	51.01	51.79	52.56	53.34	54.12	54.90	55.68	56.47	57.25	58.04	58.84	59.63	60.43	61.22
58	50.43	51.22	52.00	52.79	53.58	54.38	55.17	55.97	56.77	57.57	58.38	59.18	59.99	60.80	61.62	62.43
59	51.39	52.20	53.00	53.80	54.61	55.42	56.23	57.05	57.87	58.68	59.51	60.33	61.15	61.98	62.81	63.64
60	52.36	53.18	54.00	54.82	55.64	56.47	57.30	58.13	58.96	59.80	60.64	61.48	62.32	63.17	64.01	64.86

STEPS TO FIND THE ANNUAL PERCENTAGE RATE OF AN INSTALLMENT LOAN BY USING APR TABLES

STEP 1. Calculate the finance charge per $100.

$$\text{Finance charge per \$100} = \frac{\text{Finance charge} \times 100}{\text{Amount financed}}$$

STEP 2. From Table 13-1, scan down the Number-of-Payments column to the number of payments for the loan in question.

STEP 3. Scan to the right in that Number-of-Payments row to the table factor that most closely corresponds to the finance charge per $100 calculated in Step 1.

STEP 4. Look to the top of the column containing the finance charge per $100 to find the APR of the loan.

iStock.com/Nikada

EXAMPLE6 CALCULATING APR BY TABLES

Gary Robbins purchased a used motorcycle for $7,000. He made a down payment of $1,000 and financed the remaining $6,000 for 36 months. With monthly payments of $200 each, the total finance charge on the loan was $1,200 ($200 × 36 = $7,200 − $6,000 = $1,200). Use Table 13-1 to find what annual percentage rate was charged on Gary's loan.

▶SOLUTIONSTRATEGY

Step 1.
$$\text{Finance charge per \$100} = \frac{\text{Finance charge} \times 100}{\text{Amount financed}}$$

$$\text{Finance charge per \$100} = \frac{1,200 \times 100}{6,000} = \frac{120,000}{6,000}$$

Finance charge per $100 = $20

Step 2. Using Table 13-1, scan down the Number-of-Payments column to 36 payments.

Step 3. Scan to the right in that Number-of-Payments row until you find $20, the finance charge per $100.

Step 4. Looking at the top of the column containing the $20, you will find the annual percentage rate for the loan to be 12.25%.

▶TRYITEXERCISE 6

Erica Larsen purchased a living room set for $4,500 from Century Designs. She made a $500 down payment and financed the balance with an installment loan for 24 months. If her payments are $190 per month, what APR is she paying on the loan?

CHECK YOUR ANSWERS WITH THE SOLUTIONS ON PAGE 458.

CALCULATING APR BY FORMULA

When APR tables are not available, the annual percentage rate can be closely approximated by the formula

$$\text{APR} = \frac{72I}{3P\,(n + 1) + I\,(n - 1)}$$

where:

I = finance charge on the loan
P = principal, or amount financed
n = number of months of the loan

EXAMPLE7 CALCULATING APR BY FORMULA

Refer to Example 6, Gary Robbins' motorcycle purchase. This time use the APR formula to find the annual percentage rate. How does it compare with the APR from the table?

▶SOLUTIONSTRATEGY

$$APR = \frac{72I}{3P\,(n+1) + I\,(n-1)}$$

$$APR = \frac{72\,(1{,}200)}{3(6{,}000)(36+1) + 1{,}200\,(36-1)} = \frac{86{,}400}{666{,}000 + 42{,}000} = \frac{86{,}400}{708{,}000}$$

$$APR = .1220338 = \underline{\underline{12.20\%}}$$

Note: In comparing the two answers, we can see that using the formula gives a close approximation of the Federal Reserve Board's APR table value of 12.25%.

▶TRYITEXERCISE 7

Christina Pitt repaid a $2,200 installment loan with 18 monthly payments of $140 each. Use the APR formula to determine the annual percentage rate of Christina's loan.

CHECK YOUR ANSWERS WITH THE SOLUTIONS ON PAGE 458.

CALCULATING THE FINANCE CHARGE AND MONTHLY PAYMENT OF AN INSTALLMENT LOAN BY USING THE APR TABLES

13-7

When the annual percentage rate and number of months of an installment loan are known, the APR tables can be used in reverse to find the amount of the finance charge. Once the finance charge is known, the monthly payment required to amortize the loan can be calculated as before.

STEPS TO FIND THE FINANCE CHARGE AND THE MONTHLY PAYMENT OF AN INSTALLMENT LOAN BY USING THE APR TABLES

STEP 1. Using the APR and the number of payments of the loan, locate the table factor at the intersection of the APR column and the Number-of-Payments row. This factor represents the finance charge per $100 financed.

STEP 2. Calculate the total finance charge of the loan.

$$\text{Finance charge} = \frac{\text{Amount financed} \times \text{Table factor}}{100}$$

STEP 3. Calculate the monthly payment.

$$\text{Monthly payment} = \frac{\text{Amount financed} + \text{Finance charge}}{\text{Number of months of the loan}}$$

iStock.com/Nikada

EXAMPLE 8   CALCULATING FINANCE CHARGE BY APR TABLES

Classic Motors uses Regal Bank to finance automobile and truck sales. This month Regal is offering up to 48-month installment loans with an APR of 15.5%. For qualified buyers, no down payment is required. If Todd Martin wants to finance a new truck for $17,500, what are the finance charge and the monthly payment on Todd's loan?

▶SOLUTIONSTRATEGY

Step 1. The table factor at the intersection of the 15.5% APR column and the 48 Payments row is $34.81.

Step 2.
$$\text{Finance charge} = \frac{\text{Amount financed} \times \text{Table factor}}{100}$$

$$\text{Finance charge} = \frac{17,500 \times 34.81}{100} = \frac{609,175}{100}$$

$$\text{Finance charge} = \$6,091.75$$

Step 3.
$$\text{Monthly payment} = \frac{\text{Amount financed} + \text{Finance charge}}{\text{Number of months of the loan}}$$

$$\text{Monthly payment} = \frac{17,500 + 6,091.75}{48} = \frac{23,591.75}{48}$$

$$\text{Monthly payment} = \$491.49$$

▶TRYITEXERCISE 8

Computer Mart uses a finance company that is offering up to 24-month installment loans with an APR of 13.25%. For qualified buyers, no down payment is required. If Randy Salazar wants to finance a computer and printer for $3,550, what are the finance charge and the monthly payment on Randy's loan?

CHECK YOUR ANSWERS WITH THE SOLUTIONS ON PAGE 458.

13-8   CALCULATING THE FINANCE CHARGE REBATE AND THE PAYOFF FOR LOANS PAID OFF EARLY BY USING THE SUM-OF-THE-DIGITS METHOD

finance charge rebate
Unearned portion of the finance charge that the lender returns to the borrower when an installment loan is paid off early.

sum-of-the-digits method or **Rule of 78** Widely accepted method for calculating the finance charge rebate. Based on the assumption that more interest is paid in the early months of a loan, when a greater portion of the principal is available to the borrower.

Frequently, borrowers choose to repay installment loans before the full time period of the loan has elapsed. When loans are paid off early, the borrower is entitled to a **finance charge rebate** because the principal was not kept for the full amount of time on which the finance charge was calculated. At payoff, the lender must return, or rebate, to the borrower any unearned portion of the finance charge.

A widely accepted method for calculating the finance charge rebate is known as the **sum-of-the-digits method** or the **Rule of 78**. This method is based on the assumption that the lender earns more interest in the early months of a loan, when the borrower has the use of much of the principal, than in the later months, when most of the principal has already been paid back.

When using this method, the finance charge is assumed to be divided in parts equal to the sum of the digits of the months of the loan. Because the sum of the digits of a 12-month loan is 78, the technique has become known as the Rule of 78.

$$\text{Sum of the digits of } 12 = 1 + 2 + 3 + 4 + 5 + 6 + 7 + 8 + 9 + 10 + 11 + 12 = 78$$

The amount of finance charge in any given month is represented by a fraction whose numerator is the number of payments remaining, and the denominator is the sum of the digits of the number of months in the loan.

For a 12-month loan, for example, the fraction of the finance charge in the first month would be $\frac{12}{78}$. The numerator is 12 because in the first month, no payments have been made; therefore, 12 payments remain. The denominator is 78 because the sum of the digits of

12 payments is 78. In the second month, the lender earns $\frac{11}{78}$; in the third month, $\frac{10}{78}$. This decline continues until the last month when only $\frac{1}{78}$ remains. Exhibit 13-6 illustrates the distribution of a $1,000 finance charge by using the sum-of-the-digits method.

With the sum-of-the-digits method, a **rebate fraction** is established based on when a loan is paid off. The numerator of the rebate fraction is the sum of the digits of the number of remaining payments, and the denominator is the sum of the digits of the total number of payments.

$$\text{Rebate fraction} = \frac{\text{Sum of the digits of the number of remaining payments}}{\text{Sum of the digits of the total number of payments}}$$

Although the sum of the digits is easily calculated by addition, it can become tedious for loans of 24, 36, or 48 months. For this reason, we will use the sum-of-the-digits formula to find the numerator and denominator of the rebate fraction. In the formula, n represents the number of payments.

$$\text{Sum of digits} = \frac{n(n+1)}{2}$$

rebate fraction Fraction used to calculate the finance charge rebate. The numerator is the sum of the digits of the number of payments remaining at the time the loan is paid off; the denominator is the sum of the digits of the total number of payments of the loan.

dotshock/Shutterstock.com

Installment financing is frequently used when consumers purchase big-ticket items such as appliances and electronic equipment.

EXHIBIT 13-6 Distribution of a $1,000 Finance Charge over 12 Months

Month Number	Finance Charge Fraction	×	$1,000	=	Finance Charge
1	$\frac{12}{78}$	×	$1,000	=	$153.85
2	$\frac{11}{78}$	×	$1,000	=	$141.03
3	$\frac{10}{78}$	×	$1,000	=	$128.21
4	$\frac{9}{78}$	×	$1,000	=	$115.38
5	$\frac{8}{78}$	×	$1,000	=	$102.56
6	$\frac{7}{78}$	×	$1,000	=	$89.74
7	$\frac{6}{78}$	×	$1,000	=	$76.92
8	$\frac{5}{78}$	×	$1,000	=	$64.10
9	$\frac{4}{78}$	×	$1,000	=	$51.28
10	$\frac{3}{78}$	×	$1,000	=	$38.46
11	$\frac{2}{78}$	×	$1,000	=	$25.64
12	$\frac{1}{78}$	×	$1,000	=	$12.82

rtguest/Shutterstock.com

IN THE
Business World

This table clearly illustrates that the majority of the finance charge on an installment loan is incurred in the first half of the loan.

STEPS TO CALCULATE THE FINANCE CHARGE REBATE AND LOAN PAYOFF

STEP 1. Calculate the rebate fraction.

$$\text{Rebate fraction} = \frac{\text{Sum of the digits of the number of remaining payments}}{\text{Sum of the digits of the total number of payments}}$$

STEP 2. Determine the finance charge rebate.

Finance charge rebate = Rebate fraction × Total finance charge

STEP 3. Find the loan payoff.

$$\text{Loan payoff} = \left(\text{Payment remaining} \times \text{Payments amount} \right) - \text{Finance charge rebate}$$

iStock.com/Nikada

EXAMPLE9 CALCULATING EARLY LOAN PAYOFF FIGURES

Suzie Starr financed a $1,500 health club membership with an installment loan for 12 months. The payments were $145 per month, and the total finance charge was $240. After 8 months, she decided to pay off the loan. What is the finance charge rebate, and what is her loan payoff?

►SOLUTIONSTRATEGY

Step 1.   Rebate fraction:

Set up the rebate fraction by using the sum-of-the-digits formula. Because Suzie already made eight payments, she has four payments remaining ($12 - 8 = 4$).

The *numerator* will be the sum of the digits of the number of remaining payments, 4.

$$\text{Sum of the digits of } 4 = \frac{n\,(n+1)}{2} = \frac{4\,(4+1)}{2} = \frac{4\,(5)}{2} = \frac{20}{2} = \underline{10}$$

The *denominator* will be the sum of the digits of the number of payments, 12.

$$\text{Sum of the digits of } 12 = \frac{n\,(n+1)}{2} = \frac{12\,(12+1)}{2} = \frac{12\,(13)}{2} = \frac{156}{2} = \underline{78}$$

The rebate fraction is therefore $\dfrac{10}{78}$.

Step 2.   Finance charge rebate:

Finance charge rebate = Rebate fraction × Total finance charge

$$\text{Finance charge rebate} = \frac{10}{78} \times 240$$

Finance charge rebate = 30.7692 = $\underline{\$30.77}$

Step 3.   Loan payoff:

Loan payoff	=	(Payments remaining × Payment amount) − Finance charge rebate
Loan payoff	=	(4 × 145) − 30.77
Loan payoff	=	580.00 − 30.77
Loan payoff	=	$\underline{\$549.23}$

►TRYITEXERCISE 9

Mark Sanchez financed a $4,000 piano with an installment loan for 36 months. The payments were $141 per month, and the total finance charge was $1,076. After 20 months, Mark decided to pay off the loan. What is the finance charge rebate, and what is his loan payoff?

CHECK YOUR ANSWERS WITH THE SOLUTIONS ON PAGE 459

SECTION II 13 REVIEW EXERCISES

Note: **Round all answers to the nearest cent when necessary.**

Calculate the amount financed, the finance charge, and the total deferred payment price for the following installment loans.

	Purchase (Cash) Price	Down Payment	Amount Financed	Monthly Payment	Number of Payments	Finance Charge	Total Deferred Payment Price
1.	$1,400	$350	$1,050.00	$68.00	24	$582.00	$1,982.00
2.	$3,500	20%	_____	$257.00	12	_____	_____

	Purchase (Cash) Price	Down Payment	Amount Financed	Monthly Payment	Number of Payments	Finance Charge	Total Deferred Payment Price
3.	$12,000	10%	_____	$375.00	36	_____	_____
4.	$2,900	0	_____	$187.69	18	_____	_____
5.	$8,750	15%	_____	$198.33	48	_____	_____
6.	$5,400	$1,500	_____	$427.50	12	_____	_____

7. Anny takes out an installment loan to finance the purchase of a pickup truck costing $14,400. Her loan requires a 25% down payment and equal monthly payments of $288.00 for 60 months. Calculate the total deferred payment price.

Calculate the amount financed, the finance charge, and the monthly payments for the following add-on interest loans.

	Purchase (Cash) Price	Down Payment	Amount Financed	Add-on Interest	Number of Payments	Finance Charge	Monthly Payment
8.	$788	10%	$709.20	8%	12	$56.74	$63.83
9.	$1,600	$250	_____	10%	24	_____	_____
10.	$4,000	15%	_____	$11\frac{1}{2}\%$	30	_____	_____
11.	$17,450	$2,000	_____	14%	48	_____	_____
12.	$50,300	25%	_____	12.4%	60	_____	_____
13.	$12,300	5%	_____	9%	36	_____	_____

14. You purchase a sofa costing $1,050 by taking out a 9% add-on interest installment loan. The loan requires a 15% down payment and equal monthly payments for 4 years. How much are your monthly payments?

Calculate the finance charge, the finance charge per $100, and the annual percentage rate for the following installment loans by using the APR table, Table 13-1.

	Amount Financed	Number of Payments	Monthly Payment	Finance Charge	Finance Charge per $100	APR
15.	$2,300	24	$109.25	$322.00	$14.00	13%
16.	$14,000	36	$495.00	_____	_____	_____
17.	$1,860	18	$115.75	_____	_____	_____
18.	$40,000	60	$946.33	_____	_____	_____
19.	$6,550	24	$307.30	_____	_____	_____
20.	$17,930	48	$540.47	_____	_____	_____

Calculate the finance charge and the annual percentage rate for the following installment loans by using the APR formula.

	Amount Financed	Number of Payments	Monthly Payment	Finance Charge	APR
21.	$500	12	$44.25	$31.00	11.25%
22.	$18,600	72	$421.08	_____	_____
23.	$13,000	48	$373.75	_____	_____
24.	$100,000	72	$2,055.50	_____	_____
25.	$35,600	60	$845.50	_____	_____

26. Miguel purchased a hot tub costing $5,000 by taking out an installment loan. He made a down payment of $1,300 and financed the balance for 24 months. If the payments are $176.77 each month, use the APR formula to find the APR. Round to the nearest hundredth percent.

Calculate the finance charge and the monthly payment for the following loans by using the APR table, Table 13-1.

	Amount Financed	Number of Payments	APR	Table Factor	Finance Charge	Monthly Payment
27.	$5,000	48	13.5%	$29.97	$1,498.50	$135.39
28.	$7,500	36	12%	_____	_____	_____
29.	$1,800	12	11.25%	_____	_____	_____
30.	$900	18	14%	_____	_____	_____
31.	$12,200	24	12.75%	_____	_____	_____

32. You wish to finance purchase of a sofa for $1,100. A bank offers an APR of 11.25% on a 48-month installment loan. After first using Table 13-1 to find the finance charge, calculate your monthly payment.

Calculate the missing information for the following installment loans that are being paid off early.

	Number of Payments	Payments Made	Payments Remaining	Sum-of-the-Digits Payments Remaining	Sum-of-the-Digits Number of Payments	Rebate Fraction
33.	12	4	8	36	78	36/78
34.	36	22	_____	_____	_____	_____
35.	24	9	_____	_____	_____	_____
36.	60	40	_____	_____	_____	_____
37.	48	8	_____	_____	_____	_____
38.	18	5	_____	_____	_____	_____

You are the loan department supervisor for the Pacific National Bank. The following installment loans are being paid off early, and it is your task to calculate the rebate fraction, the finance charge rebate, and the payoff for each loan.

	Amount Financed	Number of Payments	Monthly Payment	Payments Made	Rebate Fraction	Finance Charge Rebate	Loan Payoff
39.	**$3,000**	**24**	**$162.50**	**9**	**120/300**	**$360.00**	**$2,077.50**
40.	$1,600	18	$104.88	11	_____	_____	_____
41.	$9,500	48	$267.00	36	_____	_____	_____
42.	$4,800	36	$169.33	27	_____	_____	_____
43.	$11,000	30	$440.00	20	_____	_____	_____

44. Suppose you take out a 36-month installment loan to finance a delivery van for $26,100. the payments are $986 per month, and the total finance charge is $9,396.

　　After 25 months, you decide to pay off the loan. After calculating the finance charge rebate, find your loan payoff.

45. Belinda Raven is interested in buying a solar energy system for her home. At Sun-Catchers Inc., she picks out a system for a total cash price of $1,899. The salesperson informs her that if she qualifies for an installment loan, she may pay 10% now as a down payment and finance the balance with payments of $88.35 per month for 24 months.

a.　What is the finance charge on this loan?

b.　What is the total deferred payment price of the system?

46. Meghan Pease purchased a small sailboat for $8,350. She made a down payment of $1,400 and financed the balance with monthly payments of $239.38 for 36 months.

a.　What is the finance charge on the loan?

b.　Use Table 13-1 to find what annual percentage rate was charged on Meghan's loan.

Solar Energy Although solar energy is a relatively new energy source, it may become the most important energy source of the future. Presently, available tax credits and incentives greatly reduce startup costs for solar power systems. Some of the major advantages of solar power include the fact that it is renewable, is nonpolluting, does not emit greenhouse gases, and provides free energy and heat from the sun.

Job growth in the solar energy industry is expected to remain strong.

47. Valerie Ross financed a cruise to the Bahamas with a 5% add-on interest installment loan from her bank. The total price of the trip was $1,500. The bank required equal monthly payments for 2 years. What are Valerie's monthly payments?

EXCEL 3

48. Doug Black bought a jet ski with a 9% add-on interest installment loan from his credit union. The purchase price was $1,450. The credit union required a 15% down payment and equal monthly payments for 48 months. What are Doug's monthly payments?

Timeshare is a form of ownership that provides the right to the use of a property either directly or through a "points club." Each time sharer is allotted a period of time, typically a week or longer, for a great many years or in perpetuity. The timeshare industry typically generates revenues of approximately $10 billion per annum.

Mark Winfrey/Shutterstock.com

49. Olivia Fast found a timeshare offer entitling her to 3 weeks per year in a Rocky Mountain townhouse. She had the option of paying $7,600 in cash or financing the timeshare with a 2-year installment loan. The loan required a 20% down payment and equal monthly payments of $283.73.

   a. What is the finance charge on Olivia's loan?

   b. What is the total deferred payment price of the timeshare contract?

50. Tim Houston purchased a wall unit for $2,400. He made a $700 down payment and financed the balance with an installment loan for 48 months. If Tim's payments are $42.50 per month, use the APR formula to calculate what annual percentage rate he is paying on the loan.

51. First National Bank offers a 36-month installment loan with an APR of 10.5%. Liz and Julio wish to use the loan to finance a home theater system for $2,600. Use the APR tables to calculate their finance charge and monthly payment.

52. At a recent boat show, Nautica Bank was offering boat loans for up to 5 years with an APR of 13.5%. On new boats, a 20% down payment was required. Scott Vaughn wanted to finance a $55,000 boat for 5 years.

    a. What would be the finance charge on the loan?

    b. What would be the monthly payment?

53. Find the sum of the digits of

    a. 24   b. 30

54. a. What is the rebate fraction of a 36-month loan paid off after the 14th payment?

    b. What is the rebate fraction of a 42-month loan paid off after the 19th payment?

55. Charlie Allen financed a $3,500 Nautilus home gym with an 8% add-on interest installment loan for 24 months. The loan required a 10% down payment.

    a. What is the finance charge on the loan?

    b. What are Charlie's monthly payments?

fotoinfot/Shutterstock.com

Home Gym Nautilus, Inc. is a fitness products company headquartered in Vancouver, Washington. Its principal business activities include designing, developing, sourcing, and marketing high-quality cardiovascular and strength fitness products and related accessories. Nautilus products are sold under the brand names Nautilus, Bowflex, Universal, and Schwinn Fitness. Products offered include home gyms, free weight equipment, treadmills, indoor cycling equipment, ellipticals, and fitness accessories and apparel. Typical annual revenues for Nautilus, Inc. exceed $160 million.

c. What annual percentage rate is being charged on the loan?

d. If Charlie decides to pay off the loan after 16 months, what is his loan payoff?

56. Chuck Wells is planning to buy a Winnebago motor home. The listed price is $165,000. Chuck can get a secured loan from his bank at 7.25% for as long as 60 months if he pays 15% down. Chuck's goal is to keep his payments below $3,800 per month and amortize the loan in 42 months.

a. Can he pay off the loan in 42 months and keep his payments under $3,800?

Winnebago Industries, Inc., founded in 1958 and headquartered in Forest City, Iowa, manufactures motor homes, which are self-contained recreation vehicles used primarily in leisure travel and outdoor recreation activities.

The company markets its motor homes through independent dealers under the Winnebago, Itasca, and ERA brand names in the United States and Canada. Annual revenues for Winnebago vary depending on various factors, including the state of the U.S. economy and gas prices. They typically exceed $400 million.

b. What are Chuck's options to get his payments closer to his goal?

c. Chuck spoke with his bank's loan officer, who has agreed to finance the deal with a 6.95% loan if Chuck can pay 20% down. Will these conditions meet Chuck's goal?

d. Chuck tells the seller he cannot buy the motor home at the listed price. If the seller agrees to reduce the listed price by $4,600 and Chuck pays the 20% down, will Chuck meet his goal?

BUSINESS DECISION: READING THE FINE PRINT

The advertisement for the 3-D TV at the Electronic Boutique shown below appeared in your local newspaper this morning. Answer the questions that follow based on the information in the ad.

57. a. If you purchased the TV on January 24 of this year and the billing date of the installment loan is the 15th of each month, when would your first payment be due?

   b. What is the required amount of that payment?

   c. If that payment is late or less than required, what happens and how much does that amount to?

   d. If that payment is more than 30 days late, what happens and how much does that amount to?

   e. Explain the advantages and disadvantages of this offer.

Electronic Boutique

NO INTEREST & NO PAYMENTS* FOR 12 MONTHS on all 3-D TVs

*Offer is subject to credit approval. No finance charges assessed and no monthly payment required on the promotional purchase if you pay this amount in full by the payment due date as shown on the twelfth (12th) billing statement after purchase date. If you do not, finance charges will be assessed on the promotional purchase amount from the purchase date and minimum monthly payment will be required on balance of amount. Standard account terms apply to non-promotional balances and, after the promotion ends, to promotional purchases. APR = 22.73%. APR of 24.75% applies if payment is more than 30 days late. Sales tax will be paid at the time of purchase.

$3,499 Optimax Plus
1080p true HD resolution for better picture quality. 120Hz refresh rate, dual core processor, content sharing and screen mirroring. Smart TV features let you interact and stream content from the web. Supports apps.

CHAPTER
13

CHAPTER FORMULAS

Open-End Credit

$$\text{Periodic rate} = \frac{\text{Annual percentage rate}}{12}$$

$$\text{Finance charge} = \text{Previous month's balance} \times \text{Periodic rate}$$

$$\text{Average daily balance} = \frac{\text{Sum of the daily balances}}{\text{Days in billing cycle}}$$

$$\text{Finance charge} = \text{Average daily balance} \times \text{Periodic rate}$$

$$\frac{\text{New}}{\text{balance}} = \frac{\text{Previous}}{\text{balance}} + \frac{\text{Finance}}{\text{charge}} + \frac{\text{Purchases and}}{\text{cash advances}} - \frac{\text{Payments and}}{\text{credits}}$$

Closed-End Credit

$$\text{Amount financed} = \text{Purchase price} - \text{Down payment}$$

$$\text{Down payment} = \text{Purchase price} \times \text{Down payment percent}$$

$$\text{Amount financed} = \text{Purchase price}(100\% - \text{Down payment percent})$$

$$\text{Total amount of installment payments} = \text{Amount financed} + \text{Finance charge}$$

$$\text{Finance charge} = \text{Total amount of installment payments} - \text{Amount financed}$$

$$\frac{\text{Total amount of}}{\text{installment payments}} = \frac{\text{Monthly payment}}{\text{amount}} \times \frac{\text{Number of monthly}}{\text{payments}}$$

$$\text{Total deferred payment price} = \text{Total amount of installment payments} + \text{Down payment}$$

$$\underset{(\textit{finance charge})}{\text{Interest}} = \underset{(\textit{amount financed})}{\text{Principal}} \times \text{Rate} \times \text{Time}$$

$$\text{Regular monthly payments} = \frac{\text{Total amount of installment payments}}{\text{Number of months of loan}}$$

$$\text{APR} = \frac{72I}{3P\,(n+1) + I\,(n-1)}$$

$$\text{Finance charge} = \frac{\text{Amount financed} \times \text{APR table factor}}{100}$$

$$\text{Sum of digits} = \frac{n(n+1)}{2}$$

$$\text{Rebate fraction} = \frac{\text{Sum of the digits of remaining payments}}{\text{Sum of the digits of total payment}}$$

$$\text{Finance charge rebate} = \text{Rebate fraction} \times \text{Total finance charge}$$

$$\text{Loan payoff} = (\text{Payments remaining} \times \text{Payment amount}) - \text{Finance charge rebate}$$

Chapter Summary

Section I: Open-End Credit—Charge Accounts, Credit Cards, and Lines of Credit

Topic	Important Concepts	Illustrative Examples
Calculating the Finance Charge and New Balance by Using the Previous Month's Balance Method **Performance Objective 13-1, Page 422**	1. Divide the annual percentage rate by 12 to find the monthly or periodic interest rate. 2. Calculate the finance charge by multiplying the previous month's balance by the periodic interest rate from Step 1. 3. Total all the purchases and cash advances for the month. 4. Total all the payments and credits for the month. 5. Use the following formula to determine the new balance:	Calculate the finance charge and the new balance of an account with an annual percentage rate of 15%. Previous month's balance = \$186.11 Purchases = \$365.77 Payments = \$200 Periodic rate $= \dfrac{15}{12} = 1.25\%$ Finance charge $= 186.11 \times .0125 = \underline{\$2.33}$ New balance $\quad = 186.11 + 2.33 + 365.77 - 200.00$ $\quad = \underline{\$354.21}$
Calculating the Finance Charge and New Balance by Using the Average Daily Balance Method **Performance Objective 13-2, Page 426**	1. Starting with the previous month's balance, multiply each by the number of days that balance existed until the next account transaction. 2. At the end of the billing cycle, add all the daily balances × days figures. 3. 4. 5.	Calculate the finance charge and the new balance of an account with a periodic rate of 1%, a previous balance of \$132.26, and the following activity. May 5 Purchase $\qquad$ \$45.60 May 9 Cash advance $\qquad$ 100.00 May 15 Credit $\qquad$ 65.70 May 23 Purchase $\qquad$ 75.62 May 26 Payment $\qquad$ 175.00 $\$132.26 \times 4$ days $=\qquad$ \$529.04 177.86×4 days $=\qquad$ 711.44 277.86×6 days $=\qquad$ 1,667.16 212.16×8 days $=\qquad$ 1,697.28 287.78×3 days $=\qquad$ 863.34 112.78×6 days $=\qquad$ 676.68 $\overline{31 \text{ days} \qquad\qquad \$6,144.94}$ Average daily balance $= \dfrac{6,144.94}{31} = \$198.22$ Finance charge $= 1\% \times 198.22 = \underline{\$1.98}$ New balance $= 132.26 + 1.98 + 221.22 - 240.70$ $\qquad\qquad = \underline{\$114.76}$
Calculating the Finance Charge and New Balance of Business and Personal Lines of Credit **Performance Objective 13-3, Page 428**	With business and personal lines of credit, the annual percentage rate is quoted as the current prime rate plus a fixed percent. $\quad$ Once the APR rate is determined, the finance charge and new balance are calculated as before using the average daily balance method.	What are the finance charge and new balance of a line of credit with an APR of the current prime rate plus 4.6%? Previous balance = \$2,000 Average daily balance = \$3,200 Payments = \$1,500 Loans = \$3,600 Current prime rate = 7% $\qquad$ APR $= 7\% + 4.6\% = 11.6\%$ $\qquad$ Periodic rate $= \dfrac{11.6}{12} = .97\%$ Finance charge $= 3,200 \times .0097 = \underline{\$31.04}$ New balance $= 2,000 + 31.04 + 3,600 - 1,500$ $\qquad\qquad = \underline{\$4,131.04}$

Section II: Closed-End Credit—Installment Loans

Topic	Important Concepts	Illustrative Examples
Calculating the Total Deferred Payment Price and the Amount of the Finance Charge of an Installment Loan **Performance Objective 13-4, Page 436**		Value City Furniture sold a $1,900 bedroom set to Jeremy Jackson. Jeremy put down $400 and financed the balance with an installation loan of 24 monthly payments of $68.75 each. What are the finance charge and total deferred payment price of the bedroom set? Total amount of payments = $68.75 × 24 $= \$1,650$ Finance charge = 1,650 − 1,500 = $\underline{\$150}$ Total deferred payment price = 1,650 + 400 $= \underline{\$2,050}$
Calculating the Regular Monthly Payments of an Installment Loan by the Add-on Interest Method **Performance Objective 13-5, Page 437**	1. Calculate the amount financed by subtracting the down payment from the purchase price. 2. Compute the add-on interest finance charge by using $I = PRT$, with the amount financed as the principal. 3. Find the total amount of the installment payments by adding the interest to the amount financed. 4. Calculate the monthly payment by dividing the total amount of the installment payments by the number of months of the loan.	Diane Barber financed a new car with an 8% add-on interest loan. The purchase price of the car was $13,540. The bank required a $1,500 down payment and equal monthly payments for 48 months. What are Diane's monthly payments? Amount financed = 13,540 − 1,500 = $12,040 Interest = 12,040 × .08 × 4 = $3,852.80 Total amount of installment payments $= 12,040.00 + 3,852.80 = \$15,892.80$ Monthly payment $= \dfrac{15,892.80}{48} = \underline{\$331.10}$
Calculating the Annual Percentage Rate by APR Tables **Performance Objective 13-6, Page 438**	1. Calculate the finance charge per $100 by 2. From Table 13-1, scan down the Payments column to the number of payments of the loan. 3. Scan to the right in that row to the table factor that most closely corresponds to the finance charge per $100. 4. Look to the top of the column containing the finance charge per $100 to find the APR of the loan.	Steve Moran purchased a home gym for $8,000. He made a $1,500 down payment and financed the remaining $6,500 for 30 months. If Steve's total finance charge is $1,858, what APR is he paying on the loan? Finance charge per $100 $= \dfrac{1,858 \times 100}{6,500} = \$28.58$ From Table 13-1, scan down the Payments column to 30. Then scan right to the table factor closest to 28.58, which is 28.64. The top of that column shows the APR to be $\underline{20.5\%}$.
Calculating the Annual Percentage Rate of an Installment Loan by Formula **Performance Objective 13-6, Page 442**	When APR tables are not available, the annual percentage rate can be approximated by the formula	Using the APR formula, verify the 20.5% found in the table in the previous example. $APR = \dfrac{72\,(1,858)}{3\,(6,500)\,(30+1) + 1,858\,(30-1)}$ $= \dfrac{133,776}{658,382} = .2031 = \underline{20.3\%}$
Calculating the Finance Charge and Monthly Payment of an Installment Loan by Using the APR Tables **Performance Objective 13-7, Page 443**	1. From Table 13-1, locate the table factor at the intersection of the APR and number of payments of the loan. This table factor is the finance charge per $100. 2. 3.	Appliance Mart uses Galaxy Bank to finance customer purchases. This month Galaxy is offering loans up to 36 months with an APR of 13.25%. For qualified buyers, no down payment is required. If Clark Shaw wants to purchase a $2,350 stove using a 36-month loan, what are the finance charge and monthly payment of the loan? From Table 13-1, the table factor for 36 payments, 13.25% = 21.73 Total finance charge $= \dfrac{2,350 \times 21.73}{100} = \underline{\$510.66}$ Monthly payment $= \dfrac{2,350.00 + 510.66}{36} = \underline{\$79.46}$

Section II (continued)

Topic	Important Concepts	Illustrative Examples
Calculating the Finance Charge Rebate and the Payoff for Loans Paid Off Early by Using the Sum-of-the-Digits, or the Rule of 78, Method **Performance Objective 13-8, Page 444**	1. Calculate the rebate fraction by 2. Determine the finance charge rebate by 3. Find the loan payoff by	Jill Otis financed a $2,000 riding lawn mower with an installment loan for 24 months. The payments are $98 per month, and the total finance charge is $352. After 18 months, Jill decides to pay off the loan. What is the finance charge rebate, and what is the loan payoff? $\text{Rebate fraction} = \dfrac{\text{Sum of the digits of 6}}{\text{Sum of the digits of 24}}$ $\text{Sum of the digits of 6} = \dfrac{6(7)}{2} = 21$ $\text{Sum of the digits of 24} = \dfrac{24(25)}{2} = 300$ $\text{Rebate fraction} = \dfrac{21}{300}$ $\text{Finance charge rebate} = \dfrac{21}{300} \times 352 = \underline{\underline{\$24.64}}$ $\text{Loan payoff} = (6 \times 98) - 24.64$ $= 588.00 - 24.64 = \underline{\underline{\$563.36}}$

TRY IT: EXERCISE SOLUTIONS FOR CHAPTER 13

1. $\text{Periodic rate} = \dfrac{\text{APR}}{12} = \dfrac{15\%}{12} = 1.25\%$

Finance charge = Previous balance × Periodic rate

Finance charge = $214.90 \times .0125 = \underline{\underline{\$2.69}}$

New balance = Previous balance + Finance charge + Purchases and cash advance − Payments and credits

New balance = $214.90 + 2.69 + 238.85 - 49.12 = \underline{\underline{\$407.32}}$

2. $\text{Periodic rate} = \dfrac{\text{APR}}{12} = \dfrac{18\%}{12} = 1.5\%$

Dates	Days	Activity/Amount		Unpaid Balance	Daily Balances
Aug. 1–4	4	Previous balance	$158.69	$158.69	$634.76
Aug. 5–10	6	Charge	55.00	213.69	1,282.14
Aug. 11–14	4	Payment	−100.00	113.69	454.76
Aug. 15–16	2	Charge	43.22	156.91	313.82
Aug. 17–19	3	Charge	54.10	211.01	633.03
Aug. 20–25	6	Charge	224.50	435.51	2,613.06
Aug. 26–31	6	Cash advance	75.00	510.51	3,063.06
	31				$8,994.63

$\text{Average daily balance} = \dfrac{\text{Sum of the daily balances}}{\text{Days in billing cycle}} = \dfrac{8,994.63}{31} = \$290.15$

Finance charge = Average daily balance × Periodic rate

Finance charge = $290.15 \times .015 = \underline{\underline{\$4.35}}$

New balance = Previous balance + Finance charge + Purchases and cash advance − Payments and credits

New balance = $158.69 + 4.35 + 451.82 - 100.00 = \underline{\underline{\$514.86}}$

3. APR = Prime rate + 4.5%

APR = $8.5 + 4.5 = 13\%$

$\text{Periodic rate} = \dfrac{13\%}{12} = 1.08\%$

CHAPTER 13

Dates	Days	Activity/Amount		Unpaid Balance	Daily Balances
Nov. 1–6	6	Previous balance	$12,300	$12,300	$73,800
Nov. 7–20	14	Borrowed	16,700	29,000	406,000
Nov. 21–25	5	Borrowed	8,800	37,800	189,000
Nov. 26–30	5	Payment	−20,000	17,800	89,000
	30				$757,800

Average daily balance $= \dfrac{757,800}{30} = \$25,260$

Finance charge $= 25,260 \times .0108 = \underline{\$272.81}$

New balance = Previous balance + Finance charge + Loan amounts − Payments

New balance $= 12,300.00 + 272.81 + 25,500.00 - 20,000.00 = \underline{\$18,072.81}$

4. a. Down payment = Purchase price × Down payment percent

Down payment $= 12,500 \times .15 = \$1,875$

Amount financed = Purchase price − Down payment

Amount financed $= 12,500 - 1,875 = \$10,625$

Total amount of installment payments = Monthly payment × Number of payments

Total amount of installment payments $= 309.90 \times 48 = \$14,875.20$

Finance charge = Total amount of installment payments − Amount financed

Finance charge $= 14,875.20 - 10,625.00 = \underline{\$4,250.20}$

   b. Total deferred payment price = Total amount of installment payments + Down payment

Total deferred payment price $= 14,875.20 + 1,875.00 = \underline{\$16,750.20}$

5. Amount financed = Purchase price(100% − Down payment %)

Amount financed $= 1,500 \times .9 = \$1,350$

Finance charge = Amount financed × Rate × Time

Finance charge $= 1,350 \times .06 \times 2 = \$162$

Total amount of installment payments = Amount financed + Finance charge

Total amount of installment payments $= 1,350 + 162 = \$1,512$

Monthly payments $= \dfrac{\text{Total amount of installment payments}}{\text{Number of months of loan}}$

Monthly payments $= \dfrac{1,512}{24} = \underline{\$63}$

6. Amount financed $= 4,500 - 500 = \$4,000$

Total payments $= 190 \times 24 = 4,560$

Finance charge $= 4,560 - 4,000 = \$560$

Finance charge per $100 $= \dfrac{\text{Finance charge} \times 100}{\text{Amount financed}} = \dfrac{560 \times 100}{4,000} = \$14$

From Table 13-1 APR for $14 = \underline{13\%}$

7. Total payments $= 140 \times 18 = \$2,520$

Finance charge $= 2,520 - 2,200 = \$320$

$\text{APR} = \dfrac{72I}{3P\,(n+1) + I\,(n-1)}$

$\text{APR} = \dfrac{72(320)}{3\,(2,200)(18+1) + 320\,(18-1)} = \dfrac{23,040}{125,400 + 5,440}$

$\text{APR} = \dfrac{23,040}{130,840} = .17609 = \underline{17.6\%}$

8. 13.25%, 24-month table factor = $14.38

Finance charge $= \dfrac{\text{Amount financed} \times \text{Table factor}}{100}$

Finance charge $= \dfrac{3,550.00 \times 14.38}{100} = \dfrac{51,049}{100} = \$510.49$

Monthly payment $= \dfrac{\text{Amount financed} + \text{Finance charge}}{\text{Number of months of loan}}$

Monthly payment $= \dfrac{3,550.00 + 510.49}{24} = \dfrac{4,060.49}{24}$

Monthly payment $= \underline{\$169.19}$

9. 16 months remaining; total of 36 months

Sum of the digits of $16 = \dfrac{n(n+1)}{2} = \dfrac{16(16+1)}{2} = \dfrac{272}{2} = 136$

Sum of the digits of $36 = \dfrac{n(n+1)}{2} = \dfrac{36(36+1)}{2} = \dfrac{1{,}332}{2} = 666$

Rebate fraction $= \dfrac{136}{666}$

Finance charge rebate = Rebate fraction × Total finance charge $= \dfrac{136}{666} \times 1{,}076$

Finance charge rebate = $\underline{\$219.72}$

Loan payoff = (Payments remaining × Payment amount) − Finance charge rebate

Loan payoff = $(16 \times 141) - 219.72 = 2{,}256.00 - 219.72$

Loan payoff = $\underline{\$2{,}036.28}$

CONCEPT REVIEW

1. _____ credit is a loan arrangement in which there is no set number of payments. (13-1)

2. The effective or true annual interest rate being charged for credit is known as the _____ _____ _____ and is abbreviated _____. (13-1)

3. Loans that are backed by the borrower's "promise" to repay are known as _____ loans, whereas loans that are backed by a tangible asset are known as _____ loans. (13-1)

4. Loans made on a continuous basis and billed periodically are known as _____ credit. (13-1)

5. Name the two most common methods used to calculate the finance charge of a revolving credit account. (13-1, 13-2)

6. Write the formula for calculating the average daily balance of a revolving credit account. (13-2)

7. A pre-approved amount of open-end credit is known as a(n) _____ of credit. (13-3)

8. The interest rate of most lines of credit is tied to the movement of the _____ rate. (13-3)

9. A loan made for a specified number of equal monthly payments is known as a(n) _____ loan. (13-4)

10. The portion of the purchase price of an asset paid in a lump sum at the time of purchase is known as the _____ payment. (13-4)

11. A popular method for calculating the interest on an installment loan is known as _____ interest. (13-5)

12. Write the formula for calculating the APR of an installment loan. (13-6)

13. The finance charge _____ is the unearned portion of the finance charge that is returned to a borrower when an installment loan is paid off early. (13-8)

14. The most common method for calculating the finance charge rebate of an installment loan is known as the sum-of-the-_____ method or the Rule of _____. (13-8)

ASSESSMENT TEST

1. John Dugan's revolving credit account has an annual percentage rate of 15%. The previous month's balance was $428.10. During the current month, his purchases and cash advances amounted to $281.15 and his payments and credits totaled $150.00.

    a. What is the monthly periodic rate of the account?

    b. What is the finance charge?

    c. What is John's new balance?

2. John Public has a Bank of America revolving credit account with an annual percentage rate of 12% calculated on the previous month's balance. In April, the account had the following activity.

Statement of Account

NAME	DATE	DESCRIPTION OF TRANSACTIONS	CHARGES
JOHN PUBLIC	04/01	Previous month's balance	$301.98
	04/08	Mason Gym & Health Club	250.00
ACCOUNT NUMBER	04/09	Payment	75.00
9595-55-607	04/15	Nordstrom	124.80
	04/25	Cash Advance	100.00
BILLING CYCLE	04/28	Rimrock Hotel	178.90
APRIL 1–30			

    a. What is the finance charge?

    b. What is John's new balance?

3. Charlotte Williams has a Visa account. The finance charge is calculated on the previous month's balance, and the annual percentage rate is 20%. Complete the following three-month account activity table for Charlotte.

	Month	Previous Month's Balance	Finance Charge	Purchases and Cash Advances	Payments and Credits	New Balance End of Month
a.	December	$267.00	_____	$547.66	$95.00	_____
b.	January	_____	_____	$213.43	$110.00	_____
c.	February	_____	_____	$89.95	$84.00	_____

4. Calculate the average daily balance for January of a charge account with a previous month's balance of $480.94 and the following activity.

Date	Activity	Amount
January 7	Cash advance	$80.00
January 12	Payment	$125.00
January 18	Purchase	$97.64
January 24	Credit	$72.00
January 29	Purchase	$109.70
January 30	Purchase	$55.78

Credit Card Fees Decline
As a result of the Credit Card Accountability, Responsibility, and Disclosure Act and the improving economy, the number of households paying late and over-the-limit fees has significantly declined.

Pressmaster/Shutterstock.com

5. Cindy Citizen has a Bank of America account with a 13% annual percentage rate calculated on the average daily balance. The billing date is the first day of each month, and the billing cycle is the number of days in that month.

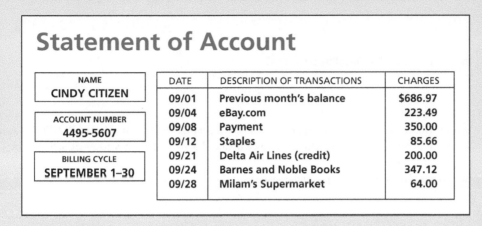

Statement of Account

NAME			
CINDY CITIZEN			

ACCOUNT NUMBER
4495-5607

BILLING CYCLE
SEPTEMBER 1–30

DATE	DESCRIPTION OF TRANSACTIONS	CHARGES
09/01	Previous month's balance	$686.97
09/04	eBay.com	223.49
09/08	Payment	350.00
09/12	Staples	85.66
09/21	Delta Air Lines (credit)	200.00
09/24	Barnes and Noble Books	347.12
09/28	Milam's Supermarket	64.00

a. What is the average daily balance for September?

b. What is the finance charge for September?

c. What is Cindy's new balance?

6. Alpine Construction, Inc. has a $100,000 line of credit with the Bow Valley Bank. The annual percentage rate is the current prime rate plus $3\frac{1}{4}\%$. The balance on June 1 was $52,900. On June 8, Alpine borrowed $30,600 to pay for a shipment of lumber and roofing materials and on June 18 borrowed another $12,300 for equipment repairs. On June 28, a $35,000 payment was made on the account. The billing cycle for June has 30 days. The current prime rate is $7\frac{3}{4}\%$.

a. What is the finance charge on the account?

b. What is Alpine's new balance?

7. George Bell bought an ultralight airplane for $29,200. He made a 15% down payment and financed the balance with payments of $579 per month for 60 months.

a. What is the finance charge on George's loan?

b. What is the total deferred payment price of the airplane?

Up, Up, and Away!
Ultralight aircraft provide an exciting and affordable flying solution for many people. They allow you to own an aircraft that doesn't require an expensive hangar or a special pilot license; and, best of all, you can haul it with your car or truck.

Ultralights are defined by the U.S. FAA as a single-seat vehicle of less than 5 U.S. gallons of fuel capacity, empty weight of less than 254 pounds, and a top speed of 64 mph. Restrictions include flying only during daylight hours over unpopulated areas. Quicksilver and Buckeye Corporations are the industry leaders in ultralight and powered parachute-type aircraft.

8. David Sporn bought a saddle from Linville Western Gear with a 9.3% add-on interest installment loan. The purchase price of the saddle was $1,290. The loan required a 15% down payment and equal monthly payments for 24 months.

    a. What is the total deferred payment price of the saddle?

    b. What are David's monthly payments?

9. Buster Blaster Recording Studio purchased a new digital recording console for $28,600. A down payment of $5,000 was made and the balance financed with monthly payments of $653.92 for 48 months.

    a. What is the finance charge on the loan?

    b. Use Table 13-1 to find what annual percentage rate was charged on the equipment loan. (Use the closest value found in Table 13-1 to find your result.)

10. Chris Manning purchased a $7,590 motorcycle with a 36-month installment loan. The monthly payments are $261.44 per month.

    a. Use the APR formula to calculate the annual percentage rate of the loan. Round to the nearest hundredth of a percent.

    b. Use the APR tables to verify your answer from part a.

11. SkyHigh Aircraft Sales uses the Executive National Bank to finance customer aircraft purchases. This month Executive National is offering 60-month installment loans with an APR of 11.25%. A 15% down payment is required. The president of Vista Industries wants to finance the purchase of a company airplane for $250,000.

    a. Use the APR tables to calculate the finance charge.

    b. What are the monthly payments on Vista's aircraft loan?

12. After making 11 payments on a 36-month loan, you pay it off.
    a. What is your rebate fraction?

    b. If the finance charge was $1,300, what is your finance charge rebate?

13. An Auntie Anne's franchise financed a $68,000 pretzel oven with a $6\frac{1}{2}\%$ add-on interest installment loan for 48 months. The loan required a 20% down payment.
    a. What is the finance charge on the loan?

    b. What are the monthly payments?

    c. What annual percentage rate is being charged on the loan?

    d. If the company decides to pay off the loan after 22 months, what is the loan payoff?

Auntie Anne's, Inc. Is a leading franchisor of snack outlets, with more than 1,050 pretzel stores located in some 45 states and 23 other countries. The stores are found primarily in high-traffic areas such as malls, airports, train stations, and stadiums.

Back in June 2006, Auntie Anne's sold its billionth pretzel! Total initial investment to purchase a franchise ranges from $197,875 to $439,100.

14. You are a salesperson for Mega Marine Boat Sales. A customer is interested in purchasing the Donzi Classic shown in the accompanying ad and has asked you the following questions.
    a. What is the APR of the loan? (Use the formula.)

    b. What is the total deferred payment price of the boat?

    c. If the loan is paid off after 7 years, what would be the payoff?

FORD MUSTANG

$6,000 DOWN - PLUS TAX, TAG, TITLE
60-MONTHS WITH APPROVED
CREDIT

INCLUDES: AUTO TRANS., AIR
COND., 2-DOOR, AM/FM WITH CD &
SIRIUS XM RADIO, POWER WINDOWS AND
LOCKS, POWER STEERING

$28,525

$557 PER MO.

Winston Luzier/Transtock Inc./Alamy

15. Joe Keener found the accompanying ad for a Ford Mustang in his local newspaper. If the sales tax in his state is 7% and the tag and title fees are $165, calculate the following information for Joe.

   a. The total cost of the car, including tax, tag, and title

   b. The amount financed

   c. The finance charge

   d. The total deferred price of the car

   e. The annual percentage rate of the loan rounded to the nearest hundredth

BUSINESS DECISION: PURCHASE VS. LEASE

Dollars AND Sense

Getting into—or out of—a lease

Sites such as LeaseTrader.com and www.Swapalease.com match people eager to escape a vehicle lease (without paying huge termination fees) with bargain hunters looking to avoid dealer fees and a down payment by assuming a lease for its remaining term.

- For sellers—Brokerage fees range from $100 to $240. Some lease companies still hold you liable for damage and unpaid fees after the transfer.
- For buyers—Some sellers will pay you to take over the lease. Check the mileage allowed and get the vehicle inspected before you sign.

Source: *AARP Magazine*, March/April 2010, Don Beaulieu, "Getting Into (or Out of) a Car Lease" page 14.

iStock.com/vreemous

16. You are interested in getting a Nissan Rogue. You have decided to look into leasing to see how it compares with buying. In recent years, you have noticed that advertised lease payments are considerably lower than those advertised for financing a purchase. It always seemed as if you would be getting "more car for the money!"

   In your research, you have found that a closed-end vehicle lease is an agreement in which you make equal monthly payments based on your estimated usage for a set period of time. Then you turn the vehicle back in to the leasing dealer. No equity, no ownership, no asset at the end! You also have the option of purchasing the vehicle at an agreed-upon price. Leasing terminology is different from that of purchasing, but they are related.

Purchase		Lease
Purchase price	=	Capitalized cost
Down payment	=	Capitalized cost reduction
Interest rate	=	Money factor
End-of-lease market price	=	Residual value

   Use the advertisement and the Purchase vs. Lease Worksheet which follow to compare the total cost of each option. The residual value of the car is estimated to be $13,650. The lease has no termination fees or charges. If you decide to purchase, your bank requires a down payment of $3,800 and will finance the balance with a 10.25% APR loan for 36 months. The sales tax in your state is 6.5%, and the tag and title charges are $75. The *opportunity cost* is the interest your down payment could have earned if you didn't purchase the vehicle. Currently, your money earns 4.5% in a savings account.

   a. What is the total purchase price of the vehicle, including tax, tag, and title?

   b. What are the monthly payments on the loan?

c. What is the total cost of purchasing?

d. What is the total cost of leasing?

e. In your own words, explain which of these financing choices is a better deal and why.

Nissan Rogue

$19,995

$249 LEASE PER MO.

36 mos.
No security deposit.
$2,500 at signing.
Plus tax, tag & title
with approved
credit.

Victor Maschek/Shutterstock.com

f. Choose an ad from your local newspaper for a lease offer on a vehicle you would like to have. Gather the necessary information needed to complete a Purchase vs. Lease Worksheet. Use local dealers and banks to find the information you need or do some research on the Internet. Report your findings and conclusions to the class.

Purchase vs. Lease Worksheet

Cost of Purchasing

1. Total purchase price, including tax, tag, and title _____

2. Down payment _____

3. Total amount of loan payments (monthly payment _____ × _____ months) _____

4. Opportunity cost on down payment (_____ % × _____ years × line 2) _____

5. Less: Expected market value of vehicle at the end of the loan _____

6. Total cost of purchasing (lines 2 + 3 + 4 − 5) _____

Cost of Leasing

1. Capitalized cost, including tax, tag, and title. _____

2. Down payment (capitalized cost reduction _____ + security deposit _____) _____

3. Total amount of lease payments (monthly payments _____ × _____ months) _____

4. Opportunity cost on down payment (_____ % × _____ years × line 2) _____

5. End-of-lease termination fees and charges (excess mileage or damage) _____

6. Less: Refund of security deposit _____

7. Total cost of leasing (lines 2 + 3 + 4 + 5 − 6) _____

COLLABORATIVE LEARNING ACTIVITY

Plastic Choices

1. Have each member of the team contact a bank, credit union, or retail store in your area that offers a credit card. Get a brochure and/or a copy of the credit agreement.

   a. For each card, determine the following:

   - Annual interest rate
   - Method used for computing interest
   - Credit limit
   - Annual fee
   - "Fine-print" features

   b. Based on your research, which cards are the best and worst deals?

2. Go to www.cardtrak.com or www.bankrate.com.

   a. Research and list the best credit card deals being offered around the country.

   b. Compare your local banks' offers with those found on the Internet.

3. Research the Internet for recent changes to the following:

   a. The Credit Card Accountability, Responsibility, and Disclosure Act (the Credit Card Act)

   b. Other financial regulations relating to consumer credit and credit cards

   c. Laws in your state relating to consumer credit and credit cards

CHAPTER 14 Mortgages

PERFORMANCE OBJECTIVES

Monkey Business Images/Shutterstock.com

SECTION I 14 MORTGAGES—FIXED-RATE AND ADJUSTABLE-RATE

real estate Land, including any permanent improvements such as homes, apartment buildings, factories, hotels, shopping centers, or any other "real" structures.

mortgage A loan in which real property is used as security for a debt.

Federal Housing Administration (FHA) A government agency within the U.S. Department of Housing and Urban Development (HUD) that sets construction standards and insures residential mortgage loans made by approved lenders.

Veterans Affairs (VA) mortgages or GI Loans Long-term, low-down-payment home loans made by private lenders to eligible veterans, the payment of which is guaranteed by the Veterans Administration in the event of a default.

conventional loans Real estate loans made by private lenders that are not FHA-insured or VA-guaranteed.

private mortgage insurance (PMI) A special form of insurance primarily on mortgages for single-family homes, allowing the buyer to borrow more by putting down a smaller down payment.

adjustable-rate mortgage (ARM) A mortgage loan in which the interest rate changes periodically, usually in relation to a predetermined economic index.

mortgage discount points Extra charges frequently added to the cost of a mortgage, allowing lenders to increase their yield without showing an increase in the mortgage interest rate.

closing A meeting at which the buyer and seller of real estate conclude all matters pertaining to the transaction. At the closing, the funds are transferred to the seller and the ownership or title is transferred to the buyer.

Real estate is defined as "land, including the air above and the earth below, plus any permanent improvements to the land, such as homes, apartment buildings, factories, hotels, shopping centers, or any other 'real' property." Whether for commercial or residential property, practically all real estate transactions today involve some type of financing. The mortgage loan is the most popular method of financing real estate purchases.

A **mortgage** is any loan in which real property is used as security for a debt. During the term of the loan, the property becomes security, or collateral, for the lender, sufficient to ensure recovery of the amount loaned.

Mortgages today fall into one of three categories: FHA-insured, VA-guaranteed, and conventional. The National Housing Act of 1934 created the **Federal Housing Administration (FHA)** to encourage reluctant lenders to invest their money in the mortgage market, thereby stimulating the depressed construction industry. Today the FHA is a government agency within the Department of Housing and Urban Development (HUD). The FHA insures private mortgage loans made by approved lenders.

In 1944, the Servicemen's Readjustment Act (GI Bill of Rights) was passed to help returning World War II veterans purchase homes. Special mortgages were established known as **Veterans Affairs (VA) mortgages** or **GI Loans**. Under this and subsequent legislation, the government guarantees payment of a mortgage loan made by a private lender to a veteran/buyer should the veteran default on the loan.

VA loans may be used by eligible veterans, surviving spouses, and active service members to buy, construct, or refinance homes, farm residences, or condominiums. Down payments by veterans are not required but are left to the discretion of lenders, whereas FHA and conventional loans require a down payment from all buyers.

Conventional loans are made by private lenders and generally have a higher interest rate than either an FHA or a VA loan. Most conventional lenders are restricted to loaning 80% of the appraised value of a property, thus requiring a 20% down payment. If the borrower agrees to pay the premium for **private mortgage insurance (PMI)**, the conventional lender can lend up to 95% of the appraised value of the property.

Historically, high interest rates in the early 1980s caused mortgage payments to skyrocket beyond the financial reach of the average home buyer. To revitalize the slumping mortgage industry, the **adjustable-rate mortgage (ARM)** was created. These are mortgage loans under which the interest rate is periodically adjusted to more closely coincide with changing economic conditions. ARMs are very attractive, particularly to first-time buyers, because a low teaser rate may be offered for the first few years and then adjusted upward to a higher rate later in the loan. Today the adjustable-rate mortgage has become the most widely accepted option to the traditional 15- and 30-year fixed-rate mortgages.

Extra charges known as **mortgage discount points** are frequently added to the cost of a loan as a rate adjustment factor. This allows lenders to increase their yield without showing an increase in the mortgage interest rate. Each discount point is equal to 1% of the amount of the loan.

By their nature, mortgage loans involve large amounts of money and long periods of time. Consequently, the monthly payments and the amount of interest paid over the years can be considerable. Exhibit 14-1 illustrates the 30-year mortgage rates in the United States from 1974 to 2010 and the monthly payment on a $100,000 mortgage at various interest rate levels.

In reality, the higher interest mortgages would have been refinanced as rates declined, but consider the "housing affordability" factor. In 1982, payments on a $100,000 mortgage were $1,548 per month, compared with $457 in 2010!

In this section, you learn to calculate the monthly payments of a mortgage and prepare a partial amortization schedule of that loan. You also calculate the amount of property tax and insurance required as part of each monthly payment. In addition, you learn about the **closing**, the all-important final step in a real estate transaction, and the calculation of the closing costs. Finally, you learn about the important components of an adjustable-rate mortgage: the index, the lender's margin, the interest rate, and the cost caps.

EXHIBIT 14-1 Mortgage Rates Varied Widely in the Four-Decade Period Shown in This Chart.

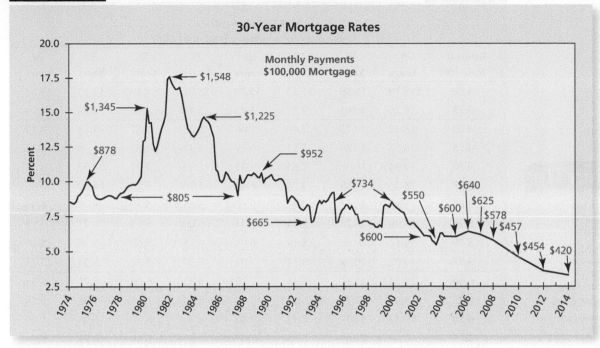

CALCULATING THE MONTHLY PAYMENT AND TOTAL INTEREST PAID ON A FIXED-RATE MORTGAGE

14-1

In Chapter 12, we learned that amortization is the process of paying off a financial obligation in a series of equal, regular payments over a period of time. We calculated the amount of an amortization payment by using the present value of an annuity table or the optional amortization formula.

Because mortgages run for relatively long periods of time, we can also use a special present-value table in which the periods are listed in years. The table factors represent the monthly payment required per $1,000 of debt to amortize a mortgage. The monthly payment includes mortgage interest and an amount to reduce the principal. (See Table 14-1.)

STEPS TO FIND THE MONTHLY MORTGAGE PAYMENT BY USING AN AMORTIZATION TABLE AND TO FIND TOTAL INTEREST

STEP 1. Find the number of $1,000s financed.

$$\text{Number of \$1,000s financed} = \frac{\text{Amount financed}}{1,000}$$

STEP 2. Using Table 14-1, locate the table factor, monthly payment per $1,000 financed, at the intersection of the number-of-years column and the interest-rate row.

STEP 3. Calculate the monthly payment.

$$\text{Monthly payment} = \text{Number of \$1,000s financed} \times \text{Table factor}$$

STEP 4. Find the total interest of the loan.

$$\text{Total interest} = (\text{Monthly payment} \times \text{Number of payments}) - \text{Amount financed}$$

> **Dollars AND Sense**
>
> As a result of declining mortgage rates in recent years, a record 68.8% of families own their own homes today. That amounts to nearly 76 million households.
>
> Purchasing and financing a home is one of the most important financial decisions a person will ever make. Substantial research should be done and much care taken in choosing the correct time to buy, the right property to buy, and the best financial offer to accept. (See Exhibit 14-2, "Mortgage Shopping Worksheet," pages 474–476.)

TABLE 14-1   Monthly Payments to Amortize Principal and Interest per $1,000 Financed

Monthly Payments
(Necessary to amortize a loan of $1,000)

Interest Rate (%)	5 Years	10 Years	15 Years	20 Years	25 Years	30 Years	35 Years	40 Years
3.50	$18.19	$9.89	$7.15	$5.80	$5.01	$4.49	$4.13	$3.87
3.75	18.30	10.01	7.27	5.93	5.14	4.63	4.28	4.03
4.00	18.42	10.12	7.40	6.06	5.28	4.77	4.43	4.18
4.25	18.53	10.24	7.52	6.19	5.42	4.92	4.58	4.34
4.50	18.64	10.36	7.65	6.33	5.56	5.07	4.73	4.50
4.75	18.76	10.48	7.78	6.46	5.70	5.22	4.89	4.66
5.00	18.88	10.61	7.91	6.60	5.85	5.37	5.05	4.83
5.25	18.99	10.73	8.04	6.74	6.00	5.53	5.21	4.99
5.50	19.11	10.86	8.18	6.88	6.15	5.68	5.38	5.16
5.75	19.22	10.98	8.31	7.03	6.30	5.84	5.54	5.33
6.00	19.34	11.11	8.44	7.17	6.45	6.00	5.71	5.51
6.25	19.45	11.23	8.58	7.31	6.60	6.16	5.88	5.68
6.50	19.57	11.36	8.72	7.46	6.76	6.33	6.05	5.86
6.75	19.69	11.49	8.85	7.61	6.91	6.49	6.22	6.04
7.00	19.81	11.62	8.99	7.76	7.07	6.66	6.39	6.22
7.25	19.92	11.75	9.13	7.91	7.23	6.83	6.57	6.40
7.50	20.04	11.88	9.28	8.06	7.39	7.00	6.75	6.59
7.75	20.16	12.01	9.42	8.21	7.56	7.17	6.93	6.77
8.00	20.28	12.14	9.56	8.37	7.72	7.34	7.11	6.96
8.25	20.40	12.27	9.71	8.53	7.89	7.52	7.29	7.15
8.50	20.52	12.40	9.85	8.68	8.06	7.69	7.47	7.34
8.75	20.64	12.54	10.00	8.84	8.23	7.87	7.66	7.53
9.00	20.76	12.67	10.15	9.00	8.40	8.05	7.84	7.72
9.25	20.88	12.81	10.30	9.16	8.57	8.23	8.03	7.91
9.50	21.01	12.94	10.45	9.33	8.74	8.41	8.22	8.11
9.75	21.13	13.08	10.60	9.49	8.92	8.60	8.41	8.30
10.00	21.25	13.22	10.75	9.66	9.09	8.78	8.60	8.50
10.25	21.38	13.36	10.90	9.82	9.27	8.97	8.79	8.69
10.50	21.50	13.50	11.06	9.99	9.45	9.15	8.99	8.89
10.75	21.62	13.64	11.21	10.16	9.63	9.34	9.18	9.09
11.00	21.75	13.78	11.37	10.33	9.81	9.53	9.37	9.29
11.25	21.87	13.92	11.53	10.50	9.99	9.72	9.57	9.49
11.50	22.00	14.06	11.69	10.67	10.17	9.91	9.77	9.69
11.75	22.12	14.21	11.85	10.84	10.35	10.10	9.96	9.89
12.00	22.25	14.35	12.01	11.02	10.54	10.29	10.16	10.09
12.25	22.38	14.50	12.17	11.19	10.72	10.48	10.36	10.29
12.50	22.50	14.64	12.33	11.37	10.91	10.68	10.56	10.49
12.75	22.63	14.79	12.49	11.54	11.10	10.87	10.76	10.70
13.00	22.76	14.94	12.66	11.72	11.28	11.07	10.96	10.90

Learning Tip

Remember that the table values represent monthly payments "per $1,000" financed. When calculating the amount of the monthly payment, you must first determine the number of $1,000s being financed, then multiply that figure by the table factor.

B-A-C-O/Shutterstock.com

EXAMPLE 1 — CALCULATING MONTHLY PAYMENT AND TOTAL INTEREST

What is the monthly payment and total interest on a $150,000 mortgage at 5% for 30 years?

►SOLUTIONSTRATEGY

Step 1. Number of $1,000s financed $= \dfrac{\text{Amount financed}}{1,000} = \dfrac{150,000}{1,000} = 150$

Step 2. Table factor for 5%, 30 years is 5.37.

Step 3. Monthly payment = Number of $1,000s financed × Table factor
Monthly payment = 150 × 5.37
Monthly payment = $\underline{\$805.50}$

Step 4. Total interest = (Monthly payment × Number of payments) − Amount financed
Total interest = (805.50 × 360) − 150,000
Total interest = 289,980 − 150,000
Total interest = $\underline{\$139,980}$

►TRYITEXERCISE 1

What is the monthly payment and total interest on an $85,500 mortgage at 4.5% for 25 years?

CHECK YOUR ANSWERS WITH THE SOLUTIONS ON PAGE 491.

PREPARING A PARTIAL AMORTIZATION SCHEDULE OF A MORTGAGE

14-2

Mortgages used to purchase residential property generally require regular, equal payments. A portion of the payment is used to pay interest on the loan; the balance of the payment is used to reduce the principal. This type of mortgage is called a **level-payment plan** because the amount of the payment remains the same for the duration of the loan. The amount of the payment that is interest gradually decreases, while the amount that reduces the debt gradually increases.

An **amortization schedule** is a chart that shows the status of the mortgage loan after each payment. The schedule illustrates month by month how much of the mortgage payment is interest and how much is left to reduce to principal. The schedule also shows the outstanding balance of the loan after each payment.

In reality, amortization schedules are long because they show the loan status for each month. A 30-year mortgage, for example, would require a schedule with 360 lines (12 months × 30 years = 360 payments).

level-payment plan Mortgages with regular, equal payments over a specified period of time.

amortization schedule A chart that shows the month-by-month breakdown of each mortgage payment into interest and principal and the outstanding balance of the loan.

STEPS TO CREATE AN AMORTIZATION SCHEDULE FOR A LOAN

STEP 1. Use Table 14-1 to calculate the amount of the monthly payment.

STEP 2. Calculate the amount of interest for the current month using $I = PRT$, where P is the current outstanding balance of the loan, R is the annual interest rate, and T is $\frac{1}{12}$.

STEP 3. Find the portion of the payment used to reduce principal.

Portion of payment reducing principal = Monthly payment − Interest

Dollars AND Sense

In most cases, mortgage interest expense is tax-deductible. To increase your deductions for the current year, make your January mortgage payment by December 20. This will allow time for the payment to be credited to your account in December, giving you an extra month of interest deduction this year.

iStock.com/Nikada

iStock.com/vreemous

STEP 4. Calculate the outstanding balance of the mortgage loan.

Outstanding balance = Previous balance − Portion of payment reducing principal

STEP 5. Repeat Steps 2, 3, and 4 for each succeeding month and enter the values on a schedule with columns labeled as follows.

| Payment Number | Monthly Payment | Monthly Interest | Portion Used to Reduce Principal | Loan Balance |

EXAMPLE2 PREPARING A PARTIAL AMORTIZATION SCHEDULE

Prepare an amortization schedule for the first three months of the $150,000 mortgage at 5% for 30 years from Example 1. Remember, you have already calculated the monthly payment to be $805.50.

▶ SOLUTIONSTRATEGY

Step 1. $805.50 (from Example 1, page 471)

Step 2. **Month 1:**

Interest = Principal × Rate × Time

Interest = $150,000 \times .05 \times \frac{1}{12}$

Interest = $625.00

Step 3. Portion of payment reducing principal = Monthly payment − Interest

Portion of payment reducing principal = 805.50 − 625.00

Portion of payment reducing principal = $180.50

Step 4. Outstanding balance = Previous balance − Portion of payment reducing principal

Outstanding balance = 150,000.00 − 180.50

Outstanding balance after one payment = $149,819.50

Step 5. Repeat Steps 2, 3, and 4, for two more payments and enter the values on the schedule.

Month 2:

Interest = $149,819.50 \times .05 \times \frac{1}{12}$ = $624.25

(*Note:* Although very slightly, interest decreased.)

Portion reducing principal = 805.50 − 624.25 = $181.25

Outstanding balance after two payments = 149,819.50 − 181.25 = $149,638.25

Month 3:

Interest = $149,638.25 \times .05 \times \frac{1}{12}$ = $623.49

Portion reducing principal = 805.50 − 623.49 = $182.01

Outstanding balance after three payments = 149,638.25 − 182.01 = $149,456.24

Amortization Schedule
$150,000 Loan, 5%, 30 years

Payment Number	Monthly Payment	Monthly Interest	Portion Used to Reduce Principal	Loan Balance
0				$150,000.00
1	$805.50	$625.00	$180.50	$149,819.50
2	$805.50	$624.25	$181.25	$149,638.25
3	$805.50	$623.49	$182.01	$149,456.24

►TRYITEXERCISE 2

Prepare an amortization schedule of the first four payments of a $125,000 mortgage at 6% for 15 years. Use Table 14-1 to calculate the amount of the monthly payment.

CHECK YOUR ANSWERS WITH THE SOLUTIONS ON PAGE 491–492.

CALCULATING THE MONTHLY PITI OF A MORTGAGE LOAN

14-3

In reality, mortgage payments include four parts: principal, interest, taxes, and insurance—thus the abbreviation **PITI**. VA, FHA, and most conventional loans require borrowers to pay $\frac{1}{12}$ of the estimated annual property taxes and hazard insurance with each month's mortgage payment. Each month the taxes and insurance portions of the payment are placed in a type of savings account for safekeeping known as an **escrow account**. Each year when the property taxes and hazard insurance premiums are due, the lender disburses those payments from the borrower's escrow account. During the next 12 months, the account again builds up to pay the next year's taxes and insurance.

PITI An abbreviation for the total amount of a mortgage payment; includes principal, interest, property taxes, and hazard insurance.

escrow account Bank account used by mortgage lenders for the safekeeping of the funds accumulating to pay next year's property taxes and hazard insurance.

STEPS TO CALCULATE THE PITI OF A MORTGAGE

STEP 1. Calculate the principal and interest portion, PI, of the payment as before, using the amortization table, Table 14-1.

STEP 2. Calculate the monthly tax and insurance portion, TI.

$$\text{Monthly TI} = \frac{\text{Estimated property tax} + \text{Hazard insurance}}{12}$$

STEP 3. Calculate the total monthly PITI.

$$\text{Monthly PITI} = \text{Monthly PI} + \text{Monthly TI}$$

EXAMPLE3 CALCULATING THE MONTHLY PITI OF A MORTGAGE

Lorie Kojian purchased a home with a mortgage of $87,500 at 7.5% for 30 years. The property taxes are $2,350 per year, and the hazard insurance premium is $567.48. What is the monthly PITI payment of Lorie's loan?

►SOLUTIONSTRATEGY

Step 1. From the amortization table, Table 14-1, the factor for 7.5%, 30 years is 7.00. When we divide the amount of Lorie's loan by 1,000, we get 87.5 as the number of 1,000s financed. The principal and interest portion, PI, is therefore 87.5 × 7.00 = $612.50.

Step 2. $\text{Monthly TI} = \dfrac{\text{Estimated property tax} + \text{Hazard insurance}}{12}$

$\text{Monthly TI} = \dfrac{2,350.00 + 567.48}{12} = \dfrac{2,917.48}{12} = \$243.12$

Step 3. Monthly PITI = PI + TI
Monthly PITI = 612.50 + 243.12
Monthly PITI = $855.62

IN THE
Business World

Typically, over the years of a mortgage, property taxes and insurance premiums rise. When this happens, the lender must increase the portion set aside in the escrow account by increasing the taxes and insurance parts of the monthly payment.

▶TRYITEXERCISE 3

Michael Veteramo purchased a home with a mortgage of $125,600 at 6.25% for 20 years. The property taxes are $3,250 per year, and the hazard insurance premium is $765. What is the monthly PITI payment of Michael's loan?

CHECK YOUR ANSWER WITH THE SOLUTION ON PAGE 492.

14-4   UNDERSTANDING CLOSING COSTS AND CALCULATING THE AMOUNT DUE AT CLOSING

title or deed The official document representing the right of ownership of real property.

closing costs Expenses incurred in conjunction with the sale of real estate, including loan origination fees, credit reports, appraisal fees, title search, title insurance, inspections, attorney's fees, recording fees, and broker's commission.

settlement or closing statement
A document that provides a detailed accounting of payments, credits, and closing costs of a real estate transaction.

The term *closing* or *settlement* is used to describe the final step in a real estate transaction. This is a meeting at which time documents are signed; the buyer pays the agreed-upon purchase price; and the seller delivers the **title**, or right of ownership, to the buyer. The official document conveying ownership is known as the **deed**.

Closing costs are the expenses incurred in conjunction with the sale of real estate. In the typical real estate transaction, both the buyer and the seller are responsible for a number of costs that are paid for at the time of closing. The party obligated for paying a particular closing cost is often determined by local custom or by negotiation. Some closing costs are expressed as dollar amounts, whereas others are a percent of the amount financed or amount of the purchase price.

At closing, the buyer is responsible for the purchase price (mortgage + down payment) plus closing costs. The amount received by the seller after all expenses have been paid is known as the proceeds. The **settlement statement** or **closing statement** is a document, usually prepared by an attorney, that provides a detailed breakdown of the real estate transaction. This document itemizes closing costs and indicates how they are allocated between the buyer and the seller.

Exhibit 14-2, "Mortgage Shopping Worksheet," can be used to compare mortgage offers from various lenders. It provides a comprehensive checklist of important loan information, typical fees, closing and settlement costs, and other questions and considerations people should be aware of when shopping for a mortgage loan.

EXHIBIT 14-2   Mortgage Shopping Worksheet

Mortgage Shopping Worksheet

	Lender 1	Lender 2
Name of Lender		
Name of Contact		
Date of Contact		
Mortgage Amount		
Basic Information on the Loans		
Type of mortgage: fixed rate, adjustable rate, conventional, FHA, other? If adjustable, see page 469		
Minimum down payment required		
Loan term (length of loan)		
Contract interest rate		
Annual percentage rate (APR)		
Points (may be called loan discount points)		
Monthly private mortgage insurance (PMI) premiums		
How long must you keep PMI?		
Estimated monthly escrow for taxes and hazard insurance		
Estimated monthly payment (principal, interest, taxes, insurance, PMI)		

(Continued)

EXHIBIT 14-2 Mortgage Shopping Worksheet (Continued)

Mortgage Shopping Worksheet

	Lender 1	Lender 2
Fees		
Different institutions may have different names for some fees and may charge different fees. We have listed some typical fees you may see on loan documents.		
Appraisal fee or loan processing fee..	_____	_____
Origination fee or underwriting fee	_____	_____
Lender fee or funding fee	_____	_____
Appraisal fee.,.,.,.	_____	_____
Attorney's fees	_____	_____
Document preparation and recording fees	_____	_____
Broker's fees (may be quoted as points, origination fees, or interest rate add-on).......................	_____	_____
Credit report fee	_____	_____
Other fees	_____	_____
Name of Lender	_____	_____
Other Costs at Closing/Settlement		
Title search/title insurance	_____	_____
For lender.......................	_____	_____
For you.......................	_____	_____
Estimated prepaid amounts for interest, taxes, hazard insurance, payments to escrow.......................	_____	_____
State and local taxes, stamp taxes, transfer taxes	_____	_____
Flood determination	_____	_____
Prepaid private mortgage insurance (PMI).......................	_____	_____
Surveys and home inspections	_____	_____
Total Fees and Other Closing/Settlement Cost Estimates	_____	_____
Other Questions and Considerations about the Loan		
Are any of the fees or costs waivable?	_____	
Prepayment penalties		
Is there a prepayment penalty?.......................	_____	_____
If so, how much is it?	_____	_____
How long does the penalty period last? (for example, three years? five years?)	_____	_____
Are extra principal payments allowed?.......................	_____	_____
	_____	
Lock-ins		
Is the lock-in agreement in writing?.......................	_____	_____
Is there a fee to lock in?	_____	_____
When does the lock-in occur—at application, approval, or another time?.......................	_____	_____
How long will the lock-in last?.,.,.	_____	_____
If the rate drops before closing, can you lock in at a lower rate?.......................	_____	_____

EXHIBIT 14-2 Mortgage Shopping Worksheet (Continued)

Mortgage Shopping Worksheet

	Lender 1	Lender 2
If the loan is an adjustable-rate mortgage:		
What is the initial rate?	_____	_____
What is the maximum the rate could be next year?	_____	_____
What are the rate and payment caps for each year and over the life of the loan?	_____	_____
What is the frequency of rate change and of any changes to the monthly payment?	_____	_____
What index will the lender use?	_____	_____
What margin will the lender add to the index?	_____	_____
Credit life insurance		
Does the monthly amount quoted to you include a charge for credit life insurance?	_____	_____
If so, does the lender require credit life insurance as a condition of the loan?	_____	_____
How much does the credit life insurance cost?	_____	_____
How much lower would your monthly payment be without the credit life insurance?	_____	_____
If the lender does not require credit life insurance and you still want to buy it, what rates can you get from other insurance providers?	_____	_____

Dollars AND Sense

The amount of interest paid and the length of a mortgage can be dramatically reduced by making **biweekly payments** (every two weeks) instead of monthly. By choosing this mortgage payment option, you are taking advantage of the all-important "time value of money" concept.

Here's an example. A 30-year, 7% mortgage for $100,000 has monthly payments of $666. The total interest you will pay on the loan is $139,509. If, instead, you make biweekly payments of $333, you would pay off the loan in 23 years and the total interest would be $103,959. The biweekly option saves you $35,550 in interest and seven years of payments!

To see how this option can be applied to your mortgage, go to www.bankrate.com and type *biweekly mortgage calculator* in the search box.

iStock.com/vreemous

EXAMPLE4 CALCULATING MORTGAGE CLOSING COSTS

Barry and Donna Rae Schwartz are purchasing a $180,000 home. The down payment is 25%, and the balance will be financed with a 25-year fixed-rate mortgage at 6.5% and 2 discount points (each point is 1% of the amount financed). When Barry and Donna Rae signed the sales contract, they put down a deposit of $15,000, which will be credited to their down payment at the time of the closing. In addition, they must pay the following expenses: credit report, $80; appraisal fee, $150; title insurance premium, $\frac{1}{2}$% of amount financed; title search, $200; and attorney's fees, $450.

a. Calculate the amount due from Barry and Donna Rae at the closing.

b. If the sellers are responsible for the broker's commission, which is 6% of the purchase price, $900 in other closing costs, and the existing mortgage with a balance of $50,000, what proceeds will they receive on the sale of the property?

▶SOLUTIONSTRATEGY

a. Down payment = $180,000 \times 25\% = \$45,000$

Amount financed = $180,000 - 45,000 = \$135,000$

Closing Costs, Buyer	
Discount points ($135,000 \times 2\%$)	$ 2,700
Down payment ($45,000 - 15,000$ deposit)	30,000
Credit report	80
Appraisal fee	150
Title insurance ($135,000 \times \frac{1}{2}\%$)	675
Title search	200
Attorney's fees	450
Due at closing	$34,255

b.

Proceeds, Seller

Sale price		$180,000
Less: Broker's commission:		
180,000 × 6%	$10,800	
Closing costs	900	
Mortgage payoff	50,000	
		−61,700
Proceeds to seller		$118,300

▶TRYITEXERCISE 4

Jonathan Monahan is purchasing a townhouse for $120,000. The down payment is 20%, and the balance will be financed with a 15-year fixed-rate mortgage at 9% and 3 discount points (each point is 1% of the amount financed). When Jonathan signed the sales contract, he put down a deposit of $10,000, which will be credited to his down payment at the time of the closing. In addition, he must pay the following expenses: loan application fee, $100; property transfer fee, $190; title insurance premium, $\frac{3}{4}$% of amount financed; hazard insurance premium, $420; prepaid taxes, $310; and attorney's fees, $500.

a. Calculate the amount due from Jonathan at the closing.

b. If the seller is responsible for the broker's commission, which is $5\frac{1}{2}$% of the purchase price, $670 in other closing costs, and the existing mortgage balance of $65,000, what proceeds will the seller receive on the sale of the property?

CHECK YOUR ANSWERS WITH THE SOLUTIONS ON PAGE 492.

CALCULATING THE INTEREST RATE OF AN ADJUSTABLE-RATE MORTGAGE (ARM)

14-5

With a fixed-rate mortgage, the interest rate stays the same during the life of the loan. With an adjustable-rate mortgage (ARM), the interest rate changes periodically, usually in relation to an index, and payments may go up or down accordingly. In recent years, the ARM has become the most widely accepted alternative to the traditional 30-year fixed-rate mortgage.

The primary components of an ARM are the index, lender's margin, calculated interest rate, initial interest rate, and cost caps. With most ARMs, the interest rate and monthly payment change every year, every three years, or every five years. The period between one rate change and the next is known as the **adjustment period**. A loan with an adjustment period of one year, for example, is called a one-year ARM.

Most lenders tie ARM interest rate changes to changes in an **index rate**. These indexes usually go up and down with the general movement of interest rates in the nation's economy. When the index goes up, so does the mortgage rate, resulting in higher monthly payments. When the index goes down, the mortgage rate may or may not go down.

To calculate the interest rate on an ARM, lenders add a few points called the **lender's margin** or **spread** to the index rate. The amount of the margin can differ among lenders and can make a significant difference in the amount of interest paid over the life of a loan.

> **Calculated ARM interest rate = Index rate + Lender's margin**

The **calculated** or **initial ARM interest rate** is usually the rate to which all future adjustments and caps apply, although this rate may be discounted by the lender during the first payment period to attract and qualify more potential borrowers. This low initial interest rate, sometimes known as a **teaser rate**, is one of the main appeals of the ARM; however, without some protection from rapidly rising interest rates, borrowers might be put in a position of not

adjustment period The amount of time between one rate change and the next on an adjustable-rate mortgage; generally one, two, or three years.

index rate The economic index to which the interest rate on an adjustable-rate mortgage is tied.

lender's margin or spread The percentage points added to an index rate to get the interest rate of an adjustable-rate mortgage.

calculated or initial ARM interest rate The interest rate of an adjustable-rate mortgage to which all future adjustments and caps apply.

teaser rate A discounted interest rate for the first adjustment period of an adjustable-rate mortgage that is below the current market rate of interest.

interest-rate caps Limits on the amount the interest rate can increase on an ARM.

periodic rate caps Limits on the amount the interest rate of an ARM can increase per adjustment period.

overall rate caps Limits on the amount the interest rate of an ARM can increase over the life of the loan.

being able to afford the rising mortgage payments. To prevent this situation, standards have been established requiring limits or caps on increases.

Interest-rate caps place a limit on the amount the interest rate can increase. These may come in the form of **periodic rate caps**, which limit the increase from one adjustment period to the next, and **overall rate caps**, which limit the increase over the life of the mortgage. The following formulas can be used to find the maximum interest rates of an ARM:

Maximum rate per adjustment period = Previous rate + Periodic rate cap

Maximum overall ARM rate = Initial rate + Overall rate cap

EXAMPLE5 CALCULATING ARM RATES

Florence Powers bought a home with an adjustable-rate mortgage. The lender's margin on the loan is 2.5%, and the overall rate cap is 6% over the life of the loan.

a. If the current index rate is 4.9%, what is the calculated interest rate of the ARM?

b. What is the maximum overall rate of the loan?

SOLUTIONSTRATEGY

a. Because the loan interest rate is tied to an index, we use the formula

  Calculated ARM interest rate = Index rate + Lender's margin

  Calculated ARM interest rate = 4.9% + 2.5%

  Calculated ARM interest rate = 7.4%

b. Maximum overall rate = Calculated rate + Overall rate cap

  Maximum overall rate = 7.4% + 6%

  Maximum overall rate = 13.4%

▶TRYITEXERCISE 5

Kate Fitzgerald bought a home with an adjustable-rate mortgage. The lender's margin on the loan is 3.4%, and the overall rate cap is 7% over the life of the loan. The current index rate is 3.2%.

a. What is the initial interest rate of the ARM?

b. What is the maximum overall rate of the loan?

CHECK YOUR ANSWERS WITH THE SOLUTIONS ON PAGE 492.

SECTION I 14 REVIEW EXERCISES

Using Table 14-1 as needed, calculate the required information for the following mortgages.

	Amount Financed	Interest Rate	Term of Loan (years)	Number of $1,000s Financed	Table Factor	Monthly Payment	Total Interest
1.	$80,000	9.00%	20	80	9.00	$720.00	$92,800.00
2.	$72,500	6.00%	30				
3.	$164,900	4.50%	25				
4.	$154,300	4.75%	15				
5.	$96,800	7.75%	30				
6.	$422,100	5.50%	20				

7. Find the monthly payment and the total interest for a mortgage of $44,000 at $5\frac{3}{4}$% for 30 years. Use Table 14-1 and give the total interest as your answer.

8. Prepare an amortization schedule for the first 3 payments of a $64,000 mortgage at 6% for 20 years. Use Table 14-1.

Payment Number	Monthly Payment	Monthly Interest	Portion Used to Reduce Principal	Loan Balance
0				$64,000.00
1	___	___	___	___
2	___	___	___	___
3	___	___	___	___

As one of the loan officers for Grove Gate Bank, calculate the monthly principal and interest, PI, using Table 14-1 and the monthly PITI for the following mortgages.

	Amount Financed	Interest Rate	Term of Loan (years)	Monthly PI	Annual Property Tax	Annual Insurance	Monthly PITI
9.	$76,400	8.00%	20	$639.47	$1,317	$866	$821.39
10.	$128,800	4.75%	15	___	$2,440	$1,215	___
11.	$224,500	5.25%	30	___	$3,506	$1,431	___
12.	$250,000	4.50%	25	___	$6,553	$2,196	___
13.	$164,500	6.75%	30	___	$3,125	$1,569	___

14. James has a mortgage of $90,500 at 6% for 20 years. The property taxes are $3,600 per year, and the hazard insurance premium is $771.50 per year. Find the monthly PITI payment.

15. Ben and Mal Scott plan to buy a home for $272,900. They will make a 10% down payment and qualify for a 25-year, 7% mortgage loan.

   a. What is the amount of their monthly payment?

   b. How much interest will they pay over the life of the loan?

16. Michael Sanchez purchased a condominium for $88,000. He made a 20% down payment and financed the balance with a 30-year, 9% fixed-rate mortgage.

    a. What is the amount of the monthly principal and interest portion, PI, of Michael's loan?

    b. Construct an amortization schedule for the first four months of Michael's mortgage.

Payment Number	Monthly Payment	Monthly Interest	Portion Used to Reduce Principal	Loan Balance
0				_____
1	_____	_____	_____	_____
2	_____	_____	_____	_____
3	_____	_____	_____	_____
4	_____	_____	_____	_____

    c. If the annual property taxes are $1,650 and the hazard insurance premium is $780 per year, what is the total monthly PITI of Michael's loan?

17. Luis Schambach is shopping for a 15-year mortgage for $150,000. Currently, the Fortune Bank is offering an 8.5% mortgage with 4 discount points and the Northern Trust Bank is offering an 8.75% mortgage with no points. Luis is unsure which mortgage is a better deal and has asked you to help him decide. (Remember, each discount point is equal to 1% of the amount financed.)

    a. What is the total interest paid on each loan?

    b. Taking into account the closing points, which bank is offering a better deal and by how much?

18. Phil Pittman is interested in a fixed-rate mortgage for $100,000. He is undecided whether to choose a 15- or 30-year mortgage. The current mortgage rate is 5.5% for the 15-year mortgage and 6.5% for the 30-year mortgage.

    a. What are the monthly principal and interest payments for each loan?

    b. What is the total amount of interest paid on each loan?

    c. Overall, how much more interest is paid by choosing the 30-year mortgage?

19. Larry and Cindy Lynden purchased a townhome in Alison Estates with an adjustable-rate mortgage. The lender's margin on the loan is 4.1%, and the overall rate cap is 5% over the life of the loan. The current index rate is the prime rate, 3.25%.

    a. What is the calculated interest rate of the ARM?
        Calculated ARM interest rate = Index rate + Lender's margin
        Calculated ARM interest rate = 3.25 + 4.1 = <u>7.35%</u>

    b. What is the maximum overall rate of the loan?
        Maximum overall ARM rate = Initial rate + Overall rate cap
        Maximum overall ARM rate = 7.35 + 5.0 = <u>12.35%</u>

20. The margin on an adjustable-rate mortgage is 3.5% and the rate cap is 5% over the life of the loan. If the current index rate is 6.8%, find the maximum overall rate of the loan.

21. Kari is purchasing a home for $210,000. The down payment is 25% and the balance will be financed with a 15-year mortgage at 8% and 3 discount points. Kari made a deposit of $20,000 (applied to the down payment) when the sales contract was signed.

    Kari also has these expenses: credit report, $80; appraisal fee, $120; title insurance premium, 1% of amount financed; title search, $200; and attorney's fees, $500. Find the closing costs.

22. You are a real estate broker for Aurora Realty. One of your clients, Erica Heston, has agreed to purchase one of the homes your office has listed for sale for a negotiated price of $235,000. The down payment is 20%, and the balance will be financed with a 15-year fixed-rate mortgage at 8.75% and $3\frac{1}{2}$ discount points. The annual property tax is $5,475, and the hazard insurance premium is $2,110. When Erica signed the original contract, she put down a deposit of $5,000, which will be credited to her down payment. In addition, at the time of closing, Erica must pay the following expenses:

Appraisal fee	$215
Credit report	$65
Roof inspection	$50
Mortgage insurance premium	$\frac{1}{2}$% of amount financed
Title search	$125
Attorney's fees	$680
Escrow fee	$210
Prepaid interest	$630

As Erica's real estate broker, she has asked you the following questions:

a. What is the total monthly PITI of the mortgage loan?

b. What is the total amount of interest that will be paid on the loan?

c. How much is due from Erica at the time of the closing?

d. If your real estate office is entitled to a commission from the seller of $6\frac{1}{2}\%$ of the price of the home, how much commission is made on the sale?

BUSINESS DECISION: BUYING DOWN THE MORTGAGE

23. The buyer of a piece of real estate is often given the option of buying down the loan. This option gives the buyer a choice of loan terms in which various combinations of interest rates and discount points are offered. The choice of how many points and what rate is optimal is often a matter of how long the buyer intends to keep the property.

   Darrell Frye is planning to buy an office building at a cost of $988,000. He must pay 10% down and has a choice of financing terms. He can select from a 7% 30-year loan and pay 4 discount points, a 7.25% 30-year loan and pay 3 discount points, or a 7.5% 30-year loan and pay 2 discount points. Darrell expects to hold the building for four years and then sell it. Except for the three rate and discount point combinations, all other costs of purchasing and selling are fixed and identical.

   a. What is the amount being financed?

   b. If Darrell chooses the 4-point 7% loan, what will be his total outlay in points and payments after 48 months?

   c. If Darrell chooses the 3-point 7.25% loan, what will be his total outlay in points and payments after 48 months?

   d. If Darrell chooses the 2-point 7.5% loan, what will be his total outlay in points and payments after 48 months?

   e. Of the three choices for a loan, which results in the lowest total outlay for Darrell?

After the "housing crisis" brought on by the recession of 2008, the Mortgage Bankers Association reported that more than 1 in 10 homeowners with a mortgage were in foreclosure or were behind in their payments. (See Exhibit 14-3.)

Despite these statistics, homeowners today may use the *equity* in their homes to qualify for a sizable amount of credit at interest rates that are historically low. In addition, under existing law, the interest may be tax-deductible because the debt is secured by the home.

A **home equity loan** is a lump-sum second mortgage loan based on the available equity in a home. A **home equity line of credit** is a form of revolving credit also based on the available equity. Because the home is likely to be a consumer's largest asset, many homeowners use these loans and credit lines only for major expenditures such as debt consolidation, education, home improvements, business expansion, medical bills, and vacations.

With home equity lines of credit, the borrower will be approved for a specific amount of credit known as the **credit limit**. This is the maximum amount that can be borrowed at any one time on that line of credit.

home equity loan A lump-sum second mortgage loan based on the available equity in a home.

home equity line of credit A revolving credit second mortgage loan made on the available equity in a home.

credit limit A pre-approved limit on the amount of a home equity line of credit.

CALCULATING THE POTENTIAL AMOUNT OF CREDIT AVAILABLE TO A BORROWER

14-6

Most lenders set the credit limit on a home equity loan or line by taking a percentage of the appraised value of the house and subtracting the balance owed on the existing mortgage. In determining your actual credit limit, the lender also will consider your ability to repay by looking at your income, debts, and other financial obligations as well as your credit history.

STEPS TO CALCULATE THE POTENTIAL AMOUNT OF CREDIT AVAILABLE TO A BORROWER

STEP 1. Calculate the percentage of appraised value.

Percentage of appraised value = Appraised value × Lender's percentage

STEP 2. Find the potential amount of credit available.

Potential credit = Percentage of appraised value − First mortgage balance

EXAMPLE6 CALCULATING POTENTIAL CREDIT OF A HOME EQUITY LOAN

Terri Alexander owns a house that was recently appraised for $115,700. The balance on her existing mortgage is $67,875. If her bank is willing to loan up to 75% of the appraised value, what is the potential amount of credit available to Terri on a home equity loan?

SOLUTIONSTRATEGY

Step 1. Percentage of appraised value = Appraised value × Lender's percentage
Percentage of appraised value = 115,700 × .75
Percentage of appraised value = $86,775

Step 2. Potential credit = Percentage of appraised value − First mortgage balance
Potential credit = 86,775 − 67,875
Potential credit = $18,900

iStock.com/Nikada

In 2010, the signing of the financial reform bill into law meant real financial reform had finally become a reality. Almost two years after the near collapse of the financial system, Congress put new rules in place to prevent the abusive lending practices responsible for the crisis. Highlights of the new law include the following:

- A Consumer Financial Protection Bureau (CFPB) to stop unfair lending practices

- Governmental authority to step in and safely shut down failing financial firms

- Prohibitions on abusive mortgage lending practices such as kickbacks for steering people into high-rate loans when they qualify for lower rates

- Stronger foreclosure prevention, including an emergency loan fund to help families at risk of losing their home because of unemployment or illness

Source: www.responsiblelending.org

►TRYITEXERCISE 6

Justin Schaefer owns a home that was recently appraised for $92,900. The balance on his existing first mortgage is $32,440. If his credit union is willing to loan up to 80% of the appraised value, what is the potential amount of credit available to Justin on a home equity line of credit?

CHECK YOUR ANSWER WITH THE SOLUTION ON PAGE 492.

EXHIBIT 14-3 Home Equity Lending

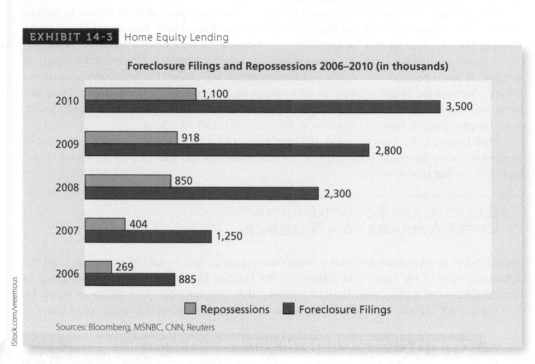

Foreclosure Filings and Repossessions 2006–2010 (in thousands)

Year	Repossessions	Foreclosure Filings
2010	1,100	3,500
2009	918	2,800
2008	850	2,300
2007	404	1,250
2006	269	885

Sources: Bloomberg, MSNBC, CNN, Reuters

iStock.com/vreemous

14-7 CALCULATING THE HOUSING EXPENSE RATIO AND THE TOTAL OBLIGATIONS RATIO OF A BORROWER

Mortgage lenders use ratios to determine whether borrowers have the economic ability to repay the loan. FHA, VA, and conventional lenders all use monthly gross income as the base for calculating these **qualifying ratios**. Two important ratios used for this purpose are the **housing expense ratio** and the **total obligations ratio**. These ratios are expressed as percents and are calculated by using the following formulas:

qualifying ratios Ratios used by lenders to determine whether borrowers have the economic ability to repay loans.

housing expense ratio The ratio of a borrower's monthly housing expense (PITI) to monthly gross income.

total obligations ratio The ratio of a borrower's total monthly financial obligations to monthly gross income.

$$\text{Housing expense ratio} = \frac{\text{Monthly housing expense (PITI)}}{\text{Monthly gross income}}$$

$$\text{Total obligations ratio} = \frac{\text{Total monthly financial obligations}}{\text{Monthly gross income}}$$

The mortgage business uses widely accepted guidelines for these ratios that should not be exceeded. The ratio guidelines are shown in Exhibit 14-4.

EXHIBIT 14-4

Lending Ratio Guidelines

Mortgage Type	Housing Expense Ratio	Total Obligations Ratio
FHA	29%	41%
Conventional	28%	36%

Note that the ratio formulas are an application of the percentage formula; the ratio is the rate, the PITI or total obligations are the portion, and the monthly gross income is the base. With this in mind, we are able to solve for any of the variables.

EXAMPLE 7   CALCULATING MORTGAGE LENDING RATIOS

Sue Harper earns a gross income of $2,490 per month. She has applied for a mortgage with a monthly PITI of $556. Sue has other financial obligations totaling $387.50 per month.

a. What is Sue's housing expense ratio?

b. What is Sue's total obligations ratio?

c. According to the Lending Ratio Guidelines in Exhibit 14-4, for what type of mortgage would she qualify, if any?

SOLUTIONSTRATEGY

a. $\text{Housing expense ratio} = \dfrac{\text{Monthly housing expense (PITI)}}{\text{Monthly gross income}}$

$\text{Housing expense ratio} = \dfrac{556}{2,490}$

$\text{Housing expense ratio} = .2232 = \underline{22.3\%}$

b. $\text{Total obligations ratio} = \dfrac{\text{Total monthly financial obligations}}{\text{Monthly gross income}}$

$\text{Total obligations ratio} = \dfrac{556.00 + 387.50}{2,490} = \dfrac{943.50}{2,490}$

$\text{Total obligations ratio} = .3789 = \underline{37.9\%}$

c. According to the Lending Ratio Guidelines, Sue would qualify for an FHA mortgage but not a conventional mortgage; her total obligations ratio is 37.9%, which is above the limit for conventional mortgages.

TRYITEXERCISE 7

Roman Bass earns a gross income of $3,100 per month. He has made application at the Golden Gables Bank for a mortgage with a monthly PITI of $669. Roman has other financial obligations totaling $375 per month.

a. What is Roman's housing expense ratio?

b. What is Roman's total obligations ratio?

c. According to the Lending Ratio Guidelines in Exhibit 14-4, for what type of mortgage would he qualify, if any?

CHECK YOUR ANSWERS WITH THE SOLUTIONS ON PAGE 493.

SECTION II 14 REVIEW EXERCISES

Note: Round all answers to the nearest cent when necessary.

For the following second mortgage applications, calculate the percentage of appraised value and the potential credit.

	Appraised Value	Lender's Percentage	Percentage of Appraised Value	Balance of First Mortgage	Potential Credit
1.	$118,700	75%	$89,025	$67,900	$21,125
2.	$124,500	70%	_____	$53,400	_____
3.	$141,200	80%	_____	$99,100	_____
4.	$324,600	75%	_____	$197,500	_____
5.	$105,000	65%	_____	$70,000	_____
6.	$1,329,000	70%	_____	$514,180	_____

7. You own a home that was recently appraised for $320,000. The balance on your existing mortgage is $116,450. If your bank is willing to loan up to 70% of the appraised value, what is the potential amount of credit available on a home equity loan?

Calculate the housing expense ratio and the total obligations ratio for the following mortgage applications.

	Applicant	Monthly Gross Income	Monthly PITI Expense	Other Monthly Financial Obligations	Housing Expense Ratio (%)	Total Obligations Ratio (%)
8.	Parker	$2,000	$455	$380	22.75	41.75
9.	Forman	$3,700	$530	$360		
10.	Martin	$3,100	$705	$720		
11.	Tajsich	$5,200	$1,300	$510		
12.	Emerson	$2,900	$644	$290		
13.	Jameson	$4,250	$1,150	$475		

14. Use Exhibit 14-4, Lending Ratio Guidelines (repeated in the next problem), to answer the following questions:

  a. Which of the applicants in Exercises 8–14 would *not* qualify for a conventional mortgage?

  b. Which of the applicants in Exercises 8–14 would *not* qualify for any mortgage?

15. Carlos earns a gross income of $5,790 per month and applies for a mortgage with a monthly PITI of $1,273.80. Carlos has other financial obligations totaling $1,001.67 per month.

    If the lending ratio guidelines are as given in the table below, what type of mortgage, if any, would Carlos qualify for?

Lending Ratio Guidelines

Mortgage Type	Housing Expense Ratio	Total Obligations Ratio
FHA	29%	41%
Conventional	28%	36%

16. Ronald and Samantha Brady recently had their condominium in Port Isaac appraised for $324,600. The balance on their existing first mortgage is $145,920. If their bank is willing to loan up to 75% of the appraised value, what is the amount of credit available to the Bradys on a home equity line of credit?

$$324,600 \times .75 = \$243,450$$
$$\underline{-145,920}$$
Available credit $\underline{\$97,530}$

17. The Barclays own a home that was recently appraised for $219,000. The balance on their existing first mortgage is $143,250. If their bank is willing to loan up to 65% of the appraised value, what is the potential amount of credit available to the Barclays on a home equity loan?

18. Ransford and Alda Mariano own a home recently appraised for $418,500. The balance on their existing mortgage is $123,872. If their bank is willing to loan up to 80% of the appraised value, what is the amount of credit available to them?

19. Michelle Heaster is thinking about building an addition on her home. The house was recently appraised for $154,000, and the balance on her existing first mortgage is $88,600. If Michelle's bank is willing to loan up to 70% of the appraised value, does she have enough equity in the house to finance a $25,000 addition?

20. Jamie and Alice Newmark have a combined monthly gross income of $9,702 and monthly expenses totaling $2,811. They plan to buy a home with a mortgage whose monthly PITI will be $2,002.

a. What is Jamie and Alice's combined housing expense ratio?

b. What is their total obligations ratio?

c. For what kind of mortgage can they qualify, if any?

d. (Optional challenge) By how much would they need to reduce their monthly expenses in order to qualify for an FHA mortgage?

Mortgage brokers are real estate financing professionals acting as the intermediary between consumers and lenders during mortgage transactions. A mortgage broker works with consumers to help them through the complex mortgage origination process.

Brokers earn commissions in exchange for bringing borrowers and lenders together and receive payment when the mortgage loan is closed.

21. You are a mortgage broker at Interamerican Bank. One of your clients, Bill Cramer, has submitted an application for a mortgage with a monthly PITI of $1,259. His other financial obligations total $654.50 per month. Bill earns a gross income of $4,890 per month.

a. What is his housing expense ratio?

b. What is his total obligations ratio?

c. According to the Lending Ratio Guidelines on page 484, for what type of mortgage would Bill qualify, if any?

d. If Bill decided to get a part-time job so that he could qualify for a conventional mortgage, how much additional monthly income would he need?

BUSINESS DECISION: DOES IT PAY TO REFINANCE YOUR MORTGAGE?

22. According to money.CNN.com, with mortgage rates near 35-year lows, you may be able to cut your payments sharply by refinancing your loan. To qualify for the best rates, you need a credit score of 740 or higher and usually at least 20% equity.

Even if you have to settle for a higher rate, a new loan may save you money. The main consideration is whether you will live in your home long enough to offset the refinance closing costs.

Your current mortgage payment is $1,458.50 per month, with a balance of $214,800. You have a chance to refinance at the Biltmore Bank with a 30-year, 5.5% mortgage. The closing costs of the loan are application fee, $90; credit report, $165; title insurance, .4% of the amount financed; title search, $360; and attorney's fees, $580.

You plan to live in your home for at least four more years. Use the Mortgage Refinancing Worksheet below to see if it makes sense to refinance your mortgage.

MORTGAGE REFINANCING WORKSHEET

STEP 1. Current monthly mortgage payment.. [ ]

STEP 2. New monthly mortgage payment if you refinance........................ [ ]

New rate _____   Current mortgage balance _____

| Table 14-1 factor _____ | × | # of 1,000s to borrow _____ |

STEP 3. Monthly savings.. [ ]

| Step 1. _____ | − | Step 2. _____ |

STEP 4. Total refinance closing costs (appraisal, title search, etc.).............. [ ]

STEP 5. Total months needed to recoup your costs.................................... [ ]

| Step 4 result | ÷ | Step 3 result |

STEP 6. Total months you plan to live in your home................................. [ ]

The Bottom Line—If you plan to live in your home longer than the result in Step 5, it makes sense to refinance.

CHAPTER FORMULAS

Fixed-Rate Mortgages

Monthly payment = Number of $1,000s financed × Table 14-1 factor

Total interest = (Monthly payment × Number of payments) − Amount financed

$$\text{Monthly taxes and Insurance (TI)} = \frac{\text{Estimated property tax + Hazard insurance}}{12}$$

Monthly PITI = Monthly PI + Monthly TI

Adjustable-Rate Mortgages

Calculated interest rate = Index rate + Lender's margin

Maximum rate per adjustment period = Previous rate + Periodic rate cap

Maximum overall rate = Initial rate + Overall rate cap

Home Equity Loans and Lines of Credit

Percentage of appraised value = Appraised value × Lender's percentage

Second mortgage potential credit = Percentage of appraised value − First mortgage balance

$$\text{Housing expense ratio} = \frac{\text{Monthly housing expense (PITI)}}{\text{Monthly gross income}}$$

$$\text{Total obligations ratio} = \frac{\text{Total monthly financial obligations}}{\text{Monthly gross income}}$$

CHAPTER SUMMARY

Section I: Mortgages—Fixed-Rate and Adjustable-Rate

Topic	Important Concepts	Illustrative Examples
Calculating the Monthly Payment and Total Interest Paid on a Fixed-Rate Mortgage **Performance Objective 14-1, Page 469**	1. Find the number of $1,000s financed by 2. From Table 14-1, locate the table factor, monthly payment per $1,000 financed, at the intersection of the number-of-years column and the interest-rate row. 3. Calculate the monthly payment by 4. Find the total interest of the loan by	What is the monthly payment and total interest on a $100,000 mortgage at 9.5% for 30 years? $$\text{Number of 1,000s} = \frac{100,000}{1,000} = 100$$ Table factor: $9\frac{1}{2}\%$, 30 years = 8.41 Monthly payment = 100 × 8.41 = $841 Total interest of the loan = (841 × 360) − 100,000 = 302,760 − 100,000 = $202,760
Preparing a Partial Amortization Schedule of a Mortgage **Performance Objective 14-2, Page 471**	1. Calculate the monthly payment of the loan as before. 2. Calculate the amount of interest for the current month using $I = PRT$, where P is the current outstanding balance of the loan, R is the annual interest rate, and T is $\frac{1}{12}$. 3. Find the portion of the payment used to reduce principal by 4. Calculate outstanding balance of the loan by 5. Repeat Steps 2, 3, and 4 for each succeeding month and enter the values on a schedule labeled appropriately.	Prepare an amortization schedule for the first month of a $70,000 mortgage at 9% for 20 years. Using Table 14-1, we find the monthly payment of the mortgage to be $630. *Month 1:* Interest = Principal × Rate × Time Interest = 70,000 × .09 × $\frac{1}{12}$ Interest = $525 Portion of payment reducing principal 630 − 525 = $105 Outstanding balance after one payment 70,000 − 105 = $69,895 An amortization schedule can now be prepared from these data.

Section I (continued)

Topic	Important Concepts	Illustrative Examples
Calculating the Monthly PITI of a Mortgage Loan **Performance Objective 14-3, Page 473**	In reality, mortgage payments include four elements: principal, interest, taxes, and insurance—thus the abbreviation PITI. *Monthly PITI of a mortgage:* 1. Calculate the principal and interest portion (PI) of the payment as before using Table 14-1. 2. Calculate the monthly tax and insurance portion (TI) by 3. Calculate the total monthly PITI by	Maureen Cassidy purchased a home for $97,500 with a mortgage at 8.5% for 15 years. The property taxes are $1,950 per year, and the hazard insurance premium is $466. What is the monthly PITI payment of Maureen's loan? Using a table factor of 9.85 from Table 14-1, we find the monthly PI for this 8.5%, 15-year mortgage to be $960.38. $$\text{Monthly TI} = \frac{1,950 + 466}{12}$$ $$= \frac{2,416}{12} = \$201.33$$ Monthly PITI = PI + TI $$= 960.38 + 201.33 = \underline{\underline{\$1,161.71}}$$
Calculating the Amount Due at Closing **Performance Objective 14-4, Page 474**	Closing costs are the expenses incurred in conjunction with the sale of real estate. Both buyer and seller are responsible for specific costs. The party responsible for paying a particular closing cost is often determined by local custom or by negotiation. Some closing costs are expressed as dollar amounts, whereas others are a percent of the amount financed or amount of the purchase price. At closing, the buyer is responsible for the purchase price (mortgage and down payment) plus closing costs. The amount received by the seller after all expenses have been paid is known as the proceeds.	*Typical Closing Costs* *Buyer:* Attorney's fee, inspections, credit report, appraisal fee, hazard insurance premium, title exam and insurance premium, escrow fee, prepaid taxes, and interest *Seller:* Attorney's fee, broker's commission, survey expense, inspections, abstract of title, certificate of title, escrow fee, prepayment penalty—existing loan, documentary stamps
Calculating the Interest Rate of an Adjustable-Rate Mortgage (ARM) **Performance Objective 14-5, Page 477**	Use the following formulas to find the various components of an ARM:	Howard Gold bought a home with an adjustable-rate mortgage. The margin on the loan is 3.5%, and the rate cap is 8% over the life of the loan. If the current index rate is 3.6%, what is the calculated interest rate and the maximum overall rate of the loan? Calculated interest rate = 3.6% + 3.5% = <u>7.1%</u> Maximum overall rate = 7.1% + 8% = <u>15.1%</u>

Section II: Second Mortgages—Home Equity Loans and Lines of Credit

Topic	Important Concepts	Illustrative Examples
Calculating the Potential Amount of Credit Available to a Borrower **Performance Objective 14-6, Page 483**	Most lenders set the credit limit on a home equity loan or line by taking a percentage of the appraised value of the home and subtracting the balance owed on the existing first mortgage. In determining your actual credit limit, the lender also will consider your ability to repay by looking at your income, debts, and other financial obligations, as well as your credit history. *Potential amount of credit available to borrower:* 1. Calculate the percentage of appraised value by 2. Find the potential amount of credit available by	The McCartneys own a home that was recently appraised for $134,800. The balance on their existing first mortgage is $76,550. If their bank is willing to loan up to 70% of the appraised value, what is the amount of credit available to the McCartneys on a home equity loan? Percentage of appraisal value = 134,800 × .70 $$= \$94,360$$ Available credit = 94,360 − 76,550 = <u>$17,810</u>

Section II (continued)

Topic	Important Concepts	Illustrative Examples
Calculating the Housing Expense Ratio and the Total Obligations Ratio of a Borrower **Performance Objective 14-7, Page 484**	Mortgage lenders use ratios to determine whether borrowers have the economic ability to repay the loan. Two important ratios used for this purpose are the housing expense ratio and the total obligations ratio. These ratios are expressed as percents and are calculated by using the following formulas:	Vickie Howard earns a gross income of $3,750 per month. She has made application for a mortgage with a monthly PITI of $956. Vickie has other financial obligations totaling $447 per month. a. What is her housing expense ratio? b. What is her total obligations ratio? c. According to the Lending Ratio Guidelines on page 484, for what type of mortgage would Vickie qualify, if any? $$\text{Housing expense ratio} = \frac{956}{3,750} = 25.5\%$$ $$\text{Total obligations ratio} = \frac{1,403}{3,750} = 37.4\%$$ According to the Lending Ratio Guidelines, Vickie would qualify for an FHA mortgage but not a conventional mortgage; her total obligations ratio is 37.4%, which is above the limit for conventional mortgages.

TRY IT: EXERCISE SOLUTIONS FOR CHAPTER 14

1. Number of 1,000s financed $= \dfrac{\text{Amount financed}}{1,000}$

Number of 1,000s financed $= \dfrac{85,500}{1,000} = 85.5$

Table factor 4.5%, 25 years $= 5.56$

Monthly payment $=$ Number of 1,000s financed $\times$ Table factor

Monthly payment $= 85.5 \times 5.56 = \underline{\$475.38}$

Total interest $=$ (Monthly payment $\times$ Number of payments) $-$ Amount financed

Total interest $= (475.38 \times 300) - 85,500$

Total interest $= 142,614 - 85,500 = \underline{\$57,114}$

2. Number of 1,000s financed $= \dfrac{125,000}{1,000} = 125$

Table factor 6%, 15 years $= 8.44$

Monthly payment $= 125 \times 8.44 = \$1,055.00$

Month 1

$I = PRT = 125,000 \times .06 \times \dfrac{1}{12} = \$625.00$

Portion of payment reducing principal $= \$1,055.00 - 625.00 = \$430.00$

Outstanding balance $= 125,000.00 - 430.00 = \$124,570.00$

Month 2

$I = PRT = 124,570.00 \times .06 \times \dfrac{1}{12} = \$622.85$

Portion of payment reducing principal $= \$1,055.00 - 622.85 = \$432.15$

Outstanding balance $= 124,570.00 - 432.15 = \$124,137.85$

Month 3

$I = PRT = 124,137.85 \times .06 \times \dfrac{1}{12} = \$620.69$

Portion of payment reducing principal $= 1,055.00 - 620.69 = \$434.31$

Outstanding balance $= 124,137.85 - 434.31 = \$123,703.54$

Month 4

$$I = PRT = 123{,}703.54 \times .06 \times \frac{1}{12} = \$618.52$$

Portion of payment reducing principal $= 1{,}055.00 - 618.52 = \$436.48$

Outstanding balance $= 123{,}703.54 - 436.48 = \$123{,}267.06$

Amortization Schedule
$125,000, 6%, 15 years

Payment Number	Monthly Payment	Monthly Interest	Portion Used to Reduce Principal	Loan Balance
0				$125,000.00
1	$1,055.00	$625.00	$430.00	$124,570.00
2	$1,055.00	$622.85	$432.15	$124,137.85
3	$1,055.00	$620.69	$434.31	$123,703.54
4	$1,055.00	$618.52	$436.48	$123,267.06

3.

Number of 1,000s $= \dfrac{125{,}600}{1{,}000} = 125.6$

Table factor 6.25%, 20 years $= 7.31$

Monthly payment (PI) $= 125.6 \times 7.31 = \$918.14$

Monthly TI $= \dfrac{\text{Property tax} + \text{Hazard insurance}}{12}$

Monthly TI $= \dfrac{3{,}250 + 765}{12} = \dfrac{4{,}015}{12} = \$334.58$

Monthly PITI $= \text{PI} + \text{TI} = 918.14 + 334.58 = \underline{\underline{\$1{,}252.72}}$

4. a.   Down payment $= 120{,}000 \times 20\% = \$24{,}000$

Amount financed $= 120{,}000 - 24{,}000 = \$96{,}000$

Closing Costs, Buyer:

Discount points $(96{,}000 \times 3\%)$	$ 2,880
Down payment $(24{,}000 - 10{,}000)$	14,000
Application fee	100
Condominium transfer fee	190
Title insurance $\left(96{,}000 \times \frac{3}{4}\%\right)$	720
Hazard insurance	420
Prepaid taxes	310
Attorney's fees	500
Due at closing	$\underline{\underline{\$19{,}120}}$

b. *Proceeds, Seller:*

Purchase price		$120,000
Less: Broker's commission		
$120{,}000 \times 5\frac{1}{2}\%$	$ 6,600	
Closing costs	670	
Mortgage payoff	$\underline{65{,}000}$	
		$-72{,}270$
Proceeds to seller		$\underline{\underline{\$47{,}730}}$

5. a. Calculated ARM rate = Index rate + Lender's margin

Calculated ARM rate $= 3.2 + 3.4 = \underline{6.6\%}$

b. Maximum overall rate = Calculated ARM rate + Overall rate cap

Maximum overall rate $= 6.6 + 7.0 = \underline{13.6\%}$

6. Percentage of appraised value = Appraised value × Lender's percentage

Percentage of appraised value $= 92{,}900 \times 80\% = \$74{,}320$

Potential credit = Percentage of appraised value − First mortgage balance

Potential credit $= 74{,}320 - 32{,}440 = \underline{\$41{,}880}$

7. a. Housing expense ratio $= \dfrac{\text{Monthly housing expense (PITI)}}{\text{Monthly gross income}}$

Housing expense ratio $= \dfrac{669}{3,100} = 21.6\%$

b. Total obligations ratio $= \dfrac{\text{Total monthly financial obligation}}{\text{Monthly gross income}}$

Total obligations ratio $= \dfrac{669 + 375}{3,100} = \dfrac{1,044}{3,100} = 33.7\%$

c. According to the guidelines, Roman qualifies for both   .

CONCEPT REVIEW

1. Land, including permanent improvements on that land, is known as _____. (14-1)

2. A(n) _____ is a loan in which real property is used as security for a debt. (14-1)

3. Mortgage _____ points are an extra charge frequently added to the cost of a mortgage. (14-1, 14-4)

4. A chart that shows the month-by-month breakdown of each mortgage payment into interest and principal is known as a(n) _____ schedule. (14-2)

5. A(n) _____ account is a bank account used by mortgage lenders to accumulate next year's property taxes and hazard insurance. (14-3)

6. Today most mortgage payments include four parts, abbreviated PITI. Name these parts. (14-3)

7. The final step in a real estate transaction is a meeting at which time the buyer pays the agreed-upon purchase price and the seller delivers the ownership documents. This meeting is known as the _____. (14-4)

8. The official document representing the right of ownership of real property is known as the _____ or the _____. (14-4)

9. List four mortgage loan closing costs. (14-4)

10. A mortgage in which the interest rate changes periodically, usually in relation to a predetermined economic index, is known as a(n) _____ rate mortgage. (14-5)

11. A home equity _____ is a lump-sum second mortgage based on the available equity in a home. (14-6)

12. A home equity _____ of credit is a revolving credit second mortgage loan on the equity in a home. (14-6)

13. Write the formula for the housing expense ratio. (14-7)

14. Write the formula for the total obligations ratio. (14-7)

ASSESSMENT TEST

You are one of the branch managers of the Insignia Bank. Today two loan applications were submitted to your office. Calculate the requested information for each loan.

	Amount Financed	Interest Rate	Term of Loan	Number of $1,000s Financed	Table Factor	Monthly Payment	Total Interest
1.	$155,900	4.50%	25 years	_____	___	_____	_____
2.	$98,500	5.25%	20 years	_____	___	_____	_____

3. Suzanne Arthurs purchased a home with a $146,100 mortgage at 6.5% for 30 years. Calculate the monthly payment and prepare an amortization schedule for the first three months of Suzanne's loan.

Payment Number	Monthly Payment	Monthly Interest	Portion Used to Reduce Principal	Loan Balance
0				$146,100.00
1	_____	_____	_____	_____
2	_____	_____	_____	_____
3	_____	_____	_____	_____

Use Table 14-1 to calculate the monthly principal and interest and calculate the monthly PITI for the following mortgages.

	Amount Financed	Interest Rate	Term of Loan	Monthly PI	Annual Property Tax	Annual Insurance	Monthly PITI
4.	$54,200	4.75%	25 years	_____	$719	$459	_____
5.	$162,100	5.50%	15 years	_____	$2,275	$1,033	_____

For the following second mortgage applications, calculate the percentage of appraised value and the potential credit.

	Appraised Value	Lender's Percentage	Percentage of Appraised Value	Balance of First Mortgage	Potential Credit
6.	$114,500	65%	_____	$77,900	_____
7.	$51,500	80%	_____	$27,400	_____
8.	$81,200	70%	_____	$36,000	_____

For the following mortgage applications, calculate the housing expense ratio and the total expense ratio.

	Applicant	Monthly Gross Income	Monthly PITI Expense	Other Monthly Financial Obligations	Housing Expense Ratio (%)	Total Obligations Ratio (%)
9.	Morton	$5,300	$1,288	$840	_____	_____
10.	Hauser	$3,750	$952	$329	_____	_____

11. As a loan officer using the Lending Ratio Guidelines on page 484, what type of mortgage can you offer Morton and Hauser from Exercises 9 and 10?

12. Dale Evans bought the Lazy D Ranch with an adjustable-rate mortgage. The lender's margin on the loan is 3.9%, and the overall rate cap is 6% over the life of the loan.

   a. If the current index rate is 4.45%, what is the calculated interest rate of the ARM?

   b. What is the maximum overall rate of Dale's loan?

13. Diversified Investments purchased a 24-unit apartment building for $650,000. After a 20% down payment, the balance was financed with a 20-year, 7.75% fixed-rate mortgage.

   a. What is the amount of the monthly principal and interest portion of the loan?

CHAPTER
14

b. As Diversified's loan officer, construct an amortization schedule for the first two months of the mortgage.

Payment Number	Monthly Payment	Monthly Interest	Portion Used to Reduce Principal	Loan Balance
0				_____
1	_____	_____	_____	_____
2	_____	_____	_____	_____

c. If the annual property taxes are $9,177 and the hazard insurance premium is $2,253 per year, what is the total monthly PITI of the loan?

d. If each apartment rents for $825 per month, how much income will Diversified make per month after the PITI is paid on the building?

14. Larry Mager purchased a ski lodge in Telluride for $850,000. His bank is willing to finance 70% of the purchase price. As part of the mortgage closing costs, Larry had to pay $4\frac{1}{4}$ discount points. How much did this amount to?

15. A Denny's Restaurant franchisee is looking for a 20-year mortgage with 90% financing to build a new location costing $775,000. The Spring Creek Bank is offering an 8% mortgage with $1\frac{1}{2}$ discount points; Foremost Savings & Loan is offering a 7.5% mortgage with 4 discount points. The franchisee is unsure which mortgage is the better deal and has asked for your help.

a. What is the total interest paid on each loan?

b. Taking into account the discount points, which lender is offering a better deal and by how much?

16. How much more total interest will be paid on a 30-year fixed-rate mortgage for $100,000 at 9.25% compared with a 15-year mortgage at 8.5%?

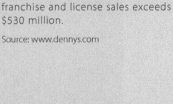

Denny's Corporation, through its subsidiaries, engages in the ownership and operation of a chain of family-style restaurants primarily in the United States. Its restaurants offer traditional American-style food. The company owns and operates its restaurants under the Denny's brand name.

In a typical year, total revenue from company restaurant sales and franchise and license sales exceeds $530 million.

Source: www.dennys.com

17. Adam Marsh is purchasing a $134,000 condominium apartment. The down payment is 20%, and the balance will be financed with a 20-year fixed-rate mortgage at 8.75% and 3 discount points. The annual property tax is $1,940, and the hazard insurance premium is $1,460. When Adam signed the original sales contract, he put down a deposit of $10,000, which will be credited to his down payment. In addition, at the time of closing, he must pay the following expenses:

Appraisal fee	$165
Credit report	$75
Attorney's fees	$490
Roof inspection	$50
Termite inspection	$88
Title search	$119
Mortgage insurance premium	1.2% of amount financed
Documentary stamps	$\frac{1}{4}$% of amount financed

As Adam's real estate agent, he has asked you the following questions:

a. What is the total monthly PITI of the mortgage loan?

b. What is the total amount of interest that Adam will pay on the loan?

c. How much is due at the time of the closing?

d. If the sellers are responsible for the 6% broker's commission, $900 in closing costs, and the existing first mortgage with a balance of $45,000, what proceeds will be received on the sale of the property?

18. Martin Ellingham is negotiating to buy a vacation cottage in Port Wenn. The seller of the cottage is asking $186,000. Martin offered him a cash deal, owner-seller (no broker) only if the seller would reduce the price by 12%. The seller agreed. Martin must pay a 10% down payment upon signing the agreement of sale. At closing, he must pay the balance of the agreed-upon sale price, a $500 attorney's fee, a $68 utility transfer fee, a title search and transfer fee of $35 plus $\frac{3}{4}$% of the selling price, and the first six months of the annual insurance of $1,460 per year. How much does Martin owe at closing?

19. The Randolphs own a home that recently appraised for $161,400. The balance on their existing first mortgage is $115,200. If their bank is willing to loan up to 70% of the appraised value, what is the amount of credit available to the Randolphs on a home equity line of credit?

20. Jonathan and Kimberly Schwartz live in a home to which they want to make major improvements. They plan to replace the existing heating and cooling system, remodel the kitchen, and add a room above the garage. To pay for this renovation, they plan to get a home equity line of credit. Their home currently appraises for $298,000. They owe $68,340 on the first mortgage. How much credit will their bank provide if the limit is 75% of their home's value?

21. Phil Armstrong earns a gross income of $5,355 per month. He has submitted an application for a fixed-rate mortgage with a monthly PITI of $1,492. Phil has other financial obligations totaling $625 per month.

    a. What is his housing expense ratio?

    b. What is his total obligations ratio?

    c. According to the Lending Ratio Guidelines on page 484, for what type of mortgage would Phil qualify, if any?

22. Magda Leon is applying for a home mortgage with a monthly PITI of $724. She currently has a gross income of $2,856 and other monthly expenses of $411.

    a. What is Magda's housing expense ratio?

    b. What is her total obligations ratio?

    c. According to the lending ratio guidelines, for what type of mortgage would Magda qualify, if any?

BUSINESS DECISION: FOR WHAT SIZE MORTGAGE CAN YOU QUALIFY?

23. You are applying for a conventional mortgage from the Americana Bank. Your monthly gross income is $3,500, and the bank uses the 28% housing expense ratio guideline.

    a. What is the highest PITI for which you can qualify? *Hint:* Solve the housing expense ratio formula for PITI. Remember, this is an application of the percentage formula, Portion = Rate × Base, where PITI is the portion, the expense ratio is the rate, and your monthly gross income is the base.

b. Based on your answer from part a, if you are applying for a 30-year, 9% mortgage and the taxes and insurance portion of PITI is $175 per month, use Table 14-1 to calculate the size of the mortgage for which you qualify. *Hint:* Subtract TI from PITI. Divide the PI by the appropriate table factor to determine the number of $1,000s for which you qualify.

c. Based on your answer from part b, if you are planning on a 20% down payment, what is the most expensive house you can afford? *Hint:* Use the percentage formula again. The purchase price of the house is the base, the amount financed is the portion, and the percent financed is the rate.

COLLABORATIVE LEARNING ACTIVITY

The Hypothetical Mortgage

Speak with the loan officers at mortgage lending institutions in your area and ask for their help with a business math class project.

Your assignment is to research the various types of financing deals currently being offered for a hypothetical condominium you plan to buy. The following assumptions apply to this project:

- The purchase price of the condo you plan to buy is $200,000.
- The condo was recently appraised for $220,000.
- You plan to make a 25% down payment ($50,000) and are seeking a $150,000 mortgage.
- You have a job that qualifies you for that size mortgage.

As a team, your assignment is to compare the current interest rates, costs, and features associated with a 15-year fixed-rate mortgage, a 30-year fixed-rate mortgage, and an adjustable-rate mortgage.

a. What are the current interest rates and discount points of the 15- and 30-year fixed-rate mortgages?

b. What are the monthly payments of the fixed-rate mortgages?

c. What is the initial (teaser) rate, discount points, adjustment period, rate caps, margin, and index for the adjustable-rate mortgage?

d. What are the fees or charges for the loan application, property appraisal, survey, credit report, inspections, title search, title insurance, and document preparation?

e. What other charges or fees can be expected at closing?

f. Which type of mortgage does your team think is the best deal at this time? Why?

g. Which bank would you choose for the mortgage? Why?

CHAPTER 15 Financial Statements and Ratios

PERFORMANCE OBJECTIVES

15

THE BALANCE SHEET

financial statements A series of accounting reports summarizing a company's financial data compiled from business activity over a period of time. The four most common are the balance sheet, the income statement, the owner's equity statement, and the cash flow statement.

Financial statements are the periodic report cards of how a business is doing from a monetary perspective. After all, money is the primary way in which the score is kept in the competitive arena of business. These important statements are a summary of a company's financial data compiled from business activity over a period of time.

The four major financial statements used in business today are the balance sheet, the income statement, the owner's equity statement, and the cash flow statement. Together they tell a story about how a company has performed in the past and is likely to perform in the near future. In this chapter, we focus our attention on the preparation and analysis of the balance sheet and the income statement. The Business Decisions at the ends of the review exercises and the Assessment Test feature actual financial statements from recent annual reports of well-known companies representing various industries. These financial statements provide an opportunity to examine real-world statements and apply your own analytical skills.

Typically, a company's accounting department prepares financial statements quarterly for the purpose of management review and government reporting of income tax information. At the end of each year, the accounting department prepares annual financial statements to present the company's yearly financial position and performance. Public corporations, those whose stock can be bought and sold by the general investing public, are required by law to make their statements available to the stockholders and the financial community in the form of quarterly and annual reports. Because it is public information, condensed versions of these reports often appear in financial publications such as the *Wall Street Journal, Business Week, Forbes,* and *Fortune.*

financial analysis The assessment of a company's past, present, and anticipated future financial condition based on the information found on the financial statements.

Financial analysis is the assessment of a company's past, present, and anticipated future financial condition based on the information found on the financial statements. Financial ratios are the primary tool of this analysis. These ratios are a way of standardizing financial data so that they may be compared with ratios from previous operating periods of the same firm or from other similar-size firms in the same industry.

Internally, owners and managers rely on this analysis to evaluate a company's financial strengths and weaknesses and to help make sound business decisions. From outside the firm, creditors and investors use financial statements and ratios to determine a company's creditworthiness or investment potential.

balance sheet A financial statement illustrating the financial position of a company in terms of assets, liabilities, and owner's equity as of a certain date.

The **balance sheet** is the financial statement that lists a company's financial position on a certain date, usually at the end of a month, a quarter, or a year. To fully understand the balance sheet, we must first examine some basic accounting theory.

financial position The economic resources owned by a company and the claims against those resources at a specific point in time.

Financial position refers to the economic resources owned by a company and the claims against those resources at a specific point in time. *Equities* is another term for *claims.* Keep in mind that a firm's economic resources must be equal to its equities. A business enterprise can therefore be pictured as an equation:

creditors Those to whom money is owed.

$$\text{Economic resources} = \text{Equities}$$

liabilities Debts or obligations of a business resulting from past transactions that require the company to pay money, provide goods, or perform services in the future.

There are two types of equities: the rights of the **creditors** (those who are owed money by the business) and the rights of the owners. The rights of the creditors are known as **liabilities** and represent debts of the business. The rights of the owners are known as **owner's equity.** Owner's equity represents the resources invested in the business by the owners. Theoretically, owner's equity is what would be left over after all liabilities were paid to the creditors. We can now enhance our equation:

owner's equity The resources claimed by the owner against the assets of a business: Owner's equity = Assets − Liabilities. Also called proprietorship, capital, or net worth.

$$\text{Economic resources} = \text{Liabilities} + \text{Owner's equity}$$

In accounting terminology, the economic resources owned by a business are known as the **assets.** Our equation now becomes

assets Economic resources (for example, cash; inventories; and land, buildings, and equipment) owned by a business.

$$\text{Assets} = \text{Liabilities} + \text{Owner's Equity}$$

accounting equation Algebraic expression of a company's financial position: Assets = Liabilities + Owner's equity.

This all-important equation is known as the **accounting equation.** The balance sheet is a visual presentation of this equation at a point in time. Some balance sheets display the assets on the left and the liabilities and owner's equity on the right. Another popular format lists the assets on top and the liabilities and owner's equity below. Remember, on a balance sheet, the assets must be equal to the liabilities plus owner's equity.

PREPARING A BALANCE SHEET

15-1

Let's begin by looking at an example of a typical balance sheet and then examining each section and its components more closely. A balance sheet for a corporation, Hypothetical Enterprises, Inc., follows. Carefully look over the statement. Then read the descriptions of the balance sheet components, which begin below, and "Steps to Prepare a Balance Sheet," page 503. Finally, follow the example and attempt the Try-It Exercise.

Hypothetical Enterprises, Inc.
Balance Sheet
December 31, 20XX

Assets

Current Assets		
Cash	$ 13,000	
Accounts Receivable	32,500	
Merchandise Inventory	50,600	
Prepaid Expenses	1,200	
Supplies	4,000	
Total Current Assets		$101,300
Property, Plant, and Equipment		
Land	40,000	
Buildings	125,000	
Machinery and Equipment	60,000	
Total Property, Plant, and Equipment		225,000
Investments and Other Assets		
Investments	10,000	
Intangible Assets	5,000	
Total Investments and Other Assets		15,000
Total Assets		$341,300

Liabilities and Owner's Equity

Current Liabilities		
Accounts Payable	$ 17,500	
Salaries Payable	5,400	
Taxes Payable	6,500	
Total Current Liabilities		$ 29,400
Long-Term Liabilities		
Mortgage Payable	115,000	
Debenture Bond	20,000	
Total Long-Term Liabilities		135,000
Total Liabilities		164,400
Stockholders' Equity		
Capital Stock	126,900	
Retained Earnings	50,000	
Total Stockholders' Equity		176,900
Total Liabilities and Stockholders' Equity		$341,300

Annual Meeting The annual meeting is a company gathering usually held at the end of each fiscal year at which the previous year and the outlook for the future are discussed and directors are elected by vote of the common stockholders.

Shortly before each annual meeting, the corporation sends out a document called a proxy statement to each stockholder. The proxy statement contains a list of the business concerns to be addressed at the meeting and a ballot for voting on company initiatives and electing the new board of directors.

BALANCE SHEET COMPONENTS

ASSETS The asset section of a balance sheet is divided into three components: Current Assets; Property, Plant, and Equipment; and Investments and Other Assets.

Current Assets Cash or assets that will be sold, used, or converted to cash within one year. The following are typical examples of current assets:

• Cash—Cash on hand in the form of bills, coins, checking accounts, and savings accounts.
• Marketable securities—Investments in short-term securities that can be quickly converted to cash, such as stocks and bonds.

- Accounts receivable—Money owed by customers to the firm for goods and services sold on credit.
- Notes receivable—Money owed to the business involving promissory notes.
- Merchandise inventory—The cost of goods a business has on hand for resale to its customers.
- Prepaid expenses—Money paid in advance by the firm for benefits and services not yet received, such as prepaid insurance premiums or prepaid rent.
- Supplies—Cost of assets used in the day-to-day operation of the business. These might include office supplies such as paper, pencils, pens, CDs, and DVDs or maintenance supplies such as paper towels, soap, lubricants, lightbulbs, and batteries.

Property, Plant, and Equipment   Also known as fixed or long-term assets. These assets will be used by the firm in the operation of the business for a period of time longer than one year. Some examples follow:

- Land—The original purchase price of land owned by the company. Land is an asset that does not depreciate (or lose its value) over a period of time.
- Buildings—The cost of the buildings owned by the firm less the accumulated depreciation (or total loss in value) on those buildings since they were new. This is known as the book value of the buildings.
- Machinery and equipment—The book value (or original cost less accumulated depreciation) of all machinery, fixtures, vehicles, and equipment used in the operation of a business.

Investments and Other Assets   This category lists the firm's investments and all other assets.

- Investments—Investments made by the firm and held for periods longer than one year.
- Other assets—A catch-all category for any assets not previously listed.
- Intangibles—Long-term assets that have no physical substance but have a value based on rights and privileges claimed by the owner. Some examples are copyrights, patents, royalties, and goodwill.

LIABILITIES AND OWNER'S EQUITY   The liabilities and owner's equity section of the balance sheet lists the current and long-term liabilities incurred by the company as well as the owner's *net worth* or claim against the assets of the business. From the accounting equation, it is the difference between the total assets and the total liabilities.

Current Liabilities   Debts and financial obligations of the company that are due to be paid within one year. Some examples follow:

- Accounts payable—Debts owed by the firm to creditors for goods and services purchased with less than one year of credit. These might include 30-, 60-, or 90-day terms of sale extended by suppliers and vendors.
- Notes payable—Debts owed by the firm involving promissory notes. An example is a short-term loan from a bank.
- Salaries payable—Compensation to employees that has been earned but not yet paid.
- Taxes payable—Taxes owed by the firm but not yet paid by the date of the statement.

Long-Term Liabilities   Debts and financial obligations of the company that are due to be paid in one year or more or are to be paid out of non-current assets. Some examples follow:

- Mortgage payable—The total obligation a firm owes for the long-term financing of land and buildings.
- Debenture bonds—The total amount a firm owes on bonds at maturity to bondholders for money borrowed on the general credit of the company.

Owner's Equity   When a business is organized as a sole proprietorship or partnership, the equity section of the balance sheet is known as owner's equity. The ownership is labeled with the name of the owners or business and the word *capital*. Some examples follow:

- Paul Kelsch, capital
- Lost Sock Laundry, capital.

　　　　　　　　　　　　　　　　　　　　　　　　503

Stockholders' Equity　When the business is a corporation, the equity section of the balance sheet is known as stockholders' equity. The ownership is represented in two categories, capital stock and retained earnings.

- Capital stock—This represents money acquired by selling stock to investors who become stockholders. Capital stock is divided into preferred stock, which has preference over common stock regarding dividends, and common stock, representing the most basic rights to ownership of a corporation.
- Retained earnings—Profits from the operation of the business that have not been distributed to the stockholders in the form of dividends.

STEPS TO PREPARE A BALANCE SHEET

STEP 1. Centered at the top of the page, write the company name, type of statement, and date.

STEP 2. In a section labeled ASSETS, list and total all of the Current Assets; Property, Plant, and Equipment; and Investments and Other Assets.

STEP 3. Add the three components of the Assets section to get Total Assets.

STEP 4. Double-underline Total Assets.

STEP 5. In a section labeled LIABILITIES AND OWNER'S EQUITY, list and total all Current Liabilities and Long-Term Liabilities.

STEP 6. Add the two components of the Liabilities section to get Total Liabilities.

STEP 7. List and total the Owner's or Stockholders' Equity.

STEP 8. Add the Total Liabilities and Owner's Equity.

STEP 9. Double-underline Total Liabilities and Owner's Equity.

Note: In accordance with the accounting equation, check to be sure that

$$\text{Assets} = \text{Liabilities} + \text{Owner's Equity}$$

EXAMPLE1　PREPARING A BALANCE SHEET

Use the following financial information to prepare a balance sheet for Royal Equipment Supply, Inc., as of June 30, 20XX: cash, $3,400; accounts receivable, $5,600; merchandise inventory, $98,700; prepaid insurance, $455; supplies, $800; land and building, $147,000; fixtures, $8,600; delivery vehicles, $27,000; forklift, $7,000; goodwill, $10,000; accounts payable, $16,500; notes payable, $10,000; mortgage payable, $67,000; common stock, $185,055; and retained earnings, $30,000.

SOLUTIONSTRATEGY

The balance sheet for Royal Equipment Supply, Inc. follows. Note that the assets are equal to the liabilities plus stockholders' equity.

Royal Equipment Supply, Inc.
Balance Sheet
June 30, 20XX

Assets

Current Assets

Cash	$3,400	
Accounts Receivable	5,600	
Merchandise Inventory	98,700	
Prepaid Insurance	455	
Supplies	800	
Total Current Assets		$108,955

Property, Plant, and Equipment		
Land and Building	$147,000	
Fixtures	8,600	
Delivery Vehicles	27,000	
Forklift	7,000	
Total Property, Plant, and Equipment		189,600
Investments and Other Assets		
Goodwill	10,000	
Total Investments and Other Assets		10,000
Total Assets		$308,555

Liabilities and Stockholders' Equity

Current Liabilities		
Accounts Payable	$16,500	
Notes Payable	10,000	
Total Current Liabilities		$ 26,500
Long-Term Liabilities		
Mortgage Payable	67,000	
Total Long-Term Liabilities		67,000
Total Liabilities		93,500
Stockholders' Equity		
Common Stock	185,055	
Retained Earnings	30,000	
Total Stockholders' Equity		215,055
Total Liabilities and Stockholders' Equity		$308,555

▶ TRYITEXERCISE 1

Use the following financial information to prepare a balance sheet as of December 31, 20XX, for Keystone Auto Repair, a sole proprietorship owned by Blake Williams: cash, $5,200; accounts receivable, $2,800; merchandise inventory, $2,700; prepaid salary, $235; supplies, $3,900; land, $35,000; building, $74,000; fixtures, $1,200; tow truck, $33,600; tools and equipment, $45,000; accounts payable, $6,800; notes payable, $17,600; taxes payable, $3,540; mortgage payable, $51,000; Blake Williams, capital, $124,695.

CHECK YOUR ANSWER WITH THE SOLUTION ON PAGE 538.

15-2   PREPARING A VERTICAL ANALYSIS OF A BALANCE SHEET

vertical analysis A percentage method of analyzing financial statements whereby each item on the statement is expressed as a percent of a base amount. On balance sheet analysis, the base is total assets; on income statement analysis, the base is net sales.

common-size balance sheets Special forms of balance sheets that list only the vertical analysis percentages, not the dollar figures. All items are expressed as a percent of total assets.

Once the balance sheet has been prepared, a number of analytical procedures can be applied to the data to further evaluate a company's financial condition. One common method of analysis of a single financial statement is known as **vertical analysis**. In vertical analysis, each item on the balance sheet is expressed as a percent of total assets (total assets = 100%).

Once the vertical analysis has been completed, the figures show the relationship of each item on the balance sheet to total assets. For analysis purposes, these percents can then be compared with previous statements of the same company, with competitors' figures, or with published industry averages for similar-size companies.

A special form of balance sheet known as a common-size balance sheet is frequently used in financial analysis. **Common-size balance sheets** list only the vertical analysis percentages, not the dollar figures.

STEPS TO PREPARE A VERTICAL ANALYSIS OF A BALANCE SHEET

STEP 1. Use the percentage formula, Rate = Portion ÷ Base, to find the percentage of each item on the balance sheet. Use each item as the portion and total assets as the base.

STEP 2. Round each answer to the nearest tenth of a percent.

Note: A 0.1% differential may sometimes occur due to rounding.

STEP 3. List the percent of each balance sheet item in a column to the right of the monetary amount.

EXAMPLE2 PREPARING A VERTICAL ANALYSIS OF A BALANCE SHEET

Prepare a vertical analysis of the balance sheet for Hypothetical Enterprises, Inc., on page 501.

►SOLUTIONSTRATEGY

Using the steps for vertical analysis, perform the following calculation for each balance sheet item and enter the results on the statement:

$$\frac{\text{Cash}}{\text{Total assets}} = \frac{13,000}{341,300} = .038 = \underline{\underline{3.8\%}}$$

Hypothetical Enterprises, Inc.
Balance Sheet
December 31, 20XX

Assets

Current Assets		
Cash	$13,000	3.8% ◄
Accounts Receivable	32,500	9.5
Merchandise Inventory	50,600	14.8
Prepaid Expenses	1,200	0.4
Supplies	4,000	1.2
Total Current Assets	101,300	29.7
Property, Plant, and Equipment		
Land	40,000	11.7
Buildings	125,000	36.6
Machinery and Equipment	60,000	17.6
Total Property, Plant, and Equipment	225,000	65.9
Investments and Other Assets		
Investments	10,000	2.9
Intangible Assets	5,000	1.5
Total Investments and Other Assets	15,000	4.4
Total Assets	$341,300	100.0%

Liabilities and Stockholders' Equity

Current Liabilities		
Accounts Payable	$17,500	5.1%
Salaries Payable	5,400	1.6
Taxes Payable	6,500	1.9
Total Current Liabilities	29,400	8.6

Learning Tip

In vertical analysis, remember that each item on the balance sheet is the *portion* and Total Assets is the *base*.

Because of rounding, the percents may not always add up to 100%. There may be a 0.1% differential.

Long-Term Liabilities		
Mortgage Payable	115,000	33.7
Debenture Bond	20,000	5.9
Total Long-Term Liabilities	135,000	39.6
Total Liabilities	164,400	48.2
Stockholders' Equity		
Capital Stock	126,900	37.2
Retained Earnings	50,000	14.6
Total Stockholders' Equity	176,900	51.8
Total Liabilities and Stockholders' Equity	$341,300	100.0%

▶ TRYITEXERCISE 2

Prepare a vertical analysis of the balance sheet for Royal Equipment Supply, Inc., on pages 503–504.

CHECK YOUR ANSWERS WITH THE SOLUTIONS ON PAGE 539.

15-3

PREPARING A HORIZONTAL ANALYSIS OF A BALANCE SHEET

comparative balance sheet Balance sheet prepared with the data from the current year or operating period side by side with the figures from one or more previous periods.

horizontal analysis Method of analyzing financial statements whereby each item of the current period is compared in dollars and percent with the corresponding item from a previous period.

Frequently, balance sheets are prepared with the data from the current year or operating period side by side with the figures from one or more previous periods. This type of presentation is known as a **comparative balance sheet** because the data from different periods can be readily compared. This information provides managers, creditors, and investors with important data concerning the progress of the company over a period of time, financial trends that may be developing, and the likelihood of future success.

Comparative balance sheets use horizontal analysis to measure the increases and decreases that have taken place in the financial data between two operating periods. In **horizontal analysis**, each item of the current period is compared in dollars and percent with the corresponding item from a previous period.

STEPS TO PREPARE A HORIZONTAL ANALYSIS OF A BALANCE SHEET

STEP 1. Set up a comparative balance sheet format with the current period listed first and the previous period listed next.

STEP 2. Label the next two columns:

Increase (Decrease)	
Amount	Percent

STEP 3. For each item on the balance sheet, calculate the dollar difference between the current and previous periods and enter this figure in the Amount column. Enter all decreases in parentheses.

STEP 4. Calculate the percent change (increase or decrease) using the percentage formula:

$$\text{Percent change (rate)} = \frac{\text{Amount of change, Step 3 (portion)}}{\text{Previous period amount (base)}}$$

STEP 5. Enter the percent change (rounded to the nearest tenth of a percent) in the Percent column. Once again, enter all decreases in parentheses.

EXAMPLE3 PREPARING A HORIZONTAL ANALYSIS OF A BALANCE SHEET

Using the following comparative balance sheet for the Supreme Construction Company as of December 31, 2018 and 2019, prepare a horizontal analysis of this balance sheet for the owner, Randy McQueen.

Supreme Construction Company
Comparative Balance Sheet
December 31, 2018 and 2019

Assets	2019	2018
Current Assets		
Cash	$ 3,500	$ 2,900
Accounts Receivable	12,450	7,680
Supplies	2,140	3,200
Total Current Assets	18,090	13,780
Property, Plant, and Equipment		
Land	15,000	15,000
Buildings	54,000	61,000
Machinery and Equipment	134,200	123,400
Total Property, Plant, and Equipment	203,200	199,400
Total Assets	$ 221,290	$ 213,180
Liabilities and Owner's Equity		
Current Liabilities		
Accounts Payable	$ 5,300	$ 4,100
Notes Payable	8,500	9,400
Total Current Liabilities	13,800	13,500
Long-Term Liabilities		
Mortgage Payable	26,330	28,500
Note Payable on Equipment (5-year)	10,250	11,430
Total Long-Term Liabilities	36,580	39,930
Total Liabilities	50,380	53,430
Owner's Equity		
Randy McQueen, Capital	170,910	159,750
Total Liabilities and Owner's Equity	$ 221,290	$ 213,180

►SOLUTIONSTRATEGY

Using the steps for horizontal analysis, perform the following operation on all balance sheet items and then enter the results on the statement.

Cash
2014 amount − 2013 amount = 3,500 − 2,900
$$= \$600 \text{ Increase}$$

$$\text{Percent change} = \frac{\text{Amount of change}}{\text{Previous period amount}} = \frac{600}{2,900} = .20689 = 20.7\%$$

Supreme Construction Company
Comparative Balance Sheet
December 31, 2018 and 2019

Assets	2019	2018	Increase (Decrease) Amount	Percent
Current Assets				
Cash	$ 3,500	$ 2,900	$ 600	20.7%
Accounts Receivable	12,450	7,680	4,770	62.1
Supplies	2,140	3,200	(1,060)	(33.1)
Total Current Assets	18,090	13,780	4,310	31.3

Property, Plant, and Equipment

Land	15,000	15,000	0	0
Buildings	54,000	61,000	(7,000)	(11.5)
Machinery and Equipment	134,200	123,400	10,800	8.8
Total Property, Plant, and Equipment	203,200	199,400	3,800	1.9
Total Assets	$221,290	$213,180	$8,110	3.8%

Liabilities and Owner's Equity

Current Liabilities

Accounts Payable	$ 5,300	$ 4,100	$ 1,200	29.3%
Notes Payable	8,500	9,400	(900)	(9.6)
Total Current Liabilities	13,800	13,500	300	2.2

Long-Term Liabilities

Mortgage Payable	26,330	28,500	(2,170)	(7.6)
Note Payable on Equipment (5-year)	10,250	11,430	(1,180)	(10.3)
Total Long-Term Liabilities	36,580	39,930	(3,350)	(8.4)
Total Liabilities	50,380	53,430	(3,050)	(5.7)

Owner's Equity

Randy McQueen, Capital	170,910	159,750	11,160	7.0
Total Liabilities and Owner's Equity	$221,290	$213,180	$ 8,110	3.8%

►TRYITEXERCISE 3

Complete the following comparative balance sheet with horizontal analysis for Calypso Industries, Inc.

Calypso Industries, Inc.
Comparative Balance Sheet
December 31, 2018 and 2019

			Increase (Decrease)	
Assets	2019	2018	Amount	Percent
Current Assets				
Cash	$ 8,700	$ 5,430	_____	_____
Accounts Receivable	23,110	18,450	_____	_____
Notes Receivable	2,900	3,400	_____	_____
Supplies	4,540	3,980	_____	_____
Total Current Assets			_____	_____
Property, Plant, and Equipment				
Land	34,000	34,000	_____	_____
Buildings	76,300	79,800	_____	_____
Machinery and Equipment	54,700	48,900	_____	_____
Total Property, Plant, and Equipment			_____	_____
Investments and Other Assets	54,230	49,810	_____	_____
Total Assets			_____	_____
Liabilities and Stockholders' Equity				
Current Liabilities				
Accounts Payable	$ 15,330	$ 19,650	_____	_____
Salaries Payable	7,680	7,190	_____	_____
Total Current Liabilities			_____	_____
Long-Term Liabilities				
Mortgage Payable	53,010	54,200	_____	_____
Note Payable (3-year)	32,400	33,560	_____	_____
Total Long-Term Liabilities			_____	_____
Total Liabilities			_____	_____

Liabilities and Stockholders' Equity	2019	2018		
Stockholders' Equity				
Common Stock	$130,060	$120,170	_____	_____
Retained Earnings	20,000	9,000	_____	_____
Total Liabilities and Stockholders' Equity			_____	_____

CHECK YOUR ANSWERS WITH THE SOLUTIONS ON PAGES 539–540.

REVIEW EXERCISES

15 SECTION I

Calculate the following values according to the accounting equation.

	Assets	Liabilities	Owner's Equity
1.	$283,000	$121,400	$161,600
2.	$548,900	$335,900	$213,000
3.	$45,300	$29,000	$16,300
4.	$657,300	$241,100	_____
5.	_____	$1,366,500	$2,117,000
6.	$830,400	_____	$210,800
7.	_____	$406,000	$2,000,200
8.	$15,909,000	$6,339,100	_____

JUMP
START
WWW

Calculate the missing items in the the balance sheet for each company below. Complete each company's column; then move on to the next column.

THE BALANCE SHEET (in millions)			
	Exercise 9	Exercise 10	Exercise 11
Company Date	Redrescue, Inc. February 2, 20XX	Weekers, Inc. December 31, 20XX	Intersec, Inc. February 1, 20XX
Current Assets	$15,279	$24,625	_____
Fixed and Other Assets—net	25,239	_____	3,419
Total Assets	_____	40,159	7,849
Current Liabilities	10,749	22,980	_____
Long-Term and Other Liabilities	17,247	_____	2,342
Total Liabilities	_____	30,413	4,787
Stockholders' Equity	_____	_____	_____

For the following balance sheet items, check the appropriate category.

		Current Asset	Fixed Asset	Current Liability	Long-Term Liability	Owner's Equity
12.	Land	____	____	____	____	____
13.	Supplies	____	____	____	____	____
14.	Marketable securities	____	____	____	____	____
15.	Retained earnings	____	____	____	____	____

		Current Asset	Fixed Asset	Current Liability	Long-Term Liability	Owner's Equity
16.	Buildings	___	___	___	___	___
17.	Mortgage payable	___	___	___	___	___
18.	Cash	___	___	___	___	___
19.	Notes payable	___	___	___	___	___
20.	Equipment	___	___	___	___	___
21.	Note receivable (3-month)	___	___	___	___	___
22.	Prepaid expenses	___	___	___	___	___
23.	Merchandise inventory	___	___	___	___	___
24.	Common stock	___	___	___	___	___
25.	Trucks	___	___	___	___	___
26.	Debenture bonds	___	___	___	___	___
27.	Accounts receivable	___	___	___	___	___
28.	Salaries payable	___	___	___	___	___
29.	R. Smith, capital	___	___	___	___	___
30.	Savings account	___	___	___	___	___
31.	Preferred stock	___	___	___	___	___

32. Perform a vertical analysis for the balance sheet entry "Accounts Payable" given below. (Round to nearest tenth.)

Liabilities and Qwner's Equity

Current Liabilities		
Accounts Payable	$11,800	???
Salaries Payable	3,200	
Taxes Payable	4,000	
Total Current Liabilities	19,000	
Long-Term Liabilities		
Debenture Bond	17,000	
Total Liabilities	36,000	
Stockholder's Equity		
Retained Earnings	47,000	
Total Liabilities and Stockholder's Equity	$83,000	

33. Perform a horizontal analysis for the balance sheet entry "Cash" given below. That is, find the amount of increase or decrease and the associated percent (rounded to the nearest tenth.)

Assets	2019	2018	Increase/Decrease Amount	Percent
Current Assets				
Cash	$ 18,600	$11,900	???	???
Accounts Receivable	22,300	18,100		
Merchandise Inventory	30,100	25,900		
Supplies	5,600	7,600		
Total Current Assets	76,600	63,300		
Property, Plant, and Equipment				
Machinery and Equipment	56,000	57,100		
Total Assets	$132,600	$120,400		

Prepare the following statements on separate sheets of paper.

34. a. Use the following financial information to calculate the owner's equity and prepare a balance sheet with vertical analysis as of December 31, 2018, for Victory Lane Sporting Goods, a sole proprietorship owned by Kyle Pressman: current assets, $157,600; property, plant, and equipment, $42,000; investments and other assets, $35,700; current liabilities, $21,200; and long-term liabilities, $53,400.

Victory Lane Sporting Goods
Balance Sheet
December 31, 2018

b. The following financial information is for Victory Lane Sporting Goods as of December 31, 2019: current assets, $175,300; property, plant, and equipment, $43,600; investments and other assets, $39,200; current liabilities, $27,700; and long-term liabilities, $51,000.

   Calculate the owner's equity for 2019 and prepare a comparative balance sheet with horizontal analysis for 2018 and 2019.

Victory Lane Sporting Goods
Comparative Balance Sheet
December 31, 2018 and 2019

35. a. Use the following financial information to prepare a balance sheet with vertical analysis as of June 30, 2018, for Stargate Industries, Inc.: cash, $44,300; accounts receivable, $127,600; merchandise inventory, $88,100; prepaid maintenance, $4,100; office supplies, $4,000; land, $154,000; building, $237,000; fixtures, $21,400; vehicles, $64,000; computers, $13,000; goodwill, $20,000; investments, $32,000; accounts payable, $55,700; salaries payable, $23,200; notes payable (6-month), $38,000; mortgage payable, $91,300; debenture bonds, $165,000; common stock, $350,000; and retained earnings, $86,300.

Stargate Industries, Inc.
Balance Sheet
June 30, 2018

b. The following financial information is for Stargate Industries as of June 30, 2019: cash, $40,200; accounts receivable, $131,400; merchandise inventory, $92,200; prepaid maintenance, $3,700; office supplies, $6,200; land, $154,000; building, $231,700; fixtures, $23,900; vehicles, $55,100; computers, $16,800; goodwill, $22,000; investments, $36,400; accounts payable, $51,800; salaries payable, $25,100; notes payable (6-month), $19,000; mortgage payable, $88,900; debenture bonds, $165,000; common stock, $350,000; and retained earnings, $113,800.

   Prepare a comparative balance sheet with horizontal analysis for 2018 and 2019.

Stargate Industries, Inc.
Comparative Balance Sheet
June 30, 2018 and 2019

BUSINESS DECISION: THE BALANCE SHEET

36. From the consolidated balance sheets giving historical data for Macy's on the following page,

   a. Prepare a horizontal analysis of the Current Assets section comparing February 2, 2013 and February 1, 2014.

   b. Prepare a vertical analysis of the Current Liabilities section for February 1, 2014.

Macy's, established in 1858, opened as a small, fancy dry goods store on the corner of 14th Street and 6th Avenue in New York City. With corporate offices in Cincinnati and New York, today Macy's is one of the nation's premier retailers. Together with its subsidiaries, Macy's, Inc. operates 850 stores in 45 states, the District of Columbia, Guam, and Puerto Rico under the names Macy's and Bloomingdale's, as well as the websites www.macys.com and www.bloomingdales.com.

The company's retail stores and websites sell a range of merchandise, including men's, women's, and children's apparel and accessories and cosmetics, home furnishings, and other consumer goods. The company, formerly known as Federated Department Stores, Inc., changed its name to Macy's, Inc. in June 2007.

DW labs Incorporated/Shutterstock.com

MACY'S, INC.
CONSOLIDATED BALANCE SHEETS
(in millions)

	February 1, 2014	February 2, 2013
ASSETS		
Current Assets:		
Cash and Cash Equivalents	$ 2,273	$ 1,836
Receivables	438	371
Merchandise Inventories	5,557	5,308
Prepaid Expenses and Other Current Assets	420	361
Total Current Assets	8,688	7,876
Property and Equipment—Net	7,930	8,196
Goodwill	3,743	3,743
Other Intangible Assets—Net	527	561
Other Assets	746	615
Total Assets	$21,634	$20,991
LIABILITIES AND SHAREHOLDERS' EQUITY		
Current Liabilities:		
Short-Term Debt	$ 463	$ 124
Merchandise Accounts Payable	1,691	1,579
Accounts Payable and Accrued Liabilities	2,810	2,610
Income Taxes	362	355
Deferred Income Taxes	400	407
Total Current Liabilities	5,726	5,075
Long-Term Debt	6,728	6,806
Deferred Income Taxes	1,273	1,238
Other Liabilities	1,658	1,821
Shareholders' Equity	6,249	6,051
Total Liabilities and Shareholders' Equity	$21,634	$20,991

THE INCOME STATEMENT

THE BOTTOM LINE

When all is said and done, the question is how well did the business do. The real score is found on the income statement. An **income statement**, also known as an **operating statement** or **profit and loss statement**, is a summary of the operations of a business over a period of time—usually a month, a quarter, or a year. For any business to exist, it must have earnings as well as expenses in the form of either cash or credit. The income statement shows the **revenue**, or earnings, of the business from the sale of goods and services; the **expenses**, the costs incurred to generate that revenue; and the bottom line **profit** or **loss**, the difference between revenue and expenses.

> **Profit (or Loss) = Revenue − Total Expenses**

where: Revenue = Earnings (either cash or credit) from sales during the period

Total expenses = Cost of goods sold + Operating expenses + Taxes

income, operating, or profit and loss statement Financial statement summarizing the operations of a business over a period of time. Illustrates the amount of revenue earned, expenses incurred, and the resulting profit or loss: Revenue − Total Expenses = Profit (or loss).

revenue The primary source of money, both cash and credit, flowing into the business from its customers for goods sold or services rendered over a period of time.

expenses Costs incurred by a business in the process of earning revenue.

PREPARING AN INCOME STATEMENT

15-4

Once again, let's begin by looking at a typical income statement. As before, we will use Hypothetical Enterprises, Inc. to illustrate. Carefully look over the following income statement and then read the descriptions of each section and its components.

profit or loss The difference between revenue earned and expenses incurred during an operating period—profit when revenue is greater than expenses; loss when expenses are greater than revenue. Profit is also known as earnings or income.

Hypothetical Enterprises, Inc.
Income Statement for the Year Ended December 31, 20XX

Revenue		
Gross Sales	$923,444	
Less: Sales Returns and Allowances	22,875	
Sales Discounts	3,625	
Net Sales		$896,944
Cost of Goods Sold		
Merchandise Inventory, Jan. 1	220,350	
Net Purchases	337,400	
Freight In	12,350	
Goods Available for Sale	570,100	
Less: Merchandise Inventory, Dec. 31	88,560	
Cost of Goods Sold		481,540
Gross Margin		415,404
Operating Expenses		
Salaries and Benefits	152,600	
Rent and Utilities	35,778	
Advertising and Promotion	32,871	
Insurance	8,258	
General and Administrative Expenses	41,340	
Depreciation	19,890	
Miscellaneous Expenses	14,790	
Total Operating Expenses		305,527
Income before Taxes		109,877
Income Tax		18,609
Net Income		$91,268

> ### Learning Tip
>
> Keep in mind that an income statement covers a *period* of time, whereas a balance sheet covers a *moment* in time.

B-A-C-O/Shutterstock.com

INCOME STATEMENT COMPONENTS

REVENUE　The revenue section of the income statement represents the primary source of money, both cash and credit, flowing into the business from its customers for goods sold or services rendered.

> Gross sales
> − Sales returns and allowances
> − Sales discounts
> ──────────────────
> Net sales

- Gross sales—Total sales of goods and services achieved by the company during the operating period.
- Sales returns and allowances—Amount of merchandise returned for cash or credit by customers for various reasons.
- Sales discounts—Cash discounts given to customers by the business as an incentive for early payment of an invoice (for example, 3/15, n/45, where a 3% extra discount is given if the invoice is paid within 15 days rather than the net date of 45 days).
- Net sales—Amount received after taking into consideration returned goods, allowances, and sales discounts.

COST OF GOODS SOLD　The cost of goods sold section represents the cost to the business of the merchandise that was sold during the operating period.

> Merchandise inventory (beginning)
> + Net purchases
> + Freight in
> ──────────────────
> Goods available for sale
> − Merchandise inventory (ending)
> ──────────────────
> Cost of goods sold

- Merchandise inventory (beginning of operating period)—Total value of the goods in inventory at the beginning of the operating period. This *beginning inventory* is last period's ending inventory.
- Net purchases—Amount, at cost, of merchandise purchased during the period for resale to customers after purchase returns and allowances and purchase discounts earned are deducted.
- Freight in—Total amount of the freight or transportation charges incurred for the net purchases.
- Goods available for sale—The total amount of the goods available to be sold during the operating period. It is the sum of beginning inventory, net purchases, and freight in.
- Merchandise inventory (end of operating period)—Total value of the goods remaining in inventory at the end of the operating period. This *ending inventory* is next period's beginning inventory.
- Cost of goods sold—Total value of the goods that were sold during the period. It is the difference between goods available for sale and the ending merchandise inventory.

GROSS MARGIN　Gross margin, also known as gross profit, represents the difference between net sales and cost of goods sold.

> Net sales
> − Cost of goods sold
> ──────────────────
> Gross margin

TOTAL OPERATING EXPENSES　Total operating expenses are the sum of all expenses incurred by the business during the operating period except the cost of goods sold and taxes. Operating expenses differ from company to company. Some typical examples are salaries and benefits, sales commissions, rent and utilities, advertising and promotion, insurance, general and administrative expenses, depreciation, and miscellaneous expenses.

INCOME BEFORE TAXES　This figure represents the money a company made before paying income tax. It is the difference between gross margin and total operating expenses.

> Gross margin
> − Total operating expenses
> ──────────────────
> Income before taxes

IN THE Business World

The phrase *all to the good* is derived from an old accounting term. The word *good* was used in the nineteenth century to mean *profit*. Thus, after expenses were taken out, the rest "went to the good!"

rtguest/Shutterstock.com

INCOME TAX   This expense figure is the amount of income tax, both state and federal, that is paid by the business during the operating period.

NET INCOME, NET PROFIT, or NET LOSS   Literally the bottom line of the income statement. It is the difference between income before taxes and the income tax paid.

Income before taxes
− Income tax
Net income (loss)

STEPS TO PREPARE AN INCOME STATEMENT

STEP 1.   Centered at the top of the page, write the company name, type of statement, and period of time covered by the statement (for example, "Year ended Dec. 31, 2019" or "April 2019").

STEP 2.   In a two-column format as illustrated on page 513, calculate:

   a.   *Net Sales:*

Gross sales
− Sales returns and allowances
− Sales discounts
Net sales

   b.   *Cost of Goods Sold:*

Merchandise inventory (beginning)
+ Net purchases
+ Freight in
Goods available for sale
− Merchandise inventory (ending)
Cost of goods sold

   c.   *Gross Margin:*

Net sales
− Cost of goods sold
Gross margin

   d.   *Total Operating Expenses:* Sum of all operating expenses

   e.   *Income before Taxes:*

Gross margin
− Total operating expenses
Income before taxes

   f.   *Net Income:*

Income before taxes
− Income tax
Net income (loss)

iStock.com/Nikada

EXAMPLE 4   PREPARING AN INCOME STATEMENT

Use the following financial information to prepare an income statement for Royal Equipment Supply, Inc. for the year ended December 31, 20XX: gross sales, $458,400; sales returns and allowances, $13,200; sales discounts, $1,244; merchandise inventory, Jan. 1, 20XX, $198,700; merchandise inventory, Dec. 31, 20XX, $76,400; net purchases, $86,760; freight in, $875; salaries, $124,200; rent, $21,000; utilities, $1,780; advertising, $5,400; insurance, $2,340; administrative expenses, $14,500; miscellaneous expenses, $6,000; and income tax, $17,335.

►SOLUTIONSTRATEGY

The income statement for Royal Equipment Supply, Inc. follows.

Royal Equipment Supply, Inc.
Income Statement
For the Year Ended December 31, 20XX

Revenue		
Gross Sales	$458,400	
Less: Sales Returns and Allowances	13,200	
Sales Discounts	1,244	
Net Sales		$443,956
Cost of Goods Sold		
Merchandise Inventory, Jan. 1	198,700	
Net Purchases	86,760	
Freight In	875	
Goods Available for Sale	286,335	
Less: Merchandise Inventory, Dec. 31	76,400	
Cost of Goods Sold		209,935
Gross Margin		234,021
Operating Expenses		
Salaries	124,200	
Rent	21,000	
Utilities	1,780	
Advertising	5,400	
Insurance	2,340	
Administrative Expenses	14,500	
Miscellaneous Expenses	6,000	
Total Operating Expenses		175,220
Income before Taxes		58,801
Income Tax		17,335
Net Income		$ 41,466

►TRYITEXERCISE 4

Use the following financial information to prepare an income statement for Cutting Edge Manufacturing, Inc., for the year ended December 31, 20XX: gross sales, $1,356,000; sales returns and allowances, $93,100; sales discounts, $4,268; merchandise inventory, Jan. 1, 20XX, $324,800; merchandise inventory, Dec. 31, 20XX, $179,100; net purchases, $255,320; freight in, $3,911; salaries, $375,900; rent, $166,000; utilities, $7,730; advertising, $73,300; insurance, $22,940; administrative expenses, $84,500; miscellaneous expenses, $24,900; and income tax, $34,760.

CHECK YOUR ANSWER WITH THE SOLUTION ON PAGE 540.

IN THE Business World

The popular business term *bottom line* literally comes from the structure of an income statement:

Total revenue
−Total expenses
Income (loss) ◄——— Bottom line

rtguest/Shutterstock.com

15-5

PREPARING A VERTICAL ANALYSIS OF AN INCOME STATEMENT

Vertical analysis can be applied to the income statement just as it was to the balance sheet. Each figure on the income statement is expressed as a percent of net sales (net sales = 100%). The resulting figures describe how net sales were distributed among the expenses and what percent was left as net profit. For analysis purposes, this information can then be compared with the figures from previous operating periods for the company, with competitors' figures, or with published industry averages for similar-size companies.

As with balance sheets, income statements with vertical analysis can be displayed in the format known as **common-size**, in which all figures on the statement appear as percentages.

common-size income statement A special form of income statement that lists only the vertical analysis percentages, not the dollar figures. All items are expressed as a percent of net sales.

STEPS TO PREPARE A VERTICAL ANALYSIS OF AN INCOME STATEMENT

STEP 1. Use the percentage formula, Rate = Portion ÷ Base, to find the rate of each item on the income statement. Use each item as the portion and net sales as the base.

STEP 2. Round each answer to the nearest tenth of a percent.

Note: A 0.1% differential may sometimes occur due to rounding.

STEP 3. List the percentage of each statement item in a column to the right of the monetary amount.

EXAMPLE5 PREPARING A VERTICAL ANALYSIS OF AN INCOME STATEMENT

Prepare a vertical analysis of the income statement for Hypothetical Enterprises, Inc., on page 513.

►SOLUTIONSTRATEGY

Using the steps for vertical analysis, perform the following calculation for each income statement item and enter the results on the income statement as follows:

$$\frac{\text{Gross sales}}{\text{Net sales}} = \frac{923,444}{896,944} = 1.0295 = \underline{103.0\%}$$

Hypothetical Enterprises, Inc.
Income Statement for the Year Ended December 31, 20XX

Revenue		
Gross Sales	$923,444	103.0% ◄
Less: Sales Returns and Allowances	22,875	2.6
Sales Discounts	3,625	.4
Net Sales	896,944	100.0%
Cost of Goods Sold		
Merchandise Inventory, Jan. 1	220,350	24.6
Net Purchases	337,400	37.6
Freight In	12,350	1.4
Goods Available for Sale	570,100	63.6
Less: Merchandise Inventory, Dec. 31	88,560	9.9
Cost of Goods Sold	481,540	53.7
Gross Margin	415,404	46.3
Operating Expenses		
Salaries and Benefits	152,600	17.0
Rent and Utilities	35,778	4.0
Advertising and Promotion	32,871	3.7
Insurance	8,258	.9
General and Administrative Expenses	41,340	4.6
Depreciation	19,890	2.2
Miscellaneous Expenses	14,790	1.6
Total Operating Expenses	305,527	34.1
Income before Taxes	109,877	12.3
Income Tax	18,609	2.1
Net Income	$ 91,268	10.2%

►TRYITEXERCISE 5

Prepare a vertical analysis of the income statement for Royal Equipment Supply, Inc., on page 516.

CHECK YOUR ANSWER WITH THE SOLUTION ON PAGE 540.

iStock.com/Nikada

15-6 PREPARING A HORIZONTAL ANALYSIS OF AN INCOME STATEMENT

As with the balance sheet, the income statement can be prepared in a format that compares the financial data of the business from one operating period to another. This horizontal analysis provides percent increase or decrease information for each item on the income statement. Such information provides a useful progress report of the company. As before, the previous or original period figure is the base.

STEPS TO PREPARE A HORIZONTAL ANALYSIS OF AN INCOME STATEMENT

STEP 1. Set up a comparative income statement format with the current period listed first and the previous period listed next.

STEP 2. Label the next two columns: $\dfrac{\text{Increase (Decrease)}}{\text{Amount} \quad \text{Percent}}$

STEP 3. For each item on the income statement, calculate the dollar difference between the current and the previous period and enter this figure in the Amount column. Enter all decreases in parentheses.

STEP 4. Calculate the percent change (increase or decrease) by the percentage formula:

$$\text{Percent change (rate)} = \frac{\text{Amount of change, Step 3 (portion)}}{\text{Previous period amount (base)}}$$

STEP 5. Enter the percent change, rounded to the nearest tenth of a percent, in the Percent column. Once again, enter all decreases in parentheses.

EXAMPLE 6 PREPARING A HORIZONTAL ANALYSIS OF AN INCOME STATEMENT

A comparative income statement for Foremost Furniture, Inc. for 2018 and 2019 follows. Prepare a horizontal analysis of the statement for the company.

Foremost Furniture, Inc.
Comparative Income Statement

	2019	2018
Revenue		
Gross Sales	$623,247	$599,650
Less: Sales Returns and Allowances	8,550	9,470
Sales Discounts	3,400	1,233
Net Sales	611,297	588,947
Cost of Goods Sold		
Merchandise Inventory, Jan. 1	158,540	134,270
Purchases	117,290	111,208
Freight In	2,460	1,980
Goods Available for Sale	278,290	247,458
Less: Merchandise Inventory, Dec. 31	149,900	158,540
Cost of Goods Sold	128,390	88,918
Gross Margin	482,907	500,029
Operating Expenses		
Salaries and Benefits	165,300	161,200
Rent and Utilities	77,550	76,850
Depreciation	74,350	75,040
Insurance	4,560	3,900
Office Expenses	34,000	41,200
Warehouse Expenses	41,370	67,400
Total Operating Expenses	397,130	425,590
Income before Taxes	85,777	74,439
Income Tax	27,400	19,700
Net Income	$ 58,377	$ 54,739

iStock.com/Nikada

▶SOLUTIONSTRATEGY

Using the steps for horizontal analysis, perform the following operation on all income statement items and then enter the results on the statement.

Gross Sales   2019 amount − 2018 amount = Amount of change
$$623,247 - 599,650 = \underline{\$23,597 \text{ increase}}$$

$$\text{Percent change} = \frac{\text{Amount of change}}{\text{Previous period amount}} = \frac{23,597}{599,650} = \underline{3.9\%}$$

Foremost Furniture, Inc.
Comparative Income Statement

	2019	2018	Increase (Decrease) Amount	Percent
Revenue				
Gross Sales	$623,247	$599,650	$23,597	3.9%
Less: Sales Returns and Allowances	8,550	9,470	(920)	(9.7)
Sales Discounts	3,400	1,233	2,167	175.8
Net Sales	611,297	588,947	22,350	3.8
Cost of Goods Sold				
Merchandise Inventory, Jan. 1	158,540	134,270	24,270	18.1
Purchases	117,290	111,208	6,082	5.5
Freight In	2,460	1,980	480	24.2
Goods Available for Sale	278,290	247,458	30,832	12.5
Less: Merchandise Inventory, Dec. 31	149,900	158,540	(8,640)	(5.4)
Cost of Goods Sold	128,390	88,918	39,472	44.4
Gross Margin	482,907	500,029	(17,122)	(3.4)
Operating Expenses				
Salaries and Benefits	165,300	161,200	4,100	2.5
Rent and Utilities	77,550	76,850	700	.9
Depreciation	74,350	75,040	(690)	(.9)
Insurance	4,560	3,900	660	16.9
Office Expenses	34,000	41,200	(7,200)	(17.5)
Warehouse Expenses	41,370	67,400	(26,030)	(38.6)
Total Operating Expenses	397,130	425,590	(28,460)	(6.7)
Income before Taxes	85,777	74,439	11,338	15.2
Income Tax	27,400	19,700	7,700	39.1
Net Income	$ 58,377	$ 54,739	$ 3,638	6.6%

▶TRYITEXERCISE 6

Complete the following comparative income statement with horizontal analysis for Timely Watch Company, Inc.

Timely Watch Company, Inc.
Comparative Income Statement

	2019	2018	Increase (Decrease) Amount	Percent
Revenue				
Gross Sales	$1,223,000	$996,500	_____	_____
Less: Sales Returns and Allowances	121,340	99,600	_____	_____
Sales Discounts	63,120	51,237	_____	_____
Net Sales	_____	_____	_____	_____
Cost of Goods Sold				
Merchandise Inventory, Jan. 1	311,200	331,000	_____	_____
Purchases	603,290	271,128	_____	_____
Freight In	18,640	13,400	_____	_____
Goods Available for Sale			_____	_____
Less: Merchandise Inventory, Dec. 31	585,400	311,200	_____	_____
Cost of Goods Sold			_____	_____
Gross Margin			_____	_____

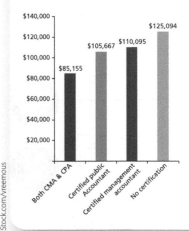

	2019	2018	Increase (Decrease) Amount	Percent
Operating Expenses				
Salaries and Benefits	215,200	121,800	_____	_____
Rent and Utilities	124,650	124,650	_____	_____
Depreciation	43,500	41,230	_____	_____
Insurance	24,970	23,800	_____	_____
Administrative Store Expenses	58,200	33,900	_____	_____
Warehouse Expenses	42,380	45,450	_____	_____
Total Operating Expenses	_____	_____	_____	_____
Income before Taxes	_____	_____	_____	_____
Income Tax	66,280	41,670	_____	_____
Net Income	_____	_____	_____	_____

CHECK YOUR ANSWERS WITH THE SOLUTIONS ON PAGES 540–541.

SECTION II · 15 · REVIEW EXERCISES

Calculate the missing information based on the format of the income statement.

	Net Sales	Cost of Goods Sold	Gross Margin	Operating Expenses	Net Profit
1.	$565,700	$244,600	$321,100	$276,400	$44,700
2.	$4,232,000	$2,362,000	$1,870,000	$1,210,500	$659,500
3.	$705,300	$398,450	$306,850	$196,525	$110,325
4.	$334,500	$132,300	_____	$108,000	_____
5.	$1,640,000	_____	$760,000	$354,780	_____
6.	_____	$257,000	$418,530	_____	$84,370
7.	$341,300	$186,740	_____	_____	$68,050
8.	$7.64 million	_____	$2.75 million	$1.68 million	_____

Calculate the missing items in the income statement for each company below. Complete each company's column; then move on to the next column.

	THE INCOME STATEMENT		
	Exercise 9	Exercise 10	Exercise 11
Company Year Ended	Maxiton, Inc. December 31, 20XX (in millions)	Coreindi Co. December 31, 20XX (in thousands)	Univast February 3, 20XX (in thousands)
Revenue	$123,133	$9,475,313	_____
Cost of Goods Sold	100,627	_____	4,696,098
Gross Margin	_____	4,934,907	2,062,139
Operating Expenses	15,278	3,104,684	_____
Income before Taxes	_____	_____	651,217
Income Tax*	3,351	_____	_____
Net Income (loss)	_____	1,069,744	389,529

*Also includes interest expense and other income and losses.

12. For the third quarter, Micro Tech had gross sales of $315,450, sales returns and allowances of $23,100, and sales discounts of $18,700. What were the net sales?

13. For August, Island Traders, Inc. had the following financial information: merchandise inventory, August 1, $244,500; merchandise inventory, August 31, $193,440; gross purchases, $79,350; purchase returns and allowances, $8,700; and freight in, $970.

   a. What is the amount of the goods available for sale?

   b. What is the cost of goods sold for August?

   c. If net sales were $335,000, what was the gross margin for August?

   d. If total operating expenses were $167,200, what was the net profit?

14. Perform a vertical analysis for the entry "Gross Sales" on the portion of an income statement shown below. (Round to nearest tenth.)

   Revenue

Gross Sales	$185,000	???
Less: Sales Returns and Allowances	11,800	
Net Sales	173,200	

   Cost of Goods Sold

Merchandise Inventory, Jan. 1	69,200
Net Purchases	58,300
Goods Available for Sale	128,450
Less: Merchandise Inventory, Dec. 31	85,000
Cost of Goods Sold	43,450
Gross Margin	129,750

15. Perform a horizontal analysis for the entry "Gross Sales" shown on the income statement portion below. (Round to nearest tenth.)

			Increase/Decrease	
	2019	**2018**	**Amount**	**Percent**
Revenue				
Gross Sales	$279,000	$200,900	???	???
Less: Sales Returns and Allowances	14,200	12,400		
Net Sales	264,800	188,500		
Cost of Goods Sold				
Merchandise Inventory, Jan. 1	31,900	33,800		
Net Purchases	60,300	55,500		
Goods Available for Sale	92,200	89,300		
Less: Merchandise Inventory, Dec. 31	43,000	60,200		
Cost of Goods Sold	49,200	29,100		
Gross Margin	215,600	159,400		

Prepare the following statements on separate sheets of paper.

16. a. As the assistant accounting manager for Jefferson Airplane Parts, Inc., construct an income statement with vertical analysis for the first quarter of 2019 from the following information: gross sales, $240,000; sales discounts, $43,500; beginning inventory, Jan. 1, $86,400; ending inventory, March 31, $103,200; net purchases, $76,900; total operating expenses, $108,000; and income tax, $14,550.

Jefferson Airplane Parts, Inc.
Income Statement
January 1 to March 31, 2019

    b. You have just received a report with the second-quarter figures. Prepare a comparative income statement with horizontal analysis for the first and second quarter of 2019: gross sales, $297,000; sales discounts, $41,300; beginning inventory, April 1, $103,200; ending inventory, June 30, $96,580; net purchases, $84,320; total operating expenses, $126,700; and income tax, $16,400.

Jefferson Airplane Parts, Inc.
Comparative Income Statement
First and Second Quarter, 2019

17. a. Use the following financial information to construct a 2018 income statement with vertical analysis for the Sweets & Treats Candy Company, Inc.: gross sales, $2,249,000; sales returns and allowances, $143,500; sales discounts, $54,290; merchandise inventory, Jan. 1, $875,330; merchandise inventory, Dec. 31, $716,090; net purchases, $546,920; freight in, $11,320; salaries, $319,800; rent, $213,100; depreciation, $51,200; utilities, $35,660; advertising, $249,600; insurance, $39,410; administrative expenses, $91,700; miscellaneous expenses, $107,500; and income tax, $38,450.

Sweets & Treats Candy Company, Inc.
Income Statement, 2018

    b. The following data represents Sweets & Treats' operating results for 2019. Prepare a comparative income statement with horizontal analysis for 2018 and 2019: gross sales, $2,125,000; sales returns and allowances, $126,400; sales discounts, $73,380; merchandise inventory, Jan. 1, 2019, $716,090; merchandise inventory, Dec. 31, 2019, $584,550; net purchases, $482,620; freight in, $9,220; salaries, $340,900; rent, $215,000; depreciation, $56,300; utilities, $29,690; advertising, $217,300; insurance, $39,410; administrative expenses, $95,850; miscellaneous expenses, $102,500; and income tax, $44,530.

Sweets & Treats Candy Company, Inc.
Comparative Income Statement, 2018 and 2019

BUSINESS DECISION: THE INCOME STATEMENT

18. The following historical data is from the consolidated income statements filed by Comcast Corporation.

    a. Prepare a horizontal analysis of the net income comparing 2012 and 2013.

    b. Prepare a vertical analysis of the costs and expenses for 2013.

COMCAST CORPORATION
CONSOLIDATED STATEMENT OF INCOME

Year ended December 31 (in millions, except per share data)	2013	2012	2011
Revenue	$64,657	$62,570	$55,842
Costs and Expenses:			
Programming and production	19,670	19,929	16,596
Other operating and administrative	18,584	17,833	16,646
Advertising, marketing and promotion	4,969	4,831	4,243
Depreciation	6,254	6,150	6,040
Amortization	1,617	1,648	1,596
	51,094	50,391	45,121
Operating Income	13,563	12,179	10,721
Other Income (Expense):			
Interest expense	(2,574)	(2,521)	(2,505)
Investment income (loss), net	576	219	159
Equity in net income (losses) of investees, net	(86)	959	(35)
Other income (expense), net	(364)	773	(133)
	(2,448)	(570)	(2,514)
Income before income taxes	11,115	11,609	8,207
Income tax expense	(3,980)	(3,744)	(3,050)
Net income	7,135	7,865	5,157
Net (income) loss attributable to noncontrolling interests and redeemable subsidiary preferred stock	(319)	(1,662)	(997)
Net Income Attributable to Comcast Corporation	$6,816	$6,203	$4,160
Basic earnings per common share attributable to Comcast Corporation shareholders	$2.60	$2.32	$1.51
Diluted earnings per common share attributable to Comcast Corporation shareholders	$2.56	$2.28	$1.50
Dividends declared per common share	$0.78	$0.65	$0.45

Comcast Corporation (Nasdaq: CMCSA, CMCSK) (www.comcast.com) is one of the world's leading media, entertainment, and communications companies. Comcast is principally involved in the operation of cable systems through Comcast Cable and in the development, production, and distribution of entertainment, news, sports, and other content for global audiences through NBCUniversal. Comcast Cable is one of the nation's largest video, high-speed Internet, and phone providers to residential and business customers. Comcast is the majority owner and manager of NBCUniversal, which owns and operates entertainment and news cable networks, the NBC and Telemundo broadcast networks, local television station groups, television production operations, a major motion picture company, and theme parks.
Source: Comcast Corporation

FINANCIAL RATIOS AND TREND ANALYSIS

15 SECTION III

financial ratios A series of comparisons of financial statement components in ratio form used by analysts to evaluate the operating performance of a company.

In addition to vertical and horizontal analysis of financial statements, managers, creditors, and investors also study comparisons among various components on the statements. These comparisons are expressed as ratios and are known as **financial ratios**.

Basically, financial ratios represent an effort by analysts to standardize financial information, which in turn makes comparisons more meaningful. The fundamental purpose of ratio analysis is to indicate areas requiring further investigation. Think of them as signals indicating areas of potential strength or weakness of the firm. Frequently, financial ratios have to be examined more closely to discover their true meaning. A high ratio, for example, might indicate that the numerator figure is too high or the denominator figure is too low.

Financial ratios fall into four major categories:

- **Liquidity ratios** tell how well a company can pay off its short-term debts and meet unexpected needs for cash.

- **Efficiency ratios** indicate how effectively a company uses its resources to generate sales.

- **Leverage ratios** show how and to what degree a company has financed its assets.

- **Profitability ratios** tell how much of each dollar of sales, assets, and stockholders' investment resulted in bottom-line net profit.

IN THE Business World

To be most meaningful, financial ratios should be compared with ratios from previous operating periods of the company and with industry statistics for similar-size companies.

This information can be found in the annual publication *Industry Norms* and *Key Business Ratios*, produced by Dun and Bradstreet, or in *The Survey of Current Business*, published by the U.S. Department of Commerce.

15-7   CALCULATING FINANCIAL RATIOS

ratio A comparison of one amount to another.

StockLite/Shutterstock.com

Managers analyze financial statement data to determine strengths and weaknesses of a business.

As we learned in Chapter 5, a **ratio** is a comparison of one amount to another. A financial ratio is simply a ratio whose numerator and denominator are financial information taken from the balance sheet, the income statement, or other important business data.

Ratios may be stated a number of ways. For example, a ratio of credit sales, $40,000, to total sales, $100,000, in a retail store may be stated as follows:

a. Credit sales ratio is $\dfrac{40,000}{100,000}$,
    or 4 to 10,
    or 2 to 5 (written 2:5).

b. Credit sales are $\dfrac{4}{10}$, or 40% of total sales.

c. For every $1.00 of sales, $0.40 is on credit.

Conversely, the ratio of total sales, $100,000, to credit sales, $40,000, in a retail store may be stated as follows:

a. Total sales ratio is $\dfrac{100,000}{40,000}$,
    or 10 to 4,
    or 2.5 to 1 (written 2.5:1).

b. Total sales are $\dfrac{10}{4}$, or 250% of credit sales.

c. For every $2.50 of sales, $1.00 is on credit.

To illustrate how ratios are used in financial analysis, let's apply this concept to Hypothetical Enterprises, Inc., a company introduced in Sections I and II of this chapter.

EXAMPLE7   CALCULATING FINANCIAL RATIOS

Calculate the financial ratios for Hypothetical Enterprises, Inc., using the data from the financial statements presented on pages 501 and 513.

►SOLUTIONSTRATEGY

Liquidity Ratios

liquidity ratios Financial ratios that tell how well a company can pay off its short-term debts and meet unexpected needs for cash.

working capital The difference between current assets and current liabilities at a point in time. Theoretically, the amount of money left over if all current liabilities are paid off by current assets.

current ratio or working capital ratio The comparison of a firm's current assets to current liabilities.

Businesses must have enough cash on hand to pay their bills as they come due. The **liquidity ratios** examine the relationship between a firm's current assets and its maturing obligations. The amount of a firm's working capital and these ratios are good indicators of a firm's ability to pay its bills over the next few months. Short-term creditors pay particular attention to these figures.

The term **working capital** refers to the difference between current assets and current liabilities at a point in time. Theoretically, it is the amount of money that would be left over if all current liabilities were paid off by current assets.

$$\textbf{Working capital = Current assets − Current liabilities}$$

Current ratio or **working capital ratio** is the comparison of a firm's current assets to current liabilities. This ratio indicates the amount of current assets available to pay off $1 of current debt. A current ratio of 2:1 or greater is considered by banks and other lending institutions to be an acceptable ratio.

$$\textbf{Current ratio} = \dfrac{\textbf{Current assets}}{\textbf{Current liabilities}}$$

Hypothetical Enterprises, Inc.:

$$\text{Working capital} = 101,300 - 29,400 = \underline{\$71,900}$$

$$\text{Current ratio} = \dfrac{101,300}{29,400} = 3.45 = \underline{\underline{3.45:1}}$$

Analysis: This ratio shows that Hypothetical has $3.45 in current assets for each $1.00 it owes in current liabilities. A current ratio of 3.45:1 indicates that the company has more than sufficient means of covering short-term debts and is therefore in a strong liquidity position.

Acid test or **quick ratio** indicates a firm's ability to quickly liquidate assets to pay off current debt. This ratio recognizes that a firm's inventories are one of the least liquid current assets. Merchandise inventories and prepaid expenses are not part of quick assets because they are not readily convertible to cash. An acid test ratio of 1:1 or greater is considered acceptable.

> **acid test** or **quick ratio** A ratio that indicates a firm's ability to quickly liquidate assets to pay off current debt.

$$\text{Quick assets} = \text{Cash} + \text{Marketable securities} + \text{Receivables}$$

$$\text{Acid test ratio} = \frac{\text{Quick assets}}{\text{Current liabilities}}$$

Hypothetical Enterprises, Inc. (*Note:* Hypothetical has no marketable securities):

$$\text{Quick assets} = 13,000 + 32,500 = \underline{\$45,500}$$

$$\text{Acid test ratio} = \frac{45,500}{29,400} = 1.55 = \underline{\underline{1.55:1}}$$

Analysis: An acid test ratio of 1.55:1 also indicates a strong liquidity position. It means that Hypothetical has the ability to meet all short-term debt obligations immediately if necessary.

Efficiency Ratios

Efficiency ratios provide the basis for determining how effectively the firm is using its resources to generate sales. A firm with $500,000 in assets producing $1,000,000 in sales is using its resources more efficiently than a firm producing the same sales with $2,000,000 invested in assets.

> **efficiency ratios** Financial ratios that indicate how effectively a company uses its resources to generate sales.

Average collection period indicates how quickly a firm's credit accounts are being collected and is a good measure of how efficiently a firm is managing its accounts receivable. *Note:* When credit sales figures are not available, net sales may be used instead.

> **average collection period** Indicator of how quickly a firm's credit accounts are being collected. Expressed in days.

$$\text{Average collection period} = \frac{\text{Accounts receivable} \times 365}{\text{Credit sales}}$$

Hypothetical Enterprises, Inc.:

$$\text{Average collection period} = \frac{32,500 \times 365}{896,944} = \frac{11,862,500}{896,944} = 13.23 = \underline{13 \text{ Days}}$$

Analysis: This ratio tells us that on average, Hypothetical's credit customers take 13 days to pay their bills. Because most industries average between 30 and 60 days, the firm's 13-day collection period is favorable and shows considerable efficiency in handling credit accounts.

Inventory turnover is the number of times during an operating period that the average inventory was sold.

> **inventory turnover** The number of times during an operating period that the average inventory was sold.

$$\text{Average inventory} = \frac{\text{Beginning inventory} + \text{Ending inventory}}{2}$$

$$\text{Inventory turnover} = \frac{\text{Cost of goods sold}}{\text{Average inventory}}$$

Hypothetical Enterprises, Inc.:

$$\text{Average inventory} = \frac{220,350 + 88,560}{2} = \underline{\$154,455}$$

$$\text{Inventory turnover} = \frac{481,540}{154,455} = 3.12 = \underline{3.1 \text{ Times}}$$

Analysis: Inventory turnover is one ratio that should be compared with the data from previous operating periods and with published industry averages for similar-size firms in the same industry to draw meaningful conclusions. When inventory turnover is below average, it may be a signal that the company is carrying too much inventory. Carrying excess inventory can lead to extra expenses such as warehouse costs and insurance. It also ties up money that could be used more efficiently elsewhere.

asset turnover ratio Ratio that tells the number of dollars in sales a firm generates from each dollar it has invested in assets.

Asset turnover ratio tells the number of dollars in sales the firm generates from each dollar it has invested in assets. This ratio is an important measure of a company's efficiency in managing its assets.

$$\text{Asset turnover ratio} = \frac{\text{Net sales}}{\text{Total assets}}$$

Hypothetical Enterprises, Inc.:

$$\text{Asset turnover ratio} = \frac{896,944}{341,300} = 2.63 = \underline{2.63{:}1}$$

Analysis: Asset turnover is another ratio best compared with those of previous operating periods and industry averages to reach any meaningful conclusions. Hypothetical's 2.63:1 ratio means that the company is generating $2.63 in sales for every $1.00 in assets.

Leverage Ratios

leverage ratios Financial ratios that show how and to what degree a company has financed its assets.

When firms borrow money to finance assets, they are using financial leverage. Investors and creditors alike are particularly interested in the **leverage ratios** because the greater the leverage a firm has used, the greater the risk of default on interest and principal payments. Such situations could lead the firm into eventual bankruptcy.

debt-to-assets ratio Ratio that measures to what degree the assets of the firm have been financed with borrowed funds, or leveraged. It is commonly expressed as a percent.

Debt-to-assets ratio measures to what degree the assets of the firm have been financed with borrowed funds, or leveraged. This ratio identifies the claim on assets by the creditors. It is commonly expressed as a percent.

$$\text{Debt-to-assets ratio} = \frac{\text{Total liabilities}}{\text{Total assets}}$$

Hypothetical Enterprises, Inc.:

$$\text{Debt-to-assets ratio} = \frac{164,400}{341,300} = .4817 = \underline{48.2\%}$$

Analysis: This ratio indicates that Hypothetical's creditors have claim to 48.2% of the company assets, or for each $1.00 of assets, the company owes $0.48 to its creditors.

debt-to-equity ratio A ratio that compares the total debt of a firm to the owner's equity. It is commonly expressed as a percent.

Debt-to-equity ratio is used as a safety-factor measure for potential creditors. The ratio compares the total debt of the firm with the owner's equity. It tells the amount of debt incurred by the company for each $1 of equity. It is commonly expressed as a percent.

$$\text{Debt-to-equity ratio} = \frac{\text{Total liabilities}}{\text{Owner's equity}}$$

Hypothetical Enterprises, Inc.:

$$\text{Debt-to-equity ratio} = \frac{164,400}{176,900} = .929 = \underline{.929{:}1 \text{ or } 92.9\%}$$

Analysis: This ratio indicates that for each $1.00 of owner's equity, Hypothetical has financed $0.93 in assets. As the debt-to-equity ratio increases, so does the risk factor to potential creditors and investors. This ratio should be compared with previous periods and industry norms.

Profitability Ratios

profitability ratios Financial ratios that tell how much of each dollar of sales, assets, and owner's investment resulted in net profit.

The **profitability ratios** are important to anyone whose economic interests are tied to the long-range success of the firm. Investors expect a return on their investment in the form of dividends and stock price appreciation. Without adequate profits, firms quickly fall out of favor with current and future investors.

gross profit margin An assessment of how well the cost of goods sold category of expenses was controlled. Expressed as a percent of net sales.

Gross profit margin is an assessment of how well the cost of goods sold category of expenses was controlled. In particular, this measure spotlights a firm's management of its purchasing and pricing functions. Gross profit margin is expressed as a percent of net sales.

$$\text{Gross profit margin} = \frac{\text{Gross profit}}{\text{Net sales}}$$

Hypothetical Enterprises, Inc.:

$$\text{Gross profit margin} = \frac{415,404}{896,944} = .463 = \underline{46.3\%}$$

Analysis: Hypothetical's gross profit constitutes 46.3% of the company's sales, which means that for each $1.00 of sales, $0.46 remains as gross margin. For a meaningful analysis, this ratio should be compared with previous operating periods and industry averages.

Net profit margin is an assessment of management's overall ability to control the cost of goods sold and the operating expenses of the firm. This ratio is the bottom-line score of a firm's profitability and is one of the most important and most frequently used ratios. Net profit margin can be calculated either before or after income tax. As with gross profit margin, it is expressed as a percent.

> **net profit margin** An assessment of management's overall ability to control the cost of goods sold and the operating expenses of a firm. Expressed as a percent of net sales.

$$\text{Net profit margin} = \frac{\text{Net income}}{\text{Net sales}}$$

Hypothetical Enterprises, Inc.:

$$\text{Net profit margin} = \frac{91{,}268}{896{,}944} = .1018 = \underline{10.2\%}$$

Analysis: This means that for each $1.00 of net sales, Hypothetical was able to generate $0.10 in net profit. Most firms today have net profit margins between 1% and 8% depending on the industry. Regardless of industry, Hypothetical's 10.2% net profit margin would be considered very profitable.

Return on investment is the amount of profit generated by the firm in relation to the amount invested by the owners. Abbreviated ROI, this ratio is commonly expressed as a percent.

> **return on investment** The amount of profit generated by a firm in relation to the amount invested by the owners. Expressed as a percent of owner's equity.

$$\text{Return on investment} = \frac{\text{Net income}}{\text{Owner's equity}}$$

Hypothetical Enterprises, Inc.:

$$\text{Return on investment} = \frac{91{,}268}{176{,}900} = .5159 = \underline{51.6\%}$$

Analysis: This ratio indicates that Hypothetical generated $0.52 in net profit for each $1.00 invested by the owners. Most investors would consider 51.6% an excellent return on their money.

▶TRYITEXERCISE 7

Use the balance sheet and income statement on pages 503–504 and 516 to calculate the financial ratios for Royal Equipment Supply, Inc.

CHECK YOUR ANSWERS WITH THE SOLUTIONS ON PAGES 541–542.

PREPARING A TREND ANALYSIS OF FINANCIAL DATA

15-8

In Sections I and II of this chapter, we used horizontal analysis to calculate and report the *amount* and *percent* change in various balance sheet and income statement items from one operating period to another. When these percentage changes are tracked for a number of successive periods, it is known as **trend analysis**. Trend analysis introduces the element of time into financial analysis. Whereas data from one statement gives a firm's financial position at a given point in time, trend analysis provides a dynamic picture of the firm by showing its financial direction over a period of time.

Index numbers are used in trend analysis to show the percentage change in various financial statement items. With index numbers, a base year is chosen and is equal to 100%. All other years' figures are measured as a percentage of the base year. Once again, we encounter the now familiar percentage formula Rate = Portion ÷ Base. The index number should be expressed as a percent rounded to the nearest tenth.

> **trend analysis** The use of index numbers to calculate percentage changes of a company's financial data for several successive operating periods.
>
> **index numbers** Numbers used in trend analysis indicating changes in magnitude of financial data over a period of time. Calculated by setting a base period equal to 100% and calculating other periods in relation to the base period.

$$\text{Index number (rate)} = \frac{\text{Yearly amount (portion)}}{\text{Base year amount (base)}}$$

For example, if a company had sales of $50,000 in the base year and $60,000 in the index year, the index number would be 1.2, or 120% (60,000 ÷ 50,000). The index number means that the sales for the index year were 1.2 times, or 120%, of the base year.

STEPS FOR PREPARING A TREND ANALYSIS

STEP 1. Choose a base year and let it equal 100%.

STEP 2. Calculate the index number for each succeeding year.

$$\text{Index number} = \frac{\text{Yearly amount}}{\text{Base year amount}}$$

STEP 3. Round each index number to the nearest tenth of a percent.

EXAMPLE8   PREPARING A TREND ANALYSIS

From the following data, prepare a 5-year trend analysis of net sales, net income, and total assets for Hypothetical Enterprises, Inc.

Hypothetical Enterprises, Inc.
5-Year Selected Financial Data

	2018	2017	2016	2015	2014
Net Sales	$896,944	$881,325	$790,430	$855,690	$825,100
Net Income	91,268	95,550	56,400	75,350	70,100
Total Assets	341,300	320,100	315,600	314,200	303,550

►SOLUTIONSTRATEGY

To prepare the trend analysis, we will calculate the index number for each year by using the percentage formula and then enter the figures in a trend analysis table. The earliest year, 2014, will be the base year (100%). The first calculation, 2015 net sales index number, is as follows:

$$2015 \text{ net sales index number} = \frac{855,690}{825,100} = 1.037 = \underline{103.7\%}$$

Trend Analysis (in percentages)

	2018	2017	2016	2015	2014
Net Sales	108.7	106.8	95.8	103.7	100.0
Net Income	130.2	136.3	80.5	107.5	100.0
Total Assets	112.4	105.5	104.0	103.5	100.0

In addition to the table form of presentation, trend analysis frequently uses charts to visually present the financial data. Multiple-line charts are a particularly good way of presenting comparative data. For even more meaningful analysis, company data can be graphed on the same coordinates as industry averages.

iStock.com/Nikada

The chart below illustrates Hypothetical's trend analysis figures in a multiple-line-chart format.

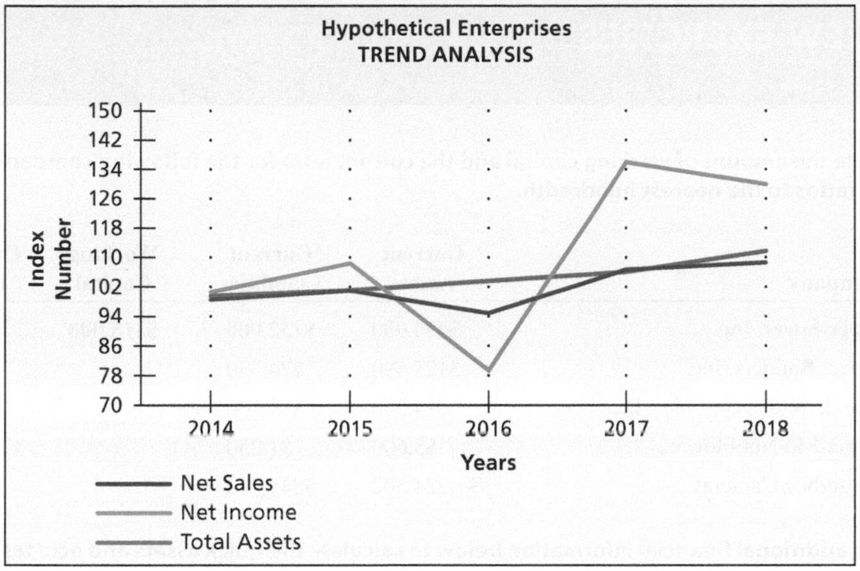

Hypothetical Enterprises
TREND ANALYSIS

Index Number (vertical axis): 150, 142, 134, 126, 118, 110, 102, 94, 86, 78, 70

Years (horizontal axis): 2014, 2015, 2016, 2017, 2018

— Net Sales
— Net Income
— Total Assets

IN THE
Business World

Tables illustrate specific data better than charts; however, charts are able to show "relationships" among data more clearly and visually.

Frequently in business presentations, tables and charts are used together, with the chart used to clarify or reinforce facts presented in a table.

►TRY IT EXERCISE 8

Prepare a trend analysis from the following financial data for Precision Engineering, Inc., and prepare a multiple-line chart of the net sales, total assets, and stockholders' equity.

Precision Engineering, Inc.
5-Year Selected Financial Data

	2018	2017	2016	2015	2014
Net Sales	$245,760	$265,850	$239,953	$211,231	$215,000
Total Assets	444,300	489,320	440,230	425,820	419,418
Stockholders' Equity	276,440	287,500	256,239	223,245	247,680

Precision Engineering, Inc.
Trend Analysis (in percentages)

	2018	2017	2016	2015	2014
Net Sales	_____	_____	_____	_____	_____
Total Assets	_____	_____	_____	_____	_____
Stockholders' Equity	_____	_____	_____	_____	_____

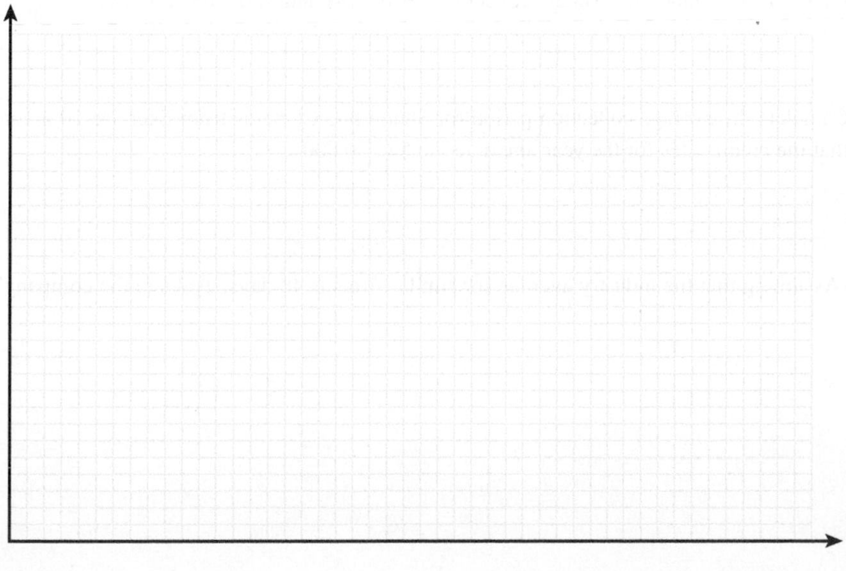

CHECK YOUR ANSWERS WITH THE SOLUTIONS ON PAGES 541–542.

SECTION III 15 REVIEW EXERCISES

Calculate the amount of working capital and the current ratio for the following companies.
Round ratios to the nearest hundredth.

Company	Current Assets	Current Liabilities	Working Capital	Current Ratio
1. Super-Saver, Inc.	$450,000	$132,000	$318,000	3.41:1
2. Impact Builders, Inc.	$125,490	$74,330	_____	_____
3. Thunderbird Electronics, Inc.	$14,540	$19,700	_____	_____
4. Forget-Me-Not Flowers	$3,600	$1,250	_____	_____
5. Shutterbug Cameras	$1,224,500	$845,430	_____	_____

Use the additional financial information below to calculate the quick assets and acid test
ratio for the companies in Questions 1–5.

Company	Cash	Marketable Securities	Accounts Receivable	Quick Assets	Acid Test Ratio
6. Super-Saver, Inc.	$39,350	$95,000	$52,770	$187,120	1.42:1
7. Impact Builders, Inc.		$30,000	$53,600	_____	_____
8. Thunderbird Electronics, Inc.	$2,690	0	$4,330	_____	_____
9. Forget-Me-Not Flowers	$1,180	0	$985	_____	_____
10. Shutterbug Cameras	$24,400	$140,000	$750,300	_____	_____

11. Calculate the average collection period for Super-Saver, Inc. from Exercise 6 assuming that
    the credit sales for the year amounted to $770,442.

$$\text{Average collection period} = \frac{\text{Accounts receivable} \times 365}{\text{Credit sales}}$$

$$\text{Average collection period} = \frac{52,770 \times 365}{770,442} = \frac{19,261,050}{770,442} = \underline{\underline{25 \text{ Days}}}$$

12. Over the previous period, your company had accounts receivable of $95,600 and credit sales of
    $581,566.67. Calculate the average collection period. (Round to the nearest day.)

13. a. Calculate the average collection period for Shutterbug Cameras from Exercise 10 assuming
    that the credit sales for the year amounted to $8,550,000.

    b. Assuming that the industry average for similar firms is 48 days, evaluate the company's ratio.

Calculate the average inventory and inventory turnover ratio for the following companies.

Company	Beginning Inventory	Ending Inventory	Average Inventory	Cost of Goods Sold	Inventory Turnover
14. High-Line Jewelers	$1,547,800	$1,366,000	$1,456,900	$6,500,000	4.5
15. Summit Gas	$90,125	$58,770	_____	$487,640	_____
16. Skyline Gifts	$856,430	$944,380	_____	$3,437,500	_____
17. Certified Fabrics	$121,400	$89,900	_____	$659,000	_____
18. Prestige Hardware	$313,240	$300,050	_____	$4,356,470	_____

19. The Organic Market had net sales of $650,000 last year. If the total assets of the company are $2,450,000, what is the asset turnover ratio?

$$\text{Asset turnover ratio} = \frac{\text{Net sales}}{\text{Total assets}} = \frac{650,000}{2,450,000} = .27 = .27{:}1$$

20. Heads or Tails Coin Shop had net sales of $1,354,600 last year. If the total assets of the company are $2,329,500, what is the asset turnover ratio?

Calculate the amount of owner's equity and the two leverage ratios for the following companies.

Company	Total Assets	Total Liabilities	Owner's Equity	Debt-to-Assets Ratio	Debt-to-Equity Ratio
21. Royal Rugs	$1,400.000	$535,000	$865,000	.38:1	.62:1
22. Gateway Imports	$232,430	$115,320	_____	_____	_____
23. Reader's Choice Books	$512,900	$357,510	_____	_____	_____
24. Café Europa	$2,875,000	$2,189,100	_____	_____	_____

Calculate the gross and net profits and the two profit margins for the following companies.

Company	Net Sales	Cost of Goods Sold	Gross Profit	Operating Expenses	Net Profit	Gross Profit Margin (%)	Net Profit Margin (%)
25. Plant World	$640,000	$414,000	$226,000	$112,600	$113,400	35.3	17.7
26. Timberline Marble	$743,500	$489,560	_____	$175,410	_____	_____	_____
27. Sundance Plumbing	$324,100	$174,690	_____	$99,200	_____	_____	_____
28. Dynamic Optical	$316,735	$203,655	_____	$85,921	_____	_____	_____

Using the owner's equity information below, calculate the return on investment for the companies in Exercises 25–28.

	Owner's Equity	Return on Investment (%)
29. Plant World	$525,000	21.6
30. Timberline Marble	$434,210	_____
31. Dynamic Optical	$397,000	_____

32. From the following data, find the 2019 Net Sales index number. (Round to the nearest tenth percent.)

International Industries—5 Year Selected Financial Data

	2019	2018	2017	2016	2015
Net Sales	491,790	459,620	488,960	461,280	431,100
Net Income	42,470	43,780	47,590	51,730	51,730
Total Assets	141,540	148,990	156,830	156,830	146,570

33. Prepare a trend analysis from the following financial data for Hook, Line, and Sinker Fishing Supply.

Hook, Line, and Sinker Fishing Supply
5-Year Selected Financial Data

	2018	2017	2016	2015	2014
Net Sales	$238,339	$282,283	$239,448	$215,430	$221,800
Net Income	68,770	71,125	55,010	57,680	55,343
Total Assets	513,220	502,126	491,100	457,050	467,720
Stockholders' Equity	254,769	289,560	256,070	227,390	240,600

Hook, Line, and Sinker Fishing Supply
Trend Analysis (in percentages)

	2018	2017	2016	2015	2014
Net Sales	_____	_____	_____	_____	_____
Net Income	_____	_____	_____	_____	_____
Total Assets	_____	_____	_____	_____	_____
Stockholders' Equity	_____	_____	_____	_____	_____

BUSINESS DECISION: FINANCIAL RATIOS

The years 2005 to 2009 were a period of rapid growth for Starbucks and the company's revenues grew by more than 50% during that period. Use the financial data for Starbucks on the following page for Exercises 34a–34e.

34. a.   Calculate the asset turnover ratio for 2008 and 2009.

   b.   Calculate the net profit margin for 2007, 2008, and 2009.

Starbucks is the world's #1 specialty coffee retailer. Its story began in 1971 when it was a roaster and retailer of whole bean and ground coffee, tea, and spices with a single store in Seattle's Pike Place Market. Starbucks Corporation was founded in 1985, and it remains based in Seattle, Washington.

Starbucks engages in the purchase, roasting, and sale of whole bean coffees worldwide. It offers brewed coffees, Italian-style espresso beverages, cold blended beverages, various complementary food items, and a selection of premium teas, as well as beverage-related accessories and equipment through its retail stores. In addition, it produces ready-to-drink beverages and ice cream for sale in retail stores.

In 2000, net revenues were $2.2 million ($2,169,218). Just 10 years later, in 2010, net revenues were $10.7 billion. Of this, beverage sales accounted for 75% of net revenues, food accounted for 19%, whole bean and soluble coffees accounted for 4%, and coffee-making equipment and other merchandise comprised 2%.

c. Calculate the return on investment for 2007, 2008, and 2009.

d. Prepare a trend analysis of the net revenue and total assets for 2005 through 2009.

e. Extra credit: Prepare a trend analysis multiple-line chart for the information in part d.

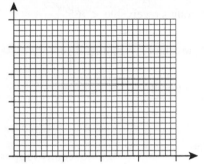

Starbucks—Selected Financial Data

(In millions, except earnings per share)

As of and for the fiscal year ended	Sept. 27, 2009 (52 wks)	Sept. 28, 2008 (52 wks)	Sept. 30, 2007 (52 wks)	Oct. 1, 2006 (52 wks)	Oct. 2, 2005 (52 wks)
Results of Operations					
Net revenues:					
Company-operated retail	$8,180.1	$ 8,771.9	$7,998.3	$6,583.1	$5,391.9
Specialty:					
Licensing	1,222.3	1,171.6	1,026.3	860.6	673.0
Food service and other	372.2	439.5	386.9	343.2	304.4
Total specialty	1,594.5	1,611.1	1,413.2	1,203.8	977.4
Total net revenues	$9,774.6	$10,383.0	$9,411.5	$7,786.9	$6,369.3
Operating income	$562.0	$ 503.9	$1,053.9	$ 894.0	$ 780.5
Earnings before cumulative effect of change in accounting principle	390.8	315.5	672.6	581.5	494.4
Cumulative effect of accounting change for asset retirement obligations, net of taxes	—	—	—	17.2	—
Net earnings	$ 390.8	$ 315.5	$ 672.6	$ 564.3	$ 494.4
Earnings per common share before cumulative effect of change in accounting principle—diluted ("EPS")	$ 0.52	$ 0.43	$ 0.87	$ 0.73	$ 0.61
Cumulative effect of accounting change for asset retirement obligations, net of taxes—per common share	—	—	—	0.02	—
EPS—diluted	$ 0.52	$ 0.43	$ 0.87	$ 0.71	$ 0.61
Net cash provided by operating activities	$1,389.0	$ 1,258.7	$1,331.2	$1,131.6	$ 922.9
Capital expenditures (additions to property, plant, and equipment)	$ 445.6	$ 984.5	$1,080.3	$ 771.2	$ 643.3
Balance Sheet					
Total assets	$5,576.8	$ 5,672.6	$5,343.9	$4,428.9	$3,513.7
Short-term borrowings	—	713.0	710.3	700.0	277.0
Long-term debt (including current portion)	549.5	550.3	550.9	2.7	3.6
Shareholders' equity	$3,045.7	$ 2,490.9	$2,284.1	$2,228.5	$2,090.3

CHAPTER FORMULAS

Liquidity Ratios

Working capital = Current assets − Current liabilities

$$\text{Current ratio} = \frac{\text{Current assets}}{\text{Current liabilities}}$$

Quick assets = Cash + Marketable securities + Receivables

$$\text{Acid test ratio} = \frac{\text{Quick assets}}{\text{Current liabilities}}$$

Efficiency Ratios

$$\text{Average collection period} = \frac{\text{Accounts receivable} \times 365}{\text{Credit sales}}$$

$$\text{Average inventory} = \frac{\text{Beginning inventory} + \text{Ending inventory}}{2}$$

$$\text{Inventory turnover} = \frac{\text{Cost of goods sold}}{\text{Average inventory}} \qquad \text{Asset turnover ratio} = \frac{\text{Net sales}}{\text{Total assets}}$$

Leverage Ratios

$$\text{Debt-to-assets ratio} = \frac{\text{Total liabilities}}{\text{Total assets}} \qquad \text{Debt-to-equity ratio} = \frac{\text{Total liabilities}}{\text{Owner's equity}}$$

Profitability Ratios

$$\text{Gross profit margin} = \frac{\text{Gross profit}}{\text{Net sales}} \qquad \text{Net profit margin} = \frac{\text{Net income}}{\text{Net sales}}$$

$$\text{Return on investment} = \frac{\text{Net income}}{\text{Owner's equity}}$$

CHAPTER SUMMARY

Section I: The Balance Sheet

Topic	Important Concepts	Illustrative Examples

Preparing a Balance Sheet
 	
Performance Objective 15-1, Page 501
	The balance sheet is a financial statement that shows a company's financial position on a certain date. It is based on the fundamental accounting equation:
	Assets = Liabilities + Owner's equity
	
	Balance sheet preparation:
	
	1. *List and total:*
	    Current assets
	    + Property, plant, and equipment
	    + Investments and other assets
	    Total assets
	
	2. *List and total:*
	    Current liabilities
	    + Long-term liabilities
	    Total liabilities
	
	3. *List and total:*
	    Owner's equity
	4. Add the Total liabilities and the Owner's equity. This total should equal the Total assets.
		International Industries, Inc.
		Balance Sheet
		December 31, 2018
		Assets

Detail of Illustrative Example:

International Industries, Inc.
Balance Sheet
December 31, 2018

Assets

Cash	$ 24,000
Receivables	92,000
Inventory	68,500
Supplies	12,100
Total current assets	$196,600
Land and building	$546,700
Fixtures & equipment	88,400
Vehicles	124,200
Total property & equipment	$759,300
Total assets	$955,900

Liabilities & Owner's Equity

Accounts payable	$ 82,400
Note payable (3-month)	31,300
Total current liabilities	$113,700
Mortgage payable	$213,400
Note payable (2-year)	65,800
Total long-term liabilities	$279,200
Total liabilities	$392,900
Owner's equity	563,000
Total liabilities & owner's equity	$955,900

Section I (continued)

Topic	Important Concepts	Illustrative Examples

Preparing a Vertical Analysis of a Balance Sheet
 	
Performance Objective 15-2, Page 504
	In vertical analysis, each item on the balance sheet is expressed as a percent of total assets.
	Vertical analysis preparation:
	
	1. Use the percentage formula,
	
	   Use each balance sheet item as the portion and total assets as the base.
	2. Round each answer to the nearest tenth of a percent.
	
	   Note: A 0.1% differential may occur due to rounding.
		International Industries, Inc.
		Balance Sheet—Asset Section
		December 31, 2018
		
		<table><tr><td>Cash</td><td>$ 24,000</td><td>2.5%</td></tr><tr><td>Receivables</td><td>92,000</td><td>9.6</td></tr><tr><td>Inventory</td><td>68,500</td><td>7.2</td></tr><tr><td>Supplies</td><td>12,100</td><td>1.3</td></tr><tr><td>Current assets</td><td>$196,600</td><td>20.6</td></tr><tr><td>Land & building</td><td>$546,700</td><td>57.2</td></tr><tr><td>Fixtures & equipment</td><td>88,400</td><td>9.2</td></tr><tr><td>Vehicles</td><td>124,200</td><td>13.0</td></tr><tr><td>Property & equipment</td><td>$759,300</td><td>79.4</td></tr><tr><td>Total assets</td><td>$955,900</td><td>100.0%</td></tr></table>

Preparing a Horizontal Analysis of a Balance Sheet
 	
Performance Objective 15-3, Page 506
	Comparative balance sheets display data from the current period side by side with the figures from one or more previous periods. In horizontal analysis, each item of the current period is compared in dollars and percent with the corresponding item from the previous period.
	
	Horizontal analysis preparation:
	
	1. Set up a comparative balance sheet format with the current period listed first.
	2. Label the next two columns:
	    Increase (Decrease)
	    Amount Percent
	3. For each item, calculate the dollar difference between the current and previous period and enter this figure in the Amount column. Enter all decreases in parentheses.
	4. Calculate the percent change using
	
	5. Enter the percent change in the Percent column. Round to the nearest tenth of a percent. Enter all decreases in parentheses.
		If the 2017 cash figure for International Industries, Inc. was $21,300, the comparative balance sheet horizontal analysis would be listed as follows:
		
		Cash
		
		<table><tr><td></td><td></td><td colspan="2">Increase (Decrease)</td></tr><tr><td>2018</td><td>2017</td><td>Amount</td><td>Percent</td></tr><tr><td>$24,000</td><td>$21,300</td><td>$2,700</td><td>12.7</td></tr></table>
		$$\frac{2,700}{21,300} = 12.7\%$$
		
		For a comprehensive example of a comparative balance sheet with horizontal analysis, see pages 507–508, Supreme Construction Company.

Section II: The Income Statement

Topic	Important Concepts	Illustrative Examples
Preparing an Income Statement **Performance Objective 15-4, Page 513**	An income statement is a summary of the operations of a business over a period of time. It is based on the equation *Income Statement preparation:* 1. Label the top of the statement with the company name and period of time covered. 2. In a two-column format, calculate a. *Net sales*	International Industries, Inc. Income Statement Year Ended December 31, 2018 (in thousands) <table><tr><td>Gross sales</td><td>$435.3</td><td></td></tr><tr><td>Sales returns</td><td>11.1</td><td></td></tr><tr><td>Sales discounts</td><td>8.0</td><td></td></tr><tr><td> Net sales</td><td></td><td>$416.2</td></tr><tr><td>Inventory, Jan. 1</td><td>124.2</td><td></td></tr><tr><td>Net purchases</td><td>165.8</td><td></td></tr><tr><td>Freight in</td><td>2.7</td><td></td></tr><tr><td>Goods available</td><td>292.7</td><td></td></tr><tr><td>Inventory, Dec. 31</td><td>118.1</td><td></td></tr><tr><td> Cost of goods sold</td><td></td><td>174.6</td></tr><tr><td> Gross margin</td><td></td><td>241.6</td></tr><tr><td>Salaries</td><td>87.6</td><td></td></tr><tr><td>Rent & utilities</td><td>22.5</td><td></td></tr><tr><td>Other expenses</td><td>101.7</td><td></td></tr><tr><td> Total operating expenses</td><td></td><td>211.8</td></tr><tr><td> Net income</td><td></td><td>$ 29.8</td></tr></table>

Section II (continued)

Topic	Important Concepts	Illustrative Examples
	b. *Cost of goods sold*	
	c. *Gross margin*	
	d. *Net income*	

Preparing a Vertical Analysis of an Income Statement
 	
Performance Objective 15-5, Page 516
	In vertical analysis of an income statement, each figure is expressed as a percent of net sales.
	
	Vertical analysis preparation:
	
	1. Use the percentage formula,
	
	  Use each income statement item as the portion and net sales as the base.
	2. Round each answer to the nearest tenth of a percent.
	
	  Note: A 0.1% differential may occur due to rounding.
		International Industries, Inc.
		Income Statement—2018 (in thousands)
		
		<table><tr><td>Gross sales</td><td>$435.3</td><td>104.6%</td></tr><tr><td>Sales returns</td><td>11.1</td><td>2.7</td></tr><tr><td>Sales discounts</td><td>8.0</td><td>1.9</td></tr><tr><td>Net sales</td><td>416.2</td><td>100.0</td></tr><tr><td>Inventory, Jan. 1</td><td>124.2</td><td>29.8</td></tr><tr><td>Net purchases</td><td>165.8</td><td>39.8</td></tr><tr><td>Freight in</td><td>2.7</td><td>.6</td></tr><tr><td>Goods available for sale</td><td>292.7</td><td>70.3</td></tr><tr><td>Inventory, Dec. 31</td><td>118.1</td><td>28.4</td></tr><tr><td>Cost of goods sold</td><td>174.6</td><td>42.0</td></tr><tr><td>Gross margin</td><td>241.6</td><td>58.0</td></tr><tr><td>Salaries</td><td>87.6</td><td>21.0</td></tr><tr><td>Rent & utilities</td><td>22.5</td><td>5.4</td></tr><tr><td>Other expenses</td><td>101.7</td><td>24.4</td></tr><tr><td>Total operating expenses</td><td>211.8</td><td>50.9</td></tr><tr><td>Net income</td><td>$ 29.8</td><td>7.2%</td></tr></table>

Preparing a Horizontal Analysis of an Income Statement
 	
Performance Objective 15-6, Page 518
	In horizontal analysis of a comparative income statement, each item of the current period is compared in dollars and percent with the corresponding item from the previous period.
	
	Horizontal analysis preparation:
	
	1. Set up a comparative income statement format with the current period listed first.
	2. Label the next two columns:
	
	  Increase (Decrease)
	  Amount Percent
	
	3. For each item, calculate the dollar difference between the current and previous period and enter this figure in the Amount column. Enter all decreases in parentheses.
	4. Calculate the percent change by using
	
	5. Enter the percent change in the Percent column. Round to the nearest tenth of a percent. Enter all decreases in parentheses.
		If the 2017 net income figure for International Industries, Inc. was $23,100, the comparative income statement horizontal analysis would be listed as follows:
		
		Net Income
		
		<table><tr><td></td><td></td><td colspan="2">Increase (Decrease)</td></tr><tr><td>**2018**</td><td>**2017**</td><td>**Amount**</td><td>**Percent**</td></tr><tr><td>$29,800</td><td>$23,100</td><td>$6,700</td><td>29.0</td></tr></table>
		$$\frac{6,700}{23,100} = 29.0\%$$
		
		For a comprehensive example of a comparative income statement with horizontal analysis, see pages 518–519, Foremost Furniture, Inc.

Section III: Financial Ratios and Trend Analysis

Topic	Important Concepts	Illustrative Examples
Calculating Financial Ratios **Performance Objective 15-7, Page 524**	Financial ratios are standardized comparisons of various items from the balance sheet and the income statement. When compared with ratios of previous operating periods and industry averages, they can be used as signals to analysts of potential strengths or weaknesses of the firm.	A company had net sales of $100,000 and net income of $10,000. Express these data as a ratio. $$\frac{100,000}{10,000} = 10$$ 1. The ratio of sales to income is 10 to 1, written 10:1. 2. Net income is $\frac{1}{10}$, or 10%, of net sales. 3. For every $1.00 of net sales, the company generates $0.10 in net income.
Liquidity Ratios **Performance Objective 15-7, Page 524**	Liquidity ratios examine the relationship between a firm's current assets and its maturing obligation. They are a good indicator of a firm's ability to pay its bills over the next few months. $$\text{Current ratio} = \frac{\text{Current assets}}{\text{Current liabilities}}$$	International Industries, Inc. Financial Ratios 2015 $$\text{Current ratio} = \frac{196,600}{113,700} = 1.73 = 1.73{:}1$$ $$\text{Acid test ratio} = \frac{24,000 + 92,000}{113,700} = 1.02 = 1.02{:}1$$
Efficiency Ratios **Performance Objective 15-7, Page 525**	Efficiency ratios provide the basis for determining how effectively a firm uses its resources to generate sales.	Credit sales for International Industries, Inc. are 50% of net sales. Average collection period = $$\frac{92,000 \times 365}{208,100} = 161 \text{ Days}$$ Inventory turnover = $$\frac{174,000}{(124,200 + 118,100)/2} = 1.44 \text{ Times}$$ $$\text{Asset turnover ratio} = \frac{416,200}{955,900} = .44 = .44{:}1$$
Leverage Ratios **Performance Objective 15-7, Page 526**	Leverage ratios provide information about the amount of money a company has borrowed to finance its assets.	$$\text{Debt-to-assets ratio} = \frac{392,900}{955,900} = .411 = 41.1\%$$ $$\text{Debt-to-equity ratio} = \frac{392,900}{563,000} = .698 = 69.8\%$$
Profitability Ratios **Performance Objective 15-7, Page 526**	Profitability ratios show a firm's ability to generate profits and provide its investors with a return on their investment.	$$\text{Gross profit margin} = \frac{241,600}{416,200} = .580 = 58.0\%$$ $$\text{Net profit margin} = \frac{29,800}{416,200} = .072 = 7.2\%$$ $$\text{Return on investment} = \frac{29,800}{563,000} = .053 = 5.3\%$$
Preparing a Trend Analysis of Financial Data **Performance Objective 15-8, Page 527**	Trend analysis is the process of tracking changes in financial statement items for three or more operating periods. Trend analysis figures can be displayed on a chart using index numbers or more visually as a line graph or bar chart.	Prepare a trend analysis for International Industries, Inc. net sales data. International Industries, Inc. Net Sales (in thousands) | 2018	2017	2016	2015	2014
---	---	---	---	---
416.2	401.6	365.4	388.3	375.1	

Section III (continued)

Topic	Important Concepts	Illustrative Examples
	Trend analysis preparation: 1. Choose a base year (usually the earliest year) and let it equal 100%. 2. Calculate the index number for each succeeding year by using 3. Round each index number to the nearest tenth of a percent. 4. *Optional:* Graph the index numbers or the raw data on a line chart.	For this trend analysis, we will use 2014 as the base year, 100%. Each subsequent year's index number is calculated by using the yearly amount as the portion and the 2014 amount as the base. For example, 2015 index number = $$\frac{388.3}{375.1} = 103.5\%$$ <table><tr><td>**2018**</td><td>**2017**</td><td>**2016**</td><td>**2015**</td><td>**2014**</td></tr><tr><td>111.0</td><td>107.1</td><td>97.4</td><td>103.5</td><td>100.0</td></tr></table> International Industries, Inc. Trend Analysis

TRY IT: EXERCISE SOLUTIONS FOR CHAPTER 15

1.

Keystone Auto Repair
Balance Sheet
December 31, 20XX

Assets

Current Assets

Cash	$5,200	
Accounts Receivable	2,800	
Merchandise Inventory	2,700	
Prepaid Salary	235	
Supplies	3,900	
Total Current Assets		$ 14,835

Property, Plant, and Equipment

Land	35,000	
Building	74,000	
Fixtures	1,200	
Tow Truck	33,600	
Tools and Equipment	45,000	
Total Property, Plant, and Equipment		188,800
Total Assets		$203,635

Liabilities and Owner's Equity

Current Liabilities

Accounts Payable	$ 6,800	
Notes Payable	17,600	
Taxes Payable	3,540	
Total Current Liabilities		$ 27,940

Long-Term Liabilities

Mortgage Payable	51,000	
Total Long-Term Liabilities		51,000
Total Liabilities		78,940

Owner's Equity

Blake Williams, Capital	124,695	
Total Owner's Equity		124,695
Total Liabilities and Owner's Equity		$203,635

2.

Royal Equipment Supply, Inc.
Balance Sheet
June 30, 20XX

Assets

Current Assets

Cash	$ 3,400	1.1%
Accounts Receivable	5,600	1.8
Merchandise Inventory	98,700	32.0
Prepaid Insurance	455	.1
Supplies	800	.3
Total Current Assets	108,955	35.3

Property, Plant, and Equipment

Land and Building	147,000	47.6
Fixtures	8,600	2.8
Delivery Vehicles	27,000	8.8
Forklift	7,000	2.3
Total Property, Plant, and Equipment	189,600	61.4

Investments and Other Assets

Goodwill	10,000	3.2
Total Investments and Other Assets	10,000	3.2
Total Assets	$308,555	100.0%

Liabilities and Stockholders' Equity

Current Liabilities

Accounts Payable	$ 16,500	5.3%
Notes Payable	10,000	3.2
Total Current Liabilities	26,500	8.6

Long-Term Liabilities

Mortgage Payable	67,000	21.7
Total Long-Term Liabilities	67,000	21.7
Total Liabilities	93,500	30.3

Stockholders' Equity

Common Stock	185,055	60.0
Retained Earnings	30,000	9.7
Total Stockholders' Equity	215,055	69.7
Total Liabilities and Stockholders' Equity	$308,555	100.0%

3.

Calypso Industries, Inc.
Comparative Balance Sheet
December 31, 2018 and 2019

			Increase (Decrease)	
Assets	**2019**	**2018**	**Amount**	**Percent**
Current Assets				
Cash	$ 8,700	$ 5,430	$ 3,270	60.2%
Accounts Receivable	23,110	18,450	4,660	25.3
Notes Receivable	2,900	3,400	(500)	(14.7)
Supplies	4,540	3,980	560	14.1
Total Current Assets	39,250	31,260	7,990	25.6
Property, Plant, and Equipment				
Land	34,000	34,000	0	0
Buildings	76,300	79,800	(3,500)	(4.4)
Machinery and Equipment	54,700	48,900	5,800	11.9
Total Prop., Plant, and Equipment	165,000	162,700	2,300	1.4
Investments and Other Assets	54,230	49,810	4,420	8.9
Total Assets	$258,480	$243,770	$14,710	6.0%

Liabilities and Stockholders' Equity	2019	2018	Increase (Decrease)	
			Amount	Percent
Current Liabilities				
Accounts Payable	$ 15,330	$ 19,650	($4,320)	(22.0%)
Salaries Payable	7,680	7,190	490	6.8
Total Current Liabilities	23,010	26,840	(3,830)	(14.3)
Long-Term Liabilities				
Mortgage Payable	53,010	54,200	(1,190)	(2.2)
Note Payable (3-year)	32,400	33,560	(1,160)	(3.5)
Total Long-Term Liabilities	85,410	87,760	(2,350)	(2.7)
Total Liabilities	108,420	114,600	(6,180)	(5.4)
Stockholders' Equity				
Common Stock	130,060	120,170	9,890	8.2
Retained Earnings	20,000	9,000	11,000	122.2
Total Liabilities and Stockholders' Equity	$258,480	$243,770	$14,710	6.0%

4.

Cutting Edge Manufacturing, Inc.
Income Statement
December 31, 20XX

Revenue		
Gross Sales	$1,356,000	
Less: Sales Returns and Allowances	93,100	
Sales Discounts	4,268	
Net Sales		$1,258,632
Cost of Goods Sold		
Merchandise Inventory, Jan. 1	324,800	
Net Purchases	255,320	
Freight In	3,911	
Goods Available for Sale	584,031	
Less: Merchandise Inventory, Dec. 31	179,100	
Cost of Goods Sold		404,931
Gross Margin		853,701
Operating Expenses		
Salaries	375,900	
Rent	166,000	
Utilities	7,730	
Advertising	73,300	
Insurance	22,940	
Administrative Expenses	84,500	
Miscellaneous Expenses	24,900	
Total Operating Expenses		755,270
Income before Taxes		98,431
Income Tax		34,760
Net Income		$ 63,671

5.

Royal Equipment Supply, Inc.
Income Statement
December 31, 20XX

Revenue		
Gross Sales	$458,400	103.3%
Less: Sales Returns and Allowances	13,200	3.0
Sales Discounts	1,244	.3
Net Sales	$443,956	100.0%
Cost of Goods Sold		
Merchandise Inventory, Jan. 1	198,700	44.8
Net Purchases	86,760	19.5
Freight In	875	.2
Goods Available for Sale	286,335	64.5
Less: Merchandise Inventory, Dec. 31	76,400	17.2
Cost of Goods Sold	209,935	47.3
Gross Margin	234,021	52.7
Operating Expenses		
Salaries	124,200	28.0
Rent	21,000	4.7
Utilities	1,780	.4
Advertising	5,400	1.2
Insurance	2,340	.5
Administrative Expenses	14,500	3.3
Miscellaneous Expenses	6,000	1.4
Total Operating Expenses	175,220	39.5
Income before Taxes	58,801	13.2
Income Tax	17,335	3.9
Net Income	$ 41,466	9.3%

6.

Timely Watch Company, Inc.
Comparative Income Statement
For the Years Ended December 31, 2018 and 2019

	2019	2018	Increase (Decrease)	
			Amount	Percent
Revenue				
Gross Sales	$1,223,000	$996,500	$226,500	22.7%
Less: Sales Returns and Allowances	121,340	99,600	21,740	21.8
Sales Discounts	63,120	51,237	11,883	23.2
Net Sales	1,038,540	845,663	192,877	22.8

Cost of Goods Sold

Merchandise Inventory, Jan. 1	311,200	331,000	(19,800)	(6.0)
Purchases	603,290	271,128	332,162	122.5
Freight In	18,640	13,400	5,240	39.1
Goods Available for Sale	933,130	615,528	317,602	51.6
Less: Merchandise Inventory, Dec. 31	585,400	311,200	274,200	88.1
Cost of Goods Sold	347,730	304,328	43,402	14.3
Gross Margin	690,810	541,335	149,475	27.6

Operating Expenses

Salaries and Benefits	215,200	121,800	93,400	76.7
Rent and Utilities	124,650	124,650	0	0
Depreciation	43,500	41,230	2,270	5.5
Insurance	24,970	23,800	1,170	4.9
Administrative Store Expenses	58,200	33,900	24,300	71.7
Warehouse Expenses	42,380	45,450	(3,070)	(6.8)
Total Operating Expenses	508,900	390,830	118,070	30.2
Income before Taxes	181,910	150,505	31,405	20.9
Income Tax	66,280	41,670	24,610	59.1
Net Income	$115,630	$108,835	$ 6,795	6.2%

7. *Royal Equipment Supply—Financial Ratios 2011*

Working capital = Current assets − Current liabilities = 108,955 − 26,500 = $82,455

$$\text{Current ratio} = \frac{\text{Current assets}}{\text{Current liabilities}} = \frac{108,955}{26,500} = 4.11:1$$

$$\text{Acid test ratio} = \frac{\text{Cash + Marketable securities + Receivables}}{\text{Current liabilities}} = \frac{3,400 + 5,600}{26,500} = .34:1$$

$$\text{Average collection period} = \frac{\text{Accounts receivable} \times 365}{\text{Net sales}} = \frac{5,600 \times 365}{443,956} = 4.6 \text{ days}$$

$$\text{Average inventory} = \frac{\text{Beginning inventory + Ending inventory}}{2} = \frac{198,700 + 76,400}{2} = \$137,550$$

$$\text{Inventory turnover} = \frac{\text{Cost of goods sold}}{\text{Average inventory}} = \frac{209,935}{137,550} = 1.5 \text{ times}$$

$$\text{Asset turnover ratio} = \frac{\text{Net sales}}{\text{Total assets}} = \frac{443,956}{308,555} = 1.44:1$$

$$\text{Debt-to-assets ratio} = \frac{\text{Total liabilities}}{\text{Total assets}} = \frac{93,500}{308,555} = .303 = 30.3\%$$

$$\text{Debt-to-equity ratio} = \frac{\text{Total liabilities}}{\text{Owner's equity}} = \frac{93,500}{215,055} = .435 = 43.5\%$$

$$\text{Gross profit margin} = \frac{\text{Gross profit}}{\text{Net sales}} = \frac{234,021}{443,956} = .527 = 52.7\%$$

$$\text{Net profit margin} = \frac{\text{Net income}}{\text{Net sales}} = \frac{41,446}{443,956} = .093 = 9.3\%$$

$$\text{Return on investment} = \frac{\text{Net income}}{\text{Owner's equity}} = \frac{41,466}{215,055} = .193 = 19.3\%$$

8.

Precision Engineering, Inc.
Trend Analysis (in percentages)

	2018	2017	2016	2015	2014
Net Sales	114.3	123.7	111.6	98.2	100.0
Total Assets	105.9	116.7	105.0	101.5	100.0
Stockholders' Equity	111.6	116.1	103.5	90.1	100.0

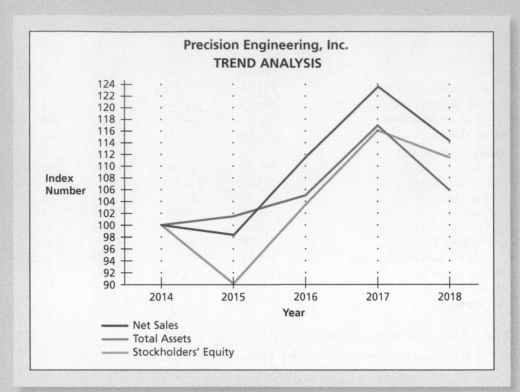

CONCEPT REVIEW

1. In accounting, economic resources owned by a company are known as _____, whereas debts or obligations of a company are known as _____. (15-1)

2. The financial statement that illustrates the financial position of a company in terms of assets, liabilities, and owner's equity as of a certain date is known as a(n) _____ sheet. (15-1)

3. The balance sheet is a visual presentation of the all-important "accounting equation." Write this equation. (15-1)

4. In vertical analysis of a balance sheet, each figure on the statement is expressed as a percent of _____ _____. (15-2)

5. A financial statement prepared with the data from the current operating period side by side with the figures from one or more previous periods is known as a(n) _____ statement. (15-3, 15-6)

6. Horizontal analysis is a method of analyzing financial statements whereby each item of the current period is compared in _____ and _____ with the corresponding item from a previous period. (15-3, 15-6)

7. A financial statement summarizing the operations of a business over a period of time is known as an income statement, an operating statement, or a(n) _____ and _____ statement. (15-4)

8. Write the formula that illustrates the structure of an income statement. (15-4)

9. In vertical analysis of an income statement, each figure on the statement is expressed as a percent of _____ _____. (15-5)

10. Name the four major categories of financial ratios. (15-7)

11. Write the formulas for the current ratio and inventory turnover. (15-7)

12. Write the formulas for the debt-to-assets ratio and return on investment. (15-7)

13. The use of index numbers to track percentage changes of a company's financial data over successive operating periods is known as _____ analysis. (15-8)

14. With index numbers, a base period is chosen and is equal to _____ percent. (15-8)

ASSESSMENT TEST

Prepare the following statements on separate sheets of paper.

Calculate the missing balance sheet items. Complete each company's column; then move on to the next column.

THE BALANCE SHEET (in millions)		
	Exercise 1	Exercise 2
Company Date	Boss Co. December 31, 20XX	Besty, Inc. January 31, 20XX
Current Assets	$2,487	$10,296
Fixed Assets	2,870	_____
Total Assets	_____	32,732
Current Liabilities	1,408	8,876
Long-Term Liabilities	2,345	_____
Total Liabilities	_____	20,879
Stockholders' Equity	_____	_____

Calculate the missing income statement items. each company's column; then move on to the next column.

THE INCOME STATEMENT (in millions)		
	Exercise 3	Exercise 4
Company Year Ended	Motomobile, Inc. December 31, 20XX	Finegans, Inc. December 31, 20XX
Revenue	$72,596	_____
Cost of Goods Sold	51,160	3,242
Gross Margin	_____	3,252
Operating Expenses	4,229	_____
Income before Taxes	_____	626
Income Tax*	15,236	_____
Net Income (loss)	_____	392

*Also includes interest expense and other income and losses.

5. **a.** Use the following financial information to calculate the owner's equity and prepare a balance sheet with vertical analysis as of December 31, 2017, for Uniflex Fabricators, Inc., a sole proprietorship owned by Paul Provost: current assets, $132,500; property, plant, and equipment, $88,760; investments and other assets, $32,400; current liabilities, $51,150; and long-term liabilities, $87,490.

Uniflex Fabricators, Inc.
Balance Sheet
As of December 31, 2017

b. The following financial information is for Uniflex Fabricators, Inc., as of December 31, 2018. Calculate the owner's equity for 2018 and prepare a comparative balance sheet with horizontal analysis for 2017 and 2018: current assets, $154,300; property, plant, and equipment, $124,650; investments and other assets, $20,000; current liabilities, $65,210; and long-term liabilities, $83,800.

CHAPTER 15

Uniflex Fabricators, Inc.
Comparative Balance Sheet
As of December 31, 2017 and 2018

6. **a.** Use the following financial information to prepare a balance sheet with vertical analysis as of October 31, 2017, for Sticks & Stones Builders Mart: cash, $45,260; accounts receivable, $267,580; merchandise inventory, $213,200; prepaid expenses, $13,400; supplies, $5,300; land, $87,600; building, $237,200; equipment, $85,630; vehicles, $54,700; computers, $31,100; investments, $53,100; accounts payable, $43,200; salaries payable, $16,500; notes payable (6-month), $102,400; mortgage payable, $124,300; notes payable (3-year), $200,000; common stock, $422,000; and retained earnings, $185,670.

Sticks & Stones Builders Mart
Balance Sheet
As of October 31, 2017

   b. The following financial information is for Sticks & Stones Builders Mart as of October 31, 2018. Prepare a comparative balance sheet with horizontal analysis for 2017 and 2018: cash, $47,870; accounts receivable, $251,400; merchandise inventory, $223,290; prepaid expenses, $8,500; supplies, $6,430; land, $87,600; building, $234,500; equipment, $88,960; vehicles, $68,800; computers, $33,270; investments, $55,640; accounts payable, $48,700; salaries payable, $9,780; notes payable (6-month), $96,700; mortgage payable, $121,540; notes payable (3-year), $190,000; common stock, $450,000; and retained earnings, $189,540.

Sticks & Stones Builders Mart
Comparative Balance Sheet
As of October 31, 2017 and 2018

7. For the second quarter, Evergreen Plant Nursery had gross sales of $214,300, sales returns and allowances of $26,540, and sales discounts of $1,988. What were Evergreen's net sales?

8. For the month of January, Consolidated Engine Parts, Inc. had the following financial information: merchandise inventory, January 1, $322,000; merchandise inventory, January 31, $316,400; gross purchases, $243,460; purchase returns and allowances, $26,880; and freight in, $3,430.

   a. What are Consolidated's goods available for sale?

   b. What is the cost of goods sold for January?

   c. If net sales were $389,450, what was the gross margin for January?

   d. If total operating expenses were $179,800, what was the net profit or loss?

Prepare the following statements on separate sheets of paper.

9. **a.** From the following third-quarter 2018 information for Woof & Meow Pet Supply, construct an income statement with vertical analysis: gross sales, $224,400; sales returns and allowances, $14,300; beginning inventory, July 1, $165,000; ending inventory, September 30, $143,320; net purchases, $76,500; total operating expenses, $68,600; and income tax, $8,790.

Woof & Meow Pet Supply
Income Statement
Third Quarter, 2018

b. The following financial information is for the fourth quarter of 2018 for Woof & Meow Pet Supply. Prepare a comparative income statement with horizontal analysis for the third and fourth quarters: gross sales, $218,200; sales returns and allowances, $9,500; beginning inventory, October 1, $143,320; ending inventory, December 31, $125,300; net purchases, $81,200; total operating expenses, $77,300; and income tax, $11,340.

Woof & Meow Pet Supply
Comparative Income Statement
Third and Fourth Quarters, 2018

10. **a.** Use the following financial information to construct a 2017 income statement with vertical analysis for Jazzline Jewelers: gross sales, $1,243,000; sales returns and allowances, $76,540; sales discounts, $21,300; merchandise inventory, Jan. 1, 2017, $654,410; merchandise inventory, Dec. 31, 2017, $413,200; net purchases, $318,000; freight in, $3,450; salaries, $92,350; rent, $83,100; depreciation, $87,700; utilities, $21,350; advertising, $130,440; insurance, $7,920; miscellaneous expenses, $105,900; and income tax, $18,580.

Jazzline Jewelers
Income Statement
For the Year Ended December 31, 2017

b. The following data represent Jazzline's operating results for 2018. Prepare a comparative income statement with horizontal analysis for 2017 and 2018: gross sales, $1,286,500; sales returns and allowances, $78,950; sales discounts, $18,700; merchandise inventory, Jan. 1, 2018, $687,300; merchandise inventory, Dec. 31, 2018, $401,210; net purchases, $325,400; freight in, $3,980; salaries, $99,340; rent, $85,600; depreciation, $81,200; utilities, $21,340; advertising, $124,390; insurance, $8,700; miscellaneous expenses, $101,230; and income tax, $12,650.

Jazzline Jewelers
Comparative Income Statement
For the Years Ended December 31, 2017 and 2018

As the accounting manager of Spring Creek Plastics, Inc., you have been asked to calculate the following financial ratios for the company's 2018 annual report. Use the balance sheet and the income statement on page 546 for Spring Creek.

11. Working capital:

12. Current ratio:

13. Acid test ratio:

14. Average collection period (credit sales are 60% of net sales):

15. Inventory turnover:

16. Asset turnover ratio:

17. Debt-to-assets ratio:

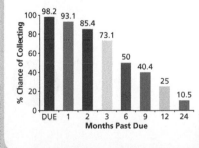

According to Burt & Associates, one of America's premiere collection agencies, the following chart illustrates the percent chance of collecting accounts receivable from financially distressed companies.

18. Debt-to-equity ratio:

19. Gross profit margin:

20. Net profit margin:

21. Return on investment:

Spring Creek Plastics, Inc.
Balance Sheet
As of December 31, 2018

Assets

Cash	$ 250,000	
Accounts Receivable	325,400	
Merchandise Inventory	416,800	
Marketable Securities	88,700	
Supplies	12,100	
Total Current Assets		$1,093,000
Land and Building	1,147,000	
Fixtures and Equipment	868,200	
Total Property, Plant, and Equipment		2,015,200
Total Assets		$3,108,200

Liabilities and Owner's Equity

Accounts Payable	$ 286,500	
Notes Payable (6-month)	153,200	
Total Current Liabilities		$439,700
Mortgage Payable	325,700	
Notes Payable (4-year)	413,100	
Total Long-Term Liabilities		738,800
Total Liabilities		1,178,500
Owner's Equity		1,929,700
Total Liabilities and Owner's Equity		$3,108,200

Spring Creek Plastics, Inc.
Income Statement, 2018

Net Sales		$1,695,900
Merchandise Inventory, Jan. 1	$ 767,800	
Net Purchases	314,900	
Freight In	33,100	
Goods Available for Sale	1,115,800	
Merchandise Inventory, Dec. 31	239,300	
Cost of Goods Sold		876,500
Gross Margin		819,400
Total Operating Expenses		702,300
Income before Taxes		117,100
Taxes		35,200
Net Income		$ 81,900

22. Prepare a trend analysis from the financial data listed below for Coastal Marine International.

Coastal Marine International
4-Year Selected Financial Data

	2018	2017	2016	2015
Net Sales	$ 898,700	$ 829,100	$ 836,200	$ 801,600
Net Income	96,300	92,100	94,400	89,700
Total Assets	2,334,000	2,311,000	2,148,700	1,998,900
Stockholders' Equity	615,000	586,000	597,200	550,400

Coastal Marine International
Trend Analysis (in percentages)

	2018	2017	2016	2015
Net Sales	——	——	——	——
Net Income	——	——	——	——
Total Assets	——	——	——	——
Stockholders' Equity	——	——	——	——

23. As part of the trend analysis for Coastal Marine International, prepare a multiple-line chart for the annual report comparing net sales and net income for the years 2011 through 2014.

EXCEL 3

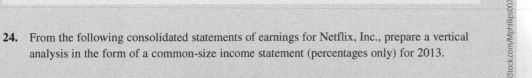

24. From the following consolidated statements of earnings for Netflix, Inc., prepare a vertical analysis in the form of a common-size income statement (percentages only) for 2013.

NETFLIX, INC.
CONSOLIDATED STATEMENTS OF OPERATIONS
(in thousands)

	Twelve Months Ended December 31, 2013
Revenues	$4,374,562
Cost of revenues	3,083,256
Marketing	503,889
Technology and development	378,769
General and administrative	180,301
Operating income	228,347
Other income (expense)	
Interest expense	(29,142)
Interest and other	(3,002)
Loss on extinguishment of debt	(25,129)
Income before income taxes	171,074
Provision for income taxes	58,671
Net income	$ 112,403

iStock.com/Mphillips007

Netflix, Inc. is the world's largest video subscription service, streaming movies, TV episodes, and original content over the Internet and sending DVDs and Blu-ray high-definition discs by mail. The company was founded in 1997 and had its first profitable year in 2003. With the rise of streaming videos, by 2010 Netflix had morphed from being the U.S. Postal Service's most rapidly growing first-class customer to being the biggest source of evening Internet traffic in North America.

CHAPTER 15

BUSINESS DECISION: EVALUATING FINANCIAL PERFORMANCE

25. In 2010, Apple introduced the iPad, and the sales of this device helped boost Apple revenues significantly. From the consolidated statements of income and balance sheets for Apple on the following page, prepare the following financial ratios for 2010 and 2011.

    a. Current ratio

    b. Acid test ratio

    c. Asset turnover ratio

    d. Debt-to-assets ratio

    e. Debt-to-equity ratio

    f. Net profit margin

    g. Return on investment

    h. Based on your calculations of the financial ratios for Apple, for each ratio, determine whether the 2011 figure was better or worse than the ratio for 2010.

    i. How would you rate Apple's financial ratios in 2010 and 2011?

Apple Inc. Apple was founded in 1976 with the goal of developing and selling personal computers. It has since expanded to offer the wide range of consumer electronics products used by many people around the world. In 2014, Apple became the first company in the world to reach a valuation (based on stock price times number of shares) of more than $700 billion.

dennizn/Shutterstock.com

Apple Inc.
CONSOLIDATED BALANCE SHEETS
(In millions, except number of shares which are reflected in thousands)

Assets:	September 24, 2011
Current assets:	
Cash and cash equivalents	$ 9,815
Short-term marketable securities	16,137
Accounts receivable, less allowances of $53 and $55, respectively	5,369
Inventories	776
Deferred tax assets	2,014
Vendor non-trade receivables	6,348
Other current assets	4,529
Total current assets	44,988

Apple Inc.
CONSOLIDATED BALANCE SHEETS
(In millions, except number of shares which are reflected in thousands)

Assets:	September 24, 2011
Long-term marketable securities	55,618
Property, plant and equipment, net	7,777
Goodwill	896
Acquired intangible assets, net	3,536
Other assets	3,556
Total assets	$ 116,371

Liabilities and Shareholders' Equity:	
Current liabilities:	
Accounts payable	$ 14,632
Accrued expenses	9,247
Deferred revenue	4,091
Total current liabilities	27,970
Deferred revenue—non-current	1,686
Other non-current liabilities	10,100
Total liabilities	39,756
Commitments and contingencies	
Shareholders' equity:	
Common stock, no par value; 1,800,000 shares authorized; 929,277 and 915,970 shares issued and outstanding, respectively	13,331
Retained earnings	62,841
Accumulated other comprehensive income/(loss)	443
Total shareholders' equity	76,615
Total liabilities and shareholders' equity	$ 116,371

CONSOLIDATED STATEMENTS
OF OPERATIONS
(In millions, except number of shares which are reflected in thousands and per share amounts)

Three Years Ended September 24, 2011	2011	2010
Net sales	$ 108,249	$ 65,225
Cost of sales	64,431	39,541
Gross margin	43,818	25,684
Operating expenses:		
Research and development	2,429	1,782
Selling, general and administrative	7,599	5,517
Total operating expenses	10,028	7,299
Operating income	33,790	18,385
Other income and expense	415	155
Income before provision for income taxes	34,205	18,540
Provision for income taxes	8,283	4,527
Net income	$ 25,922	$ 14,013
Earnings per common share:		
Basic	$ 28.05	$ 15.41
Diluted	$ 27.68	$ 15.15
Shares used in computing earnings per share:		
Basic	924,258	909,461
Diluted	936,645	924,712

COLLABORATIVE LEARNING ACTIVITY

1. How Are They Doing Now?

Work as teams to research the latest balance sheet and income statement figures for the following companies.

- Home Depot, Amazon.com, and Gap
- CVS Caremark, AutoZone, and PetSmart
- Hershey, Lowe's, Target, and Advance Auto Parts.

a. Using your favorite search engine, enter the company name and the words *investor relations* to locate the latest company 10K report filed with the Securities and Exchange Commission (SEC). This document contains the most recent company information, including balance sheet and income statement figures.

b. For each company, compare the balance sheet and income statement figures over the last three years.

c. Report your findings to the class using horizontal analysis and a visual presentation.

d. (optional) For each company, compare the earnings per share and stock price figures over the last three years. Use a trend analysis and line charts for your presentation of this data to the class.

2. Analyzing a Company

As a team, choose an industry you want to research, such as airlines, beverage, computers, entertainment, food, motor vehicles, retail, or wholesale. Then choose three public companies that directly compete in that industry.

Using the Internet, research key business ratios and other available information about that industry. This may be found in the government's publication the *Survey of Current Business* or from private sources such as Moody's Index, Dun & Bradstreet, or Standard & Poors.

Obtain the most recent annual report and quarterly report for each company from its website. This information is usually available under a section entitled "Investor Information." Based on the information your team has accumulated:

a. Calculate the current and previous years' financial ratios for each company.

b. Compare each company's ratios to the industry averages.

c. Evaluate each company's financial condition regarding liquidity, efficiency, leverage, and profitability.

d. If your team were going to invest in only one of these companies, which would you choose? Why?

Business Math JOURNAL

Identity Theft

What Is It?

According to SpendOnLife.com, identity theft is defined as "the process of using someone else's personal information for your own personal gain."

The Federal Trade Commission released information regarding identity theft in a recent year:

- Total fraud losses amounted to approximately $905 million.
- The median loss was $429.
- Younger people reported losses more often than older people. However, when people over the age of 70 had losses, the median loss was higher than for younger people.

Identity Theft Tips for Students

- Don't conduct financial transactions, manage bank accounts, or input personal information using library or shared computers.
- Log off a public computer after using it, whether it is in the school lab or in a shared dorm room or apartment.
- Don't post personal details such as your phone number and address on Facebook or other social networking sites.
- Password-protect your cell phone and laptop. Use a password that is at least six digits long and contains special characters, numbers, and letters. Never use personal information like your birth date or birth year as your password. Change passwords frequently and use a different password for each device.
- Look for a pop-up window that asks if you'd like to save your password when you log in to accounts on the computer. Never check this box, even if you are the only person who uses the computer. That way the password isn't stored.
- Download the latest updates for your antivirus software as soon as they become available. This will help keep your machine virus-free and protect it from the newest versions of malware and spyware.
- Don't trust a new roommate until you know him or her better. At least keep your personally identifiable information secure.
- Consider an identity theft protection service. Many cost only about a quarter per day. An identity protection plan is exponentially better than having no protection.

Source: www.identitytheftlabs.com

Types of Identity Theft Fraud Reports

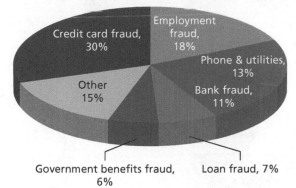

Source: Federal Trade Commission, Consumer Sentinel Network Fraud Complaints, Adapted from tables at www.ftc.gov/policy/reports/policy-reports/commission-staff-reports/consumer-sentinel-network-data-book-2017/id-theft-reports-by-type

Issues & Activities

1. If the total number of reports received was 471,748, use the chart above to find how many reports were in the credit card and employment fraud categories. Round to the nearest thousand.
2. In teams, research the Internet to find current trends in "identity theft" statistics. List your sources and visually report your findings to the class.

Brainteaser—"I See the Light"

If a digital clock is the only light in an otherwise totally dark room, at what time will the room be the darkest? The brightest?

See the end of Appendix A for the solution.

CHAPTER 16 Inventory

PERFORMANCE OBJECTIVES

INVENTORY VALUATION

As noted on howstuffworks.com, the next time you visit a mega-retailer such as Walmart, you will see one of businesses' greatest logistical triumphs: billion dollar inventory management systems. Retailers such as Target, Lowe's, Home Depot, and Best Buy stock tens of thousands of items from all over the world. Walmart alone stocks items made in more than 70 countries and at any given time manages an average of $32 billion in inventory.

With those kinds of numbers, having an effective and efficient inventory management system is imperative. Walmart's system helps it maintain its signature "everyday low prices" by telling store managers which products are selling and which are simply taking up valuable shelf and warehouse space. Inventory management systems are the rule for such enterprises, but smaller businesses and vendors use them, too. These systems ensure that customers always have enough of what they want and balance that goal against a retailer's financial need to maintain as little inventory as possible.

In business, the term **inventory** is used to describe the goods that a company has in its possession at any given time. For companies engaged in manufacturing activities, inventories are divided into raw materials (used to make other products), partially completed products (work in process), and finished goods (ready for sale to the trade).

Manufacturers sell their finished goods to wholesalers and retailers. These goods, purchased and held expressly for resale, are commonly known as **merchandise inventory**. For wholesalers and retailers, the primary source of revenue is from the sale of this merchandise. In terms of dollars, merchandise inventory is one of the largest and most important assets of a merchandising company. As an expense, the cost of goods sold is the largest deduction from sales in the determination of a company's profit, often larger than the total of operating or overhead expenses.

Interestingly, merchandise inventory is an account that is found on both the balance sheet and the income statement. The method used to determine the value of this inventory has a significant impact on a company's bottom-line results. In addition to appearing on the financial statements, the value of the merchandise inventory must also be determined for income tax purposes and insurance and as a business indicator to management.

To place a value on a merchandise inventory, we must first know the quantity and the cost of the goods remaining at the end of an operating period. Merchandise held for sale must be physically counted at least once a year. Many businesses take inventory on a quarterly or even monthly basis. This is known as a **periodic inventory system** because the physical inventory is counted periodically.

Today most companies use computers to keep track of merchandise inventory on a continuous, or perpetual, basis. This is known as a **perpetual inventory system**. For each merchandise category, the purchases made by the company are added to inventory, whereas the sales to customers are subtracted. These balances are known as the **book inventory** of the items held for sale. As accurate as the perpetual system may be, it must be confirmed with an actual physical count at least once a year.

Taking inventory consists of physically counting, weighing, or measuring the items on hand; placing a price on each item; and multiplying the number of items by the price to determine the total cost. The counting part of taking inventory, although tedious, is not difficult. The pricing part, however, is an important and often controversial business decision. To this day, accountants have varying opinions on the subject of inventory valuation techniques.

In most industries, the prices that businesses pay for goods frequently change. A hardware store, for example, may buy a dozen lightbulbs for $10.00 one month and $12.50 the next. A gasoline station may pay $1.75 per gallon on Tuesday and $1.69 on Thursday. When inventory is taken, it is virtually impossible to determine what price was paid for those items that remain in inventory. This means that the *flow of goods* in and out of a business does not always match the *flow of costs* in and out of the business.

The one method of pricing inventory that actually matches the flow of costs to the flow of goods is known as the **specific identification method**. This method is feasible only when

Dollars AND Sense

Although the material in this chapter essentially deals with accounting procedures, anyone who plans to own or manage a business involving merchandise should have a conceptual understanding of inventory valuation methods.

inventory Goods that a company has in its possession at any given time. May be in the form of raw materials, partially finished goods, or goods available for sale.

merchandise inventory Goods purchased by wholesalers and retailers for resale.

periodic inventory system Inventory system in which merchandise is physically counted at least once a year to determine the value of the goods available for sale.

perpetual inventory system Inventory system in which goods available for sale are updated on a continuous basis by computer. Purchases by the company are added to inventory, whereas sales to customers are subtracted from inventory.

book inventory The balance of a perpetual inventory system at any given time. Must be confirmed with an actual physical count at least once a year.

specific identification method Inventory valuation method in which each item in inventory is matched or coded with its actual cost. Feasible only for low-volume merchandise flow such as automobiles, boats, and other expensive items.

When a cashier scans a product being purchased, a laser reads the **Universal Product Code (UPC)**, a 12-digit bar code on each product's package or label. The digits identify the manufacturer, the product, the size, and product attributes such as flavor or color.

Originally invented by a Toyota subsidiary to track vehicles during production, **QR (Quick Response) Codes** are used for inventory control as well as advertising and many other uses. Both UPC and QR Codes are used for maintaining perpetual inventory systems.

the variety of merchandise carried in stock and the volume of sales are relatively low, such as with automobiles and other expensive items. Each car, for example, has a specific vehicle identification number, or serial number, that makes inventory valuation accurate. A list of the vehicles in stock at any given time with their corresponding costs can easily be totaled to arrive at an inventory figure.

In reality, most businesses have a wide variety of merchandise and find this method too expensive because implementation would require sophisticated computer bar-coding systems. For this reason, it is customary to use an *assumption* as to the flow of costs of merchandise in and out of a business. The three most common cost flow assumptions or inventory pricing methods are as follows:

1. **First-in, first-out (FIFO):** Cost flow is in the order in which the costs were incurred.
2. **Last-in, first-out (LIFO):** Cost flow is in the reverse order in which the costs were incurred.
3. **Average cost:** Cost flow is an average of the costs incurred.

Although cost is the primary basis for the valuation of inventory, when market prices or current replacement costs fall below the actual cost of the items in inventory, the company has incurred a loss. For example, let's say a computer retailer purchases a large quantity of DVD drives at a cost of $200 each. A few months later, due to advances in technology, a faster model is introduced costing only $175 each. Under these market conditions, companies are permitted to choose a method for pricing inventory known as the lower-of-cost-or-market (LCM) rule.

All the inventory valuation methods listed above are acceptable for both income tax reporting and a company's financial statements. As we see in this section, each of these methods has advantages and disadvantages. Economic conditions such as whether merchandise prices are rising (inflation) or falling (deflation) play an important role in the decision of which method to adopt.

For income tax reporting, once a method has been chosen, the Internal Revenue Service (IRS) requires that it be used consistently from one year to the next. Any changes in the method used for inventory valuation must be for a good reason and must be approved by the IRS.

16-1   PRICING INVENTORY BY USING THE FIRST-IN, FIRST-OUT (FIFO) METHOD

first-in, first-out (FIFO) method
Inventory valuation method that assumes the items purchased by a company *first* are the *first* items to be sold. Items remaining in ending inventory at the end of an accounting period are therefore considered as if they were the most recently purchased.

The **first-in, first-out (FIFO) method**, illustrated in Exhibit 16-1, assumes that the items purchased *first* are the *first* items sold. The items in inventory at the end of the year are matched with the costs of items of the same type that were most recently purchased. This method closely approximates the manner in which most businesses reduce their inventory, especially when the merchandise is perishable or subject to frequent style or model changes.

Essentially, this method involves taking physical inventory at the end of the year or accounting period and assigning cost in reverse order in which the purchases were received.

STEPS TO CALCULATE THE VALUE OF ENDING INVENTORY BY USING FIFO

STEP 1. List the number of units on hand at the end of the year and their corresponding costs starting with the ending balance and working *backward* through the incoming shipments.

STEP 2. Multiply the number of units by the corresponding cost per unit for each purchase.

STEP 3. Calculate the value of ending inventory by totaling the extensions from Step 2.

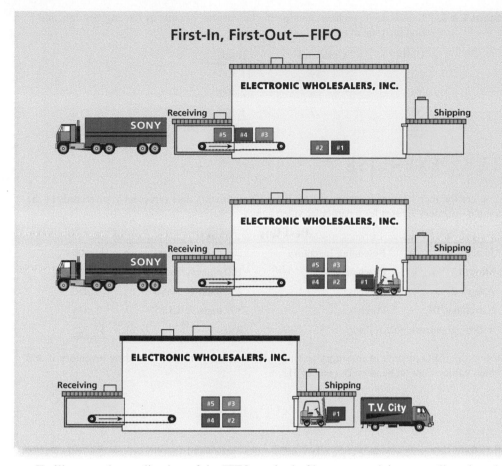

EXHIBIT 16-1
First-In, First-Out—FIFO

To illustrate the application of the FIFO method of inventory pricing as well as the other methods in this section, we will use the following annual inventory data for 8 × 10 picture frames at Target.

Target

January 1	Beginning Inventory	400 units @ $5	$ 2,000
April 9	Purchase	200 units @ $6	1,200
July 19	Purchase	500 units @ $7	3,500
October 15	Purchase	300 units @ $8	2,400
December 8	Purchase	200 units @ $9	1,800
Picture frames available for sale during the year		1,600	$10,900

Target is an upscale discounter that provides high-quality, on-trend merchandise at attractive prices in spacious and guest-friendly stores. In addition, Target operates an online business, Target.com.

The Target merchandise mix includes 23% household essentials, 22% hardlines, 20% apparel and accessories, 19% home furnishings and décor, and 16% food and pet supplies.

EXAMPLE1 PRICING INVENTORY BY USING THE FIFO METHOD

When physical inventory of the picture frames was taken at Target on December 31, it was found that 700 remained in inventory. Using the FIFO method of inventory pricing, what is the dollar value of this ending inventory?

►SOLUTIONSTRATEGY

With the assumption under FIFO that the inventory cost flow is made up of the *most recent* costs, the 700 picture frames in ending inventory would be valued as follows:

Step 1. Set up a table listing the 700 picture frames with costs in reverse order of acquisition.

200 units @ $9 from the December 8 purchase
300 units @ $8 from the October 15 purchase
200 units @ $7 from the July 19 purchase
700 Inventory, December 31

Steps 2 & 3. Extend each purchase, multiplying the number of units by the cost per unit, and find the total of the extensions.

Units	Cost/Unit	Total
200	$9	$1,800
300	8	2,400
200	7	1,400
700		$5,600 Ending inventory using FIFO

►TRY IT EXERCISE 1

You are the merchandise manager at Best Buy. The following data represent your records of the annual inventory figures for a particular video game.

Best Buy

January 1	Beginning Inventory	200 units @ $8.00	$1,600
May 14	Purchase	100 units @ $8.50	850
August 27	Purchase	250 units @ $9.00	2,250
November 18	Purchase	300 units @ $8.75	2,625
Video games available for sale		850	$7,325

Using the FIFO method of inventory pricing, what is the dollar value of ending inventory if 380 video games were on hand on December 31?

CHECK YOUR ANSWER WITH THE SOLUTION ON PAGE 580.

16-2 PRICING INVENTORY BY USING THE LAST-IN, FIRST-OUT (LIFO) METHOD

last-in, first-out (LIFO) method
Inventory valuation method that assumes the items purchased by a company *last* are the *first* items to be sold. Items remaining in ending inventory at the end of an accounting period are therefore considered as if they were the oldest goods.

The **last-in, first-out (LIFO) method**, illustrated in Exhibit 16-2, assumes that the items purchased *last* are sold or removed from inventory *first*. The items in inventory at the end of the year are matched with the cost of items of the same type that were purchased earliest. Therefore, items included in the ending inventory are considered to be those from the beginning inventory plus those acquired first from purchases.

This method involves taking physical inventory at the end of the year or accounting period and assigning cost in the same order in which the purchases were received.

STEPS TO CALCULATE THE VALUE OF ENDING INVENTORY BY USING LIFO

STEP 1. List the number of units on hand at the end of the year and their corresponding costs starting with the beginning inventory and working *forward* through the incoming shipments.

STEP 2. Multiply the number of units by the corresponding cost per unit for each purchase.

STEP 3. Calculate the value of ending inventory by totaling the extensions from Step 2.

iStock.com/Nikada

EXHIBIT 16-2
Last-In, First-Out—LIFO

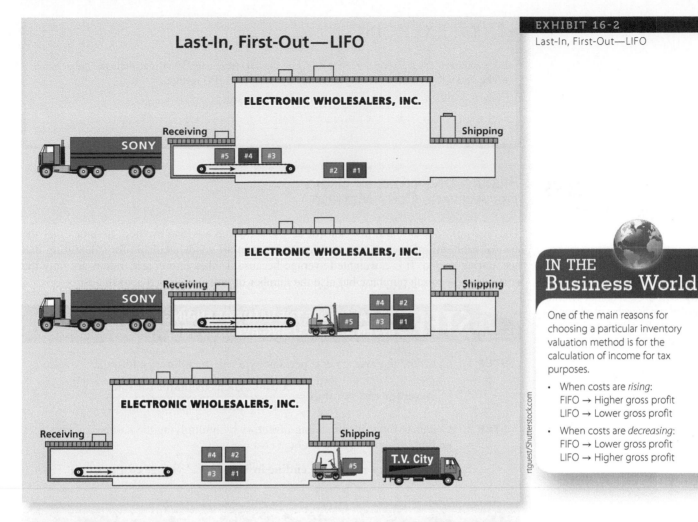

Last-In, First-Out—LIFO

IN THE Business World

One of the main reasons for choosing a particular inventory valuation method is for the calculation of income for tax purposes.

- When costs are *rising*:
  FIFO → Higher gross profit
  LIFO → Lower gross profit

- When costs are *decreasing*:
  FIFO → Lower gross profit
  LIFO → Higher gross profit

rtguest/Shutterstock.com

EXAMPLE2 PRICING INVENTORY BY USING THE LIFO METHOD

Let's return to the previous example about the 8 × 10 picture frames from Target, page 555. Once again, when physical inventory was taken on December 31, it was found that 700 remained in inventory. Using the LIFO method of inventory pricing, what is the dollar value of this ending inventory?

SOLUTIONSTRATEGY

With the assumption under LIFO that the inventory cost flow is made up of the *earliest* costs, the 700 picture frames in ending inventory would be valued as follows:

Step 1. Set up a table listing the 700 picture frames with costs in the order in which they were acquired.

400 units @ $5 from the January 1 beginning inventory
200 units @ $6 from the April 9 purchase
100 units @ $7 from the July 19 purchase
700 Inventory, December 31

Steps 2 & 3. Extend each purchase, multiplying the number of units by the cost per unit, and find the total of the extensions.

Units	Cost/Unit	Total	
400	$5	$2,000	
200	6	1,200	
100	7	700	
700		$3,900	Ending inventory using LIFO

TRYITEXERCISE 2

Let's return to Try It Exercise 1, Best Buy. Use the data from page 556 to calculate the dollar value of the 380 video games in ending inventory by using the LIFO method.

CHECK YOUR ANSWER WITH THE SOLUTION ON PAGE 580.

16-3 PRICING INVENTORY BY USING THE AVERAGE COST METHOD

average cost, or **weighted average**, **method** Inventory valuation method that assumes the cost of each unit of inventory is the average cost of all goods available for sale during that accounting period.

The **average cost method,** also known as **the weighted average method,** assumes that the cost of each unit of inventory is the *average* cost of all goods available for sale during that accounting period. It is a weighted average because it takes into consideration not only the cost per unit in each purchase but also the number of units purchased at each cost.

STEPS TO CALCULATE THE VALUE OF ENDING INVENTORY BY USING AVERAGE COST

STEP 1. Calculate the average cost per unit by using the following formula.

$$\text{Average cost per unit} = \frac{\text{Cost of goods available for sale}}{\text{Total units available for sale}}$$

STEP 2. Calculate the value of ending inventory by multiplying the number of units in ending inventory by the average cost per unit.

$$\text{Ending inventory} = \text{Units in ending inventory} \times \text{Average cost per unit}$$

EXAMPLE3 PRICING INVENTORY BY USING AVERAGE COST

Let's return once again to the example of the 8 × 10 picture frames from Target, page 555. Using the average cost method of inventory pricing, what is the dollar value of the 700 frames on hand in ending inventory?

SOLUTIONSTRATEGY

Under the weighted average cost method, the 700 frames in ending inventory would be valued as follows:

Step 1. Calculate the average cost per unit:

$$\text{Average cost per unit} = \frac{\text{Cost of goods available for sale}}{\text{Total units available for sale}}$$

$$\text{Average cost per unit} = \frac{10,900}{1,600} = \$6.81$$

Step 2. Ending inventory = Units in ending inventory × Average cost per unit
Ending inventory = 700 × 6.81 = $\underline{\$4,767}$

TRYITEXERCISE 3

Once again, let's use the Best Buy example. This time use the data from page 556 to calculate the value of the 380 video games in ending inventory by using the average cost method.

CHECK YOUR ANSWER WITH THE SOLUTION ON PAGE 580.

iStock.com/Nikada

PRICING INVENTORY BY USING THE LOWER-OF-COST-OR-MARKET (LCM) RULE

16-4

The three methods of pricing inventory discussed to this point—FIFO, LIFO, and weighted average—have been based on the cost of the merchandise. When the market price or current replacement price of an inventory item declines below the actual price paid for that item, companies are permitted to use a method known as the **lower-of-cost-or-market (LCM) rule**. This method takes into account such market conditions as severely falling prices, changing fashions or styles, and obsolescence of inventory items. The use of the LCM rule assumes that decreases in replacement costs will be accompanied by proportionate decreases in selling prices.

The lower of cost or market means comparing the market value (current replacement cost) of each item on hand with its cost, using the lower amount as its inventory value. Under ordinary circumstances, market value means the usual price paid based on the volume of merchandise normally ordered by the firm.

lower-of-cost-or-market (LCM) rule Inventory valuation method whereby items in inventory are valued at their actual cost or their current replacement value, whichever is lower. This method is permitted under conditions of falling prices or merchandise obsolescence.

STEPS TO CALCULATE THE VALUE OF ENDING INVENTORY BY USING THE LOWER-OF-COST-OR-MARKET RULE

STEP 1. Calculate the cost for each item in the inventory by using one of the acceptable methods: FIFO, LIFO, or weighted average.

STEP 2. Determine the market price or current replacement cost for each item.

STEP 3. For each item, select the basis for valuation, cost or market, by choosing the lower figure.

STEP 4. Calculate the total amount for each inventory item by multiplying the number of items by the valuation price chosen in Step 3.

STEP 5. Calculate the total value of the inventory by adding all the figures in the Amount column.

EXAMPLE4 PRICING INVENTORY BY USING THE LCM RULE

The following data represent the inventory figures of the Sundance Boutique. Use the lower-of-cost-or-market rule to calculate the extended amount for each item and the total value of the inventory.

Item	Description	Quantity	Unit Price Cost	Market	Valuation Basis	Amount
Blouses	Style #44	40	$ 27.50	$ 31.25	_____	_____
	Style #54	54	36.40	33.20	_____	_____
Slacks	Style #20	68	42.10	39.80	_____	_____
	Style #30	50	57.65	59.18	_____	_____
Jackets	Suede	30	141.50	130.05	_____	_____
	Wool	35	88.15	85.45	_____	_____
				Total Value of Inventory		_____

iStock.com/Nikada

▶SOLUTIONSTRATEGY

In this example, the cost and market price are given. We begin by choosing the lower of cost or market and then extending each item to the Amount column. For example, the Style #44 blouse will be valued at the cost, $27.50, because it is less than the market price, $31.25. The extension would be 40 × $27.50 = $1,100.00.

Item	Description	Quantity	Unit Price Cost	Unit Price Market	Valuation Basis	Amount
Blouses	Style #44	40	$ 27.50	$ 31.25	Cost	$ 1,100.00
	Style #54	54	36.40	33.20	Market	1,792.80
Slacks	Style #20	68	42.10	39.80	Market	2,706.40
	Style #30	50	57.65	59.18	Cost	2,882.50
Jackets	Suede	30	141.50	130.05	Market	3,901.50
	Wool	35	88.15	85.45	Market	2,990.75
					Total Value of Inventory	$15,373.95

▶TRYITEXERCISE 4

Determine the value of the following inventory for the Personal Touch Gift Shop by using the lower-of-cost-or-market rule.

Description	Quantity	Unit Price Cost	Unit Price Market	Valuation Basis	Amount
Lamps	75	$ 9.50	$ 9.20	_____	_____
Jewelry Boxes	120	26.30	27.15	_____	_____
16" Vases	88	42.40	39.70	_____	_____
12" Vases	64	23.65	21.40	_____	_____
Fruit Bowls	42	36.90	42.00	_____	_____
				Total Value of Inventory	_____

CHECK YOUR ANSWERS WITH THE SOLUTIONS ON PAGE 581.

SECTION I   **16**   **REVIEW EXERCISES**

1. Calculate the total number of Sonic Blu-ray players available for sale and the cost of goods available for sale from the following inventory figures at Superior Electronics.

Superior Electronics
Sonic Blu-ray Player Inventory

Date	Units Purchased	Cost per Unit	Total Cost
Beginning Inventory, January 1	40	$125	$5,000
Purchase, February 20	32	118	3,776
Purchase, April 16	30	146	4,380
Purchase, June 8	25	135	3,375
Blu-ray Players Available for Sale	127	Cost of Goods Available for Sale	$16,531

2. **When the buyer for Superior Electronics (Exercise 1) took physical inventory of the Blu-ray players on July 31, 64 units remained in inventory.**

   a. **Calculate the dollar value of the 64 Blu-ray players by using FIFO.**

Units	Cost/Unit	Total
25	$135	$3,375
30	146	4,380
9	118	1,062
64		$8,817 FIFO

   b. **Calculate the dollar value of the 64 Blu-ray players by using LIFO.**

Units	Cost/Unit	Total
40	$125	$5,000
24	118	2,832
64		$7,832 LIFO

   c. **Calculate the dollar value of the 64 Blu-ray players by using the average cost method. Round average cost to the nearest cent.**

   $$\text{Average cost} = \frac{16,531}{127} = 130.165 = \$130.17 \text{ each}$$

   Inventory value $= 64 \times 130.17 = \underline{\$8,330.88}$

Advance Auto Parts began as a two-store operation in 1932 in Virginia. It now operates over 3,700 locations in forty states plus Puerto Rico and the Virgin Islands.

3. The annual inventory of Bargain Bonanza, Inc. shows the following information for jackets:

Date		Qty	Cost	Total Cost
January 1	Beginning Inventory	400	$46	$18,400
February 14	Purchase	150	43	6,450
July 13	Purchase	250	50	12,500
September 2	Purchase	400	69	27,600
October 8	Purchase	200	58	11,600
	Total available for sale	1,400		$76,550

If 938 jackets were on hand on December 31, find the value of the ending inventory using the FIFO method of inventory pricing?

_____

_____

4. Westcoast Purveyors had 301 computer system in stock at the end of the year. Inventory records show the following information:

Date		Qty	Cost	Total Cost
January 1	Beginning Inventory	50	$1,428	$71,400
June 21	Purchase	50	1,152	57,600
August 1	Purchase	300	924	277,200
October 23	Purchase	200	1,176	235,200
November 16	Purchase	100	1,464	146,400
	Total available for sale	700		$787,800

Using the LIFO method of inventory pricing, calculate the dollar value of the ending inventory.

_____

_____

5. Southern Industries had 403 dining sets in stock at the end of the year. Inventory records show the following information:

Date		Qty	Cost	Total Cost
January 1	Beginning Inventory	50	$1,320	$66,000
April 13	Purchase	300	1,296	388,800
May 2	Purchase	300	1,248	374,400
September 7	Purchase	250	1,272	318,000
November 18	Purchase	400	1,236	494,400
	Total available for sale	1,300		$1,641,600

Using the average cost method of inventory pricing, calculate the dollar value of the ending inventory.

6. Calculate the total number of units available for sale and the cost of goods available for sale from the following inventory of oil filters for Advance Auto Parts.

Advance Auto Parts
Oil Filter Inventory

Date	Units Purchased	Cost per Unit	Total Cost
Beginning Inventory, January 1	160	$1.45	_____
Purchase, March 14	210	1.65	_____
Purchase, May 25	190	1.52	_____
Purchase, August 19	300	1.77	_____
Purchase, October 24	250	1.60	_____
Total Units Available	_____	**Cost of Goods Available for Sale**	_____

7. When the merchandise manager of Advance Auto Parts took physical inventory of the oil filters on December 31, it was found that 550 remained in inventory.

a. Calculate the dollar value of the 550 oil filters by using FIFO.

b. Calculate the dollar value of the 550 oil filters by using LIFO.

c. Calculate the dollar value of the 550 filters by using the average cost method.

8. The following data represent the inventory figures for 55-gallon fish tanks at Something's Fishy.

Something's Fishy
55-Gallon Fish Tanks Inventory

			Amount
January 1	Beginning Inventory	42 units @ $38.00	_____
March 12	Purchase	80 units @ $36.50	_____
July 19	Purchase	125 units @ $39.70	_____
September 2	Purchase	75 units @ $41.75	_____
Fish Tanks Available for Sale		**Cost of Tanks Available for Sale**	_____

a. How many fish tanks did Something's Fishy have available for sale?

b. Calculate the total cost of the tanks available for sale.

c. If physical inventory on December 31 showed 88 tanks on hand, calculate their dollar value by using FIFO.

d. Calculate the value of the 88 tanks by using LIFO.

e. Calculate the dollar value of the 88 tanks by using the average cost method.

9. **Determine the value of the following inventory for A Nose for Clothes Boutique by using the lower-of-cost-or-market rule.**

A Nose for Clothes Boutique

Description	Quantity	Unit Price Cost	Unit Price Market	Valuation Basis	Amount
Jackets	56	$124	$128	Cost	$ 6,944
Slacks	88	58	53	Market	4,664
Belts	162	19	17	Market	2,754
Blouses	125	41	45	Cost	5,125
				Total Value of Inventory	**$19,487**

True Value, headquartered in Chicago, is one of the world's largest retailer-owned hardware cooperatives. True Value's cooperative serves 54 countries with more than 5,000 stores, 12 regional distribution centers, and 3,000 associates.

A cooperative, or co-operative, is a retailer-owned buying group consisting of members. It's not a franchise, but a group of individual store owners. Collectively, store operators own their wholesale distributor, which is True Value Company. To become a member, you must purchase 60 shares of Class A common stock per store. In addition to acquiring the stock, there are other financial considerations to be made in order to cover inventory, fixtures, equipment, and start-up costs.

10. Use the lower-of-cost-or-market rule to determine the value of the following inventory for Save-Mor Merchandisers.

Item	Qty	Cost	Market	Basis	Amount
Raincoats	470	$53	$83	____	____
Birdsages	315	50	38	____	____
Radios	222	48	47	____	____
Calculators	377	17	14	____	____
Video games	467	40	33	____	____
			Total value of Inventory		====

11. Determine the value of the following inventory for the Rainbow Gardens Emporium by using the lower-of-cost-or-market rule.

Rainbow Gardens Emporium

Description	Quantity	Unit Price Cost	Market	Valuation Basis	Amount
Dish Sets	220	$36	$33	____	____
Tablecloths	180	13	14	____	____
Barbeque Tools	428	35	33	____	____
Outdoor Lamps	278	56	50	____	____
Ceramic Statues	318	22	17	____	____
			Total Value of Inventory		====

BUSINESS DECISION: IN OR OUT?

12. You are the accounting manager of Kleen and Green Janitorial Supply, Inc., of Chicago. One of your junior accountants is working on the December 31 year-end inventory figures and has asked for your help in determining which of several transactions belong in the ending inventory. From the following inventory scenarios, decide which *should* be included in the year-end inventory and which *should not. Hint:* Refer to Exhibit 7-3, Shipping Terms, page 200.

   a. An order for a floor buffer and three different floor conditioning attachments shipped on December 31, FOB Chicago, and is expected to arrive on January 4.
   b. An order for six drums of floor wax and four drums of wax stripper was shipped to a Detroit customer on December 31, FOB Detroit, and should arrive on January 2.
   c. An order for 5 foot-operated mop buckets and 12 rag mops will be shipped on January 3.
   d. A floor cleaning machine was returned on December 28 for warranty repair and is scheduled to be return-shipped on January 6.
   e. Two cases of window wipes were shipped on December 30 FOB destination and are due to arrive on January 5.
   f. A carton of 12 one-gallon bottles of window washing solution and 8 boxes of streak-free window washing cloths were ordered on December 30 and are due to be shipped on January 3.

INVENTORY ESTIMATION

16 SECTION II

In Section I of this chapter, we learned to calculate the value of ending inventory with several methods using a physical count at the end of the accounting year. Most companies, however, require inventory figures more frequently than the once-a-year physical inventory. Monthly and quarterly financial statements, for example, may be prepared with inventory estimates rather than expensive physical counts or perpetual inventory systems. In addition, when physical inventories are destroyed by fire or other disasters, estimates must be made for insurance claims purposes.

The two generally accepted methods for *estimating* the value of an inventory are the retail method and the gross profit method. For these methods to closely approximate the actual value of inventory, the markup rate for all items bought and sold by the company must be consistent. If they are not, the estimates should be calculated separately for each product category. For example, if a toy store gets a 30% markup on tricycles and 50% on bicycles, these categories should be calculated separately.

IN THE Business World

In business today, it is common practice for retail stores to use the retail method of inventory valuation, whereas manufacturers and wholesalers use the gross profit method.

ESTIMATING THE VALUE OF ENDING INVENTORY BY USING THE RETAIL METHOD

16-5

The **retail method** of inventory estimation is used by retail businesses of all types and sizes, from Walmart and Sears to the corner grocery store. To use this method, the company must have certain figures in its accounting records, including the following:

a. *Beginning inventory* at cost price and at retail (selling price)

b. *Purchases* during the period at cost price and at retail

c. *Net sales* for the period

From these figures, the goods available for sale are determined at both cost and retail. We then calculate a ratio known as the **cost to retail price ratio**, or simply **cost ratio**, by the formula:

$$\text{Cost ratio} = \frac{\text{Goods available for sale at cost}}{\text{Goods available for sale at retail}}$$

This ratio represents the cost of each dollar of retail sales. For example, if the cost ratio for a company is .6, or 60%, this means that $.60 is the cost of each $1.00 of retail sales.

retail method Method of inventory estimation used by most retailers based on a comparison of goods available for sale at cost and at retail.

cost to retail price ratio, or **cost ratio** Ratio of goods available for sale at cost to the goods available for sale at retail. Used in the retail method of inventory estimation to represent the cost of each dollar of retail sales.

STEPS TO ESTIMATE THE VALUE OF ENDING INVENTORY BY USING THE RETAIL METHOD

STEP 1. List beginning inventory and purchases at both cost and retail.

STEP 2. Add purchases to beginning inventory to determine goods available for sale at both cost and retail.

Beginning inventory
+ Purchases
―――――――――――
Goods available for sale

STEP 3. Calculate the cost ratio.

$$\text{Cost ratio} = \frac{\text{Goods available for sale at cost}}{\text{Goods available for sale at retail}}$$

iStock.com/Nikada

STEP 4. Subtract net sales from goods available for sale at retail to get ending inventory at retail.

$$\begin{array}{r} \text{Goods available for sale at retail} \\ -\ \text{Net sales} \\ \hline \text{Ending inventory at retail} \end{array}$$

STEP 5. Convert ending inventory at retail to ending inventory at cost by multiplying the ending inventory at retail by the cost ratio.

Ending inventory at cost = Ending inventory at retail × Cost ratio

EXAMPLE5　ESTIMATING INVENTORY USING THE RETAIL METHOD

Using the retail method, estimate the value of the ending inventory at cost on June 30 from the following information for Dependable Distributors, Inc.

Dependable Distributors, Inc.
Financial Highlights
June 1–June 30

	Cost	Retail
Beginning Inventory	$200,000	$400,000
Net Purchases (June)	150,000	300,000
Net Sales (June) $500,000		

►SOLUTIONSTRATEGY

Steps 1 & 2. List the beginning inventory and purchases and calculate the goods available for sale.

	Cost	Retail
Beginning Inventory	$200,000	$400,000
+ Net Purchases (June)	+ 150,000	+ 300,000
Goods Available for Sale	$350,000	$700,000

Step 3. $\text{Cost ratio} = \dfrac{\text{Goods available for sale at cost}}{\text{Goods available for sale at retail}}$

$\text{Cost ratio} = \dfrac{350,000}{700,000} = .5 = 50\%$

Remember, this 50% figure means that $.50 was the cost of each $1.00 of retail sales.

Step 4. Find ending inventory at retail.

$$\begin{array}{lr} \text{Goods available for sale at retail} & \$700,000 \\ -\ \text{Net sales} & -\ 500,000 \\ \hline \text{Ending inventory at retail} & \$200,000 \end{array}$$

Step 5. Convert the inventory at retail to inventory at cost by using the cost ratio.
Ending inventory at cost = Ending inventory at retail × Cost ratio
Ending inventory at cost = 200,000 × .5 = $100,000

►TRYITEXERCISE 5

Using the retail method, estimate the value of the ending inventory at cost on August 31 from the following information for Ripe 'N Ready Fruit Wholesalers, Inc.

Ripe 'N Ready Fruit Wholesalers, Inc.
Financial Highlights
August 1–August 31

	Cost	Retail
Beginning Inventory	$600,000	$800,000
Net Purchases (August)	285,000	380,000
Net Sales (August) $744,000		

CHECK YOUR ANSWER WITH THE SOLUTION ON PAGE 581.

ESTIMATING THE VALUE OF ENDING INVENTORY BY USING THE GROSS PROFIT METHOD

16-6

The **gross profit** or **gross margin method** uses a company's gross margin percent to estimate the ending inventory. This method assumes that a company maintains approximately the same gross margin from year to year. Inventories estimated in this manner are frequently used for interim reports and insurance claims; however, this method is not acceptable for inventory valuation on a company's annual financial statements.

From Chapter 15, remember that net sales comprises the cost of goods sold and gross margin.

gross profit or **gross margin method** Method of inventory estimation using a company's gross margin percent to estimate the ending inventory. This method assumes that a company maintains approximately the same gross margin from year to year.

> **Net sales (100%) = Cost of goods sold (%) + Gross margin (%)**

From this equation, we see that when the gross margin percent is known, the cost of goods sold percent would be its complement because together they equal net sales, which is 100%.

> **Cost of goods sold percent = 100% − Gross margin percent**

Knowing the cost of goods sold percent is the key to this calculation. We use this percent to find the cost of goods sold, which when subtracted from goods available for sale, gives us the estimated ending inventory.

STEPS TO ESTIMATE THE VALUE OF ENDING INVENTORY BY USING THE GROSS PROFIT METHOD

STEP 1. Calculate the goods available for sale.

$$\begin{array}{l} \text{Beginning inventory} \\ + \text{Net Purchases} \\ \hline \text{Goods available for sale} \end{array}$$

STEP 2. Find the estimated cost of goods sold by multiplying net sales by the cost of goods sold percent (complement of gross margin percent).

> **Estimated cost of goods sold = Net sales (100% − Gross margin%)**

STEP 3. Calculate the estimate of ending inventory by subtracting the estimated cost of goods sold from the goods available for sale.

$$\begin{array}{l} \text{Goods available for sale} \\ - \text{Estimated cost of goods sold} \\ \hline \text{Estimated ending inventory} \end{array}$$

EXAMPLE6   ESTIMATING INVENTORY BY USING THE GROSS PROFIT METHOD

Angler's Fishing Supply, Inc., maintains a gross margin of 45% on all its wholesale supplies. In April, Angler's had a beginning inventory of $80,000, net purchases of $320,000, and net sales of $500,000. Use the gross profit method to estimate Angler's cost of ending inventory.

►SOLUTIONSTRATEGY

Step 1.
Beginning inventory (April 1)	$ 80,000
+ Net purchases	320,000
Goods available for sale	$400,000

Step 2.   Estimated cost of goods sold = Net sales (100% − Gross margin %)
Estimated cost of goods sold = $500,000 (100% − 45%) = $275,000

Step 3.
Goods available for sale	$400,000
− Estimated cost of goods sold	275,000
Estimated ending inventory (April 30)	$125,000

►TRYITEXERCISE 6

Fantasy Beauty Products, Inc., maintains a gross margin of 39% on all its wholesale beauty supplies. In November, the company had a beginning inventory of $137,000, net purchases of $220,000, and net sales of $410,000. Use the gross profit method to estimate the cost of ending inventory for November.

CHECK YOUR ANSWER WITH THE SOLUTION ON PAGE 581.

SECTION II 16 REVIEW EXERCISES

1. Using the retail method, estimate the value of the ending inventory at cost on June 30 from the following information for Perfume Bazaar. Round the cost ratio to the nearest whole percent.

Perfume Bazaar
Financial Highlights
June 1–June 30

	Cost	Retail
Beginning inventory, June 1	$43,000	$92,000
Net purchases (June)	26,000	55,300
Net sales (June) $132,400		

	Cost	Retail		
Beginning inventory, June 1	$43,000	$92,000	Goods available for sale at retail	$147,300
Net purchases (June)	26,000	55,300	Net sales	− 132,400
Goods available for sale	$69,000	$147,300	Ending inventory at retail	$14,900
			Ending inventory at cost = 14,900 × 47%	

Cost ratio $= \dfrac{69,000}{147,300} = .468 = 47\%$

$= \$7,003$

2. Universal Suppliers had sales of $476,000 in the month of June. Use the retail method to estimate the value of the inventory as of June 30 given the following financial information:

Universal Suppliers
Financial Highlights
June 1–June 30

	Cost	Retail
Beginning Inventory	$302,371	$585,900
Net Purchases (June)	117,165	220,900

3. Using the retail method, estimate the value of the ending inventory at cost on September 30 from the following information for Scandinavian Furniture Designs, Inc. Round the cost ratio to the nearest tenth of a percent.

Scandinavian Furniture Designs, Inc.
September 1–September 30

	Cost	Retail
Beginning Inventory, September 1	$150,000	$450,000
Purchases (September)	90,000	270,000
Net Sales (September) $395,000		

4. **Rambo Plumbing Supply maintains a gross margin of 40% on all of its kitchen sinks and faucet sets. In November, Rambo had a beginning inventory of $178,400, net purchases of $91,200, and net sales of $215,800. Use the gross profit method to estimate the cost of ending inventory.**

Beginning inventory, Nov. 1	$178,400	Estimated cost of goods sold = 215,800(100% − 40%)
Net purchases (Nov.)	+ 91,200	= 215,800 × .6 = $129,480
Goods available for sale	$269,600	

Goods available for sale	$269,600
Cost of goods sold	− 129,480
Estimated ending inventory	$140,120

5. On July 1, the total inventory for Save-Mor Merchandisers was $614,100. Net purchases during the month were $314,900 and sales amounted to $611,400. Gross margin on sales was 62%.

Estimate the cost value of the inventory as of July 31 using the gross profit method.

6. Omni Fitness Equipment, Inc., maintains a gross margin of 55% on all its weight training products. In April, Omni had a beginning inventory of $146,000, net purchases of $208,000, and net sales of $437,000. Use the gross profit method to estimate the cost of ending inventory.

7. The following data represent the inventory figures for Hot Shot Welding Supply, Inc. Using the retail method, estimate the value of the ending inventory at cost on January 31. Round the cost ratio to the nearest tenth of a percent.

Hot Shot Welding Supply, Inc.
January 1–January 31

	Cost	Retail
Beginning Inventory, January 1	$50,000	$120,000
Net purchases (January)	90,000	216,000
Net Sales (January) $188,000		

8. You are the warehouse manager for Discovery Kitchen Supplies. On a Sunday in May, you receive a phone call from the owner. He states that the entire building and contents were destroyed by fire. For the police report and the insurance claim, the owner has asked you to estimate the value of the lost inventory. Your records, which luckily were backed up on the hard drive of your home computer, indicate that at the time of the fire, the net sales to date were $615,400 and the purchases were $232,600. The beginning inventory on January 1 was $312,000. For the past three years, the company has operated at a gross margin of 60%. Use the gross profit method to calculate your answer.

BUSINESS DECISION: OVER OR UNDER?

9. You own Bristol Marine, a retailer of boats, motors, and marine accessories. The store manager has just informed you that the amount of the physical inventory was incorrectly reported as $540,000 instead of the correct amount of $450,000. Unfortunately, yesterday you sent the quarterly financial statements to the stockholders. Now you must send revised statements and a letter of explanation.

a. What effect did the error have on the items of the balance sheet for Bristol? Express your answer as *overstated* or *understated* for the items affected by the error.

b. What effect will the error have on the items of the income statement for Bristol?

c. Did this error make the Bristol quarterly results look better or worse than they actually were?

INVENTORY TURNOVER AND TARGETS

16 SECTION III

In Chapter 15, we learned to use inventory turnover as one of the financial statement efficiency ratios. To review, **inventory turnover**, or **stock turnover**, is the number of times during an operating period that the average dollars invested in merchandise inventory was theoretically sold out or turned over.

Generally, the more expensive the item, the lower the turnover rate. For example, furniture and fine jewelry items might have a turnover rate of three or four times per year, whereas a grocery store might have a turnover of 15 or 20 times per year, or more. In this section, we revisit the concept of inventory turnover and learn to calculate it at retail and at cost.

Although a company must maintain inventory quantities large enough to meet the day-to-day demands of its operations, it is important to keep the amount invested in inventory to a minimum. In this section, we also learn to calculate target inventories for companies based on published industry standards.

Regardless of the method used to determine inventory turnover, the procedure always involves dividing some measure of sales volume by a measure of the typical or average inventory. This **average inventory** is commonly found by adding the beginning and ending inventories of the operating period and dividing by 2.

inventory, or stock, turnover The number of times during an operating period that the average dollars invested in merchandise inventory was theoretically sold out or turned over. May be calculated in retail dollars or in cost dollars.

average inventory An estimate of a company's typical inventory at any given time that is calculated by dividing the total of all inventories taken during an operating period by the number of times inventory was taken.

$$\text{Average inventory} = \frac{\text{Beginning inventory} + \text{Ending inventory}}{2}$$

Whenever possible, additional interim inventories should be used to increase the accuracy of the average inventory figure. For example, if a mid-year inventory was taken, this figure would be added to the beginning and ending inventories and the total divided by 3. If monthly inventories were available, they would be added and the total divided by 12.

CALCULATING INVENTORY TURNOVER RATE AT RETAIL

16-7

When inventory turnover rate is calculated at retail, the measure of sales volume used is net sales. The average inventory is expressed in retail sales dollars by using the beginning and ending inventories at retail. The inventory turnover rate is expressed in number of *times* the inventory was sold out during the period.

STEPS TO CALCULATE INVENTORY TURNOVER RATE AT RETAIL

STEP 1. Calculate average inventory at retail.

$$\text{Average inventory}_{\text{at retail}} = \frac{\text{Beginning inventory at retail} + \text{Ending inventory at retail}}{2}$$

STEP 2. Calculate the inventory turnover at retail. Round to the nearest tenth when necessary.

$$\text{Inventory turnover}_{\text{at retail}} = \frac{\text{Net sales}}{\text{Average inventory at retail}}$$

IN THE Business World

Inventory turnover is an important business indicator, particularly when compared with turnover rates from previous operating periods and with published industry statistics for similar-sized companies.

iStock.com/Nikada

rtguest/Shutterstock.com

RFID—Smart Shopping Long checkout lines at the grocery store are one of the biggest complaints about the shopping experience. According to howstuffworks. com, soon these lines could disappear when the ubiquitous Universal Product Code (UPC) bar code is replaced by **smart labels**, also called **radio frequency identification** (RFID) tags. RFID tags are intelligent bar codes that can communicate to a networked system to track every product that you put in your shopping cart.

Albert Lozano/Shutterstock.com

Imagine going to the grocery store, filling up your cart, and walking right out the door. No longer will you have to wait as someone rings up each item in your cart one at a time. Instead, these RFID tags will communicate with an electronic reader that will detect every item in the cart and ring each up almost instantly. The reader will be connected to a large network that will send information on your products to the retailer and product manufacturers. Your bank will then be notified and the amount of the bill will be deducted from your account. No lines, no waiting!

Source: www.howstuffworks.com

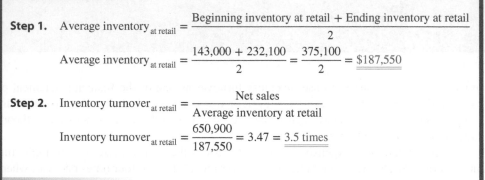

EXAMPLE7 CALCULATING INVENTORY TURNOVER RATE AT RETAIL

Hobby Town had net sales of $650,900 for the year. If the beginning inventory at retail was $143,000 and the ending inventory at retail was $232,100, what are the average inventory at retail and the inventory turnover at retail rounded to the nearest tenth?

▶ SOLUTIONSTRATEGY

Step 1. $\text{Average inventory}_{\text{at retail}} = \dfrac{\text{Beginning inventory at retail} + \text{Ending inventory at retail}}{2}$

$\text{Average inventory}_{\text{at retail}} = \dfrac{143,000 + 232,100}{2} = \dfrac{375,100}{2} = \underline{\underline{\$187,550}}$

Step 2. $\text{Inventory turnover}_{\text{at retail}} = \dfrac{\text{Net sales}}{\text{Average inventory at retail}}$

$\text{Inventory turnover}_{\text{at retail}} = \dfrac{650,900}{187,550} = 3.47 = \underline{\underline{3.5 \text{ times}}}$

▶ TRYITEXERCISE 7

Exotic Gardens had net sales of $260,700 for the year. If the beginning inventory at retail was $65,100 and the ending inventory at retail was $52,800, what are the average inventory and the inventory turnover rounded to the nearest tenth?

CHECK YOUR ANSWERS WITH THE SOLUTIONS ON PAGE 581.

16-8 CALCULATING INVENTORY TURNOVER RATE AT COST

Frequently, the inventory turnover rate of a company is expressed in terms of cost dollars rather than selling price or retail dollars. When this is the case, the cost of goods sold is used as the measure of sales volume and becomes the numerator in the formula. The denominator, average inventory, is calculated at cost.

STEPS TO CALCULATE INVENTORY TURNOVER RATE AT COST

STEP 1. Calculate the average inventory at cost.

$\text{Average inventory}_{\text{at cost}} = \dfrac{\text{Beginning inventory at cost} + \text{Ending inventory at cost}}{2}$

STEP 2. Calculate the inventory turnover at cost.

$\text{Inventory turnover}_{\text{at cost}} = \dfrac{\text{Cost of goods sold}}{\text{Average inventory at cost}}$

iStock.com/Nikada

EXAMPLE8 CALCULATING INVENTORY TURNOVER RATE AT COST

Metro Mechanical, Inc., had cost of goods sold of $416,200 for the year. If the beginning inventory at cost was $95,790 and the ending inventory at cost was $197,100, what are the average inventory at cost and the inventory turnover at cost rounded to the nearest tenth?

SOLUTIONSTRATEGY

Step 1. $\text{Average inventory}_{\text{at cost}} = \dfrac{\text{Beginning inventory at cost} + \text{Ending inventory at cost}}{2}$

$\text{Average inventory}_{\text{at cost}} = \dfrac{95,790 + 197,100}{2} = \dfrac{292,890}{2} = \underline{\$146,445}$

Step 2. $\text{Inventory turnover}_{\text{at cost}} = \dfrac{\text{Cost of goods sold}}{\text{Average inventory at cost}}$

$\text{Inventory turnover}_{\text{at cost}} = \dfrac{416,200}{146,445} = 2.84 = \underline{2.8 \text{ times}}$

TRYITEXERCISE 8

E-Z Kwik Grocery Store had cost of goods sold of $756,400 for the year. If the beginning inventory at cost was $43,500 and the ending inventory at cost was $59,300, what are the average inventory at cost and the inventory turnover rounded to the nearest tenth?

CHECK YOUR ANSWERS WITH THE SOLUTIONS ON PAGE 581.

CALCULATING TARGET INVENTORIES BASED ON INDUSTRY STANDARDS

16-9

When inventory turnover is below average for a particular size firm, it may be a signal that the company is carrying too much inventory. Carrying extra inventory can lead to extra expenses such as warehousing costs and insurance. It also ties up money the company could use more efficiently elsewhere. In certain industries, some additional risks of large inventories would be losses due to price declines, obsolescence, or deterioration of the goods.

Trade associations and the federal government publish a wide variety of important industry statistics, ratios, and standards for every size company. When such inventory turnover figures are available, merchandise managers can use the following formulas to calculate the **target average inventory** required by their firm to achieve the published industry standards for a company with similar sales volume.

$$\text{Target average inventory}_{\text{at cost}} = \dfrac{\text{Cost of goods sold}}{\text{Published inventory turnover at cost}}$$

$$\text{Target average inventory}_{\text{at retail}} = \dfrac{\text{Net sales}}{\text{Published inventory turnover at retail}}$$

target average inventory Inventory standards published by trade associations and the federal government for companies of all sizes in all industries. Used by managers as *targets* for the ideal amount of inventory to carry for maximum efficiency.

EXAMPLE9 CALCULATING TARGET INVENTORIES BASED ON INDUSTRY STANDARDS

F-Stop Photo, Inc., a wholesale photo supply business, had cost of goods sold of $950,000 for the year. The beginning inventory at cost was $245,000, and the ending inventory at cost amounted to $285,000. According to the noted business research firm Dun & Bradstreet, the inventory turnover rate at cost for a photo business of this size is five times. Calculate the average inventory and actual inventory turnover for F-Stop. If the turnover is less than five times, calculate the target average inventory needed by F-Stop to theoretically come up to industry standards.

SOLUTIONSTRATEGY

Step 1.
$$\text{Average inventory}_{\text{at cost}} = \frac{\text{Beginning inventory at cost} + \text{Ending inventory at cost}}{2}$$

$$\text{Average inventory}_{\text{at cost}} = \frac{245{,}000 + 285{,}000}{2} = \frac{530{,}000}{2} = \$265{,}000$$

Step 2.
$$\text{Inventory turnover}_{\text{at cost}} = \frac{\text{Cost of goods sold}}{\text{Average inventory at cost}}$$

$$\text{Inventory turnover}_{\text{at cost}} = \frac{950{,}000}{265{,}000} = 3.58 = \underline{3.6 \text{ times}}$$

Step 3. The actual inventory turnover for F-Stop is *3.6 times* per year compared with the industry standard of five times. This indicates that the company is carrying too much inventory. Let's calculate the target average inventory F-Stop should carry to meet industry standards.

$$\text{Target average inventory}_{\text{at cost}} = \frac{\text{Cost of goods sold}}{\text{Published inventory turnover at cost}}$$

$$\text{Target average inventory}_{\text{at cost}} = \frac{950{,}000}{5} = \underline{\$190{,}000}$$

The actual average inventory carried by F-Stop for the year was $265,000 compared with the target inventory of $190,000. This indicates that at any given time, the inventory for F-Stop averaged about $75,000 higher than that of its competition.

TRYITEXERCISE 9

Satellite Communications, Inc., had net sales of $2,650,000 for the year. The beginning inventory at retail was $495,000, and the ending inventory at retail amounted to $380,000. The inventory turnover at retail published as the standard for a business of this size is seven times. Calculate the average inventory and actual inventory turnover for the company. If the turnover is less than seven times, calculate the target average inventory needed to theoretically come up to industry standards.

CHECK YOUR ANSWERS WITH THE SOLUTIONS ON PAGES 581–582.

SECTION III 16 REVIEW EXERCISES

Assuming that all net sales figures are at *retail* and all cost of goods sold figures are at *cost*, calculate the average inventory and inventory turnover for the following. If the actual turnover is less than the published rate, calculate the target average inventory necessary to come up to industry standards. Round inventories to the nearest dollar and inventory turnovers to the nearest tenth.

	Net Sales	Cost of Goods Sold	Beginning Inventory	Ending Inventory	Average Inventory	Inventory Turnover	Published Rate	Target Average Inventory
1.	$500,000		$50,000	$70,000	$60,000	8.3	10.0	$50,000.00
2.		$335,000	$48,000	$56,000	$52,000	6.4	6.0	Above
3.		$1,200,000	$443,000	$530,000	_____	_____	3.5	_____
4.	$4,570,000		$854,000	$650,300	_____	_____	8.2	_____
5.		$258,400	$76,300	$43,500	_____	_____	5.2	_____
6.	$540,000		$133,250	$71,200	_____	_____	4.8	_____
7.	$1,329,000		$545,800	$387,120	_____	_____	2.6	_____
8.		$884,500	$224,130	$134,900	_____	_____	5.9	_____

9. Bubbles Bath Boutique had net sales of $245,300 for the year. The beginning inventory at retail was $62,600, and the ending inventory at retail was $54,200.

    a. What was the average inventory at retail?

    b. What was the inventory turnover rounded to the nearest tenth?

10. Find the inventory turnover at retail of Walker Manufacturing. The starting inventory at retail was $419,300 and the ending inventory at retail was $304,600. Sales for the year totaled $2,388,870. Round your answer to the nearest tenth.

Circle K has been one of North America's most popular and successful operators of convenience stores for more than 50 years. Today there are more than 3,300 Circle K locations across the United States and over 4,000 Circle K locations across the globe, including Japan, Mexico, China, Guam, and Vietnam.

To become a Circle K franchisee, you must have access to $100,000 in liquid assets and have a net worth of $300,000 as the initial investment. Circle K Stores, Inc., is a subsidiary of Alimentation Couche-Tard, Inc., based in Quebec, Canada. It's the second-largest convenience store operator in North America and the leader in Canada. Alimentation Couche-Tard is French for "food for those who go to bed late."

11. On January 1, Veltron International has inventory worth $599,900 at cost. At the end of the year, the cost value of the inventory was $170,200. If annual cost of goods sold was $1,309,170, find the inventory turnover at cost for the year.

    Round your answer to the nearest tenth.

12. Riverside Industries had cost of goods sold of $359,700 for the year. The beginning inventory at cost was $73,180, and the ending inventory at cost was $79,500.

    a. What was the average inventory at cost?

    b. What was the inventory turnover rounded to the nearest tenth?

13. The cost of goods sold for Veltron International last year amounted to $508,200, and the average inventory at cost was $231,000. The published inventory turnover at cost is 6.6.

    Calculate the inventory turnover at cost, and if it is less than the published rate, calculate the target average inventory at cost.

14. Kwik-Mix Concrete Corporation had cost of goods sold of $1,250,000 for the third quarter. The beginning inventory at cost was $135,000, and the ending inventory at cost amounted to $190,900. The inventory turnover rate published as the industry standard for a business of this size is 9.5 times.

   a. Calculate the average inventory and actual inventory turnover rate for the company.

   b. If the turnover rate is less than 9.5 times, calculate the target average inventory needed to theoretically come up to industry standards.

15. Trophy Masters had net sales for the year of $145,000. The beginning inventory at retail was $36,000, and the ending inventory at retail amounted to $40,300. The inventory turnover rate published as the industry standard for a business of this size is 4.9 times.

   a. Calculate the average inventory and actual inventory turnover rate for the company.

   b. If the turnover rate is less than 4.9 times, calculate the target average inventory needed to theoretically come up to industry standards.

BUSINESS DECISION: KEEP YOUR EYE ON THE FEET

16. Another way to look at the concept of inventory turnover is by measuring sales per square foot. Taking the average inventory at retail and dividing it by the number of square feet devoted to a particular product will give you *average sales per square foot*. When you multiply this figure by the inventory turnover rate, you get the *annual sales per square foot*.

   It is important to know the amount of sales per square foot your merchandise is producing, both on average and annually. These figures should be tracked monthly and compared with industry standards for businesses of similar size and type.

   You own Electron Magic, a large multi product electronics store in a regional mall. The store has 10,000 square feet of selling space divided into five departments.

   a. From the table below, calculate the average and annual sales per square foot. Then calculate the annual sales for each department and the total sales for the entire store.

Electron Magic—Annual Sales

Department	Square Feet	Average Inventory at Retail	Average Sales per Sq. Foot	Inventory Turnover	Annual Sales per Sq. Foot	Departmental Annual Sales
Televisions	3,500	$153,000	_____	5.2	_____	_____
Surround sound	2,800	$141,000	_____	4.6	_____	_____
DSLR cameras	2,100	$38,500	_____	4.1	_____	_____
Cell phones	500	$12,700	_____	2.3	_____	_____
Video gaming	1,100	$45,000	_____	4.7	_____	_____
					Total Sales	_____

   b. If industry standards for this size store and type of merchandise is $200 per square foot in annual sales, which departments are below standards? What can be done to improve the situation?

   c. (Optional) Use the Internet to research and share with the class the current "industry standard" sales per square foot and inventory turnover rates for the merchandise categories of your store.

CHAPTER FORMULAS

Inventory Valuation—Average Cost Method

$$\text{Average cost per unit} = \frac{\text{Cost of goods available for sale}}{\text{Total units available for sale}}$$

Ending inventory = Units in ending inventory × Average cost per unit

Inventory Estimation—Retail Method

$$\text{Cost ratio} = \frac{\text{Goods available for sale at cost}}{\text{Goods available for sale at retail}}$$

Estimated ending inventory at cost = Ending inventory at retail × Cost ratio

Inventory Estimation—Gross Profit Method

Estimated cost of goods sold = Net sales(100% − Gross margin %)

Inventory Turnover—Retail

$$\text{Average inventory}_{\text{retail}} = \frac{\text{Beginning inventory at retail} + \text{Ending inventory at retail}}{2}$$

$$\text{Inventory turnover}_{\text{retail}} = \frac{\text{Net sales}}{\text{Average inventory at retail}}$$

Inventory Turnover—Cost

$$\text{Average inventory}_{\text{cost}} = \frac{\text{Beginning inventory at cost} + \text{Ending inventory at cost}}{2}$$

$$\text{Inventory turnover}_{\text{cost}} = \frac{\text{Cost of goods sold}}{\text{Average inventory at cost}}$$

Target Inventory

$$\text{Target average inventory}_{\text{cost}} = \frac{\text{Cost of goods sold}}{\text{Published inventory turnover at cost}}$$

$$\text{Target average inventory}_{\text{retail}} = \frac{\text{Net sales}}{\text{Published inventory turnover at retail}}$$

CHAPTER SUMMARY

Section I: Inventory Valuation

Topic	Important Concepts	Illustrative Examples
Pricing Inventory by Using the First-In, First-Out (FIFO) Method **Performance Objective 16-1, Page 554**	FIFO assumes that the items purchased first are the first items sold. The items in inventory at the end of the year are matched with the cost of items of the same type that were purchased most recently. *Inventory Pricing—FIFO:* 1. List the number of units on hand at the end of the year and their corresponding costs starting with the ending balance and working *backward* through the incoming shipments. 2. Multiply the number of units by the corresponding cost per unit for each purchase. 3. Calculate the value of ending inventory by totaling all the extensions from Step 2.	The following data represent the inventory figures for imported jewelry boxes at The Gift Collection. Date / Units / Cost per Unit table below

Table for Illustrative Examples:

Date		Units	Cost per Unit
Jan. 1	Beg. Inv.	55	$12.30
Mar. 9	Purch.	60	13.50
Aug. 12	Purch.	45	13.90
Nov. 27	Purch.	75	14.25

On December 31, physical inventory revealed 130 jewelry boxes in stock. Calculate the value of the ending inventory by using FIFO.

Section I (continued)

Topic	Important Concepts	Illustrative Examples
		With the assumption under FIFO that the inventory cost flow is made up of the most recent costs, the 130 jewelry boxes would be valued as follows: **Date / Units / Cost per Unit / Total** Nov. 27 — 75 — $14.25 — $1,068.75 Aug. 12 — 45 — 13.90 — 625.50 Mar. 9 — 10 — 13.50 — 135.00 130 — $1,829.25
Pricing Inventory by Using the Last-In, First-Out (LIFO) Method **Performance Objective 16-2, Page 556**	LIFO assumes that the items purchased last are sold or removed from inventory first. The items in inventory at the end of the year are matched with the cost of the same type items purchased earliest. *Inventory Pricing—LIFO:* 1. List the number of units on hand at the end of the year and their corresponding costs starting with the beginning inventory and working *forward* through the incoming shipments. 2. Multiply the number of units by the corresponding cost per unit for each purchase. 3. Calculate the value of ending inventory by totaling all the extensions from Step 2.	Using the data on page 577 for The Gift Collection, calculate the value of the 130 jewelry boxes in ending inventory by using LIFO. With the assumption under LIFO that the inventory cost flow is made up of the earliest costs, the 130 jewelry boxes would be valued as follows: **Date / Units / Cost per Unit / Total** Jan. 1 — 55 — $12.30 — $ 676.50 Mar. 9 — 60 — 13.50 — 810.00 Aug. 12 — 15 — 13.90 — 208.50 130 — $1,695.00
Pricing Inventory by Using the Average Cost Method **Performance Objective 16-3, Page 558**	The average cost method, also known as the weighted average method, assumes that the cost of each unit of inventory is the average cost of all goods available for sale during that accounting period. 1. Calculate the average cost per unit by 2. Calculate the value of ending inventory by multiplying the number of units in ending inventory by the average cost per unit.	Using the average cost method of inventory pricing, what is the dollar value of the 130 jewelry boxes in ending inventory for The Gift Collection? First, we extend and sum each purchase to find the total units available and the total cost of those units available for sale. **Date / Units / Cost per Unit / Total** Jan. 1 — 55 — $12.30 — $ 676.50 Mar. 9 — 60 — 13.50 — 810.00 Aug. 12 — 45 — 13.90 — 625.50 Nov. 27 — 75 — 14.25 — 1,068.75 235 — $3,180.75 $$\text{Average cost} = \frac{3,180.75}{235} = \$13.54$$ Ending inventory = 130 × 13.54 = $1,760.20
Pricing Inventory by Using the Lower-of-Cost-or-Market (LCM) Rule **Performance Objective 16-4, Page 559**	When the market price or current replacement price of an inventory item declines below the actual price paid for the item, a company is permitted to use the lower-of-cost-or-market rule. 1. Choose the lower of cost or market as the valuation basis. 2. Multiply the number of units by the valuation basis price. 3. Add the extended totals in the Amount column to get the value of ending inventory.	From the following inventory data for small, medium, and large lamps at The Lighting Center, calculate the value of the ending inventory by using the LCM rule. **Units / Unit Price Cost / Market / Valuation Basis / Amount** Small 34 — $40 — $43 — Cost — $1,360 Medium 55 — 70 — 65 — Market — 3,575 Large 47 — 99 — 103 — Cost — 4,653 Ending inventory = $9,588

Section II: Inventory Estimation

Topic	Important Concepts	Illustrative Examples
Estimating the Value of Ending Inventory by Using the Retail Method **Performance Objective 16-5, Page 565**	When it is too costly or not feasible to take a physical inventory count, inventory can be estimated. The retail method, as the name implies, is used by retail operations of all sizes. 1. List beginning inventory and purchases at both cost and retail. 2. Add purchases to beginning inventory to determine goods available for sale. 3. Calculate the cost ratio by 4. Calculate ending inventory at retail by subtracting net sales from goods available for sale at retail. 5. Convert ending inventory at retail to ending inventory at cost by multiplying the ending inventory at retail by the cost ratio.	Estimate the value of the ending inventory at cost on July 31 from the following information for Central Distributors, Inc. <table><tr><td></td><td>Cost</td><td>Retail</td></tr><tr><td>Beg. Inv.</td><td>$300,000</td><td>$450,000</td></tr><tr><td>Net Purch.</td><td>100,000</td><td>150,000</td></tr></table>Net Sales $366,000 <table><tr><td></td><td>Cost</td><td>Retail</td></tr><tr><td>Beg. Inv.</td><td>$300,000</td><td>$450,000</td></tr><tr><td>Net Purch.</td><td>+ 100,000</td><td>+ 150,000</td></tr><tr><td>Goods Avail.</td><td>$400,000</td><td>$600,000</td></tr></table>$$\text{Cost ratio} = \frac{400,000}{600,000} = .67$$ <table><tr><td>Good avail. at retail</td><td>$600,000</td></tr><tr><td>− Net sales</td><td>− 366,000</td></tr><tr><td>Ending inventory at retail</td><td>$234,000</td></tr></table>$$\text{Ending inventory at cost} = 234,000 \times .67$$ $$= \$156,780$$
Estimating the Value of Ending Inventory by Using the Gross Profit Method **Performance Objective 16-6, Page 567**	The gross profit or gross margin method uses a company's gross margin percent to estimate the ending inventory. This method assumes that a company maintains approximately the same gross margin from year to year. 1. Calculate the goods available for sale. Beginning inventory + Net purchases Goods available for sale 2. Find the estimated cost of goods sold by multiplying net sales by the cost of goods sold percent (complement of gross margin percent). 3. Calculate the estimate of ending inventory by Goods available for sale − Estimated cost of goods sold Estimated ending inventory	The Stereo Connection maintains a gross margin of 60% on all speakers. In June, the beginning inventory was $95,000, net purchases were $350,600, and net sales were $615,000. What is the estimated cost of ending inventory using the gross profit method? <table><tr><td>Beginning inventory</td><td>$95,000</td></tr><tr><td>+ Net purchases</td><td>+ 350,600</td></tr><tr><td>Goods available</td><td>$445,600</td></tr></table>Estimated cost of goods sold = Net sales(100% − Gr. margin%) = 615,000(100% − 60%) = $246,000 <table><tr><td>Goods available</td><td>$445,600</td></tr><tr><td>− Estimated CGS</td><td>− 246,000</td></tr><tr><td>Estimated ending inventory</td><td>$199,600</td></tr></table>

Section III: Inventory Turnover and Targets

Topic	Important Concepts	Illustrative Examples
Calculating Inventory Turnover Rate at Retail **Performance Objective 16-7, Page 571**	Inventory or stock turnover rate is the number of times during an operating period that the average inventory is sold out or turned over. Average inventory may be expressed at either retail or cost. 1. Calculate the average inventory at retail by 2. Calculate the inventory turnover at retail by	Tip Top Roofing Supply had net sales of $66,000 for the year. If the beginning inventory at retail was $24,400 and the ending inventory at retail was $19,600, what are the average inventory and the inventory turnover rate? $$\text{Average inventory at retail} = \frac{24,400 + 19,600}{2}$$ $$= \$22,000$$ $$\text{Inventory turnover at retail} = \frac{66,000}{22,000} = 3 \text{ times}$$

Section III (continued)

Topic	Important Concepts	Illustrative Examples
Calculating Inventory Turnover Rate at Cost **Performance Objective 16-8, Page 572**	Inventory turnover may also be calculated at cost by using cost of goods sold and the average inventory at cost. 1. Calculate average inventory at cost by 2. Calculate the inventory turnover at cost by	Atlantic Importers had $426,000 in cost of goods sold on oriental rugs. The beginning inventory at cost was $75,000, and the ending inventory at cost was $95,400. What are Atlantic's average inventory at cost and inventory turnover rate? $$\text{Average inventory at cost} = \frac{75,000 + 95,400}{2}$$ $$= 85,200$$ $$\text{Inventory turnover at cost} = \frac{426,000}{85,200} = 5 \text{ times}$$
Calculating Target Inventories Based on Industry Standards **Performance Objective 16-9, Page 573**	When inventory turnover is below average based on published industry standards, it may be a signal that a company is carrying too much inventory. This can lead to extra expenses such as warehousing and insurance. The following formulas can be used to calculate target average inventories at cost or retail to theoretically achieve the published turnover rate.	Playtime Toys had cost of goods sold of $560,000 on stuffed animals for the year. The beginning inventory at cost was $140,000, and the ending inventory was $180,000. The published rate for a firm this size is four times. Calculate the average inventory and turnover rate for Playtime. If the rate is less than four times, calculate the target average inventory. Average inventory at cost $$= \frac{140,000 + 180,000}{2} = \$160,000$$ $$\text{Inventory turnover at cost} = \frac{560,000}{160,000}$$ $$= 3.5 \text{ times}$$ $$\text{Target average inventory} = \frac{560,000}{4}$$ $$= \$140,000$$

TRY IT: EXERCISE SOLUTIONS FOR CHAPTER 16

1. FIFO Inventory Valuation

Units	Cost/Unit	Total
300	$8.75	$2,625
80	9.00	720
380		$3,345

2. LIFO Inventory Valuation

Units	Cost/Unit	Total
200	$8.00	$1,600
100	8.50	850
80	9.00	720
380		$3,170

3. Average Cost Method

$$\text{Average cost/unit} = \frac{\text{Cost of goods available}}{\text{Total units available}} = \frac{7,325}{850} = \$8.62$$

Ending inventory = Units in inventory × Average cost per unit

Ending inventory = 380 × 8.62 = $3,275.60

4.

LCM Rule				
The Personal Touch Gift Shop				
Description	Quantity	Valuation Basis	Price	Amount
Lamps	75	Market	$ 9.20	$ 690.00
Jewelry Boxes	120	Cost	26.30	3,156.00
16" Vases	88	Market	39.70	3,493.60
12" Vases	64	Market	21.40	1,369.60
Fruit Bowls	42	Cost	36.90	1,549.80
			Total Value of Inventory	$10,259.00

5.

	Cost	Retail
Beginning inventory	$600,000	$800,000
+ Net purchases	+ 285,000	+ 380,000
Goods available for sale	$885,000	$1,180,000

$$\text{Cost ratio} = \frac{\text{Goods available for sale at cost}}{\text{Goods available for sale at retail}} = \frac{885,000}{1,180,000} = .75 = 75\%$$

Goods available at retail	1,180,000
− Net sales	− 744,000
Ending inventory at retail	$436,000

Ending inventory at cost = Ending inventory at retail × Cost ratio

Ending inventory at cost = 436,000 × .75 = $327,000

6.

Beginning inventory	$137,000
+ Net purchases	+ 220,000
Goods available for sale	$357,000

Estimated cost of goods sold = Net sales (100% − Gross margin %)

Estimated cost of goods sold = 410,000 (100% − 39%)

Estimated cost of goods sold = 410,000 (.61) = $250,100

Goods available for sale	$357,000
− Estimated cost of goods sold	− 250,100
Estimated ending inventory	$106,900

7.
$$\text{Average inventory}_{\text{retail}} = \frac{\text{Beginning inventory at retail} + \text{Ending inventory at retail}}{2}$$

$$\text{Average inventory}_{\text{retail}} = \frac{65,100 + 52,800}{2} = \$58,950$$

$$\text{Inventory turnover}_{\text{retail}} = \frac{\text{Net sales}}{\text{Average inventory at retail}}$$

$$\text{Inventory turnover}_{\text{retail}} = \frac{260,700}{58,950} = 4.4 \text{ times}$$

8.
$$\text{Average inventory}_{\text{cost}} = \frac{\text{Beginning inventory at cost} + \text{Ending inventory at cost}}{2}$$

$$\text{Average inventory}_{\text{cost}} = \frac{43,500 + 59,300}{2} = \$51,400$$

$$\text{Inventory turnover}_{\text{cost}} = \frac{\text{Cost of goods sold}}{\text{Average inventory at cost}}$$

$$\text{Inventory turnover}_{\text{cost}} = \frac{756,400}{51,400} = 14.7 \text{ times}$$

9.
$$\text{Average inventory} = \frac{\text{Beginning inventory} + \text{Ending inventory}}{2}$$

$$\text{Average inventory} = \frac{495,000 + 380,000}{2} = \$437,500$$

$$\text{Inventory turnover} = \frac{\text{Net sales}}{\text{Average inventory at retail}} = \frac{2{,}650{,}000}{437{,}500} = 6.1 \text{ times}$$

$$\text{Target average inventory} = \frac{\text{Net sales}}{\text{Published turnover}}$$

$$\text{Target average inventory} = \frac{2{,}650{,}000}{7} = \$378{,}571.43$$

CONCEPT REVIEW

1. Goods that a company has in its possession at any given time are known as _____. (16-1)

2. A(n) _____ inventory system is physically counted at least once a year to determine the value of the goods available for sale. (16-1)

3. A(n) _____ inventory system updates goods available for sale on a continuous basis by computer. (16-1)

4. An inventory valuation method in which each item in inventory is matched or coded with its actual cost is known as the specific _____ method. (16-1)

5. An inventory valuation method that assumes the items purchased by a company *first* are the *first* items to be sold is known as the _____ method. Its abbreviation is _____. (16-1)

6. An inventory valuation method that assumes the items purchased by the company *last* are the *first* items to be sold is known as the _____ method. Its abbreviation is _____. (16-2)

7. An inventory valuation method that assumes the cost of each unit of inventory is the *average* cost of all goods available for sale during that accounting period is known as the average cost or _____ average method. (16-3)

8. An inventory valuation method whereby items in inventory are valued at their actual cost or current replacement value, whichever is lower, is known as the _____ rule. Its abbreviation is _____. (16-4)

9. The two generally accepted methods for *estimating* the value of an inventory are the _____ method and the gross _____ method. (16-5, 16-6)

10. The number of times during an operating period that the average dollars invested in inventory was theoretically sold out or turned over is known as the _____ turnover or _____ turnover. (16-7, 16-8)

11. Inventory or stock turnover may be calculated in _____ dollars or in _____ dollars. (16-7, 16-8)

12. Write the formula for average inventory. (16-7, 16-8)

13. The ideal amount of inventory a company should carry for maximum efficiency is known as the _____ average inventory. (16-9)

14. When the target average inventory is calculated at *cost*, the numerator of the formula is the cost of _____ _____; when the target average inventory is calculated *at retail*, the numerator of the formula is net _____. (16-9)

ASSESSMENT TEST

1. Calculate the total number of Maytag Neptune washing machines available for sale and the cost of goods available for sale from the following inventory figures for Southern Distributors, Inc.

Date	Units Purchased	Cost per Unit	Total Cost
Beginning Inventory, March 1	24	$525	_____
Purchase, May 19	12	479	_____
Purchase, August 26	18	540	_____
Purchase, November 27	27	488	_____
Washing Machines Available for Sale = _____		**Cost of Goods Available for Sale**	_____

2. When the buyer for Southern Distributors (Exercise 1) took physical inventory on December 31, 48 washing machines remained in inventory.

   a. Calculate the dollar value of the 48 washing machines by using FIFO.

   b. Calculate the dollar value of the 48 washing machines by using LIFO.

   c. Calculate the dollar value of the 48 washing machines by using the average cost method.

3. Calculate the total number of imported silk ties available for sale and the cost of goods available for sale from the following inventory figures for Ritz Fashions, Inc.

Date	Units Purchased	Cost per Unit	Total Cost
Beginning Inventory, January 1	59	$46.10	_____
Purchase, March 29	75	43.50	_____
Purchase, July 14	120	47.75	_____
Purchase, October 12	95	50.00	_____
Purchase, December 8	105	53.25	_____
Total Units Available	____	**Cost of Goods Available for Sale**	_____

4. When the merchandise manager for Ritz Fashions (Exercise 3) took physical inventory on December 31, 128 silk ties remained in inventory.

   a. Calculate the dollar value of the 128 ties by using FIFO.

   $$105 \ @ \ 53.25 = 5,591.25$$
   $$\underline{\ 23} \ @ \ 50.00 = \underline{1,150.00}$$
   $$128$$

   b. Calculate the dollar value of the 128 ties by using LIFO.

   $$59 \ @ \ 46.10 = 2,719.90$$
   $$\underline{69} \ @ \ 43.50 = \underline{3,001.50}$$
   $$128$$

   c. Calculate the dollar value of the 128 ties by using the average cost method.

   $$\text{Average cost} = \frac{22,053.65}{454} = \$48.58 \text{ per unit}$$

   $$128 \times 48.58 =$$

5. Determine the value of the following inventory for Iberia Tile by using the lower-of-cost-or-market rule.

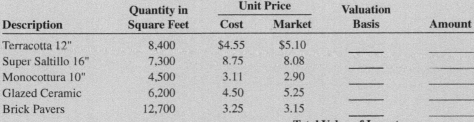

Description	Quantity in Square Feet	Unit Price Cost	Unit Price Market	Valuation Basis	Amount
Terracotta 12"	8,400	$4.55	$5.10	_____	_____
Super Saltillo 16"	7,300	8.75	8.08	_____	_____
Monocottura 10"	4,500	3.11	2.90	_____	_____
Glazed Ceramic	6,200	4.50	5.25	_____	_____
Brick Pavers	12,700	3.25	3.15	_____	_____
				Total Value of Inventory	_____

CHAPTER 16

6. Using the retail method, estimate the value of the ending inventory at cost on May 31 from the following information for Fortune Industries, Inc. Round the cost ratio to the nearest tenth of a percent.

Fortune Industries, Inc.
May 1–May 31

	Cost	Retail
Beginning Inventory, May 1	$145,600	$196,560
Purchases	79,000	106,650
Net Sales $210,800		

7. On July 24, a tornado destroyed Astro Wholesalers' main warehouse and all its contents. Company records indicate that at the time of the tornado, the net sales to date were $535,100 and the purchases were $422,900. The beginning inventory on January 1 was $319,800. For the past three years, the company has maintained a gross margin of 35%. Use the gross profit method to estimate the inventory loss for the insurance claim.

Assuming that all net sales figures are at *retail* and all cost of goods sold figures are at *cost*, calculate the average inventory and inventory turnover for Exercises 8–11. If the actual turnover is below the published rate, calculate the target average inventory necessary to come up to industry standards. Round inventories to the nearest dollar and inventory turnovers to the nearest tenth.

	Net Sales	Cost of Goods Sold	Beginning Inventory	Ending Inventory	Average Inventory	Inventory Turnover	Published Rate	Target Average Inventory
8.	$290,000		$88,000	$94,000	___	___	4.4	___
9.		$760,000	$184,000	$123,000	___	___	6.8	___
10.		$237,550	$24,670	$43,120	___	___	5.9	___
11.	$454,000		$87,900	$75,660	___	___	6.2	___

12. A Foot Locker store had net sales of $435,900 for the year. The beginning inventory at retail was $187,600, and the ending inventory at retail was $158,800.

a. What is the average inventory at retail?

b. What is the inventory turnover rounded to the nearest tenth?

c. If the turnover rate for similar-sized competitors is 3.8 times, calculate the target average inventory needed to theoretically come up to industry standards.

Foot Locker, Inc., is the world's leading retailer of athletic footwear and apparel. Headquartered in New York City, it operates approximately 3,600 athletic retail stores in 21 countries in North America, Europe, and Australia under the brand names Foot Locker, Footaction, Lady Foot Locker, Kids Foot Locker, and Champs Sports.

BCFC/Shutterstock.com

13. The Fabric Mart had cost of goods sold of $884,000 for the year. The beginning inventory at cost was $305,500, and the ending inventory at cost amounted to $414,200. The inventory turnover rate published as the industry standard for a business of this size is five times.
   a. What is the average inventory at cost?

   b. What is the inventory turnover rounded to the nearest tenth?

   c. What is the target average inventory needed to theoretically come up to the industry standard?

BUSINESS DECISION: INVENTORY VALUATION AND THE BOTTOM LINE

14. You are the chief accountant of Pan American Industries, Inc. In anticipation of the upcoming annual stockholders' meeting, the president of the company asked you to determine the effect of the FIFO, LIFO, and average inventory valuation methods on the company's income statement.
   Beginning inventory, January 1, was 10,000 units at $5 each. Purchases during the year consisted of 15,000 units at $6 on April 15, 20,000 units at $7 on July 19, and 25,000 units at $8 on November 2.

   a. If ending inventory on December 31 was 40,000 units, calculate the value of this inventory by using the three valuation methods.

   FIFO: _____   LIFO: _____   Average Cost: _____

   b. Calculate the income statement items below for each of the inventory valuation methods.

Net sales	30,000 units at $12 each
Operating expenses	$100,000
Income tax rate	30%

   Pan American Industries, Inc.

	FIFO	LIFO	Average Cost
Net sales			
Beginning inventory			
Purchases			
Cost of goods available for sale			
Ending inventory			
Cost of goods sold			
Gross profit			
Operating expenses			
Income before taxes			
Income tax			
Net income			

   c. Which inventory method should be used if the objective is to pay the least amount of taxes?

   d. Which inventory method should be used if the objective is to show the greatest amount of profit in the annual report to the shareholders?

Dollars AND Sense

This Business Decision, "Inventory Valuation and the Bottom Line," clearly Illustrates how the various inventory methods can affect a company's profit picture. Note the significant variation in net income among the three methods.

iStock.com/vreemous

COLLABORATIVE LEARNING ACTIVITY

The Counting Game!

As a team, choose two or three competitive retail stores in your area, such as supermarkets, drug stores, hardware stores, shoe stores, or clothing stores. Speak with an accounting and/or merchandise manager for each store to get answers to the following questions.

a. Approximately how many different items are carried in inventory?

b. What method of inventory valuation is being used? Why?

c. What is the store's average inventory?

d. How often is a physical inventory count taken? Who does it?

e. Does the company have a computerized perpetual inventory system? If so, how does it work?

f. What is the inventory turnover ratio? How does this compare with the published industry figures for a company that size? Where did you find the published figures?

g. Which of the companies your team researched has the most efficient inventory system? Why?

CHAPTER 17 Depreciation

PERFORMANCE OBJECTIVES

SECTION I 17 TRADITIONAL DEPRECIATION—METHODS USED FOR FINANCIAL STATEMENT REPORTING

long-term or **long-lived assets** Relatively fixed or permanent assets such as land, buildings, tools, equipment, and vehicles that companies acquire in the course of operating a business.

In Chapter 15, we learned a firm's assets are divided into three categories: current assets; property, plant, and equipment; and investments and other assets. This chapter deals with the valuation of the **long-term** or **long-lived assets** of the firm: the property, plant, and equipment. Companies acquire these relatively fixed or permanent assets in the course of building and operating a business. Some examples of these assets would be land, buildings, equipment, machinery, vehicles, furniture, fixtures, and tools.

As time goes by, the usefulness or productivity of these assets, except land, decreases. Think of this decrease as a loss of revenue earning power. Accordingly, the cost of these assets is distributed over their useful life to coincide with the revenue earned. This cost write-off is known as **depreciation**. On the income statement, depreciation is listed under operating expenses as **depreciation expense**. On the balance sheet, it is used to determine the current **book value** of an asset, whereby

depreciation, or **depreciation expense** The decrease in value from the original cost of a long-term asset over its useful life.

book value The value of an asset at any given time. It is the original cost less the accumulated depreciation to that point.

$$\text{Book value} = \text{Original cost} - \text{Accumulated depreciation}$$

Assets depreciate for a number of reasons. They may physically wear out from use and deterioration, or they may depreciate because they have become inadequate and obsolete. Four important factors must be taken into account to determine the amount of depreciation expense of an asset.

total cost, or **original basis** The total amount a company pays for an asset, including shipping, handling, and setup charges.

residual, scrap, salvage, or **trade-in value** The value of an asset at the time it is taken out of service.

useful life The length of time an asset is expected to generate revenue.

1. The **total cost**, or **original basis**, of the asset. This amount includes such items as shipping, handling, and setup charges.
2. The asset's estimated **residual value** at the time it is taken out of service. This is also known as **scrap value**, **salvage value**, and **trade-in value**.
3. An estimate of the **useful life** of the asset, or the length of time it is expected to generate revenue. To be depreciated, an asset must have a life greater than one year.
4. The method of calculating depreciation must match the way in which the asset will depreciate. Some assets depreciate evenly over the years (straight-line depreciation), whereas others depreciate more quickly at first and then slow down in the later years (accelerated depreciation). Regardless of which method a company chooses, at the end of the useful life of an asset, the total amount of depreciation expense write-off will be the same.

This chapter examines the various methods used to depreciate assets. In Section I, we learn to calculate depreciation by the four traditional methods: straight-line, sum-of-the-years' digits, declining-balance, and units-of-production. Any of these methods may be used for financial statement reporting. However, once a method has been implemented, it cannot be changed.

Frequently, the amount of depreciation reported by a company on its financial statements will differ from the amount reported to the IRS for income tax purposes because the IRS allows additional options for calculating depreciation expense. Today the most widely used method for tax purposes is known as the Modified Accelerated Cost Recovery System (MACRS). This method is covered in Section II.

Depreciation is more frequently based on time, how many years an asset is expected to last. Certain assets, however, are depreciated more accurately on the basis of some productivity measure, such as units of output for production machinery or mileage for vehicles, regardless of time. This section deals with both time- and productivity-based depreciation methods.

17-1 CALCULATING DEPRECIATION BY THE STRAIGHT-LINE METHOD

straight-line depreciation A method of depreciation that provides for equal periodic charges to be written off over the estimated useful life of an asset.

Straight-line depreciation is by far the most widely used method in business today. It provides for equal periodic charges to be written off over the estimated useful life of the asset.

Once the annual depreciation has been determined, we can set up a **depreciation schedule**. The depreciation schedule is a chart illustrating the depreciation activity of the asset for each year of its useful life. The chart shows the amount of depreciation each year, the accumulated depreciation to date, and the book value of the asset.

depreciation schedule Chart showing the depreciation activity (depreciation, accumulated depreciation, and book value) of an asset for each year of its useful life.

STEPS TO PREPARE A DEPRECIATION SCHEDULE BY THE STRAIGHT-LINE METHOD

STEP 1. Determine the total cost and salvage value of the asset.

STEP 2. Subtract salvage value from total cost to find the total amount of depreciation.

$$\text{Total depreciation} = \text{Total cost} - \text{Salvage value}$$

STEP 3. Calculate the annual amount of depreciation by dividing the total depreciation by the useful life of the asset.

$$\text{Annual depreciation} = \frac{\text{Total depreciation}}{\text{Estimated useful life (years)}}$$

STEP 4. Set up the depreciation schedule in the form of a chart with the following headings:

End of Year	Annual Depreciation	Accumulated Depreciation	Book Value

Learning Tip

On a depreciation schedule, the starting book value is the *original cost* of the asset and the last book value is the *salvage value* of the asset.

EXAMPLE1 CALCULATING STRAIGHT-LINE DEPRECIATION

Cascade Enterprises purchased a computer system for $9,000. Shipping charges were $125, and setup and programming amounted to $375. The system is expected to last 4 years and has a residual value of $1,500. If Cascade elects to use the straight-line method of depreciation for the computer, calculate the total cost, total depreciation, and annual depreciation. Prepare a depreciation schedule for its useful life.

►SOLUTIONSTRATEGY

Step 1. Total cost = Cost + Shipping charges + Setup expenses
Total cost = 9,000 + 125 + 375 = $\underline{\underline{\$9,500}}$

Step 2. Total depreciation = Total cost − Salvage value
Total depreciation = 9,500 − 1,500 = $\underline{\underline{\$8,000}}$

Step 3. $\text{Annual depreciation} = \frac{\text{Total depreciation}}{\text{Estimated useful life (years)}}$

$\text{Annual depreciation} = \frac{8,000}{4} = \underline{\underline{\$2,000}}$

Step 4.

Cascade Enterprises
Straight-Line Depreciation Schedule
Computer System

End of Year	Annual Depreciation	Accumulated Depreciation	Book Value
			(original cost) $9,500
1	$2,000	$2,000	7,500
2	2,000	4,000	5,500
3	2,000	6,000	3,500
4	2,000	8,000	(salvage value) 1,500

Expensive assets such as this construction equipment are considered long-lived assets, the value of which depreciates over time.

▶TRY IT EXERCISE 1

Wild Flour Bakery purchased a new bread oven for $125,000. Shipping charges were $1,150, and installation amounted to $750. The oven is expected to last 5 years and has a trade-in value of $5,000. If Wild Flour elects to use the straight-line method, calculate the total cost, total depreciation, and annual depreciation of the oven. Prepare a depreciation schedule for its useful life.

CHECK YOUR ANSWERS WITH THE SOLUTIONS ON PAGE 611.

17-2 CALCULATING DEPRECIATION BY THE SUM-OF-THE-YEARS' DIGITS METHOD

accelerated depreciation Depreciation methods that assume an asset depreciates more in the early years of its useful life than in the later years.

sum-of-the-years' digits A method of accelerated depreciation that allows an asset to depreciate the most during the first year, with decreasing amounts each year thereafter. Total depreciation is based on the total cost of an asset less its salvage value.

The sum-of-the-years' digits and the declining-balance methods of calculating depreciation are the two **accelerated depreciation** methods. These methods assume that an asset depreciates more in the early years of its useful life than in the later years. Under the sum-of-the-years' digits method, the yearly charge for depreciation declines steadily over the estimated useful life of the asset because a successively smaller fraction is applied each year to the total depreciation (total cost − salvage value).

This fraction is known as the **sum-of-the-years' digits** fraction. The denominator of the fraction is the sum of the digits of the estimated life of the asset. This number does not change. The numerator of the fraction is the number of years of useful life remaining. This number changes every year as the asset gets older and older. This sum-of-the-years' digits depreciation rate fraction can be expressed as

$$\text{SYD depreciation rate fraction} = \frac{\text{Years of useful life remaining}}{\text{Sum of the digits of the useful life}}$$

The denominator (the sum of the years' digits) can be calculated by adding all the digits of the years or by using the following formula:

$$\text{SYD} = \frac{n(n+1)}{2}$$

where

$$n = \text{the number of years of useful life of the asset}$$

For example, let's compute the depreciation rate fractions for an asset that has a useful life of 4 years. The denominator, the sum of the digits of 4, is 10. This is calculated by $4 + 3 + 2 + 1 = 10$ or by the SYD formula $4(4 + 1) \div 2 = 10$. Remember, the denominator does not change. The numerator of the fractions will be 4, 3, 2, and 1 for each succeeding year.

Year	Depreciation Rate Fraction	Depreciation Rate Decimal	Depreciation Rate Percent
1	$\frac{4}{10}$	.40	40%
2	$\frac{3}{10}$	.30	30%
3	$\frac{2}{10}$	.20	20%
4	$\frac{1}{10}$	.10	10%

From this chart, we can see that an asset with 4 years of useful life will depreciate $\frac{4}{10}$, or 40%, in the first year; $\frac{3}{10}$, or 30%, in the second year; and so on. The accelerated rate of 40% depreciation write-off in the first year gives the business a reduced tax advantage and therefore an incentive to invest in new equipment.

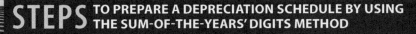

STEPS TO PREPARE A DEPRECIATION SCHEDULE BY USING THE SUM-OF-THE-YEARS' DIGITS METHOD

STEP 1. Find the total depreciation of the asset by

$$\text{Total depreciation} = \text{Total cost} - \text{Salvage value}$$

STEP 2. Calculate the SYD depreciation rate fraction for each year by

$$\text{SYD depreciation rate fraction} = \frac{\text{Years of useful life remaining}}{\dfrac{n(n+1)}{2}}$$

STEP 3. Calculate the depreciation for each year by multiplying the total depreciation by that year's depreciation rate fraction

$$\text{Annual depreciation} = \text{Total depreciation} \times \text{Depreciation rate fraction}$$

STEP 4. Set up a depreciation schedule in the form of a chart with the following headings:

End of Year	Total Depreciation	×	Depreciation Rate Fraction	=	Annual Depreciation	Accumulated Depreciation	Book Value

---

EXAMPLE2 CALCULATING SUM-OF-THE YEARS' DIGITS DEPRECIATION

Spectrum Industries purchased a delivery truck for $35,000. The truck is expected to have a useful life of 5 years and a trade-in value of $5,000. Using the sum-of-the-years' digits method, prepare a depreciation schedule for Spectrum.

▶**SOLUTION**STRATEGY

The following steps are used to prepare a depreciation schedule by using sum-of-the-years' digits:

Step 1.   Total depreciation = Total cost − Salvage value

Total depreciation = 35,000 − 5,000 = $30,000

Step 2.   Year 1: SYD depreciation rate fraction = $\dfrac{\text{Years of useful life remaining}}{\dfrac{n(n+1)}{2}}$

$$\text{SYD depreciation rate fraction} = \frac{5}{\dfrac{5(5+1)}{2}} = \frac{5}{15}$$

The depreciation rate fraction for year 1 is $\frac{5}{15}$. The depreciation fractions for the remaining years will have the same denominator, 15 (the sum of the digits of 5). Only the numerators will change, in descending order. The depreciation fractions for the remaining years are $\frac{4}{15}, \frac{3}{15}, \frac{2}{15}$, and $\frac{1}{15}$.

Note how accelerated this SYD method is: $\frac{5}{15}$, or $\frac{1}{3}$ (33.3%), of the asset is allowed to be written off in the first year. This is compared with only $\frac{1}{5}$ (20%) per year when using the straight-line method.

Step 3.   Annual depreciation = Total depreciation × Depreciation rate fraction

$$\text{Annual depreciation (year 1)} = 30,000 \times \frac{5}{15} = \$10,000$$

$$\text{Annual depreciation (year 2)} = 30,000 \times \frac{4}{15} = \$8,000$$

Continue this calculation for each of the remaining 3 years. Then prepare the schedule.

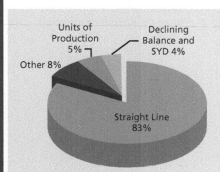

Depreciation Pie According to an Accounting Trends and Techniques survey conducted by the American Institute of Certified Public Accountants (AICPA), the above pie chart shows the breakdown of depreciation methods used by the 600 largest U.S. companies.

iStock.com/Nikada

Step 4.

Spectrum Industries
SYD Depreciation Schedule
Delivery Truck

End of Year	Total Depreciation	×	Depreciation Rate Fraction	=	Annual Depreciation	Accumulated Depreciation	Book Value
							(new) $35,000
1	$30,000	×	$\dfrac{5}{15}$	=	$10,000	$10,000	25,000
2	30,000	×	$\dfrac{4}{15}$	=	8,000	18,000	17,000
3	30,000	×	$\dfrac{3}{15}$	=	6,000	24,000	11,000
4	30,000	×	$\dfrac{2}{15}$	=	4,000	28,000	7,000
5	30,000	×	$\dfrac{1}{15}$	=	2,000	30,000	5,000

▶ **TRYITEXERCISE 2**

Bow Valley Kitchens purchased new production-line machinery for a total of $44,500. The company expects this machinery to last 6 years and have a residual value of $2,500. Using the sum-of-the-years' digits method, prepare a depreciation schedule for Bow Valley.

CHECK YOUR ANSWERS WITH THE SOLUTIONS ON PAGE 611.

17-3

CALCULATING DEPRECIATION BY THE DECLINING-BALANCE METHOD

declining-balance A method of accelerated depreciation that uses a multiple (150% or 200%) of the straight-line rate to calculate depreciation.

double-declining balance Name given to the declining-balance method of depreciation when the straight-line multiple is 200%.

The second widely accepted method of accelerated depreciation in business is known as the **declining-balance** method. This method uses a *multiple* of the straight-line rate to calculate depreciation. The most frequently used multiples are 1.5 and 2. When 1.5 is used, it is known as the 150% declining balance. When 2 is the multiple, the method is known as the **double-declining balance**.

To calculate the declining-balance rate, we first determine the straight-line rate by dividing 1 by the number of years of useful life, then multiplying by the appropriate declining-balance multiple. For example, when using the double-declining balance, an asset with a useful life of 4 years would have a straight-line rate of 25% per year ($1 \div 4 = \frac{1}{4} = 25\%$). This rate is then multiplied by the declining-balance multiple, 2, to get 50%, the double-declining rate. The following formula should be used for this calculation:

$$\text{Declining-balance rate} = \frac{1}{\text{Useful life}} \times \textbf{Multiple}$$

To further accelerate the depreciation, this declining-balance rate is applied to the original total cost of the asset. Salvage value is not considered until the last year of depreciation. When preparing a depreciation schedule by using the declining-balance method, the depreciation stops when the book value of the asset reaches the salvage value. By IRS regulations, the asset cannot be depreciated below the salvage value.

STEPS TO PREPARE A DEPRECIATION SCHEDULE BY USING THE DECLINING-BALANCE METHOD

STEP 1. Calculate the declining-balance rate by the formula

$$\text{Declining-balance rate} = \frac{1}{\text{Useful life}} \times \text{Multiple}$$

STEP 2. Calculate the depreciation for each year by applying the rate to each year's beginning book value, which is the ending book value of the previous year.

$$\text{Depreciation for the year} = \text{Beginning book value} \times \text{Declining-balance rate}$$

STEP 3. Calculate the ending book value for each year by subtracting the depreciation for the year from the beginning book value.

$$\text{Ending book value} = \text{Beginning book value} - \text{Depreciation for the year}$$

STEP 4. When the ending book value equals the salvage value, the depreciation is complete.

STEP 5. Set up a depreciation schedule in the form of a chart with the following headings:

End of Year	Beginning Book Value	Depreciation Rate	Depreciation for the Year	Accumulated Depreciation	Ending Book Value

IN THE Business World

From Chapter 15, "Financial Statements and Ratios," remember that depreciation appears on both the balance sheet and the income statement.

- *Balance sheet*—Used to determine book value of an asset.
- *Income statement*—Listed as an operating expense.

EXAMPLE3   CALCULATING DECLINING BALANCE DEPRECIATION

Allstate Shipping bought a forklift for $20,000. It is expected to have a 5-year useful life and a trade-in value of $2,000. Prepare a depreciation schedule for this asset by using the double-declining balance method.

SOLUTIONSTRATEGY

Step 1. $\text{Declining-balance rate} = \dfrac{1}{\text{Useful life}} \times \text{Multiple}$

$\text{Declining-balance rate} = \dfrac{1}{5} \times 2 = .20 \times 2 = .40 = \underline{40\%}$

Step 2. Depreciation for the year = Beginning book value × Declining-balance rate

     Depreciation: Year 1 = 20,000 × .40 = $\underline{\$8,000}$

Step 3. Ending book value = Beginning book value − Depreciation for the year

     Ending book value: Year 1 = 20,000 − 8,000 = $\underline{\$12,000}$

     Repeat Steps 2 and 3 for years 2, 3, 4, and 5.

Step 4. In year 5, although the calculated depreciation is $1,036.80 (2,592 × .4), the allowable depreciation is limited to $592 (2,592 − 2,000) because the book value has reached the $2,000 salvage value. At this point, the depreciation is complete.

Step 5.

Allstate Shipping
Double-Declining Balance Depreciation Schedule Forklift

End of Year	Beginning Book Value	Depreciation Rate	Depreciation for the Year	Accumulated Depreciation	Ending Book Value
					(new) $20,000
1	$20,000	40%	$8,000	$8,000	12,000
2	12,000	40%	4,800	12,800	7,200
3	7,200	40%	2,880	15,680	4,320
4	4,320	40%	1,728	17,408	2,592
5	2,592	40%	592*	18,000	2,000

*Maximum allowable to reach salvage value.

▶TRYITEXERCISE 3

Kelowna Air Service bought a small commuter airplane for $386,000. It is expected to have a useful life of 4 years and a trade-in value of $70,000. Prepare a depreciation schedule for the airplane by using the 150% declining-balance method.

CHECK YOUR ANSWERS WITH THE SOLUTIONS ON PAGE 611.

17-4 CALCULATING DEPRECIATION BY THE UNITS-OF-PRODUCTION METHOD

units-of-production
Depreciation method based on how much an asset is used, such as miles, hours, or units produced, rather than the passage of time.

When the useful life of an asset is more accurately defined in terms of how much it is used rather than the passage of time, we may use the **units-of-production** method to calculate depreciation. To apply this method, the life of the asset is expressed in productive capacity, such as miles driven, units produced, or hours used. Some examples of assets typically depreciated by using this method would be cars, trucks, airplanes, production-line machinery, engines, pumps, and electronic equipment.

To calculate depreciation by using this method, we begin by determining the depreciation per unit. This number is found by dividing the amount to be depreciated (cost − salvage value) by the estimated units of useful life:

$$\text{Depreciation per unit} = \frac{\text{Cost} - \text{Salvage value}}{\text{Units of useful life}}$$

For example, let's say that a hole-punching machine on a production line had a cost of $35,000 and a salvage value of $5,000. If we estimate that the machine had a useful life of 150,000 units of production, the depreciation per unit would be calculated as follows:

$$\text{Depreciation per unit} = \frac{\text{Cost} - \text{Salvage value}}{\text{Units of useful life}} = \frac{35,000 - 5,000}{150,000} = \frac{30,000}{150,000} = \$.20 \text{ per unit}$$

Once we have determined the depreciation per unit, we can find the annual depreciation by multiplying the depreciation per unit by the number of units produced each year.

$$\text{Annual depreciation} = \text{Depreciation per unit} \times \text{Units produced}$$

In the previous example, if the hole-punching machine produced 30,000 units in a year, the annual depreciation for that year would be as follows:

Annual depreciation = Depreciation per unit × Units produced = .20 × 30,000 = $6,000

STEPS TO CALCULATE DEPRECIATION BY USING THE UNITS-OF-PRODUCTION METHOD

STEP 1. Determine the depreciation per unit by using

$$\text{Depreciation per unit} = \frac{\text{Cost} - \text{Salvage value}}{\text{Units of useful life}}$$

(Round to the nearest tenth of a cent when necessary.)

STEP 2. Calculate the annual depreciation by using

$$\text{Annual depreciation} = \text{Depreciation per unit} \times \text{Units produced}$$

STEP 3. Set up the depreciation schedule in the form of a chart with the following headings:

End of Year	Depreciation per Unit	Units Produced	Annual Depreciation	Accumulated Depreciation	Book Value

---

EXAMPLE4 CALCULATING UNITS-OF-PRODUCTION DEPRECIATION

Colorcraft Manufacturing purchased a new metal stamping press for $8,500 with a salvage value of $500. For depreciation purposes, the press is expected to have a useful life of 5,000 hours. From the following estimate of hours of use, prepare a depreciation schedule for the press by using the units-of-production method.

Year	Hours of Use
1	1,500
2	1,200
3	2,000
4	500

►SOLUTIONSTRATEGY

Step 1. $\text{Depreciation per unit (hours)} = \dfrac{\text{Cost} - \text{Salvage value}}{\text{Hours of useful life}}$

$$\text{Depreciation per unit} = \frac{8,500 - 500}{5,000} = \frac{8,000}{5,000} = \underline{\$1.60 \text{ per hour}}$$

Step 2. $\text{Annual depreciation} = \text{Depreciation per unit} \times \text{Units produced}$

Annual depreciation (year 1) = 1.60 × 1,500 = $2,400

Annual depreciation (year 2) = 1.60 × 1,200 = $1,920

Continue this procedure for the remaining years.

Step 3.

Colorcraft Manufacturing
Units-of-Production Depreciation Schedule
Metal Stamping Press

End of Year	Depreciation per Hour	Hours Used	Annual Depreciation	Accumulated Depreciation	Book Value
					(new) $8,500
1	$1.60	1,500	$2,400	$2,400	6,100
2	1.60	1,200	1,920	4,320	4,180
3	1.60	2,000	3,200	7,520	980
4	1.60	500	480*	8,000	500

*Maximum allowable to reach salvage value.

►TRYITEXERCISE 4

Prestige Limousine Service purchased a limousine with an expected useful life of 75,000 miles. The cost of the limousine was $54,500, and the residual value was $7,500. If the limousine was driven the following number of miles per year, prepare a depreciation schedule by using the units-of-production method. After finding the depreciation per mile, round this dollar amount to three decimal places for use in calculating your schedule.

Year	Miles Driven
1	12,500
2	18,300
3	15,900
4	19,100
5	12,400

CHECK YOUR ANSWERS WITH THE SOLUTIONS ON PAGE 612.

SECTION I 17 REVIEW EXERCISES

Note: Round answers to the nearest cent when necessary.

Calculate the total cost, total depreciation, and annual depreciation for the following assets by using the straight-line method.

	Cost	Shipping Charges	Setup Charges	Total Cost	Salvage Value	Estimated Useful Life (years)	Total Depreciation	Annual Depreciation
1.	$45,000	$150	$500	$45,650	$3,500	10	$42,150	$4,215.00
2.	$88,600	$625	$2,500	_____	$9,000	7	_____	_____
3.	$158,200	0	$1,800	_____	$20,000	5	_____	_____
4.	$900,000	0	$15,500	_____	$100,000	12	_____	_____
5.	$220,000	$400	0	_____	$24,500	10	_____	_____
6.	$76,200	$1,600	$850	_____	$4,500	11	_____	_____
7.	$470,000	0	0	_____	$54,000	8	_____	_____
8.	$34,800	$600	$1,900	_____	$8,100	6	_____	_____

9. Mason Industries purchased a drilling rig for $75,900. Delivery costs totaled $2,880.
   The useful life is 7 years and the salvage value is $12,903. Prepare a depreciation schedule using the straight-line method.

Mason Industries
Depreciation Schedule—Drilling Rig

End of Year	Annual Depreciation	Accumulated Depreciation	Book Value
			$78,780 (new)
1	$9,411	_____	_____
2	9,411	_____	_____
3	9,411	_____	_____
4	9,411	_____	_____
5	9,411	_____	_____
6	9,411	_____	_____
7	9,411	_____	_____

10. White Mountain Supply Company purchases warehouse shelving for $18,600. Shipping charges were $370, and assembly and setup amounted to $575. The shelves are expected to last for 7 years and have a scrap value of $900. Using the straight-line method of depreciation,

a. What is the annual depreciation expense of the shelving?

b. What is the accumulated depreciation after the third year?

c. What is the book value of the shelving after the fifth year?

Complete Exercises 11–16 as they relate to the sum-of-the-years' digits method of depreciation.

	Useful Life (years)	Sum-of-the-Years' Digits	Depreciation Rate Fraction		
			Year 1	Year 3	Year 5
11.	5	15	$\frac{5}{15}$	$\frac{3}{15}$	$\frac{1}{15}$
12.	7	____	____	____	____
13.	10	____	____	____	____
14.	6	____	____	____	____
15.	15	____	____	____	____
16.	12	____	____	____	____

17. Billings Corporation purchased a wood pulp mixer for $17,204. Delivery costs totaled $464. The useful is 7 years, and the salvage value is $1,204.

Prepare a depreciation schedule using the sum-of-the-years' digits method.

Billings Corporation
SYD Depreciation Schedule—Wood Pulp Mixer

End of Year	Total Depreciation	×	Depreciated Fraction	=	Annual Depreciation	Accumulated Depreciation	Book Value
							$17,668 (new)
1	16,464		____		____	____	____
2	16,464		____		____	____	____
3	16,464		____		____	____	____
4	16,464		____		____	____	____
5	16,464		____		____	____	____
6	16,464		____		____	____	____
7	16,464		____		____	____	____

Complete Exercises 18–23 as they relate to the declining-balance method of depreciation. Round to the nearest hundredth of a percent when necessary.

	Useful Life (Years)	Straight-Line Rate (%)	Multiple (%)	Declining-Balance Rate (%)
18.	**6**	**16.67**	**200**	**33.34**
19.	10	_____	150	_____
20.	4	_____	200	_____
21.	8	_____	150	_____
22.	3	_____	150	_____
23.	20	_____	200	_____

24. Some trucks purchased by a U-Haul franchise should last 7-years. The purchase price was $175,000. Shipping costs were $5,000. The trade-in (salvage value) is $20,000. Prepare a depreciation schedule by using the double-declining-balance method for the trucks.

U-Haul
Double-Declining-Balance Depreciation Schedule
Truck Fleet

End of Year	Beginning Book Value	Depreciation Rate	Depreciation for the Year*	Accumulated Depreciation	Ending Book Balance
1	_____	_____	_____	_____	_____
2	_____	_____	_____	_____	_____
3	_____	_____	_____	_____	_____
4	_____	_____	_____	_____	_____
5	_____	_____	_____	_____	_____
6	_____	_____	_____	_____	_____
7	_____	_____	_____	_____	_____

Since 1945, **U-Haul** has been the first choice of do-it-yourself movers, with a network of more than 15,950 locations in all 50 states in the United States and in 10 Canadian provinces. The U-Haul fleet consists of more than 100,000 trucks, 78,500 trailers, and 31,100 towing devices. U-Haul also offers more than 389,000 rooms and more than 34 million square feet of storage space at more than 1,055 owned and managed facilities throughout North America.

Major competitors include Avis Budget Group, Inc.; Penske Truck Leasing; Public Storage Inc.; Extra Space Storage Inc.; and Sovran Self Storage Inc.

Complete Exercises 25–30 as they relate to the units-of-production method of depreciation. Round to the nearest tenth of a cent when necessary.

	Asset	Cost	Salvage Value	Units of Useful Life	Depreciation per Unit
25.	**Pump**	**$15,000**	**$2,800**	**100,000 gallons**	**$.122**
26.	Automobile	$27,400	$3,400	60,000 miles	_____
27.	Assembly robot	$900,000	$20,000	4,000,000 units	_____
28.	Sewing machine	$9,000	$1,800	120,000 garments	_____
29.	Air compressor	$6,500	$700	35,000 hours	_____
30.	Tour bus	$135,000	$10,000	225,000 miles	_____

31. Thunderbird Manufacturing purchases a new stamping machine for $45,000. Its useful life is estimated to be 250,000 units with a salvage value of $5,000. Prepare a units-of-production (UOP) depreciation schedule based on the given annual usage (units produced) as shown below.

Thunderbird Manufacturing
Units-of-Production Depreciation Schedule
Stamping Machine

End of Year	Depreciation per Unit	Units Produced	Annual Depreciation	Accumulated Depreciation	Book Value
					(new) _____
1	_____	50,000	_____	_____	_____
2	_____	70,000	_____	_____	_____
3	_____	45,000	_____	_____	_____
4	_____	66,000	_____	_____	_____
5	_____	30,000			

32. You are the accountant for Raleigh Industries, a manufacturer of plastic gears for electric motors. The company's production facility in Pittsburgh has a cost of $3,800,000, an estimated residual value of $400,000, and an estimated useful life of 40 years. You are using the straight-line method of depreciation for this asset.

a. What is the amount of the annual depreciation?

b. What is the book value of the property at the end of the 20th year of use?

c. If at the start of the 21st year you revise your estimate so that the remaining useful life is 15 years and the residual value is $120,000, what should be the depreciation expense for each of the remaining 15 years?

BUSINESS DECISION: REPLACING AN ASSET

33. Supreme Auto Service opened a new service center three decades ago. At the time the center was preparing to open, new equipment was purchased totaling $388,000. Residual value of the equipment was estimated to be $48,000 after 20 years. The company accountant has been using straight-line depreciation on the equipment.

a. How much was the annual depreciation for the original equipment?

b. If the hydraulic lift had originally cost $11,640, what would its residual value be after 20 years?

c. After six years of operation, the original hydraulic lift was replaced with a new model that cost $22,000. Book value was allowed for the old machine as a trade-in. What was the old hydraulic lift's book value when the replacement machine was bought?

d. What was the book value of the equipment inventory at the six-year point, substituting the new hydraulic lift for the original after the new lift had joined the inventory?

Section I of this chapter described the depreciation methods used by businesses for the preparation of financial statements. For income tax purposes, the Internal Revenue Service (IRS), through federal tax laws, prescribes how depreciation must be taken.

As part of the Economic Recovery Act of 1981, the IRS introduced a depreciation method known as the accelerated cost recovery system (ACRS), which allowed businesses to depreciate assets more quickly than they could with traditional methods. Faster write-offs encouraged businesses to invest in new equipment and other capital assets more frequently, thereby sparking needed economic growth. Essentially, ACRS discarded the concepts of estimated useful life and residual value. In their place, it required that businesses compute a **cost recovery allowance**.

After the ACRS was modified by the Tax Equity and Fiscal Responsibility Act of 1982 and the Tax Reform Act of 1984, it was significantly overhauled by the Tax Reform Act of 1986. The resulting method was known as the **modified accelerated cost recovery system (MACRS)**. This is the system we will use to calculate depreciation for federal income tax purposes.

cost recovery allowance Term used under MACRS meaning the amount of depreciation of an asset that may be written off for tax purposes in a given year.

modified accelerated cost recovery system (MACRS) A 1986 modification of the property classes and the depreciation rates of the accelerated depreciation method; used for assets put into service after 1986.

17-5 CALCULATING DEPRECIATION BY USING THE MODIFIED ACCELERATED COST RECOVERY SYSTEM (MACRS)

According to the IRS, the modified accelerated cost recovery system (MACRS) is the name given to tax rules for getting back, or recovering, through depreciation deductions the cost of property that is used in a trade or business or to produce income. These rules generally apply to tangible property placed into service *after 1986*.

Before we can calculate the amount of depreciation for a particular asset, we must determine the **basis for depreciation**, or "cost," of that asset for depreciation purposes. Sometimes the basis for depreciation is the original cost of the asset; however, in many cases, the original cost (original basis) is "modified" by various IRS rules, Section 179 deductions, and special depreciation allowances. Once the basis for depreciation has been established, the MACRS depreciation deduction can be calculated for each year and the depreciation schedule can be prepared.

Table 17-1 exhibits the nine main property classes of MACRS and their recovery periods with some examples of assets included in each class. Once the **property class** for the asset has been identified, the amount of depreciation each year can be manually calculated or found by using percentage tables. As a general rule, the 3-, 5-, 7-, and 10-year property class assets are depreciated by using the 200% declining-balance method; the 15- and 20-year classes use the 150% declining-balance method; and the 25-year property, residential rental property, and nonresidential rental property classes use straight-line depreciation.

Because these calculations were already covered in Section I of this chapter, we will focus on using one of the **cost recovery percentage** tables provided by the IRS. Table 17-2 is such a table.

Note that the number of recovery years is one greater than the property class. This is due to a rule known as the **half-year convention**, which assumes that the asset was placed in service in the middle of the first year and therefore begins depreciating at that point. Quarterly tables are listed in IRS Publication 946, How to Depreciate Property, for assets placed in service at other times of the year.

basis for depreciation The cost of an asset for MACRS depreciation purposes. This figure takes into account business usage rules, Section 179 deductions, and special depreciation allowances.

property class One of several time categories to which property is assigned under MACRS that shows how many years are allowed for cost recovery.

cost recovery percentage An IRS-prescribed percentage that is multiplied by the original basis of an asset to determine the depreciation deduction for a given year. Based on property class and year of asset life.

half-year convention IRS rule under MACRS that assumes all property is placed in service or taken out of service at the midpoint of the year regardless of the actual time.

DETERMINING THE ASSET'S BASIS FOR DEPRECIATION

The basis for depreciation of an asset is determined by the percentage of time it is used for business, Section 179 deductions, and special depreciation allowances. To qualify for depreciation, an asset must be used for business a "minimum of 50%" of the time. An asset used for business 100% of the time may be depreciated completely. If, for example, an asset is used only 75% of the time for business, then only 75% of the original cost can be depreciated.

TABLE 17-1 MACRS Property Classes (Recovery Period) General Depreciation System

3-Year Property (3 years)	**5-Year Property** (5 years)	**7-Year Property** (7 years)
Over-the-road tractors Some horses and hogs Special handling devices for the manufacture of food and beverages Specialty tools used in the manufacture of motor vehicles Specialty tools used in the manufacture of finished products made of plastic, rubber, glass, and metal	Automobiles and taxis Buses and trucks Computers and peripherals Office machinery Breeding or dairy cattle, sheep and goats Airplanes (except those in commercial use) Trailers and trailer-mounted containers Assets used in construction Assets used in the manufacture of knitted goods, textile yarns, carpets, medical and dental supplies, chemicals, and electronic components Assets used in radio and television broadcasting, and CATV	Office furniture and fixtures Railroad cars and engines Commercial airplanes Assets used in the manufacture of wood, pulp, and paper products Assets used in printing and publishing Assets used in the production of tobacco, leather, stone, and steel products Assets used in the production of sporting goods, toys, jewelry, and musical instruments Assets used in theme and amusement parks, theaters, concert halls, and miniature golf courses
10-Year Property (10 years)	**15-Year Property** (15 years)	**20-Year Property** (20 years)
Vessels, barges, and tugs Single-purpose agricultural structures Trees and vines bearing fruits or nuts Assets used in the production of grain, sugar, and vegetable oil products Assets used in petroleum refining Assets used in the manufacture and repair of ships, boats, and marine drilling rigs	Depreciable improvements made to land, such as shrubbery, fences, roads, and bridges Assets used to manufacture cement Gas and petroleum utility pipelines Industrial steam and electric generation and/or distribution systems Water taxis and ferry boats	Farm buildings Railroad structures and improvements Communication cable and long-line systems Water, electric, gas, and steam utility plants and equipment
25-Year Property (25 years)	**Residential Rental Property** (27.5 years)	**Nonresidential Real Property** (39 years)
Municipal sewers Certain water utility property integral to the gathering, treatment, or commercial distribution of water	This is any building or structure, such as a rental home (including a mobile home), if 80% of its gross rental income for the tax year is from dwelling units. A dwelling unit is a house or an apartment used to provide living accommodations.	This is property such as an office building, a store, or a warehouse that is not residential rental property.

TABLE 17-2 Cost Recovery Percentage Table MACRS

Recovery Year	Depreciation Rate for Property Class					
	3-year	5-year	7-year	10-year	15-year	20-year
1	33.33%	20.00%	14.29%	10.00%	5.00%	3.750%
2	44.45	32.00	24.49	18.00	9.50	7.219
3	14.81	19.20	17.49	14.40	8.55	6.677
4	7.41	11.52	12.49	11.52	7.70	6.177
5		11.52	8.93	9.22	6.93	5.713
6		5.76	8.92	7.37	6.23	5.285
7			8.93	6.55	5.90	4.888
8			4.46	6.55	5.90	4.522
9				6.56	5.91	4.462
10				6.55	5.90	4.461
11				3.28	5.91	4.462
12					5.90	4.461
13					5.91	4.462
14					5.90	4.461
15					5.91	4.462
16					2.95	4.461
17						4.462
18						4.461
19						4.462
20						4.461
21						2.231

Learning Tip

In MACRS, the entire asset is depreciated. There is no salvage value.

Note that the percents for any given property class in the Cost Recovery Percentage Table add up to 100%.

SECTION 179 DEDUCTIONS

As the table below shows, Section 179 deductions have varied widely over the years.

Section 179 deductions are a way for small businesses to write off in one year all or part of certain business assets that are usually depreciated over many years using MACRS. These assets include most business machinery and equipment, furniture, fixtures, storage facilities, and off-the-shelf software. Table 17-3 lists the Section 179 deductions over the past few years.

SPECIAL DEPRECIATION ALLOWANCE

The law provided additional depreciation allowances for qualified MACRS assets with a class life of 20 years or less and acquired and placed into service according to the dates in Table 17-4. This allowance is an additional deduction after the Section 179 deduction and before regular depreciation under MACRS. Certain limits and numerous restrictions apply to these depreciation tax rules. For the latest information, once again refer to IRS Publication 946, How to Depreciate Property, at www.irs.gov.

Dollars AND Sense

You can allocate the Section 179 deduction among qualifying assets in any way you want, thus reducing the basis of each of the assets. It is generally to your advantage to take the deduction on those assets that have the longest life, thus recovering your basis sooner, and use the regular depreciation methods on those assets that have short lives.

iStock.com/vreemous

TABLE 17-3 Section 179 Deductions

Year Asset Was Placed into Service	Maximum Section 179 Deduction	
1996	$17,500	
1997	$18,000	
1998	$18,500	
1999	$19,000	
2000	$20,000	
2001	$24,000	
2002	$25,000	
2003	$100,000 ◄	**Jobs and Growth Tax Relief Act**
2004–2005	$102,000	
2006	$108,000	
2007	$112,000	
2008–2010	$250,000 ◄	**The Great Recession**
2011–2017	$500,000	
2018–2022	$1,000,000	

TABLE 17-4 Special Depreciation Allowance

Certain Qualified Asset Placed into Service	Special Allowance
September 11, 2001–May 5, 2003	30%
May 6, 2003–January 1, 2005	50%
December 31, 2007–September 27, 2017	50%
September 28, 2017–December 31, 2022	100%

STEPS TO PREPARE A DEPRECIATION SCHEDULE BY USING MACRS

STEP 1. Calculate the basis for depreciation—the **cost** of the particular asset for depreciation purposes.

a. **Percent of business use:** If an asset is used for business less than 100% of the time, multiply the original cost by the business-use percentage of the asset. (*Note*: The minimum percentage for an asset to qualify for depreciation is 50%.)

Business-use basis = Original cost × Business-use percentage

iStock.com/Nikada

b. **Section 179 deduction:** Determine the amount of the Section 179 deduction you choose to take, up to the limit, and subtract that amount from the business-use basis for depreciation.

Tentative basis = Business-use basis − Section 179 deduction

c. **Special depreciation allowances:** For qualifying assets, apply any special depreciation allowances, as specified in Table 17-4, to the tentative basis for depreciation.

**Basis for depreciation =
Tentative basis(100% − Special depreciation allowance percent)**

STEP 2. Set up the depreciation schedule in the form of a chart with the following headings:

End of Year	Basis for Depreciation	Cost Recovery Percentage	MACRS Depreciation Deduction	Accumulated Depreciation	Book Value

Use Table 17-1 to determine the property class for the asset and Table 17-2 to find the cost recovery percentages for each year. Calculate the MACRS depreciation deduction for each year by multiplying the basis for depreciation by the cost recovery percentages.

**MACRS depreciation deduction =
Basis for depreciation × Cost recovery percentage for that year**

EXAMPLE5   PREPARING A MACRS DEPRECIATION SCHEDULE

On July 27, 2017, Utopia Industries purchased and placed into service new office and computer equipment costing $400,000. This equipment is used for business 100% of the time. The accountants have elected to take a $30,000 Section 179 deduction. Prepare a depreciation schedule for the new asset by using MACRS.

▶SOLUTIONSTRATEGY

We begin by calculating the basis for depreciation:

Step 1a. Because the equipment is used for business 100% of the time, the business-use basis for depreciation is the same as the original cost of the asset.

Business-use basis = Original cost × Business-use percentage
Business-use basis = $400,000 × 100% = $400,000

Step 1b. We find the tentative basis for depreciation by subtracting the section 179 deduction of $30,000 from the business-use basis.

Tentative basis = Business-use basis − Section 179 deduction
Tentative basis = $400,000 − $30,000 = $370,000

Step 1c. We find the basis for depreciation by applying the special depreciation allowance.

Basis for depreciation = Tentative basis(100% − Special depreciation allowance percent)

Basis for depreciation = $370,000(100% − 50%) = $185,000

Step 2. Let's set up the depreciation schedule. From Table 17-1, we find that office and computer equipment is in the 5-year property class. Table 17-2 provides the cost recovery percentage for each year. Note once again, the extra year is to allow for the assumption that the asset was placed in service at mid-year.

Utopia Industries
MACRS Depreciation Schedule
Office and Computer Equipment

End of Year	Basis for Depreciation	Cost Recovery Percentage	MACRS Depreciation Deduction	Accumulated Depreciation	Book Value
					(new) $185,000
1	$185,000	20.00%	$37,000	$37,000	148,000
2	185,000	32.00	59,200	96,200	88,800
3	185,000	19.20	35,520	131,720	53,280
4	185,000 ·	11.52	21,312	153,032	31,968
5	185,000	11.52	21,312	174,344	10,656
6	185,000	5.76	10,656	185,000	0

▶ TRYITEXERCISE 5

Roadway Trucking purchased and placed into service an over-the-road tractor for $135,500 in 2017. The vehicle was used for business 80% of the time. The accountant took a $20,000 Section 179 deduction for the year 2014. Prepare a depreciation schedule for this new asset by using MACRS.

CHECK YOUR ANSWERS WITH THE SOLUTIONS ON PAGE 612.

17-6 CALCULATING THE PERIODIC DEPLETION COST OF NATURAL RESOURCES

depletion The proportional allocation or write-off of the cost of natural resources to the units used up, or depleted, per accounting period. Calculated the same way as units-of-production depreciation.

wasting assets An accounting term used to describe natural resources that are exhausted, or used up, as they are converted into inventory by mining, pumping, or cutting.

Just as depreciation is used to write off the useful life of plant assets such as trucks, equipment, and buildings, depletion is used to account for the consumption of natural resources such as coal, petroleum, timber, natural gas, and minerals. **Depletion** is the proportional allocation of the cost of natural resources to the units used up, or depleted, per accounting period. In accounting, natural resources are also known as **wasting assets** because they are considered to be exhausted, or used up, as they are converted into inventory by mining, pumping, or cutting.

Depletion of natural resources is calculated the same way as the units-of-production method of depreciation for plant assets. To calculate the depletion allocation, we must determine the following:

a. *Total cost of the natural resource package*, including the original purchase price, exploration expenses, and extraction or cutting expenses.
b. *Residual or salvage value* of the property after resources have been exhausted.
c. *Estimated total number of units* (tons, barrels, and board feet) of resource available.

STEPS TO CALCULATE THE PERIODIC DEPLETION COST OF NATURAL RESOURCES

STEP 1. Compute the average depletion cost per unit by

$$\text{Average depletion cost per unit} = \frac{\text{Total cost of resource} - \text{Residual value}}{\text{Estimated total units available}}$$

(Round to the nearest tenth of a cent when necessary.)

STEP 2. Calculate the periodic depletion cost by

$$\text{Periodic depletion cost} = \frac{\text{Units produced in}}{\text{current period}} \times \frac{\text{Average depletion}}{\text{cost per unit}}$$

EXAMPLE6 CALCULATE THE PERIODIC DEPLETION COST OF NATURAL RESOURCES

Black Gold Oil, Inc., purchased a parcel of land containing an estimated 1.5 million barrels of crude oil for $16,000,000. Two oil wells were drilled at a cost of $3,400,000. The residual value of the property and equipment is $2,500,000. Calculate the periodic depletion cost for the first year of operation if 325,000 barrels were extracted.

►SOLUTIONSTRATEGY

Step 1. Average depletion cost per unit $= \dfrac{\text{Total cost of resource} - \text{Residual value}}{\text{Estimated total units available}}$

Average depletion cost barrel $= \dfrac{(16,000,000 + 3,400,000) - 2,500,000}{1,500,000} = \$11.27$ per barrel

Step 2. Periodic depletion cost $=$ Units produced in current period $\times$ Average depletion cost per unit

Periodic depletion cost $= 325,000 \times 11.27 = \underline{\$3,662,750}$

►TRYITEXERCISE 6

The Canmore Mining Company paid $5,330,000 for a parcel of land, including the mining rights. In addition, the company spent $900,000 on labor and equipment to prepare the site for mining operations. After mining is completed, it is estimated that the land and equipment will have a residual value of $400,000. Geologists estimated that the mine contains 185,000 tons of coal. If Canmore mined 15,000 tons of coal in the first year, what is the amount of the depletion cost?

CHECK YOUR ANSWERS WITH THE SOLUTIONS ON PAGE 612.

Natural resources are also known as wasting assets because they are considered to be used up when converted into inventory.

REVIEW EXERCISES

17 SECTION II

1. Ink Masters Printing purchased a new printing press for $660,000 on February 9, 2017. The press is used for business 90% of the time. As the accountant for the company, you elected to take a $100,000 Section 179 deduction. The press also qualified for a special depreciation allowance. (See Table 17-4.)

   a. What was the basis for depreciation of the printing press?

   Business-use basis $= 660,000 \times .9 = \$594,000$
   Tentative basis $= 594,000 - 100,000 = \$494,000$
   The asset qualifies for a 50% special depreciation allowance (Table 17-4).
   Basis for depreciation $= 494,000 \,(100\% - 50\%) = \underline{\$247,000}$

   b. What was the amount of the third year's depreciation using MACRS?

   Printing presses are in the 7-year property class (Table 17-1).
   Third-year depreciation $= 17.49\%$ (Table 17-2)
   $247,000 \times .1749 = \underline{\$43,200.30}$

2. Trident Developers purchased a computer system for $75,000 on April 27, 2017. The computer system is used for business 100% of the time. The accountant for the company elected to take a $10,000 Section 179 deduction, and the asset qualified for a special depreciation allowance. (see Table 17-4)

a. What was the basis for depreciation of the computer system?

b. What was the amount of the first year's depreciation using MACRS?

3. Mid-State Construction built roads and a bridge at Atlantis World in Orlando, Florida, at a cost of $15,000,000. Atlantis World uses MACRS for tax purposes. No Section 179 or special depreciation allowances were taken.

a. What is the second year's depreciation deduction?

b. What is the ninth year's depreciation deduction?

4. Johnson Industries purchased a metal-working lathe for $34,000. This item will be used for business 90% of the time. Accountants elected to take a $14,000 section 179 deduction and utilize the special depreciation allowance of 50%.

Prepare a depreciation shedule using MACRS.

Round all dollar amounts to the nearest cent.

Johnson Industries
MACRS Depreciation Schedule—Metal-working Lathe

End of Year	Basis for Depreciation	×	Recovery Percent	=	MACRS Depreciation Deduction	Accumulated Depreciation	Book Value
							$8,300.00
1	$8,300.00	×	33.33%	=	_____	_____	_____
2	8,300.00	×	44.45%	=	_____	_____	_____
3	8,300.00	×	14.81%	=	_____	_____	_____
4	8,300.00	×	7.41%	=	_____	_____	_____

5. All-That-Glitters Mining Company paid $49,250,000 for a parcel of land, including the gold mining rights. In addition, the company spent $7,462,500 to prepare the site for mining operations. It is estimated that the residual value of the asset will be $5,300,000. Geologists estimate the site contains a total of 225,000 ounces of gold.

a. What is the average depletion cost per ounce?

Total depletion = 49,250,000 + 7,462,500 − 5,300,000 = $51,412,500

$$\text{Average depletion cost per ounce} = \frac{51,412,500}{225,000} = \$228.50$$

> **b.** If 16,200 ounces were mined in the first year of operation, what is the amount of the depletion cost?
>
> First-year depletion cost = 16,200 × 228.50 = <u>$3,701,700</u>

6. Sequoia Timber Company purchased land containing an estimated 6,500,000 board feet of lumber for $3,700,000. The company invested another $300,000 to construct access roads and a company depot. The residual value of the property and equipment is estimated to be $880,000.

   a. What is the average depletion cost per board foot of lumber?

   b. If 782,000 board feet were cut in the second year of operation, what is the amount of the depletion cost for that year?

7. For $42,750,000, Wesco Developers purchased land which their experts believe to contain 28.5 million tons of copper ore. It cost $12,483,000 to develop the property, whose residual value is estimated as $5,985,000.

   Determine the current year depletion expense if annual production amounted to 4,845,000 tons. Round depletion cost per unit to the nearest cent.

BUSINESS DECISION: INTANGIBLE WRITE-OFFS

iStock.com/
MarsBars

8. As you have seen in this chapter, companies depreciate, or write off, the expense of *tangible assets* such as trucks and equipment over a period of their useful lives. Many companies also have *intangible assets* that must be accounted for as an expense over a period of time.

   Intangible assets are resources that benefit the company but do not have any physical substance. Some examples are copyrights, franchises, patents, trademarks, and leases. In accounting, intangible assets are written off in a procedure known as asset amortization. This is much like straight-line depreciation, but there is no salvage value.

   You are the accountant for Front Line Pharmaceuticals, Inc. In January 2000, the company purchased the patent rights for a new medication from Novae, Inc., for $9,000,000. The patent had 15 years remaining as its useful life. In January 2005, Front Line Pharmaceuticals successfully defended its right to the patent in a lawsuit that cost $550,000 in legal fees.

   a. Using the straight-line method, calculate the patent's annual amortization expense for the years before the lawsuit.

   b. Calculate the revised annual amortization expense for the remaining years after the lawsuit.

CHAPTER 17

CHAPTER FORMULAS

Straight-Line Method

Total cost = Cost + Shipping charges + Setup expenses

Total depreciation = Total cost − Salvage value

$$\text{Annual depreciation} = \frac{\text{Total depreciation}}{\text{Estimated useful life (years)}}$$

Sum-of-the-Years' Digits Method

$$\text{SYD depreciation rate fraction} = \frac{\text{Years of useful life remaining}}{\dfrac{n(n+1)}{2}}$$

Annual depreciation = Total depreciation × Depreciation rate fraction

Declining-Balance Method

$$\text{Declining-balance rate} = \frac{1}{\text{Useful life}} \times \text{Multiple}$$

Depreciation for the year = Beginning book value × Declining-balance rate

Ending book value = Beginning book value − Depreciation for the year

Units-of-Production Method

$$\text{Depreciation per unit} = \frac{\text{Cost} - \text{Salvage value}}{\text{Units of useful life}}$$

Annual depreciation = Depreciation per unit × Units produced

MACRS Depreciation

Business-use basis = Original cost × Business-use percentage

Tentative basis = Business-use basis − Section 179 deduction

Basis for depreciation = Tentative basis(100% − Special depreciation allowance percent)

MACRS depr. deduction = Basis for depr. × Cost recovery percentage for that year

Natural Resource Depletion

$$\text{Average depletion cost per unit} = \frac{\text{Total cost of resource} - \text{Residual value}}{\text{Estimated total units available}}$$

Periodic depl. cost = Units produced in current period × Average depl. cost per unit

CHAPTER SUMMARY

Section I: Traditional Depreciation—Methods Used for Financial Statement Reporting

Topic	Important Concepts	Illustrative Examples
Calculating Depreciation by the Straight-Line Method **Performance Objective 17-1, Page 588**	Straight-line depreciation provides for equal periodic charges to be written off over the estimated useful life of the asset. 1. Determine the total cost and residual value of the asset. 2. Subtract residual value from total cost to find the total amount of depreciation. 3. Calculate the annual depreciation by dividing the total depreciation by the useful life of the asset.	Golden National Bank purchased a closed-circuit television system for $45,000. Shipping charges were $325, and installation expenses amounted to $2,540. The system is expected to last 5 years and has a residual value of $3,500. Prepare a depreciation schedule for the system. Total cost = 45,000 + 325 + 2,540 = $47,865 Total depr. = 47,865 − 3,500 = $44,365 Annual depr. = $\dfrac{44,365}{5}$ = $8,873

Section I (continued)

Topic	Important Concepts	Illustrative Examples
	4. Set up a depreciation schedule in the form of a chart. <table><tr><td>End of Year</td><td>Annual Depreciation</td><td>Accumulated Depreciation</td><td>Book Value</td></tr></table>	<table><tr><td>End of Year</td><td>Annual Depr.</td><td>Accum. Depr.</td><td>Book Value</td></tr><tr><td></td><td></td><td></td><td>(new) $47,865</td></tr><tr><td>1</td><td>$8,873</td><td>$8,873</td><td>38,992</td></tr><tr><td>2</td><td>8,873</td><td>17,746</td><td>30,119</td></tr><tr><td>3</td><td>8,873</td><td>26,619</td><td>21,246</td></tr><tr><td>4</td><td>8,873</td><td>35,492</td><td>12,373</td></tr><tr><td>5</td><td>8,873</td><td>44,365</td><td>3,500</td></tr></table>
Calculating Depreciation by the Sum-of-the-Years' Digits Method **Performance Objective 17-2, Page 590**	The sum-of-the-years' digits method is one of the accelerated methods of calculating depreciation. 1. Find the total depreciation of the asset: 2. Calculate the SYD depreciation rate fraction for each year: 3. Calculate the depreciation for each year:	The Gourmet Diner purchased new kitchen equipment for $165,000 with a 4-year useful life and a salvage value of $5,000. Using the sum-of-the-years' digits method, calculate the depreciation expense for year 1 and year 3. Total depr. $= 165,000 - 5,000 = \underline{160,000}$ Rate fraction year 1 $= \dfrac{4}{\dfrac{4(4+1)}{2}} = \dfrac{4}{10}$ Depr. year 1 $= 160,000 \times \dfrac{4}{10} = \underline{\$64,000}$ Rate fraction year 3 $= \dfrac{2}{\dfrac{4(4+1)}{2}} = \dfrac{2}{10}$ Depr. year 3 $= 160,000 \times \dfrac{2}{10} = \underline{\$32,000}$
Calculating Depreciation by the Declining-Balance Method **Performance Objective 17-3, Page 592**	Declining-balance depreciation, the second accelerated method, uses a multiple of the straight-line rate, such as 150% or 200%. Salvage value is not considered until the last year. 1. Calculate the declining-balance rate: 2. Calculate the depreciation for each year by applying the rate to each year's beginning book value. 3. Calculate the ending book value for each year by subtracting the depreciation for the year from the beginning book value. 4. The depreciation is complete when the ending book value equals the salvage value.	The Fitness Factory purchased a treadmill for $5,000. It is expected to last 4 years and have a salvage value of $1,000. Use 150% declining-balance depreciation to calculate the book value after each year. Round your answer to dollars. Declining-balance rate $= \dfrac{1}{4} \times 1.5 = .375$ *Year 1:* Depr. $= 5,000 \times .375 = 1,875$ Book value $= 5,000 - 1,875 = \underline{\$3,125}$ *Year 2:* Depr. $= 3,125 \times .375 = 1,172$ Book value $= 3,125 - 1,172 = \underline{\$1,953}$ *Year 3:* Depr. $= 1,953 \times .375 = 732$ Book value $= 1,953 - 732 = \underline{\$1,221}$ *Year 4:* Depr. $= 1,221 \times .375 = 458$ Book value $= 1,221 - 221 = \$1,000^*$ *In year 4, the calculated depreciation is $458. Because the book value of an asset cannot fall below the salvage value, the allowable depreciation is limited to $221 (1,221 - 1,000 = 221).

Section I (continued)

Topic	Important Concepts	Illustrative Examples
Calculating Depreciation by the Units-of-Production Method **Performance Objective 17-4, Page 594**	When the useful life of an asset is more accurately defined in terms of how much it is used, such as miles driven or units produced, we may apply the units-of-production method. 1. Determine the depreciation cost per unit by using 2. Calculate the depreciation for each year by using	Vita Foods purchased a new canning machine for one of its chicken soup production lines at a cost of $455,000. The machine has an expected useful life of 1,000,000 cans and a residual value of $25,000. In the first year, the machine produced 120,000 cans. Calculate the depreciation on the machine for year 1. $$\text{Depreciation per unit} = \frac{455,000 - 25,000}{1,000,000}$$ $$= \$0.43$$ First-year depreciation cost $= 120,000 \times .43$ $= \underline{\underline{\$51,600}}$

Section II: Asset Cost Recovery Systems—IRS–Prescribed Methods for Income Tax Reporting

Topic	Important Concepts	Illustrative Examples

Calculating Depreciation by Using the Modified Accelerated Cost Recovery System (MACRS)
 	
Performance Objective 17-5, Page 600
	MACRS is used for assets placed in service after 1986. This system uses property classes, Table 17-1, and recovery percentages, Table 17-2. To determine the basis for depreciation, use the Section 179 deductions in Table 17-3 and the special depreciation allowance dates in Table 17-4.
	
	1. Calculate the basis for depreciation.
	   a. Percent of business use (Minimum 50% to qualify):
	
	   b. Section 179 deduction (Table 17-3):
	
	   c. Special Depreciation Allowances (Table 17-4):
	
	2. **MACRS depreciation deduction (Tables 17-1 and 17-2)**
		Harbor Helpers purchased a tugboat for $650,000. The boat is used for business 100% of the time. No Section 179 or special allowances were available. As the accountant, use MACRS to calculate the depreciation expense for the second and fifth year.
		   Using Table 17-1, we find that tugboats are considered 10-year property.
		MACRS Depreciation Expense:
		
		Year 2:
		   $650,000 \times .18 = \underline{\underline{\$117,000}}$
		
		Year 5:
		   $650,000 \times .0922 = \underline{\underline{\$59,930}}$

Calculating the Periodic Depletion Cost of Natural Resources **Performance Objective 17-6, Page 604**	Depletion is the proportional allocation of natural resources to the units used up, or depleted, per accounting period. Depletion is calculated the same way as the units-of-production method of depreciation. 1. Compute the average depletion cost per unit: 2. Calculate the periodic depletion cost:	The Mother Lode Mining Company purchased a parcel of land containing an estimated 800,000 tons of iron ore. The cost of the asset was $2,000,000. An additional $350,000 was spent to prepare the property for mining. The estimated residual value of the asset is $500,000. If the first year's output was 200,000 tons, what is the amount of the depletion allowance? $$\text{Avg. depl. per unit} = \frac{2,350,000 - 500,000}{800,000}$$ $$= \$2.31 \text{ per ton}$$ First-year depletion cost $= 200,000 \times 2.31$ $= \underline{\underline{\$462,000}}$

TRY IT: EXERCISE SOLUTIONS FOR CHAPTER 17

1. Total cost = Cost + Shipping charges + Setup expenses

Total cost = 125,000 + 1,150 + 750 = $\underline{\$126,900}$

Total depreciation = Total cost − Salvage value

Total depreciation = 126,900 − 5,000 = $\underline{\$121,900}$

$$\text{Annual depreciation} = \frac{\text{Total depreciation}}{\text{Estimated useful life}}$$

$$\text{Annual depreciation} = \frac{121,900}{5} = \underline{\$24,380}$$

Wild Flour Bakery
Straight-Line Depreciation Schedule
Bread Oven

End of Year	Annual Depreciation	Accumulated Depreciation	Book Value
			(cost) $126,900
1	$24,380	$24,380	102,520
2	24,380	48,760	78,140
3	24,380	73,140	53,760
4	24,380	97,520	29,380
5	24,380	121,900	(salvage value) 5,000

2. Total depreciation = Total cost − Salvage value

Total depreciation = 44,500 − 2,500 = $\underline{\$42,000}$

$$\text{SYD depreciation rate fraction} = \frac{\text{Years of useful life remaining}}{\dfrac{n(n+1)}{2}}$$

$$\text{Rate fraction year 1} = \frac{6}{\dfrac{6(6+1)}{2}} = \frac{6}{\dfrac{42}{2}} = \frac{6}{21}$$

Bow Valley Kitchens

End of Year	Total Depreciation	Rate Fraction	Annual Depreciation	Accumulated Depreciation	Book Value
					(new) $44,500
1	$42,000	$\frac{6}{21}$	$12,000	$12,000	32,500
2	42,000	$\frac{5}{21}$	10,000	22,000	22,500
3	42,000	$\frac{4}{21}$	8,000	30,000	14,500
4	42,000	$\frac{3}{21}$	6,000	36,000	8,500
5	42,000	$\frac{2}{21}$	4,000	40,000	4,500
6	42,000	$\frac{1}{21}$	2,000	42,000	2,500

3. $\text{Declining-balance rate} = \dfrac{1}{\text{Useful life}} \times \text{Multiple}$

$\text{Declining-balance rate} = \dfrac{1}{4} \times 1.5 = .375$

Kelowna Air Service

End of Year	Beginning Book Value	Depreciation Rate	Depreciation for Year	Accumulated Depreciation	Ending Book Value
					(new) $386,000.00
1	$386,000.00	37.5%	$144,750.00	$144,750.00	241,250.00
2	241,250.00	37.5%	90,468.75	235,218.75	150,781.25
3	150,781.25	37.5%	56,542.97	291,761.72	94,238.28
4	94,238.28	37.5%	24,238.28*	316,000.00	70,000.00

*Maximum allowable to reach salvage value

CHAPTER
17

4. $\text{Depreciation per unit} = \dfrac{\text{Cost} - \text{Salvage value}}{\text{Units of useful life}}$

$\text{Depreciation per unit} = \dfrac{54,500 - 7,500}{75,000} = \$0.627/\text{mile}$

Prestige Limousine Service

End of Year	Depreciation per Mile	Miles Used	Annual Depreciation	Accumulated Depreciation	Book Value
					(new) $54,500.00
1	$.627	12,500	$7,837.50	$7,837.50	46,662.50
2	.627	18,300	11,474.10	19,311.60	35,188.40
3	.627	15,900	9,969.30	29,280.90	25,219.10
4	.627	19,100	11,975.70	41,256.60	13,243.40
5	.627	12,400	5,743.40*	47,000.00	7,500.00

*Maximum allowable to reach salvage value.

5. MACRS 3-Year Property

Business-use basis = Original cost × Business-use percentage

Business-use basis = 135,500 × 80% = $108,400

Tentative basis = Business-use basis − Section 179 deductions

Tentative basis = 108,400 − 20,000 = $88,400

There are no special allowances available for this asset.

Basis for depreciation = $88,400

Roadway Trucking
Over-the-Road Tractor

End of Year	Original Basis	Cost Recovery Percentage	Cost Recovery	Accumulated Depreciation	Book Value
					(new) $88,400.00
1	$88,400	33.33	$29,463.72	$29,463.72	58,936.28
2	88,400	44.45	39,293.80	68,757.52	19,642.48
3	88,400	14.81	13,092.04	81,849.56	6,550.44
4	88,400	7.41	6,550.44	88,400.00	0

6. $\text{Average depletion cost per unit} = \dfrac{\text{Total cost} - \text{Residual value}}{\text{Estimated total units available}}$

$\text{Average depletion cost per unit} = \dfrac{(5,330,000 + 900,000) - 400,000}{185,000} = \dfrac{5,830,000}{185,000}$

$= 31.513 = \$31.51$

Periodic depletion cost = Units produced × Average depletion cost per unit

Periodic depletion cost (1st year) = 15,000 × 31.51 = $\underline{\underline{\$472,650}}$

CONCEPT REVIEW

1. The decrease in value from the original cost of a long-term asset over its useful life is known as _____. (17-1)

2. The total cost or original _____ is the total amount a company pays for an asset. The _____ value is an asset's value at any given time during its useful life. (17-1)

3. The useful _____ is the length of time an asset is expected to generate revenue. The value of an asset at the time it is taken out of service is known as its _____, scrap, salvage, or trade-in-value. (17-1)

4. _____ depreciation is a method of depreciation that provides for equal periodic charges to be written off over the life of an asset. (17-1)

5. Depreciation methods that assume an asset depreciates more in the early years of its useful life are known as _____ depreciation. (17-2)

6. _____ digits is a method of accelerated depreciation that allows an asset to depreciate the most during the first year of its useful life. (17-2)

7. Write the formula for the sum of the digits of the useful life of an asset, where *n* is the number of years of useful life. (17-2)

8. A method of accelerated depreciation that uses a multiple (150% or 200%) of the straight-line rate is known as the _____ method. (17-3)

9. Write the formula for the declining-balance rate. (17-3)

10. Write the formula for the depreciation per unit in the units-of-production method. (17-4)

11. According to the IRS, the depreciation system for getting back, or recovering, the cost of property used to produce income is known as the _____ system. This system is abbreviated as _____. (17-5)

12. The IRS system named in item 11 lists assets in various time categories known as _____ classes. Once an asset's class has been determined, a table is used to find the cost _____ percentage for the recovery year in question. (17-5)

13. The depreciation of natural resources is known as _____. The accounting term used to describe these natural resources is _____ assets. (17-6)

14. When natural resources are depleted, the average depletion cost per unit is equal to _____. (17-6)

ASSESSMENT TEST

Calculate the total cost, total depreciation, and annual depreciation for the following assets by using the straight-line method.

	Cost	Shipping Charges	Setup Charges	Total Cost	Salvage Value	Estimated Useful Life (years)	Depreciation Total	Annual
1.	$5,600	$210	$54	_____	$600	6	_____	_____
2.	$16,900	$310	0	_____	$1,900	4	_____	_____

EXCEL 2

3. Oxford Manufacturing, Inc., purchased new equipment totaling $648,000. Shipping charges were $2,200, and installation amounted to $1,800. The equipment is expected to last 4 years and have a residual value of $33,000. If the company elects to use the straight-line method of depreciation, prepare a depreciation schedule for these assets.

Oxford Manufacturing, Inc.
Straight-Line Depreciation Schedule
Manufacturing Equipment

End of Year	Annual Depreciation	Accumulated Depreciation	Book Value
		(new)	_____
1	_____	_____	_____
2	_____	_____	_____
3	_____	_____	_____
4	_____	_____	_____

Complete the following as they relate to the sum-of-the-years' digits method of depreciation.

	Useful Life (years)	Sum-of-the-Years' Digits	Depreciation Rate Fraction		
			Year 2	Year 4	Year 6
4.	8	_____	_____	_____	_____
5.	9	_____	_____	_____	_____

CHAPTER 17

6. Mr. Fix-It purchased a service truck for $32,400. It has an estimated useful life of 3 years and a trade-in value of $3,100. Using the sum-of-the-years' digits method, prepare a depreciation schedule for the truck.

Mr. Fix-It
SYD Depreciation Schedule
Service Truck

End of Year	Total Depreciation	Depreciation Rate Fraction	Annual Depreciation	Accumulated Depreciation	Book Value
					(new) _____
1	_____	___	_____	_____	_____
2	_____	___	_____	_____	_____
3	_____	___	_____	_____	_____

Complete the following as they relate to the declining-balance method of depreciation. Round to the nearest hundredth if necessary.

Years	Straight-Line Rate (%)	Multiple (%)	Declining-Balance Rate (%)
7. 9	_____	150	_____
8. 4	_____	200	_____

9. Award Makers bought a computerized engraving machine for $33,800. It is expected to have a 5-year useful life and a trade-in value of $2,700. Prepare a depreciation schedule for the *first three years* by using the 150% declining-balance method for the machine.

Award Makers
150% Declining-Balance Depreciation Schedule
Computerized Engraving Machine

End of Year	Beginning Book Value	Depreciation Rate	Depreciation for the Year	Accumulated Depreciation	Ending Book Value
					(new) _____
1	_____	___	_____	_____	_____
2	_____	___	_____	_____	_____
3	_____	___	_____	_____	_____

Complete the following as they relate to the units-of-production method of depreciation. Round answers to the nearest tenth of a cent.

Asset	Cost	Salvage Value	Units of Useful Life	Depreciation per Unit
10. Pump	$8,900	$250	500,000 gallons	_____
11. Copier	3,900	0	160,000 copies	_____

12. Screen Gems Movie Theater purchased a new projector for $155,000 with a salvage value of $2,000. Delivery and installation amounted to $580. The projector is expected to have a useful life of 15,000 hours. Complete the following depreciation schedule for the *first four years* of operation by using the units-of-production method.

EXCEL 3

Screen Gems Movie Theater
Units-of-Production Depreciation Schedule
Projector

End of Year	Depreciation per Hour	Hours	Annual Depreciation	Accumulated Depreciation	Book Value
					(new) _____
1	_____	2,300	_____	_____	_____
2	_____	1,890	_____	_____	_____
3	_____	2,160	_____	_____	_____
4	_____	2,530	_____	_____	_____

Websites such as boxoffice.com and boxofficemojo.com track box office revenue for movies playing in theaters in the United States and around the world.

StockLite/Shutterstock.com

13. Stone Age Concrete, Inc., purchased cement manufacturing equipment valued at $420,000 on March 14, 2017. The equipment is used for business 100% of the time. The firm's accountant elected to take a $100,000 section 179 deduction. You have been asked to review the depreciation figures used for this equipment.

    a. What is the basis for depreciation of this equipment?

    b. Prepare a depreciation schedule for the first five years of operation of this equipment by using MACRS.

Stone Age Concrete, Inc.
MACRS Depreciation Schedule
Cement Manufacturing Equipment

End of Year	Original Basis (cost)	Cost Recovery Percentage	Cost Recovery (depreciation)	Accumulated Depreciation	Book Value
					(new) _____
1	_____	_____	_____	_____	_____
2	_____	_____	_____	_____	_____
3	_____	_____	_____	_____	_____
4	_____	_____	_____	_____	_____
5	_____	_____	_____	_____	_____

14. The Platinum Touch Mining Company paid $4,000,000 for a parcel of land, including the mining rights. In addition, the company spent $564,700 to prepare the site for mining operations. When mining is completed, it is estimated that the residual value of the asset will be $800,000. Scientists estimate that the site contains 15,000 ounces of platinum.

    a. What is the average depletion cost per ounce?

    b. If 1,220 ounces were mined in the first year of operation, what is the amount of the depletion cost?

15. In January 2009, Marine Science Corporation was awarded a patent for a new boat hull design. The life of the patent is 20 years. The company estimates the value of the patent over its lifetime is $7,500,000. Marine Science's accountant amortizes the patent using straight-line depreciation to zero value at the end of the 20 years. In January 2017, Marine Science successfully defended its patent in a lawsuit at a legal expense of $486,000.

    a. Using the straight-line method, calculate the patent's annual amortization expense for the years before the lawsuit.

    b. Calculate the revised annual amortization expense for the remaining years after the lawsuit.

BUSINESS DECISION: A DISPUTE WITH THE IRS

16. You are the accountant for the Millenium Corporation. Last year the company purchased a $2,500,000 corporate jet to be used for executive travel. To help offset the cost of the airplane, your company occasionally rents the jet to the executives of two other corporations when it is not in use by Millenium.

When the corporate tax return was filed this year, you began depreciating the jet by using MACRS. Today you received a letter from the IRS informing you that because your company occasionally rents the airplane to others, it is considered a commercial aircraft and must be depreciated as such. The corporate lawyers are considering disputing this IRS ruling and have asked you the following questions:

a. How much depreciation did you claim this year?

b. Under the new category, how much depreciation would be claimed?

c. If the company pays 30% income tax, what effect will this change have on the amount of tax owed, assuming the company made a net profit this year?

COLLABORATIVE LEARNING ACTIVITY

Going, Going, Gone!

1. Have each member of your team choose his or her favorite vehicle and determine the price of a new one from a dealership. Then check the classified ads of your local newspaper, a publication of used vehicle prices, or the Internet to determine the price of the same vehicle at one, two, three, four, and five years old.

   a. Prepare a depreciation schedule based on the information found.
   b. Calculate the percent of the vehicle's original value that was lost each year.
   c. Construct a line graph of the five years of depreciation of the vehicle.
   d. Does it seem to be straight-line or accelerated?
   e. Compare the depreciation for each team member's vehicle. Which models depreciated the fastest? The slowest?

2. As a team, choose a local industry. Have each member of the team pick a different company within that industry and speak with an accountant who works there. Identify three major assets that are being depreciated, such as a truck, production-line equipment, a computer system, or office furniture and fixtures. For each asset, determine the following:

   a. Original purchase price
   b. Useful life
   c. Salvage value
   d. Depreciation method used for financial statement reporting
   e. Depreciation method used for income tax purposes

PERFORMANCE OBJECTIVES

SECTION I 18 SALES AND EXCISE TAXES

taxation The imposition of a mandatory levy or charge by a government unit to provide financing for public services.

Benjamin Franklin wrote that "nothing can be said to be certain except death and taxes." **Taxation** is the imposition of a mandatory levy on the citizens of a country by their government. In 1904, Supreme Court Justice Oliver Wendell Holmes, Jr., defined taxes as "the price we pay for living in a civilized society." In almost all countries, tax revenue is the major source of financing for publicly provided services. In a democracy, a majority of citizens or their representatives vote to impose taxes on themselves in order to finance, through the public sector, services on which they place value but that they believe cannot be adequately provided by market processes.

In addition to generating revenue to finance public services, taxation can be used for other objectives, such as income redistribution, economic stabilization, and the regulating of consumption of certain commodities or services. In this chapter, we will focus our attention on the three major categories of taxation: sales and excise tax, property tax, and individual and corporate income tax.

IN THE Business World

The cost of a civilized society: In a typical year federal, state, and local governments in the United States collect over $16,000 in tax revenue for every man, woman, and child in the country!

THE BUCK STOPS HERE!

FEDERAL INCOME TAX · STATE INCOME TAX · PROPERTY TAX · SALES TAX · SIN TAX · MISC TAX · MINE

sales tax A tax based on the retail selling or rental price of tangible personal property, collected by the retailer at the time of purchase, and paid to the state or local government.

A tax based on the retail selling or rental price of tangible personal property is called a **sales tax**. This tax may also be imposed on admission charges to places of amusement, sport, and recreation, as well as on certain services. Most states and many other taxing units such as cities, counties, and municipalities levy or charge a tax on sales. Businesses that purchase merchandise for resale to others are normally exempt from this tax. Only final buyers pay sales tax. Many states allow a sales tax exemption for food, prescription drugs, household medicines, and other selected items.

The liability for the sales tax is incurred at the time the sale is made. Retail merchants act as agents, collecting sales taxes and periodically remitting them to the proper tax agency. The **sales tax rate** is expressed as a percent and varies from state to state.

sales tax rate Sales tax expressed in its most common form, as a percent of the retail price of an item.

excise tax A tax levied by federal, state, and local governments on certain luxury or nonessential products and services such as alcoholic beverages, furs, tobacco products, telephone service, and airline and cruise ship tickets.

Another type of tax levied by federal, state, and local governments on certain products and services is known as an **excise tax**. This tax, which is paid in addition to the sales tax, is imposed on so-called luxury or nonessential items. Some typical examples are tires, alcoholic beverages, jewelry (except watches), gasoline, furs, firearms, certain recreational equipment and sporting goods, tobacco products, telecommunications (including telephone) services, and airline and cruise ship transportation.

18-1 DETERMINING SALES TAX BY USING SALES TAX TABLES

Many state and local governments provide retailers with sales tax tables such as those in Exhibit 18-1. These tables are used by businesses that do not have electronic cash register systems that automatically compute the proper amount of sales tax.

EXHIBIT 18-1 $6\frac{1}{2}$% Sales Tax Brackets

$6\frac{1}{2}$% SALES TAX BRACKETS

Amount of Sale		Tax	Amount of Sale		Tax	Amount of Sale		Tax	Amount of Sale		Tax
.10-	.15	.01	5.08-	5.23	.34	10.10-	10.15	.66	15.08-	15.23	.99
.16-	.30	.02	5.24-	5.38	.35	10.16-	10.30	.67	15.24-	15.38	1.00
.31-	.46	.03	5.39-	5.53	.36	10.31-	10.46	.68	15.39-	15.53	1.01
.47-	.61	.04	5.54-	5.69	.37	10.47-	10.61	.69	15.54-	15.69	1.02
.62-	.76	.05	5.70-	5.84	.38	10.62-	10.76	.70	15.70-	15.84	1.03
.77-	.92	.06	5.85-	6.09	.39	10.77-	10.92	.71	15.85-	16.09	1.04
.93-	1.07	.07	6.10-	6.15	.40						
						10.93-	11.07	.72	16.10-	16.15	1.05
1.08-	1.23	.08	6.16-	6.30	.41	11.08-	11.23	.73	16.16-	16.30	1.06
1.24-	1.38	.09	6.31-	6.46	.42	11.24-	11.38	.74	16.31-	16.46	1.07
1.39-	1.53	.10	6.47-	6.61	.43	11.39-	11.53	.75	16.47-	16.61	1.08
1.54-	1.69	.11	6.62-	6.76	.44	11.54-	11.69	.76	16.62-	16.76	1.09
1.70-	1.84	.12	6.77-	6.92	.45	11.70-	11.84	.77	16.77-	16.92	1.10
1.85-	2.09	.13	6.93-	7.07	.46	11.85-	12.09	.78	16.93-	17.07	1.11
2.10-	2.15	.14	7.08-	7.23	.47	12.10-	12.15	.79	17.08-	17.23	1.12
2.16-	2.30	.15	7.24-	7.38	.48	12.16-	12.30	.80	17.24-	17.38	1.13
2.31-	2.46	.16	7.39-	7.53	.49	12.31-	12.46	.81	17.39-	17.53	1.14
2.47-	2.61	.17	7.54-	7.69	.50	12.47-	12.61	.82	17.54-	17.69	1.15
2.62-	2.76	.18	7.70-	7.84	.51	12.62-	12.76	.83	17.70-	17.84	1.16
2.77-	2.92	.19	7.85-	8.09	.52	12.77-	12.92	.84	17.85-	18.09	1.17
2.93-	3.07	.20	8.10-	8.15	.53	12.93	13.07	.85	18.10-	18.15	1.18
3.08-	3.23	.21	8.16-	8.30	.54	13.08-	13.23	.86	18.16-	18.30	1.19
3.24-	3.38	.22	8.31-	8.46	.55	13.24-	13.38	.87	18.31-	18.46	1.20
3.39-	3.53	.23	8.47-	8.61	.56	13.39-	13.53	.88	18.47-	18.61	1.21
3.54-	3.69	.24	8.62-	8.76	.57	13.54-	13.69	.89	18.62-	18.76	1.22
3.70-	3.84	.25	8.77-	8.92	.58	13.70-	13.84	.90	18.77-	18.92	1.23
3.85-	4.09	.26	8.93-	9.07	.59	13.85-	14.09	.91	18.93-	19.07	1.24
4.10-	4.15	.27	9.08-	9.23	.60	14.10-	14.15	.92	19.08-	19.23	1.25
4.16-	4.30	.28	9.24-	9.38	.61	14.16-	14.30	.93	19.24-	19.38	1.26
4.31-	4.46	.29	9.39-	9.53	.62	14.31-	14.46	.94	19.39-	19.53	1.27
4.47-	4.61	.30	9.54-	9.69	.63	14.47-	14.61	.95	19.54-	19.69	1.28
4.62-	4.76	.31	9.70-	9.84	.64	14.62-	14.76	.96	19.70-	19.84	1.29
4.77-	4.92	.32	9.85-	10.09	.65	14.77-	14.92	.97	19.85-	20.09	1.30
4.93-	5.07	.33				14.93-	15.07	.98			

IN THE Business World

Currently, 45 states have a sales tax, with rates that range from 2.09% to 7.5%. In many areas, city and county rates add an additional 0.25% to 8.0%. According to the Tax Foundation, in a recent year states collected over $400 billion in sales tax. The five states with the highest average combined rates are Tennessee (9.44%), Arizona (9.16%), Louisiana (8.87%), Washington (8.86%), and Oklahoma (8.67%). The five states with the lowest average combined rates are Alaska (1.69%), Hawaii (4.35%), Maine (5%), Virginia (5%), and Wyoming (5.34%). Five states do not have a statewide sales tax: Alaska, Delaware, Montana, New Hampshire, and Oregon. Of these, Alaska and Montana allow localities to charge local sales taxes.

Source: www.taxfoundation.org

STEPS TO DETERMINE SALES TAX DUE ON AN ITEM BY USING SALES TAX TABLES

STEP 1. Locate the taxable retail price in the Amount of Sale column.

STEP 2. Scan to the right to locate the amount of tax due in the Tax column.

Note: Exhibit 18-1 is only a partial listing. Complete sales tax tables are available in most states from the Department of Revenue.

EXAMPLE1 USING SALES TAX TABLES

Beth Nelson purchased a bottle of aspirin at CVS Pharmacy for $3.29. Use Exhibit 18-1 to determine the amount of sales tax on this item.

▶SOLUTIONSTRATEGY

Step 1. From Exhibit 18-1, we find that the retail price of the aspirin, $3.29, falls in the range of $3.24 to $3.38.

Step 2. Scanning to the right, we find the tax due on this item is $0.22.

▶TRYITEXERCISE 1

Use Exhibit 18-1 to determine the amount of sales tax on a calculator at Office Depot with a retail price of $12.49.

CHECK YOUR ANSWER WITH THE SOLUTION ON PAGE 643.

18-2 CALCULATING SALES TAX BY USING THE PERCENT METHOD

When sales tax tables are not available, the percent method may be used to calculate the sales tax on an item or a service. Other nontaxable charges such as packing, delivery, handling, and setup are added after the sales tax has been computed.

STEPS TO CALCULATE SALES TAX AND TOTAL PURCHASE PRICE BY USING THE PERCENT METHOD

STEP 1. Calculate the sales tax by multiplying the selling price of the good or service by the sales tax rate.

$$\textbf{Sales tax} = \textbf{Selling price} \times \textbf{Sales tax rate}$$

STEP 2. Compute the total purchase price by adding the selling price, the sales tax, and any other additional charges.

$$\textbf{Total purchase price} = \textbf{Selling price} + \textbf{Sales tax} + \textbf{Other charges}$$

EXAMPLE2 CALCULATING SALES TAX

John Baker purchased a Craftsman lawn mower for $488.95 at a Sears store in Atlanta, Georgia. The store charges $25 for delivery and $15 for assembly. If the state sales tax in Georgia is 5% and Atlanta has a 1.5% city tax, what is the amount of sales tax on the lawn mower and what is the total purchase price?

SOLUTIONSTRATEGY

In this example, the sales tax rate will be the total of the state and city taxes:

$$\text{Sales tax rate} = 5\% + 1.5\% = 6.5\%$$

Step 1. Sales tax = Selling price × Sales tax rate
Sales tax = 488.95 × .065 = <u>$31.78</u>

Step 2. Total purchase price = Selling price + Sales tax + Other charges
Total purchase price = 488.95 + 31.78 + (25 + 15)
Total purchase price = <u>$560.73</u>

TRYITEXERCISE 2

Andy Bennett purchased a car for $38,600 at Auto Nation in Milwaukee, Wisconsin. If the dealer preparation charges are $240 and the sales tax rate in Wisconsin is 5%, what is the amount of sales tax on the car and what is the total purchase price?

CHECK YOUR ANSWERS WITH THE SOLUTIONS ON PAGE 643.

Learning Tip

Remember, there is no sales tax on packing, shipping, handling, or setup charges for merchandise purchased. These charges should be added *after* the sales tax has been computed.

B-A-C-O/Shutterstock.com

iStock.com/Nikada

CALCULATING SELLING PRICE AND AMOUNT OF SALES TAX WHEN TOTAL PURCHASE PRICE IS KNOWN

18-3

From time to time, merchants and customers may want to know the actual selling price of an item when the total purchase price, including sales tax, is known.

STEPS TO CALCULATE SELLING PRICE AND AMOUNT OF SALES TAX

STEP 1. Calculate the selling price of an item by dividing the total purchase price by 100% plus the sales tax rate.

$$\text{Selling price} = \frac{\text{Total purchase price}}{100\% + \text{Sales tax rate}}$$

STEP 2. Determine the amount of sales tax by subtracting the selling price from the total purchase price.

$$\text{Sales tax} = \text{Total purchase price} - \text{Selling price}$$

EXAMPLE3 CALCULATING SELLING PRICE AND SALES TAX

Arie Daniels bought a television set at Costco for a total purchase price of $477. If his state has a 6% sales tax, what were the actual selling price of the TV and the amount of sales tax?

SOLUTIONSTRATEGY

Step 1. $\text{Selling price} = \dfrac{\text{Total purchase price}}{100\% + \text{Sale tax rate}}$

$\text{Selling price} = \dfrac{477}{100\% + 6\%} = \dfrac{477}{1.06} = \underline{\$450}$

Step 2. $\text{Sales tax} = \text{Total purchase price} - \text{Selling price}$

$\text{Sales tax} = 477 - 450 = \underline{\$27}$

TRYITEXERCISE 3

At the end of a business day, the cash register at The Grove Art Gallery showed total sales, including sales tax, of $3,520. If the state and local sales taxes amounted to $8\frac{1}{2}\%$, what is the amount of the gallery's actual sales? How much sales tax was collected that day?

CHECK YOUR ANSWERS WITH THE SOLUTIONS ON PAGE 643.

CALCULATING EXCISE TAX

18-4

As with the sales tax, an excise tax is usually expressed as a percentage of the purchase price. In certain cases, however, the excise tax may be expressed as a fixed amount per unit purchased, such as $3 per passenger on a cruise ship or $0.15 per gallon of gasoline.

When both sales and excise taxes are imposed on merchandise at the retail level, the excise taxes are *not included* in the selling price when the sales tax is computed. Each tax should be calculated independently on the actual selling price.

Learning Tip

Don't tax the tax! The excise tax is *not included* in the selling price when the sales tax is computed. Each tax should be calculated *separately* on the actual selling price.

STEPS TO CALCULATE THE AMOUNT OF EXCISE TAX

STEP 1. *When expressed as a percent:* Multiply the selling price of the item by the excise tax rate.

Excise tax = Selling price × Excise tax rate

When expressed as a fixed amount per unit: Multiply the number of units by the excise tax per unit.

Excise tax = Number of units × Excise tax per unit

STEP 2. Calculate total purchase price by adding the selling price plus sales tax plus excise tax.

Total purchase price = Selling price + Sales tax + Excise tax

---

EXAMPLE 4   CALCULATING EXCISE TAX

The round-trip airfare from Miami to New York is $379. If the federal excise tax on airline travel is 10% and the Florida state sales tax is 6%, what is the amount of each tax and the total purchase price of the ticket?

SOLUTIONSTRATEGY

Step 1.   Sales tax = Selling price × Sales tax rate
Sales tax = 379 × .06 = <u>$22.74</u>

Excise tax = Selling price × Excise tax rate
Excise tax = 379 × .10 = <u>$37.90</u>

Step 2.   Total purchase price = Selling price + Sales tax + Excise tax
Total purchase price = 379.00 + 22.74 + 37.90 = <u>$439.64</u>

TRYITEXERCISE 4

An archery set at The Sports Authority in Mason, Ohio, has a retail price of $129.95. The sales tax in Ohio is 5%, and the federal excise tax on this type of sporting equipment is 11%. What is the amount of each tax, and what is the total purchase price of the archery set?

CHECK YOUR ANSWERS WITH THE SOLUTIONS ON PAGE 643.

IN THE Business World

The government "takes its cut" is a good description of the **excise**, or **tax**, charged on various goods considered luxury items.

The word *excise* is from *excidere*, Latin for "to cut out." In essence, the government cuts out its share!

In a typical year the federal government collects over $100 billion in excise tax.

Source: www.taxpolicycenter.org

SECTION I | 18   REVIEW EXERCISES

Use Exhibit 18-1 to determine the sales tax and calculate the total purchase price for the following items.

Item	Selling Price	Sales Tax	Total Purchase Price
1. Music CD	$8.95	<u>$.59</u>	<u>$9.54</u>
2. Candy bar	$.79	_____	_____
3. Mouse pad	$4.88	_____	_____
4. Hair dryer	$18.25	_____	_____
5. Ream of paper	$9.90	_____	_____
6. Backpack	$19.50	_____	_____

Calculate the missing information for the following purchases.

Item	Selling Price	Sales Tax Rate	Sales Tax	Excise Tax Rate	Excise Tax	Total Purchase Price
7. Motor	$1,440.00	7%	$100.80	3%	$43.20	$1,584.00
8. Sofa	$750.00	5	_____	0	0	_____
9. Fishing rod	$219.95	$4\frac{1}{2}$	_____	10		_____
10. Tire	$109.99	6	_____	5		_____
11. Automobile	_____	$5\frac{1}{4}$	_____	0	0	$18,785.00
12. Book	_____	8	_____	0	0	$15.12
13. Archery bow	$189.00	6.4	_____	11		_____

14. Gloria Carey purchased a refrigerator at Best Buy for $899.90. The delivery charge was $20, and the ice maker hookup amounted to $55. The state sales tax is $6\frac{1}{2}$%, and the city tax is 1.3%.

   a. What is the total amount of sales tax on the refrigerator?

   b. What is the total purchase price?

15. Mike purchases a bicycle costing $175.90. State taxes are 5% and local sales taxes are 2%. The store charges $20 for assembly. What is the total purchase price?

16. Suppose you bought a sofa for a total purchase price of $1,274.94. State taxes were 4%. What was the amount of the sales tax?

17. Sig Moline purchased supplies at Office Max for a total purchase price of $46.71. The state has a 4% sales tax.

   a. What was the selling price of the supplies?

   b. What was the amount of sales tax?

18. Last month The Sweet Tooth Candy Shops had total sales, including sales tax, of $57,889. The stores are located in a state that has a sales tax of $5\frac{1}{2}$%. As the accountant for The Sweet Tooth, calculate:

   a. The amount of sales revenue for the shops last month.

   b. The amount of sales taxes that must be sent to the state Department of Revenue.

19. Abby Duncan purchased a diamond necklace for $17,400 at Royal Jewelers. The state sales tax is 8%, and the federal excise tax on this type of jewelry is 10% on amounts over $10,000.

   a. What is the amount of the sales tax?

Because commercial airlines are subject to the federal aviation tax, they pay a reduced per-gallon excise tax compared to other aviation operations.

    b. What is the amount of the federal excise tax?

    c. What is the total purchase price of the necklace?

20. Loudoun Trucking purchases 5,850 truck tires. The federal excise tax is $0.14 per tire. Find the amount of the excise tax for this transaction.

BUSINESS DECISION: SPLITTING THE TAX

21. You are the owner of Caché, a chain of women's clothing boutiques. Your state has a sales tax of 6%, and your city has an additional sales tax of 1.5%. Each quarter you are responsible for making these tax deposits to the city and state. Last quarter your stores had total revenue, including sales tax, of $376,250.

    a. How much of this revenue was sales and how much was sales tax?

    b. How much sales tax should be sent to the city?

    c. How much sales tax should be sent to the state?

SECTION II   18   PROPERTY TAX

ad valorem or **property tax** A tax based on the assessed value of property, generally collected at the city or county level as the primary source of revenue for counties, municipalities, school districts, and special taxing districts.

real estate, or **real property** Land, buildings, and all other permanent improvements situated thereon.

personal property For ad valorem tax purposes, divided into tangible personal property such as business equipment, fixtures, and supplies and household goods such as clothing, furniture, and appliances.

Most states have laws that provide for the annual assessment and collection of ad valorem taxes on real and personal property. **Ad valorem tax** means a tax based on the assessed value of property. The term **property tax** is used interchangeably with the term *ad valorem tax*. Property taxes are assessed and collected at the county level as the primary source of revenue for counties, municipalities, school districts, and special taxing districts.

Real estate, or **real property**, is defined as land, buildings, and all other permanent improvements situated thereon. Real estate is broadly classified based on land use and includes the following:

- Single-family and multifamily residential, condominiums, townhouses, and mobile homes
- Vacant residential and unimproved acreage
- Commercial and industrial land and improvements
- Agriculture

Personal property is divided into two categories for ad valorem tax purposes:

- Tangible personal property such as business fixtures, supplies, and equipment and machinery for shops, plants, and farms
- Household goods (exempt from property tax in most states) such as apparel, furniture, appliances, and other items usually found in the home

The value of property for tax purposes is known as the **assessed value**. In some states, assessed value of the property is a specified percentage of the **fair market value**, while in other states, it is fixed by law at 100%. Typical factors considered in determining the fair market value of a piece of property are location, size, cost, replacement value, condition, and income derived from its use.

The assessed value is determined each year by the **tax assessor** or **property appraiser**. Most states allow specific discounts for early payment of the tax and have serious penalties for delinquency. The Department of Revenue in each state has the responsibility of ensuring that all properties are assessed and taxes are collected in accordance with the law.

assessed value The value of property for tax purposes, generally a percentage of the fair market value.

fair market value The value of property based on location, size, cost, replacement value, condition, and income derived from its use.

tax assessor or **property appraiser** The city or county official designated to determine assessed values of property.

CALCULATING THE AMOUNT OF PROPERTY TAX

18-5

On the basis of the fair market value, less all applicable exemptions, the property tax due is computed by applying the tax rates established by the taxing authorities in that area to the assessed value of the property.

Property tax = Assessed value of property × Tax rate

Property tax rates may be expressed in the following ways:

- Decimal or percent of assessed value—for example, .035 or 3.5%
- Per $100 of assessed value—for example, $3.50 per $100
- Per $1,000 of assessed value—for example, $35 per $1,000
- Mills (one one-thousandth of a dollar)—for example, 35 mills

Let's look at the steps used to calculate the property tax due when the same tax is expressed in each of the four different ways on a house with an assessed value of $250,000.

IN THE Business World

Property taxes vary greatly from area to area. Among the highest are Bridgeport, Connecticut; Des Moines, Iowa; Providence, Rhode Island; Newark, New Jersey; and Manchester, New Hampshire.

Among the lowest are Honolulu, Hawaii; Denver, Colorado; Birmingham, Alabama; Cheyenne, Wyoming; and New York, New York.

rtguest/Shutterstock.com

STEPS TO CALCULATE PROPERTY TAX WHEN THE TAX IS EXPRESSED AS A PERCENT

STEP 1. Convert the tax rate percent to a decimal by moving the decimal point two places to the left.

STEP 2. Multiply the assessed value by the tax rate as a decimal.

Property tax = Assessed value × Tax rate

iStock.com/Nikada

EXAMPLE5 CALCULATING PROPERTY TAX USING PERCENT

Calculate the tax due on a house with an assessed value of $250,000. The tax rate is 7.88% of the assessed value.

SOLUTIONSTRATEGY

Step 1. Convert tax percent to decimal form: 7.88% = .0788.

Step 2. Property tax = Assessed value × Tax rate
Property tax = 250,000 × .0788 = $19,700

TRYITEXERCISE 5

Calculate the tax due on a condominium with an assessed value of $160,000. The property tax rate is 6.3%.

CHECK YOUR ANSWER WITH THE SOLUTION ON PAGE 643.

Property taxes are the primary source of income for most school districts.

STEPS TO CALCULATE PROPERTY TAX WHEN THE TAX IS EXPRESSED PER $100 OF ASSESSED VALUE

STEP 1. Divide the assessed value by $100 to determine the number of $100 the assessed value contains.

$$\text{Number of } \$100 = \frac{\text{Assessed value}}{100}$$

STEP 2. Calculate the property tax by multiplying the number of $100 by the tax per $100.

$$\text{Property tax} = \text{Number of } \$100 \times \text{Tax per } \$100$$

Dollars AND Sense

According to the National Taxpayers Union, here is a checklist for homeowners planning to appeal a property tax bill:

- Take all the deductions to which you are entitled.
- Don't miss filing deadlines.
- Check the assessor's facts about your property.
- Consult experts for help.
- Find at least five comparable properties.
- Compare your assessment with those of the comparables.
- If your assessment looks unfair, lodge an informal appeal.
- If the assessor doesn't agree, file a formal appeal.

EXAMPLE6 CALCULATING PROPERTY TAX USING TAX PER $100 OF ASSESSED VALUE

Calculate the tax due on a house with an assessed value of $250,000. The tax rate is $7.88 per $100 of assessed value.

SOLUTIONSTRATEGY

Step 1. $\text{Number of } \$100 = \dfrac{\text{Assessed value}}{100} = \dfrac{250{,}000}{100} = 2{,}500$

Step 2. Property tax = Number of $100 × Tax per $100
Property tax = $2{,}500 \times 7.88 = \underline{\$19{,}700}$

TRYITEXERCISE 6

Calculate the tax due on a three-acre parcel of land with an assessed value of $50,800. The property tax rate is $3.60 per $100 of assessed value.

CHECK YOUR ANSWER WITH THE SOLUTION ON PAGE 643.

STEPS TO CALCULATE PROPERTY TAX WHEN THE TAX IS EXPRESSED PER $1,000 OF ASSESSED VALUE

STEP 1. Divide the assessed value by $1,000 to determine the number of $1,000 the assessed value contains.

$$\text{Number of } \$1{,}000 = \frac{\text{Assessed value}}{1{,}000}$$

STEP 2. Calculate the tax due by multiplying the number of $1,000 by the tax per $1,000.

$$\text{Property tax} = \text{Number of } \$1{,}000 \times \text{Tax per } \$1{,}000$$

EXAMPLE7 — CALCULATING PROPERTY TAX USING TAX PER $1,000 OF ASSESSED VALUE

Calculate the tax due on a house with an assessed value of $250,000. The tax rate is $78.80 per $1,000 of assessed value.

SOLUTIONSTRATEGY

Step 1.   Number of $1,000 = $\dfrac{\text{Assessed value}}{1,000} = \dfrac{250,000}{1,000} = 250$

Step 2.   Property tax = Number of $1,000 × Tax per $1,000
Property tax = 250 × 78.80 = $\underline{\$19,700}$

►TRYITEXERCISE 7

Calculate the tax due on a warehouse with an assessed value of $325,400. The property tax rate is $88.16 per $1,000 of assessed value.

CHECK YOUR ANSWER WITH THE SOLUTION ON PAGE 643.

STEPS — TO CALCULATE PROPERTY TAX WHEN THE TAX IS EXPRESSED IN MILLS

STEP 1.   Because mills means $\dfrac{1}{1,000}$ (.001) of a dollar, convert tax rate in mills to tax rate in decimal form by multiplying mills times .001.

Tax rate in decimal form = Tax rate in mills × .001

STEP 2.   Calculate the tax due by multiplying the assessed value by the tax rate in decimal form.

Property tax = Assessed value × Tax rate in decimal form

EXAMPLE8 — CALCULATING PROPERTY TAX USING MILLS

Calculate the tax due on a house with an assessed value of $250,000. The tax rate is 78.8 mills.

SOLUTIONSTRATEGY

Step 1.   Tax rate in decimal form = Tax rate in mills × .001
Tax rate in decimal form = 78.8 × .001 = .0788

Step 2.   Property tax = Assessed value × Tax rate in decimal form
Property tax = 250,000 × .0788 = $\underline{\$19,700}$

►TRYITEXERCISE 8

Calculate the tax due on a farm with an assessed value of $85,300. The property tax rate is 54.1 mills.

CHECK YOUR ANSWER WITH THE SOLUTION ON PAGE 643.

iStcck.com/Nikada

18-6 CALCULATING TAX RATE NECESSARY IN A COMMUNITY TO MEET BUDGETARY DEMANDS

Each year local taxing units such as counties and cities must estimate the amount of tax dollars required to pay for all government services provided. Typical examples include public schools, law enforcement, fire protection, hospitals, public parks and recreation, roads and highways, and sanitation services. The tax rate necessary to meet these budgetary demands is determined by two factors: (1) the total taxes required and (2) the total assessed value of the property in the taxing unit. The tax rate is computed by the following formula:

$$\text{Tax rate per dollar (decimal form)} = \frac{\text{Total taxes required}}{\text{Total assessed property value}}$$

As before, the tax rate may be expressed as a percent, per $100 of assessed value, per $1,000 of assessed value, or in mills.

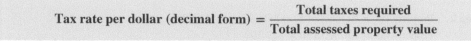

STEPS TO COMPUTE TAX RATE

STEP 1. Calculate tax rate per dollar of assessed property value by dividing the total taxes required by the total assessed property value.

$$\text{Tax rate per dollar (decimal form)} = \frac{\text{Total taxes required}}{\text{Total assessed property value}}$$

Round your answer to ten-thousandths (four decimal places). In most states, the rounding is always up, even if the next digit is less than 5.

STEP 2. *To convert tax rate per dollar to:*
- **percent**, move the decimal point two places to the right and add a percent sign.
- **tax rate per $100**, multiply by 100.
- **tax rate per $1,000**, multiply by 1,000.
- **mills**, divide by .001.

Learning Tip

When calculating tax rate per dollar, remember to round your answer to ten-thousandths (four decimal places) and always round up, even if the next digit is less than 5.

B-A-C-O/Shutterstock.com

iStock.com/Nikada

EXAMPLE9 COMPUTING TAX RATE

The budget planners for the town of Canmore have determined that $5,700,000 will be needed to provide all government services for next year. If the total assessed property value in Canmore is $68,000,000, what tax rate is required to meet the budgetary demands? Express your answer in each of the four ways.

►SOLUTIONSTRATEGY

Step 1. Tax rate per dollar $= \dfrac{\text{Total tax required}}{\text{Total assessed property value}}$

Tax rate per dollar $= \dfrac{5,700,000}{68,000,000} = .0838235 = \$0.0839$

Step 2. a. To express tax rate as a percent, move the decimal point two places to the right and add a percent sign. Tax rate = <u>8.39%</u>

b. Tax rate expressed per $100 = .0839 × 100 = <u>$8.39</u>

c. Tax rate expressed per $1,000 = .0839 × 1,000 = <u>$83.90</u>

d. Tax rate expressed in mills $= \dfrac{.0839}{.001} = $ <u>83.9 mills</u>

►TRYITEXERCISE 9

The budget planners for Mountain View have determined that $3,435,000 will be needed to provide government services for next year. The total assessed property value in Mountain View is $71,800,000. As the tax assessor, you have been asked by the city council to determine what tax rate will need to be imposed to meet these budgetary demands. Express your answer in each of the four ways.

CHECK YOUR ANSWERS WITH THE SOLUTIONS ON PAGE 643.

REVIEW EXERCISES

18 SECTION II

Calculate the assessed value and the property tax due on the following properties.

	Fair Market Value	Assessment Rate	Assessed Value	Property Tax Rate	Property Tax Due
1.	$240,000	90%	$216,000	4.1%	$8,856.00
2.	$95,500	75	$71,625	$1.80 per $100	$1,289.25
3.	$310,000	100	$310,000	$17.25 per $1,000	$5,347.50
4.	$194,460	80	$155,568	35.5 mills	$5,522.66
5.	$76,000	100	_____	3.44%	_____
6.	$125,000	100	_____	$1.30 per $100	_____
7.	$248,000	80	_____	$25.90 per $1,000	_____
8.	$54,600	30	_____	45.5 mills	_____
9.	$177,400	60	_____	$2.13 per $100	_____
10.	$2,330,000	100	_____	13.22 mills	_____
11.	$342,900	77	_____	5.3%	_____

12. You have some property which has an assessed value of $250,600. If the tax rate is 65.80 mills, calculate the tax due.

Calculate the property tax rate required to meet the budgetary demands of the following communities. *Note: When calculating budgetary demands, always round up.*

	Community	Total Assessed Property Valuation	Total Taxes Required	Property Tax Rate			
				Percent	Per $100	Per $1,000	Mills
13.	Bay Harbor	$850,000,000	$39,450,000	4.65%	$4.65	$46.50	46.5
14.	Morningside	$657,000,000	$32,300,000	____	____	____	____
15.	Bay Heights	$338,000,000	$19,900,000	____	____	____	____
16.	Ellingham	$57,000,000	$2,100,000	____	____	____	____
17.	North Shore	$880,000,000	$13,600,000	____	____	____	____

18. Chuck Wells purchased a condominium with a market value of $125,000 in The Villages. The assessment rate is 70%, and the tax rate is 19.44 mills.

   a. What is the assessed value of the condo?

   b. What is the amount of property tax?

19. Budget planners for a certain community have determined that $7,051,000 will be required to provide all government services next your. The total assessed property value in the community is $110,000,000.

   What tax rate is required to meet the budgetary demands? (Express your answer as a tax rate per $100 to two decimal places rounded up.)

20. As the tax assessor for Indian Creek County, you have been informed that due to budgetary demands, a tax increase will be necessary next year. The total market value of the property in the county is $600,000,000. Currently, the assessment rate is 45% and the tax rate is 30 mills. The county commission increases the assessment rate to 55% and the tax rate to 35 mills.

   a. How much property tax was collected under the old rates?

   b. How much more tax revenue will be collected under the new rates?

BUSINESS DECISION: EARLY PAYMENT, LATE PAYMENT

21. You own an a townhome with an assessed value of $185,400. The tax rate is $2.20 per $100 of assessed value.

   a. What is the amount of property tax?

   b. If the state offers a 4% discount for early payment, how much would the tax bill amount to if you paid early?

   c. If the state charges a mandatory $3\frac{1}{2}\%$ penalty for late payments, how much would the tax bill amount to if you paid late?

INCOME TAX

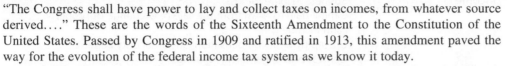

18 SECTION III

"The Congress shall have power to lay and collect taxes on incomes, from whatever source derived...." These are the words of the Sixteenth Amendment to the Constitution of the United States. Passed by Congress in 1909 and ratified in 1913, this amendment paved the way for the evolution of the federal income tax system as we know it today.

Income taxes, both personal and corporate, compose the largest source of receipts for our federal government. In a typical year, individuals pay over $1 trillion in federal income taxes and businesses pay more than $200 billion. In addition to the federal income tax, many state governments have also imposed income taxes on their citizens to finance government activities.

Income tax is a pay-as-you-go tax. The tax is paid as you earn or receive income throughout the year. As we learned in Chapter 9, payment is accomplished through income tax withholdings made by employers on wages and salaries paid to employees and through quarterly estimated tax payments made by people earning substantial income other than wages and salaries, such as interest income and business profits.

For those individuals subject to personal income tax, a **tax return** must be filed on the appropriate IRS form before midnight on April 15. The tax return pertains to income earned during the previous calendar year. As the income tax filing deadline approaches, taxpayers must begin the preparation of their tax returns. Although tax preparation services are available to help with this annual task, you still have to keep and organize the records necessary for the return. Keep in mind that even if someone else prepares your return, you are ultimately responsible for its accuracy!

Although the tax rules and forms change almost every year, the method for calculating the amount of income tax due remains generally the same. For the purpose of this chapter, we will divide the task into two components: (1) calculating the taxable income and (2) determining the amount of income tax due. The figures and tables used in this section reflect IRS requirements as this is written. For the most recent tax information and tables, consult the instruction booklet that accompanies this year's income tax forms.

income tax A pay-as-you-go tax based on the amount of income of an individual or a corporation.

tax return The official Internal Revenue Service forms used to report and pay income tax for income earned during the previous calendar year.

Federal income tax forms must be filed before midnight on April 15. In the event that the 15th falls on a Saturday, Sunday, or holiday, the forms are due on the first succeeding day that is not a Saturday, Sunday, or holiday.

CALCULATING TAXABLE INCOME FOR INDIVIDUALS

18-7

Taxable income is the amount of income to which tax rates are applied in order to calculate the amount of tax owed for the year. Exhibit 18-2 is a schematic diagram of the procedure used to calculate taxable income. Look it over carefully and then use the following steps to calculate taxable income. The standard deductions reflect IRS amounts as this is written.

taxable income The amount of income to which tax rates are applied in order to calculate the amount of tax owed for the year.

Dollars AND Sense

2018 brought significant changes to income tax laws. Exemptions for taxpayers and their dependents were eliminated but standard deductions were nearly doubled. Other changes included revisions to tax rates and tax brackets.

The current standard deductions, tax tables, and forms can be found in the IRS publication *1040 Forms and Instructions*. This and other tax forms and publications can be obtained by calling the IRS at 1-800-TAX-FORM (open 24 hours a day, 7 days a week) or by downloading the form from the website www.irs.gov/formspubs.

STEPS TO CALCULATE TAXABLE INCOME FOR INDIVIDUALS

STEP 1. Determine **total income** by adding all sources of taxable income.

STEP 2. Calculate **adjusted gross income** by subtracting the sum of all adjustments to income from total income.

STEP 3. To find taxable income, subtract the sum of the **itemized deductions** or the **standard deduction** (whichever is larger) from the adjusted gross income. The amounts below are the standard deductions in effect as this is written.

Standard Deductions

Single or married filing separately	$12,000
Married filing jointly or surviving spouse	$24,000
Head of household	$18,000

65 or older and/or blind and/or someone else can claim you (or your spouse if filing jointly) as a dependent: Varies (See www.irs.gov for information.)

EXHIBIT 18-2 Procedure to Calculate Taxable Income

Income	Wages, salaries, bonuses, commissions, tips, gratuities Interest and dividend income Rents, royalties, partnerships, S corporations, trusts Pensions and annuities Business income (or loss) Capital gain (or loss) from the sale or exchange of property Farm income Unemployment compensation, social security benefits Contest prizes, gambling winnings
	Less
Adjustments to Income such as:	Qualified alimony payments Retirement fund payments—IRA, Keogh, 401(k) One-half of self-employment tax Penalty on early withdrawal of savings
	Equals
Adjusted Gross Income	Used in determining limits on certain itemized deductions such as medical, dental, and employee expenses
	Less

Deductions: Standard or Itemized	Standard deduction
	or
	Itemized deductions as shown below.
	  Medical and dental expenses*
	  Taxes paid: state and local income taxes; real estate taxes (up to $10,000 or $5,000 for married filing separately)
	  Home mortgage interest and points*
	  Charitable contributions*
	  Casualty and theft losses*
	  Moving expenses*
	  Unreimbursed employee expenses—union dues, job travel, education*
	
	*Limitations apply. Please visit www.irs.gov for more information.

	Equals
Taxable Income	Income on which the amount of income tax is due.

EXAMPLE 10 CALCULATING TAXABLE INCOME

Doug and Beth Nelson are married and file a joint tax return. Doug is a manager and earned $43,500 last year. Beth worked as a secretary and earned $24,660. In addition, they earned $540 interest on their savings account. They each contributed $2,500 to a retirement account, and Doug paid qualified aliminony of $4,700 to his first wife. Itemized deductions were as follows: $2,340 in real estate taxes, $4,590 in mortgage interest, and $445 in charitable contributions. From this information, calculate the Nelsons' taxable income.

►SOLUTIONSTRATEGY

Step 1. Total Income:

$43,500 Doug's income
+ 24,660 Beth's income
+   540 Interest from savings account
$68,700 Total income

Step 2. Adjusted Gross Income:

$68,700 Total income
− 9,700 Deductions from total income
$59,000 Adjusted gross income

$2,500 Doug's retirement payments
+2,500 Beth's retirement payments
+4,700 Alimony payments
$9,700 Deductions from total income

Step 3. Deductions:

$2,340 Real estate taxes
+ 4,590 Mortgage interest
+   445 Charitable contributions
         (above 2% of adjusted gross income)
$7,375 Total itemized deductions

Because the total itemized deductions, $7,375, is less than the standard deduction for married filing jointly ($24,000), we will use the standard deduction amount for Doug and Beth's tax return.

$59,000 Adjusted gross income
− 24,000 Standard deduction
$35,000 Taxable income

▶ TRYITEXERCISE 10

Nick Bontempo is a single iron worker who earns $35,000 in wages per year. Last year he also earned $1,200 in cash dividends from his investments portfolio. Nick contributed $1,500 to his individual retirement account and gained $5,000 from the sale of 100 shares of Consolidated Widget stock. The stock sale was classified as a short-term sale, so it counts as ordinary income. His itemized deductions amounted to $2,945 in real estate taxes, $2,500 in mortgage interest, and $300 in charitable contributions. From this information, calculate Nick's taxable income.

CHECK YOUR ANSWER WITH THE SOLUTION ON PAGE 643.

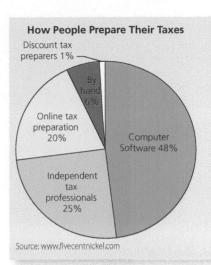

How People Prepare Their Taxes

Discount tax preparers 1%
By hand 6%
Online tax preparation 20%
Computer Software 48%
Independent tax professionals 25%

Source: www.fivecentnickel.com

IN THE Business World

According to the Tax Policy Center, in a recent year:

- 46.4% of filers paid no federal income tax

- 10% of the population paid 71% of all federal taxes

Using the Tax Rate Tables to Calculate Tax Liability

18-8

Exhibit 18-3 gives the tax rates in effect as this is written. We will use these rates for all problems in this chapter.

STEPS TO CALCULATE TAX LIABILITY USING THE TAX RATE TABLES

STEP 1. Locate the table corresponding to the appropriate filing status.

STEP 2. Read down the first column to find the range containing the taxable income.

STEP 3. Find the amount of tax by using the procedure given in the second column.

IN THE Business World

The federal individual income tax began relatively modestly in 1913 with 400 pages of rules and a basic rate of 1%. From the beginning, CCH Incorporated has published an annual collection of federal tax rules containing the tax code, tax regulations, and summaries of federal tax pronouncements. The number of pages in this publication grew from 400 in 1913 to 73,608 one hundred years later.

iStock.com/Nikada

rtguest/Shutterstock.com

rtguest/Shutterstock.com

Exhibit 18-3   Income Tax Rate Tables

Filing status: Single

Taxable income	Tax
At least $0 but not over $9,525	10% of the amount over $0
Over $9,525 but not over $38,700	$952.50 + 12% of the amount over $9,525
Over $38,700 but not over $82,500	$4,453.50 + 22% of the amount over $38,700
Over $82,500 but not over $157,500	$14,089.50 + 24% of the amount over $82,500
Over $157,500 but not over $200,000	$32,089.50 + 32% of the amount over $157,500
Over $200,000 but not over $500,000	$45,689.50 + 35% of the amount over $200,000
Over $500,000	$150,689.50 + 37% of the amount over $500,000

Filing status: Married filing jointly or Qualifying widow(er)

Taxable income	Tax
At least $0 but not over $19,050	10% of the amount over $0
Over $19,050 but not over $77,400	$1,905 + 12% of the amount over $19,050
Over $77,400 but not over $165,000	$8,907 + 22% of the amount over $77,400
Over $165,000 but not over $315,000	$28,179 + 24% of the amount over $165,000
Over $315,000 but not over $400,000	$64,179 + 32% of the amount over $315,000
Over $400,00 but not over $600,000	$91,379 + 35% of the amount over $400,000
Over $600,000	$161,379 + 37% of the amount over $600,000

Filing status: Married filing separately

Taxable income	Tax
At least $0 but not over $9,525	10% of the amount over $0
Over $9,525 but not over $38,700	$952.50 + 12% of the amount over $9,525
Over $38,700 but not over $82,500	$4,453.50 + 22% of the amount over $38,700
Over $82,500 but not over $157,500	$14,089.50 + 24% of the amount over $82,500
Over $157,500 but not over $200,000	$32,089.50 + 32% of the amount over $157,500
Over $200,000 but not over $300,000	$45,689.50 + 35% of the amount over $200,000
Over $300,000	$80,689.50 + 37% of the amount over $300,000

Filing status: Head of household

Taxable income	Tax
At least $0 but not over $13,600	10% of the amount over $0
Over $13,600 but not over $51,800	$1,360 + 12% of the amount over $13,600
Over $51,800 but not over $82,500	$5,944 + 22% of the amount over $51,800
Over $82,500 but not over $157,500	$12,698 + 24% of the amount over $82,500
Over $157,500 but not over $200,000	$30,698 + 32% of the amount over $157,500
Over $200,000 but not over $500,000	$44,298 + 35% of the amount over $200,000
Over $500,000	$149,298 + 37% of the amount over $500,000

EXAMPLE11 USING THE TAX RATE TABLES

Elizabeth Ashcroft had taxable income last year of $121,334. For income tax purposes, she files as married filing separately. Use the appropriate table to calculate her tax liability.

SOLUTIONSTRATEGY

Step 1. We'll use the table for those with filing status "Married filing Separately."

Step 2. Reading down the first column, we find Elizabeth's taxable income in the range "Over $82,500 but not over $157,500."

Step 3. Tax $= 14,089.50 + .24(121,334 - 82,500)$
$= 14,089.50 + .24(38,834)$
$= 14,089.50 + 9,320.16$
$= \$23,409.66$

▶TRYITEXERCISE 11

Mike Straus had taxable income of $56,500 last year. If he files as single, what is his tax liability?

CHECK YOUR ANSWER WITH THE SOLUTION ON PAGE 644.

CALCULATING AN INDIVIDUAL'S TAX REFUND OR AMOUNT OF TAX OWED

18-9

Once the tax liability has been determined, we must consider the final three items in income tax preparation: tax credits, other taxes, and payments. The following formula is used to complete the tax preparation process. *Note:* When the result is a positive number, it is the amount of tax owed. When the result is a negative number, it indicates a tax overpayment by that amount. When an overpayment occurs, the taxpayer has the option of receiving a refund or applying the amount of the overpayment to next year's estimated tax.

> **Refund (−) or amount owed (+) = Tax liability − Credits + Other taxes − Payments**

Tax Credits. Tax credits are a dollar-for-dollar subtraction from the tax liability. A **tax credit** of one dollar saves a full dollar in taxes, whereas a tax deduction of one dollar results in less than a dollar in tax savings (the amount depends on the tax rate). Some examples are credit for child and dependent care expenses, credit for the elderly or disabled, and the foreign tax credit.

Other Taxes. In addition to the tax liability from the Tax Table or Tax Computation Worksheet, other taxes may also be due. These taxes are added to the tax liability. Some examples would be self-employment taxes and Social Security and Medicare taxes on tip income.

Payments. This calculation involves subtracting payments such as employees' federal income tax withheld by employers, estimated tax payments made quarterly, excess Social Security and Medicare paid, and the Earned Income Credit (considered a payment and available to some taxpayers. See www.irs.gov for more information.)

tax credit Dollar-for-dollar subtraction from an individual's or corporation's tax liability. Some examples for individuals would be the credit for child and dependent care expenses, the credit for the elderly or disabled, and the foreign tax credit.

Internal Revenue Service Taxes are one of the certainties of life! As long as governments collect taxes, there will be a need for someone to review tax returns, conduct examinations, identify taxes payable, and collect overdue tax dollars.

As this is written, IRS tax examiners, collectors, and revenue agents held about 74,500 jobs at all levels of government. Half of all such workers earned $49,360 or more. The lowest 10% earned less than $29,540 and the top 10% earned more than $92,250.

Approximately 49% were employed by the federal government, 32% by state governments, and 19% by local governments.

Source: www.bls.gov

STEPS TO CALCULATE AN INDIVIDUAL'S TAX REFUND OR AMOUNT OF TAX OWED

STEP 1. Subtract total credits from the tax liability.

STEP 2. Add total of other taxes to the tax liability to get total tax.

STEP 3. If total payments are greater than total tax, a refund of the difference is due. If total payments are less than total tax, the difference is the tax owed.

EXAMPLE 12 CALCULATING TAX REFUND OR AMOUNT OWED

After preparing her taxes for last year, Emily James determined that she had a tax liability of $5,326. In addition, she owed other taxes of $575. Because of her mother, Emily was entitled to a credit for the elderly of $1,412. If her employer withheld $510 from her paycheck each month, is Emily entitled to a refund or does she owe additional taxes? How much?

▶SOLUTIONSTRATEGY

Steps 1 & 2.

	$5,326	Tax liability
	− 1,412	Tax credits
	+ 575	Other taxes
	$4,489	Total tax owed

Step 3. Payments: Federal income tax withheld was $510 × 12 months = $6,120.

	$6,120	Payments
	− 4,489	Total tax
	$1,631	Overpayment

Because Emily's payments are greater than her total tax owed, she has made an overpayment by the amount of the difference and is therefore entitled to a tax refund of $1,631.

▶TRYITEXERCISE 12

Kenya Dawson had a tax liability of $14,600 last year. In addition, she owed other taxes of $2,336. She was entitled to a credit for child care of $668 and a foreign tax credit of $1,719. If her employer withheld $270 per week for 52 weeks, does Kenya qualify for a refund or owe more taxes? How much?

CHECK YOUR ANSWERS WITH THE SOLUTIONS ON PAGE 644.

18-10 CALCULATING CORPORATE INCOME TAX AND NET INCOME AFTER TAXES

Just as with individuals, corporations are also taxable entities that must file tax returns and are taxed directly on their earnings. In Chapter 15, we learned to prepare a balance sheet and an income statement based on the operating figures of a company over a period of time. At the bottom of the income statement, the net income before taxes was determined. At the time this is written, the corporate tax rate is set at 21%.

EXAMPLE 13   CALCULATING CORPORATE INCOME TAX AND AFTER-TAX NET INCOME

Landmark Industries had net income before taxes of $7,550,000. Calculate the amount of income tax due and calculate the company's net income after taxes.

▶ SOLUTIONSTRATEGY

The corporate tax rate is 21%.

Tax liability = .21 × income before taxes

Tax liability = .21 × 7,550,000 = $1,585,500

Net income after taxes = Income before taxes − tax liability

Net income after taxes = $7,550,000 − 1,585,500 = $5,964,500

▶ TRYITEXERCISE 13

The Trough Restaurant had taxable income of $311,200 last year. Calculate the amount of income tax due and calculate the company's net income after taxes.

CHECK YOUR ANSWERS WITH THE SOLUTIONS ON PAGE 644.

rtguest/Shutterstock.com

IN THE Business World

A qualifying domestic corporation with 35 or fewer shareholders may elect to be treated as an **S-corporation**, thus eliminating all corporate liability for federal income taxes.

Instead, any taxable income or loss will be allocated proportionately among the shareholders, who will be responsible for reporting the amounts on their personal income tax returns.

REVIEW EXERCISES   18 SECTION III

As a tax return preparer for The Fernando Rodriguez Tax & Accounting Service, you have been asked to calculate the missing information for eight of the firm's tax clients. Use the standard deductions listed on page 631.

	Name	Filing Status	Income	Adjustments to Income	Adjusted Gross Income	(circle your choice) Standard Deduction	Itemized Deductions	Taxable Income
1.	O'Connell	Single	$34,300	$2,120	$32,180	($12,000)	$4,870	$20,180
2.	Lerner	Married filing jointly	____	$1,244	$47,228	____	$5,329	____
3.	Harmon	Surviving spouse	$45,670	$1,760	____	____	$3,870	____
4.	Warfield	Single	____	$3,410	$51,290	____	$13,120	____
5.	Cruz	Married filing separately	$66,210	____	$59,430	____	$2,245	____
6.	Campbell	Married filing jointly	$52,130	$1,450	____	____	$5,610	____
7.	Lee	Head of household	$88,600	____	$84,520	____	$21,230	____

8. Adela and James are married and file tax returns jointly. Last year Adela earned $48,500 and James earned $46,800 in wages.

   Additional tax information for the year is as follows: Interest earned: $1,200, State and local income taxes paid: $4,240, mortgage interest: $6,200, contributions to charity: $1,400, contributions to retirement plans: $3,350.

   From this information, calculate their taxable income.

9. Nancy Sullivan sells wholesale school supplies for Sharpie Corporation. She is single. For income tax purposes, she qualifies as a head of household. Last year she earned a total of $53,100 in salary and commission. She earned $1,200 in interest. She contributed $2,500 to her retirement plan and had the following itemized deductions: $1,231 in real estate taxes, $5,450 in mortgage interest, and $420 in charitable contributions.

   From this information, calculate Nancy's taxable income.

Use the Tax Rate Tables, Exhibit 18-3, to calculate the tax liability for the following taxpayers.

Name	Filing Status	Taxable Income	Tax Liability
10. Rua	Head of Household	$175,800	$36,554
11. Dylewski	Married, Jointly	$52,500	
12. Williams	Single	$61,300	
13. Cabral	Married, Separately	$185,188	

14. Ross is single with an adjusted gross income of $62,100, and he uses the standard deduction for single filers. After first finding his taxable income, calculate his tax liability.

As a newly hired IRS trainee, you have been asked to calculate the amount of tax refund or tax owed for the following taxpayers.

Name	Tax Liability	Tax Credits	Other Taxes	Payments	Refund/Owe (circle one)	Amount
15. Jackson	$7,525	$1,670	$840	$5,300	Refund/Owe	$1,395
16. Hayward	$3,229	$750	0	$3,130	Refund/Owe	
17. Lane	$12,280	$2,453	$1,232	$9,540	Refund/Owe	
18. Trent	$6,498	$1,221	$885	$7,600	Refund/Owe	

19. Victor and Roberta Sanchez file jointly and had a combined income of $88,700 last year. They contributed $4,200 to their retirement plan and had itemized deductions of $19,420. Their combined income tax withheld last year amounted to $9,888.

    Are they entitled to a refund or do the owe additional taxes? How much?

Calculate the amount of corporate income tax due and the net income after taxes for the following corporations.

Name	Taxable Income	Tax Liability	Net Income after Taxes
20. All City Plumbing, Inc.	$352,100	$73,941	$278,159
21. Universal Holdings, Inc.	$88,955		
22. Evergreen Corp.	$14,550,000		
23. Bioscience Labs, Inc.	$955,000,000		

24. Green Grow Energies, Inc. reported a taxable income of $87,544,200 last year. What was their net income after paying corporate income taxes?

BUSINESS DECISION: INVESTING YOUR TAX SAVINGS

25. You are a manager for Vector International. You earn $50,000 per year and are in the 28% federal income tax bracket. Each year you contribute $2,500 tax free to your individual retirement account, IRA. The account earns 8% annual interest. In addition, the amount of tax that you save each year by making these "pre-tax" contributions is invested in a taxable aggressive growth mutual fund averaging 15%.

    a. How much tax do you save each year by making the retirement fund contributions?

    b. How much will the retirement fund be worth in 30 years?

    c. Although the income from this investment is taxable each year, how much will the "tax savings" fund be worth in 30 years?

CHAPTER FORMULAS

Sales and Excise Taxes

Sales tax = Selling price × Sales tax rate

Total purchase price = Selling price + Sales tax + Other charges

$$\text{Sales price} = \frac{\text{Total purchase price}}{100\% + \text{Sales tax rate}}$$

Sales tax = Total purchase price − Selling price

Excise tax = Selling price × Excise tax rate

Excise tax = Number of units × Excise tax per unit

Total purchase price = Selling price + Sales tax + Exercise tax

Property Tax

Expressed as a Percent

Property tax = Assessed value of property × Tax rate

Expressed per $100 of Assessed Value

Property tax = Number of $100 of assessed value × Tax per $100

Expressed per $1,000 of Assessed Value

Property tax = Number of $1,000 of assessed value × Tax per $1,000

Expressed in Mills

Tax rate in decimal form = Tax rate in mills × .001

Property tax = Assessed value × Tax rate in decimal form

Community Tax Rate

$$\text{Tax rate per dollar (decimal form)} = \frac{\text{Total taxes required}}{\text{Total assessed property value}}$$

Income Tax

Refund (−) or Amount owed (+) = Tax liability − Credits + Other taxes − Payments

CHAPTER SUMMARY

Section I: Sales and Excise Taxes

Topic	Important Concepts	Illustrative Examples

Determining Sales Tax by Using Sales Tax Tables
 	
Performance Objective 18-1, Page 618
	Sales tax is a tax based on the total retail price of tangible personal property and certain services and admissions.
	    Exhibit 18-1 is an example of a $6\frac{1}{2}\%$ sales tax table.
	    Sales tax tables
	1. Locate the taxable retail price in the Amount of Sale column.
	2. Scan to the right to locate the amount of tax due in the Tax column.
		Steve Adams purchased food at Chicken Delight for a total of $16.23. The sales tax in that state is $6\frac{1}{2}\%$. Use Exhibit 18-1 to determine the amount of sales tax due on this sale.
		    From Exhibit 18-1, we find that the retail price of the food, $16.23, falls in the range of $16.16 to $16.30. Scanning to the right, we find the tax due on this sale is $\underline{\$1.06}$.

Calculating Sales Tax by Using the Percent Method
 	
Performance Objective 18-2, Page 620
	Sales tax is expressed as a percentage of the retail selling price.
	    Percent Method
	1. Calculate the sales tax by multiplying the retail selling price by the sales tax rate:
	
	2. Compute total purchase price by adding the selling price, the sales tax, and any other additional charges:
		Carl Boyd purchased a barbecue grill for $179.95 at Target. The store charged $12 for assembly. If the state sales tax is 4% and the city adds an additional $3\frac{1}{2}\%$, what is the amount of sales tax on the grill and what is Carl's total purchase price?
		
		Sales tax rate = $4 + 3\frac{1}{2} = 7\frac{1}{2}\%$
		Sales tax = $179.95 \times .075 = \underline{\$13.50}$
		Total purchase price =
		    $179.95 + 13.50 + 12.00 = \underline{\underline{\$205.45}}$

Section I (continued)

Topic	Important Concepts	Illustrative Examples
Calculating Selling Price and Amount of Sales Tax When Total Purchase Price Is Known **Performance Objective 18-3, Page 621**	When the total purchase price of an item or items, including sales tax, is known, actual selling price and amount of sales tax is calculated as follows: 1. Calculate the selling price of an item by dividing the total purchase price by 100% plus the sales tax rate: 2. Determine the amount of sales tax by subtracting the selling price from the total purchase price:	At the end of the day, the cash register at an Ace Hardware store showed total purchases, including sales tax, of \$2,251.83. If the sales tax rate in that state is 5%, calculate Ace's actual sales revenue and sales tax collected. Sales revenue $= \dfrac{2,251.83}{1.05} = \$2,144.60$ Sales tax $= 2,251.83 - 2,144.60 = \underline{\$107.23}$
Calculating Excise Tax **Performance Objective 18-4, Page 621**	An excise tax is a tax levied by federal, state, and local governments on certain products and services deemed to be luxury or nonessential items. Excise tax is paid in addition to sales tax and is expressed as a percentage of the purchase price or as a fixed amount per unit purchased. *Percentage:* *Per Unit:*	Harris Mones purchased fishing equipment for \$244. The sales tax in his state is 4%, and the federal excise tax on fishing equipment is 11%. What is the amount of each tax and the total purchase price of the equipment? Sales tax $= 244 \times .04 = \underline{\$9.76}$ Excise tax $= 244 \times .11 = \underline{\$26.84}$ Total purchase price $=$ $244.00 + 9.76 + 26.84 = \underline{\$280.60}$

Section II: Property Tax

Topic	Important Concepts	Illustrative Examples
Calculating Property Tax Due with Tax Rate Expressed: **As a Percent** **Performance Objective 18-5, Page 625**	A tax levied on the assessed value of real and certain personal property is known as property tax. *Expressed as a percent:* 1. Convert the tax rate to a decimal. 2. Calculate property tax:	The following examples illustrate how to calculate the property tax due when the same tax is expressed in each of the four different ways. A house with an assessed value of \$120,000 is subject to a property tax of 2.31%. What is the amount of property tax due? Property tax $= 120,000 \times .0231 = \underline{\$2,772}$
Per \$100 of Assessed Value **Performance Objective 18-5, Page 626**	*Per \$100 of assessed value:* 1. Calculate number of \$100: 2. Calculate property tax:	A house with an assessed value of \$120,000 is subject to a property tax of \$2.31 per \$100 of assessed value. What is the amount of property tax due? Number of \$100 $= \dfrac{120,000}{100} = 1,200$ Property tax $= 1,200 \times 2.31 = \underline{\$2,772}$
Per \$1,000 of Assessed Value **Performance Objective 18-5, Page 626**	*Per \$1,000 of assessed value:* 1. Calculate number of \$1,000: 2. Calculate property tax:	A house with an assessed value of \$120,000 is subject to a property tax of \$23.10 per \$1,000 of assessed value. What is the amount of property tax due? Number of \$100 $= \dfrac{120,000}{1,000} = 120$ Property tax $= 120 \times 23.10 = \underline{\$2,772}$
In Mills **Performance Objective 18-5, Page 627**	*Expressed in mills:* 1. Multiply tax rate in mills by .001 to get tax rate as a decimal: 2. Calculate property tax:	A house with an assessed value of \$120,000 is subject to a property tax of 23.1 mills. What is the amount of property tax due? Tax rate (decimal) $= 23.1 \times .001 = .0231$ Property tax $= 120,000 \times .0231 = \underline{\$2,772}$

Section II (continued)

Topic	Important Concepts	Illustrative Examples
Calculating Tax Rate Necessary in a Community to Meet Budgetary Demands **Performance Objective 18-6, Page 628**	1. 2. To convert tax rate per dollar to: • *Percent*—move the decimal point two places to the right and add a percent sign. • *Tax rate per $100*—multiply by 100. • *Tax rate per $1,000*—multiply by 1,000. • *Mills*—divide by .001.	Spring Valley requires $5,000,000 for its annual budget. If the total assessed property value of the town is $80,000,000, what property tax rate is needed to meet those demands? Express your answer in each of the four ways. $$\text{Tax rate} = \frac{5,000,000}{80,000,000} = .0625$$ Percent = <u>6.25%</u> Per $100 = .0625 × 100 = <u>$6.25 per $100</u> Per $1,000 = .0625 × 1,000 = <u>$62.50 per $1,000</u> $$\text{Mills} = \frac{.0625}{.001} = \underline{\underline{62.5 \text{ mills}}}$$

Section III: Income Tax

Topic	Important Concepts	Illustrative Examples
Calculating Taxable Income for Individuals **Performance Objective 18-7, Page 631**	Taxable income is the amount of income to which tax rates are applied in order to calculate the amount of tax owed for the year. Use Exhibit 18-2 and the following steps to compute taxable income. 1. Determine *gross income* by adding all sources of taxable income. 2. Calculate *adjusted gross income* by subtracting the sum of all adjustments to income from the gross income. 3. Subtract the sum of the *itemized deductions* or the *standard deduction* (whichever is larger) from the adjusted gross income. The result is *taxable income*. See www.irs.gov for additional information pertaining to certain special conditions.	Joe and Sylvia Ortiz are married. For income tax purposes, they file jointly and claim four exemptions. Last year they earned a total of $45,460. They had adjustments to income of $3,241 and itemized deductions of $12,676. What is the amount of their taxable income? $45,460 Total income <u>− 3,241</u> Adjustments to income $42,219 Adjusted gross income The standard deduction for married filers is larger than their itemized deductions, so use that value. $42,219 Adjusted gross income <u>− 24,000</u> Standard deduction <u>$18,219</u> Taxable income
Using the Tax Rate Tables to Calculate Tax Liability **Performance Objective 18-8, Page 633**	Exhibit 18-3 contains the Tax Rate Tables in use as this is written. Use the appropriate table based on filing status, find the appropriate taxable income range, then use the corresponding tax calculation information to find the tax.	Pearl Jackson had taxable income last year of $67,000. For income tax purposes, she files as married filing separately. Calculater Pearl's tax liability. Tax = 4,453.50 + .22(67,000 − 38,700) = <u>$10,679.50</u>

Calculating an Individual's Tax Refund or Amount of Tax Owed
 	
Performance Objective 18-9, Page 635
	To calculate the refund or tax owed, we must finally consider tax credits, other taxes, and payments.
	
	1. Subtract total credits from the tax liability.
	2. Add total of other taxes to the tax liability to get total tax.
	3. If total payments are greater than total tax, a refund of the difference is due. If total payments are less than total tax, the difference is the tax owed.
		After preparing his taxes, Tyson Reese determined that he had a tax liability of $7,370. In addition, he owed other taxes of $1,225 and was entitled to a tax credit of $3,420. If Tyson's employer withheld $445 each month for income tax, is he entitled to a refund or does he owe additional taxes? How much?
		
		  $7,370 Tax liability
		 <u>− 3,420</u> Tax credits
		 <u>+ 1,225</u> Other taxes
		  $5,175 Total tax

Topic	Important Concepts	Illustrative Examples
		Payments = 445 × 12 = $5,340 $$\begin{array}{rl} \$5,340 & \text{Payments} \\ -\ 5,175 & \text{Total tax} \\ \hline \$165 & \text{Tax refund due} \end{array}$$ (may be applied to next year's taxes)

Calculating Corporate Income Tax and Net Income after Taxes
 	
 Performance Objective 18-10, Page 636
	The corporate tax rate in effect as this is written is 21%.	Starpointe Enterprises, Inc., had net income before taxes of $162,000. What is the amount of income tax due and the net income after taxes?
		
		 Tax = .21 × 162,000
		    = $34,020
		
		 Net income after taxes = 162,000 − 34,020
		                      = $127,980

TRY IT: EXERCISE SOLUTIONS FOR CHAPTER 18

1. From Exhibit 18-1, sales tax on $12.49 = $.82

2. Sales tax = Selling price × Sales tax rate
   Sales tax = 38,600 × .05 = $1,930
   Total purchase price = Selling price + Sales tax + Other charges
   Total purchase price = 38,600 + 1,930 + 240 = $40,770

3. Selling price = $\dfrac{\text{Total purchase price}}{100\% + \text{Sales tax rate}}$

   Selling price = $\dfrac{3,520}{100\% + 8\frac{1}{2}\%} = \dfrac{3,520}{1.085} = \$3,244.24$

   Sales tax = Total purchase price − Selling price
   Sales tax = 3,520.00 − 3,244.24 = $275.76

4. Sales tax = Selling price × Sales tax rate
   Sales tax = 129.95 × .05 = $6.50
   Excise tax = Selling price × Excise tax rate
   Excise tax = 129.95 × .11 = $14.29
   Total purchase price = Selling price + Sales tax + Excise tax
   Total purchase price = 129.95 + 6.50 + 14.29 = $150.74

5. Tax rate = 6.3% = .063
   Property tax = Assessed value × Tax rate
   Property tax = 160,000 × .063 = $10,080

6. Number of $100 = $\dfrac{\text{Assessed value}}{100} = \dfrac{50,800}{100} = 508$
   Property tax = Number of $100 × Tax per $100
   Property tax = 508 × 3.60 = $1,828.80

7. Number of $100 = $\dfrac{\text{Assessed value}}{1,000} = \dfrac{325,400}{1,000} = 325.4$
   Property tax = Number of $1,000 × Tax per $1,000
   Property tax = 325.4 × 88.16 = $28,687.26

8. Tax rate in decimal form = Tax rate in mills × .001
   Tax rate in decimal form = 54.1 × .001 = .0541
   Property tax = Assessed value × Tax rate in decimal form
   Property tax = 85,300 × .0541 = $4,614.73

9. Tax rate per dollar = $\dfrac{\text{Total tax required}}{\text{Total assessed property value}}$

   Tax rate per dollar = $\dfrac{3,435,000}{71,800,000} = .0478412 = \$.0479$

   a. *Percent*   .0479 = 4.79%

   b. *Per $100*   .0479 × 100 = $4.79

   c. *Per $1,000*   .0479 × 1,000 = $47.90

   d. *Mills* $\dfrac{.0479}{.001} = 47.9$ mills

10. $$\begin{array}{rl} \$35,000 & \text{Wages} \\ +\ 1,200 & \text{Cash dividends} \\ +\ 5,000 & \text{Sales of stock (gain)} \\ \hline \$41,200 & \text{Total income} \end{array}$$

   $$\begin{array}{rl} \$41,200 & \text{Total income} \\ -\ 1,500 & \text{Retirement contributions} \\ \hline \$39,700 & \text{Adjusted gross income} \end{array}$$

   $$\begin{array}{rl} 2,945 & \text{Real estate taxes} \\ 2,500 & \text{Mortgage interest} \\ +\ 300 & \text{Charitable contributions} \\ \hline \$5,745 & \text{Itemized deduction} \end{array}$$

   $$\begin{array}{rl} \$39,700 & \text{Adjusted gross income} \\ -12,000 & \text{Standard deduction} \\ \hline \$27,700 & \text{Taxable income} \end{array}$$

11. From the table for single filers:

$$\text{Tax} = 4{,}453.50 + .22(56{,}500 - 38{,}700)$$

$$= 4{,}453.50 + .22(17{,}800)$$

$$= 4{,}453.50 + 3{,}916$$

$$= \$8{,}369.50$$

12.

$14,600	Tax liability
+ 2,336	Other taxes
− 668	Child care credit
− 1,719	Foreign tax credit
$14,549	Total tax

Employer withheld $270 \times 52 = \$14{,}040$

Tax owed = Total tax − Payments

Tax owed = $14{,}549 - 14{,}040 = \underline{\$509}$

13. Tax liability = .21 × income before taxes

Tax liability = .21 × 311,200 = $65,352

Net income after taxes = Income before taxes − tax liability

Net income after taxes = 311,200 − 65,352 = $245,848

Concept Review

1. A tax based on the retail selling or rental price of tangible personal property is known as _____ tax. (18-1)

2. Sales tax expressed in its most common form, as a percent of the retail price of an item, is known as the sales tax _____. (18-2)

3. Write the formula for calculating the selling price of an item when the total purchase price, including sales tax, is known. (18-3)

4. A tax levied on certain luxury or nonessential products and services such as alcoholic beverages, furs, tobacco products, and airline tickets is known as a(n) _____ tax. (18-4)

5. Another name for property tax is _____ _____ tax. (18-5)

6. The value of property for tax purposes is known as the _____ value. The value of property based on location, size, cost, and other such factors is known as the fair _____ value. (18-5)

7. What are the four methods of expressing property tax rates? (18-5)

8. As the tax assessor for your city, what formula would you use to calculate the tax rate per dollar of assessed property value necessary to provide the budgeted government services for next year? (18-6)

9. A pay-as-you-go tax based on the amount of income of an individual or a corporation is known as _____ tax. The amount of income to which tax rates are applied in order to calculate the amount of tax owed is known as _____ income. (18-7)

10. When calculating an individual's taxable income, we subtract the sum of the _____ deductions or the _____ deduction, whichever is larger, from adjusted gross income. (18-7)

11. A tax _____ is a dollar-for-dollar subtraction from an individual's or a corporation's tax liability. (18-9)

ASSESSMENT TEST

Use Exhibit 18-1 to determine the sales tax and calculate the total purchase price for the following items.

Item	Selling Price	Sales Tax	Total Purchase Price
1. Blue-ray disk	$17.88	_____	_____
2. Shampoo	$2.90	_____	_____

Calculate the missing information for the following purchases.

Item	Selling Price	Sales Tax Rate	Sales Tax	Excise Tax Rate	Excise Tax	Total Purchase Price
3. Video camera	$135.00	4.9%	_____	0	0	_____
4. Cable TV bill	$24.40	5	_____	4.2%	_____	_____
5. Fur coat	$17,550	$6\frac{3}{4}$	_____	10% (over $10,000)	_____	_____
6. Computer	_____	$7\frac{1}{2}$	_____	0	0	$1,277.10

7. Tim Meekma purchased a microwave oven for $345.88. The delivery charge was $25, and the installation amounted to $75. The state sales tax is $6\frac{1}{4}$%, and the county tax is 1.1%.

   a. What is the total amount of sales tax on the microwave oven?

   b. What is the total purchase price?

8. Yesterday Estate Jewelers had total sales, including sales tax, of $16,502.50. The store is located in a state that has a sales tax of $6\frac{3}{4}$%. As the accountant for the store, calculate:

   a. The amount of sales revenue.

   b. The amount of sales taxes that must be sent to the state Department of Revenue.

9. For its fleet of trucks, Overland Transport, Inc., purchased 580 tires rated at 50 pounds each. The tires had a retail price of $85 each. The sales tax is 4.5%, and the federal excise tax is $0.15 per pound.

   a. What are the amount of sales tax per tire and the total sales tax?

   b. What are the amount of federal excise tax per tire and the total excise tax?

   c. What is the total purchase price of the tires?

Calculate the assessed value and the property tax due on the following properties.

	Fair Market Value	Assessment Rate	Assessed Value	Property Tax Rate	Property Tax Due
10.	$92,200	80%	_____	2.33%	_____
11.	$74,430	70	_____	$12.72 per $1,000	_____
12.	$2,450,900	100	_____	$2.16 per $100	_____
13.	$165,230	50	_____	28.98 mills	_____

Calculate the property tax rate required to meet the budgetary demands of the following communities.

| | | | | Property Tax Rate | | | |
Community	Total Assessed Property Valuation	Total Taxes Required	Percent	Per $100	Per $1,000	Mills
14. Stoney Creek	$860,000,000	$32,400,000	_____	_____	_____	_____
15. Three Sisters	$438,000,000	$7,200,000	_____	_____	_____	_____

16. The Young family is considering the purchase of a home. They have narrowed the choice down to a $162,000 home in Palm Springs and a $151,200 home in Weston. With regard to property taxes, Palm Springs has an assessment rate of 90% and a tax rate of 22.45 mills, while Weston has a 100% assessment rate and a tax rate of $2.60 per $100 of assessed value. Which house has the higher property tax and by how much?

17. As the tax assessor for Barclay County, you have been informed that an additional $4,500,000 in taxes will be required next year for new street lighting and bridge repairs. If the total assessed value of the property in Barclay County is $6,500,000,000, how much will this add to property taxes?

    a. As a percent

    b. Per $100 of assessed value

    c. Per $1,000 of assessed value

    d. In mills

Calculate the missing information for the following taxpayers.

| | | | | | (circle your choice) | | |
Name	Filing Status	Income	Adjustments to Income	Adjusted Gross Income	Standard Deduction	Itemized Deductions	Taxable Income
18. Huskey	Single	$54,900	$660	_____	_____	$12,325	_____
19. Shotwell	Married filing jointly	_____	$2,180	$63,823	_____	$6,850	_____
20. Chong	Head of household	$48,100	_____	$45,650	_____	$5,930	_____

As an accountant for the Give Me A Break Tax Service, use the Tax Rate Tables given in Exhibit 18-3, to calculate the tax liability for the following clients.

Name	Filing Status	Taxable Income	Tax Liability
21. Bester	Head of household	$184,112	_____
22. Whitney	Single	$70,890	_____
23. Gamble	Married, Jointly	$54,938	_____
24. Henne	Married, Separately	$125,202	_____

Calculate the amount of tax refund or tax owed for the following taxpayers.

Name	Tax Liability	Tax Credits	Other Taxes	Payments	Refund/Owe (circle one)	Amount
25. Morton	$6,540	$1,219	0	$5,093	Refund/Owe	_____
26. Newquist	$25,112	$7,650	$2,211	$21,200	Refund/Owe	_____

27. Bob Paris is the promotions director for Power 105, a local radio station. He is single. Last year Bob earned a salary of $3,600 per month from the station and received a $3,500 Christmas bonus. In addition, he earned royalties of $3,250 from a song he wrote, which was recorded and made popular by a famous musical group. Bob's itemized deductions amounted to $1,850. If the radio station withheld $525 per month for income tax, what is Bob's:

   a. Adjusted gross income?

   b. Taxable income?

   c. Tax liability?

   d. Is Bob entitled to a refund, or does he owe additional taxes? How much?

28. You are the tax consultant for Fidelity Manufacturing, Inc. If the company had taxable income of $875,500 last year, calculate:

   a. Corporate tax liability.

   b. Net income after taxes.

BUSINESS DECISION: THE 90% RULE, HAPPY NEW YEAR!

29. Patrick Von Radesky, an engineer with Century Power and Light, earns a gross income of $6,000 per month. Patrick is single and uses the standard deduction. Throughout last year, his company withheld $600 each month from his paycheck for federal income tax.

   Today is January 4. As Patrick's accountant, you just informed him that although his tax return is due at the IRS by April 15, 90% of the income tax due for last year must be paid by January 15; otherwise, a penalty will be imposed.

   a. Calculate the amount of tax Patrick owes for the year.

   b. Did his company withhold enough from each paycheck to cover the 90% requirement?

   c. How much should Patrick send the IRS by January 15 so that he will not be penalized?

Dollars AND Sense

If the April 15 clock runs out, you can get an automatic six-month extension to file until October 15 by filing Form 4868, Application for Automatic Extension of Time to File U.S. Individual Income Tax Return. However, this extension of time to file does not give you more time to pay any taxes due. If you have not paid at least 90% of the total tax due by the April deadline, you may be subject to an estimated tax penalty.

There are three ways to request an automatic extension of time to file a U.S. individual income tax return:

- Use Form 4868 electronically by accessing IRS e-file using a computer or by using a tax professional who uses e-file.
- File a paper Form 4868.
- Use Free File at www.freefile.irs.gov.

    d. If Patrick waits until April 15 to send the balance of his taxes to the IRS, how much will he be penalized if the penalty is 18% per year, or 1.5% per month, on the shortfall up to 90%? (*Hint:* Use the simple formula $I = PRT$ with exact interest.)

    e. If Patrick gets a 10% raise, all other factors being the same, how much should he tell his payroll department to withhold from each month's paycheck so that 90% of the tax due will be deducted?

COLLABORATIVE LEARNING ACTIVITY

Your Tax Dollars at Work

The primary focus of this chapter has been on calculating the amount of taxes that are due. Now, as a team, do some research into how your local, state, and federal tax dollars are being spent.

1. <u>Local Level:</u> As we have learned, local tax dollars are generally raised from property and local sales taxes. Is this true in your area? Contact your local tax assessor's office to determine the following:

    a. What are the local taxing units: city, county, municipality, district, province, parish, other?

    b. How are local taxes derived for each unit?

    c. What are the tax rates for each unit?

    d. How have the rates changed over the past five years?

    e. What is the latest tax budget for each unit and how is the money being spent?

    f. List five major projects in your area that are currently, recently, or soon-to-be funded by your tax dollars.

    g. As a team, what is your overall opinion of "your local tax dollars at work?"

2. <u>State Level:</u> Tax revenue in most states is derived either from sales tax, state income tax, or a combination of both. Is this true in your state? As a team, contact your state taxing authority to determine the following:

    a. How are state taxes derived?

    b. What are the tax rates?

    c. How have the rates changed over the past five years?

    d. What is the latest tax budget and how is the money being spent?

    e. List five or more major projects in your state that are currently, recently, or soon-to-be funded by tax dollars.

    f. As a team, what is your overall opinion of "your state tax dollars at work?"

3. <u>Federal Level:</u> As we have learned, federal tax revenues are derived from excise taxes, individual income taxes, Social Security and Medicare receipts, and corporate income taxes. As a team, research the Internet to determine the following:

    a. What is the current year's amount of excise taxes, individual income taxes, Social Security and Medicare receipts, and corporate income taxes collected by the federal government? Where did you find this information?

    b. From the White House's Office of Management and Budget, research the president's latest federal budget. Construct or find a pie chart of the major categories of the budget by dollar amount and percent breakdown.

    c. How have the categories changed over the past five years?

    d. As a team, what is your overall opinion of "your federal tax dollars at work?"

Business Math JOURNAL

Taxes

Tax Facts

- **The Beginning**—In 1864, a 3% income tax on all incomes over $800 was enacted by the federal government to finance the Civil War. By 1872, the income tax was discontinued. The U.S. Supreme Court declared the law unconstitutional in 1894.
- **A Great Rate**—In 1913, with the adoption of the Sixteenth Amendment, the income tax as we know it today became law. From 1913 to 1915, the rate was 1%.
- **A Not-So-Great Rate**—The highest income tax rate in U.S. history was levied in 1944 by the Individual Tax Act, with a 91% tax bracket.
- **A CPA's Delight**—Since 1954, Congress has changed the tax code approximately every 15 months. The number of pages in the tax code has increased 16,775% in the past century.
- **Time Is Money**—Americans spend 7.6 billion hours and $27.7 billion each year preparing their taxes.
- **The Bean Counters**—Americans typically hire over 1 million accountants for tax help. According to the Bureau of Labor Statistics, accountants and auditors are expected to experience faster-than-average employment growth through 2018.
- **Save a Tree–Save a Buck**—The Internal Revenue Service plans to stop mailing out instructions and paper forms for annual income tax returns, saving the agency about $10 million annually as more Americans are filing online.
- **Don't Overpay**—In a recent year, the government issued 96.3 million tax refunds, totaling over $278 billion. The average refund amounted to $2,887.
- **Finally Free**—Tax Freedom Day is the date each year when the average taxpayer has finally earned enough money to pay all of his or her local, state, and federal tax obligations for the year.

Sources: www.irs.gov; www.taxfoundation.org; www.businessinsider.com

Tax Freedom Day

In a recent typical year, Tax Freedom Day was April 17, the 107th day of the year. This meant that taxpayers had to work well over three months to pay their tax obligations.

Here's another way to look at "tax freedom." If you worked an eight-hour day from 9 a.m. to 5 p.m., it took you until 11:20 a.m. each day to earn enough money to pay your taxes.

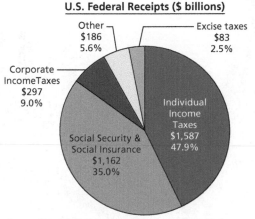

U.S. Federal Receipts ($ billions)

- Other $186 — 5.6%
- Excise taxes $83 — 2.5%
- Corporate Income Taxes $297 — 9.0%
- Social Security & Social Insurance $1,162 — 35.0%
- Individual Income Taxes $1,587 — 47.9%

Source: Data: OMB—Adapted from tables at www.whitehouse.gov/omb/historical-tables/

Issues & Activities

1. Locate the current "individual income tax" rate categories and the rate categories for last year.
   a. Compare the current rates with those for last year and calculate the dollar amount of increase or decrease for each category.
   b. Calculate the percent increase or decrease for each category.
2. Locate the latest "U.S. Federal Receipts" data published by the government's Office of Management and Budget. Compare the latest receipts with those in the pie chart above and calculate the percent increase or decrease for each category.
3. What date is Tax Freedom Day this year? Calculate the percent increase or decrease from the figure of 107 days in given above.
4. In teams, use the Internet to find current trends in "tax facts" and "IRS filings" statistics. List your sources and visually report your findings to the class.

Brainteaser—"A Taxing Situation"

In a small town, 1/3 of the tax revenue comes from property tax, 1/4 comes from sales tax, and the remaining $25 million is from business income tax. What is the total amount of taxes collected by the town?

See the end of Appendix A for the solution.

PERFORMANCE OBJECTIVES

LIFE INSURANCE

19 SECTION I

Insurance is the promise to substitute future economic certainty for uncertainty and to replace the unknown with a sense of security. It is a mechanism for reducing financial risk and spreading financial loss due to unexpected events such as the death or disability of an individual, a home or business fire, a flood, an earthquake, an automobile accident, a negligence lawsuit, or an illness. These are only a few of the uncertainties that businesses and individuals can protect against by purchasing insurance. Companies may even purchase business interruption insurance, which covers the loss of income that may occur as a result of a multitude of perils.

Insurance is a very large and important segment of the U.S. economic system. Today there are more than 6,000 insurance companies employing more than 2.3 million persons and collecting close to $240 billion in annual premiums. The insurance industry is second only to commercial banking as a source of investment funds because insurance companies invest the billions of premium dollars they receive each year in a wide range of investments.

Insurance is based on the theory of **shared risk**, which means that insurance protection is purchased by many whose total payments are pooled together to pay off those few who actually incur a particular loss. Insurance companies use statisticians known as **actuaries** to calculate the probability, or chance, of a certain insurable event occurring. Based on a series of complicated calculations, insurance rates are then set. The rates are high enough to cover the cost of expected loss payments in the future and to provide a profit for the insurance company.

This chapter covers three major categories of insurance: life insurance, property insurance, and motor vehicle insurance. Within these three categories are several hundred different products or lines. Each year companies market new insurance products to meet the needs of a changing society. Recently, for example, insurance was made available to cover the loss of communication satellites during launch, space travel, and reentry.

Let's start with some basic terminology of the insurance industry. The company offering the insurance protection and ensuring payment in the event of a loss is known as the **insurer**, **carrier**, or **underwriter**. The individual or business purchasing the protection is the **insured**, or **policyholder**. The document stipulating the terms of the contract between the insurer and the insured is the **policy**. The amount of protection provided by the policy is the **face value**, and the amount paid at regular intervals to purchase this protection is known as the **premium**. The **beneficiary** is the person or institution to whom the proceeds of the policy are paid in the event that a loss occurs.

The insurance industry is regulated by a number of authorities, including federal, state, and some inside the industry itself. This regulation is designed to promote the public welfare by maintaining the solvency of insurance companies, providing consumer protection, and ensuring fair trade practices as well as fair contracts at fair prices.

insurance A mechanism for reducing financial risk and spreading financial loss due to unexpected events.

shared risk The theory on which insurance is based; protection is purchased by many whose total payments are pooled together to pay off those few who actually incur a particular loss.

actuaries Statisticians employed by insurance companies who calculate the probability, or chance, of a certain insurable event occurring.

insurer, carrier, or **underwriter** The company offering the insurance protection and ensuring payment in the event of a loss.

insured, or **policyholder** The person or business purchasing the insurance protection.

policy The document stipulating the terms of the contract between the insurer and the insured.

face value The amount of protection provided by the policy.

premium The amount paid at regular intervals to purchase insurance protection.

beneficiary The person or institution to whom the proceeds of the policy are paid in the event that a loss occurs.

iStock.com/CEFutcher

According to statistics from industry research and consulting firm LIMRA International, the average American household carries just $126,000 in life insurance—approximately $300,000 less than they actually need. Only 61% of adult Americans have life insurance protection.

Insurance regulations, procedures, and laws vary widely from state to state. Most states have insurance commissions, departments, divisions, or boards that regulate all aspects of the insurance industry. Some of their responsibilities include premium structure and computation, insurance requirements, and salesperson education and licensing. This chapter focuses on calculating the premiums and the payouts of typical life, property, and motor vehicle insurance policies.

19-1 UNDERSTANDING LIFE INSURANCE AND CALCULATING TYPICAL PREMIUMS FOR VARIOUS TYPES OF POLICIES

life insurance A type of insurance that guarantees a specified sum of money to the surviving beneficiaries upon the death of the person who is insured.

term insurance A type of life insurance that offers pure insurance protection, paying the face value of the policy to the beneficiaries upon the death of the insured.

permanent insurance A type of insurance that combines an investment component with risk protection to provide the policyholder with both a death benefit and attractive investment returns.

Most individuals enjoy feeling that they are in control of their financial destiny. Few products are more important to that sense of security than life insurance. **Life insurance** guarantees a specified sum of money to the surviving beneficiaries upon the death of the person who is insured. Over the years, the average amount of life insurance per insured household has been steadily increasing. In 1960, for example, each insured household had an average of $13,000 in life insurance. By 1970, the average had doubled to about $26,000. By 1980, it had doubled again to more than $50,000. Today the average insured household has more than $125,000 in life insurance coverage. Exhibit 19-1 lists the top 10 life insurance companies by revenue.

There are two basic types of policies: those that pay only if the policyholder dies (**term insurance**) and those that pay whether the policyholder lives or dies (**permanent insurance**). Today many insurance policies combine an investment component with risk protection to provide the policyholder with both a death benefit if he or she dies and attractive investment returns if he or she lives. In this section, we examine five popular types of life insurance policies: term, whole life, limited payment life, endowment, and nontraditional.

TYPES OF LIFE INSURANCE

Term Insurance. This type of life insurance offers pure insurance protection, paying the face value of the policy to the beneficiaries upon the death of the insured. With term insurance, there is no investment component. All the premium goes toward purchasing the risk coverage. With most term policies, the premium increases periodically because the risk of death of the insured increases with age. Term policies may be purchased with premiums increasing every year, every 5 years, every 10 years, and so on.

Renewable term insurance allows the policyholder the option of renewing the policy for another 5- or 10-year period regardless of his or her health. The premiums on these policies

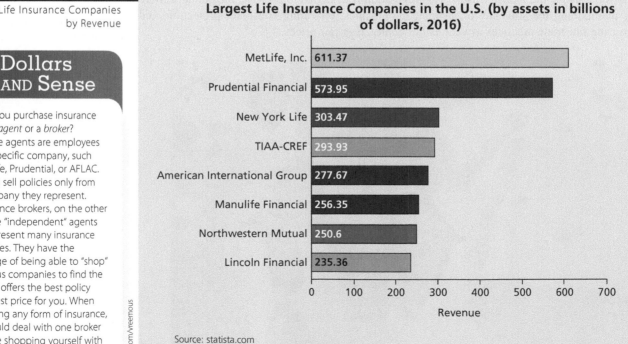

EXHIBIT 19-1
Top 10 Life Insurance Companies by Revenue

Dollars AND Sense

Should you purchase insurance from an *agent* or a *broker*? Insurance agents are employees of one specific company, such as MetLife, Prudential, or AFLAC. They can sell policies only from the company they represent.

Insurance brokers, on the other hand, are "independent" agents who represent many insurance companies. They have the advantage of being able to "shop" numerous companies to find the one that offers the best policy at the best price for you. When purchasing any form of insurance, you should deal with one broker or do the shopping yourself with several agents.

Largest Life Insurance Companies in the U.S. (by assets in billions of dollars, 2016)

Company	Revenue
MetLife, Inc.	611.37
Prudential Financial	573.95
New York Life	303.47
TIAA-CREF	293.93
American International Group	277.67
Manulife Financial	256.35
Northwestern Mutual	250.6
Lincoln Financial	235.36

Revenue (0, 100, 200, 300, 400, 500, 600, 700)

Source: statista.com

are higher than nonrenewable term insurance. Because it is impossible to predict one's future health, many persons opt for the renewable policy. Another common type of insurance, known as convertible term, allows the policyholder to trade in or convert the term policy for permanent insurance with an investment element and cash value, without having to prove his or her health status.

Whole Life Insurance.   Whole life, also known as ordinary life and straight life, is the most common type of permanent insurance. With whole life insurance, policyholders agree to pay premiums for their entire lives. Whole life insurance offers a guaranteed premium and death benefit as well as a guaranteed minimum cash value, which can be borrowed against if necessary. When the insured dies, the beneficiaries receive the face value of the policy. Having cash value is like having a savings account within the policy that grows each year. If the policyholder lives long enough, the cash value can be received as an annuity to supplement retirement income in later years.

Limited Payment Life Insurance.   Limited payment life policies have level premiums that are limited to a certain period of time. After this period, usually 10, 20, or 30 years, the policy is paid up and the insured is covered for the rest of his or her life. The premiums charged for limited payment policies are higher than premiums for whole life policies because they are paid for a shorter period of time. A variation of the limited payment policy is the Life Paid-Up at 65 policy. With this policy, the premiums are payable until the insured reaches age 65, after which no more premiums are owed.

Endowment Insurance.   Endowment insurance is a combination of life insurance and an accelerated savings plan. The emphasis of the endowment policy is the accumulation of money. Endowment insurance pays the face amount of the policy upon the death of the insured. It also pays the face amount if the insured is alive as of a specified date, known as the maturity date. Typical endowment periods are 10, 15, or 20 years or to a specified age such as 65 or 70. Traditionally, this type of insurance has been purchased by families with young children to save money for college education or by those who want to set up a retirement fund with immediate life insurance protection. Because they are designed to build cash values quickly, endowment policies have comparatively high premiums.

Nontraditional Insurance.   In recent years, certain nontraditional policies have been introduced by insurance companies. Most of these interest-sensitive products are more flexible in design and provisions than their traditional counterparts. With these policies, the basic components of a life insurance policy, insurance (protection) and savings (investment), are separated. When premium payments are made, a portion known as the *mortality charge* is deducted to pay for the insurance coverage. This mortality charge increases with the age of the policyholder each year because the probability of death increases with age. The remaining amount, after other fees are deducted, goes to the investment *side fund*.

- *Universal life* is the most popular interest-sensitive policy. It features a minimum guaranteed death benefit and flexible premiums and face amounts. The insurance company decides on the type of investments to make, with the earnings credited to the side fund.
- *Variable life* is a higher-risk interest-sensitive policy that allows the policyholder to choose how the side fund will be invested. Typical choices include stocks, bonds, money market accounts, and real estate funds. Although this policy has a guaranteed death benefit, it does not have a guaranteed cash value like universal life does.
- *Variable/universal life* is a recently introduced policy that combines features of both variable life and universal life. These policies offer flexible premiums and guaranteed death benefits, both of which can be adjusted by the policyholder. The cash value is not guaranteed and depends on the investment performance of the funds selected by the policyholder.

CALCULATING PREMIUMS

Insurance premiums are based on the age and sex of the insured as well as the type of policy being purchased. Premiums are less expensive for younger people because their probability of dying is lower than for older people. Females pay lower rates than do males of the same age because females have a longer life expectancy than males.

Life insurance is purchased in increments of $1,000 of face value. The actuaries at insurance companies generate comprehensive rate tables listing the premiums per $1,000 of insurance for males and females of all ages. Table 19-1 is a typical example of such a table.

Annual life insurance premiums are calculated by determining the number of $1,000 of insurance desired and then multiplying the number of $1,000 by the rate per $1,000 found in Table 19-1. When the insured desires to pay the premiums more frequently than annually, such as semiannually, quarterly, or monthly, a small surcharge is added to account for the increased cost of billing, handling, and bookkeeping. Table 19-2 illustrates typical **premium factors** used by insurance companies for this purpose.

premium factors Small surcharges added to the cost of insurance policies when the insured chooses to pay the premiums more frequently than annually; takes into account the increased cost of billing, handling, and bookkeeping.

TABLE 19-1 Annual Life Insurance Premiums (per $1,000 of Face Value)

| | Term Insurance | | | | Permanent Insurance | | | | | |
| | 5-Year Term | | 10-Year Term | | Whole Life | | 20-Payment Life | | 20-Year Endowment | |
Age	Male	Female	Male	Female	Male	Female	Male	Female	Male	Female
18	$ 2.32	$ 1.90	$ 4.33	$ 4.01	$13.22	$11.17	$23.14	$19.21	$33.22	$29.12
19	2.38	1.96	4.42	4.12	13.60	11.68	24.42	20.92	33.68	30.04
20	2.43	2.07	4.49	4.20	14.12	12.09	25.10	21.50	34.42	31.28
21	2.49	2.15	4.57	4.29	14.53	12.53	25.83	22.11	34.90	31.79
22	2.55	2.22	4.64	4.36	14.97	12.96	26.42	22.89	35.27	32.40
23	2.62	2.30	4.70	4.42	15.39	13.41	27.01	23.47	35.70	32.93
24	2.69	2.37	4.79	4.47	15.90	13.92	27.74	24.26	36.49	33.61
25	2.77	2.45	4.85	4.51	16.38	14.38	28.40	25.04	37.02	34.87
26	2.84	2.51	4.92	4.60	16.91	14.77	29.11	25.96	37.67	35.30
27	2.90	2.58	5.11	4.69	17.27	15.23	29.97	26.83	38.23	35.96
28	2.98	2.64	5.18	4.77	17.76	15.66	30.68	27.54	38.96	36.44
29	3.07	2.70	5.23	4.84	18.12	16.18	31.52	28.09	39.42	37.21
30	3.14	2.78	5.30	4.93	18.54	16.71	32.15	28.73	40.19	37.80
35	3.43	2.92	6.42	5.35	24.19	22.52	37.10	33.12	43.67	39.19
40	4.23	3.90	7.14	6.24	27.21	25.40	42.27	36.29	48.20	42.25
45	6.12	5.18	8.81	7.40	33.02	29.16	48.73	39.08	51.11	46.04
50	9.72	8.73	14.19	9.11	37.94	33.57	56.31	44.16	58.49	49.20
55	16.25	12.82	22.03	13.17	45.83	37.02	61.09	49.40	71.28	53.16
60	24.10	19.43	37.70	24.82	53.98	42.24	70.43	52.55	79.15	58.08

TABLE 19-2

Life Insurance—Premium Factors

Premium Paid	Percent of Annual Premium
Semiannually	52%
Quarterly	26%
Monthly	9%

STEPS TO CALCULATE LIFE INSURANCE PREMIUMS

STEP 1. Calculate the number of $1,000 of insurance desired by dividing the face value of the policy by $1,000. Round to the nearest whole $1,000.

$$\text{Number of } \$1,000 = \frac{\text{Face value of policy}}{\$1,000}$$

STEP 2. Locate the appropriate premium rate per $1,000 from Table 19-1. Choose the rate based on the type of policy desired and the age and sex of the applicant.

STEP 3. Calculate annual premium by multiplying the number of $1,000 of insurance desired by the Table 19-1 rate.

Annual premium = Number of $1,000 × Rate per $1,000

STEP 4. For premiums other than annual, multiply the appropriate Table 19-2 premium factor by the annual premium.

Premium other than annual = Annual premium × Premium factor

iStock.com/Nikada

EXAMPLE1 CALCULATING LIFE INSURANCE PREMIUMS

Claudia Mercado is 24 years old. She is interested in purchasing a whole life insurance policy with a face value of $50,000. As her insurance agent, calculate the annual and monthly insurance premiums for this policy.

▶SOLUTIONSTRATEGY

Step 1. Number of $1,000 = $\dfrac{\text{Face value of policy}}{\$1,000} = \dfrac{50,000}{1,000} = 50$

Step 2. From Table 19-1, we find the premium per $1,000 for whole life insurance for a 24-year-old woman to be $13.92.

Step 3. Annual premium = Number of $1,000 × Rate per $1,000
Annual premium = 50 × 13.92 = $696

Step 4. Monthly premium = Annual premium × Monthly premium factor
Monthly premium = 696 × .09 = $62.64

▶TRYITEXERCISE 1

Gary Foster, age 26, wants to purchase a 10-year term insurance policy with a face value of $75,000. Calculate his annual and quarterly premiums. How much more will Gary pay per year if he chooses quarterly payments?

CHECK YOUR ANSWERS WITH THE SOLUTIONS ON PAGE 679.

CALCULATING THE VALUE OF VARIOUS NONFORFEITURE OPTIONS

19-2

Because all life insurance policies (except term) build up a **cash value** after the first two or three years, they should be viewed as being property with a value. Policyholders in effect own these properties and therefore have certain **ownership rights**. For example, policyholders, or policyowners, have the right to change beneficiaries, designate how the death benefits will be paid, borrow money against the policy, assign ownership to someone else, or cancel the policy.

Let's take a closer look at what happens when a policyowner decides to cancel a policy or allows it to terminate, or **lapse**, by failing to make the required premium payments within 31 days of the due date. The amount of cash value that has accumulated to that point is based on the size of the policy and the amount of time it has been in force. Most policies give the policyowner three choices, known as **nonforfeiture options**.

Option 1—Cash Value or Cash Surrender Option.   Once a policy has accumulated cash value, the policyowner may choose to surrender (give up) the policy to the company and receive its cash value. At this point, the policy is terminated. If the insured wants to maintain the insurance coverage, the amount of the cash value may be borrowed and later repaid with interest.

Option 2—Reduced Paid-Up Insurance.   The second option is that the available cash value is used to purchase a reduced level of paid-up insurance. This policy is of the same type as the original and continues for the life of the policyowner, with no further premiums due.

Option 3—Extended Term Insurance.   With this option, the policyholder elects to use the cash value to purchase a term policy with the same face value as the original policy. The new policy will last for as long a time period as the cash value will purchase. When a policyowner simply stops paying on a policy and does not choose a nonforfeiture option, the insurance company automatically implements this extended term option.

Table 19-3 illustrates typical nonforfeiture options per $1,000 of face value for a policy issued to a woman at age 20.

cash value The amount of money that begins to build up in a permanent life insurance policy after the first two or three years.

ownership rights The rights of life insurance policyholders, including the right to change beneficiaries, designate how the death benefits will be paid, borrow money against the policy, assign ownership to someone else, or cancel the policy.

lapse To terminate. This is what happens when a policyholder fails to make the required premium payments on an insurance policy within 31 days of the due date.

nonforfeiture options The options available to the policyholder upon termination of a permanent life insurance policy with accumulated cash value; these include receiving the cash value, using the cash value to purchase a reduced paid-up insurance policy of the same type, or purchasing term insurance with the same face value as the original policy for as long a time period as the cash value will purchase.

TABLE 19-3 Nonforfeiture Options (per $1,000 of Face Value Issued to a Woman at Age 20)

	Whole Life Options					20-Payment Life Options					20-Year Endowment Options			
	1	2	3			1	2	3			1	2	3	
End of Year	Cash Value	Reduced Paid-Up Insurance	Extended Term			Cash Value	Reduced Paid-Up Insurance	Extended Term			Cash Value	Reduced Paid-Up Insurance	Extended Term	
			Years	Days				Years	Days				Years	Days
3	$ 11	$ 25	2	17		$ 29	$ 90	4	217		$ 39	$ 97	7	132
5	32	64	9	23		73	212	14	86		91	233	19	204
7	54	99	13	142		101	367	23	152		186	381	26	310
10	98	186	17	54		191	496	30	206		324	512	32	117
15	157	314	21	218		322	789	34	142		647	794	37	350
20	262	491	25	77		505	1,000	-Life-			1,000	1,000	-Life-	

STEPS TO CALCULATE THE VALUE OF VARIOUS NONFORFEITURE OPTIONS

STEP 1. Calculate the number of $1,000 of insurance by dividing the face value of the policy by $1,000.

STEP 2. *Option 1—Cash Value.* Locate the appropriate dollars per $1,000 in the Cash Value column of Table 19-3 and multiply this figure by the number of $1,000 of insurance.

Option 2—Reduced Paid-Up Insurance. Locate the appropriate dollars per $1,000 in the Reduced Paid-Up Insurance column of Table 19-3 and multiply this figure by the number of $1,000 of insurance.

Option 3—Extended Term. Locate the length of time of the new extended term policy in the Years and Days columns of Table 19-3.

EXAMPLE 2 CALCULATING NONFORFEITURE OPTIONS

Tricia Lee purchased a $30,000 whole life insurance policy when she was 20 years old. She is now 35 years old and wants to investigate her nonforfeiture options. As her insurance agent, use Table 19-3 to calculate the value of Tricia's three options.

►SOLUTIONSTRATEGY

Step 1. Number of $1,000 = $\dfrac{\text{Face value of policy}}{\$1,000} = \dfrac{30,000}{1,000} = 30$

Step 2. *Option 1—Cash Value.* From Table 19-3, we find that after being in force for 15 years, a whole life policy issued to a woman at age 20 has a cash value of $157 per $1,000 of insurance.

Number of $1,000 × Table value = 30 × 157 = <u>$4,710</u>

Tricia's cash value option is to receive $4,710 in cash from the company and have no further insurance coverage.

Option 2—Reduced Paid-Up Insurance. From Table 19-3, we find that after being in force for 15 years, a whole life policy issued to a woman at age 20 will have enough cash value to buy $314 in paid-up whole life insurance per $1,000 of face value.

Number of $1,000 × Table value = 30 × 314 = <u>$9,420</u>

Tricia's reduced paid-up insurance option is to receive a $9,420 whole life policy effective for her entire life with no further payments.

Dollars AND Sense

It is important to check your insurance coverage periodically or whenever your situation changes to be sure it meets your current needs.

Some changes that require insurance review might include increased income, change in marital status, or change in family size.

Many insurable assets are tied to inflation and therefore require periodic increases.

- Life insurance—Cost of living increases such as food, clothing, and transportation
- Property insurance—Rising real estate values and cost of replacement materials
- Health care insurance— Increases in physician, hospital, and other medical-related costs

> *Option 3—Extended Term Insurance.* From Table 19-3, we find that after being in force for 15 years, a whole life policy issued to a woman at age 20 will have enough cash value to purchase $30,000 of term insurance for a period of <u>21 years, 218 days</u>.

►TRYITEXERCISE 2

Virginia Bennett purchased a $100,000 20-payment life insurance policy when she was 20 years old. She is now 30 years old and wants to investigate her nonforfeiture options. As her insurance agent, use Table 19-3 to determine the value of Virginia's three options.

CHECK YOUR ANSWERS WITH THE SOLUTIONS ON PAGE 679.

CALCULATING THE AMOUNT OF LIFE INSURANCE NEEDED TO COVER DEPENDENTS' INCOME SHORTFALL

19-3

Evaluating your life insurance needs is a fundamental part of sound financial planning. The amount of insurance and type of policy you should purchase are much less obvious. Life insurance is needed if you run a household, support a family, have a mortgage or other major debts, or expect children to attend college. Insurance should be used to fill the financial gap a family may incur by the death or disability of the insured.

One so-called rule of thumb is that you carry between 7 and 10 times your annual income depending on your lifestyle, number of dependents, and other sources of income. Another estimator of the amount of insurance to purchase is based on a family's additional income requirements needed in the event of the death of the insured. These additional requirements are known as the **income shortfall**.

Let's say, for example, that a family has $30,000 in living expenses per year. If after the death of the insured the family's total income decreases to only $20,000, the income shortfall would be $10,000 ($30,000 − $20,000). The theory is to purchase enough life insurance so that the face value of the policy, collected by the family on the death of the insured, can be invested at the prevailing interest rate to generate the additional income needed to overcome the $10,000 shortfall. When prevailing interest rates are low, large amounts of insurance are needed to cover the shortfall. As interest rates rise, less insurance is needed.

income shortfall The difference between the total living expenses and the total income of a family in the event of the death of the insured; used as an indicator of how much life insurance to purchase.

STEPS TO CALCULATE INSURANCE NEEDED TO COVER DEPENDENTS' INCOME SHORTFALL

STEP 1. Determine the dependents' total annual living expenses, including mortgages.

STEP 2. Determine the dependents' total annual sources of income, including salaries, investments, and social security.

STEP 3. Subtract the income from the living expenses to find the income shortfall.

$$\text{Income shortfall} = \text{Total living expenses} - \text{Total income}$$

STEP 4. Calculate the insurance needed to cover the shortfall by dividing the shortfall by the prevailing interest rate (round to the nearest $1,000).

$$\text{Insurance needed} = \frac{\text{Income shortfall}}{\text{Prevailing interest rate}}$$

EXAMPLE 3   CALCULATING AMOUNT OF INSURANCE NEEDED

With a prevailing interest rate of 6%, how much life insurance is required to cover dependents' income shortfall if their living expenses amount to $48,000 per year and their total income sources amount to $33,000 per year?

►SOLUTIONSTRATEGY

Step 1. Living expenses per year are $48,000 (given).

Step 2. Dependents' total income is $33,000 (given).

Step 3. Income shortfall = Total expenses − Total income

Income shortfall = 48,000 − 33,000 = $15,000

Step 4. Insurance needed = $\dfrac{\text{Shortfall}}{\text{Prevailing rate}} = \dfrac{15,000}{.06} = \$250,000$

►TRYITEXERCISE 3

Norm Jaffe is evaluating his life insurance needs. His family's total living expenses are $54,000 per year. Kate, his wife, earns $38,000 per year in salary and receives another $5,000 per year from an endowment fund. If the prevailing interest rate is currently 5%, how much life insurance should Norm purchase to cover his dependents' income shortfall?

CHECK YOUR ANSWERS WITH THE SOLUTIONS ON PAGE 679.

SECTION I   19   REVIEW EXERCISES

Calculate the annual, semiannual, quarterly, and monthly premiums for the following life insurance policies.

	Face Value of Policy	Sex and Age of Insured	Type of Policy	Annual Premium	Semiannual Premium	Quarterly Premium	Monthly Premium
1.	$ 5,000	Male—24	Whole Life	$79.50	$41.34	$20.67	$7.16
2.	10,000	Female—35	10-Year Term				
3.	25,000	Male—19	20-Year Endowment				
4.	75,000	Male—50	20-Payment Life				
5.	100,000	Female—29	5-Year Term				
6.	60,000	Male—40	Whole Life				
7.	60,000	Male—50	Whole Life				

8. How much would Juanita's monthly premium be for a 10-year term insurance policy with a face value of $230,000, based on Tables 19-1 and 19-2? She turned 24 years old on her last birthday.

Round your answer to the nearest cent.

Calculate the value of the nonforfeiture options for the following life insurance policies.

	Face Value of Policy	Years in Force	Type of Policy	Cash Value	Reduced Paid-Up Insurance	Extended Term	
						Years	Days
9.	$ 50,000	10	Whole Life	$4,900	$9,300	17	54
10.	250,000	7	20-Year Endowment	_____	_____	____	____
11.	35,000	15	Whole Life	_____	_____	____	____
12.	100,000	3	20-Payment Life	_____	_____	____	____
13.	25,000	5	20-Year Endowment	_____	_____	____	____

14. At age 20, Kari purchased a whole life insurance policy with face value of $360,000. She is now 35 and wants to cancel her policy. Use Table 19-3 to calculate the amount of reduced paid-up insurance to which she is entitled.

15. Leroy Kirk is 35 years old and is interested in purchasing a 20-year endowment insurance policy with a face value of $120,000.

a. Calculate the annual premium for this policy.

b. Calculate the semiannual premium.

16. Rene Boyer, age 27, wants to purchase a 5-year term insurance policy with a face value of $25,000. As her insurance agent, answer the following questions:

a. What is the annual premium for this policy?

b. What is the monthly premium?

c. How much more will Rene pay per year if she chooses monthly payments?

17. Carmen Gutierrez purchased a $75,000, 20-payment life insurance policy when she was 20 years old. She is now 30 years old and wants to investigate her nonforfeiture options. As her insurance agent, calculate the value of Carmen's three options.

18. Alex Baron is evaluating his life insurance needs. His family's total living expenses are $39,800 per year. Carol, his wife, earns $23,000 per year in salary and receives an additional $4,000 per year in municipal bond interest. If the prevailing interest rate is currently 2.5%, how much life insurance should Alex purchase to cover his dependents' income shortfall?

Total living expenses = $39,800

Total income = 23,000 + 4,000 = $27,000

Income shortfall = 39,800 − 27,000 = $12,800

$$\frac{\text{Income shortfall}}{\text{Prevailing interest rate}} = \frac{12,800}{.025} = \underline{\$512,000} \text{ Insurance needed}$$

19. If Roberta's husband were to die, she and her children could live on $52,500 per year. Roberta earns $14,900 annually and estimates additional income of $3,500 from other sources. How much insurance should she purchase on her husband to cover the shortfall, assuming a 4.5% prevailing interest rate? Round to the nearest $1,000.

BUSINESS DECISION: THE CONSULTATION

20. Tina Parker, a single mother, is 20 years old. She has called on you for an insurance consultation. Her objective is to purchase life insurance protection for the next 10 years while her children are growing up. Tina tells you that she can afford about $250 per year for insurance premiums. You have suggested either a 10-year term policy or a whole life policy.

a. Rounded to the nearest thousand, how much insurance coverage can Tina purchase under each policy? *Hint*: Divide her annual premium allowance by the rate per $1,000 for each policy.

b. If she should die in the next 10 years, how much more will her children receive under the term insurance?

c. If she should live beyond the 10th year, what are her nonforfeiture options with the whole life policy?

PROPERTY INSURANCE

UNDERSTANDING PROPERTY INSURANCE AND CALCULATING TYPICAL FIRE INSURANCE PREMIUMS

19-4

Businesses and homeowners alike need insurance protection for the financial losses that may occur to their property from such perils as fire, lightning, wind, water, negligence, burglary, and vandalism. Although the probability that a particular peril will occur is small, no homeowner or business can afford the risk of not having **property insurance**. Most mortgage lenders, in fact, require that sufficient property insurance be purchased by the borrower as a condition for obtaining a mortgage.

property insurance Insurance protection for the financial losses that may occur to business' and homeowner's property from such perils as fire, lightning, wind, water, negligence, burglary, and vandalism.

In addition to the items listed above, most property insurance policies today have provisions for liability coverage, medical expenses, and additional expenses that may be incurred while the damaged property is being repaired. For example, a business may have to move to a temporary location during reconstruction or a family may have to stay in an apartment or a motel while their house is being repaired. Insurance companies offer similar policies to meet the needs of apartment and home renters as well as condominium owners.

In this section, we focus our attention on fire insurance and how these premiums are determined. Fire insurance rates are quoted as an amount per $100 of insurance coverage purchased. Rates are separated into two categories: (1) the structure or building itself and (2) the contents in the building.

A *building's* fire insurance rates are determined by a number of important factors:

- The *dollar amount* of insurance purchased on the property
- The *location of the property*—city, suburbs, and rural areas
- The *proximity* and *quality* of fire protection available
- The *type of construction* materials used—masonry (brick) or wood (frame)

The *contents* portion of the fire insurance rate is based on the following:

- The *dollar amount* or value of the contents
- The *flammability* of the contents

From this rate structure, we can see that a building made of concrete, bricks, and steel that is located 2 or 3 miles from a fire station would have a considerably lower rate than a

Jerry Sharp/Shutterstock.com

Most businesses and homeowners carry special insurance policies to protect against loss due to fire and other perils. In a recent year, the average homeowner's policy had an annual premium of $952. (Adapted from information at valuepenguin.com)

EXHIBIT 19-2 The Top Ten Most Expensive and Least Expensive States for Homeowners Insurance

Rank	Most expensive states	Homeowners average premium	Rank	Least expensive states	Homeowners average premium
1	Florida	$1,191	1	Idaho	$534
2	Louisiana	1,722	2	Oregon	576
3	Texas	1,625	3	Utah	580
4	Mississippi	1,451	4	Wisconsin	610
5	Oklahoma	1,428	5	Washington	645
6	Alabama	1,198	6	Ohio	663
7	Rhode Island	1,173	7	Delaware	684
8	Kansas	1,136	8	Arizona	695
9	New York	1,130	9	Nevada	710
10	Connecticut	1,129	10	Iowa	734

Source: http://www.valuepenguin.com/average-cost-of-homeowners-insurance

TABLE 19-4 Annual Fire Insurance Premiums (per $100 of Face Value)

Area Rating	A Building	A Contents	B Building	B Contents	C Building	C Contents	D Building	D Contents
1	$.21	$.24	$.32	$ .37	$ .38	$ .42	$ .44	$ .48
2	.38	.42	.39	.48	.43	.51	.57	.69
3	.44	.51	.55	.66	.69	.77	.76	.85
4	.59	.68	.76	.83	.87	1.04	.98	1.27
5	.64	.73	.92	1.09	1.08	1.13	1.39	1.43

building of the same value with wood frame construction located in a rural area 12 miles from the nearest fire-fighting equipment. Or for that matter, a warehouse filled with explosive chemicals would cost more to insure than the same warehouse filled with Coca-Cola.

Table 19-4 illustrates typical annual fire insurance premiums. Note that the rates are per $100 of insurance coverage. The building and contents are listed separately and divided by the structural class of the building and the location (area rating).

STEPS TO CALCULATE TYPICAL FIRE INSURANCE PREMIUMS

STEP 1. From Table 19-4, locate the appropriate rate based on *structural class* and *area rating* for both the building and the contents.

STEP 2. Calculate the number of $100 of insurance coverage desired for both the building and the contents by dividing the amount of coverage for each by $100.

STEP 3. Multiply the number of $100 for both the building and contents by the rates from Step 1 to find the annual premium for each.

STEP 4. Add the annual premiums for the building and the contents to find the total annual premium.

Total annual fire premium = Building premium + Contents premium

EXAMPLE4 CALCULATING FIRE INSURANCE PREMIUMS

What is the total annual fire insurance premium on a building valued at $200,000 with structural classification B and area rating 4 and contents valued at $40,000?

▶SOLUTIONSTRATEGY

Step 1. From Table 19-4, we find the following rates for structural class B and area rating 4:

Building—$.76 per $100 of coverage
Contents—$.83 per $100 of coverage

Step 2. Number of $100 of coverage:

$$\text{Building} = \frac{\text{Amount of coverage}}{\$100} = \frac{200,000}{100} = 2,000$$

$$\text{Contents} = \frac{\text{Amount of coverage}}{\$100} = \frac{40,000}{100} = 400$$

Step 3. Annual fire insurance premiums:

Building = Number of $100 × Table rate = 2,000 × .76 = $1,520

Contents = Number of $100 × Table rate = 400 × .83 = $332

Step 4. Total annual fire premium = Building premium + Contents premium

Total annual fire premium = 1,520 + 332 = $1,852

▶TRYITEXERCISE 4

You are the insurance agent for Diamond Enterprises, Inc. The owner, Ed Diamond, would like you to give him a quote on the total annual premium for a property insurance policy on a new warehouse in the amount of $420,000 and contents valued at $685,000. The warehouse is structural classification A and area rating 2.

CHECK YOUR ANSWERS WITH THE SOLUTIONS ON PAGE 679

CALCULATING PREMIUMS FOR SHORT-TERM POLICIES AND THE REFUNDS DUE ON CANCELED POLICIES

19-5

From time to time, businesses and individuals cancel insurance policies or require **short-term policies** of less than one year. For example, a family might sell their home two months after paying the annual premium or a business may require coverage for a shipment of merchandise that will be sold in a few months. When a policy is canceled by the insured or is written for less than one year, the premium charged is known as the **short-rate**.

short-term policies Insurance policies for less than one year.

SHORT-RATE REFUND

Table 19-5 illustrates typical short-term policy rate factors. These rate factors should be used to calculate the premiums and refunds for short-term policies canceled by the insured. Note that these rate factors are a percentage of the annual premium.

short-rate The premium charged when a policy is canceled by the insured or is written for less than one year.

STEPS TO CALCULATE SHORT-RATE REFUNDS—POLICIES CANCELED BY INSURED

STEP 1. Calculate the short-term premium using the short-rate from Table 19-5.

Short-rate premium = Annual premium × Short-rate

STEP 2. Calculate the short-rate refund by subtracting the short-rate premium from the annual premium.

Short-rate refund = Annual premium − Short-rate premium

TABLE 19-5 Property Insurance Short-Rate Schedule

Time Policy Is in Force	Percent of Annual Premium	Time Policy Is in Force (months)	Percent of Annual Premium
5 days	8	4	50
10 days	10	5	60
15 days	14	6	70
20 days	16	7	75
25 days	18	8	80
		9	85
1 month	20	10	90
2 months	30	11	95
3 months	40	12	100

iStock.com/Nikada

EXAMPLE5   CALCULATING SHORT-RATE RETURNS

A property insurance policy has an annual premium of $500. What is the short-rate refund if the policy is canceled by the insured after 3 months?

▶SOLUTIONSTRATEGY

Step 1.   Short-rate premium = Annual premium × Short-rate
Short-rate premium = 500 × 40% = $\underline{200}$

Step 2.   Short-rate refund = Annual premium − Short-rate premium
Short-rate refund = 500 − 200 = $\underline{\underline{300}}$

▶TRYITEXERCISE 5

A property insurance policy has an annual premium of $850. What is the short-rate refund if the policy is canceled by the insured after 8 months?

CHECK YOUR ANSWERS WITH THE SOLUTIONS ON PAGE 679.

REGULAR REFUND

When a policy is canceled by the insurance company rather than the insured, the company must refund the entire unused portion of the premium. This short-term refund calculation is based on the fraction of a year the policy was in force and is known as a regular refund.

STEPS TO CALCULATE REGULAR REFUNDS—POLICIES CANCELED BY COMPANY

STEP 1.   Calculate the premium for the period of time the policy was in force.

$$\text{Annual premium} \times \frac{\textbf{Days policy in force}}{\textbf{365}}$$

or

$$\text{Annual premium} \times \frac{\textbf{Months policy in force}}{\textbf{12}}$$

STEP 2.   Calculate refund by subtracting premium for period in force from the annual premium.

$$\textbf{Regular refund = Annual premium − Premium for period}$$

iStock.com/Nikada

EXAMPLE6   CALCULATING REGULAR REFUNDS

A property insurance policy has an annual premium of $500. What is the regular refund if the policy is canceled by the insurance company after 3 months?

▶SOLUTIONSTRATEGY

Step 1.   Premium for period = Annual premium × $\dfrac{\text{Months policy in force}}{12}$

Premium for period = $500 \times \dfrac{3}{12} = \underline{125}$

Step 2. Regular refund = Annual premium − Premium for period
Regular refund = 500 − 125 = $375

▶TRYITEXERCISE 6

A property insurance policy has an annual premium of $850. What is the regular refund if the policy is canceled by the insurance company after 8 months?

CHECK YOUR ANSWERS WITH THE SOLUTIONS ON PAGE 679.

UNDERSTANDING COINSURANCE AND COMPUTING COMPENSATION DUE IN THE EVENT OF A LOSS

19-6

Knowing that most fires do not totally destroy the insured property, many businesses, as a cost-saving measure, insure their buildings and contents for less than the full value. To protect themselves from having more claims than premiums collected, insurance companies write a **coinsurance clause** into most business policies. This clause stipulates the minimum amount of coverage required for a claim to be paid in full. The coinsurance minimum is stated as a percent of the replacement value of the property and is usually between 70% and 90%.

Here is an example of how coinsurance works. Let's say that a building has a replacement value of $100,000. If the insurance policy has an 80% coinsurance clause, the building must be insured for $80,000 (80% of the $100,000) to be fully covered for any claim up to the face value of the policy. Any coverage less than the required 80% would be paid out in proportion to the coverage ratio. The **coverage ratio** is a ratio of the amount of insurance carried by the insured to the amount of insurance required by the insurance company.

coinsurance clause A clause in a property insurance policy stipulating the minimum amount of coverage required for a claim to be paid in full. This requirement is stated as a percent of the replacement value of the property.

coverage ratio A ratio of the amount of insurance carried by the insured to the amount of insurance required according to the coinsurance clause of the insurance policy.

$$\text{Coverage ratio} = \frac{\text{Insurance carried}}{\text{Insurance required}}$$

If, for example, the owner had purchased only $40,000 rather than the required $80,000, the insurance company would be obligated to pay only half, or 50%, of any claim. This is because the ratio of insurance carried to insurance required was 50%.

$$\text{Coverage ratio} = \frac{40,000}{80,000} = \frac{1}{2} = 50\%$$

STEPS TO CALCULATE AMOUNT OF LOSS TO BE PAID WITH A COINSURANCE CLAUSE

STEP 1. Determine the amount of insurance required by the coinsurance clause.

Insurance required = Replacement value of property × Coinsurance percent

STEP 2. Calculate the amount of the loss to be paid by the insurance company by multiplying the coverage ratio by the amount of the loss.

$$\text{Amount of loss paid by insurance} = \frac{\text{Insurance carried}}{\text{Insurance required}} \times \text{Amount of the loss}$$

iStock.com/Nikada

EXAMPLE7 | **CALCULATING INSURANCE LOSS PAYOUT**

The Tradewinds Corporation had property valued at $500,000 and insured for $300,000. If the fire insurance policy contained an 80% coinsurance clause, how much would be paid by the insurance company in the event of a $100,000 fire?

►SOLUTIONSTRATEGY

Step 1. Insurance required = Value of the property × Coinsurance percent
Insurance required = 500,000 × .80 = $400,000

Step 2. Amount of loss paid by insurance $= \dfrac{\text{Insurance carried}}{\text{Insurance required}} \times \text{Amount of loss}$

Amount of loss paid by insurance $= \dfrac{300,000}{400,000} \times 100,000 = \underline{\underline{\$75,000}}$

►TRYITEXERCISE 7

Bravo Manufacturing, Inc., had property valued at $850,000 and insured for $400,000. If the fire insurance policy contained a 70% coinsurance clause, how much would be paid by the insurance company in the event of a $325,000 fire?

CHECK YOUR ANSWERS WITH THE SOLUTIONS ON PAGE 679.

19-7 DETERMINING EACH COMPANY'S SHARE OF A LOSS WHEN LIABILITY IS DIVIDED AMONG MULTIPLE CARRIERS

multiple carriers A situation in which a business is covered by fire insurance policies from more than one company at the same time.

Sometimes businesses are covered by fire insurance policies from more than one company at the same time, which is known as having **multiple carriers**. This situation occurs because one insurance company is unwilling or unable to carry the entire liability of a particular property or because additional coverage was purchased from different insurance companies over a period of time as the business expanded and became more valuable.

Assuming that all coinsurance clause requirements have been met, when a claim is made against multiple carriers, each carrier is responsible for its portion of the total coverage carried. To calculate that portion, we divide the amount of each company's policy by the total insurance carried. This portion is expressed as a percent of the total coverage.

For example, if an insurance company was one of multiple carriers and had a $30,000 fire policy written on a business that had a total of $200,000 in coverage, that insurance company would be responsible for $\dfrac{30,000}{200,000}$, or 15%, of any loss.

STEPS TO DETERMINE EACH COMPANY'S SHARE OF A LOSS WHEN LIABILITY IS SHARED AMONG MULTIPLE CARRIERS

STEP 1. Calculate each carrier's portion by dividing the amount of each policy by the total insurance carried.

$$\text{Carrier's percent of total coverage} = \frac{\textbf{Amount of carrier's policy}}{\textbf{Total amount of insurance}}$$

STEP 2. Determine each carrier's share of a loss by multiplying the amount of the loss by each carrier's percent of the total coverage.

Carrier's share of loss = Amount of loss × Carrier's percent of total coverage

iStock.com/Nikada

EXAMPLE8   CALCULATING MULTI-CARRIER PAYOUTS

Dynaco Development Corp. had multiple carrier fire insurance coverage in the amount of $400,000 as follows.

$$
\begin{array}{rl}
\text{Travelers:} & \$80,000 \quad \text{policy} \\
\text{State Farm:} & \$120,000 \quad \text{policy} \\
\text{Allstate:} & \underline{\$200,000} \quad \text{policy} \\
& \$400,000 \quad \text{total coverage}
\end{array}
$$

Assuming that all coinsurance clause stipulations have been met, how much would each carrier be responsible for in the event of a $50,000 fire?

▶ SOLUTIONSTRATEGY

Step 1. Carrier's percent of total coverage $= \dfrac{\text{Amount of carrier's policy}}{\text{Total amount of insurance}}$

$$
\text{Travelers} = \frac{80,000}{400,000} = \underline{20\%}
$$

$$
\text{State Farm} = \frac{120,000}{400,000} = \underline{30\%}
$$

$$
\text{Allstate} = \frac{200,000}{400,000} = \underline{50\%}
$$

Step 2. Carrier's share of loss $=$ Amount of loss $\times$ Carrier's percent of total coverage

$$
\begin{array}{l}
\text{Travelers Share} = 50,000 \times .20 = \underline{\$10,000} \\
\text{State Farm Share} = 50,000 \times .30 = \underline{\$15,000} \\
\text{Allstate Share} = 50,000 \times .50 = \underline{\$25,000}
\end{array}
$$

▶ TRYITEXERCISE 8

Savoy International had multiple carrier fire insurance coverage in the amount of $125,000 as follows.

$$
\begin{array}{rl}
\text{Aetna:} & \$20,000 \quad \text{policy} \\
\text{USF\&G:} & \$45,000 \quad \text{policy} \\
\text{John Hancock:} & \underline{\$60,000} \quad \text{policy} \\
& \$125,000 \quad \text{total coverage}
\end{array}
$$

Assuming that all coinsurance clause stipulations have been met, how much would each carrier be responsible for in the event of a $16,800 fire?

CHECK YOUR ANSWERS WITH THE SOLUTIONS ON PAGE 680.

REVIEW EXERCISES   19 SECTION II

Calculate the building, contents, and total property insurance premiums for the following policies.

	Area Rating	Structural Class	Building Value	Building Premium	Contents Value	Contents Premium	Total Premium
1.	5	D	$425,000	$5,907.50	$70,000	$1,001.00	$6,908.50
2.	4	B	$88,000	_____	$21,000	_____	_____
3.	2	C	$124,000	_____	$35,000	_____	_____
4.	1	A	$215,000	_____	$29,000	_____	_____
5.	5	D	$518,000	_____	$90,000	_____	_____

6. As the owner of a business, Karen needs fire insurance. Her building is worth $728,000 and the contents are valued at $677,000.

   Her agent placed the building in structural classification B and area rating 2. Use Table 19-4 to calculate her total premium.

   Round your answer to the nearest cent.

Calculate the short-term premium and refund for each of the following policies.

	Annual Premium	Canceled After	Canceled By	Short-Term Premium	Refund
7.	$750	2 months	insured	$225.00	$525.00
8.	$390	5 months	insurance company	$162.50	$227.50
9.	$450	3 months	insurance company	_____	_____
10.	$560	20 days	insured	_____	_____
11.	$1,280	9 months	insured	_____	_____
12.	$1,550	5 months	insurance company	_____	_____

13. If Yolanda's insurance company cancels her fire insurance policy after 208 days, how much of the $688.00 annual premium will she receive as a refund?

    Round your answer to the nearest cent.

Calculate the amount to be paid by the insurance company for each of the following claims.

	Replacement Value of Building	Face Value of Policy	Coinsurance Clause (%)	Amount of Loss	Amount of Loss Insurance Company Will Pay
14.	$430,000	$225,000	70	$150,000	$112,126.25
15.	$200,000	$160,000	80	$75,000	_____
16.	$350,000	$300,000	90	$125,000	_____
17.	$70,000	$50,000	70	$37,000	_____
18.	$125,000	$75,000	80	$50,000	_____

19. The insurance carrier used by Sharma Kennels specifies 90% coinsurance. The company recently incurred $455,000 in damages from a tornado. The building was valued at $570,000, but was only insured for $487,000.

    What will be paid by the insurance company for the loss? Round your answer to the nearest cent.

20. You are the insurance agent for Castle Mountain Furniture, Inc. The owner, Craig Ferguson, would like you to give him a quote on the total annual premium for property insurance on a new production facility in the amount of $1,640,000 and equipment and contents valued at $955,000. The building is structural classification B and area rating 4.

21. A property insurance policy has an annual premium of $1,625. What is the short-rate refund if the policy is canceled by the insured after 10 months?

22. Insignia Enterprises has a property insurance policy with an annual premium of $1,320. In recent months, Insignia has filed four different claims against the policy: a fire, two burglaries, and a vandalism incident. The insurance company has elected to cancel the policy, which has been in effect for 310 days. What is the regular refund due to Insignia?

23. A hurricane caused $185,000 in damages to a building owned by Dreamscape Landscaping. The building was insured by several carriers for a total of $460,000 and all coinsurance requirements were met.

   If Erie Insurance Group is providing $69,000 of the total coverage, what is their share of the loss?

24. Hi-Volt Electronics had multiple carrier fire insurance coverage in the amount of $500,000, as follows:

$$
\begin{array}{rl}
\text{Aetna:} & \$300,000 \quad \text{policy} \\
\text{State Farm:} & \$125,000 \quad \text{policy} \\
\text{Liberty Mutual:} & \underline{\$75,000} \quad \text{policy} \\
& \$500,000 \quad \text{total coverage}
\end{array}
$$

   Assuming that all coinsurance clause stipulations have been met, how much would each carrier be responsible for in the event of a $95,000 fire?

BUSINESS DECISION: BUSINESS INTERRUPTION INSURANCE

25. As the owner of a successful business, you have just purchased an additional type of property insurance coverage known as *business interruption insurance*. This insurance protects the profits that a company would have earned had there been no problem. Business interruption insurance covers damages caused by all types of perils, such as fires, tornadoes, hurricanes, lightning, or any other disaster except floods and earthquakes.

   This insurance pays for "economic" losses incurred when business operations suddenly cease. These include loss of income due to the interruption and additional expenses (e.g., leases; relocation to temporary facilities; overtime to keep up with production demands; recompiling of business, financial, and legal records; and even the salaries of key employees).

   Your coverage provides insurance reimbursement for 80% of any losses. Your company pays the other 20%. The annual premium is 2% of the income and extra expenses that you insure.

   a. If you have purchased coverage amounting to $20,000 per month, what is the amount of your annual premium?

   b. If a tornado put your company out of business for $5\frac{1}{2}$ months, what would be the amount of the insurance reimbursement for your economic loss?

Home-Based Business For those running a business from home, a typical homeowner's policy is not enough because it provides only $2,500 in coverage for business equipment. The insurance industry has recently created "in-home business" insurance policies. For about $200 a year, you can insure your business property for $10,000. General liability coverage is included in the policy.

   For an additional premium, a business owner can purchase $300,000 to $1 million in liability coverage. The policy also covers lost income and expenses such as payroll for up to one year if damage occurs to the house and the business is shut down.

SECTION III 19 MOTOR VEHICLE INSURANCE

19-8 UNDERSTANDING MOTOR VEHICLE INSURANCE AND CALCULATING TYPICAL PREMIUMS

motor vehicle insurance Insurance protection for the financial losses that may be incurred due to a motor vehicle accident or damage caused by fire, vandalism, or other perils.

liability A portion of motor vehicle insurance that includes payment for bodily injury to other persons and damages to the property of others resulting from the insured's negligence.

collision A portion of motor vehicle insurance that covers damage sustained by the insured's vehicle in an accident.

comprehensive Insurance coverage that protects the insured's vehicle for damage caused by fire, wind, water, theft, vandalism, and other perils not caused by accident.

deductible A premium reduction measure in collision insurance whereby the insured pays a stipulated amount of the damage first, the deductible, and the insurance company pays any amount over that; common deductibles are $100, $250, $500, and $1,000.

With the steadily increasing costs of automobile and truck repairs and replacement, as well as all forms of medical services, **motor vehicle insurance** today is an absolute necessity! In fact, most states require a minimum amount of insurance before a vehicle may be registered.

Motor vehicle insurance rates, regulations, and requirements vary widely from state to state, but the basic structure is the same. Vehicle insurance is divided into three main categories: **liability**, **collision**, and **comprehensive**.

Liability.   This category includes (1) payment for bodily injury to other persons resulting from the insured's negligence and (2) damages to the property of others resulting from the insured's negligence. This property may be other vehicles damaged in the accident or other objects such as fences, landscaping, or buildings.

Collision.   This category covers damage sustained by the insured's vehicle in an accident. As a premium reduction measure, collision coverage is often sold with a **deductible** amount, for example, $250 deductible. This means that the insured pays the first $250 in damages for each occurrence and the insurance company pays the amount over $250. As the deductible amount increases, the premium for the insurance decreases.

Comprehensive.   This insurance coverage protects the insured's vehicle for damage caused by fire, wind, water, theft, vandalism, and other perils not caused by an accident.

Most insurance companies also offer policyholders the option of purchasing policy extras such as uninsured motorist's protection and coverage while driving a rented or borrowed car. Some policies even offer to pay towing expenses in the event of a breakdown or cover the cost for a rental car while the insured's vehicle is being repaired after an accident.

Liability rates are based on three primary factors: *who* is driving the vehicle, *where* the vehicle is being driven, and the *amount* of insurance coverage desired. Table 19-6 illustrates typical annual liability premiums for bodily injury and property damage. Note that the rates are listed by driver classification (age, sex, and marital status of the driver), territory (metropolitan area, suburb, small town, rural or farm area), and amount (in thousands of dollars).

Least and Most Expensive Cars to Insure
In a recent year, the least expensive car to insure was the Ford Edge SE (averaging $1,128 per year) and the most expensive ("non-exotic") car to insure was the Mercedes-Benz CL600 (averaging $3,357 per year).

Got You Covered
State rankings of car insurance rates

State	Average rate				
Michigan	$2,484	Arkansas	$1,370		
Louisiana	$2,190	Arizona	$1,356		
Florida	$1,823	Wisconsin	$1,351		
Connecticut	$1,771	New Jersey	$1,346	Minnesota	$1,187
New York	$1,759	Georgia	$1,340	Missouri	$1,154
Kentucky	$1,752	Mississippi	$1,323	Nebraska	$1,113
Nevada	$1,746	North Dakota	$1,315	Alaska	$1,109
DC	$1,723	Texas	$1,300	New Hampshire	$1,101
Rhode Island	$1,688	Alabama	$1,299	South Dakota	$1,059
Delaware	$1,646	Oregon	$1,264	Iowa	$1,015
Oklahoma	$1,643	South Carolina	$1,260	Illinois	$1,004
Pennsylvania	$1,522	New Mexico	$1,253	Virginia	$972
California	$1,518	Kansas	$1,242	Indiana	$964
Wyoming	$1,494	Montana	$1,224	Vermont	$963
Hawaii	$1,458	Tennessee	$1,214	North Carolina	$960
Colorado	$1,404	Utah	$1,199	Ohio	$952
Maryland	$1,390	Washington	$1,191	Idaho	$941
West Virginia	$1,375	Massachusetts	$1,191	Maine	$925

Source: www.carinsurance.com /state-car-insurance-rates/

*Dollar figures shown are an average of insurance rates for a typical car and driver the 2017 model year.

TABLE 19-6 Motor Vehicle Liability Insurance Annual Premiums—Bodily Injury and Property Damage Rates

Territory	Driver Class	Bodily Injury Coverage ($000)					Property Damage Coverage ($000)				
		10/20	15/30	25/50	50/100	100/300	5	10	25	50	100
1	1	$61	$73	$88	$92	$113	$46	$49	$53	$58	$64
	2	63	75	81	94	116	48	51	55	61	66
	3	65	78	84	98	118	52	54	58	63	69
	4	69	81	86	101	121	54	56	60	65	71
2	1	66	75	83	93	114	56	63	68	73	77
	2	69	77	88	98	117	58	64	70	75	79
	3	75	82	92	104	119	59	66	71	76	82
	4	78	86	95	109	122	62	67	73	78	84
3	1	73	77	84	95	116	64	65	72	76	81
	2	78	83	86	99	119	66	69	74	80	83
	3	84	88	92	103	124	70	73	77	82	85
	4	87	93	95	106	128	72	78	81	85	89
4	1	77	81	86	99	118	76	78	83	88	92
	2	81	86	93	103	121	79	83	87	91	95
	3	87	92	100	106	126	80	84	88	93	97
	4	90	94	103	111	132	84	86	91	94	100

Motor vehicle liability coverage is typically stated in a three-number format, such as 50/100/50, with the numbers given in thousands of dollars. The first two numbers, 50/100, refer to the bodily injury portion and means the policy will pay up to $50,000 for bodily injury caused by the insured's vehicle to any one person, with $100,000 maximum per accident regardless of the number of persons injured. The third number, 50 ($50,000), represents the maximum property damage benefits to be paid per single accident.

Table 19-7 illustrates typical collision and comprehensive premiums. Note that these rates are listed according to model class (type of vehicle—compact, luxury, truck, or van), vehicle age, territory (where driven), and the amount of the deductible.

Insurance companies often adjust premiums upward or downward by the use of **rating factors**, which are multiples of the base rates found in the tables. For example, if a vehicle is used for business purposes, the risk of an accident is increased; therefore, a rating factor of, say, 1.5 might be applied to the base rate to adjust for this risk. A $200 base-rate premium would increase to $300, $200 times the rating factor of 1.5. However, a vehicle driven less than 3 miles to work each way would have less chance of having an accident and might have a rating factor of .9 to lower the rate.

rating factors Multiples of the base rates for motor vehicles; used by insurance companies to adjust premiums upward (factors greater than 1) or downward (factors less than 1) depending on the amount of risk involved in the coverage.

STEPS TO CALCULATE TYPICAL MOTOR VEHICLE INSURANCE PREMIUMS

STEP 1. Use Table 19-6 to find the appropriate base premiums for bodily injury and property damage.

STEP 2. Use Table 19-7 to find the appropriate base premiums for collision and comprehensive.

STEP 3. Add all the individual premiums to find the total base premium.

STEP 4. Multiply the total base premium by the rating factor, if any.

Total annual premium = Total base premium × Rating factor

TABLE 19-7 Motor Vehicle Insurance Annual Premiums—Collision and Comprehensive Rates

| Model Class | Vehicle Age | Territories 1 and 2 | | | | Territories 3 and 4 | | | |
| | | Collision | | Comprehensive | | Collision | | Comprehensive | |
		$250 Deductible	$500 Deductible	Full Coverage	$100 Deductible	$250 Deductible	$500 Deductible	Full Coverage	$100 Deductible
A–G	0–1	$89	$81	$63	$59	$95	$88	$67	$61
	2–3	87	79	60	57	93	84	63	58
	4–5	86	77	58	54	89	81	60	57
	6+	84	76	55	50	86	78	57	52
H–L	0–1	96	92	78	71	104	95	83	75
	2–3	93	89	76	68	101	90	80	72
	4–5	89	85	74	66	96	87	78	68
	6+	86	81	70	64	92	84	74	66
M–R	0–1	108	104	86	83	112	106	91	88
	2–3	104	101	83	79	109	104	88	82
	4–5	100	98	79	75	104	101	84	77
	6+	94	90	75	71	100	96	80	74
S–Z	0–1	120	115	111	108	124	116	119	113
	2–3	116	112	106	104	121	114	115	109
	4–5	111	107	101	99	116	110	111	106
	6+	108	103	98	96	111	107	108	101

EXAMPLE9 CALCULATING MOTOR VEHICLE PREMIUMS

Michelle Hiland wants to purchase a motor vehicle insurance policy with bodily injury and property damage coverage in the amounts of 25/50/25. In addition, she wants collision coverage with $500 deductible and comprehensive with no deductible. Michelle is in driver classification 3 and lives in territory 1. Her vehicle, a Toyota Prius, is in model class P and is 3 years old. Because she has taken driver training classes, Michelle qualifies for a .95 rating factor. As Michelle's insurance agent, calculate her total annual premium.

▶SOLUTIONSTRATEGY

Step 1.   From Table 19-6, we find the bodily injury premium to be $84 and the property damage premium to be $58.

Step 2.   From Table 19-7, we find collision to be $101 and comprehensive to be $83.

Step 3.   Total base premium = Bodily injury + Property damage + Collision + Comprehensive
Total base premium = 84 + 58 + 101 + 83 = $326

Step 4.   Total annual premium = Total base premium × Rating factor
Total annual premium = 326 × .95 = $309.70

▶TRYITEXERCISE 9

Jeff Wasserman, owner of High Performance Racing Equipment, wants to purchase truck insurance with bodily injury and property damage coverage in the amounts of 100/300/100. Jeff also wants $250 deductible collision and $100 deductible comprehensive. He is in driver classification 4 and lives in territory 3. His vehicle, a Ford F-150, is in model class F and is 4 years old. Because Jeff uses his truck to make trackside calls and haul cars to his shop, the insurance company has assigned a 2.3 rating factor to his policy. What is Jeff's total annual premium?

CHECK YOUR ANSWERS WITH THE SOLUTIONS ON PAGE 680.

IN THE Business World

Many insurance companies give money-saving *rating factor* discounts to students who have good grade point averages, usually over 3.0 out of 4.0, or safe-driving records—without tickets or accidents.

rtguest/Shutterstock.com

COMPUTING THE COMPENSATION DUE FOLLOWING AN ACCIDENT

When the insured is involved in a motor vehicle accident in which he or she is at fault, his or her insurance company must pay out the claims resulting from that accident. Any amounts of bodily injury or property damage that exceed the limits of the policy coverage are the responsibility of the insured.

EXAMPLE10 CALCULATING ACCIDENT COMPENSATION

Bill Strickland has motor vehicle insurance in the following amounts: liability, 15/30/5; $500 deductible collision; and $100 deductible comprehensive. Recently, Bill was at fault in an accident in which his van hit a car stopped at a traffic light. Two individuals in the other vehicle, Angel and Martha Diaz, were injured. Angel's bodily injuries amounted to $6,300, whereas Martha's more serious injuries totaled $18,400. In addition, their car sustained $6,250 in damages. Although Bill was not physically injured, the damage to his van amounted to $4,788.

a. How much will the insurance company have to pay and to whom?

b. What part of the settlement will be Bill's responsibility?

▶SOLUTIONSTRATEGY

Liability Portion:

Bill's liability coverage is limited to $15,000 per person. The insurance company will pay the $6,300 for Angel's injuries; however, Bill is responsible for Martha's expenses above the limit.

$18,400	Martha's medical expenses
−15,000	Insurance limit—bodily injury
$3,400	Bill's responsibility

Property Damage Portion:

The property damage limit of $5,000 is not sufficient to cover the damage to Angel's car. Bill will have to pay the portion above the limit.

$6,250	Angel's car repairs
−5,000	Insurance limit—property damage
$1,250	Bill's responsibility

The damage to Bill's van will be paid by the insurance company, except for the $500 deductible.

$4,788	Bill's van repairs
−500	Deductible
$4,288	Insurance company responsibility

▶TRYITEXERCISE 10

Jody Burnett has automobile liability insurance in the amount of 25/50/10 and carries $250 deductible collision and full-coverage comprehensive. Recently, Jody was at fault in an accident in which her Nissan went out of control on a rainy day and hit two cars, a fence, and the side of a house. The first car, a Lexus, had $8,240 in damages. The second car, a Ford Taurus, sustained damages of $2,540. The repairs to Jody's car amounted to $3,542. In addition, the fence repairs came to $880 and the house damages were estimated at $5,320.

a. How much will the insurance company have to pay and to whom?

b. What part of the settlement will be Jody's responsibility?

CHECK YOUR ANSWERS WITH THE SOLUTIONS ON PAGE 680.

As an insurance agent, calculate the annual premium for the following clients.

Name	Territory	Driver Class	Bodily Injury	Property Damage	Model Class	Vehicle Age	Comprehensive Deductible	Collision Deductible	Rating Factor	Annual Premium
1. Schwartz	2	4	50/100	25	J	3	$100	$250	None	$343.00
2. Mager	1	2	10/20	10	R	1	Full Coverage	$500	1.5	
3. Almas	3	1	25/50	5	U	5	Full Coverage	$250	3.0	
4. Denner	2	3	100/300	25	C	4	$100	$250	None	
5. Nadler	4	2	50/100	100	H	2	Full Coverage	$500	1.7	
6. Fisk	1	4	15/30	50	M	4	$100	$250	2.2	
7. Hale	2	1	10/20	10	Q	6	$100	$250	3.9	

8. Robert wishes to obtain auto insurance. He wants 10/20/5 liability coverage, $250 deductible collision, and $100 deductible comprehensive.

He lives in territory 3 and has been assigned to driver class 3 with a rating factor of 1.95.

Based on Tables 19-6 and 19-7 what would be his total premium, if his 5-year old car is in model class X?

Round your answer to the nearest cent.

9. Rick Clinton wants to purchase an automobile insurance policy with bodily injury and property damage coverage in the amounts of 50/100/50. In addition, he wants collision coverage with $250 deductible and comprehensive with no deductible. Rick is in driver classification 4 and lives in territory 3. His vehicle, a Buick Regal, is in model class B and is 1 year old. Rick has had two accidents and one ticket in the past 12 months and is therefore considered to be a high risk. Consequently, the insurance company has assigned a rating factor of 4.0 to his policy. As Rick's automobile insurance agent, calculate the total annual premium for his policy.

10. Howard Marshall's Corvette was hit by a palm tree during a hurricane. The damage was estimated at $1,544. If Howard carried $250 deductible collision and $100 deductible comprehensive, how much of the damages does the insurance company have to pay?

11. Juanita was involved in an auto accident in which she was at fault. Her own car sustained $1,236 damages and the other vehicle cost $1,500 to repair.

Juanita was not injured, but the driver of the other car required medical treatment costing $17,604 and a passenger's injuries totalled $11,993.

Juanita's policy includes 10/20/5 liability, $500 deductible collision and $100 deductible comprehensive. How much of the damages must Juanita pay?

12. Ben Hoffman has motor vehicle liability insurance in the amount of 50/100/50 and carries $250 deductible collision coverage and full-coverage comprehensive. Recently, he was at fault in an accident in which his camper hit a bus. Five individuals were injured on the bus and were awarded the following settlements by the courts: Hart, $13,500; Black, $11,700; Garner, $4,140; Williams, $57,800; and Morgan, $3,590. The damage to the bus was $12,230, and Ben's camper sustained $3,780 in damages.

    a. How much will the insurance company have to pay and to whom?

    b. What part of the settlement will be Ben's responsibility?

BUSINESS DECISION: INSURING THE FLEET

13. The Flamingo Cab Company of Cougar Creek is interested in purchasing $250 deductible collision insurance and full-coverage comprehensive insurance to cover its fleet of 10 taxicabs. As a requirement for the job, all drivers already carry their own liability coverage in the amount of 100/300/100. Cougar Creek is rated as territory 2. Five of the cabs are 4-year-old Checker Towncars, model class Y. Three of them are 2-year-old Chrysler station wagons, model class R. The remaining two are new Buick sedans, model class C. Because the vehicles are on the road almost 24 hours a day, they are considered to be very high risk and carry a rating factor of 5.2. They are, however, subject to an 18% multi-vehicle fleet discount.

    a. As the insurance agent for Flamingo Cabs, calculate the total annual premium for the fleet.

    b. When the owner saw your rate quote, he exclaimed, "Too expensive! How can I save some money on this insurance?" At that point, you suggested changing the coverage to $500 deductible collision and $100 deductible comprehensive. How much can you save Flamingo by using the new coverage?

CHAPTER 19

CHAPTER FORMULAS

Life Insurance

$$\text{Number of } \$1{,}000 = \frac{\text{Face value of policy}}{1{,}000}$$

$$\text{Annual premium} = \text{Number of } \$1{,}000 \times \text{Rate per } \$1{,}000$$

$$\text{Premium other than annual} = \text{Annual premium} \times \text{Premium factor}$$

$$\text{Income shortfall} = \text{Total living expenses} - \text{Total income}$$

$$\text{Insurance needed} = \frac{\text{Income shortfall}}{\text{Prevailing interest rate}}$$

Property Insurance

$$\text{Total annual fire premium} = \text{Building premium} + \text{Contents premium}$$

$$\text{Short-rate premium} = \text{Annual premium} \times \text{Short-rate}$$

$$\text{Short-rate refund} = \text{Annual premium} - \text{Short-rate premium}$$

$$\text{Regular refund} = \text{Annual premium} - \text{Premium for period}$$

$$\text{Coverage ratio} = \frac{\text{Insurance carried}}{\text{Insurance required}}$$

$$\text{Insurance required} = \text{Replacement value of property} \times \text{Coinsurance percent}$$

$$\text{Amount of loss paid by insurance} = \frac{\text{Insurance carried}}{\text{Insurance required}} \times \text{Amount of loss}$$

$$\text{Carrier's percent of total coverage} = \frac{\text{Amount of carrier's policy}}{\text{Total amount of insurance}}$$

$$\text{Carrier's share of loss} = \text{Amount of loss} \times \text{Carrier's percent of total coverage}$$

CHAPTER SUMMARY

Section I: Life Insurance

Topic	Important Concepts	Illustrative Examples
Understanding Life Insurance and Calculating Typical Premiums for Various Types of Policies **Performance Objective 19-1, Page 652**	Life insurance guarantees a specified sum of money to the surviving beneficiaries upon the death of the insured. It is purchased in increments of $1,000. Calculating premiums: 1. Calculate the number of $1,000 of insurance desired by dividing the face value of the policy by $1,000. 2. Locate the appropriate premium rate per $1,000 in Table 19-1. 3. Calculate the total annual premium by multiplying the number of $1,000 by the Table 19-1 rate. 4. For premiums other than annual, multiply the annual premium by the appropriate Table 19-2 premium factor.	Chelsea Anderson is 20 years old. She is interested in purchasing a 20-payment life insurance policy with a face value of $25,000. Calculate her annual and monthly premium. $\text{Number of } \$1{,}000 = \dfrac{25{,}000}{1{,}000} = 25$ Table 19-1 rate = $21.50 Annual premium = 25 × 21.50 = $537.50 Monthly premium = 537.50 × 9% = $48.38

Section I (continued)

Topic	Important Concepts	Illustrative Examples

Calculating the Value of Various Nonforfeiture Options
 	
Performance Objective 19-2, Page 655
	Life insurance policies with accumulated cash value may be converted to one of three nonforfeiture options.
	    Use Table 19-3 and the number of $1,000 of insurance to determine the value of each option.
	    Option 1—Take the cash value of the policy and cancel the insurance coverage.
	    Option 2—Reduced, paid-up amount of the same insurance.
	    Option 3—Term policy for a certain number of years and days, with the same face value as the original policy.
		Betty Price, 30 years old, purchased a $50,000 whole life insurance policy at age 20. What is the value of her nonforfeiture options?
		
		Number of $1,000 = $\dfrac{50,000}{1,000}$ = 50
		
		Option 1: 50 × $98 = $4,900 Cash
		
		Option 2: 50 × $186 =
		    $9,300 Reduced Paid-Up Insurance
		
		Option 3: 17 years, 54 days Term Policy

Calculating the Amount of Life Insurance Needed to Cover Dependents' Income Shortfall **Performance Objective 19-3, Page 657**	When one of the wage earners in a household dies, the annual living expenses of the dependents may exceed the annual income. This difference is known as the income shortfall. To calculate the amount of insurance needed to cover the shortfall, use	With a prevailing interest rate of 5%, how much life insurance will be needed to cover dependents' income shortfall if the annual living expenses amount to $37,600 and the total income is $21,200? Income shortfall = 37,600 − 21,200 = $16,400 Insurance needed at 5% = $\dfrac{16,400}{.05}$ = $328,000

Section II: Property Insurance

Topic	Important Concepts	Illustrative Examples
Understanding Property Insurance and Calculating Typical Fire Insurance Premiums **Performance Objective 19-4, Page 661**	Fire insurance premiums are based on type of construction, location of the property, and availability of fire protection. Fire insurance premiums are quoted per $100 of coverage, with buildings and contents listed separately. Use Table 19-4 to calculate fire insurance premiums:	What is the total annual fire insurance premium on a building valued at $120,000 with structural class C and area rating 3 and contents valued at $400,000? Building: 1,200 × .69 = $828 Contents: 4,000 × .77 = $3,080 Total annual fire premium = 828 + 3,080 = $3,908
Calculating Premiums for Short-Term Policies and the Refunds Due on Canceled Policies **Performance Objective 19-5, Page 663**	Fire policies for less than 1 year are known as short-rate. Use Table 19-5 for these policies. a. Short-rate refund (Policy canceled by insured): b. Regular refund (Policy canceled by insurance company):	The Evergreen Company has property insurance with State Farm. The annual premium is $3,000. a. If Evergreen cancels the policy after 2 months, what is the short-rate refund? b. If State Farm cancels the policy after 2 months, what is the regular refund? a. Short-rate refund Short-rate premium = 3,000 × 30% = $900 Short-rate refund = 3,000 − 900 = $2,100 b. Regular refund Time in force premium = 3,000 × $\dfrac{2}{12}$ = $500 Regular refund = 3,000 − 500 = $2,500

Section II (continued)

Topic	Important Concepts	Illustrative Examples
Understanding Coinsurance and Computing Compensation Due in the Event of a Loss **Performance Objective 19-6, Page 665**	A coinsurance clause stipulates the minimum amount of coverage required for a claim to be paid in full. If less than the coinsurance requirement is carried, the payout is proportionately less.	Metro Holdings, Inc., has a $150,000 fire insurance policy on a property valued at $250,000. If the policy has an 80% coinsurance clause, how much would be paid in the event of a $50,000 fire? Insurance required = 250,000 × 80% = $200,000 Amount of loss paid = $\frac{150,000}{200,000} \times 50,000 = \underline{\$37,500}$
Determining Each Company's Share of a Loss When Liability Is Divided among Multiple Carriers **Performance Objective 19-7, Page 666**	When more than one insurance company covers a piece of property, the property has multiple carriers. In the event of a claim, each company is responsible for its portion of the total insurance carried.	Lorenzo's Italian Market has multiple carrier fire insurance on its property as follows: Southwest Mutual .... $300,000 Travelers .... 100,000 　　　　　Total .... $400,000 Assuming that all coinsurance requirements have been met, how much will each carrier be responsible for in the event of a $20,000 fire? Southwest Mutual: $\frac{300,000}{400,000} \times 20,000 = \underline{\$15,000}$ Travelers: $\frac{100,000}{400,000} \times 20,000 = \underline{\$5,000}$

Section III: Motor Vehicle Insurance

Topic	Important Concepts	Illustrative Examples
Understanding Motor Vehicle Insurance and Calculating Typical Premiums **Performance Objective 19-8, Page 670**	Motor vehicle insurance is divided into three main categories: Liability—Covers bodily injury and property damage to others. Use Table 19-6 for these rates. Collision—Covers damage to the insured's vehicle from an auto accident. Use Table 19-7. Comprehensive—Covers damage to the insured's vehicle from fire, wind, water, vandalism, theft, and so on. Use Table 19-7. Rates may be adjusted up or down by multiplying the total table rate by a rating factor.	Casey Roberts wants auto liability coverage of 25/50/25, $250 deductible collision, and $100 deductible comprehensive. She is in driver class 2 and lives in territory 3. Her vehicle, a new SL 500, is in model class L and has a sports car rating factor of 1.7. What is Casey's total auto premium? 　$86　Bodily injury　　Table 19-6 　　74　Property damage　Table 19-6 　104　Collision　　　　Table 19-7 　+ 75　Comprehensive　Table 19-7 　$339　Total base 　× 1.7　Rating factor $576.30　Total premium
Computing the Compensation Due Following an Accident **Performance Objective 19-9, Page 673**	When the policyholder is at fault in an accident, his or her insurance company is responsible for all settlements up to the limits and deductibles of the policy. Any settlement amounts greater than the policy coverage are the responsibility of the insured.	Warner Bouton has auto liability coverage of 50/100/50, no deductible comprehensive, and $250 deductible collision. Recently, Warner ran a red light and broadsided Sylvia Norton's car. 　In the court settlement, Sylvia was awarded $75,000 for bodily injury and $14,500 in property damages. Warner's car sustained $7,500 in damages. How much is the insurance company responsible for paying? 　How much of the settlement is Warner's responsibility?

Topic	Important Concepts	Illustrative Examples

		Liability:
		   Warner's policy limit for bodily injury liability is $50,000.
		
		   $75,000 Court settlement
		  −50,000 Paid by insurance
		  $25,000 Paid by Warner
		
		The policy limit for property damage is $50,000; therefore, the insurance company will pay the full $14,500.
		
		Collision:
		
		  $7,500 Collision damage
		  − 250 Deductible
		  $7,250 Paid by insurance

Try It: Exercise Solutions for Chapter 19

1. Number of $1,000 = $\dfrac{\text{Face value of policy}}{1,000}$

Number of $1,000 = $\dfrac{75,000}{1000} = 75$

Table 19-1 rate = $4.92 per $1,000

Annual premium = Number of $1,000 × Rate per $1,000
Annual premium = 75 × 4.92 = $369

Quarterly premium = Annual premium × Quarterly factor
Quarterly premium = 369 × .26 = $95.94

Total payment = Quarterly payment × 4 payments
Total payment = 95.94 × 4 = $383.76
Jason will pay $14.76 (383.76 − 369) more if paid quarterly.

2. Number of $1,000 = $\dfrac{\text{Face value of policy}}{1,000} = \dfrac{100,000}{1,000} = 100$

Option 1:
Cash Value = 100 × 191 = $19,100

Option 2:
Reduced Paid-Up Insurance = 100 × 496 = $49,600

Option 3:
Extended Term Insurance = 30 years, 206 days

3. Total income = 38,000 + 5,000 = $43,000

Income shortfall = Total expenses − Total income
Income shortfall = 54,000 − 43,000 = $11,000

Insurance needed = $\dfrac{\text{Shortfall}}{\text{Prevailing rate}}$

Insurance needed = $\dfrac{11,000}{.05} = \$220,000$

4. From Table 19-4
   Building: .38
   Contents: .42

Building = $\dfrac{\text{Amount of coverage}}{100} = \dfrac{420,000}{100} = 4,200$

Contents = $\dfrac{\text{Amount of coverage}}{100} = \dfrac{685,000}{100} = 6,850$

Building = Number of $100 × Rate = 4,200 × .38 = $1,596
Contents = Number of $100 × Rate = 6,850 × .42 = $2,877

Total premium = Building + Contents
Total premium = 1,596 + 2,877 = $4,473

5. From Table 19-5, 8 months = 80%
Short-rate premium = Annual premium × Short-rate
Short-rate premium = 850 × .8 = $680
Short-rate refund = Annual premium − Short-rate premium
Short-rate refund = 850 − 680 = $170

6. Premium for period = Annual premium × $\dfrac{\text{Months in force}}{12}$

Premium for period = 850 × $\dfrac{8}{12}$ = $566.67

Regular refund = Annual premium − Premium for period
Regular refund = 850.00 − 566.67 = $283.33

7. Insurance required = Value of property × Coinsurance percent
Insurance required = 850,000 × .7 = $595,000

Amount of loss paid = $\dfrac{\text{Insurance carried}}{\text{Insurance required}}$ × Loss

Amount of loss paid = $\dfrac{400,000}{595,000}$ × 325,000 = $218,487.40

8. Carrier's percent of total $= \dfrac{\text{Amount of carrier's policy}}{\text{Total amount of insurance}}$

$$\text{Aetna} = \dfrac{20,000}{125,000} = 16\%$$

$$\text{USF\&G} = \dfrac{45,000}{125,000} = 36\%$$

$$\text{John Hancock} = \dfrac{60,000}{125,000} = 48\%$$

Carrier's share of loss $=$ Amount of loss $\times$ Carrier's percent

$$\text{Aetna} = 16,800 \times .16 = \underline{\$2,688}$$
$$\text{SF\&G} = 16,800 \times .36 = \underline{\$6,048}$$
$$\text{John Hancock} = 16,800 \times .48 = \underline{\$8,064}$$

9. Base premium = Bodily injury + Property damage + Collision + Comprehensive

Base premium $= 128 + 89 + 89 + 57 = \underline{\$363}$

Total annual premium = Base premium $\times$ Rating factor

Total annual premium $= 363 \times 2.3 = \underline{\$834.90}$

10.

a. Insurance Pays	
$10,000	Property damage
+ 3,292	Jody's car *less* deductible
$13,292	Total insurance responsibility

b. Jody Pays	
$8,240	Lexus
2,540	Taurus
880	Fence
+ 5,320	House
16,980	Total property damage
−10,000	Insurance
$6,980	Jody's portion
+ 250	Collision deductible
$7,230	Jody's responsibility

Concept Review

1. A mechanism for reducing financial risk and spreading financial loss due to unexpected events is known as _____. The document stipulating the terms of this agreement is known as a(n) _____. (19-1)

2. The amount of protection provided by an insurance policy is known as the _____ value. The amount paid to purchase the protection is known as the _____. The _____ is the person or institution to whom the proceeds of the policy are paid in the event that a loss occurs. (19-1)

3. Name the two major categories of life insurance. (19-1)

4. The _____ factor is a small surcharge added to the cost of insurance policies when the insured chooses to pay the premiums more frequently than annually. (19-1)

5. The options available to a policyholder upon termination of a permanent life insurance policy with accumulated cash value are known as the _____ options. List these three options. (19-2)

6. The difference between the total living expenses and the total income of a family in the event of the death of the insured is known as the income _____ . Write the formula used to calculate the amount of life insurance needed to cover this difference. (19-3)

7. List four perils covered by property insurance. (19-4)

8. List the four factors used to determine the fire insurance rates on a building. (19-4)

9. The premium charged when a policy is canceled by the insured or is written for less than one year is known as the _____. (19-5)

10. The clause in a property insurance policy stipulating the minimum amount of coverage required for a claim to be paid in full is known as the _____ clause. (19-6)

11. Write the coverage ratio formula used in calculating property insurance rates. (19-6)

12. A situation in which a business is covered by fire insurance policies from more than one company at the same time is known as _____ carriers. (19-7)

13. In motor vehicle insurance, _____ covers bodily injury to other persons and damages to the property of others resulting from the insured's negligence; _____ covers accident damage to the insured's vehicle; and _____ covers the insured's vehicle for damage caused by fire, wind, water, theft, vandalism, and other perils. (19-8, 19-9)

14. In motor vehicle insurance, companies often use _____ factors to adjust premiums upward or downward depending on the amount of the risk involved in the coverage. (19-8, 19-9)

ASSESSMENT TEST

Calculate the annual, semiannual, quarterly, and monthly premiums for the following life insurance policies.

	Face Value of Policy	Sex and Age of Insured	Type of Policy	Annual Premium	Semiannual Premium	Quarterly Premium	Monthly Premium
1.	$80,000	Male, 29	20-Payment Life				
2.	$55,000	Female, 21	20-Year Endowment				
3.	$140,000	Female, 40	5-Year Term				
4.	$175,000	Male, 30	Whole Life				

Calculate the value of the nonforfeiture options for the following life insurance policies.

	Face Value of Policy	Years in Force	Type of Policy	Cash Value	Reduced Paid-Up Insurance	Extended Term Years	Extended Term Days
5.	$130,000	15	Whole Life				
6.	$60,000	5	20-Payment Life				

7. Tommy Cook is 19 years old and is interested in purchasing a whole life insurance policy with a face value of $80,000.

   a. Calculate the annual insurance premium for this policy.

   b. Calculate the monthly insurance premiums.

   c. How much more will Tommy pay per year if he chooses monthly payments?

8. Mary Hall purchased a $45,000 20-year endowment life insurance policy when she was 20 years old. She is now 35 years old and wants to look into her nonforfeiture options. As her insurance agent, calculate the value of Mary's three options.

   a. Option 1   b. Option 2

   c. Option 3

9. Joe Moutran is evaluating his life insurance needs. His family's total annual living expenses are $54,500. Gloria, his wife, earns a salary of $28,900 per year. If the prevailing interest rate is 4%, how much life insurance should Joe purchase to cover his dependents' income shortfall in the event of his death?

Calculate the building, contents, and total property insurance premiums for the following property insurance policies.

	Area Rating	Structural Class	Building Value	Building Premium	Contents Value	Contents Premium	Total Premium
10.	4	B	$47,000		$93,000		
11.	2	A	$125,000		$160,000		
12.	3	C	$980,000		$1,500,000		

CHAPTER
19

Calculate the short-term premium and refund for the following policies.

	Annual Premium	Canceled After	Canceled By	Short-Term Premium	Refund
13.	$260	8 months	insurance company		
14.	$1,440	20 days	insured		

Calculate the amount to be paid by the insurance company for each of the following claims.

	Replacement Value of Building	Face Value of Policy	Coinsurance Clause (%)	Amount of Loss	Amount of Loss Insurance Company Will Pay
15.	$260,000	$105,000	80	$12,000	
16.	$490,000	$450,000	90	$80,000	

17. You are the insurance agent for Fandango Fashions, a company that imports men's and women's clothing from Europe and the Far East. The owner, Ron Harris, wants you to give him a quote on the total annual premium for property insurance on a new warehouse and showroom facility in the amount of $320,000. The building is structural classification B and area rating 4. In addition, Ron will require contents insurance in the amount of $1,200,000. What is the amount of the quote you will give Ron for the total annual premium?

18. "Movers of the Stars" has been contracted by Premier Events, Inc., to transport the stage and sound equipment for a 4-month tour by Lady Gaga. The moving company purchased property insurance to cover this valuable equipment for an annual premium of $12,500. What is the short-rate premium due for this coverage?

19. La Belle Beauty Supply had property valued at $750,000 and insured for $600,000. The fire insurance policy contained an 80% coinsurance clause. One evening an electrical short circuit caused a $153,000 fire. How much of the damages will be paid by the insurance company?

20. Pinnacle Manufacturing has multiple carrier fire insurance coverage on its plant and equipment in the amount of $2,960,000 as follows:

Kemper $1,350,000 policy
Metropolitan   921,000 policy
The Hartford   689,000 policy
                $2,960,000 total coverage

Assuming that all coinsurance clause stipulations have been met, how much would each carrier be responsible for in the event of a $430,000 fire? Round to the nearest whole percent before using them in your final calculations.

a. Kemper   b. Metropolitan   c. The Hartford

As an insurance agent, calculate the annual premium for the following clients.

Name	Territory	Driver Class	Bodily Injury	Property Damage	Model Class	Vehicle Age	Comprehensive Deductible	Collision Deductible	Rating Factor	Annual Premium
21. Reeves	3	2	50/100	25	X	1	$100	$500	0.9	
22. Chang	1	1	10/20	5	Q	4	Full Coverage	$250	2.2	
23. Lerner	2	4	100/300	100	F	7	$100	$500	1.7	

24. Karen Doyle wants to purchase an automobile insurance policy with bodily injury and property damage coverage in the amounts of 25/50/25. In addition, she wants collision coverage with $250 deductible and comprehensive with $100 deductible. Karen is in driver classification 2 and lives in territory 3. Her vehicle, a new Ford Mustang, is in model class B. Because the car has an airbag, an alarm, and antilock brakes, the insurance company has assigned a rating factor of .95 to the policy. As her auto insurance agent, calculate Karen's total annual premium.

25. Sid King has automobile liability insurance in the amount of 50/100/50. He also carries $250 deductible collision and full comprehensive coverage. Recently, he was at fault in an accident in which his car went out of control in the rain and struck four pedestrians. In an out-of-court settlement, they were awarded the following: Goya, $45,000; Truman, $68,000; Copeland, $16,000; and Kelly, $11,000. Damage to Sid's car amounted to $3,900.

   a. How much will the insurance company pay and to whom?

   b. What part of the settlement will be Sid's responsibility?

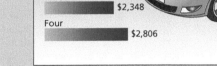

How crashes affect auto premiums
Average annual auto insurance premiums rise with each at-fault traffic accident:

No accidents $1,387
One $1,689
Two $2,041
Three $2,348
Four $2,806

Source: Insurance.com study By Ann Carey and Keith Simmons, USA Today

BUSINESS DECISION: GROUP INSURANCE

26. Many employers purchase group insurance on behalf of their employees. Under a group insurance plan, a master contract issued to the company provides life insurance, health insurance, or both for the employees who choose to participate. Most plans also provide coverage for dependents of employees. The two major benefits of group plans are lower premiums than individual insurance of the same coverage and no medical exams.

   You are the owner of Imperial Products, Inc., a small manufacturing company with 250 employees. The company has just instituted a group health insurance plan for employees. Under the plan, the employees pay 30% of the premium and the company pays 70%. The insurance company reimburses 80% of all medical expenses over the deductible. The annual rates and deductibles from the insurance company are as follows:

	Annual Premium	Deductible
Employee with no dependents	$1,200	$300
Employee with one dependent	$1,400	$500
Employee with multiple dependents	$1,800	$800

   a. If all 250 employees opt for the group health plan, what is the annual cost to the company assuming the following: 100 employees have no dependents, 80 employees have one dependent, and 70 employees have multiple dependents?

b. If your employees are paid biweekly, how much should be deducted from each paycheck for each of the three categories?

c. If Mert Wetstein, one of the employees, chooses the multiple dependent option and has a total of $3,400 in medical bills for the year, how much will be reimbursed by the insurance company?

COLLABORATIVE LEARNING ACTIVITY

Insurance for Sweetie Pie

As a team, you and your partners are going to start a hypothetical company called The Sweetie Pie Bakery, a company that makes and distributes pies, cakes, cookies, and doughnuts to restaurants and food stores in your area.

The company will have property and a building valued at $300,000, baking and production-line equipment valued at $400,000, office equipment and fixtures worth $200,000, and four delivery trucks valued at $45,000 each. The expected revenue is $50,000 per month. There will be 18 employees and 4 partners, including you.

Each team member is to consult with a different insurance agent to put together a "package" of business insurance coverage for Sweetie Pie, including property insurance, liability insurance, and business interruption insurance.

In addition, look into a health insurance program for the partners and the employees, as well as $500,000 "key man" life insurance for each partner.

a. Compare and contrast the various insurance packages quoted for Sweetie Pie.
b. Which insurance company came up with the best package? Why?
c. What other types of coverage did the insurance agents recommend?

CHAPTER 20 Investments

PERFORMANCE OBJECTIVES

financial risk The chance you take of making or losing money on an investment.

conservative investments Low-risk investments such as government bonds and certificates of deposit.

speculative investments High-risk investments such as stocks in new companies, junk bonds, and options and futures.

diversified portfolio An investment strategy that is a mixture of stocks, bonds, cash equivalents, and other types of investments.

stocks, or **equities** An investment that is an ownership share of a corporation.

Financial risk is the chance you take of making or losing money on an investment. In most cases, the greater the risk, the more money you stand to gain or lose. Investment opportunities range from low-risk **conservative investments** such as government bonds and certificates of deposit to high-risk **speculative investments** such as stocks in new companies, junk bonds, and options and futures. Selecting the right investment depends on personal circumstances as well as general market conditions. (See Exhibit 20-1.)

Investments are based on *liquidity*, which indicates how easy it is to get your money out; *safety*, how much risk is involved; and *return*, how much you can expect to earn. Investment advice is available from stockbrokers, financial planners, and many other sources. It is generally agreed that over the long run, a **diversified portfolio**, with a mixture of stocks, bonds, cash equivalents, and sometimes other types of investments, is a sensible choice. Determining the correct portfolio mix is a decision that should be based on the amount of assets available, the age of the investor, and the amount of risk desired.

In this chapter, we investigate three major categories of investments: **stocks**, also known as **equities**, which represent an *ownership share* of a corporation; bonds, or debt, which represent IOUs for money borrowed from the investor; and mutual funds, which are investment *pools* of money with a wide variety of investment goals.

20-1 UNDERSTANDING STOCKS AND DISTRIBUTING DIVIDENDS ON PREFERRED AND COMMON STOCK

shares Units of stock or ownership in a corporation.

stock certificate The official document that represents an ownership share in a corporation.

shareholder The person who owns shares of stock in a corporation.

dividends A distribution of a company's profits to its shareholders.

publicly held corporations Corporations whose stock is available to be bought and sold by the general investing public. The opposite of privately held corporations.

Corporations are built and expanded with money known as capital, which is raised by issuing and selling **shares** of stock. Investors' ownership in a company is measured by the number of shares they own. Each ownership portion, or share, is represented by a **stock certificate**. In the past, these certificates were sent to the investor, confirming the stock purchase transaction. Today, however, this confirmation comes in the form of a computerized book entry on an account statement. Exhibit 20-2 is an example of a stock certificate from many years ago.

Generally, if the company does well, the investor or **shareholder** will receive **dividends**, which are a distribution of the company's profits. If the share price goes up, the stockholder can sell the stock at a profit. Today more than 50 million persons in the United States own stock in thousands of **publicly held corporations**.

Many companies offer two classes of stock to appeal to different types of investors. These classes are known as common and preferred. With **common stock**, an investor shares directly

EXHIBIT 20-1
Risk vs. Return

Dollars AND Sense

History has demonstrated repeatedly that a well-diversified portfolio of investments based on careful planning and a focused strategy reduces risk and provides an opportunity for solid returns.

Changing investments too frequently—overreacting to daily economic data or the latest Wall Street fads—can distract investors from reaching their specific goals.

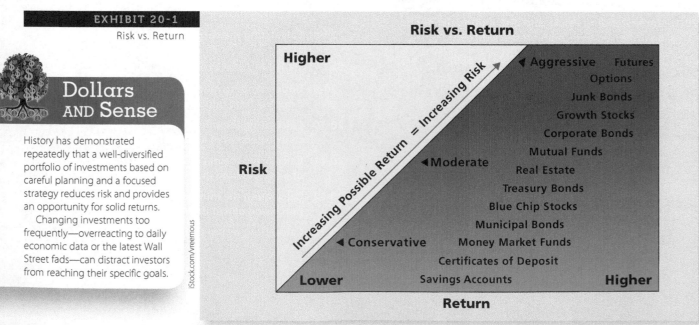

Risk vs. Return

Higher — Aggressive — Futures, Options, Junk Bonds, Growth Stocks, Corporate Bonds, Mutual Funds

Moderate — Real Estate, Treasury Bonds, Blue Chip Stocks, Municipal Bonds

Conservative — Money Market Funds, Certificates of Deposit, Savings Accounts

Increasing Possible Return = Increasing Risk

Risk: Lower / Higher
Return: Lower / Higher

EXHIBIT 20-2 Stock certificate from many years ago

in the success or failure of the business. When the company does well, the dividends and price of the stock may rise and the investors make money. When the company does poorly, it does not pay dividends and the price of the stock may fall.

With **preferred stock**, the dividends are fixed regardless of how the company is doing. When the board of directors of a company declares a dividend, the preferred stockholders are paid before the common. If the company goes out of business, the preferred stockholders have priority over the common as far as possibly getting back some of their investment.

Preferred stock is issued with or without a **par value**. When the stock has a par value, the dividend is specified as a percent of par. For example, each share of 8%, $100 par value preferred stock pays a dividend of $8 per share ($100 × .08$) per year. The dividend is usually paid on a quarterly basis, in this case, $2 each quarter. When preferred stock is **no-par value**, the dividend is stated as a dollar amount.

Cumulative preferred stock receives a dividend each year. When no dividends are paid one year, the amount owed, known as **dividends in arrears**, accumulates. Common stockholders cannot receive any dividends until all the dividends in arrears have been paid to cumulative preferred stockholders.

Preferred stock is further divided into categories known as nonparticipating, which means the stockholders receive only the fixed dividend and no more, and participating, which means the stockholders may receive additional dividends if the company does well. Convertible preferred means the stock may be exchanged for a specified number of common shares in the future.

common stock A class of corporate stock in which the investor has voting rights and shares directly in the success or failure of the business.

preferred stock A class of corporate stock in which the investor has preferential rights over the common shareholders to dividends and a company's assets.

par value An arbitrary monetary figure specified in the corporate charter for each share of stock and printed on each stock certificate. The dividend for par value preferred stock is quoted as a percent of the par value.

no-par value Refers to stock that does not have a par value. The dividend for no-par value preferred stock is quoted as a dollar amount per share.

cumulative preferred stock A type of preferred stock that receives a dividend each year. When no dividends are paid one year, the amount owed accumulates and must be paid to cumulative preferred shareholders before any dividends can be paid to common shareholders.

dividends in arrears The amount of dividends that accumulate and are owed to cumulative preferred shareholders for past years in which no dividends were paid.

STEPS TO DISTRIBUTE DIVIDENDS ON PREFERRED AND COMMON STOCK

STEP 1. If the preferred stock is *cumulative*, any dividends that are in arrears are paid first; then the preferred dividend is paid for the current period. When the dividend per share is stated in dollars (no-par stock), go to Step 2. When the dividend per share is stated as a percent (par stock), multiply the par value by the dividend rate.

Dividend per share (preferred) = Par value × Dividend rate

STEP 2. Calculate the total amount of the preferred stock dividend by multiplying the number of preferred shares by the dividend per share.

Total preferred dividend = Number of shares × Dividend per share

STEP 3. Calculate the total common stock dividend by subtracting the total preferred stock dividend from the total dividend declared.

Total common dividend = Total dividend − Total preferred dividend

STEP 4. Calculate the dividends per share for common stock by dividing the total common stock dividend by the number of shares of common stock.

$$\text{Dividend per share (common)} = \frac{\text{Total common dividend}}{\text{Number of shares (common)}}$$

EXAMPLE1 — DISTRIBUTING COMMON STOCK DIVIDENDS

Modular Manufacturing, Inc., has 2,500,000 shares of common stock outstanding. If a dividend of $4,000,000 was declared by the company directors last year, what are the dividends per share of common stock?

SOLUTIONSTRATEGY

Because the company has no preferred stock, the common shareholders will receive the entire dividend. We go directly to Step 4.

$$\text{Dividend per share (common)} = \frac{\text{Total common dividend}}{\text{Number of shares (common)}} = \frac{4,000,000}{2,500,000} = \$1.60 \text{ per share}$$

TRYITEXERCISE 1

Techron Industries, Inc., has 1,400,000 shares of common stock outstanding. If a dividend of $910,000 was declared by the company directors last year, what is the dividend per share of common stock?

CHECK YOUR ANSWERS WITH THE SOLUTIONS ON PAGE 718.

EXAMPLE2 — DISTRIBUTING COMMON AND PREFERRED STOCK DIVIDENDS

The board of directors of Silvertip Developers, Inc., has declared a dividend of $300,000. The company has 60,000 shares of preferred stock that pay $0.50 per share and 100,000 shares of common stock. Calculate the amount of dividends due the preferred shareholders and the dividend per share of common stock.

SOLUTIONSTRATEGY

Step 1. Because the preferred dividend is stated in dollars ($0.50 per share), we go to Step 2.

Step 2. Total preferred dividend = Number of shares × Dividend per share
Total preferred dividend = 60,000 × .50 = $30,000

Step 3. Total common dividend = Total dividend − Total preferred dividend
Total common dividend = 300,000 − 30,000 = $270,000

Step 4.

$$\text{Dividend per share (common)} = \frac{\text{Total common dividend}}{\text{Number of shares (common)}} = \frac{270,000}{100,000} = \$2.70 \text{ per share}$$

▶TRYITEXERCISE 2

The board of directors of Ransford Manufacturing, Inc., has declared a dividend of $2,800,000. The company has 600,000 shares of preferred stock that pay $1.40 per share and 1,000,000 shares of common stock. Calculate the amount of dividends due the preferred shareholders and the dividend per share of common stock.

CHECK YOUR ANSWERS WITH THE SOLUTIONS ON PAGE 718.

EXAMPLE3 — DISTRIBUTING COMMON AND PREFERRED STOCK DIVIDENDS

South Beach International has 100,000 shares of $100 par value, 6%, cumulative preferred stock and 2,500,000 shares of common stock. Although no dividend was declared last year, a $5,000,000 dividend has been declared this year. Calculate the amount of dividends due the preferred shareholders and the dividend per share of common stock.

▶SOLUTIONSTRATEGY

Step 1. Because the preferred stock is cumulative and the company did not pay a dividend last year, the preferred shareholders are entitled to the dividends in *arrears* and the dividends for the *current period*.

Dividend per share (preferred) = Par value × Dividend rate
Dividend per share (preferred) = 100 × .06 = $6.00 per share

Step 2. Total preferred dividend (per year) = Number of shares × Dividend per share
Total preferred dividend (per year) = 100,000 × 6.00 = $600,000
Total preferred dividend = 600,000 (arrears) + 600,000 (current year) = $1,200,000

Step 3. Total common dividend = Total dividend − Total preferred dividend
Total common dividend = 5,000,000 − 1,200,000 = $3,800,000

Step 4. Dividend per share (common) = $\dfrac{\text{Total common dividend}}{\text{Number of shares (common)}} = \dfrac{3,800,000}{2,500,000} = \$1.52$

▶TRYITEXERCISE 3

Jupiter Importers, Inc., has 300,000 shares of $100 par value, 7.5%, cumulative preferred stock and 5,200,000 shares of common stock. Although no dividend was declared for last year, a $7,000,000 dividend has been declared for this year. Calculate the amount of dividends due the preferred shareholders and the dividend per share of common stock.

CHECK YOUR ANSWERS WITH THE SOLUTIONS ON PAGE 718.

READING A STOCK QUOTATION TABLE

20-2

A stock quotation table provides investors with a summary of what happened in the stock market on a particular trading day. These tables can be found on the Internet or in the business section of most newspapers. Exhibit 20-3 is a excerpt of such a table from the wsj.com website.

EXHIBIT 20-3   Stock Quotation Table—the *Wall Street Journal Online*

(1)	(2)	(3)	(4)	(5)	(6)	(7)	(8)	(9)	(10) 52 Wk High	(11) 52 Wk Low	(12)	(13)	(14)	(15) YTD
Name	Symbol	Open	High	Low	Close	Net Chg	%Chg	Volume	High	Low	Div	Yield	P/E	% Chg
A10 Networks	ATEN	6.73	6.79	6.56	6.75	0.01	0.15	200,950	8.25	5.63	...	...	... dd	−12.56
AAC Holdings	AAC	8.55	8.81	7.80	8.65	−1.04	−10.73	640,419	13.06	6.07	...	...	... dd	−3.89
AAR Corp.	AIR	46.54	47.00	46.43	46.81	−0.10	−0.21	94,944	49.05	34.25	0.30	0.64	110.30	19.14
Aaron's Inc.	AAN	44.50	46.11	44.50	45.79	0.89	1.98	721,936	50.80	34.29	0.12	0.26	11.22	14.91
ABB ADR	ABB	22.44	22.59	22.39	22.57	−0.25	−1.10	1,893,437	28.67	21.22	0.83	3.66	21.57	−15.85
Abbott Laboratories	ABT	64.50	64.78	63.91	64.58	−0.20	−0.31	4,544,910	65.90	48.05	1.12	1.73	127.68	13.16
AbbVie	ABBV	93.58	95.86	93.41	95.12	1.21	1.29	5,874,861	125.86	69.47	3.84	4.04	23.54	−1.64
Abercrombie&Fitch	ANF	23.46	24.46	23.37	24.19	0.62	2.63	1,432,714	29.20	9.03	0.80	3.31	69.11	38.78
ABM Industries	ABM	30.98	31.12	30.71	31.12	...	...	267,275	45.12	28.17	0.70	2.25	23.18	−17.50
Acadia Realty Trust	AKR	27.14	27.35	27.12	27.19	0.03	0.11	247,409	30.63	21.34	1.08	3.97	... dd	−0.62
Accenture CI A	ACN	158.30	160.30	157.84	160.15	0.44	0.28	1,733,982	168.95	127.26	2.66	1.66	25.67	4.61
ACCO Brands	ACCO	12.70	12.88	12.60	12.70	...	...	692,722	14.63	10.60	0.24	1.89	9.84	4.10
Acorn International ADR	ATV	22.21	25.65	21.36	22.30	0.94	4.40	12,965	38.86	9.33	...	...	...	26.41
Actuant CI A	ATU	28.00	28.50	27.50	28.45	0.20	0.71	177,238	30.05	21.50	0.04	0.14	... dd	12.45
Acuity Brands	AYI	134.81	137.24	134.08	135.77	0.10	0.07	389,814	201.91	109.98	0.52	0.38	17.01	−22.86
Acushnet Holdings	GOLF	24.00	25.73	23.68	25.40	1.29	5.35	383,476	25.73	15.16	0.52	2.05	20.00	20.49
Adecoagro	AGRO	8.32	8.44	8.32	8.41	0.02	0.24	454,607	11.15	7.20	...	...	84.95	−18.67
Adient	ADNT	45.02	46.83	44.94	45.82	0.49	1.08	1,354,834	86.42	43.10	1.10	2.40	352.46	−41.78
ADT	ADT	8.88	8.91	8.56	8.62	−0.33	−3.69	2,388,176	13.02	6.93	0.14	1.62	...	...
Adtalem Global Education	ATGE	55.25	55.70	54.30	55.50	−0.05	−0.09	383,759	55.70	30.15	...	...	283.74	31.99
Advance Auto Parts	AAP	139.40	143.69	139.40	143.26	3.51	2.51	643,704	145.20	78.81	0.24	0.17	21.07	43.71

IN THE Business World

A **CUSIP number** (Committee on Uniform Securities Identification Procedures) is a unique nine-character code of both letters and numbers used to identify all registered securities in the United States and Canada. The CUSIP number acts as a sort of DNA for the security—uniquely identifying the company or issuer and the type of security—stock, bond, mutual fund, ETF, and so on.

According to Investopedia. com, the first six characters identify the issuer and are assigned in an alphabetical fashion, the seventh and eighth characters identify the type of issue, and the last digit is used as a check digit.

Let's take a column-by-column look at a particular day's listing for **Advance Auto Parts**. Stock prices in this table are listed in dollars and cents. The first step in reading the stock quotation table is to locate the alphabetical listing of the company whose stock you want to look up. Each line is divided into 15 columns, as follows.

Column 1 (**Name** Advance Auto Parts) Company name.

Column 2 (**Symbol** AAP) Symbol used to easily identify a particular stock.

Column 3 (**Open** 139.40) Opening price of the stock that trading day.

Column 4 (**High** 143.69) Highest price of the stock during the trading day.

Column 5 (**Low** 139.40) Lowest price of the stock during the trading day.

Column 6 (**Close** 143.26) The last price of the trading day.

Column 7 (**Net Change** 3.51) The difference, or net change, between the "close" price and the previous day's "close" price. Positive change is indicated in green. Negative change is indicated by a minus sign and is shown in red.

Column 8 (**%Change** 2.51) The trading day's percentage change in price. Positive change is indicated in green. Negative change is indicated by a minus sign and is shown in red.

Column 9 (**Volume** 643,704) The volume or number of shares traded during the day. On that day, 643,704 shares of Advance Auto Parts were traded.

Column 10 (**52-Week High** 145.20) Highest price of the stock during the preceding 52-week period.

Column 11 (**52-Week Low** 78.81) Lowest price of the stock during the preceding 52-week period.

Column 12 (**Dividend** 0.24) The amount of dividends paid out to shareholders in the past year. When there are no dividends, the column shows "...". (See A10 Networks.) Last year Advance Auto Parts paid shareholders a dividend of $0.20 per share.

Column 13 (**Yield** 0.17) Yield percent. Last year's dividend as a percent of the current price of the stock. When there are no dividends, the column shows "...". (See A10 Networks) Last year the dividend paid by Advance Auto Parts yielded stockholders a return of 0.17% on their investment.

Column 14 (**P/E** 21.07) Price-earnings ratio. A number that indicates investors' confidence in a stock. It is the ratio of the current price of the stock to the earnings per share for the past year. The price of Advance Auto Parts stock was selling at a multiple of 21.07 times the earnings per share.

Column 15 (**YTD %Chg** 43.71) The year-to-date percentage change in the price of the stock. Positive change is indicated in green. Negative change is indicated by a minus sign and is shown in red. In this example, the value of Advance Auto Parts stock has risen 43.71% in the past year.

EXAMPLE4 READING A STOCK QUOTATION TABLE

From Exhibit 20-3, Stock Quotation Table, explain the information listed for Abercrombie & Fitch.

▶ SOLUTIONSTRATEGY

According to the listing for Abercrombie & Fitch, the ticker symbol is ANF. That day the stock price opened at $23.46, went as high as $24.46 and as low as $23.37, and closed at $24.19. The price of the stock closed up $0.62, a 2.63% increase. During the trading day, over 1.4 million shares of the stock were traded.

In the past year, the stock price was as high as $29.20 and as low as $9.03. The company paid stockholders a dividend of $0.80 per share. That dividend provided a yield of 3.31%. On that day, the stock price of Abercrombie & Fitch was selling at a P/E ratio or multiple of 69.11 times the earnings per share. In the year to date, the stock price increased by 38.78%.

▶ TRYITEXERCISE 4

Using Exhibit 20-3, Stock Quotation Table, explain the information listed for ABM Industries.

CHECK YOUR ANSWERS WITH THE SOLUTIONS ON PAGE 718.

Stock exchanges are where brokers execute investors' requests to buy and sell shares of stock.

CALCULATING CURRENT YIELD OF A STOCK

20-3

One way to measure how well your stock is performing in terms of its ability to earn dividends is to calculate the **current yield**. In the stock quotations, this is listed in the Yield% column. The current yield is a way of evaluating the current value of a stock. It tells you how much dividend you get as a percentage of the current price of the stock. When a stock pays no dividend, there is no current yield.

current yield A percentage measure of how well a stock is performing in terms of its ability to earn dividends. It is calculated by dividing the annual dividend per share by the current price of the stock.

STEPS TO CALCULATE THE CURRENT YIELD OF A STOCK

STEP 1. Divide the annual dividend per share by the current price of the stock.

$$\text{Current yield} = \frac{\text{Annual dividend per share}}{\text{Current price of the stock}}$$

STEP 2. Convert the answer to a percent, rounding to the nearest tenth.

EXAMPLE5   CALCULATING CURRENT YIELD

Calculate the current yield of Ionosphere Corporation stock, which pays a dividend of $1.60 per year and is currently selling at $34.06 per share.

SOLUTIONSTRATEGY

$$\text{Current yield} = \frac{\text{Annual dividend per share}}{\text{Current price of the stock}}$$

$$\text{Current yield} = \frac{1.60}{34.06} = .0469759 = \underline{\underline{4.7\%}}$$

TRYITEXERCISE 5

Bentley Systems, Inc., paid a dividend of $0.68 per share last year. If yesterday's closing price was $12.84, what is the current yield on the stock?

CHECK YOUR ANSWERS WITH THE SOLUTIONS ON PAGE 718.

20-4

DETERMINING THE PRICE-EARNINGS RATIO OF A STOCK

price-earnings ratio, or **PE ratio** A ratio that shows the relationship between the price of a stock and a company's earnings for the past 12 months; one of the most widely used tools for analyzing stock.

One of the most widely used tools for analyzing a stock is the **price-earnings ratio**, commonly called the **PE ratio**. This number shows the relationship between the price of a stock and the company's earnings for the past 12 months. The price-earnings ratio is an important indicator because it reflects buyer confidence in a particular stock compared with the stock market as a whole. For example, a PE ratio of 20, or 20:1, means that buyers are willing to pay 20 times the current earnings for a share of stock.

The price-earnings ratio of a stock is most useful when compared with the PE ratios of the company in previous years and with the ratios of other companies in the same industry.

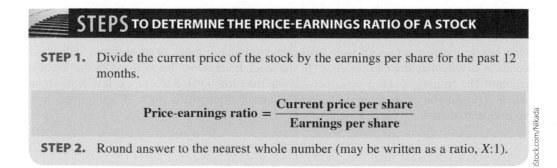

STEPS TO DETERMINE THE PRICE-EARNINGS RATIO OF A STOCK

STEP 1. Divide the current price of the stock by the earnings per share for the past 12 months.

$$\text{Price-earnings ratio} = \frac{\text{Current price per share}}{\text{Earnings per share}}$$

STEP 2. Round answer to the nearest whole number (may be written as a ratio, X:1).

EXAMPLE6 — CALCULATING PRICE-EARNINGS RATIO

Giordano International stock is currently selling at $104.75. If the company had earnings per share of $3.60 last year, calculate the price-earnings ratio of the stock.

▶SOLUTIONSTRATEGY

$$\text{Price-earnings ratio} = \frac{\text{Current price per share}}{\text{Earnings per share}}$$

$$\text{Price-earnings ratio} = \frac{104.75}{3.60} = 29.09722 = \underline{29} \text{ or } \underline{\underline{29{:}1}}$$

This means investors are currently willing to pay 29 times the earnings for one share of Giordano International stock.

▶TRYITEXERCISE 6

Sunset Corp. stock is currently selling for $37.19 per share. If the company had earnings per share of $6.70 in the past 12 months, what is the price-earnings ratio for Sunset?

CHECK YOUR ANSWERS WITH THE SOLUTIONS ON PAGE 718.

COMPUTING THE COST, PROCEEDS, AND GAIN (OR LOSS) ON A STOCK TRANSACTION

20-5

Investors take on the risks of purchasing stocks in the hope of making money. Although stocks are riskier than many other types of investment, they have shown over the years that they are capable of generating spectacular returns in some periods and steady returns in the long run. One investment strategy is to buy stocks and keep them for the dividends paid by the company each quarter. Another strategy is to make money from the profit of buying and selling the stock. Simply put, investors generally want to buy low and sell high! The gain or loss is the difference between the cost of purchasing the stock and the **proceeds** received when selling the stock.

proceeds The amount of money that an investor receives after selling a stock. It is calculated as the value of the shares less the broker's commission.

> **Gain (or loss) on stock = Proceeds − Total cost**

Stocks are generally purchased and sold through a **stockbroker**. Brokers have representatives at various **stock exchanges**, which are like a marketplace where stocks are bought and sold in the form of an auction. When you ask your broker to buy or sell a stock, the order is transmitted to the representative on the floor of the exchange. It is there that your request is *executed*, or transacted.

The charge for this service is a **commission**, which can be a percent of the cost of the transaction or a flat fee. Commission rates are competitive and vary from broker to broker.

Full-service brokers, who provide additional services such as research data and investment advice, charge higher commissions than do discount brokers, who simply execute the transactions. In recent years, as investors have become more comfortable using the Internet, online brokers have become extremely popular. Generally, online brokers charge a fixed fee, such as $7 or $8 per transaction, regardless of the size of the order.

Another factor affecting the commission is whether the number of shares purchased is a **round lot**, a multiple of 100, or an **odd lot**, less than 100. The commission rate on an odd lot is usually a bit higher than on a round lot. For example, the commission on a 400-share transaction might be 3%, while the commission on a 40-share transaction might be 4%.

stockbroker A professional in stock market trading and investments who acts as an agent in the buying and selling of stocks and other securities.

stock exchanges Marketplaces where stocks, bonds, and mutual funds are bought and sold in the form of an auction.

commission The fee a stockbroker charges for assisting in the purchase or sale of shares of stock; a percent of the cost of the stock transaction.

round lot Shares of stock purchased in multiples of 100.

odd lot The purchase of less than 100 shares of stock.

STEPS TO COMPUTE THE COST, PROCEEDS, AND GAIN (OR LOSS) ON A STOCK TRANSACTION

Cost of purchasing stock

STEP 1. Calculate the cost of the shares.

$$\text{Cost of shares} = \text{Price per share} \times \text{Number of shares}$$

STEP 2. Compute the amount of the broker's commission.

$$\text{Broker's commission} = \text{Cost of shares} \times \text{Commission rate}$$

STEP 3. Determine the total cost of the stock purchase.

$$\text{Total cost} = \text{Cost of shares} + \text{Broker's commission}$$

Proceeds from selling stock

STEP 1. Calculate the value of shares on sale.

$$\text{Value of shares} = \text{Price per share} \times \text{Number of shares}$$

STEP 2. Compute the amount of the broker's commission.

STEP 3. Determine the proceeds by subtracting the commission from the value of the shares.

$$\text{Proceeds} = \text{Value of shares} - \text{Broker's commission}$$

Gain (or loss) on the transaction

$$\text{Gain (or loss) on transaction} = \text{Proceeds} - \text{Total cost}$$

iStock.com/Nikada

EXAMPLE7 CALCULATING GAIN (OR LOSS) ON A STOCK TRANSACTION

You purchase 350 shares of Mercury Manufacturing common stock at $46.50 per share. A few months later you sell the shares at $54.31. Your stockbroker charges 3% commission on round lots and 4% on odd lots. Calculate (a) the total cost, (b) the proceeds, and (c) the gain (or loss) on the transaction.

►SOLUTIONSTRATEGY

a. *Cost of purchasing stock*

Step 1. Cost of shares = Price per share × Number of shares
Cost of shares = 46.50 × 350 = $16,275

Step 2. Broker's commission = Cost of shares × Commission rate
Round lot commission = 300 shares × 46.50 × .03 = $418.50
Odd lot commission = 50 shares × 46.50 × .04 = $93.00
Broker's commission = 418.50 + 93.00 = $511.50

Step 3. Total cost = Cost of shares + Broker's commission
Total cost = 16,275 + 511.50 = $16,786.50

b. Proceeds from selling stock

Step 1. Value of shares = 54.31 × 350 = $19,008.50

Step 2. Broker's commission = Cost of shares × Commission rate
Round lot commission = 300 shares × 54.31 × .03 = $488.79
Odd lot commission = 50 shares × 54.31 × .04 = $108.62
Broker's commission = 488.79 + 108.62 = $597.41

Step 3. Proceeds = Value of shares − Broker's commission
Proceeds = 19,008.50 − 597.41 = $18,411.09

c. Gain (or loss) on the transaction

Gain (or loss) on transaction = Proceeds − Total cost
Gain (or loss) on transaction = 18,411.09 − 16,786.50 = $1,624.59

Learning Tip

Remember, when stock is purchased, commissions are added to the cost of the stock to get total cost; when sold, the commissions are *deducted* by the brokerage firm from the sale price to get the proceeds of the sale.

▶ TRYITEXERCISE 7

You purchase 225 shares of Gulfstream Industries common stock at $44.80 per share. A few months later you sell the shares at $53.20. Your stockbroker charges 2% commission on round lots and 3% on odd lots. Calculate (a) the total cost, (b) the proceeds, and (c) the gain (or loss) on the transaction.

CHECK YOUR ANSWERS WITH THE SOLUTIONS ON PAGES 718–719.

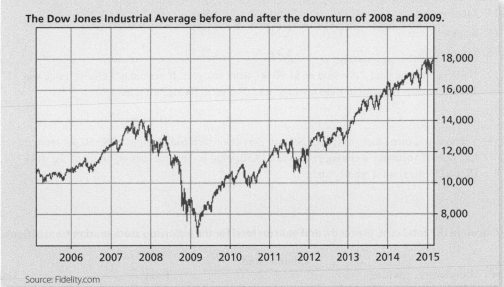

The Dow Jones Industrial Average before and after the downturn of 2008 and 2009.

Source: Fidelity.com

REVIEW EXERCISES

20 SECTION I

Calculate the preferred and common dividend per share for the following companies.

Company	Common Stock Shares	Preferred Stock Shares	Div. or Par	Cum.	Dividend Declared	Arrears	Preferred Div./Share	Common Div./Share
1. Bearing & CO.	4,000,000	1,000,000	$100 3%	yes	$8,000,000	1 year	$6.00	$.50
2. Suntech, Inc.	5,000,000		none		$3,000,000	none	___	___
3. Galaxy Corp.	10,000,000	3,000,000	$5.50	no	$25,000,000	none	___	___
4. Five Star, Inc.	6,000,000	1,000,000	$100 5%	no	$4,000,000	none	___	___
5. Fisher King, Inc.	4,000,000	1,000,000	$100 6%	yes	$15,000,000	1 year	___	___

6. The board of directors of Mountain Hotels has declared a dividend of $1,900,000. The company has 100,000 shares of preferred stock that pay $1.10 per share and 1,250,000 shares of common stock.

    After first finding the amount of dividends due the preferred shareholders, calculate the dividend per share of common stock.

Use Exhibit 20-3, Stock Quotation Table, on page 690 to fill in the blanks for Exercises 7–12.

7. **A10 Networks Symbol, Open price, Percent change: <u>ATEN, $6.73, up 0.15%</u>**

8. Abbott Laboratories High and low for the past 52 weeks: _____

9. AbbVie Ticker symbol, Close price, and PE ratio: _____

10. ADT Net change, Volume, and Dividend: _____

11. Acuity Brands 52-week low, Yield, YTD percent change: _____

12. Adient Symbol, High for the day, 52-week high: _____

Calculate the missing information for the following stocks.

Company	Earnings per Share	Annual Dividend	Current Price per Share	Current Yield	Price-Earnings Ratio
13. Huntington Corp.	**$2.18**	**$.55**	**$32.70**	**1.7%**	**15**
14. Tangiers, Inc.	$6.59	$1.60	$46.13	___	___
15. Brighton Corp.	$.77	$.24	$17.63	___	___
16. Sampson, Inc.	___	$.45	$27.50	___	21

17. National Storage paid a dividend of $1.90 per share last year. If yesterday's closing price was $37.60, what is the current yield on the stock? (Round to the nearest tenth.)

18. Suppose you own stock in Nguyen Science Services which had earnings of $0.50 per share last year. If yesterday's closing price was $19.50, what is the price-earnings ratio of the stock? (Round to the nearest whole number.)

Calculate the total cost, proceeds, and gain (or loss) for the following stock market transactions.

Company	Number of Shares	Purchase Price	Selling Price	Commissions			Total Cost	Proceeds	Gain (or Loss)
				Buy	Sell	Odd Lot			
19. Prime Time, Inc.	**200**	**$19.60**	**$24.80**	**1%**	**1%**	**—**	**$3,959.20**	**$4,910.40**	**$951.20**
20. United Gas & Oil	100	$47.20	$56.06	3%	3%		___	___	___
21. Freeport, Inc.	350	$18.42	$29.19	2%	2%	add 1%	___	___	___
22. Vector Corp.	900	$28.37	$36.25	3%	3%		___	___	___
23. Mars Distributors	775	$37.75	$34.50	1.5%	1.5%	add 1%	___	___	___
24. Capitol Mfg.	500	$25.11	$28.86	3%	3%		___	___	___

25. The Newmark Corporation has 500,000 shares of common stock outstanding. If a dividend of $425,000 was declared by the company directors last year, what is the dividend per share of common stock?

26. The board of directors of Fortune Industries has declared a dividend of $3,000,000. The company has 700,000 shares of preferred stock that pay $0.90 per share and 1,600,000 shares of common stock.

    a. What are the dividends due the preferred shareholders?

    b. What is the dividend per share of common stock?

27. Apex Developers, Inc., has 1,800,000 shares of $100 par value, 5%, cumulative preferred stock and 9,750,000 shares of common stock. Although no dividend was declared for the past two years, a $44,000,000 dividend has been declared for this year.

    a. How much is due the preferred shareholders?

    b. What is the dividend per share of common stock?

28. Bio-Science Labs stock is currently selling for $47.35 per share. The earnings per share are $3.14, and the dividend is $1.70.

    a. What is the current yield of the stock?

    b. What is the price-earnings ratio?

29. You purchase 650 shares of Sunrise Electric common stock at $44.25 per share. A few months later you sell the shares at $57.29. Your stockbroker charges 3% commission on round lots and an extra $1\frac{1}{2}\%$ on odd lots.

    a. What is the total cost of the purchase?

b. What are the proceeds on the sale?

c. What is the gain (or loss) on the transaction?

30. You purchase 350 shares of stock at $38.20 per share. Several months later you sell the shares at $34.10. Your broker charges 3% commission on round lots and 4% on odd lots.

Calculate the gain or loss on the transaction.

BUSINESS DECISION: DOLLAR-COST AVERAGING

31. Although investing all at once works best when stock prices are rising, *dollar-cost averaging* can be a good way to take advantage of a fluctuating market. Dollar-cost averaging is an investment strategy designed to reduce volatility in which securities are purchased in *fixed dollar amounts at regular intervals* regardless of what direction the market is moving. This strategy is also called the *constant dollar plan*.

You are considering a hypothetical $1,200 investment in Century Media Corporation stock. Your choice is to invest the money all at once or dollar-cost average at the rate of $100 per month for one year. Assume that Century Media allows you to purchase "fractional" shares of its stock.

a. If you invested all of the money in January and bought the shares for $10 each, how many shares could you buy?

b. From the following chart of share prices, calculate the number of shares that would be purchased each month using dollar-cost averaging and the total shares for the year. Round to the nearest tenth.

Month	Amount Invested	Cost per Share	Shares Purchased	Month	Amount Invested	Cost per Share	Shares Purchased
January	$100	$10.00	____	July	$100	$11.50	____
February	100	9.55	____	August	100	10.70	____
March	100	8.80	____	September	100	9.80	____
April	100	7.75	____	October	100	10.60	____
May	100	9.15	____	November	100	9.45	____
June	100	10.25	____	December	100	10.15	____

c. What is the average price you pay per share if you purchase them all in January?

d. What is the average price you pay per share if you purchase them using dollar-cost averaging?

BONDS

 SECTION II

UNDERSTANDING BONDS AND READING A BOND QUOTATION TABLE 20-6

A **bond** is a loan, or an IOU, where the bond buyer lends money to the bond issuer. With stock, the investor becomes a part-owner of the corporation; with bonds, the investor becomes a creditor. Bonds are known as fixed-income securities because the issuer promises to pay a specified amount of interest on a regular basis, usually semiannually. Although stock is issued only by corporations, bonds are issued by corporations and governments. The federal government, as well as states and local municipalities, issues bonds. The funds raised are used to finance general operations and specific projects such as schools, highways, bridges, and airports. An example of a bond certificate is shown in Exhibit 20-4.

Corporate bonds represent the number one source of corporate borrowing for both large and small companies. Corporations use the money raised from bonds to finance modernization and expansion programs. **Secured bonds** are backed by a lien on a plant, equipment, or another corporate asset. **Unsecured bonds**, also known as **debentures**, are backed only by the general credit of the issuing corporation. Some bonds are **convertible**, which means they can be converted into or exchanged for a specified number of shares of common stock. **Callable bonds** give the issuer the right to call or redeem the bonds before the maturity date. Calling bonds might occur when interest rates are falling and the company can issue new bonds at a lower rate.

When bonds are issued by a corporation, they may be purchased by investors at par value, usually $1,000, and held until the maturity date or they may be bought and sold through a broker on the secondary or resale market. Bonds pay a fixed interest rate, also known as the **coupon rate**. This rate is a fixed percentage of the par value that will be paid to the bondholder on a regular basis.

For example, a company might issue a $1,000 par value, 7% bond, maturing in the year 2025. The bondholder in this case would receive a fixed interest payment of $70 per year ($1,000 × .07), or $35 semiannually, until the bond matures. At maturity, the company repays the loan by paying the bondholder the par value of the bond.

bond A loan, or an IOU, in the form of an interest-bearing note in which the bond buyer lends money to the bond issuer. Used by corporations and governments to borrow money on a long-term basis.

secured bonds Bonds that are backed by a lien on specific collateral, such as a plant, equipment, or another corporate asset.

unsecured bonds, or debentures Bonds that are backed only by the general credit of the issuing corporation, not on specific collateral pledged as security.

convertible bonds Bonds that can be converted or exchanged at the owner's option for a certain number of shares of common stock.

callable bonds Bonds that the issuer has the right to call or repurchase before the maturity date. Bonds are called when interest rates are falling and the company can issue new bonds at a lower rate.

coupon rate A fixed percentage of the par value of a bond that is paid to the bondholder on a regular basis.

Somchaij/Shutterstock.com

According to whatitcosts.com, the Golden Gate Bridge in San Francisco was built over a four-and-a-half year period between 1933 and 1937. It is the second-largest suspension bridge in the United States.

The bridge cost $37 million, but it was funded by municipal bonds that cost an additional $39 million in interest. The entire cost of the bridge was paid for by tolls before the final bonds were retired in 1971. A rough estimate of the $76 million the bridge cost (including interest) in 1933 is over $1.2 billion in 2007 dollars.

EXHIBIT 20-4 Bond Certificate

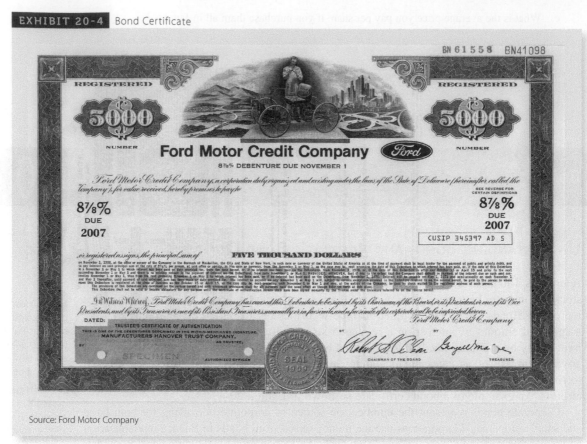

Source: Ford Motor Company

premium When a bond is selling for more than its par value, it is said to be selling at a premium. This occurs during periods when prevailing interest rates are declining.

discount When a bond is selling for less than its par value, it is said to be selling at a discount. This occurs during periods when prevailing interest rates are rising.

During the period between the issue date and the maturity date, bond prices fluctuate in the opposite direction of prevailing interest rates. Let's say you buy a bond with a coupon rate of 8%. If interest rates in the marketplace fall to 7%, newly issued bonds will have a rate lower than yours, thus making yours more attractive and driving the price above the par value. When this occurs, the bonds are said to be selling at a **premium**. However, if interest rates rise to 9%, new bonds would have a higher rate than yours, thus making yours less attractive and pushing the price down, below par. If bonds sell below par, it is known as selling at a **discount**. Remember, at maturity, the bond returns to its par value.

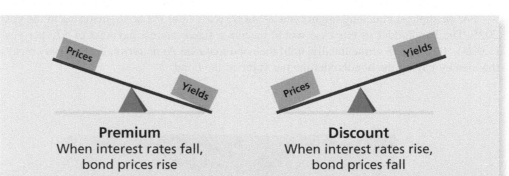

Premium
When interest rates fall, bond prices rise

Discount
When interest rates rise, bond prices fall

Learning Tip

Note that in Exhibit 20-5, the dollar amounts are rounded to tenths of a cent and percents are rounded to thousandths.

Just as with stocks, corporate bond quotations may be found on the Internet or in the financial section of most newspapers. Exhibit 20-5 is a portion of such a table reprinted from the *Fidelity.com*. Let's take a column-by-column look at the listing for **Comcast Corp**.

Column 1 (**Description** COMCAST CORP) The company name and other basic information. (Note: "CALL MAKE WHOLE" refers to information regarding the payment that must be made if the bond is paid off early, that is, if the bond is called.)

Column 2 (**Coupon** 2.350) The interest the company promises to pay based on the par value of the bond.

Column 3 (**Maturity Date** 01/15/2027) The date on which the company buys back the bond by paying the principal and the final interest payment.

Column 4 (**Next Call Date** 10/15/2026) The next date on which a bond can be redeemed early by the company. Some bonds are not callable, and in that case no date is given.

Column 5 (**Rating** A3 and A-) An assessment of the quality of the bond. For rating information consult the websites of the individual rating services.

Column 6 (**Bid – Yield** 3.899) The annual percentage yield based on the bid price.

Column 7 (**Bid – Price/Qty(min)** 88.953/100(5)) The price a buyer is willing to pay for the bond, the quantity of bonds available at that price (each bond is worth $1,000), and the minimum number of bonds to be bought at that price. **Important note:** Prices are given as a percent of par so to find the price here, multiply 1,000 × 88.953% = 1,000 × .88953 = $889.53.

Column 8 (**Ask – Price/Qty(min)** 89.123/261(2)) The price a seller is willing to accept for the bond, the quantity of bonds available for sale at that price (again, each bond is worth $1,000), and the minimum number that will be sold at that price. Note: The difference in the ask and bid prices is the "spread," and it goes to the broker handling the transaction.

Column 9 (**Ask – Yield to Worst/Yield to Sink** 3.874/--) "Yield to Worst" gives the lowest potential yield without the company actually defaulting. (Note: If the bond includes a sinking fund date, a potential yield at the next sinking fund date is given. None of the bonds shown here include a sinking fund date.)

Column 10 (**Ask – Yield to Maturity** 3.874) The rate of return an investor receives if an investment is held to the maturity date.

EXHIBIT 20-5 Corporate Bond Quotations—selected from *Fidelity.com*

(1)	(2)	(3)	(4)	(5)		(6)	(7)	(8)	(9)	(10)
				Rating		**Bid**		**Ask**		
Description	Coupon	Maturity Date	Next Call Date	Moody's	S&P	Yield	Price Qty (min)	Price Qty (min)	Yield to Worst/ Yield to Sink	Yield to Maturity
BLACK HILLS CORP NOTE CALL MAKE WHOLE3.15000% 01/15/2027	3.150	01/15/2027		BAA2	BBB	4.282	92.053 250(5)	92.810 20(2)	4.169 --	4.169
BROADCOM CORP/ BROADCOM CAYMAN3.87500% 01/15/2027 NOTE CALL MAKE WHOLE	3.875	01/15/2027		BAA2	BBB-	4.738	92.053 250(5)	94.083 28(2)	4.734 --	4.734
CBS CORP NEW NOTE CALL MAKE WHOLE2.90000% 01/15/2027	2.900	01/15/2027		BAA2	BBB	4.384	89.630 500(10)	89.901 231(12)	4.342 --	4.342
COMCAST CORP NEW NOTE CALL MAKE WHOLE2.35000% 01/15/2027	2.350	01/15/2027		A3	A-	3.899	88.953 100(5)	89.123 261(2)	3.874 --	3.874
DUKE ENERGY FLA LLC BOND CALL MAKE WHOLE3.20000% 01/15/2027	3.200	01/15/2027		A1	A	3.619	96.976 250(5)	97.498 50(20)	3.546 --	3.546
KRAFT HEINZ FOODS CONOTE CALL MAKE WHOLE4.62500% 01/30/2029	4.625	01/30/2029		BAA3	BBB	4.628	99.965 250(10)	100.120 500(10)	4.609 --	4.609
VERIZON COMMUNICATIONS INC 3.55000% 06/15/2029 MTN	3.550	06/15/2029		BAA1	BBB+	4.350	93.137 250(5)	94.938 5(5)	4.133 --	4.133

EXAMPLE 8 — READING A BOND QUOTATION TABLE

Using Exhibit 20-5, Corporate Bond Quotations, give the coupon, the ask price in dollars, and the yield to maturity for the BLACK HILLS CORP bond.

SOLUTION STRATEGY

The coupon rate is 3.150%. The ask price is $928.10 (1,000 × 0.92810). The yield to maturity is 4.169%.

TRY IT EXERCISE 8

Using Exhibit 20-5, Corporate Bond Quotations, give the coupon, the ask price in dollars, and the yield to maturity for the BROADCOM COPR/BROADCOM CAYMAN bond.

CHECK YOUR ANSWERS WITH THE SOLUTIONS ON PAGE 719.

20-7 CALCULATING THE COST OF PURCHASING BONDS AND THE PROCEEDS FROM THE SALE OF BONDS

Similar to stocks, when bonds are bought and sold, a brokerage charge is commonly added to the price of each bond. Although there is no standard commission, the charge is generally between $5 and $10 per bond. As noted earlier, bonds pay interest semiannually, such as on January 1 and July 1. When bonds are traded between the stated interest payment dates, the interest accumulated from the last payment date must be paid to the seller by the buyer. This interest due to the seller is known as the **accrued interest**.

Accrued interest of a bond is calculated by using the simple interest formula $I = PRT$, where P is the face value of the bond, R is the coupon rate, and T is the number of days since the last payment date divided by 360. When time is stated in months, divide by 12.

accrued interest When bonds are traded between the stated interest payment dates, the interest accumulated from the last payment date that must be paid to the seller by the buyer.

STEPS TO CALCULATE THE COST OF PURCHASING A BOND

STEP 1. Calculate the accrued interest on the bond since the last payment date using $I = PRT$.

STEP 2. Calculate the price to purchase the bond.

Price per bond = Current market price + Accrued interest + Commission

STEP 3. Calculate total purchase price.

Total purchase price = Price per bond × Number of bonds purchased

EXAMPLE 9 — CALCULATING THE PURCHASE PRICE OF A BOND

What is the purchase price of 10 Central Pacific bonds with a coupon rate of 9.5% and a current market price of 107? The commission charge is $5 per bond. The date of the transaction is April 1, and the bond pays interest on January 1 and July 1.

►SOLUTIONSTRATEGY

Step 1. Because the time since the last payment is 3 months, we will use $T = \dfrac{3}{12}$.

$$\text{Accrued interest} = 1{,}000 \times .095 \times \frac{3}{12} = \underline{\$23.75}$$

Step 2. Price per bond = Current market price + Accrued interest + Commission

Price per bond = $1{,}070.00 + 23.75 + 5.00 = \underline{\$1{,}098.75 \text{ per bond}}$

Note: Remember market price is given as a percent of par value.

$(1{,}000 \times 107\% = 1{,}000 \times 1.07 = \$1{,}070.00)$

Step 3. Total purchase price = Price per bond × Number of bonds

Total purchase price = $1{,}098.75 \times 10 = \underline{\$10{,}987.50}$

►TRYITEXERCISE 9

What is the purchase price of 20 Champion Industries bonds with a coupon rate of 6.25% and a current market price of 91.375? The commission charge is $10 per bond. The date of the transaction is October 1, and the bond pays interest on February 1 and August 1.

CHECK YOUR ANSWERS WITH THE SOLUTIONS ON PAGE 719.

STEPS TO CALCULATE THE PROCEEDS FROM THE SALE OF A BOND

STEP 1. Calculate the accrued interest on the bond since the last payment date by using $I = PRT$.

STEP 2. Calculate the proceeds per bond.

Proceeds = Current market price + Accrued interest − Commission

STEP 3. Calculate the total proceeds from the sale.

Total proceeds = Proceeds per bond × Number of bonds sold

EXAMPLE10 CALCULATING THE PROCEEDS OF A BOND SALE

What are the proceeds of the sale of 15 Panorama Products Corp. bonds with a coupon rate of 7.125% and a current market price of 111? The commission charge is $7.50 per bond. The date of the transaction is 71 days since the last interest payment.

►SOLUTIONSTRATEGY

Step 1. Accrued interest = $1{,}000 \times .07125 \times \dfrac{71}{360} = \underline{\$14.05}$

Step 2. Proceeds per bond = Current market price + Accrued interest − Commission

Proceeds per bond = $1{,}110.00 + 14.05 - 7.50 = \underline{\$1{,}116.55}$

Note: Remember market price is given as a percent of par value.

$(1{,}000 \times 111\% = 1{,}000 \times 1.11 = \$1{,}110.00)$

Step 3. Total proceeds = Proceeds per bond × Number of bonds sold

Total proceeds = $1{,}116.55 \times 15 = \underline{\$16{,}748.25}$

► TRYITEXERCISE10

What are the proceeds of the sale of five Neptune Corporation bonds with a coupon rate of 8.875% and a current market price of 99? The commission charge is $10 per bond. The date of the transaction is 122 days since the last interest payment.

CHECK YOUR ANSWERS WITH THE SOLUTIONS ON PAGE 719.

20-8   CALCULATING THE CURRENT YIELD OF A BOND

Just as with stocks, the current yield of a bond is a simple measure of the return on investment based on the current market price. When bonds are purchased at par, the current yield is equal to the coupon rate. For example, a bond purchased at par for $1,000 with a coupon rate of 7% pays interest of $70 per year (1,000 × .07) and has a yield of 7% $\left(\frac{70}{1,000} = .07 \right)$. If the bond is purchased at a discount (say, $875), it still pays $70; however, the yield is 8% $\left(\frac{70}{875} = .08 \right)$. If the bond is purchased at a premium (say, $1,165), it still pays $70; however, now the yield is only 6% $\left(\frac{70}{1,165} = .06 \right)$.

STEPS TO CALCULATE CURRENT YIELD OF A BOND

STEP 1. Calculate the annual interest and current price of the bond.
STEP 2. Divide the annual interest of the bond by the current market price.

$$\text{Current yield} = \frac{\text{Annual interest}}{\text{Current market price}}$$

STEP 3. Convert the answer to a percent, rounding to the nearest tenth.

EXAMPLE11   CALCULATING THE CURRENT YIELD OF A BOND SALE

Calculate the current yield of an Evergreen Corp. bond with a coupon rate of 13.5% currently selling at a premium of 107.25.

► SOLUTIONSTRATEGY

Annual interest = Par value × Coupon rate = 1,000 × .135 = $135

Current market price = Par value × Price percent = 1,000 × 1.0725 = $1,072.50

$$\text{Current yield} = \frac{\text{Annual interest}}{\text{Current market price}} = \frac{135}{1,072.50} = .12587 = \underline{12.6\%}$$

► TRYITEXERCISE 11

Calculate the current yield of a Kensington Industries bond with a coupon rate of 9.375% currently selling at a discount of 84.75.

CHECK YOUR ANSWERS WITH THE SOLUTIONS ON PAGE 719.

Learning Tip

Remember, bond interest is constant regardless of what you paid for the bond; the yield is what varies depending on the current market price of the bond.

B-A-C-O/Shutterstock.com

iStock.com/Nikada

REVIEW EXERCISES

Use Exhibit 20-5, Corporate Bond Quotation Table, on page 701 to fill in the blanks for Exercises 1–10.

1. CBS Corp—Coupon, Bid price in dollars: **2.900%, $896.30**

2. DUKE ENERGY FLA LLC—Maturity date, Yield to maturity: _____

3. Which bond has an ask price closest to par value? _____

4. CBS CORP—Ask price in dollars: _____

5. Which bond has the lowest coupon rate? _____

6. VERIZON COMMUNICATIONS INC—ratings: _____

7. COMCAST CORP—Bid price in dollars: _____

8. Which bond has the highest ask price? How much in dollars? _____

9. COMCAST CORP—Ask price in dollars: _____

10. KRAFT HEINZ FOODS—Bid price in dollars: _____

Calculate the accrued interest and the total purchase price of the following bond purchases.

Company	Coupon Rate	Market Price	Time Since Last Interest	Accrued Interest	Commission per Bond	Bonds Purchased	Total Price
11. Xerox	5.5%	86.25	2 months	$9.17	$5.00	1	$876.67
12. U.S. West	7.25	102.50	78 days	____	$4.50	15	____
13. AT&T	8.375	95.00	5 months	____	$10.00	40	____
14. Hilton	9.5	79.75	23 days	____	$9.75	15	____
15. Ford	6.625	111.875	3 months	____	$8.00	10	____

Calculate the accrued interest and the total proceeds of the following bond sales.

Company	Coupon Rate	Market Price	Time Since Last Interest	Accrued Interest	Commission per Bond	Bonds Sold	Total Proceeds
16. Textron	6.25%	91.50	21 days	$3.65	$6.00	10	$9,126.50
17. Apple	8.50	108.75	4 months	____	$8.50	4	____
18. USX	10.625	77.00	85 days	____	$12.00	15	____
19. Mobil	9.75	89.375	1 month	____	$7.25	7	____

20. Find the total proceeds from the sale of 20 bonds with a coupon rate of 7.75 and a current price of 97.375.

The commission charge is $5.00 per bond. The date of the transaction is 145 days since the last interest payment.

Calculate the annual interest and current yield of the following bonds.

Company	Coupon Rate	Annual Interest	Market Price	Current Yield
21. Kroger	6.625%	66.25	91.125	7.3%
22. Bordens	9.25	____	108.00	____
23. Blockbuster	7.50	____	125.25	____
24. McDonald's	11.875	____	73.50	____

25. Find the current yield of a bond whose coupon rate is listed as 6.625 and currently selling at a premium of 106.625.

      Round to the nearest tenth percent.

26. On March 1, Wayne Michaels bought 10 Metro Petroleum bonds with a coupon rate of 9.125%. The purchase price was 88.875, and the commission was $6 per bond. Metro Petroleum bonds pay interest on February 1 and August 1.

   a. What is the current yield of the bond as of the purchase date?

   b. What is the total purchase price of the bonds?

   c. If Wayne sold the bonds on November 1 for 93.875, what are the proceeds from the sale?

BUSINESS DECISION: TAXABLE OR TAX-FREE BONDS

27. More than 50,000 state and local governments and their agencies borrow money by issuing **municipal bonds** to build, repair, or improve schools, streets, highways, hospitals, sewer systems, and so on. When the federal income tax law was adopted in 1913, interest on municipal bonds was excluded from federal taxation. As a result, municipal bond investors are willing to accept lower yields than those they can obtain from taxable bonds.

   As part of your portfolio, you are considering investing $50,000 in bonds. You have the choice of investing in tax-exempt municipal bonds yielding 2.75% or corporate bonds yielding 4% in taxable interest income.

   a. What is the annual interest income and tax status of the municipal bond investment?

   b. What is the annual interest income and tax status of the corporate bond investment?

   c. If you are in the 30% marginal tax bracket for federal income taxes and your state and local taxes on that income amount to an additional 6%, what is the after-tax income on the corporate bonds?

   d. What is the actual percent yield realized on the corporate bonds after taxes?

MUTUAL FUNDS

UNDERSTANDING MUTUAL FUNDS AND READING A MUTUAL FUND QUOTATION TABLE

20-9

Mutual funds are a very popular way of investing. Essentially, mutual funds are professionally managed investment companies that pool the money from many individuals and invest it in stocks, bonds, and other securities. Most individual investors do not have the time or the ability to research the literally thousands of investment possibilities. By pooling the financial resources of thousands of shareholders, mutual funds can use the expertise of the country's top professional money managers.

Mutual funds are corporations known as **investment trusts**. Their assets are stocks and bonds purchased with the hope that the value of the securities will increase. Investors purchase shares of stock of the fund. If the fund is successful in its investments, it pays dividends and capital gains to its shareholders.

With mutual funds, instead of choosing individual stocks and bonds, investors pick a fund with financial goals similar to their own. These range from high-risk aggressive growth goals, such as investing in new and unproven companies and industries, to more moderate-risk goals, such as steady income and balanced growth and income, which is achieved by investing in large and established companies. Most mutual fund companies offer several different funds known as a *family*. Investors are free to move their money between the funds as their investment goals or market conditions change.

Just as with stock prices, mutual fund share prices fluctuate up and down on a daily basis and can be tracked on the Internet and in the financial section of most newspapers. Let's take a column-by-column look at a typical day's listing for a mutual fund in the **Fidelity Invest** family known as **Magellan**. Exhibit 20-6 is a portion of such a table, as listed in the *Wall Street Journal Online*.

Column 1 (**Family/Fund**) Fidelity Invest/Magellan Mutual funds are listed alphabetically by the fund's family name and in subcategories by the various funds available within that family. In this example, the family name is Fidelity Invest and the particular fund name is Magellan.

Column 2 (**Symbol** FMAGX) Symbol used to easily identify a particular fund. The symbol for the Fidelity Invest Magellan Fund is FMAGX.

Column 3 (**NAV** 58.16) Net asset value; the dollar value of one share of the fund's stock. This is the price you receive when you sell your shares of the fund. That day the net asset value for the Fidelity Invest Magellan Fund was $58.16. Positive change is indicated in green. Negative change is indicated by a minus sign and is shown in red.

Column 4 (**Change** –0.09) The difference, or net change, between the net asset value and the previous day's net asset value. That day the Fidelity Invest Magellan Fund net asset value was down $0.09. Positive change is indicated in green. Negative change is indicated by a minus sign and is shown in red.

Column 5 (**YTD %Return** –9.5) The year-to-date percentage return on investment. That day the Fidelity Invest Magellan Fund year-to-date return was down 9.5%. Positive change is indicated in green. Negative change is indicated by a minus sign and is shown in red.

Column 6 (**3-year %Change** –11.3) The 3-year percentage change in the net asset value. In the past three years, the Fidelity Invest Magellan Fund has decreased 11.3%. Positive change is indicated in green. Negative change is indicated by a minus sign and is shown in red.

mutual funds or **investment trusts** Corporations that are investment pools of money with a wide variety of investment goals.

IN THE Business World

Mutual funds are big business! In recent years, the popularity of mutual funds as an investment has skyrocketed.

According to the Investment Company Institute, in 1990, there were 3,079 different mutual funds with total net assets of just over $1 billion. Two decades later the number of U.S. mutual funds had grown to over 15,000 with more than $13 trillion in assets.

rtguest/Shutterstock.com

EXHIBIT 20-6 Mutual Fund Quotation Table in *the Wall Street Journal Online*

(1) Family/Fund	(2) Symbol	(3) NAV	(4) Change	(5) YTD % return	(6) 3-year % change
American Funds Class A					
GwthA p	AGTHX	25.53	0.01	−6.6	−7.9
ICAA p	AIVSX	23.99	0.01	−6.6	−8.6
EupacA	AEPGX	35.99	0.17	−6.1	−5.8
WshA p	AWSHX	23.60	0.02	−3.1	−9.1
CapIBA p	CAIBX	46.62	0.15	−0.8	−4.8
Fidelity Invest					
Contra	FCNTX	56.46	0.07	−3.0	−5.0
Magellan	FMAGX	58.16	−0.09	−9.5	−11.3
DivIntl	FDIVX	25.61	0.04	−8.5	−11.1
GoldInst r	FGDIX	49.26	0.69	16.3	17.7
RealEstInc r	FRIFX	10.00	0.02	10.7	3.6
John Hancock Funds A					
BondA p	JHNBX	15.52	0.01	10.5	8.7
CATxFA p	TACAX	10.60	0.01	8.9	4.9
ClassicVal p	PZFVX	13.70	0.03	−4.8	−15.8
HiYMuBdA p	JHTFX	8.30	0.01	8.6	5.1
InvGrBdA	TAUSX	10.36	0.02	9.6	7.9
PIMCO Fds Institutional					
AllAsset	PAAIX	12.30	0.01	9.4	6.3
IntlStksPLS r	PISIX	8.72	0.04	4.6	−2.4
MortBckSec r	PTRIX	11.10	0.01	8.7	8.8
VANGUARD INDEX FDS					
500 Index	VFINX	96.95	0.04	−4.7	−8.7
Europe	VEURX	23.29	0.09	−10.2	−12.0
ITBond	VBIIX	11.69	0.03	12.1	9.4
LarCapIx	VLACX	19.37	0.01	−4.6	−8.3
STBond	VBISX	10.70	0.01	4.3	5.8

IN THE Business World

For further information about stocks, bonds, and mutual funds, contact the Securities and Exchange Commission's Investor Information Service at 1-800-SEC-0330 to get free publications and investor alerts. This information is also available at www.sec.gov.

rtguest/Shutterstock.com

EXAMPLE 12
READING A BOND QUOTATION TABLE

Using Exhibit 20-6, Mutual Fund Quotation Table, explain the information listed for the Vanguard Index Funds ITBond fund.

SOLUTIONSTRATEGY

According to the listing for the Vanguard Index Funds ITBond fund, the symbol for the fund is <u>VBIIX</u>. The net asset value of the fund is <u>$11.69</u>, up <u>$0.03</u> from the previous day's net asset value. The year-to-date return on investment is up <u>12.1%</u>. The 3-year percent change in net asset value is up <u>9.4%</u>.

TRYITEXERCISE 12

Using Exhibit 20-6, Mutual Fund Quotation Table, on page 708, explain the information listed for the John Hancock Funds A, ClassicVal p fund.

CHECK YOUR ANSWERS WITH THE SOLUTIONS ON PAGE 719.

CALCULATING THE SALES CHARGE AND SALES CHARGE PERCENT OF A MUTUAL FUND

Two important terms in mutual funds are *net asset value* and *offer price*. The **net asset value (NAV)** is the dollar value of one share of a fund's stock. This is the per share price you receive when you sell the fund. The **offer price** is the per share price investors pay when purchasing a mutual fund. The offer price includes the net asset value and the broker's commission.

With mutual funds, the sales charge or broker's commission is known as the **load**. These charges vary from 1% to more than 8% of the amount invested. The load is paid when purchasing the stock, in a **front-end load**, or when selling the stock, in a **back-end load**. Some mutual funds do not charge a commission and are known as no-load funds. For load funds, the difference between the offer price and the net asset value is the sales charge.

net asset value (NAV) The dollar value of one share of a mutual fund's stock. It is the price investors receive when they sell their shares of the fund.

offer price The price per share investors pay when purchasing a mutual fund. Offer price includes the net asset value plus the broker's commission.

load The sales charge or broker's commission on a mutual fund.

front-end load The sales charge or commission on a mutual fund when it is paid at the time of purchase.

back-end load The sales charge or commission on a mutual fund when it is paid at the time of sale.

STEPS TO CALCULATE MUTUAL FUND SALES CHARGE AND SALES CHARGE PERCENT

STEP 1. Calculate mutual fund sales charge by subtracting the net asset value from the offer price.

$$\text{Mutual fund sales charge} = \text{Offer price} - \text{Net asset value}$$

STEP 2. Calculate sales charge percent by dividing the sales charge by the net asset value.

$$\text{Sales charge percent} = \frac{\text{Sales charge}}{\text{Net asset value}}$$

iStock.com/Nikada

EXAMPLE13 CALCULATING MUTUAL FUND SALES CHARGE PERCENT

The South Shore Equity BB fund has an offer price of $6.75 per share and a net asset value of $6.44. What are the sales charge and the sales charge percent?

SOLUTIONSTRATEGY

Step 1. Mutual fund sales charge = Offer price − Net asset value

Mutual fund sales charge = 6.75 − 6.44 = $0.31 per share

Step 2. $\text{Sales charge percent} = \dfrac{\text{Sales charge}}{\text{Net asset value}}$

$\text{Sales charge percent} = \dfrac{.31}{6.44} = .0481 = \underline{\underline{4.8\%}}$

TRYITEXERCISE 13

What are the sales charge and the sales charge percent for the Alta Vista SJ fund with an offer price of $9.85 per share and net asset value of $9.21?

CHECK YOUR ANSWERS WITH THE SOLUTIONS ON PAGE 719.

20-11 CALCULATING THE NET ASSET VALUE OF A MUTUAL FUND

The assets of a mutual fund consist of the total current value of the stocks or bonds that the fund owns. As stated earlier, a mutual fund's net asset value is the per share price of the fund's stock.

STEPS TO CALCULATE NET ASSET VALUE OF A MUTUAL FUND

STEP 1. Calculate net asset value by subtracting the total liabilities from the total assets of the fund and dividing by the number of shares outstanding.

$$\text{Net asset value (NAV)} = \frac{\text{Total assets} - \text{Total liabilities}}{\text{Number of shares outstanding}}$$

STEP 2. Round the answer to dollars and cents.

EXAMPLE14 CALCULATING NET ASSET VALUE

The Elite Global CX fund has total assets of $40,000,000 and liabilities of $6,000,000. If there are 12,000,000 shares outstanding, what is the net asset value of the fund?

▶SOLUTIONSTRATEGY

$$\text{Net asset value} = \frac{\text{Total assets} - \text{Total liabilities}}{\text{Number of shares outstanding}}$$

$$\text{Net asset value} = \frac{40,000,000 - 6,000,000}{12,000,000} = \underline{\$2.83 \text{ per share}}$$

▶TRYITEXERCISE 14

The Freeport Ultra A fund has total assets of $80,000,000 and liabilities of $5,000,000. If there are 17,000,000 shares outstanding, what is the net asset value of the fund?

CHECK YOUR ANSWERS WITH THE SOLUTIONS ON PAGE 719.

20-12 CALCULATING THE NUMBER OF SHARES PURCHASED OF A MUTUAL FUND

Investors frequently purchase shares of mutual funds by using lump-sum amounts of money. To accommodate this practice, most funds sell fractional shares of their stock.

STEPS TO CALCULATE NUMBER OF SHARES PURCHASED OF A MUTUAL FUND

STEP 1. Calculate number of shares by dividing the amount of the investment by the offer price of the fund. For no-load funds, use the net asset value as the denominator.

$$\text{Number of shares purchased} = \frac{\text{Total investment}}{\text{Offer price}}$$

STEP 2. Round the number of shares to thousandths (three decimal places).

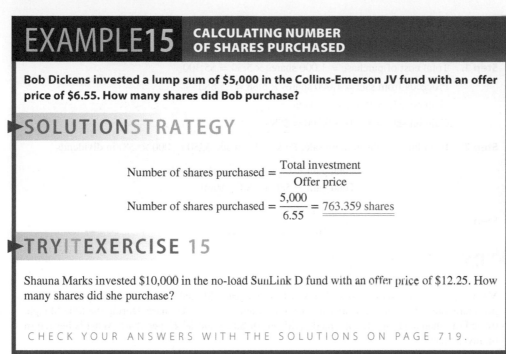

EXAMPLE15 CALCULATING NUMBER OF SHARES PURCHASED

Bob Dickens invested a lump sum of $5,000 in the Collins-Emerson JV fund with an offer price of $6.55. How many shares did Bob purchase?

►SOLUTIONSTRATEGY

$$\text{Number of shares purchased} = \frac{\text{Total investment}}{\text{Offer price}}$$

$$\text{Number of shares purchased} = \frac{5,000}{6.55} = \underline{763.359 \text{ shares}}$$

►TRYITEXERCISE 15

Shauna Marks invested $10,000 in the no-load SunLink D fund with an offer price of $12.25. How many shares did she purchase?

CHECK YOUR ANSWERS WITH THE SOLUTIONS ON PAGE 719.

CALCULATING RETURN ON INVESTMENT

20-13

Regardless of whether you are investing in stocks, bonds, or mutual funds, the basic measure of how your investments are doing is known as the **return on investment (ROI)**. This performance yardstick allows investors to compare various investments on an equal basis. Return on investment takes into account all transaction charges, such as broker's commissions and fees, as well as income received, such as dividends and interest payments. ROI is expressed as a percent rounded to the nearest tenth.

return on investment (ROI) The basic measure of how an investment is doing. Used to compare various investments on an equal basis. Calculated as a percent by dividing the total gain on the investment by the total cost of purchase.

STEPS TO CALCULATE RETURN ON INVESTMENT

STEP 1. Calculate the dollar gain (or loss) on the sale of the investment by subtracting the total cost from the proceeds of the sale.

Gain (or loss) on investment = Proceeds − Total cost

STEP 2. Compute total gain (or loss) by adding any dividends received on stocks or interest received on bonds to the gain (or loss) on sale.

Total gain (or loss) = Gain (or loss) + Dividends or interest

STEP 3. Calculate return on investment by dividing the total gain (or loss) by the total cost of purchase. Round your answer to the nearest tenth percent.

$$\text{Return on investment (ROI)} = \frac{\text{Total gain (or loss)}}{\text{Total cost of purchase}}$$

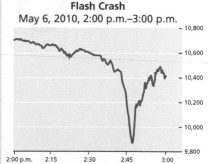

Flash Crash
May 6, 2010, 2:00 p.m.–3:00 p.m.

Flash Crash The Securities and Exchange Commission has installed new "circuit breakers" to prevent sudden stock market plunges such as the Flash Crash that occurred on May 6, 2010. On that date, the Dow Jones Industrial Average fell more than 600 points in just 20 minutes.

The new rule is that trading in certain stocks is now halted temporarily whenever their price moves more than 10% within five minutes.

EXAMPLE16 CALCULATING RETURN ON INVESTMENT

Parker Winslow purchased 1,000 shares of Classic Mutual fund for an offer price of $5.30 per share. He later sold the shares at a net asset value of $5.88 per share. During the time Parker owned the shares, Classic paid a dividend of $0.38 per share. What is his return on investment?

iStock.ccm/Nikada

SOLUTIONSTRATEGY

Step 1. Total cost of purchase = 1,000 shares × 5.30 = $5,300

Proceeds from sale = 1,000 shares × 5.88 = $5,880

Gain on sale = Proceeds − Total cost

Gain on sale = 5,880 − 5,300 = $580

Step 2. In addition to the gain on sale, Parker also made $380 (1,000 × .38) in dividends.

Total gain = Gain on sale + Dividends

Total gain = 580 + 380 = $960

Step 3. Return on investment = $\dfrac{\text{Total gain (or loss)}}{\text{Total cost of purchase}} = \dfrac{960}{5,300} = .18113 = \underline{18.1\%}$

TRYITEXERCISE 16

Maggie Flowers purchased 2,000 shares of Harley Escape Mutual fund for an offer price of $8.60 per share. She later sold the shares at a net asset value of $9.18 per share. During the time Maggie owned the shares, Harley Escape paid dividends of $0.27 and $0.42 per share. What is her return on investment?

CHECK YOUR ANSWERS WITH THE SOLUTIONS ON PAGE 719.

IN THE Business World

An Exchange Trade Fund (ETF) is a security instrument that typically tracks an index (e.g., the S&P 500) or another basket of assets. An ETF trades like a common stock, and so, unlike mutual funds, its price changes throughout the day. Operating expenses and fees for an ETF are generally lower than for a managed mutual fund.

rtguest/Shutterstock.com

SECTION III **20** **REVIEW EXERCISES**

Use Exhibit 20-6, Mutual Fund Quotation Table, on page 708 to fill in the blanks for Exercises 1–10.

JUMP START www

1. PIMCO Fds Institutional, AllAsset—Symbol and Net asset value: **PAAIX, $12.30**

2. John Hancock Funds A, HiYMuBdA p—YTD % return and 3-year % change   _____

3. Which mutual fund has the lowest net asset value? How much?   _____

_____

4. Which mutual fund has the highest YTD % return? How much?   _____

_____

5. Which mutual fund has the lowest 3-year % change? How much?   _____

_____

6. Vanguard Index Funds, 500 Index—Net asset value and Change: _____

7. Which Fidelity Invest fund has the best 3-year % change? How much?   _____

8. American Funds Class A, ICAA p—Symbol and Net asset value: _____

9. In what family is the DivIntl fund? What is the YTD % return?   _____

10. Which PIMCO fund has the symbol PTRIX? What is the NAV?   _____

Calculate the sales charge and sales charge percent for the following mutual funds.

Fund	Offer Price	Net Asset Value	Sales Charge	Sales Charge %
11. Prime Value CT	$18.25	$17.58	$.67	3.8%
12. Northstar A: MuFl A	$13.35	$12.82	___	___
13. Retire Invst Trust: Income	$15.44	$15.44	___	___
14. Rightime Group:	$26.97	$25.69	___	___

15. You purchase a mutual fund at an offer price of $10.76 per share. If the net asset value is $10.27, find the sale charge percent. Round to the nearest tenth.

Calculate the net asset value and number of shares purchased for the following mutual funds. Round shares to thousandths (three decimal places).

Total Assets	Total Liabilities	Shares Outstanding	Net Asset Value	Offer Price	Total Investment	Shares Purchased
16. $25,000,000	$6,300,000	2,000,000	$9.35	$9.92	$8,000	806.452
17. $52,000,000	$1,800,000	6,100,000	___	$9.50	$5,000	___
18. $95,400,000	$4,650,000	8,500,000	___	$11.15	$50,000	___

19. Suppose you own a mutual fund which has 14,000,000 shares outstanding. If it's total assets are $38,000,000 and it's liabilities are $9,000,000, find the net asset value of the fund. Round to the nearest cent.

20. A mutual fund has an offer price of $14.05. If you invested a lump sum of $11,000, how many shares did you purchases? Round to the nearest thousandth.

Calculate the total cost, proceeds, total gain (or loss), and return on investment for the following mutual fund investments. The offer price is the purchase price of the shares, and the net asset value is the price at which the shares were later sold.

Shares	Offer Price	Total Cost	Net Asset Value	Proceeds	Per Share Dividends	Total Gain (or Loss)	Return on Investment %
21. 300	$12.50	$3,750	$14.20	$4,260	$.25	$585	15.6
22. 500	$10.40	___	$12.90	___	$.68	___	___
23. 1,000	$4.85	___	$6.12	___	$1.25	___	___
24. 700	$7.30	___	$5.10	___	0	___	___

25. You purchased 1000 shares of a mutual fund at an offer price of $13.78 per share. Several months later you sold the shares for $14.52 per share.

During the time you owned the shares, the fund paid a dividend of $0.66. per share. What was your return on investment? Round to the nearest tenth.

26. The Victoria Growth fund has an offer price of $13.10 and a net asset value of $12.35.

    a. What is the sales charge?

    b. What is the sales charge percent?

27. The Capital MGT fund has total assets of $25,000,000 and liabilities of $3,500,000. If there are 8,600,000 shares outstanding, what is the net asset value of the fund?

28. Stuart Spector invested a lump sum of $10,000 in a mutual fund with an offer price of $14.50. How many shares did he purchase?

29. Butch Gold purchased 500 shares of Shoreline Value fund for an offer price of $8.90 per share. He later sold the shares at a net asset value of $10.50 per share. During the time that he owned the shares, the fund paid a dividend of $0.75 per share three times. What is Butch's return on investment?

BUSINESS DECISION: CAPITAL GAINS

30. There are many tax rules and regulations you should be aware of when investing—whether it be in stocks; bonds; mutual funds; real estate; or collectibles such as artwork, antiques, gems, memorabilia, stamps, and coins. **Capital gains** are proceeds derived from these types of investments. Unless they are specified as being tax-free, such as municipal bonds, you must pay capital gains taxes on these proceeds.

    Capital gains are taxed in one of two ways. If the investment is held for one year or less, this is considered **short-term** and is taxed as ordinary income at your regular income tax rate. As this is written, if the investment is held for more than one year, it is considered **long-term** and qualifies for various tax discounts, as follows for single taxpayers with earnings as shown below:

	Capital Gains Rates		
Stocks Held	**Up to $38,700**	**$38,700–$426,700**	**Over $426,700**
Over 1 year (long-term)	0%	15%	20%

    a. If you are in the 22% tax bracket for ordinary income and have a 15% capital gains rate, how much tax will you save by waiting for an investment to become long-term before selling it if your taxable profit from this investment is $25,000?

    b. How much will you save if you are in the 37% tax bracket for ordinary income and have a 20% capital gains rate?

CHAPTER FORMULAS

CHAPTER
20

Stocks

Dividend per share (preferred) = Par value + Dividend rate

$$\text{Dividend per share (common)} = \frac{\text{Total common dividend}}{\text{Number of shares (common)}}$$

$$\text{Current yield} = \frac{\text{Annual dividend per share}}{\text{Current price of the stock}}$$

$$\text{Price-earnings ratio} = \frac{\text{Current price per share}}{\text{Earnings per share}}$$

Gain (or loss) on stock = Proceeds − Total cost

Bonds

Price per bond = Current market price + Accrued interest + Commission

Proceeds = Current market price + Accrued interest − Commission

$$\text{Current yield} = \frac{\text{Annual interest}}{\text{Current market price}}$$

Mutual funds

Mutual fund sales charge = Offer price − Net asset value

$$\text{Sales charge percent} = \frac{\text{Sales charge}}{\text{Net asset value}}$$

$$\text{Net asset value (NAV)} = \frac{\text{Total assets} - \text{Total liabilities}}{\text{Number of shares outstanding}}$$

$$\text{Number of shares purchased} = \frac{\text{Total investment}}{\text{Offer price}}$$

$$\text{Return on investment (ROI)} = \frac{\text{Total gain (or loss)}}{\text{Total cost of purchase}}$$

CHAPTER SUMMARY

Section I: Stocks

Topic	Important Concepts	Illustrative Examples
Distributing Dividends on Preferred and Common Stock **Performance Objective 20-1, Page 686**	Companies raise capital by selling stock. Common stock shares in the success or failure of the business. Preferred stock receives a fixed dividend and is paid before common. Cumulative preferred receives dividends in arrears, those not paid in past years. Preferred dividends are stated as a percent of par value or as a dollar amount for no-par preferred. Dividends are distributed as follows: 1. Cumulative preferred—Arrears 2. Preferred—Current period 3. Common—Current period	Infiniti Corp. has 100,000 shares of $100 par, 7%, cumulative preferred and 300,000 shares of common stock. No dividend was declared last year. This year a $2,000,000 dividend was declared. Distribute the dividends between the two classes of stock. Preferred stockholders receive 100 × .07 = $7 per share. Preferred—Arrears: 100,000 shares × 7 = $700,000 Preferred—Current: 100,000 shares × 7 = 700,000 Total due preferred = $1,400,000 Common: 　$2,000,000　Total dividend − 1,400,000　Preferred dividend 　$600,000　Common dividend $\text{Dividend per share} = \dfrac{600,000}{300,000} = \$2$

Section I (continued)

Topic	Important Concepts	Illustrative Examples
Calculating Current Yield of a Stock **Performance Objective 20-3, Page 691**	Current yield is a percentage measure of how well your stock is performing in terms of its ability to obtain dividends.	What is the current yield of Royal Industries stock, which pays a dividend of $2.35 per share and is currently selling for $57.25? $$\text{Current yield} = \frac{2.35}{57.25} = 4.1\%$$
Determining the Price-Earnings Ratio of a Stock **Performance Objective 20-4, Page 692**	The price-earnings ratio of a stock shows the relationship between the price of a stock and the company's earnings for the past 12 months.	Escapade, Inc., stock is selling at $34.35. If the company had earnings per share of $4.27, calculate the price-earnings ratio. $$\text{PE ratio} = \frac{34.35}{4.27} = 8.04 = 8$$
Computing the Cost, Proceeds, and Gain (or Loss) on a Stock Transaction **Performance Objective 20-5, Page 693**	Stocks are purchased and sold through stockbrokers, who charge a commission for these services. Round lots are purchases in multiples of 100 shares. Odd lots are purchases of less than 100 shares. Extra commission is usually charged for odd lots.	You purchase 450 shares of Apollo Corp. common stock at $19.75 per share. A few months later you sell the shares at $27.50. Your stockbroker charges 3% on round lots and 4% on odd lots. What are the total cost, the proceeds, and the gain (or loss) on your investment? *Purchase:* Cost of shares = 450 × 19.75 = $8,887.50 Commission = $\quad$ 400 × 19.75 × .03 = $237.00 $\quad$ 50 × 19.75 × .04 = $\underline{\quad 39.50}$ $\quad$ Total commission = $276.50 Total cost of purchase = $\quad$ 8,887.50 + 276.50 = $\underline{\underline{\$9,164}}$ *Sale:* Value of shares = 450 × 27.50 = $12,375 Commission = $\quad$ 400 × 27.50 × .03 = $330 $\quad$ 50 × 27.50 × .04 = $\underline{\quad 55}$ $\quad$ Total commission = $385 Proceeds = 12,375 − 385 = $\underline{\underline{\$11,990}}$ *Gain:* $\quad$ 11,990 − 9,164 = $\underline{\underline{\$2,826}}$

Section II: Bonds

Topic	Important Concepts	Illustrative Examples
Calculating the Cost of Purchasing Bonds **Performance Objective 20-7, Page 702**	Bonds are loans to companies or governments that pay fixed interest semiannually. *Buying Bonds:* 1. Calculate accrued interest since the last payment by $I = PRT$. 2. Calculate the price to purchase the bond by 3. Calculate total purchase price by	What is the purchase price of 10 Venture bonds with a coupon rate of 5.5% and a current market price of 96.25? The commission charge is $6 per bond. The date of the purchase is November 1; the bond pays interest on January 1 and July 1. $$\text{Accrued interest} = 1,000 \times .055 \times \frac{4}{12} = \$18.33$$ Price per bond = $\quad$ 962.50 + 18.33 + 6.00 = $\underline{\underline{\$986.83}}$ Total purchase price = 986.83 × 10 = $\underline{\underline{\$9,868.30}}$

Section II (continued)

Topic	Important Concepts	Illustrative Examples
Calculating Proceeds from the Sale of Bonds **Performance Objective 20-7, Page 702**	*Selling Bonds:* 1. Calculate accrued interest since last payment by $I = PRT$. 2. Calculate the proceeds per bond by 3. Calculate the total proceeds of the sale by	Tony Stewart sold 5 Safire Corp. bonds with a coupon rate of 6.375% and a current market price of 107.75. The commission charge is $8 per bond. The date of sale is 100 days since the last interest payment. What are Tony's proceeds? Accrued interest $= 1,000 \times .06375 \times \dfrac{100}{360}$ $= \$17.71$ Proceeds per bond $=$ $1,077.50 + 17.71 - 8.00 = \$1,087.21$ Total proceeds $= 1,087.21 \times 5 = \underline{\$5,436.05}$
Calculating the Current Yield of a Bond **Performance Objective 20-8, Page 704**	Current yield is a simple measure of the return on investment based on the current market price of the bond.	Calculate the current yield of a Landmark Electronics bond with a coupon rate of 9.25% currently selling at a premium of 112.50. Annual interest $= 1,000 \times .0925 = \$92.50$ Current yield $= \dfrac{92.50}{1,125} = \underline{8.2\%}$

Section III: Mutual Funds

Topic	Important Concepts	Illustrative Examples
Calculating the Sales Charge and Sales Charge Percent of a Mutual Fund **Performance Objective 20-10, Page 709**	The mutual fund sales charge or load may vary from 1% to 8% of the amount invested. When it is paid at the time of purchase, it is known as a front-end load. It is the difference between the offer price and the net asset value of the fund.	What are the sales charge and the sales charge percent for Value Line fund with an offer price of $12.35 per share and a net asset value of $11.60? Sales charge $= 12.35 - 11.60 = \underline{\$0.75 \text{ per share}}$ Sales charge % $= \dfrac{.75}{11.60} = \underline{6.5\%}$
Calculating the Net Asset Value of a Mutual Fund **Performance Objective 20-11, Page 710**	The assets of a mutual fund are the total current value of its investments. The net asset value is the per share figure.	Diamond Equity fund has total assets of $20,000,000 and liabilities of $5,000,000. If there are 4,000,000 shares outstanding, what is the net asset value of the fund? Net asset value $= \dfrac{20,000,000 - 5,000,000}{4,000,000}$ $= \underline{\$3.75}$
Calculating the Number of Shares Purchased of a Mutual Fund **Performance Objective 20-12, Page 710**	Mutual fund stock is sold in fractional shares to accommodate those investing lump sums of money. Shares are rounded to thousandths (three decimal places). *Note*: For no-load funds, use net asset value as the denominator.	Carol Linville invested a lump sum of $10,000 in a mutual fund with an offer price of $8.75. How many shares did she purchase? Number of shares $= \dfrac{10,000}{8.75} = \underline{1,142.857}$

Section III (continued)

Topic	Important Concepts	Illustrative Examples
Calculating Return on Investment **Performance Objective 20-13, Page 711**	Return on investment is the basic measure of how your stocks, bonds, or mutual fund investments are doing. 1. Calculate the gain (or loss) on the investment by 2. Compute total gain (or loss) by 3. Calculate return on investment by	Noah Gomberg purchased 1,000 shares of Cayenne Growth fund for an offer price of $7.50 per share. He later sold the shares at a net asset value of $8.75. During the time he owned the shares, Noah was paid a dividend of $0.85 per share. What is his return on investment? Total cost = 1,000 × 7.50 = $7,500 Proceeds = 1,000 × 8.75 = $8,750 Gain = 8,750 − 7,500 = $1,250 Dividends = 1,000 × .85 = $850 Total gain = 1,250 + 850 = $2,100 $\text{ROI} = \dfrac{2,100}{7,500} = .28 = \underline{\underline{28\%}}$

TRY IT: EXERCISE SOLUTIONS FOR CHAPTER 20

1. $\text{Dividend per share} = \dfrac{\text{Total common dividend}}{\text{Number of shares}}$

$\text{Dividend per share} = \dfrac{910,000}{1,400,000} = \underline{\underline{\$0.65}}$

2. Total preferred dividend = Number of shares × Dividend per share

Total preferred dividend = 600,000 × 1.40 = $\underline{\$840,000}$

Total common dividend = Total dividend − Total preferred dividend

Total common dividend = 2,800,000 − 840,000 = $1,960,000

$\text{Dividend per share} = \dfrac{\text{Total common dividend}}{\text{Number of shares}}$

$\text{Dividend per share} = \dfrac{1,960,000}{1,000,000} = \underline{\underline{\$1.96}}$

3. Dividend per share = Par value × Dividend rate

Dividend per share = 100 × 7.5% = $7.50

Total preferred div. (per year) = Number of shares × Div. per share

Total preferred div. (per year) = 300,000 × 7.50 = $2,250,000

Total preferred div. = 2,250,000 (arrears) + 2,250,000 (this year)
= $\underline{\$4,500,000}$

Total common div. = Total div. − Total preferred div.

Total common div. = 7,000,000 − 4,500,000 = $2,500,000

$\text{Dividend per share} = \dfrac{2,5000,000}{5,200,000} = \underline{\underline{\$0.48}}$

4.

Name	ABM Industries
Symbol	ABM
Open	$30.98
High	$31.12
Low	$30.71
Close	$31.12
Net Change	none
Percent Change	0%
Volume	267,275 shares
52-Week High	$45.12
52-Week Low	$28.17
Dividend	$0.70 per share
Yield	2.25%
P/E	23.18
YTD % Change	down 17.50%

5. $\text{Current yield} = \dfrac{\text{Annual dividend per share}}{\text{Current price of stock}}$

$\text{Current yield} = \dfrac{.68}{12.84} = \underline{\underline{5.3\%}}$

6. $\text{Price-earnings ratio} = \dfrac{\text{Current price per share}}{\text{Earnings per share}}$

$\text{Price-earnings ratio} = \dfrac{37.19}{6.70} = 5.55 = \underline{\underline{6}}$

7. a. *Cost of stock:*

Cost of shares = Price per share × Number of shares

Cost of shares = 44.80 × 225 = $\underline{\$10,080}$

Broker's commission = Cost of shares × Comm. rate

Round lot = 200 × 44.80 × .02 = $179.20

Odd lot = 25 × 44.80 × .03 = $33.60

Total commission = 179.20 + 33.60 = $\underline{\$212.80}$

Total cost = Cost of shares + Commission

Total cost = 10,080.00 + 212.80 = $\underline{\$10,292.80}$

b. *Proceeds from sale:*

Value of shares = Price per share × Number of shares

Value of shares = 53.20 × 225 = $\underline{\$11,970}$

Commission:

Round lot = 200 × 53.20 × .02 = $212.80

Odd lot = 25 × 53.20 × .03 = $39.90

Total commission = 212.80 + 39.90 = $\underline{\$252.70}$

Proceeds = Value of shares − Broker's commission

Proceeds = 11,970.00 − 252.70 = $\underline{\$11,717.30}$

c. **Gain (or loss) on transaction:**

Gain = Proceeds − Total cost

Gain = 11,717.30 − 10,292.80 = $1,424.50

8. The coupon rate is 3.875%. The ask price is $940.83 (1,000 × .94083). The yield to maturity is 4.734%.

9. Accrued interest = $1{,}000 \times .0625 \times \dfrac{2}{12} = \$10.42$

Price per bond = Current market price + Accrued int. + Comm.

Price per bond = 913.75 + 10.42 + 10.00 = $934.17

Total purchase price = Price per bond × Number of bonds

Total purchase price = 934.17 × 20 = $18,683.40

10. Accrued interest = $1{,}000 \times .08875 \times \dfrac{122}{360} = \$30.08$

Proceeds per bond = Current market price + Accrued interest − Comm.

Proceeds per bond = 990.00 + 30.08 − 10.00 = $1,010.08

Total proceeds = Proceeds per bond × Number of bonds

Total proceeds = 1,010.08 × 5 = $5,050.40

11. Annual interest = Par value × Coupon rate

Annual interest = 1,000 × .09375 = $93.75

Current price = Par value × Price percent

Current price = 1,000 × .8475 = $847.50

Current yield = $\dfrac{\text{Annual interest}}{\text{Market price}}$

Current yield = $\dfrac{93.75}{847.50} = .1106 = \underline{11.1\%}$

12. Family/Fund   John Hancock Funds A, ClassicVal p fund

    Symbol   PZFVX

    Net asset value $13.70

Change   up $0.03

YTD % Return   down 4.8%

3-year % Change   down 15.8%

13. Mutual fund sales charge = Offer price − Net asset value

Mutual fund sales charge = 9.85 − 9.21 = $0.64

Sales charge percent = $\dfrac{\text{Sales charge}}{\text{NAV}} = \dfrac{.64}{9.21} = \underline{6.9\%}$

14. Net asset value = $\dfrac{\text{Total assets} - \text{Total liabilities}}{\text{Number of shares}}$

Net asset value = $\dfrac{80{,}000{,}000 - 5{,}000{,}000}{17{,}000{,}000} = \underline{\$4.41}$

15. Number of shares purchased = $\dfrac{\text{Total investment}}{\text{Offer price}}$

Number of shares purchased = $\dfrac{10{,}000}{12.25} = \underline{816.327 \text{ shares}}$

16. Total cost of purchase = 2,000 × 8.60 = $17,200

Proceeds from sale = 2,000 × 9.18 = $18,360

Gain on sale = Proceeds − Total cost

Gain on sale = 18,360 − 17,200 = $1,160

Dividends: 2,000 × .27 = $540

          2,000 × .42 = $840

Total dividends = 540 + 840 = $1,380

Total gain = Gain on sale + Dividends

Total gain = 1,160 + 1,380 = $2,540

Return on investment = $\dfrac{\text{Total gain (or loss)}}{\text{Total cost of purchase}}$

ROI = $\dfrac{2{,}540}{17{,}200} = .1476 = \underline{14.8\%}$

CONCEPT REVIEW

1. _____, or equities, are a major investment category represented by an ownership share of a corporation. (20-1)

2. A distribution of a company's profits to its shareholders is known as _____. (20-1)

3. _____ stock is a class of stock in which the investor has voting rights. A class of stock in which the investor has preferential rights to dividends and company assets is known as _____ stock. (20-1)

4. When you are reading a stock table, which two columns indicate a stock's performance in the past full year? Which column indicates how a stock has done so far in the current year? (20-2)

5. The current _____ is a measure of how well the stock is performing in terms of its ability to earn dividends. Write the formula used to calculate this measure. (20-3)

6. The _____ ratio shows the relationship between the price of a stock and the company's earnings for the past 12 months. (20-4)

7. Write the formula used to calculate the gain (or loss) on an investment in stocks. (20-5)

8. A _____ is a loan, or an IOU, in the form of an interest-bearing note in which the buyer lends money to the issuer. (20-6)

9. When you sell a bond, your proceeds from the sale are the current market price plus _____ interest minus the broker's _____. (20-7)

10. Write the formula used to calculate the current yield of a bond. (20-8)

11. _____ _____ are professionally managed collective investment accounts that pool the money from many individuals and invest it in stocks, bonds, and other securities. (20-9)

12. The dollar value of one share of a mutual fund's stock is known as the net _____ _____. (20-10, 20-11)

13. The price per share investors pay when purchasing a mutual fund is known as the _____ price. (20-12)

14. The basic measure of how well an investment is doing is known as the _____ on investment. Write the formula used to calculate this measure. (20-13)

ASSESSMENT TEST

Calculate the preferred and common stock dividend per share for the following companies.

Company	Common Stock Shares	Preferred Stock Shares	Div. or Par.	Cum.	Dividend Declared	Arrears	Preferred Div./Share	Common Div./Share
1. Granville, Inc.	22,000,000		None		$7,900,000	None	_____	_____
2. F. Drake, Inc.	4,000,000	1,000,000	$3.20	Yes	$8,200,000	1 year	_____	_____
3. High-Point, LLC	80,000,000	3,400,000	$100, 5%	Yes	$58,000,000	2 years	_____	_____

Use Exhibit 20-3, Stock Quotation Table, on page 690 to fill in the blanks for Exercises 4–7.

4. Acadia Realty Trust—Open, High, Low, and Close: _____

5. Which stock had the lowest volume? How much? _____

6. Aaron's Inc.—Dividend, Yield, P/E: _____

7. Which stock had the highest year-to-date percent change? How much? _____
_____

Calculate the missing information for the following stocks.

Company	Earnings per Share	Annual Dividend	Current Price per Share	Current Yield%	Price-Earnings Ratio
8. Windstar, Inc.	$3.20	$1.50	$69.25	_____	_____
9. Fortuna Corp.	_____	$1.12	$33.50	_____	16
10. Alliance Industries	$2.10	$.48	_____	1.2	_____
11. Big Ben, Inc.	_____	_____	$89.75	1.9	10

Calculate the total cost, proceeds, and gain (or loss) for the following stock market transactions.

Company	Number of Shares	Purchase Price	Selling Price	Commissions Buy	Commissions Sell	Commissions Odd Lot	Total Cost	Proceeds	Gain (or Loss)
12. Regal Fantasy	400	$39.25	$44.75	2%	2%	—	_____	_____	_____
13. Tip-Top Imports	630	$24.13	$19.88	3%	3%	Add 1%	_____	_____	_____
14. Apex Mining	200	$61.50	$71.25	2%	2%	—	_____	_____	_____
15. Gold Masters	850	$45.50	$53.75	1.5%	1.5%	Add 1%	_____	_____	_____

16. The board of directors of Micro-Fine Fabricators, Inc., has declared a dividend of $16,000,000. The company has 800,000 shares of preferred stock that pay $4.90 per share and 8,200,000 shares of common stock.

    a. What are the dividends due the preferred shareholders?

    b. What is the dividend per share of common stock?

17. Equinox Energy Inc. has 500,000 shares of $100 par value, 6.5%, cumulative preferred stock and 8,400,000 shares of common stock. Although no dividend was declared for the past three years, a $19,000,000 dividend has been declared for this year.

    a. How much is due the preferred shareholders?

    b. What is the dividend per share of common stock?

18. ICC Corp. stock is currently selling at $34.22 per share. The earnings per share are $2.84, and the dividend is $.93.

    a. What is the current yield of the stock?

    b. What is the price-earnings ratio?

19. You purchase 350 shares of Universal Metals common stock at $12.38 per share. A few months later you sell the shares at $9.88. Your stockbroker charges 3% commission on round lots and an extra 1.5% on odd lots.

    a. What is the total cost of the purchase?

    b. What are the proceeds on the sale?

    c. What is the gain (or loss) on the transaction?

Use Exhibit 20-5, Corporate Bond Quotation, on page 701 to fill in the blanks for Questions 20–25.

20.   BLACK IIILLS CORP—Bid price in dollars: _____

21.   COMCAST CORP – Next call date: _____

22.   VERIZON COMMUNICATIONS INC – Ask price in dollars: _____

23.   BROADCOM CORP/BROADCOM CAYMAN – Bid price in dollars: _____

24.   KRAFT HEINZ FOODS – Yield to Maturity: _____

25.   CBS CORP – Ratings: _____

CHAPTER 20

Calculate the accrued interest and the total purchase price of the following bond purchases.

Company	Coupon Rate	Market Price	Time Since Last Interest	Accrued Interest	Commission per Bond	Bonds Purchased	Total Price
26. Raven Corp.	8.25%	95.375	65 days	_____	$5.00	10	_____
27. CommScope	7.375	78.50	100 days	_____	$9.50	5	_____
28. LandStar, Inc.	5.625	105.75	3 months	_____	$7.00	15	_____

Calculate the accrued interest and the total proceeds of the following bond sales.

Company	Coupon Rate	Market Price	Time Since Last Interest	Accrued Interest	Commission per Bond	Bonds Purchased	Total Price
29. Logic-Wise	7.375%	94.50	10 days	_____	$6.00	10	_____
30. Micro Capital	8.875	109.25	4 months	_____	$5.00	20	_____
31. RAB Limited	9.25	98.00	85 days	_____	$8.00	5	_____

Calculate the annual interest and current yield of the following bonds.

Company	Coupon Rate	Annual Interest	Market Price	Current Yield
32. Asia Express Corp.	5.375%	_____	94.125	_____
33. Dynamic Ventures	9.5	_____	105.75	_____

34. On May 1, Emerson Fast bought 10 Manitoba Polar bonds with a coupon rate of 7.875%. The purchase price was 101.375, and the commission was $8 per bond. Manitoba Polar bonds pay interest on April 1 and October 1.

a. What is the current yield of the bond?

b. What is the total purchase price of the bonds?

c. If Emerson sold the bonds on August 1 for 109.50, what are the proceeds from the sale?

Use Exhibit 20-6, Mutual Fund Quotation Table, on page 708 to fill in the blanks for Questions 35–38.

35. Which mutual fund has the highest NAV? How much?   _____

36. Fidelity Invest, RealEstInc—Symbol, YTD % return: _____

37. Pimco Fds Institutional—AllAsset – NAV, Change: _____

38. Which fund has the highest 3-year % change? How much?   _____

Calculate the sales charge and sales charge percent for the following mutual funds.

Fund	Offer Price	Net Asset Value (NAV)	Sales Charge	Sales Charge%
39. Quest for Value: CA TE	$10.88	$10.36	_____	_____
40. Sentinel Group: EmGr	$5.59	$5.31	_____	_____

Calculate the net asset value and number of shares purchased for the following mutual funds. Round shares to thousandths (three decimal places).

	Total Assets	Total Liabilities	Shares Outstanding	Net Asset Value (NAV)	Offer Price	Total Investment	Shares Purchased
41.	$30,000,000	$1,800,000	4,000,000	_____	$7.80	$50,000	_____
42.	$58,000,000	$3,700,000	7,100,000	_____	NL	$25,000	_____

Calculate the total cost, proceeds, total gain (or loss), and return on investment for the following mutual fund investments. The offer price is the purchase price of the shares, and the net asset value is the price at which the shares were later sold.

	Shares	Offer Price	Total Cost	Net Asset Value (NAV)	Proceeds	Per Share Dividends	Total Gain (or Loss)	Return on Investment %
43.	100	$13.40	_____	$11.80	_____	$.75	_____	_____
44.	500	$12.65	_____	$15.30	_____	$.63	_____	_____
45.	1,000	$9.40	_____	$12.82	_____	$.96	_____	_____

46. RedRock Strategic fund has an offer price of $8.90 and a net asset value of $8.35.
   a. What is the sales charge?

   b. What is the sales charge percent?

47. Springfield Aggressive fund has total assets of $25,000,000 and liabilities of $1,500,000. If there are 2,600,000 shares outstanding, what is the net asset value of the fund?

48. Karl Hellman invested a lump sum of $20,000 in a mutual fund with an offer price of $11.80. How many shares did he purchase?

49. Kyle Pressman purchased 800 shares of Three Sisters Value fund for an offer price of $6.90 per share. He later sold the shares at a net asset value of $8.60 per share. During the time he owned the shares, the fund paid dividends of $0.24 and $0.38 per share. What is Kyle's return on investment?

BUSINESS DECISION: PAPER PROFIT

50. You have received your investment portfolio year-end statement from your broker, Rich Waldman. All investments were purchased at the January prices and held the entire year.

Portfolio Year-End Statement

Investment	Number	Dividend	Price—Jan. 1	Price—Dec. 31
FernRod Corp.	400 shares	$.30	$38.38	$45.75
Crown Realty, Inc.	500 shares	0	$74.50	$70.13
Sterling Mines	200 shares	$.24	$27.88	$29.25
SJB Enterprises	300 shares	$3.00	$68.75	$64.63
GTech 7.125% 16	20 bonds		$98.50	$101.38
Comet 9.875% 17	10 bonds		$103.88	$100.75

a. Calculate how much profit or loss you made for the year, including stock dividends and bond interest.

b. What was the total return on investment for your portfolio?

c. Using a broker's commission of 3% buying and 3% selling on the stocks and $5 buying and $5 selling per bond, how much profit or loss would you make if you liquidated your entire portfolio at the December 31 prices?

d. What would be the return on investment?

COLLABORATIVE LEARNING ACTIVITY

Yesterday, Today, and Tomorrow—An Economic Picture!

In this activity, you and your team members will research some of the more important investment and money indicators in the economy. Your best source of information for this project will be financial publications on the Internet.

a. Briefly explain what each indicator means and how it is derived.
b. Look up the current figure for each indicator and fill in the table on the following page.
c. Prepare a visual presentation (line graph or bar graph) of each indicator's performance trend using the historical data given and your current findings.
d. As a team, discuss and report to the class what each trend indicates and how it might affect your investment strategy.

Economic Indicator	October 12, 2007	August 3, 2018	Today
Dow Jones Industrial Average	14,093.08	25,430.10	_____
Standard & Poor's 500	1,561.80	2,834.94	_____
NASDAQ Composite Average	2,805.68	7,795.27	_____
30-year U.S. Treasury bond	4.76%	3.097%	_____
10-year U.S. Treasury note—Yield	4.649%	2.949%	_____
Euro (in U.S. dollars)	$1.4147	$1.16	_____
Canadian dollars (in U.S. dollars)	$1.0201	$0.77	_____
Gold (troy oz)	$740.40	$1,216.01	_____
Oil, W. Texas (per barrel)	$83.69	$69.30	_____
U.S. Prime Rate	7.75%	5.00%	_____
Certificate of deposit (6-month)	4.75%	2.15%	_____
30-year mortgage	6.30%	4.50%	_____
Consumer price index (CPI)	207.917	251.989	_____
Gross domestic product ($billions)	$13,630	$18,570	_____
Unemployment rate	4.4%	4.0%	_____
Average hourly earnings	$17.22	$27.05	_____

CHAPTER 21 Business Statistics and Data Presentation

PERFORMANCE OBJECTIVES

DATA INTERPRETATION AND PRESENTATION

INFORMATION, THE NAME OF THE GAME!

Statistical ideas and methods are used in almost every aspect of human activity, from the natural sciences to the social sciences. Statistics has special applications in such areas as medicine, psychology, education, engineering, and agriculture. In business, statistical methods are applied extensively in production, marketing, finance, and accounting.

Business statistics is the systematic process of collecting, interpreting, and presenting numerical data about business situations. In business, statistics is organized into two categories: descriptive statistics and statistical inference. **Descriptive statistics** deals with tabular, graphical, or numerical methods for organizing and summarizing information. Whereas **statistical inference** is the process of arriving at conclusions, predictions, forecasts, or estimates based on a sample drawn from the population of all data under consideration. For example, a company may contact a randomly selected sample of 250 customers and ask their opinion of a possible new product. From this sample, the company will try to infer information about the opinions of the entire population of prospective customers. In this chapter, we will concentrate on various types of descriptive statistical methods.

Business statistics starts with the collection of raw data concerning a particular business situation or question. For example, if management wants the next annual report to present a comparison chart of company sales and profit figures with current industry trends, two types of information are required. First are the company records of sales and profits. These data would be readily available from *internal* company sources. Most large corporations today use a vast array of computer systems to collect and store incredible amounts of information relating to all aspects of business activity. Management information systems are then used to deliver these data, upon request, in an electronic instant.

Information gathered from sources outside the firm, such as current industry statistics, is known as *external* data and is readily available from a variety of private and government publications. The federal government is by far the largest researcher and publisher of business data. The Departments of Commerce and Labor periodically publish information relating to all aspects of the economy and the country. Some of these publications are the *Statistical Abstract of the United States, Survey of Current Business, Monthly Labor Review, Federal Reserve Bulletin, Census of the United States*, and *Census of Business*.

Private statistical services such as Moody's Investors Service and Standard and Poor's offer a wealth of information for business decision making. Other private sources are periodicals such as the *Wall Street Journal, Fortune, Business Week, Forbes*, and *Money*, as well as hundreds of industry and trade publications, and websites.

Numerical data form the raw material on which analyses, forecasts, and managerial plans are based. In business, tables and charts are used extensively to summarize and display data in a clear and concise manner. In this section, you learn to read, interpret, and construct information from tables and charts.

business statistics The systematic process of collecting, interpreting, and presenting numerical data about business situations.

descriptive statistics Statistical procedures that deal with tabular, graphical, or numerical methods for organizing and summarizing information.

statistical inference The process of arriving at conclusions, predictions, forecasts, or estimates based on a sample drawn from the population of all data under consideration.

READING AND INTERPRETING INFORMATION FROM A TABLE

21-1

A **table** is a collection of related data arranged for ease of reference or comparison, usually in parallel columns with meaningful titles. Tables are a very useful tool in summarizing statistical data and are found everywhere in business. Once the data have been obtained from the table, they can be compared with other data by arithmetic or percentage analysis.

table A collection of related data arranged for ease of reference or comparison, usually in parallel columns with meaningful titles.

STEPS TO READING A TABLE

STEP 1. Scan the titles above the columns for the category of information being sought.

STEP 2. Look down the column for the specific fact required.

iStock.com/Nikada

Table 21-1 shows the sales figures in dollars for Magnum Enterprises over a six-month period. Magnum manufactures and sells standard and deluxe computer components. Note that the table is divided into columns representing sales per month of each product type by territory.

TABLE 21-1 Magnum Enterprises Six-Month Sales Report

	Magnum Enterprises Six-Month Sales Report										
	January		February		March		April		May		June	
	Standard	Deluxe	Standard	Deluxe	Standard	Deluxe	Standard	Deluxe	Standard	Deluxe	Standard	Deluxe
Northwest	$123,200	$86,400	$115,800	$73,700	$133,400	$91,100	$136,700	$92,600	$112,900	$65,300	$135,000	$78,400
Northeast	$214,700	$121,300	$228,400	$133,100	$246,600	$164,800	$239,000	$153,200	$266,100	$185,000	$279,300	$190,100
Southwest	$88,300	$51,000	$72,100	$45,700	$97,700	$58,300	$104,000	$67,800	$125,000	$78,300	$130,400	$74,500
Southeast	$143,200	$88,700	$149,900	$91,300	$158,400	$94,500	$127,700	$70,300	$145,700	$79,400	$162,000	$88,600

EXAMPLE1   READING A TABLE

Use Table 21-1 to answer the following questions about Magnum Enterprises.

a. What were the sales of deluxe units in April in the Northeast?
b. What were the sales of standard units in May in the Southwest?
c. What were the total sales for February and March in the Southeast?
d. What months showed a decrease in sales of deluxe units in the Northwest?
e. How much more standard sales were there company-wide in June than in January?
f. What percent of the total sales in March were deluxe?

▶SOLUTIONSTRATEGY

Questions a, b, and d can be answered by inspection. Questions c, e, and f require numerical or percentage calculations.

a. Deluxe unit sales in April in the Northeast = $153,200
b. Standard unit sales in May in the Southwest = $125,000
c. Total sales in February and March in the Southeast:
$$149,900 + 91,300 + 158,400 + 94,500 = \$494,100$$
d. Decrease in sales of deluxe units in the Northwest occurred in February and May.
e. Standard sales in January = $569,400
Standard sales in June = $706,700
$$706,700 - 569,400 = \$137,300 \text{ more in June}$$

f. To solve this problem, we use the percentage formula Rate = Portion ÷ Base. In this case, the rate is the unknown, the total sales in March is the base, and the deluxe sales in March is the portion.

$$\text{Rate} = \frac{408,700}{1,044,800} = .3911 = 39.1\%$$

▶TRYITEXERCISE 1

Use Table 21-1 to answer the following questions about Magnum Enterprises.

a. What were the sales of standard units in February in the Northeast?
b. What were the sales of deluxe units in April in the Southeast?
c. What were the total sales for May and June in the Northwest?
d. What months showed an increase in sales of standard units in the Southwest?
e. How much more deluxe sales were there company-wide in May than in April?
f. What percent of the total sales in the Northwest were standard?

CHECK YOUR ANSWERS WITH THE SOLUTIONS ON PAGE 767.

IN THE Business World

The material in this chapter presents concepts and procedures that will help you understand and evaluate statistical information that you encounter as both a consumer and businessperson.

Statistical information may be in the form of daily media such as radio and television reports or newspaper and magazine articles, or they may be business-related statistics such as company reports, presentations, budgets, and schedules.

rtguest/Shutterstock.com

READING AND CONSTRUCTING A LINE CHART

Charts are used to display a picture of the relationships among selected data. A **line chart** shows data changing over a period of time. A single glance at a line chart gives the viewer a general idea of the direction, or trend, of the data: up, down, or up and down.

The **horizontal axis**, or **x-axis**, is used to measure units of time, such as days, weeks, months, or years, whereas the **vertical axis**, or **y-axis**, depicts magnitude, such as sales dollars or production units. Frequently, the vertical axis is used to measure the percentage of something.

Line charts are actually a series of data points on a grid that are continuously connected by straight lines. They may contain a single line, representing the change of one variable such as interest rates, or they may contain multiple lines, representing the change of interrelated variables such as interest rates and stock prices or sales and profits.

line chart A series of data points on a grid that are continuously connected by straight lines and that display a picture of selected data changing over a period of time.

horizontal axis The horizontal axis of a chart usually used to measure units of time such as days, weeks, months, or years. The horizontal axis is sometimes referred to as the "x-axis."

vertical axis The vertical axis of a chart usually used to measure the quantity or magnitude of something, such as sales dollars or production units. The vertical axis is frequently used to measure the percentage of something. The vertical axis is sometimes referred to as the "y-axis."

STEPS FOR READING A LINE CHART

STEP 1. Scan either the horizontal or vertical axis for the known variable.

STEP 2. Draw a perpendicular line from that axis to the point where it intersects the chart.

STEP 3. Draw a line from that point perpendicular to the opposite axis.

STEP 4. The value of the other variable is read where the line intersects the opposite axis.

Exhibits 21-1 and 21-2 are an example of a single- and multiple-line chart, respectively.

APPLES
Wholesale Price
(per pound)

EXHIBIT 21-1
Single-Line Chart

IN THE Business World

Frequently, the word *graph* is used instead of *chart*. *Graph* is short for *graphic formula*—that is, a means of providing information graphically rather than in words. *Graph* is from the Greek *graphein*, meaning to draw.

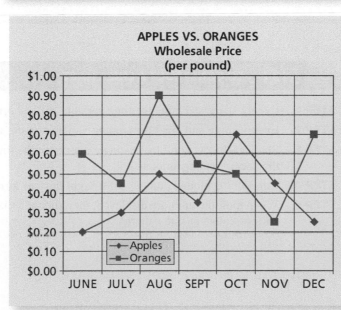

APPLES VS. ORANGES
Wholesale Price
(per pound)

EXHIBIT 21-2
Multiple-Line Chart

IN THE Business World

Tables illustrate specific data better than line charts do; however, line charts show relationships among data more clearly.

Frequently, in business presentations, tables and charts are used together, with the chart used to clarify or reinforce facts presented in the table.

EXAMPLE2   READING A LINE CHART

Use Exhibits 21-1 and 21-2 to answer the following questions.

a. In which month was the price of apples highest?

b. In which month was the price of apples higher—August or November?

c. How much lower was the price of apples in June compared with September?

d. Which fruit had a higher price in November—apples or oranges?

e. In which months was the price of apples higher than the price of oranges?

f. In August, how much lower was the price of apples than the price of oranges?

►SOLUTIONSTRATEGY

a. In Exhibit 21-1, by inspection, we find the high point on the graph. This corresponds to October on the horizontal axis.

b. In Exhibit 21-1, look vertically from the horizontal axis at August ($0.50) and November ($0.45) to find that August had the higher price.

c. In Exhibit 21-1, find the values for June ($0.20) and September ($0.35) and then calculate the difference—$0.15 ($0.35 – $0.20).

d. In Exhibit 21-2, from November on the horizontal axis, look vertically to both lines to find that apples had the higher price.

e. In Exhibit 21-2, by inspection, we find that apples had a higher price in October and November.

f. In Exhibit 21-2, locate the August price for both apples ($0.50) and oranges ($0.90). Then calculate the difference between the two prices: $0.40 ($0.90 – $0.50).

►TRYITEXERCISE 2

Use Exhibits 21-1 and 21-2 to answer the following questions.

a. In which month was the price of apples lowest?

b. In which month was the price of apples higher—July or December?

c. How much lower was the price of apples in November compared with August?

d. Which fruit had a lower price in July—apples or oranges?

e. In which months was the price of oranges higher than the price of apples?

f. In which month was the price differential between apples and oranges the greatest? How much?

CHECK YOUR ANSWERS WITH THE SOLUTIONS ON PAGE 768.

STEPS TO CONSTRUCT A LINE CHART

STEP 1. Evenly space and label the time variable on the horizontal axis.

STEP 2. Evenly space and label the amount variable on the vertical axis.

STEP 3. Show each data point by placing a dot above the time period and across from the corresponding amount.

STEP 4. Connect the plotted points with straight lines to form the chart.

STEP 5. When multiple lines are displayed, they should be labeled or differentiated by various colors or line patterns.

EXAMPLE3 CONSTRUCTING A LINE CHART

You are the manager of Handy Hardware Stores, Inc. The company has one store in Centerville and one in Carson City. The following table shows the monthly sales figures in thousands of dollars for each store last year. From this information, construct a line chart of the total sales for each month.

Handy Hardware: Monthly Sales Report ($1,000s)

	Jan.	Feb.	Mar.	Apr.	May	June	July	Aug.	Sept.	Oct.	Nov.	Dec.
Centerville	16	18	24	21	15	13	17	18	16	23	24	20
Carson City	8	11	14	12	10	16	13	13	9	13	14	17
Total	24	29	38	33	25	29	30	31	25	36	38	37

▶SOLUTIONSTRATEGY

For this chart, show the months on the horizontal axis and the sales on the vertical axis. Use a range of 0 to 40 on the vertical axis. Plot each month with a dot and connect all the dots with straight lines.

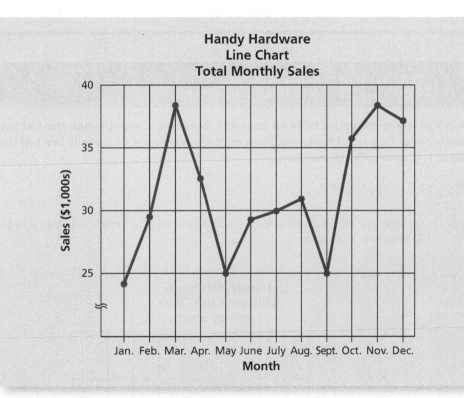

▶TRYITEXERCISE 3

The following data represent the audience statistics for a circus that performed in your town last week. Use the grid on the next page to draw a line chart of the total attendance for each day.

Circus Attendance

	Monday	Tuesday	Wednesday	Thursday	Friday	Saturday	Sunday
Adults	2,300	2,100	1,900	2,200	2,400	2,700	2,600
Children	3,300	2,600	2,400	1,900	2,700	3,100	3,600
Total	5,600	4,700	4,300	4,100	5,100	5,800	6,200

Learning Tip

Sometimes the horizontal or vertical axis of a chart is "shortened" to better display the required scale. A pair of wavy lines (≈) intersecting the axis are used to indicate when this occurs.

B-A-C-O/Shutterstock.com

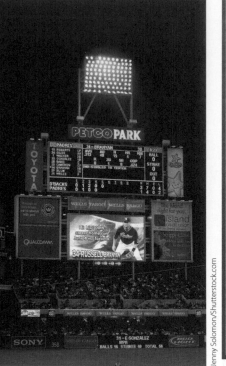

Statistical information is recorded and used in many different ways at sporting events, including measuring attendance and athletic performance.

CHECK YOUR CHART WITH THE SOLUTIONS ON PAGE 768.

EXAMPLE4   CONSTRUCTING A MULTIPLE-LINE CHART

From the Handy Hardware table on page 731, construct a multiple-line chart of the monthly sales for each of the stores. Show the Centerville store with a solid line and the Carson City store with a dashed line.

▶SOLUTIONSTRATEGY

As in the last example, the horizontal axis, time, will be months. The vertical axis should range from 0 to 25 to include all the data.

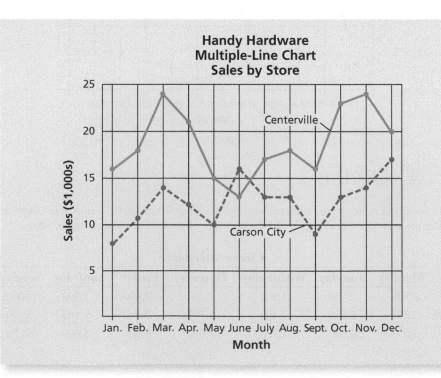

►TRY IT EXERCISE 4

From the Circus Attendance table on page 731, draw a multiple-line chart showing the number of adults and children attending the circus last week. Use a solid line for the adults and a dashed line for the children.

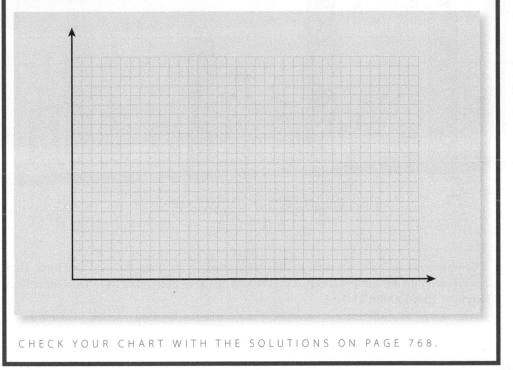

CHECK YOUR CHART WITH THE SOLUTIONS ON PAGE 768.

READING AND CONSTRUCTING A BAR CHART

21-3

Bar charts represent quantities or percentages by the length of horizontal or vertical bars. As with line charts, bar charts often illustrate increases or decreases in magnitude of a certain variable or the relationship between similar variables. Bar charts may or may not be based on the movement of time.

Bar charts are divided into three categories: standard, comparative, and component. **Standard bar charts** are used to illustrate the change in magnitude of one variable. (See Exhibit 21-3.)

Comparative bar charts are used to illustrate two or more related variables. The bars representing each variable should be shaded or colored differently to make the chart easy to read and interpret. (See Exhibit 21-4.)

bar charts Graphical presentations that represent quantities or percentages by the length of horizontal or vertical bars. These charts may or may not be based on the movement of time.

standard bar charts Bar charts that illustrate increases or decreases in magnitude of one variable.

comparative bar charts Bar charts used to illustrate the relationship between two or more similar variables.

Standard Bar Chart

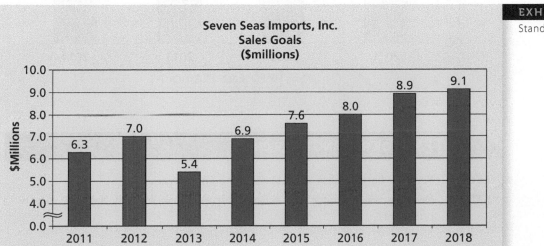

Seven Seas Imports, Inc.
Sales Goals
($millions)

EXHIBIT 21-4   Comparative Bar Chart

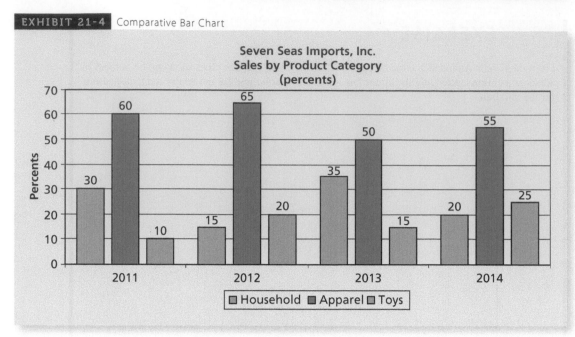

component bar charts Bar charts used to illustrate the parts of something that add to a total; each bar is divided into the components stacked on top of each other and shaded or colored differently.

Component bar charts are used to illustrate parts of something that add to a total. Each bar is divided into the components that are stacked on top of each other and shaded or colored differently. (See Exhibit 21-5.)

EXHIBIT 21-5

Component Bar Chart

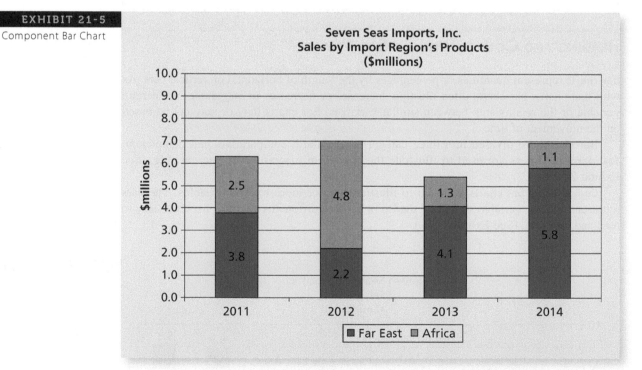

STEPS FOR READING A BAR CHART

STEP 1.   Scan the horizontal or vertical axis for a known variable.

STEP 2.   Read the answer on the opposite axis directly across from the top of the appropriate bar.

EXAMPLE5 READING A BAR CHART

Use Exhibits 21-3, 21-4, and 21-5 to answer the following questions about Seven Seas Imports, Inc.

a. What was the sales goal for 2014 for Seven Seas Imports, Inc.

b. In what year did Seven Seas have a sales goal of $8.0 million?

c. Which three product categories are being compared in Exhibit 21-4?

d. In 2012, what percent of Seven Seas' sales were toys?

e. What are the two import regions for Seven Seas?

f. In 2011, which import regions had the greatest amount of sales?

▶SOLUTIONSTRATEGY

a. In Exhibit 21-3, locate 2014 on the horizontal axis and scan up to the top of the bar to find the projected sales, $6.9 million.

b. In Exhibit 21-3, locate $8.0 million on the vertical axis and scan right until you reach the top of a bar. Look down to the horizontal axis for the answer, 2016.

c. In Exhibit 21-4, by inspection, we find the three product categories in the legend: household, apparel, and toys.

d. In Exhibit 21-4, locate 2012 on the horizontal axis. Then locate the "Toys" bar as indicated by the orange color to find the answer, 20%.

e. In Exhibit 21-5, by inspection, we find the two import regions: Far East and Africa.

f. In Exhibit 21-5, locate 2011 on the horizontal axis. Scan the bar to find that the greatest amount of sales were goods from the Far East as indicated by a larger portion of the bar represented by the dark purple color.

▶TRYITEXERCISE 5

Use Exhibits 21-3, 21-4, and 21-5 to answer the following questions about Seven Seas Imports, Inc.

a. What was the sales goal in 2012 for Seven Seas?

b. In which year was the sales goal lowest? How much?

c. In what year were the sales of household goods the lowest? What percent?

d. In 2014, what percent of Seven Seas' sales were from apparel?

e. Explain what is being illustrated in Exhibit 21-5.

f. In what year were the sales of Far East imports less than African imports?

CHECK YOUR ANSWERS WITH THE SOLUTIONS ON PAGE 769.

STEPS TO CONSTRUCT A BAR CHART

STEP 1. Evenly space and label the horizontal axis. The space between bars should be one-half the width of the bars.

STEP 2. Evenly space and label the vertical axis. Be sure to include the full range of values needed to represent the variable. The lowest values should start at the bottom of the vertical axis and increase upward.

STEP 3. Draw each bar up from the horizontal axis to the point opposite the vertical axis that corresponds to its value.

STEP 4. For comparative and component bar charts, differentiate the bars by color or shading pattern. For complex presentations, provide a key or legend that shows which pattern or color represents each variable. This will help the reader interpret the chart.

Learning Tip

The steps shown here are used to construct charts with *vertical* bars. For charts with *horizontal* bars, lay out the bars on the vertical axis and the magnitude variable on the horizontal axis.

EXAMPLE6 — CONSTRUCTING A STANDARD BAR CHART

From the Handy Hardware sales report table on page 731, construct a standard bar chart of total sales for January through June.

SOLUTIONSTRATEGY

For this chart, the time variable, January through June, is shown on the horizontal axis. A range of 0 to 40 is used on the vertical axis.

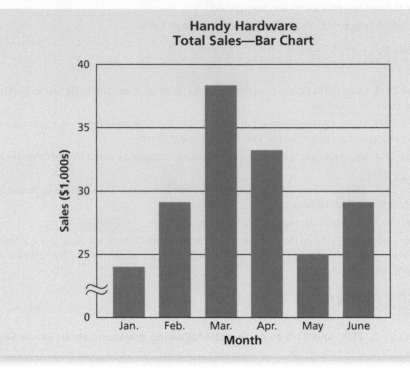

TRYITEXERCISE 6

From the table for Circus Attendance on page 731, use the following grid to construct a standard bar chart of the total attendance for each day.

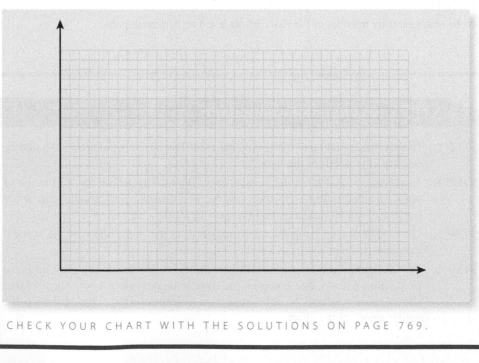

CHECK YOUR CHART WITH THE SOLUTIONS ON PAGE 769.

EXAMPLE 7   CONSTRUCTING A COMPONENT BAR CHART

From the table for Circus Attendance on page 731, construct a component bar chart that displays the number of adults and children as components of each day's total audience. Plot the number of adults at the bottom of the bars in blue shading and the number of children stacked above the adults in green shading.

▶ SOLUTION STRATEGY

For this chart, the time variable, Monday through Sunday, is shown on the horizontal axis. A range of 0 to 7,000 is used on the vertical axis.

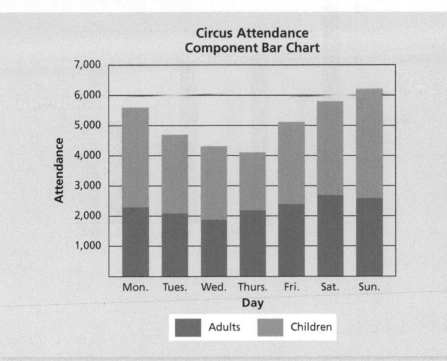

▶ TRY IT EXERCISE 7

Refer to the Handy Hardware sales report on page 731. Use a separate sheet of graph paper to construct a component bar chart that displays the Centerville and the Carson City stores as components of the total monthly sales for July through December.

CHECK YOUR CHART WITH THE SOLUTIONS ON PAGE 769.

EXAMPLE 8   CONSTRUCTING A COMPARATIVE BAR CHART

From the table below, construct a comparative bar chart of the freshman and sophomore enrollment. Let the horizontal axis represent the time variable. For each term, group the bars together and differentiate them by shading.

Interstate Business College: Annual Enrollment			
	Fall	**Winter**	**Spring**	**Summer**
Freshmen	1,800	1,400	1,350	850
Sophomores	1,200	1,200	1,150	700
Juniors	1,200	1,100	750	650
Seniors	850	700	500	400

►SOLUTIONSTRATEGY

This chart is constructed the same way as the standard bar chart except that the variables being compared are drawn side by side. The space between the bars is one-half the width of each bar. The vertical axis ranges from 0 to 2,000 students. Note that the bars are shaded to differentiate the variables and that an explanation key is provided.

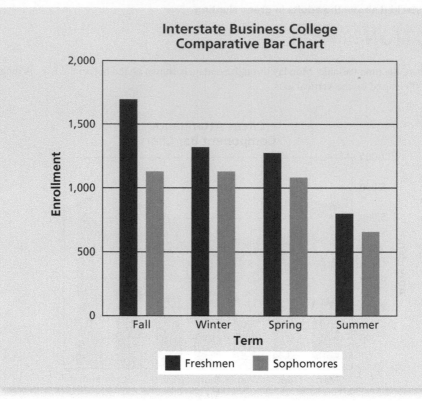

►TRYITEXERCISE 8

From the Interstate Business College enrollment figures in the table on page 737, construct a comparative bar chart of the junior and senior enrollment. Let the horizontal axis represent the time variable. For each term, group the bars together and differentiate them by shading.

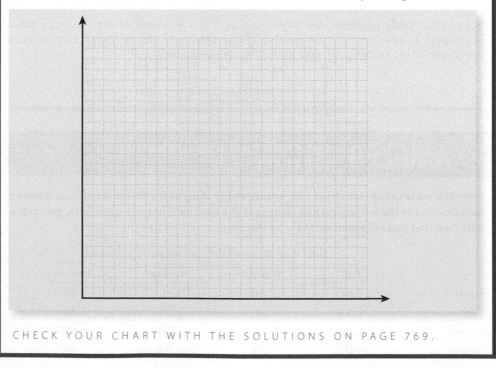

CHECK YOUR CHART WITH THE SOLUTIONS ON PAGE 769.

READING AND CONSTRUCTING A PIE CHART

21-4

The **pie chart** is a circle divided into sections representing the component parts of a whole. The whole, 100%, is the circle; the parts are the wedge-shaped sections of the circle. When this type of chart is used, the data are usually converted to percentages. The size of each section of the circle is determined by the portion or percentage each component is of the whole. Pie charts are generally read by inspection because each component of the data is clearly labeled by category and percent. Exhibit 21-6 illustrates examples of pie charts.

pie chart A circle divided into sections that are usually expressed in percentage form and that represent the component parts of a whole.

EXHIBIT 21-6 Pie Charts

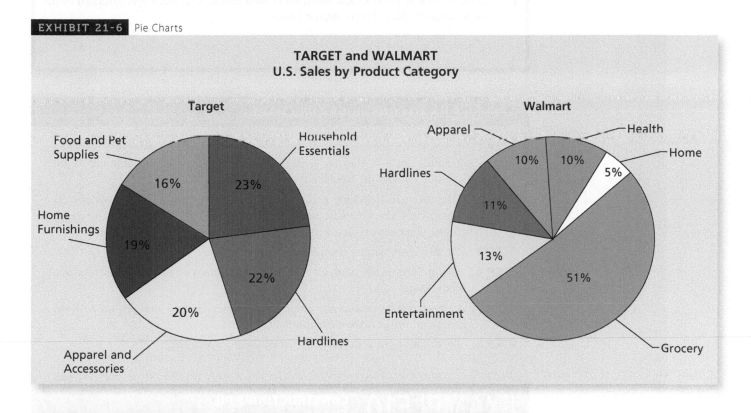

TARGET and WALMART
U.S. Sales by Product Category

EXAMPLE9 | **READING A PIE CHART**

Use Exhibit 21-6 to answer the following questions.

a. What percent of Target's sales were from food and pet supplies?

b. At Walmart, which two categories had the same percent of sales?

c. What percent were the combined sales of hardlines and household essentials at Target?

d. At Walmart, what category represented 5% of sales?

e. Considering that Target's revenue was $63.4 billion, calculate the amount of sales that the home furnishings category generated. (Round to the nearest billion.)

SOLUTIONSTRATEGY

a. By inspection, we find that food and pet supplies at Target amounted to 16% of sales.

b. At Walmart, apparel and health products had the same amount of sales.

c. At Target, the combined sales of hardlines and household essentials amounted to 45% (22% + 23%).

d. The home category represented 5% of sales at Walmart.

e. At Target, the sales in the home furnishings category were $12 (19% × $63.4).

▶TRYITEXERCISE 9

Use Exhibit 21-6 to answer the following questions.

a. What percent of Walmart's sales were from entertainment?
b. At Target, which category had the highest percent of sales? What percent?
c. What were the combined sales in percent of the hardlines and home categories at Walmart?
d. At Target, what category represented 22% of sales?
e. Considering that Walmart's sales amounted to $405 billion, how much was generated by the grocery category? (Round to the nearest billion.)

CHECK YOUR ANSWERS WITH THE SOLUTIONS ON PAGE 770.

STEPS TO CONSTRUCT A PIE CHART

STEP 1. Convert the amount of each component to a percent by using the percentage formula Rate = Portion ÷ Base. Let the portion be the amount of each component and the base the total amount.

STEP 2. Because a full circle is made up of 360° representing 100%, multiply each component's percent (decimal form) by 360° to determine how many degrees each component's slice will be. Round to the nearest whole degree.

STEP 3. Draw a circle with a compass and mark the center.

STEP 4. Using a protractor, mark off the number of degrees on the circle that represents each component.

STEP 5. Connect each point on the circle to the center using a straight line to form a segment, or slice, for each component.

STEP 6. Label the segments clearly by name, color, or shading.

EXAMPLE10 CONSTRUCTING A PIE CHART

Cycle World sold the following bicycles last week: 30 racing bikes, 20 off-road bikes, 15 standard bikes, and 15 tricycles. Construct a pie chart showing the sales breakdown for the shop.

▶SOLUTIONSTRATEGY

For this chart, we must convert the component amounts to percents and then multiply the decimal form of the percents by 360° as follows:

Racing bikes:	$\frac{30}{80} = .375 = 37.5\%$	$.375 \times 360 = 135$
Off-road bikes:	$\frac{20}{80} = .25 = 25\%$	$.25 \times 360 = 90$
Standard bikes:	$\frac{15}{80} = .1875 = 18.75\%$	$.1875 \times 360 = 67.5$
Tricycles:	$\frac{15}{80} = .1875 = 18.75\%$	$.1875 \times 360 = 67.5$

Now draw a circle and use a protractor to mark the degree points of each component. Connect the points to the center of the circle to form the segments and label each segment appropriately. The completed chart follows.

Learning Tip

Although a full circle has exactly 360°, sometimes the total of the degrees from each slice may be slightly higher or lower than 360° because of rounding.

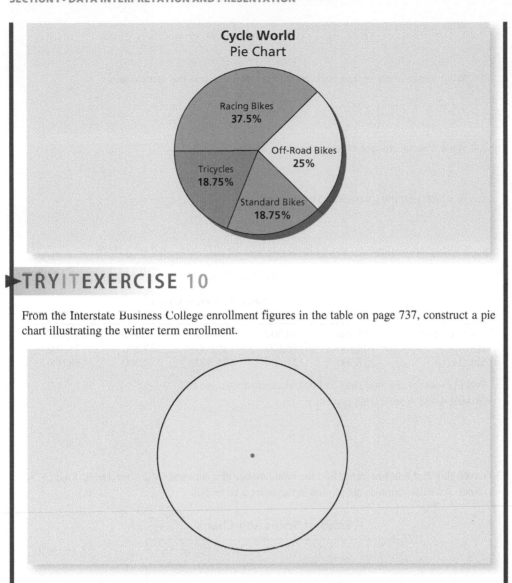

Cycle World
Pie Chart

Racing Bikes
37.5%

Off-Road Bikes
25%

Tricycles
18.75%

Standard Bikes
18.75%

►TRYITEXERCISE 10

From the Interstate Business College enrollment figures in the table on page 737, construct a pie chart illustrating the winter term enrollment.

CHECK YOUR CHART WITH THE SOLUTIONS ON PAGE 770.

REVIEW EXERCISES   21   SECTION I

1. Use the line chart "Widget Sales 2009–2016" to answer the following questions.

   a. What was the amount of widget sales in 2009?

      $0.2 billion

   b. In what year did widget sales reach $0.8 billion?

      2014

Widget Sales 2009–2016
Widget Corporation of America

$1.2
$1.0
$0.8
$0.6
$0.4
$0.2
0

$1.2

$0.2

(in billions)

'09 '10 '11 '12 '13 '14 '15 '16

JUMP
START
WWW

  c. What does this line graph represent?

  d. What variables are represented on the horizontal axis and the vertical axis?

  e. What was the amount of widget sales in 2015?

  f. In which year did sales reach $0.6 billion?

  g. Calculate how much greater widget sales were in 2016 compared with 2009.

2.

Sales on Toaster Ovens

	2004	2005	2006	2007	2008
Super Deluxe	$83,100	$140,500	$65,800	$56,100	$59,000
Deluxe	103,100	136,100	129,900	133,800	75,400
Standard	137,300	123,600	125,500	132,600	58,000

What percent of the total sales in 2004 were the deluxe model?
(Round to the nearest tenth percent.)

3. Given this multiple-line chart, find the total number of chairs and sofas sold during June.
(Note: All sales numbers are plotted to the nearest 10 units.)

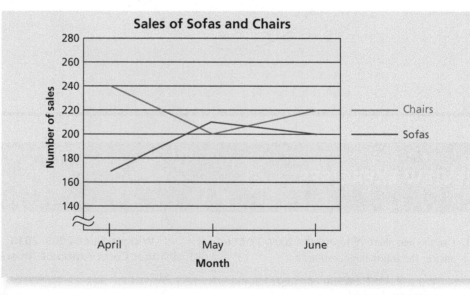

4. Use this component bar chart to find the number of tickets males received on Thursday.

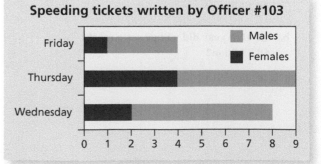

5. Use this pie chart to determine the total percent of cars sold that were European or made in the United States.

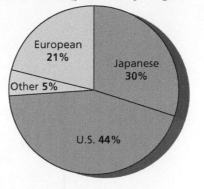

Auto Sales (percent by origin)

European 21%

Japanese 30%

Other 5%

U.S. 44%

As the sales manager for Magnum Enterprises, you have been asked by the president to prepare the following charts for the shareholders' meeting next week. Use the six-month sales report, Table 21-1 on page 728, as the database for these charts. Calculate totals as required.

6. Single-line chart of the total company sales per month

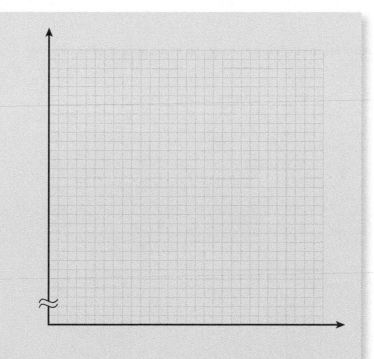

EXCEL 1

7. Multiple-line chart of the total sales per month of each model, standard and deluxe

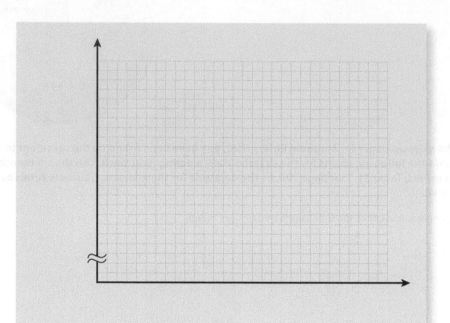

EXCEL 1

8. Standard bar chart of the deluxe sales per month in the Southeast territory

9. Component bar chart of the standard and deluxe model sales as components of total monthly sales in the Northeast territory

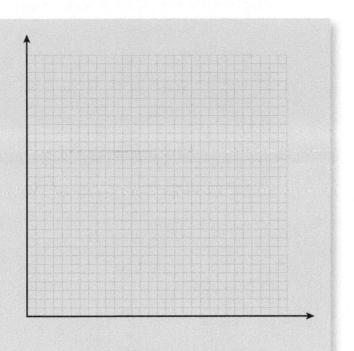

10. Comparative bar chart of the standard and deluxe model sales per month in the Northwest territory

11. Pie chart of the total six-month sales of the four territories

12. A survey of 480 households in a certain area yielded this data concerning their housing situation.

Rent apartment: 173, Rent house: 53, Own home: 206, Other: 48

Find the percent for each type of housing situation (round to the nearest whole number) and then construct a pie chart.

Housing (percent of households)

BUSINESS DECISION: CHOOSING A CHART

13. You have been asked to prepare a chart of stock prices for the upcoming semiannual stockholders' meeting for Magnum Enterprises. The following table shows Magnum's stock prices on the first day of each month. Choose and prepare a chart that best illustrates this information.

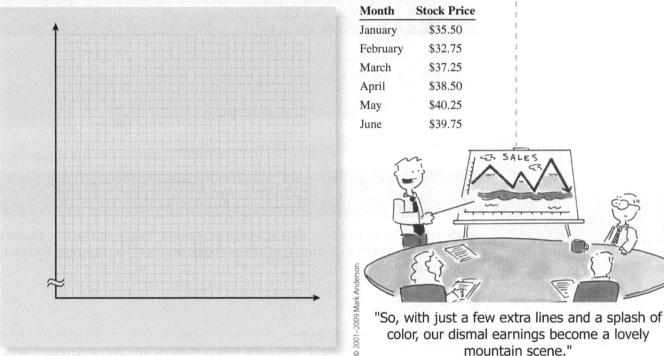

Month	Stock Price
January	$35.50
February	$32.75
March	$37.25
April	$38.50
May	$40.25
June	$39.75

"So, with just a few extra lines and a splash of color, our dismal earnings become a lovely mountain scene."

MEASURES OF CENTRAL TENDENCY AND DISPERSION—UNGROUPED DATA

21 SECTION II

A numerical average is a value that is representative of a whole set of values. In business, managers use averages extensively to describe or represent a variety of situations. Imagine a payroll director being asked to describe the hourly wages of his 650 factory workers. On the one extreme, he might produce a list of his 650 workers along with their hourly wages. This action answers the question, but it provides too much information. A more appropriate response might be to calculate the average hourly wage and report that "$9.75 was the average hourly wage of the workers."

Because an average is numerically located in the range of values it represents, averages are often referred to as **measures of central tendency**. In this section, we study the three most commonly used measures of central tendency in business statistics: the arithmetic mean, the median, and the mode. In this section, we also study a measure of dispersion known as the range.

measure of central tendency
A numerical value that is representative of a whole set of values.

21-5 CALCULATING THE ARITHMETIC MEAN OF UNGROUPED DATA

mean, or arithmetic mean The sum of the values of a set of data divided by the number of values in that set.

The **arithmetic mean** corresponds to the generally accepted meaning of the word *average*. It is customary to abbreviate the term *arithmetic mean* and refer to this average simply as the **mean**.

STEPS TO CALCULATE THE ARITHMETIC MEAN OF UNGROUPED DATA

STEP 1. Find the sum of all the values in the data set.

STEP 2. Divide the sum in Step 1 by the number of values in the set.

$$\text{Mean of ungrouped data} = \frac{\text{Sum of values}}{\text{Number of values}}$$

EXAMPLE11 CALCULATING THE MEAN

WorldWide Travel had daily sales of $4,635 on Monday, $3,655 on Tuesday, $3,506 on Wednesday, $2,870 on Thursday, $4,309 on Friday, and $5,475 on Saturday. What is the mean sales per day?

►SOLUTIONSTRATEGY

To calculate the mean (average sales per day), we find the sum of the values (sales per day) and divide this sum by the number of values (six days).

$$\text{Mean of ungrouped data} = \frac{\text{Sum of values}}{\text{Number of values}}$$

$$\text{Mean} = \frac{4,635 + 3,655 + 3,506 + 2,870 + 4,309 + 5,475}{6} = \frac{24,450}{6} = \underline{\underline{\$4,075}}$$

►TRYITEXERCISE 11

Amour, a Bernese Mountain Dog, loves her daily walks. If over a five-day period she had walks of 2.6, 1.6, 2.8, 3.7, and 2.8 miles, what was the average number of miles she walked?

CHECK YOUR ANSWERS WITH THE SOLUTIONS ON PAGE 770.

21-6 DETERMINING THE MEDIAN

median The *midpoint* value of a set of data when the numbers are ranked in ascending or descending order.

Another measure of central tendency—and a very useful way of describing a large quantity of data—is the median. The **median** of a set of numbers is the *midpoint* value when the numbers are ranked in ascending or descending order. Compared to the mean, the median is a more useful measure of central tendency when one or more of the values of the set is significantly higher or lower than the rest of the set. For example, if the ages of five individuals in a group are 22, 26, 27, 31, and 69, the mean of this set is 35. However, the median is 27, a value that better describes the set.

When there is an odd number of values in the set, the middle value is the median. For example, in a set of seven ranked values, the fourth value is the midpoint. There are three values greater than and three values less than the median.

When there is an even number of values in the set, the median is the mean of the two middle values. For example, in a set with 10 values, the median is the mean of the fifth and the sixth value.

STEPS TO DETERMINE THE MEDIAN

STEP 1. Rank the numbers in ascending or descending order.

STEP 2a. For an *odd number* of values, the median is the middle value.

STEP 2b. For an *even number* of values, the median is the mean of the two middle values.

EXAMPLE 12 DETERMINING THE MEDIAN

Determine the median for the following set of values:

$$2 \quad 8 \quad 5 \quad 13 \quad 11 \quad 6 \quad 9 \quad 15 \quad 4$$

SOLUTION STRATEGY

Step 1. Rank the data in ascending order as follows:

$$2 \quad 4 \quad 5 \quad 6 \quad 8 \quad 9 \quad 11 \quad 13 \quad 15$$

Step 2. Because the number of values in this set is *odd* (nine), there are four values less than and four values greater than the median. Therefore, the median is the fifth value, $\underline{\underline{8}}$.

TRY IT EXERCISE 12

Determine the median for the following set of values:

$$4,589 \quad 6,558 \quad 4,237 \quad 2,430 \quad 3,619 \quad 5,840 \quad 1,220$$

CHECK YOUR ANSWERS WITH THE SOLUTIONS ON PAGE 770.

EXAMPLE 13 DETERMINING THE MEDIAN

A runner preparing for the Marine Corps Marathon in Washington, D.C., had training runs of 5, 9, 23, 6, 7, and 5 miles. Find the median of these values.

SOLUTION STRATEGY

Step 1. Rank the data in ascending order:

$$5 \quad 5 \quad 6 \quad 7 \quad 9 \quad 23$$

Step 2. Because the number of values in this set is *even* (six), the median is the mean of the third and the fourth values, 6 and 7.

$$\text{Median} = \frac{6 + 7}{2} = \frac{13}{2} = \underline{\underline{6.5 \text{ miles}}}$$

Clarissa Bergeman

TRYITEXERCISE 13

Determine the median for the following set of values representing the number of plants sold at Exotic Gardens in the past 10 days.

12 33 42 13 79 29 101 54 76 81

CHECK YOUR ANSWERS WITH THE SOLUTIONS ON PAGE 770.

21-7

DETERMINING THE MODE

mode The value or values in a set of data that occur *most often*.

The **mode** is the third measure of central tendency that we consider. It is the value or values in a set that occur *most often*. It is possible for a set of data to have more than one mode or no mode at all.

STEPS TO DETERMINE THE MODE

STEP 1. Count the number of times each value in a set occurs.

STEP 2a. If one value occurs more times than any other, it is the mode.

STEP 2b. If two or more values occur more times than any other, they are all modes of the set.

STEP 2c. If all values occur the same number of times, there is no mode.

One common business application of the mode is in merchandising, where it is used to keep track of the most frequently purchased goods, as in the following example. Note that the mean and median of this set of data would provide little useful information regarding sales.

EXAMPLE14 DETERMINING THE MODE

Find the mode of the following set of values representing the wattage of lightbulbs sold at a Home Depot yesterday.

25 25 60 60 60 75 75 75 75 100 100 150

SOLUTIONSTRATEGY

From these data, we see that the mode is 75 watts because the value 75 occurs most often. This would indicate to the retailer that 75-watt bulbs were purchased most frequently.

TRYITEXERCISE 14

Calculate the mode of the following set of values representing the size, in gallons, of fish tanks sold at Aquarium Adventures.

10 10 20 10 55 20 10 65 85 20 10 20 55 10 125 55 10 20

CHECK YOUR ANSWERS WITH THE SOLUTIONS ON PAGE 770.

IN THE Business World

The *mode* is used extensively in marketing research to measure the most frequent responses on survey questions. In advertising, the mode translates into persuasive headlines, "4 Out of 5 Doctors Recommend. ..."

DETERMINING THE RANGE

Although it does not measure central tendency as the mean, median, and mode do, the range is another useful measure in statistics. The **range** is a measure of *dispersion*; it is the difference between the lowest and the highest values in a data set. It is used to measure the scope, or broadness of a set of data. A small range indicates that the data in a set are narrow in scope; the values are close to each other. A large range indicates that the data in a set are wide in scope; the values are spread far apart.

range The difference between the lowest and the highest values in a data set; used as a measure of *dispersion*.

STEPS TO DETERMINE THE RANGE

STEP 1. Locate the highest and lowest values in a set of numbers.

STEP 2. Subtract the lowest from the highest to get the range.

$$\text{Range} = \text{Highest value} - \text{Lowest value}$$

EXAMPLE15 DETERMINING THE RANGE

Determine the range of the following shirt prices at Styline Men's Shop.

   $37.95 $15.75 $24.75 $18.50 $33.75 $42.50 $14.95 $27.95 $19.95

▶SOLUTIONSTRATEGY

To determine the range of shirt prices, subtract the lowest price from the highest price:

   $$\text{Range} = \text{Highest value} - \text{Lowest value} = 42.50 - 14.95 = \underline{\$27.55}$$

Note that the range for shirts, $27.55, is relatively large. It might be said that customers shopping in this shirt department have a wide range of prices from which to choose.

▶TRYITEXERCISE 15

Determine the range of the following temperature readings from the oven at Bon Appétit Bakery.

   367°   351°   349°   362°   366°   358°   369°   355°   354°

CHECK YOUR ANSWERS WITH THE SOLUTIONS ON PAGE 770.

REVIEW EXERCISES

21 SECTION II

Calculate the mean (that is, calculate the arithmetic mean) of the following sets of values. Round to the nearest tenth when applicable.

1. 5   7   21   46   35   2   19   7

   $$\frac{5 + 7 + 21 + 46 + 35 + 2 + 19 + 7}{8} = \frac{142}{8} = \underline{17.8}$$

JUMP START WWW

2. 594   314   595   708   541   626   915

EXCEL 2

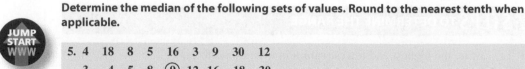

EXCEL 3

3. 324   553   179   213   423   336   190   440   382   111   329   111   397

4. 4.87   4.32   5.43   6.3   9.4   7.25   5.13

JUMP START WWW

Determine the median of the following sets of values. Round to the nearest tenth when applicable.

5. 4   18   8   5   16   3   9   30   12
    3   4   5   8   ⑨   12   16   18   30

    $\underline{\underline{9}}$ is the median.

6. 56   34   28   60   48   55
    28   34 ⟨48   55⟩ 56   60

    $\dfrac{48 + 55}{2} = \dfrac{103}{2} = \underline{\underline{51.5}}$

EXCEL 1

7. 57   38   29   82   71   90   11   94   26   18   18

8. 61   62   97   43   50   90

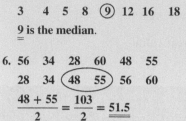

IN THE Business World

Your grade point average (GPA) is actually the *mean* of your grades. It is calculated by assigning a "value" to each grade, such as A = 4, B = 3, C = 2, and multiplying those values by the number of credits earned for each.

The sum of those values divided by the number of credits earned is your GPA.

9. 35%   51%   50%   23%   18%   67%   44%   52%

rtguest/Shutterstock.com

Determine the mode of the following sets of values.

JUMP START WWW

10. 8   3   5   6   3   7   2   1   8   2   4   3   6   2
    8 × 2 ⟨3 × 3⟩ 5 × 1   6 × 2   7 × 1 ⟨2 × 3⟩ 1 × 1   4 × 1

    Both 3 and 2 are modes in this set.

EXCEL 1

11. 21   57   46   21   34   76   43   68   21   76   18   12

12. $1,200 $7,300 $4,500 $3,450 $1,675

13. 4   9   3   5   4   7   1   9   9   4   7   1   8   1   4   7   4   9   9

Determine the range of the following sets of values.

JUMP START WWW

14. 184 237 256 359 36 71
    Highest   359
    Lowest   − 36
    Range $\underline{323}$

15. 48 42 54 28 112 76 95 27 36 11 96 196 191

16. $2.35 $4.16 $3.42 $1.29 $.89 $4.55   17. 1,099 887 1,659 1,217 2,969 790

18. The following numbers represent the gallons of chocolate fudge syrup used per month by a Dairy Queen to make hot fudge sundaes.

Jan.—225	Feb.—254	March—327	April—370	May—425	June—435
July—446	Aug.—425	Sept.—359	Oct.—302	Nov.—270	Dec.—241

  a. What is the mean of this set of data?

  b. What is the median of this set of data?

  c. What is the mode of this set of data?

  d. What is the range of this set of data?

Ice Cream According to the U.S. Department of Agriculture (USDA), U.S. production of ice cream and related frozen desserts, one of the U.S. food industry's largest sectors, amounted to more than 1.4 billion gallons in a recent year. That translates to more than 21 pounds per person.

Dairy Queen, one of the largest soft serve ice cream franchises in the world, has reported more than 5,700 stores in 19 countries, including 652 locations outside the United States and Canada.

19. You are the owner of The Dependable Delivery Service. Your company has four vehicles: a large and a small van and a large and a small truck. The following set of data represents the number of packages delivered last week.

	Monday	Tuesday	Wednesday	Thursday	Friday
Small Van	67	86	94	101	86
Large Van	142	137	153	165	106
Small Truck	225	202	288	311	290
Large Truck	322	290	360	348	339

  a. What is the mean number of packages delivered for each van?

  b. What is the median number of packages delivered for each truck?

  c. What is the mean number of packages delivered on Monday?

  d. What is the median number of packages delivered on Thursday?

e. What is the mode of all the packages delivered during the week?

f. What is the range of all the packages delivered during the week?

BUSINESS DECISION: INTERPRETING THE NUMBERS

20. You are the manager of a production plant that makes computer hard drives for Digital Storage Corporation. Last week your plant had the following production numbers during a six-day production run:

$$2,300 \quad 2,430 \quad 2,018 \quad 2,540 \quad 2,675 \quad 4,800$$

a. What is the mean, median, mode, and range of this set of production data?

b. Which measure best describes the production at your plant? Why?

SECTION III 21 FREQUENCY DISTRIBUTIONS—GROUPED DATA

ungrouped data Data that have not been grouped into a distribution-type format.

grouped data Data that have been divided into equal-size groups known as classes. Frequently used to represent data when dealing with large amounts of values in a set.

frequency The number of values in each class of a frequency distribution.

In the previous section, the values in the sets are listed individually and are known as **ungrouped data**. Frequently, business statistics deals with hundreds, even thousands, of values in a set. In dealing with such a large number of values, it is often easier to represent the data by dividing the values into equal-size groups known as classes, creating **grouped data**.

The number of values in each class is called the **frequency**, with the resulting chart called a **frequency distribution** or **frequency table**. The purpose of a frequency distribution is to organize large amounts of data into a more compact form without changing the essential information contained in those values.

21-9 CONSTRUCTING A FREQUENCY DISTRIBUTION

frequency distribution or **frequency table** The chart obtained by dividing data into equal-size classes; used to organize large amounts of data into a more compact form without changing the essential information contained in those values.

STEPS TO CONSTRUCT A FREQUENCY DISTRIBUTION

STEP 1. Divide the data into equal-size classes. Be sure to use classes that include all values in the set.

STEP 2. Use tally marks to record the frequency of values in each class.

STEP 3. Rewrite the tally marks for each class numerically in a column labeled "Frequency (f)." The data are now grouped.

EXAMPLE16 CONSTRUCTING A FREQUENCY DISTRIBUTION

From the following ungrouped data representing the weight of packages shipped by Monarch Manufacturing this month, construct a frequency distribution using classes with an interval of 10 pounds each.

13 16 65 45 44 35 22 46 36 49 56 26
68 27 35 15 43 62 32 57 48 23 43 44

▶SOLUTIONSTRATEGY

First, we find the range of the data by subtracting the lowest value, 13, from the highest value, 68. This gives a range of 55 pounds. Second, by using 10–19 for our lowest class and 60–69 for our highest class, we include all values in the set. Class intervals of 10 pounds each allow for six equal classes.

Frequency Distribution for Monarch Manufacturing

Class (lb)	Tally	Frequency (f)
10–19	III	3
20–29	IIII	4
30–39	IIII	4
40–49	IIII III	8
50–59	II	2
60–69	III	3

▶TRYITEXERCISE 16

You are the manager of The Dress Code Boutique. From the following ungrouped data representing the dollar sales of each transaction at the store today, construct a frequency distribution using classes with an interval of $10 each.

14 19 55 47 44 39 22 71 35 49 64 22 88 78 16
88 37 29 71 74 62 54 59 18 93 49 74 26 66 75

CHECK YOUR ANSWERS WITH THE SOLUTIONS ON PAGE 770.

CALCULATING THE MEAN OF GROUPED DATA

21-10

Just as with ungrouped data, we can calculate the arithmetic mean of grouped data in a frequency distribution. Keep in mind, however, that the means for grouped data are calculated by using the midpoints of each class rather than the actual values of the data and are therefore only approximations. Because the actual values of the data in each class of the distribution are lost, we must make the assumption that the midpoints of each class closely approximate the values in that class. In most cases, this is true because some class values fall below the midpoint and some above, thereby canceling the inaccuracy.

STEPS TO CALCULATE THE MEAN OF A FREQUENCY DISTRIBUTION

STEP 1. Add a column to the frequency distribution listing the midpoints of each class. Label it "Midpoints (m)."

STEP 2. In a column labeled "($f \times m$)," multiply the frequency for each class by the midpoint of that class.

STEP 3. Find the sum of the frequency column.

STEP 4. Find the sum of the $(f \times m)$ column.

STEP 5. Find the mean by dividing the sum of the $(f \times m)$ column by the sum of the frequency column.

$$\text{Mean of grouped data} = \frac{\text{Sum of (frequency} \times \text{midpoint)}}{\text{Sum of frequencies}}$$

EXAMPLE17   CALCULATING THE MEAN OF GROUPED DATA

Calculate the mean of the grouped data from the frequency distribution for Monarch Manufacturing in the previous example.

SOLUTIONSTRATEGY

Begin by attaching the Midpoint (m) and Frequency × Midpoint ($f \times m$) columns to the frequency distribution as follows:

Frequency Distribution for Monarch Manufacturing

Class (lb)	Tally	Frequency (f)	Midpoint (m)	$f \times m$
10–19	III	3	14.5	43.5
20–29	IIII	4	24.5	98.0
30–39	IIII	4	34.5	138.0
40–49	IHT III	8	44.5	356.0
50–59	II	2	54.5	109.0
60–69	III	3	64.5	193.5
		24		938.0

After finding the sum of the "Frequency" and $f \times m$ columns, use these sums to calculate the mean of the grouped data:

$$\text{Mean of grouped data} = \frac{\text{Sum of (frequency} \times \text{midpoint)}}{\text{Sum of frequencies}} = \frac{938}{24} = 39.1 \text{ lb}$$

▶TRYITEXERCISE 17

From the frequency distribution prepared in Try It Exercise 16 for The Dress Code Boutique, calculate the mean of the grouped data.

CHECK YOUR ANSWERS WITH THE SOLUTIONS ON PAGE 771.

21-11   PREPARING A HISTOGRAM OF A FREQUENCY DISTRIBUTION

histogram A special type of bar chart without space between the bars that is used to display the data from a frequency distribution.

A **histogram** is a special type of bar chart that is used in business to display the data from a frequency distribution. A histogram is drawn in the same way as a standard bar chart but without space between the bars.

STEPS TO PREPARE A HISTOGRAM OF A FREQUENCY DISTRIBUTION

STEP 1. Locate the classes of the frequency distribution adjacent to each other along the horizontal axis, increasing from left to right.

STEP 2. Evenly space the frequencies on the vertical axis, increasing from bottom to top.

STEP 3. Plot the frequency for each class in the form of a rectangular bar whose top edge is opposite the frequency of that class on the vertical axis.

EXAMPLE18 PREPARING A HISTOGRAM

Prepare a histogram from the Monarch Manufacturing frequency distribution above.

SOLUTIONSTRATEGY

On page 755 is the histogram prepared from the data in the Monarch Manufacturing frequency distribution. Note that the horizontal axis displays the adjacent classes and the vertical axis displays their frequencies.

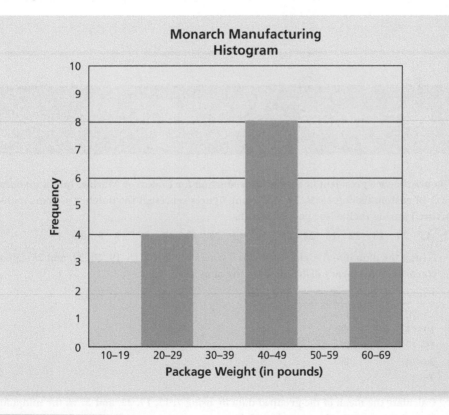

> **Learning Tip**
>
> Because a frequency distribution has classes whose numbers are continuous, the histogram bars depicting that distribution are made to look continuous by drawing them adjacent to each other—no space between them.

TRYITEXERCISE 18

Using the grid provided below, construct a histogram from the data in The Dress Code Boutique frequency distribution you prepared in Try It Exercise 16.

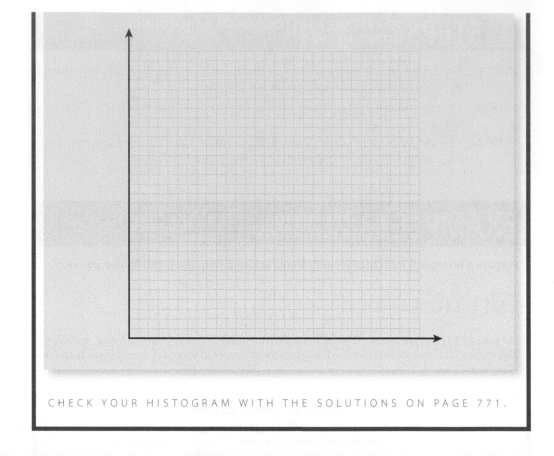

CHECK YOUR HISTOGRAM WITH THE SOLUTIONS ON PAGE 771.

SECTION III **21** **REVIEW EXERCISES**

JUMP
START
www

1. You are the vice president in charge of production for Endeavor Marine, Inc., a manufacturer of custom fishing boats. The following figures represent the number of boats manufactured during each of the past 18 months.

   12   15   24   18   22   16   21   19   10   14   26   23   17   15   21   9   28   13

   a. Group the data into five classes of equal size (5–9, 10–14, 15–19, 20–24, and 25–29) and
      construct a frequency distribution of the number of boats.

Class	Tally	Frequency
5–9	I	1
10–14	IIII	4
15–19	JHT I	6
20–24	JHT	5
25–29	II	2

   b. Calculate the mean of the grouped data by using 7, 12, 17, 22, and 27 as the midpoints.
      Round the mean to the nearest tenth if necessary.

Class	Tally	Frequency (f)	Midpoint (m)	$f \times m$
5–9	I	1	7	7
10–14	IIII	4	12	48
15–19	JHT I	6	17	102
20–24	JHT	5	22	110
25–29	II	2	27	54
		18		321

   $$\text{Mean} = \frac{321}{18} = 17.8$$

c. **Construct a histogram of these data to graphically illustrate your company's boat manufacturing figures.**

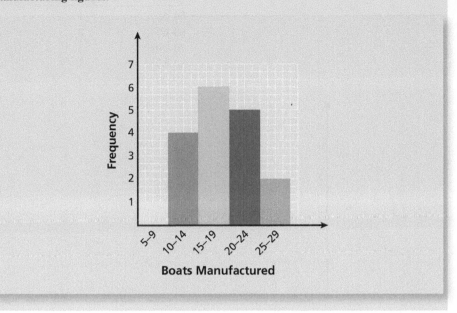

2. Using 6 classes of width 50 starting at 100, construct a frequency distribution for the following numbers:

358   384   325   221   324   366   308   355

220   394   111   288   316   217

3. Calculate the mean of the grouped data from the given frequency distribution. Round your answer to the nearest tenth.

Class	Frequency (f)
40–49	1
50–59	4
60–69	3
70–79	0
80–89	3

4. Construct a histogram for the data given in this frequency distribution.

Scores on 100-point Quiz	
Class	Frequency (f)
50–59	1
60–69	2
70–79	3
80–89	5
90–99	3

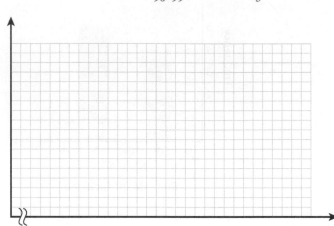

5. You are the owner of the Internet Café. As part of a marketing effort to increase the "average sale" per customer, you recently did a survey of the lunch-hour sales receipts for a busy Saturday. Following are the results of that survey.

$4.15	$5.60	$4.95	$6.70	$5.40	$7.15	$6.45	$8.25	$7.60	$6.25
$5.50	$4.90	$7.60	$6.40	$7.75	$5.25	$6.70	$8.45	$7.10	$8.80
$9.65	$8.40	$6.50	$5.25	$6.75	$8.50	$5.35	$6.80	$4.25	$9.95

a. Group the sales receipts into six classes of equal size ($4.00–$4.99, $5.00–$5.99, etc.) and construct a frequency distribution.

b. Calculate the mean of the grouped data.

Many coffee establishments provide wireless Internet connections for their customers.

c.   Using the grid provided below, prepare a histogram of the sales receipts.

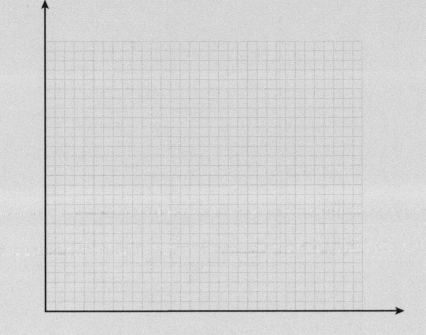

6. You are the sales manager of the Esquire Sportswear Company. Last week your 30 salespeople reported the following automobile mileage while making sales calls to retail stores around the state:

385   231   328   154   283   86   415   389   575   117   75   173   247   316   357
211   432   271   93   515   376   328   183   359   136   88   438   282   375   637

a.   Group the data into seven classes of equal size (0–99, 100–199, 200–299, 300–399, etc.) and construct a frequency distribution of the mileage.

b.   Calculate the mean of the grouped data by using 49.5, 149.5, 249.5, etc., as the midpoints.

c. Using the grid provided below, prepare a histogram of these data to illustrate your salespeoples' mileage graphically.

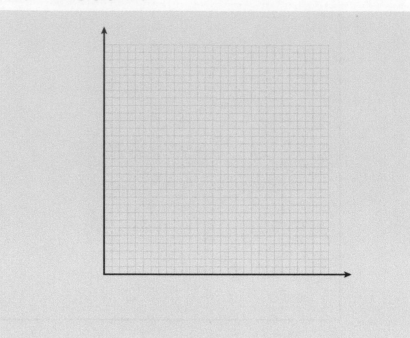

BUSINESS DECISION: RELATIVE FREQUENCY DISTRIBUTION

7. In business, percents are frequently used to represent the portion of observations falling within classes of a frequency distribution. A **relative frequency distribution** expresses the distribution as percents. To convert a frequency distribution to a relative frequency distribution, divide each of the class frequencies (portion) by the total number of observations (base). Remember, Rate = Portion ÷ Base.

a. From the frequency distribution you constructed for the Internet Café in Exercise 5a, convert each class frequency to a relative class frequency, percents. Round your answers to tenths.

b. What percent of the sales receipts were paid between $5.00 and $5.99?

c. What percent of the sales receipts were $7.00 or more?

d. What percent of the sales receipts were less than $8.00?

CHAPTER FORMULAS

Ungrouped Data

Mean of ungrouped data $= \dfrac{\text{Sum of values}}{\text{Number of values}}$

Median (odd number of values) = Middle value (Don't forget to rank scores first.)

Median (even number of values) = Mean of the middle two values (Don't forget to rank scores first.)

Mode = Value or values that occur most frequently

Range = Highest value − Lowest value

Grouped Data

Mean of grouped data $= \dfrac{\text{Sum of (frequency} \times \text{midpoint)}}{\text{Sum of frequencies}}$

CHAPTER SUMMARY

Section I: Data Interpretation and Presentation

Topic	Important Concepts	Illustrative Examples
Reading and Interpreting Information from a Table **Performance Objective 21-1, Page 727**	Tables are a collection of related data arranged for ease of reference or comparison, usually in parallel columns with meaningful titles. They are a very useful tool in summarizing statistical data and are found everywhere in business. Reading tables: 1. Scan the titles above the columns for the category of information being sought. 2. Look down the column for the specific fact required.	Apollo Auto Sales 90-Day Sales Report ($1,000s) <table><tr><td></td><td>April</td><td>May</td><td>June</td></tr><tr><td>Autos</td><td>56</td><td>61</td><td>64</td></tr><tr><td>Trucks</td><td>68</td><td>58</td><td>66</td></tr><tr><td>Parts</td><td>32</td><td>41</td><td>37</td></tr><tr><td>Total</td><td>156</td><td>160</td><td>167</td></tr></table>
Reading and Constructing a Line Chart **Performance Objective 21-2, Page 729**	Charts are used to display a picture of the relationships among selected data. Line charts show changes occurring over a period of time. They are represented on a grid by a series of data points continuously connected by straight lines. Reading line charts: 1. Scan either the horizontal or vertical axis for the known variable. 2. Draw a perpendicular line from that axis to the point where it intersects the chart. 3. Draw a line from that point perpendicular to the opposite axis. 4. The value of the other variable occurs where the line intersects the opposite axis.	*Single-Line Chart* Apollo Auto Sales Total Sales ($1,000s)

Section I (continued)

Topic	Important Concepts	Illustrative Examples
	Constructing line charts: 1. Evenly space and label the time variable on the horizontal axis. 2. Evenly space and label the amount variable on the vertical axis. 3. Show each data point by placing a dot above the time period and across from the corresponding amount. 4. Connect the plotted points with straight lines to form the chart. 5. Lines should be differentiated by various line patterns or colors.	*Multiple-Line Chart* 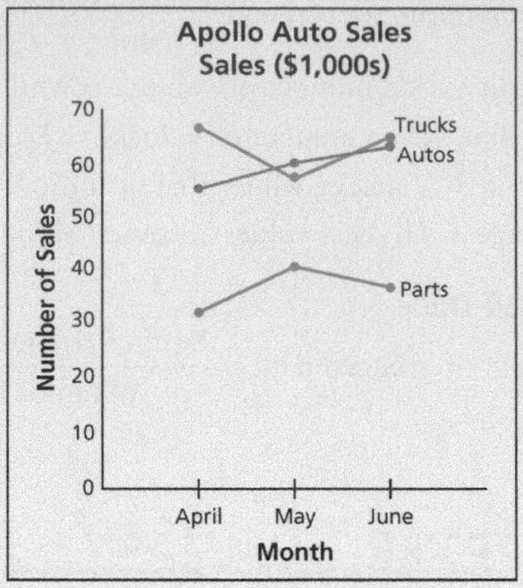

Reading and Constructing a Bar Chart
 	
Performance Objective 21-3, Page 733
	Bar charts represent data by the length of horizontal bars or vertical columns. As with line charts, bar charts often illustrate increases or decreases in magnitude of a certain variable or the relationship between similar variables.
	   Comparative bar charts illustrate two or more related variables. In this chart, the bars of the related variables are drawn next to each other but do not touch.
	   Component bar charts illustrate parts of something that add to a total. Each bar is divided into components stacked on top of each other and shaded or colored differently.
	
	Reading bar charts:
	1. Scan the horizontal or vertical axis for a known variable.
	2. Read the answer on the opposite axis directly across from the top of the appropriate bar.
	
	Constructing bar charts:
	1. Evenly space and label the horizontal axis. The space between bars should be one-half the width of the bars.
	2. Evenly space and label the vertical axis.
	3. Draw each bar up from the horizontal axis to the point opposite the vertical axis that corresponds to its value.
	4. For comparative and component bar charts, differentiate the bars by color or shading pattern.
		Standard Bar Chart 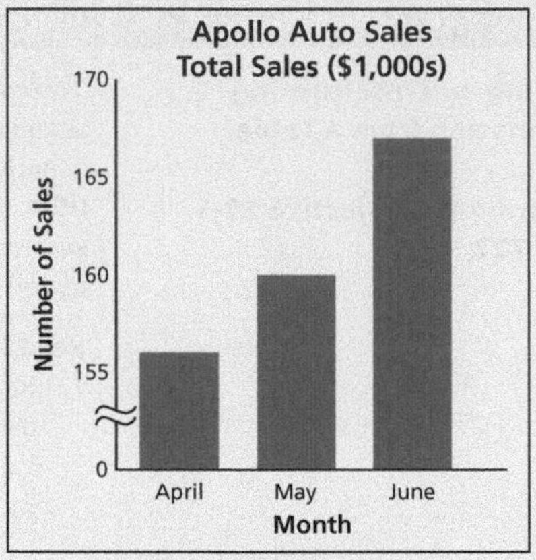
		
		Comparative Bar Chart 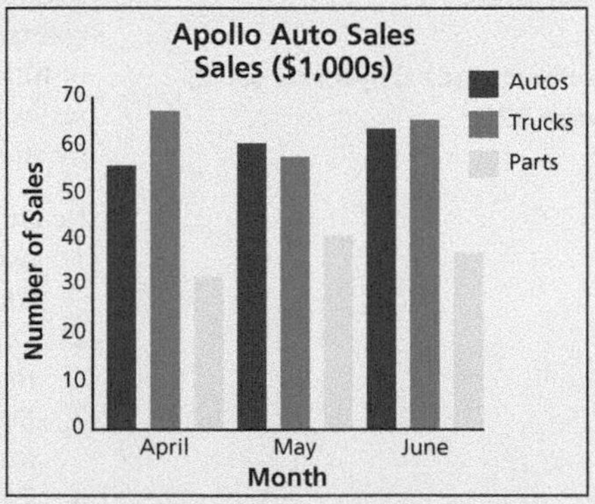
		
		Component Bar Chart 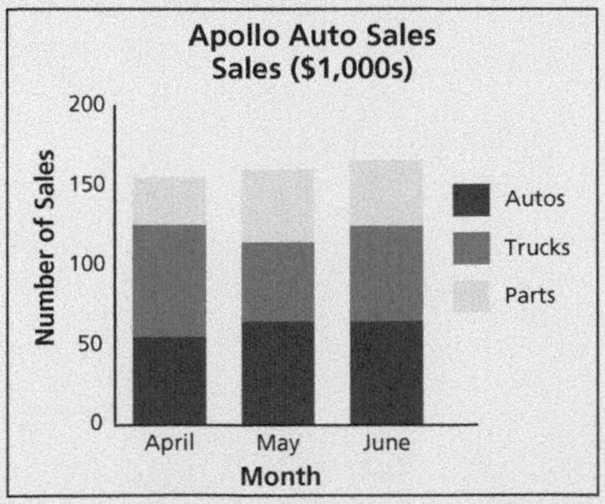

Section I (continued)

Topic	Important Concepts	Illustrative Examples
Reading and Constructing a Pie Chart **Performance Objective 21-4, Page 739**	The pie chart is a circle divided into sections representing the component parts of a whole, usually in percentage terms. Constructing pie charts: 1. Convert the amount of each component to a percent using the formula Rate = Portion ÷ Base. Let the percentage be the amount of each component and the base the total amount. 2. Because a full circle is made up of 360° representing 100%, multiply each component's percent (decimal form) by 360° to determine how many degrees each component's slice will be. Round to the nearest whole degree. 3. Draw a circle with a compass and mark the center. 4. Using a protractor, mark off the number of degrees on the circle that represents each component. 5. Connect each point on the circle with the center using a straight line to form a segment, or slice, for each component. 6. Label the segments clearly by name, color, or shading.	$\text{April} = \dfrac{156}{483} = .323 = 32.3\%$ $\text{April} = .323 \times 360° = 116°$ $\text{May} = \dfrac{160}{483} = .331 = 33.1\%$ $\text{May} = .331 \times 360° = 119°$ $\text{June} = \dfrac{167}{483} = .346 = 34.6\%$ $\text{June} = .346 \times 360° = 125°$ *Pie Chart* **Apollo Auto Sales** April 32.3% May 33.1% June 34.6%

Section II: Measures of Central Tendency and Dispersion—Ungrouped Data

Topic	Important Concepts	Illustrative Examples
Calculating the Arithmetic Mean of Ungrouped Data **Performance Objective 21-5, Page 748**	A numerical average is a value that is representative of a whole set of values. The arithmetic mean corresponds to the generally accepted meaning of the word *average*. Computing the mean: 1. Find the sum of all the values in the set. 2. Divide by the number of values in the set.	If a grocery store had sales of \$4,600 on Monday, \$3,650 on Tuesday, and \$3,500 on Wednesday, what is the mean sales for the 3 days? $\text{Mean} = \dfrac{4,600 + 3,650 + 3,500}{3}$ $= \dfrac{11,750}{3} = \$3,916.67$
Determining the Median **Performance Objective 21-6, Page 749**	Another measure of central tendency—and a very useful way of describing a large quantity of data—is the median. The median of a set of numbers is the *midpoint* value when the numbers are ranked in increasing or decreasing order. Determining the median: 1. Rank the numbers in increasing or decreasing order. 2a. For an *odd number* of values in the set, the median is the middle value. 2b. For an *even number* of values in the set, the median is the mean of the two middle values.	Find the median for the following set of values: 2 8 5 13 11 6 9 15 4 Rank the data as follows: 2 4 5 6 8 9 11 13 15 Because the number of values in the set is odd (nine), the median is the middle value, 8. Find the median for the following set of values: 56 34 87 12 45 49 Rank the data as follows: 12 34 45 49 56 87 Because the number of values in this set is even (six), the median is the mean of the third and the fourth values, 45 and 49. $\text{Median} = \dfrac{45 + 49}{2} = \dfrac{94}{2} = 47$

Section II (continued)

Topic	Important Concepts	Illustrative Examples
Determining the Mode **Performance Objective 21-7, Page 750**	The mode is the third measure of central tendency. It is the value or values in a set that occur most often. It is possible for a set of data to have more than one mode or no mode at all. Determining the mode: 1. Count the number of times each value in a set occurs. 2a. If one value occurs most often, it is the mode. 2b. If more than one value occurs the same number of times, all of the values are modes of the set. 2c. If all values occur only once, there is no mode.	Find the mode of the following set of values representing television screen sizes sold in a Best Buy store yesterday: 25 25 27 25 17 19 12 12 17 25 17 5 25 Because the value 25 occurs most often, the mode is 25 inches.
Determining the Range **Performance Objective 21-8, Page 751**	The range is a measure of dispersion equal to the difference between the lowest and the highest values in a set. It is used to measure the scope, or broadness, of a set of data. Determining the range: 1. Locate the highest and lowest values in a set of numbers. 2. Subtract these values to determine the range.	Find the range of the following hard drive prices at CompUSA: 237 215 124 185 375 145 199 Highest = \$375 Lowest = \$124 Range = 375 − 124 = \$251

Section III: Frequency Distributions—Grouped Data

Topic	Important Concepts	Illustrative Examples
Constructing a Frequency Distribution **Performance Objective 21-9, Page 754**	Business statistics frequently deals with hundreds, even thousands, of values in a set. In dealing with large amounts of values, it is often easier to represent the data by dividing the values into equal-size groups known as classes, forming grouped data. The number of values in each class is called the frequency, with the resulting chart called a frequency distribution. Constructing a frequency distribution: 1. Divide the data into equal-size classes. Be sure to use a range that includes all values in the set. 2. Use tally marks to record the frequency of values in each class. 3. Rewrite the tally marks for each class numerically in a column labeled "Frequency (f)." The data are now grouped.	The following ungrouped data represent the number of sales calls made by the sales force of Northwest Supply Company last month. Construct a frequency distribution of these data using six equal classes with an interval of 10. 13 26 65 45 44 35 46 36 49 56 16 68 27 35 43 62 32 57 23 43 44

Class	Tally	Freq (f)
10 to 19	II	2
20 to 29	III	3
30 to 39	IIII	4
40 to 49	IIII II	7
50 to 59	II	2
60 to 69	III	3

Section III (continued)

Topic	Important Concepts	Illustrative Examples
Calculating the Mean of Grouped Data **Performance Objective 21-10, Page 755**	Calculating the mean of a frequency distribution: 1. Add a column to the frequency distribution listing the midpoints (*m*) of each class. 2. In a column labeled "(*f* × *m*)," multiply the frequency for each class by the midpoint of that class. 3. Find the sum of the frequency column. 4. Find the sum of the (*f* × *m*) column. 5. Find the mean by dividing the sum of the (*f* × *m*) column by the sum of the frequency column.	Calculate the mean number of sales calls for Northwest Supply. The mean of the grouped data is computed by first attaching the Midpoint (*m*) and Frequency × Midpoint (*f* × *m*) columns to the frequency distribution as follows: Class · Freq (*f*) · Midpt (*m*) · *f* × *m* 10–19 · 2 · 14.5 · 29.0 20–29 · 3 · 24.5 · 73.5 30–39 · 4 · 34.5 · 138.0 40–49 · 7 · 44.5 · 311.5 50–59 · 2 · 54.5 · 109.0 60–69 · 3 · 64.5 · 193.5 · 21 · · 854.5 $\text{Mean} = \dfrac{854.5}{21} = 40.7 \text{ calls}$
Preparing a Histogram of a Frequency Distribution **Performance Objective 21-11, Page 756**	A histogram is a special type of bar chart that is used in business to display the data from a frequency distribution. A histogram is drawn in the same way as a standard bar chart except there are no spaces between the bars. Constructing a histogram: 1. Locate the classes of the frequency distribution adjacent to each other along the horizontal axis, increasing from left to right. 2. Evenly space the frequencies on the vertical axis, increasing from bottom to top. 3. Plot each class's frequency in the form of a rectangular bar whose top edge is opposite the frequency of that class on the vertical axis.	*Histogram* Northwest Supply Sales Calls Histogram

TRY IT: EXERCISE SOLUTIONS FOR CHAPTER 21

1. **a.** Standard sales—February—Northeast = $228,400

    b. Deluxe sales—April—Southeast = $70,300

    c. Total sales—May and June—Northwest
    May = 112,900 + 65,300 =   178,200
    June = 135,000 + 78,400 =   213,400
    Total $391,600

    d. Months with increase in standard sales—Southwest
    March, April, May, June

    e. April—Deluxe = 92,600 + 153,200 + 67,800 + 70,300 = 383,900
    May—Deluxe = 65,300 + 185,000 + 78,300 + 79,400 = 408,000
    408,000 − 383,900 = $24,100

    f. Northwest—Percent standard sales = $\dfrac{\text{Standard sales}}{\text{Total sales}}$

    Northwest—Percent standard sales = $\dfrac{757,000}{1,244,500} = .6082 = 60.8\%$

2. **a.** June

b. July

c. $0.05 ($0.50 – $0.45)

d. Apples

e. June, July, August, September, and December

f. December; $0.45 ($0.70 – $0.25)

3.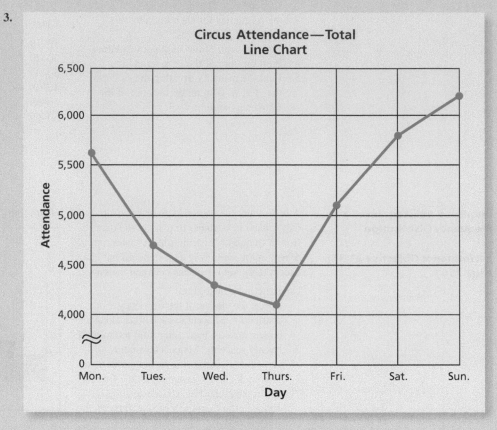

4.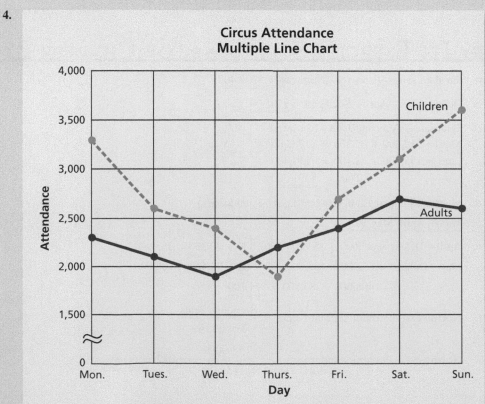

5. **a.** $7.0 million

    b. 2013; $5.4 million

    c. 2012; 15%

    d. 55%

    e. Exhibit 21-5 illustrates the annual sales breakdown of goods from each import region; Far East and Africa.

    f. 2012

6.

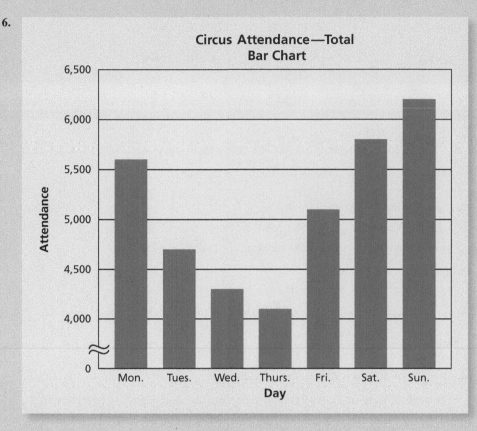

7.

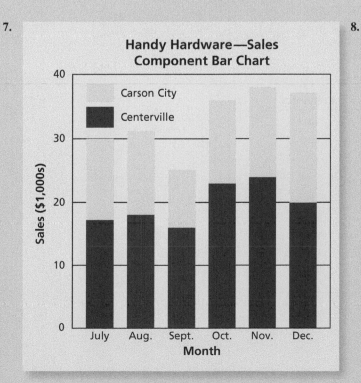

8.

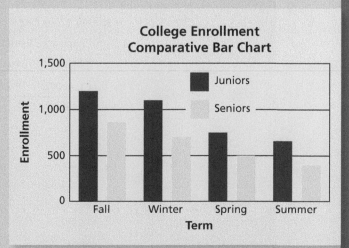

9. a. 13%

   b. Household essentials; 23%

   c. 16% (11% + 5%)

   d. Hardlines

   e. $207 billion (51% × $405 billion and then rounded to the nearest billion)

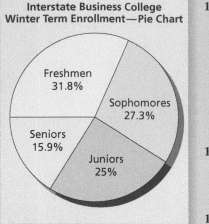

**Interstate Business College
Winter Term Enrollment—Pie Chart**

Freshmen 31.8%
Sophomores 27.3%
Seniors 15.9%
Juniors 25%

10. Freshmen $= \dfrac{1,400}{4,400} = .318 = \underline{31.8\%}$ $.318 \times 360° = \underline{114°}$

Sophomores $= \dfrac{1,200}{4,400} = .273 = \underline{27.3\%}$ $.273 \times 360° = \underline{98°}$

Juniors $\quad= \dfrac{1,100}{4,400} = .25 \ = \underline{25\%}$ $.25 \times 360° = \underline{90°}$

Seniors $\quad= \dfrac{700}{4,400} = .159 = \underline{15.9\%}$ $.159 \times 360° = \underline{57°}$

11. $\text{Mean} = \dfrac{\text{Sum of values}}{\text{Number of values}}$

$\text{Mean} = \dfrac{2.6 + 1.6 + 2.8 + 3.7 + 2.8}{5} = \dfrac{13.5}{5} = \underline{2.7 \text{ miles}}$

12. Ranked in increasing order:

1,220 2,430 3,619 ④,237 4,589 5,840 6,558

Median is the middle value of the odd number of values = $\underline{4,237}$

13. Ranked in increasing order:

12 13 29 33 42 54 76 79 81 101

For even number of values, median is the mean of the two middle values.

$\text{Median} = \dfrac{42 + 54}{2} = \dfrac{96}{2} = \underline{48}$

14. $\underline{10 = 7}$ 20 = 5 55 = 3 65 = 1 85 = 1 125 = 1

The mode of these values is $\underline{10}$ because it occurred the most number of times, seven.

15. Range = Highest value – Lowest value

Range $= 369° – 349° = \underline{20°}$

16. *The Dress Code*

Frequency Distribution

$ Sales per transaction

Class ($)	Tally	Frequency
10–19	IIII	4
20–29	IIII	4
30–39	III	3
40–49	IIII	4
50–59	III	3
60–69	III	3
70–79	IЖ̷I	6
80–89	II	2
90–99	I	1

17. *The Dress Code*

$ Sales per transaction

Class ($)	Tally	Frequency (f)	Midpoint (m)	($f \times m$)
10–19	IIII	4	14.5	58.0
20–29	IIII	4	24.5	98.0
30–39	III	3	34.5	103.5
40–49	IIII	4	44.5	178.0
50–59	III	3	54.5	163.5
60–69	III	3	64.5	193.5
70–79	IIIII	6	74.5	447.0
80–89	II	2	84.5	169.0
90–99	I	1	94.5	94.5
		30		1,505.0

$$\text{Mean} = \frac{\text{Sum of } (f \times m)}{\text{Sum of frequencies}}$$

$$\text{Mean} = \frac{1,505}{30} = 50.166 = \$50.17$$

18.

CONCEPT REVIEW

1. The systematic process of collecting, interpreting, and presenting numerical data about business situations is known as business _____. (21-1)

2. Statistical procedures that deal with the collection, classification, summarization, and presentation of data are known as _____ statistics. The process of arriving at conclusions, predictions, forecasts, or estimates based on a sample from a larger population is known as statistical _____. (21-1)

3. A collection of related data arranged for ease of reference or comparison, usually in parallel columns with meaningful titles, is known as a(n) _____. (21-1)

4. A(n) _____ chart is a series of data points on a grid that are continuously connected by straight lines that display a picture of change occurring over a period of time. (21-2)

5. The horizontal axis of a line chart is also known as the _____ and is often used to measure units of time; the vertical axis of a line chart is also known as the _____ and is usually used to measure the quantity or magnitude of something. (21-2)

6. When a bar chart is used to illustrate the relationship between two or more similar variables, it is known as a(n) _____ bar chart. When a bar chart is used to illustrate the parts of something that add to a total, it is known as a(n) _____ bar chart. (21-3)

7. To construct a pie chart, we multiply each component's percent by _____ degrees to determine how many degrees of the circle each component's slice will be. (21-4)

8. A numerical value that is representative of a whole set of values is known as a(n) _____ . It is also known as the mean or the arithmetic mean. Write the formula for the mean of ungrouped data. (21-5)

9. The _____ is the midpoint value of a set of data that is listed in ascending or descending order. Write a formula for this midpoint value when there is an even number of values in the data set. (21-6)

10. The _____ is the value or values in a set of data that occur most often. (21-7)

11. The difference between the lowest and the highest values in a data set are known as the _____ . This useful statistic is a measure of _____ . (21-8)

12. When dealing with large amounts of data in a set, it is often easier to represent the data by dividing the values into equal-size groups known as _____ . The chart obtained by this procedure is known as a frequency _____ or frequency table. (21-9)

13. Write the formula for the mean of grouped data. (21-10)

14. A(n) _____ is a special type of bar chart without space between the bars that is used to display the data from a frequency distribution. (21-11)

ASSESSMENT TEST

1. The following data represent the monthly sales figures in thousands of dollars for the New York and California branches of Universal Corporation.

EXCEL 1

	April	May	June	July	August	September
New York	121	254	218	156	255	215
California	88	122	211	225	248	260

a. Construct a multiple-line chart depicting the monthly sales for the two branches. Show the New York branch as a solid line and the California branch as a dashed line.

b. Construct a comparative bar chart for the same data. Highlight the bars for each branch differently.

2. Construct a pie chart from the following information compiled in a recent survey of the buying habits of children aged 8 to 17.

Category	Percentage
Clothing	35%
Fast food, snacks, candy	20%
Electronics products	15%
Entertainment	10%
School supplies	10%
Personal care	7%
Other	3%

3. Last month The Computer Connection sold $150,000 in desktop computers, $75,000 in notebook computers, $30,000 in software, $37,500 in printers, and $7,500 in accessories.

a. What percent of the total sales does each category of merchandise represent?

b. Construct a pie chart showing the percentage breakdown of sales by merchandise category.

4. You have just been hired as the quality control manager for Pressure Point Manufacturing, a company producing fuel injection systems for General Motors, Ford, and Chrysler. Top management has requested a status report on the number of defective units produced each day. You decide to keep track of the number of defects each day for 30 days. Following are the results of your survey.

Pressure Point Manufacturing—Defects per day—Survey 1

| 11 | 13 | 17 | 13 | 15 | 9 | 14 | 11 | 13 | 15 | 11 | 10 | 14 | 12 | 15 |
| 19 | 15 | 13 | 17 | 9 | 20 | 13 | 14 | 18 | 16 | 15 | 14 | 17 | 18 | 13 |

a. Find the mean, median, mode, and range of these data for your report to top management.

After implementing your suggestions for improved quality on the production line, you decide to survey the defects for another 30 days with the following results:

Pressure Point Manufacturing—Defects per day—Survey 2

| 11 | 9 | 12 | 7 | 8 | 10 | 12 | 8 | 9 | 10 | 9 | 7 | 11 | 12 | 8 |
| 7 | 9 | 11 | 8 | 6 | 12 | 10 | 8 | 8 | 7 | 9 | 6 | 10 | 9 | 11 |

b. Find the mean, median, mode, and range of the new data.

c. If the company's cost to fix each defective unit is $75, use the *mean* of each survey to calculate the average cost per day for defects before and after your improvements.

d. Theoretically, how much will your improvements save the company in a 300-day production year?

    e. Congratulations! The company has awarded you a bonus amounting to 15% of the first year's savings. How much is your bonus check?

5. You are the human resource director for Apollo Industries. Forty applicants for employment were given an assessment test in math and English with the following results:

$$
\begin{array}{cccccccccc}
87 & 67 & 81 & 83 & 94 & 72 & 84 & 68 & 33 & 56 \\
91 & 79 & 88 & 95 & 84 & 75 & 46 & 27 & 69 & 97 \\
69 & 57 & 66 & 81 & 87 & 19 & 76 & 54 & 78 & 91 \\
78 & 72 & 75 & 89 & 74 & 92 & 45 & 59 & 85 & 72
\end{array}
$$

    a. What are the range and mode of these scores?

    b. Group the data into nine classes of equal size (11–20, 21–30, etc.) and construct a frequency distribution.

    c. Calculate the mean of the grouped data by using 15.5, 25.5, etc., as the midpoints.

    d. If company policy is to consider only those who score *10 points higher or better* than the mean of the data, how many from this group are still being considered for the job?

e. Construct a histogram of the assessment test scores frequency distribution.

BUSINESS DECISION: BEAT THE MEAN BONUS!

6. You are the owner of The Green Machine, Inc., a car dealership specializing in pre-owned electric automobiles. You have a unique and motivating bonus plan for your salespeople that has worked well over the years.

Each quarter the mean number of cars sold is calculated. The first time a salesperson sells more cars than the mean, he or she earns a $100 bonus for each car *over the mean* in that quarter. If a salesperson exceeds the mean a second time in a year, the bonus increases to $150 per car for that quarter. If a salesperson exceeds the mean three times in one year, the bonus is $200 per car for that quarter. If anyone exceeds the mean all four quarters, the fourth-quarter bonus is $300 per car. Remember, the bonus is paid only for the number of cars over the mean.

Each year the program starts over again. All bonuses are paid once per year, in January, for the previous year. The following table represents the number of electric cars sold by your five salespeople for each quarter last year. Calculate the bonus each person should receive for last year.

	First Quarter	Second Quarter	Third Quarter	Fourth Quarter
Lugano	16	23	14	23
Gordon	12	20	16	25
Chen	15	13	26	19
Young	22	20	27	19
McIntosh	25	19	32	24

Tesla Beginning with the Tesla Roadster and continuing with the Model S and other models, Tesla was a catalyst in the development of the plug-in, all electric car industry.

Jessy Bergeman

CHAPTER
21

COLLABORATIVE LEARNING ACTIVITY

Conducting a Marketing Research Survey

You and your team members have been hired to conduct a marketing research survey for a company that is interested in advertising its products to college students in your area. The company wants to know the news media preferences of the students at your school and specifically would like answers to the following questions:

- What radio station, if any, do you listen to for news in the morning?
- What local television news program, if any, do you watch in the evening?
- What newspaper, if any, do you read each day?
- What Internet sites, if any, do you access for news each week?

a.   As a team, design a questionnaire for this research survey. For each media question, list all of the local choices, providing a place for easy check-off responses. Be sure to include "no preference" and "none of the above" as choices. For the Internet question, list the most popular news sites and include space for students to list other responses. In addition to the survey questions, design some easy check-off questions pertaining to demographics—for example, gender, age group, ethnic group, income range, and marital status.

b.   Have each member of the research team personally interview between 25 and 30 students. Questionnaires can be handed out and then collected.

c.   Tabulate the results of the surveys you conducted. As a team, total the results of each team member's surveys to arrive at the survey totals.

d.   Convert the totals for each question to percents.

e.   Calculate the mean, median, and mode for each demographic question that has numerical data.

f.   Using different types of charts, prepare a visual presentation for the class by illustrating the results of the survey questions.

g.   As a team, do you think the results of your survey are valid? Why or why not?

Business Math JOURNAL

U.S Census

Opinion Polls: What do the numbers mean?

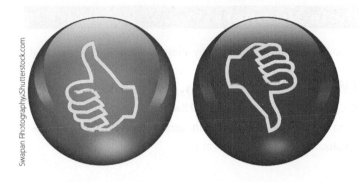

Swapan Photography/Shutterstock.com

Descriptive and Inferential Statistics

The field of statistics is broadly divided into two branches: Descriptive Statistics and Inferential Statistics.

Descriptive Statistics: Used to describe sets of data by using one or more types of procedures. These include 1) numerical calculations such as mean, median, mode, and range, 2) graphical representations such as line graphs, bar charts, and pie charts, and 3) tables such as frequency distributions.

The data available for analysis by descriptive methods typically represent information from the entire population of everything or everyone being studied.

On the other hand, sometimes it isn't possible or practical to get information from or about every element of a population being analyzed. In that case, statisticians may choose to rely on inferential statistics.

Inferential Statistics: Used to make inferences about an entire population based on a sample drawn from that population.

Opinion Polls

One type of inferential statistics that we often hear about is political *opinion polling*. For example, it isn't possible to contact every U.S. voter the morning after a political debate to see the level of approval each candidate has at that point in time. Instead, a sample (typically numbering approximately 1,000 voters) is contacted. Members of this sample provide their opinions, and then conclusions about the views of the population of all voters are inferred from this sample.

Because the approval percentage expressed by the voters in this relatively small sample cannot be expected to precisely equal the approval percentage in the population of all voters, there is some uncertainty involved in the conclusions reached based on the sample. That's why poll results are usually presented accompanied by a *margin of error*.

For example, a poll might report that 52% of voters approve of a particular politician, and it may further state that the margin of error is +4%. Since 52% − 4% = 48% and 52% + 4% = 56%, this result refers to an interval spanning 48% to 56%.

Does that mean we're certain that the true approval percentage in the population of all voters is between 48% and 56%? Unfortunately, the answer is no.

So, if we aren't 100% certain that the true population percentage falls in our interval, how certain are we? That's where inferential statistics comes in. Through scientific sampling and data collection methods, we can specify a level of certainty known as the *confidence level*.

95% is a common confidence level when polls are designed and results are calculated—although often this is not explicitly stated when results are reported. With all the above in mind, a more precise manner in which the results of the poll in our example can be expressed is this:

> "We are 95% confident that between 48% and 56% of the population of voters approve of this politician."

As you can see, inferential statistics attempts to present information about the confidence we have in our conclusions as well as the conclusions themselves.

Issues & Activities

Find the results of two recent polls as reported online, on TV, or in newspapers or magazines. Then present those results in a form similar to the statement shown in quotes above. Work in groups if possible.

"QUOTE...UNQUOTE"

"Get your facts straight first. Then you can distort them as much as you like." –Mark Twain

"An economist is an expert who will know tomorrow why the things he predicted yesterday didn't happen today." –Laurence J. Peter

Brainteaser—"The Missing Grade"

An absent-minded professor misplaced the business math test scores of his five students. However, he did remember that the mode of the five scores was 90, the median was 85, and the mean was 83. If the grades ranged from 0 to 100, what is the lowest possible grade from the missing set of scores?

See the end of Appendix A for the solution.

Answers to *Business Decisions* are not included.

1 Chapter 1: Whole Numbers

SECTION I

1. 22,938—Twenty-two thousand, nine hundred thirty-eight   **3.** 184—One hundred eighty-four   **5.** 2,433,590—Two million, four hundred thirty-three thousand, five hundred ninety   **7.** 183,622   **9.** $40,000,000,000   **11.** d   **13.** c   **15.** 1,760   **17.** 812,500   **19.** 26,000,000   **21.** 1,300,000,000   **23a.** Texas: eight thousand seven hundred ninety-seven megawatts, Iowa: three thousand, fifty-three megawatts   **23b.** Texas: 8,800 megawatts, Iowa: 3,100 megawatts

SECTION II

1. 91   **3.** 19,943   **5.** 37,648   **7.** 70,928   **9.** estimate 35,400—exact 33,361   **11a.** 7,000 Vehicles   **11b.** 6,935 Vehicles   **13.** $103,005 Grand Total   **15.** $1,627   **17.** 4,629   **19.** 278,091   **21.** $138   **23.** $94   **25.** 3,490,700   **27.** 378   **29a.** 43   **29b.** 22   **29c.** 94

SECTION III

1. 11,191   **3.** 294,300   **5.** 56,969,000   **7.** 549,564   **9.** estimate 100,000—exact 98,980   **11.** estimate 200—exact 187   **13.** $6,985,000   **15a.** $87   **15b.** $13   **17.** 128 R 20   **19.** 240   **21.** estimate 3—exact 3 R 5   **23.** estimate 682—exact 609 R 38   **25a.** 117   **25b.** 15   **27.** The Royale Hotel is more economical.   **29a.** $40,182   **29b.** $20,052   **29c.** $20,130

Assessment Test

1. 200,049—Two hundred thousand, forty-nine   **3.** 316,229   **5.** 18,300   **7.** 260,000   **9.** 99   **11.** 44 R 28   **13.** 22,258   **15.** 714   **17.** $14,365   **19a.** 19   **19b.** 25   **21a.** $11,340   **21b.** $36   **23.** $1,003   **25.** $49,260   **27.** $3,186   **29.** 15   **31.** $20

2 Chapter 2: Fractions

SECTION I

1. Mixed, Twenty-three and four-fifths   **3.** Improper, Fifteen-ninths   **5.** Mixed, Two and one-eighth   **7.** $3\frac{1}{3}$ **9.** $3\frac{6}{7}$ **11.** $1\frac{2}{31}$ **13.** $\frac{59}{5}$ **15.** $\frac{99}{8}$ **17.** $\frac{1,001}{4}$ **19.** $\frac{3}{4}$ **21.** $\frac{27}{115}$ **23.** $\frac{1}{8}$ **25.** $\frac{19}{65}$ **27.** $\frac{13}{16}$ **29.** $\frac{5}{18}$ **31.** $\frac{36}{48}$ **33.** $\frac{6}{64}$ **35.** $\frac{42}{98}$ **37.** $\frac{40}{64}$ **39.** $\frac{126}{182}$ **41.** $\frac{5}{11}$ **43a.** $\frac{1}{9}$ **43b.** $\frac{8}{9}$

1. 15 **3.** 12 **5.** 300 **7.** $1\frac{1}{3}$ **9.** $1\frac{7}{16}$ **11.** 1 **13.** $2\frac{3}{20}$ **15.** $11\frac{13}{24}$

17. $10\frac{17}{40}$ **19.** $10\frac{19}{30}$ **21.** $\frac{2}{3}$ **23.** $\frac{2}{3}$ **25.** $8\frac{4}{15}$ **27.** $26\frac{29}{45}$ **29.** $35\frac{13}{15}$

31. $21\frac{1}{8}$ **33.** $1\frac{13}{16}$

1. $\frac{8}{15}$ **3.** $\frac{2}{9}$ **5.** $\frac{10}{19}$ **7.** $2\frac{2}{5}$ **9.** $21\frac{13}{15}$ **11.** $\frac{1}{125}$ **13a.** $\frac{5}{8}$ **13b.** 2,750

15. $43\frac{15}{16}$ **17.** 15 **19.** $2\frac{2}{9}$ **21.** $2\frac{1}{10}$ **23.** $\frac{2}{5}$ **25.** $5\frac{17}{35}$ **27.** 19 **29.** $\frac{5}{14}$

31. 46 **33a.** 240 **33b.** 90 **35.** 185 **37.** 55 **39a.** $2\frac{17}{64}$ **39b.** 11

Assessment Test

1. Improper fraction, Eighteen-elevenths **3.** Proper fraction, Thirteen-sixteenths

5. 25 **7.** $\frac{65}{3}$ **9.** $\frac{2}{5}$ **11.** $\frac{18}{78}$ **13.** $\frac{1}{12}$ **15.** $5\frac{1}{3}$ **17.** $4\frac{3}{10}$ **19.** $13\frac{1}{3}$ **21.** 69

23. $23\frac{5}{8}$ **25.** $10\frac{7}{16}$ **27a.** $588,000 **27b.** $49,000 **29a.** 275 **29b.** 495

31a. 99 **31b.** 22 **31c.** $6,605

Chapter 3: Decimals

1. Twenty-one hundredths **3.** Eighty-one thousandths **5.** Ninety-eight thousand,
forty-five and forty-five thousandths **7.** Nine hundred thirty-eight hundred-
thousandths **9.** Fifty-seven and one-half hundred-thousandths **11.** .8 **13.** 67,309.04
15. 41.057 seconds, 41.183 seconds, 41.507 seconds **17.** 0.448557 = 0.45
19. 0.4813501 = 0.4814 **21.** $688.75 = $689 **23.** 88.964 = 89.0 **25.** 1.344 = 1.34

1. 58.033 **3.** $45.27 **5.** 152.784494 **7.** 16.349 **9.** $1.59
11. 116.278—One hundred sixteen and two hundred seventy-eight thousandths
13. 80.482 **15a.** $30.25 **15b.** $27.75 **17.** $11.14 **19a.** 900,000
19b. 11,800,000 **21.** 309.8922 **23.** 1,120,050 **25.** 20.0772 **27.** 33,090
29. 151.44 **31.** $2.72 **33.** 6 **35.** 217.39 **37a.** $2,480.98 **37b.** $15,590.00
37c. $230 **39a.** $250,000,000 **39b.** $2,700,000 **41a.** $2,104.32
41b. $920.06 **43.** $16 **45a.** 1,152 **45b.** $1,440 **45c.** 12-ounce size

1. $\frac{1}{8}$ **3.** $\frac{2}{125}$ **5.** $14\frac{41}{50}$ **7.** 5.67 **9.** 1.22 **11.** 58.43 **13.** 5 **15a.** 16
15b. $190.24 **17a.** $664.76 **17b.** 25.1¢ **19.** $2,520.50

Assessment Test

1. Sixty-one hundredths **3.** One hundred nineteen dollars and eighty-five cents
5. Four hundred ninety-five ten-thousandths **7.** 5.014 **9.** $16.57 **11.** 995.070
13. 4.7 **15.** $96.22 **17.** 7.7056 **19.** .736 **21.** .000192 **23.** .4 **25.** $20.06
27. $\frac{441}{10,000}$ **29.** 7.56 **31.** The box of 40 Blu-ray discs and box of 40 jewel cases is
the better buy by $4.93. **33.** $19.89 **35.** $9.25 Savings **37.** $2,161.19 Remains
39a. 160 **39b.** $6.60

4 Chapter 4: Checking Accounts

SECTION I

1. $345.54 **3.** for deposit only, Your Signature, 099-506-8, Restrictive Endorsement **5.** Pay to the order of, David Sporn, Your Signature, 099-506-8, Full Endorsement **7.** $501.03 net deposit **9a.** $479.20 bal. forward **9b.** $1,246.10 bal. forward **9c.** $1,200.45 bal. forward **9d.** $1,075.45 bal. forward **9e.** $205.45 bal. forward **9f.** $1,555.45 bal. forward **9g.** $691.05 bal. forward

SECTION II

1. $1,935.90 reconciled balances **3.** $471.84 reconciled balances

Assessment Test

1. $24,556.00 **3.** $935.79 net deposit **5a.** $463.30 bal. forward **5b.** $395.52 bal. forward **5c.** $145.52 bal. forward **5d.** $270.97 bal. forward **5e.** $590.97 bal. forward **5f.** $467.87 bal. forward **7.** $1,538.32 reconciled balances

5 Chapter 5: Using Equations to Solve Business Problems

SECTION I

1. 13 **3.** 90 **5.** 3 **7.** $7\frac{1}{2}$ **9.** 4 **11.** 3 **13.** 3 **15.** 5 **17.** 1 **19.** $5F + 33$ **21.** $HP + 550$ **23.** $8Y–128$ **25.** $\frac{3}{4}B + 40$ **27.** $X = 5B + C$ **29.** $\$5.75R = \$28.75$ **31.** $5X + 4 + 2X = X + 40$

SECTION II

1. 39 Kathy's sales **3.** $21,700 Last year's salary **5.** 24 Lower-priced speaker docks **7a.** 170 Large size, 280 Small size **7b.** Large size = $3,400, Small size = $3,920 **9.** $5,000 = Each grandchild's share, $15,000 = Each child's share, $60,000 = Wife's share **11.** 288 Total transactions **13a.** 220 Pounds of peanut butter cookies, 310 Pounds of oatmeal cookies **13b.** $352 Sales of peanut butter cookies, $403 Sales of oatmeal cookies **15.** 100 Senators, 435 Representatives **17.** $485.80 Total cost to ship order **19.** 44 Cones to be placed around the area **21.** 3,080 Pounds of fruit **23.** 21 Eggs needed for recipe **25.** 43 People per job **27.** 72 Passenger flights **29a.** 12 Pages of news, 36 Pages of advertising **29b.** 4 Pages classified, 12 Pages national, 20 Pages retail **29c.** Retail = $450,000, National = $270,000, Classified = $90,000 **29d.** $14,400 Bonus

Assessment Test

1. 43 **3.** 15 **5.** 8 **7.** 8 **9.** 15 **11.** $4R–108$ **13.** $ZW + 24$ **15.** $X = 4C + L$ **17.** $3F–14 = 38$ **19.** 14 Boats sold by Pelican Marine, 19 Boats sold by Boater's Paradise **21.** $55 Cost per phone **23.** 95 Watts for energy-saver bulb **25a.** 225 Long-sleeve shirts, 150 Short-sleeve shirts **25b.** $6,412.50 Long-sleeve shirts, $3,450.00 Short-sleeve shirts **27.** 25 Words **29.** $208,000 Equipment inventory **31.** $3\frac{1}{3}$ Quarts of water **33a.** 45 Pizzas **33b.** 180 People served

Chapter 6: Percents and Their Applications in Business — 6

SECTION I

1. .28   **3.** .134   **5.** .4268   **7.** .0005   **9.** 1.2517   **11.** 350%   **13.** 4,600%

15. .52%   **17.** 16,400%   **19.** 533%   **21.** $\frac{1}{20}$ **23.** $\frac{89}{100}$ **25.** $\frac{19}{50}$ **27.** $\frac{5}{8}$ **29.** $1\frac{1}{4}$

31. 75%   **33.** 240%   **35.** 125%   **37.** 18.75%   **39.** 35%   **41.** .57, $\frac{57}{100}$

43. .15, $\frac{3}{20}$ **45.** .05, $\frac{1}{20}$

SECTION II

1. 57   **3.** 90   **5.** 85.5   **7.** 64.77   **9.** 17.6   **11.** 32%   **13.** 250%   **15.** 13.5%
17. 29.9%   **19.** 6.2%   **21.** 460   **23.** 34.86   **25.** 363.64   **27.** 400   **29.** $53.65
31a. $59,200   **31b.** $594.50   **33.** 2,220 Square feet   **35.** 12,600   **37.** 2,820
39a. $150   **39b.** Server $111.00, Host $7.50, Bartender $9.00, Busser $22.50
41. 1,700   **43.** $61,230.75   **45.** $32.3 Billion   **47.** 60,000 Police vehicles

SECTION III

1. 37.5%   **3.** 25.2%   **5.** 60   **7.** 15   **9.** 4,100   **11.** 26.5% Decrease   **13a.** 1,105
Racquets   **13b.** Metal Alloy: 442 Racquets, Graphite: 663 Racquets   **15.** 49 Million
uninsured people   **17.** $658,762   **19.** 50%   **21a.** 32.4% Increase   **21b.** 17.35%
Decrease

Assessment Test

1. .76   **3.** .5968   **5.** .005625   **7.** 68.1%   **9.** 2,480%   **11.** $\frac{19}{100}$ **13.** $\frac{93}{1,250}$

15. $\frac{127}{500}$ **17.** 55.56%   **19.** 5,630%   **21.** 1,760   **23.** 103.41   **25.** 180%   **27.** 69

29. 2,960   **31.** 1,492   **33.** $157.48 Savings   **35a.** $72,000 Total cost
35b. $0.24 Per mile   **35c.** 25% Savings per mile   **35d.** 203% Increase
37. 21.0% Increase   **39a.** 133,695 Vehicles   **39b.** 2.9% Increase
41. 18.1% Increase   **43.** $3,016,000   **45.** $40,583.33 Total shipment
47. 158.2%   **49.** $229.9 Million

Chapter 7: Invoices, Trade Discounts, and Cash Discounts — 7

SECTION I

1. Box   **3.** Drum   **5.** Gross   **7.** Thousand   **9.** Panorama Products   **11.** June 16,
20XX   **13.** J. M. Hardware Supply   **15.** 2051 W. Adams Blvd., Lansing, MI 48901
17. Gilbert Trucking   **19.** $61.45   **21.** $4,415.12   **23.** $1,085.00

SECTION II

1. $258.00   **3.** $7.93   **5.** $44.13   **7.** $53.92, $80.87   **9.** $562.50, $687.50
11. 76%, $429.65   **13.** 87.25%, $4.01   **15.** $120.50, 34.9%   **17.** $239.99
19. $177.98   **21a.** $8,653   **21b.** $16,797   **23.** $1,512   **25.** $17

SECTION III

1. .792, $285.12   **3.** .648, $52.97   **5.** .57056, $4.14   **7.** .765, .235
9. .59288, .40712   **11.** .51106, .48894   **13.** .6324, .3676, $441.12, $758.88
15. .65666, .34334, $303.34, $580.16   **17.** .5292, .4708, $1,353.53, $1,521.42
19. .442   **21a.** .6   **21b.** $54,300   **23a.** Northwest   **23b.** $4,500 Savings per year
25a. $1,494.90   **25b.** $687.65   **25c.** $807.25   **27a.** $851.05   **27b.** $392.72

SECTION IV

1. $474.00, $15,326.00   **3.** $96.84, $2,324.16   **5.** $319.25, $8,802.19   **7.** $474.23, $870.37   **9.** $5,759.16, $1,472.92   **11.** Sept. 11, Oct. 12   **13.** 2% Feb. 8, 1% Feb. 18, Mar. 30   **15.** Jan. 10, Jan. 30   **17.** Oct. 23, Nov. 12   **19.** June 25, July 15   **21a.** April 27, May 27   **21b.** $21.24   **21c.** $1,148.76   **23a.** March 22   **23b.** April 11   **25a.** $3,298 on August 19   **25b.** $3,332 on September 3   **27a.** $32,931.08   **27b.** May 19

Assessment Test

1. Leisure Time Industries   **3.** 4,387   **5.** $46.55   **7.** $2,558   **9.** $11,562.45   **11.** $2,090   **13.** 33.76%   **15.** Fancy Footwear   **17a.** .6052   **17b.** .3948   **19a.** April 24   **19b.** May 9   **19c.** May 15   **19d.** June 4   **21.** $16,747.60

8 Chapter 8: Markup and Markdown

SECTION I

1. $138.45, 85.7%   **3.** $6,944.80, 77.8%   **5.** $156.22, $93.73   **7.** $2,149.00, 159.2%   **9.** $.75, $1.33   **11.** $85.90   **13.** $529   **15a.** $4.19   **15b.** 71.7%   **17a.** $60.63   **17b.** 104.1%   **19.** $94.50   **21.** $55   **23.** $21.88

SECTION II

1. $115.00, 43.5%   **3.** $61.36, $136.36   **5.** 37.5%   **7.** $94.74, 133%, 57.1%   **9.** $9,468.74, $24,917.74, 61.3%   **11.** 60%   **13a.** $1.74   **13b.** 34.9%   **13c.** $2.09, 41.9%   **15.** $500   **17.** $125   **19.** 81.8%   **21a.** $30.49   **21b.** 141.8%   **21c.** 58.6%

SECTION III

1. $161.45, 15%   **3.** $1.68, 23.2%   **5.** $41.10, $16.44   **7.** $80.27, 30.7%   **9.** $559.96, $1,039.92   **11a.** $800   **11b.** 17.0%   **13a.** $.70   **13b.** 41.4%   **13c.** $1.39   **15.** $39.20   **17.** $69.50   **19.** $95.07   **21.** $233.99   **23a.** $65.00, 40.6%   **23b.** $85.00, 53.1%   **23c.** $396.25   **23d.** Answers will vary.

Assessment Test

1. $19.75   **3.** $18.58   **5.** $6.28, 52.9%   **7.** $15.95   **9a.** $688   **9b.** 22.5%   **11.** $216.06   **13a.** $56.25   **13b.** $64.68   **15a.** $2,499.99   **15b.** $1,000   **15c.** 60%   **15d.** 36%

9 Chapter 9: Payroll

SECTION I

1. $1,250.00, $625.00, $576.92, $288.46   **3.** $8,333.33, $4,166.67, $3,846.15, $1,923.08   **5.** $34,800, $2,900.00, $1,338.46, $669.23   **7.** $17,420, $1,451.67, $725.83, $670.00   **9.** $1,115.38   **11.** $1,329.23   **13.** 36, 0, $313.20, 0, $313.20   **15.** 48, 8, $290.00, $87.00, $377.00   **17.** $711.90   **19.** $320.25   **21.** $1,170.90   **23.** $5,790.40   **25.** $1,565   **27.** $352.66

SECTION II

1. $51.15 Social security, $11.96 Medicare   **3a.** $694.40 Social security, $162.40 Medicare   **3b.** December   **3c.** $322.40 Social security, $162.40 Medicare   **5.** $212.16, $49.62.   **7.** $291.40, $68.15   **9.** $21.24   **11.** $430.78   **13.** $139.62   **15.** $3,370.09 Paycheck   **17.** $103.91   **19.** $523.59

1a. $282.72 Total social security, $66.12 Total Medicare **1b.** $3,675.36 Social security for the first quarter, $859.56 Medicare for the first quarter **3.** $17,184.96 **5.** $23,802.00 Social security, $1,235.40 Medicare **7a.** $378 **7b.** $42 **9.** $8,299.20 **11a.** $3,770.40 **11b.** 15% **11c.** $196,060.80 **13.** 8.9%

Assessment Test

1a. $67,200 **1b.** $2,584.62 **3.** $898.70 **5.** $656.25 **7.** $1,011.71 **9.** $6,963 **11.** $2,284.10 **13.** $44.95 Social security, $10.51 Medicare **15a.** $2,062.91 **15b.** $2,183.03 **17.** $917.57 **19a.** $1,693.03 Social security, $395.95 Medicare **19b.** $44,018.78 Social security, $10,294.70 Medicare **21a.** $378 **21b.** $42 **23a.** $58,589.20 **23b.** 20.8% **23c.** $3,046,638.40

Chapter 10: Simple Interest and Promissory Notes

10

1. $800.00 **3.** $8,250.00 **5.** $206.62 **7.** $1,602.74, $1,625.00 **9.** $1,839.79, $1,865.34 **11.** $15.16, $15.38 **13.** $30.41, $30.83 **15.** $32.88 **17.** $12,852.00, $66,852.00 **19.** $2,362.50, $36,112.50 **21.** $22,929.60, $79,129.60 **23.** $1,770.00 **25.** $1,330,000.00 **27.** $155,043.00 **29.** 98 **31.** 289 **33.** 47 **35.** December 3 **37.** June 24 **39.** February 23 **41.** October 2 **43.** $61,002.74 **45.** $403.89 **47.** $14.97

1. $1,250 **3.** $50,000 **5.** $31,440 **7.** $7,500 **9.** 4.7 **11.** 6.8 **13.** 10.3 **15.** 158 Days **17.** 308 Days **19.** 102 Days **21.** 216 Days **23.** $13,063.16, $13,403.16 **25.** $2,390.63, $27,890.63 **27a.** 166 Days **27b.** September 29 **29.** $10,000 **31.** 11.6% **33.** $66,620.99 **35.** $6,784.35 **37a.** 12.5 Years **37b.** 10 Years

1. $292.50, $4,207.50 **3.** $150, $1,850 **5.** $2,700 **7.** 84, $171.50, $4,828.50 **9.** 100, $34.31, $1,265.69 **11.** $132.30, $2,567.70, 14.72 **13.** $107.14, $3,692.86, 7.46 **15.** 7.1% **17.** Jan. 31, $4,057.78, 12, $4,037.49 **19.** Aug. 8, $8,180, 34, $8,101.20 **21.** $195, $14,805, 5.27 **23.** $964, $79,036, 4.88 **25.** 4.19% **27.** 6.13% **29a.** $484.62 **29b.** $149,515.38 **29c.** 4.21%

Assessment Test

1. $641.10 **3.** $366.47 **5.** $20,224.00 **7.** 107 **9.** Jan. 24 **11.** $20,000 **13.** 9.1 **15.** 156 **17.** 190, $13,960.00 **19.** 15.2, $2,795.00 **21.** Jan. 20, $20,088.54, $854,911.46 **23.** $10,544.72, $279,455.28, 12.35 **25.** Aug. 25, $5,642.31, 34, $5,569.30 **27.** $686.00, $27,314.00, 5.02 **29.** $99.37 **31.** 8.5% **33.** $9,393.88 **35a.** $28,970.83 **35b.** November 12 **35c.** 13.46% **37a.** $752 **37b.** $63,248 **37c.** 4.76%

11 | Chapter 11: Compound Interest and Present Value

SECTION I

1. 3, 13   **3.** 24, 4   **5.** 16, 1.5   **7.** 3, 1   **9.** $10,406.04, $406.04   **11.** $11,817.84
13. $13,950.64, $2,950.64   **15.** $95,776.50, $28,776.50   **17.** $450.86,
$50.86   **19.** 1.43077, $18,600.01   **21.** 1.54933, $53,761.75   **23.** $14,595.21
25. $80.00, 4%   **27.** $82.43, 8.24%   **29a.** 6.14%   **29b.** $4,288.50
31. $16,174.20   **33.** 97 Sheep   **35.** $5,904.40, $904.40   **37.** $3,024.73, $224.73
39. $71,875

SECTION II

1. $4,633.08, $1,366.92   **3.** $437.43, $212.57   **5.** $3,680.50, $46,319.50
7. $6,107.07, $3,692.93   **9.** $235.48, $14.52   **11.** .67165, $8,059.80   **13.** .48936,
$685.10   **15.** $9,314.85   **17a.** $2,549.58   **17b.** $950.42   **19.** $15,742,200
21. 47 Million songbirds   **23.** $3,466.02, $1,033.98   **25.** $15,643.55, $3,256.45
27a. $5,385   **27b.** $615

Assessment Test

1. $17,755.36, $3,755.36   **3.** $3,185.04, $185.04   **5.** 2.39005, $47,801.00
7. $1,078.06, 12.68%   **9.** $6,930.00, $143,070.00   **11.** $658.35, $241.65
13. .62027, $806.35   **15.** $81,392.40, $45,392.40   **17.** $17,150.85, $2,150.85
19. $92,727.70   **21a.** 12.55%   **21b.** $17,888.55   **23.** $48,545.40   **25a.** $37,243.34
25b. $14,243.34   **27.** 3.7 Million fleet miles   **29.** $25,910.82, $4,110.82
31. $11,218.11, $1,588.11   **33.** $77,380.73, $2,819.27   **35.** $2,263.80, $176.20
37. $97,129   **39.** $17,795

12 | Chapter 12: Annuities

SECTION I

1. $18,639.29   **3.** $151,929.30   **5.** $4,601.99   **7.** $13,680.33   **9.** $100,226.90
11. $2,543.20   **13.** $3,228.00   **15.** $15,934.37   **17.** $36,848.56   **19.** $42,082.72
21. $52,139.38   **23a.** $8,101.04   **23b.** $28,442.52

SECTION II

1. $2,969.59   **3.** $75,655.72   **5.** $13,089.01   **7.** $45,565.03   **9.** $156,394.74
11. $9,025.15   **13.** $380,773   **15.** $7,900.87   **17.** $5,865.77   **19.** $14,792.29
21. $21,856.03   **23.** $100,490.79

SECTION III

1. $2,113.50   **3.** $68.12   **5.** $803.25   **7.** $336.36   **9.** $1,087.48
11a. $245,770.96   **11b.** $2,135,329.28   **13a.** $3,769.04   **13b.** $2,385.76
15. $12,802.39   **17.** $53.96   **19.** $3,756.68   **21.** $155.12   **23.** $169.11
25a. $13,787.95   **25b.** $172,723

Assessment Test

1. $121,687.44   **3.** $86,445.14   **5.** $42,646.92   **7.** $12,081.04   **9.** $993.02
11. $255.66   **13.** $20,345.57   **15.** $6,081.72   **17.** $368.62   **19.** $40,012.45
21. $7,639.68   **23.** $5,431.63   **25.** $69,840.21   **27.** $32,115.31   **29.** $5,913.62
31. $2,468.92   **33a.** $11,261.18   **33b.** $12,321.12   **35.** $1,454.65

Chapter 13: Consumer and Business Credit

13

SECTION I

1. 1.5%, $2.52, $335.90   **3.** 9%, $4.54, $566.08   **5.** .75%, $25.64, $2,573.14
7. $461.94   **9.** $636.17, $11.13, $628.75   **11.** $817.08, $14.30, $684.76   **13.** $677.84
15. $158.51   **17a.** 12.4%   **17b.** 15.5%   **17c.** 14.65%   **17d.** 11%   **19.** $14,503.35

SECTION II

1. $1,050.00, $582.00, $1,982.00   **3.** $10,800.00, $2,700.00, $14,700.00
5. $7,437.50, $2,082.34, $10,832.34   **7.** $20,880   **9.** $1,350.00, $270.00, $67.50
11. $15,450.00, $8,652.00, $502.13   **13.** $11,685.00, $3,154.95, $412.22
15. $322.00, $14.00, 13%   **17.** $223.50, $12.02, 14.75%   **19.** $825.20, $12.60,
11.75%   **21.** $31.00, 11.25%   **23.** $4,940.00, 16.6%   **25.** $15,130.00, 14.71%
27. $29.97, $1,498.50, $135.39   **29.** $6.20, $111.60, $159.30   **31.** $13.82, $1,686.04,
$578.59   **33.** 8, 36, 78, $\frac{36}{78}$ **35.** 15, 120, 300, 120/300   **37.** 40, 820, 1,176,
820/1,176   **39.** 120/300, $360.00, $2,077.50,   **41.** 78/1,176, $219.94, $2,984.06
43. 55/465, $260.22, $4,139.78   **45a.** $1,709.10, $2,120.40, $411.30
45b. $2,310.30   **47.** $68.75   **49a.** $729.52   **49b.** $8,329.52
51. $442.26, $84.51   **53a.** 300   **53b.** 465   **55a.** $504   **55b.** $152.25
55c. 14.64%, 14.75%   **55d.** $1,157.52

Assessment Test

1a. 1.25%   **1b.** $5.35   **1c.** $564.60   **3a.** $4.46, $724.12   **3b.** $724.12, $12.09,
$839.64   **3c.** $839.64, $14.02, $859.61   **5a.** $694.76   **5b.** $7.50   **5c.** $864.74
7a. $9,920   **7b.** $39,120   **9a.** $7,788.16   **9b.** 14.75%   **11a.** $66,300
11b. $4,646.67   **13a.** $14,144   **13b.** $1,428   **13c.** 11.75%   **13d.** $32,906.45
15a. $30,686.75   **15b.** $24,686.75   **15c.** $8,733.25   **15d.** $39,420   **15e.** 12.75%

Chapter 14: Mortgages

SECTION I

1. 80, 9.00, $720.00, $92,800.00   **3.** 164.9, 5.56, $916.84, $110,152.00   **5.** 96.8,
7.17, $694.06, $153,061.60   **7.** $48,505.60   **9.** $639.47, $821.39
11. $1,241.49, $1,652.91   **13.** $1,067.61, $1,458.78   **15a.** $1,736.46
15b. $275,328   **17a.** Fortune Bank, $115,950; Northern Trust Bank, $120,000
17b. Fortune Bank, $121,950; Northern Trust Bank, $120,000 (Better deal, $1,950
Less)   **19a.** 7.35%   **19b.** 12.35%   **21.** $39,700

SECTION II

1. $89,025, $21,125   **3.** $112,960, $13,860   **5.** $68,250, $0   **7.** $107,550
9. 14.32, 24.05   **11.** 25.00, 34.81   **13.** 27.01, 38.24   **15.** FHA: Qualified,
Conventional: Not qualified   **17.** 0   **19.** $19,200, No to the addition
21a. 25.75%   **21b.** 39.13%   **21c.** FHA   **21d.** $425.28

Assessment Test

1. 155.9, 5.56, $866.80, $104,140.00   **3.** Month 1 loan bal.: $145,966.57, Month 2 loan
bal.: $145,832.41, Month 3 loan bal.: $145,697.53   **5.** $1,325.98, $1,601.65
7. $41,200, $13,800   **9.** 24.30, 40.15   **11.** FHA, FHA and Conventional
13a. $4,269.20   **13b.** Month 1 loan bal.: $519,089.13, Month 2 loan bal.: $518,172.38
13c. $5,221.70   **13d.** $14,578.30   **15a.** $703,639.20, $651,744.00
15b. Foremost is better by $34,457.70   **17a.** $1,230.98   **17b.** $120,236
17c. $22,557.40   **17d.** $80,060   **19.** 0   **21a.** 27.86%   **21b.** 39.53%   **21c.** FHA

15   Chapter 15: Financial Statements and Ratios

SECTION I

1. $161,600   **3.** $29,000   **5.** $3,483,500   **7.** $2,406,200   **9.** $40,518, $27,996, $12,522   **11.** $4,430, $2,445, $3,062   **13.** Current Asset   **15.** Owner's Equity   **17.** Long-Term Liability   **19.** Current Liability   **21.** Current Asset   **23.** Current Asset   **25.** Fixed Asset   **27.** Current Asset   **29.** Owner's Equity   **31.** Owner's Equity   **33.** $6,700, 56.3%

35a.

Stargate Industries, Inc.
Balance Sheet
June 30, 2018

Assets

Current Assets		Percent*
Cash	$ 44,300	5.5%
Accounts Receivable	127,600	15.8
Merchandise Inventory	88,100	10.9
Prepaid Maintenance	4,100	.5
Office Supplies	4,000	.5
Total Current Assets	268,100	33.2
Property, Plant, and Equipment		
Land	154,000	19.0
Buildings	237,000	29.3
Fixtures	21,400	2.6
Vehicles	64,000	7.9
Computers	13,000	1.6
Total Property, Plant, and Equipment	489,400	60.4
Investments and Other Assets		
Investments	32,000	4.0
Goodwill	20,000	2.5
Total Assets	$809,500	100.0%

Liabilities and Stockholders' Equity

Current Liabilities		
Accounts Payable	55,700	6.9%
Salaries Payable	23,200	2.9
Notes Payable	38,000	4.7
Total Current Liabilities	116,900	14.5
Long-Term Liabilities		
Mortgage Payable	91,300	11.3
Debenture Bonds	165,000	20.4
Total Long-Term Liabilities	256,300	31.7
Total Liabilities	373,200	46.2
Stockholders' Equity		
Common Stock	350,000	43.2
Retained Earnings	86,300	10.7
Total Stockholders' Equity	436,300	53.9
Total Liabilities and Stockholders' Equity	$809,500	100.0%

*Percents may vary by .1 due to rounding.

35b.

Stargate Industries, Inc.
Balance Sheet
June 30, 2018 and 2019

Assets	2019	2018	Increase (Decrease) Amount	Increase (Decrease) Percent
Current Assets				
Cash	$40,200	$44,300	($4,100)	(9.3)%
Accounts Receivable	131,400	127,600	3,800	3.0
Merchandise Inventory	92,200	88,100	4,100	4.7
Prepaid Maintenance	3,700	4,100	(400)	(9.8)
Office Supplies	6,200	4,000	2,200	55.0
Total Current Assets	273,700	268,100	5,600	2.1
Property, Plant, and Equipment				
Land	154,000	154,000	0	0.0
Buildings	231,700	237,000	(5,300)	(2.2)
Fixtures	23,900	21,400	2,500	11.7
Vehicles	55,100	64,000	(8,900)	(13.9)
Computers	16,800	13,000	3,800	29.2
Total Property, Plant, and Equipment	481,500	489,400	7,900	1.6
Investments and Other Assets				
Investments	36,400	32,000	4,400	13.8
Goodwill	22,000	20,000	2,000	10.0
Total Assets	$813,600	$809,500	4,100	.5
Liabilities and Stockholders' Equity				
Current Liabilities				
Accounts Payable	51,800	55,700	(3,900)	(7.0)
Salaries Payable	25,100	23,200	1,900	8.2
Notes Payable	19,000	38,000	(19,000)	(50.0)
Total Current Liabilities	95,900	116,900	(21,000)	(18.0)
Long-Term Liabilities				
Mortgage Payable	88,900	91,300	(2,400)	(2.6)
Debenture Bonds	165,000	165,000	0	0.0
Total Long-Term Liabilities	253,900	256,300	(2,400)	(.9)
Total Liabilities	349,800	373,200	(23,400)	(6.3)
Stockholders' Equity				
Common Stock	350,000	350,000	0	0.0
Retained Earnings	113,800	86,300	27,500	31.9
Total Stockholders' Equity	463,800	436,300	27,500	6.3
Total Liabilities and Stockholders' Equity	$813,600	$809,500	4,100	.5

1. $565,700, $44,700   **3.** $306,850, $110,325   **5.** $880,000, $405,220   **7.** $154,560, $86,510   **9.** $22,506, $7,228, $3,877   **11.** $6,758,237, $1,410,922, $261,688
13a. $316,120   **13b.** $122,680   **13c.** $212,320   **13d.** $45,120   **15.** $78,100, 38.9%

SECTION II

17a.

Sweets & Treats Candy Company, Inc.
Income Statement
For the Year Ended December 31, 2018

Revenue		
Gross Sales	$2,249,000	109.6%
Less: Sales Returns and Allowances	143,500	7.0
Sales Discounts	54,290	2.6
Net Sales	$2,051,210	100.0
Cost of Goods Sold		
Merchandise Inventory, Jan. 1	875,330	42.7
Net Purchases	546,920	26.7
Freight In	11,320	.6
Goods Available for Sale	1,433,570	69.9
Less: Merchandise Inventory, Dec. 31	716,090	34.9
Cost of Goods Sold	717,480	35.0
Gross Margin	1,333,730	65.0
Operating Expenses		
Salaries	319,800	15.6
Rent	213,100	10.4
Depreciation	51,200	2.5
Utilities	35,660	1.7
Advertising	249,600	12.2
Insurance	39,410	1.9
Administrative Expenses	91,700	4.5
Miscellaneous Expenses	107,500	5.2
Total Operating Expenses	1,107,970	54.0
Income before Taxes	225,760	11.0
Income Tax	38,450	1.9
Net Income	$187,310	9.1

17b.

Sweets & Treats Candy Company, Inc.
Income Statement
For the Year Ended December 31, 2018 and 2019

			Increase (Decrease)	
	2019	**2018**	**Amount**	**Percent**
Revenue				
Gross Sales	$2,125,000	$2,249,000	($124,000)	(5.5)%
Less: Sales Returns and Allowances	126,400	143,500	(17,100)	(11.9)
Sales Discounts	73,380	54,290	19,090	35.2
Net Sales	1,925,220	2,051,210	(125,990)	(6.1)
Cost of Goods Sold				
Merchandise Inventory, Jan. 1	716,090	875,330	(159,240)	(18.2)
Net Purchases	482,620	546,920	(64,300)	(11.8)
Freight In	9,220	11,320	(2,100)	(18.6)
Goods Available for Sale	1,207,930	1,433,570	(225,640)	(15.7)
Less: Merchandise Inventory, Dec. 31	584,550	716,090	(131,540)	(18.4)
Cost of Goods Sold	623,380	717,480	(94,100)	(13.1)
Gross Margin	1,301,840	1,333,730	(31,890)	(2.4)

Sweets & Treats Candy Company, Inc.
Income Statement
For the Year Ended December 31, 2018 and 2019

	2019	2018	Increase (Decrease) Amount	Percent
Operating Expenses				
Salaries	340,900	319,800	21,100	7.0
Rent	215,000	213,100	1,900	.9
Depreciation	56,300	51,200	5,100	10.0
Utilities	29,690	35,660	(5,970)	(16.7)
Advertising	217,300	249,600	(32,300)	(13.0)
Insurance	39,410	39,410	0	0
Administrative Expenses	95,850	91,700	4,150	4.5
Miscellaneous Expenses	102,500	107,500	(5,000)	(4.7)
Total Operating Expenses	1,096,950	1,107,970	(11,020)	(1.0)
Income before Income Tax	204,890	225,760	(20,870)	(9.2)
Income Tax	44,530	38,450	6,080	15.8
Net Income	$160,360	$187,310	$(26,950)	(14.4)

SECTION III

1. $318,000, 3.41:1 **3.** ($5,160), .74:1 **5.** $379,070, 1.45:1 **7.** $95,920, 1.29:1
9. $2,165, 1.73:1 **11.** 25 Days **13a.** 32 Days **13b.** 32, 16 Days faster than
competition **15.** $74,447.50, 6.6 **17.** $105,650, 6.2 **19.** .27:1 **21.** $865,000, .38:
1, .62:1 **23.** $155,390, .70:1, 2.30:1 **25.** $226,000, $112,600, $113,400, 35.3, 17.7
27. $149,410, $50,210, 46.1, 15.5 **29.** 21.6 **31.** 6.8

33.

Hook, Line, and Sinker Fishing Supply
Trend Analysis

	2018	2017	2016	2015	2014
Net Sales	107.5	127.3	108.0	97.1	100.0
Net Income	124.3	128.5	99.4	104.2	100.0
Total Assets	109.7	107.4	105.0	97.7	100.0
Stockholders' Equity	105.9	120.3	106.4	94.5	100.0

Assessment Test

1. $5,357, $3,753, $1,604 **3.** $21,436, $17,207, $1,971

5a.

Uniflex Fabricators, Inc.
Balance Sheet as of
December 31, 2017

Assets		Percent
Current Assets	$132,500	52.2
Property, Plant, and Equipment	88,760	35.0
Investments and Other Assets	32,400	12.8
Total Assets	$253,660	100.0%

Uniflex Fabricators, Inc.
Balance Sheet as of
December 31, 2017

Liabilities		
Current Liabilities	51,150	20.2
Long-Term Liabilities	87,490	34.5
Total Liabilities	138,640	54.7
Owner's Equity		
Paul Provost, Equity	115,020	45.3
Total Liabilities and Owner's Equity	$253,660	100.0%

5b.

Uniflex Fabricators, Inc.
Comparative Balance Sheet
as of December 31, 2017 and 2018

			Increase (Decrease)	
	2018	2017	Amount	Percent
Assets				
Current Assets	$154,300	$132,500	$21,800	16.5
Property, Plant, and Equipment	124,650	88,760	35,890	40.4
Investments and Other Assets	20,000	32,400	(12,400)	(38.3)
Total Assets	$298,950	$253,660	45,290	17.9
Liabilities				
Current Liabilities	65,210	51,150	14,060	27.5
Long-Term Liabilities	83,800	87,490	(3,690)	(4.2)
Total Liabilities	149,010	138,640	10,370	7.5
Owner's Equity				
Paul Provost, Equity	149,940	115,020	34,920	30.4
Total Liabilities and Owner's Equity	$298,950	$253,660	45,290	17.9

7. $185,772

9a.

Woof & Meow Pet Supply
Income Statement
Third Quarter, 2018

Revenue		
Gross Sales	$224,400	106.8
Less: Sales Returns and Allowances	14,300	6.8
Net Sales	210,100	100.0
Cost of Goods sold		
Merchandise Inventory, July 1	165,000	78.5
Net Purchases	76,500	36.4
Goods Available for Sale	241,500	114.9
Less: Merchandise Inventory, Sept. 30	143,320	68.2
Cost of Goods Sold	98,180	46.7
Gross Margin	111,920	53.3
Operating Expenses	68,600	32.7

Woof & Meow Pet Supply
Income Statement
Third Quarter, 2018

Income before Taxes	43,320	20.6
Income Tax	8,790	4.2
Net Income	$34,530	16.4

9b.

Woof & Meow Pet Supply
Income Statement
Third and Fourth Quarters, 2018

	Fourth Quarter	Third Quarter	Increase (Decrease) Amount	Increase (Decrease) Percent
Revenue				
Gross Sales	$218,200	$224,400	($6,200)	(2.8)
Less: Sales Returns and Allowances	9,500	14,300	(4,800)	(33.6)
Net Sales	208,700	210,100	1,400	.7
Cost of Goods Sold				
Merchandise Inventory, Beginning	143,320	165,000	(21,680)	(13.1)
Net Purchases	81,200	76,500	4,700	6.1
Goods Available for Sale	224,520	241,500	(16,980)	(7.0)
Less: Merchandise Inventory, Ending	125,300	143,320	(18,020)	(12.6)
Cost of Goods Sold	99,220	98,180	1,040	1.0
Gross Margin	109,480	111,920	(2,440)	(2.2)
Operating Expenses	77,300	68,600	8,700	12.7
Income before Income Tax	32,180	43,320	(11,140)	(25.7)
Income Tax	11,340	8,790	2,550	29.0
Net Income	$ 20,840	$ 34,530	(13,690)	(39.6)

11. $653,300 **13.** 1.51:1 **15.** 1.74 Times **17.** 37.9% **19.** 48.3% **21.** 4.2%

23.

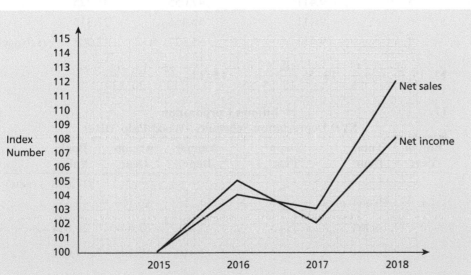

16   Chapter 16: Inventory

SECTION I

1. 127, $16,531   **3.** $55,484   **5.** $508,896.31   **7a.** $931.00   **7b.** $852.10   **7c.** $891.00   **9.** $19,487   **11.** $43,030

SECTION II

1. $7,003   **3.** $108,225   **5.** $696,668   **7.** $61,716

SECTION III

1. $60,000, 8.3, $50,000.00   **3.** $486,500, 2.5, $342,857.00   **5.** $59,900, 4.3, $49,692.00   **7.** $466,460, 2.8, Above   **9a.** $58,400   **9b.** 4.2 Times   **11.** 3.4 Times   **13.** 2.2, $77,000   **15a.** $38,150, 3.8 Times   **15b.** $29,591.84

Assessment Test

1. 81, $41,244   **3.** 454, $22,053.65   **5.** $178,159   **7.** $394,885   **9.** $153,500, 5, $111,765   **11.** $81,780, 5.6, $73,226   **13a.** $359,850   **13b.** 2.5 Times   **13c.** $176,800

17   Chapter 17: Depreciation

SECTION I

1. $45,650, $42,150, $4,215.00   **3.** $160,000, $140,000, $28,000.00   **5.** $220,400, $195,900, $19,590.00   **7.** $470,000, $416,000, $52,000.00

9.

Mason Industries
Depreciation Schedule—Drilling Rig

End of Year	Annual Depreciation	Accumulated Depreciation	Book Value	
			$78,780	(new)
1	$9,411	$9,411	69,369	
2	9,411	18,822	59,958	
3	9,411	28,233	50,547	
4	9,411	37,644	41,136	
5	9,411	47,055	31,725	
6	9,411	56,466	22,314	
7	9,411	65,877	12,903	(salvage)

11. 15, $\frac{5}{15}$, $\frac{13}{15}$, $\frac{1}{15}$ **13.** 55, $\frac{10}{15}$, $\frac{8}{55}$, $\frac{6}{55}$ **15.** 120, $\frac{15}{120}$, $\frac{13}{120}$, $\frac{11}{120}$

17.

Billings Corporation
SYD Depreciation Schedule—Wood Pulp Mixer

End of Year	Total Depr	×	Depr Frac	=	Annual Depr	Accum Depr	Book Value	
							$17,668	(new)
1	16,464	×	$\frac{7}{28}$	=	$4,116	$4,116	13,552	
2	16,464	×	$\frac{6}{28}$	=	3,528	7,644	10,024	
3	16,464	×	$\frac{5}{28}$	=	2,940	10,584	7,084	
4	16,464	×	$\frac{4}{28}$	=	2,352	12,936	4,732	

Billings Corporation
SYD Depreciation Schedule—Wood Pulp Mixer

End of Year	Total Depr	×	Depr Frac	=	Annual Depr	Accum Depr	Book Value	
5	16,464	×	$\frac{3}{28}$	=	1,764	14,700	2,968	
6	16,464	×	$\frac{2}{28}$	=	1,176	15,876	1,792	
7	16,464	×	$\frac{1}{28}$	=	588	16,464	1,204	(salvage)

19. 10.00, 15.00 **21.** 12.50, 18.75 **23.** 5.00, 10.00 **25.** $.122 **27.** .22 **29.** .166

31.

Thunderbird Manufacturing
Units-of-Production Depreciation Schedule
Stamping Machine

End of Year	Depreciation per Unit	Units Produced	Annual Depreciation	Accumulated Depreciation	Book Value
				(new)	$45,000
1	$.16	50,000	$8,000	8,000	37,000
2	.16	70,000	11,200	19,200	25,800
3	.16	45,000	7,200	26,400	18,600
4	.16	66,000	10,560	36,960	8,040
5	.16	30,000	3,040*	40,000	5,000

*Maximum allowable to reach salvage value.

1a. $247,000 **1b.** $43,200.30 **3a.** $1,425,000 **3b.** $886,500
5a. $228.50 **5b.** $3,701,700 **7.** $8,381,850

SECTION II

Assessment Test

1. $5,864, $5,264, $877.33

3.

Oxford Manufacturing, Inc.
Straight-Line Depreciation Schedule
Manufacturing Equipment

End of Year	Annual Depreciation	Accumulated Depreciation	Book Value
		(new)	$652,000
1	$154,750	$154,750	497,250
2	154,750	309,500	342,500
3	154,750	464,250	187,750
4	154,750	619,000	33,000

5. 45, $\frac{8}{45}$, $\frac{6}{45}$, $\frac{4}{45}$ **7.** 11.11, 16.67

9.

Award Makers
150% Declining-Balance Depreciation Schedule
Computerized Engraving Machine

End of Year	Beginning Book Value	Depreciation Rate	Depreciation for the Year	Accumulated Depreciation	Ending Book Value
				(new)	$33,800.00
1	$33,800.00	.3	$10,140.00	$10,140.00	23,660.00
2	23,660.00	.3	7,098.00	17,238.00	16,562.00
3	16,562.00	.3	4,968.60	22,206.60	11,593.40

11. .024   **13a.** $320,000

13b.

Stone Age Concrete, Inc.
MACRS Depreciation
Schedule Cement Manufacturing Equipment

End of Year	Original Basis (cost)	Cost Recovery Percentage	Cost Recovery (depreciation)	Accumulated Depreciation	Book Value
				(new)	$320,000
1	$320,000	5.00	$16,000	$16,000	304,000
2	320,000	9.50	30,400	46,400	273,600
3	320,000	8.55	27,360	73,760	246,240
4	320,000	7.70	24,640	98,400	221,600
5	320,000	6.93	22,176	120,576	199,424

15a. $375,000   **15b.** $415,500

18

Chapter 18: Taxes

SECTION I

1. $.59, $9.54   **3.** $.32, $5.20   **5.** $.65, $10.55   **7.** $100.80, $43.20, $1,584.00
9. $9.90, $22.00, $251.85   **11.** $17,847.98, $937.02   **13.** $12.10, $20.79, $221.89
15. $208.21   **17a.** $44.91   **17b.** $1.80   **19a.** $1,392   **19b.** $740   **19c.** $19,532

SECTION II

1. $216,000, $8,856.00   **3.** $310,000, $5,347.50   **5.** $76,000, $2,614.40
7. $198,400, $5,138.56   **9.** $106,440, $2,267.17   **11.** $264,033, $13,993.75
13. 4.65%, $4.65, $46.50, 46.5   **15.** 5.89, $5.89, $58.90, 58.9   **17.** 1.55, $1.55, $15.50, 15.5   **19.** $6.41

SECTION III

1. $32,180, $12,000, $20,180   **3.** $43,910, $24,000, $19,910
5. $6,780, $12,000, $47,430   **7.** $4,080, $18,000, $63,290
9. $33,800   **11.** $5,919   **13.** $40,949.66   **15.** $1,395   **17.** $1,519
19. Refund $3,009   **21.** $18,680.55, $70,274.45   **23.** $200,550,000, $754,450,000

Assessment Test

1. $1.17, $19.05   **3.** $6.62, $141.62   **5.** $1,184.63, $755.00, $19,489.63
7a. $25.42   **7b.** $471.30   **9a.** Sales tax per tire = $3.83, Total sales tax = $2,221.40   **9b.** Excise tax per tire = $7.50, Total excise tax = $4,350
9c. $55,871.40   **11.** $52,101, $662.72

13. $82,615, $2,394.18   **15.** 1.65%, $1.65, $16.50, 16.5   **17a.** 0.07%
17b. $0.07 per $100   **17c.** $0.70 per $1,000   **17d.** 0.7 mills   **19.** $66,003,
$24,000, $39,823   **21.** $39,213.84   **23.** $6,211.56   **25.** Owe $228
27a. $49,950   **27b.** $37,950   **27c.** $4,363.50   **27d.** Refund $1,936.50

Chapter 19: Insurance

19

SECTION I

1. $79.50, $41.34, $20.67, $7.16   **3.** $842.00, $437.84, $218.92, $75.78   **5.** $270.00,
$140.40, $70.20, $24.30   **7.** $2,276.40, $1,183.73, $591.86, $204.88   **9.** $4,900,
$9,300, 17, 54   **11.** $5,495, $10,990, 21, 218   **13.** $2,275, $5,825, 19, 204
15a. $5,240.40   **15b.** $2,725.01   **17.** Option 1: $14,325 Cash value, Option 2:
$37,200 Reduced paid-up insurance, Option 3: 30 years, 206 days Extended term
19. $758,000 Insurance needed

SECTION II

1. $5,907.50, $1,001.00, $6,908.50   **3.** $533.20, $178.50, $711.70   **5.** $7,200.20,
$1,287.00, $8,487.20   **7.** $225.00, $525.00   **9.** $112.50, $337.50   **11.** $1,088.00,
$192.00   **13.** $295.93   **15.** $75,000.00   **17.** $37,000.00   **19.** $431,939.57
21. $162.50   **23.** $27,750

SECTION III

1. $343.00   **3.** $1,125.00   **5.** $625.60   **7.** $1,146.60   **9.** $1,412   **11.** $10,097

Assessment Test

1. $2,521.60, $1,311.23, $655.62, $226.94   **3.** $546.00, $283.92, $141.96, $49.14
5. $20,410, $40,820, 21, 218   **7a.** $1,088   **7b.** 97.92   **7c.** $87.04   **9.** $640,000
11. $475.00, $672.00, $1,147.00   **13.** $173.33, $86.67   **15.** $6,057.69   **17.** $12,392
19. $153,000   **21.** $361.80   **23.** $564.40   **25a.** $103,650   **25b.** $40,250

Chapter 20: Investments

20

SECTION I

1. $6.00, $.50   **3.** $5.50, $.85   **5.** $12.00, $.75   **7.** ATEN, $6.73, up 0.15%
9. ABBV, $95.12, 23.54   **11.** $109.98, 0.38%, down 22.86%   **13.** 1.7%, 15
15. 1.4%, 23   **17.** 5.1%   **19.** $3,959.20, $4,910.40, $951.20   **21.** $6,585.15,
$9,997.57, $3,412.42   **23.** $29,723.41, $26,310.56, ($3,412.85)   **25.** $0.85 Per share
27a. $27,000,000   **27b.** $1.74 Per share   **29a.** $29,658.56   **29b.** $36,078.38
29c. $6,419.82

SECTION II

1. 2.900%, $896.30   **3.** KRAFT HEINZ FOODS   **5.** COMCAST CORP   **7.** $889.53
9. $891.23   **11.** $9.17, $876.67   **13.** $34.90, $39,796.00   **15.** $16.56,
$11,433.10   **17.** $28.33, $4,429.32   **19.** $8.13, $6,262.41   **21.** $66.25, 7.3%
23. $75.00, 6%   **25.** 6.2%

SECTION III

1. PAAIX, $12.30   **3.** John Hancock Funds A, HiYMuBdA p, $8.30   **5.** John Hancock
Funds A, ClassicVal p, down 15.8%   **7.** GoldInst r, 17.7%   **9.** Fidelity Invest, down 8.5%
11. $.67, 3.8%   **13.** $0, 0%   **15.** 4.8%   **17.** $8.23, 526.316   **19.** $2.07
21. $3,750, $4,260, $585, 15.6   **23.** $4,850, $6,120, $2,520, 52
25. 10.2%   **27.** $2.50   **29.** 43.3%

Assessment Test

1. 0, $.36   **3.** $15.00, $.09   **5.** Acorn International ADR, 12,965 shares
7. Advance Auto Parts, 43.71%   **9.** $2.09, 3.3   **11.** $8.98, $1.71   **13.** $15,665.20,
$12,142.70, ($3,522.50)   **15.** $39,277.88, $44,975.31, $5,697.43
17a. $13,000,000   **17b.** $.71 Per share   **19a.** $4,472.28   **19b.** $3,346.85
19c. ($1,125.43) Loss   **21.** 10/15/2026   **23.** $920.53   **25.** BAA2 and BBB
27. $20.49, $4,074.95   **29.** $2.05, $9,410.50   **31.** $21.84, $4,969.20
33. $95.00, 9%   **35.** Vanguard Index, 500 Index, $96.95   **37.** $12.30, up 0.01
39. $.52, 5   **41.** $7.05, $6,410.256   **43.** $1,340, $1,180, ($85.00), (6.3)
45. $9,400, $12,820, $4,380, 46.6   **47.** $9.04   **49.** 33.6%

21   Chapter 21: Business Statistics and Data Presentation

SECTION I

1a. $0.2 Billion   **1b.** 2014   **1c.** Widget sales in billions of dollars from 2009 to 2016
1d. x-axis = time from 2009 to 2016, y-axis = sales in billions of dollars
1e. $1.0 Billion   **1f.** 2013   **1g.** $1 Billion   **3.** 420   **5.** 65%

7.

	Jan.	Feb.	Mar.	Apr.	May	June
Standard	$569,400	$566,200	$636,100	$607,400	$649,700	$706,700
Deluxe	$347,400	$343,800	$408,700	$383,900	$408,000	$431,600

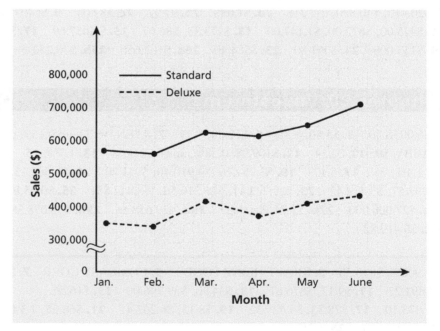

9.

	Jan.	Feb.	Mar.	Apr.	May	June
Standard	$214,700	$228,400	$246,600	$239,000	$266,100	$279,300
Deluxe	$121,300	$133,100	$164,800	$153,200	$185,000	$190,100
Total	$336,000	$361,500	$411,400	$392,200	$451,100	$469,400

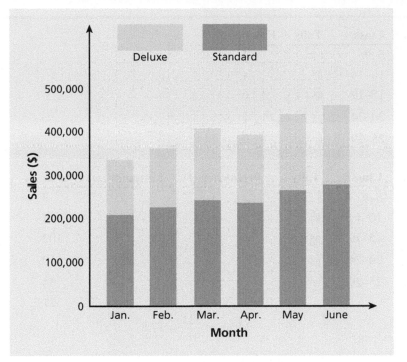

11.

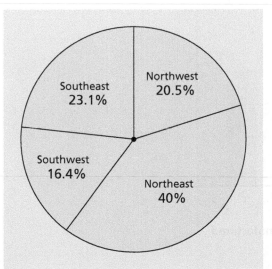

Northwest	$1,244,500
Northeast	2,421,600
Southwest	993,100
Southeast	1,399,700
Total sales	$6,058,900

Northwest $\dfrac{1,244,500}{6,058,900} = 20.5\% \times 360 = 74°$

Northeast $\dfrac{2,421,600}{6,058,900} = 40\% \times 360 = 144°$

Southwest $\dfrac{993,100}{6,058,900} = 16.4\% \times 360 = 59°$

Southeast $\dfrac{1,399,700}{6,058,900} = 23.1\% \times 360 = \dfrac{83°}{360°}$

SECTION II

1. 17.8   **3.** 306.8   **5.** 9 is the median.   **7.** 38 is the median.   **9.** 47%   **11.** 21 is the mode in this set.   **13.** Both 4 and 9 are modes in this set.   **15.** 185
17. 2,179   **19a.** Small van 5 86.8, Large van = 140.6   **19b.** Small truck = 288, Large truck = 339   **19c.** 189   **19d.** 238   **19e.** Both 86 and 290 are modes of this set of numbers.   **19f.** 293

SECTION III

1a.

Class	Tally	Frequency
5–9	I	1
10–14	IIII	4
15–19	ЖI I	6
20–24	ЖI	5
25–29	II	2

1b.

Class	Tally	Frequency (f)	Midpoint (m)	$f \times m$
5–9	I	1	7	7
10–14	IIII	4	12	48
15–19	ЖI I	6	17	102
20–24	ЖI	5	22	110
25–29	II	2	27	54
		18		321

$$\text{Mean} = \frac{321}{18} = \underline{\underline{17.8}}$$

1c.

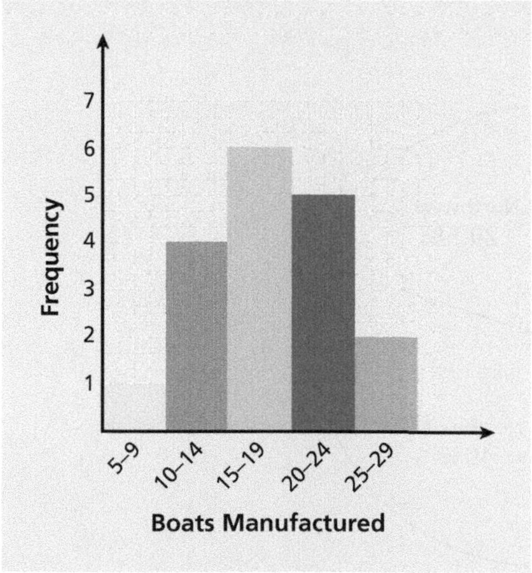

Boats Manufactured

3. 64.5

5a.

Class	Tally	Frequency
$4.00–4.99	IIII	4
$5.00–5.99	ЖI I	6
$6.00–6.99	ЖI III	8
$7.00–7.99	ЖI	5
$8.00–8.99	ЖI	5
$9.00–9.99	II	2

5b.

Class	Tally	Frequency (f)	Midpoint (m)	f × m
$4.00–4.99	IIII	4	4.495	17.980
$5.00–5.99	IIII I	6	5.495	32.970
$6.00–6.99	IIII III	8	6.495	51.960
$7.00–7.99	IIII	5	7.495	37.475
$8.00–8.99	IIII	5	8.495	42.475
$9.00–9.99	II	2	9.495	18.990
		30		201.850

$$\text{Mean} = \frac{201.85}{30} = \underline{\underline{\$6.73}}$$

5c.

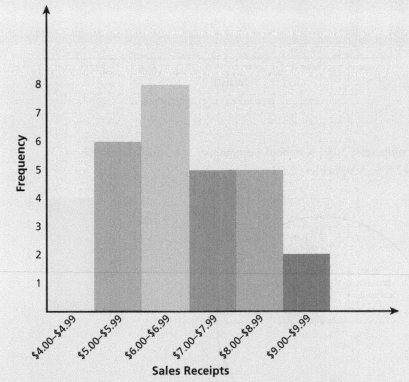

Sales Receipts

Assessment Test

1a.

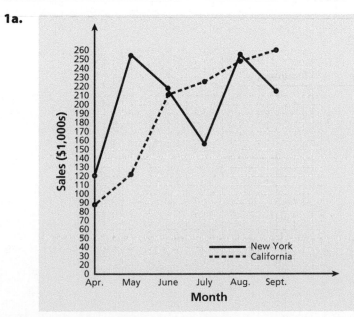

1b.

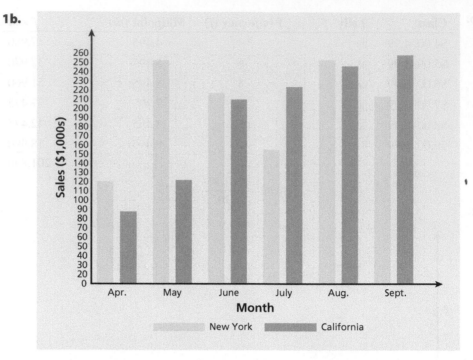

3a. Desktop computers: 50%, Notebook computers: 25%, Software: 10%, Printers: 12.5%, Accessories: 2.5%

3b.

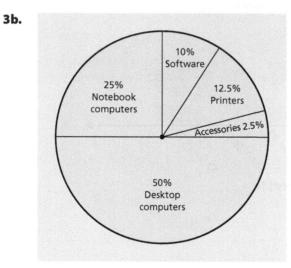

5a. Range: 78, Mode: 72

5b.

Class	Tally	Frequency
11–20	I	1
21–30	I	1
31–40	I	1
41–50	II	2
51–60	IIII	4
61–70	ЖІ	5
71–80	ЖІ ЖІ	10
81–90	ЖІ ЖІ	10
91–100	ЖІ I	6

5c.

Class	Tally	Frequency (f)	Midpoint (m)	f × m
11–20	I	1	15.5	15.5
21–30	I	1	25.5	25.5
31–40	I	1	35.5	35.5
41–50	II	2	45.5	91.0
51–60	IIII	4	55.5	222.0
61–70	IIII	5	65.5	327.5̸
71–80	IIII IIII	10	75.5	755̸.0̸
81–90	IIII IIII	10	85.5	855̸.0̸
91–100	IIII I	6	95.5	573.0̸
		40		2,900.0

$$\text{Mean} = \frac{2,900}{40} = \underline{\underline{72.5}}$$

5d. 14

5e.

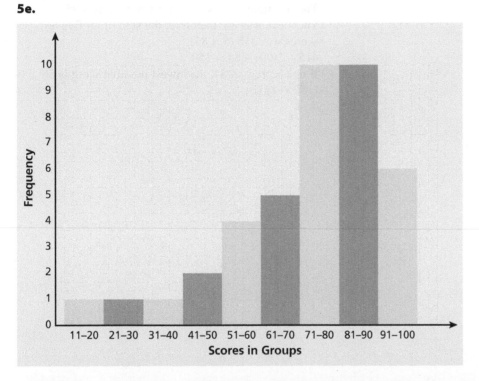

Brainteaser solutions

APPENDIX A

1. page 94   <u>A decimal point</u> 1.2

2. page 195   <u>20 nines</u> Don't forget 90, 91, 92 , 93, … 99!

3. page 311   <u>24 days</u>   Let X = days worked
Let $(30 - X)$ = days not worked
$55X - 66(30 - X) = 924$
$X = 24$ Days

4. page 419   <u>866 miles high</u>   If 4 inches equals $1 million, then a foot equals
$3 million.
A mile equals $15.84 billion (5,280 ft × $3 million)

$$\$1 \text{ trillion} = \left(\frac{1,000}{15.84}\right) = 63.13 \text{ miles}$$

$13.72 \times 63.13 = 866.14 = 866$ miles

5. page 551   Assuming the clock displays AM and PM rather than a 24-hour display,
the room will be <u>darkest at 1:11</u> and <u>brightest at 10:08.</u>

6. page 649   <u>$60 million</u>   Let X = Total taxes

$$X = \frac{1}{3}X + \frac{1}{4}X + \$25 \text{ million}$$

$$X = \frac{7}{12}X + \$25 \text{ million}$$

$$X - \frac{7}{12}X = \$25 \text{ million}$$

$$\frac{5}{12}X = \$25 \text{ million}$$

$$X = \$60 \text{ million}$$

7. page 779   <u>66</u>

The most common score (mode) was 90, so at least two scores were 90.
The middle score (median) was 85, so at least one score was 85.
The remaining two scores must be less than 85.
The mean was 83; therefore, the sum of all five test scores was 415 (5 × 83).
415 − 2(90) − 85 = 150
If one score was 84, the lowest possible score is 66 (150 − 84).

INDEX

A

AAMCO Transmissions, 599
AARP, 106
AARP The Magazine, 106
Abbreviations for invoices, 198
Accelerated cost recovery system (ACRS), 600
Accelerated depreciation, 590
Accounting equation, 500
Accounting Trends and Techniques survey, 591
Accrued interest, 702
Ace Hardware, 641
Acid test ratio, 525
ACRS. *See* Accelerated cost recovery system (ACRS)
Actuaries, 651
Addends, 7
Addition
 of decimals, 73
 defined, 7
 of fractions, 41–47, 59–60
 of mixed numbers, 44
 verification of, 7–8
 of whole numbers, 7–9, 24
Add-on interest
 calculating the regular monthly payments of an installment loan by, 437–438
 defined, 437
Adjustable-rate mortgages (ARM), 468–478, 489–490
 calculating the interest rate of, 477–478
 defined, 468
Adjusted bank balance, 111
Adjusted checkbook balance, 111
Adjustment period, 477
Ad valorem tax, 624
Advertising and display, 210
AFLAC, 652
AICPA. *See* American Institute of Certified Public Accountants (AICPA)
Airbus, 79
Alaska Department of Fish & Game, 29
Alaskan Fishing Boats, 29
Alimentation Couche-Tard, Inc., 575
Alpha Graphics, 148
Amazon.com, Inc., 243
American Association of Retired Persons (AARP), 12

American Express Card, 296
American Institute of Certified Public Accountants (AICPA), 591
Amortization, 400–404, 411–412, 468
 asset, 607
 defined, 400
Amortization payment
 calculating by formula, 403–404, 412
 calculating the amount by table, 401–402
Amortization schedule, 471
 of a mortgage, preparing a partial, 471–473
Amount, 7
 determining in increase or decrease situations, 180–183
 finding the new after a percent change, 181–183
 finding the original before a percent change, 181–183
Amount financed, 436
Amount of an annuity, 382
Annual life insurance premiums, 654, 662
Annual percentage rate (APR)
 of an installment loan, 438–441
 calculating by formula, 438–441
 defined, 421
 tables, 438–442
Annual percentage yield (APY)
 calculating, 357–358
 defined, 357
Annual premiums for motor vehicle insurance
 bodily injury and property damage rates, 671
 collision and comprehensive rates, 672
Annual rate, 357
Annual stockholders' meeting, 501
Annuities certain, 381
Annuity, 380–412
 complex, 381
 contingent, 381
 defined, 381
 future value of, 381–387, 408
 of $1 (Table), future value of an ordinary, 383–384
 ordinary, 382
 present value of, 391–397, 410
 simple, 381
 timeline illustrating present and future value of, 381

Annuity due, 381–387
 calculating the future value by formula, 386–387, 410
 calculating the future value by using tables, 385–386, 410
 calculating the present value by formula, 396–397
 calculating the present value by using table, 393–395, 410
 formula, 386–387
Anxiety, overcoming, 94
A.P. Moller–Maersk group, 91
Apple Inc., 547
APR. *See* Annual percentage rate (APR)
APY. *See* Annual percentage yield (APY)
Area rating, 662
Arithmetic mean, 748
ARM. *See* Adjustable-rate mortgages (ARM)
Assessed value, 625
Assets, 500
 amortization, 607
 basis for depreciation, determining, 600
 cost recovery systems, 600–608, 610
 current, 501–502
 intangible, 607
 investments and other, 502
 long-lived, 588
 long-term, 502, 588
 on personal balance sheet, 13–14
 replacing, 599
 tangible, 607
 wasting, 604
Asset turnover ratio, 526
Athleta, 433
ATMs. *See* Automated teller machines (ATMs)
Auntie Anne's, Inc., 463
Automated teller machines (ATMs), 96
Automatic bill paying, 96
Automotive Parts Group, 235
Average, 748
Average collection period, 525
Average cost method, 554, 558
 pricing inventory by, 558
Average daily balance
 calculating finance charge and new balance by using, 426–428
 defined, 426
Average inventory, 571

Average monthly balance, 96
Average monthly utility bills, cities with highest, 175
Avis Budget Group, Inc., 598

B

BAC. *See* Bank of America Corp. (BAC)
Back-end load, 709
Baker, Lorenzo Dow, 256
Balance
 calculating new by unpaid or previous month's balance method, 422–426
 calculating new by using average daily balance method, 426–428
Balance of business, calculating the new, 428–431
Balance sheet, 500–509, 534–535, 593
 common-size, 504
 comparative, 506
 components of, 501–504
 defined, 500
 horizontal analysis of, 506–509, 535
 personal, 13–14
 preparing, 501–504, 534
 vertical analysis, 504–506, 535
Banana Republic, 433
Bank discount, 332
 and proceeds for a simple discount note, 332
Banker's rule, 315
Banking method, preferred, 96
Bank of America Corp. (BAC), 126
Banks, 321
 largest U.S., 126
Bank statement, 109
 paper and electronic, 110
 understanding of, 109–111
Bank statement reconciliation, 111–115, 119–120
 form, 112
 preparation of, 112–115
Bank teller, 108
Bar charts
 comparative, 733, 734, 737
 component, 733, 734, 737
 defined, 733
 reading and constructing, 733–738
 standard, 733, 736, 738